THE OXFORD HANDBOOK OF

RALPH WALDO EMERSON

THE OXFORD HANDBOOK OF

RALPH WALDO EMERSON

Edited by
CHRISTOPHER HANLON

OXFORD
UNIVERSITY PRESS

Great Clarendon Street, Oxford, OX2 6DP,
United Kingdom

Oxford University Press is a department of the University of Oxford.
It furthers the University's objective of excellence in research, scholarship,
and education by publishing worldwide. Oxford is a registered trade mark of
Oxford University Press in the UK and in certain other countries

© The several contributors 2024

The moral rights of the authors have been asserted

All rights reserved. No part of this publication may be reproduced, stored in
a retrieval system, or transmitted, in any form or by any means, without the
prior permission in writing of Oxford University Press, or as expressly permitted
by law, by licence or under terms agreed with the appropriate reprographics
rights organization. Enquiries concerning reproduction outside the scope of the
above should be sent to the Rights Department, Oxford University Press, at the
address above

You must not circulate this work in any other form
and you must impose this same condition on any acquirer

Published in the United States of America by Oxford University Press
198 Madison Avenue, New York, NY 10016, United States of America

British Library Cataloguing in Publication Data
Data available

Library of Congress Control Number: 2024934364

ISBN 978–0–19–289437–3

DOI: 10.1093/oxfordhb/9780192894373.001.0001

Printed and bound by
CPI Group (UK) Ltd, Croydon, CR0 4YY

To the memory of
Joel Myerson

Contents

Preface by Christopher Hanlon   xi
Works by Emerson Frequently Cited in This Volume and Abbreviations   xxi
List of Contributors   xxiii

1. CLIMATE, OR, EMERSON AND THE ENVIRONMENTAL HUMANITIES

1. Emerson, Energy, Infrastructure   3
   JEFFREY INSKO

2. Emerson Undersea   18
   MICHELE NAVAKAS AND DOMINIC MASTROIANNI

3. "Up Again, Old Heart!": Emerson in the Anthropocene   36
   MICHELLE C. NEELY

4. The "Mute Music" in Emerson's Polarity: Generating Practical Power   54
   CHRISTINA KATOPODIS

5. Transcendental Geologies: Emerson, Antislavery, and the *Kairos* of Deep Time   71
   PATRICK MORGAN

6. The Seed of the World: Emerson's Transatlantic Transcendentalist First Philosophy   86
   DAVID GREENHAM

2. AMERICAN CIVILIZATION, OR, HEMISPHERIC EMERSONS

7. Emerson, Martí, and a Cosmopolitanism for the Americas   107
   TIMOTHY DONAHUE

8. Emersonian Figurations in Modern Hispanic Poetics   125
Ricardo Miguel-Alfonso

9. Emerson and Caribbean Emancipation   139
Martha Schoolman

3. RACE, OR, EMANCIPATION AND RESISTANCE

10. Speaking for "the Indian"   161
Drew Lopenzina and Laura L. Mielke

11. "The Calamity of the Next Ages": Emerson and Reconstruction   177
Christopher Hanlon

12. Emerson and Carlyle: Race and (Anti-)Slavery   192
Tim Sommer

13. Nature's President: Emerson on Emancipation and Executive Power   208
Michael Stancliff

14. Emersonian Legacies of Black Resistance   224
Anita Patterson

15. The "Arch-Abolitionist": Emerson, Love, and Social Justice   241
Prentiss Clark

4. WEALTH, OR, CAPITALISM AND ITS ALTERNATIVES

16. Emerson and Capitalism   261
Benjamin Pickford

17. Emerson's Market Forces   279
Andrew Kopec

18. Emerson and the Socialists: American Renaissance in the Age of Fourier   296
Holly Jackson

5. WORSHIP, OR, RELIGION AND THE SECULAR

19. Emerson among the Methodists   315
    CLAUDIA STOKES

20. Emerson and Secularism   333
    JUSTINE S. MURISON

6. PROSPECTS, OR, COMPUTATIONAL APPROACHES TO EMERSON

21. Experimenting with Emerson: A Quantitative Approach   351
    BRAD RITTENHOUSE AND MAURICE S. LEE

22. Emerson's Unoriginality and the Commonplace Books of Mary Moody Emerson and Margaret Fuller   372
    NOELLE A. BAKER

7. QUOTATION AND ORIGINALITY, OR, EMERSON'S EDITORS

23. Editing Emerson   397
    RONALD A. BOSCO AND JOEL MYERSON

24. Emerson, Nature, and Networks in the Black Press   408
    BRIGITTE FIELDER

25. Ellen Tucker Emerson: Portrait of a Daughter as Secretary, Editor, and Biographer   425
    KATE CULKIN

8. THE MAN OF THE WORLD, OR, READERS, INTERLOCUTORS, NETWORKS

26. "Fleeing to Fables": Reading Emerson in Literature for Children   443
    KRISTINA WEST

27. Emerson, Melville, Futility   460
    RACHEL BANNER

28. Emerson, Rhetoric, and Oratorical Culture — 476
    ROGER THOMPSON

29. Lydia Jackson Emerson — 489
    RANDALL FULLER

9. THE POET, OR, FROM COMMONPLACING VERSE TO POETIC PRINT CULTURE

30. Metamorphosis and Transcription: Emerson's "The Poet" and the Question of Form — 507
    MEREDITH L. MCGILL

31. Emerson's Muses, Poets, and Persons from *The Dial* to *The Atlantic Monthly* — 520
    ELIZA RICHARDS

10. "ME" AND "NOT-ME," OR, EMERSONIAN EMBODIMENTS, AFFECTS, INTIMACIES

32. "Nature Abhors the Old": Emerson's Transcendental Ageism — 543
    SARI EDELSTEIN

33. Aphasic Etymology: A Disability Poetics and the Emerson-Whitman Connection — 558
    DON JAMES MCLAUGHLIN

34. From Iconoclast to Icon: The Public Intellectual as Celebrity — 573
    BONNIE CARR O'NEILL

35. Emerson, Reluctant Feminist — 589
    LESLIE ELIZABETH ECKEL

36. Emerson and the Wildness of Friendship — 605
    EDUARDO CADAVA

    Afterword: Ralph Waldo Emerson Transfigured — 619
    CORNEL WEST

Index — 627

Preface

CHRISTOPHER HANLON

Prolific over the course of five decades, Ralph Waldo Emerson (1803–1882), American essayist, lecturer, and poet, wrote and spoke with immense range. Connecting himself with issues concerning nature, science, philosophy, religion, politics, democracy, reform, economics, politics, friendship, love, emancipation, slavery, women's rights, collective will, and individual conscience, Emerson's field of view is capacious, absorbed in literary and philosophical currents, responsive to personal experience along with the churn of national and international events; sometimes focused on the microcosm of the solitary individual, or the transitory thought; at other moments, the roiling of culture and politics; at still others, the epochal processes of the universe that make all human concerns seem tiny. And yet at some level and across this multitude of topoi, Emerson has only one thing to teach, one concern, one lesson, and that lesson is now. What he continually urges upon his reader is an insistence that the present moment is humming with possibility; that what it offers is rejuvenating, incipient, and unsettling; that *this* instant in time, exactly where you are, contains everything you could ever need—if only you can get out of your own way, overcome the patterns of avoidance through which we all so often insulate ourselves from the moment and from one another, and engage the redemptive and sublime energy of the present.

In a separate work on United States literature of the nineteenth century, one contributor to this volume, the Americanist literary historian Jeffrey Insko, describes as "romantic presentism" the habit of thought by which many antebellum writers privileged now over then, "the ever-living present" over "the dead past."[1] Within this romantic experience of American time, Transcendentalism and Emerson himself are essential. Consider this passage from near the end of his 1841 essay "Compensation," where Emerson assesses the impoverished mindset out of which "we" bind ourselves to a "beautiful yesterday":

> We cannot part with our friends. We cannot let our angels go. We do not see that they go out, that archangels may come in. We are idolators of the old. We do not believe in the riches of the soul, in its proper eternity and omnipresence. We do not believe there is any force in to-day to rival or re-create that beautiful yesterday. We linger in the ruins of the old tent, where once we had bread and shelter and organs, nor believe

that the spirit can feed, cover, and nerve us again. We cannot again find aught so dear, so sweet, so graceful. But we sit and weep in vain. The voice of the almighty saith, "Up and onward forevermore!" We cannot stay amid the ruins. Neither will we rely on the New; and so we walk ever with reverted eyes, like those monsters who look backwards. (*CW* 2:73)

Lingering in the ruins of a beautiful yesterday, for Emerson, becomes a way of foreclosing access to "eternity and omnipresence," just as remaining with our past angels inhibits the arrival of newer, more fortuitous archangels. Hindsight and retrospect are the habits that have formed part of our problem, as Emerson often finds a way to say (like in "The American Scholar," where in a similar riff he points out that "the eyes of man are set in his forehead, not his hindhead" [*CW* 1:57]). In his first major work, the 1836 essay *Nature,* an often-quoted passage reveals Emerson in yet another process of immersion in yet another now, submitting himself to the thrill of "a perfect exhilaration":

In the woods, we return to reason and faith. There I feel that nothing can befall me in life,—no disgrace, no calamity, (leaving me my eyes,) which nature cannot repair. Standing on the bare ground,—my head bathed by the blithe air, and uplifted into infinite space,—all mean egotism vanishes. I become a transparent eye-ball. I am nothing. I see all. The currents of the Universal Being circulate through me; I am part or particle of God. (*CW* 1:10)

Bathed in the blithe air, situating himself in the "there" of the woods and yet uplifted into infinite space, immersed in his own moment and surround and the conduit it offers to universal being—released from mean egotism, seeing all—Emerson both finds and founds himself.[2] In both "Compensation" and *Nature*—and at so many other junctures of his writing—Emerson invests in what is happening and divests from what is over. "There are no fixtures in nature," he writes in "Circles" (*CW* 2:179). For him, all is fluid, changing, available for revision, subject to constant transformation. "Power ceases in the instant of repose," he writes in "Self-Reliance": "it resides in the moment of transition from a past to a new state, in the shooting of the gulf, in the darting to an aim" (*CW* 2:40). There is for Emerson nothing but change, everywhere, all the time.

This is to say that Emerson is current, that he draws us into rigorous engagement with what is happening now, which is also to say that Emerson is in step with Robert Spiller's assertion that American literature itself is protean, liquid, constantly undermining itself, continually subject to transformation. Spiller—also one of the initial editors of Emerson's *Collected Works*—insisted in his 1948 *Literary History of the United States* that "each generation should produce at least one literary history of the United States, for each generation must define the past in its own terms."[3] Defining literary history in one generation's own terms means re-experiencing the past through the prerogatives of the present. It is out of respect for this Emersonian now that *The Oxford Handbook of Ralph Waldo Emerson* collects commentary from a wide variety of scholars all of whom contribute to the particular texture of Americanist literary studies today. It is Emerson's capaciousness that entwines him with the many subjects focusing the essays that follow—the environmental humanities, Black lives and emancipation, affect and intimacy, hemispheric American literary history, disability studies, the computational humanities, and print culture studies, among them—but it is his way of constantly leaning into the current moment that permits his entrée into these circles of discussion that have proven so energizing to the larger field of Americanist literary studies over the past decade.

Indeed in this very sense the writers who comprise this volume seek to address the ways in which Emerson's status in the field has become so paradoxical. Since F. O. Matthiessen's publication of the hugely influential *American Renaissance* in 1941, Emerson has generated large numbers of volumes and articles devoted to the study of his work, and yet in recent years such scholarship has become distanced from the welter of critical perspectives that have reinvigorated and redefined the field. While he is widely acknowledged as a major figure of US literary history, compared with certain others Emerson has fallen to the periphery of these circles of exchange. Melville, for example, has become a virtually necessary reference point for most of the major critical approaches that define the field currently. Climate and literature, animal studies, gender and sexuality studies, economics and literature, disability studies, transatlantic and transpacific studies—in the circles of critical exchange that constitute these subfields, scholars have re-established works such *Moby-Dick* (1851), *Bartleby, the Scrivener* (1853), or *The Confidence-Man* (1857) as necessary reading. Emerson, while frequently read and referenced as an important cultural indicator in various nineteenth-century contexts, does not seem currently as indispensable. The Modern Language Association reports 88 peer-reviewed journal articles having been published on Melville from January 2016 to July 2019; Emerson is the subject of 22 such articles during the same period. Including non-peer-reviewed venues such as edited collections, Melville outpaces Emerson at a more moderate ratio of approximately 3:1 (196 items for Melville versus 64 for Emerson).[4]

Of course, the field continues to expand and reshape its canons even as it questions productively the very paradigm of canonicity—and canonicity was in large measure the vehicle through which Emerson was enshrined initially in the syllabi, anthologies, and tables of contents that provide ballast for US literary studies. Emerson's drift from centrality in academia was registered in a signal work by Lawrence Buell, a bridge figure in Emerson criticism who noted in 2003 what appeared then as the rise of revisionary literary methodologies and new patterns of historicization within which Emerson seemed to fit awkwardly. Rather than locating a place for Emerson within then-emergent critical frames, Buell opined the work of New Americanist scholars he found patently uninterested in the "aesthetic mainstream." It's not so much that Buell challenged the insights of such critics as he described their positions as more or less obvious and iconoclastic. The "pluriform" nature of "American poetics," he wrote, has been vigorously pressed by so-called new Americanist criticism of the last two decades, which tends to see the tensions between margin and center (in particular of race, ethnicity, gender, class, and sexuality) as more central to US cultural history than any supposed aesthetic mainstream. Whereas interest in Emerson as philosopher and social criticism has increased during these years, the map of US literary history has been redrawn, at least for the nonce, to his disadvantage. No longer does it seem so self-evident that Emerson and Transcendentalism were the gateway to US literary emergence—the "American Renaissance" as F. O. Matthiessen called it. Indeed the whole notion of *an* American renaissance has come under suspicion as a facile holism that overemphasizes a small number of white male writers and artifacts of high culture. What did popular women novelists except Louisa May Alcott owe to Emerson? What indeed did virtually any American novelist in the nineteenth century except Melville and possibly Henry James? (Two very large exceptions, admittedly.) What did African American men and women of letters? What did Native American writers, like John Rollin Ridge, or the mostly Hispanophone writers of the southwestern borderlands? Even where Emersonian impress is manifest, was it really as important as has been alleged? Were not Elizabeth Barrett Browning and Christina Rossetti equally if not more important influences on Emily Dickinson, for example?[5]

Buell's analysis of the field summated "a present-day Americanist standpoint" against which he pitted Emerson—more specifically, what is "most interesting" about Emerson. "Emerson is almost always at his most interesting," he suggests as he opens the book, "when striving to free his mind from parochial entanglements of whatever sort" (4), and for him those parochial entanglements come to include most recent scholarship that "press[es]" the perspectivalism of what sound like special interests. "At best," Buell suggested, Emerson "opened up the prospect of a much more profound sense of mental emancipation, whatever one's race, sex, or nation might be. That is the Emerson most worth preserving." He goes on then to praise Emerson's prose for "its peculiar blend—of humility and assertiveness, sincerity and irony, abstraction and directness, intransigent position-taking versus infinite wariness about being pinned down to any one position." But for him, none of that, none of Emerson at his best, may be accessed through the work of literary scholars. "All this comes across best," he states, "by listening not to critics but to the sound of Emerson's words" (5).

A better model for scholarship reflects in Emerson's own, Buell suggests, since "Emerson used his favorite self-identifying term, scholar, in a disruptively antiprofessional sense" (8). Buell noticed correctly a growing gulf between much—by no means all—Emerson scholarship and the leading edges of the field. The notion behind this collection, however, is that the Emerson Buell wished to find, involved rather than distanced from the work of Americanist scholars who have pushed the field past its belles-lettres origins and toward enlivening examinations of race, gender, class (and climate change, and health, and the digital humanities) is already there in Emerson's words. The Emerson of *The Oxford Handbook of Ralph Waldo Emerson* is an Emerson whose lecture career, having been shaped by locomotives and the fossil fuels they combust, intersects with his writings on nature to make him a crucial author for current discussions of literature and climate change; whose friendship with Margaret Fuller, marriage to another first-generation feminist, and embeddedness in a community of women's rights advocates must open consideration of his place in any discussion of nineteenth-century gender and sexuality; whose writings on wealth and the economy make him an essential node in discussions of capitalism, class, and financial markets; whose considerations on race, citizenship, and national community make him a necessary figure in any account of the illiberal nineteenth-century American nation-state; whose attempt to speak for the Cherokee (whose violent removal from their ancestral lands during the 1830s outraged him) demands the attention of historians of indigeneity in the United States; whose experience of disability and whose writing on age involve him necessarily in critical exchanges over health and literature, whose resonance well beyond the United States elsewhere in the hemisphere helps scholars to continue the work of expanding the geographical scope of American Studies.

The bulk of the volume to follow disperses its examination of Emerson across ten conceptual areas. Section 1, "Climate," gathers work by environmental humanists in order to amass insight pertaining to Emerson's potential place within the environmental humanities (EH), an area somewhat untapped in Emerson scholarship. The relative paucity of work on Emerson from an EH perspective might seem curious given Emerson's obvious interest in the natural world along with his close observation of nineteenth-century infrastructures and technologies of extraction—not to mention his frequent usage of the word "energy" both to describe human and cultural vitality and literally the combustion of fossil fuels. The scholars whose insights shape this section place Emerson at the juncture of an era of natural exploitation and scientific discovery concerning the earth's climate: its changing meteorology, its oceans, its geology, its sounds, its exploitable resources, its capacity to sustain life. Chapters by Jeffrey Insko (who examines for the first time Emerson's continual involvement—professionally, philosophically, as an enthusiastic observer—with energy infrastructure), Michele Navakas and Dominic Mastroianni (who plumb the depths of Emerson's fascination with oceans, currents, and other liquid environments along with the meaning of that fascination for one of Emerson's most influential readers, Rachel Carson), Michelle Neely (who takes up Emerson's own sense for the impact of human beings on the planet, now designated in the term *Anthropocene*), Christina Katopodis (whose EH approach to Emerson explores his engagement with nineteenth-century understandings of the sounds of the planet), Patrick Morgan (who offers an assessment of Emerson's interest in geological time, in part in order to forward ongoing critical discussions of Emerson's changing sense for the temporality of reform), and David Greenham (who traces Emerson's avenues through ancient Greek philosophy in search of a "first philosophy"—a conception of which he arrived at through his study of the pre-Socratics) all provide directions for further explorations of Emerson's resonance for the Environmental Humanities.

Section 2, "American Civilization," maps the hemispheric literary and cultural networks through which Emerson and Transcendentalism have reverberated beyond the United States and Anglo-America. The section opens with a chapter by Timothy Donahue, who examines Emerson's resonance for the Cuban poet and essayist José Martí (for whom Emerson became a model of anti-imperialism and cosmopolitanism), while Ricardo Miguel-Alfonso maps a constellation of Hispanic writers from elsewhere in the Latin American and South American world such as Octavio Paz, Jorge Luis Borges, Vicento Huidobro, and Lzama Lima. Following other Americanist scholars whose venturesome work has challenged Anglocentric limitations upon our geographical, cultural, and linguistic conceptualizations of "America," Martha Schoolman then pursues Emerson's shifting profile amongst American writers in the Caribbean.

Section 3, "Race," considers Emerson's position in the cultures of emancipation and other justice struggles that formed prior to the Civil War and well beyond its conclusion. Drew Lopenzina and Laura L. Mielke open this section with a chapter that interrogates Emerson's attempts to speak on behalf of Indigenous North Americans, beginning with his open letter to President Martin Van Buren in 1838, excoriating the administration's policy of forced removal of the Cherokee from ancestral lands in what is now North Carolina, South Carolina, Georgia, and Tennessee. Building upon a depth of existing scholarship focused on Emerson's embrace of antislavery during the 1840s and 50s, Christopher Hanlon's chapter places Emerson in the setting of Reconstruction, the political struggle for Black civil rights that followed the end of the Civil War: an aspect of Emerson's public profile that can augment existing scholarship detailing Emerson's turn to abolition by estimating his capacity for visualizing deeper forms of freedom to follow literal emancipation. This is followed with a chapter by Tim Sommer on Emerson's career-long friendship with the Scottish author Thomas Carlyle, whose racism burgeoned during the years Emerson tightened his commitment to abolition. Sommer points to the Emerson/Carlyle connection as a transatlantic contest over the very notion of race and its material implications. Michael Stancliff's chapter on "Nature's President" considers Emerson's ways of conceptualizing Presidential power, from the culturally galvanizing Presidential campaign of John C. Fremont through the Lincoln presidency and Emerson's assessment of Lincoln's emancipation proclamation as a political harnessing of nature's transcendent forces. Anita Patterson's chapter follows the legacies of Emersonian resistance by tracing its resonance across the work of a series of crucial advocates for Black rights: Frederick Douglass, W. E. B. Du Bois, Booker T. Washington, Pauline Hopkins, and Anna Julia Cooper. Lastly, Prentiss Clark assesses Emerson's understanding of love as the undergirding of his social practices, connecting him in this respect to a series of more recent writer-activists such as June Jordan, bell hooks, and James Baldwin.

Emerson and his works have often been conscripted into the service of various ideologies of laissez-faire capitalism. And yet, he lived in an era of reformist attempts to envision alternative, communitarian political economies; bore witness to Karl Marx's emergence as a critic and theorist of Capital; and pondered deeply the exigencies of the market and its mechanisms. Section 4, "Wealth," describes Emerson as a public intellectual in a capitalist society by opening up these three foci of his thinking about market capitalism. The section opens with a chapter by Benjamin Pickford, who ponders Emerson's ideas on American capitalism and its alleged inevitability. Pickford juxtaposes Emerson's ideas on wealth in *The Conduct of Life* (1861) with those articulated by Marx in *Capital* (1867) and the *Grundwisse* (ca. 1857–58), works whose meditations on labor and alienation are often in striking dialogue with Emerson's own writing on the logic of capital, including its pernicious effects. The section continues with Andrew Kopec's account of Emerson's absorption—financially, interpersonally, philosophically—in the dynamism of the market forces that roiled his society and that pressured his Transcendentalist understanding. Lastly, Holly Jackson's chapter details Emerson's response to the socialist reform movement driven by American adherents to the teachings of Charles Fourier—including Emerson's famous refusal to join with the formation of a phalanx at Brook Farm, but also taking up Emerson's sometimes surprising engagements with radicals in the free-love movement.

Section 5, "Worship," pairs two chapters concerning Emerson and religion. Much scholarship has focused on Emerson's relationship with Unitarianism, the version of nineteenth-century progressive Christianity with which he enacted a public break in 1832, leaving his pulpit at the Second Church of Boston. This section begins, however, with Claudia Stokes's chapter on Emerson's influence under the theological and cultural phenomenon of Methodism, a form of revelatory Christianity whose charismatic tenor provided an alternative to what Emerson called the "corpse-cold" Unitarianism that dominated so much religious experience of the Boston-area intelligentsia. The new religious studies has taught us that the entwinement of the spiritual with the secular has conditioned the varieties of religious experience in America, and so this section continues with Justine S. Murison's chapter on Emerson and secularism, a necessary perspective from which to understand the resonance of Transcendentalism in the nineteenth century and now.

Section 6, "Prospects," breaks new ground in offering two computational approaches to Emerson and his circle. In the first, Maurice S. Lee and Brad Rittenhouse, research data facilitator of Stanford University Research Computing, present their digital corpus of Emerson—the first of its kind—incorporating Optical Character Recognition and Named Entity Recognition. "Arguments about Emerson can be especially susceptible to confirmation bias," they point out, as "sampling error, and teleological reasoning as scholars, with our variously colored critical lenses" may lead us to "paint Emerson our own hue." Through their own computational approach to Emerson's prose, Lee and Rittenhouse demonstrate the potential for digitized editions to augment—or inconveniently unsettle—our critical assessments. Their analysis is followed by Noelle A. Baker's chapter on Emerson's engagements with the commonplace books of Mary Moody Emerson and Margaret Fuller. Baker's discussion includes an overview of the digital edition of Mary Moody Emerson's Almanacks, published in *Women Writers Online*, the coding of which permits a level of analysis of her "intricate intertextuality" heretofore all but impossible.

Section 7, "Quotation and Originality," places Emerson within a constellation of nineteenth-century networks and individuals through which he now filtrates to readers and within which his thought took shape. The section opens with a statement by two of Emerson's most prolific editors, Ronald A. Bosco and the late Joel Myerson (it is to the latter's memory that this volume is dedicated). Having brought to completion the ten-volume *Collected Writings of Ralph Waldo Emerson* (1971–2013) as well as *The Later Lectures of Ralph Waldo Emerson* (2001), and having contributed to other primary-source collections of Emerson including the *Journals and Miscellaneous Notebooks* along with selections such as *The Major Prose*, Bosco and Myerson reflect on the formation of Emerson's canon—both their own role in the now-standard editions of his work and the pathbreaking contributions of others. Following this, Brigitte Fielder's chapter opens crucial new territory by investigating Emerson's circulation in the Black press, where his ideas on nature and self-reliance resonated in distinctive ways for Black editors and reviewers. Kate Culkin's chapter on Ellen Tucker Emerson describes Emerson's relationship with his eldest daughter, who late in life played a crucial role in curating, editing, and otherwise shaping his work.

Section 8, "The Man of the World," pursues some of Emerson's resonances in contexts including children's literature, Melville studies, and rhetorical studies. Kristina West's chapter maps out some of the ways Emerson has circulated within children's literature, from Louisa May Alcott's 1876 *Rose in Bloom* to Ransom Riggs's 2011 *Miss Peregrine's Home for Peculiar Children*—instances of Emerson, West argues, that provide avenues back into Emerson's own meditations on childhood in poems such as "The Sphinx" or essays such as "Self-Reliance" or "Experience." Rachel Banner follows with a chapter placing Emerson with Melville; and she is followed by Roger Thompson's chapter, which examines Emerson as a rhetorician who was steeped in the rhetorical models of his day. The section concludes with a chapter by Randall Fuller on Emerson's marriage with Lidian Jackson Emerson, whose perceptions of Emerson and the trials of her union with him offers a textured account not only of nineteenth-century marriage but of partnerships between intellectuals.

Section 9, "The Poet," offers two new considerations of Emerson's verse from two of the field's leading historians of American poetry. Meredith L. McGill opens this section with a chapter that meditates on Emerson's poetic theory, arguing (against tradition) that Emerson's poetics informs his poetic practice, and vice versa. In doing so, she draws attention to Emerson's exercises in commonplacing, a nineteenth-century practice that challenges current-day preoccupations with authorial originality. Focusing on Emerson's publication career, Eliza Richards focuses on Emerson's shifting poetics from his verse contributions to *The Dial* to those of *The Atlantic Monthly*, enfolding the former group's focus on Emerson's sense for the incapacities of poets aptly to channel the muse into the latter group's poetic interventions in the abolitionist- and war-related public spheres of the 1850s and 60s.

In his essay *Nature* (1836), Emerson famously disavows as "not-me" the body itself, a disavowal that has made Emerson seem resistant to the theories of embodiment that have been so important to the course of Americanist literary studies over the past two decades. Section 10, "'Me' and 'Not-Me,'" approaches Emersonian embodiment through a pair of chapters oriented toward the medical humanities; a third that studies Emerson as an embodiment of nineteenth-century literary celebrity; a fourth that assesses Emerson's response to the proto-feminism of his day; and finally, a chapter approaching Emerson from the angle of affect. First, Sari Edelstein writes about Emerson's "transcendental ageism," moving past consensus about Romantic childhood in order to assess his "generalizations about the life course," notions of productive adulthood also ascendent in Emerson's time as an effect of industrial capitalism. Don James McLaughlin follows with a chapter on the famed Emerson-Whitman connection focused on each writer's interest in "verbal estrangement"—not simply the kind resulting from Emerson's cognitive dysfunction late in life, but a more profound and lifelong problem of struggling with the distances that open up between language and meaning. Bonnie Carr O'Neill offers a chapter detailing Emerson's transformation from public intellectual to a literary celebrity, "the sage of Concord." The section also takes up Emerson's halting, sometimes mansplaining response to the movement for women's rights, an aspect of his public profile that has sometimes been passed over by Emerson scholars whose work seems to rationalize Emerson's milquetoast, reluctant endorsements of first-generation American feminists and their work, examined here by Leslie Elizabeth Eckel. Lastly, Eduardo Cadava discusses Emerson's understanding of the "wild" dimensions of friendship—the *fort* and *da* of its oscillations; the dialectic it stages between intimacy and unknowability—a set of Emersonian notions that offered inspiration to the Nietzsche of *The Gay Science* (1882).

Finally, this volume closes with an afterword by Cornel West, author of *The American Evasion of Philosophy: A Genealogy of Pragmatism* (1989), which places Emerson at the head of an American pragmatist tradition even while holding him accountable for his failures adequately to interrogate prevailing racist paradigms. A prolific critic of American philosophical, literary, and cultural life, West is also a widely esteemed public intellectual and advocate for political, economic, and social justice. As a thinker whose deep engagement with philosophical and aesthetic abstraction informs a life of activism and other forms of immersion in what is happening now, one might call him the Ralph Waldo Emerson of our day.

Notes

1. Jeffrey Insko, *History, Abolition, and the Ever-Present Now in Antebellum American Writing* (Oxford, 2019), 5.
2. I pay homage to the great reader of Emerson, Stanley Cavell, in whose spirit of insistence upon Emerson's abiding challenges this collection proceeds. See Stanley Cavell, *This New Yet Unapproachable America: Lectures After Emerson After Wittgenstein* (Albuquerque: Living Batch Press, 1989).
3. Robert E. Spiller et al., ed. *Literary History of the United States*, 2 vols. (New York: MacMillan, 1948), 1:vii.
4. Statistics accessed January 30, 2023, Modern Language Association International Bibliography.
5. Lawrence Buell, *Emerson* (Cambridge: Harvard University Press, 2003): 144–45.

WORKS BY EMERSON FREQUENTLY CITED IN THIS VOLUME AND ABBREVIATIONS

Ralph Waldo Emerson, *The Collected Works of Ralph Waldo Emerson*. Edited by Joseph Slater et al. 10 vols. Cambridge: Harvard University Press, 1971–2013. Abbreviated as *CW*.

———. *The Complete Works of Ralph Waldo Emerson*. Edited by James Elliot Cabot. 12 vols. Boston: Houghton Mifflin, 1883–93. Abbreviated as *CWE*.

———. *The Early Lectures of Ralph Waldo Emerson*. Edited by Stephen E. Whicher and Robert E. Spiller. 3 vols. Cambridge: Harvard University Press, 1959–72. Abbreviated as *EL*.

———. *The Journals and Miscellaneous Notebooks of Ralph Waldo Emerson*. Edited by William H. Gilman et al. 16 vols. Cambridge: Harvard University Press, 1960–82. Abbreviated as *JMN*.

———. *The Later Lectures of Ralph Waldo Emerson*. Edited by Ronald A. Bosco and Joel Myerson. 2 vols. Athens, University of Georgia Press, 2001. Abbreviated as *LL*.

———. *The Letters of Ralph Waldo Emerson*. Edited by Ralph L. Rusk and Eleanor M. Tilton. 10 vols. New York and London: Columbia University Press, 1939. Abbreviated as *LRWE*.

Contributors

Noelle A. Baker, Independent Scholar

Rachel Banner, Associate Professor of English, English Department, West Chester University of Pennsylvania

Ronald A. Bosco, Distinguished Professor of English and American Literature, Professor Emeritus, State University of New York

Eduardo Cadava, Philip Mayhew Professor of English, Princeton University

Prentiss Clark, Associate Professor, Department of English, University of South Dakota

Kate Culkin, Professor, Department of History, Bronx Community College, City University of New York

Timothy Donahue, Associate Professor, Department of English, Oakland University

Leslie Elizabeth Eckel, Associate Professor, English Department, Suffolk University

Sari Edelstein, Professor of English, Department of English, University of Massachusetts, Boston

Brigitte Fielder, Associate Professor, College of Letters and Sciences, University of Wisconsin-Madison

Randall Fuller, Herman Melville Distinguished Professor of Nineteenth-Century American Literature, University of Kansas

David Greenham, Professor of English Literature, University of the West of England

Christopher Hanlon, Professor of United States Literature, Arizona State University

Jeffrey Insko, Professor of English, Oakland University

Holly Jackson, Associate Professor of English, Interim Chair of American Studies, Bernard Bailyn Editor of The New England Quarterly, University of Massachusetts, Boston

Christina Katopodis, Senior Postdoctoral Research Associate at the CUNY Humanities Alliance, CUNY Graduate Center

Andrew Kopec, Associate Professor of English, Department of English and Linguistics, Purdue University Fort Wayne

Maurice S. Lee, Professor of English, Boston University

Drew Lopenzina, Professor, Department of English, Old Dominion University

Dominic Mastroianni, Associate Professor of English, Clemson University

Meredith L. McGill, Professor of English, Rutgers-New Brunswick

Don James McLaughlin, Assistant Professor, University of Tulsa

Laura L. Mielke, Dean's Professor, Department of English, University of Kansas

Ricardo Miguel-Alfonso, Associate Professor, Department of Modern Philology, University of Castilla-La Mancha

Patrick Morgan, Assistant Professor of English and Dr. William R. Hammond Endowed Professor in Liberal Arts, English Program, University of Louisiana Monroe

Justine S. Murison, Professor of English, University of Illinois, Urbana-Champaign

Joel Myerson, Distinguished Professor Emeritus of English Language and Literature, University of South Carolina

Michele Navakas, Professor of English, Miami University

Michelle C. Neely, Associate Professor of English, Connecticut College

Bonnie Carr O' Neill, Associate Professor, English, Mississippi State University

Anita Patterson, Professor of English, Boston University

Benjamin Pickford, Independent Scholar

Eliza Richards, Professor, Department of English and Comparative Literature, University of North Carolina, Chapel Hill

Brad Rittenhouse, Research Data Facilitator, Stanford University

Martha Schoolman, Associate Professor of English, Florida International University

Tim Sommer, Lecturer in English Literature and Culture, University of Passau

Michael Stancliff, Associate Professor of English, New College of Interdisciplinary Arts and Sciences, Arizona State University

Claudia Stokes, Professor of English, Trinity University

Roger Thompson, Associate Dean of the College of Arts and Sciences and Professor of Writing and Rhetoric, Stony Brook University

Cornel West, Dietrich Bonhoeffer Professor of Philosophy & Christian Practice, Union Theological Seminary

Kristina West, Associate Lecturer, Department of English Literature, University of Reading

1

CLIMATE, OR, EMERSON AND THE ENVIRONMENTAL HUMANITIES

CHAPTER 1

EMERSON, ENERGY, INFRASTRUCTURE

JEFFREY INSKO

In "Land," the third chapter of *English Traits* (1856), Emerson writes of the "coal smoke" that suffuses so much of the air of England's manufacturing towns. "The fine soot or *blacks*," he says, "darken the day, give white sheep the color of black sheep, discolor the human saliva, contaminate the air, poison many plants, and corrode the monuments and buildings" (*CW* 5:21). Fossil energy, in Emerson's description, is everywhere, remaking both the human and the nonhuman world. Yet rather than bemoaning what to modern eyes might just look like pollution, Emerson perceives that "the enormous consumption of coal in the island" may have a more positive effect: that of "modifying the general climate." That is, England possesses what Emerson calls, in a striking, perhaps even anachronistic-seeming phrase, a "factitious climate."

Put differently, Emerson here appears to invoke what those of us in the twenty-first century have learned to call (though not without misgivings) the Anthropocene. Setting aside, at least for the moment, important debates over the value and explanatory force of the term, the Anthropocene is meant to name a new geologic period, our period, defined by the emergence of humans as a geomorphic force—producers, among other things, of an "artificially created" climate, to quote from the OED's definition for "factitious." And yet, in 1856, Emerson's observation was hardly novel. That same year, the amateur scientist Eunice Foote published a paper for the American Society for the Advancement of Science describing carbon dioxide's heat-trapping qualities, a fact that Irish physicist John Tyndall would confirm independently just a few years later. As for England in particular, Jesse Oak Taylor has shown in *The Sky of Our Manufacture* that the artificial quality of England's climate, the result of mass domestic consumption of coal in urban centers, was a truism by the time Emerson published *English Traits*. The smoke and fog of Manchester, Birmingham, and London had by that time long since become proverbial—and a nuisance. Taylor examines, for example, the smog of England as a stock feature of Victorian fiction, as well as the Victorian interest in greenhouses, a technology designed to grow plants outside their native climates. The British adapted the latter for the famous Crystal Palace that housed the Great Exhibition of 1851. "The glasshouse," Taylor notes, "created a space that was fictive not merely in its artifice but also in its visibility, in the sense that everything that occurred within it was staged, in the manner of a scientific experiment."[1]

Emerson was, to say the least, untroubled by human alterations of the climate. In his early lecture "On the Relation of Man to the Globe," he extols the "skilfull and beneficent hand [man] has laid upon the globe." "Climate," he continues, "is ameliorated by cultivation, and not only the climate softened but the air purified and made healthful by the same cause" (*EL* 1:43). In the same vein, Emerson viewed the "staged" or factitious quality of England's climate and geography as one of the country's best traits. "A proof of the energy of the British people," he writes later in the chapter titled "Ability," "is the highly artificial construction of the whole fabric":

> The foundations of its greatness are the rolling waves; and from first to last it is a museum of anomalies. This foggy and rainy country furnishes the world with astronomical observations. Its short rivers do not afford water-power, but the land shakes under the thunder of the mills. There is no gold-mine of any importance, but there is more gold in England than in all other countries. It is too far north for the culture of the vine, but the wines of all countries are in its docks. (*CW* 5:52)

Remarkably, what Emerson offers here, seemingly unawares, is a brief sketch of the extractive history of the British empire. He means to praise British industriousness—which he calls "energy"—and its almost magical "ability" to produce in excess of what the nation's land itself has to offer. But that praise obscures the material practices, like the mining of coal and precious minerals, that made possible the thunder of the mills and the transport of gold and wine to British shores.

Of course, Emerson's celebration of the way that man, as he puts it, "keeps the world in repair" as well as his blitheness—or blindness—toward what Stacey Balkan and Swaralipi Nandi in a different context call "the off-siting of violence" (3) typical of extractive economies, past and present, is also not novel.[2] Yet it's a feature of Emerson's thought and writings that has gone largely unremarked, despite his career-long fascination with fossil fuels, coal in particular, as well as the fossil-fueled transportation infrastructures that enabled and structured his career as a transcendentalist. He marveled, for example, at the steamers that whisked by the sluggish wind-powered ship that took him on his second trip to England and he kept detailed ledgers and records documenting his travel on the Lyceum circuit, traveling mile after mile on locomotives to which he wrote paeans in both his journals and, as we'll see, his public writings and lectures. Emerson might thus be seen as a thinker of the Anthropocene, insofar as his work was both shaped by and helped to shape our understandings of and relations to what Jamie L. Jones has termed "fossil modernity."[3]

Drawing upon insights from the energy and environmental humanities and infrastructure studies, in what follows I situate Emerson's thought and writings in relation to the transformations to both the built environments and, incipiently, the Earth system over the course of Emerson's long career. Emerson was a keen and enthusiastic—from our view perhaps too enthusiastic—observer of these transformations. For that reason, Emerson, whom the historian Richard White once called "capitalism's poet/philosopher," may seem like precisely the wrong figure to turn to in order to help us contend with impending ecological catastrophe.[4] After all, Emerson perceived promise, but not failure; fruition, but not ruin; expansion, but not exhaustion; abundance, but not violence—perceptual failures that have long been constitutive features of colonial-capitalist energy and infrastructural development. But the aim here is not merely to indict Emerson. Rather, I will argue that however much we might now view his embrace of progress and national growth as smokescreens for ecological exploitation and imperial expansion, he can nevertheless help us understand and contend with the roots of our own fraught relation to the energic and infrastructural systems that have made us.

Energy Humanities and Infrastructure Studies

Neither energy nor infrastructure have figured as keywords in Emerson studies, despite Emerson's abiding interest in both. One explanation for this absence may be historical. The term "infrastructure" wasn't coined until the second decade of the twentieth century, even though many of the most significant early major projects in the US that we now recognize as infrastructural in the modern sense—the Erie canal, the transatlantic telegraph, the transcontinental railroad, and the first petroleum pipelines—were built during Emerson's lifetime. Similarly, the concept of energy as we know it now—as "a sign for fuel," the capacity to perform work—was likewise still emergent in Emerson's day. As Cara New Daggett has shown in *The Birth of Energy*, before the nineteenth-century science of thermodynamics redefined the term, "energy" was "a word predominantly for poets"[5] meant to describe unseen immaterial or spiritual forces, like, say, "the currents of the universal Being" that Emerson describes as circulating through him in the famous passage from "Nature" (*CW* 1:10). The growth and intensification of fossil fuel extraction and combustion helped redefine the concept of energy, linking it both to material sources, most especially hydrocarbons, as well as to an abstract but measurable ability to do work.

A second reason Emerson's interests in energy and infrastructure have gone largely unnoticed may have to do with their constitutive unnoticeability. That is to say, a key feature of modern energy and infrastructural assemblages is their invisibility. The prefix "infra-" means below or underneath, highlighting how many infrastructures (sewers, pipes, roads, and bridges) subtend modern social life yet also remain hidden, out of sight, often literally beneath our feet (or wheels). In this way, they resemble subterranean hydrocarbons like coal, oil, and gas, which likewise function as the material substrate of modern social arrangements, even though for many, but certainly not all, of us they go largely unseen, obscured by the vast distances, literal and metaphorical, between messy, often toxic, sites of extraction, production, and distribution (coal mines, oil wells, shipping channels) and comparatively pleasurable sites of consumption and experience (stovetops, warm showers, the sensation of speed). Energy sources and infrastructural systems and their mutual entanglements thus typically only reveal themselves at moments of failure, as when a gas pipeline explodes, cutting off supply. Otherwise, in their mundane smooth operation, they can, for many of us, simply be taken for granted.

Lastly, these strains in Emerson's writings may have been overlooked because, until recently, they have only been legible through the conceptual framework of Emerson's general relation to the technological advancements and liberal progressivism of his era, longstanding topics of interest for Emerson scholars, who have often cast him as a spokesman for manifest destiny.[6] But in the past decade or so, scholars working in the new interdisciplinary fields of the Energy Humanities and infrastructure studies have begun to turn to energy and infrastructure as sites of critical examination, identifying them, separately and together, as systems that provide the material bases of social arrangements, political longings, and aesthetic pleasures. Energy and infrastructure have thus become newly visible, as scholars have explored the roles they have played in the making of modernity, not just as engines or tools of social actors who stand apart from them, but as forces that shape social and political forms, cultural practices, and subjectivities in the first place. This critical work has thus performed what Kregg Hetherington, writing on infrastructure, describes as a "figure-ground reversal," in which the critical task is to "lay bare the wires, pipes, and foundations of a phenomenon."[7] Energy and infrastructure are thus revealed to be "dense social, material, aesthetic, and political formations that are critical both to differentiated experiences of everyday life and to expectations of the future" and that have "shaped modern forms of life and ways of being."[8]

Motivating this vibrant critical project in recent years, of course, is the planetary emergency and its "catalogs of despair"[9]—biodiversity loss, melting ice caps, acidified oceans, heatwaves, and intensified storm systems—wrought by global warming. This perilous state of affairs finds energy and infrastructure imbricated in increasingly intricate ways. So many of our modern infrastructural systems, like railroads and pipelines, developed as appurtenances of the carbon economy, built to serve and perpetuate, in various ways, the mass consumption and combustion of greenhouse gas-emitting fuel sources. Those appurtenances have helped produce a "factitious climate" on a global, not just local, scale, that now threatens all life on Earth.

Within this dire scenario, infrastructure plays the roles of victim, villain and hero alike. Climate change-related conditions and events—drought, subsidence, wildfires, hurricanes—increasingly imperil already aging infrastructures: scouring pipelines, taxing electrical grids, over-flooding sewage systems. Exacerbating these problems, carbon infrastructures nevertheless promote, sustain, and lock-in fossil fuel use (which is one reason why, for example, oil and gas pipeline projects have become powerful sites of resistance for climate activists and environmental justice advocates). And yet, infrastructure is also often promoted as the answer to the challenge of climate change. After all, the move away from the carbon economy will necessitate the investment in and development of new infrastructures: solar grids, wind farms, retrofitted homes and commercial buildings, alternative transportation systems, and a network of vehicular charging stations, for instance. Yet this promise might also be seen to emblematize just how deeply the world built by carbon and carbon infrastructure has penetrated our social and political imaginaries. After all, what a re-infrastructured world promises above all is more of the same: a continuation of the world built by fossil fuels with its promise of cheap, abundant energy, an ongoing commitment to growth and expansion, and perhaps most of all the ongoing unequal distribution of the benefits and harms of carbon consumption and carbon infrastructure.

Nineteenth-century US literary studies has only just begun to take the energic and infrastructural turns. The bulk of the literary-critical work that has taken up these topics has focused, understandably, on the twentieth and twenty-first centuries. But while the last century may have seen the greatest expansion and intensification of the energic infrastructural systems that confound us today, they have their origins, in both material and conceptual terms, in the century before. Thus I am mindful of an argument advanced recently by Laura Dassow Walls, who suggests that "looping back to the nineteenth century is the nearest way to discover the roots of both our insight and our blindness."[10] Emerson, as we'll see, offers plenty of both.

The Raw Bullion of Nature

References to energy abound across Emerson's corpus. Typically, Emerson deploys the term to signify abstract qualities he means to commend, like industriousness, or traits of character or mind he extols, like power, vitality, vigor, or even spirit. "The poet admires the man of energy and tactics" (*CW* 2:131), he writes in "Prudence." "When the spiritual energy is directed on something outward, then it is a thought" (*CW* 2:199), he says in the essay "Intellect." In "The Poet" he writes that "words and deeds are quite indifferent modes of the divine energy" (*CW* 2:6). "It is a secret which every intellectual man quickly learns," he continues in that essay, "that, beyond the energy of his possessed and conscious intellect he is capable of a new energy ... by abandonment to the nature of things" (*CW* 2:6). In keeping with his transcendentalist philosophy, Emerson understands one's inner energy to correspond with the spiritual energy of the universe. "We shall one day see," he says in the essay "Character," "that the most private is the most public energy" (*CW* 3:66). And in the essay "Nature" from his second series of essays, he writes, "If our own life flowed with the right energy, we should shame the brook" (*CW* 3:104).

The pre-scientific concept of energy at play for Emerson in all of these instances—energy as a kind of general and universally circulating life force—is one that Daggett traces back to Aristotle, who associated energy (the Greek "energeia") with dynamism and vitality. This association inflected the concept of energy with a powerful moral sense, "expressing," as Daggett puts it, "a bias toward dynamism over stasis" (16). This bias, of course, is so central to Emerson's thought that one can easily call to mind expressions of it across his essays and lectures: "this one fact the world hates," he says in

"Self-Reliance," "that the soul becomes" (*CW* 2:40). "The universe is fluid and volatile," he writes in "Circles"; "nothing is secure but life, transition, the energizing spirit" (*CW* 2:189). Following the Enlightenment period in the West, this preference for dynamism, motion, and change gets translated to amelioration and progress, the latter of which, Daggett observes, "had become an almost universal faith in the modern West" (18) by the nineteenth century. Emerson himself put it emphatically: "the world belongs to the energetic" (*CW* 8:76).

Emerson repeats that statement three times in his later essay "Resources." Fittingly, that rarely remarked upon essay displays, as much as any of his writings, Emerson's enthusiastic fascination with fossil fuels as a material resource. In doing so it helps to illustrate how, as Daggett explains, the moralism that had long constituted a feature of the pre-scientific conception of energy remained in force even as energy was transformed by thermodynamics and eventually consolidated into what Daggett calls the "energy-work nexus" (5), a coupling that would provide an empirical foundation for the organization and regulation of fuel, waste, labor, and growth. That transformation coincided with the enormous expansion of hydrocarbon extraction and consumption that took place in the US over the eight decades of Emerson's life. Abundant British coal and ample organic energy sources (wood and animal) prior to the American Revolution delayed the development of a domestic coal industry in the US. But that changed not long after independence. By the 1840s, for example, the nation's coal production and consumption doubled in the span of just seven years. In the early 1850s, the mining of coal, especially anthracite or "stone coal," also increased exponentially, as its use both in factories and as a domestic source of heat in urban areas expanded. ("Eloquence wants anthracite coal," Emerson wrote cheekily in his journal in 1846; "coldness is the most fatal quality" [*JMN* 9:360].[11]) Near the end of that decade, in 1859, oil was "discovered" in western Pennsylvania, sparking the nation's first oil boom. From there, fossil fuel extraction of both coal and petroleum quickly intensified and extended to the West, especially in the years just after the Civil War.

But even before the war, Emerson often extolled what he called in an 1851 letter to Thomas Carlyle "the raw bullion of nature" to be found in America, especially in the west, where "every acre of land has three or four bottoms; first of rich soil; then nine feet of bituminous coal; a little lower, fourteen feet of coal; then iron, or salt; salt springs with a valuable oil called petroleum floating on their surface."[12] Emerson linked this bounty both to progress—"the ancients brought the fire," he recorded in his journal in 1847, "the moderns collect coal" (256)—and to idealist philosophy—"the Pennsylvania coal-mines," he wrote in "The Fortune of the Republic," "though not idealists, gravitate in the ideal direction" (*CWE* 11:543).[13] Elsewhere, in the 1860 essay "Wealth," he said that "every basket" of coal "is power and civilization. For coal is a portable climate" (*CW* 6:46). He marveled that it could carry "the heat of the tropics to Labrador and the polar circle ... and make Canada as warm as Calcutta" (*CW* 6:46).

"Resources" may be Emerson's most fervent celebration of the country's energy abundance, enough even to make a modern oil executive blush. Based upon lectures he delivered in Boston in 1864 and 1865, the essay reflects, in part, the need to buoy a war-weary audience. But more than that, the essay strives to link the righteous cause of the war to the nation's mineral riches, as if conquering nature and conquering the slavocracy were simply coterminous. This equation is evident in the martial language Emerson deploys in the essay's opening. "Men are made of potencies," he says at the essay's outset. "I am benefited by every observation of a victory of man over Nature," he continues, "by seeing that wisdom is better than strength" (*CW* 8:72). He proceeds with what sounds like a call to arms: "We like to see the inexhaustible riches of Nature, and the access of every soul to her magazines. These examples wake an infinite hope; and call every man to emulation" (*CW* 8:72).

Emerson also invokes the war explicitly, viewing it as a sign of progress akin to the harnessing of the nation's "wealth of soil, of timber, of mines," which have been "put into the possession of a people who wield all these wonderful machines, have the secret of steam, of electricity; and have the power of invention in their brain" (*CW* 8:74). "We Americans have got suppled into the state of melioration," he continues. "Life is always rapid here, but what acceleration to its pulse in ten years,—what in the four years of the war! We have seen the railroad and telegraph subdue our enormous geography; we have seen the snowy deserts on the northwest, seats of Esquimaux, become lands of promise" (*CW* 8:74). Emerson even integrates the downfall of slavery seamlessly into his narrative of mineral extraction and infrastructural development, perceiving the shift from organic to mineral energy as emancipatory.[14] "Swarming west," he says, Americans discovered that the land is "covered with gold and silver, floored with coal" (*CW* 8:74). Then, waxing rhapsodic, he says, "we have found the Taurida"—that is, the equivalent of oil-rich Arabia—"in Pennsylvania and Ohio," where "if they have not the lamp of Aladdin, they have the Aladdin oil":

> Resources of America! why, one thinks of Saint-Simon's saying, "The Golden Age is not behind, but before you." Here is man in the Garden of Eden; here the Genesis and the Exodus. We have seen slavery disappear like a painted scene in a theatre; we have seen the most healthful revolution in the politics of the nation,—the Constitution not only amended, but construed in a new spirit ... As the walls of a modern house are perforated with water-pipes, sound-pipes, gas-pipes, heat-pipes,—so geography and geology are yielding to man's convenience, and we begin to perforate and mould the old ball, as a carpenter does with wood. All is ductile and plastic. We are working the new Atlantic telegraph. American energy is overriding every venerable maxim of political science. (*CW* 8:75)

Moulding the old ball. It's hard not to cringe at such a statement, knowing as we do now the ecological costs of the emergence of humans as a geomorphic force, a turn of events that Emerson viewed as evidence of man's divine favor. Now, we lament what Emerson celebrated. At any rate, this passage stands as a remarkable nineteenth-century instance of what those of us in the twenty-first century recognize as Anthropocene discourse—not just because of its awareness of how human activity is altering the Earth system itself, but also because of its all-too-familiar obscuring of just which humans and which activities are responsible for producing those effects.[15]

Which makes Emerson's seamless integration of revolution and the end of slavery into his dream of fossil-fueled progress especially problematic. That is, while from the point of view of the antebellum period Emerson's hope in the promise of fossil energy as a tool of liberation is understandable, from our own view his belief in the inexhaustibility of the nation's mineral resources, his faith in "melioration," and his instrumental view of nonhuman nature appear to have blinded him to the differential harms and benefits of what he calls "American energy." Others knew better. The Black radical David Walker, for example, linked New World mineral extraction not to dreams of progress and emancipation but to the long history of colonial-capitalist violence. The descendants of the peoples of Africa, Walker asserts in his famous *Appeal to the Colored Citizens of the World*, "have enriched" the United States "with our blood and tears—have dug up gold and silver for them and their children, from generation to generation."[16] By contrast, Emerson sees emancipation as a hopeful and promising expansion of capitalism, not a release from it. "The emancipation has brought a whole nation of negroes as customers," Emerson says, "to buy all the articles which once their few masters bought, and every manufacturer and producer in the North has an interest in protecting the negro as the consumer of his wares" (*CW* 8:75).

Without dismissing what from our vantage clearly appears to be a painful limitation in Emerson's understanding of energy abundance—an important blindness—I also want to emphasize what I think is one of his key insights: namely, his emphasis on fossil energy not just as a driver of so-called progress, but as an aesthetic experience. On this point, we might return to Emerson's cheeky, off-handed quip that "eloquence wants anthracite coal." In that remark, as elsewhere, Emerson highlights the kinds of sensory experiences hydrocarbons make possible. What are the ambient conditions, Emerson's joke asks, of individual expression? What kinds of bodily sensations or comforts are necessary or conducive to the production of eloquence, to the making of art? Here Emerson anticipates important insights from the energy humanities. In her book *Living Oil*, for instance, Stephanie LeMenager demonstrates how "petroleum infrastructure has become embodied memory and habitus for modern humans, insofar as everyday events such as driving or feeling the summer heat of asphalt on the soles of one's feet have become incorporating practices"—that is, those "repeated performances that become encoded in the body."[17] This is what it means to say that our relationship to hydrocarbon energy is "ultradeep," a term also employed by the energy historian Bob Johnson in *Mineral Rites*, his own examination of "the embodiment of fossil fuels," or the myriad ways that fossil energy saturates our experiences of being in the world. Johnson notes that in the premodern era, for example, "heat was scarce, limited, hard earned, and frequently visible to the eye," whereas "heat today is simply ubiquitous, assumed, and thus invisible."[18] Writing at a transitional period between these two experiences of heat, Emerson can still wonder at what so many of us simply take for granted: that Canada can feel as warm as Calcutta. What I want to suggest, then, is that the value of recalling Emerson's sense of wonder resides not in recognizing what he didn't, but in helping distance ourselves from what we might otherwise think of, simply, as the world as it is, rather than the world as it has been made by fossil fuels.

"The Earth Is Shaken by Our Engineries"

Emerson could be similarly perceptive—and similarly blithe—about his era's infrastructural developments. He possessed, for example, a keen understanding of the ways that energy and infrastructural systems are mutually reinforcing. Communication networks like the telegraph, and transportation networks, like canals and railroads, helped create and expand markets for domestically-produced coal and oil, both serving and perpetuating the fossil energy regime. Emerson puts it this way in "Wealth": "Coal carries coal" (*CW* 6:46)—an even pithier iteration of the infrastructure scholar Kregg Hetherington's observation that "carbon is the infrastructure of the infrastructure of carbon."[19] Unsurprisingly, Emerson was as buoyant about infrastructural developments as he was about resource abundance. "Who would live in the stone age, or the bronze, or the iron, or the lacustrine?" he asks in the essay "Progress of Culture," "who does not prefer the age of steel, of gold, of coal petroleum, cotton, steam, electricity, and the spectroscope?" (*CW* 8:108).

Emerson marveled at infrastructural developments of all sorts, as in the "water-pipes, sound-pipes, gas-pipes, [and] heat-pipes" he lists in "Resources." Infrastructure exemplified for him the dynamism and change, or what he calls the "newness ... the way onward," that he celebrates in "Circles." "New arts destroy the old," he writes in that essay, his phrasing quickening like the pace of change to the built environment that marked his era: "See the investment of capital in aqueducts, made useless by hydraulics; fortifications, by gunpowder; roads and canals, by railways; sails by steam; steam by electricity" (*CW* 2:180). He displays a particular reverence for engineers—"the earth is shaken by our engineries" (*CW* 7:143), he says in the later essay "Success"—about whom he also enthuses in his late essay "Works and Days":

> What of this dapper caoutchouc and gutta-percha, which make water-pipes and stomach-pumps, belting for mill-wheels, and diving-bells, and rain-proof coats for all climates, which teach us to defy the wet, and put every man on a footing with the beaver and the crocodile? What of the grand tools with which we engineer, like kobolds and enchanters, tunnelling Alps, canalling the American Isthmus, piercing the Arabian desert? ... The chain of Western railroads from Chicago to the Pacific has planted cities and civilization in less time than it costs to bring an orchard into bearing. (*CW* 7:81)

These marvels of human contrivance cause Emerson to declare at the essay's outset that "our nineteenth century is the age of tools." "These arts," he says elsewhere in the essay, "open great gates of a future" and, in a phrase that signifies today, unfortunately, in a more troubling register, "promis[e] to make the world plastic" (*CW* 7:80).

Emerson was especially taken with the railroad, which facilitated his career as a lyceum speaker, transporting him to cities and towns where he could communicate with audiences across the country. He called the railroad "highly poetic," observing in his journal in 1843 that "Americans take to the little contrivance as if it were the cradle in which they were born" (336). In his lecture, "The Young American," delivered the next year, he likens "railroad iron" to "a magician's rod, in its power to evoke the sleeping energies of land and water" (CW 1:226). Elsewhere in the address, he celebrates the railroad for "the increased acquaintance it has given the American people with the boundless resources of their own soil," adding that it has "given a new celerity to time, or anticipated by fifty years the planting of tracts of land, the choice of water privileges, the working of mines, and other national advantages" (CW 1:226). He thought infrastructures had conquered space as well, as in the passage above from "Resources": "We have seen the railroad and telegraph subdue our enormous geography" (340).

Yet once again, Emerson's zeal for his era's infrastructural developments seems generally to have dulled his critical sense. Of course, he couldn't have foreseen the "world made plastic" we know today, with its massive oceanic islands of accumulated garbage, fish bellies stuffed with plastic bags, and lakes and rivers suffused with microplastic beads. But he might have anticipated the impermanence and vulnerability of infrastructures, their tendency to fail, break down, and decay. Indeed, railroad accidents were so frequent that both Emerson and Thoreau joked about how tiresome news of them had become. Just a few short weeks after its installation in 1858, the transatlantic telegraph failed and wouldn't be reinstalled until after the Civil War. Coal mines routinely collapsed and portions of the Pennsylvania landscape were literally coated in oil from uncontrolled wells. Yet Emerson rarely acknowledges these failures. Nor does he appear to consider other ecological costs of infrastructural developments or the uneven distribution of the benefits of them—unlike Thoreau, for example, who mocked the railroad, upon which Americans are likely to "spend more on luxury than on safety and convenience," adding caustically that "it threatens without attaining these to become no better than a modern drawing room, with its divans, and ottomans, and sun-shades, and a hundred other oriental things, which we are taking west with us."[20]

Put differently, Emerson seems content not to notice the ways in which such infrastructural developments might be seen as "invasive," rather than "alimentary," to borrow terms employed, respectively, by the Tlingit scholar Anne Spice and by Deborah Cowen and Winona LaDuke (Ojibwe). Emerson's vision of infrastructural development as the "gateway to a modern future" unquestioningly promotes "capitalist exchange, reproducing and encouraging new forms of white land ownership, and cementing settler ontologies that naturalize the existence and domination of the nation-state."[21] To the contrary, insofar as Emerson registered how infrastructural networks helped create and extend the material pathways of empire, he praised, rather than condemned them. "Our eyes run approvingly along the lengthened lines of railroad and telegraph," he writes in the essay "Success." "We have gone nearest to the Pole. We have discovered the Antarctic continent. We interfere in Central and South America, at Canton and in Japan; we are adding to an already enormous territory" (CW 7:143).

The point here, however, is not simply to castigate Emerson for a failure of perception, especially from the vantage of our own historical moment, when the fragility of infrastructures is far more evident than it was in the nineteenth century—in the form of California wildfires sparked by downed powerlines, electrical grid blackouts in Texas, cancer outbreaks near refineries in Louisiana, and poisoned water mains in Flint, Michigan and Jackson, Mississippi. Yet however much it may be true that Emerson was less attuned than we might like to the ways in which, as Cowen and LaDuke put it, "energy infrastructures" would come to "constitute the contemporary spine of the settler colonial nation," his failings are nevertheless instructive. Not unlike his thinking about energy, Emerson's remarks upon infrastructure exemplify a key feature of their ontology: that they exist, as Brian Larkin argues in "The Politics and Poetics of Infrastructure," not just as "material forms that facilitate the flow of goods, people, ideas," but also as forms that help give shape to human desires and fantasies.[22]

That is to say, like energy systems, infrastructures produce affects, which include ambient experiences, like speed, the smell of asphalt or gasoline, the feel of hard concrete beneath one's feet, the glare of streetlights at night, the comforting sense of certainty (or expectation) that turning a faucet will deliver water, hot or cold as one wishes. Infrastructures also produce overlapping political affects. The sensations just described are experienced differently by different populations; not everyone, for instance, can count on warm or clean water from the tap, in which case one's interface with infrastructure might be characterized by anxiety, fear, or anger at the inequalities made evident by the infrastructural neglect that some populations have to contend with more than others. Or conversely, infrastructures might promise prosperity—as in the prospect of the new jobs that will be created by investment in a new gas pipeline or a maintenance project for a road or bridge—or hope in the form of a solution to the climate emergency proffered by high-speed rail or wind-generated electricity. All of these examples reveal how infrastructures "form us," as Larkin puts it, "as subjects not just on a technopolitical level but also through this mobilization of affect and the senses of desire, pride, and frustration, feelings which can be deeply political."[23]

So when Emerson describes the railroad as "highly poetic" and speaks of the "promise" of the nation's infrastructures or when he invites us to think of railroad iron as a kind of magic, it is no coincidence that he echoes twenty-first-century theorists of infrastructure. He understood that the railroad and the telegraph conveyed more than just passengers and messages; they also conveyed a set of affects: dreams of progress, hope for the future, wonder at human ingenuity, the promise of prosperity or freedom, the longing for a new or different world. As Larkin again puts it, infrastructures "create a sensing of modernity ... a process by which the body, as much as the mind, apprehends what it is to be modern, mutable, and progressive."[24] Emerson's writings and lectures on infrastructure helped teach his fellow citizens how to be modern, how to respond to the material changes taking place in the nineteenth-century US with assurance and exultation rather than apprehension. We might, then, read his rhetorical questions—"Who would live in the stone age, or the bronze, or the iron, or the lacustrine? Who does not prefer the age of steel, of gold, of coal petroleum, cotton, steam, electricity, and the spectroscope?"—as a kind of summons, an interpellation.

Build Back Better

Most of us see through the twenty-first-century version of that kind of ideological hailing, like the ubiquitous fossil fuel industry ads that remind us of all the luxuries and comforts the carbon economy has given us. But Emerson lived in a time of seemingly endless abundance, when so many of those luxuries were still on the horizon. Ours, by contrast, is the age of exhaustion, in which both our mineral and emotional stores have been all but depleted. As a result, it's hard to imagine experiencing the world again as Emerson did, with such confident cheer, with such optimism, with promises yet unbroken. Among the many challenges we face today is how to become re-energized—perhaps even more figuratively than literally.

President Biden has attempted to recapture some of that optimism with a massive new infrastructure initiative he has called "Build Back Better." In an address to the nation in October 2021, Biden outlined the framework, which he described as "the most significant investment to deal with the climate crisis ever" (a claim that is almost certainly true, if also mainly an indication of just how low the bar is for meaningful climate action by the government).[25] The plan called for ambitious new public investments in passenger rail, public transit, electric charging stations, wind farms, solar panels, and more. It called, too, for improvements to existing infrastructures, like bridges and interstates and water pipes and the internet—"rebuilding the arteries of our economy," as Biden put it. The rhetoric of Biden's speech at times seems to channel Emerson. The plan, Biden promised, will "turn the climate crisis into an opportunity" and in doing so will "transform the nation." "If we make these investments," he continued, "there will be no stopping us. We will own the future."

Build Back Better demonstrates one of the key paradoxes of modern infrastructure: that however much it may have been the way into the climate crisis, it will just as likely be an important part of the way out. And yet, despite what the techno-optimists (or those who still have faith that the Earth will yet again be "shaken by our engineries") might have us believe, a still deeper paradox may be that yesterday's infrastructure places constraints upon tomorrow's. That is, the lock-in effect of infrastructure is as much conceptual as it is material: just as some infrastructures lock-in future fossil fuel combustion, so do those same infrastructures, as they become embedded in our everyday lives and routines, help define the limits of what is and is not thinkable, locking us in to particular social arrangements. Here is President Biden, for example, on electric vehicles:

> We'll build out the first-ever national network of 500,000 electric vehicle charging stations all across the country. So, when you buy an electric vehicle, and you get credit for buying it—when you buy an electric vehicle, you can go all the way across

America on a "single tank of gas," figuratively speaking. It's not gas; you plug it in. Five hundred thousand of them—these stations along the way. (Biden)

Despite his rhetoric of transformation, what Biden envisions here is really more of the same; a series of substitutions (EVs for internal combustion vehicles, charging stations for gas stations) that maintain rather than alter fundamental existing social and economic orders. In material terms, Biden's vision of a highway system dotted with half a million charging stations preserves, rather than dismantles, extractive capitalism. Affectively, his vision of transcontinental mobility—"you can go all the way across America on a single tank of gas"—echoes Emerson's fantasy from almost two hundred years ago of a transportation infrastructure that promises "to subdue our enormous geography." Thus rather than a plan that promises to "transform the nation," Build Back Better, one might plausibly argue, again illustrates what Mark Simpson and Imre Szeman describe as "our constitutional inability to imagine transformation itself."[26]

At the same time, as much as I think we should work toward the end of extractive capitalism, I am wary of insisting too strenuously on a radical critique that rejects any measures that are not essentially revolutionary. To put it plainly, I *want* to build back better. I found myself energized by Biden's address, heartened by the possibility of concrete steps to reduce greenhouse gas emissions, eager to shop for a newly affordable electric vehicle. In fact, the result of Biden's ambitious initiative, the Inflation Reduction Act, will reduce US greenhouse emissions by more than 40 per cent in less than a decade—an astonishing figure given the past three decades of utter government torpor on the issue. And while that still might not be enough to prevent global temperatures from reaching the 2 degrees Celsius threshold set by the Intergovernmental Panel on Climate Change, it nevertheless constitutes the most significant action on climate to date, one that will yield measurable results. What's more, it's hard to know what other kinds of effects Biden's proposed infrastructural developments might have. After all, as much as a world of electric vehicles traversing American's interstates might still resemble a world of gas-powered vehicles traversing America's interstates, there are also significant differences. Charging takes time that pumping gas does not. What kinds of opportunities for sociality might those wait times generate? How might different rhythms of travel remake our sense of mobility, our relationship to the places we encounter? Electric stations and vehicles will also produce a whole new set of ambient experiences. What might result from the refashioning of our sensorium, as we rehabituate ourselves to the gentle hum of electric motors rather than the roar of engines? To the absence of the smell of gasoline? Might those experiences be first steps toward decarbonization? "Life," Emerson says in "Circles," "is a series of surprises" (*CW* 1:189).

I turn back to Emerson's "Circles" by way of conclusion here because it adds an important final dimension to his zeal for carbon and carbon infrastructure. Paradoxically, Emerson was just as eager—philosophically, at least—for their undoing as he was for their emergence. In "Circles," Emerson articulates a doctrine of surprise, the premise of which is that "permanence is a word of degrees" (*CW* 1:180), that all that we think of as fixed and stable—or settled, to use a key term from the essay—is in fact provisional, fugacious. The world we have, the world made by the carbon economy, was not inevitable nor is it indefinite. It's best, therefore, not to cling too tightly to it. We should seek, rather, "to be surprised out of our propriety," even if that means giving up what we've been conditioned to think of as safe, comforting, perdurable. "People wish to be settled," Emerson says; "only as far as they are unsettled is there any hope for them" (*CW* 2:189).

This kind of unsettling, it seems to me, is a crucial lesson for our thinking about the climate crisis and the prospect of decarbonization, thinking that is too often tyrannized over by notions like "our modern way of life," as if that were a thing settled, so deeply settled that other ways of being either seem impossible or like just too much sacrifice and loss (LeMenager terms this latter affective state "petromelancholia"). But Emerson offers instead a simple but powerful reversal of that concept, one that we might do well to heed if there's yet time remaining to avoid planetary catastrophe: "the way of life," Emerson writes, "is wonderful; it is by abandonment" (*CW* 2:190).

Notes

1. Jesse O. Taylor, *The Sky of Our Manufacture: The London Fog in British Fiction from Dickens to Woolf* (Charlottesville: University of Virginia Press, 2016), 23.
2. Stacey Balkan and Swaralipi Nandi, *Oil Fictions: World Literature and Our Contemporary Petrosphere* (University Park, Pennsylvania State University, 2021), 3.
3. Jamie L. Jones, *Rendered Obsolete: Energy Culture and the Afterlife of U.S. Whaling* (University of North Carolina Press, 2023), 7.
4. Richard White, *The Organic Machine: The Remaking of the Columbia River* (New York: Hill and Wang, 2011), 34.
5. Cara New Daggett, *The Birth of Energy* (Durham, NC: Duke University Press, 2019), 16, 3. Further citations appear parenthetically in the text.
6. See, for example, Leo Marx, *The Machine in the Garden: Technology and the Pastoral Ideal in America* (Oxford: Oxford University Press, 2000); and Neal Dolan, *Emerson's Liberalism* (University of Wisconsin Press, 2009).
7. Kregg Hetherington, *Infrastructure, Environment, and Life in the Anthropocene* (Durham, NC: Duke University Press, 2018), 7.
8. Nikhil Anand et al., *The Promise of Infrastructure* (Durham, NC: Duke University Press, 2018), 3; Dominic Boyer and Imre Szeman, *Energy Humanities: An Anthology* (Baltimore: Johns Hopkins University Press, 2017), 4.
9. Heather Houser, "Is Climate Writing Stuck?," *LitHub* (January 3, 2022), https://lithub.com/is-climate-writing-stuck/.
10. Laura Dassow Walls, "The Sphinx at the Crossroads: Transcendentalism Meets the Anthropocene," ESQ 67, no. 3 (2021): 697–730, 50.
11. Emerson's quip also calls to mind his remark in the essay "Eloquence" that "our Southern people are almost all speakers, and have every advantage over the New England people, whose climate is so cold that 'tis said we do not like to open our mouths very wide" (*CW* 7:34).
12. Thomas Carlyle and Ralph Waldo Emerson, *The Correspondence of Thomas Carlyle and Ralph Waldo Emerson, 1834–1872* (Boston: Ticknor and Company, 1886), 231.

13. This passage does not appear in the version of "The Fortune of the Republic" in Bosco and Myerson's *Later Lectures.*
14. Nor was Emerson unique in viewing fossil energy as a means of liberating the enslaved. On this point, see Andrew Nikiforuk, *The Energy of Slaves: Oil and the New Servitude* (Greystone Books, 2012).
15. Critiques of the Anthropocene concept are by now legion. For a rather droll survey of the term's limitations, see Dana Luciano, "The Anthropocene, 1945/1783/1610/1492–???? (or, I Wish I Knew How to Quit You)," in Timelines of American Literature, ed. Cody Marrs and Christopher Hager (Baltimore: Johns Hopkins University Press, 2019), 147–58.
16. David Walker, *An Appeal to the Coloured Citizens of the World* (Boston, 1829), 15.
17. Stephanie LeMenager, *Living Oil: Petroleum Culture in the American Century* (New York: Oxford University Press, 2014), 104.
18. Bob Johnson, *Mineral Rites: An Archaeology of the Fossil Economy* (Baltimore, Johns Hopkins University Press: 2019), 20.
19. Hetherington, *Infrastructure, Environment, and Life*, 6.
20. Henry David Thoreau, 1854, *Walden; Or, Life in the Woods*, ed. James Lyndon Shanley (Princeton, NJ: Princeton University Press, 1973), 27.
21. Anne Spice, "Fighting Invasive Infrastructures," *Environment and Society* 9, no. 1 (September 1, 2018): 40–56, 42, 45.
22. Brian Larkin, "The Politics and Poetics of Infrastructure," *Annual Review of Anthropology* 42, no. 1 (October 21, 2013): 327–43, 328.
23. Ibid., 333.
24. Ibid., 327.
25. Quotations from President Biden's speech are from Joseph Biden, "Statement by President Biden on Senate Passage of the Inflation Reduction Act," *The White House*, August 7, 2022, https://www.whitehouse.gov/briefing-room/statements-releases/2022/08/07/statement-by-president-biden-on-senate-passage-of-the-inflation-reduction-act/.
26. Mark Simpson and Imre Szeman, "Impasse Time," *South Atlantic Quarterly* 120, no. 1 (January 2021): 80.

CHAPTER 2

EMERSON UNDERSEA

MICHELE NAVAKAS AND DOMINIC MASTROIANNI

Introduction

A widely held view among scholars and other students of nineteenth-century American literature is that Emerson accepts, and even celebrates, the idea that human beings are and ought to be the possessors of the earth. Considered in this way, Emerson is more of an antagonist to contemporary environmental thinking than an ally. And there is evidence, no doubt, to support the view of Emerson as anti-environmental. Some of his early writings, including his first book, *Nature* (1836), appear to endorse the idea that human beings are the purpose for which the earth was made: "Nature is thoroughly mediate. It is made to serve. It receives the dominion of man as meekly as the ass on which the Saviour rode," Emerson reflects (*CW* 1:25). From one point of view, Emerson straightforwardly expresses that nonhuman nature is subservient to a dominant human species; as "mediate," it is not an end in itself, or even a great collective of ends. If we take this view as Emerson's primary and career-long conviction about nonhuman nature, then it is no wonder that Emerson is not more often taken up by scholars working in the Environmental Humanities.

One powerful origin of this now familiar portrait of an anti-environmental Emerson is Myra Jehlen's influential book *American Incarnation* (1986), where Jehlen posits that "Emersonian Transcendentalism is the philosophy of ... an unlimited individualism whereby the self transcends its mortal limits by taking total possession of an actual world. Emerson thus completed the development of the modern concept of individualism ... by projecting an individual who possesses the world in his own image."[1] Jehlen's book, Lawrence Buell observes in his own groundbreaking work *The Environmental Imagination* (1995), "directly linked Emerson's vision of the promise of the individual's mystical relation to nature to the middle-class myth of social contract as a compact of freeholders in a land of plenty," and thereafter Emerson's and other "literary and artistic representations of natural sublimity came to be seen as an arm of American manifest destiny." Buell himself claims that "Emerson's primary consideration" is "how nature might subserve humanity" and that, relative to Thoreau, Emerson is less "interested in defining nature's structure, both spiritual and material, for its own sake."[2] With some important recent exceptions, scholars of nineteenth-century American literature and culture have continued to reinforce this version of an anti-environmental Emerson.[3]

This anti-environmental Emerson would have been entirely unrecognizable to Rachel Carson, a careful reader of nineteenth-century literature and arguably the most influential American environmental writer of the twentieth century. Today Carson is best remembered as the author of *Silent Spring* (1962), a worldwide bestseller that exposed the far-ranging effects of chemical pesticides on nearly all forms of life, turned the tide of public opinion that led to the modern environmental movement and the founding of the EPA in the 1970s, and popularized the concept of ecology, by which we mean an understanding that all nature, human and nonhuman, is bound together by intricate relations and connections, each part inseparable from the whole.[4] Yet much of the power and appeal of *Silent Spring*, the last book that Carson published before her untimely death in 1964, derives from the ecological insights that Carson developed and refined across decades of research and writing for three earlier books about the sea: *Under the Sea-Wind* (1941), *The Sea around Us* (1951), and *The Edge of the Sea* (1955). In these less examined writings, we argue, Carson engages with, transforms, expands, and applies two distinctly Emersonian ideas, impersonality and abandonment, ultimately drawing out their vital relevance to ecological thinking and action.[5]

Upon first consideration, neither impersonality nor abandonment, at least as Emerson understands them, seems especially "environmental" in any familiar contemporary sense. At their core, both ideas relate to the nature of selfhood and being, and particularly to how the self comes to see something familiar under a new aspect. Emerson's impersonal, when manifested, can reveal the illusory nature of possession and individuality, and thereby direct us to renounce these aspects of selfhood; abandonment is that state of being created by an encounter with the impersonal. Both, as we will see, are crucial checks on any tendency toward an overconfident knowingness that would keep us from forming new perceptions of, and relations to, the world.[6] For many readers of Emerson, both ideas are admittedly difficult to understand, recognize, and imagine how to practice—let alone apply to any purpose we could call environmental.

Yet we examine how these two ideas manifest in Emerson's early and understudied descriptions of water and the sea, arguing that watery life and environments—as they appear in his lecture "Water" (1834) and in some of his writings from the early 1840s— enabled Emerson to define and recommend impersonality and abandonment with particular clarity and force.[7] We then show how Rachel Carson mines the environmental potential of each idea in her own early and underanalyzed writings on the sea.[8] An avid and lifelong reader of nineteenth-century American literature, Carson proposes that Emersonian modes of human knowledge of the self, the world, and the place of the self within the world are the first, critical steps toward understanding and acting more justly within a vast and interconnected ecology. Carson did not view human or more-than-human nature in just the ways that Emerson did; yet some of Carson's most galvanizing ecological insights may have been unthinkable without Emerson.[9]

Our chapter proceeds in two parts: the first centers on impersonality, and the second on abandonment. Each part begins with an explanation of the idea at hand as it appears in Emerson's writings, traces its development in his thoughts on water, and then explores the environmental afterlife and potential of that concept within Carson's marine reflections. A conclusion further reflects on what new understanding we gain by attending to Carson's overlooked uptake of Emerson, which obliges us, among other things, to take seriously the value of reading Emerson at the Anthropocene. Throughout, our collective approach to both writers is one of sustained reflection on the philosophical and political implications that emerge from their descriptions of the material nature of water, including tides, currents, and submarine and shore life. For another tie that binds these thinkers is their shared interest in persuading through descriptions that draw the reader toward adopting a new and unfamiliar perspective.

IMPERSONALITY

Emerson's Watery Impersonal

The impersonal goes by a number of names in Emerson's writing. More precisely, and as Sharon Cameron demonstrates, "the impersonal" is one term for a topic to which Emerson never gives a settled name, using variously "the Over-Soul," "alien energy," "identical nature," and "common heart," among other terms.[10] In the part of "The Over-Soul" (1841) where he writes of "the impersonal," he makes it sufficiently clear that for him it is equally correct to speak of "a common nature" and "God" (*CW* 2:164). So, in "Experience" (1844), Emerson calls the impersonal a "cause, which refuses to be named,—ineffable cause, which every fine genius has essayed to represent by some emphatic symbol, as, Thales by water, Anaximenes by air, Anaxagoras by (*Noûs*) thought, Zoroaster by fire, Jesus and the moderns by love" (*CW* 3:42).

The placement of Thales's "water" first in this list is instructive: it indicates an emphasis on water that Emerson confirms a few sentences later when imagining the impersonal as somehow oceanic. Emerson reflects, "In our more correct writing, we give to this generalization the name of Being, and thereby confess that we have arrived as far as we can go. Suffice it for the joy of the universe, that we have not arrived at a wall, but at interminable oceans" (*CW* 3:42). These "interminable oceans" are not things we apprehend through mystical visions that create an evanescent alternate reality, or substitute for our daily experiences on earth. Rather, as Cameron observes, Emerson's impersonal is always "incarnated" or "manifested" in a perceivable reality, "through actions, emotions, properties, only through what is actual and even at times visible."[11]

At the same time, Emersonian impersonality permits no final categorical distinction between the material and the immaterial, a distinction that he regularly refuses to make:

"[T]he act of seeing and the thing seen, the seer and the spectacle, the subject and the object, are one" ("The Over-Soul," *CW* 2:160). He puts it this way in "Compensation" (1841): "Every thing in nature contains all the powers of nature. Every thing is made of one hidden stuff" (*CW* 2:59). With these two insights as guideposts—that the impersonal must manifest itself, and that there is no absolute distinction between material and immaterial things—we will continue to explore the meaning of Emersonian impersonality by turning to Emerson's more direct reflections on water.[12]

More than it is earthy or fiery or airy, the impersonal is watery. At least, the impersonal is more often imagined by Emerson as water than as anything else. For instance, in "The Over-Soul" Emerson defines moments when the impersonal offers "manifestations of its own nature" as instances of "an influx of the Divine mind into our mind." He then underscores the watery nature of this influx: "It is an ebb of the individual rivulet before the flowing surges of the sea of life" (*CW* 2:166). As early twentieth-century scholar O. W. Firkins insightfully observes, the "impression" we get of the Over-Soul "is vast and fluid—oceanic, in short; with men as arms or inlets of the sea" (1915, 338). Emerson at times thinks of human beings as "inlets" to the impersonal. In "The Divinity School Address" (1838), for instance, he writes of a "sentiment" that manifests the impersonal to the one who feels it, "showing the fountain of all good to be in himself, and that he, equally with every man, is an inlet into the deeps of Reason" (*CW* 1:79). And in "History" (1841) we are told: "There is one mind common to all individual men. Every man is an inlet to the same and to all of the same" (*CW* 2:3).

If Emerson imagines the impersonal as water, he also insists that the impersonal shows itself in actual water. In "Nature" (1844) he writes of the impersonal as a "power" that "distils its essence into every drop of rain" (*CW* 3:113). And the particular material processes that Emerson describes in his early lecture, "Water" (1834), seem to us a particularly useful basis for understanding Emerson's later thinking about the precise nature of the impersonal.

"Water" proposes that everything breaks down into particles that are carried to the ocean, where they mix together with one another and the sea. For example, Emerson makes the following observation: "[The sea] dissolves and holds in solution a great number of substances... All animal, all vegetable, all mineral particles one after the other are continually carried down from higher levels to lower levels and finally delivered into the sea" (*EL* 1:56). All matter ("all animal, all vegetable, all mineral particles") converges in the sea. The sea, then, serves as a material epitome for Emerson's monist view that everything is made of "one stuff." Everything, moreover, falls. The image of descent that recurs in Emerson's descriptions of the impersonal seems to originate in his way of thinking about the material processes that carry all matter to the sea. With the sea in mind, Emerson pictures not a fallen world but a world of falling. On this earth, as Emerson sees it, everything falls; and to this claim he adds the audacious addendum that nothing ascends: "The fruitful field is carried down little by little into the sea as well as the mountain brought down to the field. Every thing falls down and is decomposed. Nothing ascends" (*EL* 1:55).[13]

Emerson's insistence that the impersonal "descends"—into humans, into the rest of nature—is a continuation and development of his early idea that everything travels downward in a journey to the seafloor. The opening paragraph of "The Over-Soul" imagines human beings as water and claims that we are what descends into us: "Man is a stream whose source is hidden. Our being is descending into us from we know not whence" (*CW* 2:159). Later in that essay he returns to this image of a life that descends into us. Describing the impersonal as an "inevitable nature" by which "private will is overpowered," Emerson claims that "this energy does not descend into individual life, on any other condition than entire possession" (*CW* 2:169, 171). The individual life does not possess this energy, in other words, but is possessed by it. Under this possession, a person becomes a passage through which impersonal thoughts are channeled: "Thoughts come into our minds by avenues which we never left open, and thoughts go out of our minds through avenues which we never voluntarily opened" (*CW* 2:169). One who expresses such thoughts (who has "become porous to thought") is portrayed as a sea-drinker, "bibulous of the sea of light" (*CW* 2:172).

"The Over-Soul" describes the impersonal as both a "common heart" and an oceanic blood rolling through all human beings and all of nature: "The heart in thee is the heart of all; not a valve, not a wall, not an intersection is there anywhere in nature, but one blood rolls uninterruptedly, an endless circulation through all men, as the water of the globe is all one sea, and, truly seen, its tide is one" (*CW* 2:160, 173–74). This description of impersonality echoes the moment in "Water" (1834) when Emerson pointed to "the beautiful phenomenon" of water's "eternal circulation through nature": "The circulation of the water in the globe is no less beautiful a law than the circulation of blood in the body" (*EL* 1:63).

The impersonal is thus within us while also surrounding us. It is "that Over-soul, within which every man's particular being is contained," a "deep power in which we exist." At the same time, "within man is the soul of the whole" ("The Over-Soul," *CW* 2:160). Likewise, water is both inside of us and everywhere around us. Water "circulates in our veins, is present in every function of life, grows in the vegetable, is a cement, and an engineer, and an architect, in inanimate nature"; water acts "in the pulse, in the brain, in the eye, in a plant, in mist, in crystal, in a volcano," so that we can "see the same particle in every step of this ceaseless revolution serving the life, the order, the happiness of the Universe"; "suspended waters are present in the air when it is most dry and transparent and we have not only a visible ocean at our feet but we are thus always bathed in an invisible ocean overhead, and around us" ("Water," *EL* 1:51, 68, 63). The all-pervasive nature of the impersonal, which is near us even when we do not recognize it, has as its basis this thought from "Water": "No man yet knows how many offices this element fulfills ... it hides itself very cunningly sometimes close by us, and sometimes becomes invisible, and sometimes works in places inaccessible to us that we can witness only its surface action" (*EL* 1:50–51).

What, finally, does water teach us about the impersonal in these early reflections of Emerson's? For one, water teaches the lesson of the insufficiency of the human will to human flourishing, for while we can control water in some ways, water's "unseen services, over which we have no control, are greater than all these which we direct" (*EL* 1:51). Water also usefully manifests processes of metamorphosis, dissolution, and organization—processes that are ongoing and everywhere, yet harder to perceive when it comes to other elements. And partly for these reasons, thinking about water acts corrosively and beneficially on our possessiveness and self-centeredness. For whenever we see that everything is of the same nature, that the impersonal is all-pervasive, we must also begin to abandon the perception of human beings as masters of the earth, or even ourselves.[14] Thus through Emerson's "watery impersonal" run currents of thought that connect him to Carson's sea writings and, thereby, to a more contemporary understanding of ecology itself.

Carson's "Material Immortality"

Before authoring three volumes on oceans and ocean life, Carson introduced some of her most crucial ideas about nature in "Undersea" (1937), a short essay from which, she later wrote, "everything else followed."[15] Published in the *Atlantic Monthly*, the four-page "Undersea" brilliantly blends Carson's scientific knowledge of ocean currents and marine life—gained largely through her graduate training at Johns Hopkins University and her research position with the US Fish and Wildlife Service—with the "feeling of absolute fascination for everything relating to the ocean," which Carson counted among her "earliest conscious memories."[16]

A central proposal of "Undersea" is that "every living thing of the ocean, plant and animal alike, returns to the water at the end of its own life span the materials that had been temporarily assembled to form its body."[17] And thus, the narrator observes, "there descends into the depth a gentle, never-ending rain of what once were living creatures ... Here in the sea mingle elements which, in their long and amazing history, have lent life and strength and beauty to a bewildering variety of living creatures."[18] In the essay's closing lines, this process is given a name: "material immortality."[19]

According to this "inexorable [law] of the sea," all ocean matter endures forever. For "individual elements are lost to view, only to reappear again and again in different incarnations," such that "the life span of a particular plant or animal appears, not as a drama complete in itself, but only as a brief interlude in a panorama of endless change."[20] Put otherwise, all sea bodies, from mollusks to coral, are temporary assemblages of matter, ceaselessly emerging from and contributing to other life forms.

Carson continues to develop these ideas in *Under the Sea-Wind*, which introduces readers to the sea by way of different animal protagonists—various sea birds, "Scomber" the mackerel, and "Anguilla" the eel—who do not belong to themselves. The materials that compose them might just as easily have composed the bodies of any number of other sea creatures, and will certainly go on to compose other and future bodies. Scomber, for example, began as an egg that barely escaped being "seized and eaten by the comb jellies, to be speedily converted into the watery tissue of their foe and in this reincarnation to roam the sea, preying on their own kind."[21] Mackerel become comb jellies, which are mackerel eggs, preying on other mackerel eggs, while also becoming still other ocean forms, "reclaimed for other uses by the sea," as Carson writes of the bodies of another species of jellyfish.[22] Or, as she elsewhere observes of this watery world, "one dies, another lives, as the precious elements of life are passed on and on in endless chains" (65), all "used over and over again in the fashioning of other creatures."[23]

While in "Undersea" and *Under the Sea-Wind* Carson confines "material immortality" to sea materials alone, in later sea writings she includes all matter. A particularly vivid description of this all-encompassing process appears in "The Long Snowfall," the title of Chapter 6 of *The Sea around Us*. "When I think of the floor of the deep sea," Carson reflects, "the single, overwhelming fact that possesses my imagination is the accumulation of sediments. I see always the steady, unremitting, downward drift of materials from above, flake upon flake, layer upon layer—a drift that has continued for hundreds of millions of years, that will go on as long as there are seas and continents."[24] We are all, every one of us, caught up in "the long snowfall"; the sea "encompasses all the dim origins of life and receives in the end, after, it may be, many transmutations, the dead husks of that same life. For all at last return to the sea—to Oceanus, the ocean river, like the ever-flowing stream of time, the beginning and the end."[25]

When Emerson thought of the seafloor, he imagined something very like this process. In "Water," we recall, Emerson reflects that the sea "dissolves and holds in solution a great number of substances" and that "[a]ll animal, all vegetable, all mineral particles ... are continually carried down from higher levels to lower levels and finally delivered into the sea," there to begin "forming" new "strata" (*EL* 1:56). For both writers, then, the sea makes particularly and materially imaginable something that humans have profound difficulty understanding otherwise: all, even the bodies we call "ours," is nothing personal.

And for Carson the sea not only helps us shed the illusion of exclusionary, durable possession, but it also—and consequently—helps us grasp our true relation to all being as one of lending and borrowing. In Carson's formulation, possession in a more familiar Anglo-American sense is literally unthinkable since individual elements endure *only* by passing continually to and from other entities.[26] This is why the language of borrowing and lending infuses Carson's reflections on material immortality from the concept's very first appearance in "Undersea," where she writes that "every living thing of the ocean, plant and animal alike, *returns* to the water at the end of its own life span the materials that had been *temporarily assembled* to form its body." Those materials, she continues, once "*lent* life" to other "living creatures" composed of elements "*borrowed*" from and "*returned*" to the sea.[27] All, in Carson's words, is "interlude," a temporal and/or spatial pause in between.[28] As interlude, no entity is discrete or complete in itself. Each life exists only among and because of others.

What might be the potential environmental value of perceiving ourselves, body and mind, as impersonal? According to Stacy Alaimo, one environmental importance of reading Carson's sea writings is that we come to understand that "containment is not possible," that what we do to one part of nature we inevitably do to all others, ourselves included.[29] Another is that we might begin to understand humans as "trans-corporeal,"

Alaimo's term for "a new materialist and posthumanist sense of the human as perpetually interconnected with the flows of substances and the agencies of environments."[30]

In a direction more characteristically Emersonian, however, we might come to understand that while we live we do not own matter outright, but rather hold it temporarily in trust from, and for, other beings, living and nonliving. "[I]n the sea nothing lives to itself," observes Carson memorably in her final ocean book, *The Edge of the Sea*.[31] Yet by now we know that, for Carson, all is sea, and so what she means to say is that the sea's material nature helps us perceive that "nothing lives to itself." Carson says something quite close to this in the book's opening chapter where she writes that the shore "keeps alive the sense of continuing creation and of the relentless drive of life. Each time that I enter it, I gain some new awareness of its beauty and its deeper meanings, sensing that intricate fabric of life by which one creature is linked with another, and each with its surroundings."[32] These lines frame her final ocean book as an exploration of how the sea helps us "sense," or "gain some new awareness of," things that are true for all life, all matter—possibly even consciousness itself.

The suggestion that human consciousness is subject to that same law of borrowings and lendings threads through the book's epilogue, part of which Carson requested to be read at her funeral. Gazing at the "coastal forms" of the shore, the epilogue's first-person narrator understands that "there is no finality, no ultimate and fixed reality," for "the flow of time" is always "obliterating yet containing all that has gone before."[33] "And so we come to perceive life as a force as tangible as any of the physical realities of the sea."[34] Perhaps the most expansive vision of "material immortality" in all of Carson's work, the epilogue posits that even "time" and "life" are matter and, as such, persons are interludes existing only as passage among forms.

Abandonment

Emerson's Submarine Sensibility

If for Emerson the impersonal is what overpowers private will, showing that possessiveness is delusional, then what state of being remains? One possibility is a state of abandonment. Sometimes Emerson characterizes abandonment as self-surrender. At other times he describes it as an imprudent alternative to self-possession.[35] And in "The Poet" (1844), we are told that by "abandonment to the nature of things" a person may get beyond their "possessed and conscious intellect" (*CW* 2:15). When abandonment occurs, then, we can no longer be said to possess ourselves. Abandonment is a state beyond one's own will, outside of the self's sphere of control.

When in a state of abandonment, moreover, the mind moves beyond customary limits, abandoning familiar points of view. The way to what Emerson calls "a new prospect," abandonment has three primary dimensions that we might call epistemic, social, and existential ("Circles," *CW* 2:181). First, abandonment is the relinquishment of some part of one's intellectual equipment, the letting go of a theory or mode of understanding. Abandonment is also a feeling that changes one's relation to others, a fervor that produces a temporary obliviousness to manners and customs. Finally, abandonment is a moment of faith that places the self in the care of a power superior to whatever that self privately possesses.[36]

Emerson seeks to demonstrate that thinking about water and marine life can help us develop a sensibility that is open to abandonment, what in "Nature" (1836) he calls "entire humility" (*CW* 1:39). In "Water," for example, Emerson connects the way we think about sea creatures to what he would later call abandonment when he presents and comments on a lengthy passage from the work of French naturalist Georges Cuvier that portrays life undersea as an exercise in bodily and especially in sensory deprivation. Observing that this portrayal of the impoverished sensuous life of sea creatures contains something "almost pathetic," Emerson quotes Cuvier's account, which includes the following claims: sea creatures' "vital energy" is "less than in Mammals and Birds"; relative to "all vertebrated animals," fish "have the least apparent signs of sensibility"; "all those sentiments awakened or sustained by the voice have remained unknown to them"; their inflexible bodies "do not leave them any power of ... expressing their emotions"; ears are nearly useless to those "destined to live in the empire of silence"; their eyes produce no tears, and so on (*EL* 1:61–62). Emerson admits what appears to be the expressive and emotional poverty of sea creatures: "Truly the ocean children seem to be in a destitute condition" (*EL* 1:63). But this apparent destitution may reflect the limitations of human senses and mental powers, more than the reality of life undersea: "These creatures judged by our senses and powers in the upper air seem to be the creatures of privation." Here Emerson suggests that sea creatures only "seem" to lack the necessities of a good life because "our senses and powers in the upper air" are poorly suited to the task of understanding life undersea (*EL* 1:61).

Emerson seems to be well aware that the pathos in Cuvier stems from an illusion: when we read about fish, we imagine not fish but human beings who have known a rich life of sensibility and an exquisite power of expression, and then found themselves suddenly deprived of these things. After quoting Cuvier, Emerson writes: "[B]ut as men say one half the world does not know how the other half lives, much more is it true that one species have no organs for detecting the powers and satisfactions which exist in other species and are denied to itself." Here Emerson effects a cool turn from Cuvier, a quiet rebuke. Making a point we will find in Carson, Emerson insists that human beings cannot experience the world as fish do, and cannot understand their pleasures or desires: we simply "have no organs" for doing so. Emerson concludes this portion of the lecture by portraying human beings as creatures of privation: we do not merely lack, but are "denied" the "powers and satisfactions which exist in other species" (*EL* 1:63).

If human beings cannot know the powers or satisfactions enjoyed by marine animals, such animals can still help us think about our capacity for transformation and the profound changes we sometimes undergo. In "Compensation" (1841), Emerson imagines abandonment by portraying souls as shellfish: "Every soul is by this intrinsic necessity [of growth] quitting its whole system of things, its friends, and home, and laws, and faith, as the shell-fish crawls out of its beautiful but stony case, because it no longer admits of its growth, and slowly forms a new house." Emerson portrays this wholesale abandonment as something that happens to everyone, a period in the life of "every soul." But phases of crustaceous metamorphosis are more "frequent" for some people than for others. Emerson imagines a "happier mind," happier presumably than any he knows of, in which "these revolutions ... are incessant, and all worldly relations hang very loosely about him, becoming, as it were, a transparent fluid membrane through which the living form is seen, and not as in most men an indurated heterogeneous fabric of many dates, and of no settled character, in which the man is imprisoned" (*CW* 2:72).

Abandonment here is liberation from imprisonment, is a state of being whose frequency correlates with what Emerson calls happiness. In the often-cited final paragraph of "Circles," Emerson makes it clear that abandonment is all-desirable: "The one thing which we seek with insatiable desire, is to forget ourselves." The alternative to abandonment is death, since abandonment is the way of life: "The way of life is wonderful: it is by abandonment" (*CW* 2:190). In other words, abandonment is the way in which a human life is energized by an encounter with the impersonal. Abandonment is the way to open oneself to "life," understood as the influx of an impersonal vital energy: the way to achieve a sense of aliveness and what in "Experience" (1844) Emerson calls "superfluity of spirit for new creation" (*CW* 3:27). In "Circles" he imagines the struggle between life and the boundary that would "hem in the life" as a drama playing out on the deep sea: "If the soul is quick and strong, it bursts over that boundary on all sides, and expands another orbit on the great deep, which also runs up into a high wave, with attempt again to stop and to bind. But the heart refuses to be imprisoned" (*CW* 2:181).

As an intellectual transformation, abandonment is both the acceptance of a watery impersonal and the relinquishment of a misguided curiosity. In "The Over-Soul" Emerson recommends a practice of abandoning what he calls low curiosity, a crudely sexualized desire to know what we cannot know. Impelled by a debased curiosity, the mind may seek answers to certain "sensual questions" or "questions which we lust to ask"; these include "how long men shall exist, what their hands shall do, and who shall be their company, adding names, and dates, and places" (*CW* 2:167–68). The appropriate response to this ordinary but, to Emerson, vicious Augustinian curiosity is to practice an abandonment which is also an acceptance: "The only mode of obtaining an answer to these questions of the senses, is, to forego all low curiosity, and, accepting the tide of being which floats us into the secret of nature, work and live, work and live" (*CW* 2:168). Later in the essay Emerson suggests that the way to such abandonment is to become "lowly and simple," with a willingness to "put off what is foreign and proud" (*CW* 2:171). This means to practice "entire humility"—a stance Emerson recommends to even "the best read naturalist"—or, as he later describes it, to "hold hard" to a certain "poverty" ("Nature," *CW* 1:39; "Experience," *CW* 3:46).

To abandon a sense of epistemic mastery of the natural world, Emerson suggests, one should imagine that world as thoroughly watery.[37] A journal entry that he used in composing "The Method of Nature" (1841) depicts a strangely flowing, liquid universe. Emerson describes walking in a dream with someone who told him: "As the river flows, & the plant flows (or emits odors), and the sun flows (or radiates), & the mind is a stream of thoughts, so was the universe the emanation of God." Reminding us that to emanate is, etymologically, to flow out, Emerson continues: "Every thing is an emanation, & from every emanation is a new emanation, & that from which it emanates is an emanation also. If anything could stand still, it would be instantly crushed and dissipated by the torrent which it resisted, & if it were a mind, would be crazed" (*JMN* 7:449). Emerson articulates an epistemological stance according to which we cannot perfectly know, or express, anything; all statements exaggerate or communicate partially. So it is misguided to try to say something with complete truth, to imagine that our claims could encapsulate a world whose nature is flux. Thinking is like sailing, where course corrections are normal and we zigzag from one place to another.[38]

Carson's "Temporary Abandonment"

"Who has known the ocean?"[39] Thus begins Carson's "Undersea," that short essay from which "everything else followed." When the essay appeared in print in 1937, oceanographic knowledge, even among scientists such as Carson, was sparse. Diving equipment was not yet commercially available. Much of the seafloor remained unmapped and unexplored. Its geological history was relatively unknown.[40] Yet "Undersea" proposes that, however advanced human technology becomes, the sea will always elude complete human knowledge. "Neither you nor I" can ever fully know the ocean and its myriad life forms, she proposes, because we can never entirely escape "our earth-bound senses."[41]

Nonetheless, the project of trying to know the sea is of significant epistemic value because it requires one to try the experience of shedding something of the self. "To sense this world of waters known to the creatures of the sea we must shed our human perceptions of length and breadth and time and place, and enter vicariously into a universe of all-pervading water."[42] In the foreword to her first ocean volume (1941) Carson would give this practice a name: "temporary abandonment." "To get the feeling of what it is like to be a creature of the sea requires the active exercise of the imagination and the temporary abandonment of many human concepts and human yardsticks," she reflects, such as "time measured by the clock or the calendar."[43] Yet as we make these "adjustments in our thinking," "we must not depart too far." Sensing the sea appears to require actively abandoning human senses, while always remembering that full abandonment and complete knowledge of the sea are impossible to achieve. Put another way, temporary abandonment is a practice of continually checking our tendency toward an overly certain knowingness, which would prevent us from attaining any knowledge of the sea at all.

But how can we come to grasp and enact this active, always incomplete sensory abandonment for the sake of sensing the sea? Arguably the entire project of Carson's sea books is to show how the sea helps us in that project, which in turn is foundational to comprehending a reality that most humans struggle to conceptualize: all of nature, ourselves included, is one ecological system.

Carson helps readers pursue "adjustments" toward abandonment by adopting different narrative points of view, a stylistic choice that encourages us to feel the limits of, and sometimes decenter, a more traditionally Anglo-American understanding of the more-than-human world as separate from and less important than humans. In "Undersea," for example, the narrator surveys the sea from the unusual perspective of an underwater eye *watching* an underwater eye perceive.[44] About halfway into "Undersea" the narrator introduces the figure of "an undersea traveler," "dropping downward" to the seafloor, "a land where the noonday sun is swathed in twilight blues and purples, and where the blackness of midnight is eerily aglow with the cold phosphorescence of living things."[45] Readers then follow this figure among "rock ledges," through "deep ravines" of the continental shelf, over "undersea plateaus" and "submerged islands," as they see through seawater the "crystal cones" of sea snails, "spine-studded urchins," the "sessile forms of life" affixed to rock formations, a bewildering variety of fishes.[46]

It is possible to forget that we are seeing all of this through the eyes of the traveler. But we cannot forget for long. By punctuating the most engrossing and sonorous descriptions of the undersea with references to the traveler, and to what they are, would be, or could be seeing, the essay creates an overall experience of imaginative immersion that expands and then stops short by turns. It thus allows us to practice an always increasing, though never complete, sensory renunciation. For we never quite see exactly what the traveler sees: we know that we are seeing them seeing, that they see what we cannot, and that, however much they see, they cannot see it all. Carried along by Carson's seductive writing we indeed "shed our human perceptions of length and breadth and time and place"[47] yet remember, too, that full renunciation and complete knowledge are impossible, which the traveler may forget.

In *Under the Sea-Wind*, Carson replaces the human "traveler" with a succession of various sea creatures with names. We understand what we can of the sea by imagining the perceptions of sea birds Rynchops, Blackfoot, and Silverbar; Scomber the mackerel; and Anguilla the eel. Carson explains this narrative device as a kind of strategic anthropomorphism that enables what sea knowledge it is possible for humans to attain. By encouraging us to identify with nonhuman life, sometimes by describing their struggles in human terms of fear or desire, the protagonist-driven narrative of *Sea-Wind* continually lures us beneath the surface to sense marine rhythms of survival and reproduction. But it also repeatedly checks that immersion with reminders that sea time and scale and being are not human.[48] Embryonic mackerel survive nearly impossible odds only to fall prey to passing "hordes" of "enemy" glassworms, which are "terrible as dragons" to "smaller beings" though miniscule "as men measure."[49] Silver eels, in their annual passage from rivers to sea, pass also "from human sight and almost from human knowledge" (139); "no one can trace the path of the eels."[50] The abyssal reaches of the Atlantic are best measured in "ages of geologic time"[51] that human minds cannot fathom. Thus Carson brings the sea into human experience and understanding—as no book had before—partly to help us feel the contours and constraints of "earth-bound senses"[52]

In her final ocean volume, *The Edge of the Sea* (1955), Carson offers a practical way to practice temporary abandonment: look into a tide pool. The book was supposed to be a nature guide, something like the Audubon guides one uses to identify trees, but Carson refuses the genre's convention of describing each facet of nature in isolation from the others, instead striving to achieve what Sue Hubbell calls a new "way of looking," an ecological perspective that produces a truer understanding of organisms in relation to one another and their environments.[53] In *Edge of the Sea* the perceiver is the narrator who, sometimes sliding into first-person, brings readers into the shore's various, interconnected worlds that always verge on other worlds. "Tide pools contain mysterious worlds within their depths, where all the beauty of the sea is subtly suggested and portrayed in miniature," begins Carson's remarkable and extensive reflection on these places at the shore.[54] As microcosms of the sea, tide pools offer us the chance to practice finding and feeling the limits of human vision. They are remarkably adapted to this purpose because they are so seemingly visible and accessible to us.

Accordingly the narrator moves across several tide pools in memory, concluding with the smallest and most apparently comprehensible. "I remember one that occupied the shallowest of depressions; as I lay outstretched on the rocks I could easily touch its far shore" and observe the living beings therein, for "the water in which they lived was so clear as to be invisible to my eyes."[55] The narrator touches the water's surface, below which sunlight "reached down and surrounded" all within, illuminating the most minute body parts of each of the interdependent "tiny beings," the shell of each mussel, each Sertularian hydroid's miniscule "crown of tentacles."[56] Yet that sense of direct, unmediated access to this world suddenly stops short: "On what, I wondered, were these Sertularians feeding? From their very abundance I knew that whatever creatures served them as food must be infinitely more numerous than the carnivorous hydroids themselves. Yet I could see nothing."[57] So, she looks *even more closely*:

> Somewhere in the crystal clarity of the pool my eye—or so it seemed—could detect a fine mist of infinitely small particles, like dust motes in a ray of sunshine. Then as I looked more closely the motes had disappeared and there seemed to be once more only that perfect clarity, and the sense that there had been an optical illusion. Yet I knew it was only the human imperfection of my vision that prevented me from seeing those microscopic hordes that were the prey of the groping, searching tentacles I could barely see. Even more than the visible life, that which was unseen came to dominate my thoughts, and finally the invisible throng seemed to me the most powerful beings in the pool. Both the hydroids and the mussels were utterly dependent on this invisible flotsam of the tide streams...[58]

The knowledge produced by looking into and touching the "crystal clarity" (116) of this "shallowest of depressions" (115), then, is that no amount of human looking—of adjusting one's vision and scale, of zooming in ever more closely—can yield full knowledge of what one sees.

But in that way the experience can yield self-knowledge of a kind. By seeking closer and closer contact with the tide pool, the narrator gains what may be the fullest possible human understanding of it, while also gaining an understanding of the limits of her perception. For what finally comes to "dominate" her mind is the "unseen," the knowledge that beings and forces ultimately "invisible" to her are indispensable to this site and the life therein.

Conclusion

Both Emerson and Carson were latecomers to the sea, and both became sea thinkers.[59] For each, water is the matter that enables humans to perceive their actual relation to, and place within, the rest of the natural world. The sea in particular teaches a kind of skepticism toward human knowledge, vision, and mastery. After all, what stops Carson's tide pool narrator in the wake of her intense and intimate looking—what causes her to say "I could see nothing"—is a sudden conviction that the tide world is not complete unto itself, but rather dependent upon, and in turn sustaining, countless other "worlds" that she can see either partially or not at all.

For Carson, that conviction is the basis of more ethical human action toward the more-than-human world. As Neil W. Browne has recently observed, Carson's implicit proposal that "this world is something we can barely sense" (2007, 105) enjoins "an ethical imperative" that we handle ourselves with "renewed respect and restraint" toward all of nature since we cannot know how actions that affect one part of the natural world may also affect the rest.[60] In fact, few readers of Carson would contest the idea that she recommends "respect and restraint" toward the more-than-human world, particularly because that is the relatively explicit thesis of her final book, *Silent Spring*.[61] Carson ultimately wove Emersonian philosophical concepts into her most resonant environmental claim: humans act within, and are responsible toward, a larger ecological system that we do not fully understand.

A comparison of the early sea thinking of Carson and Emerson, then, illuminates otherwise imperceptible currents in each, currents that draw us toward a new understanding of both. Reading Carson alongside Emerson deepens our understanding of Carson's philosophical, literary, and ethical complexity, alerting us that she arrived at her later and most well-known environmental insights only after decades of wrestling with many of the ideas about self, being, and the true relation between humans and the more-than-human-world that Emerson also wrestled with across his own writing life. In turn, the prospect of a wholly unexamined American transcendentalist genealogy of some of Carson's more radical environmental proposals indicates that Emerson may rightly belong to a much longer tradition of American ecological thinking than most readers of Emerson have suspected. By attending to Emerson's immersion in the sea's rhythms, the habits of its minute creatures, and its submarine cycles of birth and death, we broaden our understanding of the workings and reach of his thought. We may also arrive at the ontological and epistemological insights that we most need for navigating our own moment of unprecedented, human-driven environmental peril.

Notes

1. Myra Jehlen, *American Incarnation: the Individual, the Nation, and the Continent* (Cambridge, MA: Harvard University Press, 1986), 77.
2. Lawrence Buell, *The Environmental Imagination: Thoreau, Nature Writing, and the Formation of American Culture* (Cambridge, MA: Harvard University Press, 1995), 35, 117. More recently Laura Dassow Walls traces similar views of nature in some of Emerson's early lectures, writing that there Emerson at times presents "a view confident almost to the point of smugness" in his understanding of the universe as "so benign, so utterly in and for our possession, that it cannot seriously threaten us with real danger." See Laura Dassow Walls, *Emerson's Life in Science: The Culture of Truth* (Ithaca, NY: Cornell University Press, 2003), 93. See also Louise Hutchings Westling, *The Green Breast of the New World: Landscape, Gender, and American Fiction* (Athens: University of Georgia Press, 1996), 42–53; and Matthew A. Taylor, "The Nature of Fear: Edgar Allan Poe and Posthuman Ecology," *American Literature* 84, no. 2 (2012): 353–79, 354–55.
3. Among such exceptions, the work of Susan L. Dunston, *Emerson and Environmental Ethics* (Lanham, MD: Lexington Books, 2018) stands out: "Emerson's writings are not included in environmental ethics anthologies, though his own 'iron string' (*CWE* 2:28) would have vibrated to the new fields of environmental ethics and studies," Dunston persuasively argues (18). Also see James C. McKusick, *Green Writing: Romanticism and Ecology* (New York: St. Martin's Press, 2000), who laments a general refusal, among scholars, to heed Emerson's "challenge to conventional ways of understanding the place of humankind in the natural world" and argues for "Emerson's fundamental importance to the formation of an authentically ecological conception" of nature (136). And more recently Andrea Knutson and Kathryn Dolan ("Fugitive Environmentalisms," *The Journal of the Midwest Modern Language Association* 49, no. 1 [Spring 2016]: 7–24) find Emerson vital to defining "fugitive environmentalisms," while Michael P. Branch and Clinton Mohs (*The Best Read Naturalist: Nature Writings of Ralph Waldo Emerson* [Charlottesville: University of Virginia Press, 2017]) locate an "environmental Emerson" in his natural history writings, rather than in "his more canonical essays" (xxvii). These interpretations of Emerson resonate with recent scholarship on Melville and ecology, and particularly Tom Nurmi's analysis of Melville as a writer "attuned to the intricate entanglement of human and nonhuman realms ... in terms we now recognize as hallmarks of ecology" (see Tom Nurmi, *Magnificent Decay: Melville and Ecology* [Charlottesville: University of Virginia Press, 2020], 1–2).
4. For a discussion of some origins and complex meanings of "ecology" in American thought and letters more broadly, see Sharon E. Kingsland, *The Evolution of American Ecology, 1890–2000* (Baltimore: Johns Hopkins University Press, 2005). Carson's particular contributions to ecology and ecological thinking are usefully discussed by Linda Lear (*Rachel Carson: Witness for Nature* [New York: Henry Holt, 1997]), Sue Hubbell ("Introduction," in *The Edge of the Sea* [Boston: Mariner Books, 1998], xv–xxi), Linda Nash (*Inescapable Ecologies: A History of Environment, Disease, and Knowledge* [Berkeley: University of California Press, 2006]), Philip Cafaro ("Rachel Carson's Environmental Ethics," in *Rachel Carson: Legacy and Challenge*, ed. Lisa H. Sideris and Kathleen D. Moore [Albany: State University of New York Press, 2008], 60–78), and Lorraine Code ("Thinking Ecologically: The Legacy of Rachel Carson," in *The Environment: Philosophy, Science, Ethics*, ed. William P. Kabasenche, Michael O'Rourke, and Matthew H. Slater [Cambridge: MIT Press, 2012], 117–35).

5. Overall, Carson's sea writings have received less attention than *Silent Spring*. For thoughtful studies that have influenced us, however, see note 8.
6. On Emerson's interest in working against such knowingness, see Dominic Mastroianni, *Politics and Skepticism in Antebellum American Literature* (New York: Cambridge University Press, 2014), 27–60.
7. Our approach to Emerson is informed by Branka Arsić's account of Emerson's "ontology of water," according to which everything can be said to be water, and her particular discussion of the centrality of water to Emerson's abandonment. See Arsić, *On Leaving: A Reading in Emerson* (Cambridge, MA: Harvard University Press, 2010), 4; 3–6. We are also indebted to Christopher Hanlon's articulation of "the continuum Emerson draws between currents of the sea and currents of intellection" in *Emerson's Memory Loss: Originality, Communality, and the Late Style* (Oxford: Oxford University Press, 2018), 89.
8. Our approach to Carson's sea writings is informed by the work of a small number of scholars who interpret these writings as philosophically innovative, including Susan Power Bratton on Carson's "trans-ecotonal sea ethic" ("Thinking Like a Mackerel: Rachel Carson's *Under the Sea-Wind* as a Source for a Trans-Ecotonal Sea Ethic," in *Rachel Carson: Legacy and Challenge*, ed. Lisa H. Sideris and Kathleen D. Moore [Albany: State University of New York Press, 2008], 79–93); and Marnie M. Sullivan on Carson's preference for process instead of progress, and her reflections on the limits of human vision ("Shifting Subjects and Marginal Worlds: Revealing the Radical in Rachel Carson's Three Sea Books," in *Feminist Ecocriticism: Environment, Women, and Literature*, ed. Douglas A. Vakoch [Lanham, MD: Lexington Books, 2012], 77–91, 86–89). See also Lawrence Buell (Environmental Imagination; and *The Future of Environmental Criticism: Environmental Crisis and Literary Imagination* (Malden, MA: Blackwell, 2005); Neil W. Browne, who deems the sea writings "parts of an ecological literary project" exploring the complex relations among subjects and objects (*The World in Which We Occur: John Dewey, Pragmatist Ecology, and American Ecological Writing in the Twentieth Century* [Tuscaloosa: University of Alabama Press, 2007], 79); Stacy Alaimo, who traces Carson's "marine environmentalisms" (*Exposed: Environmental Politics and Pleasures in Posthuman Times* [Minneapolis: University of Minnesota Press, 2016], 122); and Hester Blum on Carson and deep time ("'Bitter with the Salt of Continents': Rachel Carson and Oceanic Returns," *WSQ: Women's Studies Quarterly* 45, no. 1 and 2 (Spring/Summer 2017): 287–91).
9. It is more than likely that Carson read Emerson. She owned a volume of his essays and she was exposed to his ideas through several channels. Carson's early education was immersed in the nature-study movement (see Lear, *Rachel Carson*, 13–15), which Emerson greatly influenced. Later in life Carson majored in English at Pennsylvania College for Women (later Chatham College) under the presidency of Cora Coolidge who was deeply interested in the work of the Transcendentalists (ibid., 28). As an adult Carson frequently expressed her abiding fascination with the work of several nineteenth-century US writers influenced by Emerson, including Melville and Thoreau (see Paul Brooks, *The House of Life: Rachel Carson at Work* [Boston: Houghton Mifflin, 1972], 5). And Maria Popova notices an Emersonian cast to Carson's work in *Figuring* ([New York: Pantheon Books, 2019], 423, 488). The formative role of literature in Carson's ecological thinking is the main subject of Navakas's current research.
10. Sharon Cameron, *Impersonality: Seven Essays* (Chicago: University of Chicago Press, 2007). Cameron's choice of the single term "the impersonal" is useful because it helps us connect Emerson to other thinkers interested in impersonality and personhood. Emerson himself uses the term "impersonality" at least twice ("Literary Ethics," *CW* 1:101; "Fate,"

CW 6:14) and writes of "the impersonal" in both "The Over-Soul" (*CW* 2:164) and "Circles" (*CW* 2:186).
11. See Cameron, *Impersonality*, 85–86.
12. Cf. Mark Noble, *American Poetic Materialism from Whitman to Stevens* (New York: Cambridge University Press, 2014), 85–86.
13. Of Emerson on water more generally, Arsić observes that "forms are always in the making," matter always "rebuilt as something else, giving life to a new form" (*On Leaving*, 4–5). Also cf. "Experience" (*CW* 2:27) and "The Fortune of the Republic" (*LL* 2:320).
14. See Cameron, *Impersonality*, 80.
15. Quoted in Linda Lear, ed., *Lost Woods: The Discovered Writing of Rachel Carson* (Boston: Beacon Press, 1998), 88.
16. Ibid., 8.
17. See Rachel Carson, "Undersea," *Atlantic Monthly* 160 (September 1937): 325.
18. Ibid., 325.
19. Ibid., 325.
20. Ibid., 325.
21. See Rachel Carson, 1941, *Under the Sea-Wind* (New York: Penguin, 2007), 75.
22. Ibid., 96.
23. Ibid., 65, 156–57.
24. Rachel Carson, 1951, *The Sea around Us* (Oxford: Oxford University Press, 2018), 75.
25. Ibid., 212.
26. As Carol M. Rose observes, durability has historically been central to common Anglo-American conceptions of property: "the very claim of property is that it is something lasting. Indeed, duration is an important element in making a claim *property*, as opposed to a merely temporary usufruct." See Rose, *Property and Persuasion: Essays on the History, Theory, and Rhetoric of Ownership* (Boulder, CO: Westview Press, 1994), 272; italics in original.
27. Carson, "Undersea," 325, italics added.
28. Ibid., 325.
29. See Alaimo, *Exposed*, 128. Relatedly, Buell reflects that Carson's nature writing is centrally guided by "the discovery that there is no space on earth immune from anthropogenic toxification" (see Buell, *Environmental Imagination*, 41).
30. Alaimo, *Exposed*, 112.
31. Rachel Carson, 1955, *The Edge of the Sea* (Boston: Mariner Books, 1998), 37.
32. Ibid., 2.
33. Ibid., 249.
34. Ibid., 250.
35. In "Art" (1870), Emerson states that "the term *abandonment* ... describe[s] the self-surrender of the orator" (*CW* 7:25); in "The Method of Nature" (1841) he writes: "Never self-possessed or prudent, [love] is all abandonment" (*CW* 1:133).
36. On these three senses of abandonment, see Stanley Cavell, *Emerson's Transcendental Etudes*, ed. David Justin Hodge (Stanford: Stanford University Press, 2003), 18.
37. According to Arsić, Emerson maintained the view that "in one way or another, everything is water," that water epitomizes what she calls "leaving," and that "in Emerson's oceanic ontology everything is in migration, mutation, and metamorphosis" (*On Leaving*, 4; 6).
38. Cf. "Self-Reliance" (1841), *CW* 2:34.
39. Carson, "Undersea," 322.

40. For more on the state of ocean knowledge at the time Carson wrote see various essays in the illustrated commemorative edition of *The Sea Around Us* (Oxford: Oxford University Press, 2003).
41. Carson, "Undersea," 322.
42. Ibid., 322.
43. See Carson, *Under the Sea-Wind*, 5.
44. Lear claims that the narrator of "Undersea" "surveys ... the sea from the immediate perspective of an underwater eye" (see Lear, *Lost Woods*, 23–24), yet in fact the narrator watches a traveler, rather than perceiving from their perspective.
45. Carson, "Undersea," 323.
46. Ibid., 324.
47. Ibid., 322.
48. This reading of Carson builds on and also departs from Buell's claim that "Carson incipiently humanizes her creatures" (*Environmental Imagination*, 206).
49. Carson, *Under the Sea-Wind*, 76.
50. Ibid., 153.
51. Ibid., 156.
52. Carson, "Undersea," 322.
53. Hubbell, "Introduction," xvi.
54. Carson, *Edge of the Sea*, 110.
55. Ibid., 115.
56. Ibid., 116.
57. Ibid., 116.
58. Ibid., 116–17.
59. While Carson would write that a "feeling of absolute fascination for everything relating to the ocean" was among her earliest memories (quoted in Lear, *Rachel Carson*, 8), she grew up in Pennsylvania and did not so much as set eyes on the sea until after graduating from college. Emerson claimed that from childhood onward he had "kept a sort of grudge" against the sea, and that his attraction to the sea came later in life (LRWE 2:422).
60. Browne, *World in Which We Occur*, 105, 103.
61. In particular, *Silent Spring* traces how the chemical pesticides that humans once sprayed to preserve trees from insects made their way invisibly into the wider ecological system, poisoning and killing birds, and eventually accumulating in human body tissue where they could disrupt essential biological processes.

CHAPTER 3

"UP AGAIN, OLD HEART!"
Emerson in the Anthropocene

MICHELLE C. NEELY

> People wish to be settled: only insofar as they are unsettled is there any hope for them.
>
> Ralph Waldo Emerson, "Circles" (*CW* 2:188)

GRIEVING GRIEF

IN September of 2020, as devastating forest fires raged across the western United States, the eminent environmental writer Terry Tempest Williams penned a moving "Obituary for the Land" for the *New York Times* podcast "The Daily." The obituary insists upon grief as an "open-hearted," consciousness-expanding experience of pain and defiance because ultimately, "grief is love."[1]

> I will never write your obituary because even as you burn, you are throwing down seeds that will sprout and flower. Trees will grow and forests will rise again as living testaments to how one survives change. Let this be a humble tribute, an exaltation, an homage, an open-hearted eulogy to all we are losing to fire, to floods, to hurricanes, and tornadoes, and the invisible virus that has called us all home and brought us to our knees. We are not the only species that lives and loves and breathes on this planet called Earth. May we raise a fistful of ash to other lives lost that it holds. Grief is love. How can we hold this grief without holding each other? I will mark my heart with an "X" made of ash that says, "The power to restore life resides here." The future of our species will be decided here, not by facts, but by love and loss. Let us cry every day like rain in the desert. Penned on my heart, I pledge of allegiance to the only home I will ever know.[2]

"How can we hold this grief without holding each other?" Williams asks, in a question that seems rhetorical. In her formulation, we cannot. Grief is a portal to interspecies interconnection, a welcome end to what the beginning of the obituary calls the "terminal disease where humans put themselves at the center of the universe." "Grief is love" for life in all its forms, and a commitment to use our deep well of sadness to combat climate disaster ("the power to restore life resides here"). For Williams, to not feel grief fully, and powerfully, at this moment in history is to fail in a morally significant manner:

> I think it's a wonder we're not all in bed because it's—we are not neutral bodies. I mean, we are feeling that. And I just went outside and all of the patio furniture is covered in ash. And you just think that ash—those are trees. Those are bodies. That's fur. That's feathers. It's everything, and we're covered in it. And anyone who says they're fine, they are dead to this world that is really dying. And in grief, I feel like it's a raven on my shoulder. I just walk with it every day. And that is the truth.[3]

To be "dead to this world that is really dying," to all that "we are losing to fire, to floods, to hurricanes, and tornadoes, and the invisible virus that has called us all home and brought us to our knees," and not only us humans, but the entire living world—this is both a sin and a form of living death, for Williams. We must feel what has come to be known as climate grief fully, allow it to consume us like fire to make room for the new world that will emerge from the "seeds that will sprout and flower" in the fire's wake. "The future of our species will be decided here, not by facts, but by love and loss. Let us cry every day like rain in the desert," Williams concludes.

While Williams' formulation of climate grief is powerful, it is hardly unique. Environmental scholars pen thoughtful essays entitled "Climate Grief: Our Greatest Ally?," popular opinion pieces promise that "Taking Action Can Cure Your Climate Grief," and an organization called the "Good Grief Network" offers a ten-step program that promises, for $600, to help participants process their climate grief.[4] In short, grief has come to be seen by many as not only inevitable but a necessary and even useful response to the climate crisis. In the words of visual artist Chris Jordan:

> When we hold grief at a distance, our love becomes inaccessible; and when we embrace grief, we reconnect with the essential aspect of our being that has gone missing lately. I believe that if we could summon the courage to grieve together, on a collective scale, for all that is being lost in our world, then our love would return and, along with it, our generosity, joy, and peace. And if we were to step through that door together, there is no knowing how many of the world's problems we could solve, and fast.[5]

Jordan, like Williams, links grief with love, and suggests that a failure to feel one is a failure to feel the other. The loss of both stymies our ability to take action on the "the world's problems." Indeed, the only alternatives would seem to be denial (the unfeeling "dead to this world" that Williams excoriates) or the kind of privileged and cynical, self-serving "bad grief" of climate fatalists like Jonathan Franzen or Roy Scranton, who insist that there's no possible action left except "learning to die in the Anthropocene." Both denial and climate fatalism are perhaps at root linked by a mutual "reification of despair."[6] As Andreas Malm has argued, climate fatalism in particular "does not passively reflect a certain distribution of probabilities but *actively affirms it* ... The more people who tell us that a radical reorientation is 'scarcely imaginable,' the less imaginable it will be."[7] Such grief insists that there are no meaningful actions left to take, and encourages those with wealth to enjoy their luxury emissions while they still can. In the "good grief" formulation, then, we must either grieve the world as lost, or lose it through denial or climate fatalism.

I have no quibble with those able to find a spur to climate activism in their grief, or with the idea that grief itself is an appropriate response to the devastation capitalism and empire are ceaselessly wreaking on the planet.[8] As Jennifer James argues in her masterful "Ecomelancholia," grieving in an ongoing way under these circumstances is to "refus[e] to take consolation in fantasies of rectification while destruction occurs unabated."[9] It is, in this sense, an act of resistance against the quietist pablum that the status quo will yet be redeemed. James' activist grief is a meaningful, justice-oriented response to our destructive status quo.

Yet, inevitably, not all climate grief points toward action. Moreover, we should be troubled by how much of the climate grief conversation recalls Harriet Beecher Stowe's conclusion to *Uncle Tom's Cabin*, in which "every individual" is called upon to "feel right" as a first (and potentially final) step toward ending the horrors of US slavery:

> There is one thing that every individual can do,—they can see to it that *they feel right*. An atmosphere of sympathetic influence encircles every human being; and the man or woman who *feels* strongly, healthily and justly, on the great interests of humanity, is a constant benefactor to the human race. See, then, to your sympathies in this matter! Are they in harmony with the sympathies of Christ? or are they swayed and perverted by the sophistries of worldly policy?[10]

Those who have embraced climate grief, too, insist that the person "who *feels* strongly, healthily and justly, on the great interests of humanity, is a constant benefactor to the human race." Williams' obituary, or Jordan's op-ed, also command us to "see, then, to [our] sympathies in this matter." "Are they in harmony with the sympathies of" environmentalism? "Or are they swayed and perverted by the sophistries of worldly" consumer capitalism? Of course, the spuriousness of feeling right as a political act has long since been exposed. Lauren Berlant, in "Poor Eliza," observes that:

> Because the ideology of true feeling cannot admit the nonuniversality of pain, its cases become all jumbled together and the ethical imperative toward social transformation is replaced by a civic-minded but passive ideal of empathy. The political as a place of acts oriented toward publicness becomes replaced by a world of private thoughts, leanings, and gestures.[11]

James Baldwin, in "Everybody's Protest Novel," argues something similar; to focus only on "feeling right" about pain and suffering, as Stowe does in *Uncle Tom's Cabin*, is to "leave unanswered and unnoticed the only important question: what it was, after all, that moved her people to such deeds." Far from an excess of feeling, such "sentimentality" is actually "the mark of dishonesty, the inability to feel; the wet eyes of the sentimentalist betray his aversion to experience, his fear of life, his arid heart."[12] The danger is that, in cultivating our emotional responses to tragedy and injustice we may become like Lawrence Sterne's protagonist in *A Sentimental Journey*: so lost in our tears over the spectacle of a bird begging for its freedom that we forget to open the door to the cage. If, as Berlant and Baldwin warn, we lose sight of "the nonuniversality of pain," climate grief may lead us into passivity, or even solipsism.

Emerson's "Experience" suggests a related, but different problem with grief: that it might not actually transform us, or bring us into closer contact with the real. However painful a great loss may be, "Experience" suggests a chasm between the loss and one who is bereaved: "I cannot get it nearer to me." While Williams, Jordan, and others suggest that grief is a powerful, actionable transformation of love, Emerson instead insists, "The only thing grief has taught me, is to know how shallow it is. That, like all the rest, plays about the surface, and never introduces me into the reality, for contact with which, we would even pay the costly price of sons and lovers." In Williams' "grief is love," there's an insistence that, to the extent that we truly cared for our lost beloved, with equal emotional intensity and "power" we will grieve their loss. But Emerson suggests that we are always, however against our will, distanced from the things we love—in life and in death. Our "souls never touch their objects. An innavigable sea washes with silent waves between us and the things we aim at and converse with." Our grief and our love may both disappoint us, both prove unable to transform us, to pull us out past the shallows of life. "I grieve that grief can teach me nothing," Emerson writes, "nor carry me one step into real nature" (*CW* 3:29). Grief, unfortunately, does not change Emerson. It "leave[s] me as it found me—neither better nor worse" because, in some essential way, "it does not touch me."

Putting Emerson's grief into conversation with climate grief might seem to suggest that there is something spurious about eco-grief. Baldwin finds an ugly insincerity in sentimentality, and Emerson also suggests that there is some dishonesty, or at least self-deception, in big emotional displays: "People grieve and bemoan themselves, but it is not half so bad with them as they say." It is all "scene-painting and counterfeit" (*CW* 3:29). Those of us who feel any measure of climate grief know it is not mere "scene-painting and counterfeit," but perhaps Emerson's mistrust of grief can suggest the way in which, no matter how much we grieve, it must be inadequate to the loss of our planet. In Lucille Clifton's ecopoem "grief," the speaker commands herself and readers to "imagine" the anthropogenic pain of the living world, beginning with "the grass" that bore the weight of Adam at the moment of creation, a thought experiment across time and space that takes us "to now, to here, / to grief for the upright / animal, grief for the / horizontal world" (Clifton). Having arrived at grief, the repeated command the speaker issues is not to grieve, or lament, or wallow, but to "pause." We pause first for "the human / animal" and then for "the myth of america," both potent causes of the more-than-human pain readers are being invited to contemplate. But then we pause for "the girl /

with twelve fingers" (a recurring figure for Clifton herself) "who never learned to cry enough / for anything that mattered."

> not enough for the fear,
> not enough for the loss,
> not enough for the history,
> not enough
> for the disregarded planet.
> (Clifton)

Clifton's poem ends in "the garden of regret / with time's bell tolling grief"—"grief for what is born human / grief for what is not." Grief is clearly a meaningful emotion, but it is insufficient alongside the temporal and physical scale of the destruction that "the human animal" and "the myth of america" have wrought. The "girl with twelve fingers" seems to feel sadness, but it is "not enough." Emerson suggests that Clifton's "not enough" is simply the human condition: "The dearest events are summer-rain, and we the Para coats that shed every drop." No matter how much we grieve the loss of the planet that we've known, and hopefully loved, our experience of grief might still leave us with the feeling that the full import of the loss has nevertheless, in some meaningful way, resisted us, glided past us, slipped through our fingers. "Experience" calmly deplores this reality of grief: "I take this evanescence and lubricity of all objects, which lets them slip through our fingers when we clutch hardest, to be the most unhandsome part of our condition" (*CW* 3:29). For Stanley Cavell, this clutching and grasping happens "when we seek to deny the standoffishness of objects by clutching at them; which is to say, when we conceive thinking ... as grasping something."[13] Grief does not let us grasp material reality, does not put us into meaningful contact with the more-than-human world. It cannot "carry [us] one step into real nature," as Emerson observes.

How can we even "clutch" at a loss as huge and unthinkable as the loss of our planet? Especially when grief, as much as any other human emotion, confuses us such that, as Emerson puts it, "all things swim and glimmer"? Emerson begins "Experience" with a sense of dislocation that could serve as grief's *cri de coeur*: "Where do we find ourselves?" This is the essential, but unanswerable, question because in grief, "our life is not so much threatened as our perception" (*CW* 3:27). That grief alters our perception, and not always in beneficial ways, is simply true. Joan Didion, in her grief memoir, *The Year of Magical Thinking*, writes of "the power of grief to derange the mind," a power she observes has been "exhaustively noted" in medical literature and psychological work on grieving, as early as Freud's "Mourning and Melancholia." As Didion herself grieves, she is repeatedly "unsettled" as she notices in herself "those cognitive defects that came with either stress or grief... Would I ever be right again? Could I ever trust myself not to be wrong?"[14] Grief's potential to warp cognition and perception receives little mention from the "good grief" wing of climate activists, but Emerson's "Experience" suggests we would be foolish to ignore it. The climate movement needs, at the very least, acute perception of the climate crisis, and to foster the collectivities and communities that can build the infrastructure we need to survive. Yet grief can muddle our minds and isolate us, sap the meaning from our experiences and make us feel that right action is impossible. Caught in the grip of grief, we may feel, with Emerson, that:

> Dream delivers us to dream, and there is no end to illusion. Life is a train of moods like a string of beads, and, as we pass through them, they prove to be many-colored lenses which paint the world their own hue, and each shows only what lies in its focus. From the mountain you see the mountain. We animate what we can, and we see only what we animate. (*CW* 3:30)

This kind of grief pulls us toward nihilism and despair; it is hardly the raised fist call to action that Williams' was.

From the perspective of Emerson's grief, climate crisis may be rendered subjective and unreal, a "mood" we are passing through, painting the world in its hue. Or perhaps it's a mountain we're climbing and cannot see beyond. Either way, the problems of climate crisis take on a seductive air of impermanence and unreality. Grief risks becoming an obstacle to perspicuity, not the avenue to it. "Our life is not so much threatened as our perception," says Emerson, but in the case of climate grief, it might be both.

"Experience" invites readers to be cautious about what grief can do to our perception not merely of discrete events, but also to our existential understanding of human life itself. Having survived the loss of Waldo, his son, Emerson describes love, loss, and the very human experience of reality as illusory, evanescent. Sharon Cameron writes that in "Experience," Waldo's death makes "all things swim and glitter because everything is transient, either a loss in its own right or subject to loss."[15] Ultimately, she says, "mourning does its work in that the loss and grief initially attached to a single experience ultimately, impersonally, pervade the perception of all experience so that everything is susceptible to the same disappointment."[16] In Cameron's reading, Emerson's deep grief "dissolves" all other experience into itself; far from a clarity of perspective, Cameron argues Emerson's grief is characterized by nothing so much as "disassociation."[17]

It is not only our perspective that is threatened by grief, but our resilience. In an emotional economy in which grief (for a person, for the planet we are losing) is valued as an act of devotion, our capacity to recover from or repress (however temporarily) our grief cannot help but be devalued. If grief is love, to survive or even thrive after the loss of the beloved is to somehow betray our love for them or it, and thus resilience, one of the most widely touted twenty-first century environmental virtues, becomes itself "unhandsome." Resilience curdles in the context of grief, becomes proof that we didn't love enough, and don't feel our loss deeply enough. Resilience is a betrayal of our love. But of course, resilience and grief are at odds in more ways than this. In *The Year of Magical Thinking*, Didion writes that "I also notice that I do not have the resilience I had a year ago. A certain number of crises occur and the mechanism that floods the situation with adrenaline burns out. Mobilization becomes unreliable, slow or absent."[18] Grief can sap our ability to respond appropriately to crisis, and even diminish our experience of the crisis itself. We see that in Emerson: "what opium is instilled into all disaster! It shows formidable as we approach it, but there is at last no rough rasping friction, but the most slippery sliding surfaces" (*CW* 3:28). Emerson here suggests something about crisis that Octavia Butler's *Parable of the Sower* maps onto climate crisis specifically. In Butler's prescient dystopian novel, there's no single big event. Disaster has been a slow creep.[19] The crisis has not felt enough like a crisis to mobilize an adequate response; American life has adapted to the gradual climatic, social, and political shifts, and horrible though life becomes for most, it goes on.

Whether we are already suffering the havoc of climate crisis and the progress of the "sixth extinction" ourselves or watching it unfold at some distance, Emerson creates space for that grief not to be profound enough, for the probability that our grief simply cannot be commensurate with the planetary, multispecies tragedies and extinctions that are and will continue to play out. Like Clifton's twelve-fingered girl, we will never learn to cry enough, and "Experience" suggests that we could benefit from acknowledging this "most unhandsome part of our condition": the reality that the majority of us (especially but not only in the Global North), no matter how alarmed or caring we are, cannot feel enough, and have not been thoroughly incapacitated. Most of us keep going to work and flying on airplanes and raising children, however bad we feel. *Pace* ecocritics who see embracing climate grief as a form of attachment that could move us to action, the inadequacy of our grief seems just as likely to convince us of the inadequacy of our love for life on earth. The "good grief" conversation can only class the persistence of ordinary life as unfeeling denialism, but what if we instead acknowledge, with Emerson, "what opium is instilled into all disaster," and realize that there may never be a "rough rasping friction" that stops most of us in our tracks? If our subjective perception of fundamental aspects of our climate crisis—how much time we have left to act, the scale of the crisis—is compromised by the active or subterranean grief most of us feel, then such grief will not be a portal to meaningful learning, let alone action. In that case, we must take action on climate crisis *despite* the inadequacy of our subjective experience of it, *despite* the "innavigable sea" that "washes with silent waves between us" and all other living beings. In the context of climate grief, in other words, "Experience" suggests that as much as we need to "process" our grief, we may also need to bracket our emotional experiences of the crisis as an inadequate, unreliable guide in the fight for a thriving, multispecies future.

Unchopping Our Trees

Whatever the quality of the sadness we may feel, conceptualizing our sorrow over the climate crisis as grief implies that we have suffered a discrete loss, one that is singular, temporally delimited (it has already happened, it is in the past), defined, and articulable. Yet few of these qualities seem to apply to the climate crisis, which does peculiar things to our notions of time and space. Climate crisis is variously something that has already occurred, is unfolding in the present, or is yet to come—sometimes all three of these things at once. Timothy Morton coined the term "hyperobject" to describe the way that climate change has been unfolding at a temporal and spatial scale that defies human comprehension, while Rob Nixon has used "slow violence" to describe a "violence of delayed destruction that is dispersed across time and space," as environmental violence so often is.[20] The vast temporal and spatial scales of our environmental crisis resists an emotion like grief, and so too does the historical location of the crisis, which is dispersed and recursive, quite different from the pinpointable, singular type of loss humans are used to grieving. As Kyle P. Whyte has written, from the point of view of many Indigenous peoples who suffered through the horrors of European and US colonialism, the world has already ended, many times and for the same reasons that we are now living through a planetary climate crisis: settler-colonialism, capitalism, and imperialism. To insist upon the singularity of twenty-first-century crisis is to remain within a warped, settler-colonial sense of safety that was always dependent upon centuries of unacknowledged human and nonhuman violence and genocide.[21]

Still, our contemporary crisis is real, and we have limited time left to effectively respond to it. With each passing day, the action demanded of us becomes more radical, more and more divergent from the status quo. Tweaks to our economic and political systems might have sufficed forty years ago, but any adequate response at this late hour will need to be more thoroughly transformative. The good news is that there is broad consensus on the steps to take, but as David Wallace-Wells has written, "that the solutions are obvious, and available, does not mean the problem is anything but overwhelming."[22] For many of those of embedded in settler cultures like the United States, what we are confronting might be best described as a crisis of faith; to paraphrase Frederic Jameson, it's easier to imagine the end of the world than to imagine large numbers of people acting to change the systems that must now be transformed.

Emerson writes that "the use of literature is to afford us a platform whence we may command a view of our present life, a purchase by which we may move it." We need literature that will encourage us not only to embrace things as they are, but also as they must come to be. We need literature that can help us accept the destruction of certainties and constants we have organized our lives around. At his best, Emerson does this, "claps wings to the sides of all the solid old lumber of the world" and makes it possible to imagine dramatic change and meaningful action, to imagine "choosing a straight path in theory and practice" (*CW* 2:185). Imagining and believing in change at this scale is arguably the biggest obstacle many in the Global North face in addressing the climate crisis. Emerson's willingness to "unsettle all things" and "simply experiment, an endless seeker, with no Past at my back" might embolden those who continue to benefit from the status quo yet feel an ethical call to take action now, when we are out of time for half measures, and must rapidly remake our world to enact climate solutions (*CW* 2:188).

Emerson acknowledges that to live constantly in a state of "alert acceptance" of change and the new is very difficult. It requires intellectual humility, the ability to embrace "the intrepid conviction" that so many of our certainties, our "past apprehension[s] of truth," must be "superseded and decease" if humanity, and not only humanity, is to "stand":

> Valor consists in the power of self-recovery, so that a man cannot have his flank turned, cannot be outgeneralled, but put him where you will, he stands. This can only be by his preferring truth to his past apprehension of truth; and his alert acceptance of it from whatever quarter; the intrepid conviction that his laws, his relations to society, his christianity, his world, may at any time be superseded and decease. (*CW* 2:183)

To embrace intellectual revolutions requires a quality of imagination capable of distancing us from the hegemony of the actual: "the things which are dear to men at this hour, are so on account of the ideas which have emerged on their mental horizon, and which cause the present order of things as a tree bears its apples." Our "mental horizon" seems both determined by and to determine the "present order of things." A shift in perspective, a brave mental leap or the welcoming of another person's such leap, is thus transformative. Suddenly "the facts which loomed so large in the fogs of yesterday,—property, climate, breeding, personal beauty, and the like, have strangely changed their proportions. All that we reckoned settled, shakes and rattles; and literatures, cities, climates, religions, leave their foundations, and dance before our eyes" (*CW* 2:184). It is unsettling to be radically open to perspectival transformation, but it's joyful, too. Things may "shak[e] and rattl[e]" as they "leave their foundations," but then they "dance before our eyes."

In some of Emerson's writing, such unsettling can sound almost melancholic. There's something culturally salutary yet existentially bleak about the way his poem "Hamatreya" decenters the human, for instance. The poem begins with a list of six surnames of local landowners, and the seriality and lack of distinguishing descriptors makes the men seem interchangeable, diminishing their particularity and importance: "Bulkeley, Hunt, Williard, Hosmer, Meriam, Flint, / Possessed the land which rendered to their toil, / Hay, corn, roots, hemp, flax, apples, wool, and wood." The third line of the poem, with its list of the products that the land "rendered" the landowners, reinforces the deindividuation of the landowners by echoing the form of line 1, thereby implying that the landowners and their crops are of equal stature, similarly evanescent and interchangeable. Surveying their property, these landlords gloat, " 'Tis mine, my children's, and my name's" as they "fancy these pure waters and the flags / Know me, as does my dog: we sympathize" (*CW* 9:68). The narcissism of the repeated possessive pronouns ("mine," "my," "my") undermines the somewhat poetic description of the topography, as does the anticlimactic comparison of the relation of the landlord with his land to his genial mastery of his dog. As the poem continues, generations of landlords' possessive relationships with the land they own are shown to be nothing more than a "fond" "fancy" as they die and are replaced by other men who labor and expire under the same delusions. "Ah! the hot owner sees not Death, who adds / Him to his land, a lump of mould the more" (*CW* 9:69). Ultimately, the human perspective is decentered entirely by a strange "Earth-Song" that erupts in the middle of the poem. Mocking the brief, mortal lives of men who presume to claim ownership over land, the Earth concludes:

> They called me theirs,
> Who so controlled me;
> Yet every one
> Wished to stay, and is gone.
> How am I theirs,
> If they cannot hold me,
> But I hold them?
> (CW 9:70)

From the deep time perspective of Earth, humanity's self-important attempts to own and control land during their brief lives is rendered ridiculous. A human narrator returns for four short lines at the end of the poem only to express a newfound sense of the pointlessness of worldly human pursuits. "When I heard the Earth-song, / I was no longer brave; My avarice cooled / Like lust in the chill of the grave" (CW 9:70). The expanded, nonhuman perspective of "Hamatreya" ridicules private property and wealth accumulation in light of the brevity of human life. The poem leaves room for other, more meaningful ways of relating to the earth, but does not supply them.

Emerson does suggest some of what a meaningful relation to the Earth might entail elsewhere. Take "The Method of Nature." In this essay, a right understanding of nature also suggests the diminished significance of the human:

> When we behold the landscape in a poetic spirit, we do not reckon individuals. Nature knows neither palm nor oak, but only vegetable life, which sprouts into forests, and festoons the globe with a garland of grasses and vines.
>   That no single end may be selected and nature judged thereby, appears from this, that if man himself be considered as the end, and it be assumed that the final cause of the world is to make holy or wise or beautiful men, we see that it has not succeeded. (*CW* 1:125)

Here, unlike in "Hamatreya," the diminished importance of the human individual is part of a "poetic" experience of the world that is remarkably vibrant. Perceived correctly, nature is "a work of *ecstasy*," Emerson writes (*CW* 1:125). The decentering of the human makes way for the "impression" that nature "does not exist to any one or any number of particular ends, but to numberless and endless benefit, that there is in it no private will, no rebel leaf or limb, but the whole is oppressed by one superincumbent tendency, obeys that redundancy or excess of life which in conscious beings we call *ecstasy*" (*CW* 1:126–27). Emerson's dense syntax conveys formally the riotous superabundance he claims for nature. Tuning in to nature's ecstatic thriving accentuates its miraculous essence.

> Who shall dare think he has come late into nature, or has missed anything excellent in the past, who seeth the admirable stars of possibility, and the yet untouched continent of hope with all its mountains in the vast West? I praise with wonder this great reality which seems to drown all things in the deluge of its light. (*CW* 1:136–37)

Readers today cannot celebrate with Emerson "the yet untouched continent of hope with all its mountains in the vast West." The optimism of "the vast West" that Emerson references was significantly dimmed, if not destroyed, by the colonial human and environmental violence that attended the "settling" of western lands in the decades that followed "The Method of Nature." More recently, the wilderness logic of "untouched" has been "troubled" by environmental historian William Cronon, who has delineated the historical processes of inventing wilderness, as well as the unjust and anti-ecological uses to which the ideal has been put. Even if we set aside Cronon's work, our planetary climate crisis in the "Anthropocene" means nothing on the planet is now "untouched"— not rainwater, which is globally contaminated by "forever chemicals"; not the farthest reaches of the ocean, which are contaminated by microplastics; not the polar ice caps, which are melting from human-caused warming. But can we still "[see] the admirable stars of possibility"? Can we imagine that we have not "come late into nature" and so "praise with wonder this great reality which seems to drown all things in the deluge of its light"? And what might be the use of such praise, of trying to channel the "wisdom" "to see the miraculous in the common" even now, or especially now, under our current, bleak circumstances?

Wonder for the natural world, of the kind that Emerson evokes in "The Method of Nature" and elsewhere, might keep us focused on love and repair, rather than simply loss. One more objection to embracing grief as an environmental paradigm is that the finality of the loss implied by grief erases the ways in which the living world remains present, all around us, available for relationships of care. Robin Wall Kimmerer gets at this when, in *Braiding Sweetgrass*, she admonishes readers that:

> It is not enough to weep for our lost landscapes; we have to put our hands in the earth to make ourselves whole again. Even a wounded world is feeding us. Even a wounded world holds us, giving us moments of wonder and joy. I choose joy over despair. Not because I have my head in the sand, but because joy is what the earth gives me daily and I must return the gift.[23]

Grief suggests an end to a relationship, but our relationship with the earth has not ended; in fact, it must be insisted upon—nurtured, strengthened, and prioritized—now more than ever. We need to deepen our relationship with the living world, not mourn its loss. We need to embrace performing the care that the world needs, and to become ever more conscious of and grateful for the care and joy we daily receive in return, the feeding, holding, and wonder Kimmerer invites us to ground ourselves in. Unlike an isolating, potentially anthropocentric dwelling in loss, this is a relational orientation that responds to the ongoing liveliness of the world, its persistence and needs in the present, which most of us are not doing much to honor or meet. To move toward this kind of relationship Kimmerer suggests, for one thing, acting to repair harm humans have done to the more-than-human world. "Like other mindful practices, ecological restoration can be viewed as an act of reciprocity in which humans exercise their caregiving responsibility for the ecosystems that sustain them," Kimmerer writes. "We restore the land, and the land restores us."[24] In this way:

> Restoration is a powerful antidote to despair. Restoration offers concrete means by which humans can once again enter into positive, creative relationship with the more-than-human world, meeting responsibilities that are simultaneously material and spiritual. It's not enough to grieve. It's not enough to just stop doing bad things.[25]

To commit to reparative action rather than grief or apocalyptic despair is to refuse to reify the present. As Emerson urges in "Circles," we need not "accept the actual for the necessary" (*CW* 2:189). The killing status quo of contemporary capitalism and everything that follows from it need not be inevitable.

However positive and creative a commitment to restoration may be, it can also be painful, and, yes, might involve anger, perhaps even grief. Yet this blend of wonder, care, and righteous anger might serve as a more powerful goad than grief alone, as we see in W. S. Merwin's poem "Unchopping a Tree," a quiet jeremiad against the thoughtlessness of environmental destruction. In this poem, Merwin asks readers to commit to repair of the nonhuman world, even as he invokes the awful, even insurmountable scale of the reparative work before us. Merwin's prose poem is written in paragraph form and adopts the familiar, didactic tone of a mid-twentieth-century instruction manual for DIY work. Despite the fact that "unchopping a tree" is a logical impossibility, the step-by-step imperatives of the instructions insist that we perform the necessary actions. "Start with the leaves, the small twigs, and the nests that have been shaken, ripped, or broken off by the fall; these must be gathered and attached once again to their respective places," the poem begins. This first instruction, daunting but possibly achievable, is built upon, paragraph by paragraph, in dizzying detail. Bees' and wasps' nests that occupied the hollows of the tree must be rebuilt. Spiders' webs must be rewoven and replaced, even though:

> we do not have the spiders' weaving equipment, nor any substitute for the leaf's living bond with its point of attachment and nourishment. It is even harder to simulate the latter when the leaves have once become dry—as they are bound to do, for this is not the labor of a moment. Also it hardly needs saying that this is the time to repair any neighboring trees or bushes or other growth that may have been damaged by the fall. The same rules apply. Where neighboring trees were of the same species it is difficult not to waste time conveying a detached leaf back to the wrong tree. Practice, practice. Put your hope in that.[26]

"It is hard," "we do not have"—such instructions emphasize the difficulty of the tasks, and the inadequacy of the human beings who must do them. As the paragraphs of steps and tasks pile up, the painful impossibility of following the instructions for "unchopping a tree" oppresses the reader. The original chopping of the tree becomes increasingly sickening as the poem draws attention to the myriad miraculous details of the ordinary and anonymous tree that must now be repaired. The tree's leaves, branches, trunk, joints, chips, sawdust, and so on can only be reassembled in the crudest possible manner, through the unstinting labor of many years, and all of it, if it could even be done, would still only leave you with a "skeleton" standing where a living tree once was.[27] The poem ends on a note of fear. The tree has been "unchopped," but:

> You cannot believe it will hold. How like something dreamed it is, standing there all by itself... You are afraid the motion of the clouds will be enough to push it over. What more can you do? What more can you do?
>   But there is nothing more you can do.
>   Others are waiting.
>   Everything is going to have to be put back.[28]

Throughout the step-by-step instructions for "unchopping a tree," the speaker insists that the work of repair must be done, even if it is overwhelming, and even though it is wholly inadequate to undo the destruction that necessitated it. The impossibility of unchopping even a single tree turns the entire living world into something unspeakably precious, and beyond human skill to manufacture or replicate. The poem is thus a fierce attack on the vision of "cheap," disposable nature that has driven several centuries of capitalist activity and expansion.[29] It is also a strange call to action on behalf of the "wounded world" Kimmerer asks us not to grieve but to take responsibility for restoring. Merwin's final line—"everything is going to have to be put back"—could be read as a threat. To imagine putting "everything" back could be to imagine some final, apocalyptic end to our current world order. Or, as in "Circles," it could be an expansion, a circumscription, "a new degree of culture [that] would instantly revolutionize the entire system of human pursuits" (*CW* 2:184).

The power of Merwin's poem is its ability to convey how taking responsibility for restoration is also a path to increased wonder for the nonhuman world. As the reader contemplates the repair of each detail of the chopped tree, it becomes clear that this ordinary tree, and therefore every tree, and every living being, is a miracle, "a work of *ecstasy*," just as Emerson claims. Writers who bring us into this experience of ecstasy—as Emerson, Kimmerer, Merwin, and others variously do—are creating literature of the kind Emerson calls for, that which "afford[s] us a platform whence we may command a view of our present life, a purchase by which we may move it." Moving our "present life," transforming it radically, transcending its status quo in the way that Emerson celebrates in "Circles" is not something we can afford to cynically reject as impossible. If the "mood" of grief encourages us to do so, we must ignore it and commit to repair of the world in the spirit of Emerson's claim that "every thing is impossible, until we see a success" (*CW* 3:40). Dominic Mastroianni, writing of "moods and the secret cause of revolution in Emerson," observes that for Emerson, changing our mood, or perspective, or the zeitgeist—indeed all forms of radical change—are not fully within our control: "the task of the citizen is to unleash a revolutionary force capable of destroying an existing world and constituting a new one," and yet "such force cannot be summoned at will. But by doing things we know how to do, Emerson suggests, we can hope to create conditions that favor its coming."[30] Restoration, repair—these are things we know how to do, even if they are also, or would also be, in our current mood, something of a miracle. But we are called upon to make that miracle, to "once again enter into positive, creative relationship with the more-than-human world, meeting responsibilities that are simultaneously material and spiritual," as Kimmerer puts it. "Do not craze yourself with thinking," Emerson advises in "Experience," but "go about your business anywhere," including here, in the disaster of the Anthropocene (*CW* 3:35).

Conclusion

Emerson's relevance to social justice has long been debated in the context of antislavery and women's rights; where critics like John Carlos Rowe have reprimanded Emerson's Transcendentalism for its reactionary tendencies (finding it "at fundamental odds with the social reforms" in question), others, including Maurice S. Lee, acknowledge Emerson's racism, "hypocrisy," and so on, while painting a more complicated portrait of Emerson's uneven investments in social reform.[31] This essay has been meditating on the positive value of reading Emerson in the Anthropocene, as a thinker with something to offer the climate justice movement in the dismaying place we find ourselves. In so doing, I do not mean to suggest that all of Emerson's work, or even most of it, is essential reading for the environmentally minded; my sense of his relevance is closer to what Andrea Knutson and Kathryn Dolan have termed his partial, "fugitive" relevance to environmentalism.[32] Fugitive at best, some might say, given how easy it would be to assemble evidence against Emerson's relevance to contemporary environmental thought.[33]

For the Environmental Humanities, as our problems continue to deepen, why read a writer who romanticizes some of their sources, as Emerson often seems to do in his later work especially, extolling what we would now call "toxic individualism," settler-colonial development, and the prosperity gospel of capitalism? In fact, by *The Conduct of Life* (1860), Emerson not only espouses some of the most environmentally damaging aspects of American culture; he makes them sound seductive, and frequently, natural. Take this passage from "Power":

> There is always room for a man of force, and he makes room for many. Society is a troop of thinkers, and the best heads among them take the best places. A feeble man can see the farms that are fenced and tilled, the houses that are built. The strong man sees also the possible houses and farms. His eye makes estates, as fast as the sun breeds clouds. (*CW* 6:31)

While some readers may be tempted to scoff at the Manichean contrasts Emerson makes between the visionary, heroic "strong man" who dominates and develops the nonhuman world, and the "weaker" men he controls and leads, such a world view is hardly irrelevant in the twenty-first century. In fact, it is characteristic of many of the staunchest, most denialist forces currently arranged against environmental protection and repair. When Emerson writes of coal that "every basket is power and civilization," he gives voice to many in power today.[34] Such individuals, and corporate boards, and politicians and lobbyists, might easily see their beliefs reflected in Emerson's insistence that:

> It is of no use to argue the wants down: the philosophers have laid the greatness of many in making his wants few; but will a man content himself with a hut and a handful of dried pease? He is born to be rich. He is thoroughly related; and is tempted out by his appetites and fancies to the conquest of this and that piece of nature, until he finds his wellbeing in the use of his planet, and of more planets than his own. (*CW* 6:47)

We may feel disgusted by words like these in our present moment, and wish to bury them. Yet there is value in critically reading even this Emerson, as we reflect on the seductive appeal of environmentally destructive ideas and attitudes that still largely define huge swaths of US culture (and not only US culture).

The transformation of Emerson from the thinker who penned fiery criticisms of capitalism and inequality in some of his early work[35] into the one who could lecture that "commerce is a game of skill, which every man cannot play, which few men can play well … there is always a reason, *in the man*, for his good or bad fortune, and so, in making money" is worth considering, and learning from. One thing we might observe is the central role of Emerson's cynicism about political reform in this transformation: "We are incompetent to solve the times," he intones at the outset of *The Conduct of Life* (*CW* 6:1). The Emerson who writes these words has ceased to hold space for radical change in the present, for the possibility of viable alternatives to the economic, social, or cultural status quo. Emerson here sounds the notes of defeatism that we hear in the work of the well-off contemporary writers who insist transformation is impossible, who invite us to stop fighting and relax into "learn[ing] to die in the Anthropocene."[36]

We are most of us vulnerable to the kind of despair that might turn us against belief in the ongoing possibility of transformation—of ourselves, of the political and economic systems that govern our lives. Throughout his career, Emerson recognized as well as anyone how difficult it is to make the best, highest use of the present when there are so many tempting diversions. As his brief poem "Days" depicts, too often we abandon our ideals, "forget our morning wishes," and are satisfied instead with "a few herbs and apples" (shopping, alcohol, memes, streaming TV…), much to our shame (*CW* 9:423). The mere passage of time does not make us wiser, or braver, or more likely to grow or mature. As Emerson writes in "Climacteric," "I am not wiser for my age, / Nor skillful by my grief; / Life loiters at the book's first page,— / Ah! Could we turn the leaf" (*CW* 9:533).

Tempting as it may be to retreat into a safer, disappointment-proof, worldly cynicism, the Emerson of "Experience" remains wedded to a vulnerable sincerity. We could learn from sitting with the hard-won notes of optimism that Emerson sounds toward the end of that essay. Defeat and grief are inevitable, but even still: "Nevermind the ridicule, never mind the defeat: up again, old heart!—it seems to say,—there is victory yet for all justice; and the true romance which the world exists to realize, will be the transformation of genius into practical power" (*CW* 3:49). Like Emerson, however much we have already lost, and however much more we will see destroyed, we need the resilience to say to ourselves, "Onward and upward!," to exist in one of those "liberated moments" when "we know that a new picture of life and duty is already possible" (*CW* 3:43). When we know that political transformation of the present continues to be possible.

Notes

1. Terry Tempest Williams, interview with Bianca Giaever, The Daily, podcast audio, September 18, 2020, https://www.nytimes.com/2020/09/18/podcasts/the-daily/western-wildfires.html. The claim that "grief is love" means anyone who is not currently grieving the planet does not love it is not unique to Williams. It's impossible to pinpoint a single source for this widespread notion, but Joanna Macy, an influential activist and teacher, is often mentioned in conjunction with it (Joanna Macy and Chris Johnstone, *Active Hope: How to Face the Mess We're in with Unexpected Resilience and Creative Power* (San Francisco: New World Library, 2012).
2. Williams, ibid.
3. Ibid.
4. See Jennifer Atkinson, "Climate Grief: Our Greatest Ally?," *Resilience*, accessed January 3, 2022, https://www.resilience.org/stories/2020-08-27/climate-grief-our-greatest-ally/; Ellen Airhart, "Taking Action Can Cure Your Climate Grief," *Scientific American*, accessed January 3, 2022, https://www.scientificamerican.com/article/taking-action-can-cure-your-climate-grief/; and The Good Grief Network, accessed January 3, 2022, https://www.goodgriefnetwork.org/.
5. Chris Jordan, "This Image Shows the Tragedy of Mass Consumption—But Change is Possible," *HuffPost*, https://www.huffpost.com/entry/tragedy-of-mass-consumption-change-is-possible-chris-jordan-albatross_b_5a4b6d4ae4b025f99e1d6caa/.
6. Andreas Malm, *How to Blow Up a Pipeline: Learning to Fight in a World on Fire* (London: Verso Books, 2021), 141.
7. Ibid., 142.
8. Britt Wray's *Generation Dread* has the most complete evaluation of climate grief's mixed efficacy. While she leaves room for climate grief as a potentially necessary emotion (as, I hope, do I), Wray notes a study showing that "eco-anger" appears to be the affect more likely to provoke climate activism, while grief can lead to isolation, inaction, and despair. See Wray, *Generation Dread: Finding Purpose in an Age of Climate Crisis* (Toronto: Knopf, 2022), 121, 154–58.
9. Jennifer C. James, "Ecomelancholia: Slavery, War, and Black Ecological Imaginings," in *Environmental Criticism for the Twenty-First Century*, ed. Stephanie LeMenager, Teresa Shewry, and Ken Hiltner (New York: Routledge, 2011), 163–78, 167.
10. Harriet Beecher Stowe, *Uncle Tom's Cabin*, ed. Elizabeth Ammons (New York: Norton Critical Editions, 2017), 317.
11. Lauren Berlant, "Poor Eliza," *American Literature* 70, no. 3 (September 1998): 635–68, 641.

12. James Baldwin, "Everybody's Protest Novel," in *Notes of a Native Son* (Boston: Beacon Press, 1955), 13–23, 14.
13. Stanley Cavell, *This New yet Unapproachable America: Lectures after Emerson after Wittgenstein* (Chicago: Chicago University Press, 1989), 86.
14. Joan Didion, *The Year of Magical Thinking* (New York: Knopf, 2005), 214.
15. Sharon Cameron, *Impersonality: Seven Essays* (Chicago: Chicago University Press, 2007), 57.
16. Ibid., 65.
17. Ibid., 57, 68.
18. Didion, *Year of Magical Thinking*, 211.
19. Octavia Butler, *Parable of the Sower* (New York: Grand Central Publishing, 1993).
20. Timothy Morton, *Hyperobjects: Philosophy and Ecology after the End of the World* (Minneapolis: University of Minnesota Press, 2013); Rob Nixon, *Slow Violence and the Environmentalism of the Poor* (Cambridge, MA: Harvard University Press, 2011).
21. Kyle P. Whyte, "Indigenous Science (Fiction) for the Anthropocene: Ancestral Dystopias and Fantasies of Climate Change Crises," *Environment and Planning E: Nature and Space* 1 (2018): 224–42.
22. David Wallace-Wells, *The Uninhabitable Earth: Life After Warming* (New York: Tim Duggan Books, 2019), 227.
23. Robin Wall Kimmerer, *Braiding Sweetgrass: Indigenous Wisdom, Scientific Knowledge, and the Teachings of Plants* (Minneapolis: Milkweed Editions, 2013), 327.
24. Ibid., 336.
25. Ibid., 328.
26. W. S. Merwin, "Unchopping a Tree," in *The Essential W. S. Merwin*, ed. Michael Wiegers (Port Townsend: Copper Canyon Press, 2017), 142–45, 142.
27. Ibid., 143.
28. Ibid., 144–45.
29. Raj Patel and Jason Moore, *A History of the World in Seven Cheap Things: A Guide to Capitalism, Nature, and the Future of the Planet* (Berkeley: University of California Press, 2018).
30. Dominic Mastroianni, *Politics and Skepticism in Antebellum American Literature* (New York: Cambridge University Press, 2014), 31.
31. John Carlos Rowe, *At Emerson's Tomb: The Politics of Classic American Literature* (New York: Columbia University Press, 1997), 21; Maurice S. Lee, *Slavery, Philosophy, and American Literature, 1830–1860* (Cambridge: Cambridge University Press, 2005), chapter 5. Lee, interestingly for my purposes, reads "Experience" as part of the "long foreground of Emerson's [antislavery] activism" (191). Mastroianni, in a related vein, sees Emerson as "ask[ing] for a revolution with profound social and political consequences—even if the words *social* and *political* do not fully encompass the meaning of such a revolution" (*Politics and Skepticism*, 58).
32. Fugitive is a term Knutson and Dolan take from Emerson himself, who uses it "to express the (divine) strength of forms of expression that escape, resist, or challenge the oppressive stability of hardened 'fact' and discursive truths" See Andrea Knutson and Kathryn Dolan, "Fugitive Environmentalisms," *Journal of the Midwest Modern Language Association* 49, no. 1 (Spring 2016): 7–24, 10. For Knutson and Dolan, despite his uneven legacy, "Emerson's idea of dislocation and its power to reveal fugitive meanings [might] guide us" (15).

33. And this has indeed been done. For a thorough review of some of the anti-environmental charges against Emerson, see the essay "Emerson Undersea" by Michele Navakas and Dominic Mastroianni in this volume.
34. See Naomi Klein, *This Changes Everything: Capitalism vs. the Climate* (New York: Simon & Schuster, 2015), chapter 1.
35. See Milder, "The Radical Emerson?," in *The Cambridge Companion to Ralph Waldo Emerson*, ed. Joel Porte and Saundra Morris (New York: Cambridge University Press, 1999), 49–75.
36. See Roy Scranton, *Learning to Die in the Anthropocene: Reflections on the End of a Civilization* (San Francisco: City Lights Books, 2015).

CHAPTER 4

THE "MUTE MUSIC" IN EMERSON'S POLARITY

Generating Practical Power

CHRISTINA KATOPODIS

DURING a January sunset, Emerson watches pink clouds divide and subdivide in the air, modulating in "tints of unspeakable softness," a delicate undulation, and the leafless trees becoming "spires of flame in the sunset," everything contributing to the "mute music" (*CW* 1:14). By introducing the concept of "mute music," or music we cannot hear, he upends typical habits of listening with one's ears. Our world is alive with vibrations beyond the audible range of humans, some mechanical (e.g., sound waves), and some electromagnetic (e.g., radio waves). Though the human ear cannot hear it, Earth itself hums at approximately fifteen octaves below middle C (it oscillates between 2 and 7 millihertz).[1] Emerson listened with what he referred to in his journal as his "musical eyes" (*CW* 7:152). For him, "mute music" describes nature's dynamism—or *mutability*—its vast activities which enchant and compel him to dilate toward the sublime, from its jitters at the scale of an atom to Earth's rotation on its axis.

Emerson offers us a method of radical listening to nature's visible and invisible pulses, requiring deep attunement, meaning an adjustment of one's posture or activity to match or resonate with another. To him, we are "made of the same atoms as the world is," and enjoy an "original relation to the universe," a kindred relationship to our nonhuman neighbors (*CW* 8:128; 1:7). That consanguinity bears with it a mutual responsibility to care for the world.[2] If we are, as Emerson muses in *Nature* (1836), both "part and particle" of God, of Universal Being, then we ought to throw ourselves "joyfully into the sublime order," as he counsels in *The Conduct of Life* (1860): conduct ourselves in agreement (which is to say in *harmony*) with nature (*CW* 1:10; 8:128).

Emerson's process of attunement is twofold. First, he advocates close attention to physical nature and obeying natural laws within (the body's rhythms) through self-reliance. Listening to the sound of his own heartbeat and blood circulation in *Nature* (1836), he writes, "all mean egotism vanishes"; his own heart's pulse becomes the foundation of his connection to "the *currents* of Universal Being" (emphasis added) that "circulate" through him (*CW* 1:10). The fact of feeling, vibrating, *being* throughout nature is affirmed for him in that pulsation. He would later develop this inward listening practice into a method of self-reliance: writing, "Trust thyself: every heart vibrates to that iron string" (*CW* 2:28). Second, Emerson advises conducting ourselves, metaphorically, in alignment with the natural order. In *The Conduct of Life*, he plays with the word *conduct*, referring both to human behavior and to the transmission of energy between surfaces, revealing Michael Faraday's profound influence. Human bodies are, as music theorist Nina Sun Eidsheim writes, "points of transmission," able to transfer energy from one to another—an idea Emerson intuited through his exposure to both Faraday's electromagnetism and Margaret Fuller's extensive writings on music's gyrations which have an electrifying, positive effect on body and mind.[3] Across his oeuvre, Emerson focuses on self-trust that radiates outward: transmitting compassion, gained from attunement to nature, into a platform for action to do good for the greatest number. He asserts that the "power of delight" in nature "does not reside in nature, but in man, or in a *harmony of both*" (*CW* 1:10, emphasis added). If we revert to mean egotism and fail to listen and respond in reciprocal action to nature's signals, then we violate natural symbiosis. We offset that precious harmonic balance of elements that allow for human life on Earth.

Reception is a key facet to Emerson's radical listening. There is a long tradition of treating Emerson's phrase, "all I know is reception" (*CW* 3:48), in the framework of asceticism following Sharon Cameron's work on impersonality and Buddhism.[4] However, I contend that Emerson's posture of reception, his deep listening, is more about a sense of feeling and resonance *with* nature—the "occult relation" he felt "between the very worm, the crawling scorpion and man" during his visit to the Museum of the Jardin des Plantes in Paris (*CW* 10:512). When we compare Emersonian self-reliance with various Buddhist traditions, we find the greatest overlap with Tibetan Buddhist meditations on awakening the "Heart Wish," which is about accessing our genuineness of feeling and growing that outward into compassion for others, not about self-emptying in an ascetic sense.[5] It's time we reevaluate where impersonality becomes counterintuitive to Emerson's larger project.

In the following essay, I argue we gain more from studying Emerson's humility and deep listening, especially if we treat them as part of an anticolonialist relationship to soundscapes, than we do giving airtime to his alleged indifference and impersonality. Unchecked self-emptying—what Emerson describes as "reception without due outlet" (*CW* 3:54)—runs counter to Emersonian self-reliance in a democratic society dependent on willful participation. Across his essays, Emerson persistently points to the growing *problem* of an impersonal relationship to nature; or, as he calls it, "what discord is between man and nature" (*CW* 1:39). In our present climate crisis, the discordance between human and nonhuman nature remains grim. The environmental humanities tend to focus on visible climate changes such as mass accumulations of human waste. However, this chapter focuses on attending to the vibrancy (both the health and the physical vibrations) of various soundscapes; Emerson's active listening as a model of care for the entangled relations in which we live; what I call the *sonic occupation* of space as an act of claiming territory (preventing its use by other people, animals, and so on); and questions of impersonality and colonialism that have interested scholars in Emerson studies and environmental studies alike. Emerson believed in the divine reality behind the Humboldtian web of relations that connects every vibrating being and orb in the cosmos. A central claim is that Emerson processes contemporaneous science about electromagnetism in terms of the rhetoric and wandering style he develops. Focusing especially on music, by which I mean *vibration*, brings forward the pedagogue behind every essay, one who eludes us and refuses to be pinned down, affording room for his readers to find themselves in the magnetic fields of his essays. I propose that when we recognize spaces which may *look* unoccupied are, in fact, vibrant sonic territories critical to our thriving, then we may move toward a habitable future and toward a just and altogether *sound* ecology.

The Discord between Us and Our House, Nature

More than a century ago, observing the wake of the Industrial Revolution, Emerson sensed our growing disconnect from the songs of animals, writing in *Nature* (1836): "As we degenerate, the contrast between us and our house is more evident. We are as much strangers in nature as we are aliens from God. We do not understand the notes of birds. ... Yet this may show us what discord is between man and nature" (CW 1:39). He celebrated nature's regenerative power and portended catastrophe during the rise of America's industrial era. Early on, he identified our inattention to and inability to understand animal song—song being an indicator of a joyful, unstressed, vibrant ecology. Today, his words about our estrangement from nature and its sonic evidence ring truer than ever: sound recording artists report entire wild soundscapes that have been desiccated of song; they have lost their biodiversity, and no longer buzz as vibrantly, foreboding what Rachel Carson ominously called a "silent spring."[6]

I return to Emerson's environmentalism with a particular ear to what I call a sound ecology: the entanglement of humans and nonhumans making vibrations in overlapping sonic territory. Of note, as Laura Dassow Walls and Eric Wilson have shown, is that Emerson was absorbed by emerging sciences, especially Faraday's electromagnetism.[7] He followed new developments and discoveries as closely as he read non-Western literature such as the *Bhagavad Gita* and both informed his theories of self and nature. Hindu and Indigenous philosophies, which embrace a radically decentered self, contributed to what Cornel West calls Emerson's "rapacious individualism and relentless expansionism of the self."[8] Emerson's shedding of selfishness cultivates a radically personal, even sacred relationship to nature centered on listening to the heart's rhythms and thereby coming to learn the heart's wish. This centripetal force, always pointed toward the heart, the center of all motion, is consonant with contemporary anticolonial, Indigenous ways of regarding humans as participants in divine nature—not as conquerors but as consequences and reciprocators of nature's gifts.

Emerson invites us through the concept of "mute music" to listen with our whole selves, to reinsert the specificity of the body into the field of inquiry. Attention to the body—the author's, the interpreting scholar's—reinstates its potential to act, to resonate with others (human and nonhuman), and to move in sync with the land toward a mutually-aligned, more sustainable course. What I am calling an *ecology of reading* introduces a complementary centrifugal force to literary analysis, driving us to think more expansively about Emersonian scholarship and what it means to us as scholars, as people accountable to our response-able world.[9] An ecology of reading situates both Emerson *and* his readers as feeling, breathing listeners in a world of pulsing relations. Emerson's essays often demand readers use inward listening to orient themselves, especially when he places them in liminal spaces like the middle of a stair: some initial disorientation can serve to cultivate their self-determination in the roaming fields of his essays. Developing a habit of deep listening through reading Emerson can train the scholar (intended for the young American scholar especially) in self-trust, to question and interrogate impersonal, oppressive traditions and assumptions, and advocate transformation based on the compassion of the heart that feels rhythmic consanguinity with others—another human, a horse, a bean garden, a cricket, a pond.

Deliberate listening can begin to restore our familiarity with our house, nature, because we become, in part, what we attend and receive. Our bodies are always listening, receiving signals from the invisible waveforms that pass through them. Listening is a highly personal experience: what starts *out there* transforms into what we feel and know *in here*. Emerson confides in "Experience" that all he knows is what he has received: "I am and I have: but I do not get, and when I have fancied I had gotten anything, I found I did not" (*CW* 3:48). His epistemology of reception frames knowledge not as extraction but in terms of a gift economy, much like what Robin Wall Kimmerer proposes in *Braiding Sweetgrass* (2013): "When all the world is a gift in motion, how wealthy we become."[10] Giving compels reciprocation: in the act of receiving, the gift—like a sound wave—is also transmitted, becoming a part of who "I am" and what I then "have" to pass on and give further.

I conceive of Emersonian reception as a deliberate activity of embodied and situated listening, a willful posture of *welcoming in* outside knowledge no matter how soft the vibrations, however mute the music.[11] In music, reception is akin to active listening: practiced band and orchestral musicians waiting to enter the score both count time and *feel* the moment when their sound is needed, like a guttural summons or beckoning to join in collaborative, democratic creation. Active listening may seem—on the outside—to be passive, but it requires alertness and care, and it has the potential to radically change dominant structures by making room for traditionally marginalized voices. Emerson intended reception to lead to transformation: "life stagnates from too much reception without due outlet" (*CW* 3:54). Growth occurs when we convert energy received into action, what he elsewhere calls "practical power" (*CW* 3:49). True transformation requires acting on what was received, choosing to carry one's part in resonance with other vibrating beings.

Navigating Emerson's Circles: Magnetic and Mechanical Waves

Lyellian science, and the expanded temporality of geologic time that came with it, supplanted notions of Biblical time and surfaced a variety of extinction stories, a sociocultural phenomenon Ursula K. Heise outlines in *Imagining Extinction* (2016). Following sustained industrialization around 1800 came the new cultural dominant: "the sense that humans were endangering nature on a grand scale, rather than the other way around."[12] At sea, commercial whalers all but extinguished bowheads in the Bering Strait.[13] In the States, the public bore witness to declining populations of bison and passenger pigeons. Before the turn of the century, mammologist and ornithologist Joel A. Allen (1838–1921) published the first inventory of endangered species.[14] In the nineteenth century and now, an expanded temporality enables us to guess our own end, not in the hands of an angry god but at the mercy of a dying star—if not sooner due to human-driven climate changes.

Through meditating on developments in science—Humphry Davy's electrochemistry, Faraday's electromagnetism, and Ernst Chladni's sound node experiments—Emerson attuned himself to the planet's constant activity and movement in polarity, "the harmony of the centrifugal and centripetal forces," the magnetic field generated by the Earth's core, the electric frequencies that charge the air (*CW* 3:107). Emerson described Chladni's demonstrations—for instance, of sand strewn on glass that will then organize into symmetrical patterns in response to the musical tones of a violin bow—as "central" to understanding the nature of the universe. Indeed, sound waves proved an adaptable cognitive model, significantly influencing Faraday's observation of electromagnetic induction, Charles Wheatstone's acoustic experiments, and Robert Mallet's seismology.[15] Responding to Chladni, Emerson surmised music's role in the natural order: "Sing, and the rocks will crystallize; Sing, and the plant will organize."[16] Likewise, his intense focus on Faraday's electromagnetism ought to inform how we read his reflections on power and polarity. Wilson frames Emerson's electric rhetoric in *Emerson's Sublime Science*, stating that as we apprehend "the electrical undercurrent in Emerson's thought, we now suspect that when he praises 'energy,' 'life,' 'force,' 'attraction,' 'spirit,' he may well have specific scientific information in mind."[17] Our bodies, Emerson understood, are immersed in electromagnetic and mechanical (e.g., sound) waves. As he speculates in his second essay under the title "Nature" (1844): "Without electricity the air would rot" (*CW* 3:107).

Emerson called Faraday "the most exact of natural philosophers," and he understood from Faraday that our bodies are constantly subjected to forces beyond our perception. Faraday studied the relationships between invisible power sources—electricity, magnetism, light—and by examining their interrelations, he discovered the principles behind later, major inventions such as the electric motor, the generator, and the transformer. One of his most important findings is that magnetic filings organized into circular rings around poles signal undulating waves, radiating outward. Earth, for instance, is itself a magnet *and* generates an invisible yet powerful magnetic field. Today, this fact is common knowledge: we know this field is what protects us from cosmic rays. In Emerson's lifetime, the insights of wave science proliferated scientific possibilities, and ethical ones, too: he writes in "Circles" that this figure, the circle, is repeated without end throughout nature: "the heart refuses to be imprisoned; in its first and narrowest pulses, it already tends outward with a vast force, and to immense and innumerable expansions ... There is no outside, no enclosing wall, no circumference to us" (*CW* 2:181). Similarly in "Experience," he compares human beings to "globes" and "spheres," constantly turning (*CW* 3:44), and in *The Conduct of Life* this motion leads to generating power.

After witnessing a magnet align a jumble of steel filings in June 1827, a visual result similar to Chladni's sound node experiments, Emerson seized the metaphor of polarity to describe nature's undulations which bring to our world its simultaneous unity and differences. Walls describes the visible figure of the magnet as "only half the picture" which Emerson saw. Waveforms are often drawn as lines, but they are circular. Operating beyond our perception is the energy, Walls continues, "that circulates in the figure's environment, connecting pole to pole and orienting everything surrounding the magnet along its lines of force. Thus, the polar figure organizes an entire environment around itself *and* sets the components of that environment in motion."[18] For Emerson, this realization meant that Earth's creatures are affected by the undulating forces passing through us—even those forces we cannot see. Migratory songbirds, creatures far more attuned to fluctuations in sound and light than humans, have a highly sophisticated magnetic sensitivity and use it to navigate vast swaths of land, like an internal compass.[19] By the same token, Emerson reasons in "Nature" (1844) that the same "aboriginal push" at the creation of the universe, "propagates itself through all the balls of the system, and through every atom of every ball" (*CW* 3:107). He proceeds to account for every positive charge, or energy source: "to every creature nature added a little violence of direction in its proper path, a shove to put it on its way; in every instance, a slight generosity, a drop too much" (*CW* 3:107).

Emerson transforms Faraday's demonstrations of magnetic fields into a method of living in tune with nature's pulsations. He writes in "Compensation" (1841):

> Polarity, or action and reaction, we meet in every part of nature; in darkness and light; in heat and cold; in the ebb and flow of waters; in male and female; in the inspiration and expiration of plants and animals; in the equation of quantity and quality in the fluids of the animal body; in *the systole and diastole of the heart; in the undulations of fluids, and of sound*; in the centrifugal and centripetal gravity; in electricity, galvanism, and chemical affinity. (*CW* 2:57, emphasis added)

The activity of polarity is in "the undulations of fluids, and of sound," regardless of our ability to hear or see the mechanical waves (produced by charged particle vibrations), and the push-pull forces of electromagnetic waves (which differ from mechanical waves in their ability to transfer energy through a vacuum), all of which fall under Emerson's metaphor of polarity. While he keenly followed developments in wave science, Emerson strove to attune himself to all vacillations in nature, from "the inspiration and expiration of plants and animals" to "centrifugal and centripetal gravity." Meanwhile, he added his own insight, observing the principle of oscillation at work in all matters of the heart, from its physical impulses, "the systole and diastole," to "their analogy in the ebb and flow of love," as he writes in his essay, "Friendship" (*CW* 2:116).

Polarity is more than a static theory, as Emerson discusses. In a world in which "nothing solid is secure; every thing tilts and rocks," he recognized that following the same paths as those who came before is not enough to orient oneself to present realities (*CW* 1:121). Even Earth's magnetic poles fluctuate (flows of molten liquid iron in the planet's core move Earth's magnetic field); according to NASA, "magnetic pole reversal happens all the (geologic) time."[20] In the mid-nineteenth century, the north magnetic pole floated further south, "roaming around" Canada.[21] Emerson continually challenges alignments, sometimes within the same breath of an essay, and he has been known to adjust his actions in changing social currents, avoiding any easy replication of his own roaming path.

Emerson's rhetoric generates a magnetic field in writing, one that his reader is meant to chart using self-reliance (or self-tuning) as a guide. In some cases, the push-pull forces in Emerson's oeuvre might be construed as contradictions: in his essay "Compensation," "the world is thus dual," and yet it is singular in his essay on "The Over-Soul": "as the earth lies in the soft arms of the atmosphere; that Unity, that Over-soul, within which every [hu]man's particular being is contained and made one with all other" (*CW* 2:57; 2:160). William James later takes up this debate of "The One and the Many" in *Pragmatism* (1907). Some of Emerson's own tilts and shifts have to do with changing views at different periods of his life (for instance, his own progress toward advocating for abolition). I suggest that belying these oppositions is Emerson's polarity doing its work, asking the reader to find their own way, "to stand wistful and admiring before this great spectacle [nature]" and its "circular power" (*CW* 1:54).[22]

Emerson recognized, above all, the power of narrative form, as he explains in "The Poet": "it is not metres, but a metre-making argument, that makes a poem,—a thought so passionate and alive, that, like the spirit of a plant or an animal, it has architecture of its own, and adorns nature with a new thing" (*CW* 3:6). His sentences contain the spirit and architecture of electromagnetic and mechanical waves, requiring readers to confront and embrace instability, finding themselves somewhere in the lines of force between poles, or between the sound nodes of a wave. We are required to situate ourselves without Emerson's full aid as he seeks to find his own footing, all the while poised to engage in what he calls "this globe of action" (*CW* 1:60).

When nearly every Emersonian sentence could stand alone as a topic sentence, as Stanley Cavell has framed them, we might treat each one as an atom exchanging ionic charges with those in front and those behind it (Adam Hodder likewise compares his sentences to atoms).[23] Equally, we could treat each idea as a sound wave frequency passing through us, among other, simultaneous waves of ideas concerning such large and unwieldy topics as his essay titles suggest: "History," "Circles," and the like. Fittingly, Emerson in "The American Scholar" encourages readers to locate what speaks to their "own nature" in his essays, to inhabit moments in which they realize, "This is my music: this is myself" (*CW* 1:63). He demands that we steady ourselves in an essay's environment by seeking what resonates with our own habits and rhythms, finding where we stand in relation to Emerson's ideas, through "self-trust" (*CW* 1:63).

Centering the reader's embodied self-trust is, following Roland Barthes's reader-response theory, a useful method for interpreting Emerson's oscillations (as well as our own) across his long and dense oeuvre. Barthes comments, "it is the very rhythm of what is read and what is not read that creates the pleasure of the great narratives."[24] In Emerson, one finds solid ground in one essay only to lose it in another—here he is personal, there impersonal, and elsewhere he exudes "impersonal intimacy"; thus a reader constructs, deconstructs, and reconstructs an idea *with* Emerson, as if thinking alongside him, in perpetuity.[25] As Cavell writes, "wherever he [Emerson] is we are—otherwise how can we hear him?"[26] Emerson calls conversation "a game of circles" and reading him is to turn back and forth as in a wave, or a conversation each of us has with Emerson. Moreover, this activity of vibrating to and fro can be, as Barthes would say, a form of immense pleasure.

We might take Emerson's theory of polarity—both physical and metaphorical—as inspiration for an environmental sustainability movement not of conflict but of flexible and generative collaboration across communities with different, even opposing needs. This kind of collaboration, born out of difference, means finding what Angela Y. Davis and Audre Lorde would call "unity," which is not to say "sameness."[27] Sustainable solutions require balancing many disparate needs, listening willingly, welcoming in the new and then acting with purpose—to grow into a movement based on sound allyship and unity, a movement for all people, not just the privileged few. It's not easy but Emerson prepares us for the difficult task at hand when he humbles us, placing readers in paradox such that we have no choice but to listen.

Ecomusicology in Metaphor and Action

On shore, listening to the crash and spray of ocean waves, what goes on below the sea's surface seems as silent to us as outer space, yet that aqueous world is replete with a variety of mechanical and electromagnetic undulations just as space is awash with cosmic rays. Emerson offers a deep meditation on waveforms: "From the earth, as a shore, I look out into that silent sea. I seem to partake its rapid transformations: the active enchantment reaches my dust, and I dilate and conspire with the morning wind" (*CW* 1:13). Gravity produces the "active enchantment," the musical activity or the undulation of the "silent sea" that reaches, transforms, and dilates him while also calling him back to his body, activating it to sense his earliest state of being, his "dust." What on the surface looks like a visual spectacle, is actually a physical, material movement that washes over him in a "silent" but nevertheless musical sea. This is Emerson's sound ecology, his ability to expand his sensitivity through meditation on divine nature and suspend in imagination a global and even cosmic *umwelt*.

Emerson offers us a model for widening our perception and broadening the boundaries of what we conceptually call "kin" and "home." Early in his career, he felt a closeness with the nonhuman world, a "sonic intimacy" (to borrow a phrase from Dominic Pettman) with the vibrating world he—and we—receive through our bodies.[28] His felt kinship with animals, insects, and plants contributed to his unusual formulations that locate "frozen music" in the likeness between the "human hand" and the "flipper of the fossil saurus" (*CW* 1:27). Emerson's textual soundscape, essays he hopes will "resound with the hum of insects" (*CW* 1:34), aids readers in coming to know our climate in an embodied way. Lyellian science, and the radical expansion of human knowledge that came with it, worked its way into Emerson's writings on two registers of equal import: the literal and the metaphorical, which operate in tandem like music, as bass and treble clefs do—not in a binary or a hierarchy but in agreed, collective, multi-faceted action. Both registers, what he calls the "ground-tone" of common life and the loftier conclusions about living a life in harmonic alignment with nature, are essential to understanding Emerson's sound ecology.

Emerson's main thesis across his oeuvre, outlined in his 1833 lecture on "The Uses of Natural History," and again in 1841 in the essay "History," is to make communing with nature a habit of both mind and body: "Man is the broken giant, and in all his weakness he is invigorated by *touching* his mother earth, that is, by habits of conversation with nature" (*CW* 2:18, emphasis added). The reference is to the Greek god Antaeus, who drew his strength from his mother, Gaia. Antaeus was, as Emerson notes, "suffocated by the gripe [sic] of Hercules," who wrestled him so as to keep his feet off the ground (*CW* 2:18). To bring embodiment into focus, I want to emphasize the vibrational exchange that occurs in the *touch* of "conversation" with nature. To converse means to turn (Latin, *vertere, versare*) with (Latin, *con-*), so we might consider Emerson to mean turning with Earth, synchronizing our movements with and drawing our strength from the forces of nature. In this passage, the body's vitality depends on attunement: learning the rhythms of others and responding in kind to move in sync together, as true allies and wrestlers do, dancing in time with one another and in direct contact with the land.

Responding to a newly industrialized society, Emerson affirms we are part and parcel of nature's long and perpetual creation: we "participate the invention of nature," meaning we possess some of nature's power of invention (*CW* 3:15). We likewise participate in—and even possess (e.g., nuclear power)—its destruction. Now many environmental scientists call this epoch of human production the Anthropocene. Humans have accumulated so much pollution and waste as to have colonized large portions of air, land, and sea. Max Liboiron connects the problem of pollution to its long and lingering existence in Lyellian terms: "You can't 'clean up' plastics because they exist in geological time," "you can't recycle them out of the way" when "there is no 'away.'"[29] Pollution, thus considered, resonates with Emerson's insight that "Nature, in its ministry to man, is not only the material, but is also the process and the result" (*CW* 1:11). Our results thus far—thousandfold increases in global extinctions, a net loss of North American birds approaching three billion—are ominous at best.[30]

Today, popular environmentalist arguments rely heavily on visual evidence of environmental threats (e.g., footage of miles-wide plastic wastelands floating in the sea). Pollution's sound effects are given far less attention. Some noise pollution escapes land-dwellers entirely. Underwater sonic territory used by blue whales, right whales, and other marine animals for hunting and finding mates is shrinking: the documentary *Sonic Sea* chronicles innumerable whales beaching themselves with bleeding eardrums after sonic blasting.[31] 90 per cent of global trade is conducted by sea, producing noise at low-level frequencies that travel a greater distance in water than in air. This large-scale sonic occupation effectively colonizes underwater territory, preventing marine life from flourishing in the noise. We can think bigger about what we do within earshot of whales (e.g., ban sonic blasting and reduce dependence on propeller cavitation for shipping vessels), and what noise we produce above sea level: in short, shift our imagination, as Lyell, Darwin, and Emerson did, to attend to vibrations and migrations on a global scale. Indeed, some marine biologists are using sound recordings of healthy coral reefs to rehabilitate underwater ecosystems devastated by storms: they're finding that playing recordings of healthy marine soundscapes attracts more fish and encourages oysters to settle and attach themselves.[32]

If we attend only to visible borders and boundaries—of nations, of property lines—then we fail to perceive the interconnectedness of global soundscapes. We are accustomed to tuning out the noise around us as part of everyday life, an aggravating undersong, even though it has been directly linked by the US Environmental Protection Agency (EPA) to stress-induced illnesses.[33] When we listen and attend, the interference becomes more frequent, top of mind, and increasingly difficult to ignore, calling greater attention to industry's sonic occupation of our house, nature. Moreover, various health problems, such as high blood pressure, are caused by noises—from loud factories and construction sites to increased air traffic—which disproportionately impact low-income communities.

Attunement is about expanding the human perceptual register, enlarging what Baltic German biologist Jakob Johann von Uexküll named our *Umwelt*: the subjective reality of our environment, comprised of our perceptual world (*Merkwelt*) and our active world (*Wirkwelt*).[34] Most translate *umwelt* to mean environment or, literally, "self-centered world," and this is precisely the dominant view of environment that could use some Emersonian "relentless expansionism of the self," to recall West.[35] Listening alone is not enough: by Emerson's own reckoning, reception needs a due outlet, and how we go about transmitting what we receive is of the utmost importance to a man devoted to ethics. I foreground an Emersonian concept of self: meant to obey the impulses of the individual heart and to go beyond the concerns of the ego, moving from individual reflection on nature to communal action, becoming an engaged citizen and steward of land. Self-expansion, enacted through the heart wish, isn't viable if we maintain an impersonal regard for nature and all living things. For Emerson, an impersonal or impartial posture of reception is meant to be temporary.

For example, a frequent critique of Emerson is his slowness to activism. Yet when he finally rises to the occasion, he speaks with fervent conviction, aiming to anger up the blood in calls for human sympathy and action—again, he reminds us of our humanity, both in his faults and through the expression of his heart's wish. Emerson's radical listening is reflected in his meditations on the polarizing issues of his time, namely slavery and Jacksonian Indian Removal. Eight years after the Indian Removal Act (1830), Emerson wrote a public letter to President Van Buren protesting Cherokee removal. In his letter, we can hear his discerning ear and attention to the politics of sound. He had read Cherokee newspapers, and "witnessed with sympathy" for some time, concluding that those few "pretended" agents acting falsely as "deputies [who] did by no means represent the will of the [Cherokee] nation" had brokered a "sham treaty" with the US government. His call to dissolve the fraudulent treaty is far from impersonal, unfeeling or disinterested:

> Almost the entire Cherokee Nation stand up and say, "This is not our act. Behold us. Here are we. Do not mistake that handful of deserters for us;" and the American President and the Cabinet, the Senate and the House of Representatives, neither hear these men nor see them, and are contracting to put this active nation into carts and boats, and to drag them over mountains and rivers to a wilderness at a vast distance beyond the Mississippi. (*CW* 11:91)

Emerson's appeal to listen calls on the US President, his cabinet, and the public to recognize the Cherokee as an "active nation" deserving of attention as well as a response: "such deafness to screams for mercy were never heard of in times of peace and in the dealing of a nation with its own allies and wards, since the earth was made" (*CW* 11:92). Emerson was, by his own account, "slow to believe" the possibility of such "a needless act of terror," however once he determined the truth, he converted reception, or what I call *active listening*, into practical power and published this letter. Emerson conducts his self-reliance like electricity into action: whatever positive charge he gains, he eventually loses by charging others with it, transferring it, and passing it on.

On the one hand, impersonality makes sense as a moral structure in the Buddhist context employed by Sharon Cameron because it is about practicing self-discipline and moderation to achieve a morally superior state of being. On the other hand, misreadings of it in a US context reinforce a colonialist consciousness. There is a profound difference between cultures that hold nature intimately close—as "sacred," "personal," and "enchanted" (borrowing terms from Sandy Grande, Tariq Banuri, and Morris Berman, respectively)—and those cultures that regard nature with secular indifference, as a material resource used for fuel, for example.[36] The belief in reality, "as impersonal, secular, material, mechanistic, and relativistic," as Grande illumines in *Red Pedagogy* (2004), and "having no special relationship with human existence or divine reality" undergirds a colonialist consciousness.[37] Moreover, this impersonality favors and perpetuates a capitalist mindset in legislation that focuses on property lines without consideration for how activities like drilling and fracking will impact neighboring people's lives. Lands that seem, to a foreigner's eye, empty or unoccupied, are in fact alive with vibrant, interconnected, collective activity coordinated across a scale of time well beyond human perception. A theory of American impersonality is more accurately and productively employed by Banuri, Berman, and Grande as a critique of colonialism.

Environmentalist scholarship, like theories of the American impersonal, can too easily, if unintentionally, reinforce colonialism embedded in Emerson's thought, especially when it "assume[s] entitlement to Indigenous Land," to borrow Liboiron's definition.[38] While an important messenger, Emerson wrote mostly for white settler audiences and relied on the homogenizing trope of the "ecologically noble savage," as Grande aptly phrases it.[39] His emphasis on cultivating habits of conversation with nature, while making the argument for equal and free access to natural spaces, is founded on the presumption that those spaces are readily available, uninhabited by humans. It's important for us to keep these tangled knots in mind: Emerson was an advocate *and* he could not escape his own white power, privilege, casual racism, and colonialist mindset.[40] An ecology of reading acknowledges Emerson's complexities and tensions and underscores that we, Emerson's readers, are also historically bounded—holding us accountable to our present moment, to our living neighbors, and to our unsustainable course.

From Extinction Grief to Action, Converting Polarity into "Practical Power"

Musical analysis offers a new framework for reading Emerson's essay "Experience" as a physical act in writing and a mental exercise, one in which Emerson moves from being paralyzed by grief into feeling once again through resuming activity. Ecomusicology affords some guidance, through Emerson's recovery of his sensibility, on a course we might chart from grieving what we have lost to locating a sound ecology on the planet we have now.

Scholars often refer to Emerson's famous line, "We live amid surfaces, and the true art of life is to skate well on them," as an example of impersonality, self-emptying or detachment, but when we consider the motion in it, the message radically changes (*CW* 3:35). Skating, typically read as a reference to ice skating, is not as straightforward as it seems, and the author who loved the thirteenth and fourteenth definitions of words surely meant it to carry as many meanings as possible. Briefly, "to skate," derived from "stilt" (via Dutch *schaats*, Middle Dutch *schaetse*, and Old French *escache*), is related to the Old English word *sceacan*, which in its many iterations means "to shake," "to vibrate," "to tremble," and "to go" or "to glide" (*OED* and *Merriam-Webster*). Moreover, the Germanic root for "stilt" (*stelt-*) is also represented in Middle High German *stolzen*, meaning "to limp," and Swedish *stulta*, meaning "to totter, stagger" (*OED*), both of which convey a sense of trembling between two points. These etymological connections, especially the latter two, suggest vibrating between two points, which corresponds with Emerson's location (and the reader's) at the outset of "Experience" between two ends on a stair, as well as the difficulty in navigating between two extremes.

I read Emerson to mean in the above sentence that shaking and vibrating *well*—in other words, to feel, move, and vibrate with the physical world the best we can from the surfaces we are given—is "the true art of life." More generally read in musical terms, "Experience" suggests widening perception to become like a tuning fork in the world: to allow oneself to be struck, to be moved, to feel the way when the path cannot be seen clearly. We might think of Emerson as the broken giant, Antaeus, struggling to find his footing, to touch Gaia. This is the Emerson I hear, a man striving to vibrate so well as to resonate and move with the music, to converse with nature and turn as Earth does.

Turning, or circulation, assists the author's pivot in the essay from grief and dissociation to idealism and willful association. He treats movement as inevitable and natural—we must move, it is in our nature to move, to take a leap of faith: "Nature hates calculators; her methods are saltatory and impulsive. Man lives by pulses; our organic movements are such; and the chemical and ethereal agents are undulatory and alternate; and the mind goes antagonizing on, and never prospers but by fits" (*CW* 3:39). Emerson argues that humankind proceeds in leaps—the word "saltatory" connotes both dancing and leaping, from the Latin *saltare*, meaning "to leap" (*OED*)—rather than by slow, linear transitions. Humankind "lives by pulses," natural circulations link us to the natural order, nature's volcanic eruptions and spontaneous evolutions.[41]

The essay, by way of moving and feeling, fulfills Emerson's defiant promise that "grief too will make us idealists" (*CW* 3:29). If a central problem is Emerson's inability to touch or to feel his grief, as Sharon Cameron suggests, then movement—reaching or tilting to touch—offers a way beyond. When Emerson cannot see either end of the stairs in "Experience," when "night hovers all day" and "sleep lingers...about our eyes," he lowers his threshold of sensation to receive the imperceptible, to explore other means of feeling, and learn where he is (*CW* 3:27). If he cannot touch Gaia to regain his strength, he must converse or turn with nature in tandem, in harmony, in a long meditation reconnecting to the heart. Emerson recalls himself to his body in, of, and as nature, re-membering it (Cavell likewise interprets the essay as a "series of remembering") methodically until, in a final move, the author places his heart back into his chest and wills it to beat again, to re-sound and re-verb. The human pulse, especially its persistent life-giving rhythm, represents time and again the vital element or the miracle of life in literature; we need look no further than Mary Shelley's *Frankenstein* for an example. Emerson ultimately wills his "old heart" "up again" to beat the pulse of life into his perception (*CW* 3:49).

This move marks the active role the body and its feelings play in renewing idealism, strength, and vigor.

He writes near the midpoint of "Experience" from "firmer" ground: "Without any shadow of doubt, amidst this vertigo of shows and politics, I settle myself ever the firmer in the creed that we should not postpone and refer and wish, but do broad justice where we are" (*CW* 3:35). Thus no matter where one finds oneself, the conversion of energy, the transformation of inward listening into doing *justice*, movement itself generates the reliable, steadying center. When we reach into the deepest registers of our heart's wish, according to the Tibetan Buddhist Lama Shenpen Hookam, "we are not going to be fully satisfied until all beings are happy."[42]

We ought to consider Emerson's knowing by way of reception as a posture of conductivity, a means to shed mean egotism and transform inward listening into resonance with others, touching into feeling, listening into sounding, reaching into turning. By now it will come as no surprise that to Emerson, "Power," in his 1860 essay of that title, is an electric current, "an element with which the world is so saturated,—there is no chink or crevice in which it is not lodged,—that no honest seeking goes unrewarded"; power is "a sharing of the nature of the world" (*CW* 6:28, 30). The electric currents which saturate the world bring all matter into relation and into movement. Moreover, Emerson writes that a mind "parallel with the laws of nature will be in the *current* of events and strong with their strength" (*CW* 6:30, emphasis added). This strength is generated by investing in the kinetic action we may take, together, in an expressive, diverse, democratic soundscape. For Emerson, what music is "mute" in polarity becomes audible in conversation, set to motion in taking turns; through sharing, a tongue may be "framed to music," and the heartbeat becomes the ruling "will" (*CW* 6:28). Voicing is to participate in nature's democratic process: "By obeying each thought frankly, by harping, or, if you will, pounding on each string, we learn at last its power. By the same obedience to other thoughts, we learn theirs, and then comes some reasonable hope of harmonizing them" (*CW* 6:2). His musical lexicon offers the reader a method in metaphor for practical action: to harp or to sound each thought and learn its power before we deploy the instruments to make our music.

This idealism could, too easily, go awry in the wrong hands, so I would like to return, one last time, to "Compensation," an essay that is truly about karma.[43] Hinduism had a tremendous impact on Emerson, often called the Sage of Concord, who was the first public intellectual in the United States to openly embrace Eastern religion and philosophy. Texts like the *Bhagavad Gita* influenced Emerson's empathy for enslaved men and women, his admiration for John Brown, and even his firm resolve on the necessity of abolition, as Nikhil Bilwakesh has shown.[44] As Emerson writes in "Compensation": "You cannot do wrong without suffering wrong. … Treat men as pawns and ninepins and you shall suffer as well as they. If you leave out their heart, you shall lose your own" (*CW* 3:65). While harmony seems a lofty ideal, Emerson is really calling for a more spiritual way of life, a method of acting and moving in agreement with nature, the cosmos, and humanity which is encoded in the sound themes and expressive messages of the Vedas; Tatyana Elizarenkova writes about the last hymn of the Ṛg Veda: "a call for harmony of minds and intentions is the real 'message' of the hymn."[45] For Emerson, music is like the creative force at work in nature and in each individual: "Creative force, like a musical composer, goes on unweariedly repeating a simple air or theme now high, now low, in solo, in chorus, ten thousand times reverberated, till it fills earth and heaven with the chant" (*CW* 4:62). The creative force in nature is a unified, democratic expression of *all* life "in chorus" whose music depends on each individual having sufficient sonic territory to express themselves "in solo" and to trust in their unique power. This power is, of course, generated by the heart that aligns itself with the pulses of Earth and all vibrant beings.

Notes

1. Douglas Kahn, *Earth Sound Earth Signal: Energies and Earth Magnitude in the Arts* (Berkeley: University of California Press, 2013), 177.
2. For more on Emerson's environmental ethics, see Susan L. Dunston, *Emerson's Environmental Ethics* (Lanham: Lexington Books, 2018).
3. Nina Sun Eidsheim, *Sensing Sound: Singing & Listening as Vibrational Practice* (Durham, NC: Duke University Press, 2015), 18; Christina Katopodis, "The Music of the Spheres in Emerson, Fuller, and Thoreau: Lyell's Principles and Transcendental Listening," *ISLE: Interdisciplinary Studies in Literature and Environment* 28, no. 3 (Autumn 2021): 839–67.
4. Sharon Cameron, *Impersonality: Seven Essays* (Chicago: University of Chicago Press, 2007); Branka Arsić, ed., *American Impersonal: Essays with Sharon Cameron* (New York: Bloomsbury, 2014).
5. Lama Shenpen Hookam, "What Is the Heart Wish?" *Buddha Within: The Teachings of Lama Shenpen Hookam*, July 31, 2019, https://buddhawithin.org.uk/2019/07/31/heart-wish/.
6. Rachel Carson, *Silent Spring: Fortieth Anniversary Edition* (Boston: Houghton Mifflin, 2002); Bernie Krause, *The Great Animal Orchestra: Finding the Origins of Music in the World's Wild Places* (New York: Back Bay Books, 2012).
7. Laura Dassow Walls, *Emerson's Life in Science: The Culture of Truth* (Ithaca, NY: Cornell University Press, 2003); Eric Wilson, *Emerson's Sublime Science* (New York: Palgrave, 1999).
8. Cornel West, *The American Evasion of Philosophy: A Genealogy of Pragmatism* (Madison: University of Wisconsin Press, 1989), 11.
9. See a discussion of "response-ability" in Karen Barad, "On Touching—The Inhuman That Therefore I Am," *Differences: A Journal of Feminist Cultural Studies* 23, no. 2 (Fall 2012): 206–23, 206..
10. Robin Wall Kimmerer, *Braiding Sweetgrass: Indigenous Wisdom, Scientific Knowledge, and the Teachings of Plants* (Minneapolis: Milkweed, 2013), 31.
11. Situated listening is my adaptation of Donna Haraway's situated knowledge(s). See Donna Haraway, "Situated Knowledges: The Science Question in Feminism and the Privilege of Partial Perspective," *Feminist Studies* 14, no. 3 (Fall 1988): 575–99.
12. Ursula K. Heise, *Imagining Extinction: The Cultural Meanings of Endangered Species* (Chicago: University of Chicago, 2016), 6.
13. Bathsheba Demuth, *Floating Coast: An Environmental History of the Bering Strait* (New York: W. W. Norton, 2019), 15–70.

14. Mark V. Barrow, Jr., *Nature's Ghosts: Confronting Extinction from the Age of Jefferson to the Age of Ecology* (Chicago: University of Chicago Press, 2009), 5, 81–82.
15. Edward J. Gillin, "Seismology's acoustic debt: Robert Mallet, Chladni's figures, and the Victorian science of earthquakes," *Sound Studies* 6, no. 1 (2020): 65–82.
16. *LL* 1:120. See also Sarah Ann Wider, "Chladni Patterns, Lyceum Halls, and Skillful Experimenters: Emerson's New Metaphysics for the Listening Reader," in *Emerson Bicentennial Essays*, ed. Ronald A. Bosco and Joel Myerson (Boston: Massachusetts Historical Society, 2006), 86–114.
17. Wilson, *Emerson's Sublime Science*, 95.
18. Walls, *Emerson's Life in Science*, 127–29.
19. Jingjing Xu et. al., "Magnetic Sensitivity of Cryptochrome 4 from a Migratory Songbird," *Nature* 594 (2021): 535–40.
20. NASA Content Administrator, "2012: Magnetic Pole Reversal Happens All the (Geologic) Time," *NASA*, November 30, 2011, accessed July 20, 2020, www.nasa.gov/topics/earth/features/2012-poleReversal.html.
21. Shannon Hall, "The North Magnetic Pole's Mysterious Journey Across the Arctic," *The New York Times*, February 4, 2019, accessed July 20, 2020, www.nytimes.com/2019/02/04/science/north-magnetic-pole-model.html/..
22. For more on Emerson's contradictions, see Russell B. Goodman, "Paths of Coherence through Emerson's Philosophy: The Case of 'Nominalist and Realist,'" in *The Other Emerson*, ed. Branka Arsić and Cary Wolfe (Minneapolis: University of Minnesota Press, 2010), 41–58; Mildred Silver, "Emerson and the Idea of Progress," *American Literature* 12, no. 1 (March 1940): 1–19.
23. Adam Hodder, *Emerson's Rhetoric of Revelation: Nature, the Readers, and the Apocalypse Within* (University Park: Pennsylvania University Press, 1989), 121. See also Mark Noble, "Emerson's Atom and the Matter of Suffering," *Nineteenth-Century Literature* 64, no. 1 (June 2009): 16–47.
24. Roland Barthes, *The Pleasure of the Text*, trans. Richard Miller (New York: Hill and Wang, 1975), 11.
25. Joan Richardson, "Bookforum Talks with Stanley Cavell," *Bookforum*, April 1, 2011, accessed July 20, 2020, https://www.bookforum.com/interviews/bookforum-talks-with-stanley-cavell-7169.
26. Stanley Cavell, "Finding as Founding: Taking Steps in Emerson's 'Experience,'" in *Emerson's Transcendental Etudes* (Stanford: Stanford University Press, 2003), 110–40, 122.
27. Angela Davis, "Audre Lorde: A Burst of Light Symposium," March 22, 2014, Medgar Evers College, accessed July 20, 2020, https://www.youtube.com/watch?v=EpYdfcvYPEQ.
28. Dominic Pettman, *Sonic Intimacy: Voices, Species, Technics (Or, How to Listen to the World)* (Stanford: Stanford University Press, 2017).
29. Max Liboiron, *Pollution is Colonialism* (Durham, NC: Duke University Press, 2021), 17.
30. Kenneth V. Rosenberg et. al., "Decline of the North American Avifauna," *Science* 366, no. 6461 (October 2019): 120–24, accessed September 27, 2021, https://science.sciencemag.org/content/366/6461/120.
31. C. W. Clark et al., "Acoustic Masking in Marine Ecosystems: Intuitions, Analysis, and Implication," *Marine Ecology Progress Series* 395 (2009): 201–22; T. W. Cranford and P. Krysl, "Fin Whale Sound Reception Mechanisms: Skull Vibration Enables Low-Frequency Hearing," *PLoS ONE* 10, no. 1 (2015): doi:10.1371/journal.pone.0116222.
32. Elizabeth Preston, "Playing Recordings of a Healthy Ocean Can Help Restore Marine Ecosystems," *Smithsonian Magazine*, November 30, 2021, accessed October 14, 2021,

33. "Clean Air Act Title IV—Noise Pollution," *Environmental Protection Agency (EPA)*, July 16, 2019, accessed April 16, 2024, https://www.epa.gov/clean-air-act-overview/clean-air-act-title-iv-noise-pollution.
34. Brett Buchanan, *Onto-Ethologies: The Animal Environments of Uexküll, Heidegger, Merleau-Ponty, and Deleuze* (New York, NY: State University of New York Press, 2008), 2.
35. Buchanan, *Onto-Ethologies*, 4–6.
36. Grande weaves together Banuri, Berman, and Anthony Giddens's work beautifully in Sandy Grande, *Red Pedagogy: Native American Social and Political Thought* (Lanham: Rowan & Littlefield, 2004), 67.
37. Grande, *Red Pedagogy*, 69.
38. Liboiron, *Pollution is Colonialism*, 9.
39. Grande, *Red Pedagogy*, 65.
40. For more on the interconnection of Emerson's colonialist and environmental legacies, see Lawrence Buell, *The Environmental Imagination: Thoreau, Nature Writing, and the Formation of American Culture* (Cambridge, MA: Harvard University Press, 1995), 15; Roderick Nash, *Wilderness and the American Mind* (New Haven, CT: Yale University Press, 1967), 85–86.
41. To read more on Emerson's embrace of the new, see Goodman, "Paths of Coherence," 41–58.
42. Hookam, "What Is the Heart Wish?"
43. Phillip Goldberg, *American Veda: From Emerson and the Beatles to Yoga and Meditation: How Spirituality Changed the West* (New York, NY: Three Rivers Press, 2010), 33.
44. Nikhil Bilwakesh, "Emerson, John Brown, and Arjuna: Translating the *Bhagavad Gita* in a Time of War." *ESQ* 55, no. 1 (2009): 27–58, 29.
45. Tatyana J. Elizarenkova, *Language and Style of the Vedic Ṛṣis*, ed. Wendy Doniger (Albany: State University of New York Press, 1995), 147.

CHAPTER 5

TRANSCENDENTAL GEOLOGIES

Emerson, Antislavery, and the Kairos *of Deep Time*

PATRICK MORGAN

> He is its head and heart, and finds something of himself ... in every mountain stratum.
>
> Ralph Waldo Emerson, *Nature* (*CW* 1:40)

When it comes to Ralph Waldo Emerson's relation to antislavery, timing is everything. And that timing is slow. Indeed, scholars are constantly reaching for new ways to describe Emerson's sluggish activism, from Maurice S. Lee's "reluctant, uneven move"[1] to Jeffrey Insko's apt characterization of scholarly consensus: "Emerson was a kind of slow-footed laggard, his arrival to abolitionism belated."[2] Scholars generally agree that with his first major antislavery address—"On the Anniversary of the Emancipation of the Negroes in the British West Indies," delivered on August 1, 1844—Emerson's activism accelerated. The question, though, is over the rate of acceleration. Len Gougeon[3] and Robert D. Richardson[4] see a clear demarcation from mere antislavery to committed abolitionism, while Maurice S. Lee,[5] Martha Schoolman,[6] and Jeffrey Insko[7] dampen that demarcation. According to Insko, it was not until the 1850 Fugitive Slave Law that Emerson transformed from a gradualist to a "full-throated immediatist" abolitionist.[8] What is often underappreciated within these discussions of Emerson's antislavery tempo is another kind of slowness: the slowness of deep geologic time.

An attention to deep time directly reconfigures the most innovative recent readings of Emerson's 1844 West Indies address—readings that tend to complicate the gradualist-immediatist divide by foregrounding other temporalities. These readings hinge on this line from Emerson's address: "So now, the arrival in the world of such men as ... the Haytian heroes ... outweighs in good omen all the English and American humanity" (*CW* 10:325). Schoolman positions the main accomplishment of the address in terms of seeing emancipation as a historical process, highlighting the way Emerson "grants full acknowledgement to African American leadership, not only in Haiti but also in Barbados and Jamaica, as an independent historical force."[9] Insko locates immediatist resonances even within the 1844 address, arguing that this reference to the Haitian revolution "links the West Indies address to the most unsettling ... elements of his abolitionist and historiographical immediatism."[10] It turns out, however, that this most forward-looking moment in Emerson's address connects with his most backward-looking gaze, as he reveals in the draft of the address in his journal: "The use of geology has been to wont the mind to a new chronology. The little dame school measures by which we had gauged everything, we have learned to disuse, & break up our European & Mosaic & Ptolemaic schemes for the grand style of nature & fact" (*JMN* 9:123). Deep time invites Emerson to gauge his life and thoughts by a new standard—a temporality that provincializes Europe and creates an openness to new intellectual and social formations. It is precisely the way Emerson connects deep time with the breaking up of old forms of thought that allows him to reach for these more enlightened moments in his 1844 West Indies address. It is no coincidence that the section of Emerson's address that grows out of this geological beginning is also the section scholars emphasize as innovative. Schoolman writes that, in this 1844 address, "Emerson endeavored productively to imagine conditions otherwise."[11] Geological time was just such a method of imagination.

Evidently, Emerson so thoroughly "wonted"—or accustomed—his mind to a new chronology as he revised his address that he no longer needed to explicitly refer to that line, but rather, could briefly narrate a deep history of life on Earth. What is significant is that the published address contains echoes of that original geological mindset Emerson was in when he wrote the speech, and he reaches for this deeper sense of time precisely when he recognizes Black agency within the West Indies emancipation: "I add, that in part it is the earning of the blacks. They won the pity and respect which they have received, by their powers and native endowments. I think this a circumstance of the highest import. Their whole future is in it. Our planet, before the age of written history..." (*CW* 10:324). He then launches into his progressive geological history of life, from "the generations of sour paste" to the emergence of antislavery, as illustrated by the Haitian heroes (*CW* 10:324–25). He continues to refer to the "grand style of nature, her great periods," showing that he is still reflecting on that original geological reference in his journal—still using geological time to break up old thoughts (*CW* 10:324).

Although it may seem fitting, in his 1844 West Indies address, to align Emerson's gradualism with his devotion to deep time, that is not what is happening here. Rather, Emerson's deep commitment to geological time grounds his radical commitment to the present. Insko is right when, in his stirring study, he argues that Emerson sought to unsettle the past in order to make it "immediately accessible."[12] Insko, however, does not go far enough. Emerson did not just render the historical—that is, human—past immediately accessible: he also rendered the geological past immediately accessible. Emerson did this by practicing geologic presentism, or what I call deep *kairos*: a traversing of deep time in the human mind, embodying in the present moment the progressive thrust of Earth's history. *Kairos* here refers to the apprehension of the present moment as a time of action, a time of fulfillment. This is a geology not of waiting, but of acting: a geologic *now*. Nowhere in his 1844 West Indies address does Emerson invoke geologic time to advocate for a gradual unveiling of freedom in the present moment. Freedom certainly did unveil across geologic time, but *now*—the moment in which he is speaking—is a time of action, and this present moment carries the heft of the entirety of Earth's time. Geological processes are slow, but when the conditions are right, the result can be rupture. When considering the way the immense past—timespans beyond human fathoming—lead up to this present moment, one cannot help but feel a sense of urgency and a sense of responsibility. Deep time lends immensity to the present moment. This is why, after asserting his belief that the active role the enslaved played in emancipation is a "circumstance of the highest import," Emerson then reaches for immense timespans: first the future, then the deep geological past (*CW* 10:324). It is why he speaks of "now" and "the arrival in the world," and that "those moments"—the moments when "men might be forgiven, who doubted"—"are past" (*CW* 10:325–27). It is also why, in his draft—when geological time was foremost in his mind—he writes that "the time arrived when they can strike in with force & effect & take a master's part" (*JMN* 9:125). He omits the word "force" in the published address, but the message is clear: his progressive Earth history is not some mealy-mouthed gradualism, but rather, deeply connected with present action.

All of these geological resonances—both the sense of a progressive Earth history and a commitment to geologic presentism—reach their ecstatic peak with these words on slavery, the final sentences of Emerson's 1844 West Indies address:

> The Intellect, with blazing eye, looking through history from the beginning onward, gazes on this blot, and it disappears. The sentiment of Right, once very low and indistinct, but ever more articulate, because it is the voice of the universe, pronounces Freedom. The Power that built this fabric of things affirms it in the heart; and in the history of the First of August, has made a sign to the ages, of his will. (CW 10:327)

When he invokes "history" here, Emerson is not merely talking about human history, but rather a deeper sense of time. This deeper time grows out of the geological origins of the address, the progressive geological history he conjures within the speech, and is also implied when the sentence travels back to the "fabric of things." Indeed, these culminating words epitomize deep *kairos*: there is a geologic presentism at play here, as the Intellect traverses deep time to view slavery *now*. And this immediatism is closely related to progressive Earth history insofar as the sense of Right amplifies from inarticulate feeling to declaration of Freedom, a present-tense pronouncement summarizing Emerson's narrative of Earth history. Thus deep time is not conjured for its slowness, but for its endless momentum: the ability to feel it now ("in the heart"). There is a sense of time as fulfillment here, a cosmic sense of sacredness, as the Power that built Earth's history from its origins affirms freedom in this nineteenth-century moment of emancipation. Emerson's use of geological time here is not mere rhetoric; it grows out of a heartfelt belief in geologic presentism, as he slowly wonted his mind to a new chronology in the decades leading up to his 1844 West Indies address.

In telling this story of Emerson's commitment to the geologic now, a question remains: how *did* Emerson wont his mind to a new chronology? Although there are many ways to answer this question, a major influence for Emerson was the way the geological theories of his day resonated with a sense of the present moment. Indeed, the two major components of Emerson's deep *kairos*—the progression of Earth history and geologic presentism—connect back to his earliest readings of the works of the influential geologist Charles Lyell. Lyell gave Emerson an understanding of geologic time that went beyond mere duration—an understanding that deeply resonated with Emerson's sense of sacred time and the present moment—and it is *this* multidimensional quality of geologic time that Emerson marshals against slavery. This origin story of Emerson's present-oriented geology is significant because it reconfigures the discussion over the timing of Emerson's antislavery, showing how precisely he was able to attach the time of Earth with the time of dismantling the trade in human beings. Geological time, at least in the 1844 West Indies address, is not a recipe for tepidness, but rather, grows out of an abiding commitment to geology that is closely related to the kind of immediatism Insko observes in the speech. For Emerson, the result of wonting the mind to a new chronology is a new appreciation for the present moment.

Emerson's Two Lyells: Earthly Progression and the Present Moment

Emerson's 1844 West Indies address culminates in deep *kairos*: a traversing of deep time in the human mind, embodying in the present moment the progressive thrust of Earth's history. Although Emerson's conception of a progressive Earth history and a present-oriented geology come together in this 1844 piece, he acquired these two strands of deep *kairos* in two stages over the course of a decades-long fascination with Lyell's writings. In the first stage, Emerson encountered Lyell's 1820s writings, and was particularly struck by the progression of Earth history. In the second stage, he read Lyell's 1830s writings, focusing in particular on the ability of the human mind—in the present moment—to grasp geological time. By analyzing passages from Lyell's writings that Emerson singled out as particularly significant, we can see how the two Lyells—the 1820s version and the 1830s version—impact Emerson, informing the conception of Earth and geological time that he deploys in his 1844 antislavery address.

Although the focus is on Lyell's impact on Emerson, it is important to keep in mind the larger context here, as earthly progression and the mind's ability to apprehend geological time grew out of humanity's deepening realization of Earth's immense timespan. "The feebleness of the human mind was, in some sense," according to literary scholar Wai Chee Dimock, "the central discovery of the nineteenth century."[13] Indeed, historian of geology Martin J. S. Rudwick explains that there was a "common anxiety that the vast scale of geohistory reduced the human species to a cosmically insignificant latecomer."[14] In response to this anxiety over the inconsequentiality of the human, deep time acquired certain characteristics that allowed humans to compensate for their diminishment. Two of the most common compensations became visible in discourses over stratigraphic progress, on the one hand, and the celebration of the human intellect on the other. By locating progress—whether biological or any other kind of directionality, such as changes in Earth's physical qualities—in the ever-ascending succession of strata, humans positioned themselves as the endpoint toward which Earth history was pointing. Thus humans could temper their temporal infancy with the thought that these vast stretches of nonhuman nature were ripening toward humanity. The human mind's ability to even grasp this global ripening—the history of changes recorded in the crust—revealed another compensation. Lyell saw humanity's mental power as the key trait compensating for deep time, per Rudwick: "For the rational power to *know* the deep prehuman past—in Cuvier's phrase, 'to burst the limits of time'—then became in Lyell's perspective a proof of human cognitive 'dominion' over the vast spaces of cosmic history, and therefore proof of ultimate human significance."[15] Humans, in other words, were able to take up the world into their minds, and thus transform it—and for Lyell, this set humanity apart, conferring a patina of distinction upon the human.

In the mid-1820s, Emerson encountered a progressive Earth history when he read Lyell's first major geological work, an anonymous synthesis of the latest geological sciences published in the *Quarterly Review*. (Thus Emerson read Lyell before he *realized* he read Lyell.) Lyell gave Emerson a clear conception of crustal care: a view of Earth whose strata—reaching ever higher—embodied consciously designed progress. Lyell's 1826 contribution to the *Quarterly Review* is the substratum on which Emerson imagines geology for decades. The Lyell of 1826 confirmed many of Emerson's deepest held beliefs, and manifested them in the deep structures of the Earth. In his lifelong pursuit to reconcile the moral and material, the physical and the spiritual, Emerson discovered a line of relation through Lyell's article—an article whose thoughts intensely impressed him, and to which he returned years later. Lyell provided a geology closely connected with the human mind, articulating intimate, strange relations between humans and the deep nonhuman past—an underlying unity—that necessarily elevated the mind. Through these revelations, Lyell also gave Emerson a conception of geological time that resonated with sacred time: the concept of a ripening earthly time that Emerson would return to in his 1844 antislavery address.

Literature and science scholars have long argued for the significance of Lyell's review in Emerson's understanding of geology. Laura Dassow Walls[16] sees it as one of the key initial texts giving Emerson a conception of geologic time, while Dennis Dean suggests that the article inspired Emerson's fascination with geology.[17] But it was a particular section of Lyell's essay that resonated with Emerson. In October 1826, Emerson, writing in his journal, took note of "the 68th number of the Quarterly Review for some prodigiously fine remarks at the close of the Geological article" (*JMN* 3:51). He not only identifies the specific periodical, but he also singles out the ending as the part that particularly struck him. Dean calls this journal entry "the most precise citation of periodical literature in all" of Emerson's journals.[18] At this time, Emerson was an aspiring minister, writing these lines during the same month he was licensed to preach, subsequently closing his school in Cambridge.[19] As far as he knew, as he cracked open the pages, he was merely reading a recent review (published just weeks before, in the June and September 1826 issue) of a two-year-old book, the 1824 *Transactions of the Geological Society of London*. But it turns out this review also held special significance to Lyell, and it is in light of this significance that we can appreciate this autumn 1826 transatlantic crossing of geologic time.

While Emerson was preparing for a life in the ministry, Lyell was a lawyer.[20] In 1826, both young professionals were in their twenties, and both were a few years away from their transformative European tours in which Emerson would return a Transcendentalist and Lyell a full-fledged uniformitarianist.[21] After writing a couple essays in which he advocated for educational reform, Lyell turned to "his favorite science," geology.[22] The review is significant for Lyell because it represents, as Rudwick explains, "his first public attempt to synthesize" the field of geology.[23] What is significant for Emerson, though, is that he encountered a Lyell who was specifically trying to reach a wide audience. Emerson read a highly humanized geology that resonated with his belief that science should relate to the human, what he would later call the "humanity of science" (*EL* 2:22). Lyell incorporated literary quotations throughout his piece—Horace, Milton, Shakespeare—and sought "to write what would not only contribute to debates among savants, and particularly geologists, but also reach the influential social and political elites."[24] "'I must write what *will be read*,' he told Mantell; and he wanted to be read by just those whom he had defined (when writing to Cuvier) as '[both] geological and literary readers.'"[25] Little did Lyell know, Emerson was waiting for this precise approach—this melding of science and the human—across the Atlantic.

What precisely *were* these "prodigiously fine remarks at the close" of Lyell's article (*JMN* 3:51)? Throughout the article, Lyell paints a picture of dynamism, progress, and occult relation between human and the deep nonhuman. Lyell sees no reason to doubt that Earth's layers reveal "a gradual and progressive scale" starting with the "simplest forms" and "ending at length in the class of animals most related to man."[26] Much of his article is focused on sharing details about these creatures and the earthly changes they lived through, including—toward the close of the article—one of Emerson's favorite topics: how coal buried deep in the Earth was made readily available to humans, and thus Earth's temporalities teach humans to recalibrate their sense of values insofar as violent, destructive forces serve an ultimate good:

> If we pause for a moment and consider how intimately the degree of moral advancement, and the comparative political power of our own and many other countries is thus shown to be connected with the former existence of a race of plants now extinct,

which bore but a faint analogy to living species, and flourished at periods of immense antiquity, probably under a climate and in a state of the earth widely distinct from the present, the mind is elevated to an exalted conception of the magnificent extent of the whole system of nature, and of the wonderful relations subsisting between its remotest parts.[27]

A contemplation of strata and the way it relates across deep geological time to the present leads, for Lyell, to a state of mental elevation—a transcendental geology. Comparing past and present in the mind, one realizes the extraordinary degree to which present life—including morality—relies upon former beings from immensely long timespans ago. Both destruction and construction are a part of Earth's ripening. This progressive Earth is not merely a biological mechanism: in order to even conceive this reality, one must have a conception of time—deep time—that can accommodate progress. Progress must be seen to adhere to time—to be a quality of time itself, lending time a spiritual aspect of providential earthly unfolding.

Just as time leads to something, this geologic passage builds up—as the article closes—beyond mere mental exaltation. Lyell gives Emerson earthly layers that not only relate the deep past with the human, but also lead to God: not only a sense of ripening into the human, but also a sense of fulfilled divinity. He gives him an Earth that incarnates the divine mind. The previous passage's sense of occult relation leads Lyell to consider how "successive races of distinct plants and animals have inhabited this earth," and they "all belong to genera, families, or orders established for the classification of living organic productions."[28] Here the fact that the same categories apply to both present and past is crucial: genera, families, and orders are the occult relations on which Lyell is able to see a through line in deep time. As he continues, he writes a key passage that evidently struck Emerson, connecting as it does some of Emerson's foundational and cherished readings in natural theology with the latest research in geological sciences:

> It is therefore clear to demonstration, that all, at whatever distance of time created, are parts of one connected plan. They have all proceeded from the same Author, and bear indelibly impressed upon them the marks of having been designed by One Mind. ... Ascending in the scale from the lowest of the vertebrated class to the most perfect, we find at length, in the mammalia, all the most striking characters of osteological structure, and all the leading features of the physiology of the human frame fully displayed. ... [Thus] the remarks of Bishop Butler on the connection of the course of things which come within our view, with the past, the present, and the future, are forcibly recalled to our recollection: "We are placed (he observes) in the middle of a scheme, *not a fixed but a progressive one*, every way incomprehensible—incomprehensible in a manner equally with respect to what has been, what now is, and what shall be hereafter."[29]

What is key here is that stratigraphic progress is the foundation on which Lyell hangs the single authorship of the world: the two thoughts are closely juxtaposed in his piece. Going back into immense time, humans can trace lines of relation— however faint—from early layers to now, and these layers flower into humanity, testifying to the one mind emanating throughout the cosmos. Lyell so effectively conveyed the reality of crustal progress—deeming it a fact—and so thoroughly invoked the human and spiritual implications, that Emerson would never let go of this concept of stratigraphic progress even after Lyell dispensed with it in the 1830s. Crustal progress and One Mind were forever melded together. A sense of time as fulfillment adhered to Earth's time, and this simultaneously sacred and earthly temporal rhythm applies—as Butler indicates—to the past and present, but also to the future. In giving Emerson a concrete awareness of Earth timing that included progress, but also progress with a purpose—fulfillment—Lyell gave Emerson a crucial component of his 1844 antislavery address: a building block for deep *kairos*.

As Lyell's article remained in Emerson's mind during the following years, it is evident that strata and progress so thoroughly aligned that, when he needed an image for Providence, geology—and Lyell's review in particular—provided one of his central illustrations. On Friday, February 12, 1830, Emerson was preparing his Sunday sermon for Boston's Second Church. His goal was to preach on Luke 12:6–7, sharing his thoughts on the lines, "Are not five sparrows sold for two farthings and not one of them is forgotten before God? But even the hairs of your head are all numbered" (*CS* 2:138). Contemplating divine care, he evidently remembered those "prodigiously fine remarks" in the *Quarterly Review* article from four years prior (*JMN* 3:51). Thus he travelled to the Boston Athenaeum that Friday and checked out the issue.[30] When he needed an image for God's immanence—for the incursion of the divine into the world—he reached for geology. This connection between Lyell's 1826 text and Emerson's 1830 sermon is significant because—aside from undergirding the connection between time and progress—it serves as an important link between Emerson the minister and Emerson the Transcendentalist, as Emerson would return to Lyell for some of his early transcendental essays. In addition, it reveals what particularly Emerson believed were the "prodigiously fine remarks" in Lyell's piece. Scholars thus far have surmised, based on Emerson's journal passage, what aspect particularly struck him—but the correspondence between the sermon's date and his visit to the Athenaeum reveals what fascinated him.

Indeed, Emerson was so closely basing his sermon off of Lyell's essay that he borrows some of the language. Emerson writes: "The belief in God being thus gotten, the doctrine of Providence is the application of that belief to the government of the world" (*CS* 2:139). Likewise, in a key elaboration upon Butler that connects the moral and physical worlds, Lyell writes about the "constitution and government of the natural and moral worlds."[31] It is evident that this particular passage of Lyell's piece especially spoke to Emerson, as he then provides illustrations of physical and moral realms growing in tandem, showing that "as man's knowledge enlarges, that is, as his mind applies itself to a larger piece of the universe, he sees the unbroken prevalence of laws" (*CS* 2:139). Yet so far, the main aspect progressing is knowledge—not the Earth itself.

The sermon illustrates that Emerson shares the dynamic view of geology Lyell gave him, how geology is focused on strata—"the structure of the Earth"—and that "prior to the period when God created man upon the Earth, very considerable changes have taken place in the planet" (*CS* 2:140). In the subsequent several paragraphs, Emerson encapsulates key geological changes, emphasizing strata being laid down and then "broken and raised" (with all its Christological connotations) by volcanoes and earthquakes. Similar to Lyell, the key image of this progress-through-destruction is coal, "the relic of forests that existed at an unknown antiquity before the era of the creation of mankind" (*CS* 2:140). The events that humans normally associate with negative connotations—convulsions and the quaking of the ground—are actually, in light of deep time, ministering to civilization, to humanity's melioration. Thus reflecting on Lyell's 1826 article, Emerson can conclude: "The lesson it teaches me is that what men call the disorders of nature, as earthquakes and floods, are yet contained in a high Order and are ministering to good, remote yet certain—and that all the changes are guided by Providence" (*CS* 2:141). Geology, in other words, teaches that even destruction can lead to progress—that Earth's ripening is not only seen in its fossilized animals progressing over time, but also in the forces of nature that strike fear in humanity. These too are part of Earth's unfolding: a material unfolding as strata are broken and shared with humanity, but also a temporal unfolding in which the materials of immense antiquity are made to intersect with humans at the right time. Deep time and Providential care—a movement of the Earth toward the good—are so interwoven that the Earth's temporalities move to the rhythm of sacred time: the unfolding time of progressive geology.

Emerson evidently continued to think about Lyell's 1826 article into the 1830s, for the geological sections of his sixty-sixth sermon are incorporated into "The Uses of Natural History" (1833) and "On the Relation of Man to the Globe" (1834). Lyell's 1826 article appears to be crucial to Emerson's Transcendentalism, for it is able to traverse both Emerson's sermons and his Transcendentalist writings. The occult relations within Earth's strata provide a way of envisioning material and spiritual progress that acts as a textual *Jardin des Plantes* moment for Emerson. These occult relations, strewn across geological time, prepare Emerson for his transformative experience in Paris, when he experienced the interconnectedness of life, thus serving as a bridge to his Transcendentalism. In short, Lyell's 1826 article is the through line from the 1820s Emerson to the 1830s Emerson.

If the 1820s Lyell gave Emerson a concrete conception of a ripening, fulfilling deep geologic time, the 1830s Lyell gave Emerson a method for feeling that progress in the mind—intersecting deep time and the human to a degree Lyell was only beginning to articulate in the 1820s. Together, these two halves—the progressive Earth and a present-oriented geology—compose Emerson's deep *kairos*: his ability to envision Earth's temporalities as in line with the temporalities of antislavery: the capacity to see geological time as fulfilling, and humanity as the incarnation of immense temporal unfoldings.

Lyell's 1830s writings are charged throughout with a presentist view of the Earth. Indeed, the present moment is key to Lyell's theory of Earth—uniformitarianism—as it means that present geologic forces have the same intensity throughout Earth history. Yet most geologists already practiced a weak form of uniformitarianism called actualism, which uses present-day observations to interpret the past and vice versa. There could be no geology without this basic sense that what we see now can be used to envision the past.

Lyell brought the theory further by stating that Earth's geologic processes were uniform, having the same intensity throughout time. Lyell elegantly spread a way of envisioning deep time insofar as one requires an imagination—however limited—of immense time in order to conceive of our present, everyday earthly forces eroding and building the strata on which we stand. The central paradox of uniformitarianism, however, is that the process that *necessitates* deep time (i.e., that current forces over long periods make considerable changes) is the very process that allows one to *traverse* deep time. For humans now have access to the vast past insofar as present forces fully account for the entirety of Earth history—and it is this special cognitive access, bestowed upon the human, that so enthralled Lyell and Emerson. Thus uniformitarianism carries within it both a conception of deep time *and* humanity's coping mechanism for grappling with deep time. This way of bringing deep time into the mind—of using one's self-reliant sense of cause-and-effect to imaginatively enter the geologic past—profoundly impacted Emerson.

Once again, Emerson found some prodigiously fine remarks at the end of a Lyell piece, this time the last sentence of Chapter 4 of *Principles of Geology*: "Meanwhile the charm of first discovery is our own, and as we explore this magnificent field of inquiry, the sentiment of a great historian of our times may continually be present to our minds, that 'he who calls what has vanished back again into being, enjoys a bliss like that of creating.'"[32] The specific part that struck Emerson is evident in what he recorded in his October 27, 1836 journal entry: "'He who calls what has vanished back again into being enjoys a bliss like that of creating.' Hare & Thirlwall's Niebuhr ap. Lyell" (*JMN* 5:231). In these words, Lyell sums up the essence of uniformitarianism. It struck Emerson so thoroughly that he meditates on it many times in his journal, and incorporates a version of this quotation—however faint and distantly inspired—in many of his major essays.

Lyell essentially taught Emerson that the Earth has never not been modern. The past is not other. The deep geological past can be seen through living eyes, interpreted through current observations. Calling the vanished back—taking the geological into the mind—confers a special ability on the human akin to creating. In a work focused on the immensity of time, Emerson picked out the part that focused on the human mind's grasp of deep time as an assertion of ultimate significance. This geologic presentism, in other words, counterbalances humanity's shallow temporality with depth of thought. And it resonates with the "strong present tense" that Insko explores, embracing an Emerson that unsettles the past, insisting upon the past's "availability across time."[33] Lyell gave Emerson an embodied geology: a means of experiencing the deep pre-human past of Earth's history.

Transcendental Geologies: Deep *Kairos* and Antislavery

These two geologic strands—a progressive and present-oriented geology—unite for Emerson in his 1844 West Indies address in the form of deep *kairos*: a traversing of deep time in the human mind, embodying in the present moment the progressive thrust of Earth's history. A geology of action, not of waiting. Insko writes that "Emerson's immediatism ... lies at the heart of his conception of history."[34] Modifying Insko, we can now say, Emerson's immediatism lies at the heart of his conception of geology. Indeed, to the extent that geologic time only exists insofar as it is a breaking from the past, geology acts as a record of immediatism. One can look at geological history and focus on slowness, or one can foreground the ruptures: the ever-emerging new forms and layers throughout Earth's immense timespan. When he wonts his mind to a new chronology, Emerson is not reaching for stagnation or slowness, but rather, for a breaking open of thought.

Emerson certainly was belated in his abolitionism, but his geology—in itself—was not part of that slowness, at least as far as the 1844 West Indies address is concerned. Scholars tend to write off the longer timespans in the speech as illustrations of Emerson's lethargic activism, associating the slowness of amelioration with the slowness of gradualism.[35] Even Insko, whose entire book is founded on the idea of breaking from the past, cannot help but sunder "the pace of slow, gradual, incremental change, a blind trust in the progressive tide of history" from the "rash quickening advocated by immediatists."[36] Emerson, however, was so committed to the present moment that he even used the deep past for present ends. Progressive Earth history was a compass for the present, charging the moment with all the momentum of the planet's immense timespan. As his decades-long engagement with Lyell attests, Emerson's invocation of deep time in his 1844 West Indies address derives from his deep commitment to geology, rather than any kind of tepidness toward antislavery. The sense of a progressive and presentist geology—a deep *kairos*—united for Emerson in 1844, allowing him to use geologic time as a call to action *now*.

Beyond questions of Emerson's antislavery tempo, though, there is a larger implication regarding the diminishment of our scholarly perception of deep time. This focus on the disruptive possibilities of Emerson's geology resonates, in part, with Walls's analysis of his antislavery lectures, when she argues that "Emerson goes global, even planetary, reaching into the deep time of evolutionary change ... to align the constitution of the universe against" slavery.[37] When scholars invoke deep time, though, they do so in order to supplant a shorter form of duration with something much more extensive. As Walls sets up her major foray into Emerson's cosmic antislavery, for instance, she situates her conception of geological time using Dimock's writings: "Wai Chee Dimock proposes 'a more extended duration for American literary studies, planetary in scope' that she calls '*deep time*,' an historical depth that predates the adjective 'American' and 'denationalizes' space."[38] Yet there are qualities of deep time that go beyond duration—that resonate with conceptions of progress beyond the forms of progress that depend upon biological mechanisms; indeed, this conception of time is the necessary precondition to imagine evolutionary change, and it can be seen on its own as a quality of geological time, rather than being severed from geology and reduced to biological process.

Virtually all scholarly portrayals of deep time are fixated on deep *chronos* (time as duration). But Emerson's geological time reveals a conception of time that is just as much *kairos* as it is *chronos*. The term *kairos* is usually situated in rhetorical theory, and defined as "right timing" or "appropriate measure." It has this ephemeral, immediate sense in which a speaker knows when to speak at the right time. Yet it also has deeper ontological and theological meanings. The philosopher John E. Smith defines *chronos* "as measure, the *quantity* of duration, the length of periodicity, the age of an object or artifact."[39] *Kairos*, in contrast, is qualitative time: it points to "the special position an event or action occupies in a series, to a season when something appropriately happens that cannot happen at 'any' time, but only at 'that time,' to a time that marks an opportunity which may not recur."[40] When Emerson envisions a ripening Earth that bodies forth—at this moment—a time of emancipation, he is going beyond rhetoric to conceive of an earthly time that is ontologically *kairotic*. Earth's very being—its ontology—has shifted at this precise time, changed utterly from what it once was.

Beyond rhetoric and ontology, *kairos* has a theological dimension that deeply resonates with Emerson. It is here—in time as fulfillment—that *kairos* takes on its full cosmic import. Literary scholar Frank Kermode summarizes this theological dimension of *kairos* as "time filled with significance, charged with a meaning derived from its relation to the end."[41] Emerson, from his ministerial studies, would have been familiar with this conception of time. For the scriptures and "the Hebraic tradition," as Smith explains, "had from the outset a vivid sense of the historical order and of the course of history as a medium of divine disclosure."[42] Engaging with the work of the theologian Paul Tillich, Smith elaborates:

> The underlying religious meaning of *kairos* is found, for the Judaic tradition, in the critical times of religious history, when the mundane temporal order intersected with the sacred order in the form of a disclosure of the divine will. From Moses to the last of the great prophetic figures there is a series of "presents" or special times when the voice of the sacred stood in judgment on secular affairs. These times were opportunities for transformation and reformation, a return from waywardness to truth and righteousness. In Christianity, *kairos* was focused on the central event of Christ, who is said in the biblical writings to have come *en kairo*, sometimes translated as "the fullness of time"—implying a culmination in a temporal development marked by the manifestation of God in an actual historical order.[43]

Emerson singled out the emancipation of the British West Indies as such a moment, marked by the incursion of the divine—or deep time—into the human. He himself takes on the mantle of the prophetic figure in his address, singling out a crisis that necessitated a decision in order to body forth the fulfillment of cosmic justice. Thus reading Emerson's geologies through the multi-disciplinary scholarship on *kairos* reconfigures the traditional antagonism between geological time and biblical time. It is a scholarly commonplace to contrast shallow biblical time with deep geological time, but that contrast only works if one's conception of deep time is defined by *chronos*. Emerson certainly did—eventually—reject shallow biblical time, but he retained deep *kairos*, a conception of Earth's temporality that deeply resonated with his sense of the sacred and his early readings in the scriptures. Instead of a geological time that solely distances him from biblical time, it turns out that the sacred is a medium through which he apprehends geological time.

This multifaceted, overlapping nature of *kairos* is crucial for Emerson's 1844 address—the way *kairos* functions simultaneously as ontology, theology, and rhetoric provides the underlying energy for his first major antislavery speech. For if the Earth is unfolding, as Emerson conceives it, that means humans can point out certain milestones: *kairotic* moments in which earthly temporalities and cosmic justices manifest in the human. It is precisely because Emerson's Earth is *kairotic* that his imagination of it aligns so well with rhetorical *kairos* and social reform: the foundational temporalities that inform his conception of the Earth resonate with his tactics for social change, and thus he invokes Earth during these crisis moments when decisions must be made. Deep *kairos* is what allows Emerson to translate geology into action.

Having thoroughly wonted his mind to geologic time, Emerson is able to conceive—by the end of his 1844 West Indies address—that slavery disappears in the vision of deep time because the Earth's strata are progressive, guided by One Mind that bends all strata toward justice. And the Intellect can envision this—can participate in the creative capacities of the cosmos—precisely because past and present fully intersect in the human. It is no coincidence that the start of the geologic passage in Emerson's address coincides with the speech's turn to Black agency: as we have seen, Emerson practiced a presentist geology that allowed him to embody the progressive thrust of Earth's immense time spans, harnessing the deep past for present purposes. Thus it makes sense, given what Christina Katopodis calls Emerson's "vibrational epistemology," that during this *kairotic* moment—this moment in which the human enacts a transition in deep time, claiming one's emancipation—Emerson invokes that most *kairotic* of art forms: music.[44] He writes "that, in the great anthem which we call history, a piece of many parts and vast compass, after playing a long time a very low and subdued accompaniment, they perceive the time arrived when they can strike in with effect, and take a master's part in the music" (*CW* 10:325–26). This music metaphor epitomizes deep *kairos*: through the immediacy (and immediatism) of music, it reveals how the geologic time undergirding this address is meant to be enacted now, at the present moment. To give adequate language to this emancipatory transformation, Emerson made recourse to the qualities of immense time that deeply resonated with his sense of sacred time and the present moment, reaching back decades to his first transformative encounters with Lyell's transcendental geologies. Emerson, it appears, required an echo of the past to feel the true weight of the present—and the future.

Notes

1. Maurice Lee, *Slavery, Philosophy, and American Literature, 1830–1860* (New York: Cambridge University Press, 2005), 178.

2. Jeffrey Insko, *History, Abolition, and the Ever-Present Now in Antebellum American Writing* (New York: Oxford University Press, 2018), 96.
3. Len Gougeon, *Virtue's Hero: Emerson, Antislavery, and Reform* (Athens: University of Georgia Press, 2010), 85.
4. Robert Richardson, *Emerson: The Mind on Fire* (Berkeley: University of California Press, 1995), 395.
5. Lee, *Slavery, Philosophy, and American Literature*, 179.
6. Martha Schoolman, *Abolitionist Geographies* (Minneapolis: University of Minnesota Press, 2014), 84.
7. Insko, *History, Abolition, and the Ever-Present Now*, 95.
8. Ibid.
9. Schoolman, *Abolitionist Geographies*, 96.
10. Insko, *History, Abolition, and the Ever-Present Now*, 119.
11. Schoolman, *Abolitionist Geographies*, 97.
12. Insko, *History, Abolition, and the Ever-Present Now*, 113.
13. Wai Chee Dimock, *Through Other Continents: American Literature across Deep Time* (Princeton, NJ: Princeton University Press, 2006), 54.
14. Martin J. S. Rudwick, *Worlds Before Adam: The Reconstruction of Geohistory in the Age of Reform* (Chicago: University of Chicago Press, 2008), 256.
15. Ibid.
16. Laura Dassow Walls, *Emerson's Life in Science: The Culture of Truth* (Ithaca, NY: Cornell University Press, 2003), 65.
17. Dennis Dean, *Ralph Waldo Emerson's Knowledge and Use of Geology* (master's thesis, Stanford University, 1962), 19.
18. Dean, *Knowledge and Use of Geology*, 18.
19. Ralph Waldo Emerson, *Complete Sermons*, 4 vols., ed. Albert J. von Frank (Columbia: University of Missouri Press, 1989–93), 1:41. Hereafter cited parenthetically as *CS*.
20. Rudwick, *Worlds Before Adam*, 256.
21. Ibid., 266, 281.
22. Ibid., 202–3.
23. Ibid., 203.
24. Ibid.
25. Ibid.
26. Charles Lyell, "Art. IX.—*Transactions of the Geological Society of London*," *The Quarterly Review* 34, no. 68 (June and September 1826): 513.
27. Ibid., 536–37.
28. Ibid., 538.
29. Ibid., 538–39.
30. Kenneth Walter Cameron, *Ralph Waldo Emerson's Reading* (New York: Haskell House, 1966), 17.
31. Lyell, *Transactions*, 539.
32. Charles Lyell, *Principles of Geology*, vol. 1 (Chicago: University of Chicago Press, 1990), 74.
33. Insko, *History, Abolition, and the Ever-Present Now*, 93, 113.
34. Ibid., 112.
35. Lee, *Slavery, Philosophy, and American Literature*, 179–80.
36. Insko, *History, Abolition, and the Ever-Present Now*, 4–5.

37. Laura Dassow Walls, "'As Planets Faithful Be': The Higher Law of Science In Emerson's Antislavery Lectures," *Nineteenth-Century Prose* 30, no. 1 and 2 (Spring/Fall 2003): 172.
38. Walls, "As Planets Faithful Be," 172.
39. John E. Smith, "Time, Times, and the 'Right Time': *Chronos* and *Kairos*," *The Monist* 53, no. 1 (January 1969): 1.
40. Ibid., 1.
41. Frank Kermode, *The Sense of an Ending: Studies in the Theory of Fiction* (New York: Oxford University Press, 2000), 47.
42. Smith, "Time, Times, and the 'Right Time,'" 8.
43. John E. Smith, "Time and Qualitative Time," in *Rhetoric and Kairos: Essays in History, Theory, and Praxis*, ed. Phillip Sipiora and James S. Baumlin (Albany: State University of New York Press, 2002), 55.
44. Christina Katopodis, "The Music of the Spheres in Emerson, Fuller, and Thoreau: Lyell's *Principles* and Transcendental Listening," *ISLE: Interdisciplinary Studies in Literature and Environment* 28, no. 3 (Autumn 2021): 840.

CHAPTER 6

THE SEED OF THE WORLD

Emerson's Transatlantic Transcendentalist First Philosophy

DAVID GREENHAM

RALPH Waldo Emerson, delighting in his earliest transatlantic philosophical forebears in an 1841 journal entry, remarks, "I am present at the sowing of the seed of the world" (*JMN* 7:413). The philosophers that "gleam across [his] brain" (413) at this moment hail from the classical Greek world: the pre-Socratics, Platonists, and Neoplatonists. If we are to take seriously, as we should, the "deep time" of American literature proposed by Wai Chee Dimock, which "bind[s] continents and millennia into many loops of relations," we need to take account of these first thinkers, restoring, in Dimock's words, American literature's *"longue durée,"* as well as "enlarg[ing] its spatial compass."[1] This temporal and geographical expansion becomes more urgent when we also listen carefully to Emerson's seed-sowing metaphor, hearing in it an ecological motif. As Laura Dassow Walls has recently noted in her important work on transcendentalism and the Anthropocene, there is a "foundational dualism" in Western thought that sees "the concept of nature as outside the human."[2] Walls correctly identifies Emerson as an exemplar of this position (715). The seed sowing metaphor, which places Emerson as a spectator of nature, is, as we shall see, more than merely illustrative. Walls locates the codification of the concept of external nature in the European Renaissance and Early Modern period, in Galileo and Descartes (713). It is Emerson, though, who says of the earliest Greek thinkers that they "have marked once for all the distinctions which are inherent in the sound mind, and which we must henceforth respect."[3] Following Emerson's lead, we should perhaps take Walls's genealogy of the Anthropocene further back than the early seventeenth century, where, as she observes, the philosophies of Galileo and Descartes coincide with the beginning of the Indigenous holocaust in the Americas by Emerson's ancestors, and even beyond what Walls identifies as the separation of nature and culture during the Roman conquest of Europe (711, 713), to several centuries before Christ, when, as Emerson understands and celebrates, man and nature are first separated in the Greek thought of the pre-Socratics. In relocating Emerson amidst this "irregular duration and extension" (Dimock, 4) of deep time and setting him against the most unsettling question of our own time, the climate crisis marked by the Anthropocene, I am positing a new and disturbing origin story for American literature.[4]

The pre-Socratics, fifth- and sixth-century BCE Greek thinkers whose remaining philosophical fragments precede the systematic legacies of Plato and Aristotle, are enigmatic figures whom we can only glimpse in the written record. We can see the founding importance of the pre-Socratics in Emerson's great 1844 essay "Experience." Here, three years after he has imagined the spectacle of the world growing from the seed of classical Greek thought, Emerson further reflects upon that origin story, and finds himself "baffled" before a "[first] cause, which refuses to be named," but which "every fine genius has essayed to represent by some emphatic symbol, as, Thales by water, Anaximenes by air, Anaxagoras by (*Noûs*) thought, Zoroaster by fire, Jesus and the moderns by love: and the metaphor of each has become a national religion" (*CW* 3:42). Thales, Anaximenes, and Anaxagoras are three of the earliest pre-Socratic philosophers. Their "emphatic symbols" of that elusive Cause are "water," "air," and "thought." Emerson's striking observation is that these "metaphors" (along with those of the more famous religious founders Jesus and Zoroaster) have become by turns "a national religion." Indeed, for Emerson, the pre-Socratics "have somewhat so vast in their logic, so primary in their thinking, that it seems antecedent to all the ordinary distinctions of rhetoric and literature, and to be at once poetry & music & dancing & astronomy & mathematics" (*JMN* 7:413). In their fragments, Emerson finds the earliest available conceptualizations of the world that precede distinctions of disciplines and forms—from rhetoric to dance. These first concepts—water, air, thought—are, crucially, metaphorical. As George Lakoff and Mark Johnson suggest, the earliest philosophers used metaphor to conceptualize the essential mystery of "what is": Being itself.[5] Metaphors are not merely rhetorical: they undertake cognitive work, conceptualizing the unfamiliar through the familiar. Thales's water, Anaximenes's air, and Anaxagoras's thought each belong to everyday experience, and, as Emerson has recognized, these pre-Socratics used their understanding of the everyday to provide shapes and forms for what they didn't understand, namely the mysteries of Being itself. In so doing, as Emerson concludes, they placed metaphor at the very root of thinking. Moreover, Emerson's "Experience" shows us that, when face to face with the "ineffable" (*CW* 3:42), the first great minds of the European philosophical tradition initially reached for elemental metaphors (water, air), and then moved to human metaphors (thought). These metaphors were not fleeting moments of high rhetoric or poetry: they founded worldviews that would last millennia, and, as I shall show, generated the polarized concepts of man, nature, and God that were not only the conditions for Emerson's Transcendental first philosophy as proposed in his crucial 1836 essay *Nature*, but which may also be determinate for our modern ecological crisis.

Prima philosophia

Emerson's acquaintance with his transatlantic intellectual forebears, the pre-Socratics, begins early but is hardly auspicious. In the sixteen-year-old Emerson's "College Theme Book" of 1819, Heraclitus and Pythagoras are the malign products of a greater age (*JMN* 1:167–68). In the research for his 1820 Bowdoin Prize dissertation "On the Character of Socrates," Anaxagoras is more positively regarded as "the philosopher who taught the purity and grandeur of divinity" (*JMN* 1:208). A couple of years later, in 1822, "Heraclitus was a fool, who wept always for the miseries of human life" (*JMN* 2:59–60), and in 1825 Pythagoras, along with druids and hermits, is accused of attempting, wrongly, to overturn tradition through the "pursuit of novel hypotheses" (*JMN* 2:332); efforts that Emerson would come to have more sympathy with by and by. His sources for early Greek philosophy are not clear at this stage, though as a lifelong reader of the Roman historian Plutarch, his *Lives* and *Morals* would have provided glimpses into the characters of the ancient world.[6] But it wasn't until 1830, when Emerson first studied a systematic account of the pre-Socratics, that he would have the opportunity to understand them as more than characters from the past. The four-volume *Histoire comparée des systèmes de philosophie* by Baron Marie Joseph de Gérando, published in 1822–23, was possibly recommended to Emerson by the free-thinking Frenchman Achille Murat, a nephew of Napoleon, whom Emerson had met while staying in Florida for his health in 1826 (*JMN* 3:111n).[7] If so, Emerson did not follow up Murat's recommendation for several years.

In January of 1830 Emerson withdrew the first two volumes of the *Histoire* from the Boston Athenaeum, but it was not until October 27 that he started a new notebook recording his remarks on de Gérando's first volume, which gives a thorough history and interpretation of pre-Socratic philosophy from Thales to Hippocrates. However, as Emerson's first note reads, "This leads me in the outset back to Bacon" (*JMN* 3:360). De Gérando's introduction begins with a long quotation from Francis Bacon's *De augmentis scientiarum* of 1623, a Latin translation of his 1605 *On the Advancement of Learning*, in which Bacon calls for a "complete and universal literary history," including all the sciences and arts that have flourished throughout time, considering their origins, their migrations, their peaks and troughs, their methods, and their different sects (*Histoire*, ix).[8] De Gérando aims to undertake this task for philosophy by tracing the development of its most basic questions across history. In his journal Emerson translates de Gérando's ambition as follows:

> If ... there are in philosophy a small number of questions which lying at the foundation of all the rest, should exercise over them a natural influence, & which should furnish the last data necessary to their solution; if the opinions which philosophers have formed respecting this small number of primary questions [*questions primitive*] ought to determine by a secret or manifest consequence the whole after course of their opinions by fixing the direction of their ideas, if these fundamental

questions I say could be known, enumerated, strictly defined, we should have found a simple & sure means of marking in a general manner the primary conditions, the essential characteristics of each doctrine, we might then find the terms which compose one of the most important laws of the intellectual world. (*JMN* 3:362; *Histoire*, xiv–xv)

De Gérando's aim, as Emerson recognizes, is to find the "small number" of *questions primitive* that establish the "first conditions" of the major doctrines of philosophy. These primitive or primary questions will also be the most general, recurring again and again in "different aspects" (xvii). In following their development, de Gérando will map "the progress of the human spirit" (xvii). Additionally, as these questions "determine the most general causes" (xviii–xix) of progress before it divides into different sects and disciplines, de Gérando will discover the common origin of all the arts and sciences.

De Gérando sees himself as presenting a "true FIRST PHILOSOPHY" on Bacon's terms. By "first philosophy" or *prima philosophia*, Bacon meant, as Emerson puts it, "the great principles that are true in all sciences, in morals & in mechanics" (*JMN* 3:360). Bacon's examples in the *Advancement* are: "if equals are added to unequals the wholes will be unequal"—which is "an axiom of justice as well as of the mathematics"; also, "Things that are equal to the same are equal to each other," which is derived from mathematics, but underlies logical syllogisms; and "all things change but nothing is lost," which Bacon contends is a philosophical and a theological truth about eternal nature.[9] As such axioms suggest, first philosophy is not so much prior in *time* as it is prior in *generality*, whenever it's discovered, and it applies across a wide range of areas: mathematics, morality, philosophy, and theology. *Prima philosophia* becomes, and again Emerson quotes from the *Advancement*, "a receptacle for all such profitable observations & axioms as fall not within the compass of any of the special parts of philosophy or Sciences but are more common & of a higher stage" (*JMN* 3:360). The pre-Socratics, as Emerson noted above, play a special role in first philosophy as their writings, coming from the time before the division of philosophy into "special parts," are both earlier and more general. Rhodri Lewis explains: "As Bacon ruminated ... before Socrates divorced philosophy from rhetoric 'the p[ro]fessors of wysdome in Greece did p[re]tend to teach an vniversall Sapience and knowledg[e] both of matter & words.' This 'vniversall Sapience and knowledg[e]' was exactly what *philosophia prima* sought to reconfigure, and according to the [*Advancement*], it was to be considered as a kind of wisdom."[10] The pre-Socratics belong to the "stem" of knowledge, rather than to its many branches, to borrow Bacon's tree metaphor (Bacon, *Advancement*, 93). Their truths will concern knowledge of man, nature, and God equally, "for all things are marked and stamped with this triple character, of the power of God, the difference of nature, and the use of man" (Bacon, *Advancement*, 93; cf. *Histoire*, xxi). A *prima philosophia*, then, will cast light upon the development of the concepts of Nature, God, and Man, because it will be prior to any division of knowledge that considers them separately.[11]

Analogies of Experience

Philosophy commences with the element of water. Thales, the first pre-Socratic mentioned by Emerson in "Experience," who lived and thought in Ionia, now the Mediterranean coast of Turkey, around 600 BCE, "begins the catalogue of acknowledged Philosophers" (*JMN* 3:363). His most famous fragment is "Water was the beginning [*principe*] of all things" (*JMN* 3:363; *Histoire*, 339). Thales, as de Gérando puts it, draws on "analogy deduced from experience" (*Histoire*, 340) to arrive at his proposition. Analogy works in the same way as metaphor: we use something we understand to give a shape and structure to something we don't understand. A living example of metaphor would be the way we use *space* to understand *time*. For example, such familiar linguistic expressions as "a *long* time," or "you have a great future *ahead* of you," or "the weekend is *coming*." In each case *time* is conceptualized in terms of *space*: length, projection, or movement towards. It's very hard to think about time without using rich spatial metaphors. We typically say that these kinds of metaphors are "dead"; but often what we think of as dead metaphors contain our most deeply buried conceptual structures—our *prima philosophia*. Thales's "analogy," or, as Emerson said, his "metaphor," is water, which de Gérando suggests is part of his "experience." He uses his elemental metaphor to structure the complex and elusive idea of material origins.

Water has a range of experiential qualities that make it an apt metaphor for Thales. It is essential for life; it moves of itself as rain, rivers, and oceans; as the latter it surrounds the known world, and, according to Greek myth, exists under it too; water transforms what it touches, washing away land and dissolving minerals; also, water changes its state from solid to liquid to gas, while remaining what it is. As such, to Thales, water's variety offers an apt analogy for the variety of nature itself. In exploring this, de Gérando picks up on water's ability to change its state and uses that to map changes in matter more generally: "in the liquid state, matter has no shape yet; it is by passing to the solid state that it receives the various forms under which organization presents it to us" (*Histoire*, 339). Here two different forms of water, liquid and ice (though water also passes to a solid state when it becomes living things such as plants and animals), are used to conceptualize different states of matter: the formless and the formed. Water here is not just a figure; it grounds Thales's two state concept of the material world: formed and formless. Thus, "water is the principle of everything." Crucially, from Thales's metaphor, Emerson learns that we can conceptualize the universe and its principles from *within* our own experience, without recourse to authority or tradition. Thales's use of nature to conceptualize what "is" takes Emerson from "speculation to experience," which makes Thales the first "physician opposed to metaph[ysician]" (*JMN* 3:363).[12]

After conceptualizing nature, Thales, according to de Gérando, sought to define the human soul, also through experience, or, as we are coming to see, through metaphor. As Emerson writes: "Next great principle of Thales—*The essence of the soul is motion*, κινητικόν τι [something moving], αεικινητικόν [always moving], αυτοκινητικόν [self-moving]" (*JMN* 3:363; *Histoire*, 342). Movement is one aspect of Thales's experience of water, but different types of movement provide different concepts of the soul. Movement alone can't give a very complex idea of the soul, merely distinguishing it from that which is at rest—perhaps the most basic distinction between life and death. "Continuous" movement takes this further, suggesting something ever or always moving, something eternal. Finally, "self-moving" places the cause of the movement within the soul itself. De Gérando's entailment from Thales's metaphors, once he has worked through the "imperfections of language," is that the soul consists in "free-activity" (*Histoire*, 342). Nothing tells it what to do and it acts of itself. Or, as Emerson puts it in his gloss, "we can make mouse mean mountain everywhere" (*JMN* 3:363). The soul is free to makes its own meanings, its own laws, and it is self-determined.

Thales, then, has used his experience of the elemental to analogize nature and man. However, as de Gérando laments, Thales doesn't have an adequate analogy for the divine. His "principle," water, does not, as Emerson notes, "mean both *element* and *cause* but only *element*" (*JMN* 3:364). His metaphors "supply ... second causes for all particular phenom[ena]" (*JMN* 3:364), but they leave out the *first* cause. As such, philosophical history accuses Thales of "Atheism" (*JMN* 3:364). However, in his third century BCE account of Thales, the Greek biographer Diogenes Laertius tells Emerson that for Thales, "the universe is full of gods" (*Histoire*, 342). These "gods" are also aligned by de Gérando with the metaphors of movement, for they are "beings gifted with their own mobility, possessing movement by themselves and able to transmit it" (*Histoire*, 345). Thus, the gods, while still *in* nature, have a *causal* role, transmitting their free activity to nature, causing it to change. Thales's propositions present, through metaphors, principles that are fundamental for God, nature, and man—they are conceptually homologous self-causing consequences of their own free activity. Of course, there's no evidence to suggest that Thales thought he was using metaphor in this way. He was taking his metaphors literally, and really did believe that everything derived from water and that soul was movement, rather than that these were conceptual metaphors taken from experience. Thales's belief amounts to what Lakoff and Johnson call an "ontological commitment" that turns a "metaphor into a metaphysical statement" (Lakoff and Johnson, *Philosophy in the Flesh*, 353); that is, taking metaphors literally turns metaphors into metaphysics—or into first philosophy. What this means for Emerson, we'll see as this chapter proceeds.

THE FIRST CAUSE

The next pre-Socratic Emerson reckons with, though not mentioned later in "Experience," is Anaximander, another Ionian a few years younger than Thales. In his notes Emerson cites his maxim, "*Nothing can come of nothing*" (*JMN* 3:364; *Histoire*, 351; Emerson's italics), a ripe candidate for an axiom of first philosophy. De Gérando recognizes this as a statement on which Greek philosophy "pivots" (an expression which amused Emerson's wife, Ellen, then very ill with the tuberculosis that would kill her just a few months later; presumably, she saw the ridiculous in taking the metaphor literally—*JMN* 3:364). What the axiom asserts is that there are no origins, everything must always already have been here. Whereas Thales called his self-creating "everything" water, Anaximander's metaphor is at a higher level of abstraction: "The infinite, he said, is the beginning [*principe*] of all things" (*JMN* 3:364; *Histoire*, 350). "Infinite" translates the Greek *apeiron*: limitless, boundless, or unpassable. Emerson's translation of *principe* as "beginning," then, is a mistranslation if we take it to mean a single point of origin, a "first cause." Rather, as de Gérando explains, there is no point outside of, or beyond the infinite, for a beginning to take place. Thus Anaximander, like Thales, "confounds the notion of *cause* and that of *element*" (*Histoire*, 350); that is, he remains a materialist, using nature to conceptualize what is. In Anaximander's infinite universe, matter is in constant motion, creating and destroying itself in a "continual revolution" (*Histoire*, 352). Emerson also mistakes de Gérando's materialist account when, after interpreting the "infinite" as a "beginning," he concludes: "surely such transcendentalism shows how close is the first & last step of philosophy" (*JMN* 3:364). Emerson's early use of "transcendentalism" here, a term that will come to define him even as he defines it, implies a *transcendent* or *immaterial* state from which creation departs and then returns; a first and last cause beyond the mundane that unifies man, nature, and God. For Anaximander, there could be no such departure or return, for all is one immensity.

Both Thales and Anaximander fail for de Gérando because, despite Emerson's readings, they can't find an apt metaphor for what is beyond matter: an incorporeal God. Anaximenes, the sixth-century Ionian mentioned by Emerson in "Experience," considered the principle of things to be "air," to which "he attributed life, movement, and even thought" (*Histoire*, 354). In the progression towards a conceptualization of the incorporeal, "air" is a useful metaphor. Air's significant negative connotations—invisible, rarefied, weightless, and insubstantial—contrast it with the solidity of matter. Air also becomes an important metaphor for the concept of the "soul"—the Greek terms *psyche* and *pneuma*, and the Latin *spiritus*, are all drawn from words that mean "air" or "breath." De Gérando, however, doesn't have much to say on Anaximenes, and Emerson leaves a blank space under his name in his notebook. Instead, he moves on to perhaps the most important pre-Socratic for understanding his first philosophy and its profound ecological consequences: Anaxagoras.

It was Anaxagoras, the last pre-Socratic mentioned in "Experience," who in establishing his doctrine on "the first cause" marks a "principal epoch in the history of philosophy" (*Histoire*, 357) and in the genealogy of the Anthropocene. Anaxagoras was also Ionian, living a generation after his forerunners. Like them, "he searched for the explanation of phenomena in analogies furnished by experience" (*Histoire*, 357–58); that is, Anaxagoras used metaphor to understand the complexity of nature. But unlike Thales, Anaximander, and Anaximenes, he did not find causation itself *in* nature. Rather, Anaxagoras separates *cause* from *caused*. Emerson translates de Gérando on Anaxagoras as follows:

> Whilst the system of emanations, the systems of pantheism, the opinions of the first Ionians themselves had associated the elementary matter of all things to the first

cause of all production & thus conceived the Divinity as the *universal soul, the soul of the world*, the world itself is an animated whole identical in some sort with its author, Anaxagoras first detached, separated with precision & neatness, those two notions until then confounded. The universe is in his eyes an effect wholly distinct from its cause. (*JMN* 3:365; *Histoire*, 358–59; italics in the originals)

The earlier Ionians were pantheists, and nature was an animated emanation of a divine cause of which it remained a part: God saturated nature as a "universal soul" and the principle of self-movement was the metaphor that tied everything together. For Anaxagoras, however, cause and caused are distinct; God separates from man and nature. The metaphor that underlies the paradigm shift in de Gérando's account is that of the "author." This is a nuanced elaboration of a more basic metaphor of causation that is worth exploring.

In experience, when anything moves, we are typically aware that something moves it: the hand moves the cup of water, the mother picks up the child, the child knocks over the building blocks, and so on. We are also aware that each of these movements happened for a reason: someone wanted a drink of water, someone wanted comfort, someone was angry. We are also aware that there is a consequence: someone slakes their thirst, someone is comforted, someone feels better. This three-part structure of wanting something to happen, the thing happening, and the consequence of that happening forms the basic structure for metaphors of causation. When used as a metaphor, the familiar causal structure applies to situations where we don't know the cause, and we only experience the caused. Say the wind blows, then the causation metaphor implies an *intelligence* or *reason* that desires the wind to blow prior to its blowing; the wind's movement fulfils that desire. Inferences from causal metaphors account for animistic world views, where intelligence and fulfilment map onto natural but inexplicable events. The metaphor also entails a timeline, where intelligence is necessarily *before* action and the action is *before* the result. In de Gérando's "author" metaphor, the three-part structure becomes the intention to write, the writing, and the written artefact—the "book" of nature. For the Ionians, he laments, author and work are the same, but after Anaxagoras the distinction between author and work is clear and results in a crucial new concept of the divine. As Emerson's translation continues:

This Cause has nothing common with the rest of beings. It hath its peculiar nature, one, eternal, acts on the world as workman on materials. So the idea of the first Cause which until then was essentially defined by the attribute of *Power* was determined by Anaxagoras to receive chiefly the attribute of *intelligence*. (*JMN* 3:365; *Histoire*, 359; italics in originals)

Cause and caused are distinct for the first time, as workman from the work. The workman, or author, part of the metaphor, becomes something immaterial—intelligence itself, distinguished from the matter it makes. The three-part structure of the causation metaphor lies behind the elaborations of its use here: a maker wants to make something, what the maker makes is the intentional consequence of a maker's intelligent wish, the outcome is that which the maker wanted. Scaled up to the maker of all nature, the causal metaphor creates a concept of God as an intelligent and foresighted Being; creation is what God's reason has made. Indeed, Anaxagoras's divine principle of nature, as Emerson noted in "Experience," is apparently less corporeal than Anaximenes's air: it is *noûs* or thought.

Emerson recognizes that Anaxagoras's metaphors present for the first time an idea of an external Cause that moves the universe in a purposive and ordered way. "Maker" and "author" tropes strongly imply not just an original creative force, but also a creative aim—causal metaphors are implicitly purposive—and as such Anaxagoras's causation is "teleological" (*Histoire*, 361), with an end in mind (*noûs*) at the outset. As de Gérando's sources put it: "There must exist, outside of this material universe, this chaos of elements, a cause which effects their movement, gives them a form, coordinates them. This cause is supreme intelligence; for only intelligence can be a principle of order; and all that is good, beautiful, and regular, emanates from it alone" (*Histoire*, 365). Order no longer exists in nature, as its own principle. Matter is mere chaos. Order, beauty, and goodness are the result of intelligent creation; they are the *purpose* of creation. Nature no longer has the principle of its own movement, nor is it understood on its own terms. With this metaphorical reconceptualization nature is now a second-order creation, a mere book. It is the Author that matters.

Even though Anaxagoras "never uses the word *God*" (*Histoire*, 367; de Gérando's italics), for Emerson the implication is clear: Anaxagoras has "reasoned out" an "idea of God" that would elsewhere be "revealed" (*JMN* 3:365). As he concludes: "*one order* reigns. that [sic] its Unity supposes one mind which ordains it" and "Anaxagoras was able to make this demonstration of God over all" (*JMN* 3:365; Emerson's italics). Anaxagoras, Emerson learns, frees Greek philosophy from superstition and pantheism, from having a God *in* nature, to having a God *outside* and *before* nature. In so doing, his metaphors "established an absolute distinction between intelligence and matter" (*Histoire*, 365), removing the first cause from nature itself, making it invisible to the senses which can only interact with the result. From now on sensation cannot access the divine, only infer it from sensation. The ontological commitment to Anaxagoras's metaphors is crucial for our genealogy of the Anthropocene, leading to the hierarchical dualism between matter and spirit, between what can be known by the senses and what can be known by the intelligence. This dualism, as Walls noted in her discussion of the Anthropocene, marks western philosophy from Plato to Kant. But Emerson helps us to locate this division even earlier, in the pre-Socratic separation of the concepts of God, Man, and Nature. A division that, as we shall see, is definitive for Emerson's first philosophy (*Histoire*, 370) and the idea of the Transcendental.

THE ONE

Emerson then turns, finally, to the sixth-century BCE Eleatics: Xenophanes, Parmenides, and Heraclitus. The Eleatics differed from their forerunners in seeking answers to their questions "in the soul only" (*JMN* 3:368); that is, they were the first philosophers to approach questions *a priori*, using reason and pure speculation before facts (*Histoire*, 453). Beginning with Anaximander's principle that "nothing can come of nothing," their *a priori* speculations led them to believe that change itself was impossible, for not only can nothing come of nothing, but, according to Xenophanes, "one thing can never come of another thing," and "Like must produce like" (*JMN* 3:368; *Histoire*, 453). The fact that we evidently do perceive change did not dissuade Xenophanes. Rather it fed the dualist theory of Anaxagoras: "None perceives by the senses things as they are; we must not then begin from these opinions[,] got we know not how[,] but from what is stable, from what reason discovers" (*JMN* 3:368; *Histoire*, 460). Change, Emerson notes, is merely apparent; the real world, the world of "thought," is changeless and "eternal" (*JMN* 3:368; *Histoire*, 456).

As such, Xenophanes utterly removes the idea of God from analogies of experience, that is, from metaphorical conceptions. As Emerson translates and glosses: "'God is one; there can be but one God. He is always like himself. He cannot be conceived under the human form; He is perfect; we can't apply to him either motion or limit. But he is not immovable or infinite' i.e., motion & limit as they belong to matter have no relation to God's attributes" (*JMN* 3:368; *Histoire*, 456). All we can know of God is his unity and self-relation, derived *a priori* from Xenophanes's principle: if a thing can only come from something like it, then God can only come from himself; and as such, he is unique. He also cannot be like anything phenomenal (human, mobile, finite), nor constrained by their negation (inhuman, immobile, infinite). Even these last negative analogies, often used to define divine "attributes," cannot apply to God as they still derive from matter. Xenophanes, then, in a further Anthropocene moment, distinguished "the physical world from the intellectual world [and] entirely isolated the one from the other" as objects of two distinct ways of knowing (*Histoire*, 459). He relegated the physical world to a lower value and raised the intellectual world accordingly (*Histoire*, 459–60), paralleling Anaxagoras and shaping the history of philosophy. Despite this explicit dualism, Xenophanes believed in an absolute unity that belonged to the intellectual world of God and of thought (*Histoire*, 459). As Emerson translates it, "Whichever side [Xenophanes] looked, all ran to unity—there was but one substance" (*JMN* 3:369; *Histoire*, 461), an idea of unity developed by Parmenides.

Emerson only quotes one line from Parmenides, who lived in Elea in the fifth and fourth centuries BCE, but it is a crucial one: "Thought & the object of thought are but one" (*JMN* 3:369; *Histoire*, 466). The phrase appears in the *Histoire* amidst de Gérando's translation into French of the remains of Parmenides's philosophical poem *On Nature*. Emerson juxtaposes the quotation with de Gérando's general criticism of the Eleatics: "These philosophers had confounded the abstract notion of being with its objective reality & thought they could conclude from one to the other" (*JMN* 3:369; *Histoire*, 468). De Gérando's point is that through their *a priori* approach, the Eleatics have mistaken their ideas (abstract notions) for reality (there is nothing but abstraction), and argued from one to the other, dismissing the world of facts and experience that was all around them. Thought and the object of thought can be one, not because thought reaches to the real, objective world, but because the object of thought is just as "ideal" as the thought. As Emerson goes on to note, "This mistake has misled numbers of metaphysicians down to Descartes himself" (*JMN* 3:369; *Histoire*, 468). The Eleatic retreat from the world into the mind led to "the first philosophical dispute[,] concerning the senses and the existence of matter" (*JMN* 3:369). Matter and spirit are not just distinct; there is now doubt over whether matter exists at all.

Luckily for Emerson, the Eleatic dualism between an intellectual world of unity and stability, and a dubious phenomenal world of multiplicity and change was, at least in part, reconciled by Heraclitus of Ephesus, who lived in Ionia a century after Thales. De Gérando accounts Heraclitus part of the Eleatic tradition, and he almost certainly knew Xenophanes's work, if not that of his contemporary, Parmenides. For Heraclitus, phenomenal particulars are not separate from a divine unity, but rather, "All nature is governed by constant laws. The phenomena themselves which appear discordant concur in the harmony of the whole. It is an accord which results from discords" (*JMN* 3:369; *Histoire*, 482). The whole, then, as Emerson would have read in de Gérando, is a unity of many parts; those parts may be diverse and even discordant, but together they form a harmonious whole under a set of laws (*Histoire*, 483). Heraclitus's unifying metaphor of "law" draws on the legislative domain, the implication being that the divine is a kind of judge, imposing laws throughout nature. Importantly, though, this legal metaphor enables the divine and the material to reunite with each other, the "legal" framework organizing nature's variety into a whole.

The Heraclitan whole is not static, and its parts are always moving. Emerson's brusque note, "Meantime all change" (*JMN* 3:369), summarizes de Gérando's more expansive quotation from the sources: "However, all beings are subject to continual variation; each instant no longer finds them as they were at the preceding instant; it is a torrent which incessantly rolls its waves" (*Histoire*, 483–84). Thales's water metaphor is reused to conceptualize change. But Heraclitus's metaphor of law gives a new kind of unity to that change. In Emerson's laconic notes, this is the law of "Attraction Repulsion" (*JMN* 3:369), which abbreviates de Gérando's: "In the middle of these revolutions ... nature follows a constant path; the elementary and indivisible particles combine and separate; attraction and repulsion works this double change, resulting in a sort of condensation and evaporation" (*Histoire*, 484). Particles of matter are constantly changing, turning from solid to liquid to gas and back again, from living to dead or dead to living, or from light to dark, but our senses are not misleading us. Rather, we must use our reason to access the law (Emerson's "attraction-repulsion") which underlies this constant metamorphosis. The senses are only able to tell us about the sensible world, for "the same cannot be conceived except by the same" (*JMN* 3:370; *Histoire*, 486), but we can still use "divine reason" to ascertain the truth (*Histoire*, 487).

Heraclitus here builds upon one final Eleatic, Pythagoras. According to the Pythagoreans, "like can only be known by like" (*Histoire*, 421). This "consanguinity" with the universe, divine, and natural, is "reason," which "contemplates all nature" because "it has a certain affinity [*analogie*]" (*JMN* 3:367; *Histoire*, 421) with it. The implication of Pythagoras's idea is that the senses can only know matter (the eye knows light, the ear knows sound, etc.) because of their "affinity"; likewise, the mind as reason can know the "universality of nature" (*Histoire*, 421). Heraclitus's law unifies this distinction, and our senses become "open canals through which we inhale divine reason" (*JMN* 3:370; *Histoire*, 487); and this spiritual knowledge, though uncertain, can aid our intellectual understanding; and we can reach the truth. Our senses, then, give us access to a divine law that is spread amongst the many parts of nature; our reason can fathom that law from these particulars, and, crucially for what will become Emerson's first philosophy, we can get closer to divine truth: "Man breathes the universal soul [and is] united without obstacle to this supreme intelligence" (*Histoire*, 486–87).

In summary, Thales "water" gives Emerson the idea that metaphors drawn from experience can reshape the understanding of nature, man, and God. Anaximenes's "air" and Anaximander's "infinite" approach incorporeality. Anaxagoras's metaphors definitively separate the First Cause from the caused, the maker from the made, mind from matter, man and nature from God, marking a crucial first step in the movement towards the Anthropocene. Xenophanes and Parmenides bring everything back to the One, sacrificing the many, and putting what *is* above what *appears*, that is reason above nature. Pythagoras tells Emerson that like can only know like, further separating man and nature. Heraclitus reunites the one and the many, reconnects man to matter, sense to intellect, and the human to the divine, through the metaphor of "law." Emerson learns something from each of these metaphorical first philosophies as he develops his Transcendentalist approach. His last word on de Gérando, though, is not metaphysical, it is pragmatic: "Always utility gives the medal, even tho' philosophers are the school committee" (*JMN* 3:370). Metaphors as metaphysics need to work, they need to answer the questions that are posed; they need to be useful if they are to last, ground "national religions," and sustain the thought of millennia. If they are not useful, Emerson the pragmatist implies, they will not last despite the efforts of the academy of philosophers, here reduced emphatically to a "school committee."

First Philosophy

In June of 1835 Emerson sat down at his journal to "endeavour to announce the laws of First Philosophy" (*JMN* 5:270; cf. *JMN* 5:50). Realizing, perhaps, that this was a little too much for a thirty-two-year-old ex-minister of little reputation, he struck out the first words and began again in a more neutral tone: "By the First Philosophy, is meant the original laws of the mind. It is the Science of what *is*, in distinction from what *appears*" (*JMN* 5:270; Emerson's italics). There is no explicit reference to Bacon or to de Gérando here, but even so this line contains buried references to the *Advancement* and the pre-Socratics. The allusion to the *prima philosophia* becomes clearer when Emerson evokes the universality of these "original laws": "They resemble great circles in astronomy, each of which, in what direction soever it be drawn, contains the whole sphere. So each of these implies all truth" (*JMN* 5:270). As with Bacon's quest for summative maxims that precede disciplinary difference, Emerson's laws entail all truth. The pre-Socratics, as we have seen, provide a genealogy of the difference between what *is* and what *appears* with ultimately epochal significance. However, by 1835, Emerson is a very different man than he was in 1830. His beloved first wife has tragically died, and he has remarried. He has travelled across Europe from Italy to Scotland. He has resigned the ministry and become a professional lyceum lecturer. He has read more widely and deeply in the philosophical tradition of his time, in particular the post-Kantian Romanticism of Samuel Taylor Coleridge and Thomas Carlyle. Thus, when Emerson sets out his Transcendentalist first philosophy, it is not in the terms of de Gérando's pre-Socratics whose elemental and homocentric metaphors showed him the way, it is in the terms borrowed from Coleridge and Carlyle, and the Eleatic distinction between what *is* and what *appears* is now that between the "Reason" and the "Understanding" (*JMN* 5:270).[13]

From Anaxagoras to Heraclitus, in de Gérando's account, the pre-Socratics had marked the difference between what could be known by the senses and what could be known by the mind, and this difference directly mapped onto their distinction between the material world of the body and the incorporeal world of the spirit. As like could only be known by like, only spiritual knowledge—divine reason—gave access to God. This pre-Socratic settlement is analogous to Emerson's evocation of Reason:

> As our Earth & its system are found to lie in the deep thicket of spheres that compose the Milky Way, so the mind finds its place to be in the region of grandest Nature, namely, in union with the Supreme Being. Our compound nature differences us from God, but our Reason is not to be distinguished from the divine Essence. (*JMN* 5:270)

Emerson's metaphors separate out the concept of the human and the divine even while uniting them, separating both from the mere matter of "nature" with a small *n*. Though we have a "compound" or material nature, we share "our Reason" with the "divine Essence." His astronomical metaphor deploys a material analogue, albeit on a galactic scale, to conceptualize our small but important place in the vastness of divine being ("Nature" with a capital *N*). Science, though limited to scraping around in matter, can yet provide useful metaphors for spiritual knowledge, or Reason.

Indeed, as with the later pre-Socratics, our material knowledge when used for its own sake, which Emerson now calls the "Understanding," is necessarily misleading. The Understanding is "the hand of the mind. It mediates between the soul & inert matter. It works in time & space, & therefore successively. It divides, compares, reasons, invents. It lives from the Reason, yet disobeys it. It commands the material world, yet often for the pleasure of the sense" (*JMN* 5:272). Emerson's bodily metaphor for the Understanding, the "hand of the mind," is telling, conceptualizing it as a corporeal faculty: it gets things done, it moves civilization forward, but in parts, and for merely sensual reasons. What matters, however, is immortal, out of time and space, connected directly to the divine in a single permanent moment of Parmenidian "Eternal Beatitude" (*JMN* 5:272). Even our individuality is a mistake of the Understanding. In reality, as Reason directly intuits, we are one with the divine. The Understanding, Emerson argues, clumsily accounts for this intuition, creating works of art and even ideas of a future Heaven, to try to capture what it can of Reason. But these are mere "fables of its own" and cannot reveal the proper truth—which is that Heaven is *now*, if only Reason is harkened to (*JMN* 5:273).

With his newfound Romantic articulacy recasting *prima philosophia* and the pre-Socratic dualist settlement, Emerson embarks on his first masterpiece, the short monograph *Nature*, published in 1836 (his title resonating with Parmenides's poem, *On Nature*). Emerson's "Introduction" states that "All science has but one aim, namely to find a theory of nature," but he laments that knowledge is divided, and "religious teachers dispute and hate each other." What we need, Emerson writes, is a "true theory [that] will be its own evidence. Its test is, that it will explain all phenomena" (*CW* 1:8). Emerson's "true theory" will, like Bacon's *prima philosophia*, have a generalizing authority. Indeed, a subsequent part of *Nature* directly echoes Bacon's examples of first philosophy cited above, "if equals are added to unequals the wholes will be unequal," which for Bacon was "an axiom of justice as well as of the mathematics." Emerson generalizes this further, with an unacknowledged reference to Germaine de Staël's phrase, "The axioms of physics translate the laws of ethics" (*CW* 1:21; cf. *JMN* 3:255). What Emerson takes from Bacon and de Staël is a primary analogy between the laws of nature, as proposed in mathematics and physics, and moral laws: they have the same structure. "Thus," he writes, "'the whole is greater than its part'; 'reaction is equal to action'; 'the smallest weight may be made to lift the greatest, the difference in weight being compensated by time'; and many the like propositions, which have an ethical as well as physical sense" (*CW* 1:21–22). What Emerson adds to Bacon and de Staël is his insight that such primary analogies work because our conceptualizations of the spiritual, moral, and ethical spheres are fundamentally metaphorical. As he writes: "all spiritual facts are represented by natural symbols" (*CW* 1:19). This, for Emerson, is a *fact* of first philosophy. Bacon's example is merely illustrative. As he goes on: "The whole world is emblematic. Parts of speech are metaphors because the whole of nature is a metaphor of the human mind" (*CW* 1:21). The material or natural world, for Emerson as for de Gérando's pre-Socratics, is a resource for us to understand ourselves; "a reserve of useful commodities and beautiful allegories" (699), as Walls puts it. Our experience of nature provides the concepts we need to articulate the mind and its relationship to the divine. Thus, nature has become a resource for man's self-discovery. But, crucially, nature is not relegated thereby to mere matter, because, as for Thales and Anaximander, for Emerson God is *in* Nature. As such, the metaphorical transference of meaning is a powerful creative act enabling us to find God in nature and in ourselves. "It is," as Emerson puts it, "the working of the Original Cause through the instruments it has made" (*CW* 1:21). Nature's end, for Emerson, is to provide a language that takes us back to the beginning—the First Cause—and that language is metaphor.

This metaphorical conceptualization is not arbitrary, as though anything could symbolize anything. There is a necessary connection between nature's material "commodities" and the idea of the self. As Emerson puts it:

> This relation between mind and matter is not fancied by some poet, but stands as the will of God... There seems to be a necessity in the spirit to manifest itself in material

forms; and day and night, river and storm, bird and beast, acid and alkali preëxist in necessary Ideas in the mind of God, and are what they are by virtue of preceding affections in the world of spirit. (*CW* 1:22)

Though now overlain with Swedenborg's correspondence theory, where natural facts correspond directly to spiritual facts, this is essentially a consequence of Pythagoras's and Heraclitus's doctrine of like knowing like. We can know God in Nature because it is *like* him; when we use metaphors drawn from nature, we are returning matter to the spirit whence it came. The ends of nature, which the causal metaphor tells us are also its beginnings, are to provide access from spirit to spirit; from God to the human soul and back again; from the various parts of nature back to the one that is their cause—that is, from like to like. As Emerson puts it in *Nature*, with direct reference to the pre-Socratics this time:

Herein is especially apprehended the Unity of Nature,—Unity in Variety,—which meets us everywhere. All the endless variety of things makes a unique, an identical impression. Xenophanes complained in his old age, that, look where he would, all things hastened back to Unity. He was weary of seeing the same entity in the tedious variety of forms. The fable of Proteus has a cordial truth. Every particular in nature, a leaf, a drop, a crystal, a moment of time, is related to the whole, and partakes of the perfection of the whole. (*CW* 1:27)

Xenophanes's weary admission of what Emerson later calls a "tyrannising unity" (*CW* 1:39) in variety, is possible because we share a common origin and a common end, and everything is related to everything else, making up one whole. It directly recalls Heraclitus's view that nature gives reason access to the laws that order that unity: "the solid seeming block of matter has been pervaded and dissolved by a thought; this feeble human being has penetrated the base masses of nature with an informing soul, and recognised itself in their harmony, that is, seized its law" (*CW* 1:34). Together, these pre-Socratic insights cast their light on the deep time that stands behind *Nature*'s famous Transcendental epiphany: "Standing on the bare ground,—my head bathed by the blithe air, and uplifted into infinite space,—all mean egotism vanishes. I become a transparent eye-ball. I am nothing. I see all. The currents of the Universal Being circulate through me; I am part or particle of God" (*CW* 1:10). The epiphany is an ecstatic restatement of de Gérando's summary of Heraclitus cited above: "Man breathes the universal soul [and is] united without obstacle to this supreme intelligence" (*Histoire*, 486–87). The partiality of the individual returns home to its source in the whole—the first and final cause. In his 1830 notes, Emerson wrongly attributed this "transcendentalism" to the Ionians; it is rather a label that rightly fits the Eleatics. The dualism of matter and mind, man, and God, has been overcome in a moment of unity. The unity of man, nature, and God is the very epitome of Emerson's Transcendentalist vision.

Unity, though, cannot hold; the vision fades; man resolves back into matter. This, however, is essential and saves the Transcendentalist from the skepticism of pure idealism that we saw in Parmenides. The ideal world of the pure circulation of spirit may be "perfect," but it is also a "divine dream, from which we may presently awaken to the glories and certainties of day" (*CW* 1:37). As Emerson's crucial point about metaphor makes clear, and it is a point exemplified by the pre-Socratics, we need matter to understand spirit, but we also need to understand what matter, or nature, really is to "account for the consanguinity which we acknowledge to it" (*CW* 1:38). Matter is not some inert stuff; rather, like Emerson in his highest moments, nature too is "part and particle" of God. *Nature*'s God, as for the Ionians, is both *cause* and *element*: "behind nature and throughout nature, spirit is present" (*CW* 1:38). We too are part of that nature: "The Supreme Being does not build up nature around us, but puts it forth through us, as the life of the tree puts forth new branches and leaves through the pores of the old" (*CW* 1:38). Nature, what was the *not me*, the mere body, is now very much the *me* (*CW* 1:8). And that is because the *not me* and the *me* are both God, both cause and end; a circulation of pantheistic power that is creation itself.

Emerson's causal God, then, is not, as for Parmenides or Anaxagoras, a static being, distinct from an everchanging nature—a one alone. Rather, as with Heraclitus, God's unity is itself a process of creation as nature. Emerson's everchanging nature in all its particularity properly represents God's spiritual laws: "Nature is not fixed but fluid. Spirit alters, moulds, makes it. The immobility or bruteness of nature, is the absence of spirit; to pure spirit, it is fluid, it is volatile, it is obedient" (*CW* 1:44). Metaphors of motion, significantly taking Emerson back to Thales, define the spirit as nature, man, and God. As such, we should always find ourselves in nature. As he writes, recalling his famous 1833 visit to the Jardin des Plantes in Paris:

> In a cabinet of natural history, we become sensible of a certain occult recognition and sympathy in regard to the most unwieldy and eccentric forms for beast, fish and insect. [Man] finds something of himself in every great and small thing, in every mountain stratum, in every new law of color or fact of astronomy, or atmospheric influence which observation or analysis lay open. (*CW* 1:40)

We see ourselves everywhere; thus, when Emerson returns one last time to the pre-Socratic maxim of first philosophy, like can only know like, he rewrites it as "What we are, that only can we see" (*CW* 1:45); but as we are everything, like *and* unlike—bird, beast, fish, mountain, colour, air—more fully explaining Xenophanes's weariness in finding unity everywhere.

We cannot, then, to paraphrase the Latin motto *ne te quaesiveris extra* that precedes Emerson's 1841 essay "Self-Reliance" (*CW* 2:25), *seek ourselves outside of ourselves*: we are "part and particle" of everything. As Emerson learned from Anaximander, there is no outside: God's work, nature, is an *apeiron*, a boundless, limitless, infinite creative power. As Emerson puts it in "The American Scholar," one year after *Nature*: "There is never a beginning, there is never an end, to the inexplicable continuity of this web of God, but always circular power returning into itself. Therein it resembles [the scholar's] own spirit, whose beginning, whose ending, he never can find,—so entire, so boundless" (*CW* 1:54). Man and God, then, for Emerson are strictly homologous. Both are infinite;

both are creative. With man as a part of God's whole, only the scale distinguishes them. Also, Emerson's metaphors show God's causality to be immanent, as with Thales and the early pre-Socratics. God has priority but not exteriority, and if God is the first maker, then man is the ultimate maker, the point through which God works his creation. It needs, Emerson argues, the poet or the philosopher to recognize, and above all to *use*, this creative power; to reject tradition, to see the "miraculous in the common" (*CW* 1:44), and to employ this everyday resource for their metaphors, obeying Emerson's quasi-divine imperative to "build, therefore, your own world" (*CW* 1:45). The poet must find a language fit for the always primitive questions of the given moment in the "wonders ... brought to our own door" (*CW* 1:44). The American poet is in a peculiarly powerful position, for he has "new lands, new men" and can thus have "new thoughts" (*CW* 1:7). Escaping, perhaps, Xenophanes's ennui, the New World provides original answers to the primitive questions about the First Cause, the principle of the soul, the nature of God, appearance and reality, the one and the many. Indeed, if we take this as an origin point of American literature, then Whitman's leaf of grass, "a uniform hieroglyph,"[14] is a symbol of man, nature, and God, that echoes Emerson; but Dickinson's bird with eyes "like frightened beads"[15] renders nature strange to us. Melville's "whiteness of the whale"[16] marks a sublime terror in nature to be hunted and destroyed; but Thoreau's all too measurable Walden pond returns nature to itself, eluding man's clumsy symbolism.[17] But for Emerson, and this maybe his best answer to our current crisis, nature can never be other to the self it exists to represent. As he writes of nature in his poem "The Sphinx," "Who telleth one of my meanings, / Is master of all I am" (*CW* 9:125). The metaphors of Emerson's first philosophy, Transcendentalism, though cast in Romantic terms, as I have shown, flow from the pre-Socratics' anthropocentric polarization of God and nature, a significant tributary of the Anthropocene. In Emerson's hands, their metaphors become a co-creation with their divine source: God *is* everchanging nature, nature *is* an everchanging source of metaphor, metaphor allows us to constantly recreate ourselves and our world, and in such a way is God's creative power, "the seed of the world," actuated in, as, and by man.

Notes

1. Wai Chee Dimock, *Through Other Continents: American Literature Across Deep Time* (Princeton, NJ: Princeton University Press, 2006), 3–5.
2. Laura Dassow Walls, "The Sphinx at the Crossroads: Transcendentalism Meets the Anthropocene," *ESQ: A Journal of Nineteenth-Century American Literature and Culture* 67, no. 3-4: 713.
3. Ralph Waldo Emerson, *The Topical Notebooks of Ralph Waldo Emerson*, vol. 2, ed. Ronald A. Bosco (Columbia, University of Missouri Press, 1993), 346.
4. The influence of the pre-Socratics on Emerson, and in particular the importance of Baron de Gérando as transmitter, has not gone entirely unnoticed. One of the earliest examples is a short piece by Carl F. Strauch, "Gérando: A Source for Emerson," *Modern Language Notes* 58, no. 1 (January 1943): 64–67, which examines a possible source for Emerson's poem "Empedocles." Kenneth Cameron also notes de Gérando's importance in his

comprehensive *Emerson the Essayist*, Vol. 1 (Hartford: Transcendental Books, 1945), 1–36; Sacvan Bercovitch makes a further claim for the importance of Empedocles in his "The Philosophical Background to the Fable of Emerson's 'American Scholar,'" *Journal of the History of Ideas* 28, no. 1 (1967): 123–28. More recently, Herwig Friedl has made a significant claim for the importance of the pre-Socratics in Emerson's mature thought, focusing on Heinrich Ritter's *The History of Ancient Philosophy*, translated into English in 1838 and probably read by Emerson in the early 1840s. Freidl's phenomenological reading is profound, but underplays the crucial formative influence of the pre-Socratics on Emerson's first philosophy that I argue for here. See Herwig Friedl, *Thinking in Search of a Language: Essays on American Intellect and Intuition* (London: Bloomsbury, 2018), 30–53 and 126–39. Robert D. Richardson's *Emerson: The Mind on Fire* (Berkeley: University of California Press, 1995), 102–107, and Urbas's *Emerson's Metaphysics* (Lanham: Lexington, 2016), 70–77, also make claims for the importance of de Gérando and the pre-Socratics for Emerson's first philosophy that support the arguments I make in this chapter.

5. George Lakoff and Mark Johnson, *Philosophy in the Flesh: The Embodied Mind and its Challenge to Western Thought* (New York: Basic Books, 1999), 358–59. Throughout this chapter I will be drawing on the methodological insights and conclusions of Conceptual Metaphor Theory (CMT), though I will be deliberately eschewing the method's technical vocabulary. I have fully explored Emerson's metaphors using CMT in my *Emerson's Metaphors* (Lexington: Lanham, 2023). For the key texts of CMT see: Lakoff and Johnson, 1980, *Metaphors We Live By* (Chicago: University of Chicago Press, 2003); Mark Johnson, *The Body in the Mind* (Chicago: University of Chicago Press, 1987); George Lakoff, *Women, Fire and Dangerous Things* (Chicago: University of Chicago Press, 1987); George Lakoff and Mark Turner, *More Than Cool Reason: A Field Guide to Poetic Metaphor* (Chicago: University of Chicago Press, 1989); Raymond Gibbs, Jr., *The Poetics of Mind: Figurative Thought, Language and Understanding* (Cambridge: Cambridge University Press, 1994); George Lakoff, "The Contemporary Theory of Metaphor," in *Metaphor and Thought*, 2nd ed., ed. Andrew Ortony, (Cambridge: Cambridge University Press, 1995), 202–51; Zoltán Kövecses, *Metaphor: A Practical Introduction* (Oxford: Oxford University Press, 2010).

6. The references to his reading of Plutarch in the journals suggest that Emerson probably didn't read his more philosophical essays until his own philosophical position was fairly settled. See Edmund G. Berry, *Emerson's Plutarch* (Cambridge, MA: Harvard University Press, 1961), 40–42.

7. The journal entry mentions Murat, but the usually reliable Richardson says the *Histoire* was William Ellery Channing's recommendation (Richardson, *Mind on Fire*, 102). It's possible that both are right.

8. M. de Gérando, *Histoire Comparée des Systèmes de Philosophie*, vol. 1, 2nd ed. (Paris: Alexis Eymery, 1822), ix–xi. Hereafter referred to parenthetically as *Histoire*. All translations not attributed to Emerson are my own.

9. Francis Bacon, *The Works of Francis Bacon*, 10 vols. (London: Baynes and Son, 1824), 1:95.

10. Rhodri Lewis, "Francis Bacon, Allegory and the Uses of Myth," *Review of English Studies* 61, no. 250 (June 2021): 386–87. Lewis's interpolations.

11. For an exploration of Bacon's first philosophy in the contexts of Emerson's metaphorical use of Natural History tropes, see my *Emerson's Metaphors*, 145–6.

12. The editors of the journal passage interpolate "metaph[ysics]" here, but metaphysician seems to make more sense, and the editors agree with that interpolation on the following page.

13. See my *Emerson's Transatlantic Romanticism* (London: Palgrave, 2012), 35–57.
14. Walt Whitman, *Leaves of Grass and Other Writings*, ed. Michael Moon (New York: Norton, 2002), 30.
15. Emily Dickinson, *The Complete Poems of Emily Dickinson*, ed. Thomas H. Johnson (London: Faber and Faber, 1975), 156.
16. Herman Melville, *Moby-Dick*, ed. Hershel Parker and Harrison Heywood (New York: Norton, 2002), 165.
17. Henry David Thoreau, *Walden and Civil Disobedience* (Harmondsworth: Penguin, 1986), 335.

2

AMERICAN CIVILIZATION, OR, HEMISPHERIC EMERSONS

CHAPTER 7

EMERSON, MARTÍ, AND A COSMOPOLITANISM FOR THE AMERICAS

TIMOTHY DONAHUE

José Martí once listed the events he wanted to include in a never-completed memoir titled *Los momentos supremos*. At the top of that list is "la tarde de Emerson" ("the afternoon of Emerson").[1] It was in no sense out of character for the Cuban writer and revolutionary to count a few hours spent reading Emerson as amongst life's supreme moments. In the 1880s and 1890s, Martí wrote essays about Emerson, referred to him in his journalism, reflected on him in his journals, and translated his poetry.[2] This engagement with Emerson's work, a longtime topic of interest for Latin Americanists, has recently also drawn the attention of scholars in American and hemispheric studies. These bodies of scholarship offer varying assessments of what drew Martí to Emerson and of how intense his admiration was, but there recurs across them a shared assumption: that Emerson embodies US culture. In the mid-twentieth century, Félix Lizaso observed that, for Martí, Emerson and his circle represented "lo más puro y fuerte de las letras de los Estados Unidos" ("the purest and strongest of US letters"), and in the early twenty-first century, Laura Lomas found in "Martí's reading of Emerson" a critical assessment of a "United Statesian tradition" of literature.[3] On such readings, Emerson's Americanness allows Martí's writing about him to serve as a reflection on the promise and perils of US society.

But was Martí's Emerson all that American? Although critics often place Emerson at the center of a US literary canon, Emerson was, as Lawrence Buell notes, "an intermittent nationalist at best."[4] Martí himself goes further still: "Ni fue hombre de su pueblo, porque lo fue del pueblo humano" ("he was not a man of his nation; he was a man of the human nation") (*OC* 13:20; *SW* 119). These words cast Emerson not as a citizen of the US but rather as a citizen of the world. Martí's Emerson is best considered, accordingly, as a cosmopolitan figure. Distancing Martí's Emerson from the US need not depoliticize his Emersonian engagement. Far from it: this chapter will show how Martí's engagement with a worldly Emerson—a figure whose reflections on selfhood, nature, and community unfold on scales both smaller and larger than the nation—allows Martí to envision alternatives to a global order marked by the rise of US empire and the peripheralization of Latin America. My examination of this critical Emersonianism focuses on two of Martí's major essays: "Emerson" (1882), a stylistically complex literary eulogy, and "Nuestra América" ("Our America," 1891), a reflection on hemispheric culture and politics. In these texts, Martí draws on the thought of a far-from-American Emerson to develop a cosmopolitan perspective of his own; he reflects not just on the relation of an increasingly imperious US to his still-colonized Cuban homeland, and to Latin America more broadly, but also on the place of that nation, colony, and continent in a world growing ever more globalized.

To recognize the Emersonian qualities of Martí's cosmopolitan and anti-imperial outlook is to bring together, and extend, two strands of scholarship. On one hand, there are the many readers of Martí who have emphasized his deep appreciation of Emerson, but who have done so without foregrounding issues of empire. On the other lie the readers who have framed Martí as a powerful critic of Euro-American imperialism, albeit without emphasizing his affinity with Emerson.[5] However, as I will explain in this chapter, Martí's embrace of Emerson and his anti-imperialism often go hand in hand. To be sure, Martí's relation to Emerson and empire challenges a more familiar model of literary relations between metropolitan and colonial writers. Often, colonial writers are taken as expressing their anti-imperialism through agonistic struggles with metropolitan figures. That critical framework has generated ample insights, but it doesn't readily accommodate Martí's engagement with Emerson. Martí took Emerson as an object of neither critique nor emulation. Emersonian thought and style served him, rather, as resources, as conceptual tools for formulating responses to the cultural and political inequities confronting the Americas. Because Emerson's work proved an asset for Martí's anticolonialism, their literary relationship also challenges accounts of Emerson that suggest his philosophical thought is at odds with progressive politics.[6] Indeed, this chapter aims to show how both Emerson and Martí remain vital resources for those in pursuit of more just futures within and beyond the Americas.

Martí's Emerson

Two of Martí's most extended discussions of Emerson were composed upon the latter's death and printed in Caracas's *La opinión nacional*, for which Martí regularly wrote while living in New York City. The newspaper printed the essay "Emerson" on May 19, 1882; four days later, Martí's recurring "Seccion Constante" column included a shorter obituary. Martí was not the only Latin American writer to respond to Emerson's passing; remembrances published by the Argentine author and politician Domingo Sarmiento and the Cuban intellectual Enrique José Varona suggest that Emerson had at least a modest hemispheric readership.[7] These Emerson eulogies, and their many US counterparts, took stock of the North American's life and work in admiring terms. Martí notes in "Emerson," for instance, "Se oía su voz, como la de mensajero de lo futuro, que hablese de entre nube luminosa" ("his voice was heard as if it were the voice of a messenger from the future, speaking from amid incandescent clouds," *OC* 13:19; *SW* 18). Yet if such laudatory assessments were common, Martí's response remains distinct from those of his US and Latin American contemporaries because of how he understood Emersonian thought. In the Gilded Age, many readers sought to domesticate the thinker once known for his unconventional thought and radical abolitionism by associating him with solidities, like sovereign individualism, a stable nature, and eternal spiritual truths.[8] Even an obituary as otherwise nuanced as Charles G. Ames's glossed Emerson's take on "Personal Conduct and Social Aims" as "Be a brick and there will be a place for you in the wall."[9]

By contrast, Martí's Emerson resembles the dynamic thinker brought into focus in recent decades by Richard Poirier, Sharon Cameron, and Branka Arsić, among others.[10] For such an Emerson, Arsić explains, "the great formula" of his thought is "migration, mutation, metamorphosis."[11] This protean Emersonianism is on display in the Emerson texts that mattered most to Martí. For instance, *Nature* (1836), considered by Martí to be Emerson's "mejor libro" ("best book," *OC* 13:23; *SW* 122), at one point ponders whether it is even possible for a person to "look upon a river" and not be "reminded of the flux of all things."[12] One place Emerson lays out what such universal fluctuation entails is his *Essays: First Series* (1841), especially "Circles" and "Self-Reliance," which Martí alludes to and quotes from in "Emerson."[13] In "Circles," Emerson contends that we live in a world where ontological instability prevails: "the universe is fluid and volatile," so there are "no fixtures in nature" and "literatures, cities, climates, religions" are all liable to "leave their foundations and dance before our eyes" (*EPP* 174, 178). In "Self-Reliance," Emerson casts the individual self as comparably unfixed; when he declares that "the soul *becomes*" without specifying the object of that becoming (*EPP* 129, italics in-text), he describes a self in an unending process of transition, a self so protean that it approaches illegibility *as* a self.[14] For Emerson, inhabiting a self and world of constant change proves challenging, since "people want to be settled," but such unceasing change also carries salutary effects: "only insofar as [people] are unsettled, is there any hope for them," since unsettlement allows for the transformation of the world (*EPP* 181). This sense of all-encompassing fluctuation was not expressed solely in Emerson's earliest essays. In "Quotation and Originality," from the 1876 collection *Letters and Social Aims*—a book Martí describes as covering "casi todo los asuntos importantes que requieren en la tierra la atención del hombre" ("almost all the issues on Earth that require man's attention," *OC* 23:305)—Emerson asserts that "all things are in flux" (*EPP* 329).

Emerson's concern with selves and worlds in motion may have been part of his appeal to Martí, who was, as Laura Lomas has shown, a "migrant Latino subject" who moved through the Americas without plans to settle.[15] Martí's notebooks, in any case, attest to his understanding of Emersonian thought as centrally concerned with transition. In several undated notebook entries, Martí reflected on "la tarde de Emerson" that he wanted to write about in his *Los momentos supremos* memoir. One entry describes a pleasurable scene of reading in Martí's New York City apartment: "el único placer absolutamente puro que hasta hoy he gozado fue el de aquella tarde en que desde mi cuarto medio desnudo vi a la ciudad postrada, y entreví lo futuro pensando en Emerson" ("the only absolutely pure pleasure that I have enjoyed up to today was that afternoon in which from my room, half-naked, I saw the prostrate city, and I glimpsed the future, thinking of Emerson," *OC* 22:323). This passage foregrounds states of change—Martí, "medio desnudo," is caught amidst states of dress and undress, and his glimpse of the future draws him out of his prostrate present—so it documents how Martí's reading generated an Emersonian experience of a self in transformation.[16] Another entry draws a still more pronounced connection between reading Emerson and the experience of transitory selfhood: Martí describes "la tarde de Emerson" as "cuando pierde el hombre el sentido de sí, y se transfunde en el mundo" ("when man loses the sense of himself, and transfuses himself into the world," *OC* 19:370). Here, Martí goes beyond remarking upon the self's plasticity. His volition initiates the self's worldly transfusion but something else causes the loss of self that occasions it, which is to say that Martí's agency ebbs and flows over the course of the statement; as such, the passage recalls the moments of "ravishment," in which impersonal forces annihilate personal structures of selfhood, that Sharon Cameron finds across Emerson's writing.[17] Indeed, the statement's effacement of selfhood is amplified by its presentation of its subject in general terms, as "el hombre," and not as Martí himself. Yet Martí's entry unsettles more than just a sense of a durable self: the description of the self's transfusion into the world puts those two entities and the boundary between them in a state of flux, while the present tense of the ostensibly retrospective passage dissolves the temporal distinction between the moments of Martí's reading and writing about Emerson.

If these notebook entries indicate that an experience of protean selfhood and worldliness attended Martí's reading of the North American thinker, the essay "Emerson" describes its subject and his milieu in similarly dynamic terms. That piece is one of the chronicles of North American life for which Martí is well-known. These works of *modernista* literary journalism describe US culture to Latin American readers with notable aesthetic and intellectual complexity. "Emerson" is no exception. The essay's characterization of its subject constantly shifts; for instance, within the space of a paragraph, Emerson goes from being a person who lived as if the sun were "su propio sol, y él patriarca" ("his own sun, and he a patriarch") to an individual attending his guests like "un siervo" ("a servant," *OC* 13:18–19; *SW* 117–18). While such shifting descriptions put the selfhood of the essay's title figure in flux, Martí locates a parallel plasticity in Emerson's surroundings: "Uvas secas parecen los libros que poco ha parecían montes" ("the books that seemed mountains a short while before now look like shriveled grapes," *OC* 13:21; *SW* 120). At work both in Martí's account of reading Emerson and in his touchstone description of that author, then, there is a distinctly Emersonian sense of the self's and the world's instability.

Scholars have only unevenly registered how Martí's writing takes up such an Emersonian outlook; he tends to be read as drawing from Emerson either a concept of transitory selfhood, or a notion of worldly fluctuation, but not both. If one critic has Martí finding in Emerson an "unsettling" of the self, another holds that for Martí Emerson's work suggests "a fully sovereign individual standing above a rapidly changing world."[18] These partial assessments of Martí's investment in a dynamic Emersonianism are, perhaps, a consequence of the way "Emerson" often represents its title figure's protean thinking. That piece features ample "troping"—a destabilization of meaning achieved through the "turning of a word in directions or detours it seems destined otherwise to avoid"—which Richard Poirier has identified as a "constant" in Emerson's work.[19] Martí in fact highlights this Emersonian tendency for turning language and ideas in unexpected directions: "así revuelve este hombre gigantesco la poderosa mente" ("thus the powerful mind of this gigantic man turns and turns," *OC* 13:27; *SW* 126). This observation follows and describes what may be the most pronounced instance of troping in the essay. In a lengthy paragraph that does not so much describe Emerson as ventriloquize thoughts that could be associated with him, Martí initially offers comments that seem to affirm an anthropocentric sense of sovereign selfhood: "El universo es siervo, y rey el ser humano" ("the universe is the servant and the human being is the king," *OC* 13:26; *SW* 125). Yet as that paragraph approaches its conclusion, Martí turns it in a different direction, posing a question that destabilizes the foregoing propositions about human mastery: "¿Y se moverá [el mundo] como se mueve hoy perpetuamente, o se evaporá, y mecidos por sus vapores, iremos a confundirnos, en compenetración augusta y deliciosa, con un ser de quien la naturaleza es mera aparición?" ("And will it [the world] always move ahead as it moves today or will it evaporate, and will we, floating on its vapors, become one in august and delicious commingling with a being whose nature is mere appearance?" *OC* 13:26–27; *SW* 126). By suggesting the twinned prospects of the world's evaporation and humanity's commingling with the entity whose being was expressed as nature, this question tropes and undermines the foregoing commentary. Martí's essay thus introduces the idea of Emerson's investment in a sovereign self and a mastered world only to undermine it.

In "Emerson," then, Martí adopts the destabilizing intellectual and literary style of the essay's namesake. That stylistic overlap attests to the oft-recognized affinity between the two authors.[20] Indeed, although I've been showing Martí's Emerson to be more of a radical anti-foundationalist than critics have tended to recognize, my aim here is not to counter the longstanding critical assessment of Martí's deep appreciation of Emerson. Notable to my eye, rather, is with what Martí did with Emerson's work. What kinds of social and political thought emerged out of Martí's encounter with a destabilizing Emersonianism? Martí himself invites this line of inquiry, we might say, for he calls attention to Emerson's own activism regarding abolition: "Cuando vio hombres esclavos, y pensó en ellos, habló de modo que pareció que sobre las faldas de un nuevo monte bíblico se rompían de nuevo en pedazos las Tablas de la Ley" ("when he saw or thought of men who were enslaved, he spoke—and it was as if the Tablet of Law were once again being smashed at the foot of a new biblical mountain," *OC* 13:19; *SW* 118). These comments on Emerson speaking defiantly against slavery indicate how Martí saw Emerson's philosophical thought as being accompanied by an investment in worldly justice. In the next section, in turn, I consider how Martí draws on the affordances of

Emersonian thought in his own efforts to reckon with inequality within and beyond the Americas.

"Emerson" and the World

Martí's "Emerson," as my discussion of it has so far suggested, quotes, paraphrases, and stylistically echoes the work of its subject. As José Ballón puts it, the essay amounts to a "mosaico literario" ("literary mosaic"), a "collage" of Martí's and Emerson's thought and writing.[21] A number of critics have emphasized how Martí's employment of that mosaicist compositional method blurs the line between his speech and Emerson's in such a pronounced fashion that, at times, the distinctiveness of Martí's authorial persona dissolves.[22] I would further observe that the vacillating voice that Martí creates via this literary collage has an Emersonian quality itself, reflecting as it does the model of transitory selfhood visible in "Self-Reliance" and other essays. Martí uses this Emersonian erosion of selfhood's edges to formulate a cosmopolitan perspective, one he uses to challenge the cultural peripheralization of Latin America.

Such an elision of the line between author and subject occurs in other Martí essays profiling North Americans—for example, extensive quotation and paraphrase produce a comparable effect in "El poeta Walt Whitman" (1887)—but nowhere is it as pronounced as in "Emerson." The vocal blurring in that essay is notable not just for its intensity but also because it is accompanied by a cosmopolitan contextualization of its subject. Emerson's reading, we learn, was global in scope, encompassing work by Montaigne, Swedenborg, Plotinus, Hindu philosophers, and Plato (*OC* 13:21; *SW* 120). Indeed, Martí ascribes to Emerson a central position in an international cultural field akin to what Pascale Casanova has termed "world literary space," "a literary universe relatively independent of the everyday world and its political divisions" with its own center-periphery hierarchy.[23] "Emerson" does so by associating its namesake with authors who, for many denizens of the nineteenth-century Americas, had a classic status that located them at or near the center of the literary world: Emerson "tiene de Calderón, de Platón, y de Píndaro. Tiene de Franklin" ("had in him something of Calderón, of Plato, and of Pindar, and something of Franklin too," *OC* 13:29; *SW* 128). Martí points up Emerson's prominence in world literary space still more directly when he asks, "Quién fue ese que ha muerto?" ("Who was this man who died?") and answers, "Pues lo sabe toda la tierra" ("the whole world knows who he was," *OC* 13:18; *SW* 117, translation modified). By offering such a worldly contextualization of Emerson while at the same time dissolving the distinction between his persona and his subject, Martí claims for himself a position in the heart of world literary space. This occupation of Emerson's position is no agonistic bid on Martí's part to supplant a predecessor; rather, Martí's sliding into Emerson's space reflects his investment in the North American's conception of selfhood as flexible and transitory.

In an Emersonian fashion, then, "Emerson" casts both its author and subject as cosmopolitans participating in a global culture. This turn to cosmopolitanism is not exceptional, either in Martí's work or in turn-of-the-century Latin American literature. Martí's 1882 essay "Oscar Wilde" expressly argues that Latin Americans ought to adopt a cosmopolitan outlook. Before describing an Oscar Wilde lecture in New York City, Martí claims, "Conocer diversas literaturas es el medio mejor de libertarse de la tiranía de algunas de ellas" ("knowing diverse literatures is the best way to liberate oneself from the tyranny of some of them," *OC* 15:361). This statement, Mariano Siskind explains, is "the first Latin American world literary discourse"—the first suggestion that Latin Americans invest themselves in a universal literary field coterminous with the world—and a number of other Latin American authors would offer like-minded commentaries in the ensuing decades.[24] Siskind argues that these writers situated themselves in the field of world literature as a strategy for "work[ing] through" the "traumatic aspects" of Latin America's marginalization in the field of global culture; they endeavored to emancipate themselves from localities often deemed "backward," he argues, and in turn claim a "modern subjectivity."[25]

Martí's valorization of Emerson's cosmopolitanism, along with his own embrace of a cosmopolitan position in world literary space, thus reflect broad patterns in late nineteenth-century Latin American culture. In an important sense, though, "Emerson" stands distinct from the body of cosmopolitan commentaries that Siskind describes. Within that discourse, "there was nothing foreign" about the world literature field that Latin American intellectuals sought to inhabit.[26] Yet "Emerson" makes plain that there is a substantial geocultural space that Martí must traverse in order to occupy Emerson's position; that attention to geographical and cultural distinction in turn allows the essay to offer a more critical cosmopolitanism, one that not only ushers Latin Americans into world literature but also reconfigures that literary field. The essay marks out this geocultural difference in the moments when Martí's and Emerson's voices remain distinguishable. We see Emerson situated in a Concord likened to Cicero's Tusculum, while Martí is associated with Latin America, and especially Cuba, via the "palmas frescas" ("green palm fronds") he figuratively bears to Emerson's grave (*OC* 13:20, 30; *SW* 119, 129).[27] The essay thereby establishes that someone hailing from a culturally and politically marginalized territory is moving into a space formerly occupied by a metropolitan figure.

This acknowledgement of the different positions of author and subject has been interpreted as a moment of critique, as Martí "provincializing Emerson" and exposing the limits of the perspective afforded by his "mountainous" and "lofty position."[28] However, while "Emerson" does count its subject as one of the world's "hombres montañosos" ("mountain-like men"), being a lofty peak does not necessarily warrant critique for Martí, who writes in his *Versos sencillos* (1891) that "En los montes, monte soy" ("in the mountains, mountain I am," *OC* 13:18, 16:63; *SW* 117, 273, translations modified). Indeed, given Martí's willingness to adopt the mountain-like position of Emerson, his essay is perhaps best taken not as an effort at provincializing but rather as an instance of what Judith Butler has termed "restaging the universal," in which a subject "excluded" by the universalizing paradigms of western modernity takes up those concepts and creates "unconventional formulations of universality that expose the limited and exclusionary features of the former one."[29] When Martí in his essay steps into Emerson's place, a position whose centrality in a global field lends it universality, that gesture imaginatively reforms world literary space, leaving its center-periphery hierarchy intact but centering the culture of Cuba and Latin America. Such reimagining makes legible the Eurocentric features of common understandings of the world literary field. Even as Martí measures his distance from Emerson, then, the essay does not critique its title figure so much as the habits of thinking about global culture that would construe his writing as a timeless marker of universal literary value—a construal indeed at odds with Emerson's own aspiration, avowed in "Circles," to "unsettle all things" (*EPP* 180).

The essay thus showcases Martí's creative engagement with Emerson, for in it Martí avails himself of the affordances of his subject's thought in order to interrogate the hierarchies of world literary space and offer a revised model of that cultural field, one that redresses its marginalization of Latin America. At a few points in the essay, though, there emerges a vision of a still more far-reaching renovation of the world literature field, in which Martí is not re-inhabiting the center but dissolving the very structure that generates centrality. This vision is perhaps most legible in a passage describing Emerson's understanding of worldly interconnection. Emerson, Martí writes, holds:

> que hay una unidad central en los hechos,—en los pensamientos, y en la acciones; que el alma humana, al viajar por toda la naturaleza, se halla a sí misma en toda ella; que la hermosura del Universo fue creada para inspirarse el deseo, y consolarse los dolores de la virtud, y estimular al hombre a buscarse y hallarse; que "dentro del hombre está el alma del conjunto, la del sabio silencio, la hermosura universal a la que toda parte y partícula está igualmanete relacionada: el Uno Eterno." La vida no le inquieta: está contento, puesto que obra bien: lo que importa es ser virtuoso: "la virtud es la llave de oro que abre las puertas de la Eternidad" ... (*OC* 13:24)

> that there is a central unity in events, thoughts, and actions; that the human soul, as it journeys across nature, finds itself everywhere; that the beauty of the Universe was created to inspire desire and assuage the pain of virtue, and stimulate man to seek and find himself; that "within man is the soul of the whole; of the wise silence, the universal beauty to which every part and particle is equally related; the Eternal One." Life does not dismay him; he is content, given that he does what is right; the important thing is to be virtuous: "virtue is the golden key that opens the doors of eternity" ... (*SW* 123, translation modified)

This passage features Martí's Emersonian troping, for he mentions the anthropocentric prospect of a human soul finding itself everywhere only to trouble a moment later the notion of humanity's exceptional status, by suggesting the equal relation of "toda parte y partícula" to the soul underlying the world. As Martí carries out that troping, he's also bringing English-language writing into his Spanish prose with purpose. Some of that language is clearly marked out as Emerson's, like the translated quotation from "The

Over-Soul" (1841) beginning "dentro del hombre," while some is not, as with the words "unidad central," a translation of a phrase from *Nature*'s fifth chapter (*EPP* 164, 42); such textual borrowings generate the vocal blurring through which Martí claims a central position in world literary space.[30]

But the last sentence in the above-cited passage unsettles that cultural field by another measure. It does so by translating and quoting as if from Emerson a line authored by John Milton. *Nature*'s seventh chapter features that line, originally from Milton's *Comus* (1637): "The golden key / Which opes the palace of eternity" (*EPP* 50). There, it's clearly distinguished from Emerson's prose, not only by being set off as a block quotation, but also because its archaic poeticization, "opes," associates it with an earlier era. Martí thus makes several translational interventions as he carries these lines from English to Spanish. He makes the lines more Emersonian, presenting them as Emerson's own speech and redrawing "eternity" as a dynamic entity, as something with "puertas" (doors), as opposed to a palace. More consequentially, Martí renders the past-recalling English of the Milton lines as up-to-date Spanish. By removing that archaism, Martí flattens out the temporal distinctions prevailing within the world literature field. That flattening of time is no small matter, since the center-periphery spatial hierarchy of world literary space is commonly viewed as being subtended by temporal structures; as Casanova explains, the most central spaces in that global field are those considered to have been producing "classic" literature the longest, and an author can move from periphery to center by writing work so modern and up-to-date that it (ironically enough) earns classic status.[31] As such, while much of "Emerson" serves to redraw world literature's hierarchies, a moment like Martí's occlusion of Milton does something more radical: it dissolves the temporal structure of world literary space and thus projects a field of culture without hierarchy.

This image of a flattened field of culture resembles the cosmopolitan community for which Emerson himself advocated. Emerson's cosmopolitanism, several scholars have lately shown, is given particularly full expression in a piece long taken as an index of his nationalism, "The American Scholar" (1837).[32] That text, ultimately uninterested in affirming its title figure, closes by envisioning a "nation of men" (*EPP* 69), a post-national community that is constituted when people eschew cultural and political conventions and embrace a dynamic nature. When one considers this vision alongside like-minded contemporaneous reflections of Emerson's such as the lecture "Home" (1838), Branka Arsić argues, one can recognize Emerson's writing as conceptualizing a "community beyond sovereignty."[33] Such a community—in which, as Emerson puts it in "Home," the "citizen of the world" can "domesticate him[self] in every fact and event that transpire in nature" (*EL* 3:31, 29)—doubtless holds a certain appeal as a political ideal.

However, notwithstanding the glimmer of this sort of vision in "Emerson," such a model of cosmopolitanism did not ultimately prove compelling to Martí, especially not at the later points in his career when his attention fell on the increasingly colonial relations of Cuba and Latin America to the US and the broader world-system. A cosmopolitanism so free of structure as to make it seem like "all places are alike," as "Home" has it (*EL* 3:29), would have had limited appeal to Martí, invested as he was in the specificities of Latin America's place in the modern world. Moreover, such a "community beyond sovereignty" would have been a less than attractive ideal to an intellectual committed to Latin American nations' achievement and maintenance of sovereignty in the face of Euro-American geopolitical encroachments. Martí, after all, concerned himself not just with the cause of Cuban independence but also with struggles for political autonomy elsewhere in the hemisphere. He was for instance sensitive to the plight of Mexico in the wake of the US-Mexico War—especially the way, as he put it in an 1886 essay, that even decades after "la invasion Americana de 1848," many in the US viewed Mexican independence as "una mera concesion de los Estados Unidos" ("a mere concession of the United States," OC 7:46–47). Such concerns led Martí, by the early 1890s, to develop a cosmopolitan outlook distinct from Emerson's that moved beyond redrawing the field of world culture and imagining a post-sovereign society to elaborating the kind of supranational community that would allow for Latin America's political self-determination in the face of hemispheric and global power imbalances. However, while the later Martí does not ultimately advocate an Emersonian cosmopolitanism, neither does he wholly reject Emersonian thought; rather, much like in "Emerson," Martí draws on Emerson's thinking about nature's constant motion to devise a cosmopolitanism for the Americas. That cosmopolitanism is perhaps nowhere clearer than in "Nuestra América," an essay to which I now turn.

Emerson, Cosmopolitanism, and "Nuestra América"

"Nuestra América," published in the New York magazine *La revista ilustrada* in 1891, is not often considered as a text reflecting Martí's engagement with Emerson. One might even be tempted to take the essay itself as discouraging such an approach. When Martí affirms a Latin American identity and critiques Euro-American imperialism, he observes, "Ni el libro europeo, ni el libro yanqui, daban la clave del enigma hispanoamericano" ("no Yankee or European book could furnish the key to the Hispanoamerican enigma," OC 6:20; SW 293–94). But considering the place of Emersonian ideas in "Nuestra América" does not ultimately amount to casting Yankee writing as the key to a Latin American text because, as I've noted, Emerson was not for Martí a figure primarily associated with the US. Martí's own writing from the late 1880s and early 1890s in fact suggests that there is good reason to count Emerson as one of the eclectic group of writers—like Simón Bolívar, Charles Perrault, and José María Torres Caicedo—whose thought is reflected in "Nuestra América."[34] Martí's inclusion of an adaptation of Emerson's 1831 poem "A Mountain Grave" in the 1891 collection *Versos sencillos* attests to his ongoing interest in the North American's writing.[35] Moreover, Martí often draws on an Emersonian lexicon in his discussion of a key context for

"Nuestra América," the inter-American conferences on hemispheric political economy staged by the US.

Martí attended the Pan-American Conference of 1889 to 1890, and the International Monetary Conference of 1891. His journalism describes how the gestures of hemispheric solidarity the US made in those gatherings masked an aspiration to establish an imperial relationship to Latin America. He expresses that critical assessment in Emersonian terms: an article on the first conference calls for Latin Americans to resist US domination by saying, "Para eso es el genio: para vencer la fuerza con la habilidad" ("that is what genius is for: to overcome force with ability"); a piece on the second urges readers to see the imperial self-interest embedded in the US rhetoric of Pan-American cooperation, asserting, "A lo que se ha de estar no es a la forma de las cosas, sino a su espíritu" ("it is not the form of things that must be attended to but their spirit," *OC* 6:54, 158; *SW* 305).[36] These statements employ recognizably Emersonian language and ideas—an ascription of agency to "genius" like in "Self-Reliance" and other essays, an investment in moving beyond "form" as in "The Poet" and "Politics"—but they are not translations of particular Emerson phrases. Rather, in these articles, Martí uses an Emersonian style of writing and thinking in his own way, to address a scenario of hemispheric inequality unanticipated in Emerson's body of work.[37] "Nuestra América" features a parallel dynamic. There, Martí adapts Emerson's thought on cultural differentiation from Europe and on nature's plasticity in order to envision a Latin American community both cosmopolitan and anti-imperial, one that sets Latin American nations in relation to not just one another but also the US and the broader world.

The Emerson essay whose echoes are most perceptible in "Nuestra América" is "The American Scholar." Recalling Emerson's declaration that "we have listened too long to the courtly muses of Europe" (*EPP* 68), Martí decries "la importacíon excesiva de las ideas y fórmulas ajenas" ("the excessive importation of foreign ideas and formulas"); he insists that "la universidad europea ha de ceder a la universidad americana" ("the European university must yield to the American university," *OC* 6:19, 18; *SW* 293, 291). Moreover, Martí's "hombre natural" ("natural man"), who achieves knowledge by "derriba[ndo] la justicia acumulado de los libros" ("overthrow[ing] the authority that is accumulated in books," *OC* 6:18; *SW* 291), appears quite like Emerson's "Man Thinking," who, by "div[ing] into his privatest, secretest presentiment," comes to know what is "most acceptable, most public, and universally true" (*EPP* 64). Martí's essay thus follows Emerson's in understanding intellectual dependence on Europe as being best remedied via an inward turn away from received knowledge. But "Nuestra América" also substantially recasts that line of thinking.[38] When Emerson's intellectual turns from Europe's courtly muses, "the huge world will come round to him"; he will enter the cosmopolitan community Emerson terms "a nation of men" (*EPP* 68–69). By contrast, when Martí's "hombre natural" overthrows his European cultural inheritance, "el pensamiento empieza a ser de América" ("the thinking begins to be from América"); what comes round to him is not a global community but "el pais" ("the country"), by which he means, roughly, Latin America (*OC* 6:20, 18; *SW* 293, 291). Martí, then, substantially decreases the scale of the community into which the rejection of European influence affords entry.

For that reason, critics have sometimes viewed "Nuestra América" as arguing against cosmopolitanism.[39] The essay, though, is more productively read as distinguishing between salutary and problematic turns from the local.[40] Martí's censure of those who eschew their culture to embrace that of metropolitan societies is certainly clear, nowhere more so than in his representation of an earlier era of Latin American culture as an absurdly dressed figure: "Eramos una máscara, con las calzones de Ingleterra, el chaleco parisiense, el chaquetón de Norteamérica, y la montera de España" ("we were a whole fancy dress ball, in English trousers, a Parisian waistcoat, a North American overcoat, and a Spanish bullfighter's hat," *OC* 6:20; *SW* 293). But alongside that description of a hodge-podged internationalism, Martí offers a remarkably stringent critique of parochialism. After all, Martí opens his essay by bemoaning how "cree el aldeano vanidoso que el mundo entero es su aldea" ("the prideful villager thinks his hometown contains the whole world"), how such a villager remains unaware of imperial threats as powerful as "gigantes que llevan siete leguas en las botas" ("giants in seven-league boots"), and how it remains for the towns of such villagers to "conocerse" ("become acquainted," *OC* 6:15; *SW* 288); by doing so, he calls for both more solidarity within Latin America and more awareness of the potentially dangerous world beyond it. Through these moments, Martí differentiates what contemporary critical theorists refer to as "old" and "new" cosmopolitanisms. He derides an "old" cosmopolitanism that claims a Diogenes-like world-citizenship via "detachment" from local circumstances, and instead valorizes a "new" one, whose subject manages "multiple attachments" to different global sites, in pursuit of membership in a community larger than the nation but smaller than the world.[41]

Indeed, Martí's attention to both regional attachments and supranational dynamics yields an internationalism best characterized as a new cosmopolitanism *avant la lettre*. Even Martí's sentences orchestrate the confluence of multiple localities into a single supranational community; stretching grammar to its limits, he repeatedly has a singular "patria" comprise the plural "repúblicas dolorosas de América" ("long-suffering American republics," *OC* 6:16, 18; *SW* 289, 291). That American community, stretching "del Bravo a Magallanes" ("from the Río Bravo to the Straits of Magellan," *OC* 6:22; *SW* 296), is itself less than global in scope, but Martí draws a broader global whole to situate it in. In "Nuestra América," he recalls Latin American nations' independence movements as the moment when they entered the "mundo de naciones" ("world of nations," *OC* 6:18; *SW* 291, translation modified). And his journalistic account of the International Monetary Conference, published just months after "Nuestra América," expresses an even more pointed concern with Latin America's relation to the world. There, as Martí warns that a political and economic bond with the US against Europe carries the risk of subjection to the former, he argues for "la union, con el mundo, y no con una parte de él; no con una parte de él, contra otra" ("union with the world, and not a part of it; not with a part of it, against another," *OC* 6:160; *SW* 307, translation modified). This desire for union with the world reflects less an old cosmopolitan impulse to escape the constraints of one's local circumstances and more a commitment to securing Latin American self-determination in an increasingly globalized world. Martí's cosmopolitanism thus hinges upon the coordination of cultural, political, and economic relationships on multiple spatial scales; his ideals of Latin American unity and self-determination are to be achieved through the consolidation of different localities and nations into a single continental community, that community's resistance of the imperial designs of its hemispheric neighbor, and its achievement of equitable standing within a global political economy.

This cosmopolitanism certainly differs from Emerson's, but it nonetheless retains a distinctly Emersonian quality, since Martí makes nature central to his conception of a worldly Latin America whilst understanding nature in a manner much like Emerson. Against the idea, promoted most notably by Sarmiento's *Facundo: Civilización y barbarie* (1845), that Latin America should embrace European civilization, Martí holds that Latin Americans ought to cultivate community on their own terms by embracing their shared nature—hence "Nuestra América"'s allusive riposte, "No hay batalla entre la civilización y la barbarie, sino entre la falsa erudición y la naturaleza" ("the battle is not between civilization and barbarism, but between false erudition and nature," *OC* 6:17; *SW* 290). This appeal to nature has occasionally been read as an invocation of an autochthonous essence that would stabilize Latin American identity.[42] Such a conception of nature as stability-affording would certainly be at odds with the thinking of the Emerson who wrote (in Martí's favorite book of his, *Nature*) that "Nature is not fixed but fluid" (*EPP* 54). The nature of "Nuestra América," though, proves quite protean and indeed Emersonian.[43] Consider the naturalistic language of Martí's call, near the essay's opening, to resist the encroachments of US empire: "¡Los árboles se han de poner en fila, para no pase el gigante de las siete leguas! ... y hemos de andar en cuadro apretado, como la plata en los raíces de los Andes" ("the trees must put themselves in line, to block the giant in seven-league boots! ... and we must move in lines as compact as the veins of silver that lie at the root of the Andes," *OC* 6:15; *SW* 289, translation modified). Trees and geology might figure stability and stasis, but not here: Martí sets his trees-as-Latin-Americans in motion and evokes silver not as an anchor but to characterize the coordination of the trees' anti-imperial movement. By placing this Emersonian dynamism into the nature that is to bring Latin America together, Martí creates a model of community that is at once cohesive and flexible, indeed always in the process of formation.

When Martí ascribes a similar dynamism to the human biological nature he sees the denizens of "Nuestra América" as sharing, the political implications of his protean understanding of nature come into focus. Martí turns to the language of blood as he enjoins his readers to create their own lively identity: "¡Con el fuego de corazón deshelar la América coagulada! ¡Echar, bullendo y rebotando, por las venas, la sangre natural del país!" ("Melt, with the heat of fire, the coagulated América! Pour through the veins the country's natural blood, boiling and rebounding!" *OC* 6:21, my translation; cf. *SW* 294). The reference to "la América coagulada" recalls blood's common invocation as a metaphor for a natural bond solidifying a community, but in this case such consolidation is presented as a problem, something América's denizens must "deshelar" away. In an ironic figurative inversion, blood, "bullendo y rebotando," is also cast as the agent that will undo such coagulated petrifaction—a function indeed fitting in the context of the essay, since for Martí the natural blood of the country would be "mestizo," itself reflecting dynamic blending, not a fixed essence (OC 6:17). This rendering of the shared blood subtending Latin American community as ever-changing and multifarious yokes together earlier and later points in literary history. For one, assigning an unconventional dynamism to blood—and likewise to the aforementioned trees and silver—constitutes a case of Emersonian troping, a rhetorical twist that contributes to the essay's representation of nature in Emersonian terms, as more fluid than fixed. At the same time, Martí's foregrounding of mestizaje in his conception of a transamerican community anticipates the thought of a border theorist like Gloria Anzaldúa, who views Latinx and Chicanx identity to have emerged through the intermarriage of "Spanish, Indian, and mestizo ancestors."[44] Indeed, since Anzaldúa recognizes that such cultural blending stands at odds with the longstanding "policy of racial purity white America practices," discerning the alignment of Martí's thinking with hers suggests how his Emerson-recalling paradigm of Spanish American community counters the racial thought underwriting acts of US racism and colonialism from the expansionism of 1848 to Trump-era wall-building.[45]

What Martí achieves by endowing his conception of nature with an Emersonian plasticity is a conception of Latin American community at once anti-imperial and processual. This way of thinking proves responsive to the exigencies of the essay's moment of composition. When writing "Nuestra América," Martí confronted difficulties on several of the spatial scales his cosmopolitanism sought to navigate. US imperial designs on the hemisphere alarmed him, but so did political divisions within Latin America. In particular, he grew frustrated at how Latin American nations' failure to advocate for Cuba's independence left his homeland marginalized within the emergent regional bloc and thus exposed to the risk of US annexation.[46] The Emersonian flux of Martí's Latin America allows for the redress of those problems. For Martí, the US domination of Latin America was not yet inevitable, and US aggression might be checked if that nation could be made to recognize the increasing historical motility of a united Latin America, "vencedora veloz de un pasado sofocante" ("swift conqueror of a smothering past," OC 6:22, my translation; cf. SW 295). Latin America's dynamic constitution also affords a remedy for the Antilles' exclusion from continental community, as we see in the essay's last sentence, when Martí imagines how the Great Cemi, a Taíno spirit, has scattered "por las naciones del continente y por las islas dolorosas del mar, la semilla de la América nueva" ("the seed of the new America across the romantic nations of the continent and the suffering nations of the sea," OC 6:23; SW 296, translation modified). Martí calls to mind the plasticity of Latin American nature by suggesting its ongoing growth from a seed, and that seed's singular number suggests the overcoming of Cuba's marginalization within Latin America, which Martí alludes to by differentiating between continental and island localities. These passages thus underscore how Martí's cosmopolitan outlook responds to power differentials in the hemisphere and to uneven levels of colonial emancipation in Latin America. Moreover, they indicate how those inequities appear in Martí's work as surmountable—and his ideals of Latin American self-determination and unity as thereby achievable—precisely because he sees nature and community in Emersonian terms as ontologically unstable.

Martí's insistence on his América's ontological restlessness also carries a broader hemispheric significance. As the Mexican philosopher and historian Edmundo O'Gorman argues in *The Invention of America* (1961), the "fundamental issue" to recognize in the European conquest of the Americas, and the histories following from it, is "the ontological understanding of America," that is, the notion that the hemisphere has an unchanging and knowable mode of being.[47] The lands that Europeans began encountering in 1492 possessed no shared, fixed essence, but, O'Gorman explains, Europeans still invented one for them, based on what they saw in their own history and identity. Hence America was "invented in the image of its inventor," and that notion that the continent's environments and peoples should be fit into and measured against a European model, as opposed to allowed to live on their own terms, has underwritten colonial, racial, and environmental violence from the fifteenth century to today.[48] In a way that suggests its utility in struggles for a more just world, Emersonian thinking proves a resource to Martí as he challenges this Eurocentric way of apprehending the hemisphere. Martí's presentation of Latin America's internal constitution and external relations as continually fluctuating belies any notion of a fixed American being and thus allows for the denizens of the Americas to pursue their own historical paths. Amongst the signal achievements of Martí in "Nuestra América," then, is that he undoes the invention of America.

Notes

Thanks to Frances Negrón-Muntaner and Carlos Alonso for their comments, years ago, on the earliest version of this essay, and to John Hay and Gania Barlow for their feedback on this one.

1. José Martí, *Obras Completas*, vol. 18 (La Habana: Editorial Nacional de Cuba, 1964), 288, hereafter cited parenthetically by volume and page as *OC*; José Martí, "Undated Fragment," *José Martí: Selected Writings*, trans. Esther Allen (New York: Penguin, 2002), 78, hereafter cited parenthetically by page as *SW*. All translations not otherwise attributed are my own.
2. For an overview of these Emerson references, see Anne Fountain, *José Martí and U.S. Writers* (Gainesville: University Press of Florida, 2003), 27–46.
3. Félix Lizaso, "Emerson visto por Martí," *Humanismo* 23 (1954): 31–38, 34; Laura Lomas, "José Martí's 'Evening of Emerson' and the United Statesian Literary Tradition," *Journal of American Studies* 43, no. 1 (2009): 1–17, 6.
4. Lawrence Buell, *Emerson* (Cambridge, MA: Harvard University Press, 2003), 272. My inquiry into Emerson's American-ness extends Buell's question: "How American was Emerson's 'American Scholar'?" (43).
5. On Martí's affinity with Emerson, see José C. Ballón, *Autonomía cultural americana: Emerson y Martí* (Madrid: Editorial Pliegos, 1986); and Fountain, *José Martí*, 27–46. On Martí and anti-imperial critique, see Roberto Fernández Retamar, "Caliban: Notes toward a Discussion of Culture in Our America," in *Caliban and Other Essays*, trans. Edward Baker (Minneapolis: University of Minnesota Press, 1989) 3–45; and Jeffrey Belnap and Raúl Fernández, eds., *José Martí's "Our America": From National to Hemispheric Cultural*

Studies (Durham, NC: Duke University Press, 1998). For a counterpoint to my own analysis, see Laura Lomas on Martí's anti-imperial commitments leading him to disidentify with Emerson, in *Translating Empire: José Martí, Migrant Latino Subjects, and American Modernities* (Durham, NC: Duke University Press, 2008), 130–76.

6. See, e.g., John Carlos Rowe, *At Emerson's Tomb: The Politics of Classic American Literature* (New York: Columbia University Press, 1997).
7. John E. Englekirk, "Notes on Emerson in Latin America," *PMLA* 76, no. 3 (1961): 227–32.
8. This domestication is described in Len Gougeon, "Looking Backwards: Emerson in 1903," *Nineteenth-Century Prose* 30, no. 1/2 (2003): 66; and Branka Arsić, *On Leaving: A Reading in Emerson* (Cambridge, MA: Harvard University Press, 2010), 6–7. Manifestations of this domestication includes William James, *Memories and Studies* (New York: Longman, Green, 1917), 25–26; and George Santayana, *Interpretations of Poetry and Religion* (1900; New York: Charles Scribner's Sons, 1924), 233.
9. Charles G. Ames, "Obituary Notice of Ralph Waldo Emerson," *Proceedings of the American Philosophical Society* 20, no. 112 (1882): 498–503, 500.
10. See Richard Poirier, *The Renewal of Literature: Emersonian Reflections* (New Haven, CT: Yale University Press, 1987); Sharon Cameron, *Impersonality: Seven Essays* (Chicago: University of Chicago Press, 2007); and Arsić, *On Leaving*, whose account of Emerson scholarship informs my own description of that critical history.
11. Arsić, *On Leaving*, 6.
12. Ralph Waldo Emerson, *Nature*, in *Emerson's Prose and Poetry*, ed. Joel Porte and Saundra Morris (New York: W. W. Norton, 2001), 27–55, 35. Hereafter cited parenthetically by page as *EPP*.
13. Ballón documents Martí's allusion to "Circles" (*Autonomía*, 42). Fountain describes Martí's quotation from "Self-Reliance" (*José Martí*, 34).
14. My reading here follows Richard Poirier, *Poetry and Pragmatism* (Cambridge, MA: Harvard University Press, 1992), 23–28.
15. Lomas, *Translating Empire*, 35–37.
16. Critics have observed this passage's depiction of dynamic selfhood, but without noting its continuities with Emersonian selfhood. See Lomas, *Translating Empire*, 140–41; and Oscar Montero, *José Martí: An Introduction* (New York: Palgrave MacMillan, 2004), 121.
17. Cameron, *Impersonality*, 92–93.
18. Montero, *José Martí*, 116; Lomas, *Translating Empire*, 171. For an analysis that casts Martí as finding in Emerson both transitory subjectivity and worldly fluctuation, albeit with different emphases than my own, see Andrew Taylor, "Reading Resistances in Ralph Waldo Emerson and José Martí," *Journal of American Studies* 55, no. 4 (2021): 841–62.
19. Poirier, *Renewal of Literature*, 85, 131.
20. See Lizaso, "Emerson," 35; Mary Cruz, "Emerson por Martí," *Anuario del Centro de Estudios Martianos* 5 (1982): 86; Ballón, *Autonomía*, 23; Fountain, *José Martí*, 46; and Taylor, "Reading Resistances," 20.
21. Ballón, *Autonomía*, 55, 44.
22. See Ballón, *Autonomía*, 12; Fountain, *José Martí*, 29; Montero, *José Martí*, 106; and María Fernanda Pampín, "La tradicíon norteamericana en José Martí entre filosofía y literatura," *Anales de Literatura Hispanoamericana* 45 (2016): 61.
23. Pascale Casanova, *The World Republic of Letters*, trans. M. B. DeBevoise (Cambridge, MA: Harvard University Press, 2004), xii, 12. Ballón somewhat similarly argues that Martí locates Emerson in a great writers' "panteón" ("pantheon"), albeit without emphasizing, as I do, the spatial dimensions of Martí's contextualization (*Autonomía*, 49).

24. Mariano Siskind, *Cosmopolitan Desires: Global Modernity and World Literature in Latin America* (Evanston: Northwestern University Press, 2014), 109.
25. Ibid., 10, 105, 104.
26. Ibid., 122.
27. On the symbolic link between the essay's palms and Cuba, see Lomas, *Translating Empire*, 174.
28. Ibid., 158–59, 171, 167.
29. Judith Butler, "Restaging the Universal: Hegemony and the Limits of Formalism," in *Contingency, Hegemony, Universality: Contemporary Dialogues on the Left*, ed. Judith Butler, Ernesto Laclau, and Slavoj Žižek (New York: Verso, 2000), 11–43, 39–40.
30. Fountain documents these two textual borrowings (*José Martí*, 31, 34).
31. Casanova, *World Republic*, 82, 91.
32. See Kenneth Sacks, *Understanding Emerson: "The American Scholar" and His Struggle for Self-Reliance* (Princeton, NJ: Princeton University Press, 2003), 31; Buell, *Emerson*, 46; and Arsić, *On Leaving*, 257. These analyses aim to overturn an older critical tradition that sees Emerson as having, in John Jay Chapman's words, "America in his mind's eye all the time" ("Emerson," in *Emerson and Other Essays* [New York: Charles Scribner's Sons, 1898], 3–108, 38).
33. Arsić, *On Leaving*, 271–72.
34. On the way "Nuestra América" reflects the thinking of Bolívar and Perrault, see Cintio Vitier, "Las imágenes en 'Nuestra América,'" *Anuario del Centro de Estudios Martianos* 14 (1991): 160–76, 165, 168; on Martí's engagement with the thinking of Torres Caicedo, see Roberto Fernández Retamar, "El credo independiente de la América nueva," *Anuario del Centro de Estudios Martianos* 14 (1991): 151–59, 154–55.
35. On Martí's reworking of Emerson's poem, see Ballon, *Autonomía*, 108–18.
36. The translation of the first quotation is, slightly modified, from Martí, *Inside the Monster: Writings on the United States and American Imperialism*, trans. Elinor Randall et al., ed. Philip S. Foner (New York: Monthly Review Press, 1975), 352.
37. Emerson was not unconcerned with the hemispheric politics of his own time, as Martha Schoolman shows in *Abolitionist Geographies* (Minneapolis: University of Minnesota Press, 2014), 34, 44, but the political conjuncture he confronted and his mode of response remain distinct from Martí's.
38. My analysis here diverges from that of Paul Giles, who suggests in one of the few readings of this essay to consider its Emersonian qualities, that "Our America" is a "corollary" of Emerson's essay ("The Parallel Worlds of José Martí," *Radical History Review* 89 [2004]: 185–90, 188).
39. See, e.g, Jeffrey Belnap, "Headbands, Hemp Sandals, and Headdresses: The Dialectics of Dress and Self-Conception in Martí's 'Our America,'" in *José Martí's "Our America*,*"* 191–209, 192; and Siskind, *Cosmopolitan Desires*, 115.
40. Here my analysis affirms and extends Gerard Aching's argument that "Martí did not oppose the development of a cosmopolitan readership" so much as the "unreflective incorporation of a fetishistic cosmopolitanism that distorted" the region's self-image ("Against 'Library-Shelf Races': José Martí's Critique of Excessive Imitation," in *Geomodernisms: Race, Modernism, Modernity*, ed. Laura Doyle and Laura Winkiel [Bloomington: Indiana University Press, 2005], 151–69, 157).
41. On these cosmopolitanisms, see Bruce Robbins, "Introduction Part I: Actually Existing Cosmopolitanism," in *Cosmopolitics: Thinking and Feeling Beyond the Nation*, ed. Robbins and Pheng Cheah (Minneapolis: University of Minnesota Press, 1998), 1–19, 1, 2, 5–6.

42. See, e.g., Julio Ramos, *Divergent Modernities: Culture and Politics in Nineteenth-Century Latin America*, trans. John D. Blanco (Durham, NC: Duke University Press, 2001), 257.
43. I thus concur with Giles' claim that Martí's essay is "fluctuating," but I take that to reflect not Martí's writerly "inconsistency" so much as his thinking about nature ("Parallel Worlds," 187).
44. Gloria Anzaldúa, *Borderlands/La Frontera: The New Mestiza*, 4th ed. (San Francisco: Aunt Lute Books, 2012), 27.
45. Ibid., 99.
46. Enrico Marío Santí, " 'Our America,' The Gilded Age, and the Crisis of Latinamericanism," in *José Martí's "Our America,"* 179–90, 184, 180.
47. Edmundo O'Gorman, *The Invention of America: An Inquiry in the Historical Nature of the New World and the Meaning of Its History* (Bloomington: Indiana University Press, 1961), 46.
48. Ibid., 140.

CHAPTER 8

EMERSONIAN FIGURATIONS IN MODERN HISPANIC POETICS

RICARDO MIGUEL-ALFONSO

> That tall American man
> closes his Montaigne book and goes out
> searching for another, equally precious
> joy, the afternoon exalted by the plain.
> Towards the deep west in its decline,
> towards the frontier that this west paints in gold,
> he walks through the fields in the same way
> he walks through my memory.
> He thinks: I've read all the essential books
> and I have written more books that the dark oblivion
> should not erase. A god has granted me
> with everything mortals can know.
> My name traverses the continent;
> I haven't lived. I'd rather be another man.
>
> Jorge Luis Borges, "Emerson"; my translation

THIS opening poem is one of the very few readings of Emerson that Jorge Luis Borges ever published throughout his career. Aside from a brief and generally detached description in his *An Introduction to American Literature* and the prologue to his own translation of *Representative Men* and Carlyle's *On Heroes*, references to Emerson are scarce in his work. Borges's interest in the literature of the United States—and world literature generally—usually concentrated on fiction writers and poets, and only rarely did it include essayists or philosophers. Even though he has been often branded a "philosophical novelist," his interest in abstract speculation was always limited. "Emerson wrote," he says, "that 'arguments convince nobody' and that it is sufficient to state a truth for it to be accepted. This conviction gives his work a disconnected character. It abounds in memorable sayings, sometimes full of wisdom, which do not proceed from what has come before nor prepare for what is to come."[1]

However partial Borges's interest in figures such as Emerson, the fact is that the poem offers an image that accurately symbolizes certain Spanish American visions of Emerson as a cultural and political icon for the continent. The sage of Concord appears here as a figure of the past brought to the present by Borges's memory, a memory that is in fact a fiction, since Borges never met Emerson; yet his memory seems to recall his figure closing his book and going out to find "other joys" and suddenly reflecting on himself as a cultural symbol. As it emerges in this brief fictional remembrance, Emerson's self is divided between the self-sufficient scholar who has read "all the essential books" and knows "everything mortals can know," on the one hand, and the man who would "rather be another man," on the other. The clash of images suggests an unhappiness, a sense of unfulfillment, a view which is not only intensely personal but also public: Emerson realizes he hasn't "lived" after acknowledging that his name traverses not the US, but "the continent." The greater his fame, the more disappointed he seems to be with his life's career.[2] Still, when I say that this poem represents certain visions of Emerson in Hispanic America, I mean that the idea that Emerson's name actually traversed the continent is true, and it did so precisely as someone who had "read the essential books" and had something different to offer: an idea of America different from the image that the European mind had constructed for centuries. His contribution in this sense was mostly *a posteriori*, since the influence of Emerson in the disputes around the possibilities of a Pan-American vision was felt more powerfully in the decades after his death, especially during the modernist generation.[3] This means that although it is true that "Emerson rarely explored the literary possibilities afforded by inter-American political relations and cultural crossings; nor was he, as were other writers covered in this book, a great reader of Caribbean or Latin American literature,"[4] his presence was nevertheless certified by a series of translations[5] that maintained the hemispheric vision of Borges's poem. His example, and others such as Whitman, suggested the possibility of a common American literature.

* * *

At the beginning of the 1990s, Gustavo Pérez Firmat edited a collection of essays whose very title raised a question that, like Emerson's name in Borges's poem, had traversed North and South American literary culture for decades, in fact more than a century: do the Americas have a common literature? Whether or not the answer is affirmative, to ask such a question demands, then and now, that we search beyond national boundaries for common traits between both hemispheres, a work that has been carried out seriously only in the last few decades (at least, in comparison with the long traditions of both northern and southern American nations). But more importantly, it also implies an intuition that there are actual lines of influence and adaptation between the cultures of both hemispheres often kept apart by their respective political institutions and histories. As Pérez Firmat claimed in his introduction to the volume, he wanted to leave behind the already customary neglect of scholars on both hemispheres by "adopting a North-South orientation and looking at New World literature in a Pan-American or inter-American context."[6] In doing so, he was attempting to overcome a whole tradition of criticism often characterized by isolation, misunderstanding and stereotypical thinking that reinforced the colonizer/colonized duality without investigating how each one of these states permeated the other. The situation was not new. In fact, it derived from the cultural and literary exceptionalism towards Spanish literature of nineteenth-century scholars such as William H. Prescott and George Ticknor. As Helmbrecht Breinig has argued more recently, "with the exception of Melville, whose primary thematic focus lies elsewhere, the [nineteenth-century] writers show a conspicuous inability to give the subject [the nature of the colonized peoples] the complexity it deserves."[7] None of the essays in Firmat's collection, however, addressed directly the influence of Emerson in the literature of Latin America. Then and now, Poe and Whitman seem to remain the favorite targets in the study of literary relations between both subcontinents.

There are several reasons for this, but two of them stand out as revealing of this disconnect: on the one hand, the most important Spanish translations of Emerson's works appeared only in the early twentieth century, depriving most nineteenth-century Spanish-speaking writers from contact with his work; second, and this is probably the most important motive, Emerson has often appeared to Latin American literary audiences as a representative of the kind of cultural imperialism and the ideology of Manifest Destiny they were trying to avoid as an influence. His apparent lack of concern with any country south of Mexico and his unfamiliarity with Hispanic culture and literature generally have contributed to strengthen the image of the isolated, self-absorbed metaphysician that has dominated the work of more than a few scholars of Transcendentalist culture.[8] The presence of Emerson in Latin American poets, then, has to be studied in terms of an "imagined presence," rather than an actual one.

This is one of the reasons why it is important to understand that the reception and use of Emerson's work in Spanish American poetics is more a question of individual efforts than a collective work. And this is also why I choose to talk about "figurations" rather than direct "influences" or "translations." The three readings of Emerson I will use here combinedly—those of José Lezama Lima, Octavio Paz and Vicente Huidobro—are outstanding for their strength but also for their rarity. None of them belongs to a particular school or movement (Huidobro invented a term of his own, *Creacionismo*, to refer to himself), they never formed anything like an intellectual or poetic group, and they certainly have very different styles. Still, both their poetic theories and practices reveal connections to the US philosopher that go beyond mere adaptation and suggest processes of creative reading that transform and expand Emerson's thinking into a Pan-American thinker.

Before exploring these readings of Emerson, I want to stop to discuss briefly an important distinction made recently by Jeffrey Lawrence about the different between the literature of the United States and that of Latin American countries. Although his interest is primarily twentieth-century literature, I think the distinction holds for nineteenth-century writers as well. In his words:

Two dominant subject positions structure canonical twentieth-century literature in the Americas: in the United States, the subject position of the writer as *experiencer*, and in Latin America, the subject position of the writer as *reader* [*lector*]. I maintain that these subject positions have been embedded, in turn, within two cultural formations I refer to throughout this book as the "US literature of experience" and the "Latin American literature of the reader."[9]

In drawing this distinction between a "literature of experience" and a "literature of the reader," Lawrence is doing two things. On the one hand, he is suggesting the existence of two literatures (and two kinds of reading) that focus on different objects and therefore have different constructive aims: the literature of experience aims at registering and organizing a new reality, one different from the one at hand, while the literature of the reader aims at using books as a guide to what Emerson called "the conduct of life." On the other hand, Lawrence is at the same time establishing a logical and chronological order between the first and the second, giving experience a priority over reading. In doing so, he divorces "reading" from other kinds of "experience" and creates a second-order literature whose material is books and literary representations. "In Emerson's eyes," Lawrence says, "the best way for the American writer to defy Old World traditions was to look to experience instead of books,"[10] while Latin American writers could build up on the experiences already codified in books to create a new reality (or regenerate the current one). This order is not necessarily true, for there is a literature of readers before the literature experience. In fact, the spirit of cultural independence of Emerson and others comes from an already established Latin American tradition of rejection of the European muses that starts with Andrés Bello's famous "Allocution to Poetry" (1823), which precedes Emerson:

> Divine poetry...
> it is time for you to leave effete Europe,
> no lover of your native rustic charms,
> and fly to where Columbus's world
> opens its great scene before your eyes.
> There heaven respects the laurel, ever green
> with which you crown men's valor.[11]

America appears here not only as the place of freedom, but also as the *poetic* continent, the place where the regenerative power of poetry to shape the world is opposed, very much as it was in the aesthetics of the eighteenth century, to the dry philosophical reason of the Old Continent:

> Oh goddess, do not stay
> in that region of wretchedness and light,
> where your ambitious rival, Philosophy,
> subjecting virtue to calculation,
> stripped you of mortals' worship...[12]

This idea will reappear in Emerson several times—most famously when he reminds his readers that "We have listened too long to the courtly muses of Europe" (*CW* 1:69)— and, in turn, will return to influence Latin American poetics again towards the end of the nineteenth century, when his poetic mode of thinking was not only adopted but even more valued than his philosophical theories. Apart from the fact that, in the Spanish speaking world, Emerson has been more often than not received as a poet and an educator rather than a philosopher,[13] his wish to approach nature "with distinct but most poetical sense in the mind" (*CW* 1:9) was especially suitable for Latin American poetics for two reasons: first, as I have mentioned, because of the widespread belief in the idea that America is the poetic continent *par excellence*; second, because for many Latin American writers, poetic (or aesthetic) reality is the ultimate reality, based as it is on the imagination and the ability to maintain (and translate) the myths of the past. More than a century later, the Chilean poet Vicente Huidobro argued in similar terms that "poetry is a challenge to Reason, the only challenge Reason can accept, since the former creates its reality in the world that *is* and the latter in the world that *is being*" and that "poetry is a challenge to Reason, which is why she is the Over-Reason."[14]

This confidence in poetry as the path to discover a reality beyond natural objects, which is one of the tenets of Emerson's early philosophy, especially in *Nature* and "The Poet," returns in Emerson's late work in another form. In *Natural History of Intellect*, Emerson returns to some of the topics of his earlier work but from a less idealistic, more materialistic angle. The former relation between objects, words, and ideas is now a more direct (less expansive) relation between the first two. "Every object in Nature," Emerson argues, "is a word to signify some fact of the mind. But when that fact is not yet put in English words ... they are by no means unimpressive" (*CWE* 12:5). The correlation object (or natural fact) > word > idea (or spiritual fact) that characterized Emerson's earlier work (see *CW* 1:17–23) has now been transformed into a different one, and so have the relations between its terms. Now objects are not simply represented or evoked by words—they *are* words. This fusion of the real and the linguistic creates a different, hybrid form of materiality: objects have a voice of their own and excite the mind in order to get transformed into facts of the mind. And even though these facts remain impressive (that is, they make an impression on the mind), it is only when they are put into words that they come into existence. Reality acquires its full meaning when the objects of Nature are "put into English words" (*CWE* 12:5), that is, when it is *expressed*.[15]

The changes in this scheme are important in order to understand not only the shift in Emerson's philosophy, but also to comprehend the ways in which his poetics has been adapted by the Latin American writers I will deal with later. In a way, Emerson de-transcendentalizes his own earlier conception of Nature and language by replacing the relation of analogy between objects and words with an identification between them, thereby freeing language from its representational function and endowing it with the ability of embodying reality. Words and objects are one and they lead to mental facts rather than ideas, Emerson argues. So powerful is the intervention of language that "the thought that was in the world, part and parcel of the world, has disengaged itself and taken an independent existence" (*CWE* 12:6).[16]

To identify objects with words also entails that the world—and not only the text—becomes *readable*. That is, it becomes a language. And both myth and poetry become its grammar. This analogy between a new world and a blank page has been already used by Edmundo O'Gorman in his famous book *The Invention of America*. In the whole process of conquest, he argues, "there is no entity to be found to which the being of America may be assigned, nothing that can have that peculiar meaning or significance."[17] The discovery and colonization is, among other things, a process of reading and interpreting reality. The objects and peoples of the unknown and unconquered land need to be addressed and described. They are "objects" that haven't become words yet.

However, the truth is that these objects and peoples had actual names, many of them already "put in English words." As O'Gorman has argued, before its independence America as a continent had been already *created* in the European mind, it had been already imagined and, consequently, subjected to preconceptions and stereotypes of different kinds. This applies to both North and South America. The American land already had an identity—in fact, a poetic identity—yet not the one many of its inhabitants identify with. Following Bello, the (poetic) invention of America had materialized in a series of metaphors, many of them undesired, that the European mind had solidified into a philosophy of the nature and life of the American continent. What is required is a new invention, a new poetic act that provides the land and its people with a renovated meaning and a true self-definition. In short, as Emerson had suggested for his own country after independence, it needed to find a new correspondence between objects and words different from the one they had been handed. Since language is "fossil poetry" (*CW* 3:13), to use Emerson's famous expression, what is needed is to free the American reality of that second nature that has been imposed by the already fossilized language of its conquerors. And that, as José Lezama argues, is a collective task and has to be undertaken by looking at the very beginnings of its history: "The history of American cultural politics, in its expressive dimension, even more than in the Western world, must be regarded as a totality," he maintains.[18] Against the "attitude of atomization typical of the Spanish, whether in their country or as colonizers,"[19] Lezama argues that the history of America is to be regarded (and projected) as unitary in its essence, and that the process of liberating it from the "fossil poetry" of the past is trans-hemispheric. This process is yet another manifestation of a universal tendency that Lezama labels "man in his struggle with form."[20] The battle between expressive forms (languages, their metaphors) is what signals the change from one historical period to another.

Still, although Lezama insists that the struggle between images (historical and poetic) is the mark of transformation, the American character remains the same. In the face of historical change, the national character remains unchanged. As the vessel of a culture inherited throughout time, despite all its renovations, the subject's identity remains constant, being as it is part of a reality in flux whose defining language is a struggle among images. Using what we may call an Emersonian metaphor, Lezama recognizes that "man is a bottle of river water floating on a big, wide river."[21] The bottle itself is the only separation between the river water inside and outside, just like in the Emersonian metaphor of the transparent eyeball one can see everything because it is part of the whole (inner and outer) he inhabits. In fact, the self works as both frontier and mirror between the two. Emerson's famous claim that "I am nothing; I see all; the currents of the Universal Being circulate through me" (*CW* 1:10) is repeated in Lezama's metaphor of the bottle in the river as a symbol of the most primary identification between the self and its background and, especially, the analogy between inner and outer reality. In both metaphors, the material embodiment of the self—whether an eyeball or a bottle—stands between two identical worlds, its fragility symbolized by its transparency. Two apparently different worlds can look at each other through the lens of the poetic vision. The power of the true poet/creator lies in finding the connections between the two. As Vicente Huidobro argues, "creation consists in making two things that are parallel in space meet in time, and vice versa."[22]

Emerson and many modern Latin American poets met in space, an imaginary Pan-American space, but not in time. The common point between them was the renovation of both languages—Spanish and English—after their respective processes of revolution and independence while maintaining a sense of commonality. The first step in erasing the old language is the revision of history and the ways in which its representations have come to be expressed. This erasure mirrors Nietzsche's imperative to free language from its shell of fossilized meaning so that it can be used to address the world in a new, refreshing way. That this renovation has to start from the field of history means two things: first, the language in which history is told helps construct national identity, thereby providing people with a stable vision of themselves and a story of origins (and often destiny); second, since these visions and stories quickly become myth, it is necessary to rethink them in terms of present circumstances and needs. History and language work against poetry by trying to freeze meaning into images that soon become stereotypes.

In order to get rid of the old language, and assuming that a certain American identity remains unchanged, this vision requires that history must be somehow started anew. And not just history: it also requires that we rethink the history of language and the language of history. Only by modifying the metaphors of the past can a new identity be surmised.

As Octavio Paz has suggested, following O'Gorman's thesis:

> One ought rather to speak of the *invention* of America than its discovery. If America is a creation of the European spirit, it begins to emerge from the sea-mists centuries before the expedition of Columbus. And what the Europeans discover when they reach these lands is their own historic dream. Reyes has devoted some lucid pages to this subject: America is a sudden embodiment of a European utopia. The dream becomes a reality, a present; America is a present: a gift, a given of history. But it is an open present, a today that is tinged with tomorrow. The presence and the present of America are a future; our continent is, by its nature, the land which does not exist on its own, but as something which is created and invented. Its being, its reality or substance, consists of being always future, history which is justified not by the past but by what is to come. Our foundation is not what America was but what it will be. America never was; and *it is, only if it is utopia*, history on its way to a golden age.[23]

The present of America is its future, the way it can become a model for others, as Emerson would claim throughout his career, repeating an old myth that goes back to the idea of the "City upon the Hill." The absolute futurity of being only justified by "what is to come" reminds us not only of the optimistic faith in the future of Emerson's idealist philosophy, but also of the necessity of never looking back in order to recreate an identity that begins with Puritanism itself. This forward-looking movement implies denying the very (material) existence of the past, disregarding the work of memory and the possibility of learning from it. But it also comes from a mistake, idealism's mistake—that is, thinking that the harmony of the world lies within itself rather than in the language we use to represent it to ourselves. The mistake of the philosophers lies in confusing the language of reality with the language of men. As Paz elsewhere explains:

> The philosophers had thought of the world as rhythm; the poets heard the rhythm. It was not the language of the spheres—although they thought it was—but the language of men.[24]

But how can the past be erased in a continent whose (colonial) past is so explicit and historically determined? The way out of this conundrum, for Paz, lies in positing the work of history against the work of Nature. Herein lies the essential difference between North and South.

> There were no complex Indian cultures there, nor did Roman Catholicism erect its vast nontemporal structures: America was—if it was anything—geography, pure space, open to human action. Lacking historical substance—old class divisions, ancient institutions, inherited beliefs and laws—reality presented only natural obstacles. Men fought, not against history, but against nature. And where there was an historical obstacle—as in the Indian societies—it was erased from history and, reduced to a mere act of nature, action followed as if this were so. The North American attitude can be condemned in these terms: all that does not have a part in the utopian nature of America does not properly belong to history: it is a natural event and, thus, it doesn't exist; or it exists only as an inert obstacle, not as an alien conscience. Evil is outside, part of the natural world—like Indians, rivers, mountains, and other obstacles which must be domesticated or destroyed; or it is an intrusive reality (the English past, Spanish Catholicism, monarchy, etc.).[25]

Against the already domesticated reality brought about by the metaphors of the Old World, there is still a Nature to be vindicated in America, one that opposes history as a mode of being in the world. And the distinction between the two is not only physical but also moral. However, they must be divorced if the national culture is to survive. A series of dualities ensue: good/evil, interior/exterior, natural/historical ... In order to reaffirm the exceptionalism of American reality, whatever stands in opposition is imagined to be alien, non-American, and therefore eliminated. The alien obstacles are then dehumanized (they are inert obstacles), while the "national" traits become the constitutive part of history. Evil is conceived as belonging to the exterior and goodness to the interior (to the nature) of national culture, giving rise to the dualities that have founded the traditional dialectics between the American hemispheres, especially in their political relations. And whatever cannot be reduced to this kind of dialectics loses its identity as "American" and its potential future, which, according to Paz, means losing its primary condition of possibility:

> If American [US] reality is the reinvention of itself, whatever is found in any way irreducible or unassimilable is not American. In other places the future is a human attribute: because we are men, we have a future; in the Anglo-Saxon America of the last century, the process is inverted and the future determines man: we are men because we have a future. And whatever has no future is not man. Thus, reality leaves no gap at all for contradiction, ambiguity, or conflict to appear.[26]

This view is important in so far as it reminds us of the dynamic, linguistic and otherwise, at work in the history of America, North and South. Since the age of the different European colonizations of the continent, mostly English and Spanish, we have seen how language has been instrumental for the construction of paradigms of exclusion and in the organization of reality according to a binary logic: civilized vs. savage, Christian vs. unbeliever, and so on. (Even the North/South distinction has helped to support imperialist attitudes in the twentieth century.) What Octavio Paz argues here is that in the US this logic not only requires a certain American identity and a sense of purpose, but also an inversion of terms. The "human" quality of people has been subjected to the assumption that there is a common future for them ("we are men because we have a future"). Ironically, coherence and identity are provided by something that lies ahead of people, something that does not exist, something that is imagined rather than real. To say that "we're men because we have a future" means suspending all claims to the present and leaving it to the future to find out what we are. This is the logic Paz identifies as typical of modern "Anglo-Saxon America," and which is based on a previous and more important dilemma: how do we know when the future has been fulfilled? What happens if it is not fulfilled? Do American men cease to be men?

Neither Emerson nor the writers I am discussing were able to give a precise answer to these questions. For all of them the problem of the past was repressed as a historical issue and acquired an abstract poetic nature. The idea of renovating language became the umbrella term under which other necessary changes (social, political) fell. As we have seen, the sense of beginning—of historical beginning—seems to stem from the writer's own time: Emerson represses the legacy of Puritanism and (often) the racial problems of his own Transcendentalist times; Paz locates the rise of the spirit of futurity in the America of his century (1850–1950). The coincidence is not accidental: for both of them the future begins at almost the same time. This connection testifies not only to Emerson's influence, but also to the use of the same strategy to erase the influence of the past on the present.

This erasure of history and the renovation of the metaphors—and images, as Lezama would say—of language find their best expression in the poetics of Vicente Huidobro, which I have elsewhere labeled "transcendental Modernism." Huidobro adopts Emersonian poetics directly, with almost no mediation but that of translation (he didn't read Emerson in English but in Spanish and French) and used his essays, notably "Self-Reliance" and "The Poet," in formulating his *Creacionismo*, a poetic movement intended to show the possibility of a pure poetics free from history and free from the representational and the expressive theories of traditional literary aesthetics. *Creacionismo* is the most relevant revival of Emersonianism in the twentieth century.[27] This *Creacionismo* is intended to be the latest stage in the progressive abandonment of European visions of poetry, including the modernist ones of Huidobro's time, and the emergence of a truly pan-American poetics whose point of departure is Emerson's thinking and whose culmination is Huidobro's own poetry, especially his long poem *Altazor*.

In order to complete the erasure of European, hegemonic history and tradition, Huidobro resorts to several of Emerson's ideas about poetry, composition and the role of the poet. The first one, as we have seen in Lezama, is to free language from its fossilized shell in order to be able to comprehend its true meaning. "Poetry," he argues,

> is language free from any prejudice; the created and creating verb, the recently born word. She develops in the first dawn of the world. Its precision does not lie in naming things but in not getting too far from that dawn.[28]

If Lezama recommended going back to the native, pre-Columbian myths in order to understand how the American identity had emerged before becoming corrupted, Huidobro uses the figure of the "dawn" in the same sense. His Emersonian claim that "poetry is the language of Creation"[29] also suggests a return to the past that should help recuperate the freshness of poetry and serve as the basis for a new conception of composition. This past, again, is more mythical than real, retreating as it does into a prehistorical age of unknown origins.

Besides the intensely subjective tone of his ideas (we achieve originality "by retreating into ourselves,"[30] he argues), in fact the poet appears as a medium, the mind who is capable of transforming personal perception into objective reality. And he does so not by recoding his experience but by following impersonally the creative processes of nature: "It's not about imitating nature but to act like her; not to imitate its external forms but its power to externalize."[31] To use Jeffrey Lawrence's terminology, we can say that Huidobro urges poets to be readers of the experiences of others, especially Emerson's, and to transform them into a variety of creative methods.

This is how poetry can really *contribute* to reality, to *construct* in the sense of adding new knowledge. Following Emerson's famous claim that a poem "adorns nature with a new thing" (*CW* 3:6), Huidobro believes that:

> [A poem] shows a new fact, one that is independent from the external world, disconnected from any other reality except its own, separated and distinct from the rest of phenomena.[32]

Poetry is therefore analogous to any other process of creation:

> In this case [the manufacturing of a car], Man has created something without imitating the appearances of Nature, but following its internal laws. And it is curious to grasp how he has followed the same order as Nature, not only in its constructive mechanism, but also in its chronological order.[33]

Imitating the natural "chronology" of creation does not endow the poem with historicity. Huidobro clearly separates the product of creativity from its past and present context. He seems to suggest that the poem is organically connected to its historical time, but only as a witness of the constructive powers of people in a specific age. In so doing, he is reminding us how a poem is a product, as much the result of a creative act as an electric appliance can be. By providing the poem with a chronology, as Emerson had done in "The Poet," Huidobro approximates poetry to the world in general, the world of its own time, and therefore separates it from the past. As long as each era has its own expressive devices, its poetry will also be different. Historical continuity is then disrupted and history (at least, the history of poetry) becomes a sequence of moments of exceptional national self-expression. The connection among these moments is left unexplained.

In the end, the question is not so much—as one might expect—the creation of beauty but the discovery of the expressive potential of a language and to see its importance in the evolution of humanity. Art in any of its manifestations, Huidobro argues, is basically a special use of expressive power rather than the ability to move the audience or even simply to represent the world outside.

> It is not a matter of making "Beauty"; it is a matter of making "Man." I don't believe in beauty. The works of art of all time are, for me, simple human documents. I never opened a book or went to a museum in order to find beauty, but rather in order to learn how men expressed themselves in the different ages of history.[34]

As we can see, whether in a poem or a museum, for Huidobro historicity is unimportant. In fact, in the end it is only a matter of expressivity and therefore it remains confined to the realm of language. If we take the poem to be a unique creation but no different from any other commodity, then its historical significance, whether in literary history or in our social world, becomes irrelevant. The history of poetry (or literature in general, for that matter) has never been the story of a commodity. But for Huidobro poetry had to remain outside history if it was to be appreciated *as* poetry. Lezama and Paz repeated the same idea in different terms. But rather than a misunderstanding of Emerson, this is the natural consequence of the modernist reading of a romantic idealist, and the ultimate step in the modernist isolation of poetry from social life. It is also the way in which these writers, each one in his particular way, "figured" Emersonian poetics once the historical dimension of experience was reduced to language.

* * *

To sum up, the Latin American "figurations" I have explored propose—each one in its particular way—new ways of understanding Emerson not only as a Pan-American poet, but also the (unaware) architect of Pan-Americanism itself. Whether as a preserver of hemispheric unity or the renovator of language that constitutes true poetry, they all assume Emerson's work as a "contact zone" in which Northern and Southern American poetics interact. His texts emerge as the inspiration of a generation of "poets of readers." The urgency of Emerson's claims to cultural autonomy and independence, together with his disenchantment with modernity, make the perfect combination for a group of writers looking for a renovation that leads them beyond romantic self-absorption (what George Santayana called the "poetry of barbarism").

And here I return briefly to Jeffrey Lawrence's distinction between the literature of experience (in the US) and the literature of the reader (in Latin America). The process of reception of Emerson confirms this division while at the same time constituting a bridge between the two. In fact, I would suggest that Emerson's literature of experience, of close contact with the world, was directly translated into a literature of readers, some of them strong readers of the sage of Concord, in Harold Bloom's terms (both Huidobro and Paz have confessed repeatedly to being avid readers of his work). In many ways, it was through his work that Latin American poetics came to be. Paradoxically, it is by adopting Emersonian poetics and transforming it into a more radical, introvert version of itself that Latin American poetics achieves its modernity. Emerson may not have been in agreement with some of these readings, but his work served the purpose of *creating* something new. As in Borges's poem, in their work Emerson seems to actually have left his Montaigne book and gone out looking for a world in which his books can really be useful.

Notes

1. See Jorge Luis Borges, *An Introduction to American Literature*, trans. L. Clark Keating and Robert O. Evans (Lexington: University Press of Kentucky, 1971), 26.
2. Such characterization is not really unfaithful to Emerson's actual personal development. The best study of this process of disenchantment is David M. Robinson's *Emerson and the Conduct of Life: Pragmatism and Ethical Purpose in the Late Work* (Cambridge: Cambridge University Press, 1993), which traces the transition from the idealism of Emerson's younger years to his more mature (and disillusioned) works as a naturalist.
3. Coincidentally, the first Spanish translations of Emerson appeared in the 1900s, at the very beginning of the modernist period. Although Spanish publishers such as La España Moderna [Modern Spain] published several volumes of Emerson's works, from *Nature* to *The Conduct of Life*, it was mostly *Nature* and the two series of *Essays* (notably, "Self-Reliance") that attracted the attention of Spanish-speaking audiences.
4. Anna Brickhouse, *Transamerican Literary Relations and the Nineteenth-Century Public Sphere* (Cambridge: Cambridge University Press, 2004), 17–18.
5. Here I don't mean just "textual" translations in the sense of transferring a text from one language to another. I am making reference to the adaptation and expansion of a whole

set of visions and ideas (and their metaphors) to another reality, spatially and temporally different but connected by a common culture.
6. Gustavo Pérez Firmat, ed., *Do the Americas Have a Common Literature?* (Durham, NC: Duke University Press, 1990), 3.
7. Helmbrecht Breinig, "Invasive Methods: The Opening of Latin America in Nineteenth-Century US Literature," *Amerikastudien* 53 (2008): 13–36, 32.
8. What I am suggesting here is that Emerson's work has been, both in its earliest idealist phase and in his later naturalist one, a source of inspiration (or an inspiring reading) in the emergence of modern Latin American poetics.
9. Jeffrey Lawrence, *Anxieties of Experience: The Literatures of the Americas from Whitman to Bolaño* (New York: Oxford University Press, 2018), 8.
10. Ibid., 58.
11. Andrés Bello, *Selected Writings*, trans. Frances M. López-Morillas, ed. Iván Jaksic (Oxford: Oxford University Press, 1997), 7.
12. Ibid., 8.
13. See John Englekirk, "Notes on Emerson in Latin America," *PMLA* 76 (June 1961): 227–32, 229.
14. Vicente Huidobro, *Manifiestos* (Santiago de Chile: Mago, 2009), 28, 111.
15. This lack of awareness is not entirely accurate. Although it is clear that Emerson was more attracted to certain European and Asian cultures than others, he was not ignorant either of Spain or of its imperial history. As Jan Stievermann has noted, "The Louisiana territory the United States purchased from Napoleon the year Emerson was born had belonged to Spain before the latter was conquered by the French. Between 1808 and 1822, independence movements swept South America and Mexico. When Emerson traveled to St. Augustine in 1826 to restore his health, the United States had just secured the remaining western parts of Florida, the last vestiges of Spanish colonialism on the American continent." Perhaps his refusal to acknowledge the importance of Spain in history was an unconscious desire to leave behind its "old" imperial vision. See Jan Stievermann, "Europe," in *Ralph Waldo Emerson in Context*, ed. Wesley T. Mott (Cambridge: Cambridge University Press, 2014), 31–39, 32.
16. The most extreme form of this materialistic poetic use of words and/as objects is the calligram, an originally French and Latin American poetic subgenre.
17. Edmundo O'Gorman, *The Invention of America* (Bloomington: Indiana University Press, 1961), 73.
18. José Lezama Lima, *La expresión americana* (Madrid: Alianza, 1969), 111. See also Nora Catelli, *La expresión americana de José Lezama Lima* (PhD dissertation, University of Barcelona, 1996), 256.
19. Lezama Lima, *La* expresión americana, 111.
20. Ibid., 161.
21. See José Lezama Lima, *Escritos de estética*, ed. Pedro Aullón de Haro (Madrid: Dykinson, 2010), 199. Christopher Hanlon has recently argued that metaphors like these anticipate William James's famous notion of the "stream of consciousness." See Hanlon, *Emerson's Memory Loss: Originality, Communality, and the Late Style* (Oxford: Oxford University Press, 2018), 86–117.
22. Huidobro, *Manifiestos*, 97.
23. Octavio Paz, *On Poets and Others*, trans. Michael Schmidt (New York: Arcade, 1986), 9.

24. Paz, *Children of the Mire: Modern Poetry from Romanticism to the Avant-Garde*, trans. Rachel Phillips (Cambridge, MA: Harvard University Press, 1974), 64.
25. Paz, *On Poets and Others*, 10.
26. Ibid.
27. Although this *Creacionismo* is basically Huidobro's invention, its influence extended beyond his time and had a strong influence on later Latin American poets. Octavio Paz, for one example, was using the former's ideas when he argued that "the transmuting operation works as follows: the materials leave the blind of nature to enter the world of works, that is, of meaning," or that "in the poem language recovers its pristine originality, mutilated by the subjugation imposed on it by prose and everyday speech (Octavio Paz, *The Bow and the Lyre*, trans. Ruth L. C. Simms [New York: McGraw-Hill, 1975], 11.). The similarity to Emerson's ideas is again clear.
28. Huidobro, *Manifiestos*, 27.
29. Ibid., 28.
30. Ibid., 16.
31. Ibid., 39.
32. Ibid., 65.
33. Ibid., 42.
34. Ibid., 112.

CHAPTER 9

EMERSON AND CARIBBEAN EMANCIPATION

MARTHA SCHOOLMAN

> The history of mankind interests us only as it exhibits a steady gain of truth and right, in the incessant conflict which it records, between the material and the moral nature.
>
> Ralph Waldo Emerson, "Address on the Anniversary of the Emancipation of the Negroes in the British West Indies"

EMERSON's first major antislavery address, the "Address on the Anniversary of the Emancipation of the Negroes in the British West Indies," delivered on Emancipation Day in Concord on August 1, 1844, makes clear that, after some years of mild and easily overstated internal friction over the place of the antislavery cause within his larger Transcendentalist intellectual project, Emerson had managed to reframe the struggle for emancipation not as a distraction from the real work of transcendentalizing, but rather as an incontrovertible dialectical mover in the unfolding of idealist history. "In this cause," he writes, "no man's weakness is any prejudice; it has a thousand sons; if one man cannot speak, ten others can; and whether by the wisdom of its friends, or by the folly of its adversaries; by speech and by silence; by doing and by omitting to do, it goes forward" (*CW* 10:301–2). Whereas the Emerson of "Self-Reliance" (1841) has seemed to some readers to waver over whether "this bountiful cause of Abolition" (*CW* 2:30) constituted a hobbling, compromising partisanship according to which a person "is weaker by every recruit to his banner" (*CW* 2:30, 50), or rather an instance in which one must "accept the place the divine providence has found for you, the society of your contemporaries, the connexion of events" (*CW* 2:30, 50, 28), in the 1844 emancipation address it is clear that Emerson means to class abolitionism with the latter. The abolitionist cause, Emerson assures his readers in the address, is not a party, but a historical force—an instance in which history transitively *interests us*. As such, it doesn't so much solicit support as it sweeps all proximate human endeavor into its ideological singularity. By doing and omitting to do, it goes forward.

The big story Emerson tells in the address starts with the claim that British emancipation constituted "the settlement, as far as a great Empire was concerned, of a question on which almost every leading citizen in it had taken care to record his vote" (*CW* 10:301). It concludes with the narratively satisfying statement that "the sentiment of Right, once very low and indistinct, but ever more articulate, because it is the voice of the universe, pronounces Freedom. The Power that built this fabric of things affirms it in the heart; and in the history of the First of August, has made a sign to the ages, of his will" (*CW* 10:327). As a matter of oratory, this crescendo works, even as the lecture itself instantiates in both form and content the incessant conflict of dialectical history pursued across boundaries of nation and empire. The British story can certainly be framed as one of capital-*F* Freedom's triumph, from the Somerset decision of 1772 declaring Britain free soil, through the activism and parliamentary deliberations leading to the abolition of the slave trade in 1807, to the passage of the Emancipation Act of 1833, emancipation itself in 1834, and the final cancellation in 1838 of the ill-conceived compromise of "apprenticeship" according to which the formerly enslaved were expected to perform a mixture of paid/voluntary and unpaid/forced labor for either an additional four or six years depending on whether they were categorized as "nonpraedial" (domestic) or "praedial" (agricultural) workers. However, the reason for telling it there and then is the ongoing fact of enslavement in much of the American plantation zone, including in the US South as well as in parts of Latin America and the non-British Caribbean. The lecture thus has plenty to say about situations in which the sentiment of right went, and continues to go, unheeded, even to the point of threatening its own narrative of progress: the British West Indian colonial legislators who howled at the injustice of planters' loss of access to the forced labor of Africans (*CW* 10:309); the enslavers under apprenticeship for whom "the habit of oppression was not destroyed by a law and a day of jubilee" (*CW* 10:311); the "Virginian [who] piques himself on the picturesque luxury of his vassalage" (*CW* 10:302); and New England legislators from the supposedly free states who "are schooled and ridden by the minority of slaveholders" (*CW* 10:320), when they should be defending and expanding the New England emancipation process.

The 1844 emancipation address is a bold (though speculative) announcement of the inevitability of emancipation and a testament to its incompleteness. It is embedded in the conflict whose outcome it attempts to predict. Such is arguably the beauty and the tragedy of most abolitionist writing: it always risks being at least a little bit wrong when it attempts to conjure social transformations that have not yet occurred. Probing that vulnerability, some of the most searching recent critiques of Emerson's abolitionism have examined how that precise activist urge to anticipate—to presume outcomes that cannot be assured—can impose paradoxical limits on the very possibility of liberation.[1] Jared W. Hickman in *Black Prometheus: Race and Radicalism in the Age of Atlantic Slavery* (2017) argues that, by articulating a vision of freedom framed in terms of an ultimate submission to a version of the Hegelian Absolute (i.e., "the sentiment of right," "the voice of the universe," "his will"), Emerson's apparent rejection of the slaveholder's cause reinstalls mastery on a cosmic scale.[2] This characterization identifies an important element of Protestant moral dramaturgy in Emerson's antislavery that is limited to the perspective of the White emancipator. As Emerson writes in a key passage:

> This event was a moral revolution. ... Here was no prodigy, no fabulous hero, no Trojan horse, no bloody war, but all was achieved by plain means of plain men, working not under a leader, but under a sentiment. Other revolutions have been the insurrection of the oppressed; this was the repentance of the tyrant. It was the masters revolting from their mastery. The slave-holder said, I will not hold slaves. (CW 10:320)

This passage, while offering a reasonable description of the unglamorous tedium of the work of social reform (plain means, plain men), also fleshes out the very model of transcendence of which Hickman is most critical. It appears to posit emancipation in terms of the moral refinement of the enslaver with little concern for the actions or the perspective of the enslaved.[3] That the passage is in a number of senses factually false— the enslaved in the British Caribbean resisted their oppression for centuries, including numerous recorded cases of quotidian resistance, organized insurrection, and generational *marronage*; and no actual West India proprietor said any such thing—seems to provide a clear example of what Hickman criticizes (and Emerson in effect celebrates) as the idealist inclination to discover the moral abstraction sought, regardless of the so-called facts on the ground.

What Hickman promotes in place of such an idealist Christian "orthodox antislavery" is a category of Romantic metaphysical resistance that he names "heretical antislavery." Such a label may sound likewise idealist in its orientation towards the cosmic, but it functions in Hickman's system to scramble the very high-low dialectic that Emerson presumes by describing emancipation's history as an "incessant conflict between the material and the moral nature." Whereas the story sketched out in the "moral revolution" passage emphasizes White moral struggle, Hickman asks (to rework Frederick Douglass's famous query), what to the slave is such abstract moral grappling?[4] The operation of "heretical antislavery" in Hickman's view is to dismantle the Christian tendency to place desired outcomes at the level of a distant divine will and rather bring them (back) down to the level of human creativity.

"Heretical antislavery" as Hickman delineates it thus aligns with expressions of the emancipation struggle less reassured by the current moral and philosophical order. Hickman tends to class Black abolitionism—whether explicitly Christian or not—within the category of "heretical antislavery." This category can include work by Black radicals such as David Walker who appeals to "the God of Justice" in his *Appeal* (1829), and his disciple Henry Highland Garnet who in the "Address to the Slaves of the United States" (1848) posits a "God of heaven [who] would smile on every effort which the injured might take to disenthrall themselves."[5] While such statements clearly resemble Emerson's anticipatory rhetoric, for Hickman they engage as much with Afrocentric heresy as with what might otherwise be assimilated to a White Christian piety. "Heretical antislavery" can moreover include discourse that is neither Black nor explicitly abolitionist—such as some of the poetry of Percy Bysshe Shelley (Hickman, 220–39)—as well as acts of resistance that are not principally discursive, such as slave revolts. Indeed, for Hickman, as for many radical interpreters of the antislavery tradition, the Haitian Revolution offers the clearest proof of concept. As Hickman argues, the Haitian Revolution represented a decided rejection of conventional Christian morality in favor of an "immanent creation of autonomy."[6] The Haitian Revolution created a new cosmos to meet its revolutionary aims, rather than appealing to any preexisting regnant divine power.

In a somewhat similar vein, though one more constitutively invested in the abolitionism of the abolitionists that Hickman minimizes as "orthodox," Jeffrey Insko in *History, Abolition, and the Ever-Present Now in Antebellum American Writing* (2018) argues that the radical position within the larger antislavery project coincided with an antiteleological view of history which, like Hickman's "heretical antislavery," rejected ideas of liberation as residing beyond human agency to reshape material conditions. Combining William Lloyd Garrison's call for "immediate emancipation" and a historical sensibility that he describes as "Romantic presentism," Insko locates within the Romantic movement an alternative to the abstraction of slavery and abolition into narratives of orderly historical (or cosmological) progress.[7]

Like Hickman, Insko tests his theory of Romantic presentism against Emerson's writing related to slavery and abolition, though with notably different results. Working carefully and creatively between Emerson's Transcendentalist writings and his movement writings (if such a distinction indeed holds up), Insko argues that certain of Emerson's pre-1844 essays "delineate a heterodox view of history that might be described as Emerson's preabolitionist immediatism, which just so happens to coincide with what many scholars describe as the period of his preimmediatist abolitionism."[8] That is, for Insko, Emerson understood history in "presentist" and therefore "immediatist" terms, which he then imported into his abolitionism as he became more enmeshed in movement work. Whereas he may appear to have come late to abolitionism, Emerson—perhaps appropriately—did not come late to immediatism. As Insko demonstrates with a particularly compelling reading of "Circles," for Emerson in the era of the *First Series* essays (1841), "imagining a future, any future, inevitably entails accepting and responding to change in the present. Therefore, as an antidote to so desperately clinging to the past, Emerson advocates upsetting, rather than stabilizing 'foundations.' In doing so, he embraces and revels in the very terrors that beleaguer conservatives of all kinds."[9]

Extending Insko's argument just a bit, it could be said that whereas abolitionism was the exigency that brought radicals such as Elizabeth Heyrick (1824) and William Lloyd Garrison (1829) to immediatism, it was *immediatism* itself that was epistemic for Emerson, with abolitionism trailing behind.[10] But when Emerson's antislavery radicalism assumes its final form in the wake of the broadly radicalizing Compromise of 1850, it is expressed precisely in terms of a zeal for temporal derangement that Insko calls "presentism," a formation that also starts to sound a great deal like a political expression of Hickman's "heretical antislavery." For example, Emerson's 1851 "Address to the Citizens of Concord" rails against the ruinous conservatism that led Daniel Webster to rationalize the Compromise of 1850 as historically ordained by the founding documents, asserting instead the importance of "extemporizing a government."[11] And, as Insko finds in a lesser-known variant of the same lecture, the expression of an even clearer political analogue to Hickman's "heretical antislavery": "as the people have made a government, they can make another."[12] In that way, Insko discovers a radical, anti-teleological Emerson that Hickman is not particularly seeking. But, notably, Insko finds that dynamic only incidentally present in the 1844 emancipation address, because, as I have already illustrated, so much of the address appears devoted to the kind of objective historicizing against which Insko's own abolitionist analytical paradigm is arrayed, *even though that history is a history of the abolition of slavery*.

That Emerson's abolitionism could fail to qualify as such, even when applying analytical terms that his work helps us to theorize, even as it was taking shape in the Garrisonian-immediatist context of the 1844 Emancipation Day celebration in Concord, would seem to be the kind of logical blind alley that could serve to justify Hickman's general methodological impatience with movement abolitionism. However, it is a contradiction that Insko accepts with serenity: "Just as Emerson's history of British emancipation seems at odds with Emerson's sense of history, so might it seem to be at odds with his abolitionism."[13] Insko's reading then goes on to highlight the parts of the 1844 Emancipation Day lecture that would meet the criteria of epistemic-immediatist abolitionism within the apparently more generally inadequate project of Emerson's pre-1850 abolitionism. Insko locates such glimmers of another, epistemologically abolitionist abolitionism where Emerson acknowledges those aspects of the antislavery struggle that appear to lie beyond his own powers of metahistorical sense-making. Those include the important acknowledgement that slavery *itself* does not develop or improve: "Language must be raked, the secrets of slaughter-houses and infamous holes that cannot front the day, must be ransacked, to tell what negro-slavery has been."[14] And, perhaps more importantly, his acknowledgment of the emancipatory forces beyond the control or the comprehension of the White advocate: "So now, the arrival in the world of such men as Toussaint, and the Haytian heroes, or the leaders of their race in Barbadoes and Jamaica, outweighs in good omen all the English and American humanity. The antislavery of the whole world, is dust in the balance before this,—is a poor squeamishness and nervousness: the might and right are here: here is the anti-slave: here is man: and if you have man, black or white is an insignificance."[15]

For Insko, who doesn't belabor the point much, "the brief reference to the Haitian Revolution marks an important culminating point in Emerson's performance, one that links the West Indies address to the most unsettling (a term I use here deliberately) elements of his abolitionist and historiographical immediatism."[16] For Hickman, however, likely because it is the point upon which his whole characterization stands or falls, this moment is one of dire political and cosmological inadequacy, precisely "squeamish and nervous":

> Out of context, this is a moment when the black revolutionary's assertion of immanent authority comes into view as the truest self-reliance. It is the breathtaking

revelation of a black Prometheus unbound who embodies a radical autonomy. But the framing of this moment—the showy mediation of black revolutionary immanence by a transcendental narrative of race in which the Haytian heroes' success is made attributable to some divinely appointed world-historical sea-change—preempts such a reading, keeping the black Prometheus bound.[17]

For me, the very heterogeneity of the passage—is it more important as an acknowledgement of primacy of the abolitionism of the enslaved and formerly enslaved ("here is the anti-slave") or is any such acknowledgment too rapidly undermined by the homogenizing imperatives of White manhood ("if you have man, black or white is an insignificance")?—provides an indication of the horizon of both critics' normative models of properly abolitionist epistemology in a hemispheric context of staggered, uneven, still-imperfectly-realized emancipations.

Both critics' radical visions of a properly abolitionist abolitionism require that emancipation be viewed in wholly revolutionary terms. From the perspective of our own era of stubbornly uncompleted emancipation, there is something deeply correct about such a characterization. But Emerson and anyone participating in a First of August commemoration, or indeed anyone else inclined to consider the enormous volume of reportage on abolition and emancipation in Haiti and the British Caribbean in that era, would likely be positioned as "mediating black revolutionary immanence" not only through equal and opposite assumptions about the organic wholeness of the cosmic/historical order and the converse historical rupture signaled by Hickman's "radical autonomy," but materially and ideologically in a heterogeneous context in which flashes of revolutionary immanence/imminence jostle for notice alongside the more mundanely semi-unfree present conditions in the variously contested post-emancipation societies that followed those variously gradual or revolutionary changes in status.

In other words, then as now, aspirations to an abolitionist abolitionism are ever shadowed by the partial, often reversible, nature of emancipation, and apparently never more so than when US thinkers attempt to fix in time a dynamic, living Caribbean history in order to posit a desirable future for the stubborn racial conservatism of the continental North. So the question to be tackled at this point is not how Emerson fails to solve this as-yet-unsolved problem, but rather how best to capture the full historical, political, philosophical texture of what I want to put forward as an effort to interpret the meaning of emancipation from the perspective of the radically in-between moment of 1844, in which revolutionary and non-revolutionary (or material and moral) abolition stood hopelessly intermingled in a way that even the most revolutionary actors and thinkers found challenging to parse.

What Hickman and Insko (and many other critics besides) seek and find in the archive of Atlantic slavery and antislavery is the epistemic potential for radical incipience, a posture toward the future expressed in terms of a particular aesthetic, religious, philosophical, and political repertoire. However, such were the broader frameworks of quotidian resistance, structural change, and racial-capitalist cunning in the mid-nineteenth century as to make the fully revolutionary abolition thus anticipated not so much unthinkable, as unexampled, *even as the institution of slavery itself was falling throughout the hemisphere*. Hickman and Insko's critical abolitionism emphasizes a version of what the historical sociologist Mimi Sheller describes as the "cathartic" model of abolition, such that "the violence of self-liberation is seen as a necessary and cathartic process, much like Frantz Fanon's understanding of the violent catharsis necessary for decolonization" as explored in *Black Skin, White Masks*.[18] (Sheller, 25). However, in practice the abolition of slavery was effected by a range of military and political means, from legal emancipation in individual states of the US North, the British Caribbean, and the French Caribbean apart from Haiti; to the cathartic war of liberation in Haiti; to liberal anticolonial revolution as in Mexico; to multiracial civil war in the US. Logically, a particular abolition formation's degree of radical impact would seem to depend on the presence of objectively revolutionary characteristics such as speed and violence. But, in practice, a reassertion of racialized exploitation has followed abolition in all cases so far, *regardless* of the path taken to that formal legal threshold.

Although there are now and were then significant intellectual and political satisfactions involved in imagining otherwise, the stubborn partiality of abolition as it unfolded across the hemispheric nineteenth century needs to be understood as an important part of the story told in and through the situation of the 1844 emancipation address, even when it does not always appear to be the address's animating claim, and even when the address seems to will itself into a discourse of agentless inevitability of which Hickman and Insko are rightly suspicious. Without diminishing the analytical importance of contemporary abolitionism's radical implacability or the value of calling attention to the weaknesses and disappointments of Emerson's early abolitionism, it is important to recognize the extent to which Emerson's writing in the first emancipation address both reflects and confronts the state of the hemispheric emancipation process as it stood in 1844, not so much as a matter of limiting "context" but as one of political specificity. While the bare chronology employed by both Emerson and his critics would consign certain phases of Caribbean abolition to the completed past—forty years past as in Haiti or ten years as in the British Caribbean—the details in both cases were complicated and temporally unruly before any literary abolitionist arrived on the scene to further disarrange them. Haiti, the abolitionist republic, was in 1844 nearing the end of a *second*, and ultimately thwarted, revolutionary era. The British Caribbean, emancipation's empire, had just concluded its *second*, apparently successful, emancipation era with the abolition of apprenticeship in 1838, although, as would become clear in the coming decades leading up to the Morant Bay Rebellion in 1865, without any deeper agreement among the parties about the ideal shape of freedom.

This for the moment skeletal Caribbean context begins to provide us (and Emerson) with the critical distance to recognize that similar dynamics of incompletion and repetition were in play in the United States. The US was of course some decades away from the era of its own *second* "unfinished Revolution," but the failures of the first were eminently clear to abolitionists, who loved to quote the US Declaration of Independence with what Frederick Douglass called "scorching irony," even as their non-abolitionist White fellows were in the habit of loudly trumpeting the miracle of their own liberation.[19] Slavery had been abolished mostly through a patchwork of gradual emancipations in the Northern coastal states, while remaining a constitutionally protected Southern sectional institution. In that poorly regionalized guise, slavery endured a number of challenges from above, below, within, and without, challenges at that point managed by systemic repression, as variously applied locally, sectionally, and nationally, to the enslaved, to White and Black Northern abolitionists, to free African Americans living in the North and South, and even to members of the US Congress endeavoring to make abolition a matter of open debate.

From the perspective of 1844 then, abolition stands as a matter for both the past and the future, of success and failure, of moral clarity shaded by persistent racist violence and untrammeled greed. In this rather more fallen context, we could (re)revisit the "Haytian heroes" passage as registering this specific phase of simultaneously pre- and post-emancipation contention. It invokes Toussaint, as radical abolitionism often did, as evidence of Black excellence and Black capacity for self-liberation. But beyond the level of basic abolitionist tropology, Emerson's language invokes pluralized "heroes" and "leaders" in order to (prospectively, experimentally) consign "anti-slavery" to the "dust" of history, while elevating in its place the embodied commonality of *current* Black struggle across the variously-structured communities in the post-emancipation world. "The anti-slavery of the whole world," as Emerson is seemingly aware, is perpetually in the dark concerning its own influence, apart from the always-denigrated and backlash-prone job of preparing the groundwork of otherwise indifferent public opinion for the end of plantation slavery. On the other hand, the protracted work of emancipation itself is acknowledged when Emerson lets "anti-slavery" recede before the "might and right" represented by "Toussaint, and the Haytian heroes, or of the leaders of their race in Barbadoes in Jamaica." That shift in agency may not be as fully "breathtaking" as Hickman would require, but it does at least entail a shift in the geographical theater of action. In Emerson's deictic statement that "the might and the right are here: here is the anti-slave," it is notable that the "here" indicated is precisely the "now" of the post-emancipation Caribbean and not any time or yet-identifiable place on the North American continent.

With these observations, I am shifting focus from abolition as a singular act that could (still potentially) be achieved with finality given the correct configuration of personnel, thought and action, to emancipation as an uneven process and, as such, like freedom, "a constant struggle."[20] Put another way, I am shifting focus from abolitionist radicalism as an abstract ideal that shone with occasional purity over the course of the emancipation era, to the abolitionist movement's confrontation with a proliferation of semi-emancipated resistance formations that we can see repeated and revised across the long hemispheric nineteenth century, from the 1770s to the 1880s, from Massachusetts to Brazil. For even in Haiti, which came as close as any post-emancipation society to the still philosophically and politically salient desideratum of abolishing whiteness along with slavery, and to doing so precisely with the radical precipitancy of a "revolution ... not preceded or even accompanied by an explicit intellectual discourse," as Michel-Rolph Trouillot famously put it, what Emerson called the planter's "habit of oppression" managed to hold sway.[21] As Emerson likely would have known, Haiti by 1844 was a society actively revising its still-new political institutions, while operating under strain caused not only by the external reassertion of white supremacy in the form of the ruinously extractive 1825 indemnity treaty with France, but also by internal resistance to the race/class/caste politics that continued forced labor within postrevolutionary Haiti by other means.

Although this history is relatively well known, literary scholars don't generally approach the Haitian Revolution with those contradictions of emancipation in mind.[22] Characteristically in that sense, Hickman bases his interpretation of the Haitian Revolution as a Promethean event—one that "opened new cosmic-political possibilities" (Hickman, 244)—on a rather partial reading of the 1804 Haitian Declaration of Independence. Hickman demonstrates that the Haitian Declaration eschews the liberal language of God-given rights found in its US predecessor, emphasizing instead the rights Haitian citizens and soldiers secured *for one another* by "forever renounc[ing] France," and vowing "to die rather than to live under its domination."[23] The document clearly embodies the idea of non-transcendent liberation that Hickman theorizes around it. As he summarizes, "To derive revolutionary energy from endogenous rather than exogenous sources—from the human rather than the divine, from the black ancestors rather than the white oppressors—constitutes yet another resistance of the transcendental and enactment of immanence" (Hickman, 255).

However, and escaping Hickman's comment, the document itself wavers on whether the triple abolition of whiteness, slavery, and French rule should constitute the abolition of domination generally toward which the Promethean rebel is supposed to aspire. Written in the voice of General Jean-Jacques Dessalines, the Declaration addresses the "Natives of Haiti" with the hope that "I have been so fortunate as to return to your hands the sacred trust you confided to me," thus appearing to establish a refusal to hoard the authority that inevitably accrues to a general in war. However, just a few sentences later, the language of the Declaration appears to hand the power right back to Dessalines:

> If ever you refused or grumbled while receiving those laws that the spirit guarding your fate dictates to me for your own good, you would deserve the fate of an ungrateful people. But I reject that awful idea; you will sustain the liberty that you cherish and support the leader who commands you. Therefore vow before me to live free and independent, and to prefer death to anything that will try to place you back in chains.[24]

Here, in other words, Dessalines addresses the Haitian people by issuing a version of the paradoxical call for submission to freedom so widely diagnosed—and most recently by Hickman—as a central contradiction of *Emerson's* thought. The Declaration asserts the autonomy that the Revolution had already enacted, before immediately subsuming that radical democratic ferment to a disciplined national authority "commanded" for the people's "own good." Such is not of course either to excuse Emerson's racial and political limitations, or indeed to offshore them to emancipation's most obviously radical site, but rather to suggest that, when it comes to the abolitionist archive, the disappointments and imperfections—like the hopes and possibilities—are everywhere subject to celebration, to critique and, as Paul Gilroy might say, to "transfiguration."[25]

As Sheller demonstrates, the coercive model of state power figured in the Declaration turns out to have been predictive. Post-revolutionary Haiti's inability or unwillingness to demobilize its military became the nation's main obstacle to building a society based on a truly revolutionary popular democracy.[26] The assertion of elite authority backed by state violence that characterized Haiti's postrevolutionary era indeed directly contravened what Hickman aptly describes as the revolution's most Promethean elements, including, Sheller notes, African religion:

> [D]espite its revolution and the powerful political symbolism of the rebel slave, the African religion of Voudou was not tolerated (except during the regime of Emperor Soulouque [1847–1859]). ... Despite religious tolerance in the early constitutions of Haiti, Voudou was outlawed and forced into hiding.[27]

This repression of folk religion, and precisely for its antiauthoritarian capacity, corresponded with a repression of the folk more generally that became the rather-less-acknowledged model for purportedly free labor across the hemispheric nineteenth century:

> Boyer's 1826 *Code Rural* provided for the "protection and encouragement of agriculture" by a strict regime of rural police surveillance and regulation of work contracts and trade. ... [I]t declared that agricultural workers were not allowed to leave the countryside and go to the towns or cities without authorization from a Judge of the Peace, nor could their children be apprenticed in the towns. Mobility was tightly restricted by a pass system, and cooperative ownership of land was outlawed.[28]

Extending the commitment to forced labor that can be found throughout the St. Domingue/Haiti revolutionary archive, the *Code Rural* transformed a revolutionary peasant class back into something like slavery.[29] By enacting it, the "Haytian heroes" transformed *themselves* from the non-transcendent gods that Hickman posits, into power-seeking men, and did so precisely by reclaiming the cosmos from the folk.

I raise this more to extend than to debunk Hickman's excellent argument by way of suggesting that the current critical tendency of reading for abolitionist abolitionism against the grain of nineteenth-century abolitionist writing may miss some of the subtleties of which the historical subjects in question are in fact aware. Such is especially the case when we attempt to read Haitian—and, I will argue, British West Indian—history over the shoulders of nineteenth-century literary abolitionists. For although it is a close-to-reflexive critical move to read White abolitionists, even self-professed radicals, as phobically triggered by Black autonomy in general and the contours of life and governance in postrevolutionary Haiti in particular, the Garrisonian abolitionism with which Emerson was aligned mostly does not appear to bear out this characterization. In the pages of Garrison's *Liberator* we find generally admiring, and approaching boosterish, support of the Haitian state in its successive postrevolutionary guises. The *Liberator* regularly carried news from Haiti, including letters by and mostly positive accounts of the administration of Jean-Pierre Boyer, Haitian President from 1818 to 1843.[30] To take just one minor but telling detail, an advertisement for items on offer for the Eighth Massachusetts Antislavery Fair in December of 1841 featured a medal "framed of Petion [Haitian President 1807–1818] and Boyer," suggesting that the mostly White shoppers at the fair were expected to be interested in decorating their homes with the likenesses of Haitian politicians, and well beyond the widely produced, and still-recognizable images of Toussaint Louverture, who died in 1803.[31]

It is moreover clear that the *Liberator*'s generally supportive stance toward Haiti did not require that it remain under the leadership of one or another admired political figure or indeed be preserved in amber at the moment of revolution to retain Garrisonian abolitionist admiration. During the 1843–44 revolt,[32] for example, in which the peasants oppressed by the *Code Rural* and educated urbanites shut out from the political process by the military elite rose together to claim additional rights, thus deposing Boyer, the *Liberator* wrote approvingly of the insurgency as follows:

> The revolution in Hayti, by which Boyer is deposed and banished, appears to be complete. It is the triumph of the people over usurpation and misrule, consummated with scarcely the shedding of a drop of blood, in the most decisive and popular manner. The page of history does not record an overturn of this kind, and to this extent, more remarkable in its character, or more honorable to those by whom it has been achieved.[33]

That the *Liberator* contributor was inclined to call an event outside the 1791–1804 era "the revolution in Hayti" gives some indication of their awareness of emancipation as an iterative process, rather than a moment of rupture after which something called freedom, wholly distinct from slavery, takes hold. Whereas a more conservative view of Haiti would (and still does) dwell on its periods of instability as indication of a kind of postcolonial racial failure, and a less attentive approach would be content with appreciative gestures toward the military prowess of Toussaint, this piece, like Sheller's contemporary work, notices Haiti specifically for its experiments in popular democracy. Adopting the prospective hopefulness of this very particular (and rapidly foreclosed) moment, the *Liberator* commentary further notes that "it not only shews [sic] that the Haytians are making rapid advances in republican reform, but it demonstrates their right to be acknowledged as a free and independent republic." The language of "rapid advances" could of course be read in the spirit of racial assessment that surfaces in Emerson's 1844 emancipation address in moments of condescending appreciativeness toward "the civilization of the negro" (*CW* 10:323). However, the overall tone of the piece suggests that a more plausible reading would be to view Haiti as an example held up to inspire much-needed "republican reform" on US soil, which was, of course, central to *The Liberator*'s own political project.

It may be a reach to claim, based at least on internal evidence from the 1844 emancipation address, that Emerson was as engaged in Haitian affairs as the *Liberator* contributors whose work he may or may not have been reading, although there is some evidence that Emerson's generally scholarly approach to the archive of abolition did extend to contemporary reportage about Haiti.[34] More central to Emerson then, and more peripheral to criticism now, is the way similar lessons around the complexity of emancipation and the persistence of forced labor took shape in the British Caribbean, which became a particular focus of anglophone abolitionist attention in the period between August 1, 1834 and August 1, 1838, or between the abolition of slavery and the abolition of apprenticeship. During that period chroniclers including the British abolitionists Joseph Sturge and Thomas Harvey and their US counterparts James A. Thome and Horace Kimball traveled to the British Caribbean to study the emancipation process, paying particular attention to its differential unfolding in Antigua, where the local planters decided to forego the semi-emancipated phase of apprenticeship, and Jamaica and Barbados, where they did not.

The two texts, both of which Emerson mentions in the 1844 address (*CW* 10:310, 324), and both of which had a clear influence on his thinking, are superficially quite similar. They record visits paid during the same months in the Winter–Spring of 1836–37, as is indicated not only by the dates listed in the respective travelogues but also by the fact that Sturge and Harvey record running into Thome and Kimball, "on a tour of inquiry like our own," not once but twice, in Antigua in December of 1836 and then in Kingston in March of 1837.[35] Two studies that resulted—Sturge and Harvey's *The West Indies in 1837* and Thome and Kimball's *Emancipation in the West Indies*—both collate anecdotal data to the political project of immediate abolitionism. However, they do so through very different interpretive frameworks. Thome and Kimball proffer the evidence they gather in order to argue for what they emphasize as the prospective "safety of immediate emancipation" in the US South.[36] Sturge and Harvey, by contrast, use the same evidence to argue that British Emancipation itself, under what they call "the measure so undeservedly termed an Act for the Abolition of Slavery" (319), has not yet occurred.

Observing as they were the same places at more or less the same times, the striking contrast can be seen, via Insko's work, as a matter of temporal perception as much as of political sensibility. While associated with the immediatist Garrisonian American Antislavery Society, which published their findings in 1838, Thome and Kimball are in a way the abolitionists that Hickman and Insko warn us about. Their goal is clearly as much to gather reassurance that the post-emancipation future would closely resemble the pre-emancipation past as to do the work of justice. In Antigua, offered as the model for the advisability of immediate rather than gradual emancipation, masters are portrayed as emphatically still the masters, and the formerly enslaved, while technically free, are represented as assuming a posture of subservience described variously as innate and voluntary.

Thome and Kimball extend this general sense of Black geniality to a supposed willingness among the emancipated to continue working in difficult, starvation-wage agricultural jobs regardless of the other, less market-oriented alternatives that might present themselves. Whereas Haitian officials anticipated resistance to continued field labor by compelling it, Thome and Kimball—or really Thome, a Kentucky-born Presbyterian minister and recent Oberlin graduate who wrote up the pair's findings after Kimball became too ill with tuberculosis to complete the project—assured readers that mission education provided sufficient soft coercion to achieve the same object. Although they (as well as Sturge and Harvey) celebrate Black intellect and capacity for advanced educational attainment, they note that: "We were induced to believe that the education of the negro children would not, by fostering habits of idleness, be prejudicial to the agricultural interests. The instructions of the schools are directly calculated to inspire respect for labor. Idleness is ever represented as a vice and a crime, sinful in the sight of God, and injurious to society."[37] Acknowledging, and indeed catering to the increasing cultural consensus that extractive agriculture was necessary to capital, and furthermore required labor arrangements that workers would in the very best case be forced to choose, Thome and Kimball assert, with great liberal optimism, that such profitable extraction will continue in post-emancipation societies purely through the combined disciplinary forces of religion and education.

As Hickman would predict, such is part and parcel of a repressive transcendentalization of freedom. Thome and Kimball repeatedly emphasize the spiritual narrative of emancipation as a gift from God, rather than as a form of material-social transformation achieved through human struggle. This kind of framing clearly made an impression on Emerson, who quotes at length in the 1844 emancipation address from a passage in Thome and Kimball narrating the (second-hand) spectacle of Black gratitude in Antigua on August 1, 1834. That passage is used to demonstrate what Emerson calls the "touching ... moderation of the negroes" (CW 10:309): "The clergy and missionaries throughout the island were actively engaged, seizing the opportunity to enlighten the people on all the duties and responsibilities of their new relation, and urging them to the attainment of that higher liberty with which Christ maketh his children free" (CW 10:310; Thome and Kimball, 146).

However, as much as Emerson seems inclined to celebrate with Thome and Kimball, or, as Hickman suggests, show "relief,"[38] at the formerly enslaved's decorous reception of the news of their emancipation, it does not necessarily follow that such a position requires or even accepts the kind of deference to the mastery of masters to which Thome and Kimball seem startlingly subject. Despite Emerson's appreciation of the supposed spiritual passivity of the emancipated, with its connection to what Stowe (and Alexander Kinmont) liked to celebrate as the natural Christian meekness of Black folk, Emerson doesn't appear to harbor any particular admiration or hope for the spiritual or material condition of the former enslavers, whom he describes variously as greedy, childish, selfish, sinful, immoral, ill-humored, sulky, and generally beyond redemption.[39] The profit motive of planters is rational, if not laudable, Emerson concedes. But the slaveholder is distinguished by a will to dominate that cannot be so easily excused or extinguished. To take one concentrated example:

> I may here express a general remark, which the history of slavery seems to justify, that it is not founded solely on the avarice of the planter. We sometimes say, the planter does not want slaves, he only wants the immunities and the luxuries which the slaves yield him; give him money, give him a machine that will yield him as much money as the slaves, and he will thankfully let them go. He has no love for slavery, he wants luxury, and he will pay even this price of crime and danger for it. But I think experience does not warrant this favorable distinction, but shows the existence, beside the covetousness, of a bitter element, the love of power, the voluptuousness of holding a human being in absolute control. (CW 10:311)

If Emerson's only source on slavery, apprenticeship, and emancipation were Thome and Kimball, he could certainly arrive at this characterization of the enslaver by reading them ever so slightly against the grain, as for example when they record of an Antigua planter "when asked to specify the advantages of freedom over slavery, he named emphatically and above all others *the abolition of flogging*. Formerly, he said, it was 'whip—whip—whip—incessantly,' but now we are relieved from this disagreeable task,"[40] as if such violence were anything but voluntary on the enslaver's part. But with the inclusion of Sturge and Harvey, who are reporting not simply on slavery, but on the failure of the initial stages of emancipation to emancipate anyone *but* the planters from their own transgressions as well as their own obligations to the formerly enslaved, the planter's greed, violence, and love of power are matters of animating concern.

When Sturge and Harvey write of Antigua, they emphasize the planters' commitment to retaining power and profit, while leaving the formerly enslaved, especially children and the elderly, subject to abuse, re-enslavement elsewhere in the Caribbean, and the general attitude of careless privation that Christopher Taylor has aptly named the "Empire of Neglect."[41] As they shift their attention from Antigua to Barbados and Jamaica, Sturge and Harvey find the situation more dire still. They discover by collecting the testimonies of apprentices and visiting plantations in every Jamaican parish that apprenticeship is in many ways *worse* than slavery given the levels of abuse to which embittered planters subject those in whose future life and health they believe themselves to have no rational financial stake. The discovery that the supposed advance of partial emancipation could bring greater oppression was clearly radicalizing for Sturge and Harvey. This is especially noticeable when they write of Jamaica, and with particular emphasis on Black self-determination, on the subtle workings of racialized coercion, and the formerly enslaved's justified (and implicitly compensatory) claims to use the land on which they were living as they saw fit, and without disruption by the planters.

Indeed, their extensive commentary on the last point provides an intriguing context for Emerson's characterization of the behavior and preferences of the emancipated as well as a potential rejoinder to Hickman's model of cosmic abolition. Sturge and Harvey, anticipating Sheller, pay particular attention to the way the apprentices fought to determine the shape of their own freedom in a way that did not entail the *destruction* of their old world, but rather would enable them to build upon the forms of collective autonomy that they had managed to secure under slavery, particularly by exercising their new legal right to negotiate terms of employment with their former enslavers. The former enslavers, as Sturge and Harvey document quite exhaustively, fought these changes by manipulating the apprentices into performing unpaid work and attempting further to coerce labor by making it impossible for the formerly enslaved to feed themselves without wages. As they document not only in *The West Indies in 1837* but also in the well-known pamphlet *A Narrative of Events, Since the First of August, 1834, by James Williams, An Apprenticed Laborer in Jamaica*, which also resulted from their investigatory visit, Jamaican planters pushed the boundaries of their legal power over the apprentices by restricting access to their provision grounds, pulling down apprentices' houses, and allowing livestock to trample their cultivated fields.

Whereas the enslaved were often allotted provision grounds to provide sustenance to themselves and their extended local kin networks while relieving the enslavers of the obligation to provide food for them, those same provision grounds came to be viewed as a threat to the profitable transition to wage labor, lest the formerly enslaved lack incentive to join the cash economy. As Sturge and Harvey well understood, from the perspective of the formerly enslaved, the provision grounds had both practical and cultural value as sites for the construction of rural peasant identity, *alongside* but *apart from* the world of the planters. This fact of local attachment could be spun in different ways, depending on the perspective of the interpreter. On the one hand, the inclination among the formerly enslaved to stay put could be read as evidence of their willingness to continue performing plantation labor. From the perspective of the formerly enslaved, however, the provision grounds served as the material basis for constructing a world on their own terms, though on soil already cultivated by themselves, rather than, as the US mythos of freedom would have it, on wholly new ground.

Sturge and Harvey attempt perhaps too optimistically to synthesize the two perspectives when they write of the Jamaican apprentices, "when free, which they might be to-morrow, they should be glad to remain on the estate and work for wages, rather than leave their houses and grounds and *begin the world again*."[42] But in the process of accounting for the formerly enslaved's view of their own world, they do convincingly render their desire to engage in collective (or as Sheller might say, radical democratic) projects of self-determination building from their known worlds, rather than to presume their desire to be liberated by a destroyer god that would bring, to borrow a phrase from the US emancipation process, "nothing but freedom."

If we return to Emerson's own account of West Indian history following this brief and selective tour through his likely archive, it would seem that he has only partially digested the news that the presumed advance of apprenticeship was in some ways an intensification of slavery, and the arrival of supposed new freedoms also brought with them new forms of coercion. As a matter of politics, he would indeed have ample motivation for glossing over these details. After all, the whole point of the August First occasion was to commemorate West Indian emancipation and to celebrate it as an important, if flawed, precedent for future emancipations. For that particular object, the distinction among the multiple, iterable "August Firsts" may not be especially significant. Yet given that Emerson's archive for the occasion of the 1844 address was the archive of the emancipation *process,* it is notable that his account seems to register the difficulty of keeping the various stages distinct. For example, in one particular passage in which he catalogues the horrors of slavery, the salient enormity—"pregnant women set in the treadmill for refusing to work" (*CW* 10:304)—appears to come not from the archive of slavery, but from the archive of emancipation. The image of the treadmill surfaces with almost obsessive regularity in Sturge and Harvey's accounts of apprenticeship, in the James Williams narrative, as well as in a widely-reproduced engraving of women being whipped on the treadmill entitled "An Interior of a Jamaican House of Correction," through which Sturge and Harvey worked to as it were "memeify" the most sensational of their findings.[43]

When reframed in these temporally and politically complex transnational terms, we can see Emerson's early declaration of a preference for the "steady gain of truth and right" over "incessant conflict" as a wishful abstraction even in context. On closer examination, Emerson's explicit statements and formal choices in the 1844 emancipation address reflect the tendency of emancipation to become a matter not so much of historical rupture as of a repetitive positing of the possibility of transformation looped through a complex iterability of emancipation itself. Although we were led to expect otherwise, the 1844 address never really offers a linear story of British emancipation. Rather, it narrates the story of British emancipation not once, but multiple times over the course of the lecture, searching, it seems, both for the hopeful narrative arc from slavery to freedom upon which the lecture provisionally lands, as well as for the precise moment that the US fell away from the seeming upward trend that its own intellectuals had once believed themselves to be leading.

The first half of the lecture (approximately twelve pages out of twenty-five) recounts the British story chronologically, from the earliest construction of "the negro ... [as] an article of luxury to the commercial nations" (*CW* 10:303), to Granville Sharp's activism (*CW* 10:304–5), the Somerset decision (*CW* 10:305), to Quaker agitation (*CW* 10:305–6), to the anti-slave trade activism of Clarkson and Wilberforce (*CW* 10:306), through the emancipation debates of the 1830s (*CW* 10:308–9), ending with the words of Jamaican governor Charles Metcalfe in 1840 celebrating, perhaps still prematurely, British emancipation's success (*CW* 10:313). Then begins what I would call the "Deuteronomy" phase of the lecture, with a paragraph commencing, appropriately, "I said" (*CW* 10:313), which *retells* the story of British emancipation as a story of transatlantic anglophone culture's market-oriented "shopkeeping civility" (*CW* 10:314), the amoral greed of which eventually "ripened" (*CW* 10:315) into a moral revulsion against slavery that thinkers such as Wilberforce (*CW* 10:316) and, implicitly, Adam Smith, successfully reframed as bad morals *and* bad business.

The next section serves as a somewhat odd break in the action, shifting focus from the British triumph to US failure: "Whilst I have read of England," Emerson writes, "I have thought of New England" (*CW* 10:317). But the topic of this section, which occasions a furious three-page-long paragraph, is not New England emancipation or Southern

US plantation slavery, but rather the seemingly ancillary scandal of free Black mariners from Massachusetts being held and sometimes illegally enslaved when their ships landed in ports in "South Carolina, Georgia, and Louisiana" (*CW* 10:317–18). Like Sturge and Harvey, Emerson appears to be radicalized by this particular *failure* of emancipation, which brings him to the boldest radical statement of the lecture, "the Union is already at an end, when the first citizen of Massachusetts is thus outraged" (*CW* 10:319), sounding, as Insko comments, "like a true Garrisonian disunionist."[44] However, it is also abundantly clear that correcting this particular extralegal practice would not contribute much to the abolition of slavery, but rather beat back a particularly egregious form of stealth slave *trading*, which was allegedly abolished in Britain in 1807 and internationally in 1808 as the result of the Wilberforce-led phase of the movement, and thereby only slightly reduce the total number of US slavery's contemporary victims. But Emerson's surprisingly heavy emphasis on this particular example, and to the exclusion of any other contemporary examples of the abuses of slavery where it is still officially practiced, does begin to indicate that Northern emancipation (and perhaps any emancipation) is marked by a fragility that threatens to make it fully reversible if it is not defended. The Union may be at a *metaphorical* end when the first citizen of Massachusetts is thus outraged, but it is slave trade abolition—allegedly abolitionism's greatest *past* success—as well as Northern emancipation itself that is gravely compromised by the ease with which Black freedom is sacrificed in this, and most other cases, to extralegally tolerated White greed.

That excursus on the ill treatment of Black citizens of Massachusetts then gives way to a third retelling, this time reemphasizing Emerson's preferred story of moral improvement, including, as previously noted, the slave-holder who said "I will not hold slaves" (*CW* 10:320), "the great geniuses of the British Senate" (*CW* 10:321), "Franklin, Jefferson, Washington in this country" (*CW* 10:321), and those on both sides of the Atlantic who have (he hopes) learned that "the stream of human affairs flows its own way, and is very little affected by the activity of legislators" (*CW* 10:322). The fourth and final retelling then centers what Emerson calls "a new element in modern politics, namely, the civilization of the negro" (*CW* 10:323), which he narrates from the enormity of the *Zong* murders (1781), to the rise of Wilberforce and Clarkson (again), through the testimonies to Black decorum of White West Indian travelers and colonists "of Sturge, of Thome and Kimball, of [Quaker activist Joseph John] Gurney, of [Baptist missionary James] Phillippo" (*CW* 10:323–24), before at last landing on "the arrival in the world of such men as Toussaint" (*CW* 10:325) and "the proud discovery, that the black race can contend with the white" (*CW* 10:325), and then concluding the lecture.

If we were to bend the rules of Insko's "presentist" preference for the productively radical unmooring of contexts, we could regard Emerson's spiral narrative strategy here as evidence of his analysis itself being unmoored precisely by the contradictions of his own, difficult-to-characterize mid-antebellum moment. It is clear that Emerson *wants* to tell a classic Transcendentalist story of sustained organic growth and moral betterment, but the best the material at hand can supply is a tentative recursivity. Such recursive change could eventually yield something like gradual progress, from "Troglodytes" (*CW* 10:303) to Toussaint, from enslavers to liberators, or it could look more like the hopelessly repetitive cycle of unfulfilled promise that history continues to deliver, from Wilberforce, to Wilberforce, to Wilberforce.

Notes

1. The relation between freedom and limitation is a longstanding problem in Emerson studies, from Steven E. Whicher's *Freedom and Fate: An Inner Life of Ralph Waldo Emerson* (Philadelphia: University of Pennsylvania Press, 1953), to Christopher Newfield, *The Emerson Effect: Freedom and Submission in America* (Chicago: University of Chicago Press, 1996). What sets these contemporary critics apart is the intellectual seriousness with which they center the historical (as opposed to metaphorical) struggle over slavery in this context.
2. Jared W. Hickman, *Black Prometheus: Race and Radicalism in the Age of Atlantic Slavery* (New York: Oxford University Press, 2017), 244.
3. I offer a different, close to diametrically opposed reading of this passage as operating within the frame of Garrisonian radicalism according to which Northern US (and metropolitan British) complicity was regarded as a form of "slaveholding" that had to be renounced, in Martha Schoolman, *Abolitionist Geographies* (Minneapolis: University of Minnesota Press, 2014), 87–90.
4. I refer here to Douglass's famous "What to the Slave is the Fourth of July? An Address Delivered in Rochester, New York, on 5 July 1852," in *The Frederick Douglass Papers. Series One: Speeches, Debates and Interviews. Volume 2: 1847–1854*, ed. John Blassingame (New Haven: Yale University Press, 1982), 359–88. As Hickman remarks in the context of discussing Douglass's *My Bondage, My Freedom* (1855), "The slave need not—indeed, must not—admit any measure of sinfulness in his opposition to the master" (Hickman, *Black Prometheus*, 230).
5. David Walker, *David Walker's Appeal to the Colored Citizens of the World*, ed. Peter P. Hinks (University Park, PA: Penn State University Press, 2000), 14; Henry Highland Garnet, "An Address to the Slaves of the United States," in *The Rise of Aggressive Abolitionism*, ed. Stanley Harrold (Lexington: University Press of Kentucky, 2004), 184.
6. Hickman, *Black Prometheus*, 258.
7. Jeffrey Insko, *History, Abolition, and the Ever-Present Now in Antebellum American Writing* (New York: Oxford University Press, 2018), 96.
8. Ibid., 112.
9. Ibid., 122.
10. Elizabeth Heyrick, *Immediate, Not Gradual Abolition; Or, An Inquiry Into the Shortest, Safest, and Most Effectual Means of Getting Rid of West Indian Slavery* (J. Hatchard and Son, 1824). *Slavery and Anti-Slavery, A Transnational Archive*, #GALE|DS0103691627. Henry Mayer discusses Heyrick's influence on Garrison's immediatism in *All on Fire: William Lloyd Garrison and the Abolition of Slavery* (New York: W. W. Norton, 1998), 70.
11. Ralph Waldo Emerson, *Emerson's Antislavery Writings*, ed. Len Gougeon and Joel Myerson (New Haven, CT: Yale University Press, 1995), 67.
12. Insko, *History, Abolition, and the Ever-Present Now*, 98.
13. Ibid., 115.
14. *CW* 10:303; Insko, *History, Abolition, and the Ever-Present Now*, 116.
15. *CW* 10:325; Insko, *History, Abolition, and the Ever-Present Now*, 119.

16. Insko, *History, Abolition, and the Ever-Present Now*, 119.
17. Hickman, *Black Prometheus*, 252.
18. Mimi Sheller, *Democracy after Slavery: Black Publics and Peasant Radicalism in Haiti and Jamaica* (Gainsville: University Press of Florida, 2001), 25.
19. Douglass, "Fourth of July," 371. I refer here to Eric Foner, *Reconstruction: America's Unfinished Revolution, 1863-1877* (New York: HarperCollins, 1988).
20. "Freedom is a Constant Struggle" is a well-known freedom song from the civil rights movement published by Roberta Slavitt in 1965. A recent book of interviews and lectures by Angela Y. Davis has brought the phrase back into wide circulation: Angela Y. Davis, *Freedom is a Constant Struggle: Ferguson, Palestine, and the Foundations of a Movement*, ed. Frank Barat (Chicago: Haymarket Books, 2016).
21. Michel-Rolph Trouillot, *Silencing the Past: Power and the Production of History* (Boston: Beacon Press, 1995), 88.
22. Rather more routine, as Colleen C. O'Brien notes, is the examination of nineteenth-century literary figures' tendency to romanticize and oversimplify the Haitian Revolution: O'Brien, *Race, Romance, and Rebellion: Literatures of the Americas in the Nineteenth Century* (Charlottesville: University of Virginia Press, 2013), 23 and 167, n. 7 and n. 9.
23. The declaration is available in French from the UK National Archives, CO 137/111/1, https://discovery.nationalarchives.gov.uk/details/r/C12756259, and in translation in Laurent Dubois and John D. Garrigus, eds., *Slave Revolution in the Caribbean: A Brief History with Documents* (New York: Bedford/St. Martin's, 2006), 188–91.
24. Dubois and Garrigus, *Documents*, 191.
25. Paul Gilroy, *The Black Atlantic: Modernity and Double Consciousness* (Cambridge, MA: Harvard University Press, 1993).
26. Sheller, *Democracy after Slavery*, 91–92.
27. Ibid., 105–6.
28. Ibid., 96.
29. Particularly notable examples collected in Dubois and Garrigus's *Documents* include Léger Félicité Sothonax, "Decree of General Liberty," 120–5; Toussaint Louverture, "A Refutation of Some Assertions [. . .]," 147–53.
30. See, for example, "Independence of Haiti," *Liberator* 12, no. 3 (January 21, 1841); "Commerce with Haiti," *Liberator* 8, no. 45 (November 9, 1838); "Prejudice Against People of Color," *Liberator* 3, no. 42 (October 19, 1833).
31. "The Eighth Massachusetts Anti-Slavery Fair," *Liberator* 11, no. 17 (December 1841): 67.
32. Also described in Sheller, *Democracy after Slavery*, 111–42.
33. "Revolution in Hayti," *Liberator* (April 28, 1843): 67.
34. Colleen O'Brien documents that in 1848 Emerson lent a set of books on Haiti to the radical Garrisonian Wendell Phillips, and his brother Charles Chauncy Emerson (who died in 1836) published an admiring essay on the Haitian Revolution in 1835. Insko also notes the latter connection (Insko, *History, Abolition, and the Ever-Present Now*, 120).
35. Joseph Sturge and Thomas Harvey, *The West Indies in 1837; Being the Journal of a Visit to Antigua, Montserrat, Dominica, St. Lucia, Barbadoes, and Jamaica; Undertaken for the Purpose of Ascertaining the Actual Condition of the Negro Population of those Islands* (London: Hamilton, Adams, 1838), 61, 289.
36. James A. Thome and J. Horace Kimball, *Emancipation in the West Indies. A Six-Months Tour in Antigua, Barbadoes, and Jamaica, in the Year 1837* (American Anti-Slavery Society, 1838), 73.

37. Ibid., 131.
38. Hickman, *Black Prometheus*, 251.
39. On the Stowe-Kinmont connection see George M. Fredrickson, *The Black Image in the White Mind: The Debate on Afro-American Character and Destiny, 1817–1914*, 2nd ed. (Hanover, NH: University Press of New England, 1987), 97–129.
40. Thome and Kimball, *Emancipation in the West Indies*, 58, emphasis original.
41. Christopher Taylor, *Empire of Neglect: The West Indies in the Wake of British Liberalism* (Durham: Duke University Press, 2018).
42. Sturge and Harvey, *West Indies in 1837*, 224, emphasis added.
43. The treadmill engraving and its political use is discussed in Diana Paton's introduction to James Williams, *A Narrative of Events, Since the First of August, 1834, by James Williams, An Apprenticed Laborer in Jamaica*, ed. Diana Paton (Durham: Duke University Press, 2001), xxxviii.
44. Insko, *History, Abolition, and the Ever-Present Now*, 118.

3

RACE, OR, EMANCIPATION AND RESISTANCE

CHAPTER 10

SPEAKING FOR "THE INDIAN"

DREW LOPENZINA AND LAURA L. MIELKE

> Wherever the truth is injured, defend it. You are there on that spot within hearing of that word, within sight of that action as a Witness, to the end that you should speak for it.
>
> *JMN* 4:271, March 28, 1834

> I am determined... to call upon men to turn and live.
>
> William Apess, *A Son of the Forest*, 2nd edition (1831)

In a widely printed letter of April 23, 1838 to President Martin Van Buren, Ralph Waldo Emerson protests the federal government's treatment of the Cherokee Nation, and in particular its enforcement of the "sham treaty"[1] that would result in the forced expulsion of the Cherokee across the deadly winter of 1838–39. The letter stands for many as a foretaste of Emerson's turn toward political engagement—namely, an embrace of abolitionism—in subsequent years.[2] It is certainly fiery with indignation, alternately withering and pathetic in its language. But at its heart is a troublesome metaphor: that of ignored Indigenous speech.

Some two years earlier, on January 26, 1836, a lesser-known figure by the name of William Apess, a Methodist minister and Native of the Pequot tribe, spoke before a full house at the Odeon Theater in Boston. Apess's speech, published later that year as a *Eulogy on King Philip*, is also critical of the federal government's removal policies. But whereas Emerson's letter expressed incredulity at the federal government's intentions, claiming such acts would make the "name of this nation, hitherto the sweet omen of religion and liberty ... stink to the world" (3), Apess's speech positions the removal of the Cherokee within a consistent framework of historical abuse against Indigenous peoples reaching all the way back to colonial times. As he proclaims on the stage of the Odeon, "there is a deep-rooted popular opinion in the hearts of many that Indians were made, etc., on purpose for destruction, to be driven out by white Christians, and they to take their places; and that God had decreed it from all eternity."[3]

Both Emerson and Apess were important public figures of their era, commanding large audiences with their provocative ideas and powerful rhetoric. To suggest, however, that their careers ran along parallel paths would be to assume they performed on an equal playing field or faced similar sets of opportunities and obstacles. Emerson would come to be recognized as one of the most gifted men of his age—a "major figure in nineteenth-century literary studies" as the editor of this volume has it. Apess, on the other hand, following his scorching 1836 performance, would fade into obscurity, his fascinating career, his reputation, and his body of printed works subsumed by the nation's obsession with rendering Native lives invisible, silencing their collective voices, and fixing their cultural identity to a primitive state seen as incompatible with both literacy and modernity.

Nevertheless, the careers of Emerson and Apess converged on this point of opposition to Cherokee removal, suggesting a brief moment of possibility in the early years of the republic that the sovereign identities of Indigenous people's might be acknowledged and embraced by prominent and influential white thinkers such as Emerson. This hope was buttressed, perhaps, by the Supreme Court's 1832 decision in *Worcester v. The State of Georgia*, which challenged the constitutionality of Congress's 1830 Indian Removal Act.[4] Emerson articulated the sentiments of many, including the highest court, when he wrote that, rather than forcing the Cherokees into "carts and boats, and to drag them over mountains and rivers to a wilderness at a vast distance" from their homes, Native peoples should instead "taste justice and love from all to whom we have delegated the office of dealing with them" (2).

As this essay argues, however, any examination of where the careers of Emerson and Apess overlap also exposes the epistemological gaps in settler-colonial rhetoric that rendered hope of peaceful coexistence on the continent all but impossible. That Emerson himself was unwittingly complicit in long-standing patterns of discursive violence against Indigenous peoples becomes readily apparent when one weighs his writings against those of Apess. Throughout hundreds of public appearances in the 1830s and in five published texts, William Apess illumined the settler-colonial design of oppression against Native peoples as one delineated in mainstream rhetorical practices. Emerson, despite his attempt to align himself with Native interests in his 1838 letter, was, himself, prone to engage in such practices, forwarding a discourse of sympathy that, nevertheless, fails to make space for Indigenous speech.

Emerson's letter to Van Buren, inspired, quite likely, by his recent participation at a Concord gathering on behalf of the Cherokee Nation,[5] establishes not only his tentative engagement with the political struggles surrounding Native American sovereignty, but also his inability to conceive of that struggle without fixating on *voice,* and in particular, that of "the Indian." The letter's aural emphasis is evident from the start. Emerson opens by requesting "a short hearing" (1), claiming of the Cherokee that "the American President and the Cabinet, the Senate and the House of Representatives, neither hear these men nor see them" (2). Insisting that "principle ... in its coarsest form" is "a regard to the speech of men," Emerson contrasts the willingness of his Concord neighbors to listen to the protests of the Cherokees with the seeming unwillingness of the Van Buren administration. "Such a dereliction of all faith and virtue, such a denial of justice, and *such deafness to screams for mercy,*" he declares, "were never heard of in times of peace and in the dealing of a nation with its own allies and wards, since the earth was made" (3, emphasis ours).

On the surface, Emerson's evocation of ignored Indigenous speech reflects the political reality of the late 1830s. In December 1835, a small Cherokee delegation, headed by Elias Boudinot, signed the Treaty of New Echota, acquiescing, in the face of enormous federal pressure, to government terms of removal. A vast majority of the Cherokee nation, however, protested the ratification of this "sham treaty," and it is their voices that are so conveniently ignored.[6] Called on to amplify Cherokee protests, Emerson substitutes his own voice, filling what he perceives as a tragic absence. That Emerson draws upon the rhetorical application of the unheeded Indigenous voice, while simultaneously rendering that voice mute, is not surprising given the symbolic stature of Native American speech in antebellum oratorical culture. But it remains problematic given Emerson's awareness—referenced in the very same letter—of Cherokee literacy, evidenced in "their newspapers" (1) and their attendance "in our schools and colleges" (2). As Bethany Schneider points out in her analysis of the letter, Emerson is only too ready to resort to "bodily metaphorics" that replace Native citizens with white ones.[7] Rather than citing Indigenous rhetors such as Apess or his Cherokee contemporaries, John Ridge, Elias Boudinot, or John Ross, Emerson's generation gathered to themselves the privilege of speaking *for* the Indian.

In what follows, we explore Emerson's complicated and often paradoxical negotiations with Indigenous history and identity. More specifically, we read together two epideictic orations of the late Jackson administration, one by Emerson and one by Apess, in order to interrogate how the sublimation of Indigenous speech produces the seemingly inevitable establishment of settler culture. In his 1835 address celebrating Concord's bicentennial, Emerson insists, "No man spake for the Indian," lamenting, "Alas for them—their day is o'er" (*CW* 10:36–37). Apess's *Eulogy*, however, enacts a future of impactful Native speech, by reimagining the legacy of King Philip or Metacom, a seventeenth-century figure of pan-Indian resistance whose memory "yet lives in [the] hearts" of Native peoples (Apess, 277). Both Emerson and Apess purposefully evoke settler violence. However, as we find by reading their texts together, Emerson's desire to "speak for the Indian," paired with an inability to credit the existence of impactful Native American speakers, tracks the overall narrowness of America's vision for an Indigenous future.

Emerson, Webster, and the Age of Oratory

Emerson does not exaggerate when, in his 1838 letter, he describes the Van Buren administration's unwillingness to attend to all but the most plaintive of Cherokee expressions. Yet, one finds a powerful link between Emerson's characterization of ignored Cherokee speech and the oratorical culture in which he practiced his own craft.[8] From the postrevolutionary through the antebellum eras, elocutionary practice claimed a central place in education, with the understanding that oratorical skill was essential to the functioning of the young republic. As Emerson himself proclaims in "Eloquence" (first published in 1847 and derived from a lecture), "If there ever was a country where eloquence was a power, it is in the United States" (*CW* 8:70). When writing to Van Buren, Emerson appeals to what he assumes is their shared understanding of eloquence or, more specifically, what makes for decorous expression and why attentiveness to speech is a moral and political imperative.

More to the point, Emerson operates within elocutionary culture's common understanding of Native Americans as practicing an admirably "natural" or essentialized oratorical craft. Readers, students, and politicians across Euro-America regularly encountered examples of heroic expression by Indigenous leaders, both real and imagined. Yet praise for "Indian Orations" in periodicals, plays, novels, and textbooks was persistently paired with a sense that Native cultures achieved oral aptitude in the absence of textual practices, resulting in a hopelessly antiquated expression prophesying fated vanishing. Consider the treatment of Native American speech in Hugh Blair's influential and perpetually reprinted *Lectures on Rhetoric and Belles Lettres* (1783). Blair asserts that "languages are most figurative in their early state."[9] Though Blair likely never heard a Native speak, he conjectures, "This is the character of the American and Indian languages; bold, picturesque, and metaphorical; full of strong allusions to sensible qualities, and to such objects as struck them most in their wild and solitary life. An Indian chief makes a harangue to his tribe, in a style full of stronger metaphors than a European would use in an epic poem" (Blair, 137). Throughout Blair's *Lectures*, descriptions of Indigenous eloquence assume a stadial framework, wherein its striking characteristics are deemed "figurative to excess" and evidence of retrograde culture (60).

Emblematic of this, perhaps, was "Logan's Lament," a speech attributed to the eighteenth-century Cayuga leader whose family was massacred by English forces in 1774. Logan is recorded as having queried his white audience "if ever he entered Logan's cabin hungry, and he gave him not meat; if ever he came cold and naked, and he clothed him not." The speech was widely disseminated in print—most famously by Thomas Jefferson in *Notes on the State of Virginia*—and culminates in the doleful question, "who is there to mourn for Logan?—Not one."[10] Such examples of Indigenous eloquence were ghosted by a tragic flaw—perceived as out of step with modernity, the words could stimulate emotion but not change non-Native hearts. Whether or not Logan ever actually spoke the words attributed to him, his lament is prized not for its intellectual persuasiveness, but for how it foreshadows the overall demise of Indigenous peoples, thereby marking the end of Indigenous speech. It was incapable of altering the outcome of settler dominance.

Blair's influential framework for understanding Native American expression helps us grasp a critical context for Emerson's description of unheeded Native voices. In a moment when eloquence was considered a source of social potency, Indigenous speech was an exception to the rule. Its force and beauty were appreciated, even celebrated, within white-dominated culture, but it was also set apart like a cranial specimen emblematic of an early stage of human development. This is exemplified by the section on "Language" in Emerson's seminal 1836 essay *Nature*, where he posits that speech, in its purest, most originary form, stands in direct correlation to a natural fact. "Children and savages use only nouns or names of things," he observes, "which they continually convert into verbs, and apply to analogous mental acts" (*CW* 1:18). Thus, "as we go back in history, language becomes more picturesque, until its infancy, when it is all poetry" (*CW* 1:19). A man with recourse to the "picturesque" language of children and savages, Emerson maintains, is "a man in alliance with truth and God" (*CW* 1:20). This erroneous notion that Indigenous languages lack sophistication or complexity, as though formed within a state of cultural infancy, conjures for Emerson an uncorrupted mode of primitive expression allowing for bursts of poetic eloquence, but nevertheless temporalized as incapable of rising to the level of western signification.

Emerson's infantilization of Indigenous speech left him, in fact, feeling perplexed upon seeing the Cherokee orator John Ridge speak in early 1832 at the Federal Street Church in Boston. Relating the event to his brother Charles, Emerson noted how Ridge promised to "speak like an Indian" and "plain, right on, & fine Indian eloquence it was." But what Emerson found "most strange" was how Ridge seemed to fully understand "the oratorical advantages of his situation—the romance—& availed himself to the full thereof" (*LRWE* 1:346). Emerson cannot readily comprehend Ridge's eloquence as studied or strategic: the performance is one of *mimicry* in which the Indian projects white expectations of Indian-ness back at his audience, a disorienting effect of which Emerson is vaguely cognizant, yet finds "strange." Emerson takes to calling Ridge "Mr. Walker on the Mountains"—intended as a complimentary reference, perhaps, but one that works to resituate Ridge's persona as one shaped by elemental rather than intellectual forces. Although the style of Ridge's oratory is lauded, the contents of his speech, and the political plea attached to it, are silenced in Emerson's recounting. If Ridge speaks "like an Indian" it is still Emerson who must speak "for the Indian." The unheeded Cherokee voice in settler discourse remains a reflection of a lived political reality and a powerful political ideology—a rhetorically common and *highly figurative* way of asserting settler dominance.

An enlightening touchstone for understanding the figurative language at the heart of American settler oration is Daniel Webster, another son of New England, an early influence on Emerson, and a conscious foil for Apess as he addressed 1830s audiences.[11] As Craig R. Smith explores, across the 1820s and 1830s, Webster spoke into being "a civil religion that transcended the political agenda of the times."[12] Serving in the House, Senate, and cabinet, Webster crafted a sacred vocabulary for American nationalism not only through deliberative oratory, but also through celebrated epideictic addresses commemorating prominent whites and events of proto-national significance. His orations worked on audiences in large part through their religiously inflected nationalism, the distillation of the United States of America into a set of moments and men that constituted a holy governing canon.

Webster's *First Settlement of New England* (1820) in particular served as an important precursor for both Emerson's Concord speech and Apess's *Eulogy*, each of which take up in their own ways the historical vision and figurative language of the man known as "the Yankee Demosthenes."[13] Webster delivered the two-hour address on December 22, 1820, at the First Church of Plymouth, Massachusetts, as part of the celebration of the bicentennial of the Pilgrims' arrival.[14] *First Settlement* communicates a nationalistic narrative of human progress, a vast merging of time and space in reverent affirmation of Euro-American dominance. Webster moves from an heroic past shaped by the Pilgrims to a celebration of present accomplishments in science, the arts, and literature, to a prophetic vision of a peaceful, persistent national union.[15] In figurative language, he compels his audience near the start of the address to "see" and "hear" the heroic Pilgrims in their daily struggles (8). By the end, he harnesses his audience's perceptions as they hail the generations to come and welcome them "to the great inheritance which we have enjoyed" (49).

Native Americans are mentioned only a handful of times in *First Settlement*, and each time they matter insofar as they represent the antithesis to progress, to the present. Webster elaborates how the Pilgrims landed "in a vast extent of country, covered with a wilderness, and peopled by roving barbarians" (Webster, 7–8), and how across the next one hundred years, the English immigrants and their descendants faced "bloody Indian wars" (27). Following the Revolution, however, the region's "tracts of unpenetrated forest" (31) became peopled by resourceful white New Englanders, "the fear of Indian hostilities on the frontiers being now happily removed" (33). Looking back, Webster sees a land at once unclaimed and populated by a menacing foe, yet his sweeping vision includes no present or future for Native Americans.

Webster, it turns out, was present in September of 1835 when Emerson delivered his Historical Discourse at Concord, as was Edward Everett, another widely celebrated Massachusetts orator.[16] The Concord speech was the first major secular performance of Emerson's career and, in preparation, he had spent a good deal of time thinking about the stylistic strategies of composition and delivery employed by these two luminaries of the nineteenth-century political stage. He had discovered a pomposity in Everett, noting at one event how he "spoke as ill as usual, & sitting down as if one wd say the mind of man can scarce steadily contemplate the grandeur of my effort" (*LRWE* 1:346). Webster, on the other hand, was admired for his "simplicity & common natural emotion to which he instinctively & consciously adheres" (*JMN* 5:33). And yet Emerson still located a "sterility of thought" in Webster, "and the curious fact that, with a general ability that impresses all the world, there is not a single remark, not an observation on life and manners, not a single aphorism that can pass into literature from his writings" (*LL* 1:337). Emerson was deeply concerned with not only the appearance of speaking with authenticity, but of forging an oratorical style that resonated from the space wherein truth resided—that inner repository of universal forms absorbing and reflecting back the world in its most pure and lucid state. He thereby resolved to himself to "never utter the truism, but live it among men" (*JMN* 5:21).

Given this concern, there were, perhaps, aspects of the invitation to speak at Concord that troubled Emerson at this early stage of his career. To what extent could he fully commit to the expected praise and pageantry of such an orchestrated event? In preparation for the speech, he combed through musty town records and conversed with equally musty Revolutionary War veterans (*JMN* 5:82). Two weeks prior, he walked the grounds of the old Concord battlefield, where the first shots for independence were presumably fired. His companions, George Ripley and Edward Taylor, pointed out to Emerson which famous events and landmarks need be included in his talk. Emerson apparently confessed some ambivalence to all this when he later mused in his journal, "It shall be a rule in my Rhetoric,—Before you urge a duty, be sure it is one. Try Patriotism, for example" (*JMN* 5:87). Despite such hesitations concerning patriotic pomp, the Concord speech ultimately adheres to a teleological format made wildly popular by the likes of Webster and Everett, in which settler history is recounted in heroic strains. Emerson calls out the names of the first settlers of Concord in the presence of their living descendants and recollects how they fled religious persecution in England and, in 1635, made their "dangerous journey through an uninterrupted wilderness" to establish their township (*CW* 10:19).

This so-called wilderness space, only twenty miles out from the Massachusetts Bay Colony settlement, was, in fact, the Native village of Musketaquid. Dominant historical narratives, of the sort in which Emerson was engaged, have instructed us not to find paradox in such depictions, but Indigenous peoples of the Northeast did not live in anything like a wilderness state. Musketaquid would have been characterized by a large number of domiciles of both domestic, civic, and ceremonial use, some of them capable of sheltering over a hundred people and supported by extensive cultivated fields of corn, beans, squash, and other crops watered by the nearby Musketaquid River.[17] The forest leading up to this site, described by Emerson as mired in thicket and swamp, would have, in fact, been cleared by the Indigenous practice of controlled burns. William Wood, among the first Englishmen to visit the area of Musketaquid sometime around 1633, observed how the forests were not dense and overgrown as one might expect, but rather "in many places diverse acres being clear so that one may ride ahunting in most places of the land."[18] Lemuel Shattuck's *History of the Town of Concord*, published the same year as Emerson's oration, also spoke of the Native village as containing "large quantities of open land, which bore some resemblance to the prairies of the western country. These plains were annually burned or dug over for the purposes of hunting" or, as he phrased it, for "the rude culture of corn."[19] Recent archaeological research confirms the productivity of Musketaquid as a cultural center where "varied foodstuffs were apparently plentiful for a considerable period of time—from up to about 5,000 years ago onwards."[20]

The rhetorical act of producing a desert wilderness out of Native population centers was an expectation of the genre in the town histories proliferating throughout New England in the early decades of the nineteenth century. Historian Jean O'Brien (White Earth Ojibwe) writes that, although "these histories of small places likely were intended for local and limited audiences, the project in which they participated was grand and helped produce grave consequences for Indian peoples whose places they claimed as their own." New England town histories implied that "authentic history begins with the arrival of English people in the place ... and further, they might be taken to suggest that these places remained unpeopled until these momentous 'settlements' came to be."[21] Although the settler-colonial narrative might pause long enough to note a prior Indian settlement or record a vague deed of transfer between Native and settler inscribed in some town record book, the dispossession of Indigenous lands is "mundanely dispensed with as prefatory to the real history that begins with the advent of English transformation of the land."[22] As we will see, Emerson manages to adhere precisely to this generic script in his evocation of the town's founding.

After describing the hardships of the "first" settlers arriving at the "wilderness" location, Emerson shifts without hesitation to the negotiations between Musketaquid and English peoples. He relates how the Squaw Sachem of the existing village and an Indian man named "Nimrod" sold six square miles of land to the settlers in exchange for some fathoms of wampum and a few hatchets, hoes, knives, and cotton shirts. The old Colony Records recount how the lands secured by the English in this transaction included "all the planting-ground which hath been formerly planted by the Indians," again contradicting the more prevalent assertion of Musketaquid as a wilderness space.[23] Indigenous historians today question the nature of such recorded deeds, noting that Indigenous negotiators probably understood the transaction as a diplomatic agreement of shared space.[24] The exchange of wampum was often understood by the English as a monetary transaction (clearly Emerson interprets it as such), but within Indigenous societal structures wampum was used for diplomatic and ceremonial purposes, serving as a record of such events. Something of that diplomatic purpose is recalled by Emerson's claim that, in "remembrance of their unity one with another, and of their peaceful compact," the English "named their forest settlement CONCORD" (*CW* 10:22–23). Worth noting, however, is that the particulars of the treaty Emerson cites were taken from the testimony of settlers given some fifty years after the fact, when any Indigenous person who might dispute the claim of a land "sale" had been effectively silenced by the crushing defeat of King Philip's War.[25] Such records, and the refusal to legitimate Indigenous records (such as wampum), were yet another space where the settler frequently rose to speak *in place* of the Native.

Once having recorded the transfer of lands, the celebrated "concord" between settler and Native is quickly and unceremoniously abandoned in Emerson's oration. Enumerating the endless challenges of establishing a new plantation, he asserts, "The wolf was to be killed; the Indian to be watched and resisted; wells to be dug; the forest to be felled..." (*CW* 10:26). Native peoples, whom Emerson previously refers to as partners in peace and as "open as a child to kindness and justice" (*CW* 10:22), are now placed in the same rhetorical category of wolves in need of extermination and forests in need of felling. No specific action on the part of the Massachusett Natives of Musketaquid precipitates this alchemical conversion. It is simply a discursive imperative that Native peoples are deemed unfit occupiers of the land and made to seem responsible for their own eventual removal. They are nothing less than the "'ruins of mankind'" (*CW* 10:30), and as Emerson relates, the English "truly feel that they are lords of the soil" (*CW* 10:29).

Emerson's oration pauses to take one final rhetorical pass at the Natives of Musketaquid when he describes the 1646 mission of John Eliot to the Indians. This chapter in colonial lore is significant enough that neighboring towns such as Natick and Newton, to this day, bear crude reproductions of Eliot's outreach on their official town seals. The original colonial charters were primed with language of Indian conversion, placing an altruistic sheen over their scheme of conquest. It should come as no surprise, however, that people the English associated with forest beasts were ultimately considered unripe candidates for redemption. Emerson relates that despite his almost "perfect form," a Native's "irregular virtues" were found "joined to a dwindled soul." "He seemed," Emerson continues, "part of the forest and the lake, and the secret of his amazing skill seemed to be, that, he partook of the nature and fierce instincts of the beasts he slew" (*CW* 10:30). This racialized language concerning Indigenous people left little doubt as to the potential success of their conversion, and Emerson concludes that "the hunters of the tribe were found intractable at catechism" (*CW* 10:30). Here Native souls, like Native speech acts, are tragically terminated, afforded no afterlives.

Throughout the Concord speech, Emerson's rhetoric hews to a pattern of admiration for the presumably noble qualities of the savage red man, alongside an acknowledgement of his irrevocably violent nature—a stance that resolves itself in a posture of remorse that the favors of civilization could not find lodgment in the breast of the Native. Though "savage" hearts might melt at the "voice of love" heard "under the rubbish and ruins of barbarous life" (*CW* 10:30), it was merely a matter of time before the tribes of New England began to "grind their hatchets" and prepare for the disastrous King Philip's War. Emerson studiously rehearses the highlights of that conflict, but it is only in the aftermath of that war, marked by Philip's death, with the strength of the Native tribes "irrecoverably broken," that Emerson finally gives voice to the mournful afterthought, opining that "the worst feature in the history of those years, is, that no man spake for the Indian" (*CW* 10:36–37). Only at this remove can a tone of regret begin to enter the discourse. To this end, Emerson cites an 1830 verse by Charles Sprague:

> Alas for them—their day is o'er,
> Their fires are out from hill to shore,
> No more for them the wild deer bounds,
> The plough is on their hunting grounds.
> (*CW* 10:37)

The poem serves as a trite melancholy portal through which the chapter of Indigenous presence in Massachusetts is relegated to the past, allowing Emerson to now, as he says, "turn gladly to the progress of our civil history" (*CW* 10:37).

This brand of settler-colonial narrative has been long acknowledged by Indigenous Studies scholars as partaking in what anthropologist Renato Rosaldo refers to as "imperialist nostalgia"[26] and engaging in what Indigenous scholars Eve Tuck and K. Wayne Yang refer to as "settler moves to innocence."[27] Emerson's move to innocence rests on a narrative in which good whites with altruistic intentions were unable to uplift, and failed to speak on behalf of, a people lost to time. Emerson's account of history, as Schneider observes regarding Emerson's 1838 letter to Van Buren, "effectively transposes the tragedy" onto whites, both by mourning a lost opportunity and by eliding colonialism's inherent brutality, thereby producing "a grotesque sympathy separated from any hope of political efficacy."[28]

King Philip's War had the highest mortality rate of any war in US history in relation to percentage of population at the time, and it was Native people who were on the losing end of that statistical milestone. Many of those who weren't killed were either sold into slavery in the West Indies or driven to outlying regions.[29] Yet in the Concord address, Emerson insists, "English alcohol had proved more fatal to [Native peoples] than the English sword" (*CW* 10:21). Alcoholism, as Apess would remind his audiences, was one of the undeniable ills of colonialism, but there were worse repercussions, including the loss of culture, abject poverty, the binding out of Native children to labor on white-owned farms, and the sexual violation of Indigenous women. Emerson, for his part, bemoans, "We who see in the squalid remnants of the twenty tribes of Massachusetts, the final failure of this benevolent enterprise, can hardly learn without emotion, the earnestness with which the most sensible individuals of the copper race, held on to the new hope they had conceived, of being elevated to equality with their civilized brother" (*CW* 10:31). Nothing, it seems, could be said or done to forestall dispossession, degradation, and death.

Was Emerson speaking for the Indian? Could he?

Speaking as an Indian

Emerson seems never to have taken note of Apess's brief, brightly burning, career. He notes in the Concord oration that "the Pequots, the terror of the farmer, were exterminated in 1637," opening new lands for settlement and rendering Apess's existence demographically impossible (*CW* 10:32). But the Pequot tribe, as it turns out, managed to mend itself to some extent in the period following the 1636–37 Pequot War, and Apess was living proof of their tenacity as a people. Though decimated by settler-colonial violence, the Pequots still understood themselves as a discrete nation in the 1830s when Apess received his ordination to the Protestant Methodist church, was assigned as preacher to the Pequots, and began in earnest his career of public advocacy for Native peoples throughout New England.

Another reason Apess may have remained invisible to Emerson, however, is that while Emerson mostly shied away from political theater and the great human and civil rights debates unfolding during the 1830s, Apess had no such luxury—his very presence in the public sphere was always already political. As he noted in his 1835 book *Indian Nullification* (speaking of himself in the third person):

> The causes of the prevalent prejudice against his race have been his study from his childhood upward... The author has often been told seriously, by sober persons, that his fellows were a link between the whites and the brute creation, an inferior race of men to whom the Almighty had less regard than to their neighbors and whom he had driven from their possessions to make room for a race more favored. (Apess, 168–69)

This, in fact, was not dissimilar to arguments Emerson had forwarded that same year in his Concord address, and because such beliefs were so widespread, Apess pitched his public performances as living proof of the intellectual and moral capacities of Indigenous peoples.

While Emerson in the 1830s was privately rehearsing his position against slavery in his journals, Apess was at the forefront of the abolitionist movement and a frequent featured speaker at Franklin Hall—a Boston venue patronized also by Maria W. Stewart and William Lloyd Garrison.[30] Apess's sermons and speeches were firmly antislavery, and he lobbied even more energetically for the rights of Native peoples who lived under an oppressive system of state-appointed overseers and were denied basic civil rights. Had Emerson, who was staying in Boston on April 15, 1834, picked up a newspaper, he would have read of the petition of the Mashpee Natives of Cape Cod, arguing for their rights that day before the Massachusetts state legislature. Apess had been the prominent instigator in that movement, employing strategies of civil disobedience (a decade before Thoreau ever wrote on the subject), campaigning tirelessly at churches and town halls throughout the region, and even enduring a month in prison as he expertly manipulated public media to keep the Mashpee struggle before the press all that year.

Eulogy on King Philip (1836) is the last of Apess's published works and, perhaps, the most intriguing for its confrontational reenvisioning of colonial history. Emerson had presented the town of Concord with a celebration of itself as the providential culmination of settler toil in a wilderness once occupied by a people with admirable natural traits but "dwindled" souls. Apess prepared an oration similarly sweeping in historical range, albeit this time enabling that history be told from an Indigenous perspective, instructing all "lovers of liberty" on the subject of King Philip or Metacom, whose admirable leadership of the 1675–78 Indian revolt made him a greater hero than even George Washington (277). If the mass of town histories appearing in the 1830s were generically designed to compartmentalize Indigenous peoples in a long ago past, dismissing them as savages incompatible with Christian values and the demands of modernity, Apess's *Eulogy* reversed the genre's expectations by carrying the thread of Native history through to the present, decentering the memorializing proclamations of nationhood uttered by Webster, Everett, and Emerson. Rather than celebrate familiar touchstones of settler-colonial possession such as Plymouth Rock (site of the famous 1820 Webster oration), Apess asked that we bury such monuments along with all the unjust laws and weapons of war, recognizing these symbolic sites of settler nationhood to be every bit as destructive as hatchets, guns, and cannons (306).

The first portion of the *Eulogy* methodically catalogues a series of abuses committed against the Natives at the hands of the first New England colonists, allowing the settlers' archive to serve as evidence of their own crimes. Although ostensibly an oration, even the printed version of Apess's *Eulogy* retains an aural quality similar to Emerson's 1838 letter, as Apess cries, "Oh hear! In the following manner, and their own words, we presume, they will not deny!" (280). Apess deftly reverses configurations of colonial history such as Emerson and Webster had promulgated, offering a de facto deconstruction of the term "savage" and bringing into question the practices and motives of those "pretended Christians" responsible for so many demonstrable acts of savagery themselves. He debunks the notion that Native peoples lived in a "wilderness" or lacked agricultural acumen. Recalling how the Pilgrims were first given instruction by the local Wampanoag chiefs on how to plant in this foreign soil, Apess observes that they were "showing the Pilgrims how to live in their own country and find support for their wives and little ones; and for all this, they were receiving the applause of being savages" (281). Of the original reception the Pilgrims were shown by the Wampanoag sachem Massasoit, Apess concludes "this good old chief exercised more Christian forbearance than any of the governors of that age or since. It might well be said he was a pattern for the Christians themselves; but by the Pilgrims he is denounced" (283).

As he builds his list of hypocrisies, one atop the other, Apess seizes on the kind of historical touchstones of settler possession that proved so compelling when illumined by the likes of Webster or Everett. He narrates:

> December (O.S.) 1620, the Pilgrims landed at Plymouth, and without asking liberty from anyone they possessed themselves of a portion of the country, and built themselves houses, and then made a treaty, and commanded them [the Natives] to accede to it. This, if now done, it would be called an insult, and every white man would be called to go out and act the part of a patriot, to defend their country's rights; and if every intruder were butchered, it would be sung upon every hilltop in the Union that victory and patriotism was the order of the day. (280)

Apess upends the dominant rhetorical models celebrating the nation's "founding," demonstrating how, far from bringing a hope of Christian light to the Indigenous peoples of New England, the settlers brought "rum and powder and ball, together with all the diseases, such as the smallpox and every other disease imaginable, and in this way sweep off thousands and tens of thousands" (286). The missionaries "have injured us more than they have done us good," Apess asserts, "by degrading us as a people, in breaking up our governments and leaving us without any suffrages whatever, or a legal right among men" (287).

The problem, as Apess understands it, is not that Natives are a degraded or puerile race, incapable of making forward progress, but that they have been subjected to a corrupt and hypocritical settler regime that preached benevolence on the one hand, but pursued a litany of violent and repressive ends on the other. Apess fully realizes how settler anniversaries and other public commemorations and monuments carry colonial violence forward into the present. "Although in words they deny it," he chastises, "yet in their works they approve of the inequities of their fathers" (287).

Apess's rhetorical recounting of the past—as with Emerson's Concord address, Webster's *First Settlement*, and indeed a wide array of nineteenth-century epideictic addresses—has its eye on the present. Instead of conjuring that historical precipice from which Native people can be unceremoniously dropped so the orator may "turn gladly to the progress of our civil history" (*CW* 10:37), Apess carries the identities of Native peoples into the current moment. "Our groves and hunting grounds are gone," he says, "our dead are dug up, our council fires are put out, and a foundation was laid in the first Legislature to enslave our people, by taking from them all rights, which has been strictly adhered to ever since" (306). Apess does not express resignation in the face of this long history of oppression but uses it to fuel his critique of current policy:

> Look at the disgraceful laws, disenfranchising us as citizens. Look at the treaties made by Congress, all broken ... Yea, every charter that has been given was given with the view of driving the Indians out of the states, or dooming them to become chained under desperate laws ... even the president of the United States tells the Indians they cannot live among civilized people, and we want your lands and must have them and will have them. (306–7)

Ultimately, Apess, the living, speaking "son of the forest," calls for an end to this "spirit of avarice and usurpation" (308) and draws upon his recasting of local history to suggest that the work of healing, if it is to be successful, "must begin here first, in New England" (310). For history itself needs mending if the violence of the past is to be properly comprehended, if Native humanity is to be properly acknowledged, and if a process of reconciliation is to be properly begun.

Apess crafts his oration within the context of a white oratorical culture that simultaneously recalls Native historical presence and imagines an empty wilderness. Further, as we've seen, he delivers his oration in the context of a white oratorical culture that appropriates the Indigenous voice and preemptively strips it of efficacy. Apess grounds his contemporary eloquence in that of his ancestor and his ancestor's just cause in the ongoing struggle for Indigenous rights. Further, he seizes the white voice in moments of damning ventriloquy, paraphrasing President Jackson: "'We want your land for our use to speculate upon; it aids us in paying off our national debt and supporting us in Congress to drive you off'" (307). In closing, Apess imagines his audience asking, "'What do they, the Indians, want?'" He directs their eyes and hearts and speaks for them: "you have only have to look at the unjust laws made for them and say, 'They want what I want,' in order to make men of them, good and wholesome citizens" (310).

Native American speech provided models of effective expression across the colonial and early national periods even as Euro-Americans repeatedly interpreted that speech as the ineffective predecessor to their own practice. The elision of Indigenous history and discounting of Indigenous words even before they were uttered, written, and circulated had profound political consequences for Indigenous nations negotiating for their survival in the face of federal removal policies. Emerson did not create this ideological Gordian Knot, but neither did he apply his Transcendental knife to it. Writing to Van Buren, Emerson gives voice to his conscience in a manner rare among his white contemporaries. Yet when Emerson complains to Van Buren that no one listens to the Cherokee, and when he laments in his Concord address that no one "spake for Indians," he employs the figure of Indigenous abjection enshrined in settler historiography and oratorical culture. Reading the Van Buren letter and Concord address together complicates our understanding of Emerson's relationship to the oratorical culture of his era and to the rights of the Cherokee nation.

Further, reading these texts in the company of Apess's *Eulogy* allows us to see the alternative Emerson could not. Having navigated the waters of white elocutionary culture and the histories it floated, Apess articulates a Native critique of New England colonization, past and present, and it is damning: "this is the course that has been pursued for nearly two hundred years. A fire, a canker, created by the Pilgrims from across the Atlantic, to burn and destroy my poor unfortunate brethren" (306). But Apess also envisions a just future and places the language of justice in the reach of his audience. Interpretations of Indigenous eloquence and activism as beautiful but futile—and tragically so—persist in the twenty-first century, from the classrooms where we teach the works of Emerson and Apess to the news coverage of social justice movements. We look, then, to Apess, who spoke for himself, insisted that the audience hear him, and continues to speak for what Emerson called the injured truth.

Notes

1. Ralph Waldo Emerson, *Emerson's Antislavery Writings*, ed. Len Gougeon and Joel Myerson (New Haven, CT: Yale University Press, 1995), 2. Subsequent citations in text.
2. In *Virtue's Hero: Emerson, Antislavery, and Reform* (Athens: University of Georgia Press, 1990), Len Gougeon finds in the letter the key arguments Emerson would subsequently employ in his abolitionist arguments (57–59).
3. William Apess, *On Our Own Ground: The Complete Writings of William Apess, a Pequot*, ed. Barry O'Connell (Amherst: University of Massachusetts Press, 1992), 287. Subsequent citations in text.
4. In the 1832 *Worcester v. Georgia* case, the Supreme Court found that Indigenous nations are sovereign entities, as indicated by the existence of treaties with the United States government, overruling the state of Georgia's claims to Cherokee lands. Georgia ignored the ruling. See Theda Perdue and Michael Green, eds., *The Cherokee Nation and the Trail of Tears* (New York: Viking, 2007), 68–75.
5. Gougeon, *Virtue's Hero*, 57.

6. See Perdue and Green, *Cherokee Nation*, 137–44.
7. Bethany Schneider, "Boudinot's Change: Boudinot, Emerson, and Ross on Cherokee Removal," *ELH* 75, no. 1 (2008): 170. On the letter's expression of sympathy for the Cherokee Nation as intermixed with racist nationalism and paternalism, see also Floyce Alexander, "Emerson and the Cherokee Removal," *ESQ* 29, no. 3 (1983): 127–37; and T. Gregory Garvey, "Mediating Citizenship: Emerson, the Cherokee Removals, and the Rhetoric of Nationalism," *The Centennial Review* 41, no. 3 (1997): 461–69.
8. For a treatment of Emerson's engagement with oratorical culture through the figure of *voice*, see Andrew C. Hansen, "Reading Sonic Culture in Emerson's 'Self-Reliance,'" *Rhetoric and Public Affairs* 11, no. 3 (2008): 417–37.
9. Hugh Blair, *Lectures on Rhetoric and Belles Lettres*, 13th American edition (New York, 1824), 136, https://catalog.hathitrust.org/Record/011542285. Subsequent citations in text. On this passage's reference to Iroquois and Illinois treaty negotiations as treated in Cadwallader Colden's *History of the Five Indian Nations* (1727), see Sean P. Harvey, *Native Tongues: Colonialism and Race from Encounter to the Reservation* (Cambridge: Harvard University Press, 2015), 60.
10. Quoted in Thomas Jefferson, *Notes on the State of Virginia*, ed. William Pederson (Chapel Hill: University of North Carolina Press, 1982), 63. The speech circulated in popular textbooks, serving as fodder for student performances of Logan as "the tragic hero." See Gordon Sayre, *The Indian Chief as Tragic Hero: Native Resistance and the Literatures of America, from Moctezuma to Tecumseh* (Chapel Hill: University of North Carolina Press, 2005), chapter 5.
11. On Emerson's admiration for Webster in the 1830s, see Sandra Gustafson, *Eloquence is Power: Oratory and Performance in Early America* (Chapel Hill: University of North Carolina Press, 2000), 101. Barry O'Connell, in his introduction to *On Our Own Ground*, argues convincingly that Apess responds in *Eulogy* to Webster's erasure of Native Americans in addresses celebrating the founding of Plymouth colony (1820), the battle of Bunker Hill (1825), and the lives of *John Adams and Thomas Jefferson* (1826) (xx–xxi, 286, n. 15).
12. Craig R. Smith, *Daniel Webster and the Oratory of Civil Religion* (Columbia: University of Missouri Press, 2005), 4.
13. Smith, *Daniel Webster*, 27.
14. On the occasion and reception of the address, see Smith, *Daniel Webster*, 55–63.
15. Daniel Webster, *The Works of Daniel Webster*, vol. 1 (Boston: Little, Brown, 1851), 5. Subsequent citations in text. Smith also points to this passage to underscore Webster's rhetorical use of time.
16. "Celebration at Concord," *Columbian Centinel* 5365, September 12, 1835, 2. Readex: America's Historical Newspapers.
17. In an account of an early meeting of the Puritan missionaries with the Massachusett Natives in the area of Musketaquid, Thomas Shepherd describes the "principall Wigwam" of the village leader Waaubon as being able to accommodate "men, women, and children from all quarters round about." "The Day-Breaking if not the Sun-Rising of the Gospel with the Indians of New-England," in *The Eliot Tracts*, ed. Michael P. Clark (Westport, CT: Praeger, 2003), 83.
18. Quoted in William Cronon, *Changes in the Land: Indians, Colonists, and the Ecology of New England* (New York: Hill and Wang, 1983), 25.
19. Lemuel Shattuck, *History of the Town of Concord, Middlesex County Massachusetts, from its Earliest Settlement to 1832* (Concord: Russell, Odiorne, 1835), 3.

20. Ivan Gaskell, "Concord Migrations," in *Cultural Heritage, Ethics, and Contemporary Migrations*, ed. Cornelius Holtorf, Andreas Pantazatos, and Geoffrey Scarre (London and New York: Routledge, 2019), 91.
21. Jean O'Brien, *Firsting and Lasting: Writing Indians out of Existence in New England* (Minneapolis: University of Minnesota Press, 2010), 1–2.
22. O'Brien, *Firsting and Lasting*, 2.
23. Shattuck, *Town of Concord*, 6.
24. Lisa Brooks, *The Common Pot: The Recovery of Native Space in the Northeast* (Minneapolis: University of Minnesota Press, 2008), 32–37.
25. Shattuck, *Town of Concord*, 7.
26. Renato Rosaldo, "Imperialist Nostalgia," *Representations* 26, Special Issue: Memory and Counter-Memory (Spring 1989): 107–122.
27. Eve Tuck and K. Wayne Yang, "Decolonization Is Not a Metaphor," *Decolonization: Indigeneity, Education & Society* 1, no. 1 (2012): 1.
28. Schneider, "Boudinot's Change," 170–71. In an analysis of *English Traits* (1856), Susan Castillo writes that over the course of the 1840s and 50s, Emerson "seems to have accepted the existence of permanent racial divisions and (more perniciously) that these differences somehow legitimized the advancement and political hegemony of the 'superior' Caucasians." Susan Castillo, "'The Best of Nations'? Race and Imperial Destinies in Emerson's *English Traits*," *The Yearbook of English Studies* 34, no. 1 (2004): 108.
29. Neal Salisbury, in his introduction to Mary Rowlandson's 1682 Captivity narrative, notes that King Philip's War remains the bloodiest war in the history of the North American continent with a fatality rate of roughly 40 per cent of the population for Native peoples and 5 per cent for the colonists. Mary Rowlandson, *The Sovereignty and Goodness of God by Mary Rowlandson with Related Documents*, 2nd edition, ed. Neal Salisbury (Boston: Bedford St. Martins, 2018), 1. See also Lisa Brooks, *Our Beloved Kin: A New History of King Philip's War* (New Haven, CT: Yale University Press, 2018).
30. Drew Lopenzina, *Through an Indian's Looking-Glass: A Cultural Biography of William Apess, Pequot* (Amherst: University of Massachusetts Press, 2017), 191. Subsequent biographical information on Apess from this work.

CHAPTER 11

"THE CALAMITY OF THE NEXT AGES"

Emerson and Reconstruction

CHRISTOPHER HANLON

BEYOND abolition, what did Black lives mean to Emerson? Many white abolitionists had viewed emancipation as a necessary if not sufficient circumstance for national union, but after the war found it difficult to envision life in a country where Black people—or even only Black men—participated fully. Whitman, for example, was purportedly dismayed in postwar Washington, DC, where as Ed Folsom has detailed, after the passage of the Fifteenth Amendment to enfranchise Black men, Whitman "worried about ignorant freedmen having their votes bought and voting in a bloc."[1] Whitman is also on record as having complained that slavery harmed whites more than it did Black people (more harmful, apparently for him, in its power to atomize white conscience and connectedness than its power literally to destroy Black bodies, families, and lives)[2]—an approach to the matter in some ways as oblique as Emerson's claim, which he voiced in his 1841 essay "Compensation," that "if you put a chain around the neck of a slave, the other end fastens itself around your own" (*CW* 2:64). But as scholars have documented, Emerson's views on slavery changed greatly over the course of the 1840s and 50s. Did his development permit him to imagine—apart from whatever salutary affects it might have on white people—the effects of emancipation upon Black people later, during a postwar United States?

Another way to put my opening question: aside from his support for the literal emancipation of Black people, what was Emerson's investment in the possibility of actual multiracial democracy in the United States? Elsewhere in this volume, Brigitte Fielder points out that opposition to slavery is the barest, most minimal measure of a nineteenth-century white American's capacity to ally themselves with some notion of racial justice. Emerson's eventual public embrace of the movement for abolition—which developed beyond the liberal, gradualist abolitionism he articulated in a speech he would deliver in August of 1844 to the more radical, immediatist stance he took during the 1850s—comprised a constellation of speeches through which he aligned himself with antislavery activists such as William Lloyd Garrison, Wendell Phillips, Lysander Spooner, and Harriet Martineau. (As Derrick R. Spires might suggest, it may be that as Emerson endured the 1850s, he too came to channel the "spirit of '56" that further enflamed abolitionists such as Frances Ellen Watkins Harper as the decade trended downward.[3]) Still, many nineteenth-century abolitionists were also bigots who held patronizing, racist views of Black people; is that also true of Emerson? Beyond the landmark antislavery and wartime events of the Emancipation Proclamation, the Thirteenth Amendment, and the surrender of the Confederacy at Appomattox (events over which he enthused in his public writings and private journals and correspondence), was Emerson motivated not simply by the sectional conflict over slavery but by the prospect of racial justice in America?

It's a question that might prompt us to reapproach the last outpouring of Emerson scholarship that gained traction well beyond the work of Emerson specialists—scholarship focused on Emerson, in other words, but that proved absorbing to still larger swaths of the community of nineteenth-century Americanists. That critical turn occurred approximately twenty-five years ago and, indeed, concerned Emerson's abolitionism. One effect of that discussion was to resituate focus on previously underplayed texts out of the Emerson archive—lectures and speeches that had largely been excluded from anthologies of United States literature—which along with new, signal studies of Emerson himself now pushed Americanist literary historians in directions that were in keeping with larger trends in nineteenth-century literary studies, a field that was then reorienting around questions concerning both the racism of the nineteenth century and that attending the formation of the field.

In Emerson's corner of that critical exchange, particular controversies came to the fore, driven by interest in understanding the interplay between Transcendentalism and the atmosphere of protest leading up to the Civil War. Was Emerson abolitionist enough, soon enough? Did Emerson's embrace of immediate abolition after 1850 and in response to the passage of the Fugitive Slave Law of that year signal his abandonment of the more gradual process of emancipation (namely, compensated emancipation) he had envisioned in 1844? Could Emerson's Transcendentalism keep up with his activism, or did his suddenly public role in the movement require him to abandon or at least bracket the abstract idealism of his early essays and lectures? Or—another possibility—is there a way to read Emerson's abolitionism as the logical expression of the unsettling, nonconforming, socially disruptive tenor of Transcendentalism itself? Such questions energized an exchange of essays, chapters, and monographs by scholars such as Cornel West, Len Gougeon, John Carlos Rowe, Gregg Crane, Maurice S. Lee, Jeffrey Insko, and Martha Schoolman among many others including myself. From West, for whom Emerson's evasion of European philosophical traditions nevertheless left him susceptible to notions of Anglo-Saxon supremacy;[4] to Rowe, who argued that Emerson never learned how to be political and philosophical at the same time;[5] to Gougeon, whose deeply textured account of Emerson's engagement with the antislavery movement countered the view of Emerson as a detached intellectual;[6] to Anita Haya Patterson, who connected Emerson's politics to his rhetoric of contradiction that would gain fuller expression with Martin Luther King;[7] to Schoolman, who depicted Emerson as a Garrisonian rhetor even as early as 1841, when Emerson had urged that "the doctrine of hatred may be preached as the counteraction of the doctrine of love, when that pules and whines";[8] to Crane, who traced Emerson's shifting understanding of the Constitution in its relation to slavery;[9] to Lee, who finds in the pivotal essay "Experience" a philosophical working-through that underwrites Emerson's embrace of abolition;[10] to Insko, who argues that Emerson's emphasis on the present instant underwrote his swerve from gradualist to immediatist abolition[11]—scholars such as these debated the content of Emerson's Transcendentalist thought and its relationship with his political work.[12]

One important effect of this outpouring of scholarship on Emerson's abolitionism is that it displaced a much older account of Emerson—such as that forwarded in Stephen E. Whicher's 1953 *Freedom and Fate*—that had revered him as a model of detachment, a figure of reverie at the center of the US intellectual tradition who stands aloof from the merely social or political. This is to say that unlike Whicher, who had revered Emerson for allegedly having made himself "invulnerable to all the exterior life,"[13] each of the literary scholars I mention presents an Emerson who wrestled with the impulse to agitate and to join with others similarly disposed. But something else to notice about the exchange I describe is that in encapsulating Emerson's advocacy for racial justice within his work as an abolitionist, this fruitful conversation about Emerson versus the Slave Power also participated in what Christopher Hager and Cody Marrs have described as the problem with any US literary historiography that privileges the Civil War as the turning-point of the nineteenth century—or still worse, the apex of all struggles for Black emancipation. In a much-cited essay titled "Against 1865: Reperiodizing the Nineteenth Century" (2015), Hager and Marrs contest what they call "the Civil War's status as a terminus in American literary history," a mythos that instills, they say, "a chronology of phased evolution that is belied by the fluid and multilinear patterns of literary history."[14] Such an emphasis on the Civil War, for example, as an apogee that terminates an era of heady romanticism that would now—after an experience of national, mind-expanding violence—give way to a more sober and clear-sighted period of postwar realism tends to obscure two salient facts: first, that romantic expression continued to flourish and still does; and second, that those who lived through the Civil War did not see it as an end. It was certainly not an end to the struggle for full emancipation, which would intensify after 1865; for in its most simplistic implications, the myth of the Civil War Hager and Marrs criticize installs a tale of instantaneous national redemption that obscures the relationship between what occurred in the decade afterward and the still-traumatized and racially violent United States of the twenty-first century.

We can also notice that Hager and Marrs attribute part of this faulty periodization that places the Civil War at the center of things to Emerson. In April of 1862, they point out, Emerson called the war "an eye-opener," which to them is a way of describing the war as a singularly climactic moment that changed everything (Hager and Marrs, 273).[15] (Though they don't mention it, that's a metaphor in line with Emerson's bitter assessment in 1851 that the Fugitive Slave Law had similarly opened eyes, revealing the hypocrisy at the core of antebellum democracy with what he called "the illuminating power of a sheet of lightning" [*LL* 1:261]). However frequent such optically revelatory moments are in Emerson, Hager and Marrs find "Emerson's intimations" that the war constituted a sudden illumination of US moral and political reality "leading Americans out of Plato's cave" to be part of a larger cultural narrative that contrasts ante- against postbellum in emphasizing the end of the war as the end of US slavery and in that sense a kind of reboot for US democracy (Hager and Marrs, 274).

Of course, the implications of this argument touch far more than Emerson. Just such an assignment of exaggerated significance for 1865 and the end of the Civil War structured the typical American literature survey sequence delivered in US universities after the Second World War; which is to say that after 1941–45, 1861–65 became the hinge connecting one half of our national literary history (the Puritans followed by the Enlightenment followed by the Romantics) to the next (the Realists followed by the Naturalists followed by the Moderns and Black Renaissance ...). And yet an historiography focused not on legal enslavement so much as the barriers to standing and citizenship that persisted after the war would hold that, though slavery itself was unconstitutional by 1865 (and though this eventuality was a remarkably swift development in light of the deep uncertainty even as late as 1862 concerning whether slavery would end), actual emancipation for the formerly enslaved, as well as for free Black people in the North—access to the ballot, for example, as well as the safeguarding of other civil rights—would not be forthcoming for at least a hundred years, if indeed one can say it has yet fully arrived. The break implied in 1865 underwrites a false continuity, and our traditional ways of periodizing United States literary history have been complicit.

I think Hager and Marrs draw our attention to something crucial about United States literary history, though I also think they are mistaken to contend that Emerson subscribed to the mythos that presents the Civil War as the end of the struggle for racial justice. In what remains of this chapter I want to show the extent to which he rejected that notion. But in an embrace of their larger point about Americanist literary studies, I also want to point out that the discussion around Emerson's writings on racial justice has formed within an account of Black emancipation that elides the postbellum struggle we now call Reconstruction—the initially transformative but then scuttled project of developing a truly multiethnic United States in which Black people would enjoy access to ballots and equal protections under the Thirteenth, Fourteenth, and Fifteenth Amendments. Emerson certainly delivered many lectures focused on ending slavery, including a frequently-examined big three he delivered in Boston, Concord, and New York in 1851, 1854, and 1855, and as well as their more moderate precursor of 1844, and including responses to flashpoint events such as the assault in Congress of Senator Charles Sumner or the arrest and sentencing of John Brown. But by late 1862—at a dark period in the Union war effort, actually, when to many it seemed implausible to imagine an end to the war that also entailed an end to slavery—Emerson pivoted to projecting a postbellum democracy that included Black people.

Here I want to develop a few observations about what I will call Emerson's Reconstruction writings, but the paradox in thus categorizing these texts is that

Emerson wrote none of these works prior to Lee's surrender at Appomattox in 1865. (By that point, in fact, Emerson was beginning to succumb to the cognitive changes that would impede his ability to produce new texts independently—a factor, I would suggest, that prevented him from having clarified even more considerably his views on postwar Black civil rights.) And yet we might consider these works to constitute a kind of postbellum Emerson canon because, though he wrote them during the war, in each he peers forward to envision American life after the conflict, arguing that the war will have meant nothing if it does not come to have produced conditions for the enfranchisement and empowerment of Black people.

One of them comes to us in challenging form, a text bearing Emerson's name titled "Perpetual Forces." As an essay, it was published originally in the September 1877 issue of the *North American Review*, for which it was arranged by Emerson's eldest daughter, Ellen Tucker Emerson, and his literary executor, James Elliot Cabot, out of two lectures Emerson gave in 1862, some notebook entries he made later that year and the following, and passages from his 1870–71 Harvard lecture series *Natural History of Intellect*. (Later, Cabot included it in still-further altered form for inclusion in *The Complete Works of Ralph Waldo Emerson* in 1883.) Read in its 1877 rendition, the text seems only eventually concerned with the political state of the country in 1862, though it also develops themes that would inform other texts more obviously focused on the denouement of the war and questions concerning what forms of racial justice might follow. But in his own remembrance Edward Emerson connects the lecture of 1862 to another his father delivered under the title "Moral Forces" on a national day of fasting and prayer called by President Lincoln for April 13 of that year, when such perpetual or moral forces were "a subject on which his mind dwelt especially then, for in the war he saw the revulsion due to these forces heralding better days, and in his lectures during the darker days which followed, he dwelt on their sure action, to encourage the people" (*CW* 10:526).[16]

Particularly as a piece of wartime writing, the essay swirls with Transcendentalist phrasing of the sort Rowe argues Emerson had to abandon as he began speaking to abolitionist audiences. The title of "Perpetual Forces" (hereafter cited as "PF") describes a churning welter of planetary, climatological, and other natural energies, all of which for Emerson conspire in a cosmic synergy that reaches from the fundamental dynamisms of the universe into every individual's daily experience. "What agencies of electricity, gravity, light, affinity, combine to make every plant what it is," Emerson muses, "and in a manner so quiet that the presence of these tremendous powers is not ordinarily suspected" ("PF" 272; *LL* 2:291). Most of "Perpetual Forces" surveys a constantly transforming, "flowing" world in order to convey the systemic functioning both of human and non-human existence—"cosmical powers," Emerson explains at the pivot of the essay, that ought to provide "a doctrine of consolation in the dark hours of private or public fortune" that "shows us the world alive, guided, incorruptible; that its cannon cannot be stolen, nor its virtues misapplied" ("PF" 280; *LL* 2:299[17]). There is intimation in the text published in the *North American Review* that Emerson's reference to "dark hours" included the dark hours of 1862. If, for example, Emerson's audience that year would have been preoccupied with Union defeats at Bull Run, the first battle at

Lexington, or Ball's Bluff, where 550 Union troops were captured—not to mention the national disaster of secession itself—"Perpetual Forces" configures those catastrophes as the outcome of longer histories of injustice and unfreedom:

> All our political disasters grow as logically out of our attempts in the past to do without justice, as the sinking of some part of your house comes of defect in the foundation. One thing is plain; a certain personal virtue is essential to freedom; and it begins to be doubtful whether our corruption in this country has not gone a little over the mark of safety, so that when canvassed we shall be found to be made up of a majority of reckless self-seekers. The divine knowledge has ebbed out of us, and we do not know enough to be free. ("PF" 281; LL 2:299[18])

"Things are saturated with the moral law," Emerson insists in the *North American Review* version of the essay ("PF" 280). If the United States had been built on a defective foundation, had up until late 1862 been composed of a majority of reckless self-seekers who misunderstood how to be free, at least one effect of the national convulsion was to undermine sanguine narratives oblivious to what Emerson called "the real & lasting questions." In the midst of the draft materials of "Perpetual Forces" that appear in Emerson's Journal VA, he writes, "There never was a nation great except through trial. . . . A civil war sweeps away all the false issues on which it began, & arrives presently at real & lasting questions . . ." (*JMN* 15:298). During this period Emerson articulates frustration over Lincoln's hesitancy to act on abolitionist principles, though just as repeatedly he imagines that "such is the saturation of things with the moral law, that you cannot escape from it. You may call the preachers of it, but innumerable preachers of it survive . . . every cause in nature is nothing but a disguised missionary" (*JMN* 15:296).

We can pause here to notice how effortlessly Emerson slides between Transcendentalist musings over the perpetual forces of the planet and his assertion that emancipation is itself the crescendo of those energies—for him there is no distance between the dynamics of the physical, natural world and the political travails of human beings. We could even say that the essay articulates Emerson's sense of what practically it *means* to be a Transcendentalist in 1862; as it became clear that the war would not be short and as fervor in the North thus began to flag, Emerson recalls the effort against the Confederacy to what he insists are its metaphysical bearings. But perhaps more interestingly, the essay as published later in the *North American Review* may speak to Ellen Emerson's and James Cabot's sense of what it means to be a Transcendentalist in 1877—as Rutherford Hayes, in fulfillment of his bargain to become President in a contested election, withdrew Federal troops from the South and thus ended the Reconstruction era in a capitulation to former Confederates. Consider for instance the essay's emphasis on human labor as the channel of the incipient and redemptive forces of the universe. "We are surrounded by human thought and labor," Emerson writes. "Where are the farmer's days gone? See, they are hid in that stone-wall, in the excavated trench, in the harvest grown on what was shingle and pine-barren. He put his days into carting from the distant swamp the mountain of muck, which has been trundled about until now it makes the cover of fruitful soil" ("PF" 275; *LL* 2:294; *JMN* 15:275). In this depiction, the farmer becomes the instrument of more extensive energies, like those that perform their labor on more massive scales at all moments. "There is no porter like gravitation," he writes, "who will bring down any weight you cannot carry, and if he wants aid, knows how to find his fellow-laborers. Water works in masses, sets his irresistible shoulder to your mill or to your ships, or transports vast boulders of rock neatly packed in his iceberg a thousand miles" ("PF" 271; *LL* 2:290[19]). We can notice how, in his habit of aligning the massive ecological and geological forces of the Earth with human work, "Perpetual Forces" intersects with the free labor activism of the 1850s and 60s which for example Thoreau had championed. "Labor hides itself in every mode and form," he insists: "It is massed and blocked away in a stone house for five hundred years:—It is twisted and screwed into fragrant hay which fills the barn;—it surprises in the perfect form and condition of trees, clean of caterpillars and borers, rightly pruned, and loaded with grafted fruit. It is under the house, in the well; it is over the house, in slates, and copper, and water spout; it grows in the corn; it delights in the flower bed; it keeps the cow out of the garden, the rain out of the library, the miasma out of the town" (*LL* 2:294). But for that matter, it also speaks to the concerns Northern Republicans brought to the end of Reconstruction, concerns over the potential reestablishment of a white supremacist section in which Black Americans would literally become bereft of their rights under the Fifteenth Amendment, all but literally denied the protections of the Thirteenth, and become little more than hewers of wood and carriers of water.

The Transcendentalism of "Perpetual Forces" not only depicts human labor as a conduit of universal energies; it does so using language that emphasizes awesomely synergetic processes. "No force but is his force," Emerson writes:

> He does not possess them; he is a pipe through which their currents flow. If a straw be held still in the direction of the ocean-current, these will pour through it as through Gibraltar. If he should measure strength with them, if he should fight the sea and the whirlwind with his ship, he would snap his spars, tear his sails, and swamp his bark; but by cunningly dividing the forces, tapping the tempest for a little side-wind, he uses the monsters, and they carry him where he would go. ("PF" 274; *LL* 2:293[20])

For pages Emerson develops this theme according to which power and genius are indicators of the individual's receptivity to the epochal sweep of massive forces. Part of his notion is that labor models that depart from these synergistic arrangements are perversions of or departure from Nature itself. "The secret of the world," he writes later in the essay,

> is that its energies are *solidaires*; that they work together in a system of mutual aid, all for each and each for all; that the strain made on one point bears on every arch and foundation of the structure. But if you wish to avail yourself of their might, and in like manner if you wish the force of the intellect and the force of the will, you must take their divine direction, not they yours. Obedience alone gives the right to

command. It is like the village operator who taps the telegraph-wire and surprises the secrets of empires as they pass into the capital. So this child of the dust throws himself by obedience into the circuit of the heavenly wisdom, and shares the secret of God. ("PF" 279[21])

It is crucial to note that for Emerson and his listeners, all this emphasis on the system of "mutual aid" installed in the world's perpetual forces sounded like good news for the Union and its effort to correct the racist imbalances of the country. Evidence from the review history of "Perpetual Forces" suggests that audiences heard in the 1862 lecture a clear chorus of sectional, abolitionist, and emancipatory tones. Charles Sumner, who was present for the lecture on its first delivery at Tremont Temple in Boston in November 1862, would take from Emerson's delivery assurance that "there are forces working for us which cannot be resisted. The God of Battles is on our side and will prevail" (quoted in *LL* 2:288). Sumner seems to have heard in Emerson encouragement on the war effort itself, but even a hostile reviewer for Albany's *Atlas-Argus*, responding to Emerson's delivery there on December 26, 1862, heard in "Perpetual Forces" a set of projections for Black emancipation beyond the war and beyond abolition: "There were some who ... hoped to hear a discourse with Abolition left out; but they were disappointed, for the subject was 'Perpetual Forces,' and Emerson was the lecturer, and with him the negro is a perpetual impelling power" (quoted in *LL* 2:288). The reviewer continued: "When he argued in favor of forcible emancipation, a few old ladies and gentlemen applauded; but when he insisted that the negro should have 'an equal chance in society with the white man,' even they were indignantly silent" (quoted in *LL* 2:288).

Perhaps that Albany reviewer heard a rendition of the lecture more specifically targeted at New York's Democratic political establishment. Early drafts of the lecture in Emerson's Journal AZ name New York Democratic politicians such as Fernando Wood (former New York City mayor and Southern sympathizer who would oppose the Thirteenth Amendment) and Joel Park (elected Governor of New York that year, and self-proclaimed "War Democrat" who carped about states' rights and "fanatics on both sides"). Such politicians who wanted to separate the effort to preserve the Union from the push to abolish slavery were on Emerson's mind as he composed "Perpetual Forces." They were on his mind as he confessed, "I hope better of the state" ("PF" 281; *LL* 2:299). And they were on his mind as he asked, "How then to reconstruct?"

> I say, this time go down to the pan. See that your wheels turn on a jewel. Do not lay your cornerstone on a shaking morass: that will let down the superstructure into a bottomless pit, again.
> Leave slavery out. Since nothing satisfies men but justice, let us have that, and let us stifle our prejudices against commonsense and humanity, and agree that every man shall have what he honestly earns, and, if he is a sane and innocent man, have an equal vote in the state, and a fair chance in society. (*LL* 2:300)

This passage comes from an entry from Emerson's Journal VA, where Emerson also insists that "if the plan of your fort is right it is not so much matter that you have got a rotten beam or a cracked gun somewhere, they can by & by be replaced by better without tearing your fort to pieces. But if the plan is wrong, then all is rotten, & every step is added to the ruin. Then every screw is loose, and all the machine is crazy. The question stands thus, reconstruction is no longer matter of doubt" (*JMN* 15:301). But even the excised version as Emerson delivered it in 1862 Ellen Emerson and James Cabot left off from the version of the text they published in 1877, as if in recognition that the question of legalized slavery, at least, had been settled by then. That later version of "Perpetual Forces" reads as if curated to speak to an audience for whom the abolition of slavery was a fait accompli but for whom the potential for a rejuvenated national social contract—for instance, in the enforcement of the remaining Reconstruction civil rights amendments and their establishment of "an equal vote in the state, and a fair chance in society"—very much hangs in the balance.

Published in the April 1862 issue of the *Atlantic Monthly*, Emerson's "American Civilization" borrows a motif from "Perpetual Forces" in its focus (again) on labor as a conduit of transcendent natural forces.[22] One of those transcendent forces, Emerson argues in "American Civilization," is "morality," upon which "civilization depends" ("AC" 504; *CW* 10:398). "All our strength and success in the work of our hands depend on our borrowing the aid of the elements," Emerson writes. "You have seen a carpenter on a ladder with a broad-axe chopping upward chips and slivers from a beam. How awkward! at what disadvantage he works! But see him on the ground, dressing his timber around him. Now, not his feeble muscles but the force of gravity brings down the axe; that is to say, the planet itself splits his stick" ("AC" 504; *CW* 10:398–99). Here again, human work joins with massive natural or perpetual forces, but like the axe that leverages the force of the planet, in April of 1862 Emerson imagines that emancipating enslaved people will harness similar momentums, creating a Black insurgency within the Confederacy that will sap the CSA of needed frontline resources. "In this national crisis," he writes, "it is not argument that we want, but that rare courage which dares commit itself to a principle, believing that Nature is its ally" ("AC" 508; *CW* 10:405). His way of thinking speaks directly to President Lincoln's executive power to announce a policy of emancipation, a maneuver, Emerson contends, that would marshal the very forces of nature. "That is the way we are strong," Emerson contends: "by borrowing the might of elements" ("AC" 505; *CW* 10:399). For most of "American Civilization" Emerson develops the case for emancipation along such lines that draw from the expediency of what would in effect be a war policy, a strategy, but toward the end of the essay he begins looking beyond the war toward a postbellum economic sphere in which, again, emancipation aligns with other forces and interests. "The power of emancipation," he contends, "is ... that it alters the atomic social constitution of the Southern people. Now their interest is in keeping out white labor; then, when they must pay wages, their interest will be to let it in, to get the best labor, and, if they fear their blacks, to invite Irish, German, and American laborers. Thus, whilst Slavery makes and keeps disunion, Emancipation removes the whole objection to union. Emancipation at one stroke elevates the poor white of the South, and identifies his interest with that of the Northern laborer" ("AC" 510; *CW* 10:408).

This is a sanguine prophecy, as anyone familiar with the history of Reconstruction and Jim Crow knows. Still, it's noteworthy again that Emerson doesn't suspend his Transcendental conjectures in order to engage bellum *or* postbellum racial politics: if anything he intensifies them. In the coming months, in fact, Emerson would develop this way of thinking about not only abolition but civil rights after the war. There's much to connect "American Civilization" to the speech he would deliver the following year on Lincoln's Emancipation Proclamation, where he imagines that even the components of Lincoln's executive style that had been so frustrating for abolitionists—his gradualism, his prior hesitance to liberate enslaved people in the border states—now appear in retrospect to have calibrated perfectly within larger sequences of events to produce the executive order. For Emerson (as Michael Stancliff demonstrates elsewhere in this volume), Lincoln becomes a conduit of Nature, a channel for forces far greater than the presidency. In "American Civilization," much emphasis falls on emancipation itself, as Lincoln had yet to commit the Union to abolition. Emancipation, he argues, is a force of nature inasmuch as by adopting it as a war policy, the Union can effectively create an allied army behind the lines of the Confederacy ("then the slaves near our armies will come to us," he writes, while "those in the interior will know in a week what their rights are, and will, when opportunity offers, prepare to take them" ["AC" 509; *CW* 10:407]). But Emerson also intones phrases he would refocus, later, in the call for Black civil rights that would form the ballast of "Fortune of the Republic": "Morality," he states, "is the object of government. We want a state of things in which crime shall not pay" ("AC" 511; *CW* 10:409–10; *LL* 2:335). "In this national crisis," he writes, "it is not argument that we want, but that rare courage which dares commit itself to a principle, believing that Nature is its ally, and will create the instruments it requires, and more than make good any petty and injurious profit which it may disturb" ("AC" 508; *CW* 10:405–6). "Why cannot the best civilization be extended over the whole country," he asks, "since the disorder of the less civilized portion menaces the existence of the country?" ("AC" 507; *CW* 10:404.)

Or, to use paradoxical language Emerson would deploy the year after "American Civilization," emancipation is an "eternal effervescence of nature" (*LL* 2:334). That phrase emerges in a last and most powerful instance of Emerson's Reconstruction writing, the lecture he began giving in December of 1863 called "Fortune of the Republic," where Emerson already practically speaks of abolition in the past tense. "The slavery is broken," he states there, "and, if we use our advantage, irretrievably. For such a gain,—to end once and for all that pest of all free institutions,—one generation might well be sacrificed,— perhaps it will be,—that this continent be purged, and a new era of equal rights dawn on the universe. ... The revolution is the work of no man, but the eternal effervescence of nature" (*LL* 2:334). The lecture's emphasis, as its title would imply, falls on what kind of United States might emerge after slavery—the chronology of Emerson's address is thus a kind of future anterior—where Emerson invites his listener to imagine a state of looking forward to then look back. What will future generations see when they apprehend the history of what Emerson later calls "the present time"?

Part of this temporal dislocation of this "present time" has to do with the textual history of the document, which like "Perpetual Forces" comes to us in a form later reassembled by Ellen Emerson and James Cabot in a process of communal composition I have documented elsewhere.[23] This fact of the text freights its various references to "the present time," as with Emerson's statement that "at every moment, some one country more than any other represents the sentiment and future of mankind," a claim he follows with the assessment, "At the present time, none will doubt that America occupies this place in the opinion of nations" (*LL* 2:322). To which "present time" does "Fortune of the Republic" most aptly refer here? Is it the "present time" of December 1, 1863, when Emerson first delivered the lecture; or the succeeding "present time"s of Emerson's frequent redeliveries of the address during the remaining months of the war or indeed after? Or is "the present time" 1878, when "Fortune of the Republic" first came into print under the editorship of Ellen Tucker Emerson and James Elliot Cabot, who reworked it for publication as *Fortune of the Republic* with Houghton and Osgood? That historical moment occurred barely a year after Hayes became President, agreeing to withdraw federal troops from the former Confederacy in abandonment of the Republican promise of African American civil rights in the South. This later context might freight with a rueful tone he could not have anticipated Emerson's statement, also spoken from the position of future anteriority, that "we are settling for ourselves and our descendants questions, which, as they shall be determined in one way or another, will make the peace and prosperity, or the calamity of the next ages" (*LL* 2:322).

Out of this present-tense but future-prophetic disposition he leans further forward still, insisting that "it is the young men of the land, who must save it: It is they to whom this wonderful hour, after so many weary ages, dawn: the Second Declaration of Independence, the proclaiming of liberty, land, justice, and a career for all men, and honest dealings with other nations" (*LL* 2:323). For what "we want," he says, is "a state of things in which crime will not pay, a state of things which allows every man the largest liberty compatible with the liberty of every man" (*LL* 2:335). The moments of this address's first delivery and its first publication juxtapose an instant of hope—a dark hour of private or public fortune, as he had imagined in 1862, for which perpetual forces offer consolation—with the ignominious closure of Reconstructive policies in a disastrous failure thwarting Emerson's prophecy of a new era of equal rights dawning on the universe.

The review history of "Fortune of the Republic" reveals that his audiences heard clearly Emerson's call for far-reaching policies to respect and safeguard the civil rights of Black people. A reviewer for the *Brooklyn Daily Eagle* covering Emerson's delivery before the Mercantile Library Association in Brooklyn on December 21, 1863 (a writer otherwise challenged to sum up a speech by one whose "peculiarity of style makes his lectures difficult to report") nevertheless described Emerson's emphasis on "civil ... liberty" for liberated Black people, relaying that "the lecturer spoke of all the elements of prosperity and greatness we possessed, those of our political institutions, guaranteeing civil and religious liberty to all."[24] After Emerson's delivery of "Fortune of the Republic" in Bangor on January 15, 1864, coverage in the *Bangor Whig and Courier* complimented him for "working out for America a future of freedom and great moral elevation—to become what God intended it to be, a country for the production of Exalted Manhood—to aid in the regeneration of the world by raising social ideas to the highest moral standard—to show the old nations a country where prevails the largest liberty compatible with the best good of all—to hold the continent for the benefit of all mankind—to break off the shackles of the slave, and make our land the paradise of *labor*."[25]

Conversely, Democrats who would go on to oppose civil rights legislation were offended by "Fortune of the Republic." Samuel Sullivan Cox, Congressman of Ohio (later, of New York), who would vote against the Thirteenth Amendment, excoriated Emerson for "giving new youth and beauty to the State by dismembering it." In his Broadway address to the Young Men's Union Democratic Association on January 13, 1863, Cox lambasted Emerson as a starry-eyed advocate for racial equality. Transcendentalism, a dumbfounded Cox exclaimed, "absorb[s] God and nature in man, and makes the soul all in all." (It's actually not a bad definition.) Speaking in a hall "crowded … to their fullest capacity, so that all the aisles and entrances were filled," Cox denounced Emerson: "Do you wonder, therefore, that he makes the negro a part of himself and his equal?" To the guffaws and cheers of the Young Men's Union Democratic Association, Cox went on to describe the "coterie of transcendentalism around Boston, whose most clever exponent is Emerson," whose "processes of unification … proved black and white to be 'all one thing.'"[26]

The Emerson such respondents experienced was not, as Rowe has suggested, an example of merely "aesthetic dissent," and nor did he appear to such listeners to be moonlighting from his Transcendentalist day work. Rowe argues that "when he [Emerson] endorses a liberal political position, he must abandon transcendental principles; when he embraces transcendentalism, his politics are as patronizing and impractical as the formula for 'reform' in *Nature* and his other early writings. In short, Emersonian transcendentalism and political activism in mid-nineteenth-century America were inherently incompatible."[27] And yet for Cox and other opponents of Black civil rights, as well as those more disposed to imagine a changed America in which "a new era of equal rights" might dawn "on the universe," Emerson was not only sounding revolutionary tones; he was doing so out of the Transcendentalist lexicon and worldview for which he was known. And needless to say, none of this history from Emerson's career sits with the assessment articulated influentially by Whicher, who in *Freedom and Fate* would summate Emerson's great achievement in his (alleged) realization that "the opposite and the enemy of the sovereign self … is the community."[28]

We are living in the "calamity of the next ages" Emerson prophesied, the United States to result from a failed postwar Reconstruction. Emerson himself surmised our possible present as he opined, in his entry for November 5, 1865 in Journal DL, what struck him as the timidity of the Republican victors after Appomattox and Lincoln's assassination: "We hoped that in the Peace, after such a war, a great expansion would follow in the mind of the country: grand views in every direction,—true freedom in politics, in religion, in social science, in thought. But the energy of the nation seems to have expended itself in the war, and every interest is found as sectional & timorous as before" (*JMN* 15:77–78). By the end of the war Emerson had expected bold, transformative measures to be undertaken on behalf of the civil rights of Black Americans; "the task before us," he wrote as early as 1862, was "to accept the benefit of the War: it has not created our false relations, they have created it. It simply demonstrates the rottenness it found.

We watched its course as we did the cholera, which goes where predisposition already existed, took only the susceptible, set its seal on every putrid, & on none other, followed the limestone, & left the granite" (*JMN* 15:300).

Emerson's writings during the Civil War projected an enlarged national community in which Black people enjoyed the full rights of nineteenth-century citizenship; for him, the War would have meant little if not to secure that national future. Failing to accomplish such social and political transformation, he states explicitly, would amount to national disaster, "calamity"; moreover, it would represent an attempt to work against what he called "the laws of the world," the perpetual forces of Nature itself, the "rule," as he describes it in "Fortune of the Republic," "that holds in economy as well as in hydraulics, that you must have a source higher than your tap" (*LL* 2:320). His call for civil rights is drawn out of Transcendentalist creed, as if in delivery of what "Experience" calls "the transformation of genius into practical power" or what "Self-Reliance" calls "the triumph of principles" (*CW* 3:49; 2:51). When in the essay *Nature* Emerson imagines that "[a] correspondent revolution in things will attend the influx of the spirit" (*CW* 1:45); when in "The American Scholar" he suggests that "as the world was plastic and fluid in the hands of God, so it is ever to so much of his attributes as we bring to it" (*CW* 1:64); when in "Circles" he insists that "our culture is the predominance of an idea which draws after it this train of cities and institutions" (*CW* 2:179); when he states, in "Compensation," that "the history of persecution is a history of endeavors to cheat nature, to make water run up hill, to twist a rope of sand" (*CW* 2:69); and when he urges us, in *Nature,* to "know then, that the world exists for you.... Build, therefore, your own world" (*CW* 1:44–45), he offers in so many embryonic forms the radical style of thinking he would bring to the open question of what meaning a Union victory might draw from the Civil War—what national fortune he could envision as Emerson tried to influence whatever would happen next.

Notes

1. Ed Folsom, "'A Yet More Terrible and More Deeply Complicated Problem': Walt Whitman, Race, Reconstruction, and American Democracy," *American Literary History* 30, no. 3 (Summer 2018): 531.
2. Ibid.
3. In Spires's account, an increasing critique of sentimentalism marks a break between Harper's poetry of 1854 and before and the verse she would publish in 1857, part of what Spires describes as "an explosion of rhetoric in black writing that embraced slave rebellions as *the* site of revolutionary citizenship not simply in deed but, more important, as sites of citizenship theorizing." See Derrick R. Spires, *The Practice of Citizenship: Black Politics and Print Culture in the Early United States* (University of Pennsylvania Press, 2019), 210.
4. Cornel West, *The American Evasion of Philosophy: A Genealogy of Pragmatism* (Madison: University of Wisconsin Press, 1989).
5. John Carlos Rowe, *At Emerson's Tomb: The Politics of Classic American Literature* (New York: Columbia University Press, 1996).

6. Len Gougeon, *Virtue's Hero: Emerson, Antislavery, and Reform* (Athens and London: University of Georgia Press, 1990).
7. Anita Haya Patterson, *From Emerson to King: Democracy, Race, and the Politics of Protest* (Oxford and New York: Oxford University Press, 1997).
8. Martha Schoolman, "Emerson's Doctrine of Hatred," *Arizona Quarterly* 63, no. 2 (Summer 2007): 1–26.
9. Gregg D. Crane, *Race, Citizenship, and Law in American Literature* (Cambridge and New York: Cambridge University Press, 2002).
10. Maurice S. Lee, *Slavery, Philosophy, and American Literature, 1830–1860* (Cambridge and New York: Cambridge University Press, 2005).
11. Jeffrey Insko, *History, Abolition, and the Ever-Present Now in Antebellum American Writing* (Oxford and New York: Oxford University Press, 2019).
12. Moreover, other prominent scholars have taken Emerson to task for his writing on race apart from his abolitionist texts. For Nell Irvin Painter, Emerson was his era's most eloquent Saxonist, which also makes him one of America's more venerable racists. See Nell Irvin Painter, "Ralph Waldo Emerson's Saxons," *Journal of American History* 95, no. 4 (March 2009): 977–85. And indeed, Cornel West describes in *The American Evasion of Philosophy* an Emerson who "was inclined to explain the human past, present, and future in terms of some long-range destiny implicit in the racial seed and the fated cycle of circumstance" (35). See West, 28–35.
13. Stephen E. Whicher, *Freedom and Fate: An Inner Life of Ralph Waldo Emerson* (Philadelphia: University of Pennsylvania Press, 1953), 50.
14. Christopher Hager and Cody Marrs, "Against 1865: Reperiodizing the Nineteenth Century," *J19* 1, no. 2 (Fall 2013): 259–84, 260, 266.
15. The sentence "the War is an eye-opener" appears first in a journal entry of 1862, though its context there affords a slightly different reading from that Hager and Marrs ascribe: "The war is an eye-opener; and a reconciler, forgetting our petty quarrels as ridiculous" (*JMN* 15:202). Written not long after Emerson's visit to Washington and his meetings with Republican leadership such as Lincoln, Sumner, and Seward, Emerson seems to refer to the irrelevance by that time of previously deep gulfs between Northern unionists and abolitionists.
16. Gougeon notes "Moral Forces" as indicator of Emerson's "optimism" concerning the direction of the Lincoln administration and the country (Gougeon, *Virtue's Hero*, 281–82). Edward Emerson surmises that the publication of "Perpetual Forces" in the *North American Review* was "made no doubt from the two lectures" and "reinforced" from notebook entries Emerson had made in 1863 (*CW* 10:527). Also see the complete history of the lecture Emerson delivered on November 18, 1862 compiled by Bosco and Myerson in *Later Lectures* (*LL* 2:287).
17. The version published in *Later Lectures* replicates the passage up until the last sentence, which reads instead, "It shows us the long Providence, the safeguards of rectitude" (*LL* 2:299).
18. The version published in *Later Lectures* reads: "And now, when canvassed, we shall be found to be made up of a majority of reckless self-seekers: the divine knowledge has ebbed out of us, and we do not know enough to be free" (*LL* 2:299).
19. The version published in *Later Lectures* reads: "There is no porter like gravitation, who will bring down any weight which you cannot carry, and, if he wants aid, knows where to find his fellow-laborers. Water works in masses, sets his irresistible shoulder to your mills, or

to your ships, or transports vast boulders of rock nicely packed in his iceberg a thousand miles" (*LL* 2:290).

20. The version published in *Later Lectures* reads: "He does not possess them: he is a pipe through which their currents flow. If a straw be held still in the direction of the ocean-current, these will pour through it as through Gibraltar. But the whole ocean can't sink a cork. If he should measure strength with them, if he should fight the sea, and the whirlwind, with his ship, he would snap his spars, tear his sails, and swamp his bark, but by cunningly dividing the forces, and tapping the tempest for a little side wind, he uses the monsters, and they carry him where he would go" (*LL* 2:293).

21. The rendition published in *Later Lectures* reads: "The secret of the world,—that its energies are *solidaires*; that they work together in a system of mutual aid, *all for each and each for all*; that the strain made on one point bears on every arch and foundation of the structure; that is to say, every atom is a little world, representing all the forces. But if you wish to avail yourself of their might, and, in like manner, if you wish the force of the intellect, and the force of the will, you must take their divine direction, not they yours. Obedience alone gives the right to command" (*LL* 2:298).

22. "American Civilization" emerged from a lecture dating from April 23, 1861 titled "Civilization at a Pinch," though the later, published version had been shaped by later events (most obviously, Lincoln's announcement of his emancipation policy, which prompted Emerson to add a paragraph to the end of the *Atlantic* piece). See Bosco's textual and delivery history for "American Civilization" (*CW* 10:740–45) as well as Emerson's documentation of his delivery of "Civilization at a Pinch" (*JMN* 15:xi).

23. See Christopher Hanlon, *Emerson's Memory Loss: Originality, Communality, and the Late Style* (Oxford and New York: Oxford University Press, 2018), 1, 132–33.

24. "The Fortune of the Revolution—Lecture by Ralph Waldo Emerson," Brooklyn Daily Eagle, December 22, 1863, 2.

25. "Mr. Emerson's Lecture," *Bangor Whig and Courier* 30, no. 168 (January 16, 1864): 3.

26. "Puritanism in Politics," *Newark Advocate* 7, no. 26 (23 January 1863): 1.

27. Rowe, *At Emerson's Tomb*, 1, 21.

28. Whicher, Freedom and Fate, 60.

CHAPTER 12

EMERSON AND CARLYLE
Race and (Anti-)Slavery

TIM SOMMER

Towards the end of his 1856 book *English Traits*, Emerson recounts a visit to Stonehenge he had made in the company of a British friend of his in the summer of 1848. He recalls how the two of them "walked in and out, and took again and again a fresh look at the uncanny stones," a shared experience of the prehistoric sublime that "put our petty differences of nationality out of sight" (*CW* 5:157). In the original journal entry on which the later reminiscence is based, Emerson had written of Stonehenge as the "old ark of the race" (*JMN* 10:431) and he returns to the idea of racial identity in the concluding chapter of *English Traits*, presenting it as a key element of the unity between the British and the Americans. Both to him belong to the same "old race" that in "Stonehenge" guarantees cultural dialogue across national boundaries (*CW* 5:177). "Race" is what informs and structures the nineteenth-century present but also what, as Emerson's choice of words implies, points back to antiquity and ancestry. "Race is everywhere in *English Traits*" both as a term and as a concept,[1] but it surfaces perhaps nowhere more explicitly than in the separate chapter that Emerson devotes to its discussion—a text that has become the single most important point of reference for recent critical discussions of Emerson's thought on race. The chapter opens with an acknowledgement of the vast popularity that notions of "the power of blood or race" were enjoying with contemporary audiences (*CW* 5:25). Pointing instead to the "limitations of the formidable doctrine of race," Emerson suggests that "blood or race" are "frail boundaries" that ultimately fail to explain historical developments or cultural dispositions (*CW* 5:27). If he goes on to explain English material success through recourse to racial Anglo-Saxonism, he does so with the caveat that "we must use the popular category ... for convenience, and not as exact and final" (*CW* 5:29).

Emerson seems to be torn here between a desire "to deconstruct the idea of race as a 'real' category"[2] and a lingering tendency to stick with a mode of thinking that provides the structural ambivalence of the book as a whole with the methodological framework of a cultural hermeneutics. Julie Ellison has noted how in *English Traits* Emerson works within an "idealistic logic that seeks out traits, tendencies, generalities ... but does so in such a way that he is disgusted by the after-image of his allegory."[3] The fluidity of Emerson's writing on race has been characterized either as a "consistent pattern of contradiction" or, quite simply, as a "conceptual mess."[4] The tensions that lurk beneath the serpentine argumentative shifts of the "Race" chapter point to the complexity of the subject, but they also contain in themselves a condensation of the conflicting views about race held by Emerson's nineteenth-century contemporaries.

English Traits represents the result of a lifetime of thinking through the larger problems which race served as a terminological shorthand to describe. Emerson is struggling with a conflict between idealism and materialism, with the question of whether to privilege the spiritual or the embodied, and also ultimately with the implications of thinking for acting, with the relationship between philosophical speculation and social reform. Since the publication of Philip Nicoloff's classic *Emerson on Race and History* (1961), a wealth of critical discussions of Emerson's take on the question of race has emerged. Over the past three decades, Emerson has variously been described as "a rather liberal 'racist'" with "an unusually sophisticated sense of race" who championed "a cosmopolitanism of blood"[5] or, alternatively, as "the philosopher king of American white race theory" who at his worst appears to be a believer in "herrenvolk democracy among the best white strains."[6] The minimal consensus across these divergent readings seems to be that Emerson was, if anything, "deeply interested in the question of race"[7]—an interest that translated into the wide range of viewpoints he promulgated over the course of his career (covering the whole ground from biological determinism to social constructivism). The continuing vibrancy of this critical debate attests to the fact that race is a key area in which Emerson's writing resonates with contemporary concerns.

I am less interested here in systematizing Emerson's "philosophy" of race than in grounding abstractions in historical and material particulars. The passages from *English Traits* with which this chapter has opened point to at least three more specific backgrounds that are key to the ways in which Emerson engaged race over the course of his career. The first of these relates to the simple fact that Emerson's most extensive discussion of race forms part of a book on England. The transatlantic relationship, and the Anglo-American discourse of Anglo-Saxonism that in the nineteenth century defined and sustained it, was the chief coordinate along which Emerson oriented his racial thinking. The second inference which the textual evidence of *English Traits* suggests is that Emerson's notion of race emerged as the result of a dialogue with Thomas Carlyle, the British friend who features as his combative interlocutor in the "Stonehenge" chapter. Carlyle to some extent "infected" the younger Emerson "with 'we Saxon' jargon,"[8] but over the years his writings did more to confront Emerson with the ugly consequences of racial supremacism than to confirm his belief in its validity. In what follows, I will show how Emerson's and Carlyle's writings about race implicitly take the form of a debate about the concept and its concrete sociopolitical ramifications. The third question to which *English Traits* gives a sense of urgency is that of the media environments in whose context these writings originally appeared. A book printed and sold on both sides of the Atlantic, *English Traits* itself points to the sphere of international publishing, a recurring theme in Carlyle's and Emerson's correspondence and a crucial building block in their friendship. Oral discourse was an equally important framework for Emerson and Carlyle to voice their opinions on race, be it in public addresses and lectures or the essayistic reenactments of these formats (Emerson's musings on the British as the "old race" in the final chapter of *English Traits*, for example, are part of a revised transcript of a dinner speech he had given in Manchester in the winter of 1847).

These three interconnected aspects—the transatlantic relationship, the intellectual exchange with Carlyle, and the media culture of the spoken word—were key factors that shaped Emerson's take on race, and they provide the lens through which this chapter approaches the subject. No approach to nineteenth-century racialist thought, however, can be complete without taking slavery into account—the one historical reality that nineteenth-century Anglo-American race discourse inevitably had to address, whether implicitly or explicitly. How closely intertwined the abstract discourse of race was with the concrete challenge of slavery can also be gauged from *English Traits*, whose "Race" chapter in fact does not begin with Emerson's deconstruction of the category but with a series of striking observations on population figures and the geopolitics of domination. Emerson here notes that "the British Empire is reckoned to contain (in 1848) 222,000,000 souls,—perhaps ... forty of these millions are of British stock," and he goes on to say: "Add the United States of America, which reckon (in the same year), exclusive of slaves, 20,000,000 of people, ... and you have a population of English descent and language, of 60,000,000, and governing a population of 245,000,000 souls" (*CW* 5:24). Emerson has no qualms about counting the population of the United States as "of English descent and language," but his sweeping transatlantic tabulation is ultimately not inclusive enough to take into account a slave population whose racial alterity to him renders it statistically insignificant. The remainder of the chapter presents a more conflicted view of race that eschews the numerical positivism and the categorizing violence of census logic and thus offers a more accurate representation of Emerson's views on slavery in the mid-1850s. He had become an outspoken critic of the institution, turned against the moral duplicity of the Fugitive Slave Law, and would go on to defend the activism of John Brown and celebrate Lincoln's Emancipation Proclamation.

Emerson's abolitionist trajectory has come into clearer focus since the publication of Len Gougeon's *Virtue's Hero: Emerson, Antislavery, and Reform* (1990), which did much to revise the image of Emerson as a politically aloof intellectual. Subsequent scholarship has continued to work towards a nuanced description of the tension between Transcendentalist idealism and social reform.[9] What has been largely absent from such discussions, however, is an awareness of Carlyle's key role in the story of Emerson's struggle with that tension and of his eventual conversion to immediatist abolition. From the early 1840s onwards, Carlyle presented himself as a controversial defender of racial hierarchy and he gradually became one of the most prominent Victorian apologists of slavery. What I want to show here is how closely the development of Carlyle's escalating rhetoric correlates with the emergence of Emerson's abolitionist commitment.

This chapter uses two key texts to illustrate the influence Emerson and Carlyle exerted on each other in their thinking about race and slavery: Emerson's 1844 "Address on the

Anniversary of the Emancipation of the Negroes in the British West Indies" and Carlyle's 1849 "Occasional Discourse on the Negro Question." My close readings of these texts are prefaced by a brief biographical sketch of the history of the friendship and by a discussion of the predominantly culturalist racial Anglo-Saxonism that marks Emerson's and Carlyle's earlier writing and continues to inform their later stances on slavery and abolition. The chapter concludes with a discussion of their ongoing disagreements during the 1850s and 60s, as political tensions and armed conflict in the US were bringing questions of racial identity newly to the fore on both sides of the Atlantic.

A Transatlantic Friendship

English Traits is a rich source for reconstructing Emerson's views on race at the peak of his career, but the book also provides a point of entry for understanding the pivotal role that Carlyle played in his intellectual development. Emerson, an avid reader of British periodicals, had fallen under Carlyle's spell early on. In the retrospective opening chapter of the 1856 book, entitled "First Visit to England," he recalls how, touring Europe in the early 1830s, he sought out Carlyle in rural Scotland—finding in him a friend and ally with whom he could "walk over long hills" and "[talk] of the immortality of the soul" (*CW* 5:9). After he had returned to the United States, Emerson soon took up a correspondence with Carlyle—an epistolary dialogue that would last into the 1870s. This exchange was steady and productive especially during the first decade of the friendship (the mid-1830s to the mid-1840s), when both assisted each other with the publication of their works abroad.

When Emerson returned to Britain for an extended lecture tour in 1847–48, the serenity of the first meeting gave way to a sense of mutual irritation—some of which was later captured in the verbal exchanges documented in the "Stonehenge" chapter of *English Traits*, the book that eventually grew out of the trip. Much of this alienation had to do with the fact that Emerson and Carlyle, now middle-aged and well-established, were no longer just conversing about "the immortality of the soul" but had turned to more pressing contemporary social and political concerns—suffrage and abolition chief among them, but soon also the revolutions that were shaking the foundations of the European political system during Emerson's stay. Kenneth Marc Harris, in a classic reading of the Carlyle-Emerson relationship, suggests that the "respect" and "sympathy" between the two "survived and strengthened while Emerson was in England,"[10] but more recent scholarship on Emerson's European tour has emphasized that the "friendship was never the same after this visit."[11] If the quantitative evidence of the correspondence is any indication, there was indeed a noticeable cooling off from the late 1840s onwards. Letters between the two crossed the Atlantic much less regularly than they had done in the early years and the near silence continued throughout the Civil War years. Both in private and in public, Emerson and Carlyle were championing positions that many of their contemporaries found to be in open conflict with one another.

Anglo-Saxonism in the Early Emerson and Carlyle

Race plays a decisive role in the history of the friendship not only because it formed the kernel of many of the later disagreements but also because it was one of the areas in which Emerson and Carlyle had found much common ground during the early years of their exchange. As a term as well as a concept, "race" throughout much of the nineteenth century was not "anchored in any precise meaning at all" but served a number of different, and sometimes contradictory, purposes in different contexts.[12] It worked as a shorthand for national identity, furnished a method for explaining cultural difference, became the subject of anatomical-ethnological taxonomies, and featured in debates about political domination and economic exploitation. This "comprehensive grammar of race" surfaces with varying emphases across Emerson's and Carlyle's careers.[13] In their early writing, race mainly figures in the first two of these senses, while from the mid-1840s its political, social, and economic implications become increasingly prominent.

Many of Emerson's and Carlyle's early texts are marked by a concern with Saxon or Anglo-Saxon identity, a popular nineteenth-century category that shares with the more general racial discourse of the period a "confusion over race, language, culture, and nationality."[14] When in his first letter to Carlyle, written in May 1834, Emerson describes him as "now the best Thinker of the Saxon race," he uses the term "race" in such an expansive sense.[15] What dominates in his usage here and elsewhere is a culturalist notion of Saxonism. The "Saxon race" to Emerson is a synonym for an ethnically defined transatlantic community united by a common language and shared cultural dispositions. There is also a sense of the political hovering in the background already in the early Emerson, however. In a poem presented to Harvard's Phi Beta Kappa Society three months after the Carlyle letter, Emerson again emphasizes Anglo-American racial continuity, but this time he does so in the context of celebrating the triumphs of European settler colonialism in North America. Emerson here envisions westward expansion as a comprehensive campaign for "transplant[ing] the Saxon germ to ... Pacific's shore," a geopolitical strategy that he sees as firmly reuniting "the elder England & the New."[16]

At around the same time that he was writing these lines, Emerson took up the lecturing profession as a result of his break with the Unitarian ministry. While his interest in the politics of transatlantic Anglo-Saxonism remained, at the lyceum lectern it again took on a more restrained culturalist tone. In a lecture series delivered in Boston in the winter of 1835–36, for example, Emerson uses racialist language—he speaks of the English and "the active mind of th[eir] race" and highlights what he perceives to be the strong relationship between "this race and their descendants" across the Atlantic—as a conceptual backdrop for a discussion of English literary history (*EL* 1:243). Borrowing from European Romanticism and its understanding of race as a "combination of language, soul, and culture,"[17] Emerson here mobilizes the concept less as a political or biological category than as a term for describing the characterological and stylistic idiosyncrasies of different nations and their intellectual histories.

Labouring under similar Romantic influences, Carlyle in his early writings likewise mainly brought race to bear on the domains of literary criticism and cultural history. In his 1827 essay "State of German Literature"—which was among the *Edinburgh Review* pieces that the young Emerson so admired—he thinks of the characteristics of the German tradition as intimately bound up with questions of racial identity. Where Emerson deploys race to highlight transatlantic contact between the British and the Americans, Carlyle follows an analogous logic to bring home the virtues of German literature to his anglophone readers. German writers, he suggests, "speak" to him and his British audience "in the hard, but manly, deep, and expressive tones of that old Saxon speech, which is also our mother-tongue."[18] As in Emerson's Boston lectures, language, race, and nationhood to Carlyle are part of the same semantic field, at times bordering on the synonymous.

By the time he writes *Chartism* (1840), a little more than a decade later, Carlyle has turned to a more explicitly political concept of race that foreshadows the general drift of his later writing. Mainly concerned with the challenge of pauperism, which continued to occupy him throughout the "hungry forties," Carlyle here thinks of a global extension of the British Empire as capable of creating means of subsistence for Englishmen abroad. Championing colonization as a solution to the problem of domestic mass poverty, he legitimizes imperialist expansion with recourse to the language of racial strength. "The Saxon British" feature in *Chartism* as an "indomitable rock-made race of men" that appears globally, "in all quarters, in the cane-brake of Arkansas, in the Ghauts of the Himmalayha [sic], no less than in London." Coupled to this celebration of Saxon ability is its dialectical Other, the debasement of non-Saxon alterity. The outlines of the supremacist worldview that Carlyle's later writings would propagate are already fully in place in *Chartism*, where his praise of British resilience comes at the expense of those he metonymically dismisses as "the stupid black African man."[19] By the early 1840s, Carlyle had thus abandoned the soft culturalist connotations of race for a hard rhetoric of political power that combined celebration and invective and that by the end of the decade he began to apply to the conflict over slavery.

Emerson on Emancipation (1844)

Emerson was familiar with Carlyle's increasingly violent rhetoric thanks to their correspondence, but he was also aware more specifically of the arguments advanced in *Chartism*, which he helped to prepare for publication in the United States. He wrote to Carlyle after having read the book in April 1840, letting him know that what he had voiced in the text was "strongly said," with "words" that Emerson described as "barbed" (*CEC* 266). Such praise sounds like diplomatic understatement, given that Emerson himself had by and large stuck with a more moderate notion of race as culture. The full extent of how his vision of race differed from the one Carlyle was beginning to formulate became apparent four years later, when Emerson delivered the first of his more outspokenly reformist speeches. The "Address on the Anniversary of the Emancipation of the Negroes in the British West Indies," read at the Concord courthouse on August 1, 1844, marks Emerson's "transition from antislavery to abolition."[20] Over the past three decades, a series of important readings have provided a historical contextualization of the address within the larger trajectory of Emerson's antislavery thought, analysed the liberalist roots of his argument, and shed light on the hemispheric geography that his commentary on slavery in the Caribbean references.[21] My focus in the following will be more specifically on the racialist undercurrent of Emerson's remarks and on their distinctly transatlantic dimension, which takes the form of an anglophile veneration of the British as an abolitionist example held up for emulation.

Emerson opens his address by celebrating the first of August as "the anniversary of an event singular in the history of civilization."[22] The developmental narrative that frames the text follows the outlines of a Whig notion of historical progress. That the British have gradually worked their way from being one of the chief forces behind the establishment of the Atlantic slave system towards firmly advocating the abolition of slavery is a phenomenon that he reads as evidence for the gradual victories of the Enlightenment (embodied in the grand ideas of "civilization," "reason," and "humanity" referenced at the very beginning of the speech) (*AW* 7). For roughly the first half of the address Emerson plays the role of the historian, detailing the evolution of British abolitionism and the legal, economic, political, religious, and philosophical debates that accompanied the larger underlying questions of racial identity and racial (in)equality that abolitionism raised. Emerson describes such questions—and the history of emancipation, in general—as strongly linked to England and English manners, customs, and history. What he retells over long stretches of the text are the landmarks of a specifically English history of emancipationist thought and action (from the efforts of Granville Sharp and Lord Mansfield's decision in the Somerset case to Thomas Clarkson's antislavery writing and the legislative campaigning of William Wilberforce).

Apostrophizing nineteenth-century Britain as "a great Empire" and "the strongest of the family of existing nations," Emerson at the same time restates his former emphasis on transatlantic continuity (the Americans, he declares, "are the expansion of that people") (*AW* 7, 20). The historical fact of abolition "reflects infinite honor on the people and parliament of England," who "refused to give the support of English soil, or the protection of the English flag" to the "disgusting violations of nature" that Emerson sees embodied in the interrelated histories of slavery and colonial exploitation (*AW* 22–23). Emerson's Anglophilia makes him maintain a tactful silence about Britain's own historical involvement with Atlantic slavery but it also allows him to hold up a mirror to his compatriots. Out of this favourable image of transatlantic abolitionism develops his presentist application of such ethical standards to his own US context, which he finds morally lacking. Following a crucial volta in which he turns from the role of the historian to that of the cultural critic, Emerson offers a direct comparison in which the shining moral example of English antislavery action puts American double standards to the blush. As Jeffrey Insko has pointed out, the latter part of the address highlights that "slavery's history continues into the present."[23] "Whilst I have read of England," Emerson now says, "I have thought of New England. Whilst I have meditated in my solitary walks on the magnanimity of the English Bench and Senate, ... I have found myself oppressed by other thoughts" (*AW* 23). Against British "magnanimity" he pits American "tameness and silence" (*AW* 25).

Race is a key component of the Anglo-American framework in which Emerson is moving here, but it also surfaces prominently in the way in which he describes enslaved and newly emancipated people. Within a single paragraph towards the beginning of the address, he first uses a geographical denominator ("the African"), then engages the discourse of contemporary racial science ("a race of men"), and finally ends up describing what sounds like a political rather than an ethnic community ("the negro nation") (*AW* 8). Here and elsewhere, "race" to Emerson is thus less a fully-fledged analytical category than an element in a set of synonyms that describe what he perceives as ethnic or cultural difference. The terminological fuzziness that ten years later would cause conceptual problems in *English Traits* already makes itself felt here. It returns in the final three paragraphs of the address, in which Emerson keeps using the term "race" but is characteristically flexible in his use of adjectival premodification. At one point he speaks of "the black race," at another point of "the human race" at large, before ultimately returning to his idea of the constitutional liberalism of "the Saxon race" (*AW* 31–33).

Emerson plays on these shifting semantics of race in the peroration of his address, which zooms out from the concrete politics and history of British abolition to look at emancipated slaves and their new status within "the human family" (*AW* 29). Although this perspective is inextricably linked to notions of racial difference, it is at the same time predicated on an overarching sense of racial equality. To Emerson the philosophical idealist, what ultimately matters is not material or phenomenal alterity but identity on a higher level. And yet, as in the "Race" chapter of the later *English Traits*, the tension between these two positions is left far from resolved in the final paragraphs of the address, which move back and forth between gestures of universalization and othering.

Emerson begins by suggesting that the decade since the legal abolition of slavery has demonstrated that "the negro race is ... susceptible of rapid civilization" (*AW* 30)—a statement which in the context of his liberalist frame of reference is meant as praise, but which simultaneously reaffirms the notion that formerly enslaved people are a separate ethnic group with a distinct history of its own. The address accordingly goes on to spell out the extreme ramifications of thinking of race as civilizational progress along such lines:

> If the black man is feeble, and not important to the existing races not on a parity with the best race, the black man must serve, and be exterminated. But if the black man

carries in his bosom an indispensable element of a new and coming civilization, for the sake of that element, no wrong, nor strength, nor circumstance, can hurt him: he will survive and play his part. (*AW* 31)

Emerson's argument starts out in the mode of a "barbed" Carlylean rhetoric of white domination but quickly morphs into something that more closely resembles a celebration of Black power and resistance. What the passage illustrates, in Laura Dassow Walls's words, is that "the same theories of development that others used to rationalize slavery and racial inequality became, in Emerson's hands, new weapons in the fight against racism."[24] If the *avant-la-lettre* social Darwinism of the first half of the statement sees Emerson speaking as a materialist, in the paragraph that follows the above passage he changes back into idealist gear, with the scales tipping in the opposite direction. What he highlights now, in a spirit of cross-ethnic solidarity, is that "man is one," that "you cannot injure any member, without a sympathetic injury to all the members" (*AW* 32). Seen from this ontological vantage point, race appears as a merely phenomenal form of difference that camouflages a more fundamental underlying unity. Emerson's primarily philosophical argument implicitly responds to midcentury racial science, to the extent that his ideas about racial unity go against the polygenism championed by contemporaries such as Louis Agassiz or Josiah Nott and instead sit well with the monogenetic emphasis on a single origin and common descent for humanity as a whole. It is only fitting that Emerson at this point in his remarks refers to defenders of slavery as "the enemies of the human race," thereby extending the term "race" to overturn the exclusionary connotations that it carries in earlier parts of the text (*AW* 32).

This is not the note on which Emerson chooses to end his address, however. After yet another volta, he returns to a particularist position that encapsulates the "Anglo liberalism" characteristic of the speech as a whole.[25] In the final paragraph, he declares that "the genius of the Saxon race" is "friendly to liberty," that "the enterprise, the very muscular vigor of this nation, are inconsistent with slavery" (*AW* 33). Emerson's terminology is once again inconsistent. The "Saxon race" is simultaneously a "nation," and the precise referent of the phrase—whether it be Victorian Britain, the antebellum United States, or the global "Saxon" diaspora of empire—remains unclear. To readers like Nell Irvin Painter, the passage provides evidence for the assumption that "Emerson's disapproval of slavery in no way reflected racial egalitarianism" and that his endorsement of emancipation thus remained fundamentally flawed.[26] Others have highlighted the extent to which Emerson's "idea of a transhemispheric liberty-loving Anglo-Saxon continuum" was in fact less exclusionary than his formulation seems to suggest.[27] As Elisa Tamarkin has demonstrated, "black Anglophilia" and the idea of a "color-blind Anglo-Saxonism" allowed for appropriating liberalist language and expanding its reach to emphatically include enslaved and formerly enslaved people.[28] That Emerson's gesturing towards this emancipatory potential is ultimately tentative mainly has to do with the fact that what Gougeon calls his "transition from antislavery to abolition" remained informed by the ways in which he had used the concept of race in his earlier writings on Anglo-American character.

Carlyle on Slavery and Servitude (1849)

If Emerson's address stops short of systematically embracing "racial egalitarianism," his celebration of emancipation does, after all, vigorously refute ideological defences of slavery built around assertions of racial inferiority. Increasingly championing that latter position, Carlyle in his later writing provides the photographic negative to Emerson's argument. He was familiar with the 1844 address and had in fact been among its first British readers. As Emerson was preparing his manuscript for publication in Boston, he received a letter from John Chapman, a young London publisher eager to print his works in Britain. Emerson sent Chapman the Boston sheets of the emancipation address and asked Carlyle to help with overseeing the printing. The book contributed significantly to Emerson's popularity with an abolitionist and reform-minded British audience—readers of whose political persuasions Carlyle disapproved. Rather than make his opinions about the address known to Emerson at the time, Carlyle vented them in the form of an essay entitled "Occasional Discourse on the Negro Question," a vitriolic attack on philanthropism published in *Fraser's Magazine* in December 1849. The criticism that the "Occasional Discourse" levelled at reformers as "windy sentimentalists that merely have speeches to deliver" was a thinly veiled attack on Emerson's emancipation address and his new identity as an abolitionist public intellectual.[29]

In contrast to the contextual specificity of Emerson's text (whose full title upon publication was *An Address Delivered in the Court-House in Concord, Massachusetts, on 1st August, 1844, on the Anniversary of the Emancipation of the Negroes in the British West Indies*), Carlyle's essay is conspicuously devoid of spatial or temporal reference—an evasiveness that, as Edward Said has pointed out, allows Carlyle to employ "a language of total generality, anchored in unshakable certainties about the essence of races, peoples, [and] cultures."[30] The "Occasional Discourse" appeared anonymously, with its concrete "occasion" deliberately effaced. The text is prefaced by a two-paragraph notice which declares that the manuscript of the "discourse" in question had found its way to the editorial office with "no speaker named, no time or place assigned" ("OD" 670). The notice concludes with a disclaimer in which Carlyle, speaking under the collective guise of the editorship of *Fraser's*, avers that the "Discourse" was being printed "without in the least committing ourselves to the strange doctrines and notions shadowed forth in it" ("OD" 670).

This distancing device notwithstanding, the provenance of the text was in fact quite clearly marked. The presence of Carlyle's stylistic idiosyncrasies made it clear to most readers on both sides of the Atlantic whose discourse they were following. There was also significant overlap between the content of the "Discourse" and Carlyle's own thoughts on slavery and racial hierarchy. Well before the publication of the text, he had made "outrageous declamation[s] in favour of slavery" in private conversations and "declared the tyranny of the Anglo-Americans to be a natural and just aristocracy, that of race indicated by colour."[31] In 1840, he had given a group of visiting antislavery activists a lukewarm welcome at his home in Chelsea, bluntly telling the American members of the delegation that he "considered their black-slave concern a business lying in *their* parish, not in mine."[32] Elizur Wright, a Boston abolitionist who met Carlyle in London four years later, noted that nothing was easier than "to sound him on the subject of chattel slavery."[33]

Despite its editorial framing as a fictional speech event outside of time and space, the "Occasional Discourse" was thus after all grounded in historical particulars. This applies not only to Carlyle's own identity as the author of the text, but also to its theme and its location—both of which point back to Emerson. Like the 1844 address, the "Discourse" is concerned with emancipation in the British West Indies, a subject that continued to resonate with British abolitionists as they were taking aim at American slavery in the 1840s. Carlyle's unnamed orator compulsively invokes Exeter Hall, a London venue that had witnessed a series of reformist rallies in the recent past. It was the place where the members of the Society for the Extinction of the Slave Trade and of the British and Foreign Anti-Slavery Society, whom Carlyle had dismissed in 1840, congregated. Appearing more than a dozen times in the "Discourse," the phrase "Exeter Hall" works for Carlyle as a satirical target to attack what he caricatures as the "rosepink Sentimentalism" of "modern Philanthropisms" ("OD" 670-71). The editorial assertion in the short preface that the "Discourse" had originally been delivered "seemingly above a year back" ("OD" 670) creates an implicit reference to Emerson, who was widely known to have delivered a course of lectures at Exeter Hall in June 1848 (his final public appearances during his British lecture tour, which were followed by the visit to Stonehenge in Carlyle's company and his departure for the United States in mid-July).

Read with these connections in mind, the "Occasional Discourse" represents a critique of Emerson's abolitionism. Some of Carlyle's argument, however, harkens back to views that Emerson himself had held until the early 1840s. One of the main strands of the "Discourse" is a withering attack on telescopic philanthropy, an attitude that the Emerson of the 1841 *Essays* had similarly sought to expose, dismissing the abolitionist as an "angry bigot" who, instead of caring for those "at home," was interested in the "last news from Barbadoes" and the welfare of "black folk a thousand miles off" (*CW* 2:30). Whereas Emerson subsequently came to realize that the issues at stake in the campaign against slavery in fact lay closer to home, Carlyle took the argument to a new rhetorical extreme, employing what J. Hillis Miller has described as his trademark style of "hyperbolic elaboration" to relativize—and, indeed, to ridicule—the human suffering experienced by those exploited under the slave system.[34] In Carlyle's view of things, emancipation has turned the West Indies into an Edenic idyll while sending Britain itself down the abyss of pauperism. Where Emerson's 1844 address celebrates emancipation as the triumph of the moral sentiment over the sinister powers of despotism, Carlyle perverts the reformist rhetoric of human rights to suggest that "no Black man ... has the smallest right" to be treated on equal terms but instead a "perpetual right to be compelled" to be taken advantage of as a cheap source of labour ("OD" 673).

Carlyle's "Discourse" is strongly invested in ideas of ethnic difference and social hierarchy. It advances an unapologetically supremacist argument that takes centre stage especially in the second half of the text, which sees Carlyle defending a white-man's-burden type of imperialism. The idea of racial inequality is a key building block in his legitimation of the British colonial presence in the Caribbean. Championing a Victorian "discourse of conquest" that "romanticizes... racial hegemony of whites over blacks,"[35] he advances an argument that follows one of the standard narrative templates of the imperialism of the time. The colonies had been "waste savageries" ("OD" 675) inhabited by "the idle black man" prior to the providential arrival of "the European white man" ("OD" 674), who managed to make "the jungles ... become arable" through industry and efficient management, which in turn establishes the colonizers' present-day legal, political, and moral claims to being "the real proprietors" of land and people ("OD" 673). Writing history from an affirmatively colonialist perspective, Carlyle suppresses the history of Black exploitation that Emerson in his 1844 address had sought to recover and make visible.

Like Emerson's address, the "Occasional Discourse" works towards racial Anglo-Saxonism as its vanishing point, but the definitions of Saxonism that emerge in both texts and their commentaries on slavery and abolition differ significantly. To Emerson, Saxon identity is a chiffre for a liberalism that endorses abolition as an extension of the liberal project across the colour line. Carlyle, on the other hand, insists on biological determinism and racial hierarchy. The "Discourse" idolizes the British colonizers as "heroic white men, worthy to be called old Saxons" ("OD" 676) at the same time that it demonizes Black people, who appear in it only as caricatures—a marked contrast to Emerson's image of the post-emancipation "anti-slave" who makes "black or white... an insignificance" (*AW* 31).

Emerson had formed a general idea of Carlyle's views about slavery from his experience as an attentive reader of the earlier writings, but in a letter Carlyle wrote in the spring of 1849 he received a more explicit preview of the opinions the "Occasional Discourse" would end up expressing. Carlyle wrote again after an epistolary silence of almost a year, sensing that the publication of the essay had alienated Emerson, who obstinately refrained from commenting on it. Carlyle acknowledged "what a great deep cleft divides us, in our ways of practically looking at this world"—implicitly suggesting that Emerson's abolitionist views were precisely not "practical" when it came to translating his lofty idealism into new social, political, and economic realities—but he was at the same time eager to emphasize that "the rock-strata, miles deep, unite again; and the two poor souls are at one" (*CEC* 459). Carlyle, in other words, was inviting Emerson "to forswear his resentment" but himself did "not forswear his opinions."[36] If Emerson decided not to respond to the "Occasional Discourse," many of his contemporaries felt urged to do so. In a reply published in *Fraser's Magazine* a month after the essay had appeared in print, John Stuart Mill chided Carlyle for his "damnable" ideology "that one kind of human beings are born servants to another kind."[37] William Wells Brown, addressing an audience in Leeds during an abolitionist speaking tour of England, likewise denounced Carlyle's "absurd doctrine of ... the inferiority of the negro race."[38] The liberal *Westminster Review*, edited by Emerson's London publisher Chapman, was concerned that through his "Discourse" Carlyle "gave the American slave-driver the only aid which genius has given or ever will give him."[39] Indeed, commentators in the American South saw in the text a corroboration of their own views on racial inequality. Framed as "a piece of pungent satire" against "pseudo philanthropists" from the pen of a major British writer, the "Discourse" was reprinted in Southern periodicals and used as argumentative ammunition to discredit abolitionist activism as "Northern fanaticism."[40]

THE CIVIL WAR AND BEYOND

The "Occasional Discourse" was the first in a series of public interventions through which Carlyle, over the course of the 1850s and 60s, was probing "the acceptable limits of free speech,"[41] sharpening his profile as a critic of liberal democracy and intensifying his racist rhetoric. Texts such as his anti-egalitarian *Latter-Day Pamphlets* (1850), the enlarged and retitled version of the *Discourse* (1853), and the essay "Shooting Niagara: And After?" (1867) fed into his political allegiances at home and abroad. During the Civil War he sympathized with the South rather than with the Union, and in the legal aftermath of the 1865 Morant Bay rebellion he spoke out in defence of government violence as a means of suppressing Black resistance to British colonial rule in the West Indies. If Emerson did not take Carlyle to task openly, his turn towards immediatist abolition and his vocal support of the North during the War in its own way represented a form of response. His mounting unease with domestic racial inequality occasioned a revision of his own earlier take on Anglo-Saxonism. In an address on the Fugitive Slave Law delivered in New York in March 1854, he complained acerbically that where actual political decisionmaking was concerned, the exalted rhetoric of Anglo-Saxon liberty was ultimately nothing but empty talk. Taking stock of a devastating Anglo-American record of denying support to revolutionary struggles abroad, he notes that "the Anglo-Saxon race is proud and strong, but selfish. They believe only in Anglo-Saxons.... England goes for trade, not for liberty" (*LL* 1:345).

Such disillusionment notwithstanding, Emerson periodically continued to subscribe to a more affirmative rhetoric of racialized liberalism. At around the same time that he attacked the moral duplicity of the Anglo-Saxonist ideology of freedom, he was touring the lecture circuit with material that matched the panegyric enthusiasm of some of his earlier texts. In one of these lectures, "The Anglo-American"—delivered between 1852 and 1855 on various occasions and under the alternative titles "The Anglo-Saxon" and "Anglo-Saxon Race"—he once again speaks affirmatively of the "industrious liberty-loving Saxon" (*LL* 1:293). Where in the Fugitive Slave Law address the "selfish" Anglo-Saxons figure as the enemy of democratic revolutions, in the lecture they are characterized by a "decided preference ... for civil liberty" (*LL* 1:293). Even as Emerson was growing uncomfortable with the wider implications of racially inflected self-congratulation, he never fully turned his back on the transatlantic Anglo-Saxonism that had informed his thinking since the early 1830s.

Likely motivated by a "willingness to avoid acerbic personal confrontations on issues of disagreement,"[42] Emerson decided against publicly challenging Carlyle on the inhumanity of his worldview. In the 1863 lecture "Fortune of the Republic," he notes disapprovingly that Carlyle's failure to support the Union during the War demonstrated that he was "politically a fatalist," but this criticism is drowned out in Emerson's praise of Carlyle as Britain's "ablest living writer" (*AW* 141). In a journal entry the following year, he excuses Carlyle's "proslavery whim" for similar reasons as a "puerility" for which allowances needed to be made "on the credit of ... [his] talent" (*JMN* 15:429). It was in the 1856 *English Traits* that Emerson had come closest to a refutation of Carlyle's views. With all its conflicted provisionality, the book's treatment of race called into question the axiomatic certainties about racial purity, superiority, and power that the "Occasional Discourse" propounded. When Emerson presents himself as Carlyle's interlocutor in the "Stonehenge" chapter, his common-sense engagement with the latter's idiosyncratic musings stages a performative enactment of argumentative resistance. As such, it pays tribute to Emerson and Carlyle's lifelong conversation, a transatlantic exchange in which race played a key role as an abstract discourse with tangible socio-political consequences.

Notes

1. Christopher Hanlon, "'The Old Race Are All Gone': Transatlantic Bloodlines and *English Traits*," *American Literary History* 19, no. 4 (2007): 800–23, 804.
2. Laura Dassow Walls, *Emerson's Life in Science: The Culture of Truth* (Ithaca, NY: Cornell University Press, 2003), 184.
3. Julie Ellison, "The Edge of Urbanity: Emerson's *English Traits*," *ESQ* 32, no. 2 (1986): 96–109, 103.
4. Anita Haya Patterson, *From Emerson to King: Democracy, Race, and the Politics of Protest* (New York: Oxford University Press, 1997), 145; Johannes Voelz, *Transcendental Resistance: The New Americanists and Emerson's Challenge* (Hanover, NH: Dartmouth College Press, 2010), 224.
5. Cornel West, *The American Evasion of Philosophy: A Genealogy of Pragmatism* (Madison: University of Wisconsin Press, 1989), 34; Neal Dolan, *Emerson's Liberalism* (Madison: University of Wisconsin Press, 2009), 265; Ian Finseth, "Evolution, Cosmopolitanism, and Emerson's Antislavery Politics," *American Literature* 77, no. 4 (2005): 729–60, 731.
6. Nell Irvin Painter, *The History of White People* (New York: Norton, 2010), 151; Christopher Newfield, *The Emerson Effect: Individualism and Submission in America* (Chicago: University of Chicago Press, 1996), 193.
7. Len Gougeon, "Race," in *Ralph Waldo Emerson in Context*, ed. Wesley T. Mott (Cambridge: Cambridge University Press, 2014), 196–203, 197.
8. Painter, *History of White People*, 159.
9. See, for example, the contributions collected in T. Gregory Garvey, ed., *The Emerson Dilemma: Essays on Emerson and Social Reform* (Athens: University of Georgia Press, 2001).
10. Kenneth Marc Harris, *Carlyle and Emerson: Their Long Debate* (Cambridge, MA: Harvard University Press, 1978), 109.
11. Daniel R. Koch, *Ralph Waldo Emerson in Europe: Class, Race, and Revolution in the Making of an American Thinker* (London: I. B. Tauris, 2012), 18.

12. Robert J. C. Young, *The Idea of English Ethnicity* (Malden, MA: Blackwell, 2008), 43.
13. Peter J. Kitson, "Race," in *A Handbook of Romanticism Studies*, ed. Joel Faflak and Julia M. Wright (Malden, MA: Wiley-Blackwell, 2012), 289–306, 291.
14. Reginald Horsman, *Race and Manifest Destiny: The Origins of American Racial Anglo-Saxonism* (Cambridge, MA: Harvard University Press, 1981), 302.
15. Emerson and Carlyle, *The Correspondence of Emerson and Carlyle*, ed. Joseph Slater (New York: Columbia University Press, 1964), 100 (hereafter cited parenthetically as *CEC*).
16. Emerson, *Collected Poems and Translations*, ed. Harold Bloom and Paul Kane (New York: Library of America, 1994), 350.
17. Ivan Hannaford, *Race: The History of an Idea in the West* (Baltimore, MD: Johns Hopkins University Press, 1996), 244.
18. Carlyle, "State of German Literature," *Edinburgh Review* 46, no. 92 (October 1827): 304–51, 351.
19. Carlyle, *Chartism* (London: James Fraser, 1840), 30, 75, 108.
20. Len Gougeon, *Virtue's Hero: Emerson, Antislavery, and Reform* (Athens: University of Georgia Press, 1990), 85.
21. See, respectively, Gougeon, *Virtue's Hero*, 73–85; Dolan, *Emerson's Liberalism*, 194–221; and Martha Schoolman, *Abolitionist Geographies* (Minneapolis: University of Minnesota Press, 2014), 83–97.
22. Emerson, *Antislavery Writings*, ed. Len Gougeon and Joel Myerson (New Haven, CT: Yale University Press, 1995), 7 (hereafter cited parenthetically as *AW*).
23. Jeffrey Insko, *History, Abolition, and the Ever-Present Now in Antebellum American Writing* (New York: Oxford University Press, 2018), 116.
24. Walls, *Emerson's Life in Science*, 187.
25. Dolan, *Emerson's Liberalism*, 221.
26. Painter, *History of White People*, 186.
27. Lawrence Buell, *Emerson* (Cambridge, MA: Harvard University Press, 2003), 261.
28. Elisa Tamarkin, *Anglophilia: Deference, Devotion, and Antebellum America* (Chicago: University of Chicago Press, 2008), 236, 240.
29. Carlyle, "Occasional Discourse on the Negro Question," *Fraser's Magazine* 40, no. 240 (December 1849): 670–79, 672 (hereafter cited parenthetically as "OD").
30. Edward W. Said, *Culture and Imperialism* (London: Chatto and Windus, 1993), 123.
31. Henry Crabb Robinson, *On Books and Their Writers*, ed. Edith J. Morley, 3 vols. (London: Dent, 1938), 2:542 (Crabb Robinson recalls a dinner spent in Carlyle's company in 1837).
32. Carlyle, *The Collected Letters of Thomas and Jane Welsh Carlyle*, ed. Charles Richard Sanders et al., 50 vols. (Durham, NC: Duke University Press, 1970–2022), 12:254.
33. Elizur Wright, "Thomas Carlyle," *Congregational Journal* 6, no. 276 (23 April 1846): 1.
34. J. Hillis Miller, "'Hieroglyphical Truth' in *Sartor Resartus*: Carlyle and the Language of Parable," in *Victorian Perspectives: Six Essays*, ed. John Clubbe and Jerome Meckier (Basingstoke: Macmillan, 1989), 1–20, 2.
35. Jude V. Nixon, "Racialism and the Politics of Emancipation in Carlyle's 'Occasional Discourse on the Nigger Question,'" *Carlyle Studies Annual* 16 (1996): 89–108, 91.
36. Elisa Tamarkin, "Why Forgive Carlyle?," *Representations* 134 (2016): 64–92, 67.
37. John Stuart Mill, "The Negro Question," *Fraser's Magazine* 41, no. 241 (January 1850): 25–31, 29.
38. "Slavery in America," *Leeds Mercury*, 19 January 1850, 7.

39. William Edward Forster, "British Philanthropy and Jamaica Distress," *Westminster Review* 59, no. 115 (April 1853): 171–89, 177.
40. "Carlyle on West India Emancipation," *DeBow's Review* 8, no. 6 (June 1850): 527–38, 527.
41. Helen Small, "Speech beyond Toleration: On Carlyle and Moral Controversialism Now," *New Literary History* 48, no. 3 (2017): 531–54, 531.
42. Len Gougeon, "Emerson, Carlyle, and the Civil War," *New England Quarterly* 62, no. 3 (1989): 403–23, 423.

CHAPTER 13

NATURE'S PRESIDENT

Emerson on Emancipation and Executive Power

MICHAEL STANCLIFF

WHEN news of Lincoln's Emancipation Proclamation reached the Boston Music Hall late on January 1, 1863, Emerson marked the occasion by reading "Boston Hymn." The conceit of the poem receives and responds to the proclamation as the "word of the Lord," hyperbolically casting the president himself in a divine light. And yet, his praise of Lincoln forms an idiosyncratic thread within the tradition of Lincoln love, ensconcing the president in Emerson's canon of representative men. The political recreation myth of "Boston Hymn" evokes Lincoln only by implication, so perfectly does the executive order channel nature's dictates; in this poem, Lincoln is a conduit for awesome forces to which even his exceptional individual personhood is epiphenomenal. The inspired political word reveals the larger script of a primordial geographic creation, "which I hid," the divine voice declares, "of old time in the West" (*CW* 9:381). This essay dwells in part on Emerson's praise for Lincoln as a representative man for democracy, a figure in whom he discerns the embodied convergence of natural forces and the spirit of emancipation. The Western orientation of the poem's geography, however, recalls a previous presidential figure Emerson admired before his embrace of Lincoln, John C. Fremont, whose Western exploits as explorer, naturalist, and militarist in the 1840s and 50s captured the attention of an extensive reading public and the new Republican Party seeking its first presidential candidate. Though he did not record the matter either in his journal or his extant letters, Emerson was appointed an alternate Massachusetts delegate for the 1856 Republican Convention in Philadelphia, which nominated Fremont. Despite the urging of his friend, poet and Republican organizer John Greenleaf Whittier, Emerson did not attend the convention.

Nor does Emerson seem to have offered a public endorsement of Fremont, but that election year, the expansionist platform of the 1856 Republican Party certainly aligned with Emerson's anatomy of "English genius" in his volume *English Traits*, a book that legitimated—if obliquely—the Republican free-soil platform as the continuance of Anglo-Saxon global preeminence in industry, trade, and colonial geopolitics (*CW*

5:229). Finding the precedent for North American free-soil democracy and imperial expansion in the figure of the English Saxon cultivator of lands and assimilator of cultures, Emerson enacts a striking variation of the antebellum historiographic framework Christopher Hanlon has delineated as "Atlantic sectionalism" by lights of which Unionists and Confederates assumed political identities and made appeals to moral authority on the basis of "complicated engagements with various constructions of English history, race, geography and political economy."[1] Published four years later, on the brink of civil war, *The Conduct of Life* extends his study of North Atlantic character, tacitly affirming the geopolitical power politics Fremont exemplified for Republican campaigners in 1856. In the chapter titled "Power," Emerson invites a new kind of politician, an outsider from the Western territories, thus harkening back to Fremont's domineering example and also towards Lincoln, whom Emerson would denominate as a Westerner.

Beginning the story of Emerson's ambivalent Republicanism with Fremont's candidacy writes large the intertwining of Republicanism, Western expansionism, and genocide under a certain Emersonian legitimation, which demonstrates more fully the (de)colonial stakes of Emerson's emancipationist ceremony in "Boston Hymn." The poem's canonization of Lincoln obscures the history of settler-colonial violence, as does our ongoing culture of emancipationist exceptionalism.[2] Of course, Emerson had long held to nature's overmastering of political distinctions. As he claims in the 1844 essay, "Politics," "Nature is not democratic nor limited-monarchical, but despotic, and will not be fooled or abated of any jot of her authority." Such maxims evince a cold clarity regarding the violence of nature as a relational arbitrator. Even as Emerson made his tentative way first as a free-soiler and then as a Republican, he found political legitimacy not in democratic consensus, and certainly not in any political party but in the power and potential of the North American continent itself.

In *Conduct of Life*, Emerson returns repeatedly to the moral duty of reconciling the "despotism of race with liberty," a gesture with little rhetorical force in comparison to the layered metaphors by which he conveys the violence of "Providence" and its "rude" manner of unfolding through human agency, the attributes of which he likens to the "habit of snake and spider, the snap of the tiger and other leapers ... You have just dined, and however scrupulously the slaughterhouse is concealed in the graceful distance of miles, there is complicity, expensive races,—race living at the expense of race" (*CW* 6:4).

Emerson's canny slaughterhouse metaphor of 1860 registers the violent displacement Fremont's biographers elided in 1856. A paramilitary instigator of the United States' war against Mexico and the perpetrator of genocidal violence against Indigenous peoples in California, Fremont was nonetheless celebrated in Republican campaign biographies as an exemplar of frontier diplomacy and racial egalitarianism. Whatever ineffectual scruples regarding Indigenous dispossession and war against Mexico he espoused over the course of the 1830s and 40s, any account of Emerson's theory of democracy must address his reverence for power, its affective forces, and its spatial elaboration. The portraits of Fremont drawn by several Republican biographers in 1856 wax Emersonian in their admiration for the arts of exploration, a martial conception of democratic progress unfolding in the West, reaching for superlatives the attributes of great-man magnetism. For one, biographer and Republican Party founder John Bigelow praises Fremont as a martial force for democracy, a hero who "emancipated an empire from Mexican tyranny" and who by biographer Charles W. Upham's account "subdued by his talk and manner" Indigenous interlocutors otherwise bent on "attacking the whites."[3] In what follows, I focus on similar linkages of emancipation and Indigenous dispossession, which shaped key themes in Emerson's late writing.

A longer view of Emerson's embrace of emancipation remains a subject of limited critical attention, the study of his political writing and oratory being overwhelmingly devoted to his abolitionism. My goal is to refocus the conversation in order to trace Emerson's engagement with a line of thinking that connects Fremont to Lincoln with regard to the co-functionally of emancipation and Western expansion. This chapter thus places Emerson in the context of the early Republican Party's agenda—at the intersection, in other words, of emancipation and settlement in the West. This perspective on Emerson's democratic thought responds to Nell Irvin Painter's assertion that his Anglo-Saxonism would contribute to modern formations of racial whiteness. Emerson's Republican affiliations offer a race-critical lens on the transition from abolitionism to emancipation and from Anglo-Saxon "chauvinism" (using Painter's preferred term in her analysis of Emerson's 1856 *English Traits*) to the legal codes of race in post-emancipation democracy.[4]

Free-Soil (Race) Nationalism

Whittier's letter urging Emerson to attend the National Republican Convention suggests the sense of fervent possibility Republican organizers and partisans placed in Fremont's candidacy. Whittier charges Emerson with the "public duty" of attending the convention. "I drop this line to urge thee to go [Massachusetts governor, George Boutwell's] his place," he writes: "It is a great occasion; the most important public duty which can occur in a life-time. By all means go."[5] He closes by offering Emerson a "thousand thanks" for his speech a month earlier at a Concord meeting held in response to the beating on the senate floor of Charles Sumner by South Carolina Representative, Senator Preston Brooks. Judging from the text of Emerson's speech and his support of the proposed resolution, Whittier's appeal was timely. As Eric Foner notes, Brooks's caning of Sumner proved a tipping point for Republicans Whiggishly reluctant to support Fremont. Emerson's Concord speech decries the Brooks assault in the stark terms of an historic conflict.[6] "I do not see how a barbarous community and a civilized community can constitute one state," Emerson declares, partaking of the escalating end-of-the-republic recriminations that animated the election of 1856 amidst intensifying sectional conflict in the Kansas Territory (*CWE* 11:247).

Prior to Lincoln's Preliminary Emancipation Proclamation of 1862 and Emerson's passionate praise for this executive order, he criticized Lincoln as a compromising, tentative commander-in-chief. During the same period, Emerson's journal entries recall Fremont's candidacy in 1856 as an exemplar with which the Lincoln administration compared unfavorably. Emerson records his estimation of Fremont in his journal in November of 1862 at a moment when Lincoln, at least publicly, still opposed emancipation. In August of the previous year, as Military Commander of the West, Fremont had declared martial law in Missouri, stipulating that "slaves ... are hereby declared free men." Lincoln would remand the order, subsequently removing Fremont from command. Emerson's journal entry registers the president's tendencies in rueful tones. "When he puts one into office as Fremont he takes care to neutralize him" with the appointment of "a democrat or a Kentuckian who will thwart him" (*JMN* 15:297). After emancipation and the vindication of Lincoln's virtue, at least in his journal, Emerson would still reflect on Fremont's prescience. "Fremont was ... superseded in 1861, for what his superseders are achieving in 1863."[7] In his public praise Emerson casts Lincoln as the figurehead of a moral vanguard; but in his journals at the advent of emancipation, Lincoln is late for destiny, and Fremont is right on time.

Whittier might have been encouraged in his attempt to organize Emerson by the latter's support of John Gorham Palfrey's 1851 run for a Congressional seat as a free-soil candidate, which Len Gougeon documents. In 1851, Emerson had delivered his "The Fugitive Slave Law" address in his own Middlesex district.[8] His free-soil confidence, one predictive trajectory of this speech, proclaims an expansive national genius much like the one he would ascribe to Fremont in 1862. "Everything invites emancipation. The grandeur of the design, the vast stake we hold." In answer to those who consider emancipation beyond political, social, or economic plausibility, Emerson declares that "nothing is impracticable to this nation, which it shall set itself to do. Were ever men so endowed, so placed, so weaponed? Their power of territory seconded by a genius equal to every work. By new arts the earth is subdued, roaded, tunnelled, telegraphed." The nation capable of "subduing the earth" is thus also capable, in Emerson's estimation, of ending slavery.

This claiming of the "power of territory" as the precondition for national moral distinction recalls Emerson's 1838 "remonstrance" of Martin Van Buren for his role in the removal of Cherokee people from their Southeastern lands. Emerson's 1838 open letter builds its voice around the affective stance of disbelief, as if Emerson cannot quite accept that the federal government under Van Buren would actually follow through on former President Jackson's policy of removal. Despite this prior defense of Indigenous rights, only a few years later, Emerson became fascinated with Fremont's accounts of his own considerable role in other theaters of displacement and genocide. He owned a copy of Fremont's *A Report of the Exploring Expedition to Oregon and North California, in the Years 1843–'44*, though he did not include it in the list of titles for his personal library.[9] By way of apologizing for his delay in returning the copy of Fremont's *Report* he had borrowed along with other books from his friend, Charles Sumner, Emerson explains that "the only reason why they have been kept so long is that they were found so good" (*CW* 8:272). If we take Emerson at his word, we might ask what "good" he found in Fremont's narrative. Possibly Emerson's interest in Fremont stemmed from the latter's narrative and geographic opening of the uncharted West, a reconnaissance of interest to naturalists, free-soilers, and Transcendentalists alike.

Emerson was not alone in his admiration for Fremont's venturesome accounts. In 1856 the new Republican Party invested in Fremont's reputation as a Western hero; "the Pathfinder" was needed to guide the nation through intensifying sectional conflict. Charles W. Upham's 1856 *Life, Explorations, and Public Services of John Charles Fremont* stands out as particularly Emersonian, despite Upham's staunch Unitarian rationalism two decades earlier (when he assailed Transcendentalism as a threat to the Unitarian doctrine, speaking cuttingly after Emerson's delivery of the Divinity School Address).[10] Now Upham assessed Fremont in practically Emersonian terms. "Considering that we live in what is called a utilitarian age," Upham wrote, "and that [Fremont's] line of occupation has itself been eminently practical it is remarkable how much that is romantic and almost marvelous is spread over it."[11] This didactic reconciling of the practical and the transcendent as praiseworthy original action operates within the discourse of representative men in which Emerson was so prominent.

Mountains serve as an emblem of a West conquerable for democracy in Fremont's 1856 campaign literature. Precisely that connection between Western settlement and the prospect of emancipation would appear in the landscape metaphorics of "Boston Hymn." The poem recalls Emerson's wistful recollections of a heroic Fremont in 1862, when Lincoln still hesitated to commit to emancipation, syncing the Transcendentalist poetics of 1863 with the campaign literature of 1856. "Nevada!" Emerson now exclaims, "coin thy golden crags / With Freedom's image and name." A lyric to Fremont in the *Republican Campaign Songster* of 1856 had similarly connected western landscapes with the Republicans' antislavery objectives, praising Fremont for making "the wide Pacific free ... the *Golden land* ... / With Freedom all its treasures crowned." Urging readers to join the campaign, the poet apostrophizes, "Oh! 'tis worth a campaign's toil / To win an *Empire of Free Soil!*" (original emphasis). The poem's Western sublime resonates with Emerson's continental view of emancipation. The *Songster* poet enthuses:

> Who scaled the splintered crags which rise
> Cloud-girdled in the Western skies,
> And to the lands beyond them bore
> The Freedom of the Atlantic shore![12]

Like "Boston Hymn," "Hail to Fremont" soars visually from coast to coast through clouds that frame Western, mapping a moral and political force as it expands across a Western geography continent. Both poems proclaim the destiny of freedom's triumph. Figured as "Freedom's sword," the subject of "Hail Fremont" shares the moral power of continental reshaping with Emerson's angel of freedom. Both sword and angel serve as commanding figures of martial democracy. Emancipation elicits from the god who voices part of "Boston Hymn" a grand revelation of continental scope rendered in the language of the Columbiad, as if nature itself recognizes the explorer's "discover[y]" of prehistorical creation, the rugged coast's "rocks / which dip their foot in the seas."

Cultivators of the land, and builders of infrastructure upon it, Saxon Westerners on Emerson's historicist model feature prominently in the eleventh-hour campaign poem Whittier rushed to publish, "The Panorama" (1856), which employs the dramatic frame of the panorama show and its "moving canvas" to reveal vivid images of prehistoric Western territory. The poem maps a ground of limitless potential and sublime grandeur, "the new Canaan of our Israel." The "Showman," who narrates the scenes moving before the audience's eyes, presents two possible futures, one opening to a free labor culture made by emigrants transplanting the "homely old-time virtues of the North" and the other to the degenerating force of Southern slavery: "The land of promise to the swarming North, / Which, hive-like, sends its annual surplus forth," or "the poor Southeron on his worn-out soil, / Scathed by the curses of unnatural toil." The poem juxtaposes two potential socio-agricultural futures: one conditioned by "unnatural" labor relations and the other offering "the keys of thrifty life,—the mill-streams fall, / The engine's pant along its quivering rails." Whittier's sensory evocation of these "quivering rails" gestures to the Republican platform's seventh resolution: "That a railroad to the Pacific Ocean, by the most central and practicable route, is imperatively demanded by the interests of the whole country, and that the Federal Government ought to render immediate and efficient aid to its construction." Fremont's 1855 letter to the Philadelphia Pacific Railroad Company conveys just such a route charted during his Western reconnaissance, which in addition to passable routes to the Pacific Ocean through the mountains highlights vast areas of "land fit for cultivation."[13] By his 1860 volume *The Conduct of Life*, Emerson came to incorporate homesteading into the poetic vision of the "man of power" and his great future nation of annexed and improved landscapes. "A feeble man can see the farms that are fenced and tilled, the houses that are built. The strong man sees the possible houses and farms. His eye makes estates, as fast as the sun breeds clouds" (*CW* 6:31).

"The Panorama" aligns imagistically and geographically with "Boston Hymn" in its tropes of revelation and discovery and its claiming of Western lands in the name of liberty and free labor. Whittier's densely figural Western tableau maps the future promised in the 1856 Republican platform—the expansion of free labor into the plains of Kansas and a railroad to the Pacific. Accordingly, Whittier narrates the expansionist plan for a free-labor West: "Where'er our banner flaunts beneath the stars / Its mimic splendors and its cloudlike bars, / There shall Free Labor's hardy children stand / The equal sovereigns of a slaveless land." Emancipation—the flag flying over a free labor utopia—assures sovereignty over Western lands in Whittier's vision. As a relational form, "equality," presumably of the "Hesper-led ... fair-haired children" of Europe, justifies the "wave upon wave, the living flood," that eventually breaks on the highlands of the Western mountains, as "lonely Shasta listening hears the tread,"[14] as if the land itself recognizes the heavy footstep of Anglo-American destiny.

Whittier's romantic vision of free-labor society grounds the moral claims of Republicans in 1856. The broadside phrasing "Free Soil, Free Speech, Free Men, Fremont"—such was the incessant punning on the candidate's name in campaign literature—succinctly conveys the braiding of abolition, expansion, and individual liberty embraced by the new Republican Party. This rallying cry makes plain the cofunctional relation of Western settlement and Republican antislavery politics in 1856. Similarly, Emerson's Westward-facing vision of nature's design legitimates his investments in the expansionist politics of prewar homesteading before the Civil War.

Indeed, Emerson's free-soil abolition appears also to anchor much of his 1856 *English Traits*, a colonialist retrospective that extols a domineering Saxon genius for conquest and landscape alteration. A utopia of self-sufficiency, "England is a huge phalanstery," he asserts, a resource-utopic land of "comfort and plenty." Emerson's garden metaphorics, deployed at just the moment he was taking in the Republican Party's vision of the preternatural resources of the West, share historicist precepts with another vision of utopian abundance put forward in *The Garden of the World, or the Great West*, which Missouri senator, Manifest Destiny zealot, and father-in-law of John C. Fremont, Thomas Hart Benton also published in 1856. "With resources such as Nature has vouchsafed to no other clime," Benton gushes, "blessed with a race of men who are no idlers in their vineyard, but chaining all elements into their services until there seems no limit to their acquisitions, there cannot fail to be set up along its mighty rivers and over its broad prairies a pavilion of human progress which shall bless mankind."[15] In *English Traits*, British Saxons make up the "proud and ingenious race" Emerson hailed as ideal cultivators. Though Emerson may not have been a Manifest Destinarian with Benton's fervor and credentials, he might equally have uttered these sentiments, fixed as they are on the mastery of vast natural resources through the human arts.

At linked moments across its chapters, *English Traits* charts the Anglo-Saxon origins of a free-soil ethic, the moral geography of which Republican poets heralded in the West. The chapter "Land" presupposes the legitimacy of Saxon conquest and the mastery of land and races ostensibly subordinated by nature. Through those living out the geographic and historical trajectories of racial traits and possessed of constructive ingenuity, "art conquers nature, and transforms a rude, ungenial land into a paradise of comfort and plenty." England, Emerson explains, is a nation composed of an "ingenious race" that "has turned every rood of land to its best use, has found all the capabilities, the arable soil, the quarriable rock, the highways, the byways, the fords, the navigable waters ..." (*CW* 5:18). England's sovereignty is secured through the cultivation and mastery of the material world.

"Land" and "Race" bear an important relation to one another, and as scholars have amply demonstrated, these are in fact mutually dependent categories. Despite his admiration of England—this "phalanstery" or "garden"—Emerson avers that upon returning home, he is certain he will "lapse at once into the feeling, which the geography of America inevitably inspires." This feeling by which Emerson would seem impelled drives the final sentence of *English Traits*, where Emerson imagines "the courage of England" now relocated "on the Allegheny ranges, or nowhere" (*CW* 5:117)—Emerson's claim to commonality and lineage is somewhat disrupted by a nationalist brag—"we play the game with immense advantage." The national feeling into which Emerson is certain he will "lapse" upon returning to North American soil is nonetheless only coherent in the long history of Saxon cultivation and conquest, for as Emerson claims, "the centre of the British race" has migrated to North America. Emerson likens the "exhausted old island" to aging parents who see their strength transmitted to their offspring.

Emerson's 1862 essay for the *Atlantic Monthly*, "American Civilization," develops further the ligature by which he imagines Western expansion in North America as a form of Saxon progress, ensconcing emancipation in the ongoing present tense of nature as legislated, proclaimed, and secured through the aegis of a longer English history. Emancipation in the US is "preeminent" on this recursive timeline driven by the forces of labor, commerce, and democracy. Emancipation is an immanent development along a trajectory towards civilization, the landmark events of which include (as Emerson would itemize in an additional *Atlantic* piece he published in November the same year): "the plantation of America, the English Commonwealth of 1648, the Declaration of American Independence in 1776, the British emancipation of slaves in the West Indies, the passage of the Reform Bill, the repeal of the Corn-Laws, the Magnetic Ocean-Telegraph, though yet imperfect, the passage of the Homestead Bill in the last Congress" (*CW* 10:432). In this linkage of emancipation in the United States with other moments of reform in the wider Anglophone world, the anti-tariff Corn Laws become continuous with Lincoln's soon-to-be-issued Emancipation Proclamation (as "American Civilization" went to press in the *Atlantic*, Emerson was compelled to add a paragraph to acknowledge the announcement). As an echo of this timeline of civilization, we might recognize the godlike voice of "Boston Hymn" as it issues a commandment to homesteaders to found a nation.

All of which is to say that for Emerson, certainly by 1862, the future freedoms of free-soil democracy require a racially enabling past. In contrast to the Western free labor society of Whittier's "Europe's fair-haired children" now arising along the path of the transcontinental railroad, Indigenous people are figured as merely transitory. "The lank nomads of the wandering West," Whittier writes,

> Who, asking neither, in their love of change
> And the free bison's amplitude of range,
> Rear to log-hut, for present shelter meant,
> No future comfort, like an Arab's tent.[16]

Indigenous peoples are rendered a fungible presence in this version of the "vanishing Indian" trope, which insinuates a dispositional consent, a "love of change." Both Whittier and Emerson assume a racial historicism that makes a claim to Saxon sovereignty in the North American West. Both assume the ungroundedness of the roaming Native, as in the lines above, dismissing the possibility of any Indigenous counterclaim as an essential impossibility. In this shared rhetoric, the relative positions of races are figured as home structures. "Thus, the effect of a framed or stone house is immense on the tranquility, power, and refinement of the builder," Emerson states. "A man in a cave, or in a camp, a nomad, will die with no more estate than the wolf or the horse leaves" (*CW* 7:10). Emerson, like Whittier, associates Indigenous people with animals and indeed part of nature's still unarticulated flow amidst the rising moral and material infrastructure of civilization as transacted by its established agents. Emerson thus recoups the violence of expansion and dispossession as an element of the racial history he began developing in *English Traits*. It is important to note a differentiation Emerson makes in "American Civilization." Beyond what he takes to be the rightness of its historical moment, emancipation is laudable because it frees Black laborers to emulate market-models of civilization, which convey the edifying forces of nature. By contrast, in the broad strokes of his Romantic historicism, Indigenous people are left to venture, or not, from their "wigman[s]" into the light of racial and historical progress (*CW* 10:395).

Perhaps no portion of *English Traits* resonates more with campaign depictions of Fremont as an agent of both emancipation and Saxon domination than the chapter titled "Ability." Here Emerson defines the English by their ingenuity and practical inventiveness, explaining that "the bias of the nation is a passion for utility. They love the lever, the screw, and pulley, the Flanders draught-horse, the waterfall, wind-mills, tide-mills; the sea and the wind to bear their freight-ships ... Now, their toys are steam and galvanism" (*CW* 5:46). Uniformly, Fremont's campaign profiles extol the candidate's genius as an engineer and naturalist as well as a military figure and frontier icon. All the biographers of 1856 praise Fremont's part in the founding of the Army Corps of Engineers. For Emerson, technological utility puts nature's forces to work as a point of application for practical genius and original action. Consider, for example, Bigelow's inclusion in his biography of Fremont's lavish account of his repair of a broken barometer while surveying California, ostensibly demonstrating Fremont's "facility of resources and his habitual self-reliance."[17]

In *Conduct of Life*, people of power embody Nature's forces and in so doing emerge as drivers of progress and leaders who "by the force of their sympathetic attractions carry nations with them" (*CW* 10:28). Fremont did not carry the nation with him in 1856, but he seems still to be on Emerson's mind in "Power," a chapter with references to explorers, engineers, and military men referenced as examples of the particular attributes of individual power. The attributes therein identified for the man of energy and action—primarily, his physicality and disposition—would seem to characterize Fremont precisely as he was lauded in the campaign narratives of 1856 as a man possessed of preternatural energy and courage and immense practical knowledge and ability. Powerful men, Emerson writes, "pine for adventure, and must go to Pike's Peak; had rather die by the hatchet of a Pawnee, than sit all day and every day at a counting-room desk." Fremont's reconnaissance memoir, *Exploring Expedition to the Rocky Mountains, Oregon, and California*, makes numerous references to Pike's Peak, which his company sighted "luminous and grand" and which appeared to them on their Western course as "the face of an old friend."[18] The image of Fremont planting a flag atop the mountain circulated widely.[19] Western mountains and Indigenous antagonists make the proving ground for the potent masculinity Emerson imagines, the violence of which Emerson displaces onto its target in the figure of the hatchet-wielding Pawnee.

Because of, rather than despite their natural penchant for the active life and violent conflict, men of power nonetheless strike Emerson as good candidates for political office. And in a way, that notion allows Emerson to shake off at least some of whatever Anglophilia conditions his sense for Saxon progress. In "Power," he supposes "as long as our people quote English standards they will miss the sovereignty of power; but let these rough riders,—legislators in shirt-sleeves,—Hoosier, Sucker, Wolverine, Badger,—or whatever hard head Arkansas, Oregon, or Utah sends, half orator, half assassin, to represent its wrath and cupidity at Washington." Deferring to an ostensibly changing political will, Emerson assesses the limits of existing political forms:

> The instinct of the people is right. Men expect from good Whigs, put into office by the respectability of the country, much less skill to deal with Mexico, Spain, Britain, or with our own malcontent members, than from some strong transgressor ... who first conquers his own government, and then uses the same genius to conquer the foreigner. (*CW* 6:34)

Emerson invites a new type of politician in this passage, a man who masters political institutions to assert "the instinct of the people." Even if he is not Emerson's intended touchstone, Fremont seems an obvious exemplar for Emerson's character sketch of the outsider politician with the fortitude to "deal with Mexico," a likely reference to Fremont's paramilitary actions in California, which instigated, instigating war with Mexico during the so-called "Bear Flag Revolt" of 1846, a crucial part of the campaign narrative in 1855 and '56. Embodying "wrath and cupidity ... half orator, half assassin," Fremont did indeed disrupt the mild and decorous Whigs, no longer holding the trust of those who joined the Republican Party in 1856. The "necessity" of geopolitical maneuver and "keeping at bay the startling majorities of migrants and natives" transforms the organic politicians from the West. Biographies of Fremont, which repeatedly dramatize the martial courage and frontier diplomacy of its title character and his exploration party, also elide Fremont's prominence in genocidal violence against Indigenous peoples in California.[20] And yet, returning to "American Civilization" through the lenses of *English Traits* and *The Conduct of Life*, we see more readily how Emerson now lionizes the very processes of displacement he had long before decried in his letter to Van Buren concerning the Cherokee. "When the Indian trail gets widened, graded, and bridged to a good road," he now writes, "there is a benefactor, there is a missionary, a pacificator, a wealth-bringer, a maker of markets, a vent for industry" (*CW* 10:395).

Nature's President at Emancipation

The Western politician Emerson would ultimately hail as nature's own president was not Fremont of course but Lincoln, who affirmed idealist notions of governance that Emerson had held over decades. Indeed, in one sense Emerson's Lincoln seems to have stepped out of the pages of *Conduct of Life*, a product of frontier endeavor.

Emerson's heralding of Lincoln as a representative man makes a claim of indigeneity, "a quite native, aboriginal man," a status earned, it seems, as a consequence of the very mechanisms of expansion and conquest that lead as if by nature's design to the presidency and thence emancipation. Emerson's Lincoln is "Kentuckian born, working on a farm, a flatboatman, a captain in the Black Hawk War, country lawyer, a representative in the rural legislature of Illinois" (CW 10:395–96). The inclusion of the "Black Hawk War" as a part of the practical education of Lincoln's genius lends a democratic aura to the emancipation-era Republican project of Western expansion and the genocidal violence of which Fremont was such a deadly agent.

Lincoln the Indian fighter and rural politician is for Emerson a characterological descendant of "the planters of this country," whose "impatience of arbitrary power ... brought from England, forced them to a wonderful personal independence and to a certain heroic planting and trading." From Emerson's Eastern vantage point, "the solitudes of the West," self-reliance migrates from England, first to the Puritan colony, then to the Western frontier. In this imagined geography, "a man is made a hero by the varied emergencies of his lonely farm, and neighborhoods must combine against the Indians, or the horse-thieves, or the river rowdies, by organizing themselves into committees of vigilance." In the long association of Protestantism and colonial conquest, the frontier vigilance committee makes a jarring if predictable figure for the continuation of the nonconformist Puritan mission and the expansion of political liberty. The genocidal violence of this process registers only obliquely in Emerson's canon, which embraces the mainstream free-soil doctrine of conquest-as-development.

And yet, especially in Emerson's writings on Lincoln's Emancipation Proclamation, the value of emancipation derives from its fidelity to "Nature's law," and its enactment has profound implications for the moral status of nature's vanguard whom Emerson hails in the moment of redemption he finds in Lincoln's executive action. Emerson construes emancipation as a boon to White democrats; the act "paroles all the slaves in America" and "relieves our race once and for all of its crime and false position. ... We have recovered ourselves from our false position, and planted ourselves on a law of Nature" (CW 10:435). The moral recovery of "our race" is thus world-historical and makes a nature-abiding nationalism possible for Emerson. Drew Lopenzina and Laura L. Mielke trace Emerson's appropriative engagement/disengagement with Indigenous perspectives and his complicity in a particular hybrid tropology of voice, "that of 'the Indian' paired with that of the white sympathizer."[21]

Seeking to convey the "electric" dynamics between the magnetic leader and his people, Emerson employs an extended simile to delineate the intersubjective dialectics of the President as a representative of an emerging moral society. "It is as when an orator," Emerson writes, "having ended the compliments and pleasantries ... and having run over the superficial fitness and commodities of the measure he urges, suddenly, lending himself to some happy inspiration, announces with vibrating voice the grand human principles involved." In such an instance, Emerson explains, the audience, shaken from routine discourse, "are surprised and overawed" in the formation of "a new audience ... found in the heart of the assembly—an audience hitherto passive and unconcerned, now at the last so searched and kindled that they come forward, every one a representative of mankind, standing for all nationalities." The simile giving structure to this imagined alchemy of embodiment articulates an intersubjective event, an interaction between orator and audience that is spiritual, intellectual, and physiological. Responsive to his hailing, the people hear the call of the great man who speaks their values.

In the Lincoln eulogy, Emerson trades the distance of simile for an assertion of direct embodiment: "[Lincoln] *is* the true history of the American people in his time," he now emphasizes. "Step by step he walked before them, slow with their slowness, quickening his march by theirs, the true representative of this continent; an entirely public man; father of his country, the pulse of twenty millions throbbing in his heart, the thought of their minds articulated by his tongue." His "pulse" less his own than the systole and diastole of the nation, Lincoln embodies representational power that conveys the will of a people. As Dana Luciano argues, Emerson's eulogy for Lincoln partakes in "the affective rhetoric exhibited in 1865," which "exhibits an especially developed capacity for feeling."[22] Luciano captures precisely the felt temporality of the intersubjective state of feeling Emerson describes, arguing that Emerson's Lincoln "both kept pace with American history, and moved, predictively, ahead of it."[23]

Emerson's Lincoln is the subject of a form of transcendental praise that celebrates the particular only to dissolve individual identity and to abstract the President as a complex representational figure. In the conceit of "Boston Hymn," the Proclamation delivers commandments and intermittent, visionary flashes of nature's design; the poem intones the law of natural rights, which is "tired of kings" and "tyrants great and tyrants small" (*CW* 9:381). As Cadava argues, "Boston Hymn" demands a reformation of the Protestant errand and a perfectionist revision of the national values of the American Revolution.[24] "Boston Hymn" enacts a reception consistent with the interpretive function of Emerson's longstanding poetics which charges the poet with reading the times and the patterns of nature's impulses where others discern an unenchanted material world.

Like the dictates of a wartime commander-in-chief, the moral vision of "Boston Hymn" revels in a democratic ethic free from the constraints of deliberation and consensus. The geographic orientation of the poem aligns nature and the expansionist designs of the Republican Party platform in a god's-eye moral mapping of the continent. The moment of emancipation demands a new form of allegiance, no less absolute than the divine right of kings the poem abolishes: not fealty to Lincoln, but to the idea he embodies.

> My angel,—his name is Freedom,
> Choose him to be your king;
> He shall cut pathways east and west,
> And fend you with his wing.
> (*CW* 9:381)

The poet here displaces the divine right of earthly kings, elevating Lincoln's executive order to the realm of ideas and declaring a paradoxical monarchy of freedom whose agent is a warlike angel. And here is the abiding tension of the poem and of Emerson's Transcendentalist political theory which assumes the democratic channeling of primordial natural power. Ancient energies surge through the world, and yet when governments attune to them, the result is a rough, organic democracy. The poem decrees the raising of "a pine state-house," a governmental structure hewn roughly from nature's materials. The men "cho[sen] to rule / in every needful faculty, / In church, and state, and school" are called to be as "faithful" as "planets" to the gravitational forces revealed through the act of emancipation (*CW* 9:381–82). The poem demands obedience to nature, and indeed, imagines an obedient citizenry. Christopher Newfield calls "obedience" a core Emersonian virtue.[25] Benjamin Park arrives at a similar conclusion, positing Federalism as a model of centralized power informing Emerson's theory of nature. Certainly Emerson's assessments of presidential virtues assumes the "energetic executive" recommended in The Federalist No. 70.[26]

The prophetic register of "Boston Hymn" does not disappear in Emerson's broader reception of emancipation, which he calls "the demand of civilization," as Emerson asserts in "American Civilization." Referring to emancipation, Emerson writes, "That is a principle; everything else is an intrigue" (*CW* 10:406). Attempting a definition of civilization, Emerson imagines a characterological process modeled on the formation of the self-reliant individual, with "each nation grow[ing] after its own genius ... a civilization of its own" (*CW* 10:394). Here Emerson will not disenchant civilization, which "imports a mysterious progress." The importance of emancipation exceeds this strategic utility rising to the ideals of civilization. "The American Executive ranges itself for the first time on the side of freedom," and is "advanced" in original action in comparison to a backward "Congress" (*CW* 10:406). Emerson sounds here the time register of the "untried future." The lauding addendum Emerson added to "Civilization" after Lincoln issued his preliminary proclamation—and which comprised his first public comments on Lincoln—suggests a strong identification with one who "speaks his own thought in his own style" in the manner Emerson once recommended in his 1841 "Self-Reliance." The proclamation is "the President's individual act, done under a strong sense of duty." Recognizing the president as a self-reliant agent of original (political) action, worthy of epideictic praise, he can formally address a national audience thus: "All thanks and honor to the Head of the State!" (*CW* 10:410). George M. Fredrickson's assertion that emancipation made nationalism palatable for Emerson finds warrant in ceremonial lines like these.[27]

This depersonalized, universal figurehead derives nonetheless from the particulars of region, geography, and socioeconomics, the time and space of Lincoln's Western emergence. Emerson pronounces: "This middle-class country had got a middle-class president, at last ... A man of the West. The representative man of the middle class." Emerson's representative politician arrives on nature's schedule, as an embodied representative of the land that formed him and the genius he embodied as ideal sovereign stewards (*CW* 5:141). Noting Lincoln's surprise nomination as the Republican Party presidential candidate at the 1860 convention—beating out frontrunner William Seward, then "in the culmination of his good fame ... the favorite of the Eastern States." Emerson says of his region, "we heard the result coldly and sadly. It seemed too rash, on a purely local reputation, to build so grave a trust in such anxious times" (*CWE* 11:330). The emergence of a representative man, however, requires precisely the demand of the times, in this instance, the guiding star of the "frontier." Emerson thus registers his own initial misrecognition of Lincoln as a racial representative, one of the "people of Illinois and the West," a region whose people offered a "profound good opinion" of the candidate during the 1860 election. More germane for Emerson in 1862 is the moral economy of the president's self-reliant action. "More and better than the President has spoken shall, perhaps, the effect of this Message be,—but, we are sure, not more or better than he hoped in his heart, when, thoughtful of all the complexities of his position, he penned these cautious words" (*CW* 10:410). Emerson now rethinks his own impatience with the pre-emancipation Lincoln: "The extreme moderation with which the President advanced to his design—his long-avowed expectant policy, as if he chose to be strictly the executive of the best public sentiment of the country, waiting only till it should be unmistakably pronounced—so far a mind that none ever listened so patiently to such extreme variation of opinion—so reticent that his decision has taken all parties by surprise, while yet it is just the sequel of his prior acts" (*CW* 10:433). Original action, then, is definitive of the nature coming into being, the emergent present with all its potential for revolutionary moments.

Post-Emancipation Nationalism

With the issuance of the Emancipation Proclamation, Lincoln became Nature's President—less the canny, populist political agent depicted in *English Traits* and *Conduct of Life* than the ideally-calibrated embodiment of universal moral and practical forces. These two executives merge in Emerson's last political writings. By the following year, as he began delivering the lecture, "Fortune of the Republic," Emerson would weave democratic triumphalism into a colonizers' creed in limning the parameters of the "state of melioration" into which the US has been "suppled" by war; emancipation, he now states, has given rise to "politics" and "social frames" that "are almost ideal." The emergence of a reform state now permits Emerson to prophesy that "we shall be a nation" rather than simply "a multitude of people." The future, imagined as a field of interracial competition and collaboration, is giddy with possibility:

> Opportunity of civil rights, of education, of personal power, and not less of wealth; doors wide open. If I could have it,—free trade with all the world without toll or custom-houses, invitation as we now make to every nation, to every race and skin, white men, red men, yellow men, black men; hospitality of fair field and equal laws to all. Let them compete, and success to the strongest, the wisest and the best. The land is wide enough, the soil has bread for all. (*CW* 11:541)

Emerson conceives an expansive institutional system in which the "melioration" of civil rights and free market systems undergird a multiracial democracy. "Hospitality of fair field" and the open door of opportunity remain powerful figural topoi in the paradigm of individual rights underwriting US democracy. In this formulation of racial equality as a "fair field" of equivalences and competition, nature's raw, potentially undemocratic power finds its ideal system for Emerson in his imagined trajectory of institutional life.

In this summative comment declaring the emergence of the post-emancipationist state, Emerson introduces another melioration resultant from the political changes wrought in war and the rise of interracial democracy. "Nature works in immense time, and spends individuals and races prodigally to prepare new individuals and races. The lower kinds are one after one extinguished; the higher forms come in." Emerson's economic metaphorics, this figuration of the racial cost of nature's unfolding, registers something of the inevitable racial violence the democratic triumphalism of his late career elides. The "revolution" of nature's enactment through emancipation demands the competitive logic of free-labor democracy as moral proving ground. And, of course, by the 1860s it was clear—certainly to Republicans like Fremont, Lincoln, and Emerson—that free-labor democracy was bound up with processes of continental domination, of securing the land as Nature's ground for the post-emancipation exceptionalist state, as articulated in a December 1864 lecture delivered at the Parker Fraternity and lightly revised for the 1876 *Letters and Social Aims*:

> ... to know the vast resources of the continent; the good will that is in the people; their conviction of the great moral advantages of freedom, social equality, education, and religious culture, and their determination to hold these fast, and, by them, to hold fast the Country and penetrate every square mile of it with this American civilization. (*CW* 8:56)

Such commonplaces regarding the providential bounty of America locate Emerson in the mainstream of postwar patriotism, though his insistence on "social equality" as a grounding resource in that vision signals his Radical Republican commitments. Emerson's 1864 statement seeks a national equilibrium beyond politics grounded in natural resources and the projection of a collective "good will" fostered by schools and churches. How easily this formulation of liberty twines with aggression and violence. As I have argued, from the inception of emancipation, Emerson viewed American civilization as an invasive or "penetrat[ing]" moral force, expansive and expansionist. In this imagined Emersonian future, political rights and social equality are both manifestations of nature elaborated through democratic culture but made and unmade by nature's racial meliorations.

Notes

1. Christopher Hanlon, *America's England: Antebellum Literature and Atlantic Sectionalism* (Oxford: Oxford University Press, 2013), xi.
2. Eduardo Cadava, "The Nature of War in Emerson's 'Boston Hymn,'" *Arizona Quarterly* 49 (Autumn 1993): 28.

3. Charles W. Upham, *Life, Exploration, and Public Service of John C. Fremont* (Boston: Ticknor and Field, 1856), 242.
4. Nell Irvin Painter, *The History of White People* (New York: W. W. Norton, 2010), 172–74.
5. John Greenleaf Whittier, *The Letters of John Greenleaf Whittier*, ed. John B. Pickard, vol. 2 (Cambridge, MA: Harvard University Press, 1975), 288–89.
6. Eric Foner, *Free Soil, Free Labor, Free Men: The Ideology of the Republican Party Before the Civil War* (Oxford: Oxford University Press, 1995), 202–3.
7. Ralph Waldo Emerson, *Journals of Ralph Waldo Emerson, 1820–1876*, ed. Edward Waldo Emerson (Cambridge, MA: Riverside Press, 1913), 9:573.
8. Len Gougeon, *Virtue's Hero: Emerson, Antislavery, and Reform* (Athens: University of Georgia Press, 1990), 167–69.
9. Kris Fresonke, *West of Emerson: The Design of Manifest Destiny* (Berkeley: University of California Press, 2003), 104.
10. Robert Habich, "Emerson's Reluctant Foe," *The New England Quarterly* 65, no. 2 (June 1992): 232.
11. Upham, *John Charles Fremont*, 336.
12. *The Republican Campaign Songster* (New York: Miller, Orton, and Mulligan, 1856), 57. https://digital.library.pitt.edu/islandora/object/pitt%3A31735061820837/viewer#page/2/mode/2up/
13. John Bigelow, *Memoir of the Life and Public Services of John Charles Fremont* (New York: Derby & Jackson, 1856), 402–3.
14. John Greenleaf Whittier, *The Works of John Greenleaf Whittier* (New York: Houghton Mifflin, 1892), 3:198–99.
15. Thomas Hart Benton, *The Garden of the World, or the Great West* (Boston: Wentworth, 1856), 15.
16. Whittier, *Works of John Greenleaf Whittier* 3:195.
17. Bigelow, *John Charles Fremont*, 49.
18. John Charles Fremont, *The Expeditions of John Charles Fremont*, ed. Donald Jackson and Mary Lee Spence (Urbana: University of Illinois Press, 1970), 1:719.
19. Virginia Scharff, *Empire and Liberty: The Civil War and the West* (Oakland: University of California Press, 2015), 33–35.
20. Benjamin Madley, *An American Genocide: The United States and the California Indian Catastrophe* (New Haven, CT: Yale University Press, 2016), 45–48.
21. See Drew Lopenzina and Laura L. Mielke, in this volume.
22. Dana Luciano, Arranging Grief: Sacred Time and the Body in Nineteenth-Century America (New York and London: New York University Press, 2007), 216.
23. Ibid.
24. Cadava, "The Nature of War," 32.
25. Christopher Newfield, *The Emerson Effect: Individualism and Submission in America* (Chicago: University of Chicago Press, 1996), 23.
26. Benjamin Park, "Transcendental Democracy: Ralph Waldo Emerson's Political Thought, the Legacy of Federalism, and the Ironies of America's Democratic Tradition," *Journal of American Studies* 48 (May 2014): 490–91.
27. George M. Fredrickson, *The Inner Civil War: Northern Intellectuals and the Crisis of the Union* (Chicago: University of Illinois Press, 1993), 178.

CHAPTER 14

EMERSONIAN LEGACIES OF BLACK RESISTANCE

ANITA PATTERSON

Introduction

THANKS to key works of scholarship published in the 1990s, Emerson's growing interest and involvement in the antislavery campaign are beyond dispute.[1] We now know that, despite his early hesitancy, Emerson joined his network of ministerial colleagues in support of abolitionism and other humanitarian causes, ranging from peace and temperance movements to women's rights and prison reform. Relatively less, however, has been said about how Emerson's philosophy of resistance has been creatively engaged by Black American authors. This neglect is understandable, for at least three reasons. First, Emerson's move to Concord, Massachusetts, in 1834—where he was first introduced to the Concord Female Anti-Slavery Society, the Concord Lyceum, and a social circle deeply sympathetic to abolitionism—severely limited his contact with the Boston Black community.[2] Furthermore, many of his most widely read works were published during the late 1830s and 1840s, a time when Emerson openly criticized reformers for being "bitter, sterile people" who attempted to suppress creativity and free thought by demanding ideological conformity.[3] Finally, as Philip Nicoloff, Cornel West, and others including myself have shown, although Emerson refuted the "old indecent nonsense about the nature of the negro" in his celebrated 1844 emancipation address, during the 1850s and especially in *English Traits* he still considered the possibility of racial difference and inferiority, and increasingly expressed views associated with Romantic racial nationalism.[4]

What makes West's *The American Evasion of Philosophy: A Genealogy of Pragmatism* such a pivotal moment in Emerson studies is that at the same time as West acknowledges Emerson's racism, he also contends that Emerson is the "appropriate starting point" for a pragmatist tradition that includes William James, John Dewey, W. E. B. Du Bois, and West himself.[5] Since the publication of West's book in 1989—which explored how

Emerson prefigures prevailing themes in American pragmatism, including the inseparability of knowledge and action, where there is no isolated consciousness or mind-body problem but only the "dynamic character of selves and structures"—Richard Poirier, Frank Lentricchia, Ross Posnock, Joseph Urbas, and others have identified Emerson as a pragmatist originator.[6] In what follows, I will explore how Emerson's writings were also foundational to Black philosophies of resistance developed by Frederick Douglass, Booker T. Washington, Du Bois, Anna Julia Cooper, and Pauline Hopkins. As we shall see, the creative inheritance of Emerson's legacy presented by these authors situates their acts of philosophical reflection and literary creation in the midst of what West aptly describes as "quotidian human struggles for meaning," a method that poses a serious challenge to narrow conceptions of philosophy and favors a view of knowledge arising from action directed toward the attainment of freedom, race and gender equity, and social justice.[7] Their shared engagement with Emerson sheds new light on cross-racial dialogue, intertextual revision, and hidden conceptual commonalities that, taken together, subvert exclusionary boundaries of cultural inheritance.

Emerson and Frederick Douglass: Naming the Anti-Slave

Len Gougeon has vividly documented an Emersonian strain in Frederick Douglass's philosophy of resistance, reminding us that Douglass attended and spoke at the same August 1844 event sponsored by the Concord Female Anti-Slavery Society where Emerson delivered "An Address on the Anniversary of the Emancipation of the Negroes in the British West Indies."[8] In his address, Emerson ardently calls for resistance by the slaves themselves. Stating that the slaves' responsibility for achieving their own freedom outweighs anything abolitionist reformers might do on their behalf, he celebrates the rise of the "anti-slave":

> So now, the arrival in the world of such men as Toussaint, and the Haytian heroes, or of the leaders of their race in Barbados and Jamaica, outweighs in good omen all the English and American humanity. The anti-slavery of the whole world is dust in the balance before this,—is a poor squeamishness and nervousness: the might and right are here: here is the anti-slave: here is man: and if you have man, black or white is an insignificance.[9]

In a persuasive rejoinder to John Carlos Rowe—who claims that racial divisions and gender hierarchies effectively impeded Emerson's influence on Douglass—Gougeon demonstrates that Douglass was "both a model of and inspired by that avatar of resistance as Emerson conceived of and presented him." As supporting evidence he offers an impressive litany of historical details, including the fact that Douglas was seated on the stage with Emerson and his name is actually mentioned in the original draft of Emerson's address; that Emerson would have had many opportunities to learn about Douglass through their shared network of acquaintances, including William Lloyd Garrison and Wendell Phillips; and that in preparing for his address, Emerson borrowed several books from his friend and former Harvard classmate, Ellis Gray Loring, a reformist lawyer who had arranged for Douglass to be purchased from Hugh Auld in 1846. Indeed, Douglass was so intensely aware of Emerson's antislavery activities that in his personal diary, alongside notices of his own addresses, he transcribed the *Liberator*'s account of Emerson's attack on racial prejudice in an 1845 emancipation address delivered in Waltham, Massachusetts; and, in February 1850, he wrote to Emerson requesting a copy of *Representative Men*.[10] As Lawrence Buell and Albert von Frank have noted, Douglass praised Emerson's January 1855 "Lecture on Slavery" in the March issue of *Frederick Douglass' Paper* just a month before he and Emerson spoke in the same lecture series sponsored by Boston's Vigilance Committee, a group charged with sheltering fugitive slaves who sought refuge in the city. Thus it should come as no surprise that decades later, in *The Life and Times of Frederick Douglass*, Douglass praised Emerson's boycott in November 1845 of the New Bedford Lyceum for its racist policy that excluded people of color, including Douglass himself. "Notwithstanding the just and humane sentiment of New Bedford three-and-forty years ago," he recalls, "the place was not entirely free from race and color prejudice.... For instance, though white and colored children attended the same schools and were treated kindly by their teachers, the New Bedford Lyceum refused till several years after my residence in that city to allow any colored person to attend the lectures delivered in its hall. Not until such men as ... Ralph W. Emerson ... refused to lecture in their course while there was such a restriction was it abandoned."[11]

Emerson's decision to drop any mention of Douglass in the final version of his address raises a question about whether he did so because he believed that Douglass was not of "pure blood": as Henry Louis Gates, discussing Emerson's reference to Douglass in his original draft, contends, "For a black man to signify on the world's stage as 'the anti-slave,' Emerson seems to insist, he would have to be 'pure' in order to demonstrate the inherent capacities of the African people." Nonetheless, given Douglass's high esteem for Emerson, and that Emerson was so deeply impressed by Douglass's abilities as to have him in mind when he conceived of the anti-slave, it makes perfect sense that there is an intertextual signifyin(g) relationship, a call and revisionary response, between Emerson's address and Douglass's first autobiography, the 1845 *Narrative*, which Douglass commenced writing shortly after he heard Emerson deliver his address.[12] Numerous scholars have examined how Emerson's concept of self-reliance figures in Douglass's writings. Gates explores how Emerson's celebration of the anti-slave in 1844 affirms the importance of Douglass's act of writing as the exercise of self-reliant agency insofar as "black people have no choice but to achieve their subjectivity by themselves, by fashioning a self through writing, by writing themselves into the discourse of being ... but also by representing that self, as Emerson expressed it in the climax of his speech, 'in their own form.'"[13] Gougeon and Hugh Egan have observed Douglass's congruence with Emerson in his 1853 novella, *The Heroic Slave*, in scenes where his Black protagonist Madison Washington resolves to save himself; and Paul Giles and Joseph Fichtelberg have shown how Douglass achieves formal integration in his *Narrative* with an Emersonian pattern of self-reliance where, for example, his battle against Mr. Covey teaches him the reality of his own agency, and dramatizes his written act of self-fashioning as a heroic exemplar.[14] Another illustrative passage in the *Narrative* occurs when Douglass recalls his departure from Colonel Lloyd's plantation as the "most interesting" in a series of events that culminate in his act of writing himself into the discourse of history. Echoing Emerson's memorable aphorism—"Trust thyself ... Accept the place the divine providence has found for you"—Douglass avers:

> I may be deemed superstitious, and even egotistical, in regarding this event as a special interposition of divine Providence in my favor. But I should be false to the earliest sentiments of my soul, if I suppressed the opinion. I prefer to be true to myself, even at the hazard of incurring the ridicule of others, rather than to be false, and incur my own abhorrence.[15]

Freely expressing his latent conviction is a marked departure from the other slaves on Colonial Lloyd's plantation who are, as Douglass observes, "almost universally" afraid to speak out when asked about their condition and the character of their masters. Self-reliant, accepting the consequences of telling the truth in his *Narrative* rather than suppressing it, Douglass boldly endorses Emerson's celebration of Black agency and the heroism of slaves who acted to secure their freedom in his 1844 emancipation address; responding to Emerson's statement that "a man is added to the human family," Douglass proves himself to be part of that family.[16]

Elsewhere, in "The American Scholar," Emerson memorably insists that books should be transmuted by the inspired, active soul from dead fact into living thought, where thought ripens into truth through action, and there is also abundant evidence that Douglass, in seeking to define the philosophical basis for his own liberation and resistance, did so in part through his creative, revisionary engagement with Emerson's 1837 address. This same inextricable intertwining of books, thought, and action is affirmed by Douglass when, in his 1855 autobiography, *My Bondage and My Freedom*, he depicts his experience of reading the *Columbian Orator*, figuratively comparing the transformation of words on the page into speech and action to the militaristic movement of soldiers whirled into orderly ranks. He writes, "The intense desire, now felt, to be *free*, quickened by my present favorable circumstances, brought me to the determination to act, as well as to think and speak. ... That (to me) gem of a book, *The Columbian Orator*, with its eloquent orations and spicy dialogues, denouncing oppression and slavery—telling of what had been dared, done and suffered by men, to obtain the inestimable boon of liberty—was still fresh in my memory, and whirled into the ranks of my speech with the aptitude of well trained soldiers, going through the drill."[17]

There are many other examples of Douglass's creative adaptation of Emerson's philosophy, but I will end with their shared regard for nature as a source of education and a manifestation of divine self-reliant power. Gougeon has argued that the root in

Douglass's first autobiography, which psychologically fortifies him in the struggle against Covey, is an Emersonian symbol of the "natural world to which ... we are all spiritually connected" as represented in the transparent eyeball passage from *Nature*. The recollection of Emerson's *Nature* is apt when we consider how, just before Emerson's famous description of himself as a transparent eyeball, he describes the woods where there is eternal youth as symbolic "plantations of God" that present a resonant contrast with the literal horrors of Southern slavery; and Douglass would also have been aware that in Emerson's 1844 emancipation address, this same trope of transparency is reworked to condemn the common racist belief in Black inferiority: "The intellect,— that is miraculous! Who has it, has the talisman: his skin and bones, though they were the color of night, are transparent, and everlasting stars shine through, with attractive beams."[18]

What is important to note, in addition, is how Douglass's intertextual acknowledgement of Emerson's *Nature* forms the basis for a powerful revisionary critique. As Jeannine DeLombard has argued, his emphasis on embodiment marks a crucial point of difference from Emerson: whereas the transparent eyeball in Emerson's *Nature* represents universal subjectivity, in his 1845 *Narrative* Douglass refers to a scene where, defending himself against an attack by white racist apprentices in a Baltimore shipyard, his left eye is wounded by a "powerful kick ... [and] ... seemed to have burst," calling attention to the visibility, vulnerability, and injury of his body in order to communicate the brutality of slavery and racial violence.[19] An analogous but more complex critique of Emerson's transparent eyeball is undertaken a decade later in *My Bondage and My Freedom*. Describing his battle with Mr. Covey, in a deliberate revision of Emerson's claim, "I am nothing. I see all," Douglass writes, "I was a changed being after that fight. I was *nothing* before; I WAS A MAN NOW ... He only can understand the effect of this combat on my spirit, who has himself incurred something, hazarded something, in repelling the unjust and cruel aggressions of a tyrant."[20] Whereas, in 1845, Douglass's reference to his wounded eyeball emphasizes his embodied subjectivity and traumatized perspective, unequivocally affirming his difference from Emerson, in 1855 there is a new emphasis on the psychological and historical necessity of Black resistance as an affirmation of selfhood and manhood, underscoring his identification with Emerson's militant anti-slave. Recalling and revising Emerson, Douglass proves his humanity and thus the need for Black resistance.

Emersonian Inflections: W. E. B. Du Bois and Booker T. Washington

Three decades after groundbreaking analyses by West, Dickson Bruce, Werner Sollors, and Brian Bremen, Du Bois's revisionary engagement with Emersonian "double-consciousness" has gained wide acceptance.[21] Emerson's earliest characterization of double-consciousness occurs in "The Transcendentalist," an 1842 lecture at the Masonic Temple in Boston, where he describes the contradictory relation between "two lives" or "states of thought" that "diverge at every moment, and stand in wild contrast": the understanding of what Gates describes as an active self dwelling in the "here and now" and the soul or "reflective self" existing in the divine realm of ideas.[22] Eighteen years later, the role of the active or public self would be articulated in terms that reflect the racialism of Emerson's later writings. In "Fate" Emerson describes "double-consciousness" as a "stupendous antagonism" that exhibits the creative tension between race and rights, involuntary determinism and freedom. "To hazard the contradiction,—freedom is necessary," he writes. "To offset the drag of temperament and race, which pulls down, learn this lesson, namely, that by the cunning co-presence of two elements, which is throughout nature, whatever lames or paralyzes you, draws in with it the divinity, in some form, to repay."[23]

Interrogating the reductive assumption that Emerson's philosophy and poetics simply mirrored prevailing supremacist values and ideals, scholars have variously examined the similarities and differences between Emerson and Du Bois. West, for example, argues that whereas for Emerson double-consciousness means "having a European culture in an un-European environment" and an "occasion to exercise human powers to solve problems," Du Bois revises and critiques Emerson by exploring double-consciousness as a "sense of always looking at one's self through the eyes of others," which West identifies as "the *cause* of a problem, a problem resulting precisely from the exercise of white human powers celebrated by Emerson"; and Bremen claims that Du Bois reformulates Emerson's concept in order to "make the fate of both races hang upon the mutual 'revelation' of each other's worth."[24] In *From Emerson to King*, I tried to show how, despite and even because of his racism, Emerson proved to be a crucial cultural resource for Du Bois's philosophy of resistance and conception of double-consciousness. For Emerson, rights such as freedom are insufficient to represent the self and his ideal vision of America. Dissatisfied with the atomism of democratic society, Emerson eventually abandoned the utopian possibilities of friendship as the basis for social cohesion in favor of a scientific concept of race. Although democracy and racialism imply opposing views of the self and society, the two are not at cross-purposes in Emerson's thought. Instead, they are dialectically reconfigured, at once supplementing and critically correcting each other, generating a new concept of identity as double-consciousness that was to prove extremely productive for Du Bois, who was tasked with reconciling racial and national identity in America.

Throughout *The Souls of Black Folk*, Du Bois's invocation of what he calls the Negro race represents his reevaluation of its inferior status according to the prevailing dogma, and his critical recuperation of Emerson's concept of double-consciousness—his refusal to disavow either the claims of race or a universal rights-based discourse of democratic citizenship—is a deliberate gesture that allows him to acknowledge the limitations and possibilities of each.[25] "After the Egyptian and the Indian, the Greek and Roman, the Teuton and Mongolian," he writes,

> the Negro is a sort of seventh son, born with a veil, and gifted with second-sight in this American world,—a world which yields him no true self-consciousness, but only lets him see himself through the revelation of the other world. It is a peculiar sensation, this double-consciousness, this sense of always looking at one's self through the eyes of others, of measuring one's soul by the tape of a world that looks on in amused contempt and pity. One ever feels his two-ness—an American, a Negro; two souls, two thoughts, two unreconciled strivings; two warring ideals in one dark body, whose dogged strength alone keeps it from being torn asunder.[26]

Effectively recasting the Emersonian antagonism, Du Bois's conception of double-consciousness simultaneously expresses the painful burdens as well as the possibilities of insight resulting from biculturality. Although it fails to be "true" self-consciousness, double-consciousness brings a gift of clearer "second-sight." Although in this memorable statement Du Bois never clarifies whether double-consciousness is a fixed racial given or a sociohistorical construct, this question would be more directly addressed in his second autobiography, *Dusk of Dawn: An Autobiography of a Race Concept*. On the one hand Du Bois insists, "My tie to Africa is strong. On this vast continent were born and lived a large portion of my direct ancestors going back a thousand years or more. The mark of their heritage is upon me in color and hair." However, with a self-conscious, self-contradictory gesture, Du Bois also transcends and works against his biologism by also referring to a sociohistorical basis for kinship: "the physical bond is least and the badge of color relatively unimportant save as a badge; the real essence of this kinship is its social heritage of slavery; the discrimination and insult; and this heritage binds not simply the children of Africa, but extends through yellow Asia and into the South Seas."[27] Following Emerson, Du Bois relies on the liberal discourse of rights to extend equity and political participation to Black Americans, while at the same time he resists these conceptual parameters and invokes a race concept that generates a coherent oppositional identity and expresses withdrawal from the US as an existing and unjust state.

Whereas Du Bois's place in the genealogy of Emersonian pragmatism is generally accepted, there is still ongoing debate as to whether Booker T. Washington should also be included among Black public intellectuals whose lineage includes Emerson. Questioning Posnock's contention that Washington was a pragmatist "in the colloquial sense but the virtual antithesis of a philosophical pragmatist," Wilson J. Moses has recently tried to situate Washington in the pragmatist tradition by calling attention to Washington's acknowledgement of Emerson in an 1891 commencement address. According to Louis Harlan, "Washington presented himself as possessing all the virtues extolled by ... Ralph Waldo Emerson," and the fact that Washington consistently used Emerson as a touchstone to advance his educational philosophy suggests that his ideological controversy with Du Bois has been overstated.[28] Confirming studies by Houston Baker and others exploring similarities between Du Bois and Washington, Du Bois himself acknowledges such commonalities when, for example, in his third autobiography, composed at the ripe old age of 90, he concedes that their "theories of Negro progress were not absolutely contradictory."[29] In *From Emerson to King*, I argued that in their ongoing debate about education, Washington and Du Bois were emphasizing two different aspects of Emerson's philosophy, because the term "cultivation" in "Self-Reliance" where Emerson describes a man's education as a process in which "no kernel of nourishing corn can come to him but through his toil bestowed on that plot of ground which is given him to till" ambiguously refers *both* to intellectual self-cultivation as a figuratively rendered process of spiritual unfolding, *and* to literal, agricultural labor.[30] Here again, as in Emerson's conception of double-consciousness, the stark opposition between intellectual and agricultural labor has been dialectically reconfigured to represent a generative relation of sustained, reciprocal critique. Although I concur with Charles Mitchell's claim that "the debate between Du Bois and Washington may be framed, in part, as a clash between two conflicting appropriations of Emerson's thought," I disagree with his dismissal of Washington's concept of self-reliance as being "narrow" and solely materialistic.[31] We have yet to understand the full complexity and depth of Washington's engagement with Emerson in *Up From Slavery*. On the one hand, Emerson suggests that self-culture is necessary for the protection of what Du Bois calls "higher individualism," where the toil of educating oneself results in the discovery and acceptance of one's own uniqueness.[32] But on the other, Emerson also suggests that actual physical labor itself has educational value, a view shared by Washington in *Up From Slavery* when he recalls, "At Hampton, for the first time, I learned what education was expected to do for an individual ... I learned ... to love labour, not alone for its financial value, but for labour's own sake and for the independence and self-reliance which the ability to do something which the world wants done brings." Washington's nuanced interpretation of Emerson underscores the importance of self-reliance, broadly construed, as self-discovery and creative individuality, in addition to financial independence.[33]

Emerson's "The American Scholar" is another shared influence that helps to mediate the controversy between Washington and Du Bois. Mitchell has extensively discussed Du Bois's revisionary adaptation of Emerson's address in "Does Education Pay?," a speech delivered by Du Bois before the National Colored League of Boston that was published in the *Boston Courant* in March 1891, where Du Bois not only invokes Emerson by name, but also quotes from Emerson's poetry and suggestively alludes to "The American Scholar" over the course of his remarks.[34] It is also likely that Washington had Emerson in mind when, in his Atlanta address—which was, by his own account, deliberately crafted to appeal to a racially mixed audience that included "Northern whites as well as Southerners"—he uses the Emersonian trope of "the hand ... divided into fingers" to address the vexed issue of racial segregation. Emerson underscores how the division of labor and false identification of men with their professions results in a "*divided or social state*" where "Man is thus metamorphosed into a thing, into many things," tacitly foregrounding the causal connection between capitalism and New World slavery. For Washington, by contrast, the divided social state is acceptable and explicitly based on racial as well as professional differences, where "in all things that are purely social we can be as separate as the fingers, yet, one as the hand in all things essential to mutual progress. There is no defence or security for any of us except in the highest intelligence and development of all."[35]

Fitzhugh Brundage has studied Washington's "adroit use of equivocation" in this speech, and the passage is indeed notable for its ambiguity: what, precisely, does Washington mean by "things that are purely social" as opposed to "things essential to mutual progress"?[36] Du Bois, understandably, attacked Washington's acquiescence to Jim Crow segregation, sharply criticizing his surrendering of the demand for civil and political rights, and dubbing this speech the "Atlanta Compromise," a moniker that endures to this day.[37] Nonetheless, David Levering Lewis reminds us that Du Bois sent a telegram and followed up with a letter to Washington praising the speech; and historians have shown that, despite his conciliatory stance, Washington protested and fought, both publicly and behind the scenes, against lynching, unfair voting qualifications, segregated housing legislation, and discrimination by labor unions.[38] Most important of all for the purposes of this discussion, Washington ardently supported and protected Black education at a time when lawmakers sought to impose national limits on funding, and Black educators in the South regularly encountered violent opposition.[39]

Emerson and Black Feminism at the Turn of the Century: Pauline Hopkins and Anna Julia Cooper

The years between 1890 and 1910 have been identified as "The Black Women's Era," and one of the most important works during this period is Pauline Hopkins's *Contending Forces: A Romance Illustrative of Negro Life North and South*. The novel opens with an epigraph from Emerson's 1844 emancipation address—"The civility of no race can be perfect whilst another is degraded"—prompting C. K. Doreski, Sean McCann and Sydney Bufkin to examine the influential presence of Emerson in Hopkins's writings.[40] A primary reason Emerson's writings are central to Hopkins's *Contending Forces* is, as Hazel Carby has observed, that she attempts to "question the boundaries of inheritance" by demonstrating that not only her irreducibly hybrid, multiracial protagonists, but indeed Hopkins herself, are true inheritors of Emerson's legacy.[41] Hopkins, whose father was a migrant from Virginia and whose mother was from Exeter, New Hampshire, was born in Portland, Maine, but grew up in Boston. Writing two decades before the New Negro Renaissance, she envisioned a Black renaissance in Boston, hoping her turn-of-the-century novel would rekindle the political agitation and resistance of the antislavery movement in New England during the antebellum period.

Contending Forces memorably dramatizes what was, in 1900, an emerging controversy between Washington and Du Bois. Whereas Arthur Lewis, president of a Black industrial school in Louisiana who believes "industrial education and the exclusion of politics will cure our race troubles," is modeled after Washington, Will Smith, like Du Bois, "laughed at the idea of Latin and Greek being above the caliber of the Negro and likely to unfit him for the business of bread-getting ... With him Latin and Greek represented but tools which he used to unlock the storehouse of knowledge."[42] Hopkins was aligned with Du Bois in her advocacy of higher education for Blacks and full political participation, and created a global network in her campaign against colonial oppression in Africa and racial tyranny in the US. Her refusal to sacrifice race politics to achieve fiscal stability for the magazine made her, as Lois Brown has shown, "especially vulnerable in the increasingly volatile and male-dominated intraracial war that pitted spirited antiaccommodationists ... against the allies of Booker T. Washington." By November 1904, Washington and his supporters had her removed from her position as the editor of the *Colored American Magazine*, appointing Roscoe Conkling Simmons, a nephew of Washington's third wife, as her replacement.[43] Despite Hopkins's profound disagreement with many of Washington's ideas, her representation of the relationship between Smith and Lewis highlights their mutual respect, and her strategic use of the marriage plot works effectively to establish a familial unity that transcends their ideological differences: when Lewis marries Dora Smith, Will Smith's sister, he and Smith become brothers-in-law, indicating an ability to work together despite their differences.

The primary reason Emerson is invoked throughout *Contending Forces* is to highlight and consolidate the philosophical tradition that brings together Douglass, Du Bois, and Washington; and where, as Bufkin astutely observes, "Emerson's presence serves as a linchpin of sorts in this act of synthesis and mediation."[44] The character Will Smith is a fictional stand-in for Du Bois who is also consistently associated with Emerson. Hopkins's narrator tells us that he attends Harvard and a course in Heidelberg after graduation, recalling Du Bois's studies at Harvard and the University of Berlin, and that "Emerson's words on character were an apt description of the strong personality of this man." Smith's speech at the Canterbury Club borrows extensively from Emerson's 1844 emancipation address without attribution and only minor modifications: "If men are rude and foolish, down they must go. When at last in any race a new principle appears, an idea, *that* conserves it. Ideas only save races. If the black man is feeble and impotent, unimportant to the existing races—not on a parity with the best races, the black man must serve and be exterminated. *But*, if he carries within his bosom the element of a new and coming civilization, he will survive and play his part." Hopkins's appropriation of Emerson's antislavery address in this instance highlights his political alliance with Frederick Douglass, whom Will Smith invokes by name just a few pages later; and, in doing so, "represents a clear intellectual path that stretches back not only to abolitionists like William Lloyd Garrison and Frederick Douglass, but also to a broader intellectual movement that played a foundational role in New England intellectual tradition."[45]

Another less studied but equally significant allusion to Emerson in *Contending Forces* occurs when Mrs. Willis, the widow of a Black politician, gives a lecture on "the place which the virtuous woman occupies in upbuilding a race" at the community Sewing Circle, Hopkins's fictional version of the Black women's club movement, as part of a fundraising event to support interracial social justice initiatives in the Episcopal church for the city of Boston. Identifying Emerson, without naming him, as "a good man," Mrs. Willis adds the word "happiness" to a quotation which Emerson, in his 1844 emancipation address, attributed to Blacks as a testimony to their moderation: "Now let me close this talk by asking you to remember one maxim written of your race by a good man: 'Happiness and social position are not to be gained by pushing.'"[46] This simultaneous interest in the "Woman Question" and abolitionism on the part of Mrs. Willis should also be interpreted as part of Hopkins's dialogue with Emerson: in "Woman," a lecture given at the Woman's Rights Convention in Boston on September 20, 1855, Emerson claimed that the antislavery movement "has, among its other effects, given Woman a feeling of public duty and an added self-respect," revealing how support for abolitionism among Black and white women in the North was historically linked to the rise of feminism in the US (*CWE* 11:417).[47]

Mrs. Willis's reference to Emerson's 1844 emancipation address brings to mind the work of Anna Julia Cooper, a formidable Black scholar whose academic training, like that of Du Bois, was deeply rooted in the intellectual tradition of Western philosophy and the classics. Like Booker T. Washington, Cooper was born a slave in Raleigh, North Carolina, in 1858. Having earned her BS and MA degrees from Oberlin College, and a PhD from the University of Paris-Sorbonne, Cooper went on to serve as a teacher, professor, high school principal, college president, and leading Black spokeswoman of her time. In 1892, she published *A Voice from the South by a Black Woman of the South*, a foundational contribution to Black feminist thought that repeatedly refers to Emerson's writings. In "Womanhood A Vital Element in the Regeneration and Progress of a Race," Cooper recalls Emerson as saying, "I have thought that a sufficient measure of civilization is the influence of good women," a slightly modified version of his statement in "Woman" that "women are, by this and their social influence, the civilizers of mankind. What is civilization? I answer, the power of good women" (*CWE* 11:409).[48]

It is likely that Hopkins would have been aware of Cooper's engagement with Emerson insofar as Cooper's text also creatively revises Emerson's conception in "Fate" of antagonistic or "contending" historical forces, arguably the central theme of Hopkins's novel given its title.[49] Whereas Emerson depicts an incessant process of competitive conflict, claiming that, in the book of Nature, "there is complicity, expensive races—race living at the expense of race," and "when a race has lived its term, it comes no more again," Cooper believes that in America, this "irrepressible clash" of races is "predestined" to be followed by what she describes as a "stable equilibrium of opposition." In the chapter titled "Has America a Race Problem?" she concludes, "Exclusive possession belongs to none. … There was never a time since America became a nation when there were not more than one race, more than one party, more than one belief contending for supremacy. Hence no one is or can be supreme."[50] The equilibrium of these contending forces, according to Cooper, shows the importance and necessity of cultural diversity and difference as the foundation for vigorous democracy.

Hopkins's revisionary practice of allusion to Emerson's writings, which allows her to consolidate a philosophical legacy of Black resistance where differences are mediated and even celebrated, is nowhere more apparent than in her numerous references to the passage in *Nature* where Emerson becomes a transparent eyeball on the Boston Common. We have already seen how Douglass is psychologically fortified by this

Emersonian trope of transparency, and that his revisionary engagement with Emerson in his autobiographies results in a powerful critique of Emerson, foregrounding the embodiment of Black subjectivity as well as the psychological and historical necessity of resistance. In *Contending Forces*, Hopkins—who names Douglass when, at the Canterbury Club, Smith seems to be recalling his 1869 speech on "Composite Nationality," while also alluding to Emerson's transparent eyeball—advances a crucial signifyin(g) intertextual revision of both Douglass and Emerson. Whereas Emerson transcends embodiment, and whereas Douglass's selfhood, manhood, and insistence on the psychological and historical necessity of Black resistance are ultimately affirmed by an act of violence, Hopkins suggests how the blurring of racial boundaries through interracial marriage, nonviolent interculturality, and hybrid physiognomy figure in what Mrs. Willis describes, in the same scene where she quotes from the "good man" Emerson, as a beautified way of life in a "civilization of the future." We see this clearly when Jesse consents to an interracial marriage. Son of Charles Montfort, a slaveholder who relocated his plantation from Bermuda to North Carolina in the 1790s, Jesse was enslaved after Charles was murdered by Anson Pollack who, after being sexually rejected by Jesse's mother, Grace, sought revenge by killing her husband, spreading a rumor that she was of African descent, subjecting her to horrific violence as his slave, driving her to suicide, and claiming her sons as property. Fleeing from North Carolina to Massachusetts, Jesse stops briefly "beside the stone wall that enclosed the historic Boston Common" before voluntarily consenting to marry a Black woman from New Hampshire, Elizabeth Whitfield. In a variation of Emerson's phrase "I am part or particle of God," Hopkins's narrator describes their happy consensual union with sardonic and telling irony: "Thus he was absorbed into that unfortunate race of whom it is said that a man had better be born dead than to come into the world as part and parcel of it."[51]

Underscoring the significance of what might be considered just a coincidental, vague echo of Emerson, Hopkins includes two subsequent scenes, also set on the Boston Common, that, taken together, affirm her deliberate practice of allusion to the transparent eyeball in *Nature*, implicitly contrasting Grace's violent subjugation to the gradually maturing love that culminates in the marriage of her mulatto protagonists, Will Smith and Sappho Clark. The first is the scene where Will experiences a moment of transcendence as he takes Sappho's hand: "Across the heavens the Northern Lights streamed in radiance. Meteors bright and shooting stars added to the beauty of the night ... The wind whispered amidst the leafless branches of the huge old trees on the Common and Public Garden as they passed them on their homeward way." Another equally clear and even more compelling allusion occurs when Sappho, who conceals her true identity as Mabelle Beaubean throughout most of the novel, chooses to acknowledge her son, Alphonse. The daughter of Monsieur Beaubean, a wealthy "colored" Louisiana planter, and a quadroon mother, Mabelle gave birth to Alphonse in a New Orleans convent after being incestuously raped by her father's white half-brother. Leaving her baby in the care of her relative, Aunt Sally, and changing her name to Sappho Clark, she moved to Boston, where she resided in a boarding house run by Ma Smith, supported herself as a typist, and met Will, the man she would eventually marry. In contrast to Grace

Montfort, who commits suicide as a result of her subjection, Sappho instead chooses life, overcoming past trauma through the healing experience of maternal love. Sappho's vow to fulfill her duty to her son, despite the stigma of his birth, is taken just before she walks through the Boston Public Garden near the Common. Motherhood is compensatory, in Emerson's sense: "The mother-love chased out all the anguish that she had felt over his birth," Hopkins writes. "In this new and holy love that had taken possession of her soul was the compensation for all she had suffered." The Emersonian moment of being "part and parcel of God" has been adapted to represent a mother's transformative experience of love as a source of resilience that helps her to survive against all odds: "but for the child [she] would've broken down."[52]

Conclusion

It is clear from what we have seen that Emerson's writings significantly informed the development of very different Black philosophies of resistance. Inspired by Emersonian "self-reliance" and his concept of the "anti-slave" as an avatar of resistance, Douglass unequivocally asserted that the slaves' responsibility for achieving their own freedom outweighs anything abolitionist reformers might do on their behalf, and his battle against Mr. Covey as well as his own act of writing should be regarded as exercises of self-reliant agency. In both Douglass and Emerson, books should be transmuted by the inspired, active soul from dead fact into living thought, and nature is a cherished source of education and a manifestation of divine self-reliant power.

Du Bois's revisionary critique of Emerson questions the reductive assumption that Emerson's philosophy and poetics simply mirrored prevailing supremacist values and ideals. Adapting Emerson's concept of "double-consciousness" he draws on the liberal discourse of rights to extend equity and political participation to Black Americans, while at the same time resisting these conceptual parameters by invoking a race concept that generates a coherent oppositional identity and expresses withdrawal from the US as an existing and unjust state. Furthermore, in their ongoing debate about education, Washington and Du Bois were emphasizing two different aspects of Emerson's philosophy, because the term "cultivation" in "Self-Reliance" ambiguously refers *both* to intellectual self-cultivation as a figuratively rendered process of spiritual unfolding, *and* to literal, agricultural labor. Washington's nuanced interpretations of Emerson suggest that his ideological controversy with Du Bois has been overstated, underscoring the importance of self-reliance, broadly construed, as self-discovery and creative individuality, in addition to financial independence. Adapting the Emersonian trope of the hand divided into fingers, Washington addresses the vexed issue of racial segregation in terms that Du Bois would sharply criticize as surrendering the demand for civil and political rights, but despite these and other significant concerns raised in the assessment of Washington's politics, the shared engagement with Emerson on the part of Washington and Du Bois indicates their neglected commonalities.

Finally, the epigraph drawn from Emerson's 1844 emancipation address, as well as numerous allusions to Emerson in Hopkins's *Contending Forces*, highlight and consolidate the philosophical tradition of Black resistance that brings together Douglass, Du Bois, and Washington. The novel memorably dramatizes what was, in 1900, an emerging controversy between Washington and Du Bois. Despite Hopkins's profound disagreement with many of Washington's ideas, her representation of the relationship between Smith and Lewis highlights their mutual respect, and her strategic use of the marriage plot works effectively to establish a familial unity that transcends their ideological differences. The title of Hopkins's novel draws attention to Cooper's *A Voice from the South by a Black Woman of the South*, a foundational contribution to Black feminist thought that repeatedly refers to Emerson's writings, including Emerson's conception in "Fate" of "contending" historical forces. Whereas Emerson depicts an incessant process of competitive racial conflict, Cooper avers that in America, this "irrepressible clash" of races is "predestined" to be followed by what she describes as a "stable equilibrium of opposition." Hopkins's mediation and celebration of cultural differences are achieved in numerous allusions to the passage in *Nature* where Emerson becomes a transparent eyeball on the Boston Common; and, in doing so, she advances a crucial signifyin(g) intertextual revision of both Douglass and Emerson. Whereas Emerson transcends embodiment, and whereas Douglass's selfhood, manhood, and insistence on the psychological and historical necessity of Black resistance are ultimately affirmed by an act of physical violence, Hopkins suggests how the blurring of racial boundaries through interracial marriage, nonviolent interculturality, and hybrid physiognomy will be central to the civilization of the future.

Notes

1. Len Gougeon, *Virtue's Hero: Emerson, Antislavery, and Reform* (Athens: University of Georgia Press, 1990); Robert D. Richardson, Jr., *Emerson: The Mind on Fire* (Berkeley: University of California Press, 1995); Albert J. von Frank, *The Trials of Anthony Burns: Freedom and Slavery in Emerson's Boston* (Cambridge, MA: Harvard University Press, 1998).
2. Richardson, *Mind*, 208–14.
3. *JMN* 14:166.
4. Philip Nicoloff, *Emerson on Race and History: An Examination of* English Traits (New York: Columbia University Press, 1961); Cornel West, *The American Evasion of Philosophy: A Genealogy of Pragmatism* (Madison: University of Wisconsin Press, 1989); Anita Patterson, *From Emerson to King: Democracy, Race, and the Politics of Protest* (New York: Oxford University Press, 1997).
5. West, *American Evasion*, 6.
6. West, *American Evasion*, 5, 6, 10; Richard Poirier, *Poetry and Pragmatism* (Cambridge, MA: Harvard University Press, 1992); Frank Lentricchia, *Modernist Quartet* (Cambridge: Cambridge University Press, 1994); Ross Posnock, *Color and Culture: Black Writers and the Making of the Modern Intellectual* (Cambridge, MA: Harvard University Press, 1998); James Albrecht, *Reconstructing Individualism: A Pragmatic Tradition from Emerson to Ellison* (New York: Fordham University Press, 2012); Joseph Urbas, "How Close a Reader

of Emerson is Stanley Cavell?," *The Journal of Speculative Philosophy* 31, no. 4 (2017): 557–74; Douglas Anderson, *Philosophy Americana: Making Philosophy at Home in American Culture* (New York: Fordham University Press, 2006); Jonathan Levin, *The Poetics of Transition: Emerson, Pragmatism, and American Literary Modernism* (Durham, NC: Duke University Press, 1999).

7. West, *American Evasion*, 76.
8. Len Gougeon, "Militant Abolitionism: Douglass, Emerson, and the Rise of the Anti-Slave," *The New England Quarterly* 85, no. 4 (December 2012): 622–57, 623.
9. Ralph Waldo Emerson, *Emerson's Antislavery Writings*, ed. Len Gougeon and Joel Myerson (New Haven, CT: Yale University Press, 1995), 31.
10. John Carlos Rowe, *At Emerson's Tomb: The Politics of Classic American Literature* (New York: Columbia University Press, 1997), x, 7; Gougeon, "Militant Abolitionism," 623, 632, 639–40, 642.
11. Lawrence Buell, *Emerson* (Cambridge, MA: Harvard University Press, 2003), 368; von Frank, *Trials*, 325; Gougeon, "Militant Abolitionism," 648; Frederick Douglass, *Autobiographies*, ed. Henry Louis Gates, Jr. (New York: Library of America, 1994), 655–66.
12. Richardson, *Mind*, 398; Henry Louis Gates, Jr., "Frederick Douglass's Camera Obscura: Representing the Antislave 'Clothed and in Their Own Form,'" *Critical Inquiry* 42 (Autumn 2015): 31–60, 41.
13. Gates, "Douglass's Camera Obscura," 43.
14. Gougeon, "Militant Abolitionism," 643, 647; Hugh Egan, "'On Freedom': Emerson, Douglass, and the Self-Reliant Slave," *ESQ* 60, no. 2 (2014): 183–208, 197; Gates, "Camera Obscura," 43; Paul Giles, "Narrative Reversals and Power Exchanges: Frederick Douglass and British Culture," *American Literature* 73, no. 4 (December 2001): 779–810, 783; Joseph Fichtelberg, *The Complex Image: Faith and Method in American Autobiography* (Philadelphia: University of Pennsylvania Press, 1989), 148, 116–17.
15. *CW* 2:28; Douglass, *Autobiographies*, 36; Egan, "'On Freedom,'" 201.
16. Douglass, *Autobiographies*, 27; Emerson, *Antislavery Writings*, 29.
17. *CW* 1:55, 56, 59; Douglass, *Autobiographies*, 305–6.
18. Gougeon, "Militant Abolitionism," 635–36; *CW* 1:10; Emerson, *Antislavery Writings*, 31.
19. Jeannine DeLombard, "'Eye-Witness to the Cruelty': Southern Violence and Northern Testimony in Frederick Douglass's 1845 *Narrative*," *American Literature* 73, no. 2 (June 2001): 245–75, 245; Douglass, *Autobiographies*, 81–82.
20. *CW* 1:10; Douglass, *Autobiographies*, 286.
21. West, *American Evasion*, 142–43; Dickson Bruce, "W. E. B. Du Bois and the Idea of Double Consciousness," *American Literature* 64, no. 2 (June 1992): 299–309; Werner Sollors, "Of Mules and Mares in a Land of Difference: or, Quadrupeds All?," *American Quarterly* 42, no. 2 (June 1990): 167–190; Brian Bremen, "Du Bois, Emerson, and the 'Fate' of Black Folk," *American Literary Realism* 24, no. 3 (Spring 1992): 80–88.
22. *CW* 1:213; Henry Louis Gates, Jr., "The Black Letters on the Sign: W. E. B. Du Bois and the Canon," in *The Souls of Black Folk*, by W. E. B. Du Bois, ed. Gates (New York: Oxford University Press, 2007), xii–xxv, xiv.
23. *CW* 6:12, 25–26.
24. West, *American Evasion*, 142–43; Bremen, "'Fate' of Black Folk," 81.
25. Patterson, *Emerson to King*, 160–65, 169–70.
26. W. E. B. Du Bois, *The Souls of Black Folk*, ed. Henry Louis Gates, Jr. (New York: Oxford University Press, 2007), 3.

27. W. E. B. Du Bois, *Dusk of Dawn: An Autobiography of a Race Concept*, ed. Henry Louis Gates, Jr. (New York: Oxford University Press, 2007), 59.
28. Posnock, *Color and Culture*, 36; Wilson J. Moses, "More Than an Artichoke: The Pragmatic Religion of Booker T. Washington," in *Booker T. Washington and Black Progress: Up From Slavery 100 Years Later*, ed. W. Fitzhugh Brundage (Gainesville: University of Florida Press, 2003), 107–30, 113; John Blassingame and Louis Harlan, eds., *The Booker T. Washington Papers: Autobiographical Writings* (Urbana: University of Illinois Press, 1972), 1:xxxvi.
29. Houston A. Baker, Jr., *Long Black Song: Essays in Black American Literature* (Charlottesville: University Press of Virginia, 1972), 95, 99–103; Kevin Gaines, *Uplifting the Race: Black Leadership, Politics, and Culture in the Twentieth Century* (Chapel Hill: University of North Carolina Press, 1996), 2, 35, 154; Wilson Jeremiah Moses, *The Golden Age of Black Nationalism, 1859–1925* (New York: Archon Books, 1978), 101–2; W. E. B. Du Bois, *The Autobiography of W. E. B. Du Bois: A Soliloquy on Viewing My Life from the Last Decade of its First Century*, ed. Henry Louis Gates, Jr. (New York: Oxford University Press, 2007), 150.
30. *CW* 2:27–28; Patterson, *Emerson to King*, 172–73.
31. Charles Mitchell, *Individualism and Its Discontents: Appropriations of Emerson, 1880–1950* (Amherst: University of Massachusetts Press, 1997), 136.
32. Du Bois, *Souls*, 52.
33. Booker T. Washington, *Up From Slavery*, ed. William L. Andrews (New York: Norton, 1996), 38.
34. Mitchell, *Appropriations of Emerson*, 137–38.
35. Washington, *Up From Slavery*, 96, 100–101; *CW* 1:53.
36. W. Fitzhugh Brundage, "Introduction: 'An Exemplary Citizen,'" in *Up from Slavery by Booker T. Washington with Related Documents*, ed. Brundage (Boston: Bedford/St. Martins, 2003), 1–35, 22.
37. Du Bois, *Souls*, 22, 27.
38. David Levering Lewis, *W. E. B. Du Bois: Biography of a Race, 1868–1919* (New York: Henry Holt, 1993), 175.
39. Robert Norrell, "Booker T. Washington: Understanding the Wizard of Tuskegee," *Journal of Blacks in Higher Education*, no. 42 (Winter 2003–2004): 96–109, 103, 104, 107.
40. Henry Louis Gates Jr., "Foreword: In Her Own Write," in *Contending Forces: A Romance Illustrative of Negro Life North and South*, by Pauline E. Hopkins, ed. Gates (New York: Oxford University Press, 1988), xii–xxv, xvi; Emerson, *Antislavery Writings*, 32; C. K. Doreski, "Inherited Rhetoric and Authentic History: Pauline Hopkins at the Colored American Magazine," in *The Unruly Voice: Rediscovering Pauline Elizabeth Hopkins*, ed. John Cullen Gruesser (University of Illinois Press, 1996), 71–97; Sean McCann, "'Bonds of Brotherhood': Pauline Hopkins and the Work of Melodrama," *ELH* 64 (1997): 789–822; Sydney Bufkin, "*Contending Forces'* Intellectual History: Emerson, Du Bois, and Washington at the Turn of the Century," *Arizona Quarterly* 69, no. 3 (August 2013): 77–98.
41. Hazel Carby, *Reconstructing Womanhood: The Emergence of the Afro-American Woman Novelist* (New York: Oxford University Press, 1997), 128.
42. Hopkins, *Contending Forces*, 124, 167.
43. Lois Brown, *Pauline Elizabeth Hopkins: Black Daughter of the Revolution* (Chapel Hill: University of North Carolina Press, 2008), 235, 456.
44. Bufkin, "*Contending Forces'* Intellectual History," 78.

45. Hopkins, *Contending Forces*, 168, 295, 300; Bufkin, "*Contending Forces*' Intellectual History," 79.
46. Hopkins, *Contending Forces*, 152, 146.
47. Len Gougeon, "Emerson and the Woman Question: The Evolution of His Thought," *New England Quarterly* 71, no. 4 (December 1998): 581.
48. Anna Julia Cooper, *A Voice From the South by a Black Woman of the South*, ed. Henry Louis Gates, Jr. (New York: Oxford University Press, 1988), 66.
49. Janice Fernheimer, "Arguing from Difference: Cooper, Emerson, Guizot and a More Harmonious America," in *Black Women's Intellectual Traditions: Speaking Their Minds*, ed. Carol Conoway and Kristen Waters (Lebanon: University Press of New England and University of Vermont Press, 2007), 287–305, 289.
50. *CW* 6:4; Cooper, *A Voice*, 164.
51. Hopkins, *Contending Forces*, 79; *CW* 1:10.
52. Hopkins, *Contending Forces*, 140, 345–47.

CHAPTER 15

THE "ARCH-ABOLITIONIST"
Emerson, Love, and Social Justice

PRENTISS CLARK

Every man has his own voice, manner, eloquence, and, just as much, his own sort of love, and grief, and imagination, and action.

Ralph Waldo Emerson, Sermon 90 (*CS* 2:265)

The wild & untameable word of God—who is likely to speak that, but he that loveth much?

Emerson to Caroline Sturgis (*LRWE* VII:440)

EMERSON "undervalues the Affections," Theodore Parker said of his contemporary. "This defect appears in his ethics, which are a little cold, the ethics of marble men."[1] "Here is, undoubtedly, the man of ideas," Margaret Fuller reflected in her review of Emerson's *Essays: Second Series* (1844), "but we want the ideal man also; want the heart and genius of human life to interpret it, and here our satisfaction is not so perfect."[2] "Mr. Emerson's errors," Herman Melville wrote in the margin of Emerson's "The Poet" (1844), "or rather, blindness, proceeds from a defect in the region of the heart"[3] (*Marginalia*). In similar terms, in the twentieth century, John Jay Chapman refers to Emerson's "anemic incompleteness of character"[4]; George Henry Calvert finds that Emerson's "intellect is busier than his feeling"[5]; Alan Hodder says Emerson "flees from intimacy"[6]; and Lawrence Buell describes an "affective deficit"[7] in the essay "Friendship" (1841). Emerson himself offers equally severe self-criticisms. "How can I hope for a friend to me who have never been one?" (*JMN* 7:204), he asks in his journal. "Here I sit alone from month to month filled with a deep desire to exchange thoughts with a friend who does not appear—yet shall I find or refind that friend?" (*JMN* 3:272). He laments his "honorable prison"—the "quarantine of temperament wherefrom I deal courteously with all comers, but through cold water" (*LRWE* 2:239)—and he often expresses a sense of discomfort and inadequacy in interpersonal interactions: "I cannot well say what I found at Plymouth, beyond the uneasiness of seeing people. Every person of worth, man or woman whom I see, gives me a pain as if I injured them, because of my incapacity to do them justice in the intercourse that passes between us" (*JMN* 8:439–40).

Much has been written along these lines, contributing to a narrative of Emerson's emotional coldness, intellectualism, and various failures to acknowledge and reciprocate the affections of friends and family. His daughter Edith, commenting on one of the biographies published after his death, protests the beginnings of this narrative:

> Father is so often represented so cold and thin-blooded, reserved and living in far heights of philosophy without human interests ... I am quite sure that only a quarter part of the man is shown unless it is known what an *enchanting* father he was[,] what a sweet playful loveable house-mate he was, how full of human sympathy for everyone—what respect he had for every class of people.[8]

Scholarship exploring Emerson's reverence for and theory of friendship to some extent offers a corrective to the partial portraits Edith laments, as does scholarship recounting the formative interlocutors, especially women, who shaped Emerson's life and thought: his aunt Mary Moody Emerson, his first wife Ellen Tucker, Margaret Fuller, and Caroline Sturgis.[9] Yet much remains to be written about the "loveable" and loving Emerson; more specifically, the "part of the man" sensitive to the affective dimensions of human existence and civic life, and especially to the transformative power—at once deeply personal and broadly social—of love. For "the arch-abolitionist," he declares in the final sentence of his 1860 speech at a John Brown relief meeting, "older than Brown, and older than the Shenandoah mountains, is love, whose other name is justice" (*CW* 10:393).

The politics of affect—ranging from sentimentalism to disaffection, and particularly in the contexts of nationalism, activism, citizenship, and humanitarian and environmental crises (local as well as global)—continue to animate scholarship on nineteenth-century US literature and culture. A fuller portrait of the "loveable" and loving Emerson enriches these conversations, provoking questions about the forms love takes, the ways in which it affects one's engagement with the world, and the practices it requires and makes possible. Accordingly, this essay takes as its guide Emerson's observation in Sermon 90 that "every man has his own voice, manner, eloquence, and, just as much, his own sort of love, and grief, and imagination, and action."[10] What "sort of love" might we find in Emerson? How does love express itself in his writing, thinking, and living? How does love inform his politics and approach to social justice? The following pages recount how love appears throughout Emerson's oeuvre, often in surprising ways and in pivotal places such as at the ends of *Nature* (1836) and "Politics" (1844) and in lectures from the 1850s and 1860s. This essay then shows how the relationship between love and perception defines Emerson's sense of love at work in the world and enables us to begin reading him among writers and activists who consider love vital to social justice.

Emerson's writing, at heart, is an act of love. "Thy love must be thy art," he counsels himself in his journal, "Thy words must spring from love, and every thought touched with love" (*JMN* 7:386). "I would like to write as a man who writes for his own eye only,"[11] he notes on the first page of a sermon manuscript, confiding a desire to commit himself as openly and wholeheartedly to the public as he would commit himself to his private journal. "You must never lose sight," he reminds himself, "of the purpose of helping a particular person in every word you say" (*JMN* 4:381). "The true preacher can be known by this, that he deals out to the people his life,—life passed through the fire of thought" ("Divinity School Address," *CW* 1:86). Yet more telling than sentences such as these defining Emerson's writing as a labor of love—a work of wholehearted commitment to words and the world—are the many sentences revealing how his way of seeing the world may be read as his "own sort of love."

When Emerson asks in "The American Scholar" (1837), "What would we really know the meaning of?" and goes on to reply, "the meal in the firkin; the milk in the pan; the ballad in the street; the news of the boat; the glance of the eye; the form and the gait of the body," he not only affirms the value of matters "near," "common," and "familiar" (*CW* 1:67)—the ordinary, as scholars such as Stanley Cavell have recounted—but also shows himself to be a keen observer. He sees "the glance" and "the gait," and that these finer forms of human life promise a needed and more intimate understanding of the world. He delights in "the wonderful expressiveness of the human body" ("Behavior," *CW* 6:94). He reads "silent and subtle language" "in the figure, movement, and gesture of animated bodies" and he describes how "nature tells every secret" in human beings "by form, attitude, gesture, mien, face, and parts of the face" (89, 90). He knows how a particular tone of voice can be experienced as a miracle—"I do not wonder at the miracles which poetry attributes to the music of Orpheus, when I remember what I have experienced from the varied notes of the human voice" (*Lectures on the Times*, *CW* 1:169)—and he knows how "there is confession in the glances of our eyes; in our smiles; in salutations; and the grasp of hands" ("Spiritual Laws," *CW* 2:92). He knows "the forced smile which we put on in company where we do not feel at ease in answer to conversation which does not interest us" ("Self-Reliance," *CW* 2:32) and he knows the equally embodied experience of being touched by intimate address: "Were you ever instructed by a wise and eloquent man?" he asks; "remember then, were not the words that made your blood run cold, that brought the blood to your cheeks, that made you tremble or delighted you,—did they not sound to you as old as yourself?" (*JMN* 2:425).

These sentences hum with life and love. They also caution us against conflating Emerson's supposed emotional and interpersonal failings with indifference or incapacity, for together these sentences evidence a sensitive knowledge of "not *what*, but *how*" human life expresses ("Behavior," *CW* 6:89). As Carl F. Strauch rightly suggests, "Emerson was a sympathetic and even profound student of human relations, not lacking in sentiment despite his superficial coldness."[12] "We are tenderly alive to love and hatred," Emerson says in his lecture "The Heart" (1838); "the most selfish, the most able, the most solitary man will find his being woven all over with a delicate net—vital in every part—of fears, and hopes, loves, and regrets that respect other men" (*EL* 2:280). Lines in his journal echo this sentiment in more personal terms: "I am full of tenderness, and born with as large hunger to love and be loved as any man can be, yet its demonstrations are not active and bold, but are passive and tenacious. My love has no flood and no ebb, but is always there under my silence, under displeasure, under cold, arid, and even weak behavior" (*JMN* 5:565). This constant love expresses itself in the way Emerson sees the world and translates it "through the fire of thought" into writing.

Consider the quality of attention evident in phrases such as "the telltale body" and "the ocular dialect" ("Behavior," *CW* 6:94); "jets of affection" ("Friendship," *CW* 2:114); "silent melancholy" ("New England Reformers," *CW* 3:158); "the subtle streams of influence that pass from man to man" ("Introductory," *EL* 2:10); "these extraordinary enlargements of my little heart" (*LRWE* 2:332). Or consider the way a journal entry observes children in the street: "The boys in the streets say to each other 'Dick, toss the ball to me, *you know me*,' which seems to argue a confidence of each child in its own worthiness of love. If it was known to the bottom it must be loved. It is not less, I suppose, true of men[;] if they were known out & out[,] through & through[,] they would be more loved than now, many dark steps would be explained" (*JMN* 3:309–10). Or note the way the essay "Behavior" describes "communication by the glance": "Eyes are bold as lions,—roving, running, leaping, here and there, far and near. They speak all languages. What inundation of life and thought are discharged from one soul into another, through them!" (*CW* 6:95). Emerson in this catalogue of examples is his own best interpreter, teaching us to look elsewhere than his undemonstrative temperament and to observe how he sees the world lovingly.

In short, "as much love, so much perception" ("Success," *CW* 7:157). Emerson's first book *Nature* (1836) tells the story of this relationship. Generally considered a Transcendentalist manifesto which contains, as Barbara L. Packer rightly notes, "condensed versions of every major Emersonian theme,"[13] the book opens with the famous charge, "Why should not we also enjoy an original relation to the universe?" (*CW* 1:7). *Nature*'s first seven chapters attempt to reclaim this relation by asking, "To what end is nature?" and proceeding with the uncharacteristically systematic method of "enumerating the values of nature and casting up their sum" (*CW* 1:8). Yet after working through theories, for example, of beauty, language, commodity, and the limitations of empiricism and idealism, Emerson discovers that an "original relation to the universe" requires something more, and other. Love, in the eighth and final chapter, works an ontological, epistemological, and ethical revolution that transforms the aim and method of the book. Rather than seek to "recite correctly the order and superimposition of the strata" and measure things with the "half-sight of science" (*CW* 1:41) and "wintery light of the understanding" (44) alone, Emerson seeks a more intimate awareness of "that wonderful congruity which subsists between man and the world" (*CW* 1:40). He describes this awareness at the beginning of the book when he compares "superficial seeing" to seeing with love: "Most persons do not see the sun. At least they have a very superficial seeing. The sun illuminates only the eye of the man, but shines into the eye and the heart of the child. The lover of nature is he whose inward and outward senses are still truly adjusted to each other" (*CW* 1:9). More than naïve prelapsarian longing, this sentence differentiates between seeing with eyes alone and seeing with both "the eye and heart"; that is, perceiving the world with love, openheartedly, such that one "sees" in all senses of the word—understands as well as observes. The end of *Nature* returns to and realizes this opening insight.

"I only wish to indicate the true position of nature in regard to man," Emerson writes, recasting the question "to what end is nature?" as an attempt to "attain" the "ground" constituting the "connection" between humankind and the natural world (*CW* 1:36). *Nature*'s final chapter demonstrates how attaining this ground requires aligning one's "axis of vision" with "the axis of things," studying nature not from the hierarchical distance of the detached scientific observer but from a position of a "lover of nature … whose inward and outward senses are still truly adjusted to each other" (*CW* 1:9).

> The ruin or the blank, that we see when we look at nature, is in our own eye. The axis of vision is not coincident with the axis of things, and so they appear not transparent but opake. The reason the world lacks unity, and lies broken and in heaps, is, because man is disunited with himself. He cannot be a naturalist, until he satisfies all the demands of the spirit. Love is as much its demand, as perception. Indeed, neither can be perfect without the other. (*CW* 1:43)

Love aligns one with the world because it entails a way of being in the world—receptively, responsively—rather than a methodology to which one subjects the world. For "the best read naturalist," Emerson concludes, "who lends an entire and devout attention to truth, will see that there remains much to learn of his relation to the world, and that it is not to be learned by any addition or subtraction or other comparison of known quantities, but arrived at by untaught sallies of the spirit, by a continual self recovery, and by entire humility" (*CW* 1:39). The "best read naturalist," learning what the lover learns, finds that love works a revolution at once local and global.

"So shall we come to look at the world with new eyes," Emerson concludes, ". . . without more wonder than the blind man feels who is gradually restored to perfect sight" (*CW* I:44). In effect, love wed with the "half-sight of science" transforms one's relationship to the world, human as well as non-human. "What is a day? What is a year? … What is woman? What is a child? … To our blindness, these things seem unaffecting" (*CW* 1:44). Love brings "these things" home: "These wonders are brought to our own door … Man and woman, and their social life, poverty, labor, sleep, fear, fortune are known to you. Learn that none of these things is superficial" (*CW* 1:44). *Nature* thus offers a lesson in how matters once "unaffecting" claim concern, become "the miraculous in the common" (*CW* 1:44), the things "we would really know the meaning of."

The essay "Love" (1841) calls this transformed relationship to the universe—this attunement of one's heart and mind to "the common"—"the real marriage." "Love" notably precedes the essay "Friendship" in Essays: First Series, (reversing the commonplace that friendship precedes love), and it opens with Emerson's response to critics who say his "reverence for the intellect" makes him "unjustly cold to the personal relationships." "I almost shrink at the remembrance of such disparaging words," he writes, affirming how "persons are love's world," how "the oldest cannot recount the debt of the young... to the power of love," and how "no man ever forgot the visitations of that power to his heart and brain, which created all things new... when a single tone of one voice could make the heart bound, and the most trivial circumstance associated with one form, is put in the amber of memory: when he became all eye when one was present, and all memory when one was gone" (CW 2:101–2). Yet this opening defense is more than a simple response to the charge of injustice to "personal relationships." It helps readers to see that such relationships, for Emerson, are the beginning of, and condition for, love in its fullest and most socially consequential form.

Unsurprisingly, many readers thus find that the essay falls flat as an account of passionate interpersonal love. "There is a word or two in the essay on Love which seems to show that the inner and diaphanous core of this seraph has once, but not for long, been shot with blood: he recalls only the pain of it," John Jay Chapman concludes.[14] This reading, however, misses not only the way the essay, in Branka Arsić's terms, locates "the truth of love ... in actual eroticism"[15] (177) but also the way the essay gives equal attention to a "union" other than the normative "two-as-one intimacy of the couple form"[16] (*Desire/Love*, 6), to borrow terms from Lauren Berlant. More specifically, the essay celebrates the "real marriage" that love makes possible: "the purification of the intellect and heart, from year to year, is the real marriage" (109); that is, the ongoing instruction of mind and heart. "We are put in training for a love which knows not sex, nor person, nor partiality," Emerson says, "but which seeks virtue and wisdom everywhere, to the end of increasing virtue and wisdom" (CW 2:109). In other words, *Nature*'s account of how "love is as much its [the Spirit's] demand, as perception ... neither can be perfect without the other," becomes, in "Love," the "real marriage" that is "the purification of the intellect and heart, from year to year" (109). Both formulations make clear that love refines how one sees, thinks, and feels. "Love is fabled to be blind," Emerson notes in his journal, "but to me it seems that kindness is necessary to perception, that love is not an ophthalmia but an electuary" (*JMN* 5:294). Love, in effect, enhances one's faculties for engaging with the world. "In the procession of the soul from within outward, it enlarges its circles ever" (CW 2:107), Emerson says; the "lover ascends to the highest beauty, to the love and knowledge of the Divinity" (CW 2:106).

Readers often stop here. In Alan Hodder's terms, "for Emerson as for Plato, love serves an entirely spiritual purpose."[17] "If love and real relations are the starting point, the direction is upward and the end impersonal," Joseph Urbas contends, "Emerson's *scala amoris* leads to the Impersonal."[18] Sharon Cameron has written extensively on "Emerson's impersonal," a state attained by relinquishing personal identity and all its particulars to a "radical commonness" (224) and exemplified by "the most famous example"[19] from "The Over-Soul" (1841): "Persons themselves acquaint us with the impersonal" (CW 2:164). Yet when reading the essay "Love" (1841) and considering concepts such as the "impersonal" within the context of Emerson's oeuvre, the "end impersonal" is not an end but, as it was in *Nature*, a new beginning. Love between individuals indeed "leads to the Impersonal"—to "a love which knows not sex, nor person, nor partiality"— yet in this process love becomes newly personal as well: it becomes an operative power in individuals' perceptions and actions; it transforms one's "relation to the universe" and how one conducts one's life.[20] "For, it is the nature and end of this relation, that they [lovers] should represent the human race to each other," Emerson says; "all that is in the world that is or ought to be known, is cunningly wrought into the texture of man, of woman" (CW 2:108).[21]

The early lecture "Love" (1838) catalogues how this process is deeply personal and broadly social in consequence. As it "works a revolution in [a person's] soul and body," love "unites him to his race, pledges him to the domestic and civic relation, carries him with new sympathy into nature; enhances the power of the senses; gives him new eyes, and new ears ... and then at last proves only introductory to more expansive and divine affection" (EL 3:52). A moral, emotional, spiritual, and civic education, the "end of this relation" is not acquaintance with a higher world of ideal forms but discovering how the world may be read "in the texture of man, of woman." Lovers "are to teach each other by experiment the whole law of Ethics" (EL 3:66). Knowledge in particular amounts to general knowledge better able to discern particulars, and the "more expansive and divine affection" to which love "at last proves only introductory" means an ever greater capacity for seeing the world with love. Put simply, a love story, for Emerson, is not exclusively a story about a person's relationship to another person, nor is it a conventional narrative of heteronormative marriage that fits one for prescribed domestic and civic duties. A love story, for Emerson, is also, and equally, a story about a person's transformed relationship to the universe, a romance with the world.

"In fact in the spiritual world we seem to change sexes every moment," he writes in his journal.

> You love the worth that is in me[,] therefore am I your husband[;] but it is not me but the worth that really fixes your love ... that which is in me is but a drop of the Ocean of Worth that is behind me. Meantime I adore the greater worth that is in another; so I become his wife & he again aspire to a higher worth which dwells in another spirit & so is wife or receiver of that spirit's influence. Every soul is a Venus to every other soul. (JMN 7:532–33)

Even as love inevitably carries individuals outward and onward, one doesn't "lose any genuine love" (CW 2:125) for the person loved, as Emerson clarifies in "Friendship"—"we need not fear that we can lose any thing by the progress of the soul" ("Love," CW 2:110)—for this process is an education that brings home "the worth" of persons, the self as well as others. One might say love, for Emerson, is as impersonal as the sun and as personal as the sun on my face: it shines into my eyes and into my heart, such that the world is no longer "opake" and such that the "unaffecting" things of the world are brought home and newly seen.

This transformative process, as "Love" (1838, 1841) and *Nature* make clear, not only changes who one is but how one is. One begins to be otherwise, and for Emerson, a personal revolution carries with it the potential for revolutionary social change. He uses just these terms in "Self-Reliance" (1841) when he describes how "a greater self-reliance must work a revolution in all the offices and relations of men; in their religion; in their education; in their pursuits; in their modes of living; in their association; in their property; in their speculative views" (*CW* 2:44). Love informs Emerson's politics, in other words, in the same way "self-reliance" and the "moral sentiment" inform his politics: by affecting, and in many cases changing, how one conducts one's life, how one answers the ethical question "How shall I live?" ("Fate," *CW* 6:1). Put differently, at the heart of Emerson's politics is his sense that, in the final analysis, changing the world requires changing our relationship to it; that is, changing how we see it, understand it, and engage with it.

The essay "Politics" (1844) makes this point explicitly. It opens with a pointed reminder about the nature of "the State":

> Its institutions are not aboriginal, though they existed before we were born ... they are not superior to the citizen ... every one of them was once the act of a single man: every law and usage was a man's expedient to meet a particular case ... they all are imitable, all alterable; we may make as good; we may make better. (*CW* 3:117)

Institutions, laws, usages, and the government itself, he suggests, are made, sustained, and can be changed by persons, evidenced not least in the way political parties often "degenerate into personalities" (122) and in the way even "admirable law-forms and political forms" (*LL* 1:262) can become empty forms, abused by people in power or unthinkingly followed. "Treat men as pawns and ninepins," he cautions, "and you shall suffer as well as they. If you leave out their heart you shall lose your own" ("Society," *EL* 2:107). An often-debated passage in "Self-Reliance" (1841) more explicitly criticizes the consequences of these performative actions, or what Emerson calls "the service of calculation" rather than "the service of love" ("The Heart," *EL* 2:282):

> If an angry bigot assumes this bountiful cause of Abolition, and comes to me with his last news from Barbadoes, why should I not say to him, "Go love thy infant; love thy wood-chopper: be good-natured and modest: have that grace; and never varnish your hard, uncharitable ambition with this incredible tenderness for black folk a thousand miles off. Thy love afar is spite at home." Rough and graceless would be such greeting, but truth is handsomer than the affectation of love. (*CW* 2:30)

Hard words, here, in this account which doesn't question the "cause of Abolition" but the fact that "malice and vanity wear the coat of philanthropy" and go unquestioned. In effect, this angry bigot's "incredible tenderness for black folk a thousand miles off" is not only an "affectation of love" that objectifies its recipients but also "spite" toward the persons "at home" nearest to him.[22]

"Emersonian politics," in Jennifer Gurley's account, "is the practice of living a life that regards other citizens: not in theory or on occasion, but in fact, everyday"[23] (348). This practical regard—seeing fellow citizens as fellow persons rather than the "pawns and ninepins" they can become in even the most well-intentioned social justice efforts—depends, as this essay has been suggesting, on love as well as perception. W. E. B. Du

Bois, in "The Individual and Social Consciousness" (1905), calls this practical regard an "active and animate heart-to-heart knowledge of your neighbors" and he insists that "it means ... a reverent listening, not simply to the first line but to the last line of Emerson's quatrain: 'There is no great, no small, / To the Soul that maketh all; / Where it cometh, all things are—/ And it cometh everywhere.'" One might say seeing "the Soul" in all things everywhere is the broadest social consequence of love wed with perception, a union enabling "the active and animate heart-to-heart knowledge of your neighbors."[24]

Emerson envisions this way of being at the end of "Politics" (1844) when he describes a "movement" toward "the idea of self-government" which "separates the individual from all party, and unites him, at the same time to the race." This imagined community of individual citizens existing as neighbors "promises a recognition of higher rights than those of personal freedom, or the security of property": a person, he says, "has a right to be employed, to be trusted, to be loved, to be revered. The power of love, as the basis of a State, has never been tried" (*CW* 3:128). These "higher rights" depend for their realization as much on the lived interactions of individuals as they do on the laws that can never fully guarantee them. If, as Alan M. Levine and Daniel S. Malachuk suggest, the "most effective political change," for Emerson, "begins with an ethical change in one's self," then love is one way, among many, toward realizing such change.[25] Fittingly, the essay "Politics" (1844) ends with the possibility "that thousands of human beings might share and obey each with the other the grandest and truest sentiments, as well as a knot of friends, or a pair of lovers" (*CW* 3:129). Rather than exist primarily in relationship to the State, individuals here exist in relationship to each other; a "knot of friends, or a pair of lovers" become models for a citizenry in which people might exercise among themselves "the grandest and truest sentiments." For Emerson, building a better world was fundamentally a matter of ethics, a matter of how persons conduct their lives together. The "highest end of government is the culture of men: and if men can be educated, the institutions will share their improvement, and the moral sentiment will write the law of the land" (*CW* 3:120).

The radically unjust institutions, laws, and usages of the 1850s and 1860s made increasingly clear the need for this kind of individual as well as social action. Emerson's lectures during this period reiterate in the context of national crises his faith in the political and moral power held by, and required of, individuals. His 1854 lecture against the Fugitive Slave Law, revised and more militant than his 1851 version, proclaims, "No forms, neither constitutions, nor laws, nor covenants, nor churches, nor bibles, are of any use in themselves ... There is no help but in the head, and heart, and hamstrings of a man." "To make good the cause of Freedom," he insists, "... You must be citadels and warriors, yourselves Declarations of Independence" (*LL* 1:342). A year later in "American Slavery" (1855) he more explicitly calls on individuals to confront "this evil government": "When the public fails in its duty, private men take its place" (*LL* 2:10). He clarifies that he does "not cripple but exalt the social action"—he acknowledges that "exterminate[ing] slavery" is a "right social or public function which one man cannot do, which all men must do" (*LL* 2:13)—yet he continues to uphold "the doctrine of the independence and inspiration of the individual" (*LL* 2:11). "Men inspire each other. The affections are Muses. Hope is a Muse, Love is, Despair is not" (*LL* 2:13).[26] Right collective action begins here, with persons acting according to principle; or in Emerson's terms, "we have a great debt to the brave and faithful men who ... made their protest for the themselves and their countrymen by word and deed" (*LL* 2:10). Five years later he honored radical abolitionist John Brown, "a representative of the American Republic" (*CW* 10:387), in a speech with an impassioned conclusion about the "arch-abolitionist" love.[27]

He spoke "with the power, the overwhelmingness, of an avalanche," Walt Whitman said of Emerson speaking at relief meetings for Brown's family.[28] His 1860 speech accounts for why people "sympathize with [Brown]"—"it is impossible to see courage, and disinterestedness, and the love that casts out fear, without sympathy"—and then declares what he considers assured justice. "Nothing is more absurd than to complain of this sympathy, or to complain of a party of men united in opposition to Slavery" (*CW* 10:393), for the absurdity lies in the fact that the objectors contend against the power of love:

> Our blind statesmen go up and down, with committees of vigilance and safety, hunting for the origin of his new heresy. They will need a very vigilant committee indeed to find its birthplace, and a very strong force to root it out. For the arch-abolitionist, older than Brown, and older than the Shenandoah mountains, is love, whose other name is justice, which was before Alfred, before Lycurgus, before Slavery, and will be after it. (*CW* 10:393)

Love here is an impersonal power predating and outlasting individuals (even "the Shenandoah mountains") and working ever for right. It is also and equally a power exercised by particular individuals throughout history—Alfred, Lycurgus—and here today in the person of John Brown and in the "party" of men and women "united in opposition to Slavery." One might say "the arch-abolitionist" names the way Emerson sees love working in and on individuals no less than in and on the world: it frees us, individually and collectively, to be otherwise. It enlivens and increases one's perceiving—"as much love, so much perception"—and it enables one to perceive again, and differently—"he that loves sees newly every time he looks at the object; for love is an entrance into the object loved or a reception of that" (*JMN* 8:494)—and it offers continual instruction: "the remedy for all blunders, the cure of blindness, the cure of crime, is love ... The superiority that hath no superior; the redeemer and instructor of souls, as it is their primal essence, is love" ("Worship," *CW* 6:116). As he imagines in "Man the Reformer" (1841), "there will dawn ere long on our politics, on our modes of living, a nobler morning than that Arabian faith, in the sentiment of love. This is the one remedy for all ills, the panacea of nature" (*CW* 1:158).

While Emerson's faith in the universe working ultimately for right—that "Nature is not so helpless but it can rid itself at last of every crime" ("American Slavery," *LL* 2:8)—has sometimes been taken as pacifism, equivocation, or naïve faith in progress, his lectures from the 1850s onward make clear that faith does not take the place of action but supports and advances it.[29] "I hope we have come to an end of our unbelief," he said in the final sentence of his 1854 Fugitive Slave Law address, and "have to come a belief that there is a Divine Providence in the world which will not save us but through our own cooperation" (*LL* 1:347). This "cooperation," for Emerson, took the form of continued writing, speaking, and hosting at his home with Lidian abolitionists such as William Lloyd Garrison, Sarah and Angelina Grimké, and Wendell Phillips. One might say, to borrow a term from Paul Ramsey, it took the form of "neighborly-love," a term "stressing what love ought to be" rather than "the expression 'love for neighbor,' which puts the emphasis on who the neighbor is."[30] Or one might say it took the form of what Derrick Spires terms an "ethics of neighborliness, a civic ethos animated by a sensibility made material or 'real' through concrete actions."[31] For "in our idea of progress," Emerson notes in the introduction to *Lectures on the Times*, "we do not go out of this personal picture. We do not think the sky will be bluer, or honey sweeter, or our climate more temperate, but only that our relation to our fellows will be simpler and happier" (*CW* 1:168)—in other words, more just—for in "our relation" to others, including our "relation to the universe," we build, maintain, and change our forms of life. As Spires writes, "While ... neighborliness ultimately manifests in concrete actions between individuals, its logics have implications for how civic institutions take shape. Neighborly practices ultimately produce neighborly institutions; the ethos and actions that characterize the neighborly citizen also characterize the neighborly state."[32] "The state and the aspiration," Emerson observes in his early lecture "Politics" (1840), "no matter how powerful this looks and how faint that, the state always follows close on the track of the hope and the sentiment of the people" (*EL* 3:242). He believed that "the affirmative of affirmatives is love" (*CW* 7:157); "love, imperious love, that great Prophet & Poet, that Comforter, that Omnipotency in the heart" (*LRWE* 7:460).

The "sort of love" one finds modeled in Emerson's thinking, writing, and living is neither sentimentalism, that "enduring—though often disavowed—rhetoric, genre, cultural mode, set of material relations, ideology, and episteme," in Xine Yao's terms, long debated in studies of US literature and culture, nor the universal love called agape, nor a virtue one preforms.[33] The "sort of love" one finds modeled in Emerson's thinking, writing, and living is a way of being in the world, practiced daily. He experienced acutely the challenges of this practice, which says as much about what makes love profoundly and painfully human as it does about Emerson, personally. For example, the fact that love involves uncertainty, requires trust, can fail, and, as Emerson particularly knew, entails vulnerability, hurt, and loss. "Shall I ever dare to love anything again?" he wrote to Margaret Fuller following the death of his son Waldo (*LRWE* 3:8). Or as he tellingly records in his journal, "It is not that you should avoid men, but that you should not be hurt by them" (*JMN* 2:326); and, "I am cold because I am hot,—cold at the surface only as a sort of guard & compensation for the fluid tenderness of the core" (*JMN* 7:368). He was especially aware of his "Stygian limitations," which he acknowledges in a revealing letter to his wife Lidian. "Ah," he writes, "you still ask for that unwritten letter always due, it seems, always unwritten, from year to year, by me to you, dear Lidian,—I fear too more widely true than you mean,—always due & unwritten by me to every sister & brother of the human race. I have only to say that I also bemoan myself daily for the same cause" (*LRWE* 4:33). This private letter remarkably captures in life Emerson's theory of love and its limitations. His love is at once love for a particular individual—"dear Lidian"—as well as love for "every sister & brother of the human race," and his "poverty of nature" ever limits his ability to fully express it. He goes on in more painful terms to repeat, "the trick of solitariness never never can leave me"; "my own pursuits & calling often appear to me like those of an 'astronomer royal' whose whole duty is to make faithful minutes which have only value when kept for ages, and in one life are insignificant" (*LRWE* 4:33). For better and worse, Emerson lived his belief that "the universe is the bride of the soul"; bride and husband alike, considering the innumerable and diverse individuals who have husbanded his "faithful minutes" through the decades. One could argue that his lamented "unwritten" love letter to the world is in fact realized in his body of work, living proof that one expression of his "sort of love" was his service as a public intellectual who "deal[t] out to the people his life,—life passed through the fire of thought" ("Divinity School Address," *CW* 1:86).

One of his most provocative thoughts, particularly in the face of today's global humanitarian and environmental crises, is that love can help to build a better world by transforming our relationship to it; that is, to ourselves, others, the non-human world, and beyond. Emerson is not alone in voicing this perspective, a perspective that has been variously voiced by writers and activists for centuries and has been considered, by turns, necessary, naïve, conservative, radical, severely limited, and potentially transformative. "Where is the love?" June Jordan asked in 1978 at Howard University on the pioneering panel "Black Women Writers and Feminism":

> As I think about anyone or any thing—whether history or literature or my father or political organizations or a poem or a film—as I seek to evaluate the potentiality, the life-supportive commitment/possibilities of anyone or any thing, the decisive question is, always, *where is the love?* . . . it is always the love that will carry action into positive new places.[34]

In fact, bell hooks wrote decades later, "all the great movements for social justice in our society have strongly emphasized a love ethic. Yet young listeners remain reluctant to embrace the idea of love as a transformative force."[35] Undoubtedly, much can be said against love. Like anything—like language—it can be used to police, repress, coerce, and tyrannize. "In the Name of Love," to borrow terms from Sara Ahmed, individuals and institutions commit injustices. "How does politics involve a struggle over who has the right to declare themselves as acting out of love?" Ahmed asks; "what does it mean to stand for love by standing alongside some others and against other others?"[36] Lauren Berlant recounts the "long history of using the abstractions and institutions of love as the signs and sites of propriety" and how these "tacit proprieties have been used to justify the economic and physical domination of nations, races, religions, gays, lesbians and, women."[37] Xine Yao contributes to unsettling this history with a call for embracing "disaffection" as a "tool we can use to tear down dominant structures of feeling to build anew." She suggests that "marginalized unfeeling"—which includes affects ranging from "disregard" to "refusing to care" to "dissociation"—"is the unrecognized underside of universalized feelings of the dominant" and thus "dissents from the biopolitics of feeling, hinting at other ways of organizing life that might be suppressed, overlooked, adjacent, incipient, insurgent, resurgent, or still to be imagined."[38]

Yet just as much can be said for love, in support of it and its possibilities. Berlant follows a summary of how love justifies forms of domination and violence with a return to how "despite everything, desire/love continue to exert a utopian promise": "the project of this book [*Desire/Love*] is also to reopen the utopian to more promises than have yet been imagined and sustained" (112). Jennifer C. Nash, recounting a long tradition of black feminist love-politics, describes how "love is a labor of actively reorienting the self, pushing the self to be configured in new ways that might be challenging or difficult."[39] This labor "reshapes the public sphere by offering a distinctive conception of remedy. Rather than looking to the state for remedy ... black feminist love-politics asks how affective communities can themselves be a site of redress."[40] Similarly, Martha Nussbaum writes extensively about the relationship between love and justice, concluding her book *Political Emotions* with a response to objectors who say a "demand for love" is "unrealistic given the present state of politics in more or less every country":

> The objector presumably thinks that nations need technical calculation: economic thought, military thought, good use of computer science and technology. So, nations need those things, but they do not need the heart? ... do they not need the sort of daily emotion, the sympathy, tears, and laughter, that we require of ourselves as parents, lovers, and friends, or the wonder with which we contemplate beauty?[41] (396–97)

"When I was very young," James Baldwin recalls, "and was dealing with my buddies in those wine- and urine-stained hallways, something in me wondered, *What will happen to all that beauty?*"[42] Baldwin, who like Emerson left the pulpit to minister in a different way, emphasized, also like Emerson, the way love clarifies and challenges and changes. "I was being forced to see that real love involves real perception," his character Jimmy discovers in *Just Above My Head* (1979), "and that perception can bring joy, or terror, or death, but it will never abandon you to the dream of happiness. Love is perceiving and perceiving is anguish."[43]

If this roll call of writers, activists, and scholars transgresses the boundaries of periodization, historical context, and academic convention, then it does so in demonstration of love, of the way love challenges boundaries and frees us to be otherwise. As David A. J. Richards writes in *Why Love Leads to Justice: Loves Across the Boundaries* (2016), love "crosses boundaries, and thus is condemned by the social norms that are so effective at setting up boundaries in the first place."[44] A "key to understanding transformative ethical resistance," he suggests, "is the connection between the experience of love across the boundaries patriarchy imposes and the freeing of ethical voice."[45] "The wild & untameable word of God," Emerson wrote to Caroline Sturgis, "who is likely to speak that, but he that loveth much?" (*LRWE* 7:440). Love also exposes these boundaries. Emerson declares, "Our chief want in life is somebody who shall make us do what we can ... How he flings wide the doors of existence!"; "we come out of our eggshell existence into the great Dome, and see the zenith over and the nadir under us" ("Considerations by the Way," *CW* 6:145, 144). For Baldwin as well as for Emerson, artists serve as lovers who can fling open "the doors of existence." About the shared "role of the artist and the role of the lover," Baldwin writes,

> If I love you, I have to make you conscious of the things you don't see. Insofar as that is true, in that effort, I become conscious of the things that I don't see. And I will not see without you, and vice versa, you will not see without me ... The only way you can get through it is to accept that two-way street which I call love ... An artist is here not to give you answers but to ask you questions.[46]

Emerson calls it provocation.

"We must be lovers," he writes from within a nation heading toward civil war, "and instantly the impossible becomes possible" ("Man the Reformer," *CW* 1:158). "I know what I am asking is impossible," James Baldwin concludes from within a nation warring for civil rights, "but in our time, as in every time, the impossible is the least that one can demand." He grounds this faith in "the spectacle of human history"—especially "American Negro history"—because "it testifies to nothing less than the perpetual achievement of the impossible":

> If we—and now I mean the relatively conscious whites and the relatively conscious blacks, who must, like lovers, insist on, or create, the consciousness of the others—do not falter in our duty now, we may be able, handful that we are, to end the racial nightmare, and achieve our country, and change the history of the world.[47]

Emerson, in his own very different time and with "his own voice, manner, eloquence, and, just as much, his own sort of love, and grief, and imagination, and action," insists on this radical act of love: seeing the world with love as well as with perception and committing to the consciousness it makes possible. "Let our affection flow out to our fellows," he says in "Man the Reformer" (1841), "it would operate in a day the greatest of all revolutions," for "love will creep where it cannot go, will accomplish that by imperceptible methods ... which force could never achieve" (*CW* 1:158–59). In effect, against the protean forms of systemic and institutional force, Emerson would hold up the human face. As his final sentence of "Politics" (1844) affirms, "I have just been conversing with one man, to whom no weight of adverse experience will make it for a moment appear impossible, that thousands of human beings might share and obey each with the other the grandest and truest sentiments, as well as a knot of friends, or a pair of lovers" (*CW* 3:129).

Notes

1. Theodore Parker, "The Writings of Ralph Waldo Emerson," *Massachusetts Quarterly Review* (March 1850): 200–256, 220.
2. Quoted in Robert E. Burkholder and Joel Myerson, eds., *Critical Essays on Ralph Waldo Emerson* (Boston: G. K. Hall, 1983), 94–95.
3. Herman Melville, *Melville's Marginalia Online*, ed. Steven Olsen-Smith and Peter Norberg, accessed January 1, 2023, http://melvillesmarginalia.org.
4. John Jay Chapman, *The Selected Writings of John Jay Chapman*, ed. Jacques Barzun (New York: Farrar, Straus, and Cudahy, 1957), 184.
5. George Henry Calvert, 1853, "Ralph Waldo Emerson," in *Critical Essays on Ralph Waldo Emerson*, ed. Robert E. Burkholder and Joel Myerson (New York: G. K. Hall, 1983), 155–62, 158.
6. Alan Hodder, "'Let Him Be to Me a Spirit': Paradoxes of True Friendship in Emerson and Thoreau," in *Emerson and Thoreau: Figures of Friendship*, ed. John T. Lysaker and William Rossi (Bloomington: Indiana University Press, 2010), 127–50, 139.
7. Lawrence Buell, *Emerson* (Cambridge, MA: Harvard University Press, 2003), 82.
8. Quoted in Robert Habich, *Building Their Own Waldos: Emerson's First Biographers and the Politics of Life-Writing in the Gilded Age* (Iowa City: University of Iowa Press, 2011), 134.
9. For scholarship on Emerson and friendship see Thomas Constantinesco, "Discordant Correspondence in Ralph Waldo Emerson's Friendship," *New England Quarterly* 81, no. 2 (2008): 281–51; Caleb Crain, "The Unacknowledged Tie: Young Emerson and the Love of Men," in *American Sympathy: Men, Friendship, and Literature in the New Nation* (New Haven: Yale University Press, 2003), 148–76; Jeffrey S. Cramer, *Solid Seasons: The Friendship of Henry David Thoreau and Ralph Waldo Emerson* (Berkeley: Counterpoint, 2019); Carl F. Strauch, "Hatred's Swift Repulsions: Emerson, Margaret Fuller, and Others," *Studies in Romanticism* 7, no. 2 (Winter 1968): 65–103; and the essays by Lawrence Buell, Russell B. Goodman, Alan Hodder, John T. Lysaker, Barbara L. Packer, and David M. Robinson in John T. Lysaker and William Rossi, eds., *Emerson and Thoreau: Figures of Friendship* (Bloomington: Indiana University Press, 2010). For scholarship on Emerson and formative female interlocutors see Phyllis Cole, *Mary Moody Emerson and the Origins of Transcendentalism: A Family History* (New Haven: Oxford University Press, 1998); Christopher Hanlon, "Knowing by Heart," in *Emerson's Memory Loss: Originality, Communality, and the Late Style* (New York: Oxford University Press, 2018), 46–85; Kathleen Lawrence, "The 'Dry-Lighted Soul' Ignites: Emerson and His Soul-Mate Caroline Sturgis as Seen in Her Houghton Manuscripts," *Harvard Library Bulletin* 16, no. 3 (Fall 2005): 37–67; and Christina Zwarg, *Feminist Conversations: Fuller, Emerson, and the Play of Reading* (New Haven: Cornell University Press, 1995). Lawrence finds that in Emerson's exchanges with Caroline Sturgis he "transcended his sterile image to become as radical in person as he was in thought. The cold and inept sage becomes a passionate lover and friend, deeply in need, hungry for her presence and her poetry" (66). Lawrence's forthcoming book *Caroline Sturgis, Emerson's Lost Muse* will help to reclaim this neglected relationship.
10. Ralph Waldo Emerson, *The Complete Sermons of Ralph Waldo Emerson*, ed. Albert J. von Frank et al., 4 vols. (Columbia: University of Missouri Press, 1989–1992), 2:265. Further citations appear parenthetically as *CS*.
11. Quoted in Arthur Cushman McGiffert, Jr., *Young Emerson Speaks: Unpublished Discourses on Many Subjects* (Boston: Houghton Mifflin, 1938), xxxiv.

12. Carl F. Strauch, "Hatred's Swift Repulsions: Emerson, Margaret Fuller, and Others," *Studies in Romanticism* 7, no. 2 (Winter 1968): 65–103, 67.
13. Barbara L. Packer, *Emerson's Fall: A New Interpretation of the Major Essays* (London: Continuum, 1982), 25.
14. Chapman, *Selected Writings*, 71.
15. Branca Arsić, *On Leaving: A Reading in Emerson* (Cambridge, MA: Harvard University Press, 2010), 177.
16. Lauren Berlant, *Desire/Love* (punctum books, 2012), 6.
17. Hodder, "Paradoxes of True Friendship," 128.
18. Joseph Urbas, *Emerson's Metaphysics: A Song of Laws and Causes* (Lanham, MD: Lexington Books, 2016), 174.
19. Sharon Cameron, *Impersonality: Seven Essays* (Chicago: University of Chicago Press, 2007), 224, 80.
20. In Branka Arsić's terms, "In an almost phenomenological way 'Love' will proceed to describe the material (sensual) effects produced by passion ... specifically the changes it induces in perception and imagination." See Arsić, On Leaving, 177.
21. Emerson's poem "Give all to Love" clarifies, in Albert von Frank's words, how "the worthy injunction to 'give all to love' has ... to be discriminated from the unworthy injunction to 'give all to the beloved'" (*CW* 9:179).
22. For an extended reading of this passage, its critical reception, and its relationship to Emerson's abolitionism, see Martha Schoolman, "Emerson's Doctrine of Hatred," *Arizona Quarterly* 63, no. 2 (Summer 2007): 1–26.
23. Jennifer Gurley, "Emerson's Politics of Uncertainty," *ESQ* 53, no. 4 (2007): 323–59, 348.
24. W. E. B. Du Bois, "The Individual and Social Conscience" [originally untitled], *Proceedings of the Third Annual Convention of the Religious Education Association*, February 12–16, 1905, accessed January 1, 2023, www.webdubois.org/dbIASC.html.
25. Alan M. Levine and Daniel S. Malachuk, "Introduction," in *A Political Companion to Ralph Waldo Emerson*, ed. Levine and Malachuk (Lexington: University Press of Kentucky, 2014), 1–39, 5.
26. As Henry David Thoreau put it: "just in proportion as I regard [the State] as not wholly a brute force, but partly a human force, and consider that I have relations to those millions as to so many millions of men, and not of mere brute or inanimate things, I see that appeal is possible." See Thoreau, *Walden, Civil Disobedience, and Other Writings*, ed. William Rossi, 3rd ed. (New York: Norton, 2008), 242.
27. For another reading of the relationship between Emerson's affective life and his politics after 1850 see Hanlon, *Emerson's Memory Loss*. Hanlon demonstrates "a continuum between the barriers that more or less ended Emerson's friendship with [Margaret] Fuller and the blockages Emerson overcame as he took to the abolitionist stump after 1850" (53).
28. Quoted in Robert D. Richardson, *Emerson: The Mind on Fire* (Berkeley: University of California Press), 498.
29. David Robinson says Emerson "saw more and more clearly that one could not easily or confidently assume the triumph of the good, unless one became an agent of the good" (*Political Emerson*, 15). In Joseph Urbas's reading, Emerson's abolitionism "should be seen as Emerson himself saw it—as a historical application of his metaphysical doctrine, a real-world test of its truth in a time of national crisis." See Urbas, *Emerson's Metaphysics*, 179.
30. Paul Ramsey, *Basic Christian Ethics* (New York: Charles Scribner's Sons, 1950), 93.

31. Derrick R. Spires, *The Practice of Citizenship: Black Politics and Print Culture in the Early United States* (Philadelphia: University of Pennsylvania Press, 2019), 66.
32. Ibid., 66–67.
33. Xine Yao, *Disaffected: The Cultural Politics of Unfeeling in Nineteenth-Century America* (Durham, NC: Duke University Press, 2021), 8.
34. June Jordan, "Where is the Love?," in *Some of Us Did Not Die: New and Selected Essays* (London: Civitas Books, 2003), 268–74, 269.
35. bell hooks, *All About Love: New Visions* (New York: William Morrow, 2000), xix.
36. Sara Ahmed, "In the Name of Love," in *The Cultural Politics of Emotion*, 2nd ed. (Edinburgh: Edinburgh University Press, 2004), 122–43, 122.
37. Berlant, *Desire/Love*, 112.
38. Yao, *Disaffected*, 210, 11, 8.
39. Jennifer C. Nash, "Practicing Love: Black Feminism, Love-Politics, and Post-Intersectionality," *Meridians* 11, no. 2 (2011): 1–24, 11.
40. Ibid., 15.
41. Martha Nussbaum, *Political Emotions: Why Love Matters for Justice* (Cambridge, MA: Harvard University Press, 2013), 396–97.
42. James Baldwin, 1963, *The Fire Next Time* (New York: Vintage International, 1993), 104.
43. James Baldwin, 1979, *Just Above My Head* (New York: Random House, 2000), 370–71.
44. David A. J. Richards, *Why Love Leads to Justice: Love Across the Boundaries* (New York: Cambridge University Press, 2016), 2.
45. Ibid., 223.
46. James Baldwin, *Conversations with James Baldwin*, ed. Fred L. Standley and Louis H. Pratt (Columbia: University Press of Mississippi, 1989), 155–56.
47. Baldwin, *Fire*, 104–5.

4

WEALTH, OR, CAPITALISM AND ITS ALTERNATIVES

CHAPTER 16

EMERSON AND CAPITALISM

BENJAMIN PICKFORD

> The merchant has but one rule, *absorb and invest*: he is to be capitalist: the scraps and filings must be gathered back into the crucible; the gas and smoke must be burned, and earnings must not go to increase expense, but to capital again. Well, the man must be capitalist. Will he spend his income, or will he invest? His body and every organ is under the same law.
>
> Emerson, "Wealth," *The Conduct of Life* (CW 6:67)

THE purpose of this chapter is to elaborate the remarkable suggestions that Emerson makes in the epigraphic excerpt above. Emerson's subject at this point in "Wealth" is ostensibly the merchant, whose "economy is a coarse symbol of the soul's economy" (*CW* 6:67), but coarse symbolism swiftly gives way to an imperative and a universalization that demand careful and subtle consideration. "The man"—for which I will substitute the term *person*, to modernize Emerson's vocabulary, but also for reasons that will be clearer as I proceed—"*must* be capitalist" (*CW* 6:67). What justifies this imperative? Is Emerson saying, like the late Mark Fisher, that there is *no alternative* to capitalism, not simply as an economic system, but as an epistemological and even an ontological structure that not only delimits, but may be the very structure that permits, personal life and experiences?[1] From his universalization (that "his body and every organ is under the same law") Emerson seems to be saying not only this, but something more: that capitalism is (or has become) in some way part of our nature, a conclusion that has later been drawn by many writers in Marx's legacy, from Georg Lukács to Michel Foucault.[2]

These comparisons may seem unlikely, even implausible, given the positions expressed by most modern critics on Emerson's relation to capitalism. Typically, critics of Emerson's politics find him to be a witting or unwitting accomplice to the undesirable developments of capitalism in nineteenth-century America. Some, like John Carlos Rowe, see Emerson's complicity as muted but nevertheless insidious, his philosophical concerns underwriting "the legitimation of those practices of intellectual abstraction required to rationalize the contradictions of the new industrial economy." Others, like Christopher Newfield, have been more forthright, asserting that Emerson's essays "ring with a call to free-market commitment," while "at nearly every point" his "official views" on the capitalist mode of production "conformed to laissez-faire orthodoxy."[3] Such claims are only updated versions of a critical stance that has a long history in American letters. As Randall Fuller has written, the "Sage of Concord" in the American popular imagination was a construction of Emerson's genteel admirers and biographers in the Gilded Age, an Emerson who served as "a kind of shorthand for a range of associations and interests that included the devotion to an idealistic version of culture" disengaged from the politics and social pressures of the late nineteenth century. This production of an "American saint" who was "easily appropriated by industrial capitalism," whose "aphorisms... were embraced by artists and business tycoons alike," explains the modern readiness to read Emerson as an ideologist of capital, but it tells only a partial story.[4]

In this essay, my purpose is not to revisit this tradition but rather to offer an entirely new perspective by interrogating the broader meanings of Emerson's capitalist imperative. In doing so, I will draw out unexpected resonances between Emerson and his contemporary Karl Marx, the nineteenth-century political economist who continues to shape and determine the cultural studies of economic and social forms in our era. Emerson is like and unlike Marx simultaneously, resonant and yet discordant, and by elaborating and amplifying Emerson's subtle theory of production in this light I hope to clarify his position relative to our preconceptions about the development and predominance of capitalism since the nineteenth century. The essay "Wealth," my principal focus here because it is Emerson's most explicit engagement with political economy, was published as part of the volume *The Conduct of Life* in 1860. *The Conduct of Life* cannot be considered a conventional work of political economy. It is, however, a coherent volume, distinctive for a self-reflexive awareness that ties its essays together, and by taking "Wealth" to be its explanatory core I seek to demonstrate that the essays congeal into an economic thesis.[5] The conclusion I will draw is that the majority of Emerson's critics who have declared him an advocate for capitalism are right, in principle. What's important, however, is not the mere fact of this advocacy, but rather Emerson's justification of his position.

Emerson explicitly notes his concern in *Conduct* on its opening page. After listing a "chance," an "odd coincidence," and a happenstance, he offers the following lines:

> To me, however, the question of the times resolved itself into a practical question of the conduct of life. How shall I live? We are incompetent to solve the times. Our geometry cannot span the huge orbits of the prevailing ideas, behold their return and reconcile their opposition. We can only obey our own polarity. 'Tis fine for us to speculate and elect our course, if we must accept an irresistible dictation. (*CW* 6:1–2)

Emerson is alluding widely here, and historicist readers have identified his prevailing ideas and questions of the times as belonging to the fraught period leading up to the

American Civil War in which *Conduct* was composed.[6] As well as historically-specific readings, however, many broader socioeconomic and political forces may be understood as irresistible and capable of programming their human subject. The project of the volume is explicitly invoked in relation to this tolerance of the irresistible: it is an inquiry into "the conduct of life," posed subjectively ("How shall I live?"), that is "practical" in nature. Emerson's inquiry comes with a caveat—"we are incompetent to solve the times" (*CW* 6:1) —which at once points to the "odious" (*CW* 6:19) injustices and sociopolitical problems of his day, and implies the hopelessness of revolutionary and utopian thinking for the duration of our "incompetence."

This caveat is incumbent throughout Emerson's appraisals of individual and social life under capitalism, but it does not foreclose the possibility of social change. Emerson, after all, declares us "incompetent," *not* impotent. So how does the individual person, who is the victim not only of a natural world that is "inconsiderate of persons" but also of innumerable odious manmade inequalities, arrive at an understanding of her practical agency (*CW* 6:17)? How might one understand the scope and potential of personal power amidst the "colossal systems" (*CW* 6:23) of the capitalist world of which one is a component, and by doing so ascertain the conduct that is best suited to negotiating, and possibly even ameliorating, those systems? The final answer to these questions will not only account for why Emerson remarks that the person "must be capitalist," but also why many of Marx's twenty-first-century critics, and even Marx himself—in writings that depart from his orthodox views—would agree with Emerson.

Imbecility and Mixed Instrumentalities

Twice in the opening two pages of "Fate," Emerson uses the metaphor of "our geometry" to describe the inherent shortcomings of the individual person to "span the huge orbits" and "extreme points" of the intellectual, technological, and political positions of "the times" (*CW* 6:1, 2). Such remarks imply an inherent shortcoming in the constitution of persons relative to the systems of modern society, and in "Power," the second essay in the volume, Emerson affirms this implication. He describes a condition that ails not only his contemporaries, but is "the key to all ages," as "imbecility; imbecility in the vast majority of men, at all times, and, even in heroes, in all but certain eminent moments; victims of gravity, custom, and fear" (*CW* 6:29). Emerson's choice of the term "imbecile," repeated for emphasis, demands consideration. It indicates weakness or incapacity, of course, but the word's contested etymology allows for a clarifying interpretation. The Latin term *imbecillus* is often understood to describe the state of being without a *baculum* or walking staff.[7] In this context, competence to power depends on being equipped with the requisite tools to compensate for an innate incompetence, a prosthesis that becomes (paradoxically) essential to one's "habit of self-reliance or original action" (*CW* 6:29).

What constitutes or serves as an example of such a prosthesis? In the context of "Power," the immediate example is causality, "belief" in which confers meaning on the facts of existence and thus renders the world intelligible; in making this argument, Emerson appears to have had David Hume's critique of epistemology in mind.[8] But by expanding the frame to survey *Conduct* more widely, more compelling and significant examples of prostheses and auxiliaries that ameliorate personal incompetence come into view.

In "Power," and on two occasions in "Fate," Emerson uses a consistent set of terms that indicate a more radical claim about the constitutional inadequacy of the person posed in *Conduct*. In "Power" he asserts, "all power is of one kind, a sharing of the nature of the world … One man is made of the same stuff of which events are made" (*CW* 6:30). The first part of this quotation, before the ellipsis, is not especially distinctive among nineteenth-century theories of human development; sixteen years earlier, Karl Marx had described a similar concept under the term of a "human species-being" which adopts the world as its "inorganic body" in his Parisian notebooks.[9] The second part of the quotation is where Emerson becomes radical, however, and it is this more radical point that Emerson stresses on two other occasions in "Fate": "The secret of the world is, the tie between person and event. Person makes event, and event person"; soon afterwards, Emerson elaborates further in noting "thus events grow on the same stem as persons; are sub-persons" (*CW* 6:21, 22). These claims have profound consequences for Emerson's practical question of how a person should live, because he does not merely draw an analogy between the history-making efficacy of persons and events, but a categorical equivalence. The only implied caveat in this equivalence is that complete identity cannot be established between person and event, presumably because an event is unable to become conscious of its agential status. Otherwise, Emerson indicates that the agency of the sub-personal event is no less pronounced than that of the person.

By noting this structure, I want to engage with one of the richest traditions in Emerson criticism and place its epistemological lessons in relation to the structures of capitalism. "Sub-personal" is an unconventional term, but elsewhere in "Fate" Emerson uses an alternative to describe the "rousing" qualities of an event or an encounter on personal intellect: "the impersonality, the scorn of egotisms" (*CW* 6:14). Oscillating and submitting to one another, the person and the impersonal event are tied in a centrifugal, developmental process in Emerson's thought, so that, as Branka Arsić has put it, "impersonal life traverses and inhabits us," meaning that "the impersonal in Emerson does not … cancel out the personal but instead contrives it."[10] Arsić gives a relatively straightforward and benign presentation of a concept that remains a point of contestation amongst Emerson's critics. For Sharon Cameron, whose work catalyzed the study of Emerson's impersonal, his pursuit of what may be defined "a materialist epistemology"[11] is problematic because it is too extreme in its displacement of the normative personal. Cameron insists that, because personal being is "being in the only form in which we think we know it," if Emerson's essays "seductively promise access" to an "experience of impersonality," it is an experience that cannot be realized.[12] But for others working after Cameron, there are distinctive and pragmatic "assets" (to use Johannes Voelz's word) that attend Emerson's concept of an empirically inaccessible impersonal.[13]

Something closer to Voelz's reading is manifestly at work in *Conduct*, where Emerson poses the practical question of *how* a person should conduct their life while depending on impersonal "tools and auxiliaries" (*CW* 6:47), and while passively tolerating the "mixed instrumentalities" (*CW* 6:4) that shape history and social processes. In this respect Emerson anticipates modern philosophers of personhood, like Roberto Esposito, for whom the concept of the person is constitutionally paradoxical, bridging fundamentally dissimilar categories and conceptual paradigms in such a way that modern personhood must be understood to intersect with, overlap, and be co-constituted by the impersonal.[14] And when posed in these terms, one may recognize this same line of thought in Marx, who—though he seldom deployed a lexicon translatable into English through the poles of personality/impersonality—nevertheless attested throughout his work that under capitalism our personal lives are *not* our own, but are lived under and shaped by conditions of impersonal domination.[15]

Like many other theorists of the development of social relations in the context of capitalism, Emerson looks back to a putative unsocialized individual who is compelled to tolerate the untamed natural world. He develops this theme by conspicuously presenting the person as entirely subject to natural forms of impersonal domination. In "Fate," natural processes are given to be "inconsiderate of persons" (*CW* 6:3). "Diseases, the elements, fortune, gravity, lightning, respect no persons," while an event like the 1857 Basilicata earthquake killed "ten thousand persons ... in a few minutes" (*CW* 6:4). In "Culture," later in the volume, Emerson develops his remarks on impersonal forces in nature. The individual can neither overcome such forces, nor protect herself from them, and for the sake of survival "Nature has secured individualism, by giving the private person a high conceit of his weight in the system" (*CW* 6:71) in more precarious periods of human history. In the context of the nineteenth century, however, "the pest of society is egotists," and the tropes Emerson deploys to conceptualize individualism—"a metaphysical ... malady," a "distemper," a "goitre of egotism" (*CW* 6:70–71)—once again stresses his conviction that this quality which occurs *naturally* in human consciousness (it is, after all, an "organic egotism" [*CW* 6:73]) becomes a debilitating ailment when it prevails in social contexts.

The purpose and end of culture, Emerson argues, is socialization: acculturation degrades this organic individualism and presses the person into a recognition of the impersonal factors of their social constitution. Culture is given to "correct the theory of success," "redress" the "balance" of competing forces in the individual mind, and to "succor" the person "against himself" (*CW* 6:69, 72). The many forms of acculturation depicted in the essay all serve the same epistemological function, which is to apply the impersonalizing power of abstraction to the practice of selfhood. Writing that "we must have an intellectual quality in all property and in all action, or they are naught" (*CW* 6:84), Emerson argues that we are compelled to place the familiar at an unfamiliar distance, to estrange or alienate ourselves, in other words, so that "events," a "social state and history," and such material factors of social life seem "accessories," the "value" of which comes in recognizing them to be "contingent and rather showy possessions" (*CW* 6:84). Practicing abstraction at the level of personhood will, of course, alter the form of personhood as it was previously understood. Marx's theory of alienation typifies this alteration insofar as it describes the spoiling of pre-capitalist personhood and social relations. But the fact that Marx evokes a secular fall of man, followed perhaps by a secular eschatology of revolutionary redemption, also subtly parallels Emerson as the latter figures the process through a prelapsarian trope, borrowing from Milton: "Half-engaged in the soil, pawing to get free, man needs all the music that can be brought to disengage him" (*CW* 6:88).[16] The acceleration effected by the impersonal aids characterized here as "music" serves Emerson's argument, with rich personhood being founded on disengagement from the organic state. From the point of view of the nominally sovereign person, this means disengagement, or estrangement, from oneself.

Wealth and Labor

In spite of this imperative to self-estrangement, and though Emerson will insist in "Wealth" that the person *must* be capitalist, *Conduct* nevertheless foregrounds the pernicious aspects of capitalism, and in particular modes of economic determinism and their impositions on mental and social life that we, after Marx and his interpreters, describe using the term "ideology." Emerson notes that he and his readers are "complicit," whether they like it or not, in the colossal systems of nineteenth-century capitalism, "however scrupulously the slaughterhouse is concealed in the graceful distance of miles" (*CW* 6:4). Emerson's critics have read this "slaughterhouse" as referring broadly to the systems of exploitation prevalent up to 1860, including chattel slavery, and his point in raising it is patently that while distanciation hides from view the exploitation on which our social relations rely, it does not absolve one from responsibility for such exploitation.[17] Emerson makes his critique of exploitation in the history of American settlement more overt in what follows, writing that "the German and Irish millions, like the Negro, have a great deal of guano in their destiny" (*CW* 6:9). The labor of these people is what "make[s] corn cheap," but the effect of such labor on the worker, as Marx and Engels also noted, is the shortening of life.[18] The "ditch[ing]" and "drudg[ing]" labors these people undertake will be the cause of their "premature" deaths, and—on occasion—Emerson makes palpably Marxist points, including the following observation on the mental and physical consequences of manual labor for the person compelled by economic necessity to undertake it: "Ask the digger in the ditch to explain Newton's laws. The fine organs of his brain have been pinched by overwork and squalid poverty from father to son, for a hundred years" (*CW* 6:6).[19]

When Emerson takes up the work of impersonal auxiliaries and their importance in developing individual and social competencies in "Wealth," however, such readings of the merely egregious nature of exploitation in economic contexts disappear. In their place, Emerson defines "wealth" as an abundance of impersonal auxiliaries that extend human potency, suggests that such auxiliaries should be understood as analogous to capital, and describes the capitalist system as the socialization and institutionalization of this necessary instrumentality. This is consistent throughout Emerson's various definitions in the essay. First, "men of sense esteem wealth to be the assimilation of nature to themselves, the converting of the sap and juices of the planet to the incarnation and nutriment of their design" (*CW* 6:49–50). Just as Marx had defined the species-being of humanity as its compulsion to objectify its conscious activity in the physical world and conform the material world to that of consciousness, Emerson speaks of irresistible compulsions to such engagements: "Men are urged by their ideas to acquire the command over nature" (*CW* 6:51). But from this point, a crucial difference emerges between Emerson and Marx. As Marx famously wrote, this instrumentality of the world for the enrichment and development of the human individual is subverted by capital as the form of wage labor alienates or estranges the person from their activity and labor. Emerson remarks on the same mechanism in "Wealth" and elsewhere, but his presentation is starkly different. Regarding the exploitation of labor, for instance, Emerson blithely writes that "he is the richest man who knows how to draw a benefit from the labors of the greatest number of men, of men in distant countries, and in past times" (*CW* 6:47). This remark echoes through Emerson's other work of the 1850s, but—while other instances often highlight the *cultural* logic of alienated and exploited labor—this example fits the concerns of "Wealth" by indicating not only the rich man's reliance on the accumulated social labor of generations of deceased workers, but also on a global workforce in the emerging world-system of capitalism in Emerson's era.[20] In these examples, Emerson's stance is distinctive. On one hand, he seems to recognize some fundamental elements of Marx's critique of capital, but at the same moment he declines to embrace the fundamental moral objection that Marx shared with other nineteenth-century critics of capitalism in opposition to a system that extracts value through exploitation and dispossession.

Emerson's justification for his position sustains his discordant resonance with Marx. He takes up the subject of money in "Wealth," which is of course "representative" both as a mediator of value in general, but also in its Marxist sense as an embodiment of abstract labor. Emerson introduces a farmer whose concerns are faintly Marxist:

> The farmer is covetous of his dollar, and with reason. It is no waif to him. He knows how many strokes of labor it represents. His bones ache with the day's work that earned it. He knows how much land it represents;—how much rain, frost, and sunshine. He knows that, in the dollar, he gives you so much discretion and patience, so much hoeing, and threshing. (*CW* 6:54)

To the farmer, the dollar is representative of the toil of which it is the product. In capitalism, however, money is an abstraction of value indifferent as to how that value is accumulated. The farmer's dollar has the identical monetary value as the dollar tabled as part of a stock trade or a financial exchange, but "in the city, where money follows the skit of a pen, a lucky rise in exchange, it comes to be looked on as light" (*CW* 6:54). Emerson acknowledges that this abstract equivalence seems unjust: "I wish the farmer held it dearer, and would spend it only for real bread; force for force" (*CW* 6:54). But such a highly personal labor theory of value is, Emerson implies, no more than wishful thinking. In the disquisitions on the fluctuations in the value of the dollar that follow, Emerson deploys some unorthodox terms and approaches, but his general concerns—demographic change and emigration, scarcity and abundance, crime and corruption—all contribute to reinforcing his ultimate claim: "The value of a dollar is social," not personal, and the farmer who cannot see past the personal value of his dollar would inevitably be obliged to sell himself short in exchange.

This does not render labor irrelevant as an economic or a productive factor in *Conduct*. On the contrary, as I will illustrate in the closing sections of this essay, labor will take on fundamental significance in the volume, particularly in the essay "Worship." But this must be understood within the parameters of labor's decentralized place in the circuits of production and innovation to which Emerson gives expression in "Wealth." There Emerson twice insists that intellectual and technological developments exceed labor as a source of value. First, "intimate ties subsist between thought and all production; because a better order is equivalent to vast amounts of brute labor" (*CW* 6:46); later, "cultivated labor drives out brute labor. An infinite number of shrewd men, in infinite years, have arrived at certain best and shortest ways of doing, and this accumulated skill in arts, cultures, harvestings, curings, manufactures, navigations, exchanges, constitutes the worth of our world today" (*CW* 6:53). "Brute labor," which I take to mean proletarian labor, or what Marx calls "labor in the direct form,"[21] is marginalized in these formulations, and Emerson postulates in its place a future-oriented model of productive development that embodies the qualities he locates in acculturation, relying on collective, impersonal, congealed knowledges and competencies, which might in time "drive out brute labor" in a wider sense. Since capitalism is the economic system which relies on the abstraction of concrete labor for its foundation, and since capitalism fosters further division of labor, labor-saving technologies, and innovation toward productive benefits as part of its internal logic, we are close to understanding why the person *must* be capitalist in Emerson's thinking. But we have reached a stage where Emerson must seem radically indifferent to the moral critiques of capitalism and industrialization common in his era, and far from the conventional doctrines of Marxism. In the concluding section of this chapter, I will illustrate how Emerson's reflections on capitalism ultimately align with Marxist developments of the late twentieth and early twenty-first centuries that emphasize the emancipatory force of technology and capitalist acceleration.

General Intellect and Emerson's Fragment on Machines

In early 1858, while Emerson was continuing to deliver the lectures on which the chapters of *The Conduct of Life* would be based, Marx wrote the following lines in his notebooks for the project that would culminate in the 1867 publication of *Capital*:

Nature builds no machines, no locomotives, railways, electric telegraphs, self-acting mules etc. These are products of human industry; natural material transformed into organs of the human will over nature, or of human participation in nature. They are *organs of the human brain, created by the human hand*; the power of knowledge, objectified. The development of fixed capital indicates to what degree general social knowledge has become a *direct force of production*, and to what degree, hence, the conditions of the process of social life itself have come under the control of the general intellect and been transformed in accordance with it.[22]

These lines, published in the twentieth century in the *Grundrisse*, form the centerpiece of the now famous "Fragment on Machines," and feature the sole deployment in Marx's work of the equally famous, but ambiguous, concept of "general intellect." Marx's point is that technological developments radically change the role of the worker in capitalist production. Fixed capital—in the excerpt, knowledge objectified in machine technology—embodies the total general knowledge and technological skill of a society, and represents the motor of production. This "general intellect" takes over as the principal productive force, supplanting "direct labor" and marginalizing the input of human workers. Marx speculates that this course will eventually catalyze revolutionary social change, because the worker's liberation from necessary labor will open up an irresolvable contradiction so long as capitalism persists in "posit[ing] labor time ... as sole measure and source of wealth," and the contradiction will eventually provoke the collapse of the entire system.[23]

Recent interpreters of Marx have focused on how the "Fragment on Machines" "sustain[s] ... a thesis which is not at all very 'marxist' [*sic*]: abstract scientific knowledge ... tends to become, precisely by virtue of its autonomy from production, nothing less than the principal productive force, thus relegating repetitive and compartmentalized labor to a residual position."[24] Pushing concrete human labor—and, by extension, the lives and concerns of the individuals who would undertake such labor—to a marginal or residual position poses obvious challenges to traditional understanding of Marxism, and to the modes of activism based on such understanding. But, more importantly for my concerns, the marginalization of concrete labor places Marx in close alignment with Emerson's reflections on the capitalist mode of production. When Emerson stands "cultivated labor" against "brute labor" in "Wealth," he asks his reader to consider the meaning of cultivation, and then proceeds to guide them (indeed, through his chapter titled "Culture") to recognize the impersonal and abstract form of cultivated labor. Cultivated labor is defined socially, collectively, and historically—by "infinite men" in "infinite years"—and is rooted in the surpassing of direct individual labor through technological development. Emerson uses personification to illustrate the interweaving of personal and impersonal agencies in technologized production. Steam he personifies as "the workman [that British railway engineers] were in search of" (*CW* 6:18), while the epigraphic poem that opens "Wealth" provocatively names "galvanic wires [and] strong-shouldered steam" as the "new slaves" fulfilling the "dreams" of nineteenth-century progress (*CW* 6:45), and such personifications of patently *impersonal* embodiments of technological knowledge function as demonstrations not only of how new technologies displace workers, but also how those technologies feed back into the determination of emergent capitalist personhood. As Virno and other commentators on Marx's general intellect have noted, embodied knowledges operate as machines in a metaphorical sense as automated "facult[ies] of thought," and the persons who incorporate such predefined faculties in their cognitive development are compelled to submit to their structures and conditions, so that general intellect can be understood as a factor of social domination which "constitute[s] the epicenter of social production and preordain[s] all aspects of life."[25] This has direct, unambiguous consequences for personhood as it is conventionally understood—and still lived—in contemporary capitalism. Virno reflects that putting general technological knowledge—"that is, what is common"—to "work" in production "renders the impersonal technical division of labor" less overt than might have been the case in the nineteenth-century factory. In its place, however, "a viscous personalization of subjection" emerges as impersonal faculties of thought are realized and embodied in the minds, intellects, and language of other persons. For Virno, this entire process represents a deleterious step in the development of capitalism toward new forms of cognitive coercion and an interweaving of impersonal and personal modes of domination that "subdue[s] the whole person."[26] Virno's reading accurately reflects Marx's general points in the "Fragment," but both Emerson and Marx nevertheless voice an acceptance of this arguably inevitable process as part of the development of a richer sense of personhood that is the direct product of capitalism.

In "Behavior," the fifth chapter of *The Conduct of Life*, Emerson notes that "a complete man should need no auxiliaries to his personal presence" (*CW* 6:96). Emerson refers in the first sense to the "auxiliary" behaviors and manners that shape and thus socialize the individual, but the processes of socialization enacted by the capitalist mode of production already discussed in this chapter permit a richer interpretation, rendering this line a reflection on the inadequacy of the inherent competencies of personhood for the modern world. Personhood as conventionally understood, described by Emerson as "organic," is constitutionally incomplete—imbecilic—and the person compelled to conduct her life amidst the colossal systems of the capitalist epoch will be rounded out only in the uptake of impersonal auxiliary knowledges, akin to those described by Marx as general intellect, which, historically, have been most effectively developed through the innovations and technological advances endemic to the capitalist mode of production. In the *Grundrisse*, a subtle but significant thread offers a means of elaborating this element of Emerson's thought. Marx writes there of how the capitalist mode of production must be acknowledged to possess a "great civilizing influence," which is "the cultivation of all the qualities of the social human being" through the "utility" that an increasingly universal human individual draws from nature conceived as "an object for humankind."[27] Marx is clear that this process is historical and will entail generations of subjugation, because "the severe discipline of capital, acting on succeeding generations" must first cultivate its human subjects, "develop[ing] general industriousness as the general property of the new species."[28] For those persons compelled to conduct their lives under the "severe discipline of capital," such discipline can only be felt as alienation.[29] But this cannot be helped, nor can its historical development be significantly short-circuited. If Marx is right in the *Grundrisse* in seeing capital's endpoint in its "flourish[ing] to the stage where the possession and preservation of general wealth require[s] lesser labor time of society as a whole, and where the laboring society relates scientifically [which is to say, by incorporating general intellect into the mental processes of the individual mind] to the process of its progressive reproduction," then the gradual cognitive coercion of human persons by capitalist development is not to be resisted, but tolerated.[30] The person here *must* be capitalist, because only "capital's ceaseless striving towards the general form of wealth drives labor beyond the limits of its natural paltriness, and thus creates the material elements for the development of the rich individuality,"[31] which, Guido Starosta adds, "is fully and objectively conscious of the social determinations of his/her individual powers and activity."[32] Rich individuality should therefore be understood as collective or social individuality, and the lived recognition of this form of individual existence necessarily transcends personhood as it is commonly understood.

This dimension of Marx's thought is celebrated by Starosta and others for its scientific rigor and projection of a postcapitalist future immanent in the belly of capitalism as it existed in the mid-nineteenth century. As commentators on the *Grundrisse* have noted, the theoretical overcoming of capitalism that it presents differs from Marx's other discussions of revolution by placing that overcoming at "a very advanced stage of development," far beyond the levels reached in Marx's lifetime.[33] Emerson's approach in *Conduct* is different principally because, as I emphasized earlier, he addresses his argument to the person extant in 1860, and to a conduct of life appropriate to those conditions. But the anticipation of emancipation from "brute labor" through the development of forms of "cultivated labor" which incorporate impersonal embodied knowledges and technological innovations implies eventual revolutionary social change, and in "Worship," the sixth essay of *Conduct*, Emerson takes up the question of how persons might apprehend their labor as a contributory factor in the fostering of this world-to-come. Happiness, Emerson writes, comes to the person who "looks into his work for a reply, not into the market, not into opinion, not into patronage." He continues: "Work is victory. Wherever work is done, victory is obtained" (*CW* 6:120). Finally, in "learning the greatness of humility," one learns to "work in the dark, work against failure, pain and ill-will ... In the greatest destitution and calamity," Emerson claims, such a commitment to return to work "surprises men with a feeling of elasticity which makes nothing of loss" (*CW* 6:124). Elasticity stands out in this last sentence, and provides the clue which illustrates that Emerson's advocacy of work is neither paternalistic sentimentality nor a fetishization of the dignity of proletarian labor, but rather an extension of the theory of production developed throughout *Conduct*. The "elasticity" the worker feels in her work "surprises" her, both terms suggesting that the significance and usefulness of the work undertaken may exceed the expectations and awareness of the worker herself. This echoes Emerson's remark about "working in the dark," and the broader consequences of this condition can be read in "Wealth."

Early in that essay, the person's dependence on the impersonal auxiliaries defined as *wealth* is noted: "Every man is a consumer, and ought to be a producer. He fails to make his place good in the world, unless he not only pays his debt, but also adds something to the common wealth" (*CW* 6:45). A few pages later, Emerson returns to the same point with a little more clarity, asserting that "they should own who can administer ... they whose work carves out work for more, and opens a path for all" (*CW* 6:52). In both cases, against the position of the covetous farmer described earlier, and against the notion of ownership as such, Emerson praises work that is conducted with a view to its inevitable abstraction, work which disengages from its agent to create opportunities, foster potentialities, and found possibilities for *other* persons in non-contiguous contexts. Such work is inherently social and fosters further socialization of the persons who take it up and work upon it. As Emerson articulates it in "Worship," properly speaking "we are ... not to work, but to be worked upon; ... To this sentiment belong vast and sudden enlargements of power" (*CW* 6:113).[34] The practical meaning of Emerson's ideal is clarified through his deployment of a number of exemplary exponents of this mode of cultivated labor in his own era, all of whom are speculative capitalists. Emerson indicates that he was well aware that he was posing a provocative argument: "The agencies by which events so grand as the opening of California, of Texas, of Oregon ... are effected are paltry,—coarse selfishness, fraud, and conspiracy ... most of the great results of history are brought about by discreditable means." Nevertheless, this remains the exemplary beneficence Emerson would highlight: "What is the benefit done by a good King Alfred ... or Elizabeth Fry, or Florence Nightingale ... compared with the involuntary blessing wrought on nations by the selfish capitalists who built the Illinois, and Michigan, and the network of the Mississippi valley roads" (*CW* 6:136). In each example, two things are crucial. First, an elasticity of prospects is opened out by new technological apparatuses which permit expansion and innovation in the general productive force of American society. But second, the elasticity of prospects opened out is *involuntary*: accidental benefits "vastly exceed ... any intentional philanthropy on record" (*CW* 6:136.) precisely because they are abstracted from the purposes and interests of the capitalists whose work fostered their development.

When, near the end of "Illusions" and the end of the volume, Emerson writes that "we must work and affirm, and have no guess of the value of what we say or do" (*CW* 6:171), he encapsulates the limited personal vantage on the consequences and effects of one's labor that defined his era, and which continues to define our own. The potentialities or valorific developments of human labor are defined and realized in social, not individual, contexts. Since, as Marx observed, "capital ... announces from its first appearance a new epoch in the process of social production,"[35] its development must be attended, the person *must* remain capitalist, and Emerson's remark in "Wealth" that "the basis of political economy is noninterference" (*CW* 6:56) can be seen in a new light not as advocacy of free market economics for personal gain, but rather as a statement coherent with Emerson's enthusiasm for the productive enhancements catalyzed by abstraction and an anticipation of the heretical revolutionary theses of accelerationism.[36] Indeed, this leads me to my closing remarks, which concern the possibility of revolutionary change in Emerson's purview of capitalism. In general, Emerson's concern with the person and the amelioration of personal competencies via the abstractive logic of capitalist production places him at a distance from Marx, whose subject is the form and development of capitalism itself, and thus no scientifically rigorous exposition of the manner of revolutionary development should be expected in *Conduct*. Yet Emerson does speak of revolution in the text, albeit explicitly at the level of the personal. "When the state is unquiet," Emerson writes, "personal qualities are more than ever decisive." Emerson does not say what qualities he means, but, since his next sentence reads, "Fear not a revolution which will constrain you to live five years in one" (*CW* 6:86), the qualities alluded to are presumably those which mitigate the distempers of organic egotism, qualities such as tolerance and patience, which might lighten the burden on the individual compelled to await such a revolution. And these same qualities of tolerance in attending the development of technological development that will eventually "drive out brute labor" entirely, potentially emancipating the worker from the specific pressures of proletarian labor, are espoused in one of the most remarkable (if critically unremarked) passages in *Conduct*.

The concluding passage in the essay "Power" should, in terms of the structural logic of *Conduct*, prepare the reader for "Wealth," the following essay in the volume. If it is read on these terms, it sheds light on the hopes and expectations that the subjugated worker might harbor in the future of capitalist development, though the same worker will not be absolved of the obligation to patiently attend the development of general intellect which will provide the means of emancipation. In the passage, Emerson offers his own fragment on machines:

> I know no more affecting lesson to our busy, plotting New England brains, than to go into one of the factories with which we have lined all the watercourses in the States. A man hardly knows how much he is a machine until he begins to make telegraph, loom, press and locomotive, in his own image. But in these he is forced to leave out his follies and hindrances, so that when we go to the mill, the machine is more moral than we. Let a man dare go to a loom and see if he be equal to it. Let machine confront machine, and see how they come out. The world-mill is more complex than the calico-mill, and the architect stooped less. In the gingham-mill, a broken thread or a shred spoils the web through a piece of a hundred yards, and is traced back to the girl that wove it, and lessens her wages. The stockholder, on being shown this, rubs his hands with delight. Are you so cunning, Mr. Profitloss, and do you expect to swindle *your* master and employer, in the web you weave? A day is a more magnificent cloth than any muslin, the mechanism that makes it is infinitely cunninger, and you shall not conceal the sleazy, fraudulent, rotten hours you have slipped into the piece; nor fear that any honest thread, or straighter steel, or more inflexible shaft, will not testify in the web. (*CW* 6:43)

Emerson's machines, these accumulations of the "the power of knowledge, objectified," threaten or "arise in antithesis to living labor."[37] The girl in the gingham mill cannot rely on the machine—this "*animated monster*," which renders the worker "as an animated individual punctuation mark, as its living isolated accessory"[38]—to conceal her human error from the foreman's oversight. At one time, she might have relied on the comradeship of a coworker whose capacity for empathy exceeds that of machine technology, but in the context of the nineteenth-century factory social productivity has surpassed these more immediate forms of organization. All of the initial benefits of such developments flow to the capitalist while intensifying the subjugation of the worker, as Emerson notes in the relish of the stockholder who withholds wages for unproductive labor.[39] But Emerson's "more affecting lesson" in confrontations with objectified knowledge is not simply that it is monstrously and alienatingly efficient, but that it is "more moral than we." As Virno and other critics of the *Grundrisse* have noted, the compulsion on persons to live and work with forms of embodied social knowledge means not only to have their working lives and economic habits, but also their social and ultimately their mental worlds defined and constituted by them. This may be understood as a pervasive mode of dominating and programming the person insofar as the machine reveals to its human onlooker those "follies and hindrances" that inhere in her personal intellect, but which are left out of the distilled, impersonal general intellect. But in Emerson's suggestive and ambiguous conclusion, emancipatory consequences may follow the person's recognition of her mental identity with the embodied knowledge of the machine.

What, or perhaps whose, are "the sleazy, fraudulent, rotten hours you have slipped into the piece"? An extension of the metaphor of the "day" of our lifetimes, soiled by the time we lose to capitalist forms of labor? Or perhaps the hours that would likely have felt fraudulently purloined from the point of view of the girl in the gingham mill? Either way, in positing a compensatory logic in the last lines of the essay, Emerson suggests that the same technologies that first serve the factory owner will inevitably expose his cheapening of human life, if only at some future and undisclosed moment. The last few clauses of the passage are particularly ambiguous, but it does seem that—like Marx and many others who wrote in his legacy—the vast increases in social productivity facilitated by embodied knowledges will eventually redound to the benefit of the worker, and Emerson's "honest thread, or straighter steel, or more inflexible shaft" ultimately bears emancipatory, even revolutionary potential. If there is an implied revolution here, it has not yet come to pass, but then nor has Marx's speculative future described in the "Fragment." At least, the final lines of Emerson's "Power" point to where the worker is to look for signs of the change to come, while "Wealth" and the other elements of economic thinking present in *Conduct* help to articulate a conduct of life that is appropriate to anticipate such a revolution. In the meantime, however, in Emerson's era—and apparently still in our own—the person *must* be capitalist.

Notes

1. Fisher synthesizes Marxist critique and the ideological mantras of neoliberalism in his characteristically unflinching portrayal of the logic of "capitalist realism." See Mark Fisher, *Capitalist Realism: Is There No Alternative?* (Winchester: Zero Books, 2009).
2. Georg Lukács described a "second nature" created by and through capitalism that displaces preexisting first nature in "Reification and the Consciousness of the Proletariat." (See Lukács, 1923, *History and Class Consciousness: Studies in Marxist Dialectics*, trans. Rodney Livingstone [Cambridge: MIT Press, 1971], 128.) Michel Foucault's thought on the

interweaving of biological life and capitalist social forms is found in his work touching on biopower and biopolitics.

3. See John Carlos Rowe, *At Emerson's Tomb: The Politics of Classic American Literature* (New York: Columbia University Press, 1997), 5; and Christopher Newfield, *The Emerson Effect: Individualism and Submission in America* (Chicago: University of Chicago Press, 1996), 178–79. The positions taken on Emerson in the 1990s by Rowe and Newfield are symptomatic of the politically-motivated iconoclasm of New American studies, and, though Emerson is still commonly held to be an advocate for capitalism, in more recent years others have taken widely different approaches to this aspect of Emerson's thought. Emerson frequently noted the pernicious aspects of industrial production in his era, and Len Gougeon amplifies such concerns to offer an apologia that renders Emerson a bourgeois, sentimental critic of capitalism and venerator of the "dignity of labor" (see Len Gougeon, "Emerson, Great Britain, and the International Struggle for the Rights of the Workingman," in *A Power to Translate the World: New Essays on Emerson and International Culture*, ed. David LaRocca and Ricardo Miguel-Alfonso [Hanover, NH: Dartmouth College Press, 2015], 83–84). Meanwhile, in a broad but somewhat vague sense, Branka Arsić finds Emerson to agree with Marx, though my argument to follow here has little in common with Arsić's claim that labor in Emerson becomes a "non-alienated ... sensuous activity" (see Branka Arsić, *On Leaving: A Reading in Emerson* [Cambridge, MA: Harvard University Press, 2010], 83–85). Two works exist which more closely align with the argument I will make about Emerson's interest in innovation and the creative tendencies of capitalism: Thomas D. Birch's "Toward a Better Order: The Economic Thought of Ralph Waldo Emerson," *New England Quarterly* 68, no. 3 (September 1995): 385–401, and Philip Fisher, *Still the New World: American Literature in a Culture of Creative Destruction* (Cambridge, MA: Harvard University Press, 1999), 15–20.

4. Randall Fuller, *Emerson's Ghosts: Literature, Politics, and the Making of American Literature* (New York: Oxford University Press, 2007), 53, 56.

5. *The Conduct of Life* comprises nine chapters, only one of which—"Illusions," the ninth and final chapter—had been previously published (in the *Atlantic Monthly* for November 1857). On numerous occasions in the text, Emerson speaks of the volume as a whole, or describes relationships between its themes, indicating that the essays function as a coherent ensemble. See *CW* 6:69, 106–7, 108.

6. For a detailed account of the context of *Conduct*'s composition and its bearing on the themes and content of the text, see Barbara Packer's "Historical Introduction" in the *Collected Works* edition (*CW* 6:xv–lxvii).

7. This etymology remains common in modern dictionaries, although some philologists reject the ascription as fanciful (the *OED*, for instance, has listed the word as being "of unknown origin" since its first edition). The etymology nevertheless has a long history, and Emerson may well have been aware of its articulations in ancient texts. St. Isidore of Seville includes it in his *Etymologiae* of the early seventh century: "Weak (*imbecillus*), as if the term were 'without a walking-stick (*baculum*),' fragile and unsteady." See Stephen A. Barney et al., eds. and trans., *The Etymologies of Isidore of Seville* (Cambridge: Cambridge University Press, 2006), 10.1.128.

8. Hume infamously refuted the law of causation in the *Enquiry Concerning Human Understanding*, but causality in that argument was only one instrument used to inform his definition of belief as a mechanism of human cognition and of the exertion of intellectual power, which gives ideas "more weight and influence; makes them appear of

greater importance; enforces them in the mind; and renders them the governing principle of our actions." For Hume, causality is an enabling fiction that conveys power to human conceptions of agency and historical processes. See David Hume, 1748, *An Enquiry Concerning Human Understanding*, ed. Peter Millican (New York: Oxford University Press, 2007), 36, 24, 42.

9. See Karl Marx, *Economic and Philosophic Manuscripts of 1844*, in *Marx and Engels: Collected Works*, ed. and trans. Jack Cohen et al., vol. 3 (London: Lawrence & Wishart, 1975), 275, where species-being describes not only "living on inorganic nature," but also making such nature "a part of human consciousness" so that man becomes universal, "the universality which makes all nature his inorganic body."

10. Arsić, *On Leaving*, 94.

11. Branka Arsić, "Introduction," in *American Impersonal: Essays with Sharon Cameron*, ed. Branka Arsić (New York and London: Bloomsbury, 2014), 1–26, 3.

12. Sharon Cameron, "The Way of Life by Abandonment: Emerson's Impersonal," *Critical Inquiry* 25, no. 1 (Autumn 1998): 30, 31.

13. Voelz describes Emerson's non-empirical portrayal of impersonality as a philosophical and epistemological "asset" in his writing on the basis that such a presentation "helps overcome the person of the reader," enabling that reader to recognize herself as socially constituted, and "limitless[ly] connect[ed]." (See Johannes Voelz, "The Recognition of Emerson's Impersonal: Reading Alternatives in Sharon Cameron," in *American Impersonal: Essays with Sharon Cameron*, ed. Branka Arsić [London: Bloomsbury, 2014], 73–97, 80.)

14. Esposito elaborates the "category of person," finding it to bridge the biological, social, and political at every moment, the "gaping chasm between the concept of human being and that of citizen," and "the two spheres of law and humanity." At all points, therefore, the category of person is co-constituted by the impersonal: "the impersonal is its [the person's] alteration, or its extroversion into an exteriority that calls into question and overturns its prevailing meaning." See Roberto Esposito, 2007, *Third Person: Politics of life and philosophy of the impersonal*, trans. Zakiya Hanafi (Cambridge: Polity Press, 2012), 3, 4.

15. For instance, in the *Grundrisse* Marx strongly suggests that the abstractive logic which underwrites the capitalist mode of production is impersonal in nature: "These *objective* dependency relations also appear, in antithesis to those of *personal* dependence ... in such a way that individuals are now ruled by *abstractions*, whereas earlier they depended on one another." See Karl Marx, 1939, *Grundrisse: Foundations of the Critique of Political Economy* (Rough Draft), trans. Martin Nicolaus (London: Penguin, 1993), 164.

16. The allusion is to Milton's portrayal of the herbivorous, prelapsarian animals of Genesis 1:29–30, still immanent with the soil from which they had been formed, and in *Paradise Lost* it appears as "the Tawnie Lion, pawing to get free." Emerson alludes to this episode more explicitly in his journals (*JMN* 8:372). For the episode in *Paradise Lost*, see John Milton, 1667, *Paradise Lost*, ed. Stephen Orgel and Jonathan Goldberg (New York: Oxford University Press, 2004), bk. 7, ll. 463–66.

17. For examples of such critical readings, see Eduardo Cadava, "The Guano of History," in *The Other Emerson*, ed. Branka Arsić and Cary Wolfe (Minneapolis: University of Minnesota Press, 2010), 107, 109; and Stanley Cavell, "Emerson's Constitutional Amending: Reading 'Fate,'" in *Philosophical Passages: Wittgenstein, Emerson, Austin, Derrida* (Cambridge: Blackwell, 1995), 18. In evoking distanciation and the concealment it effects, Emerson is making use of a trope on which Marx also relied heavily. Perhaps the most famous

example is from chapter 1 of *Capital*. In defining how exploited labor is abstracted in the commodity form, Marx writes, "We *put out of sight* both the useful character of the various kinds of labor embodied in [commodities], and the concrete forms of that labor; there is nothing left but what is common to them all; all are reduced to one and the same sort of labor, human labor in the abstract." See Karl Marx, 1867, *Capital Volume 1*, in *Marx and Engels: Collected Works*, ed. and trans. Jack Cohen et al., vol. 35 (London: Lawrence & Wishart, 1996), 48, emphasis added.

18. Engels described the labor conditions of the urban poor in England, under which "they can neither retain health nor live long," as "social murder" (Friedrich Engels, 1845, *The Condition of the Working Class in England*, in *Marx and Engels: Collected Works*, ed. and trans. Jack Cohen et al., vol. 4 [London: Lawrence & Wishart, 1975], 295–596, 394). Later, in the "Working Day" chapter of *Capital*, Marx defines capital itself as "dead labor" that, "vampire-like, only lives by sucking living labor," consuming the life of the worker in its production of value. See Marx, *Capital*, 241.

19. Marx defined alienated labor in the *Economic and Philosophic Manuscripts* as that which "mortifies [the worker's] body and ruins his mind." See Marx, *Economic and Philosophic Manuscripts*, 274.

20. In "Power," Emerson makes a similar remark in cultural contexts: "Shakespeare was theatre manager, and used the labor of many young men, as well as the play books" (*CW* 6:31). This echoes numerous reflections on how culture is built out of (and upon) the texts and works of past times in *Representative Men*, but in each case Emerson still uses the term labor to explain this revivification of past work. See *CW* 4:8, 24, 110. The same fundamental idea also underlies Emerson's great late essay "Quotation and Originality."

21. See Marx, *Grundrisse*, 705.

22. Marx, *Grundrisse*, 706 (emphasis original).

23. In more detail, Marx clarifies that capitalism is distinctive because "it wants to use labor time as the measuring rod for the giant social forces" released by its mode of technologized production, and to use the measure of labor time to "confine" those forces "within the limits required to maintain the already created value as value." If, in maintaining this structure, it also uses machine technology to minimize the quantity of concrete human labor actually required by the productive process, it sets in train a contradictory process that undermines this structure and provides the "material conditions to blow this foundation sky-high." See Marx, *Grundrisse*, 706.

24. Paolo Virno, "Notes on the 'General Intellect,'" trans. Cesare Casarino, in *Marxism Beyond Marxism*, ed. Saree Makdisi, Cesare Casarino, and Rebecca E. Karl (New York and London: Routledge, 1996), 265–72, 265.

25. See Virno, "Notes," 266; and Virno, "General Intellect," trans. Arianna Bové, *Historical Materialism: Research in Critical Marxist Theory* 15, no. 3 (2007): 3–8, 6. Virno tends to define the compulsion for the individual to cognitively incorporate general intellect as Marx's prescient foresight of the conditions of post-Fordist knowledge economies, but Tony Smith argues that the concept should be understood more broadly as a force endemic throughout the history of capitalism: "The general intellect as Virno defines it ... has been an expansion of collective social labor throughout the history of capitalism," and the specific embodiment of "the powers of capitalism fixed in machinery" is merely "a fetishized form of the powers of collective social labor." See Tony Smith, "The 'General Intellect' in the *Grundrisse* and Beyond," *Historical Materialism: Research in Critical Marxist Theory* 21, no. 4 (2013): 235–55, 248.

26. Virno, "General Intellect," 8.
27. See Marx, *Grundrisse*, 409–10.
28. Ibid., 325.
29. As Marx notes, human social relations in any given epoch are "a historic product ... belong[ing] to a specific phase of [social] development. The alien and independent character in which it presently exists *vis-à-vis* individuals proves only that the latter are still engaged in the creation of the conditions of their social life, and that they have not yet begun, on the basis of these conditions, to live it" (Marx, *Grundrisse*, 162).
30. See Marx, *Grundrisse*, 325.
31. Ibid.
32. Guido Starosta, "The System of Machinery and Determinations of Revolutionary Subjectivity in the *Grundrisse* and *Capital*," in *In Marx's Laboratory: Critical Interpretations of the* Grundrisse, ed. Riccardo Bellofiore, Guido Starosta, and Peter D. Thomas (Leiden: Brill, 2013), 233–63, 260.
33. John E. Elliot, "Marx's *Grundrisse*: Vision of Capitalism's Creative Destruction," *Journal of Post-Keynesian Economics* 1, no. 2 (Winter 1978–79): 148–69, 162.
34. This model is repeatedly articulated throughout *Conduct*, finding expression as early as "Fate" when Emerson reflects on how impersonal structures of thought define our cognitive capabilities in writing that "it is not so much in us as we are in it" (*CW* 6:14). As such, when Cameron writes that "to live in synch with [the impersonal] is to become indifferent to any fate one might conceivably call 'mine'" and that this is "the point ultimately made by the essay 'Fate,'" she is quite right; the caveat, of course, is that indifference to the social meaning, purpose, and fate of one's activities conceived as labor is a constitutive factor of the capitalist mode of production (Cameron, "Emerson's Impersonal," 3).
35. Marx, *Capital*, 135.
36. For a rich overview of the historical development of the "political heresy" of accelerationism, which insists "that the only radical political response to capitalism is not to protest, disrupt, or critique" the capitalist mode of production, "but to accelerate its uprooting, alienating, decoding, abstractive tendencies," see Robin Mackay and Armen Avanessian, "Introduction," in *#Accelerate: The Accelerationist Reader*, ed. Robin Mackay and Armen Avanessian (Falmouth: Urbanomic, 2014), 1–46.
37. Marx, *Grundrisse*, 705, 832.
38. Ibid., 470.
39. For Marx as for Emerson: "All the progress of civilization, or ... in the *productive powers of labor itself*—such as results from science, inventions, divisions and combinations of labor ... machinery etc.—enriches not the worker but rather *capital*; hence it only magnifies again the power dominating over labor" (Marx, *Grundrisse*, 308).

CHAPTER 17

EMERSON'S MARKET FORCES

ANDREW KOPEC

In his contribution to the first issue of *Hunt's Merchants' Magazine and Commercial Review*, the premier periodical "devoted to commercial subjects" in the nineteenth-century United States,[1] Edward Everett celebrated capitalist institutions' role in the character formation of the merchant. For Everett, one such organization, the Mercantile Library Association of Boston, served the "elevated purpose" of enlightening the businessman, this "intelligent friend of social advancement, the benefactor of his race."[2] Focusing on the themes of "accumulation, property, capital, and credit," he extols the advance of commerce as a civilizing force. Everett, whom Robert D. Richardson dubs Ralph Waldo Emerson's "first intellectual hero [and] for a time, his personal idol," arrived in Cambridge, Massachusetts, as a professor of Greek literature at Harvard University in 1819.[3] A tenacious scholar, Everett brought the Higher Criticism from the University of Göttingen in Germany to Harvard and led students to subject classical texts like the Homeric epics and the Bible to historical scrutiny. Having first arrived in the Boston area at the outset of a nationwide economic depression set off by the Panic of 1819, now in the aftermath of the Panic of 1837, he would supplement his scholastic pedagogy with the moral education of the merchant.

Everett's twin belief in exchange as a site of self-culture and market forces as moral ones informs Emerson's work as well. This liberalism, as Neal Dolan has argued, is of a piece with both men's class dispositions,[4] and in 1837 Emerson prodded his audience, typically "heedless of the instruction" of their work (*EL* 2:231), to see it anew. He wanted them to seize "the wisdom which has proceeded from other sources" in the "little strokes of the tool, little portions of time, little particles of stock and small gains" (*EL* 2:243). Even if Emerson in the December 1837 lecture, "Doctrine of the Hands," worries that political economy can degrade "man [into] a pair of hands, a useful engine" (*EL* 2:230), only later in "Wealth" (1860) to embrace the discipline "as good a book wherein to read the life of man and the ascendancy of laws over all private and hostile influences" (*CW* 6:54), there is continuity across his long career. This shift in attitude toward the science of market forces can be misleading, indeed—as I will show in this essay, it obscures

Emerson's enduring belief in the market's role in self-culture from the depression of the late 1830s to the Civil War era.

In the context of "Emerson and economics,"[5] from early twentieth-century intellectual history to late twentieth-century historicism, scholars have struggled to reconcile "Emerson's philosophical and political work."[6] Here I aim if not to reconcile then to clarify Emerson's sustained approach to the market through the lens of what is known today as the new history of capitalism. Research in this subfield of US historiography offers more than "an account of transaction costs, economies of scale, and diminishing returns, but of social habits, cultural logics, and the conditions of system-building as well."[7] And to consider Emerson's conception of capitalism in relation to that mode's "transformation into an 'ism' "[8]—that is, into a psychological regime with particular affective intensities, logics, laws, and identity categories—can suggest the convergence of his Transcendentalism and economics. Market forces can be wielded by the self—any self, not just merchants. To be self-reliant, he concludes, is to make one's enterprise the risking of that self. For Emerson, this preoccupation with self-making in the context of financial uncertainty was a distinctive project.[9] Even "if [he] never mounts a systematic critique of liberal capitalism," his writing, both "early" and "late," reveals an abiding interest in market forces as a context in which character emerges and stabilizes.[10] Rather than disjointed "job-work," such a theme represents a "line of [Emerson's] career" (*CW* 6:60).

New History of Capitalism and the Wave of Social Life: Emerson's "Finance Faculty"

According to John Lauritz Larson, "historians and economists argue bitterly over the meaning of these terms ["capitalism," for example] and when they apply to early American society."[11] Like others working in the new history of capitalism, he grounds his analysis in "the lives of antebellum Americans, [who] came to believe (correctly or not) that impersonal market forces had disabled the fabric of personal, familial, and cultural connections by which people earlier had tried to mitigate the hard facts of material life."[12] A major theme of this scholarship has been the speedy dissolution by such powers of "longstanding hierarchies and traditional forms of authority." "Capitalism," as Michael Zakim and Gary J. Kornblith pithily conclude, "became America's revolutionary tradition."[13]

This cultural tendency toward creative destruction or disruption gains legibility in the shifting assessment of individual risk-taking. In 1848, Marx and Engels in the *Communist Manifesto* described capitalism as an "uninterrupted disturbance of all social conditions, everlasting uncertainty and agitation."[14] American commentators would focus on the implications of this uncertainty for the self. As Judge Joseph Hopkinson would put it in the late 1830s in remarks to the same institution, the Mercantile Association, addressed by Edward Everett above, "The life of a merchant is, necessarily, a life of peril. He can scarcely move without danger."[15] What stands out in the antebellum era's discourse, then, is the degree to which Americans normalized risk ("peril") as an opportunity to win an identity, a rhetorical move that made clear that "uncertainties and anxieties ... had to be managed and coped with, perhaps even capitalized upon."[16] Previously confined to the field of maritime insurance, the cultural meaning of risk tilted, the historian Jonathan Levy shows, as everyday Americans became increasingly enmeshed in finance through "insurance policies, savings accounts, government debt markets, mortgage-backed securities, bonds markets, futures markets, and stock markets."[17] In step with these material conditions, liberal ideologies of selfhood would "come to mean mastery over personal financial 'risk.' "[18] Through risk taking, nineteenth-century Americans would not simply trust or rely on the self, but assert that self in the first place.

If risk, in Levy's formulation, "has a biography," so, too, do the related identity categories, success and failure.[19] In pursuing a history of the latter category, Scott Sandage's *Born Losers* (2006) charts how "the misfits of capitalism" remind us that, "with few exceptions, the only identity deemed legitimate in America is a capitalist identity; in every walk of life, investment and acquisition are the keys to moving forward and avoiding stagnation."[20] This is an ideology of achieved identity, and Transcendental literary culture was caught up in these psychocultural changes. Indeed, if the biography of risk leads Levy to Walt Whitman's "Passage to India,"[21] that of failure leads Sandage to Thoreau—or, rather, to Emerson's eulogy of his younger friend, "Thoreau" (1862). Citing this text at the outset of his monograph, Sandage latches on to Emerson's claim that "I cannot help counting it a fault in [Thoreau] that he had no ambition" and, therefore, had failed (*CW* 10:429). For Maurice S. Lee, these "ungenerous" words reflect Emerson's "own insecurities" over having "regretfully strayed from his youthful" idealism.[22] But whether looking outward to Thoreau's life or inward to his own, Emerson here hooks the ambition to strive amid uncertainty to an identity outcome. If we can imagine Thoreau as indifferent to the rigors of capitalist subjectivity, Emerson struggled to let them go.

My point is that a historiographical investigation into the cultural "matrix of achieved identity" prompts us to see Emersonian idealism as a program of risk management for riding the "wave" of social life.[23] With the word *wave*, I borrow here Emerson's metaphor from "Self-Reliance" (1841), which expresses his exasperation with the masquerade of social progress: "society is a wave," he counsels, which "moves onward, but the water of which it is composed does not" (*CW* 2:49). Earlier in "Self-Reliance," Emerson denigrates society as a "joint-stock company," a corporate form at the center of modernity's capitalization of risk (*CW* 2:29). "The great early modern joint-stock corporations," Levy writes, "pooled investor capital, lightening potential risk."[24] But perhaps what is good for the gander is bad for the goose, and Emerson understands success in such a venture as a failure of self-reliance.

If an explicit economic context seems missing from the second line of critique in "Self-Reliance" I mention above—"society is a wave"—Emerson follows that paragraph immediately with one that warns against the "reliance on Property" as "the want of self-reliance" (*CW* 2:49). Likewise drawn to this imagery in order to contemplate property relations in the midcentury United States, Nathaniel Hawthorne, in *The House of the Seven Gables* (1851), had mused: "In this republican country, amid the fluctuating waves of our social life, somebody is always at the drowning point."[25] A feature of capitalist psychology, the individual drama of self-making was of tremendous interest to Hawthorne. "Self-Reliance" eschews this prurience, though, to define "living property" as that which accrues value precisely because of its proximity to risk. Such property is vulnerable to flux ("revolution" or "robb[ery]" [*CW* 2:50]) and, therefore, anticipates it; it "does not wait the beck of ... bankruptcies, but perpetually renews itself wherever the man breathes" (*CW* 2:50). Such rhetoric can seem like a romantic flight from the market—idealist property is perhaps sheltered from unrest, not subjected to it. But the threats to property demand careful knowledge of the self and that self's relation to ideal laws if one is to secure it. And, in one more figure of speech taken from business enterprise, in the very act of exposing property to risk in order to protect it, Emerson finds that one redeems one's nature from widespread "insolven[cy]" (*CW* 2:43).[26]

This search for a form of property that can withstand external dislocations quietly appears in Everett's 1838 address cited at the outset of this essay too, in which his liberal faith in the market runs up against the era's boom-bust cycle. On the one hand, he wants to celebrate how capital "must go forth like a mighty genius" to "diffuse its inestimable moral, social, and economic blessings through the land, canals, rail-roads, and steamboats."[27] On the other one, he acknowledges that "these benefits, public and private, are not without some counterbalancing risks" that must be managed morally.[28] Everett sees the constant potential for economic volatility to be dampened through individual culture; to this end, he arrives on the "recent embarrassments of the commercial world," a euphemism for the Panic of 1837, which had beset the United States in May 1837.[29] Here Everett approaches, but never explicitly engages, the era's ideologically diverse panic discourse, which spread from the New England pulpit to the presidential dais. The main debate was whether to blame the crisis on President Andrew Jackson's refusal to recharter the US central bank or the greed of bankers.[30] But whereas the one-time Transcendentalist Orestes Brownson saw the panic as a harbinger of a class reckoning,[31] Whiggish writers like Everett saw it as a chance to improve capitalism, not replace it. For Brownson, like Marx and Engels, the wave of social life would be inalterably changed by the internal contradictions of the market. For Everett, these problems might be avoided in the future with moral discipline: "Let us hope that hereafter [US merchants] will keep themselves more beyond the reach of the fluctuations in business and the vicissitudes of affairs."[32]

Despite his use of the language of commercial enterprise as seen above, one common view of Emerson is that he was very much "beyond the reach" of this turbulent business world. (What can one learn of economy and finance while "uplifted into infinite space" [*CW* 1:10]?) This portrait is doubly wrong. First, Emerson turns out to be just one more investor whose portfolio suffered in the late 1830s. With the death of his father in 1811,

Emerson felt the perils of capitalism, as he took on the role of "family banker" in 1824 when his eldest brother, William, left to study in Germany.[33] The loss of his first wife, Ellen Louisa Tucker, would alter his financial reality, however. Once her estate was settled, Emerson "was assured of an annual income of about $1,200."[34] The trouble was that the settlement of the estate, although initiated in 1834, was not legally concluded until 1837—"just in time for the Financial Panic of 1837, when interest from the [estate's bank] stocks dried up."[35] Further, in addition to the bad timing of the settlement of Ellen Tucker's estate, his eagerness to help his brother William with real estate investments in Staten Island added to his stress. Emerson questioned the "prudence" of his brother's venture—his (Waldo's) lawyer "impress[ed] me with the prudence ... of not diminishing or risking the capital" of the Tucker settlement on William's scheme (*LRWE* 2:86). But he helped William nevertheless—as William wrote him in 1838, "you have been so good as to financier for me."[36] And yet there was a limit to this financiering; as Emerson writes in 1838, "I can raise no money here, having quite exhausted my financial faculty" (*LRWE* 2:136).

So, Emerson, the Sage of Concord, spent much of the 1830s and 40s fretting over "the occasional failure of the banks to pay dividends on [his] stock"—if we are to believe his statement in 1838—to the point of exhaustion. (The financial instruments that might have enabled his uplifting into infinite space would remain in flux.) But, and second, if his correspondence with William reflects his familiarity with bank stocks, mortgages, and insurance contracts, Emerson's journals offer a portrait of his evolving philosophical response to the ups and downs of the market. On May 10, 1837, precipitating the panic, New York City banks suspended payment to depositors in gold and silver. Just ten days later, Emerson wonders: "Is the world sick? Bankruptcy in England & America ... these are the morning's news" (*JMN* 5:331). The next day, with a clearer sense of the event's impact on the larger economy gleaned from the Boston newspapers, he expounds: "Young men have no hope. Adults stand like daylaborers idle in the streets. None calleth us to labor ... The present generation is bankrupt of principles & hope, as of property" (*JMN* 5:331–32).

The Panic of 1857 spurred Marx toward writing *Capital*; similarly, the 1837 disruption stirred something profound in Emerson. And in the same May 20, 1837, entry cited above, one can already discern that he would embrace the crisis as an intellectual opportunity—it would become a symbol of the "causal bankruptcy ... that the ideal should serve the actual." We find Emerson nearly triumphant in this passage, as he looks askance at "Prudence [which] itself is at her wits' end." He is "forced to inquire if the Ideal might not also be tried. Is it to be taken for granted that it is impracticable?". In a culmination of this energy, he concludes, "Let me begin anew. Let me teach the finite to know its Master. Let me ascend above my fate and work down upon my world" (*JMN* 5:332). The soaring disembodied eye would join the world below, determined to integrate the actual and the ideal. Not hoping to put the self "beyond the reach of the fluctuations in business," as Everett, Emerson experienced volatility in finance firsthand and, even still, embraced it as a vibrant philosophical context.

"The Morning after an Earthquake": The Scholar and Risk

As he surveyed the uprooted social landscape in May 1837, Emerson would "learn geology the morning after an earthquake" (*JMN* 5:333). That is, he read market forces as symbols and, in doing so, set out for a "remedy" (his term from "The American Scholar" [1837, *CW* 1:69]) for the times. He believed that in tending to one's work—what Emerson elsewhere called one's "foreordained" pursuit (*EL* 2:113)—one discovers "Culture." This is true of all forms of work because "each art is a whole in itself" (*EL* 2:234). As Emerson states in "Doctrine of the Hands," even (perhaps especially) manual labor, if attended to properly, alerts one to the "radical agreement and correspondence between these properties of matter and the properties of the soul" (*EL* 2:233). But, in one of the few critical studies of Emerson's early lecture series from 1836–1838, Carolyn R. Maibor (2004) sees works like "Trades and Professions" and "Doctrine of the Hands" to show how Emerson enlightens especially those young people primed to engage the bourgeois professions of nineteenth-century capitalism. He presumes that "our vocations provide us with the basis for our knowledge of the world, our ethical education and our self-development,"[37] but this is an insight for those educated "young men of the fairest promise" who must equip themselves for the waves of social life (*CW* 1:69).

Just prior to delivering "The American Scholar" at Harvard, Emerson gave the dedication address to the coeducational students and faculty (including Margaret Fuller, who taught there for two years) of the Greene Street School in Providence, Rhode Island. The institution was founded by Hiram Fuller (no relation to Margaret Fuller) on the principles of Bronson Alcott's Temple School in Boston. Emerson's speech was not a local success; as (Margaret) Fuller would write, his "'good words' ... fell ... on stony soil."[38] The relevant point here is that whether well received or not, the June 1837 address indicates Emerson's sense of obligation in instructing young people on the make for life within the turbulence of capitalism—a lesson, he explains in a likely reference to the Panic of 1837, that is "afford[ed] [by] great calamities" (*EL* 2:195).

Recycling his journal entries for the address, Emerson grounded his thoughts, once again, in the revelatory language of seismic rupture: "In exploring the relations of social man at a period of calamity and alarm, I seek to learn geology the morning after an earthquake" (*EL* 2:196). And in what followed, he identified the institution of education as a site in which to oppose the materialism that the panic had exposed. Lamenting the incompleteness of "Man," he lands upon a jeremiad targeting the interrelation between the self and the economy. He establishes, first, that man wrongly "regards wealth ... a profession ... and the office of power [as the] absolute value." Indeed, man "is a money chest" (*EL* 2:196). This insolvency of the self predicted financial bankruptcy, as the merchant's overgrown "desires" "drew [the farmer] into the fever of the market. They even infected the brain of the scholar and the clerk and tinged the removed dreams of the poet with some hope of the realization of his aims out of mechanical force" (*EL*

2:197). And second, as an antidote to this problem, he offers education, the "great object of [which] should be commensurate with the object of life. It should be a moral one; to each self-trust; to inspire the youthful man with an interest in himself" (*EL* 2:199).

The two domains—moral and financial—dovetail in Emerson's pun here, in which he lauds the idealist's self-interest, rather than the merchant's investment in the market. Of course, Emerson wasn't alone in bringing these domains into collision. For the historian of risk, Levy, "the thread that runs most consistently through risk's history is a moral one."[39] The problem, that is, was to define acceptable risks within individual culture, not to banish risk-taking. Similarly, in addition to the rhetoric of "interest," the "Address on Education" demonstrates Emerson's yoking of risk to morality in its critique of imprudent market activity that aims narrowly, feverishly, at accumulating mere property. But even here the address aims to recuperate risk, not eliminate it: "Thus a man may well spend many years of life in trade. It is a constant teaching of the laws of matter and of mind; no dollar of property can be created without some direct communication of nature, and of course, some acquisition of knowledge and practical force" (*EL* 2:201). "The office of a true Education," then, links commercial hazard and living—it awakens the "higher faculties of the individual" in any domain of life and thus can prevent "degenerat[ion] into the mere love of money," a contamination of work that is the same as if one "dieth daily" (*EL* 2:202).[40]

Delivered later that summer in Cambridge, "The American Scholar" is the most familiar of Emerson's attempts to persuade young people to live—that is, to align moral and business cultures. As in his speech at the Greene Street School, the panic still hangs in his thoughts in August, as he states, "Our anniversary is one of hope, and, perhaps, not enough of labor" (*CW* 1:52). At the same time, more confident in his own "remedy" for the times—idealism—he proceeds optimistically, aiming to embolden the young scholars to divorce their senses of self from the cost-benefit calculus of the market. Indeed, the scholar must "defer never to the popular cry" as he prepares to "guide men by showing them facts amidst appearances" (*CW* 1:63, 62).

In turning against such deference, Emerson co-opts the culture's narratives of enterprise to reveal to his audience that US citizens have become too risk averse. Recurring to the liberal principle of the "freeman," he states, "The spirit of the American freeman is already suspected to be timid, imitative, tame. Public and private avarice make the air we breathe thick and fat. The scholar is decent, indolent, complaisant." The era's bankrupt morality, expressed symbolically in the Panic of 1837, has deformed the scholar's ingenuity, daring, and freedom. It has desiccated his ambition. "The mind of this country," after all, "taught him to aim at low objects" and, accordingly, "there is no work for any but the decorous and the complaisant" (*CW* 1:69).

To alter this low estimation of enterprise seems daunting, but Emerson raises the stakes, as he did in the "Address on Education," by framing the issue of risk aversion ("complaisan[cy]") as a matter of life or death. He observes, "Young men of the fairest promise, who begin life upon our shores, inflated by the mountain winds, shined upon by all the stars of God, find the earth below not in unison with these." Earlier we saw Emerson move down to the world after his panic-induced epiphany; it is this trajectory from somnolence to wakefulness that he tries to model for the audience here. For these "promis[ing]" "young men" "are hindered from action by the disgust which the principles on which business is managed inspire, and turn drudges, or die of disgust—some of them suicides." The solution to death is a risk taking that aligns truth and work. Rather than "crowding to the barriers for the career," rather than following the cut path to death, "the single man [ought to] plant himself indomitably on his instincts, and there abide." Earlier in "The American Scholar," Emerson had painted a bleak portrait of the scholar's labor—it is lonely, unremunerated, and so on. Here, though, this labor defies death and leads to "infinite life," the "conversion of the world" (*CW* 1:69). If, as the president of Smith College William Allan Nielson observed at the centennial of the Cambridge address, there Emerson "feels profoundly the risk of men's becoming mere functionaries" in the modern economy (151), it is equally true that Emerson saw risk as something worth repurposing—as an affective charge to "walk on our own feet; ... work with our own hands; ... speak our own minds" (*CW* 1:70).

PRUDENCE, TRUE AND SPURIOUS

As I imply above, whether drawing from the eulogy of Thoreau or, as is more likely for modern scholars, the meditation on "wealth" from *The Conduct of Life* (1860), historiographers of capitalism prefer "late" Emerson. And yet, as we have seen, his attempts at redefining the culture of the market inform his early work too, including his first major essay series in 1841. In an apt formulation for an era characterized by booms and busts, he concludes in "Circles" (1841) that "life is a series of surprises" (*CW* 2:189). Character reveals itself in responding to such convulsions—in fact, character *stabilizes* amid unrest. "The great man," he writes, "is not convulsible or tormentable"; he does not make a monument to "calamity." Rather, "true conquest is the causing of the calamity to fade and disappear." From this perspective, greatness emerges in a disregard for previously failed enterprises, and its sign is, "in short," the ability "to draw a new circle" around one's experience (*CW* 2:190).

If "Circles" presents in this "true conquest" a model for managing the self, "Prudence" (1841) more directly tackles the commercial themes countenanced in the "Address on Education" and "The American Scholar." Developed from journal entries in the 1830s, the essay seems notably interested in the world beyond the self. If prudence can be derided as the "virtue of the senses," as Emerson states (*CW* 2:131), in Christopher Hanlon's recent reevaluation, it is also "for Emerson in 1841 the genius of managing outward reality with an eye to its betterment, and doing so requires us to give social, economic, and political circumstances its due."[41] Of course, still committed to idealism, this essay demands that people pay attention to the undercurrents of nineteenth-century capitalism as a context shaping—and, Emerson hoped, shaped by—Transcendentalism.

This is not to ignore the soaring rhetoric of Emerson's idealist philosophy in "Prudence." But, when framed as part of his engagement with midcentury capitalist identity formations, along with the earlier lecture series, the essay insists on the inextricable link between "the world of the senses" and spiritual laws: "a true prudence or law of shows recognizes the co-presence of other laws, and knows that its own office is subaltern; knows that it is surface and not centre where it works" (*CW* 2:131–32). Whereas one might use "the proverbs and acts and winkings of a base prudence" to secure life's necessities and pursue its wants, this is a "spurious prudence" (*CW* 2:133). But, and at the same time, the essay partakes in the era's risk culture to instill that lessons in "private economy" are indeed lessons in idealism. In a catalog of the teachings of a true prudence, Emerson lingers with financial language. "Money," he writes, "if kept by us, yields no rent, and is liable to loss." "Our Yankee trade," he continues further in the paragraph, "takes bank notes ... and saves itself by the speed with which it passes them off. Iron cannot rust, nor beer sour, nor timber rot, nor caligoes go out of fashion, nor money stocks depreciate, the few swift moments in which the Yankee suffers any one of them to remain in his possession. In skating over thin ice our safety is in our speed." Earlier, we heard Judge Hopkinson note that the merchant lives a life "necessarily ... of peril." Such rhetoric papers over what, from a Marxian perspective, is an internal contradiction of capitalist growth, as if individual morality can eliminate "peril." But Emerson approaches enterprise, too, as a rich source of meaning; he wants to translate—and quickly—financial ingenuity into the language of the soul (*CW* 2:138).[42]

The search for commercial profits, then, can train one's eye on social "betterment."[43] This means careful attention to the immediate problems of the present. In Levy's history of risk, he traces its emergence out of "the financial arena of marine insurance" and finds that "the image of the ship on stormy waters became a powerful metaphor for the perils and possibilities of life under capitalism."[44] And Emerson adapts this image in "Prudence" to underscore Transcendentalism's potential as a lifeline on the stormy seas of capitalism. Toward the end of the essay, he writes:

> When he sees a folded and sealed scrap of paper float round the globe in a pine ship, and come safe to the eye for which it was written, amidst a swarming population, let him likewise feel the admonition to integrate his being across all these distracting forces, and keep a slender human word among the storms, distances, and accidents, that drive us hither and thither, and, by persistency, make the paltry force of one man reappear to redeem its pledge, after months and years, in the most distant climes. (*CW* 2:139)

The passage nods to the concept of risk's genealogical relation to insurance by, tellingly, imagining the individual "eye," or soul, as a product of maritime commerce—a posted letter, in this example. The analogy between the "scrap of paper" safely delivered and the soul well "integrate[d]" in the present, despite the distances of time and place, draws attention to the potentially disruptive "forces" that separate a letter from its addressee, an individual and their soul. The safely delivered missive, then, offers a lesson in unity amid uncertainty: "among the storms, distances, and accidents," the "paltry force of man" endures through "persistency." Such a force can be imminently—and immanently—insured, that is, so as ever to secure value.

To think of self-trust as insurance, as I am doing so here, must acknowledge moments of seeming resistance in Emerson's earlier work against this maneuver by denouncing insularity. In "New England Reformers" (1844), for example, he wonders, "Am I not too protected a person?" (*CW* 3:152). There reflecting on his bourgeois identity within a society that favors commerce over manual labor, he laments the fact that market forces mediate social relations. Such mediation, indeed, denigrates human relationships: in buying a good or service, one is "prone to count myself relieved of any responsibility to behave well and nobly to that person whom I pay with money" (*CW* 3:152). A purchase in the market, that is, renders sociability dilatory, perhaps even impossible; exchange actually "defraud[s]" the self of "my best culture" (*CW* 3:152). Obedience to market forces thus creates a distance that protects the self from others and, in doing so, levies a "destructive tax" (*CW* 3:152).[45]

What Emerson fears in "New England Reformers," finally, is risk *avoidance*—an insurance that is too self-assured. Students of nineteenth-century US literature and culture might well think in this context of Herman Melville's monomaniacal Captain Ahab in *Moby-Dick*.[46] There, in the chapter "The Chart," the sea captain who surely experienced "the storms, distances, and accidents, that drive us hither and thither" (*CW* 2:139) "pondered over his charts ... with a view to the more certain accomplishment of that monomaniac thought of his soul."[47] In defiance of "reality" (in the narrator Ishmael's term), Ahab held a fast faith in a "time or place ... when all possibilities would become probabilities, and ... every possibility the next thing to a certainty."[48] Such narrow-minded faith is akin to madness. Emerson's "New England Reformers" thus exposes Ahab's self-belief as a partial one. And such men "lose their way; in the assault on the kingdom of darkness they expend all their energy on some accidental evil, and lose their sanity and power of benefit" (*CW* 3:261). A certainty in one's protection, as this cruel irony has it, leads necessarily to loss.

Capitalism and Emerson's Abolitionism

The problem with protection is that, with its offer of a safe distance from risk, it allows one to misunderstand market forces as disconnected from ideal ones. It permits, in other words, imprudence. This same worry about severing ties between inward and outward worlds as an economic problem informs Emerson's abolitionism too. A group of twenty-first-century scholars working within the new history of capitalism has started to "provide an empirical basis for challenging slavery's presumptive remoteness to the main story of innovation, entrepreneurship, and finance at the heart of American capitalism."[49] Scholarship in Emerson studies has similarly reevaluated enslavement's centrality to his thought.[50] In the 1840s and 1850s Emerson "had little difficulty grasping slavery's capitalism."[51] And to further challenge the idea that Emerson came to a more radical (immediatist) position only after the Compromise of 1850 and the Fugitive Slave Law, a focus on his stance toward commercial enterprise makes a throughline across his abolitionism more visible.[52]

Like those of other midcentury abolitionists, Emerson's speeches in celebration of Emancipation Day in the British West Indies disputed claims that US enslavement "was merely a regional institution."[53] Indeed, he stridently criticizes the intermingling of enslavement and US capitalism. In a lesser-known Fourth of July address in 1846 delivered in Dedham, Massachusetts, for example, Emerson understands Northern financial (and industrial) institutions as complicit with human bondage. He does so by criticizing the moderate affects that Jeffrey Insko, in a temporal critique of Emerson's antislavery writings and its resonance with his (Emerson's) philosophy of history, rightly attributes to gradualists.[54] But Emerson specifically links this inhibiting affective stance to an American commercial ethos; he concludes, "Hence, though slaveholders are apt to have a bad temper ... a strong desire to keep the peace ... is felt not only by the financial authorities in State street and Wall street, but also ... by every description of Northern salesmen."[55] When read in relation to his earlier critique of the self amid financial uncertainty, this address that predates the Compromise of 1850 revolves around a related question: how to end enslavement when so many financial institutions, and presumably the people that fill them up, profit so vastly from it?

The better-known 1844 memorial, "An Address on the Anniversary of the Emancipation of the Negroes in the British West Indies," delivered in Concord, expatiates on the connection between enslavement and national economic complacency. After providing a historical account of the British government's Slavery Abolition Act (1833), Emerson ponders the impediments to abolition in the United States. He targets the United States' "civility," which is "that of a trading nation; it is a shopkeeping civility." As revealed in a catalog of action verbs, this means that Americans "peddle, we truck, we sail, we row, we ride in cars, we creep in teams, we go in canals—to market, and for the sale of goods." Inevitably, "the national aim and employment streams into our ways of thinking, our laws, our habits and our manners" (*CW* 10:314). In a speech notable for "a more or less straightforward recounting of the available facts surrounding the decades-long efforts by which the British eliminated first the slave trade and finally slavery throughout the Empire," here Emerson catalogs actions that are never quite that.[56] They are, rather, malaise-inspiring routines, figures of busyness, passing for activity—they are strengths masquerading as weaknesses, near lifelessness.

But if the habits of shopkeeping lead to contentment, they might lead to a less comfortable liberation as well. And to conclude his speech Emerson deploys a Whiggish faith in the market that, as Martha Schoolman writes, "fits emancipation into a progressive narrative."[57] For his abolitionism, Emerson's conflation of the moral and the mercantile begins on the premise that enslavement is stasis: "Slavery is no scholar, no improver; it does not love the whistle of the railroad; it does not love the newspaper, the mail-bag, a college, a book," and so on. In fact, it "decay[s]" enterprise, in addition to suffocating liberty. To the contrary, to yearn for an improvement that is forestalled by enslavement is to effect wakefulness and vigor. To reach this alert state requires a nod to prudence: "It was easy for manufacturers [in the West Indies] to see that if the state of things in the islands was altered, if the slaves had wages, the slaves would be clothed, would build houses, would fill them with tools ... In every naked negro of those thousands, they saw a future customer" (*CW* 10:315). And it is "these considerations [that] opened the eyes of the dullest in Britain" (*CW* 10:316). Emerson is careful to hedge about commercial forces functioning as the primary engine of abolition. In concluding his remarks in 1844, though, he cannot help but, once again, assert the incompatibility of enslavement and "the enterprise, the very muscular vigor of this nation," the United States. Finally, he wonders to what extent a commercial ethos not only limits the "sentiment of Right" but perhaps, on an Atlantic scale, brings it to fruition (*CW* 10:327).

The Laws of Success

Emerson's Dedham, Massachusetts, address on the Fourth of July in 1846 that I reference above contained a further sign of how entwined finance was with his abolitionism. In their steadfast vision of a "sublime" law "that the right will conquer," "the Abolitionists" leave Emerson a "debtor": "I am a debtor, in common with all well-meaning persons, to this association." This "common" debt owed the abolitionists arises from their modeling how to channel a power that "as readily and irresistibly pours itself from one man." They embolden others, in a term with further financial resonance, to "repudiate" "the solemn nonsense of existing things" (*AW* 44).

That Emerson employs financial rhetoric to establish that self-reliant people ("association") can alter the mindset of a single person illustrates how the market can be a venue in which the ideal "pours itself from one man" to another. This belief informs the "late" Emerson of such interest to the new historiographers of capitalism. Writing of the lecture series that would become *The Conduct of Life*, the biographer Robert Richardson acknowledges the "unfortunate" reception of the book by "the publicists of the Gilded Age" who see Emerson as "not wholly repudiat[ing] American business and workaday success."[58] Neither robber barons nor would-be Ragged Dicks but modern scholars, including Sandage, Jeffrey Sklansky, and Michael Zakim, too, see Emerson to codify the culture of the market. And yet, in drawing considerably from the essay "Wealth," included in *The Conduct of Life* and long a target of those critical of Emerson's accommodation of capitalism, Sandage's *Born Losers* recognizes that "Emerson's [work] combined market logic and moral creed," even as it silos this essay from Emerson's larger body of work. Sandage is right to see "Wealth" as part of a "powerful ideology, a canon of cultural beliefs and practices that shaped the ordeal and aftermath of economic loss," but work remains to understand Emerson's evolving engagement with, to use the title of his opening lecture in the *Conduct of Life* series, the "laws of success."[59]

In 1837, Emerson had an inkling that a "single man" could "plant himself indomitably on his instincts," effect the "conversion of the world," and, thereby, redeem US culture's imprudence (*CW* 1:69). By the time "Wealth" is published as an essay in 1860, he revives the old complaint and begins with the premise that "society is barbarous until every industrious man can get his living without dishonest customs." But he further specifies his vision of economy here by defining terms like "wealth" as an intimacy "between thought and all production"; later, he states, pithily, "Wealth is in applications of the mind to nature" (*CW* 6:45). What was prospective in the 1830s is poised to be actualized in the 1860s. More confident about how the human intellect applies itself to produce value in the material world, indeed, Emerson celebrates "the craft of the merchant," his ability in "bringing a thing from where it abounds to where it is costly" (*CW* 6:46), as evidence of this success.

In doing so, he unfortunately overlooks market-based wealth's complicity with the linked issues of ecological and economic crises. Thus coal mining, and its attendant transportation infrastructure, is celebrated for making possible a "portable climate," where labor recedes behind the screen of the commodity as "coal carries coal, by rail and by boat, to make Canada as warm as Calcutta" (*CW* 6:46). Moreover, capital wealth's relation to the ongoing event of settler colonialism is obscured, as it requires "the freedom of the city, the freedom of the earth, traveling, machinery," and so on, for its production and maintenance (*CW* 6:47). But, in the context of connecting early and late Emerson and his view of the economic, I am drawn to "Wealth" for two other (contradictory) reasons. First, it furthers Emerson's thinking from the late 1830s, in which he adapts the Puritan work ethic to capitalist culture—wealth, after all, "begins with ... articles of necessity" and concludes with "the rich man who can avail himself of all men's faculties" (*CW* 6:47): with a single person knowing their work well. Second, it presents an intriguing sleight of hand in its seeming focus on the genius of the single "merchant." Wealth is not only the product of (long) time but also the coordinated effect of many who apply their intellects to the material world. He presents, in short, an expansive vision, temporally and spatially, of an economy "on the higher plane" (*CW* 6:68).

This coordination works through a dialectic of the singular and the average intellects applied to market activities. In contemplating the industrial revolution, for example, he finds the successes of "the monomaniacs who talk up their projects in marts and offices." This "*speculative* genius is the madness of a few for the gain of the world. The projectors are sacrificed, but the public is the gainer" (Emerson's emphasis). But the question is not only "how did our factories get built?" in an act of single-focused "sacrifice" but also "how do they stay running?" (*CW* 6:50). How does wealth continue to grow? The answer lies, surprisingly, not in the extraordinary person but one "who has the just average of faculties" (*CW* 6:54). If the "*speculative* genius" gets a mass moving, the average merchant maintains that momentum.

Here Emerson comes full circle from "The American Scholar," in which he urges the young men to enact a theory of ideal vocation, to what he sees as its realization a generation later—people with the "just average of faculties" lifting an economy to a "higher plane." In other words, what he sought in vain in 1837, he normalizes in 1860. And in turning to the laws of physics to understand the laws of success in "Wealth," he anticipated his fullest expression of this normative economy, the Civil War address "Perpetual Forces" (1862), which later appeared as a standalone essay in *Atlantic Monthly*. For there, Emerson outlines a vision of economy in which market forces operate over a long period of time, flowing through any number of people. This is a patient, "average" view of market activity, in which the "young men of the fairest promise" have succeeded en masse.

"Perpetual Forces" finds Emerson once more dwelling upon, to reference again his terminology from "Wealth," one's ability to "insure himself in every transaction" (*CW* 6:53). The problem to solve remains how to produce value through risk-taking that is at the same time that activity's guarantor. "Wealth" sought to link one man's small work to "gigantic results, without any compromise of safety" (*CW* 6:54). This severe single-mindedness leads to an increase in "power," Emerson declares in the early 1860s: "The power of a man increases steadily by continuance in one direction" (*LL* 2:283). The trick is to work "obedience into the circuit of the heavenly wisdom" (*LL* 2:298)—that is, to acknowledge that "things work to their ends, not to yours" (*LL* 2:299). Finally, then, for Emerson market forces bend to justice, with each man slowly figuring out the "just average" and, in doing so, aligning work and "heavenly wisdom." This process is not merely in the service of today—it should not be grasped as a "short success" (*LL* 2:300). Rather, the fulfillment of true wealth in the market "works in long periods." If prudence in investing is a virtue, that is because prudence ("success") "consists in close appliance to the laws of the world" (*CW* 6:54).

Such abstraction from Emerson about market forces, which across the nineteenth century in the United States resulted in widespread disparity along gender, racial, social, and ecological axes, can seem uncompelling to modern critics. But given the remarkable consistency across his career, it is impractical to turn only to the "late" Emerson to anchor such concerns. Indeed, market forces, for the body of Emerson's work, are just that—forces—and, as such, "the laws of force" apply in the economic domain as in any other. And this means, further, that market forces "are in an ascending series"—they move toward "a higher plane" (*LL* 2:292). Thinking within a liberal progressivism that, indeed, the history of global capitalism has made seem untenable, Emerson imagined people suffering not the lives of quiet desperation his friend Thoreau opined, but more skillfully matching their moral sense to the tasks at hand. Seeing the market as an arena in which to insure the self against the risks of materialism, in obeying "the laws of force," Emerson approached commerce as yet one more path "on the way to the highest" good (*CW* 6:68).

Notes

1. Elizabeth Hewitt, "Romances of Real Life; or, the Nineteenth-Century American Business Magazine," *American Periodicals* 20, no. 1 (2010): 1–22, 5.
2. Edward Everett, "Accumulation, Property, Capital, and Credit," *Hunt's Merchants' Magazine* 1, no. 1 (1839): 29–37, 29.
3. Robert D. Richardson, Emerson: The Mind on Fire (Berkeley: University of California Press, 1995), 13.
4. Neil Dolan, Emerson's Liberalism (Madison, University of Wisconsin Press, 2009).
5. I borrow the phrase from Alexander Kern, "Emerson and Economics," *New England Quarterly* 13, no. 1 (December 1940): 678–96.

6. See Maurice S. Lee, *Slavery, Philosophy, and American Literature, 1830–1860* (Cambridge: Cambridge University Press, 2005), 167. See also Jeffrey Insko, *History, Abolition, and the Ever-Present Now in Antebellum American Writing* (New York: Oxford University Press, 2018), 95 for an overview of this scholarly debate.
7. Michael Zakim and Gary J. Kornblith, "Introduction: An American Revolutionary Tradition," in *Capitalism Takes Command: The Social Transformation of Nineteenth-Century America*, ed. Zakim and Kornblith (Chicago: University of Chicago Press, 2012), 1–12, 2.
8. Ibid., 1.
9. This project is distinct from Everett's and thus complicates Emerson's liberalism (Dolan, *Emerson's Liberalism*; see also Insko, *History, Abolition, and the Ever-Present Now*). In his remarks to the Mercantile Association, for example, Everett aims at the moral education of the merchant so as to "counterbalance" market "risks" ("Accumulation, Property, Capital, and Credit," 35). Emerson, true to his idealism, worries about protection from turmoil in the first place. More on this below.
10. Lee, *Slavery, Philosophy, and American Literature*, 167.
11. See John Lauritz Larson, *The Market Revolution in Early America: Liberty, Ambition, and the Eclipse of the Common Good* (Cambridge: Cambridge University Press, 2009), 8.
12. Ibid., 9.
13. Zakim and Kornblith, "Introduction," 2.
14. See Karl Marx and Friedrich Engels, *Manifesto of the Communist Party*, 1848, in *The Marx-Engels Reader*, ed. Robert C. Tucker, 2nd ed. (New York: Norton, 1978), 469–500, 476.
15. Joseph Hopkinson, "Lecture on Commercial Integrity," *Hunt's Merchants' Magazine* 1, no. 5 (1839): 376–90, 380.
16. Jonathan Levy, *Freaks of Fortune: The Emerging World of Capitalism and Risk in America* (Cambridge, MA: Harvard University Press, 2012), 1.
17. Ibid., 4.
18. Ibid., 5–6.
19. Ibid., 3.
20. Scott Sandage, *Born Losers: A History of Failure in America* (Cambridge, MA: Harvard University Press, 2006), 5.
21. Levy, *Freaks of Fortune*, 1.
22. Lee, *Slavery, Philosophy, and American Literature*, 205.
23. Sandage, *Born Losers*, 47.
24. Levy, *Freaks of Fortune*, 36.
25. Nathaniel Hawthorne, *The House of the Seven Gables*, ed. Fredson Bowers (Columbus, OH: Ohio State University Press, 1965), 38.
26. As for society, though, that's possibly too far gone. As Emerson writes in "Wealth," "society can never prosper, but must always be bankrupt, until every man does that which he was created to do" (*CW* 6:60).
27. Everett, "Accumulation, Property, Capital, and Credit," 32.
28. Ibid., 35.
29. Ibid.
30. Larson, *Market Revolution in Early America*, 34–35.
31. Orestes A. Brownson, Babylon is Falling (Boston, 1837).
32. Everett, "Accumulation, Property, Capital, and Credit," 35.
33. Ronald A. Bosco and Joel Myerson, *The Emerson Brothers: A Fraternal Biography in Letters* (New York: Oxford University Press, 2006), 316.

34. Richardson, *Mind on Fire*, 135.
35. Bosco and Myerson, *Fraternal Biography*, 328.
36. Quoted in Bosco and Myerson, *Fraternal Biography*, 330. Here William Emerson explains that, in eagerness to mitigate risk to his brother, he has added him (Waldo) as the beneficiary to a life insurance policy.
37. Carolyn R. Maibor, *Labor Pains: Emerson, Thoreau, and Alcott on Work, Women, and the Development of the Self* (London: Routledge, 2003), 59.
38. Quoted in Laraine R. Fergenson, "Margaret Fuller in the Classroom: The Providence Period," Studies in the American Renaissance (1987): 131–42, 133.
39. Levy, *Freaks of Fortune*, 5.
40. For a provocative account of the rhetoric of somnolence in Emerson, both early and late, and its links to Emerson's abolitionism, see Insko, *History, Abolition, and the Ever-Present Now*. More on Emerson, abolition, and finance below.
41. Christopher Hanlon, *Emerson's Memory Loss: Originality, Communality, and the Late Style* (New York: Oxford University Press, 2018), 82.
42. That Emersonian prudence in 1841 means justifying the superficial and the deep might complicate how we understand a text like "Experience" (1844), in which he writes, "We live amid surfaces, and the true art of life is to skate well upon them" (*CW* 3:35). My thanks to Christopher Hanlon for pointing me to this passage.
43. Hanlon, *Emerson's Memory Loss*, 82.
44. Levy, *Freaks of Fortune*, 1, 2.
45. See also Hanlon, *Emerson's Memory Loss*, 75.
46. Levy credits Melville's father-in-law, Lemuel Shaw, the Chief Justice of the State of Massachusetts Supreme Court, for "invit[ing] risk inland" in his ruling *Farwell v. Boston and Worcester R.R. Corp.* (1842), 7. Farwell, an engine man for the Boston and Worcester Railroad, lost the use of his hand in an industrial accident. Turning to maritime risk insurance for precedence, Shaw and the court denied his claim and held that Farwell assumed an inherent risk in his role.
47. Herman Melville, *Moby-Dick*, ed. Hershel Parker, 3rd ed. (New York: Norton, 2018), 158.
48. Ibid., 160.
49. Sven Beckert and Seth Rockman, "Introduction: Slavery's Capitalism," in Slavery's Capitalism: A New History of American Economic Development, ed. Beckert and Rockman (Philadelphia: University of Pennsylvania Press, 2016): 5.
50. See, for instance, Lee, *Slavery, Philosophy, and American Literature*; Insko, *History, Abolition, and the Ever-Present Now*; Hanlon, *Emerson's Memory Loss*; and Martha Schoolman, *Abolitionist Geographies* (Minneapolis: University of Minnesota Press), 2014.
51. Beckert and Rockman, "Introduction," 5.
52. See Insko, *History, Abolition, and the Ever-Present Now*, 95 and 113.
53. Beckert and Rockman, 5.
54. Insko, *History, Abolition, and the Ever-Present Now*, 95.
55. Ralph Waldo Emerson, "Antislavery Speech at Dedham," in Emerson's Antislavery Writings, ed. Len Gougeon and Joel Myerson (New Haven, CT: Yale University Press, 1995), 42.
56. Insko, *History, Abolition, and the Ever-Present Now*, 115.

57. Martha Schoolman, "Emerson's Doctrine of Hatred," *Arizona Quarterly* 63, no. 2 (2007): 1–26, 14. In seeing Emerson's argument to embrace a progressive philosophy of history founded in commercial evolution, here I depart from Insko's reading of this address (*History, Abolition, and the Ever-Present Now*, 119).
58. See Richardson, *Mind on Fire*, 491.
59. Sandage, *Born Losers*, 46.

CHAPTER 18

EMERSON AND THE SOCIALISTS

American Renaissance in the Age of Fourier

HOLLY JACKSON

IN his 1852 *Love vs. Marriage*, Marx Edgeworth Lazarus cites a range of authorities to condemn monogamous marriage and advocate instead "variety in love"—that is, having more than one sexual or romantic partner, either serially or simultaneously. This tome offers classical allusions, historical precedents, and arguments resting on religious, economic, political, legal, and feminist grounds. Though his frame of reference is wide-ranging, Lazarus, like most American free-lovers in the 1850s, derives much of his perspective and expression from the work of the late philosopher Charles Fourier; the final chapters conclude that society must be rearranged into phalansteries, the communal palaces that the French socialist theorized, for truly free and equal love relations to be realized. But Lazarus is clear that his preference for multiple partners does not come from scholarly research and social theory alone, but stems from his individual insight and experience as well. He cites another of his major influences to argue that these inner truths must be honored despite society's inherited prejudices: "I have only to say with Emerson, if I am the devil's child, I will do the devil's work. Why should we disown ourselves?"[1]

This paraphrase of "Self-Reliance" is not the only citation of Ralph Waldo Emerson in this paean to polyamory; Lazarus reprints portions of the poems "To Rhea" and "Threnody" as well. Many other prominent free-lovers of the period also presented their views as expressions of Emersonian individualism: Thomas Low and Mary Gove Nichols reprinted his poem "Each in All" in their monthly periodical in 1855; he is cited in the July 1877 issue of Ezra Heywood's *Word*; and the anarchist free-love paper *Lucifer, the Light-Bearer*, run by Moses Harmon in Kansas in the final decades of the century, mentioned or discussed Emerson more than a dozen times.[2]

Perhaps it comes as no surprise that a fringe thinker like Lazarus would find inspiration in the most prominent intellectual of his time, particularly given the nonconformist bent of Emersonian philosophy. What may be more surprising is that Emerson read Lazarus and other free-lovers too, and may have found in their writings fuller expression of sentiments he himself had entertained, if only in private. Emerson's journal mentions *Love vs. Marriage* and another of Lazarus's books, along with work by Stephen Pearl Andrews, and two French Fourierist volumes, one of which, *Love in the Phalanstery*, had been translated by his friend, Henry James. He took careful notes on the other, transcribing the free-love maxim, "marriage is the tomb of love," an idea he had mulled over for many years (*JMN* 13:210–11).

Emerson's engagement with Fourier and his followers, though deeply ambivalent, was serious and sustained, enduring for over a decade and shaping his philosophy. Though his published writings on Fourierist socialism tend to lampoon, reject, and misread these ideas to emphasize by contrast his own doctrine of individualism, the two hewed closer than he cared to admit, which is perhaps why he denied them so strenuously. This conflicted but crucial interchange raises again the question of Emerson's relationship to radical thought in his time, and more specifically to the activists who sought to live out ideas they attributed to Emerson himself.

Critics have long upheld some version of Henry Steele Commager's evocative 1960 claim that Emerson was "the cow" from which all antebellum reformers "drew their milk."[3] Though he habitually characterized all reformers in an unflattering light—as "partial," conceited, attention-seeking, ineffectual, odious bores—scholars have emphasized how his philosophy was embraced and revered by activists and thus constituted a major contribution to the pivotal social reform movements of his day.[4] But Emerson drew his milk from these radicals more than we have acknowledged. His ultimate disavowal of their critiques of capitalism and marriage (though he privately shared them to a surprising degree) shaped the inactive liberal progressivism that lies uneasily beside the liberatory elements of his philosophy. Moreover, tracking his encounters with Fourier's unabashedly flamboyant, disruptive, and far-fetched ideas reveals an important struggle in Emerson's thought more broadly over the social utility of philosophy. From "Man the Reformer" to *Representative Men*, he sternly rejects real-life applications of Transcendentalism and casts doubt on the very possibility of social change. Ultimately, the reformist collectivity of the Fourierist zeitgeist in the United States embraced forms of public exposure that Emerson found unbearable, giving rise to a reactionary counter-utopianism that informs a range of major works of the American Renaissance.

***

Fourierist socialism arrived in the United States at a moment when the public was uniquely poised to receive it, due in part to the impact of both social justice activism and Emersonian Transcendentalism in the previous decade, as well as dire economic conditions. The 1830s saw the rise of the radical antislavery movement and organized labor, activist critiques of American society that also brought women into public life in unprecedented ways. In the religious and philosophical realms, Transcendentalism's controversial rejection of Unitarian tradition evinced a similar hunger for "the newness." The Panic of 1837 and the long ensuing economic depression were watershed events that seemed to indicate the graphic failure of existing systems and stoked desires for transformative change. The preceding decades had been capitalist boom times, the Jacksonian "market revolution" of rapid economic expansion that relied on unregulated speculation, leading to a disastrous bust. Capitalism had seemed to promise the limitless growth and wealth creation that would allow for the meritocratic mobility and equality of white American men. But after 1837, it was clear that this volatile system relied on exploitation and extreme social inequalities. People were starving on the streets in the land of plenty.[5]

Reflecting on this state of affairs in his journal that year, Emerson wrote, "The world has failed." In the news that sixty thousand more laborers were about to lose their jobs, he heard "loud cracks in the social edifice," the makings of a mob that might attack the rich and overthrow the government. "The young men have no hope," he observed. Yet in this economic crisis, Emerson also saw the opportunity for transformative change that would not be possible otherwise: "I see a good in such emphatic and universal calamity as the times bring, that they dissatisfy me with society. Under common burdens we say there is much virtue in the world, and what evil co-exists is inevitable ... but when these full measures come, it then stands confessed—society has played out its last stake; it is checkmated." Specifically, he suggests that this widespread dissatisfaction with capitalism called for utopian experimentation: "I am forced to inquire if the ideal might not also be tried. Is it to be taken for granted that it is impracticable?" (*JMN* 5:332).

The publication of Albert Brisbane's *Social Destiny of Man* in 1840 seemed to many precisely this needed new direction, a plan somehow both "ideal" and "practicable." In response to the exploitation, waste, and ugliness of industrial capitalism, Brisbane forecasted not a violent class war but rather a process of social and even geological evolution resulting in a utopic future called Harmony, a translation of the teachings of the French philosopher Charles Fourier. Having studied under Fourier in Paris, Brisbane became his leading American acolyte, translating his ideas for the most sympathetic and proactive audience they would ever find. In the throes of the worst economic downturn the young country had experienced, antebellum Americans flocked to his plans for a more cooperative and beautiful world.

Brisbane called for nothing less than a wholesale reorganization of society and life, starting from the premise that work could and must be made attractive and pleasurable. Workers would cycle through a variety of useful labors in a single day, moving quickly from shepherding to gardening to fishing, according to their attractions. Their days would be structured to gratify a catalogue of desires, with special attention to sensual enjoyment, fulfilling work, and near-constant socializing. At the core of his philosophy were "the passions," or individual desires and drives, which he believed should not be repressed as civilization then demanded but rather utilized to create social bonds, propelling people to make fulfilling contributions to their communities. Brisbane argues that "isolated man without social interests and sympathies is, like a single note in music, valueless. We must combine and associate large masses to develop the harmonies of human nature." Thus, the unique composition and contributions of individuals would achieve their highest expression and value in their combined effect. They would live in groups of 1,620 in communal palaces called phalanxes; nuclear families in independent dwellings, the idealized core organization of American private life, would be abandoned.[6] "The cabin, the cottage, or the dwelling house of civilization, with its monotony, with the daily repetition of its petty and harassing cares, with its antisocial spirit, its absence of emulation, debilitates the energies of the soul and produces apathy and intellectual death, where all should be life and exaltations!" Americans must crawl out of their cramped existence in the private home, Brisbane declared, into gorgeous palaces devoted to the collective realization of their desires.[7]

The impact of Fourier's thought on this period has been underestimated, surely in part because it is difficult to believe that people took his extravagant claims seriously. He asserted, for example, that his proposed changes to work and home life would make the earth's climates more agreeable, that seawater would turn to lemon soda, helpfully revised animals like the "antilion" would roam the earth, and people would be seven feet tall and amphibious, sporting a long tail with a hand at the end.[8] But Brisbane did not include Fourier's most outlandish or sexual visions in his 1840 translation. Though Marx and Engels's later classification of Fourier as a "utopian socialist" is undoubtedly apt, Brisbane's proposal for "Association" was presented and received as a practical reform blueprint, taken up by workers and labor organizers, including thousands who joined model phalanxes and Fourier Clubs, and perhaps most robustly by the progressive Northern intellectual vanguard of which Emerson was a part. The review of Brisbane's book in the Transcendentalist *Dial* notes, "The name of Fourier may be placed at the head of modern thinkers, whose attention has been given to the practical evils of society and the means of their removal." They describe it as a systematic plan for addressing material issues related to the important questions of labor and capital.[9]

The Transcendentalists' interest in Fourier reflected the similarities in their philosophies and also the fact that some of them were looking for real social applications of their critiques of industrial society and the spiritual damage it had wreaked. As Association gained steam the year following the publication of Brisbane's major work, Emerson's essays amply demonstrate his grappling with capitalism as an exploitative system creating vast social disparities that undermined both democracy and personal morality. But in direct opposition to his friends who cast off their comfortable, ordinary lives in an attempt to change the world, many inspired by Fourier, he asserts that taking action on these issues is not only futile but absurd.

Emerson's 1841 lecture "Man the Reformer" critiques the American economy as "a system of selfishness," shot through with abuses and theft, "a system of distrust, of concealment, of superior keenness, not of giving but of taking advantage" (*CW* 1:148). Importantly, Emerson admits his own role in this system of exploitation and suggests that each individual American is trapped in a web of complicity: "We are all implicated, of course, in this charge; it is only necessary to ask a few questions as to the progress of the articles of commerce from the fields where they grew, to our houses, to become aware that we eat and drink and wear perjury and fraud in a hundred commodities" (*CW* 1:147). He poses the difficult questions of culpability and agency for subjects of a systemically exploitative economic system: "every body partakes" and "yet none feels himself accountable. He did not create the abuse; he cannot alter it. What is he? an obscure private person who must get his bread. That is the vice,—that no one feels himself called to act" (*CW* 1:148). This is the crux of Emerson's position at this time: he diagnoses inequalities and yet does not feel called to correct them. For the very rare person who refuses to benefit from the misery of others, "nothing is left him but to begin the world anew" (*CW* 1:147), which is, of course, exactly what his Transcendentalist colleagues George Ripley and Bronson Alcott aimed to do by disentangling from mainstream society and crafting new socially conscious collectives.

"Man the Reformer" provides a template that Emerson's writings on reform and reformers tends to follow: he agrees with their ideas but rejects their activism as ineffectual and foolish. He lays out in this essay the risks of taking social justice consciousness too far: "I do not wish to be absurd and pedantic in reform. I do not wish to push my criticism on the state of things around me to that extravagant mark, that shall compel me to suicide, or to an absolute isolation from the advantages of civil society" (*CW* 1:155). These concerns about seeming silly and losing the benefits of conformity might strike us as strange coming from the arch-individualist. Furthermore, though Emerson repeatedly criticized reform projects as "partial," his gripe here seems to be with their perfectionism: "If we suddenly plant our foot, and say,—I will neither eat nor drink nor wear nor touch any food or fabric which I do not know to be innocent, or deal with any person whose whole manner of life is not clear and rational, we shall stand still. Whose is so? Not mine; not thine; not his" (*CW* 1:155). But of course, many people at this time and in Emerson's own circle were committed to the attempt to live in just this way, a lifestyle of protest and sacrifice that he pretends here is unimaginable. His remark brings to mind two activist strains in particular: in the Free Produce movement, begun by African Americans and Quakers years earlier, people boycotted the products of slave labor; Garrisonian Non-Resistants refused all entanglement with the US government—refusing to vote, serve on juries, or perform militia duties, and so on—because it sanctioned slavery. These projects were not dreamy utopianism but rather practical strategies to undermine systems of oppression and, at the very least, to withdraw the allegiance and contributions of dissenting individuals.

Emerson's conclusions here about the inconvenience of shunning society and the impossibility of living according to one's conscience are difficult to square with his signature articulation of his philosophy of individualism. "Self-Reliance" presents even more starkly his rejection of social responsibility ("Are they my poor?" [*CW* 2:30]), and yet bears a striking resemblance in many instances to the style and substance of Association. Emerson argues that a corrupt society deforms us and make us hypocrites, a critique remarkably similar to Fourier's. Moreover, Emerson's description of the inner truths that ought to drive us sound like the individual "passions" that would form the basis of Association: "These are the voices which we hear in solitude, but they grow faint and inaudible as we enter into the world" (*CW* 2:29). Indeed, Emerson uses jargon that would soon become endemic in the writings of Fourierist free-lovers when he confirms his obligation only to those who he belongs by "spiritual affinity" rather than traditional family and marital relations. He declares, "I will not hide my tastes or aversions. I will so trust that what is deep is holy, that I will do strongly before the sun and moon whatever inly rejoices me, and the heart appoints," making it clear why Lazarus cited this essay in his apologia for heterodox sexual relations (*CW* 2:42).

A final essay from that pivotal year of 1841, "Lecture on the Times," offers a clear synthesis of his position at this time that reform impulses are always utopian and indeed should remain untried. He notes that "purists" are inquiring into the church, private property, slavery, and also "growing uneasy on the subject of Marriage." He describes this social justice foment as a relentless kind of looking, obscene in its insistence to reveal: "so it goes up and down, paving the earth with eyes, destroying privacy." He says that throughout history, all reforms boil down to "the comparison of the idea with the fact. Our modes of living are not agreeable to our imagination. We suspect they are unworthy." Thus, activism is the hope "that the thoughts of the mind may yet, in some distant age, in some happy hour, be executed by the hands." It is right to wish that the world might someday align with the ideals we imagine, but taking action toward this end, setting "your heart and face against society when you thought it wrong," is pointless. It amounts to nothing more lasting "than the passing of your hand through the air ... The world leaves no track in space, and the greatest action of man no mark in the vast idea" (*CW* 1:175–76). Perhaps this is why he had yet showed little interest in the radical antislavery movement gaining momentum throughout the 1830s, even though his grandfather, aunt, younger brother, wife, and a number of his closest friends were committed to the cause. He had published a letter opposing "Indian removal" in 1835 but, as Cornel West has observed, seemed immediately to regret it.[10] Emerson's wholesale rejection of any hope for social progress is staggering, and restates an earlier lecture's admonition against the practical application of ideas: "All philosophy, all theory, all hope are defeated when applied to society" (*EL* 2:176).

Of course, this emphasis in his 1841 essays emerged most directly as a rebuttal not of Brisbane but of his Transcendentalist colleagues who were plunging into collective projects aimed at extricating themselves from the exploitation economy and realizing the more immediate relationship to the material world they had discussed in the parlors of Concord and Cambridge. When Ripley invited Emerson that year to join them in their attempt to begin the world anew, Emerson refused, though he made this decision, in his own words, "very slowly and I may almost say with penitence." Ripley's letter of invitation to him explaining the community's aims seems to echo Emerson's "American Scholar" directly: "a more natural union between intellectual and manual labor than now exists; to combine the thinker and the worker, as far as possible, in the same individual." But Emerson's response declares, "All I shall solidly do, I must do alone, and I am so ignorant and uncertain in my improvements that I would fain hide my attempts and failures in solitude." He was clearly wrestling with the question of applying his philosophy to his life, of how he personally fit into the projects taking off around him that were inspired in part by his own ideas.[11]

While scholars have noted his insistence on individualism even to the point of "solitude" in reaction to the communitarian activist projects of this moment, his focus here on failure and the necessarily public character of social action are key. His letter hinges on the view that attempts to improve the world should not be grand enough to hazard the embarrassments of exposure. By his own admission, Emerson wanted to contribute to the world only in the realm of thought. He was aware of what he called his "inefficiency to practical ends," his constitutional aversion to action in the world: "I was born a seeing eye not a helping hand" (*JMN* 5:298). Though he had rejected in "American Scholar" this very dichotomy between seeing and doing, theorizing wrongs and aiming to right them ("the so-called 'practical men' sneer at speculative men, as if, because they speculate or *see*, they could do nothing"), Emerson ultimately affirms this binary, insisting that utopian speculation is distinct from practical action and superior to it. Though his colleagues who set out to redeem the world at Brook Farm, Hopedale, Fruitlands, and elsewhere have been called utopian, they were in fact devoting themselves to working out solutions to the problems that Emerson had also diagnosed. Their communes were very real attempts to take their beliefs out of the realm of theory and live them, to work out new rather than traditional relationships to food, housing, infrastructure, work, kin systems, and the like. The critical insistence has been that Emerson rejected these projects because they were collective, but he did not launch a solo experimental living project like Thoreau. He was opposed to taking action in response to the social problems he critiqued, insistently rejecting pragmatic applications of his philosophy as silly, threatening, indecent, and bound to fail.

Many critics have noted that the founding of Brook Farm was a turning point for Emerson, marking his move away from critiques of capitalism toward an embrace of the free market, his apotheosis of the individual worked out in contrast to communalism.[12] But less examined is how Emerson's oeuvre responded to the basic premise of the reform foment, namely that ideas, beliefs, and critiques should be applied to society in the hope of some pragmatic result. Emerson defends philosophy as a utopian pursuit and rejects applications aimed at social reform, many of them inspired by his own philosophy, as pointless. Ironically enough, Fourierist socialism served as Emerson's straw man after this point in his defense of utopian speculation from his fellow Transcendentalists who sought a pragmatist philosophy.

Emerson met Brisbane in 1842 in New York City, dining with him and Horace Greeley, the leaders of the Association movement at that time, and heard about their plans first hand. Afterwards, he wrote to his wife: "I foresaw in the moment when I encountered these two new friends here, that I cannot content them. They are bent on popular action: I am in all my theory, ethics & politics a poet and of no more use to them in their New York than a rainbow or firefly ... One of these days shall we not have new laws forbidding solitude; and severe penalties on all separatists & unsocial thinkers?" As William Hall Brock notes, "Emerson paints these utopian dreamers as pragmatists, and himself as the fanciful idealist" in this letter—a useless poet, unsocial separatist, a lovely rainbow with no material existence—while the Fourierists wanted action. He wrote about this encounter in the *Dial*, his first mention of Fourier in print and indicative of the peculiar mix of admiring interest, patronizing bemusement, misreading, and avoidance that would characterize his engagements with his troubling philosophical interlocutor for many years to come.[13]

In "Fourierism and the Socialists," Emerson notes the "increasing zeal and numbers of the disciples of Fourier" and offers a brief overview of some of their ideas. Moving from mild sarcasm to direct criticism, he says that their program shows the same failing that he finds in "so many projects for reform with which the brain of the age teems." He claims that in all his minute plans, Fourier "treats man as a plastic thing, something that may be put up or down, ripened or retarded, moulded, polished, made into solid, or fluid, or gas, at the will of the leader," and that he "skipped no fact but one, namely, Life ... which spawns and scorns system and system-makers, which eludes all conditions, which makes or supplants a thousand phalanxes and New-Harmonies with each pulsation."[14] His conflation of Robert Owen with Fourier here extends beyond his reference to their respective communal living projects to a wildly inaccurate characterization of Fourier's philosophy. While it is true that Owen was a devout social constructionist who believed that people were the products of their environment, Fourier, on the other hand, regarded each individual as the bearer of distinct desires and needs that society must be arranged to honor.

Emerson closes the essay with a quotation from Brisbane, which he leaves ambiguously unparsed: "What is more futile than barren philosophical speculation, that leads to no great practical results?" It is unclear what light Emerson wants to cast on this question, but given his letter to Lidian imagining that the Associationists would make solitude and "unsocial" thought illegal, he likely means to defend what Brisbane dismisses as "futile" and "barren" philosophy, namely theory detached from social applications. Emerson staunchly took up the banner of inactive speculation, even in the face of humanitarian crisis, rejecting and even mocking his activist contemporaries who tried, with varying levels of commitment and success, to do something about it. In his engagements with reform on paper, in his faint critiques of injustice, in his theories of the relationship of the nonconforming individual to a corrupt society, Emerson skipped no fact but one, namely, life.

* * *

Association gained firmer footing in the Boston reform scene with a major convention in December 1843 and a follow-up in January 1844, attended not only by communitarians from Brook Farm, Hopedale, and the Northampton Association, but also William Lloyd Garrison, Frederick Douglass, Elizabeth Cady Stanton, and others. Like Emerson, Ripley regarded protest movements like antislavery to be "partial," but he believed that Association had the unique potential to be a total reform—freeing enslaved people, women, workers, and all others from the web of capitalist oppression. In 1844, Ripley's Transcendentalist commune at Brook Farm converted to a model phalanx, organized into series and groups as Fourier had instructed, with rounds of attractive labor and regular lectures from Brisbane, joining eighteen others in operation around the country. The New England Fourier Society in Boston became one of fifteen such clubs at that time from Maine to Wisconsin to Ohio.[15]

With the Fourierist zeitgeist in full swing, Emerson published two major essays that year addressing communitarian projects directly, "New England Reformers" and "The

Young American," both of which disparage reformers and set up Association to serve his intensifying idealization of individualism and capitalism. But two other essays in his Second Series, also published in 1844, reveal a more nuanced longing for an even more utopian vision of society than the protest movements of his time offered, specifically because of their insistence on action, evincing a paired longing for a harmonic society to replace the modern state and contempt for those who attempt to effect that change.

In "Politics," he imagines governments of force replaced with a society based on "right and love." He seems to have the Associationists in mind when he remarks, "Such designs, full of genius and full of fate as they are, are not entertained except avowedly as air-pictures. If the individual who exhibits them, dare to think them practicable, he disgusts scholars and churchmen; and men of talent, and women of superior sentiments, cannot hide their contempt" (*CW* 3:129). Despite his apparent regret that those who attempt to put social theory into practice meet with contempt, in "Experience," he declares: "Hankering after an overt or practical effect seems to me an apostasy" (*CW* 3:48). Abolitionists and other social radicals were willing to hazard public exposure and failure, to say nothing of violence, in the name of their ideas; Emerson insisted in contrast that ideas were valuable in themselves—and only in themselves—untried, entertained inwardly for the benefit of the individual's intellectual fulfillment and growth.

"New England Reformers" presents much the same argument. Emerson credits "the great activity of thought and experimenting" as the defining character of the region for the past twenty-five years, naming as some examples "temperance and non-resistance societies," "ultraists" who champion animal rights, homeopathy, hydropathy, mesmerism, phrenology, and those who attack "the institution of marriage, as the fountain of social evils," as well as "movements of abolitionists and of socialists" (*CW* 3:149, 150). He attacks this "soldiery of dissent" on the grounds that "they are partial; they are not equal to the work they pretend. They lose their way; in the assault on the kingdom of darkness, they expend all their energy on some accidental evil, and lose their sanity and power of benefit" (*CW* 3:154, 149). He insists that only an individual in solitude has the power to effect change, and suggests vaguely that once each man regenerates his own life then he might be able to improve society, but only insofar as he remains "isolated" (*CW* 3:157), a word anathema to Association since Brisbane's screeds against the "isolated household."

The April 1844 issue of the *Dial* showcases two essays that seem strategically arranged to counter and contain the growing influence of Association with Emerson's futurist idealization of capitalist individualism. His essay "The Young American" appears as a companion piece to Elizabeth Palmer Peabody's "Fourierism," and signals a final parting of ways between versions of Transcendentalism defined by their divergent relation to collective politics and reform. In her lengthy article, Peabody reports on the recent Fourier conventions in Boston and explains for readers, in language as clear as possible given the complex metaphysics intrinsic to the philosopher's thought, the main currents of his plans for Association, reviewing his theory of the passions, the amelioration of climates, the new form of social organization in the phalanx, even, if euphemistically, the Associationists' intention to "purify the institution of marriage." Ultimately, she rejects the materialist solutions of socialism, but offers this intriguing final paragraph: "We understand that Brook Farm has become a Fourierist establishment. We rejoice in this, because such persons as form that association will give it a fair experiment. We wish it God-speed. May it become a University where the young American shall learn his duties, and become worthy of this broad land of his inheritance."[16] This strange vision of a Fourierist phalanx as the college for the training of nationalists feeds directly on the next page into Emerson's "The Young American," perhaps the most fervent tract of capitalist utopianism in his oeuvre. Emerson echoes Peabody in positioning the transnational socialist movement as somehow a promising stage in the evolution of American destiny.[17]

Abandoning his acknowledgement of the exploitation of labor in "Man the Reformer," this essay offers full-throated advocacy for capitalism as the basis of American equality rather than an obstacle to it. As Sacvan Bercovitch has argued, Emerson masterfully contains and even assimilates the socialist challenge into the narrative of capitalism's role in America's utopian greatness, noting that "trade is also but for a time, and must give way to somewhat broader and better, whose signs are already dawning in the sky," and points to the socialist communes in Massachusetts and elsewhere based on the "noble thought of Fourier" as indications of what will come after capitalism. Bercovitch details how he subsumes socialism here to present American liberalism as a revolutionary force, indicating how Emerson's philosophy can "absorb the radical communitarian vision it renounces" and "be nourished by the liberal structures it resisted." He further notes the implications of this move for the construction of American nationalism more broadly: "It demonstrates the capacity of the culture to shape the subversive in its own image, and thereby, *within limits* to be shaped by the radicalism it seeks to contain." Emerson's engagement with the socialist communes concludes with the idea that their value is in forecasting that a revolution is on the way, strangely distancing these projects and their live challenge by imagining them as an outcome to be desired in the distant future rather than presently underway.[18]

This issue of the *Dial* was the final installment in this iteration of the publication, and it was precisely this model of Transcendentalism that Ripley rejected when he began publishing the *Harbinger*, the country's leading Fourierist periodical, the following year at the Brook Farm Phalanx. Having previously served as an editor of the *Dial*, his opening editorial explicitly positions his new publication against the old one in its devotion to social justice action: "The interests of Social Reform will be considered as paramount to all others, in whatever is admitted into pages of the *Harbinger*. We shall suffer no attachment to literature, no taste for abstract discussion, no love of purely intellectual theories, to seduce us from our devotion to the cause of the oppressed, the down trodden, the insulted and injured masses of our fellow men ... we labor for the equal rights of All." This vow that the *Harbinger* will not confuse art and philosophy for activism, and a description of these pursuits as seductive escapism from pressing social matters, is a pointed critique of its Transcendentalist predecessor. Though it would be written by literary men, the *Harbinger* was devoted to "the radical movement for the benefit of the masses, which is the crowning glory of the nineteenth century," and sought a readership comprised of both "refined and educated circles" and "the swart and sweaty artisan."[19] Thus, while I agree with John Carlos Rowe that "Emersonian transcendentalism and political activism in mid-nineteenth-century America were inherently incompatible," it is essential to note that Ripley and others aimed to fulfill the promise of Transcendentalism in practice, departing from Emerson's pointedly utopian philosophy.[20]

The list of contributors to the *Harbinger* indicates the overlaps between Transcendentalism, Association, labor reform, and an increasingly vocal movement for free love; Emerson refused to contribute to the publication because he found it too "sectarian" and too "French."[21] Indeed, leaders of Association like Ripley and Horace Greeley would soon stop keeping such company as increasingly, Fourier's name unavoidably carried with it the taint of sexual heterodoxy. The publication in 1845 of his *Oeuvres Complètes* made a broader selection of his thought available and kicked off a renewed wave of interest among the cultural elite, including the Transcendentalist set.[22] Again, the appeal for this group of thinkers may have been the many similarities between Fourier's ideas and their own; Orestes Brownson wrote at this time that "Fourierism is simply an attempt to realize in society the leading principles of Transcendentalism."[23] But after this time, public interest in Fourier shifted from his ideas about the reorganization of industry to the "secret doctrines" about sex and marriage that the philosopher had always been rumored to hold. Philip Gura states a critical commonplace in noting that "Fourier's ideas about sexuality unnerved [Emerson]," but we should clarify that this is not because he disagreed. Despite commenting in his journal that Fourier was "one of those salacious old men" who behaved as if it were "universal rutting season," critiques of monogamous marriage may have particularly discomfited Emerson because he had similar notions himself.[24] Because these controversial ideas echoed thoughts that Emerson entertained privately for years, the next wave of Fourierist radicalism presented yet another test of his commitment to the philosophy associated with his name—that man should be guided by insight, disdaining tradition and public opinion—and provided further opportunities for articulating his antipragmatist position that philosophy constituted an ideal realm importantly apart from social life, finally the only site of utopia.

* * *

In 1841, when his wife, Lidian, was pregnant with their third child, Emerson had confided to his journal a number of strikingly bleak assessments of the marriage relation. In one entry, he wrote: "It is not the plan or prospect of the soul, this fast union of one to one." He wrote at the top of the page: "Mezentian marriage," a phrase suggesting that lifelong monogamy was comparable to a mythical form of torture in which a living person was tied face-to-face with a corpse. "Plainly marriage should be a temporary relation," he declared, and when two people have exhausted "the good which they held for the other," or were "drawn to new society," then "they should part," letting the new love serve as "the balm to prevent a wound from forming where the old love detached."[25] Numerous antebellum free-lovers advocated and practiced this model of serial relationships dictated by affinity rather than legal compulsion. But Emerson was convinced that his private feelings about marriage should not be applied to real life because it would result in disruptive, structural change. He wrote in his journal, "we cannot rectify marriage because it would introduce such carnage into our social relations." He felt that all women were to some extent in danger from male lust but that the marriage institution checked it. "Therefore it will not do to abrogate the laws which make Marriage a relation for life, fit or unfit" (*JMN* 8:34, 95).

This concern about the dangers that Fourier's plan for a "new amorous world" would pose for women was a leading reason that Emerson repeatedly voiced opposition to free love ideas. But this seems both ironic and baldly paternalistic when we consider the responses of some of the women Emerson knew personally. Brisbane had argued that women had the most to gain from a reorganization of society away from private domesticity and into the phalanx, and many American women agreed. Elizabeth Cady Stanton, for one, credited Fourier with her realization that the oppression she felt as a wife and mother was systemic rather than personal, inciting her to organize the Seneca Falls convention. Moreover, of Emerson's many friends who were interested in Fourier, Margaret Fuller and Caroline Sturgis may have been the most intrigued by his proposed interventions into private life, and he discussed these ideas with each of them at length.

Indeed, Megan Marshall has suggested that his "intimate working relationship" with Fuller in 1841 "may have been the root cause of Emerson's increasingly dark thoughts on the subject of marriage" in his journal that year.[26] Robert Richardson has gone so far as to describe Emerson as engaged in an "open marriage" at this time, at least "emotionally."[27] On Fuller's visits to the Emerson home, they would walk through the Walden woods discussing the institution, with Fuller no doubt voicing at times variations on her claim that "all the marriages she knew were a mutual degradation." This would have included, of course, that of her hosts. Fuller studiously avoided Lidian Emerson and noted that nothing made her feel "so anti-marriage" as talking to her. Indeed, though Fuller did not think the constitutionally chilly philosopher capable of an "intimate union," she felt she might be "more his companion" than his wife, since Emerson's real life was intellectual rather than embodied. One journal entry hints that the two may have had a painful discussion about whether their passion should remain purely cerebral; Emerson wrote, "You would have me love you. What shall I love? Your body? The supposition disgusts you." Perhaps this is why Lidian hid in her bedroom during at least one of Fuller's visits and burst into tears at the sight of her.[28]

Four years later, Emerson was engaged in an immersive correspondence with young Caroline Sturgis. She lent Emerson Fourier's *Oeuvres* in 1845 and he reported that he read it "with surprising ease, considering what courage it cost to begin."[29] Sturgis tried to encourage him to shed his repression and embrace the freer life Fourier imagined. He responded, "I am somewhat puritanical in my way of living, you will think ... but I am not in my theory." His letter praises Fourier as a "new Napoleon, so able, so equal, so full of resources, & so just in his criticism on existing society." But he makes it clear that ideas of this kind must remain in the utopian realm of thought: "If we were permitted to make experiments, I would enlist for five years ... But there is an immense presumption against every experiment in morals. We must not overstep our sphere or system to gratify hopes & wishes which as such decorate our days like rainbows but could only be realized by violence." He said the interventions into private life Fourier proposed "smelled furiously of the guillotine."[30]

Emerson's distinction between his puritanical "way of living" and his liberated "theory" suggests again that what was threatening and alluring about Fourierism to Emerson was that it goaded one to embrace what his philosophy advocated: to be a nonconformist, to reject all that was false to man's inner self. In "Self-Reliance," he proclaims his readiness to "shun father and mother and wife and brother," and a desire to form relations in "a new and unprecedented way" (CW 2:30, 42). Yet while he admits that wishful dreaming about the fall of marriage and the private home might light up our imaginations "like rainbows," just as his emotional intimacy with women outside of his marriage seemed to brighten his life, he cautions that open departures from the institution would result in revolutionary violence and therefore feels that he is not "permitted to make experiments."

And yet Emerson continued reading the Fourierists even as they became more explicit in their sex radicalism. Indeed, as Emerson worked on *Representative Men*, "he was still struggling with the representative status of Fourier," according to Christina Zwarg, who notes that "an early listing of the table of contents in one of his notebooks shows that he considered ending his book with a chapter on Fourier."[31] Though ultimately, Fourier did not get his own chapter, Emerson's intense engagement with him in the essay on Montaigne displays again his intolerance for action, his lack of confidence in social change, the tension once again between what can be imagined and practically achieved.

In this essay, Emerson offers a close reading of a well-known Fourierist motto: "The attractions of man are proportioned to his destinies." He glosses this phrase to mean "that every desire predicts its own satisfaction," in other words that all of one's desires are destined to be fulfilled (CW 4:103). But Fourier meant instead that our passions will lead us to the contributions we should make and the lives we should live, that the individual must precede society just as Emerson himself had said in essays like "Ethics" ("each man has his own calling;" his "call to do any particular work ... is, his fitness to do that thing he proposes" [EL 2:147]) and "Trades and Professions" ("to each man is his calling foreordained in his faculty ... The brain and the body of man is adapted to the work that is to be done in the world" [EL 2:113–14]). Indeed, he had noted in his journal that "all that is valuable in the phalanstery comes of individualism" (JMN 10:154); he clearly understood that the unique inner truths, preferences, desires, and insights of individuals were the basis of Fourier's social vision.

But rather than recognizing in Fourier's axiom his own belief that one's inner compass must guide the way, Emerson departs here from his conviction in the limitless capacity of the individual man to dramatize the uselessness of all great ambition and of action itself. He rejects Fourier's theory of the passions, claiming simply that our reach always exceeds our grasp: "All experience exhibits the reverse of this; the incompetency of power is the universal grief of young and ardent minds." He says that desire is "raging, infinite" while our actual power is "a single drop, a bead of dew," that every man has an "appetite that could eat the solar system like a cake; a spirit for action and passion without bounds," but soon discovers that he cannot marshal the force to accomplish his aims: "On the first motion to prove his strength,—hands, feet, senses gave way, and would not serve him." He describes human experience as trying to tackle acres of ambition by moving only a millimeter a day, exposing "the yawning gulf between the ambition of man and his power of performance." This is not simply a critique of Fourier but a truly revealing statement about the necessarily utopian nature of all social justice desire, and Emerson's surprising claim that individuals lack the capacity to realize in life their vaunted inner impulses.

In the essay on Goethe that concludes *Representative Men*, the spot he had initially contemplated for Fourier, Emerson offers a final warning to "the fiery reformer" and those who would emulate him against the dangers of social activism: "A certain partiality, a headiness and loss of balance, is the tax which all action must pay. Act, if you like,—but you do it at your peril. Men's actions are too strong for them. Show me a man who has acted and who has not been the victim and slave of his action." Still, he insists "the speculative and the practical doctrines are one" (*CW* 4:154). Returning to this dichotomy, which he had sought to deconstruct many years before in "American Scholar," it is even clearer in this iteration that his message is not that intellectuals like himself should take on the practical labor required to change the world. Rather, he defends speculation itself as action enough.

* * *

I take the subtitle of my essay from one of the "important books" that F. O. Matthiessen did not write. In the introduction to his canon-making study *American Renaissance: Art and Expression in the Age of Emerson and Whitman*, Matthiessen acknowledges that his investigation of the American literary "masterpieces" published in rapid succession "in one extraordinarily concentrated moment of expression" neglects an important question, namely "the economic, social, and religious causes *why* this flowering came in just these years." He describes another book that would undertake this investigation, an imaginary book he calls *American Literature in the Age of Fourier*, which would "concentrate on how discerning an interpretation our great authors gave of the economic and social forces of the time." This unwritten book would consider not just socialism but all the radical foment of this period, which "probably gave rise to more movements of reform than any other decade in our history; they marked the last struggle of the liberal spirit of the eighteenth century in conflict with the rising forces of exploitation."[32]

Matthiessen's mention of Fourier in this field-founding work offers an intriguing glimpse of an alternative cultural genealogy, an American Renaissance rooted in the countercultural zeitgeist of the 1840s. We might consider this provocation alongside John Carlos Rowe's claim "that the scholarly reliance on such Emersonianism to interpret (even *organize*) the modern American literary tradition has effectively depoliticized that tradition."[33] Restoring Emersonian philosophy and other works of the American Renaissance to their context in "the Age of Fourier" might involve reckoning with the fact that depoliticization was sometimes their aim, bringing into focus a reactionary counter-utopianism deeply shaped by the radical projects they reject.

And yet the citations from Lazarus and other free-lovers suggest that they embraced some version of Emerson as an intellectual fellow traveler, despite his repeated insistence that trying to apply his ideas to social problems was pointless, to say nothing of his personal ambivalence about sexual freedom, the equality of women, the poor, African Americans, and other people of color. Ultimately, Emerson's insistence that philosophy is a realm distinct from activism calls us to a frank evaluation of the particular contributions of that realm, its limitations in times of humanitarian crisis, and its complex, often unaccountable relationship to social change. Indeed, it offers a model for acknowledging the contribution of Fourier, not in the long-gone phalanxes in which the Associationists placed their hope, but rather in his surprisingly enduring castles in the air, his wild notions and novel descriptions, his ability and audacity to imagine the world otherwise, and his palimpsestic imprint on the literature and culture of antebellum America.

Notes

1. Marx Lazarus, *Love vs. Marriage* (New York: Fowler and Wells, 1852), 313.
2. *Nichols Monthly* (August and September 1855), 216; *Word* (July 1877). References to Emerson in *Lucifer, the Light-Bearer* include June 1, 1882; May 18, 1882; May 4, 1882; October 9, 1902; March 23, 1888; May 11, 1882; June 4, 1903; March 17, 1904; January 12, 1883; June 25, 1898; August 15, 1890; September 14, 1888. The Boston-based free-love anarchist periodical *Liberty* also favorably cited Emerson, reprinted his poetry, and claimed him as an inspiration and fellow-traveler; see especially "Emerson, the Reformer," Liberty 1, no. 20 (May 13, 1882): 3.
3. Henry Steele Commager, *The Era of Reform, 1830–1860* (Ann Arbor: University of Michigan Press, 1960), 7. Also see Peter Wirzbicki, *Fighting for the Higher Law* (Philadelphia: Penn Press, 2021); David Robinson, *Emerson and the Conduct of Life* (Cambridge: Cambridge University Press, 1993); and T. Gregory Garvey, *Creating the Culture of Reform in Antebellum America* (Athens: University of Georgia Press, 2006).
4. On Emerson and antislavery see Len Gougeon, *Virtue's Hero: Emerson, Antislavery, and Reform* (Athens: University of Georgia Press, 1990). On Emerson's racism see Nell Irvin Painter, *The History of White People* (New York: Norton, 2010) and Cornel West, *The American Evasion of Philosophy* (Madison: University of Wisconsin Press, 1989).
5. On the Panic of 1837, see Alisdair Roberts, *America's First Great Depression: Economic Crisis and Political Disorder After the Panic of 1837* (Ithaca: Cornell University Press, 2012); Jessica Lepler, *The Many Panics of 1837* (Cambridge: Cambridge University Press, 2013). The definitive source on Fourierism in the United States and the arrival of Association in this economic context is Carl J. Guarneri, *The Utopian Alternative: Fourierism in Nineteenth-Century America* (Ithaca, NY: Cornell University Press, 1991).

6. Jonathan Beecher, *Charles Fourier: The Visionary and His World* (Berkeley: University of California Press, 1986), 281, 132.
7. Albert Brisbane, *Social Destiny of Man; Or, Association and Reorganization of Industry* (Philadelphia: Stollmeyer, 1840), 131.
8. Beecher, *Charles Fourier*, 340.
9. "Select List of Recent Publications," *Dial* 1, no. 2 (October 1840): 265–66. On the utopianism of mainstream American culture in this moment see Christopher Clark, *The Communitarian Moment: The Radical Challenge of the Northampton Association* (Amherst: University of Massachusetts Press, 1995), 10, and Guarneri, *Utopian Alternative*, 147.
10. West, *American Evasion*, 21. Emerson's 1837 speech on antislavery is lost, but record of the disappointment of abolitionists in his audience survives. See Len Gougeon, "Abolition, the Emersons, and 1837," *The New England Quarterly* 54, no. 3 (September 1981): 345–64.
11. Ripley to Emerson, November 9, 1840. Emerson to Ripley, December 1840. Lawrence Buell, ed., *The American Transcendentalists: Essential Writings* (New York: Random House, 2006), 202–6.
12. Neal Dolan argues that Emerson was pro-market even during his supposedly radical period, in contrast to scholars including Bercovitch, Michael T. Gilmore, and Stephen E. Whicher who see Emerson as more critical of capitalism before 1843, and to James Albrecht and Alexander Kern, who hold that he was a consistent critic of capitalist excess but never anticapitalist. See Neal Dolan, "Property in Being: Liberalism and the Language of Ownership in Emerson's Writing," in *A Political Companion to Ralph Waldo Emerson*, ed. Alan Levine and Daniel S. Malachuk (Lexington: University of Kentucky Press, 2011), 343–82, 361. Others like Jean Mudge have argued that Emerson turned to activism at this time based on the fact that he delivered a public antislavery lecture at long last in 1844, then condemned the imperialist war on Mexico, and later defended John Brown. Jean Mudge, *Mr. Emerson's Revolution* (Cambridge: Open Book Publishers, 2015), xvii.
13. William Hall Brock, "Phalanx on a Hill: Responses to Fourierism in the Transcendentalist Circle" (PhD dissertation, Loyola University of Chicago, 1995), 163. Ralph Waldo Emerson to Lidian Emerson, March 1, 1842, *LRWE* 3:18.
14. Ralph Waldo Emerson, "Fourierism and the Socialists," *Dial* 3, no. 1 (July 1846): 86–90.
15. See Guarneri's appendices, *Utopian Alternative*, 407–9.
16. Elizabeth Palmer Peabody, "Fourierism," *Dial* 4, no. 4 (April 1844): 473–83, 478, 483.
17. Ralph Waldo Emerson, "The Young American," *Dial* 4, no. 4 (April 1844): 484–507.
18. Sacvan Bercovitch, "Emerson, Individualism, and Liberal Dissent," in *The Rites of Assent* (New York: Routledge, 1993): 307–52. Bercovitch notes that the term "individualism" was coined by the French socialists, for whom it was negative. Thus Emerson's adaptation and embrace of this signal concept itself is part of how Fourier shaped his work.
19. On the *Harbinger* see Octavius Brooks Frothingham, *Transcendentalism in New England* (New York: Putnam, 1886) and Sterling Delano, *The Harbinger and New England Transcendentalism: A Portrait of Associationism in America* (Vancouver: Fairleigh Dickinson University Press: 1983).
20. John Carlos Rowe, *At Emerson's Tomb: The Politics of Classic American Literature* (New York: Columbia University Press: 1997), 21.
21. *LRWE* 3:289; also George Willis Cook, John Sullivan Dwight: A Biography (Boston: Small, Maynard, 1898), 103–5.
22. Philip Gura, *American Transcendentalism: A History* (New York: Farrar, Straus, and Giroux, 2008), 169.

23. Orestes Brownson, "Transcendentalism, or the Latest Form of Infidelity," *Brownson's Quarterly Review* 2, no. 3 (July 1845): 273–323, 310.
24. Gura, 174.
25. Megan Marshall, *The Peabody Sisters: Three Women Who Ignited American Romanticism* (New York: Houghton Mifflin, 2005), 426; and Megan Marshall, *Margaret Fuller: A New American Life* (New York: Houghton Mifflin, 2013), 192–97. Also on Emerson's relationships with Fuller, Sturgis, and Samuel Gray Ward in relation to his restless, antimarriage brooding, see Caleb Crain, *American Sympathy: Men, Friendship, and Literature in the New Nation* (New Haven, CT: Yale University Press, 2008).
26. Marshall, *Peabody Sisters*, 426.
27. Robert D. Richardson, Jr., *Emerson: The Mind on Fire* (Berkeley: University of California Press, 1995), 329.
28. *JMN* 7:400; Marshall, *Fuller*, 191–92.
29. Gura, *American Transcendentalism*, 173.
30. Emerson to Caroline Sturgis, February 6, 1845, *LRWE* 8:4–8.
31. Christina Zwarg, *Feminist Conversations: Fuller, Emerson, and the Play of Reading* (Ithaca: Cornell University Press, 2018), 223.
32. F. O. Matthiessen, *American Renaissance: Art and Expression in the Age of Emerson and Whitman* (Oxford: Oxford University Press, 1941), viii–ix.
33. Rowe, *At Emerson's Tomb*, 25.

5

WORSHIP, OR, RELIGION AND THE SECULAR

CHAPTER 19

EMERSON AMONG THE METHODISTS

CLAUDIA STOKES

It is a long-overlooked fact that, in the first half of the nineteenth century, Methodism was the single biggest instigator of religious change in the United States. As the primary religious movement at the center of the Second Great Awakening, Methodism grew exponentially in this period, rapidly expanding from a contested eighteenth-century minority sect to the nation's largest denomination; by 1850, nearly three million Americans identified as Methodists, comprising over a third of American affiliated Christians.[1] Methodism attracted worshippers with its signature camp meetings, promotion of hymnody, and advocacy of Arminianism, the theological belief that human beings may elect salvation and the popularity of which contributed directly to the decline of Calvinist orthodoxy.[2] The meteoric rise of Methodism thus corresponds with a parallel decline in mainline denominations, which for decades denounced Methodism as heretical but which, by the second quarter of the nineteenth century, were willing to implement some Methodist practices in an attempt to remain viable. For instance, in 1824 theologian William Ellery Channing urged Unitarian ministers to adapt to these changes, arguing that Christians now "want a religion which will take a strong hold upon them. ... It is objected to Unitarian Christianity that it does not possess this heart-stirring energy" characteristic of Methodism.[3] Numerous other Protestant denominations made similar concessions, and, through the widespread adoption of its signature customs and beliefs, Methodism gradually became mainstream and permanently changed the practice and disposition of American Christianity.

Ralph Waldo Emerson generally took interest in contemporary religious developments, but he remained indifferent to Methodism throughout his life. Despite the extraordinary religious sea change occurring around him, Emerson had little to say about it or the denomination that sparked it. In his many writings, he mentions Methodism and its founder, John Wesley, rarely and only in passing, and all evidence suggests that he never engaged in a serious inquiry into Methodist theology or practice: his personal library contained no publications by or about Wesley, and his voluminous journals register no sustained consideration of Methodism. Furthermore, one of Emerson's rare explicit comments on Methodism was wholly contemptuous: in 1827, he expressed revulsion at the "monstrous absurdities of the Methodists at their Camp Meetings" (*JMN* 3:115).[4] Perhaps because Emerson's documented response to Methodism was so limited, it has seldom been incorporated into scholarly efforts to understand the larger religious culture that both framed and informed his work. The influences on Emerson of Calvinism, Hinduism, Quakerism, and Swedenborgianism are well chronicled, but the impact of Methodism, the most influential denomination of Emerson's own time, remains largely overlooked in our estimation of Emerson's engagement in contemporary religious matters. One might readily take Emerson's indifference at face value and presume that Methodism provided nothing of substance in the constitution of Emerson's own ideas. However, that presumption is inaccurate, and this essay seeks to show that some of Emerson's major religious ideas have a clear origin in Methodism, a denomination that merits inclusion among the diverse array of Emerson's documented religious influences. The omission of any significant discussion of Methodism among his papers suggests that Emerson himself was likely unaware of the sectarian inflection of these ideas, and he may have unconsciously followed the lead of fellow mainline clergy in adapting and absorbing some popular features of Methodism. Emerson nevertheless encountered some of the foundational tenets of Methodism through several esteemed social acquaintances whom he repeatedly cited as instrumental to his own developing religious ideas: Edward Thompson Taylor, a famed Methodist preacher whose unorthodox sermons influenced Emerson's ideas about public oratory, and Tarbox, a farm worker whom Emerson briefly encountered toward the end of his seminary studies. Taking inspiration from both these figures, Emerson embraced some of their distinctively Methodist teachings, packaged them as denominationally neutral, and propounded them to the elite social demographic that was most critical of Methodist populism. As I will show, Methodist teachings also influenced Emerson's own oratorical style as well as his renowned comments about the importance of personal experience in rhetoric.

This influence implicitly challenges an enduring scholarly narrative that construes some of the major events of Emerson's early career in the 1830s—such as his 1832 resignation from the pulpit of Boston's Second Church and his controversial 1838 address at Harvard's Divinity School—as heralding a decisive break with organized religion, a rupture that critics have characterized as both emancipatory and requisite for Emerson's subsequent promotion of an intellectual and literary independence unconfined by denominationalism. According to such eminent critics as Lawrence Buell, Alfred Kazin, Richard Poirier, and David Reynolds, Emerson's break with sectarianism was a necessary precondition for his lifelong advocacy of nonconformist individualism.[5] It has likewise served as a cornerstone in the secularization thesis of American history by seemingly evidencing a major defection from organized religion in pursuit of greater philosophical wisdom. Richard A. Grusin has contested this narrative by showing that Emerson's rupture with organized religion was neither as absolute nor as liberatory as has been suggested: Emerson continued to perform ministerial duties for years after his resignation, and he kept abreast of contemporary theological developments, such as the new mode of exegesis known as the "Higher Criticism."[6] Emerson's embrace of numerous foundational Methodist tenets further complicates our understanding of his relationship with organized religion, for it affirms that his promotion of individualism by no means necessitated the rejection of denominational, creedal precepts. On the contrary, Emerson's advocacy of individualism was deeply indebted to Methodism, which supplied numerous sectarian beliefs central to Emerson's developing ideas about the religious authority of the common individual. In keeping with recent scholarly reevaluations of the secularization thesis, such as Justine S. Murison's important contribution to this collection, this essay argues that Emerson's public contestation of mainline Protestant practice was rooted in sectarian influence, not sectarian disavowal.[7]

Edward Taylor and Methodist Oratory

Today Methodism is a respectable Protestant denomination, but for the first half of the nineteenth century it was a controversial movement widely denounced by mainline clergy. Founded in eighteenth-century England by John Wesley, Methodism emerged in response to the emotional dispassion and social elitism that Wesley observed in religious worship, and it was designed to activate intense religious ardor and bypass any hindrances that might keep the worshipper at an emotional distance. Pulpit oratory, religious ritual, and even the physical spaces of worship all underwent transformation at the hands of Methodism, which sought to make Christian faith accessible and appealed to people on the social margins. Methodism eliminated pew fees, a common requirement that made church attendance available only to the affluent, and it likewise moved worship services into the public sphere, in makeshift tents, open plazas, and meeting halls. Methodism also did away with conventional pulpit oratory, which was typically formulaic and cerebral, and it replaced dry scriptural exegesis with an informal rhetorical style designed to be apprehensible to all auditors, regardless of education or class. Methodist populism extended even to its clergy: in the late eighteenth and early nineteenth centuries, Methodism did not require clergy to attend seminary, and for many years its leadership in North America was comprised of volunteers without any formal training in theology, scripture, or oratory.[8] The Methodist spirit of populist inclusiveness reached its fullest expression in the setting of the camp meeting, which dismantled conventional social hierarchy and enabled people across social strata—laborers, middle-class women, enslaved persons, and children—to commingle in the spirit of collective worship. In contrast with the decorum of mainline worship, the Methodist camp meeting was famous for its intemperate rowdiness, as preachers incited participants to public weeping, confession, and exhortation.

Unsurprisingly, all these features met with disapproval from conservatives, who denounced the ignorance of Methodist clergy, its dissolution of conventional social hierarchy, and its promotion of a religious frenzy that critics claimed would produce only enthusiastic, insincere conversions and backsliding. With his 1827 denunciation of the "monstrous absurdities of the Methodists at their Camp Meetings," Emerson intoned the conventional opinion of mainline clergy, and yet there is no discounting the foundational precedent of Methodism, which put into wide circulation numerous ideas that Emerson himself would promote in his lectures and essays. For example, in condemning conventional religious ritual as "dry, sore, creaking formalism," Emerson was echoing the similar claims leveled by Wesley and his Methodist followers, a position that resulted in innovative new religious practices, such as the Love Feast, and the allocation of some rites to the laity in an effort to impart vitality to these rituals (*JMN* 7:21).[9] Similarly, his repeated assertion that religious belief should both ennoble and pervade everyday life affirms the pietism already popularized by Methodism, which encouraged adherents to suffuse their workaday lives with religious devotion.

The influence of some of these Methodist tenets was likely discursive rather than direct, but some of Emerson's signature ideas can be traced directly to his personal encounters with Edward Thompson Taylor, a famed Methodist preacher renowned for his inventive oratory.[10] Emerson first met Edward Taylor in 1831 when he attended a service at Taylor's congregation, the Seaman's Bethel in Boston, and Emerson was dazzled by Taylor's eccentric sermons, which afforded him wide international renown. The two men maintained a warm friendship for decades, with Emerson occasionally substituting for Taylor during Sunday worship services and hosting Taylor when he preached in Concord in 1845. Commentators such as Dorothy Bedford, David Reynolds, and Austin Warren have noted Emerson's longstanding admiration for Taylor, but this relationship was more than just another example of the broadmindedness of Emerson's enthusiasms, as Robert D. Richardson has suggested.[11] Rather, Taylor's preaching was a major source of influence and inspiration, as evidenced by Emerson's journals of the 1830s and 40s, which are rife with commentaries on Taylor's style and rhetoric. Indeed, it was through these private reflections on Taylor that Emerson would come to develop his landmark ideas about the intellectual import and persuasive powers of personal experience as well as his growing skepticism about the shortcomings of mainline homiletic convention. Emerson was aware of Taylor's Methodist affiliation, but he did not seem to have recognized that what he found so appealing in Taylor's sermons were their distinctively Methodist form and style. Consequently, the philosophy of oratory that Emerson developed in response to Taylor was keenly, if inadvertently, informed by the habitual practices of the Methodist pulpit. In essays and speeches in which Emerson promoted an oratorical style grounded in personal experience and liberated from generic convention, he implicitly urged audiences to emulate not only Taylor's own oratorical habits but also the common practices of Methodist preachers. In this way, Emerson's most incisive public critiques of mainline religious custom derived from the customs of another competing religious denomination. David Reynolds has argued that Emerson in these writings privileged "artistry and humanity above Christianity," but these journal entries reveal that Emerson instead implicitly advocated exchanging the oratorical practices of one Protestant denomination for another.[12]

A former sailor who ministered to the many transient seamen of Boston's thriving port, Taylor was famous for his ability to deliver engaging sermons pitched to the educational level of his working-class audience. He was particularly renowned for his rich repertoire of maritime metaphors comparing life's struggles to the travails of the seaman, a figurative register that struck home with his seafaring audience and delighted his more educated listeners with its freshness and inventiveness. Taylor's sermons attracted such august auditors as Charles Dickens, Jenny Lind, and Harriet Martineau; Walt Whitman described Taylor as the "one essentially perfect orator" he had ever heard. Herman Melville was also awed by Taylor and used him as the inspiration for the character Father Mapple in *Moby-Dick*.[13] Emerson concurred with these opinions and frequently wrote in his journals about Taylor's sermons, as with his 1834 description of Taylor as a "godly poet" and "the Shakspeare [sic] of the sailor & the poor" (*JMN* 5:287).[14] Emerson did not hesitate to make this admiration public: in his essay "Eloquence," he hailed Taylor as an exemplar of oratorical brilliance, extolling his rhetoric as "all glittering and fiery with imagination" (*CW* 8:61). Similarly, in "The Problem," Emerson's autobiographical poem about his 1832 decision to resign from the pulpit, he portrayed Taylor as the ideal minister—eloquent, noble, and inspiring—whose formidable example justified Emerson's own resignation: the last verse concludes by praising "Taylor, the Shakspeare [sic] of divines. / His words are music in my ear, / I see his cowled portrait dear; / And yet, for all his faith could see, / I would not the good bishop be" (*CW* 9:22).

Celebrated by audiences of diverse religious backgrounds and renowned for his ecumenical inclusiveness, Taylor's own affiliation was patently Methodist. One biographer described him as a "Shouting Methodist," a term used to describe Methodists particularly inclined to the jubilant exclamations and public declarations that became characteristic of camp meetings and that shocked more temperate mainline clergy.[15] Largely illiterate, untrained, and unfamiliar with the finer points of theology, Taylor began preaching while held as a prisoner of war during the War of 1812, spurred by fellow prisoners frustrated by the incompetence of the Calvinist chaplain, and he quickly acquired appreciative audiences stirred by his inventive metaphors and heartfelt rhetoric. After having already achieved renown as a preacher, Taylor attended seminary only briefly, dropping out in frustration at his educational deficits, but he acquired official standing by delivering a sermon before the Methodist quarterly conference. Because of his illiteracy, Taylor left behind no correspondence or written sermons, and he delivered weekly homilies extemporaneously, without any notes or textual support other than the chosen Bible reading. Even Taylor's knowledge of the Bible remained tenuous, and one chronicler described how he once began a sermon by admitting that he didn't know the exact location of his chosen biblical text: he declared, "'Praise the Lord,' that's my text: it's somewhere between these two covers. I can't tell you exactly where; but that's it, so hold on to it. 'Praise the Lord.'"[16]

Taylor lacked the conventional educational credentials of his mainline peers, but these deficits directly contributed to his effectiveness as an orator. Having never studied homiletics or attended church until his own conversion as a young man, Taylor remained unaware of the formal features of the sermon, and he employed an energetic, improvisational style dependent upon instantaneous inspiration instead of prewritten remarks. Audiences did not condemn Taylor as unprepared or ignorant but instead warmed to the freshness of his style, taking it as evidence of Taylor's own faith and quicksilver intellect. To compensate for his lack of biblical knowledge, Taylor enlisted what he and his customary audience did know—seafaring life—and his sermons contained countless references to nautical matters. For instance, in one sermon, he described Jesus Christ as a lifeboat; in another he urged his audience to throw Satan overboard. He habitually referred to his pulpit as his quarterdeck, and on one occasion, when he lost the thread of his sermon, he exclaimed, "Hard down the helm! hard down the helm! I've lost my reckoning—we're in the region of icebergs!"[17] He even employed a maritime metaphor in his characterization of Transcendentalism, comparing it to a sea bird: "It is like a gull,—long wings, lean body, poor feathers, and miserable meat."[18]

There is nothing particularly Methodist about this figurative repertoire other than its unorthodoxy and association with the working class, but the essential kernel of Taylor's technique—namely, the enlistment of the preacher's own personal ken—was indeed characteristically Methodist in nature. While orthodox clergy employed "similitudes," or comparisons to daily life, to enliven their sermons and demonstrate the applications of their lessons, Methodist clergy used everyday speech, excised the cerebral exegesis characteristic of orthodox oratory, and focused instead on the emotional and the personal, qualities that rendered their sermons riveting and readily apprehensible. Orthodox oratory ran the risk of presenting Christianity as a rarified intellectual puzzle comprehensible only to a knowledgeable elite, but Methodist oratory instead characterized Christianity as the province of the everyday and the broader populace, and it did so by way of preachers who actively discussed the effects of Christianity on their own lives. Methodist oratory was thus distinctively experiential in nature, and preachers often made their own lives the central text of their sermons, publicly discussing their own histories and conversion experiences. Famed Methodist preacher Francis Asbury summarized the experiential character of Methodist preaching by urging clergy to "preach as if you had seen heaven and its celestial inhabitants and had hovered over the bottomless pit and beheld the tortures and heard the groans of the damned": preachers should draw on their own lived experiences in their sermons and describe Christian cosmology with the vividness of personal experience, rendering it with the same detail and intensity as their own lived encounters.[19] The Methodist emphasis on personal experience was thus at the very center of Taylor's distinctive style. In lieu of the theological knowledge or generic convention that would otherwise form the basis of sermons in the mainline tradition, Taylor substituted his personal history as a sailor, and nautical rhetoric—rather than the Bible—figured as the primary textual source of his sermons. In so doing, he forged a shared frame of reference designed to make Christianity inclusive and accessible to his maritime audience.

Taylor's oratory was a revelation to Emerson, who studied homiletics at seminary and whose own sermons were marked by their formality, cerebral nature, and generic regularity. In innumerable journal entries, Emerson attempted to analyze the successes of Taylor's oratory, and he came to endorse the inclusion of personal experience characteristic of Methodist rhetoric. For instance, as early as 1832, just a few weeks after Emerson's resignation from the pulpit, Taylor's example contributed directly to Emerson's growing insistence on the credentialing powers of experience in animating a speaker's statements, noting that remarks unmoored in personal experience tended to fall flat. He wrote, "I have heard a man call himself a practical man & yet he said nothing to the purpose; but a mere recluse that could not tie a beau knot threw out the very word; forth it came, alive & ran from mouth to mouth[,] from street to street & the whole city obeyed it." Language, he concluded, is persuasive and compelling only if it derives from—and is thus animated by—the orator's personal experience: the speaker's energy and conviction implicitly corroborate the validity of his claims and elicit the listener's confidence. The succeeding sentence attests to the derivations of these observations in Emerson's encounters with Edward Taylor, for he expressly names Taylor as the exemplar of the successful, experientially-grounded orator he lauds and whose compelling, personal oratory confirms Emerson's new belief that "all Truth is practical" (*JMN* 4:59).[20] In describing the spread of these remarks from "mouth to mouth [and] from street to street," Emerson invoked the oral transmission of Methodism, which circulated not by way of printed pamphlets or tracts but through the spoken word of believers.

Two years later, in 1834, Emerson's esteem for Taylor resulted in his growing impatience with mainline clergy. Emerson wrote in his journal:

> If I were called upon to charge a young minister, I would say Beware of Tradition: Tradition which embarrasses all life & falsifies all teaching. The sermons that I hear are all dead to that ail. The preacher is betrayed by his ear. He begins to inveigh against some real evil & falls unconsciously into formulas of speech which have been said & sung in the church some ages & have lost all life. They never had any but when freshly & with special conviction applied ... Not so with Edward Taylor that living Methodist[,] the Poet of the Church. (*JMN* 4:380–81)[21]

Emerson's denunciation of religious oratorical "Tradition" may initially suggest a rejection of established sectarian tradition altogether, but his later remarks confirm his endorsement of distinctively Methodist practice. This comparison between the "living" rhetoric of Taylor and the lifelessness of clerical "Tradition" confirmed to Emerson the perils of conventional pulpit oratory, which indicate a passive reliance on the inheritances of custom and throw into question whether the minister has actually experienced the religious precepts he propounds. If the minister cannot speak with personal conviction about the religious truths of his teachings, Emerson presumes, then neither he nor his teachings are credible. By contrast, Taylor's style confirms the potency of these religious teachings in causing regeneration, for Taylor's fresh, inspiring oratory evidences the extraordinary transformations that faith may engender.

Emerson's statement that the "preacher is betrayed by his ear" likewise references the improvisational orality of Taylor's rhetoric, which, because he was illiterate and untrained, was governed not by reliance on written scripts or convention but by his ability to improvise in response to the reactions of his auditors. Emerson implicitly pits these two modes of address in opposition to each other—the written, the prescribed, and the conventional against the oral, improvised, and experiential mode characteristic of both Taylor and Methodism more generally—and he resoundingly endorses the latter as the more effective technique. And though this journal entry predates by four years Emerson's famed address at Harvard's Divinity School, this entry's premise, in which Emerson imagines instructing a young minister in this unorthodox sermonic style, suggests that Emerson was already planning to use Taylor's example to intervene in conventional seminary training and offer the lessons of Taylor's oratory to a broader audience of young clergy.

Another journal entry, from 1837, affirms Taylor's influence on Emerson's developing ideas about oratory as well as on Emerson's own writing style. In response to hearing Taylor preach on temperance, Emerson jubilantly proclaimed Taylor "a perfect orator," insisting that Taylor's "utter want & loss of all method, the ridicule of all method" imparts such "splendor." It remains unclear whether Emerson's repetition of the word "method" indicates his awareness that Taylor's rhetorical unconventionality was prototypically Methodist in character, but Taylor nonetheless confirmed for Emerson the benefits of oratorical nonconformity. What follows is a series of exclamatory proclamations that diverges from Emerson's own characteristic prose style of elaborately subordinated sentences: "what sweetness! what richness[,] what depth! what cheer! How he conciliates[,] how he humanizes! how he exhilarates & ennobles! Beautiful philanthropist! godly poet!" (*JMN* 5:287).[22] Emerson's ecstatic reaction certainly corroborates Taylor's capacity to inspire his audience, causing this particular auditor to erupt in exclamations of praise. It likewise suggests that Taylor's improvisational style inspired Emerson himself to experiment somewhat with his own prose, his fragmentary exclamations imitating the outbursts and colloquial speech of the renowned Shouting Methodist.[23]

In his two famed lectures at Harvard in the 1830s, Emerson promoted the Methodist oratorical style he encountered in Edward Taylor. The institutional setting for these remarks is not incidental, for Emerson chose his own alma mater, the site of his own training in homiletics, as the venue for these iconoclastic remarks, which denounced convention and lauded instead knowledge derived from direct personal experience. Emerson's 1837 Phi Beta Kappa lecture, "The American Scholar," addressed educational matters rather than religious ones, but Emerson nonetheless incorporated these ideas in his comments about the paramount importance of personal experience: he described experience as the "raw material out of which the intellect moulds her splendid products" and insisted, "I learn immediately from any speaker how much he has already lived, through the poverty or the splendor of his speech. Life lies behind us as the quarry from whence we get tiles and copestones for the masonry of to-day" (*CW* 1:59, 61). Emerson's remarks on the virtues of experiential learning—rather than learning through secondhand reading or rote memorization—have exerted considerable influence on American philosophies of education, but these statements, in echoing his prior comments on Taylor's oratory, also affirm the underlying influence of Methodism on

Emerson's ideas about the intellectual value and persuasiveness of experience, without which one cannot be an effective teacher or preacher.

In his lecture at Harvard's Divinity School the following year, Emerson propounded an alternative model of pulpit oratory expressly derived from Taylor's Methodist influence. The lecture is best remembered for his acerbic criticism of moribund religious ceremony and routinized clergy, but at the heart of the lecture is a lengthy argument about the importance of personal experience in pulpit oratory. As Emerson describes it, the qualities that elevated clergy and made them members of the social elite—such as their advanced education and rarified knowledge—had no power whatsoever in sparking religious feeling in their audiences. Effective preaching, Emerson asserted, derives not from established convention or biblical exegesis but from the minister's own life, for, without it, the preacher's lessons register as perfunctory and flat. In stark opposition to the homiletic mode taught at Harvard, Emerson boldly declaimed, "The true preacher can be known by this, that he deals out to the people his life,—life passed through the fire of thought": the minister's own life should be the central text of his sermon, Emerson asserted (*CW* 1:86). By way of example, Emerson recounted an anecdote about listening to a dry, conventional preacher who offered abstract religious lessons without the invigorating proof of personal narrative. As Emerson recounts the story, he found himself bored by the sermon and passed the time by staring through the window at the snowstorm outside. The sermon's primary defect, Emerson notes, was its omission of any personal experience attesting to the merits of the preacher's lesson. In this anecdote, Emerson himself employed the same experiential oratorical technique he promotes here, for he substantiates and enlivens his remarks with a personal tale about his own experience with the tedium of conventional pulpit oratory. And in this respect, Emerson himself adopted the experiential oratory characteristic of Methodism and implicitly emulated Taylor's rhetorical style.

Emerson was not prevaricating in this anecdote. In his 1838 journal, Emerson recounted his experience attending the Sunday service led by Rev. Barzillai Frost, the junior minister of the Concord Unitarian church, and in his journal he commented on the absence of personal experience in Frost's sermon. Emerson did not expressly mention Edward Taylor in the Divinity School address, but this journal entry confirms Taylor's influence on this speech, for in the succeeding paragraph Emerson references Taylor both directly and indirectly. Readers familiar with the Divinity School address will recognize some of its phrasings in this 1838 journal entry:

> I shrink & wince as soon as the prayers begin & am very glad if my tailor has given me a large velvet collar to my wrapper or cloak, the prayers are so bad. ... Tell them that a true preacher can always be known by this, that he deals them out his life, life metamorphosed; as Taylor, Webster, Scott, Carlyle do. But of the bad preacher, it could not be told from his sermon, what age of the world he fell in, whether he had a father or a child, whether he was a freeholder or a pauper, whether he was a citizen or a countryman, or any other fact of his biography. But a man's sermon should be rammed with life. (*JMN* 5:464–65)

In describing Frost's service, Emerson uses a suggestive pun in describing his appreciation for the protective work of his "tailor," who has equipped him with protection against Frost's tedious sermon, thereby both referencing Edward Taylor's modest working-class origins and suggesting that Taylor's robust rhetoric shields him from the numbing effects of the service. This pun is born out in Emerson's later explicit reference to Edward Taylor, whom he names first in a list of contemporary rhetoricians who serve as counterpoints to Frost and whose example Emerson would later publicly imitate and encourage Unitarian seminarians to emulate.

Unitarian clergy responded to Emerson's Divinity School address with public outrage, and this underlying context suggests that sectarian rivalry (as well as the resentments of the social elite) may have contributed to their response. Emerson did not expressly name Taylor or Methodism in his lecture, but he nonetheless stepped into the fray by tacitly acknowledging the oratorical superiority of competing denominations and urging Unitarians to join their fellow mainline denominations in adopting revivalist technique. Emerson amplified this sectarian rivalry by invoking typology, as with his assertion that the "true preacher ... deals out to the people his life," a statement that characterized the Methodist orator as Christlike in his willingness to rhetorically offer up his own life for the sake of his followers. Similarly, his assertion that the successful sermon is "life metamorphosed" into text references the theological understanding of Christ, as articulated in the Gospel according to John, as the Word made flesh. The Methodist sermon, he suggests, is the obverse—fleshy experience proffered through the oratorical word. To employ Methodist pulpit technique, Emerson intimates, is to reproduce the ministerial work of Christ. By extension, he insinuated that the Unitarian insistence on homiletic convention was more in keeping with Pharisaical formalism, an implication that surely caused severe offense. It is little wonder that Emerson was for decades barred from speaking at Harvard, for, in promoting a movement that threatened Unitarianism, he committed a stark public betrayal of both the institution and the denomination that trained him.

Tarbox and Methodist Arminianism

Edward Taylor was not the only Methodist figure who influenced Emerson's ideas. Throughout his life, Emerson also repeatedly mentioned a shadowy figure who taught him a crucial lesson that Emerson would promote throughout his life. In the summer of 1825, when Emerson was in his early twenties, he spent a summer working on his uncle's farm, where he came into contact with a Methodist farm worker named Tarbox who conveyed a bit of religious wisdom that left a lasting impression. According to Emerson's account, Tarbox informed him that "*men were always praying*, and ... *their prayers were answered*"[24] (emphasis in original). Little is known about Tarbox—including his first name, which Emerson never recorded—but, because of this single statement, Emerson cited Tarbox repeatedly as one of the major influences on his life. For instance, in a journal entry dated September 1842, Emerson included "my Methodist Tarbox" alongside Bronson Alcott and Emanuel Swedenborg in his list of the "company of people who travel with me in the world" (*JMN* 7:465).[25] Tarbox's remark made an immediate impact on Emerson's ideas about prayer. Following this exchange, Emerson wrote a quatrain in his journal in which he clarified his interpretation of Tarbox's remark. He wrote, "And, tho' thy knees were never bent, / To heaven thy hourly prayers are sent, / And whether formed for good or ill, / Are registered & answered still" (*JMN* 2:388). Emerson interpreted Tarbox's statement as an important reinterpretation of prayer, which is typically understood as a mindful, intentional appeal to the divine. Tarbox, however, asserted instead that the deity heeds all our thoughts and that our unconscious musings operate as a form of direct intercourse with an attentive deity. While it is nothing new to declare that the deity attends to all our thoughts and desires, Tarbox offered a new contribution to this formulation: the deity not only "registered" all our thoughts but also "answered" them. Our thoughts, wishes, and desires—regardless of their righteousness—receive some kind of rejoinder from the divine, though the precise nature of that response remains undefined.

Tarbox's remark exerted direct influence on Emerson's first sermon, which he delivered on July 25, 1826, and preached fourteen additional times. Many years later, Emerson acknowledged Tarbox as the inspiration of this sermon: Tarbox, he recalled, "said to me that men were always praying, and that all prayers were granted. I meditated much on this saying, and wrote my first sermon therefrom."[26] The sermon's immediate scriptural source was the text "pray without ceasing" from 1 Thessalonians 5:17, but the sermon ruminates on the implications of Tarbox's statement that the deity heeds and answers all our thoughts, as with Emerson's statement that "*every desire of the human mind, is a prayer uttered to God and registered in heaven*" (emphasis in original), a declaration nowhere present in the passage from Thessalonians.[27] Emerson's indebtedness to Tarbox is particularly evident in the sermon's assertion that "the true prayers are the daily, hourly, momentary desires, that come without impediment, without fear, into the soul, and bear testimony at each instant to its shifting character. And these prayers are granted."[28] Elaborating on Tarbox's statement, Emerson asserts that all our desires, conscious and unconscious, constitute a form of prayer to a receptive deity, who grants these unspoken wishes. Emerson found this sermon—and, by extension, the lesson from Tarbox—to be so significant that, several months later, he delivered it before the Middlesex Association of Ministers to secure his license to preach.[29]

The Methodist nature of Tarbox's lesson was not limited to the incidental fact that its original purveyor had been a known adherent of Methodism. Rather, Tarbox conveyed to Emerson a sophisticated amplification of a central feature of Methodist theology. At its core, Tarbox's teaching affirms that human wishes and desires matter deeply: they are both monitored and gratified by a responsive deity, and our thoughts thus have the power to influence our lives and the world around us. Thoughts, Tarbox instructed, are not confined to the immaterial domain of consciousness but may have worldly, empirical consequences. Half a century later, a similar belief would become the cornerstone of Christian Science, as formulated by Mary Baker Eddy in *Science and Health with Key to the Scriptures* (1875) and the New Thought movement of the late nineteenth century, but in the 1820s this belief in the spiritual potency of the human will was a contested, heretical belief with a marked Methodist pedigree. In the Calvinist reformed tradition, individuals have no influence whatsoever on divine action or their own salvation, but sixteenth-century Dutch theologian Jacobus Arminius developed a countervailing theology arguing that human beings possess considerable influence on divine acts and on their own fates. This theology, which has come to be known as Arminianism, contends that human beings need not be passive bystanders of divine providence, as Calvinism argued, but they may instead direct the course of their own lives and salvation. In this theology, the mere desire to become converted and saved is sufficient to sway the divine will and may initiate religious regeneration: we may wish or pray ourselves into the fold of the converted, and this belief by implication suggests that the divine heeds and answers at least some of our desires. As a theology of human agency, Arminianism suggests that our salvation may be of our own making and derives from the divine execution of our innermost desires and thoughts.

Long deemed heretical in the Calvinist orthodox tradition, Arminianism was a central tenet of Methodism from the very outset: the name "Methodism" derives from John and Charles Wesley's early efforts to develop a systematic method of activating intense religious ardor and effecting conversion. Transatlantic missionary efforts brought Arminianism to North America, though it was only in the aftermath of the American Revolution that this theology found purchase among American Protestants. The new climate of political self-governance rendered the Arminian belief in religious self-determination newly appealing and relevant, and the popularity of Arminianism contributed directly to Methodism's exponential growth in the early national period.[30] Perry Miller has described Arminianism as "wholly American" because of its promotion of a religious egalitarianism that makes salvation accessible to all: as Miller put it, "everybody *can* help it."[31]

Emerson was already familiar with Arminianism before his encounter with Tarbox: it had long been the subject of lively theological debate among Unitarians, and Emerson's own father was known to have been a proponent.[32] However, it was Tarbox's particular distillation of Arminianism that Emerson would elaborate on throughout his life. Tarbox's lesson underlies, for instance, the Divinity School address, in which Emerson not only propounded Methodist oratory but also offered a similar vision of human interactions with the divine. Like Tarbox, Emerson contends that the commonplace acts of everyday life have spiritual reverberations that confirm their essential moral tenor. Emerson elaborated on this teaching with the assertion that "he who does a good deed, is instantly ennobled. He who does a mean deed, is by the action itself contracted" (*CW* 1:78, 76). And in accord with Tarbox's claims about the spiritual consequences of everyday life, Emerson asserts here that the ordinary acts of daily life are of immense importance, for "divine laws" mandate that their ethical character is replicated ad infinitum in our lives: like causes like, and in this way the morality of our actions directly determines the nature of the world we experience (*CW* 1:77, 76). Emerson's lecture also expands the particulars of Tarbox's lesson with a discussion of the specific repercussions of our thoughts and actions. For instance, Emerson wrote:

> If a man dissemble, deceive, he deceives himself, and goes out of acquaintance with his own being. ... a man is made the Providence to himself, dispensing good to his goodness, and evil to his sin. ... As we are, so we associate. The good, by affinity, seek the good; the vile, by affinity, the vile. Thus of their own volition, souls proceed into heaven, into hell. (*CW* 1:78, 76–77)

The ethical character of our actions directly attracts people with corresponding ethics, so our social circles thereby convey our own moral natures. The Methodist origins of this formulation are also evident in Emerson's assertion that this moral, cosmic unity renders "a man ... Providence to himself," an unambiguous declaration of Arminian sympathy. Our fates are determined not by the inscrutable judgment of an aloof deity, he insists, but are instead of our own making, our salvation or damnation enabled through the moral character of our own actions and through the consequences effected by a receptive deity.

Emerson's published corpus bears overwhelming testimony to Tarbox's lasting influence, for Emerson repeatedly elaborated on this teaching and propounded it widely, urging his audiences to recognize the moral symmetry between actions and reactions, as enabled by an attentive deity. However, in all his numerous instances in which he publicly promoted this belief, he never once characterized it as sectarian, an omission that suggests that Emerson himself failed to recognize the denominational origins of this belief and which likely contributed to the receptivity of mainline Protestant audiences to these remarks. This influence, for instance, is evident in Emerson's 1841 collection, *Essays: First Series,* which contains several essays that reflect on the implications of Tarbox's lesson. The collection's most famous essay, "Self-Reliance," amply registers this influence in his remarks about prayer, which he characterizes not as a deliberate appeal to the divine but as an unconscious product of daily life, as with his assertion that there is "prayer in all action" (*CW* 2:44). The essay's central argument that we should rely more fully on the truth of our own convictions is likewise indebted to the Methodist climate of populism and Arminian autonomy, which invests the common person with religious authority and renders the individual responsible for his or her own fate. Ordained clergy and established theological convention, he insists, are false idols, and we should instead recognize that "all persons that ever existed are ... forgotten ministers," a statement that vested common people with the wisdom of sages and derives from the Methodist democratization of religious authority (*CW* 2:39). The essay's concluding remarks are noticeably influenced by Arminianism, which can be construed as the apogee of theological self-reliance: "Nothing can bring you peace but yourself," Emerson contended, and "nothing can bring you peace but the triumph of principles," a final assertion that the ethical reciprocity engendered by our actions may allows us to achieve fulfillment (*CW* 2:51).

The collection's third essay, "Compensation," similarly attests to Emerson's continuing efforts to interpret Tarbox's lesson. The essay does not discuss Methodism per se, but its opening references the populist uprising against both clericalism and orthodoxy that characterized the Second Great Awakening and enabled the rise of Methodism. Emerson begins by summarizing Calvinist teachings about worldly compensation, which argue that virtue is rewarded with poverty and sin with wealth, an arrangement that Calvinists claim will be reversed in the afterlife. Such a belief is altogether devoid of common sense, Emerson insists, and he frames his essay as an attempt to offer an opposing theory anchored in personal experience rather than theology. The essay begins as follows: "Ever since I was a boy, I have wished to write a discourse on Compensation: for it seemed to me when very young, that on this subject life was ahead of theology, and the people knew more than the preachers taught" (*CW* 2:55). This account offers several explanations at once: in addition to describing the origin of the essay itself, it also describes both the early childhood sources of Emerson's adult resignation from the clergy and metonymically recounts the social changes underlying Methodism's growth and Calvinism's decline. He articulates growing opinion that orthodox clergy are out of touch, and the essay begins by joining Methodist efforts to elevate common people as worthy sources of religious wisdom.

The essay provides Emerson's fullest elaboration on Tarbox's lesson, arguing in great detail that the ethical character of our ambitions, actions, and thoughts directly determines their outcomes. Envisioning the correspondence between action and reaction as a balance sheet, Emerson insists, "Take what figure you will, its exact value, nor more nor less, still returns to you" (*CW* 2:60). What we put into the world, Emerson asserts, will come back to us, in precisely the same character and with comparable consequences, effecting in us what we hoped to effect in the world. "Every act rewards itself," he wrote, and he considers at length how goodness yields only comparable goodness and vice generates only more vice (*CW* 2:60). "Love, and you shall be loved," Emerson wrote, and the thief likewise "steals from himself. The swindler swindles himself" (*CW* 2:68, 66). It bears stressing that Emerson does not envision a moral universe governed entirely by human actions. Rather, he concurs with Tarbox in his assertion that "there is a third silent party to all our bargains," who heeds all our desires and ensures "the fulfillment of every contract" (*CW* 2:69). However, the divine role is primarily reactive to the actions and wishes of the individual, and Emerson concludes his essay with an affirmation of the Methodist Arminian belief in the power of the individual to direct his or her own fate: "Thus do all things preach the indifference of circumstances. The man is all" (*CW* 2:70).

Tarbox's influence by no means diminished with the passing of time but seems only to have intensified. In 1860, twenty-five years after this original encounter and during Emerson's late mid-life, Emerson made Tarbox's remarks the centerpiece of his essay "Fate." The essay takes up a topic of immediate relevance to Tarbox's remark: the nature of our fates and the roles we play in determining our lives. Emerson contends that our fates are of our own making, made possible by our constant reciprocal intercourse with the divine, which is receptive to our wishes. He writes, "The soul contains the event that shall befall it, for the event is only the actualization of its thoughts; and what we pray to ourselves for is always granted. … Events are the children of his body and mind" (*CW* 6:21–22). This statement paraphrases Tarbox's original statement that "men were always praying, and … their prayers were answered," and it asserts both that our thoughts and actions constitute a form of prayer and that our actions directly influence future events. What happens to us is not fated by an external third party but is the direct result of our own thoughts and deeds.

In all these ways, Tarbox's 1825 remark figures as an unacknowledged source text underlying numerous essays and lectures, just as significant as Edward Taylor's oratory in providing content for some of Emerson's most influential writings. As the contributions of these two men illustrate, Methodism provided important precedents for Emerson's ideas about the potent significance of the individual, whose personal experiences have extraordinary persuasive power and who is capable of determining his or her own fate. However, the invisibility of Methodism in the history of these ideas demonstrates the unfortunate historiographical consequences of relying primarily on written, printed materials in our reconstruction of the past. This medium necessarily commemorates the lives and contributions of a privileged sector of the population, those who have the standing and education to leave written, preserved records. It also omits a significant sector of the population who were either incapable of writing—such as the illiterate Taylor, who influenced countless lives but left behind no papers—or who, like Tarbox, left no historical paper trail. The written archive will always be incomplete, but this is particularly the case with populist movements that operated in the oral medium, with instruction passed "from mouth to mouth [and] from street to street," with few surviving written transcriptions of these important exchanges. Even Emerson recorded only a single sentence from his conversation with Tarbox, with the rest lost to history.

Reliance on the spoken word did not prevent Methodism from permeating American culture, but it did result in the omission of Methodism from our understanding of Emerson, whose avid, documented reading has directed the researches of scholars but who seems never to have read or written about Methodism. As a result, Methodism is underrepresented both in the written archive of the period and in Emerson's own vast written corpus. In his journals, Emerson frequently acknowledged the importance of these two Methodist men, and to track their influence is both to recognize the vast gaps in the historical written record and to wonder what other vital populist influences have also been overlooked in the annals of American intellectual history.

This genealogy has several other important implications, for it provides a vital data point in nineteenth-century American intellectual and religious history. In the first place, it suggests that Transcendentalism was more heavily influenced by the events of the Second Great Awakening than we have previously recognized and that its immediate religious sources were not restricted to such regional sects as Unitarianism and Calvinist orthodoxy.[33] The populist leanings of Transcendentalism were thus not limited to merely promoting individualism and the rejection of hierarchical convention but also entailed the enlistment of anti-authoritarian religious ideas circulating among the public.[34] In Emerson's encounters with Taylor and Tarbox, one might realistically expect the more educated, affluent man to occupy the tutelary role and offer instruction to his less cultivated counterpart. However, in both cases Emerson was the recipient, not the purveyor, of religious teaching. While this trajectory comports with Emerson's lifelong willingness to glean insight from figures across the social spectrum, it also reveals the bottom-up circulation of some major ideas of the nineteenth century, which originated not amid the learned cerebrations of the seminary or the Transcendental Club but in the open-air tents of the revival meeting. In this case, eminent New Englanders were not at the forefront of progressive developments in religious belief, as we might expect, but instead were late arrivals to a populist movement already well underway.

This genealogy also illuminates the circumstances of Methodism's rapid spread in the first half of the nineteenth century, when it moved from the religious periphery to the Protestant mainstream, its teachings and practices so widely assimilated that, by the end of the century, these sectarian features lost all lingering associations with this denomination.[35] To trace the influence of Methodism on Emerson is to affirm his involvement within this larger national context, as his writings both registered and contributed to the integration of Methodist teachings within mainstream American culture. That Emerson would unwittingly embrace Methodist doctrine in his own work suggests that these teachings were already well on their way to becoming conventional. At the same time, these writings demonstrate that Emerson actively participated in this process: in offering cogent defenses of Methodist precepts and refining this denomination's often rough public presentation, Emerson imparted intellectual respectability to Methodist doctrines and enabled them to circulate in more privileged social spheres than they might have otherwise reached. Emerson's promotion helped Methodist tenets to shed their populist associations and to be received as vehicles of self-improvement and high-minded refinement, a transition that aided their adoption among the educated elite and absorption into the Protestant mainstream.

Notes

1. Roger Finke and Rodney Stark, *The Churching of America, 1776–2005: Winners and Losers in Our Religious Economy* (New Brunswick: Rutgers University Press, 2005), 56, 71, 121.
2. Finke and Stark, *Churching*, 56.
3. William Ellery Channing, 1882, "The Demands of the Age on the Ministry," in *The Works of William Ellery Channing* (New York: Lenox Hill, 1970), 273; Daniel Walker Howe, *The Unitarian Conscience: Harvard Moral Philosophy, 1805–1861* (Cambridge, MA: Harvard University Press, 1970), 163.
4. Emerson recorded this entry on March 1, 1827.
5. Lawrence Buell, *Literary Transcendentalism: Style and Vision in the American Renaissance* (Ithaca, NY: Cornell University Press, 1978), 21–22; Alfred Kazin, *An American Procession* (New York: Vintage, 1985), xiii; Richard Poirier, *A World Elsewhere: The Place of Style in American Literature* (New York: Oxford University Press, 1966), 63–64; David S. Reynolds,

Beneath the American Renaissance: The Subversive Imagination in the Age of Emerson and Melville (New York: Knopf, 1988), 16–24.
6. Richard A. Grusin, *Transcendentalist Hermeneutics: Institutional Authority and the Higher Criticism of the Bible* (Durham, NC: Duke University Press, 1991), 57, 61ff.
7. Such work includes Peter Coviello and Jared Hickman, "Introduction: After the Postsecular," *American Literature* 86, no. 4 (2015): 645–54; Tracy Fessenden, *Culture and Redemption: Religion, the Secular, and American Literature* (Princeton, NJ: Princeton University Press, 2007); Michael W. Kaufmann, "The Religious, the Secular, and Literary Studies: Rethinking the Secularization Narrative in Histories of the Profession," *New Literary History* 38, no. 4 (2007): 607–28; John Lardas Modern, *Secularism in Antebellum America* (Chicago: Chicago University Press, 2011); Ashley Reed, *Heaven's Interpreters: Women Writers and Religious Agency in Nineteenth-Century America* (Ithaca: Cornell University Press, 2020).
8. By the second quarter of the nineteenth century, however, Methodism would establish institutions of higher learning. Perhaps because of a perceived sympathy for Methodist doctrine in his writings, Emerson would receive an invitation to lecture at one such school, Wesleyan University, in 1845. An account of Emerson's address, as well as its poor reception, was printed in the *Zion's Herald* under the title, "Emerson among the Methodists," a name that is indeed the forerunner of this essay.
9. This entry derives from Journal D, 1838.
10. David Reynolds has written about Taylor's influence on Emerson, though he overlooks the distinctively sectarian character of Taylor's oratory and instead deems it evidence of the "secularization of religious discourse" (*Beneath the American Renaissance*, 21).
11. Dorothy Anna Bedford, *Ralph Waldo Emerson and Father Taylor* (master's thesis, Pennsylvania State University, n.d.); Reynolds, *Beneath the American Renaissance*, 21–22; Austin Warren, *New England Saints* (Ann Arbor: University of Michigan Press, 1956), 111; Robert D. Richardson, Jr., *Emerson: The Mind on Fire* (Berkeley: University of California Press, 1995), 120.
12. Reynolds, *Beneath the American Renaissance*, 23.
13. Boston Port and Seamen's Aid Society, *Life of Father Taylor the Sailor Preacher* (Boston: Boston Port and Seamen's Aid Society, 1904), lxvii. Whitman's essay "Father Taylor and Oratory" was originally published in *Century* in February 1887.
14. This entry derives from Journal C, March 4, 1837.
15. Rev. Gilbert Haven and Rev. Thomas Russell, *Father Taylor, The Sailor Preacher. Incidents and Anecdotes of Rev. Edward T. Taylor, for Over Forty Years Pastor Seaman's Bethel, Boston* (Boston: B. B. Russell, 1871), 29.
16. Warren, *New England Saints*, 109.
17. Haven and Russell, *Father Taylor*, 171. This anecdote is also repeated in Warren, *New England Saints*, 109.
18. *Life of Father Taylor*, xxxvii.
19. Nathan O. Hatch, *The Democratization of American Christianity* (New Haven, CT: Yale University Press, 1989), 137.
20. This entry derives from Journal Q, November 14, 1832.
21. This entry derives from Journal A, December 28, 1834.
22. This entry derives from Journal C, March 4, 1837.
23. Julie Ellison has noted Emerson's tendency to imitate writers or speakers he admired. See Julie Ellison, *Emerson's Romantic Style* (Princeton, NJ: Princeton University Press, 1984), 17.

24. Ralph Waldo Emerson, *Journals of Ralph Waldo Emerson*, ed. Edward Waldo Emerson and Waldo Emerson Forbes, vol. 2 (Boston: Houghton Mifflin, 1909), 98, n. 1.
25. This entry was composed on September 4, 1842.
26. Quoted in Richardson, *Emerson*, 64.
27. Ralph Waldo Emerson, *The Complete Sermons of Ralph Waldo Emerson*, vol. 1, ed. Albert J. Frank (Columbia: University of Missouri Press, 1989), 57.
28. Emerson, *Complete Sermons* 1:57.
29. Emerson, *Complete Sermons* 1:55; Ralph L. Rusk, *The Life of Ralph Waldo Emerson* (New York: Scribner's, 1949), 117.
30. William G. McLoughlin, *Revivals, Awakenings, and Reform: An Essay on Religion and Social Change in America, 1607–1977* (Chicago: University of Chicago Press, 1978), 98.
31. Perry Miller, *The Life of the Mind in America: From the Revolution to the Civil War* (New York: Harcourt, Brace, 1965), 32.
32. David Robinson, *Apostle of Culture: Emerson as Preacher and Lecturer* (Philadelphia: University of Pennsylvania Press, 1982), 30; David M. Robinson, "Emerson and Religion," in *A Historical Guide to Ralph Waldo Emerson*, ed. Joel Porte (New York: Oxford, 2000), 152; Conrad Wright, *The Beginnings of Unitarianism in America* (Boston: Starr King, 1955), 3.
33. This context receives only passing mention in a few studies. See, for instance, Miller, *Life of the Mind*, 14; Robinson, *Apostle of Culture*, 12. Barry Hankins's study of Transcendentalism and the Second Great Awakening largely summarizes these parallel movements but declines to show the intellectual and discursive overlaps between them. Barry Hankins, *The Second Great Awakening and Transcendentalism* (Westport: Greenwood, 2004).
34. Nancy Ruttenburg has shown the significant contributions of nineteenth-century American literature to the construction of the era's populism, showing in particular Emerson's involvement in the creation of a national "democratic personality." See Nancy Ruttenburg, *Democratic Personality: Popular Voice and the Trial of America Authorship* (Stanford: Stanford University Press, 1998), 290–97.
35. Nathan Hatch terms this process the "democratization of American Christianity." Amanda Porterfield's recent study contests some of Hatch's claims about the politics of this process, but she nonetheless confirms this larger national religious shift. See Hatch, *Democratization of American Christianity*; Amanda Porterfield, *Conceived in Doubt: Religion and Politics in the New American Nation* (Chicago: University of Chicago Press, 2012).

CHAPTER 20

EMERSON AND SECULARISM

JUSTINE S. MURISON

"The doctrines of the Over-Soul, Correspondence, and Compensation seem nowadays to add up to shallow optimism and insufferable smugness. Contemporary criticism reflects this distaste, and would lead us to prize these men, if at all, for their incidental remarks, their shrewd observations upon society, art, manners, or the weather, while we put aside their premises and their conclusions, as notions too utterly fantastic to be any longer taken seriously."[1] So wrote Perry Miller in 1940 in his field-defining essay, "Jonathan Edwards to Emerson." It would seem that picking and choosing from Emerson's epigraphic writing for a reader's own purposes is not simply a postmodern response. We might even say that Emerson's writings encourage this type of selective—and, as I will advance here, secular—reading habit. In the larger essay, Miller famously argued that the two strands of seventeenth-century Calvinism—the rational strand urging social conformity and the ecstatic strand finding in nature the evidence of God and Providence—secularized into Unitarianism and Transcendentalism. According to Miller, Edwards's ecstasy flowed—likely to his horror, were he to know—into Emerson's "transparent eye-ball," a mellowing of Calvinism from theological urgency to what would seem to be infidelity: that we can all be "part or particle of God." This is the secularization narrative in a nutshell, the progress narrative that imagines modernity as marked by the sequestration to the private sphere and then the ultimate disappearance of "irrational" religiosity. Miller's version of this narrative in "Edwards to Emerson" became, for quite a long time, not just a way to interpret Emerson's religiosity (or lack thereof) but the very terms by which the literary history of the United States was narrated.

It is this secularization thesis that has been declared dead—at least in part—by current scholars of nineteenth-century American literature. But, of course, as Peter Coviello and Jared W. Hickman argue—riffing on the first line of Charles's Dickens's *A Christmas Carol* that "Marley was dead: to begin with"—the secularization thesis never really dies. Its ghosts are always reappearing to haunt literary scholars: "it is our sense that, here in the aftermath of the demise of the secularization thesis, we are only now beginning to grasp how deeply we remain in it: how shaped our conceptual frameworks are, down to their most elemental premises, by secularization."[2] Indeed, as both Michael Kaufmann, for literary studies, and José Casanova and Robert Orsi, for religious studies, have argued trenchantly, those conceptual frameworks are built into the very institutions and disciplines—housed in the modern, secular university system—through which this research is pursued.[3]

Emerson (the writer) and Emerson studies are a case in point. As one of the foremost of canonical figures upon which an American literary canon was built—positioned first in F. O. Matthiessen's *American Renaissance* (1941)—Emerson, for much of the twentieth century, *was* American literary studies. If Emerson proved too "religious"—too much in line with a feminized religious sentimentality of the likes of Harriet Beecher Stowe, Susan Warner, or Maria Susanna Cummins—his ability to shore up a secular literary canon would come under question. Emerson scholars since Miller have been embroiled in interpreting the degree to which this former minister was religious and the degree to which scholars can claim him for secularity.[4] While Harold Bloom positioned Emerson as *the* source for what he sweepingly dubbed a secularized "American religion," Phyllis Cole's monumental *Mary Moody Emerson and the Origins of Transcendentalism* (1998) recreates through rich archival sources the role that Emerson's aunt, Mary Moody Emerson, played in providing Emerson "a culture of Puritan vision through ancestral stories" and modeling the unflinching confrontation with that culture that came out in her writing in notes of "religious ecstasy and dissenting vision."[5]

Not all Emerson scholars have been so comfortable with Emerson's relation to religiosity, however. George Kateb, for one, asked, "should [Emerson's] religiousness interfere with our reception of him? It is a horror to say so, but it may be rather wasteful to study Emerson unless one shares his religiousness."[6] Kateb fretted about the traces of religiousness in Emerson's writing, but he optimistically decided that "our hope is that his religiousness, though sincere, is so minor as not to pose an insuperable obstacle to our secular reception of him."[7] As Lawrence Buell summed it up, "Emerson has had to be rescued several times from the clutches of religion. The first time he rescued himself. Since then, the rescuers have been Emersonians seeking to extricate him from the taint of religiocentrism."[8]

Emerson studies has therefore long been preoccupied with Emerson's relation to religion and the secular. That said, Emerson has strangely been a marginal figure in postsecular studies of nineteenth-century American literature. Postsecular studies is an interdisciplinary field that, according to Tracy Fessenden, takes as its given a scholarly "environment in which the categories of the religious and the secular no longer divide the world cleanly between them" and searches for better, more analytic categories.[9] Scholars such as Talal Asad and Saba Mahmood, both social scientists, have led this endeavor, turning the secular gaze of the academy on assumptions and formations of the secular itself. For the humanities, again to cite Fessenden, "the problem of the postsecular—the inadequacy of either secular or religious frames to wholly compass lived experience—is felt as an existential and not merely analytic predicament."[10] This predicament is especially acute for literary studies because, as Michael Kaufmann explains, literary study as a discipline has long depended on a secularization narrative that assumed that literature, in the tradition of Matthew Arnold, replaced religion for Western culture, a narrative "so entrenched," according to Kaufmann, that "it now functions more as a rhetorical gesture than a deliberative argument."[11]

At the heart of nineteenth-century literary studies after the postsecular turn there remains a tension between the analysis of the secular, which promises "an epistemological and methodological reorientation from which history might look different" (to cite Coviello and Hickman), and the desire to capture the excess—religious, queer, spiritual, and so on—left to the side in a canon and field long organized by the secularization thesis.[12] Nineteenth-century American literary studies has thus concentrated on, among other topics, limning the indebtedness of US secularism to the ideological power of white Protestantism, the flourishing of spiritual, social, and sexual experiments like Mormonism, the relation between credulity and secularism in such practices as Mesmerism, and rethinking the relationship between gender, religiosity, and authority, especially in the work of women writers.[13] For the most part, if there is a canonical writer in nineteenth-century American secular studies it is not Emerson but Herman Melville, of whom Nathaniel Hawthorne opined in his journal, "[he] can neither believe, nor be comfortable in his unbelief."[14]

Why is Emerson—whose relative religiousness and secularity are much-discussed topics among Emerson scholars—not a significant part of the debates around the secular and secularism for the larger field of nineteenth-century American literary studies? My wager in this essay is that Emerson stands for the relation to religion that is at once too central to the development of a secular literary canon but that does not provide, despite George Kateb's discomfort with Emerson's religiosity, the frisson of *difference* that announces that scholars are departing from secular norms or challenging the secularization thesis. As David Faflik has argued, Emerson's lifelong commentary on religion and the spiritual "will hardly strike today's readers as revelatory, unless they recognize that the reflexive skepticism now informing academic criticism derives in part from the religion practiced by Emerson and the members of his antebellum generation."[15] In this essay, I advance two arguments about Emerson and secularism. First, I position Emerson as a participant in and influence on the development of basic tenets of the secularization thesis, the main narrative at the heart of secularism as an ideology of Western modernity. Second, in examining how he articulates the dialectic between religion and the secular we can see a further historical shift in which he played a part: the emergence of American forms of "spirituality," including a category of belief now termed "spiritual but not religious."

"First, Soul, and Second, Soul, and Evermore, Soul"

To understand how central Emerson was and remains to secularism in the United States (and to its structural importance to antebellum American literary study) requires seeing him not just as an object through which we might interpret formations of the secular but as a participant in their construction. Though much-scrutinized today, the secularization thesis (that modernity is marked by progress away from credulity and religious belief and toward rationality and secularity) long held sway as a collective assumption in both literary studies and religious studies. Two related assumptions of this thesis are of particular use for this argument. First, as Charles Taylor elaborated, this narrative is shaped by what he calls "subtraction stories": the idea that one could subtract religion from a society (or, more accurately, sequester it to a private sphere) and that what is "left" is the secular, which can be considered simply the "underlying features of human nature which were there all along, but had been impeded by what is now set aside."[16] Secularism is the ideological belief in this subtraction story: that the relocation of religion to the private sphere constitutes progress and modernity, and as religion disappears from the public sphere, we discover something natural and true that religion has obscured.[17]

Equally important, secularism's favored version of privatized religion sounds a lot like mainstream white Protestantism, with its emphasis on propositional belief and its easy divorce from church institutions and public rites. As Robert Orsi explains, secular scholars and US law both tend to equate religion with belief. In doing so, both assume that "to 'believe in' a religion means that one has deliberated over and then assented to its propositional truths, has chosen this religion over other available options, a personal choice unfettered by authority, tradition, or society. What matters about religion from this perspective are its ideas and not its things, practices, or presences. This is not necessarily how Americans actually are religious, of course, but this account of religion carries real normative force."[18] According to Orsi, this version of religion has been positioned as "good" in both academic studies and in liberal secular thought more generally. Tracy Fessenden has usefully called this the "unmarked" Protestantism at the center of American secularism. As she explains, Protestantism shaped secular institutions and assumptions about religion without being marked *as religion* itself.[19] The way these assumptions became unmarked—advanced as commonsense or generalizable morality—can be seen in a variety of conflicts over religion in the nineteenth century, from state legislation requiring the teaching of the Protestant Bible in public schools as a source of nondenominational moral truths to the majority decision in *Reynolds v. United States* (1878), which outlawed plural marriage as practiced by Mormons.[20]

As scholars like Orsi and Fessenden clarify, one cannot define "secular" or "religious" without the other term, for they are dialectically intertwined. Emerson's impact on this dialectic is often hard to see because he both expressed and influenced the type of religion that has the greatest purchase in the academy and in liberal circles more broadly—religion as private, belief-oriented, ecstatic, and spiritual. And Emerson—as well as his readers—can take it up, reject it, or adopt parts as they see fit, exactly the type of belief that Orsi notes gets coded as salvageable in the academy. This version of religion has its roots both in the Protestant Reformation and anti-Catholicism. Among the many things Reformed Protestants targeted about the Church were its hierarchy, sacraments, and figures of mediation—that is, the institution, saints, and rituals that mediated between a believer and God. One result was the promotion of vernacular translations of the Bible. Another was a strand of anti-institutionalism running from seventeenth-century Antinomianism through to arguments for disestablishment and Transcendental writings. We can see this version of good religion quite visibly in Kateb's argument: "Emerson does not think that modern people need church religions to be moral. To the contrary, the moral kernel has now to be extracted from church religions to be kept safer. He is a critic of church religions because, in part, they sully the motive to morality and its content."[21] Kateb pursues distinctions very familiar to scholars of gender and religious studies: secularity is "strong" whereas religion, thus coded as the secular's feminine antithesis, is weak—simply an ephemeral "gesture." Moreover, Emerson can be saved from his own religiosity by distinguishing it from institutional religion ("church religions"), a distinction that comes out of centuries of Protestant anti-Catholicism.

Foremost in many arguments against church establishments in the new nation was an argument that "religion" constituted—or should constitute—exactly what Orsi names as "good belief" and that if the state has any role in religion, it is to sequester it to the private sphere and thus preserve it from corruption. Take for instance James Madison's "A Memorial and Remonstrance," which he presented to the General Assembly of Virginia in 1785 to argue for the disestablishment of the state's church. In an idiom infused with both revolutionary and anti-Catholic rhetoric, Madison asked, "What influence in fact have ecclesiastical establishments had on Civil Society? In some instances they have been seen to erect a spiritual tyranny on the ruins of the Civil authority; in many instances they have been seen upholding the thrones of political tyranny: in no instance have they been seen the guardians of the liberties of the people."[22] One of the main arguments driving the disestablishment of state churches—a complicated, state-by-state process that formally ended in 1833 when Massachusetts disestablished the Congregational Church—can be glimpsed in Madison's anti-Catholicism: that institutionalized religion, when wedded to a state, encourages corruption. Conversely, as can be seen in arguments from Madison, Thomas Jefferson, and Thomas Paine made in the 1780s and 1790s to defenses of privatized religion in the nineteenth century from even "conservative" figures like Lyman Beecher, private religion was imagined as promoting purity of belief.[23]

Unitarianism and other liberal Protestants in the early nineteenth century made this equation between institutional religion and corruption integral to their vision of religion itself. In his final sermon as a Unitarian minister, Emerson ruminated on the problem of institutionalized forms in religion. Considering the weekly ritual of communion, in commemoration of the Last Supper, he admits that "forms are as essential as bodies," but that "to exalt particular forms, to adhere to one form a moment after it is out-grown, is unreasonable, and it is alien to the spirit of Christ." What makes Christianity superior, he continues, is that it is a "moral system" that "presents men with truths which are their own reason, and enjoins practices that are their own justification."[24] Theodore Parker echoed this sentiment, declaring that "true religion is always the same thing" across history, but what he dubs "the Christianity of the Pulpit" "has never been the same thing in any two centuries or lands, except only in name."[25] Yet, he confesses with "Sorrow," these "transient things form a great part of what is commonly taught as Religion. An undue place has often been assigned to forms and doctrines, while too little stress has been laid on the divine life of the soul, love to God, and love to man."[26] In short, institutions corrupted Christianity.

Emerson and Parker both picked up on themes established by William Ellery Channing, the most influential Unitarian minister on the Transcendental generation. In "A Discourse at the Ordination of the Rev. Frederick A. Farley" (1828), popularly known as "Likeness to God," Channing asked, "But what, let me ask you, is the Christian religion?" and his answer was straightforward: "A spiritual system, intended to turn men's minds upon themselves, to frame them to watchfulness over thought, imagination, and passion, to establish them in an intimacy with their own souls. What are all the Christian virtues, which men are exhorted to love and seek? I answer, pure and high motions or determinations of the mind. That refinement of thought, which, I am told, transcends the common intellect, belongs to the very essence of Christianity."[27] Later in the sermon, he calls for Christianity to "rise above the technical, obscure, and frigid theology which has come to us from times of ignorance, superstition, and slavery. Let it penetrate the human soul, and reveal it to itself. No preaching, I believe is so intelligible, as that which is true to human nature, and helps men to read their own spirits."[28] Here we have the coming together of two definitions of religiousness: first, propositional belief, that religion happens by the "determinations of the mind"; but we also see that language of purity so central to Reformed Protestantism and disestablishment, that the "very essence of Christianity" consists in transcending the "common intellect" and refining thoughts in the "pure and high motions" of the mind, and that the goal for ministers is to allow their parishioners to "read their own spirits."

As Channing, Parker, and Emerson, among others, defined religion as spiritual, they fit seamlessly into the secularization thesis: that religion is best and modern when sequestered to the private realm and the mind. Yet it would surprise both Channing and Emerson that they played such a pivotal role in defining religion for secularism. That, of course, was not their intention. Emerson's "Divinity School Address" is, in fact, a *lament* on secularization and an attempt to shore up enthusiasm, ecstasy, and revelation as bulwarks against what Emerson saw as a triumph of organized, and to him deadened, religion. Here in Emerson's early, controversial lecture, he laid out what he saw as the crisis facing the ministry in the 1830s: rational Protestantism and especially Unitarianism encouraging or at least not countering the decay of belief.[29] As Emerson claims, the "creed" of the Puritans "is passing away, and none arises in its room. I think no man can go with his thoughts about him, into one of our churches, without feeling, that what hold the public worship had on men is gone, or going" (*CW* 1:88). This history comprises the classic secularization thesis of American studies, focused entirely on Calvinism in New England.

Emerson asks his audience, "What shall we do?" to confront this secularizing force (*CW* 1:92). As would Parker, Emerson voices a possible solution through the growing distinction between "true" belief and what Kateb dubbed "church religions." Emerson wonders how to inspire religion with life such that it can confront the "the universal decay and now almost death of faith in society" (*CW* 1:84). Emerson dismisses the ability to forge a fully new religion. Contriving a new system would be "as cold as the new worship introduced by the French to the goddess of Reason,—to-day, pasteboard and fillagree, and ending to-morrow in madness and murder" (*CW* 1:92). His answer instead is to "let the breath of new life be breathed by you through the forms already existing. For, if once you are alive, you shall find they shall become plastic and new. The remedy to their deformity is, first, soul, and second, soul, and evermore, soul. A whole popedom of forms, one pulsation of virtue can uplift and vivify" (*CW* 1:92).

Emerson's answer to how ministers can respond to the "death" and "decay" of faith has two elements I want to foreground. First, we again see the anti-institutionalism and anti-Catholicism in which "church religions" are described as a "whole popedom of forms" and thus absent any true religiosity. This conflation is not unique to Emerson, though it should probably be no surprise that advancing it in an address to graduating ministers would ruffle some institutional feathers. Second, the answer to the transformation of belief into institutions and forms is, as it was with Channing, what we might call "spiritual": "first, soul, and second, soul, and evermore, soul." Something immaterial and, in the logic of the address, anti-institutional ("soul") counters formalized and—because formalized—dead religion. In keeping with the individualism that Emerson would develop elsewhere, the onus to spark regeneration of belief is on the individual; once it is organized into a church, it loses its vitality.

Ultimately the argument running through "The Divinity School Address," though it may have seemed controversial for its occasion and era, became a standard theory of secularization in the nineteenth-century United States: the waning of Calvinism, a historical narrative that equally structured this address as it did such domestic fiction as Stowe's *The Minister's Wooing* (1859). In other words, Emerson was at the vanguard of telling a specific and eventually quite mainstream story: that in the first half of the nineteenth century, the religious spirit in the US was disappearing and what was left was a more secular society. This was not factually true and certainly required ignoring the great flourishing of evangelical revivals, the prominence of Black churches like the African Methodist Episcopal Church, and other religious inventions in what historian Jon Butler has called the "hothouse" of antebellum spirituality like Mormonism, Spiritualism, and Christian Science.[30] But Calvinism *was* losing its strong grip in New England. Emerson's "Divinity School Address" thus augurs two things: first, the individualizing and spiritualizing of belief, especially for mainstream liberal Protestantism, such that we can see the roots of a secular category prominent in the contemporary United States, "spiritual but not religious." And second, the elements that would lead to the realignment of "spirituality" with, as opposed to against, materialism and embodiment.

Spiritual but not Religious

Channing, Parker, and Emerson contrasted spiritual Christianity with "church religions," that is, the institutionalization of faith or belief. Running through their exhortations was certainly an inherited anti-Catholicism, but what I want to highlight is how their arguments presage a future development: though all three claimed to be delineating a true *religious* orientation, they collectively gave language to the eventual cleaving of the "spiritual" from the "religious" that culminated in the contemporary identity known as "spiritual but not religious." In other words, the difference between Channing's liberal Unitarian conflation of Christianity with spirituality and what would be implied by "spirituality" in the twenty-first century is the repositioning of spiritual *as opposed to religious* rather than aligned with it. We see one significant part of this dissociation in Emerson's and Parker's suspicion of organized religions. In this section I will limn Emerson's further emphasis on direct mystical experience, placing him as a significant voice in the emergence of what Catherine L. Albanese has called "American metaphysics," which emphasized an individualism that "leans toward the attainment of states of contentment, self-possession, and mastery, with the successful religionist an exemplar of the 'spiritual' instead of either a missionary or established social contributor."[31]

The emergence in the late twentieth century of the category of "spiritual but not religious" has its roots in this epochal shift of the nineteenth, in which Emerson played a profound role as an influence on the New Thought movement and other later nineteenth-century metaphysical seekers.[32] Consider the stirring opening lines of "The Over-Soul" in this regard: "There is a difference between one and another hour of life, in their authority and subsequent effect. Our faith comes in moments; our vice is habitual. Yet there is a depth in those brief moments which constrains us to ascribe more reality to them than to all other experiences" (*CW* 2:159). In this passage, we see how Emerson locates faith in passing moments and in the individual. Vice is ever-present; the hour that provides the experience of faith is ephemeral, even if its impact is profound. Faith thus arises from individual experience in brief but profound moments. We hear echoes here of Emerson's *Nature*: "Standing on the bare ground,—my head bathed by the blithe air, and uplifted into infinite space,—all mean egotism vanishes. I become a transparent eye-ball; I am nothing; I see all; the currents of the Universal Being circulate through me; I am part and particle of God" (*CW* 1:10). In both, faith is individualized, stripped of institutions and experienced in solitude. As he puts it later in "The Over-Soul," "The faith that stands on authority is not faith. The reliance on authority measures the decline of religion, the withdrawal of the soul" (*CW* 2:174). Emerson celebrates a central tenet of mysticism, originally "the ecstatic experience in the Christian life." As Leigh Eric Schmidt argues, however, after the eighteenth century and particularly through the influence of Emanuel Swedenborg on Transcendentalism, mysticism came to emphasize individual religious experience as ahistorical and universal, not tied to any one faith or theology.[33]

The second transformation that led to today's definition of "spirituality" was built on the first and involved the influence of Eastern religions. If the first primary shift was the cleaving of "spiritual" from "religious," the second was to associate "spirituality" with embodiment. In his "Likeness to God," Channing assumed that a "spiritual system" not only watches over the passions and imagination, but that system is defined against its traditional other, embodiment and materiality: "Man has animal propensities as well as intellectual and moral powers. He has a body as well as mind" and therefore "to such a being, religion, or virtue, is a conflict, requiring great spiritual effort, put forth in habitual watchfulness and prayer."[34] For Channing, the "spiritual" is aligned with religion and both are opposed to the body and materialism. "Likeness to God" thus usefully marks a point before "spiritual" underwent an enormous transformation in meaning. Emerson's earliest forays into thinking about faith and religious experience likewise strip spirituality of material embodiment. *Nature* exemplifies this. In it, we see how faith is pure soul—the speaker becomes transparent, all-seeing but immaterial.

While certain Protestant spiritual disciplines would have been familiar to both Channing and Emerson—such as private prayer, diary writing, Bible reading, and so on—there is a marked distinction between these and the types of embodied practices "spirituality" invokes today. As Boaz Huss argues, "the binary opposition between the spiritual on the one hand and the corporeal and material on the other has become blurred in the current definitions and usages of the term; instead, a new dichotomy has emerged, juxtaposing spirituality with the category it was previously closely related to: the religious." What is more, as Huss explains, spirituality has become a term aligned with, as "opposed to materiality and corporeality" and "it is frequently associated with physical and corporeal domains."[35] By the twenty-first century, to announce oneself to be "spiritual" often means as much a relentless attention to physical health—through fitness culture, diet, and alternative medicine—as it does practices such as meditation and mindfulness. Spiritual bodywork encompasses, as Courtney Bender has tracked, a host of alternative health practices like acupuncture, Reiki, and yoga.[36]

We can see this endpoint as beginning with Emerson and the Transcendentalists as they infused a version of Eastern religions into their own writings and influenced the next generation's encounter with such religious practices. As Arthur Versluis has ably shown, Emerson, Thoreau, and other early Transcendentalists read deeply about Eastern religious practices and beliefs. Versluis traces Emerson's developing thought, from early readings that were as much routed through Orientalist researchers' accounts as they were direct readings (in translation) of the Bhagavad Gita or the Upanishads to the later decades, in which "he read primarily Eastern works when concerning himself with religious matters."[37] Emerson's reading in Eastern religions infused such essays as "The Over-Soul" and poems like "Brahma." The effect of this reading was much more than Emerson's participation in the growing field of "comparative religions," though.[38] As Jan Stievermann has argued, it helped Emerson develop his basic definition of "religion" for a secular age. Combined with his emphasis on individualism, religion would mainly be "concerned with self-knowledge and realization of the true 'inner self' as an individual participation in the divine through a continuous quest for higher spiritual things and moral self-improvement."[39] Indeed, as Versluis explains, Emerson was "interested in divine inspiration, not ritual, in the blasting light of mysticism, not in form, in ethical responsibility, not in adherence to any particular religion."[40] This more or less encapsulates Orsi's definition of "good" religion. All religions are available for mystical experience and ethical precepts, with that which makes theologies or rituals particular left to the side.

Schmidt's *Restless Souls* and Albanese's *A Republic of Mind & Spirit* canvass the route from Emerson's encounters with Eastern religions to the great flourishing of spiritualities in the later nineteenth century, including the importation and appropriation of Hinduism, Zen Buddhism, and such practices as yoga and meditation. Anti-institutional forms of religious experience and Transcendental mysticism would meet up, especially following the World's Parliament of Religions in Chicago in 1893, with Hinduism as introduced by Swami Vivekanánda, and Buddhist devotional and meditative practices by the Sri Lankan monk Anagarika Dharmapala and Japanese Zen Buddhism through D. T. Suzuki (who also wrote an essay on Emerson in 1896).[41] While Emerson's development of a concept of "religion" depended on Eastern sources, as Stievermann has ably shown, he, in turn, influenced such figures as Vivekanánda and Suzuki.[42]

The 1893 World's Parliament of Religions, held at the Chicago World's Fair, was pivotal in bringing meditative and devotional practices drawn from Buddhism and Hinduism into more prominent circulation in the United States. These practices found their way into New Thought and other movements via figures like Vivekanánda and Dharmapala, who, during their tours of the United States, visited Sarah Farmer's summer community Greenacre in Eliot, Maine, which became a conduit for Eastern practices to influence the New Thought movement. As Arielle Zibrak explains, New Thought was "an umbrella term for many distinct variants of Mental science, all connected through a central belief in the power of the mind to influence outcomes in the physical world," drawing from such disparate sources in liberal Protestantism as Mary Baker Eddy's Christian Science and, significantly, the Transcendentalism of Emerson.[43]

The specific alignment of the spiritual with the physical and corporeal was certainly not central either to Emerson or the New Thought movement.[44] Yet as Zibrak notes about the Arts and Crafts movement, and as Schmidt, Albanese, and Stievermann show about the influence of Eastern practices on Transcendentalism and New Thought, the body and the material world would find a place in spiritual seeking before the twenty-first century, and we can find elements of it already apparent in Emerson's writings. For the most part, Emerson's writings are largely in keeping with thinking of the spiritual as opposed to the body, as we saw in Channing's "Likeness to God." Yet in both "The Over-Soul" and his chapter on Swedenborg in *Representative Men*, the division between soul and body—and spiritual and material—begins to break down, in a way that anticipates the epistemological shift that Huss identifies and Bender explores in depth. Emerson writes of the soul, "All goes to show that the soul in man is not an organ, but animates and exercises all the organs; is not a function, like the power of memory, of calculation, of comparison, but uses these as hands and feet; is not a faculty, but a light; is not the intellect or the will, but the master of the intellect and the will; is the background of being, in which they lie,—an immensity not possessed and that cannot be possessed" (*CW* 2:161). While the soul is certainly not conflated with the body in this passage, it has a quality of being infused in and through it; you cannot locate the soul in one place. It is instead everywhere. This description edges into exactly the rhetoric Huss and Bender identify: if the soul infuses the whole body, body work is also soul work.

In his chapter "Swedenborg; or, the Mystic" in *Representative Men* (1850), Emerson brings together his critique of church religion, his critique of lifelessness in theology, and his affirmation of mystical experience. Emerson, as William James would later, elevates ecstatic experience as the definition of religious experience. For those who seek to be "a holy and godlike soul," the path is "difficult, secret, and beset with terror" (*CW* 4:55). As he explains, "The ancients called it *ecstasy* or absence,—a getting out of their bodies to think. All religious history contains traces of the trances of saints,—a beatitude, but without any sign of joy, earnest, solitary, even sad; 'the flight,' Plotinus called it, 'of the alone to the alone'" and finally, in Greek, "the closing of the eyes, whence our word Mystic" (*CW* 4:55). Though his descriptive opening to the chapter cites ecstasy as a "getting out" of the body, as he pivots to Swedenborg, the material emerges as central to Swedenborg's mystical achievement. Specifically, Emerson cites his training as an engineer, his study of mines and smelting works, not as incidental biographical information but as important to the mystical insights he would develop. In his ecstasies, Swedenborg had "pass[ed] the bounds of space and time; venture[d] into the dim spirit-realm, and attempt[ed] to establish a new religion in the world" but he did so by beginning his "lessons in quarries and forges, in the smelting-pot and crucible, in shipyards and dissecting-rooms" (*CW* 4:58). Emerson here celebrates how the material was the basis of and the undergirding for Swedenborg's ecstatic revelation.

That said, much of the chapter is also a critique of Swedenborg's mystical vision. Emerson faults its lifelessness, its tendency toward homogeneity: "All his types mean the same few things. All his figures speak one speech. All his interlocutors Swedenborgize" (*CW* 4:75). His great fault is a "want of individualism. The thousand-fold relation of men is not there" (*CW* 4:74). And ultimately this inability to grasp the actual ways that people are, the individual quirks of life that compile into the multiplicity of liveliness, is a fault of institutionalization. "The vice of Swedenborg's mind is its theologic determination," Emerson explains. "Nothing with him has the liberality of universal wisdom, but we are always in a church" (*CW* 4:75). Emerson brings these together for his ultimate appraisal: "The genius of Swedenborg, largest of all modern souls in this department of thought, wasted itself in the endeavor to reanimate and conserve what had already arrived at its natural term, and, in the great secular Providence, was retiring from its prominence, before western modes of thought and expression. Swedenborg and Behmen both failed by attaching themselves to the Christian symbol, instead of to the moral sentiment, which carries innumerable christianities, humanities, divinities, in its bosom" (*CW* 4:76).

Here we see a distinct shift from his "Divinity School Address." In 1838, Emerson imagined a reinvigoration of belief through Christianity with his gesture to the French Revolution sealing off the invention of a new belief system to replace the old. Here he faults Swedenborg not just for being churchy but for failing to shed Christian symbolism entirely; Swedenborg missed an opportunity to hitch his mystical vision to the "moral sentiment" that Christianity promulgates, a sentiment Emerson hastens to add is not particular or unique to Christianity itself (though Emerson's elevation of the moral sentiment above all else betrays the continued influence of Protestantism in his definition of "good" religion). In other words, Swedenborg failed to grasp the zeitgeist of secularization. Emerson ties together Swedenborg's tendency to make everyone feel as if they're at church with this inability to see past institutionalized religions. Swedenborg fails because he puts too much stock in Christianity, and his revelation returns everyone to the "dullness" of a church service. As Emerson has made clear since the "Divinity School Address," individualism, anti-institutionalism, moral sensibility, and embodied vitality are all tied together.

George Kateb asked, "should [Emerson's] religiousness interfere with our reception of him?" The answer is that Emerson's religiousness—and his secularism—has shaped our reception of him. His thinking is central to the development and, in the academy especially, the popularity of the secularization thesis in the United States. The secularization thesis operates through a fantasy that one can "subtract" religion and what is left is the rational, credulous secular. Emerson's religiousness is not subtractable from his secularism; indeed, the two are inextricably intertwined, as they are for American culture more broadly. To put this differently, we can't see Emerson's individualism or his politics without seeing the connection to his critique of church religions; and conversely, we can't see his celebration of Eastern philosophies without glimpsing an unfolding historical process that would change the mainstream, secular definition of "spirituality" in the United States. Viewed in the context of that historical process, we can see Emerson as one major starting point that would end with the emergence of the term "spiritual but not religious"—a category that is so beholden to the nineteenth-century redefinition of religiousness by liberal Protestantism that it almost becomes a full-blown contradiction in its very enunciation.

That Emerson's influence—perhaps overstated by Emerson scholars but also undeniably important—has been most pronounced in the arenas of "spirituality" and "spiritual but not religious" is also likely why Emerson has not yet been a central focus in postsecular studies. Too canonical and famous in his era to fill out a missing religious history that can help us understand popular religion or popular religious fiction, Emerson also articulated what would become such a mainstream version of spirituality for liberal circles for much of the twentieth century (anti-institutional, individualist, and ecstatic) that it in many ways disappears as a category of "religion." What we gain by seeing Emerson in relation not just to *religion* but also to *secularism* is therefore twofold: first, a more accurate understanding of what we mean when we talk about his or any author's "religiousness"; and second, the reason to return to an extremely canonical figure like Emerson for this type of historical analysis. So fully at the center of the emergence of secularism as to be nearly rendered invisible to scholars in the field now, Emerson's writings still help us understand the roots of today's religious landscape and the way our popular and public modes of religiosity—and their relation to the history of the academy—are inextricably linked to the emergence of United States secularism in the nineteenth century.

Notes

1. Perry Miller, "Jonathan Edwards to Emerson," *The New England Quarterly* 13, no. 4 (1940): 589–617, 590.
2. Peter Coviello and Jared W. Hickman, "Introduction: After the Postsecular," *American Literature* 86, no. 4 (2015): 645–54, 646.

3. See Michael W. Kaufmann, "The Religious, the Secular, and Literary Studies: Rethinking the Secularization Narrative in Histories of the Profession," *New Literary History* 38, no. 4 (2007): 607–28; Robert Orsi, *Between Heaven and Earth: The Religious Worlds People Make and the Scholars Who Study Them* (Princeton, NJ: Princeton University Press, 2005).
4. In this overview I purposely highlight some of the most visible or bombastic claims. Recent scholarship on Emerson has expanded our understanding of his relation to religion, including the influence of his training for the ministry, his rejection of Unitarianism, and the relation of his philosophy to other Romantic-era religious movements like Mormonism. For more recent work on Emerson in relation to Joseph Smith and Mormonism (especially in the convergences between Smith's stress on divine revelation and Emerson's denunciation of church religions), see Evan Carton, "American Scholars: Ralph Waldo Emerson, Joseph Smith, John Brown, and the Springs of Intellectual Schism," *The New England Quarterly* 85, no. 1 (2012): 5–37; Claudia Jetter, "Continuing Revelation and Institutionalization: Joseph Smith, Ralph Waldo Emerson and Charismatic Leadership in Antebellum America," *Studies in Church History* 57 (2021): 233–53; and Benjamin E. Park, "'Build, Therefore, Your Own World': Ralph Waldo Emerson, Joseph Smith, and American Antebellum Thought," *Journal of Mormon History* 36, no. 1 (2010): 41–72; for recent work considering the relation of Puritanism to Emerson's thinking (particularly the radicalness of this legacy), see Kenyon Gradert, "Swept into Puritanism: Emerson, Wendell Phillips, and the Roots of Radicalism," *The New England Quarterly* 90, no. 1 (2017): 103–29; for more on Emerson and specters of unbelief, see Robert Milder, "Emerson and the Fortunes of Godless Religion," *The New England Quarterly* 87, no. 4 (2014): 573–624.
5. Phyllis Cole, *Mary Moody Emerson and the Origins of Transcendentalism* (New York and Oxford: Oxford University Press, 1998), 11, 5.
6. George Kateb, *Emerson and Self-Reliance* (Thousand Oaks, London, and New Delhi: Sage Publications, 1995), 65.
7. Kateb, *Emerson and Self-Reliance*, 76.
8. Lawrence Buell, *Emerson* (Cambridge, MA: Harvard University Press, 2003), 158.
9. Tracy Fessenden, "The Problem of the Postsecular," *American Literary History* 26, no. 1 (2014): 154–67, 156.
10. Fessenden, "Problem of the Postsecular," 156.
11. Kaufmann, "Religious, Secular, and Literary Studies," 616.
12. Coviello and Hickman, "Introduction: After the Postsecular," 646.
13. For work on how white Protestantism shaped the US secular, see Tracy Fessenden, *Culture and Redemption: Religion, the Secular, and American Literature* (Princeton, NJ: Princeton University Press, 2007); and John Lardas Modern, *Secularism in Antebellum America* (Chicago: Chicago University Press, 2011); for how secularism has obscured the queer sexualities of the nineteenth century, see Peter Coviello, *Make Yourselves Gods: Mormons and the Unfinished Business of American Secularism* (Chicago: University of Chicago Press, 2019); for an understanding of secularism as it was shaped by popular cultural practices like Mesmerism, see Emily Ogden, *Credulity: A Cultural History of US Mesmerism* (Chicago: Chicago University Press, 2018); for more on secularism and literary history, see Ashley Barnes, *Love and Depth in the American Novel: From Stowe to James* (Charlottesville, VA: University of Virginia Press, 2020); and Dawn Coleman, "The Spiritual Authority of Literature in a Secular Age," *Christianity & Literature* 67, no. 3 (June 2018): 519–20; finally, for scholarship on secularism, postsecularism, religion, and women's writing, see Gretchen Murphy, *New England Women Writers, Secularity,*

and the Federalist Politics of Church and State (Oxford: Oxford University Press, 2021); Ashley Reed, *Heaven's Interpreters: Women Writers and Religious Agency in Nineteenth-Century America* (Ithaca: Cornell University Press, 2020); and Claudia Stokes, *The Altar at Home: Sentimental Literature and Nineteenth-Century American Religion* (Philadelphia: University of Pennsylvania Press, 2014).

14. Nathaniel Hawthorne, *The English Notebooks* (New York: Russell & Russell, 1962), 433.
15. David Faflik, "Critique, Belief, and the Negative Tendencies of New England Transcendentalism," *ESQ* 66, no. 3 (2020): 518–31, 519. For a far-reaching study of how Transcendentalism emerged out of Unitarianism at Harvard, and how it "multiplied, rather than removed, the available spiritual possibilities among New Englanders" (5), see David Faflik, *Transcendental Heresies: Harvard and the Modern American Practice of Unbelief* (Amherst: University of Massachusetts Press, 2020).
16. Charles Taylor, *A Secular Age* (Cambridge, MA: Harvard University Press, 2007), 22.
17. For trenchant analyses of the political problems the United States faces from this conflation of private religion with freedom and modernity, see Finbarr Curtis, *The Production of American Religious Freedom* (New York: New York University Press, 2016); and Tracy Fessenden, "'The Secular' as Opposed to What?," *New Literary History* 38, no. 4 (2007): 631–36.
18. Orsi, *Between Heaven and Earth*, 18. In chapter 6 of the book, Orsi elaborates on how and why this definition of "good religion" developed in the discipline of Religious Studies and examines its impact on current scholarship.
19. Fessenden, *Culture and Redemption*, 3.
20. For more on the controversies around Bible teaching in public schools, see Fessenden, *Culture and Redemption*, chapter 3; for more on the *Reynolds* decision and its logic, see Sarah Barringer Gordon, *The Mormon Question: Polygamy and Constitutional Conflict in Nineteenth Century America* (Chapel Hill: University of North Carolina Press, 2002).
21. Kateb, *Emerson and Self-Reliance*, 92.
22. James Madison, "To the Honorable the General Assembly of the Commonwealth of Virginia. A Memorial and Remonstrance," ca. June 20, 1785, Founders Online, National Archives, http://founders.archives.gov/documents/Madison/01-08-02-0163.
23. For more on the history of disestablishment, see Steven K. Green, *The Second Disestablishment: Church and State in Nineteenth-Century America* (New York: Oxford University Press, 2010); and Carl H. Esbeck and Jonathan J. Den Hartog, eds., *Disestablishment and Religious Dissent: Church-State Relations in the New American States, 1776–1833* (Columbia, MO: University of Missouri Press, 2019), especially their introduction; for more on the growing ideological relation between private, noninstitutional religion and "pure" religion, see Justine S. Murison, *Faith in Exposure: Privacy and Secularism in the Nineteenth-Century United States* (Philadelphia: University of Pennsylvania Press, 2023), chapter 1; for more on the effect of disestablishment on women's writing, see Murphy, *New England Women Writers*.
24. Ralph Waldo Emerson, "The Lord's Supper," originally given on September 9, 1832, at Boston's Second Church, accessed February 2, 2022, https://archive.vcu.edu/english/engweb/transcendentalism/authors/emerson/essays/lordsupper.html.
25. Theodore Parker, "A Discourse of the Transient and Permanent in Christianity," in *The Critical and Miscellaneous Writings of Theodore Parker*, 2nd ed. (Boston: Little, Brown, 1856), 152–189: 156.
26. Parker, "Transient and Permanent," 141.

27. William Ellery Channing, "A Discourse at the Ordination of the Rev. Frederick A. Farley," in *American Sermons: The Pilgrims to Martin Luther King, Jr.* (New York: Library of America, 1999), 551–71: 567–68.
28. Channing, "Discourse," 568.
29. For more on the fallout from the "Divinity School Address," see Robert D. Richardson Jr., *Emerson: The Mind on Fire* (Berkley: University of California Press, 1995), 298–300.
30. See Jon Butler, *Awash in a Sea of Faith: Christianizing the American People* (Cambridge, MA: Harvard University Press, 1990), chapter 8.
31. Catherine L. Albanese, *A Republic of Mind and Spirit: A Cultural History of American Metaphysical Religion* (New Haven, CT: Yale University Press, 2007), 7.
32. For more on Emerson's influence on New Thought, see Leigh Eric Schmidt, *Restless Souls: The Making of American Spirituality*, 2nd edition (Berkeley: University of California Press, 2012), 199–200; and Albanese, *Republic of Mind and Spirit*, 162, 395.
33. Schmidt, *Restless Souls*, 14–15, 53–54.
34. Channing, "Discourse," 568.
35. Boaz Huss, "Spirituality: The Emergence of a New Cultural Category and its Challenge to the Religious and the Secular," *Journal of Contemporary Religion* 29, no. 1 (2014): 47–60, 50.
36. For more on the way in which contemporary "spirituality" and alternative medicine are entangled in beliefs, practices, and institutional settings, see Courtney Bender, *The New Metaphysicals: Spirituality and American Religious Imagination* (Chicago: Chicago University Press, 2010), chapter 1.
37. Arthur Versluis, *American Transcendentalism and Asian Religions* (New York: Oxford University Press, 1993), 54, 63–67, and chapter 3 more broadly.
38. For more on the rise of "world religions" and "comparative religions," see Tomoko Masuzawa, *The Invention of World Religions: Or, How European Universalism was Preserved in the Language of Pluralism* (Chicago: University of Chicago Press, 2005); and Toni Wall Jaudon, "The Compiler's Art: Hannah Adams, the *Dictionary of All Religions*, and the Religious World," *American Literary History* 26, no. 1 (Spring 2014): 28–41.
39. Jan Stievermann, "Emersonian Transcendentalism and the Invention of Religion(s) in the Nineteenth Century," *ESQ* 67, no. 3–4 (2021): 533–70, 549.
40. Versluis, *American Transcendentalism and Asian Religions*, 78.
41. Schmidt weaves the World's Parliament of Religions throughout *Restless Souls*, but see especially chapter 4 on meditation; see Albanese, chapter 6, for more on the World's Parliament of Religions, Vivekanánda, Dharmapala, and the influence of Asian religious practices on US metaphysical religions.
42. Stievermann, "Emersonian Transcendentalism," 560–63.
43. Arielle Zibrak, "Power of Body/Power of Mind: Arts and Crafts, New Thought, and Popular Women's Literature at the Fin de Siècle," *American Literature* 93, no. 4 (2021): 601–28, 603. Zibrak's article usefully corrects a historiography that has generally focused on men in both the Arts and Crafts and New Thought movements, clarifying the central role of women teachers, writers, and organizers in both.
44. See Zibrak on how New Thought positioned the body as that which was to be "overcome" through mind science, 610–12.

6

PROSPECTS, OR, COMPUTATIONAL APPROACHES TO EMERSON

CHAPTER 21

EXPERIMENTING WITH EMERSON

A Quantitative Approach

BRAD RITTENHOUSE AND MAURICE S. LEE

Introduction

One measure of an author's vitality is how readily they drive or become the subject of emerging subfields and methods. Judging Emerson by this standard renders mixed results, for if he continues to figure in literary discussions of aesthetics, transnationalism, and science—and if he retains a lively interdisciplinary presence in philosophy, political theory, and religious studies—Emerson scholarship has been slow to engage some developments, including those in the digital humanities. This is especially true for the kind of large-scale quantitative projects sometimes lumped under the term *distant reading*. Such work tends to focus on claims and corpora that exceed the scope of author-centric study, and Emerson's oeuvre can seem particularly ill-suited to the affordances of data-based methods. Whereas the novel is the preferred genre of distant reading, Emerson's favored forms—essays, speeches, and journals—are more difficult to classify and collect at culture-wide scales, while his poetry is not his primary legacy and constitutes a relatively small corpus for statistical analysis.

The romantic strains of Emerson's imagination might also seem at odds with computational methods. When "Self-Reliance" (1841) disparages the "slavish respect for numbers," Emerson not only resists the tyranny of the majority but also the disarticulating, deracinating logic of an increasingly quantitative age.[1] Much of the skepticism directed at the digital humanities from more traditional critical quarters shares an outlook often associated with Emerson that sets subjectivity, unknowability, beauty, and intuition over and against computational discourses of objectivity, transparency, instrumentality, and reason. As if anticipating critiques of distant reading, Emerson often resists classificatory systems and the reduction of experience to facts. He complains in "The Superlative" (1884): "We are unskillful definers. From want of skill to convey quality, we hope to move admiration by quantity" (*CWE* 10:160). There is no substitute for close reading Emerson if one seeks the finer textures of his style and thought, and Emerson's ethos can indeed seem incommensurate with algorithmic methods of analysis.

And yet incommensurability, for Emerson, is almost always a passing mood. As scholars such as Lee Rust Brown and Laura Dassow Walls have emphasized, Emerson found much to admire in the natural sciences, including the wonders of classification.[2] He was even surprisingly open to data-driven efforts to produce what we might call literary knowledge. In *Representative Men* (1850), he takes a judicious view of the "laborious computations" of Edmond Malone, the eighteenth-century scholar who used basic quantitative methods to determine the authorship of plays attributed to Shakespeare.[3] Elsewhere, Emerson's article "Books" (1858) refers to "the arithmetical rule of Permutation and Combination" when conceptualizing the problem of choosing what to read from the immense number of available texts (*CW* 7:96). This is the Emerson who in "Fate" (1860) praises "the new science of Statistics" for showing that even geniuses like Jenny Lind and Napoleon are born according to "fixed calculation" (*CW* 6:9). Curious, experimental, and unbounded by discipline, an Emersonian ethos need hardly be opposed to computational literary criticism. Rather, one question for Emerson and Emerson studies is how best to apply quantitative methods to humanist enterprises while recognizing the limitations of such projects.

Computational criticism may even be distinctively helpful when trying to understand Emerson. Because many of the methods used in the digital humanities were first developed for the shorter utterances of business and technical forms such as tweets and user reviews, and because such methods struggle to register novelistic features like perspective and dramatic irony, they may actually be better suited for expository expression, even richly complex prose such as Emerson's. Moreover, Emerson—who as often as any American writer can become something like what Foucault called an "author function"—may benefit from the extensive capacities of computational analysis. Scholars, of course, attend to Emerson's biography and explicate his individual texts, but "Emerson" frequently comes to stand for a constellation of ideas or a mosaic-like figure composed of a selection of anecdotes and quotes that stand in for a broader mind and corpus. Which is inevitable and fine—indeed, often much better than fine—but is complicated by Emerson's prolific inconsistencies. Is he an egalitarian champion of democracy or a founding father of Anglo-Saxon racism?[4] Is he a devotee to universal moral principles or a herald of antifoundational philosophy?[5] Or to turn toward questions that this chapter explores: What are the patterns and proportions of Emerson's intellectual influences? To what extent should we regard him as a regional, national, or international figure? How can we generalize about his varied body of work spread over half a century?

The capaciousness and contradictions of Emerson's writings allow for much interpretive license, and so arguments about Emerson can be especially susceptible to confirmation bias, sampling error, and teleological reasoning as scholars, with our variously colored critical lenses, paint Emerson our own hue. Computational literary analysis does not solve this problem (which might not even be a problem under Emerson's philosophy insofar as the multiple meanings generated by subjectivity are as much a feature as a bug). But if we, like Emerson, are sometimes drawn toward harder empirical truths, quantitatively modeling his work at a large scale offers new opportunities for argument and speculation. What follows uses computational techniques to provide an account of Emerson's oeuvre not typically possible through close reading. In doing so, we confirm and sharpen some existing views of Emerson (for example, his commitments to western intellectual history; the Transcendentalism of his most canonical texts), qualify some arguments (e.g. the centrality of certain figures to his work; his status as a global thinker), and offer some new claims (such as the anomalous roles that Hafiz, Napoleon, and Jesus play in his writings). The focus throughout is on Emerson's references to people and places, as well as links between the two, with the goal of sketching some maps, figurative and literal, of his intellectual influences and geographic coordinates. Finally, this chapter is not driven by a single thesis but serves as something of a pilot study—an initial attempt to model Emerson's corpus quantitatively and see what this new approach might (and might not) accomplish.

Background and Process

The critical history of computational studies of Emerson starts early but is quite thin. It begins with Lucius Adelno Sherman, a philologist and professor of English at the University of Nebraska, who in 1893 published *Analytics of Literature: A Manual For the Objective Study of English Prose and Poetry*. Sherman and his students took up a number of stylometric projects, including tabulating Emerson's subordinate clauses (he uses them less frequently than most canonical essayists) and measuring the average length of Emerson's sentences (shorter than those of most of his peers). For Sherman, such data reflects an Emersonian style that echoes the "ordinary intercourse of men" and is "almost colloquial in structural simplicity."[6] Current students may disagree, but eighty years after Sherman, Donald Ross, Jr. came to a similar finding when using "word-class-distribution statistics" to show that Emerson's *Nature* (1836) uses modifiers less frequently than the "Spring" chapter of Thoreau's *Walden* (1854).[7] More recently, Amy Earhart and Augusta Rohrbach have written on Emerson and digital pedagogy, but there remains little computational analysis of Emerson's writings and, aside from a blog post from Eric Lease Morgan in 2015, nothing since the digitization of his collected works.[8]

Some of the factors that complicate editing Emerson also obtain when creating a digital corpus of his writings. Collected versions of some Emerson texts differ from their originally published forms, and—as Christopher Hanlon has discussed—Ellen Emerson and James Elliot Cabot collaborated with the fading Emerson to revise and even posthumously assemble certain works.[9] It is not always clear which version of an Emerson text is primary, how to date some texts, and whether to attribute them solely to Emerson. And because his publications frequently draw from journal entries and lectures written decades before, tracking the growth of Emerson's mind or the evolution of his style across time has always been a challenge. Acknowledging these dynamics, and setting aside some initial aspirations for chronological analysis, we assembled our corpus using The Liberty Fund's digitized version of the Centenary Edition of *The Complete Works of Ralph Waldo Emerson* (1903–1904), itself a close copy of the Riverside Edition (1883) with some materials added after Emerson's death. This source text does not contain all of the works that Emerson published during his life, and the data generated from it are imperfect for a number of technical reasons, but we take our corpus as sufficiently representative of Emerson's oeuvre and the datasets as sufficiently large to average out anomalous errors. We also decided to omit Emerson's collected poems from the corpus and focus on the more robust body of his prose, if only because Emerson's verse seems a different mode of expression with a different linguistic logic. Future projects might choose differently and collaborate with copyright holders to assemble a more comprehensive corpus of Emerson's texts.

To prepare our corpus for analysis, we attached metadata to texts so trends could be analyzed in relation to information such as publication dates, genres, and venues. We then cleaned the texts, correcting common Optical Character Recognition (OCR) errors and removing publication boilerplates.[10] From there, we performed standard Natural Language Processing (NLP) tokenization and divided the texts on a paragraph level, after which we performed Named Entity Recognition (NER), identifying Persons, Geopolitical Areas, Organizations, and Groups, among several other categories, while also establishing links among entities that appear in the same paragraph.[11] For the sake of convenience, when we refer to an entity such as a person or place being mentioned (say) twenty-three times, we mean that the entity appears at least once in twenty-three different paragraphs (that is, multiple references within a single paragraph are counted only once).

One aspect of our method worth emphasizing is its capacity to model relationships between entities. Computational textual analysis often relies on word counts, but as many practitioners and their critics note, word frequencies in and of themselves fail to capture relationships between words and thus miss much semantic richness. This limitation can be mitigated, though of course not eliminated, by tracking links between entities to provide additional insights into Emerson's patterns of thought and the topography of his knowledge. Consistent collocations of entities suggest associations between references in Emerson's mind, allowing for inferences about his sense of philosophical, literary, historical, and geographical lineages and formations.

The graphing of links was produced from the initial NER analysis, but it is important to note that certain link patterns appear to be duplicated in reverse (for instance, Shakespeare -> Bacon, Bacon -> Shakespeare). This is in some ways an artifact of the data structure, but it also encodes important information about Emerson's referential semantics. For the purposes of knowledge graphing and social network analysis, a link is only recorded once, typically with the first entity mentioned connecting to later entities. So if Emerson were to list "Shakespeare, Bacon, and Milton," Shakespeare would serve as the origin with destinations to Bacon and Milton. To avoid "double-counting" such linkages in reverse, the links are only recorded for the first entity, though Bacon would also be linked directly to Milton. Thus the categorization of entities into origins and destinations encode a directionality of linkages that can represent real world directionality (Person A sent a letter to Person B) or syntactic directionality (entity A performed an action on entity B). In our case, directionality simply records the occurrence of one entity before another, which interpreted over the breadth of Emerson's writings can indicate how he thought about people and places in relation to each other. For instance, as we shall see, Person A may consistently come before Person B for reasons of chronology or prominence.

To further measure relationships between words, we used an additional technique: word embedding. This entailed tokenizing the corpus with the Penn Treebank Tokenizer and performing a skip-gram word embedding with Google's Word2Vec algorithm through the gensim Python library.[12] We chose skip-gram because it tends to work well on small datasets like our corpus; and indeed, qualitative review of the results, we think, proves the method to be relatively accurate in representing Emerson's semantics. In contrast to establishing links based on NER, word embedding allows for measuring the collocation of any word with other words, whether or not such words are tagged as entities. It also allows more flexibility in setting parameters for measuring the proximity of words.

With data in hand, we performed various quantitative analyses and generated numerous exploratory and explanatory visualizations. Data on entities and the relationships between words through entity links and word embedding may not constitute statistically significant proof, but they are useful in forming hypotheses about Emerson's writings and can support critical inferences in ways that close reading cannot. The methods adopted here reflect Emerson's conviction that (in Branka Arsić's words) "everything is ... relational."[13] Or as Emerson writes in "Poetry and Imagination" (1872): "Science was false by being unpoetical. It assumed to explain a reptile or mollusk, and isolated it,—which is hunting for life in graveyards. Reptile or mollusk or man or angel only exists in system, in relation."[14]

Results and Discussion: Overview

Beginning broadly, we examined the general contours of the dataset by calculating measurements such as the number of entities mentioned per year in the corpus, the number of words per year, and the ratio between the two measures, which we call the "entity rate" (Figure 21.1). At first glance, the pattern of entity usage across Emerson's career does not seem particularly illuminating, as it mainly reflects his total word usage with predictable spikes in the years in which he published books.

However, closer examination of the data reveals some interesting inflection points. For instance, 1841, 1844, and 1860 have high total word counts but low entity rates. These years saw the publication of *Essays: First Series* (1841), *Essays: Second Series* (1844), and

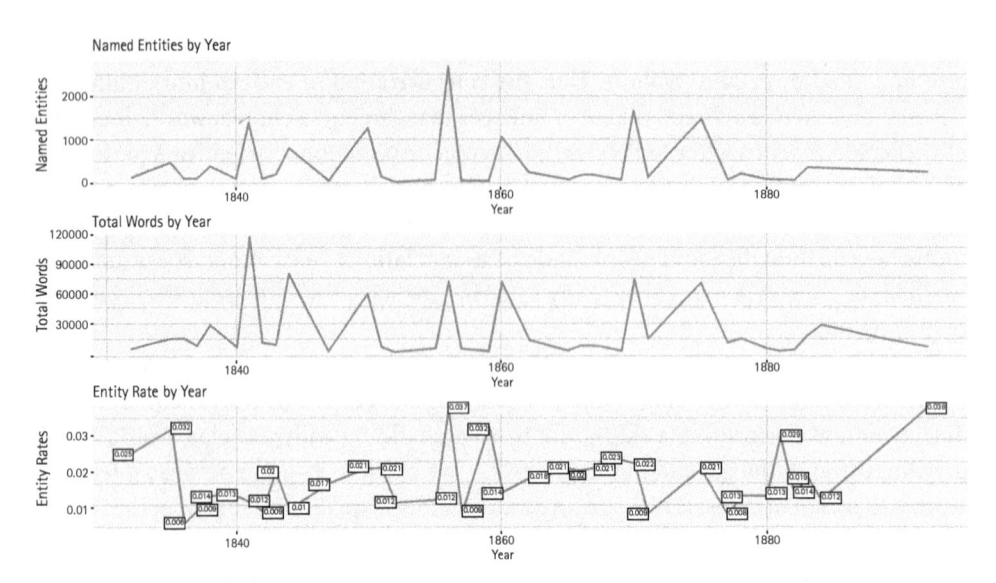

FIGURE 21.1: Total Entities per Year

The Conduct of Life (1860)—volumes that include some of Emerson's most canonical essays and that tend to be more abstract, philosophical, and (in a word) Transcendental compared to the rest of the corpus. Of the thirty texts that appear in the three essay collections, all but two–"History" (1841) and "Heroism" (1841)—fall below the corpus's median entity rate; and of the 126 total texts in the corpus, 8 of the 10 with the lowest entity rates come from the three essay collections. Similarly, *Nature* (1836) has a low entity rate: in championing originality, it largely avoids explicit references to other thinkers; and as one of Emerson's most conceptual texts, it seldom names specific places, organizations, or events.

Conversely, years in which Emerson published other books—1850 (*Representative Men*), 1870 (*Society and Solitude*), 1875 (*Letters and Social Aims*), and especially 1856 (*English Traits*)—show higher than average entity rates, which makes sense for volumes that include such entity-rich genres as scholarly articles, biographical sketches, travel writings, and occasional speeches. Other spikes in entity rates reflect single texts that dominate small samples, such as "Historical Discourse" in 1835 and "Europe and European Books" in 1843. In general, the entity rates of Emerson's corpus correspond with genre and accord with the sense of many scholars that *Nature* and Emerson's collected essays are among his most Transcendental texts. It is encouraging that our data reflect these characteristics and intriguing when specific texts violate expectations. For example, the seemingly "untranscendental" texts "Lecture on the Times" (1842), "Agriculture of Massachusetts" (1843), and "Farming" (1870) rank in the lowest quartile of entity rates, suggesting that Emerson treated even current events abstractly (at least in 1842) and that agriculture throughout his life was a largely theoretical pursuit (just ask Thoreau).

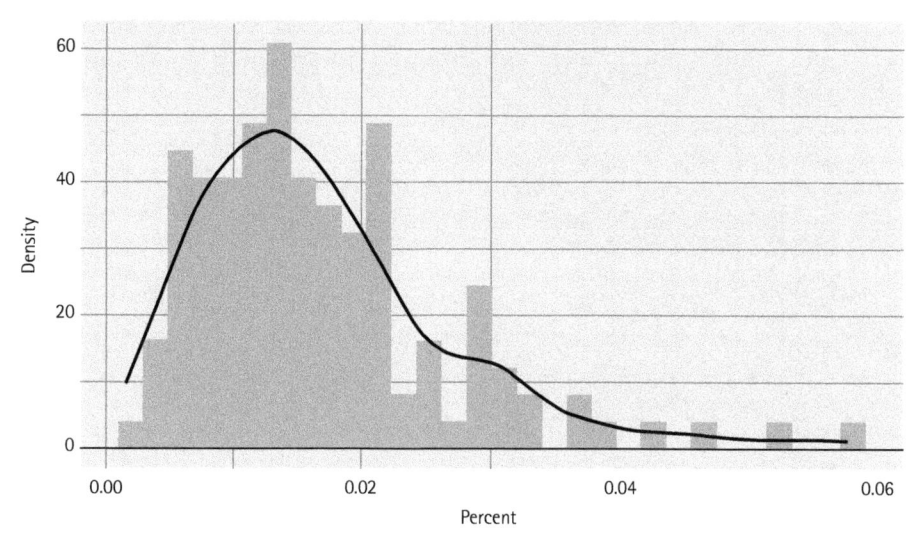

FIGURE 21.2: Histogram of Entity Percentages

Another useful measure of Emerson's entity rates describes variances within the corpus. Taking Emerson's texts individually, entity rates tend to fall within a narrow band from 0.6 per cent to 3.8 per cent. But in Figure 21.2, we can see that the distribution is right-skewed with a normal distribution shape giving way to a long tail.

This means that Emerson's texts generally refer to entities at a relatively consistent rate, except in a number of outlying texts in which entities are highly concentrated. Z-scores of the dataset further confirm this finding. Z-scores measure a data point's relationship to the mean value of a dataset such that a score of 1 would mean one standard deviation above the mean, while a score of -2 indicates two standard deviations below. Typically, a normal range for z-scores is 3 to -3, but the entity rates of Emerson's texts range between just over 4 to a little less than -1.5. The -1.5 score is relatively close to the mean because in English it is unlikely that one would write more than a few paragraphs with no named entities. However, the ceiling for Emerson's most entity-rich works such as "Europe and European Books," "Books," and "Walter Scott" (1871) rise well beyond the expected 3 to -3 standard deviations. Just as Emerson's canonical essays tend to have low entity rates, the most entity-rich texts in the corpus often go unread, perhaps because they are regarded as insufficiently transcendental.

Moving toward more specific analysis, we also surveyed Emerson's most mentioned entities, which gives some idea of the people, places, groups, and organizations that are most salient to his thought (Figure 21.3). We also calculated average links per entity type and found that, compared to the average link per entity (14.5), Person entities averaged 13.9 links and Geopolitical entities averaged 20.1 links. Such data provide a broad context for thinking about Emerson's networks of people and places.

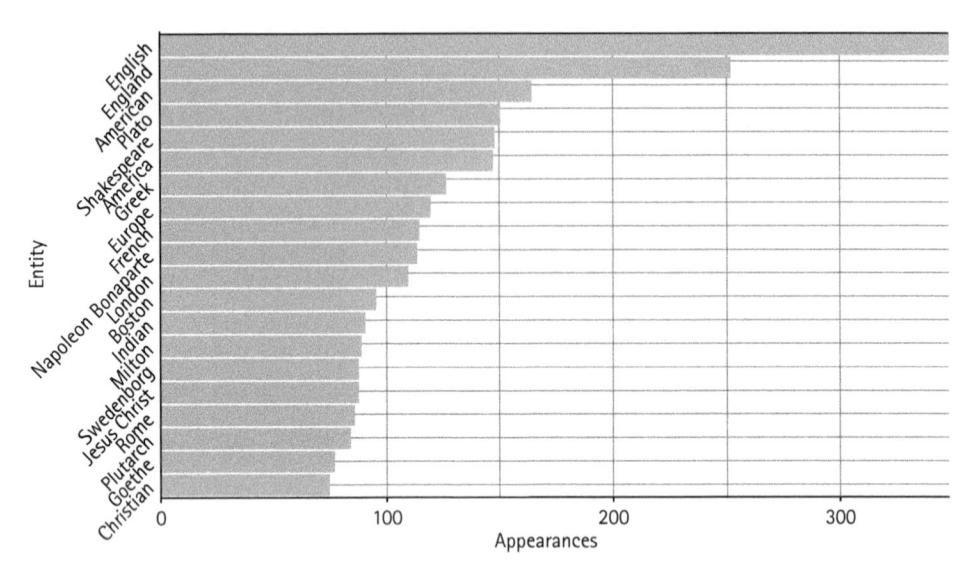

FIGURE 21.3: Top 20 Entities

Persons

In many ways, Emerson was not a people person. He valued his privacy, resented social obligations, and was accused by many who knew him best of being emotionally distant. His insistence in "Self-Reliance" that "I shun father and mother and wife and brother, when my genius calls me" is not hyperbole, nor is it a coincidence that word embedding shows that the top ten words in his corpus most likely to be collocated with "solitude" include "riches," "blessing," and "nobleness."[15] The three Emerson texts that refer least frequently to Person entities are "Friendship" (1841), "Love" (1841), and "Gifts" (1844)—topics that might be expected to invoke specific people and relationships but that Emerson treats in largely abstract ways. As Lawrence Buell and John T. Lysaker have argued, Emerson can idealize love and friendship so scrupulously that intimacy seems unsustainable to the point of impossibility.[16] Emerson acknowledges this moody isolation in "Experience" (1844): "Let us treat the men and women well: treat them as if they were real: perhaps they are."[17]

And yet Emerson's writings are chock full of people, who far outnumber any other entity type (Figure 21.4), inviting the question: How might we characterize his references to and, by extension, the influences of other people?

The following Person entities appear most frequently in the corpus:

1. Plato (147 times)
2. Shakespeare (145)
3. Napoleon (113)

4. Milton (88)
5. Jesus (87)
6. Swedenborg (86)
7. Goethe (77)
8. Plutarch (72)
9. Homer (59)
10. Bacon (57)
11. Newton (55)
12. Socrates (54)
13. Wordsworth (50)
14. Dante (46)
15. Hafiz (40)
16. Burke (37)
17. Carlyle (34)
18. Montaigne (33)
19. Michael Angelo (31)
20. Aristotle (30)

Representative Men is obviously a powerful determinant here, as are Emerson's essays on Milton, Plutarch, Carlyle, Michael Angelo, and Persian poetry. On the whole, the

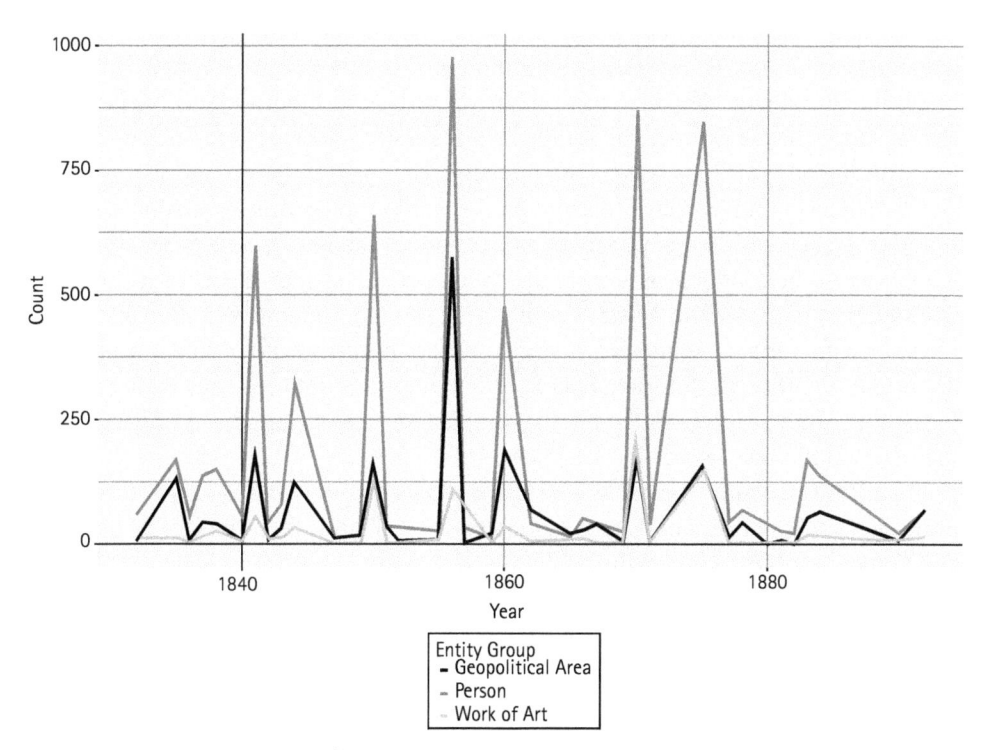

FIGURE 21.4: Most Mentioned Entities

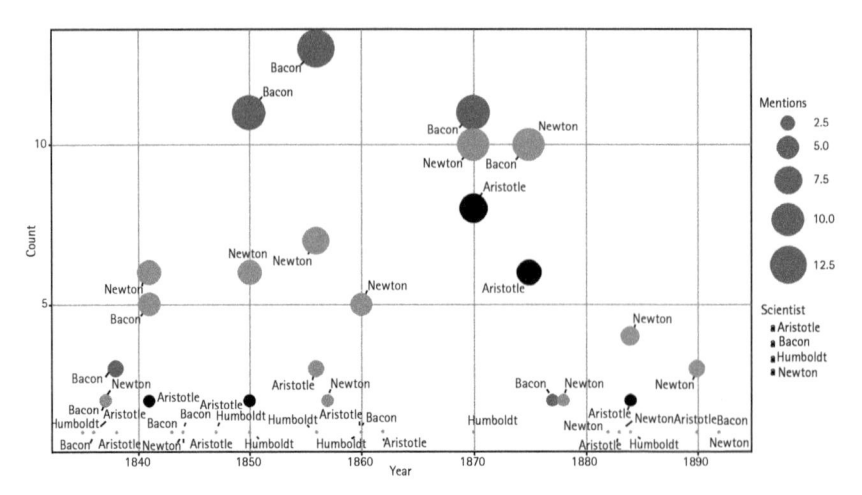

FIGURE 21.5: Mentions of Scientific Thinkers across the Corpus

list of top twenty people is dominated by canonical figures from literary and intellectual history, nearly all of them Western men. Despite his calls for originality and disdain for convention, Emerson's touchstones are, with a few exceptions, quite traditional for a college-educated person of his time with interests in the increasingly enshrined Romantic movement.

That said, the data reveal some surprising strains of influence. The conservative Edmund Burke is represented prominently in the corpus, though the MLA International Bibliography lists no scholarship with both Emerson and Burke as key terms, suggesting that Emerson studies has generally preferred to associate its subject with liberal traditions. Emerson's frequent references to Bacon and Newton may also be somewhat unexpected, despite recent work emphasizing Emerson's scientific interests. Tracking his references to scientific thinkers can indicate the proportions and tendencies of their influences, even if the data is complicated by the fact that Emerson admired Bacon's essays and Aristotle's ethics (Figure 21.5). Here we see Bacon occupying Emerson's attention most intensely in the middle of his career, while Newton is a more consistent presence. By contrast, Humboldt's influence is not especially evident in the data, particularly when compared to that of Aristotle, who occupies a significant place in Emerson's thought, especially near the end of his career.

Some less frequently mentioned Person entities are also worth noting. Of modern philosophers, Kant ranks highest at #43 (16 mentions) but is followed closely by Locke and Voltaire (15 each), suggesting that Emerson's investment in Transcendental idealism is not as exclusive or predominant as sometimes supposed. Indeed, references to Kant are concentrated in the first half of the corpus, whereas Locke has a more durable presence, suggesting (as does some of the data on scientists) a growing commitment to empiricism (Figure 21.6).

Locke and Kant (1836–1860)

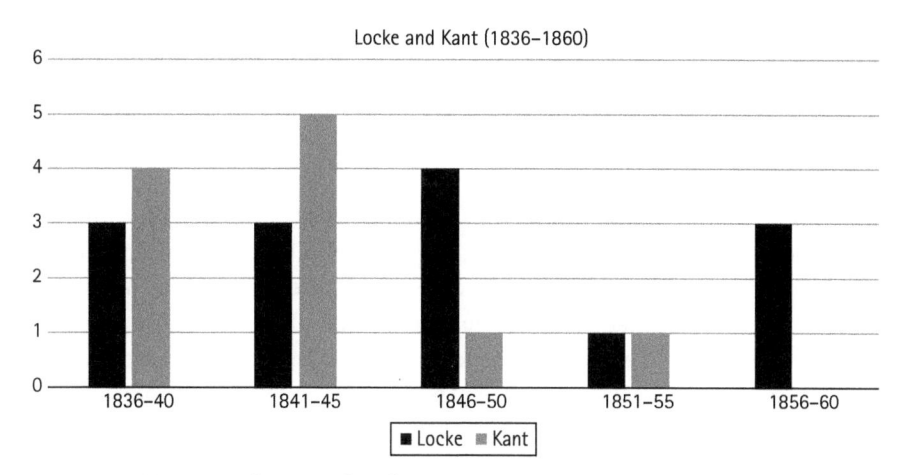

FIGURE 21.6: Mentions of Kant and Locke

Moving away from canonical thinkers, the women highest on the Person entity list are Mary (#121, 7 times), Queen Elizabeth (6), and Margaret Fuller (5), as well as Madame de Staël, George Sand, Jenny Lind, and Minerva (4 each). After Hafiz, the most cited non-Western figures are Confucius, Mahomet, and Saadi (tied at #60, 13 references each). The most frequently mentioned Americans are Daniel Webster at #25 (26 times), followed closely by Benjamin Franklin (24), George Washington (19), and John Brown (19). Of people with whom Emerson had more than a passing acquaintance, Carlyle appears most frequently, followed distantly by friends that Emerson eulogized in print—Thoreau (14 times) and Theodore Parker (9). These data indicate that as intensely as Emerson interacted with his circle of New England intellectuals, the Person entities cited most frequently in the corpus reflect his reading, not his social milieu. Borrowing from the title of Michael Colacurcio's recent book, people in Emerson's published writings function most often as "Other Minds."[18] This confirms Emerson's recognized dedication to literary and intellectual history, though quantifying his references can sharpen our sense of proportion. For example, Calvin appears in the corpus only four times, Hawthorne twice, and Jonathan Edwards and Descartes only once.

Individual references matter, though also revealing is how Emerson relates and configures the people that he mentions. Tracing such networks through conventional reading is difficult, for Emerson is an avid dropper of names whose many catalogs of people are not always organized by nationality, chronology, or obvious intellectual affinity. For instance, *Representative Men* eschews literary-historical logic when listing "Bacon, Milton, Tasso, [and] Cervantes" as great authors;[19] and even "Books," which offers a curated plan for reading, often strays from discernible order, as when Emerson includes the following list: "Froissart's Chronicles; Southey's Chronicle of the Cid;

Cervantes; Sully's Memoirs; Rabelais; Montaigne; Izaak Walton; Evelyn; Sir Thomas Browne; Aubrey; Sterne; Horace Walpole; Lord Clarendon; Doctor Johnson; Burke" (*CW* 2:101). Here and elsewhere, Emerson sometimes lists people in the way he lists the "lords of life" in "Experience": "I dare not assume to give their order, but I name them as I find them in my way."[20]

Yet if Emerson prefers impressionistic associations to taxonomic or linear logic, his references to people are often related—and unrelated—in meaningful ways. Quantitatively, links across Emerson's corpus indicate that he is not especially committed to listing thinkers in chronological order. Though he always mentions Homer before Chaucer, he mentions Chaucer before Shakespeare only 66 per cent of the time, Shakespeare before Milton 61 per cent of the time, and Milton before Wordsworth 54 per cent of the time. He is actually less likely to mention Socrates before Plato (38 per cent), perhaps a function of their relative importance in his mind, which can also explain why Shakespeare appears before his contemporary Francis Bacon 75 per cent of the time. Emerson's essay "History" shows that he typically understands the subject less as a diachronic chain of events and more as a series of anecdotes that exemplify universal truths. The ordering of Person entities in the corpus evince a similar outlook and—combined with Emerson's composition practices and essays on influence such as "Quotation and Originality" (1875)—suggests that he conceived of his voluminous reading less as a historical narrative in the manner of Hippolyte Taine and more as a playground or workshop of ideas.

All this said, Emerson's clustering of people is not random, and even anomalous links have explanatory value. Certain pairings of Person entities make good sense: Behmen's links with Swedenborg (10) far exceed his second most frequent pairings (with Fox and Socrates, 3 times each); Beaumont and Fletcher form the tenth highest pairing in the corpus, but both rank significantly lower on the list of individual references (#67 and #78, respectively). As we might expect, Socrates is paired most often with Plato (13 times), but his next highest pairings are with Shakespeare (8), Pythagoras (7), Jesus (6), and Swedenborg (4), while Aristotle, who has 106 total links to other people, is paired with Socrates only once.

Another curious figure is Hafiz, who appears 40 times in the corpus, has 89 total links to other people, but is not paired with any single figure more than twice. One possible explanation for this flat distribution is that Emerson, who in all cases makes some wild associations, had even less desire or capacity to locate Hafiz within a settled network of other people. In "Persian Poetry" (1875), Emerson vaguely compares Hafiz's verse to that of "Pindar, Anacreon, Horace and Burns," but he finds no place for Hafiz in his intellectual scaffolding, perhaps because Emerson sets "Oriental life and society ... in violent contrast with ... the Western nations."[21] In "Persian Poetry" and our linkage data, Hafiz—like some kind of cosmopolitan—has connections with a wide range of people but with none of them consistently.

So, too, with Napoleon, the third-most mentioned Person entity, whose links are also flatly distributed. Napoleon's most frequent connections are to Caesar (8 times), Nelson (6), and Shakespeare (6)—low numbers given his 286 total links. These links measure Person entities appearing in the same paragraph, while word embedding, which counts collocations with all words, further shows that Napoleon's connections with other people are low. Taking the top ten most frequently mentioned people in the corpus, and looking at the twenty words most likely to be collocated with each, we generally find an extremely high concentration of people: the top twenty words proximate to Shakespeare, Plato, Milton, Homer, and Bacon are all people (or in several cases, titles associated with people such as "Lord" or "St."), while for Swedenborg, Goethe, and Plutarch, people constitute 19 out of the 20 most proximate words. This reflects Emerson's habit of clustering intellectuals together, as if he is making seating arrangements for a banquet of great thinkers. Napoleon, however, does not always make the guest list, as only 12 of his 20 most proximate words refer to people, suggesting that Emerson does not include him in his pantheon of Other Minds and regards him instead as a "Man of the World."[22] Indeed, Napoleon's network of people is distinctive, including many links to military figures and political leaders who do not figure prominently in the corpus (for instance, of Napoleon's most frequent links, Caesar ranks #25 on the Person entity list and Nelson only #92).

But the greatest anomaly in terms of linkage data is Jesus, the fifth most mentioned person in the corpus. Jesus's most frequent links are to John and Paul (7 times each, a relatively low number given his 188 total links). And while even Napoleon's top twenty collocations include 12 people, Jesus's top twenty include "prayer," "almighty," "wisest," and "faithful" but not a single person. In a corpus where people tend to exist in dense networks of other people, Jesus often stands on his own, though why this is so requires some speculation. Despite his formal religious training, Emerson's publications seldom engage explicitly in theology or exegesis. "The Lord's Supper" (1832) is an obvious exception, but even if it mentions Jesus twenty-three times, and even if it has a high density of Person entities, the sermon—when compared to the rest of Emerson's corpus—has a very low percentage of unique entities (entities that are mentioned only once in the text). That is, Jesus is mentioned often in "The Lord's Supper" but exists in a relatively small cluster of people (almost entirely constituted by Matthew, Mark, Luke, and John, whom Emerson discusses in the same order that they appear in the New Testament). As Emerson's earliest work in the corpus and the only one written while he was still a minister, "The Lord's Supper" is a legible anomaly—more organized and tightly networked than the rest of Emerson's writings, and more likely to associate Jesus with a consistent group of people. Within the context of our corpus, "The Lord's Supper" is outweighed by texts that locate Jesus in flatter distribution patterns, reflecting what scholars have recognized as Emerson's growing tendencies toward pantheism and pluralism.

Another reason for the lack of people collocated with Jesus may be that Emerson does not think of Jesus as a person in the same way he thinks of figures like Plato, Shakespeare, Hafiz, or even Napoleon. In the "Divinity School Address" (1838), Emerson complains of "Historical Christianity": "It has dwelt, it dwells, with noxious exaggeration about the person of Jesus." It is not that Emerson did not think of Jesus as a man, for he also complains in the "Divinity School Address" that Jesus was "a true man" who has been turned into a "Mythus."[23] Jesus, however, remains distinct for Emerson as a figure who stands "alone in all history" and so remains incomparable to other people. To expect the linkage and word-embedding data on Jesus to look like those of other top-ranking Person entities may be, for the computational analyst, worse than infidelity. It might be a category error.

Geopolitical Entities

If Person entities help to map the proportions and networks of Emerson's intellectual sources, another type of entity encoded in the corpus generates more literal maps. Geopolitical Areas are a common categorization in NER processes, typically referring to politically established places in the world. They differ from another category, Locations, which usually refer to ostensibly nonincorporated places such as mountains and streams. Obviously, boundaries between the two categories can blur, but upon mapping Locations and Geopolitical Areas in the corpus, we found that the latter were more likely to correlate with geocoding entries. Geocoding is a process by which a place reference is algorithmically associated with data about the place, including latitude and longitude, essential information for creating maps. The process is not perfect. For instance, Emerson's references to "Paradise" are mapped to "Paradise, Texas"; and geocoding tends to be more accurate at larger scales insofar as continents, nations, and states are easier to identify than more specific locations that may not appear on coding indexes or can be taken to refer to multiple places (such as Cambridge, Massachusetts and Cambridge, England). By and large, however, the geocoding and mapping of Geopolitical Areas within the corpus were accurate enough to make some observations about the shape of Emerson's world.

Emerson has been variously viewed as a sage of Concord, a son of Massachusetts, a New England intellectual, an American scholar, and a citizen of the world. Franklin B. Sanborn, Carlos Baker, and Phyllis Cole have emphasized the rich influences of Emerson's immediate environs, while Octavius Frothingham, Van Wyck Brooks, and Buell place him in the broader intellectual culture of New England.[24] This regional focus takes on metonymic force under a paradigm that takes Emerson as a seminal figure of American literary history, even if F. O. Matthiessen and Perry Miller knew better than some of their followers that Emerson draws heavily on transatlantic traditions.[25] Subsequent scholarship from Robert Weisbuch, Paul Giles, and Wai Chee Dimock elaborates a more international Emerson and theorizes more capacious global frameworks.[26] But as with Emerson's listing of people, his many references to places are difficult to conceptualize using conventional reading practices, and so computational methods offer new ways to represent some geographic dimensions of his work.

A top-layer map of the Geopolitical Areas cited in Emerson's corpus indicate a preponderance of references to Europe (1369) and the United States (782), as compared to the rest of the world (159 total) (Figure 21.7).

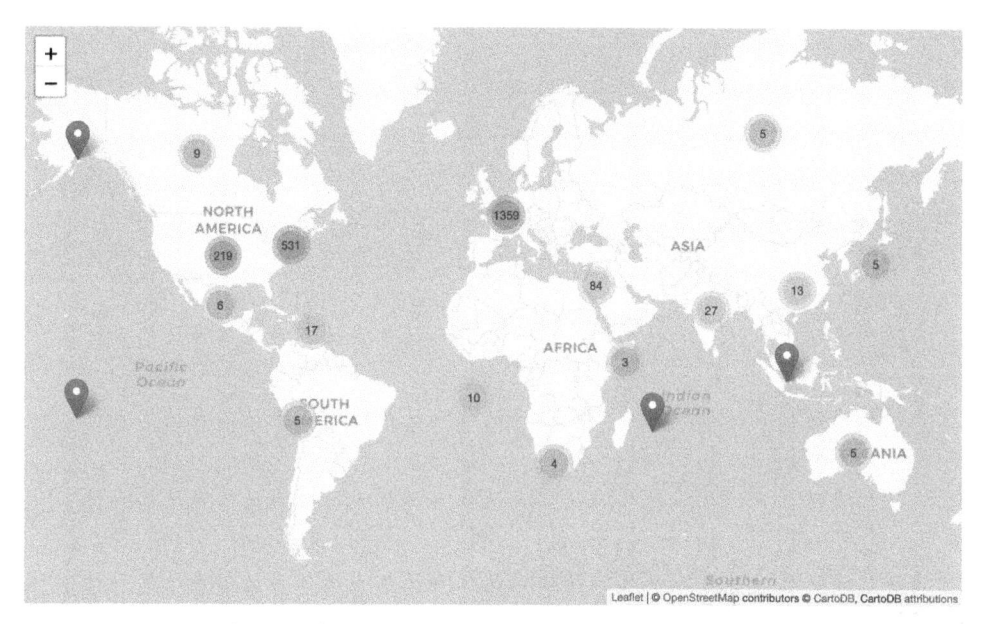

FIGURE 21.7: Distribution of Emerson's Geopolitical Mentions—Global (pins indicate a single reference)

While Emerson is certainly interested in global perspectives and events, and though in Transcendental moods, he feels "the currents of the Universal Being circulate through [him]," when it comes to naming Geopolitical Areas, he gravitates toward coordinates in the United States and Europe.[27]

Lower-level mappings of place names in the corpus show more granular concentrations of Emerson's references. Of Geopolitical Areas named within the United States, roughly 60 per cent are in the Northeast, 45 per cent are in New England, and 23 per cent are in the Greater Boston area (Figure 21.8).

The most frequently mentioned states are Massachusetts (59 times), California (18), Virginia (18), Kansas (16), and Maine (10) with "New York" appearing 46 times as either a city or a state. Clearly Emerson was most familiar with and felt allegiances to New England and Massachusetts, though the data also indicate additional foci. References to California typically involve either the Gold Rush or panoramas of the nation, while the high number of references to Virginia and Kansas point toward Emerson's engagement with the slavery crisis. Both states appear 9 times each in the handful of texts devoted primarily to slavery.[28] Moreover, word embedding shows that the top twenty collocated words with Kansas include "planter," "troops," "battles," and "freedman." Just as the slavery crisis in general and "Bleeding Kansas" in particular forced many Americans to think about far-off states, Emerson admits in "The Fugitive Slave Law" (1854): "Slavery in Virginia or Carolina was like Slavery in Africa or the Feejees to me" until the Compromise of 1850 revealed that chattel bondage "very seriously touches me."[29]

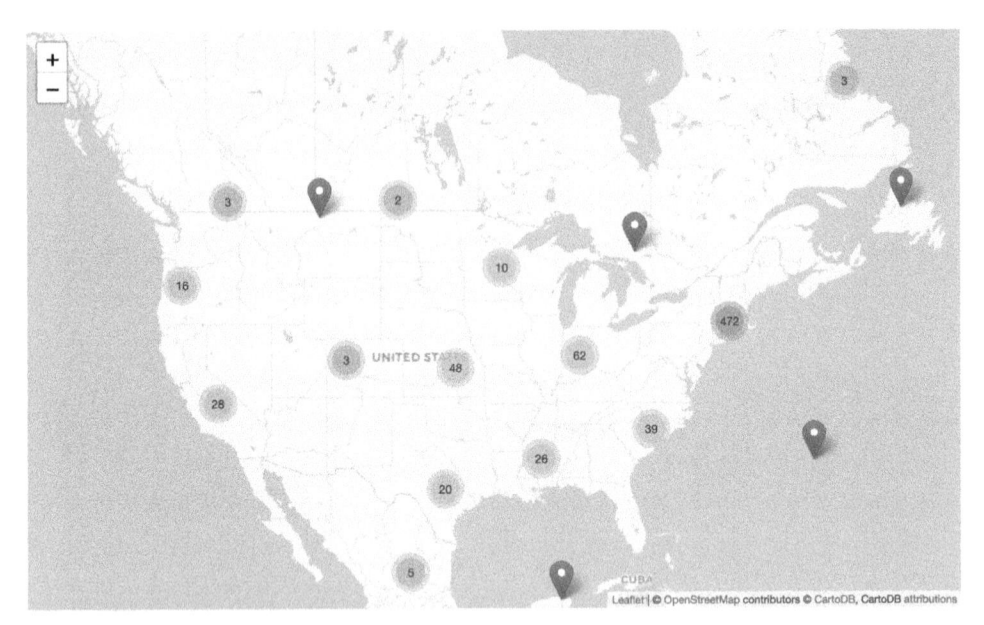

FIGURE 21.8: Distribution of Emerson's Geopolitical Mentions—US and Northeast (pins indicate a single reference)

As for US cities (omitting New York), Boston is mentioned 103 times, followed by Concord (50), Washington (23), New Orleans (9), Philadelphia (8), Baltimore (6), and Charleston (6). Such data can bolster the case for a more provincial Emerson, though it is worth noting that of the 50 times that Emerson mentions Concord, 32 come from "Historical Discourse," his history of the town. No text has a comparable concentration of references to Boston, which of all cities most consistently sits at the center of Emerson's America as it appears in his published works.

Students trained to think of Emerson as a national figure who scorns the courtly muses of Europe may be surprised by the corpus's high proportion of references to Geopolitical Areas in Europe (including Britain). At the level of nation, England leads the way with 252 citations, followed by France (67), Greece (42), Italy (39), Germany (26), Spain (21), and Scotland (18). These data make sense given the length of *English Traits*, Emerson's commitments to British thinkers and print markets, and what Elisa Tamarkin has discussed as the Anglophilia of many Americans of the time.[30] That France outranks Greece and Italy might seem to suggest that Emerson's interest in modern nations outweighs his passion for classical settings, though Rome, often used of course to denote the Roman Empire, appears 85 times in the corpus.

Ratios between national and smaller-scale Geopolitical Areas further indicate how Emerson maps Europe in his writings. He traveled widely in Italy in 1833 and lectured extensively in England and Scotland in 1847 and 1848. Accordingly, he names a range of English cities—London (105), Cambridge (20), Oxford (17), Liverpool (12), Manchester (9), Birmingham (6), and many more. He also mentions many Italian places in addition to Rome—Florence (15), Naples (13), Venice (7), Sicily (6), and so on. This pattern holds for Scotland but not for France, for while France is mentioned 67 times in the corpus, the only cities mentioned more than once are Paris (48) and Toulouse (twice). This reflects how Emerson's two trips to France prior to 1872 were limited to its capital city. Though Paris left some strong impressions on Emerson, most notably his visit to the Jardin des Plantes, his 1854 lecture "France, or Urbanity" (not included in the corpus) is characterized more by anecdotes and generalizations about French culture than by vivid and varied place descriptions. In the absence of wider, firsthand experiences, Paris often stands in for all of France.

Emerson's tendency toward geographic generalization is most pronounced for countries outside North America and Europe. Within this category, Emerson most frequently cites Egypt (33), India (24), Persia (10), China (9), Cuba (8), Jamaica (5), and Japan (5). Not only are such references sparse, the corpus seldom mentions smaller-scale Geopolitical Areas within these countries. Only two specific place names are cited in India (Calcutta and Delhi, once each) and Persia (Ispahan and Shiraz, once each). Havana is the only specific place mentioned in Cuba, and none are cited in Egypt, China, Jamaica, or Japan. By contrast, Canada is mentioned 9 times with 7 specific places in the country appearing a total of 10 times. Though the sample sizes are small, such data suggest that low frequencies of specific place names correlate with low levels of personal experience with, proximity to, and specific knowledge of certain countries.

All of which points toward Emerson's orientalism. The most prominent non-Western entity in the corpus is "Indian," which homographically refers to Emerson's interests in both South Asian philosophy and indigenous North Americans. But interest is not the same as understanding. In Nan Z. Da's words, Emerson often treats non-Western cultures with "cringe-inducing reductivism," as when he writes in "Persian Poetry": "Life in the East is fierce, short, hazardous, and in extremes.... The desert, the simoon, the mirage, the lion and the plague endanger it."[31] Word embedding suggests similar dynamics at a larger scale: the top twenty collocations for "Asia" include "colonies," "temples," and "legends," and for "Persia" include "villas," "crusades," "skull," and "musk." For Africa and South America, geographic references are too infrequent to suggest much beyond notional representations. Only 8 Geopolitical Areas in the corpus are in South America; and outside of Egypt, Africa has only 9 references (or 16, if one counts St. Helena, where Napoleon was imprisoned). That Emerson's writings focus on Europe and the United States is to be expected, but the patterns and proportions of Geopolitical entities show that, for all his global and Transcendental commitments, Emerson's sense of place is overwhelmingly Western.

People and Places

To synthesize the two previous sections, linkage data between Person and Geopolitical entities in the corpus reveal patterns in how Emerson spatially situates literary and intellectual history. Many high-frequency pairings associate people with predictable places: Shakespeare with England; Socrates with Athens; Michael Angelo with Florence and Rome. It also makes sense that worldly actors are most likely to be associated with the areas of their exploits: Alexander with Persia, Africa, and Greece; Columbus with America and Spain; Napoleon with Europe, Italy, Paris, France, Spain, and the Alps. Also broadly distributed, but for different reasons, are the Geopolitical links for two of Emerson's most frequently cited people. Plato is paired with England (6), Europe (5), America, Asia, France, and London (3 times each), Athens, Egypt, Germany, India, and New England (twice each), as well as 25 other locations (once each). As Emerson wrote of Plato, "Thinkers of all civilized nations are his posterity and are tinged with his mind."[32] Jesus's pairings are similarly widespread, suggesting a figure who is everywhere and nowhere at once; he is linked with Rome (3), Egypt (2), Europe (2), Jerusalem (2), and once each with 15 other locations from Africa to India to Panama to Persia. That 36 per cent of Plato's references are linked to a Geopolitical entity, compared to only 24 per cent for Jesus, suggests that Emerson thinks of Plato as a global figure and Jesus as more of a transcendent one.

Given Emerson's prominent role in narratives of American literary history, linkage data between American people and places may be of particular interest. When examining the Americans paired most frequently with Geopolitical entities, 67 per cent of George Washington's place links are in the United States, compared to 64 per cent for Thoreau, 65 per cent for Daniel Webster, and 100 per cent (34 out of 34) for John Brown. Given that only 33 per cent of place names in the corpus are in the United States, Emerson is thus especially likely to associate Americans with their home nation—a predictable pattern perhaps, but one that does not hold in other cases such as Napoleon, Goethe, Dante, and Burke (the last of whom is linked to English places only 19 per cent of the time as compared to 33 per cent for US locales). In Emerson's corpus, Americans seem more nation-bound than other frequently cited people. This makes sense in the case of Thoreau (whom Emerson described as "referring everything to the meridian of Concord"), as well as for Washington, Webster, and Brown (figures known primarily for their roles in domestic politics).[33] As an exception that helps indicate the rule, the more cosmopolitan Benjamin Franklin, among the top five most frequently mentioned Americans and the most likely of the group to be seen as a contributor to intellectual history, is only linked to Geopolitical entities four times, none of them in the United States. Taken together, the data suggest that Emerson associates Americans with national events more than the wide world of ideas, a broader tendency at a time when American culture was widely viewed as provincial, materialist, and practical. Just as Emerson sometimes complained that America, for all its promise, was an inhospitable place for Transcendentalism, our data suggest that Emerson often found his intellectual coordinates elsewhere.

There is more to be said about the entity data we have gathered, but this essay will end where it began—by thinking metacritically about what it might mean to study Emerson quantitatively. Empiricism does not lend itself to grand or tidy conclusions, which puts it at odds with Emerson's transcendental urge to reach for unity and synthesis. Yet Emerson's attentiveness to experience and open-ended experimentation can also incline him toward empiricism. In this sense, computational literary analysis comports with an Emersonian spirit, particularly when quantitative methods are practiced with appropriate skepticism. Modeling Emerson's corpus, tabulating entities and links, tracking word counts and collocations across time and texts—such data-driven efforts hardly settle questions about Emerson's influences, interests, and world views, but they offer new ways for evaluating old arguments and imagining original claims under a logic of interpretation, not proof. The process here has been dialectical (moving between explication and distant reading), collaborative (between an Emerson and digital humanities specialist), fallible (no interpretation or model is definitive), partial (there is, of course, much more to study beyond Emerson's people and places, and much more to explore within these domains), and experimental (no scholarship to our knowledge has studied Emerson's corpus quantitatively). As an experiment, we hope this essay opens new paths to understanding Emerson and helps to put us in what he calls a "right relation with magazines of facts."[34]

Notes

1. Ralph Waldo Emerson, *Essays and Lectures*, ed. Joel Porte (New York: Library of America, 1983), 281.
2. Lee Rust Brown, *The Emerson Museum: Practical Romanticism and the Pursuit of the Whole* (Cambridge, MA: Harvard University Press, 1997); Laura Dassow Walls, *Emerson's Life in Science: The Culture of Truth* (Ithaca: Cornell University Press, 2003).
3. Emerson, *Essays and Lectures*, 713.
4. George Kateb, *Emerson and Self-Reliance* (Thousand Oaks, CA: SAGE Publications, 1994) (democracy); Nell Irvin Painter, "Ralph Waldo Emerson's Saxons," *The Journal of American History* 95, no. 4 (March 2009): 977–85 (racism).
5. Lawrence Buell, *Emerson* (Cambridge, MA: Harvard University Press, 2003) (moral principles); Stanley Cavell, *Emerson's Transcendental Etudes*, ed. David Justin Hodge (Stanford: Stanford University Press, 2003), and Branka Arsić, *On Leaving: A Reading in Emerson* (Cambridge, MA: Harvard University Press, 2010) (antifoundational philosophy).
6. Lucius Adelno Sherman, *Analytics of Literature: A Manual for the Objective Study of English Prose and Poetry* (Boston: Ginn, 1893), 284, 298.
7. Donald Ross, Jr., "Emerson and Thoreau: A Comparison of Prose Styles," *Language and Style* 6 (1973): 185–95: 185.
8. Amy Earhart, "Emerson and the Digital Humanities," in *Approaches to Teaching the Works of Ralph Waldo Emerson*, ed. Mark C. Long and Sean Ross Meehan (New York: Modern Language Association of America, 2018), 164–68; Augusta Rohrbach, "Nineteenth-Century Literary History in a Web 2.0 World," in *Teaching with Digital Humanities: Tools and Methods for Nineteenth-Century American Literature*, ed. Jennifer Travis and Jessica DeSpain (Urbana: University of Illinois Press, 2018), 44–56; Eric Lease Morgan, "Some Automated Analysis of Ralph Waldo Emerson's Works," http://sites.nd.edu/emorgan/2015/06/automated-emerson/.
9. Christopher Hanlon, *Emerson's Memory Loss: Originality, Communality, and the Late Style* (Oxford: Oxford University Press, 2018).

10. OCR stands for Optical Character Recognition, the process by which computers interpret text or writing and convert it into machine-encoded text, enabling further analysis.
11. Links could be determined by various heuristics, such as appearing within the same sentences or within a sliding window of *x* sentences. The first, we felt, would be too small a window (especially considering Emerson's motile writing style) to quantify a connection; and the latter, though it may have yielded better results, would have been more computationally costly. We performed these processes with the Hugging Face machine learning tool utilizing the OntoNote model, which we chose because it provides a wide variety of entity-type tags that we could use to analyze Emerson's references in a categorical fashion.
12. Word embeddings generate "vectors" or coordinates for words in a particular word-space, with the coordinates representing the semantic similarity of words within that space. Coordinates are given in very large dimensional space (ours was 100 dimensions) and reduced to human-readable dimensions (2 or 3) by various processes of factor reduction (we used PCA or Principal Component Analysis). Vectors are usually generated through two primary methods, either skip-gram or CBOW (continuous bag of words).
13. Arsić, *On Leaving*, 9.
14. Ralph Waldo Emerson, *The Works of Ralph Waldo Emerson*, vol. 8, *Letters and Social Aims* (Boston: Fireside Edition, 1909), 15.
15. Emerson, *Essays and Lectures*, 262.
16. Lawrence Buell, "Transcendental Friendship: An Oxymoron?," in *Emerson and Thoreau: Figures of Friendship*, ed. John T. Lysaker and William Rossi (Bloomington: Indiana University Press, 2010), 17–32; John T. Lysaker, "On the Faces of Emersonian 'Friendship,'" in *Figures of Friendship*, 86–106.
17. Emerson, *Essays and Lectures*, 479.
18. Michael Colacurcio, *Emerson and Other Minds*, 2 vols. (Waco, TX: Baylor University Press, 2021).
19. Emerson, *Essays and Lectures*, 725.
20. Emerson, *Essays and Lectures*, 491.
21. Emerson, *Letters and Social Aims*, 232, 226.
22. Emerson, *Essays and Lectures*, 727.
23. Emerson, *Essays and Lectures*, 80–81.
24. Franklin B. Sanborn, *Emerson and His Friends in Concord* (Boston: New England Magazine, 1890); Carlos Baker, *Emerson among the Eccentrics: A Group Portrait* (New York: Penguin, 1997); Phyllis Cole, *Mary Moody Emerson and the Origins of Transcendentalism: A Family History* (Oxford: Oxford University Press, 1998); Octavius Frothingham, *Transcendentalism in New England* (New York: G. P. Putnam's Sons, 1876); Van Wyck Brooks, *The Flowering of New England, 1815–1865* (New York: E. P. Dutton, 1936); Lawrence Buell, *New England Literary Culture: From Revolution through Renaissance* (Cambridge: Cambridge University Press, 1986).
25. F. O. Matthiessen, *American Renaissance: Art and Expression in the Age of Emerson and Whitman* (London: Oxford University Press, 1941); Perry Miller, ed., *The Transcendentalists: An Anthology* (Cambridge, MA: Harvard University Press, 1950).
26. Robert Weisbuch, *Atlantic Double-Cross: American Literature and British Influence in the Age of Emerson* (Chicago: University of Chicago Press, 1989); Paul Giles, "Transnationalism and Classic American Literature," *PMLA* 118, no. 1 (2003): 62–77; Wai Chee Dimock, *Through Other Continents: American Literature across Deep Time* (Princeton, NJ: Princeton University Press, 2008).

27. Emerson, *Essays and Lectures*, 10.
28. These texts include "Emancipation in the British West Indies" (1844), "The Fugitive Slave Law" (1854), "The Assault Upon Mr. Sumner" (1856), "Speech on Affairs in Kansas" (1856), two speeches on John Brown (1859 and 1860), and "The Emancipation Proclamation" (1862).
29. Ralph Waldo Emerson, *The Works of Ralph Waldo Emerson*, vol. 11, *Miscellanies* (Boston: Fireside Edition, 1909), 215, 206.
30. Elisa Tamarkin, *Anglophilia: Deference, Devotion, and Antebellum America* (Chicago: University of Chicago Press, 2008).
31. Nan Z. Da, *Intransitive Encounter: Sino-U.S. Literatures and the Limits of Exchange* (New York: Columbia University Press, 2018), 70; Emerson, *Letters and Social Aims*, 226.
32. Emerson, *Essays and Lectures*, 633.
33. Emerson, *Lectures and Biographical Sketches*, 437.
34. Ralph Waldo Emerson, *The Works of Ralph Waldo Emerson*, vol. 7, *Society and Solitude* (Boston: Fireside Edition, 1909), 17.

CHAPTER 22

EMERSON'S UNORIGINALITY AND THE COMMONPLACE BOOKS OF MARY MOODY EMERSON AND MARGARET FULLER

NOELLE A. BAKER

> The foregoing generations beheld God and nature face to face; we, through their eyes. Why should not we also enjoy an original relation to the universe? Why should not we have a poetry and philosophy of insight and not of tradition...?
>
> Ralph Waldo Emerson, *Nature* (1836)[1]

THIS chapter considers the significance of the commonplace book as a genre, its gendered expressions, and the uses of unoriginality for Mary Moody Emerson (1774–1863) and Margaret Fuller (1810–1850), the aunt and friend, respectively, of Ralph Waldo Emerson. Distinguished by conversational gifts, intellectual aspiration, and firm rejection of gendered cultural restrictions, they figure essentially in the origins and development of Transcendentalism, as well as its female genealogies.[2] They are essential in understanding Waldo's development, and moreover, their commonplace books suggest the extent to which popular, conventional, and unoriginal genres shaped the movement.

Waldo demonstrated his esteem for both women when he commonplaced from and curated their manuscripts, producing composites Jerome J. McGann might refer to as "social texts"—meaning that in these instances Waldo's homage was a form of textual recovery amounting to an approximation of collaboration.[3] Waldo contributed to their commonplace books, kept his own, theorized the genre's proliferation in his 1840 *Dial* essay "New Poetry," and in paying tribute also altered both women's manuscripts—sometimes radically. These practices are noteworthy for a writer famously associated with originality even as they indicate the crucial types of influence Mary Emerson and Margaret Fuller exerted upon Waldo through their own commonplacing.

A series of questions concerning Mary Emerson and Margaret Fuller thus also concern Ralph Waldo Emerson. How did they interact with their commonplace books, comprised of quotations from their reading? How might their reading and writing practices inform fresh approaches to the cultural, literary, reformist, and spiritual movement later characterized as "the Newness"? How might their unpublished notebooks help us reassess the ostensible exceptionality of Transcendentalist experiments in friendship, conversation, and "*Verses of the Portfolio*" within the context of analogous reading and writing conventions?[4]

To explore these questions I will begin with an overview of commonplace books and their gendered variants, proposing that the unoriginal intertextuality and dispersal of agency found therein promote dialogic modalities, manuscript circulation, self-development, and kinship. Turning to Mary Emerson, I will suggest that computational analysis can unpack her intricate intertextuality. After examining the ways in which Fuller synthesized gendered commonplace book expressions to serve professional and interpersonal objectives, I conclude by considering Ralph Waldo Emerson in the framework of social-text editorial practices and his late career publication *Parnassus* (1874)—a poetry anthology that at first glance passes for what Nikhil Bilwakesh has called "a definitively 'unoriginal' work by a writer famous for instigations to originality."[5] Reading this text through the lens of the sentimental friendship album exposes the revelatory ways in which *Parnassus* overlaps with Mary Emerson and Margaret Fuller's methods of excerpting from their reading—or "commonplacing."

Oddly enough, in advancing tributes to both women, Waldo anticipated the editorial labors of his children and literary executor, James Elliot Cabot, who published his late works with increasingly little assistance from Waldo. As Christopher Hanlon argues in *Emerson's Memory Loss*, these collaboratively authored publications articulate a model of collective intellection, affect, and memory, a perspective from which Hanlon reads "backwards" into Emerson's earlier writings, developing a compelling case for reconsidering the ejection of Emerson's late publications from the Emersonian canon.[6] In his analysis of Emerson's "late style," Hanlon illustrates the "provisional and unavoidably faulty nature of all curations."[7] Moreover, other scholarship similarly reconfigures our understanding of the ways in which antebellum literary culture shaped Transcendentalist reading, writing, and editorial practices. Claudia Stokes suggests that in publications such as "The American Scholar" and *Nature* Waldo represents a relatively anomalous voice in calling for a break with European literary culture; more to the point, antebellum literary critics and readers prized emulation and European tradition. Similarly, Fuller (and Poe) figured as the rare literary critics deriding European imitation. "Unoriginality used to be a sound career move," Stokes observes in her trenchant analysis of Longfellow's self-conscious cultivation of antiquarian-style verse.

Conversely, prior to the late nineteenth century "originality ... connoted irregularity, sensationalism, and vulgarity" and elicited rank "skepticism and distaste."[8] Just as Stokes adds insight into contemporaries' critiques of the Newness, the group's reliance on unoriginality complicates our estimation of their textual productions.

Commonplace Books and Their Gendered Expressions

An exceptionally old and fluid genre, since antiquity the commonplace book had offered a means of professional advancement and societal mobility for (largely) male rhetoricians, statesmen, authors, and ministers. Such men copied passages from source texts to enhance their publications, speeches, and sermons.[9] By the eighteenth century, users augmented the efficacy of commonplace books as reference works by indexing and ordering their transcriptions under subject headings according to John Locke's prescription, such that commonplace books resembled a database, or—in Ralph Waldo Emerson's mature assessment—a "Savings Bank."

Waldo's reading and writing practices were not always so professional. In his early "Wide World" journals Waldo spun out whimsical drawings and creative mythologies in verse and prose. Similarly, during his courtship of the terminally ill, teenage Ellen Louisa Tucker (1811–1831), the smitten Waldo—who at age twenty-five became for the couple her "Grandpa" to his "Ellinelli"—penned love-note quotations in her friendship album. Waldo's earnest contributions to a conventional feminine genre likely derived from the magic of his three-year union with an ephemeral and charming poet-partner who styled herself "Lady Penseroso" and "Lady Frolick," depending upon her mood.[10] But after Ellen's death and Waldo's gradual turn from minister to public intellectual and lecturer, his journaling aligned with the male-gendered, professional generic tradition, especially as he began to arrange his journals "in alphabetical order, to buy rather than to make them, to choose books of relatively uniform size for his records, and to increase his somewhat sporadic indexing into a major activity," as Alfred R. Ferguson documents (*JMN* 4:249). In 1833, Waldo marked this shift in his reading and writing practices explicitly. "This Book is my Savings Bank," he declares. "I grow richer because I have somewhere to deposit my earnings; and fractions are worth more to me because corresponding fractions are waiting here that shall be made integers by their additions" (*JMN* 4:249, 250–51). Waldo's analogy was hardly unique; instead, it underscores the financial and professional viability the male commonplace tradition proffered implicitly. In his *Index Rerum: or Index of Subjects; Intended as a Manual to Aid the Student and the Professional Man, in Preparing Himself for Usefulness* (1835), the Reverend John Todd also evidences the notion that the commonplace book "equates material 'saving' with the collection of knowledge."[11]

By the nineteenth century this male-gendered genre figured within a spectrum of evolving, related, and coexisting genres in America. Ronald J. and Mary Saracino

Zboray detail the ways in which an account book or diary "could easily morph into a scrapbook or a scrapbook into a commonplace book," revealing a "common transgression or disregard of form or genre."[12] Across this continuum men and women put unoriginal material to new purposes, but female-gendered mutations, such as the popular and conventional sentimental friendship album, relied on and enriched dialogic social networks, rather than professionally-oriented public works. In a related manner, after moving to Philadelphia in 1838 to become the editor of the Quaker antislavery paper the *Pennsylvania Freeman*, John Greenleaf Whittier joined a collective of male and female Quaker activists and poets for whom the circulation of single poems and manuscript books of verse and illustrations was collaborative and centered on "acts of reading, transcribing, circulating and giving poems." Many of these poems were copied into wider circles' commonplace books, and the combined sets of reading and writing conventions establish the numerous ways in which creative "*exchanges of poems* literally brought people together*" in friendship and reform—and thereby uniting gendered generic traditions in a manner Fuller would also pursue.[13] Indeed, in Michael C. Cohen's estimation the vast majority of antebellum poetry was unpublished and resided in such albums. "Poetry albums," Cohen remarks, "inculcated a kind of writing predicated on rereading and remembrance, where secondariness and not originality made poems valuable for giver and receiver."[14] Such exchanges thrived within a "gift economy"[15] in several settings for antebellum practitioners. Although men such as Whittier and academy graduates participated in these collectives, unmarried women and schoolgirls were the most common keepers of American friendship albums, a genre that originated in sixteenth-century Germany; in them, individuals transcribed verse quotations and original verse, produced botanical drawings, laid in pressed leaves of flowers and plants, and pasted etchings on their pages, frequently adding signatures.[16]

Despite their divergences, both gendered genres decenter the model of single-author agency upon which canon building and modern textual scholarship have relied. Reflecting forms of collaborative authorship and dispersal of agency, commonplace books and their variants also generate a dialogic modality that synchronized well with the oral and written conversation in which Fuller and Mary Emerson excelled, although they experimented with genre and gender distinctively. Fuller's education rendered her more conversant with the male-gendered commonplace book, but she also explored its popular feminine variants, whereas the self-taught Mary Emerson reworked the male tradition—knowingly or unconsciously—to suit her goals as a writer engaging with public sphere discourse.

Both women contributed to Waldo Emerson's awareness of the significance of unpublished writings. Positing an increasing pace in Americans' commitment to letter writing, diary keeping, versifying, and commonplacing in "New Poetry," Waldo attributes this seemingly fresh abundance to "democratical" "tendencies of the time," in which public discourse becomes the right of all, rather than the sole purview of ministers or statesmen. "Every child has been taught the tongues," he exults, while also suggesting that "each person, who is moved to address any public assembly, will speak from the floor."[17] Waldo discloses that "a friend" (likely Fuller) had intensified his appreciation of such portfolio verses by placing examples in his hands.[18] After meeting Fuller in 1836, Waldo was enchanted with "letters, poems, journal entries, critical essays, prints, and books and periodicals" that Fuller circulated in "pacquets" from, in his words, a "covenanted" circle of friends who theorized platonic and erotic love, intimacy, marriage, and friendship—among them Emerson, Caroline Sturgis, Samuel Gray Ward, Anna Hazard Barker, and Ellery Channing.[19]

Ironically, in assembling the Fuller *Memoirs*, Waldo and co-editors William Henry Channing and James Freeman Clarke performed an unfortunate reverberation of the ways in which Fuller disarticulated and combined unpublished and multi-generic writings for her captivating pacquets. As Fuller's manuscripts testify in various repositories, homage and curation wreaked havoc on her papers, not only rendering her journals as incoherent shards but also generating multi-generic misrepresentations, in which, for example, a transcription of Fuller's commonplacing in another hand with accompanying commentary from the *Memoirs* is pasted onto an authentic journal fragment and defaced with inked out lines and substituted words (see Figure 22.1). Such textual splinters and malformations are all that remain for readers who seek insight into Fuller's extant journals—a lamentable reality that underscores Jerome M. McGann's contention that textual scholarship is a foundational component of literary interpretation.[20]

Moreover, and as Phyllis Cole demonstrates, dating from his college years, Waldo mined Mary's "Almanack" commonplace books to inform his themes, sermons, and publications. Surfacing a financial metaphor exemplifying professional commonplacing while pleading for Mary's Almanacks in 1827, Waldo confessed, "I grow more avaricious of this kind of property like other misers with age, and like expecting heirs would be glad to put my fingers into the chest of 'old almanacks' before they are a legacy." Of his entreaty Cole remarks dryly, "This request came simultaneously with his critique of a minister who was 'all of clay & not of tuneable metal,' who plagiarized from the common stock of knowledge instead of creating anew."[21]

Mary and Waldo Emerson's manuscript exchanges inhabited a more mutually productive bent suggestive of the gift economy as they traded fictionalized letters to and from Plato, extracted commonplaces from Coleridge in her Almanack, and—less so—when Waldo produced with son Edward three volumes of Almanack extracts, some of which informed his late lecture, "Amita," and the subsequent essay "Mary Moody Emerson," a social text coauthored by Mary, Waldo, his children, and Cabot.[22] Whereas this curation wrought less damage upon the Almanacks than Waldo's interventions in Fuller's papers, it produced gaps in her manuscripts. Moreover, as much as Waldo's extracts can supply text that is missing today in the heavily damaged Almanacks and offer dating that Mary did not furnish, his curation also misrepresents her content. In generating word clouds from Waldo's 1821 Almanack excerpts and from Mary's 1821 Almanack, one finds that the most prominent substantive word is "life" in Waldo's anthology; in Mary's Almanack, it's "nature."

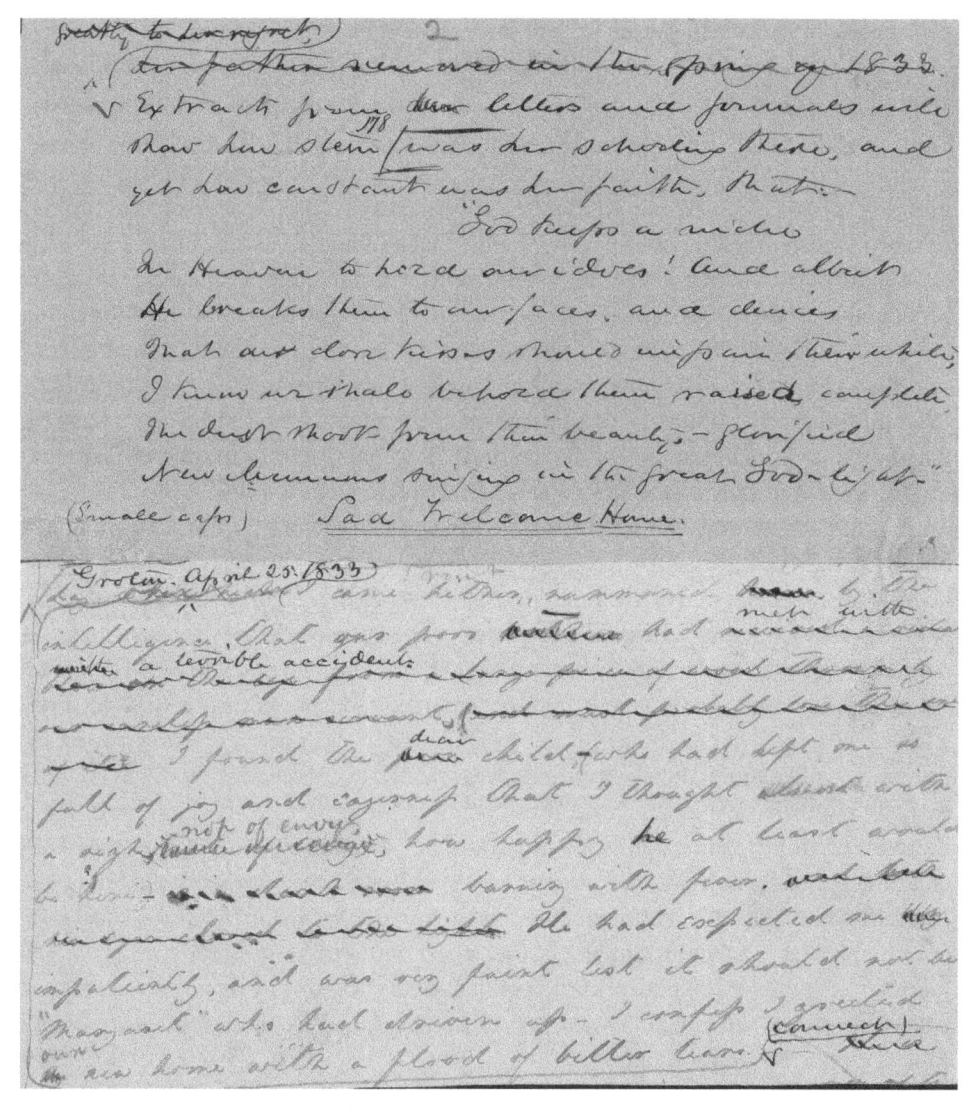

FIGURE 22.1: Assembled page for the Fuller Memoirs. MS Am 1086 (55), Houghton Library, Harvard University

Mary Moody Emerson, Intertextual Gestures, and Computational Analysis

Although Mary Emerson published essays early and late in life, her Almanacks (ca. 1804–1858) represent her zenith as a writer. Long regarded as an originating figure in Transcendentalist studies, Emerson and her complex intertextual expressions merit further study. Descending from generations of New England ministers, Emerson laid claim to that heritage in one of the few ways possible for an early American, self-educated woman. "Old maids may realize the publick spirit of Plato's republic," she pronounced in 1821: "no female attachment."[23] Renouncing wedlock and maternity, Emerson read voraciously, refused marriage proposals, and as a single woman cherished her right to own property in Waterford, Maine, where she established a literal and metaphorical room of her own to foster reading, writing, and intellectual growth. Well known to her nephew's contemporaries as a formidable thinker and conversationalist, after the death of Waldo Emerson, they also recognized his intellectual debt to his aunt, which one anonymous biographer described as their "remarkably similar" "mode of thought and expression." For others Mary Emerson embodied Transcendentalist aspiration. She was to William Channing Gannett "an imperious, glowing soul," a woman "who transcendentalized the fiery faith into a poetic worship of the infinite."[24] Resonating with vibrant intertextuality, the Almanacks display this accomplishment, fifty years in the making.

Spanning over one thousand pages, Emerson's Almanacks are commonplace books that also comprise spiritual and philosophical diaries, poetry, original essays, genealogies, letters, prayers, commemorative parcels, graphic texts, and a booklet that conflates and reimagines the generic features of the horoscope, classical epic, and dramatic dialogue. They do not, however, resemble the discursive database her nephew would describe as his savings bank. Instead, Emerson repurposes, distills, and converses with the authors of her reading; moreover, on singular occasions she does so in a graphic fashion.[25] Unlike professional commonplaces selected to enhance later work, Almanack extracts are their own desired end product, an experience of reading and writing in themselves. In fact, Emerson rarely called out her source texts and only occasionally cited the names of authors she was reading. In the latter case, typically she addressed them directly. Likewise, although Emerson regularly circulated Almanack leaves to enrich epistolary conversations, she seldom composed them in order to support, remember, or honor social networking and affectionate bonding in verse, in the feminine friendship album style. Waldo and his brother Charles were the atypical recipients of Mary's version of the gift economy.[26]

In her Almanacks commonplacing emerges as a creative act distinguished by "intertextual gestures"—including but not restricted to allusion, misquotation, and paraphrase—that may alter the meaning of her source.[27] It must be said, however, that when Emerson "re-author[ed]" an extract she mirrored related transatlantic reading and writing conventions; in their friendship albums, for instance, British women also played with authorial agency: retitling poems, selecting only the commonplacer's favorite verses, or providing alternate wording—sometimes producing variations that "radically alter the meaning of the poem."[28] Margaret Fuller's verse extracts also manifest these characteristics. In one example from her journal "S. M. Fuller's Bouquet," after commonplacing from the poet George Herbert's "Employment," Fuller notes, "I have only taken the best stanzas of this poem"; she frequently extracted a few verse lines, affixing her own title.

In our digital edition of the Almanacks, published in *Women Writers Online* (*WWO*), Sandra Harbert Petrulionis and I reconstruct the text's chronology and pagination and restore missing words, sentences, and larger blocks of text. The Almanacks exhibit extensive damage and disorder due to their circulation and to the 1872 fire that ravaged "Bush," Waldo's home, but transcriptions from Waldo Emerson and George Tolman enable our textual remediation. Annotations also provide Mary Emerson's sources in full for readers to compare against Emerson's commonplaces from them; nevertheless, the intricacies of such intertextual gestures remain formidable. The affordances of computational analysis can render these references more legible, however, and our Women Writers Project (WWP) collaborators have designed an open-access visualization interface that enriches such examinations, in concert with distant and close reading. Based upon code by Sarah Campbell and Zheng-yan Yu, "Intertextual References in the Almanacks of Mary Moody Emerson: Visualization for Close and Distant Reading" expresses both subtle and complex information concerning Emerson's intertextuality (see Figure 22.2).[29] The interface's data is extracted from the markup of annotations identifying her Almanack references, following the Guidelines of the Text Encoding Initiative (TEI). Aided by keyword searching, the interface not only offers accessible ways of engaging with the intellectual content of the Almanacks, but also entices readers to experience visually and then experiment with manuscripts whose disorder, extraordinary length, recursive structures, noncanonical genres, and linguistic and intellectual density might otherwise prove impenetrable.

Exercising distant and close reading, interface users can interpret the ways in which Emerson experiments with intertextuality by decade, genre, or reference—or by some

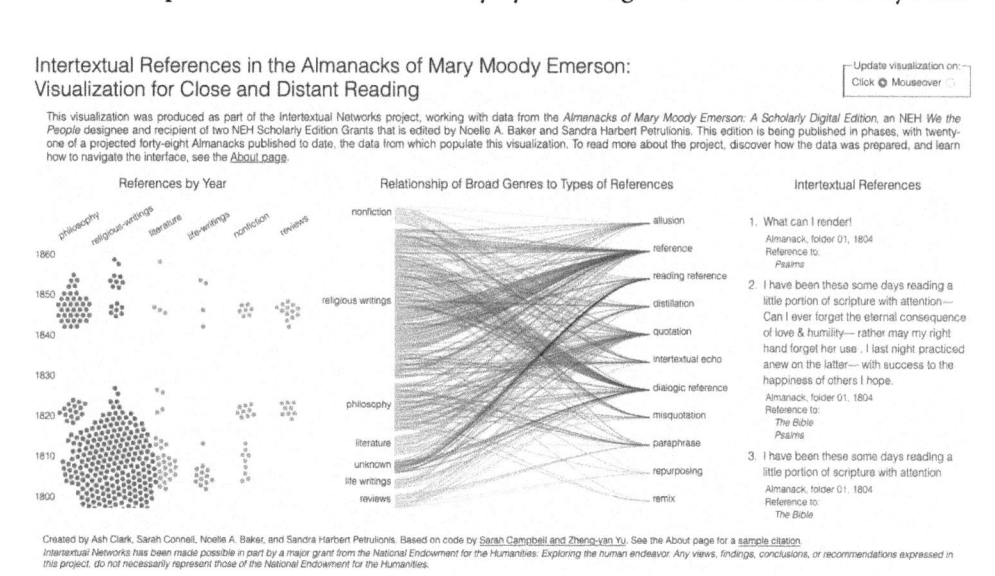

FIGURE 22.2: "Intertextual References in the Almanacks of Mary Moody Emerson: Visualization for Close and Distant Reading [1]." Northeastern University Women Writers Project. https://wwp.northeastern.edu/lab/emerson-networks/index.html

combination of these categories. For example, readers can filter their search by choosing the "repurposing" intertextual gesture, a selection that alters the visualization such that individual commonplace "bubbles" brighten within their decade and are identified by genre in panel one. In panel two the filter reveals that Emerson repurposed texts of religious writings, nonfiction, philosophy, and reviews. The third panel exhibits the commonplaces that reflect this repurposing, including one from Emerson's "folder 32" Almanack, nomenclature derived from Houghton Library cataloguing (see Figure 22.3). This Almanack passage finds Emerson commonplacing from a review published in the *Edinburgh Review*, "Art. III.—Six Discourses Delivered before the Royal Society" (1827). After turning to folder 32 in *WWO*, readers can examine the editors' introduction to this Almanack for context before analyzing this intertextual gesture.

As the editors' introduction elaborates more fully, folder 32 is an Almanack composed between December 1846 and March 1847 while Emerson was residing at "Elm Vale," her Maine property. Only sporadically dated and damaged by fire, water, and mildew, this Almanack is missing text on every page, producing fraught pagination and chronology. However, Emerson's correspondence yields significant information about her selection criteria for commonplacing during these months. These letters enumerate the considerable personal challenges she was facing that winter—the details of which scarcely emerge in folder 32. In addition to struggling with financial and legal setbacks based upon relatives' competing claims to the ownership of Elm Vale, Emerson was debilitated by an attack of the chronic erysipelas she often endured. In this case she suffered from lesions covering her face and one eye with painful swelling, from insomnia and nightmares induced by her abolitionist concerns regarding "the sufferings of slavery," and from compounded psychological distress that caused her to question her sanity.[30]

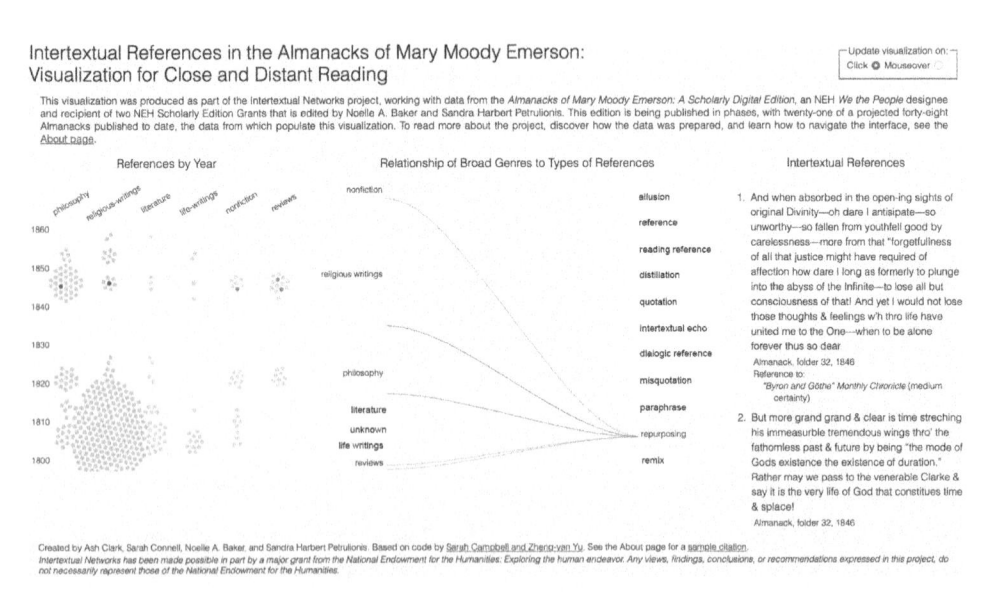

FIGURE 22.3: "Intertextual References in the Almanacks of Mary Moody Emerson: Visualization for Close and Distant Reading [2]." Northeastern University Women Writers Project. https://wwp.northeastern.edu/lab/emerson-networks/index.html

This correspondence also discloses that Emerson's commonplacing fails to reflect the entirety of her reading. For instance, letters document that Mary received and returned books from Waldo's library via Elizabeth Palmer Peabody's Boston bookshop—including Waldo's newest publication, *Poems* (1846). "I can't get interested in this Poet. the little I've looked over," she confessed to Lidian Emerson privately. Conversely, other missives exhibit Emerson's praise for George Sand's feminist novel *Consuela* (1842) and dismissive estimation of Nathaniel Hawthorne's *Mosses from an Old Manse* (1846). Emerson chose not to excerpt these three texts but instead concentrated upon Johann Gottlieb Fichte, Samuel Clarke, Dugald Stewart, Baruch Spinoza, Thomas Brown, Sir Humphrey Davy, Ralph Cudworth, Lord Byron, William Ellery Channing, Edward Young, William Wordsworth, and Thomas Taylor's translations of Plotinus, demonstrating her preference for selecting works of philosophy, science, and verse (excepting Waldo's) at this time.[31]

Following up on a previous consideration of the relationship between divinity, time, and space in this Almanack, in a late March 1847 entry Emerson commonplaced from a speech by Sir Humphrey Davy published in the *Edinburgh Review*. As president of the Royal Society of London for Improving Natural Knowledge, Davy delivered this address when awarding the society's Royal Medal to British mathematician James Ivory. A close reading of the Almanack and of the editors' reproduction of Davy's original speech in *WWO* indicates that although Emerson recognized Davy's debt to the writings of Samuel Taylor Coleridge, she disagreed with the ways that Davy applied Coleridge's terminology. As a result, Emerson repurposed his text to align with her thinking—and with her preceding discussion of divinity, time, and planetary space.

At the heart of her argument with Davy is Emerson's conception of Coleridge's distinction between "reason"—the intuiting of universal, higher truths—and "understanding," cognitive analysis. As her editorializing and intertextual gestures specify, Emerson believed that Davy mistakes understanding for reason and found his estimation of the potency and artifacts of human intellect insufficiently cognizant of what was—to her—the true source of Coleridgean reason, divine authority. In truth, Davy was indebted to Coleridge's characterization of reason and understanding—and to Coleridge's scientific methods, which "comprehended nature by replacing the creative mind of God with the creative mind of man," as Laura Dassow Walls observes.[32] Davy's similar belief in the human mind's inventive power undergirded the celebration of human ambition and achievement that Emerson would dilute or eliminate from her commonplacing from Davy's oration.

Emerson cherry-picked and recontextualized discrete sections of the address to enable them to orchestrate with her earlier Almanack entry and then rejected Davy's terminology; further, she deleted his preamble, in which Davy announces that "the nature of mathematical science or its results" ranks among "the noblest of human pursuit and ambition." Analogous to her elimination of the preamble, Emerson tinkered further with authorial intention by substituting "&ccc" for Davy's discussion of the mechanistic "results" of "mathematical science" on the earth—such as the development of new technologies that drive industry and transportation. Emerson also obscured Davy's discussion of the ways in which "data" enables aspiring humanity to gauge the laws of planetary motion and their relation to time. A final, subtle revision undercut both human and authorial agency. Emerson delivered a token nod to Davy's intentionality by transcribing Davy's "monuements" of the earth—an acknowledgment of some human accomplishment. That said, Davy's actual text reads "monuments of its power," a phrase in which "its" represents the "intellectual creation" fueled by the human mind. This revision further attenuated Davy's belief that the scientific method recognizes in humanity an intellectual creativity equal to that of divinity. What remains in the Almanack commonplace is reconfigured and abbreviated source material that illustrates Emerson's spiritual view and reaffirms Hanlon's insights into curation's inherent fissures:

> The nature of magnitudes is gradually formed into an instrument of pure reason, (I should say understanding) of the most refined kind. Applying to & illustrating all the phenomena of nature & art, & embracing the whole system of the visible universe &ccc leaving the earth filled with its monuements it ascends to the stars & measures & weighs the sun & planets." Now it does nothing with the "pure reason which discovers the nature of the soul and mounts to its divine Author ... yet the mind prepared by it for high induction should value it—[33]

Similar to her revisions of this address, Emerson argued with Davy by quibbling with his theories and their ability to encompass spirit and science. She broke into her quotation of Davy's remnants to do so. "(I should say understanding)," she harrumphs initially after quoting Davy's "instrument of pure reason." Further, she concluded the extract by contending that Davy "does nothing" with her own view of Coleridgean " 'pure reason," an intuition that should disclose "the nature" of the human soul and enable it to ascend "to its divine Author." The "mind prepared by" reason "should value it," she scolds. In the end, although Emerson was sympathetic to Coleridge's philosophy and fascinated by scientific discoveries, her approach to science skews towards spirituality—Western or Eastern scripture. In the process, she recast unoriginal material and wrested agency from the authors of her reading.[34]

Although Emerson enjoyed the privilege of home ownership and self-cultivation, she also signals the ways in which a female autodidact could dispute male-dominated, public-sphere discourse with nothing more than borrowed books, paper scraps, and pens. Further, in addition to displaying extraordinary creativity, the Almanacks' intertextual gestures emphasize that Emerson commonplaced in order to reread her unoriginal curations, rather than the works of great men. Mary Moody Emerson didn't require a database. She wanted conversation with the wider world.

Margaret Fuller: Synthesizing Gender-Based Genres

Over thirty years younger than Mary Emerson and the eldest child of an exacting father keen to educate an intelligent daughter, Margaret Fuller underwent a rigorous course of study equivalent to that of nineteenth-century men; even as a schoolgirl she gained a reputation for erudition. Armed with this atypical instruction and natural talent, Fuller became the first woman granted reading privileges at Harvard. Exceptionally charismatic to men and women, gifted in languages and in conversational skills, and distinguished by a searching ambition that a self-educated woman of Emerson's generation could not hope to bring to fruition, Fuller was accepted as an equal among the Newness's male leaders.

After teaching in several settings, Fuller gained influence as an author, journalist and critic, editor of the *Dial: A Magazine for Literature, Philosophy, and Religion* (1840–1844), translator of the writings of Goethe and German Romantics, and feminist leader of a Boston "Conversation" series intended primarily for women's personal and intellectual development (1839–1844) for which she was remunerated at the level of male lecturers. Having achieved acclaim within New England Transcendentalist circles, in 1844 Fuller moved to New York at the invitation of Horace Greeley to become an author of columns, essays, and reviews in magazines, newspapers, and literary journals. There she contributed front-page columns for two years to Greeley's *New York Tribune* before moving to Europe for the *Tribune* to serve as the first female foreign correspondent for a major paper and—in Rome—hospital superintendent during the 1848 wave of revolutions convulsing Europe, including the dramatic rise and fall of the Roman Republic (1848–1849). In Rome she met Giovanni Angelo Ossoli, the man whom she may have married, likely after bearing his child, Angelo Eugene Philip Ossoli. In May 1850 they embarked upon the *Elizabeth* to return to America, where Fuller hoped to support them financially. In a stunning turn of events the *Elizabeth* was shipwrecked off the coast of Fire Island, New York. All three drowned in plain sight of shoreline inhabitants and looters.

Fuller left a legacy on several fronts, including five books, poetry, an extensive archive of journals and letters, newspaper columns, and reviews on literature, music, art, foreign affairs, and social reform. Her essay "The Great Lawsuit" (1843), a feminist tract, was followed by and expanded upon in *Woman in the Nineteenth Century* (1845). These are foundational sources for the women's rights movement that was mobilizing at the time of her death. Demonstrating Fuller's theorizing on gender fluidity, these publications antedate Virginia Woolf's fictional explorations of gender and twenty-first-century academic gender theories.

Like Mary Emerson, Margaret Fuller kept numerous commonplace books; she experimented with genre and gender differently, however. Typically, Fuller recorded her source text and/or author in the manner of the male-gendered commonplace tradition, and sometimes even relevant volume and page numbers for future use, as in, for example, her early plans to write a biography of Goethe. Akin to other commonplace books, Fuller's "reading" journals slip into other genres and then back again—among them, diary, original verse, and dialogues—and, because of her linguistic acuity, not infrequently passing from English to German, Italian, or French.

One such undated, bound commonplace journal of 194 pages with marbled boards, which Fuller entitled "S. M. Fuller's Bouquet.—" (ca. 1836–1837), enacts this generic mutation, in this case shifting multiple times between a commonplace book and an informal friendship album. The publication dates of Fuller's published commonplace sources, references to her thwarted plans to travel to Europe in 1836, and her transcriptions from Amos Bronson Alcott's 1837 journal suggest this dating. Visual and verse contributions in "S. M. Fuller's Bouquet" by Fuller and others include drawings by Fuller's friend and former student, Caroline Sturgis, unoriginal verse offerings by Sturgis, several other poetic extracts in unidentified hands, and an unsigned original verse contribution, "Each in All," in the hand of Waldo Emerson.[35] Fuller had first visited with Emerson in July 1836, so this journal annotates the early stages of their friendship, including overtures such as this one. Other forms of friendship, gifting, and exchange harmonize its pages similarly. In it Fuller had extracted both Waldo's and Alcott's journals, and she also copied numerous poems from George Herbert, gifts from Sturgis. When thanking Sturgis for the volume in a June 1837 letter, Fuller exclaimed, "George Herbert" is "constantly at my elbow."[36]

At first glance, Waldo's interaction with this feminine genre fails to align neatly with his own reading and writing practices at this time, so one wonders how Fuller enticed him to participate in the gendered and generic dynamics of the friendship album. His willingness to partake was perhaps occasioned by her compelling presence. As he enthused in an August 1836 letter to brother William after her first Concord visit, "It is always a great refreshment to see a very intelligent person. It is like being set in a large place. You stretch your limbs & dilate to your utmost size" (*LRWE* 1:32). Joseph M. Thomas's remarks also bear repeating in this context, however. Emerson "willingly left open his mature practice to influence from persons around him," Thomas observes, "and in ways that may surprise readers who associate him exclusively with Romantic individual genius." Citing alliances with friends, family, and publishers from the 1830s forward, Thomas adds, "at the heart of his authorship lay a sociability that entertained advice and influence from many quarters," an attitude reflected in *Parnassus*.[37]

Conspicuously, "more than half" of the verse populating this anthology—for which Waldo had been accumulating poetry notebooks for nearly fifty years with daughter Edith Emerson Forbes—had been altered, retitled, excised, and expanded upon in the manner of contributors to antebellum poetry notebooks and friendship albums. Although he relegates Edith's role to that of a "secretary and copyist," Ronald A. Bosco maintains that such re-authoring represents an extension of Waldo's "theory of textual integrity," in which Emerson "absorbed" and "assimilated" unattributed prose borrowings and regarded them as his own, a phenomenon Cole also denotes in regard to Waldo's entreaties for Mary's Almanacks. Moreover, in justifying such editorial liberties, Bosco asserts that in two essays from *Letters and Social Aims* (1876)—"Quotation and Originality" and "Poetry and Imagination"—Waldo articulates a theory of the "reader bard" who integrates his perspective on textual integrity, also in the manner of Shakespeare, who had been charged with excessive reliance upon his sources. "Yet he was more original than his originals," Emerson insists, quoting Walter Savage Landor in "Quotation and Originality." "He breathed upon dead bodies and brought them into life."[38]

Characterizing these reader-bard, freestyle alterations as Waldo Emerson's "late compositional style" of "decomposition," or "long-assayed theory of quotation *as* creation," Nikhil Bilwakesh also attends to aspects of *Parnassus* that, in my estimation, resemble generic features of the sentimental friendship album. Referencing Leon Jackson's *The Business of Letters*, Bilwakesh observes that in producing *Parnassus* Waldo was rejecting the increasingly commercialized poetry anthologies that were replacing the gift economy—"writers' personal webs of connection, created through gifting, ... or lending books," gestures of intimacy also witnessed within "S. M. Fuller's Bouquet" and other antebellum poetry albums. Bilwakesh describes Emerson's refutation of a mass-produced and market-driven anthology with the more "intimate commerce" reflected in *Parnassus*, while also detailing the "inclusion of mediocre poems by friends and local figures not generally known as poets"—including Henry Thoreau, Edward Bliss Emerson, James Freeman Clarke, Frederic Hedge, Franklin B. Sanborn, and Daniel Webster. Bosco similarly identifies the anomalous appearance of this "odd lot" of "new poets."[39] In fact, such contributions from his friends bring to mind the portfolio versifiers Waldo welcomes in "New Poetry." Reflecting upon the dubious quality of verse sourced from Waldo's networks, Bilwakesh regards *Parnassus* "as a 'miscellany' in the guise of an anthology, presenting local novelties alongside canonical poets"[40]—or, in another light, presenting in the manner of original and unoriginal verse in friendship albums, a generic kin to manuscript miscellanies. Whether Waldo and Edith crafted this generic resemblance deliberately or unconsciously, its sentimental-friendship styling may illuminate the "literary and financial success" *Parnassus* achieved in the nineteenth century, despite its "undistinguished reputation" today.[41]

Irrespective of the contexts that may have informed Waldo's use of unoriginality in his poetry notebooks and in *Parnassus*, both the friendship album and commonplace book portions in "S. M. Fuller's Bouquet" anticipate Fuller's later experiments in theorizing the fluidity of gender, in placing genres in conversation, in cultivating new forms of friendship through pacquet circulation, and in convening Conversations dedicated to mutual cultivation. The friendship album portions fall into occasional clusters, and within other parts of the journal they appear scattered amidst commonplaces—particularly excerpts in Fuller's hand from Emerson and Alcott's journals. As the foregoing biographical information intimates, multiple elements within "S. M. Fuller's Bouquet" situate a Margaret Fuller poised on the cusp of a personally and professionally enriching Transcendentalist phase in New England. Fuller had grown acquainted with Alcott while teaching in his Boston Temple School between December 1836 and April 1837; then or shortly thereafter she had borrowed Alcott's 1837 journal, returning it in May.[42] At the Temple School she also encountered his dialogic pedagogical style, a methodology she would bring to her subsequent Providence posting at the Greene Street School and to her Boston Conversations. In the future, they would share an interest in professional Conversations as a means of advancing Transcendentalist forms of personal enrichment.

Generic attributes of the friendship album figure and gift economy emerge prominently in portions of "S. M. Fuller's Bouquet." They include, as noted above, unoriginal or original verse in others' hands, drawings, an emphasis on the florilegium, a common trope representing poetry albums as "a bouquet of flowers,"[43] and an implicit intentionality to affirm affectionate ties and remembrance, yet amidst these generic features Fuller intermingled prose and verse commonplacing from her friends' gifts or loans of books and journals. Consequently, and unlike some of her other commonplace books, in "S. M. Fuller's Bouquet" an affectionate tonality connects and permeates the two gendered genres and emphasizes the ways in which commonplace excerpts from others' gifts figured in her professional interests as an emergent leader and friend within the Newness.

As much as Waldo Emerson, Sturgis and several other unidentified people appear to have contributed verse and illustrations in the friendship album convention, the nature of their offerings largely fails to accord with elements common to the genre, deviations that may suggest that Fuller and her participants understood that this bouquet was not a typical friendship album, but instead an experiment influenced by the genre, as was potentially the case with *Parnassus*. For instance, the verse does not seem to allude to their friendship with Fuller, or to Fuller as an individual, components standard to friendship albums. Waldo offered his original verse draft, "Each in All," a poem from his poetry Notebook P (1834–1845) that he published in 1839 as "Each and All."[44] The poem advances a philosophical argument derived from his reading of Goethe and Coleridge's natural history writings, but in so doing, many of its lines also allude to the ways in which found materials such as seashells on a beach or plants and animals in their natural environment lose their special aura when taken out of the context of their original setting, or "perfect Whole."[45] An ironic resonance may be accidental, but arguably the lines could be interpreted as a rejection or criticism of the genre to which he was contributing—one in which verse removed from its primary situation and placed in a new milieu is deemed significant.[46] Curiously, however, this poem also derives in part from Waldo's 1834 Journal A, where he records a childhood memory that emphasizes the sociality of the first encounter:

> I remember when I was a boy going upon the beach & being charmed with the colors & forms of the shells. I picked up many & put them in my pocket. When I got home I could find nothing that I gathered—nothing but some <old> dry ugly mussel & snail shells. Thence I learned that Composition was more important than the beauty of individual forms to effect. On the shore they lay wet & social by the sea & under the sky. (JMN 4:291)

In rekindling this past revelation Waldo accentuates the aesthetic and philosophical milieu of the "perfect Whole" from "Each in All," but he also emphasizes that snail and mussel shells and sand and water "lay wet and social," companionable and in that way analogous to the nature of friendship albums, in which multiple poems and authors coexist in an ecology that prizes kinship, shared ideas, conjoined memories, collaborated words. In a related gesture, Fuller sought Alcott, Sturgis, Emerson, and others to reify and witness "S. M. Fuller's Bouquet" as a textual homage to friendship that juxtaposes images, words, and gendered genres; conspicuously, however, shared autonomy and Fuller's multi-generic creation produce a disarray that rejoins Hanlon's sense of the provisional and inherently faulty nature of curation. As an exhibit, the disjointed placement of disparate commonplace and friendship album components betrays perhaps the most distinct irregularity, second only to the offerings Sturgis brings to the journal's front cover. Penned over the decorative enclosure, her contributions appear difficult to comprehend. "Farewell," she submits mysteriously from the marbled design to one or to all, along with an unclear flourish and a drawing of a female head in profile.

Having inscribed her valediction rather peculiarly at the onset of any reader's experience with Fuller's journal, Sturgis also added two unsigned verse extracts: Crashaw's "The Two Mites," and Tennyson's "The Mystic." Her first of two other drawings, another woman's head in profile, find no apparent connection to its surrounding text or to the generic features of the friendship album. However, the second illustration appears under Fuller's excerpt of "The Pulley"—one of many Herbert poems Fuller copied into this journal. In placing her drawing alongside Herbert's verse Sturgis may gesture to the florilegium, to which Fuller also alluded in naming the journal "S. M. Fuller's Bouquet." Tellingly, Sturgis embodied the trope by sketching a portrait of a young girl clutching a handful of flowers.[47]

Fuller's use of Waldo Emerson's journals and library, along with other Transcendentalist bequests, in "S. M. Fuller's Bouquet" replicates the intimate generosity of the gift economy Sturgis's illustrations address. Further, Fuller's commonplaces testify to the fact that Waldo shared his journals with her, just as Mary Emerson and he had exchanged their own journals from the time of his Harvard days. After borrowing Alcott's journal, Fuller replied with her own gift, a poem signed and dated May 18, 1837, her translation of Schiller's "Light and Warmth." Appropriate to the friendship album, this translation expressed shared values and a recognition of the individual to whom the poem is bestowed. Fuller's first poetic lines responded to commonplaces she gleaned from Alcott's journal, passages in which Alcott outlines his aspirations for Temple School Conversations. Significantly, the verse praises his objectives:

> The noble man walks forth,
> Untroubled by low fear or doubt,
> Visions which in his soul have birth
> He hopes to meet without;
> And consecrates, with generous feeling warm,
> To do his faith's behests, a faithful arm.[48]

Alcott received Fuller's offering gratefully, copying it into his journal.

Whereas generic elements of the feminine friendship album and the masculine commonplace book mingle to produce one of Fuller's early experiments in friendship and manuscript circulation, other commonplaces in this journal reflect the male generic heritage of professional growth. Notably, Fuller selected passages from her friends' bequests whose subject matter anticipated goals she would outline for her

Conversations. In an 1839 letter to Sophia Ripley Fuller characterized her proposed Conversations as stimuli that would enable women to "ascertain what pursuits are best suited to us in our time and state of society, and how we may make best use of our means for building up the life of thought upon the life of action." "Could a circle be assembled in earnest desirous to answer the great questions," she proposes. "What were we born to do? How shall we do it?"[49]

Several of the commonplaces from "S. M. Fuller's Bouquet" resonate with these questions and may have enabled her plans two years later as she embarked upon her professional life as a Transcendentalist proto-New Woman. Moreover, Fuller's transcriptions from Waldo's library reveal continuities with Boston Conversations that would prompt women to ask, "What were we born to do? How shall we do it?" She returned several books to Waldo in May 1837,[50] and internal evidence in "S. M. Fuller's Bouquet" suggests that Coleridge's *Letters, Conversations and Recollections* (1836) lay among these gifts.[51] Scattered in her commonplace extracts from Coleridge is his prospectus for a biographical and historical lecture series. Coleridge advises that because the course material will not cover "logical subtleties" and metaphysics, participants would need no special preparation to follow the lectures. Instead, attendants would require only:

> a due interest in questions of deepest concern to all, and which every rational creature, who has arrived at the age of reflection, must be presumed ... to have put to his own thoughts: What, and for what am I made? What can I, and what ought I to make of myself? and in what relations do I stand to the world and to my fellow men?[52]

These commonplaces detail the remarkable ways in which assays in friendship and manuscript exchange sculpted Margaret Fuller. Reciprocally, in combining gendered and generic forms of unoriginality, Fuller instantiated early forms of the dialogic and relational experiments that would characterize the Newness. Equally provocative, they resonate with and illustrate the ways in which Waldo Emerson engaged with female-gendered, unoriginal genres.

Similar to Mary Emerson in her privilege, Fuller's generic expressions derived from exercises that served professional and affectionate objectives. For other antebellum writers on the margins without this luxury, unoriginality was a necessity. For these aspiring authors, quotation, epigraphs, and commonplacing "signaled respectability and ambition ... [and attested to] the significant struggles of white women and writers of color to find a place for themselves amid a crowded literary market that required ample proof of their professional bona fides and declined to make room for ... alternative voices."[53] Despite such tangible differences and due to the innate flexibility of commonplace books and their gendered variants, the reading and writing conventions of Fuller and other transatlantic women enabled them to claim unoriginality for mutual cultivation and kinship in a predominantly white, male culture, according to individual need. Fuller's individual need signified as a conjoined search for love, truth, and purpose, and that want is manifested aptly in her reliance upon the gendered polarities of the commonplace tradition in "S. M. Fuller's Bouquet": the ostensibly masculine professional commonplace book and the ostensibly feminine sentimental friendship album.

Unlocking the Savings Bank/Recovering the Shards

Although the rationales that inform editors of primary texts are extensive, broadly speaking, they vary between two poles. The textual critic of a digital or print curation may aim to establish a "product" at a distinct moment in time, such as a particular edition judged to be closest to an author's intention, a photographic facsimile or faithful "diplomatic" transcription of a manuscript, or an "eclectic," ideal text composed of "substantive" readings and "accidentals" (punctuation, capitalization, and the like) derived from selected versions of a work. The intentionalist rationale has shaped the Emerson canon of *Collected Works*, and this splendid achievement imagines an author who actively and self-consciously crafts his texts based on objectives that can be distinguished clearly—and perhaps also in the spirit of self-reliant originality with which Waldo Emerson's antebellum publications are often identified.

Alternatively, those engaged in the recovery of cultural materials may prefer to examine the text as a "process," in which the significance of authorial intentionality recedes and digital affordances are particularly germane. In such cases, practitioners may highlight the role of revision, data and keywords, sociocultural milieu, or of the implicit social contract between author(s), publisher, family members, posthumous editors, poet bards, and readers, as well as the materiality of the text(s) (including paratextual elements such as book covers, illustrations, paper choice, and font). One could argue that the rich history of social-text constructions in Emersonian circles represents a proposal for such an undertaking.

Similarly, digital resources can offer granular and nuanced means of parsing social-text materials. However, and as Brad Rittenhouse and Maurice S. Lee assert in this volume, Emerson studies have been slow to take a digital turn. Their preliminary work in computational criticism demonstrates the fresh ways in which computational aggregation and analysis can illuminate the writings of Ralph Waldo Emerson. A fascinating example of their findings reveals that the three texts most devoid of reference to people are the essays "Friendship," "Love," and "Gifts"—underscoring the potential that in the 1840s intimacy existed most comfortably for Waldo in theory. Conversely, social-text partnerships generating literary productions may have offered more palatable options.

A significant framework for the preceding observation is the apparently widespread familiarity with which antebellum Americans experienced literary imitation, emulation, and tradition. In their experiments with gender, genre, and unoriginality Mary Emerson and Margaret Fuller joined a majority of white women and writers of color, would-be poets, poet bards, academy students, male and female reformers, Waldo Emerson, and other members of the Newness. Conspicuously, however, these participants relied on decentered and communal forms of authorship that subverted singular models of authority in favor of collectivity, a companionate ecosystem in which agency is disbursed and acts of unoriginality shared, producing a relation to the universe that echoes with cascades of voices drawn from other settings. Shall we salvage these imperfect remnants of late style Waldo Emerson publications and of Mary Emerson and Margaret Fuller's commonplace book manuscripts—each exemplifying the vestiges of curated and nominally "perfect Wholes"? Likewise, is it time to further explore the dialogic and communal modalities that were so deeply interwoven into the production of their literary expressions? In a hopeful spirit of commonplacing, I quote Fuller for prophecy: "Persist to ask and it will come."[54]

Notes

1. *CW* 1:7.
2. Phyllis Cole, *Mary Moody Emerson and the Origins of Transcendentalism: A Family History* (New York: Oxford University Press, 1998); Jana L. Argersinger and Phyllis Cole, eds., *Toward a Female Genealogy of Transcendentalism* (Athens: University of Georgia Press, 2014); Charles Capper, *Margaret Fuller: An American Romantic Life*, 2 vols. (New York: Oxford University Press, 1992–2007); Megan Marshall, *Margaret Fuller: A New American Life* (Boston: Houghton Mifflin Harcourt, 2013).
3. Jerome J. McGann, *The Textual Condition* (Princeton, NJ: Princeton University Press, 1991); D. F. McKenzie, *Bibliography and the Sociology of Texts* (Cambridge: Cambridge University Press, 1999).
4. Ralph Waldo Emerson, "New Poetry," *Dial* 1, no. 2 (October 1840): 220–32, 221; Larry J. Reynolds, "From *Dial* Essay to New York Book: The Making of *Woman in the Nineteenth Century*," in *Periodical Literature in Nineteenth-Century America*, ed. Kenneth M. Price and Susan Belasco Smith (Charlottesville: University Press of Virginia, 1995), 17–34 ("pacquet"); Charles Wesley Grady, "A Conservative Transcendentalist: The Early Years (1805–1835) of Frederic Henry Hedge," *Studies in the American Renaissance* (1983): 58; Charles R. Crowe, "Transcendentalism and 'The Newness' in Rhode Island," *Rhode Island History* 14, no. 2 (April 1955): 33–46; Caleb Crain, *American Sympathy: Men, Friendship, and Literature in the New Nation* (New Haven, CT: Yale University Press, 2001), 177–237; William Rossi, "Performing Loss, Elegy, and Transcendental Friendship," *New England Quarterly* 81, no. 2 (June 2008): 252–77; Lawrence Buell, *Literary Transcendentalism: Style and Vision in the American Renaissance* (Ithaca: Cornell University Press, 1973), 75–101 (conversation).
5. Nikhil Bilwakesh, "Emerson's Decomposition: *Parnassus*," *Nineteenth-Century Literature* 67, no. 4 (2013): 520–45, 528.
6. Christopher Hanlon, *Emerson's Memory Loss: Originality, Communality, and the Late Style* (New York: Oxford University Press, 2018).
7. Hanlon, *Emerson's Memory Loss*, 130.
8. Claudia Stokes, *Old Style: Unoriginality and Its Uses in Nineteenth-Century U.S. Literature* (Philadelphia: University of Pennsylvania Press, 2022), 172 (career move), 1 (irregularity), 2 (skepticism and distaste).

9. Earle Havens, *Commonplace Books: A History of Manuscripts and Printed Books from Antiquity to the Twentieth Century* (New Haven, CT: University Press of New England, 2001); Todd S. Gernes, "Recasting the Culture of Ephemera," in *Popular Literacy: Studies in Cultural Practices and Poetics*, ed. John Trimbur (Pittsburgh: University of Pittsburgh Press, 2001), 107–27.

10. *JMN* 1:158, Plates III, IV, VI, VIII–XI; Evelyn Barish, *Emerson: The Roots of Prophecy* (Princeton, NJ: Princeton University Press, 1989); Edith W. Gregg, ed., *One First Love: The Letters of Ellen Louisa Tucker to Ralph Waldo Emerson* (Cambridge, MA: Harvard University Press, 1962), 26, 27, 166–68, 19.

11. Susan Miller, *Assuming the Positions: Cultural Pedagogy and the Politics of Commonplace Writing* (Pittsburgh: University of Pittsburgh Press, 1998), 46; Stokes, *Old Style*, 85, 87.

12. "Ronald J. Zboray and Mary Saracino Zboray, "Is It a Diary, Commonplace Book, Scrapbook, or Whatchamacallit? Six Years of Exploration in New England's Manuscript Archives," *Libraries & the Cultural Record* 44, no. 1 (2009): 101–23, 102.

13. Michael C. Cohen, *The Social Lives of Poems in Nineteenth-Century America* (Philadelphia: University of Pennsylvania Press, 2015), 76, 89, original emphasis.

14. Michael C. Cohen, "Album Verse and the Poetics of Scribal Circulation," in *A History of Nineteenth-Century American Women's Poetry*, ed. Jennifer Putzi and Alexandra Socarides (Cambridge: Cambridge University Press, 2017), 68–86, 68, 83.

15. Leon Jackson, *The Business of Letters: Authorial Economies in Antebellum America* (Stanford: Stanford University Press, 2008), 99.

16. Jackson, *Business of Letters*, 102; Gernes, "Recasting the Culture of Ephemera," 121.

17. Emerson, "New Poetry," 220.

18. Emerson, "New Poetry," 222.

19. Reynolds, "*Dial* Essay to New York Book," 20 (pacquets); *JMN* 7:404 ("covenanted"); David M. Robinson, "'In the Golden Hour of Friendship': Transcendentalism and Utopian Desire," in *Emerson and Thoreau: Figures of Friendship*, ed. John T. Lysaker and William Rossi (Bloomington: Indiana University Press, 2010), 53–69, 55 (intimacy).

20. Jerome M. McGann, "The Monk and the Giants: Textual and Bibliographical Studies and the Interpretation of Literary Works," in *Women Editing/Editing Women: Early Modern Women Writers and the New Textualism*, ed. Ann Hollinshead Hurley and Chanita Goodblatt (Newcastle: Cambridge Scholars Publishing, 2009), 55–74, 57.

21. Quoted in Cole, *Mary Moody Emerson*, 204; *JMN* 1:208.

22. Ronald A. Bosco and Joel Myerson, *The Emerson Brothers: A Fraternal Biography in Letters* (Oxford: Oxford University Press, 2006), 195–96.

23. Noelle A. Baker and Sandra Harbert Petrulionis, eds., *The Almanacks of Mary Moody Emerson: A Scholarly Digital Edition*, folder 40. Women Writers Online, Women Writers Project, Northeastern University, https://www.wwp.northeastern.edu/wwo/. *Women Writers Online* requires a subscription; it offers free one-month trial subscriptions upon request. Editorial interventions signaled by braces and other keys in the edition are eliminated here for a "reading' version of the text.

24. William Channing Gannett, "Ralph Waldo Emerson," in *Appleton's Cyclopaedia of American Biography* (New York: Appleton, 1887), 2:343; W[illiam]. C[hanning]. G[annett]., "Ralph Waldo Emerson: A Life Sketch," *Unity* 21, no. 11 (May 12, 1888): 140–42.

25. Noelle A. Baker, "'Somthing More Than Material': Nonverbal Conversation in Mary Moody Emerson's Almanacks," *Resources for American Literary Study* 35 (2010): 29–67; Baker, "'Let Me Do Nothing Smale': Mary Moody Emerson and Women's 'Talking'

Manuscripts," in *Towards a Female Genealogy of Transcendentalism*, ed. Jana L. Argersinger and Phyllis Cole (Athens: University of Georgia Press, 2014), 35–56.
26. Baker and Petrulionis, *Almanacks of Mary Moody Emerson*, Introduction to folder 42.
27. Noelle A. Baker, Sarah Connell, and Sandra Harbert Petrulionis, "Mary Moody Emerson as Reader and Reviewer," *Women Writers in Context* (2017), https://wwp.northeastern.edu/context/#bakpet.emerson.xml.
28. Corin Throsby, "Byron, Commonplacing and Early Fan Culture," in *Romanticism and Celebrity Culture, 1750–1850*, ed. Tom Mole (Cambridge: Cambridge University Press, 2009), 227–44, 236.
29. Ash Clark, Sarah Connell, Noelle A. Baker, and Sandra Harbert Petrulionis, "Intertextual References in the Almanacks of Mary Moody Emerson: Visualization for Close and Distant Reading," Women Writers Project, https://wwp.northeastern.edu/lab/emerson-networks/index.html.
30. Baker and Petrulionis, *Almanacks of Mary Moody Emerson*, Introduction to folder 32.
31. Baker and Petrulionis, *Almanacks of Mary Moody Emerson*, Introduction to folder 32.
32. Laura Dassow Walls, *Emerson's Life in Science: The Culture of Truth* (Ithaca: Cornell University Press, 2003), 59.
33. Baker and Petrulionis, *Almanacks of Mary Moody Emerson*, folder 32.
34. Baker and Petrulionis, *Almanacks of Mary Moody Emerson*, Introduction to folder 32.
35. MS Am 1086 (98), Houghton Library, Harvard University.
36. Margaret Fuller, *The Letters of Margaret Fuller*, ed. Robert N. Hudspeth (Ithaca: Cornell University Press, 1983–1994), 1:285.
37. Joseph M. Thomas, "Poverty and Power: Revisiting Emerson's Poetics," in *Emerson Bicentennial Essays*, ed. Joel Myerson and Ronald A. Bosco (Boston: Massachusetts Historical Society, 2006), 213–46, 237–38.
38. Ronald A. Bosco, "'Poetry for the World of Readers' and 'Poetry for Bards Proper': Poetic Theory and Textual Integrity in Emerson's *Parnassus*," *Studies in the American Renaissance* (1989): 257–312, 305, 269, 297, 298, 300 (more than half), 269 (secretary), 297, 298 (theory of textual integrity, absorbed and assimilated, reader bard), 300 (Shakespeare, quoted); *CW* 8:100.
39. Bosco, "Poetry for the World of Readers," 267 (new poets), 268 (odd lot).
40. Bilwakesh, "Emerson's Decomposition," 521 (decomposition), 531 (rejecting commercialism), 540 (long-assayed theory), 531, n. 23 (miscellany).
41. Bosco, "Poetry for the World of Readers," 259 (undistinguished), 268–69 (success).
42. Larry A. Carlson, "Bronson Alcott's 'Journal for 1837' (Part One)," *Studies in the American Renaissance* (1981): 130, n. 166; Fuller, *Letters of Margaret Fuller*, 1:274.
43. Cohen, "Album Verse and the Poetics of Scribal Circulation," 77.
44. Ralph Waldo Emerson, *The Poetry Notebooks of Ralph Waldo Emerson*, ed. Ralph H. Orth et al. (Columbia: University of Missouri Press, 1986), 16, 20–21, 778–89.
45. MS Am 1086 (98), Houghton Library, Harvard University; *CW* 9:12–14.
46. MS Am 1086 (98), Houghton Library, Harvard University; on the inherent tensions in gifting within friendship albums, see Jackson, *Business of Letters*, 89–109.
47. MS Am 1086 (98), Houghton Library, Harvard University. I am indebted to Sarah Wider for conversations confirming that these unsigned offerings are in Sturgis's hand and typical of her drawings.
48. Larry A. Carlson, "Bronson Alcott's 'Journal for 1837' (Part Two)," *Studies in the American Renaissance* (1982): 53–167, 80–81.

49. Fuller, *Letters of Margaret Fuller* 2:87.
50. Fuller, *Letters of Margaret Fuller* 1:277.
51. Walter Harding, *Emerson's Library* (Charlottesville: University Press of Virginia, 1967), 64.
52. MS Am 1086 (98), Houghton Library, Harvard University.
53. Stokes, *Old Style*, 67.
54. Margaret Fuller, *Woman in the Nineteenth Century*, in *The Essential Margaret Fuller*, ed. Jeffrey Steele (New Brunswick: Rutgers University Press, 1995), 247–378, 349.

7

QUOTATION AND ORIGINALITY, OR, EMERSON'S EDITORS

CHAPTER 23

EDITING EMERSON

RONALD A. BOSCO AND JOEL MYERSON

Most authors have been edited in their lifetimes by friends, spouses, agents, copyeditors, and publishers, but rarely has an author's extended family been so involved and important as has Ralph Waldo Emerson's. The family's editorial intervention provided late nineteenth- and early twentieth-century readers with three, and perhaps four, more books attributed to the Emerson we inherit; the Emerson family's stewardship also ensured publication of the many modern editorial projects that have appeared in their current, comprehensive forms. This essay discusses the editing of Emerson's printed and manuscript texts and those of his family, beginning in the mid-nineteenth century, and up to the present.

Printed Texts

Like most authors, Emerson's writing was edited by copyeditors and compositors, mostly with his acquiescence (especially in regard to punctuation), although in early years he paid particular attention to reading proofs, mostly because unauthorized British publishers routinely took the liberty of "altering" his texts to their audiences' preferences. Rare among his contemporaries, he also controlled the copyrights to his books. He paid for production costs (composition, stereotyping, printing, and binding) and gave the publisher and booksellers a percentage of sales on the copies they distributed. By 1850, when he began to accept straight royalties of 20 per cent, he required publishers to advance him the full amount of his profit for each book immediately upon publication, thus limiting his own financial risk. In all instances, Emerson retained the copyright to his books and, after stereotyping was introduced, he paid for and thus owned the plates used to print his books, so that all future reprintings would generate revenue for him, not the publisher. It was not until 1860, when he signed a contract with Ticknor and Fields (later Houghton Mifflin), who were booksellers and distributors, that he took standard royalties on all his works.[1]

By 1860 Emerson had become such a popular author that his publishers marketed his works in a "collected edition." Such multivolume sets, available in different bindings (and at different prices), marked established authors of the time, and were also useful for interior decorating, as means to show off to visitors the literary aspirations of the owners. They also created an incentive for new volumes to be added, and this phenomenon drove Emerson's editors and publishers from the 1870s through 1914.

The fire in July 1872 that nearly destroyed Emerson's house in Concord affected his cognitive abilities,[2] so that after that date his writings were often a collaboration between him and his daughters Edith[3] and Ellen, son Edward Waldo, and literary executor James Elliot Cabot (for *Letters and Social Aims* [1876]).[4] The latter group edited Emerson's previous publications and "reconstructed" unpublished works from remaining manuscripts to add three more volumes to the Emerson bibliography (and to his collected works): *Miscellanies* (1884), *Lectures and Biographical Sketches* (1884), and *Natural History of Intellect and Other Papers* (1893). These four volumes and all of Emerson's previous works were again re-edited for "the modern reader" in the 1903–1904 *Complete Works of Ralph Waldo Emerson*, often referred to as the "Centenary Edition."

Those last four volumes, as well as ones appearing as late as 2015, would not have been possible had it not been for a family that valued and safeguarded its papers. Ralph Waldo Emerson saved his father's papers and those of his aunt Mary Moody Emerson (1774–1863). In the 1872 fire at his house (called by the family "Bush"), one of the first rooms whose contents were saved was that containing those papers and the papers of his mother Ruth Haskins Emerson (1768–1853) and those of his brothers, Charles Chauncy (1808–1836), Edward Bliss (1805–1834), and William (1801–1868). Rebuilt, Bush housed the family papers for many years. Ellen Tucker Emerson (1839–1909), Waldo's daughter, saved the papers of her mother, Lidian Jackson Emerson (1802–1892), and continued living in Bush until her own death in 1909. Waldo's other children, Edith Emerson Forbes (b. 1841) and Edward Waldo Emerson (b. 1844), died in, respectively, 1929 and 1930. In the latter year, the Emerson heirs formed the Ralph Waldo Emerson Memorial Association, which oversaw Bush, its land and household and barn contents, and Emerson's library, manuscripts, and personal belongings. By the late 1930s, family papers were still housed in Bush, among descendants, and in a vault at Harvard's Fogg Museum, where Edward Waldo Forbes (Waldo's grandson [1873–1969]) had been director since 1909, a position he held until 1944. When the Houghton Library was opened in 1942 across Quincy Street from the Fogg, the family deposited almost all its collections there, and in 1992, formally gifted Emerson's journals and notebooks to Harvard University. Every printed and electronic edition of Emerson's published and unpublished writings and those of family members derive from these collections, which had been added to over the years by subsequent donations from the family.

The other major cache of family papers belonged to William Emerson, Waldo's brother. Consisting of the correspondence between William, his other brothers, and both William and Waldo's families, these papers were first collected by Haven Emerson, William's grandson. Eventually, they were housed at the Peconic Bay home on Long Island, NY, of Dr. Ethel Emerson Wortis, William's great-granddaughter. Before her death in 1995, her son Dr. Michael Wortis and his wife, Ruth Emerson Wortis, deposited (1993) and then donated (2003) the Emerson Family Papers to the Massachusetts Historical Society.[5]

Although there had been collected editions of Emerson's writings in 1876 (Little Classics Edition) and 1883 (Riverside Edition),[6] the 1903–1904 Centenary Edition served as the basic Emerson text for nearly a century. While this was edited according to then-standard practices by Edward Waldo Emerson, the text was modernized and diverged significantly from the works as originally published.

A new edition, edited according to modern textual practices, was clearly needed, and in 1971 the first volume of *The Collected Works of Ralph Waldo Emerson* appeared with Robert E. Spiller as general editor and Alfred R. Ferguson as textual editor. Unfortunately, the textual policy at the beginning was unusual and was routinely altered as the edition proceeded.[7] Modern editorial practice is to use the earliest manuscript or printed form of the text, because the more times a text is printed, the greater the chances for printers' or compositors' errors to enter into it. But the editors of the first volume of *Collected Works* dealt with texts that had been revised between six and thirteen years after their original publication, and their solution, faced with a choice between printing the earlier Emerson his initial audience read, or the later Emerson, versions of which were read by different audiences at different times, was to present a text that never existed: as explained by Spiller in his introduction to the first volume, "revisions in later editions which increased the original or clarified it without excision are accepted; revisions which reduced the original are refused" (*CW* 1:xxxi–xxxiii). In other words, the practice adopted by Spiller and Ferguson amounted to editing by weighing the changes rather than by evaluating them.

This farrago of a textual policy was abandoned in the next volume of *The Collected Works, Essays: First Series* (1979), with this statement: "all revisions identifiable as Emerson's will ordinarily be accepted," but here too, changes in the text made decades later were accepted as revisions in the original text and, again, the editors created a procrustean text that stretched over several decades, beginning three years later with a new edition in 1847. This unfortunate editorial policy of producing eclectic texts drawn from many sources over many decades (1850, 1865, 1870, and 1876) continued to be followed in the next volume of *Essays: Second Series* (1983), both of the latter having Joseph Slater as general editor and as textual editors Ferguson (who died in 1974) and his daughter Jean Ferguson Carr. Thirteen years elapsed between the publication of these three volumes. The length of time devoted to producing the early editions caused both the press and Emerson scholars to doubt openly the viability of the edition.

Later volumes in the edition hewed to a more conservative editorial policy. Slater enlisted a former college classmate, Douglas Emory Wilson, as general editor and textual editor, posts he held from 1987 to 2003, during which time three more volumes were published: *Representative Men* (1987), *English Traits* (1994), and *Conduct of Life* in 2004. Although better than it was at the edition's start, the pace of production was judged unacceptable by the press, the edition's funding sources, and the academic community. In 2003, Wilson proposed a meeting with the press and asked Ronald A. Bosco to join him in that meeting, which included the press's new incoming representative to the edition, John Gregory Kulka, who asked in advance for a schedule toward completion of the edition. Bosco produced a schedule for the completion of the edition by 2012. The press was open to the proposal, but required Wilson to conduct a search for a new General Editor for the edition. When Wilson notified the board of the outcome of that visit, they accepted his recommendation that the board name Bosco General Editor. Bosco, in turn, asked Albert J. von Frank to join the edition and, with Thomas Wortham as textual editor, to see volume 9, Emerson's *Poems*, through the press. After Wilson died in 2005, Bosco asked Joel Myerson to join the edition as textual editor, and Glen M. Johnson as an editor.

Two volumes of *Collected Works* deserve further comment. Volume 9, *Poems*, not only established the texts for Emerson's poetry but, building on von Frank's work in compiling the notes for *Poetry Notebooks*, discussed the composition and publication history for each poem as well as variant readings in subsequent editions, including the 1876 edition of *Selected Poems* which underwent significant revisions, not all attributed to Emerson.[8] *Uncollected Prose Writings: Addresses, Essays, and Reviews* (2012) not only brought together 108 of Emerson's fugitive prose pieces and provided a rationale for including each, but also discussed at some length the posthumously published *Miscellanies, Lectures and Biographical Sketches*, and *Natural History of Intellect and Other Papers*. For the latter three books, the editors demonstrated how Cabot, the Emerson family, and friends of either the Emerson or the Cabot families constructed "new" works by Emerson: an earlier Emerson lecture, or draft of a work, or miscellaneous manuscript fragments cohering around a single topic served as the basis for an essay that was fleshed out by adding materials from Emerson's lectures, fragments of his prose, or journal passages, occasionally with transitional materials supplied by the editors. The resulting works were collaborations in which Emerson may have been consulted during the composition process, or even induced to add new material, but the result was the production of an editorial team, not a work over which the author had complete and coherent control. In general, *Uncollected Prose Writings* authenticates the works over which Emerson was able to control the printing, proofing, and publication, and lists those for which the editors lacked evidence of such authorial control.[9]

Manuscript Texts

Letters

The first group of Emerson's letters to be published consisted of his correspondence with Thomas Carlyle. In 1870 Emerson had his letters from Carlyle copied and bound and, after Carlyle's death in 1881, at the request of Edith Emerson Forbes, Carlyle's executors returned Emerson's letters to his family. Edited by Charles Eliot Norton, the Emerson-Carlyle correspondence appeared in two volumes in 1883 (A 39), with a supplementary volume in 1886 (A 43).[10] Editions of less extensive correspondences appeared over the next decades: with the British poet John Sterling in 1897 (A 46), Emerson's friend the poet and banker Samuel Gray Ward in 1899 (A 47), the German literary critic Herman Grimm in 1903 (A 49), his lifelong friend and minister in Philadelphia William Henry Furness in 1910 (A 53), and the British poet Arthur Hugh Clough in 1934 (A 56).

The publication of *The Letters of Ralph Waldo Emerson* in six volumes in 1939 (A 59) marked a turning point in Emerson scholarship. Ralph L. Rusk's edition provided the first extended glimpse into Emerson's private life without family concerns or censorship affecting what was to be printed.[11] The edition presents unmodernized texts of the letters, including significant revisions made by Emerson, fully annotates the texts, and provides a comprehensive index. Because of space limitations, Rusk referenced but did not publish letters that had appeared in print earlier.[12]

Rusk began editing Emerson's letters as the prelude to writing a biography of him and worked mainly at Bush and the Fogg Museum before the Emerson materials were moved to the Houghton Library. For both projects, he annotated over fourteen thousand 4" x 6" index cards documenting his research on Emerson. Before his death in 1962, he gave these cards to Eleanor M. Tilton to use in the preparation of her supplemental edition of Emerson's letters, which appeared in four volumes between 1990 and 1995 (A 59). Tilton included the texts of those previously published letters only referenced in Rusk's edition and provided comprehensive annotations.[13] However, she did not reprint letters in the final significant edition of Emerson's letters, Joseph Slater's 1964 *The Correspondence of Emerson and Carlyle* (*CEC*; A 68).[14]

Sermons

Published in 1938 by Houghton Mifflin and edited by Arthur Cushman McGiffert, Jr., *Young Emerson Speaks: Unpublished Discourses on Many Subjects* printed twenty-five sermons, and introduced Emerson as minister to a new audience of readers. As McGiffert notes in his introduction, Emerson's preaching and ministerial habits during the early years of his pastorship at Boston's Second Church came as a pleasant surprise to the membership, especially his recognition of the need for the congregation and its preacher to be active in the community—an unexpected turn applauded by members of a church once overseen by Increase and Cotton Mather.

McGiffert's volume was eventually subsumed by *The Complete Sermons of Ralph Waldo Emerson* (ed. Albert J. von Frank, Chief Editor; Andrew H. Delbanco; Ronald A. Bosco; Teresa Toulouse; and Wesley T. Mott, 4 vols., Columbia: University of Missouri Press, 1989–1992). These volumes, which appeared as "An Approved Edition," by the Committee on Scholarly Editions of the Modern Language Association, is the definitive record of Emerson's career in the pulpit. The edition is introduced by a substantial essay on Emerson in the pulpit by David M. Robinson, "The Sermons of Ralph Waldo Emerson: An Introductory Essay."

Lectures

As of this printing, Emerson's extensive career as a lecturer is documented in six collections. *Uncollected Lectures*, edited by Clarence Gohdes (New York: William Edwin Rudge, 1932), included such lectures as "Public and Private Education," "Social Aims," "Resources," "Table-Talk," "Books," "Character," and "Natural Religion." *The Early Lectures of Ralph Waldo Emerson* (ed. Stephen E. Whicher, Robert E. Spiller, and Wallace E. Williams, 3 vols., Cambridge, MA: Harvard University Press, 1959–1972) established the standard edition for lectures Emerson delivered between 1835 and 1842. This three-volume edition was followed by *The Later Lectures of Ralph Waldo Emerson* (ed. Ronald A. Bosco and Joel Myerson, 2 vols., Athens and London: University of Georgia Press, 2001), which presented lectures Emerson delivered from 1843 to 1871.

A major set of lectures not included in these editions, however, is *Natural History of Intellect*, the series Emerson delivered at Harvard in 1870 and then again in 1871. Albert J. von Frank's *An Emerson Chronology* (2 vols., 2nd ed., Albuquerque, NM: Studio Non Troppo, 2016) contains a convenient guide to these lectures. Moreover, Ronald A. Bosco's "His Lectures were Poetry, His Teaching the Music of Spheres: Annie Adams Field and Francis Greenwood Peabody on Emerson's 'Natural History of the Intellect' Lectures at Harvard in 1870" (*Harvard Library Bulletin* 8, no. 2, 1997) provides two first-person accounts of the lectures written by Fields and Greenwood, who attended their first iteration. Lastly, William Charvat's *Emerson's American Lecture Engagements: A Chronological List* (New York: New York Public Library, 1961), though now displaced by Albert J. von Frank's two-volume *An Emerson Chronology*, contains extensive research into Emerson's lecture engagements for which it has withstood the test of time.

Journals and Notebooks

The success of the Centenary Edition of Emerson's writings, as well as the publication in 1906 of a fourteen-volume edition of Henry David Thoreau's *Journal*, led to *The Journals of Ralph Waldo Emerson*, edited in ten volumes by Emerson's son Edward and nephew Waldo Emerson Forbes (1879–1917) between 1909 and 1914 (A 52). Like many contemporary editions of private papers, the *Journals* were circumspect in dealing with Emerson's private life and concentrated on providing a portrait of him as a Victorian intellectual. Sections from Emerson's journals that were later used in published writings were not reproduced. Annotations were sparse but did have the advantage of including Edward's personal recollections.

Half a century later, work began on a new edition, one that would record the compositional features of the manuscript journals by reporting revisions such as cancellations and insertions. Annotations included the sources Emerson used in quotations and other borrowings, as well as his use of journal passages in his own published works and lectures through 1842.[15] The general editor of *The Journals and Miscellaneous Notebooks of Ralph Waldo Emerson* was William H. Gilman.[16] As co-editor of Melville's letters,

Gilman was a self-trained textual scholar who enlisted the help of three other University of Wisconsin PhDs who had studied with Stanley T. Williams: Merrell R. Davis, his co-editor on the Melville letters; George P. Clark, whose dissertation was on James Russell Lowell; and Alfred R. Ferguson, whose dissertation was on Edward Rowland Sill, whose poetry he later edited. The first volume of *JMN* was published in 1960, the second in 1961, but the original editorial team shrank from four to two: Clark resigned, and Davis died in 1961. Gilman recruited two more fellow Wisconsin grads: Merton M. Sealts, Jr. and Harrison M. Hayford, both of whom had, like Gilman and Davis, written dissertations on Melville, and had proved their textual skills by editing *Billy Budd*.[17]

This team formed the backbone of the edition for the next dozen years. In addition, Gilman chose three of his recent PhDs: Ralph H. Orth, whose dissertation was on Emerson's journal "Encyclopedia," which, with other similar journal volumes, formed volume 6; A. W. ("Bill") Plumstead, a Canadian who was then teaching at the University of Saskatchewan, was paired with Hayford on volume 7 and, later, with Gilman on volume 11; and J. E. ("Jay") Parsons was paired with Gilman on volume 8. Sealts, who preferred to work alone, accepted sole responsibility for editing volumes 5 and 10.

At the beginning, the edition was funded through the University of Rochester, but in the 1960s it began to receive funding from the National Endowment for the Humanities. By then the future of the edition had been plotted out to volume 14: volume 12 was assigned to Linda Allardt, who was on the editorial staff at Rochester; 13 to Ferguson and Orth; and 14 to Hayford and Susan Sutton Smith, the latter being another of Gilman's former doctoral students. Only the last two volumes of the sixteen contracted for with Harvard University Press were left unassigned.

The edition's forward progress then slowed due to death and defection. Ferguson died in May 1974. Sealts and Hayford declined doing more volumes and went off on other, Melville-related projects. Parsons disappeared without a trace. Plumstead resigned a full professorship at the University of Massachusetts to return to Canada and open a fishing lodge. After Gilman's death in 1976 the editorial staff consisted of Orth as general editor, Allardt, and Smith. Orth advertised for new editors, one to assist Allardt on volume 15 and two to edit volume 16. Applicants were given a test document to edit, and of the dozen individuals who had responded to the advertisement Orth chose Bosco, who had edited the seventeenth-century unpublished manuscript of Cotton Mather's autobiographical *Paterna* in an edition that received the MLA's seal as "An Approved Edition," and who, later, had edited the transatlantic and Italian correspondence between Robert and Elizabeth Barrett Browning and Elizabeth C. Kinney, wife of William Burnet Kinney, American Minister to the Court of Victor Emanuel in Turin, and, by an earlier marriage, the mother of Edmund Clarence Steadman; and Glen M. Johnson whose dissertation had been on Emerson. Bosco and Johnson would edit volume 16, which appeared in 1982. Allardt proposed David W. Hill, who was in an editing program at Rochester, and he assisted with her volume. From start to finish the *JMN* published sixteen volumes in twenty-five years under the general editorships of Gilman and Orth. Although the Harvard University Press had promised the surviving editors that they would be able to produce a one-volume selected edition of Emerson's journals, the press decided instead to select one of their own for the task.[18]

Although the appearance of *The Poetry Notebooks of Ralph Waldo Emerson* (ed. Ralph H. Orth et al., Columbia: University of Missouri Press, 1986) came as a happy surprise to many students of Emerson, the volume represents a major achievement that established the conditions for serious scholarly attention to Emerson as a poet, and the eventual publication of volume 9 of the *Collected Works: Poems: A Variorum Edition*. Similarly crucial was the publication of *The Topical Notebooks of Ralph Waldo Emerson* (ed. Ralph H. Orth, Susan Sutton Smith, Ronald A. Bosco, and Glen M. Johnson, 3 vols., Columbia and London: University of Missouri Press, 1990–1994). Emerson began keeping a substantial number of *Topical Notebooks* in the early 1850s; his purpose was twofold: to have at hand records on specific subjects from his own journals, miscellaneous notebooks, and voluminous readings to draw upon as invitations to lecture on specific subjects came his way; they also served as a testing ground for new subjects for either lectures or essays, or both.

Although the notebooks differ in content, collectively, they adhere to common patterns of reportage: Volume 1 printed seven of Emerson's topical notebooks from the 1850s and early 1860s: "Naturalist"; EO ("Fate"), LO ("Beauty and Art"); IT ("Natural History of Intellect"); EA ("England and America"), XO ("Reality" and "Illusion" and "Inexorable"), and WA ("Country Life"). Of these, "Naturalist," "Fate," and "Country Life" have attracted the most scholarly attention. Volume 2 printed five of Emerson's substantial topical notebooks from the 1850s through the late 1860s: "Orientalist"; RT ("Rhetoric"); LI ("Literature"); PY (subtitled "Theory of Poetry" by Emerson); and PH ("Philosophy"). Of these, "Orientalist," "Theory of Poetry," and "Philosophy" have attracted the most scholarly attention. Volume 3 printed four of Emerson's topical notebooks. OP ("Gulistan") alludes to the *Gulistan* of the Persian poet Hafiz, one of the poets Emerson most admired. This portion of the volume, however, is devoted mainly to the character of Emerson's family members and friends, including Longfellow, Henry James, Sr., Ellery Channing, Henry Thoreau, Bronson Alcott, Mary Moody Emerson, Elizabeth Sherman Hoar, and others. Notebook S ("Salvage") collects journal and notebook material from the 1840s through the late 1860s. Emerson drew extensively from this notebook when arranging portions of both *Society and Solitude* and *Letters and Social Aims* for publication. Notebook ZO collects journal, notebook, and other available writings that contribute to "Farming," "Success," and "Old Age" in *Society and Solitude* and thoughts on "Immortality" published in *Letters and Social Aims*.

A major collection of Emerson's manuscript materials remaining to be edited is Emerson's *Account Books*. At the time of Joel Myerson's death, he and Bosco held exclusive permission from the Emerson family and the Houghton Library to edit and subsequently publish Emerson's account books. Bosco has identified partners to undertake the project and see it through to conclusion.

Emerson began entering the eleven notebook volumes in 1828 and continued until his last years. Frugal New Englander that he was, he wrote down every expense, so that as they now stand, collectively the account books constitute a type of financial social history concerning the prices of commodities (the Emerson family went through a lot of butter). They are also invaluable for demonstrating how Emerson supported his friends (Alcott and Thoreau, for instance, received monies for their work on projects Emerson assigned them), his role as the family's banker (including monies given or loaned to Lidian and his brother William), his travel expenses for his lectures and his receipts from them, and the instructions he gave his publishers, including when to reprint his works and in how many copies, and his receipts from them.

Emerson Family Papers

The descendants of Ralph Waldo Emerson not only kept his papers together for future generations to study; they also helped edit parts of them. Amelia Forbes Emerson (1888–1979), who had married Edward Waldo Emerson's son Raymond (1886–1977), edited the *Diary and Letters of William Emerson 1743–1776*, Waldo's grandfather (Boston: Thomas Todd, 1972). Edith W. Gregg, Waldo's great-granddaughter, contributed editions of letters by his first wife, *One First Love: The Letters of Ellen Louisa Tucker to Ralph Waldo Emerson* (Cambridge, MA: Harvard University Press, 1962; she lived 1811–1831, and had married Waldo in 1829), and his elder daughter, *The Letters of Ellen Tucker Emerson* (2 vols., Kent, OH: Kent State University Press, 1982).

Many of the letters from Emerson's first wife were used, along with materials then in the possession of Dr. Wortis, in Henry F. Pommer's *Emerson's First Marriage* (Carbondale: Southern Illinois University Press, 1967). The private writings of Emerson's second wife, Lidian, who married Waldo in 1835, have appeared in Delores Bird Carpenter's editions of Lidian's daughter Ellen's *The Life of Lidian Jackson Emerson* (Boston: Twayne, 1980), and *The Selected Letters of Lidian Jackson Emerson* (Columbia: University of Missouri Press, 1987).

Emerson's aunt Mary Moody Emerson had been portrayed variously as a somewhat difficult figure until the revisionist work by Phyllis Cole, *Mary Moody Emerson and the Origins of Transcendentalism: A Family History* (New York: Oxford University Press, 1998), argued for her centrality in her nephew's intellectual growth. Two editions have continued to demonstrate her importance: *The Selected Letters of Mary Moody Emerson* (ed. Nancy Craig Simmons, Athens: University of Georgia Press, 1993), and the ongoing *The Almanacks of Mary Moody Emerson: A Scholarly Digital Edition* (ed. Noelle A. Baker and Sandra Harbert Petrulionis, documented by Baker in this volume).

The correspondence among the four Emerson brothers is quoted from liberally in *The Emerson Brothers: A Fraternal Biography in Letters* (ed. Bosco and Myerson, New York: Oxford University Press, 2006); transcripts of the letters themselves (except for Waldo's) are on the website of the Ralph Waldo Emerson Society ("The Correspondence of Charles, Edward, and William Emerson"). Edward's letters written in Spanish and his journal of travels in the Caribbean are in José G. Rigau-Pérez's *Edward Bliss Emerson: The Caribbean Journal and Letters, 1831–1834* (2013).

Notes

1. For further information on Emerson's career in publishing, see Joel Myerson, "Ralph Waldo Emerson's Income from His Books," in *The Professions of Authorship: Essays in Honor of Matthew J. Bruccoli*, ed. Richard Layman and Myerson (Columbia: University of South Carolina Press, 1996), 135–49.
2. See *CW* 8:clx–ccxi, for an extended discussion of the fire, its aftermath, its impact on Emerson's wellbeing, and the publication of Emerson's later works. Bosco's "Historical Introduction" traces in detail Emerson's loss of memory and cognitive abilities.
3. For Edith's work in preparing *Parnassus*, see Ronald A. Bosco, "'Poetry for the World of Readers' and 'Poetry for Bards Proper': Poetic Theory and Textual Integrity in Emerson's *Parnassus*," *Studies in the American Renaissance* (1989): 257–312.
4. For Cabot, see Nancy Craig Simmons, "Arranging the Sibylline Leaves: James Elliot Cabot's Work as Emerson's Literary Executor," *Studies in the American Renaissance* (1983): 335–89.
5. The Emerson Family Papers were used primarily by Rusk in his biography of Emerson and his edition of Emerson's letters, Henry Pommer in his biography of Ellen Louisa Tucker Emerson, and Bosco and Myerson in *The Emerson Brothers* (see below for full citations).
6. Both editions continued through 1893 with the addition of the *Natural History of Intellect* volume.
7. For a discussion of some issues raised concerning the editorial practices of the first two volumes of the *Collected Works*, see *Ralph Waldo Emerson: The Major Prose*, ed. Bosco and Myerson (Cambridge, MA: Harvard University Press, 2015), xxxv–xxxix, as well as a review of the edition's evolving editorial theories in Robert N. Hudspeth's "The Collected Works of Ralph Waldo Emerson," *Nineteenth-Century Prose* 40, no. 2 (Fall 2013): 1–104. Another issue in some volumes was the reliance on what the editors called Emerson's "correction" copies and/or lists of what he called "Consideranda." Unfortunately, they often adopted these readings instead of evaluating them, as did Emerson, as revisions to be considered or evaluated (see *Poems* in *CW*, where the editors state these "potential emendations" amounted to "nothing more than memoranda to be acted upon or not at such time" as the work might be reprinted *(CW* 9:cxiii–cxiv).
8. For *Selected Poems*, see also Joseph M. Thomas, "Late Emerson: *Selected Poems* and the 'Emerson Factory,'" *ELH: English Literary History* 65 (Winter 1998): 971–94.
9. See the "Textual Introduction" to *Uncollected Prose Writings* for a full discussion of the editorial principles involved.
10. Rather than give full publication information for the many editions to be cited hereafter, we use the numbers assigned these works in Myerson's *Ralph Waldo Emerson: A Descriptive Bibliography* (Pittsburgh: University of Pittsburgh Press, 1982).
11. Some comments still thought to be sensitive in 1939 were left out at the family's request. They were restored in Tilton's edition (see below). For more on Rusk, see Glen M. Johnson's biographical and critical sketch in the *Dictionary of Literary Biography* 103:241–49.
12. Nor did he publish those letters included in his 1934 edition of Emerson's correspondence with Clough (A 56) and 1939 edition of those to the poet Emma Lazarus (D 207). He did, however, publish selected letters from Waldo's brothers, Margaret Fuller, and Caroline Sturgis (Tappan). The substantial but unpublished Emerson-Sturgis correspondence is currently being edited for publication by Bosco and Sarah Ann Wider.
13. The press and the readers who examined proof for the edition were unaware that Tilton was suffering from cognitive decline and errors appeared, including dropping a sentence

from the famous "I Greet You at the Beginning of a Great Career" letter to Whitman. Students and scholars who reference letters from this edition in what they propose to be serious scholarship would be wise to visit the library holding the original or purchase a copy of the original.

14. We have made no attempt to record the various smaller editions or magazine and journal appearances of Emerson's letters. They are listed in Myerson's *Ralph Waldo Emerson: A Descriptive Bibliography* and its *Supplement* (New Castle, DE: Oak Knoll Press; Pittsburgh: University of Pittsburgh Press, 2005).
15. The cutoff date of 1842 was chosen because that is where the lectures published in *EL* concluded.
16. Much of the history of *JMN* is drawn from Ralph H. Orth, "William Gilman: A Reminiscence," *Emerson Society Papers* 32, no. 1 (Spring 2021): 1, 5–8.
17. The *JMN* practice of presenting a genetic text, one which reproduced Emerson's revisions by using symbols, was praised by most scholars but also attacked, most famously by Edmund Wilson in the January 18, 1967 *New York Review of Books*, where he complained that Emerson's manuscript revisions were seen "through a barbed wire entanglement of diacritical marks," concluding, "Nothing has been lost by this process—except Emerson" ("Emerson Behind Barbed Wire"). Numerous measured responses pointed out that the *JMN* produced an authoritative edition that would allow subsequent users of the texts to create a clear reading text.
18. For a comprehensive collection from the Journals see Ralph Waldo Emerson, *Selected Journals*, ed. Lawrence Rosenwald, 2 vols. (New York: Library of America, 2010).

CHAPTER 24

EMERSON, NATURE, AND NETWORKS IN THE BLACK PRESS

BRIGITTE FIELDER

Over the past twenty years many scholars such as Len Gougeon, Joel Myerson, Martha Schoolman, and Christopher Hanlon have focused on Emerson's antislavery activism, which began in 1844 with Emerson's August 1 address on the abolition of slavery in the British Caribbean and which grew in intensity after Congress's passage of the Fugitive Slave Law in 1850. This body of scholarship effectively recovered Emerson as a public-minded thinker who invested himself in struggles over racial justice, and much of it has focused on Emerson's relations with other white abolitionists such as William Lloyd Garrison, Wendell Phillips, Theodore Parker, Henry Thoreau, and John Brown. Among treatments of Emerson's relationship to race, Nell Irvin Painter has productively taken up Emerson's approach to whiteness.[1] While much scholarly attention has been given to Emerson's writings both on slavery and on race, far fewer have considered approaches to his work from Black perspectives and in Black contexts.

And yet, interest in Emerson's position in the constellation of race and racial justice extends not only from his abolitionism, and not only from his occasional failure to transcend the racialist paradigms of his day, but by way of the quite separate matter of nineteenth-century Black interests in nature and networks. For instance, one absence conspicuous in Emerson scholarship is an assessment of the ways Emerson circulated in the Black press during the years prior to or following the Civil War. This chapter will address this significant gap in our understanding of Emerson's public profile by attending to the ways Black writers and readers engaged Emerson in Black print contexts. But by eschewing, rather than centering, slavery as the topic for Black engagements with this thinker, I reach beyond the most predictable topics of interest in Emerson.

Examining the ways Emerson generated meaning within the authorial circles and editorial spaces within and among which his work circulated—and taking up related

Black writing with which we might productively read him—I here explore a useful methodology for acknowledging racially diverse readerships even of white writers. This approach acknowledges the breadth of Black intellectualism that has been irresponsibly downplayed in nineteenth-century scholarship, accentuating the ways in which not only Emersonian abolitionism, but also Emersonian Transcendentalism, spoke to Black writers, editors, and readers. It also allows us to more fully explore the Black literary and intellectual culture that is often masked by disproportionate attention to white writers.

The work I treat here is not the usual writing for considering Emerson's relationship to Black readers; it is writing without an obvious antislavery message. I take for the occasion of my analysis an extended discussion of Emerson's poetry in the Black press, a discussion of Emerson's 1867 collection *May-Day and Other Pieces*, published in the June 1 *Christian Recorder* of that year. The newspaper reprinted an excerpt from the first two pieces in this collection, "May-Day" and "The Adirondacs," along with a brief reading of each. Approaching Emerson as a well-known though variously celebrated poet, the analysis features Emerson's poetic bridging of sensations in the natural world and the expansion of communication technology networks.

While this may initially seem an unexpected treatment of Emerson, more closely examining this context for reading Emerson amid Black attention to both nature and networks allows us to surmise what appeal these particular poems may have had for the paper's readers. I take up this discussion of Emerson's poetry, contextualized alongside the various genres and conversations that appeared in the antebellum and Reconstruction-era Black press with which we might put Emerson's writing into conversation. This reading shows that Emerson's poetry resonated alongside not only his antislavery work but within a longer context of Black freedom struggle. Thus, this chapter appropriates Emerson's work for contexts (and perhaps for purposes) different than Emerson himself may have intended and within which few scholars have considered him.

Beyond Abolitionism

Emerson's abolitionism has been widely noted, in part because white abolitionists have been given disproportionate attention in academic and popular discussions of antislavery history. Accordingly, scholars have overwhelmingly discussed him in relation to other white abolitionists. But indeed, treating Emerson's abolitionism within a strictly white context is part of a larger framing of American abolitionism as a project undertaken by white actors on behalf of Black victims of slavery. Rather, the history of abolitionism is a chronicle of Black advocacy, organizing, and publishing. As scholars such as Kellie Carter Jackson and Manisha Sinha have noted, recognizing the centrality of Black abolitionists to emancipation movements helps to put white antislavery efforts into perspective, particularly within a longer history of Black freedom efforts.

In fact, when one considers white abolitionists within this larger scope and history, one might say that white abolitionists seem less exceptional. While white antislavery advocates are often lauded for even moderate antislavery positions, the bar is set low. In her discussion of Black literary theory, Koritha Mitchell notes "how often white mediocrity is treated as merit."[2] White abolitionism might be one such form of mediocrity. Opposition to enslavement is a basic prerequisite for human decency that is overrepresented in conversations about abolition, and which displaces other orientations to racial justice.[3] This is not to say that Emerson was, himself, mediocre as a thinker or writer, or to discount the fact of white abolitionism as an exceptional (i.e., unusual) position for nineteenth-century white thinkers. But to reframe abolitionism in these terms allows one to look beyond the framing of white abolitionist exceptionalism for understanding Black interest in Emerson.

If we regard an antislavery stance not as exceptional but as requisite, one might take the finer points of Emerson's abolitionism and compare him to his other antislavery contemporaries. In doing so, to compare him only to white abolitionists would, of course, compress artificially the discursive and political spaces in which he worked. Situating Emerson within the context that includes the work and the words of Black abolitionists puts him alongside activists for whom abolition was not an ultimate goal, but merely a necessary one amid a variety of other (and more radical) steps toward Black freedom. Because many Black intellectuals were noted abolitionists, and because too many white nineteenth-century thinkers failed to engage Black intellectualism beyond abolition, we must consider how Black abolitionists were not simply in conversation with mainstream white abolitionism, but more consistently drove the movement toward various forms of radical equality beyond the literal abolition of slavery. Further, if we trace the flow of abolitionist discourse to its origins in Black activism and intellectualism, we might better understand how Black thinkers may have related to white abolitionists like Emerson. For while Black thinkers often praised white antislavery advocates for their efforts, they also critiqued them.

Given his importance as a public intellectual, it is perhaps unsurprising that antebellum Black newspapers noted Emerson's antislavery work. Editors of periodicals such as the *Christian Recorder, The North Star, Frederick Douglass' Paper, The Provincial Freeman,* and the *Weekly Anglo-African* reprinted and reported on Emerson in antislavery contexts, noting him among other white abolitionists, though discussions of Emerson with regard to abolition have overshadowed the history of this engagement. One primary result of this gap in the scholarship has been to emphasize Emerson's relationship to the anonymous enslaved rather than to free Black people who were not only his contemporaries but potential interlocutors.

Moreover, Black abolitionists were always engaged beyond this necessary but insufficient movement toward Black emancipation. Manisha Sinha, for example, describes abolition as a movement "which addressed the entrenched problems of exploitation and disenfranchisement in a liberal democracy and anticipated debates over race, labor, and empire."[4] Black abolitionism was always intertwined with other complex intellectual, literary, and activist engagements. In this, abolitionism was not an entryway for Black thinkers into white intellectual discourse; rather, antislavery thought offered white agents such as Emerson a potential entryway into conversation with Black thinkers. In other words, Black interests extended beyond the limitations of white antislavery actors, a fact that might refocus away from antislavery activism when considering Emerson's relation to Black intellectual discourse.

Even if his antislavery stance may have been an entryway for or even a prerequisite to Black engagement with the popular white thinker, Black engagement with Emerson beyond his abolitionism is unsurprising. Scholars such as Carla Peterson, Eric Gardner, Daniel Hack, and Matt Sandler have discussed the various ways that nineteenth-century Black intellectuals engaged white thinkers and writers, reading broadly and contributing to interracial literary conversations even while the majority of their white contemporaries failed to engage nonwhite interlocutors. Even beyond abolitionism, it is no surprise that Emerson is among the white writers who engaged Black readers and writers in Black contexts. For unlike the majority of their white counterparts, Black intellectuals capaciously reached across racial lines in their engagement.[5]

Because their intellectual investments extended beyond abolition, Black thinkers were also interested in Emerson beyond his antislavery politics. Black readers (like white readers) of Emerson were interested in a multitude of things, even while abolition was key. Therefore, antislavery discussions formed only one context in which Emerson was given attention in the Black press. Black writers praised Emerson's intellect, naming him in their litany of public intellectual figures and laudable writers. They also showed how Black investments both in and beyond abolition dovetailed with Transcendentalist thought.

Transcendentalism was not an exclusively white intellectual philosophical/social movement. While this fact may be unsurprising to scholars of Black studies, it requires stating in discussions of intellectual discourse that have overwhelmingly centered white thinkers, giving them disproportionate attention while obscuring others. Some scholars have included Black intellectualism in conversations about Emerson's potential interlocutors. As Peter Wirzbicki has noted, Black Transcendentalists such as William Cooper Nell and others associated with the Adelphic Union (a Boston lyceum and intellectual club that was a center for Black thought) were in conversation with white Transcendentalists such as Emerson.[6] Eric Gardner reads Edmonia Highgate's engagement with Transcendentalist thinkers, Emerson included.[7] And Matt Sandler connects Emerson's "seething brain" figure of speech to midcentury Black Romantic poets such as Joshua McCarter Simpson, Elymas Payson Rogers, James Monroe Whitfield, George Boyer Vashon, James Madison Bell, and Frances Ellen Watkins Harper in what he describes as "dissonant and revolutionary lyrics, aimed at both sensuality and intellect."[8]

To give just one example, we might take James Whitfield's poem, "Self Reliance," which first appeared in the *North Star* in December 1849.[9] The poem begins, "I love the man whose lofty mind / On God and its own strength relies."[10] This is not explicitly an antislavery poem (though it may be read in this vein) as it alludes to worldly struggles alongside relations to an Almighty force, to which individual strength is tied. Whitfield's subject is confident, "But trusting in the aid of Heaven, / And wielding, with unfaltering arm, / The utmost power which God has given." One might say this sentiment is Emersonian, echoing Emerson's coupling of individual and Divine power. Whitfield's poem, though not quoting directly from Emerson, seems to share the white writer's sentiment that "God will not have his work made manifest by cowards" (*CW* 2:28). But these sentiments aren't exclusively Emersonian. As Robert S. Levine and Ivy G. Wilson note in their edition of Whitfield's poetry, Emerson did not invent the phrase or the concept of "self-reliance," which the Oxford English Dictionary dates as early as 1833.[11] Rather, Emerson and Whitfield were both part of a broader landscape of literary intellectualism that evidences the participation of Black thinkers and writers beyond simply responding to white ones.

I turn briefly to this work in order to situate Black engagement with Emerson in a larger context of Black Transcendentalism and to show how Transcendentalist ideas might also be read alongside other prominent forms of Black thought. Wirzbicki notes that, even as many historians have sidestepped considering what Black activists thought about Transcendentalism, "even fewer have asked what Transcendentalism might have learned from black intellectuals."[12] What they might learn, too, extends beyond abolitionism. My next section will take up the decidedly Transcendentalist theme of union with nature by exploring the Black intellectual and creative musings that engaged with Emerson in the Black press.

May-Day's "Sultry Morning": Nature Writing in the *Christian Recorder*

The most extended treatment of Emerson in the *Christian Recorder*, the official publication of the African Methodist Episcopal Church, was not about his abolitionism but a treatment of his writing about nature and technology. It is not surprising to find Emersion in this venue, even when abolitionism is not the topic. As Eric Gardner notes, "the *Recorder* published a range of material about transcendentalism, including a large excerpt from *Walden*—'A Battle between Ants'—in March 1863, an extended extract from Thoreau's 1842 *Dial* piece 'Natural History of Massachusetts' in May 1864, and brief quotes from several transcendentalists."[13] While Emerson is mentioned specifically in various places in this paper, this is his most extended (extant) treatment in this venue and therefore merits attention.

Just as abolitionism and Transcendentalism were not exclusively white movements or discourses, neither was engagement with nature the sole purview of white literature. However, Black engagements with nature have often been ignored in white contexts. In the introduction to her anthology, *Black Nature: Four Centuries of African American Nature Poetry,* Camille T. Dungy notes that, while African Americans are "fundamental to the natural fabric of this nation," they "have been noticeably absent from tables of contents" in conversations on topics such as ecocriticism and ecopoetics.[14] Dungy's collection traces Black engagement with the natural world as early as the eighteenth century, via Phillis Wheatley's poem "On Imagination," included in her 1773 *Poems on Various Subjects, Religious and Moral*, in which "Show'rs may descend, and dews their gems disclose, / And nectar sparkle on the blooming rose." Such examples show that African American nature writing is not new and illustrate that we miss much when we leave out Black writing on nature.[15]

African American people engaged with nature from their own distinctly racialized perspectives, even as these perspectives are often excluded from discussions of nature writing—including in Transcendentalism. As with Black interests beyond abolitionism, discussions of nature were not isolated from but intertwined with other Black interests. Dungy discusses nature poetry in the Western intellectual canon that spans from Virgil to the Transcendentalists as informing "prevailing views of the natural world as a place of positive collaboration, refuge, idyllic rural life, or wilderness." She takes up the pastoral in her discussion of Black nature poetry, noting that "the poetry of African Americans only conforms to these [white] traditions in limited ways."[16] But Black engagements with nature (like other Black intellectual engagements) were not as racially isolated as white ones.

Emerson's 1867 "May-Day" and "The Adirondacs" were both excerpted and discussed in the June 1 *Christian Recorder* of that year. I will turn to the latter in my next section. I take up the first of these in order to illustrate how, even in historical contexts of anti-Black violence and Black resistance, Black discourse on nature included its celebration. In the pages of the *Christian Recorder*, we read engagement with Emerson's nature poetry in a larger Black print context that also engaged nature. In this we see some hint (as Dungy has it) of "the natural world as a place of positive collaboration, refuge, idyllic rural life, or wilderness."[17] We can also read here a distinctly Black nature writing context, as nature is examined and reflected on and celebrated in the larger context of Black efforts for and beyond abolition.

The *Christian Recorder*'s discussion of "Emerson's New Poems" begins with praise. Asserting universal appreciation among "all who have carefully read his essays or his poems," the piece includes Black people among these careful readers, taking African Americans' engagement and understanding of these as a given.[18] As Eric Gardner notes, the newspaper's assessment "assumes some reader familiarity with Emerson and transcendentalism."[19] It cites Emerson's 1836 essay *Nature* without attribution, suggesting that readers recognize these lines as Emerson's own vision that "man imprisoned, man crystallized, man vegetative, unconscious man, speaks to man impersonated who is self-conscious nature." As much as his antislavery writing, these musings of the "philosopher-poet" are of interest to the *Christian Recorder*'s Black readers.

This piece is also an occasion to introduce Emerson's new work, the volume recently published by Ticknor and Fields. The piece goes on to quote twenty-seven lines from Emerson's title poem. While the *Christian Recorder* (like other nineteenth-century newspapers) often reprinted poetry from a variety of authors and sources, editors did not always choose to reprint that work, even while recommending it to their readers.[20]

The space devoted to Emerson's nature poetry in the *Christian Recorder*'s pages is one indication of the extent of the newspaper's treatment of his work.

The *Christian Recorder*'s discussion of "May-Day" leads with an interest in nature writing.[21] Describing Emerson's teachings as "philosophic Pantheism," the article also offers what seems like an aesthetic assessment of his poetics, in which "the grass, the flower, the fruit, and the birds, are made to speak their own thoughts rather than those supplied to them by the interpreter." This poetic prowess seems a vehicle for realizing both nature's divinity and human connections to the natural divine. The sense given here is that, via these poems, nature is experienced, rather than interpreted, and this is Emerson's key accomplishment. The piece not only presents this new example of nature writing but presents it as a prime example. We read that "the leading poem ... is decidedly the best which we remember ever to have seen from Mr. Emerson's pen—indeed, portions of it have seldom been surpassed in power of description and delicacy of delineation of the sensations (if we may use the paradox) of inanimate nature."[22] Reproducing these opening lines, the *Christian Recorder*'s editors give its readers access to these "powerful sensations" themselves.

"May-Day" was not alone in the *Christian Recorder*'s nature writing; it appeared as part of a clearing-house of such romantic treatments of the natural world in which readers encountered other nature poetry treating themes of flora, and fauna, and seasons. I turn now to read "May-Day" alongside examples from elsewhere in the *Christian Recorder* in order to situate this reading of Emerson within this context for Black nature writing. Reading "May-Day" alongside "the grass, the flower, the fruit, and the birds," we might begin with the perennial, a marking of time's recurrence that we also read in Emerson's poem. This piece's reprinting of Emerson's title poem begins mid-stanza, juxtaposing the coming day with the change of seasons.

> But soft! A sultry morning breaks;
> The cowslips make the brown brook gay;
> A happier hour, a longer day.
> Now the sun leads in the May,
> Now desire of action wakes,
> And the wish to roam.

Coupling the lengthening days with the changing seasons, the shift from winter to spring is joyous, bringing "happier hours" and waking "desire of action." The *Christian Recorder* describes these "lines on the awakening influences of opening spring" as "very suggestive"—though suggestive of what, the piece does not say. Reading these reprinted lines in the context of the post-emancipation African American press reveals the convergence of nature poetry and politicized writing for a Black audience.

Readers considering Emerson's description of a "sultry morning" breaking in this early moment in the process of Reconstruction may well have read resonances of different temporal scales in this presentation of "morning." Elsewhere I have similarly discussed the significance of *Christian Recorder* readers being directed to Emily

Dickinson's "Morning" in *St. Nicholas* magazine in May of 1891.[23] Just as readers might have read Dickinson's opening question, "Will there really be a morning?" with a mixture of skepticism and faith in this late-century moment of the nadir, the breaking of a morning in 1867 signified more than a new day, but a moment of historical shift and continuing engagement. As Black men approached their imminent (though soon-to-be-thwarted) enfranchisement and as Black women continued to lobby for their own voting rights, Emerson's line, "Now desire of action wakes," resonates with a fatigue over deliberation and an accompanying yearning for change. We also see hope in Emerson's poem, that "wakes the wish in youngest blood / To tread the forfeit Paradise" to which they will return. A similar linking of natural, cyclical change and revolutionary change appear in William C. Nell's "The Morning Dawns," where morning is not only expected but achieved through action. Not divorced from nature, but intermingled with and interested in it, we might read these Black engagements with Emerson, reframed within the context of the Black press, as giving racialized meaning to these musings on the natural world. The second half of this *Christian Recorder* piece about Emerson's poetry, a reading of his "Adirondacs," further illustrates African American interests in topics for which mainstream white discourse often erases Black thought and counters false dichotomies that would separate the natural from the technological.

"Thought's New Found Path": Cables and Other Black Communication Networks

"Emerson's New Poems" turns from its discussion of "May-Day" to "the Cable of 1858" and Emerson's "Adirondacs," also included in his 1867 volume. "Adirondacs," this piece holds, "differs widely from 'May-Day' in style as in subject, but it has some fine passages."[24] As with "May-Day," the writer devotes space in the paper to reproducing much of the poem. (Indeed, while giving more commentary on "May-Day," the editor reprints more of "Adirondacs"—thirty-two lines total.) Unlike with "May-Day," the *Christian Recorder*'s quotation begins late in this poem, several pages into Emerson's lines. The newspaper begins with the lines that reveal the cable itself:

> With a vermilion pencil mark the day
> When of our little fleet three cruising skiffs
> Entering Big Tupper bound for the foaming Falls
> Of loud Bog River, suddenly confront
> Two of our mates returning with swift oars,
> One held a printed journal waving high
> Caught from a late arriving traveler,
> Big with great news, and shouted the report

> For which the world had waited, now firm fact,
> Of the wire cable laid beneath the sea ...

The *Christian Recorder*'s reprinted lines continue for the entire thirty-two-line stanza. These lines take up more than a page and a half of Emerson's original volume.

The juxtaposition of "May-Day" and "Adirondacs" in the *Christian Recorder* gives some sense of the breadth of possible interest in Emerson's writing beyond abolition. Like the displacement of Black thought on nature, there has been a long history of white erasure of Black contributions to and interest in science and technology. Rayvon Fouché notes, for example, the undervaluation of both Black technological contributions and experiences. He describes both the "historical reduction" that "robs black inventors of their humanity ... and produces disembodied icons celebrated merely for their patented material production" and histories that have "ignored technology as an institutional force that marginalizes black people within American society and culture."[25] As *Christian Recorder* readers, like Emerson, marveled at the "wire cable laid beneath the sea ... pulsating / With ductile fire," one wonders whether readers may have interpreted the stanza's last line, "Let them hear well! 'tis theirs as much as ours" in terms of rights or access to this technological development. Black interest in this communication technology and Emerson's discussion of it are unsurprising when we contextualize the cable's significance for periodicals like the *Christian Recorder*. Newspaper referents to the cable as an infrastructure of print echo Emerson's description of the "printed journal waving high."

Various commentary on cable technology appeared in the *Christian Recorder* between its 1858 completion and in the aftermath of the second transatlantic cable, laid in 1865, and third, in 1866. These included comments on the cable's cost, labor, and materials, as well as its use-value.[26] This conversation on the implications of rapid communication centers on information's control. The question of how the telegraph will affect relations of global trade involves what information will be transmitted by this mechanism, to whom, and when. Reading about the telegraph in Black contexts raises clear questions about how this information technology would become a contribution to African American networks for print communication. Christopher Hanlon describes how domestic and transatlantic discussions of the telegraph interrogated its implications for slavery, given international and regional divides regarding abolitionism and notions of technology as a harbinger of progress.[27] Here we see the question of the telegraph's potential uses either in opposition to slavery or in its support and with its benefit.

At the same time, the technology could also contribute to Black communication networks. African American newspapers served as one such network. Interest in the new telegraphic technology that Emerson celebrates was also noted in the pages of the Black press. *The Self-Elevator*'s first issue, for example, described itself as a periodical to be "Published Semi Monthly, and is devoted to the subject of General elevation among the Colored People of this country. It will also contain the latest intelligence by telegraph and the mails, and all local news of the week, up to the time of putting the paper to press."[28] The *Christian Recorder* also noted the usefulness of the transatlantic cable. There, a brief notice in February of 1867 noted the use of the cable in the newspaper's correspondence, explaining that "our readers will find on our second and third pages, a full summary of political news, both home and foreign including the latest dispatches by the *Atlantic Cable*."[29] In these print contexts, the potentially political uses of the telegraph become apparent.

Like Transcendentalism itself, the technology of the telegraph was not divorced from Black discourses of abolition. When considering Black interest in this communication technology, we might first acknowledge the specifically racialized importance of communication networks. James Redpath discussed a different kind of telegraph in his narrative of encounters with enslaved people as he traveled in the south between 1854 and 1856. In his assessment of the "thriving" Underground Railroad, Redpath also described what he called an "Underground Telegraph," the "secret and rapid modes of communication among the slave population of the South," a careful system of movement and communication by which information was transmitted.[30] According to Redpath, this network was a key part of abolitionist efforts but this was not its only purpose. It was meant also to facilitate everyday Black life, a product of a natural desire to maintain relationships, growing out of "social desires ... love of gossip and wish to meet their friends and relatives."[31] Recounting his encounters near Charleston, Redpath notes the rapidity of the telegraph as information was "passed from plantation to plantation."[32] He is awed by the accuracy of information transmitted in this way. He notes also its span across geographic regions, connecting even free Canada to the "Slave States." In this context for information's transmission and control, he notes also the danger of the telegraph in its potential use for insurrection. Black communication networks were, so to speak, a technology for emancipation.

In this context of Black communication, we read about the cable as a celebratory technology. While this is quite usual for discussions of telegraph technology in the midcentury, it counters popular misreadings of technology's racial resonances in what Louis Chude-Sokei describes as "the all-too-easy assumption that ... blacks are either in an adversarial relationship to technology or fundamentally opposed to it due to lack of access or differential conceptual and political priorities."[33] While the *Christian Recorder* includes some critique of the cable's cost and concerns about its upkeep, the newspaper's discussions were more often favorable. An item in the "News of the Week" in the May 25 issue lauded the cable's ability to connect people across the globe. This read, "THE *ATLANTIC CABLE* has almost brought the extremities of the earth together. It is announced from Newburyport, Massachusetts, that a merchant of that city recently received a telegram from Calcutta, which had been but two days and five hours on its passage. This dispatch cost $500, and had traveled over 13,000 miles."[34] The paper's introduction to Emerson's poem similarly notes a celebration that has been augmented by the cable's continued operation, describing his poem in which "the exultant outburst of triumphant joy on learning that the Atlantic cable had been successfully (?) laid, can now be read with better appreciation than any of the intervening years since the time of which the poem treats."[35] This is a poem that hopefully celebrates the cable as utility, wherein "thought's new found path / Shall supplement henceforth all trodden ways" as the cable might be employed to speak to the breadth of Black interests. The parenthetical question mark following "successfully" signals the tentative (i.e., uncertain) nature of this hope for technological success.

But even recognizing its utility, we might understand Black interest in the cable as a technological wonder approaching something like the sublime. In this, the coupling of the natural with the technological in Emerson's work—and in Black interest—is evident. We see this in the connections between utility and nature that appear elsewhere in the newspaper. Although technological development has at times been imagined in opposition to nature, an idealist consideration of technology also includes appreciation that extends beyond use-value. This much is suggested by this and the paper's other musings on the technological, and is reinforced by a juxtaposition that appears on the same page as "Emerson's New Poems." In the adjacent column to the right, readers find a piece called "The Utility of Flowers," which reprinted a selection from Joseph Breck's 1866 *New Book of Flowers*.[36] The brief piece includes about a page of Breck's text, interspersed with brief lines from white Romantic poet Horace Smith's poem "Hymn to the Flowers" that were also included in the original. "The Utility of Flowers" begins by questioning the prioritization of utility: "There is a class of men who would pare down everything to the mere grade of *utility*, who think it the height of wisdom to ask, when one manifest enthusiasm in the culture of flowers, 'of what use are they?' With such we have no sympathy." This piece speaks specifically to the aesthetic value of nature, characterized as "luminously displayed … perfections of the Creator." Here nature and the divine are connected (a point to which I return below). Moreover, this excerpt challenges the notion that appreciation and cultivation of natural beauty necessitates neglecting "the necessary," refusing to put nature in opposition with utility. In its last line, "The Utility of Flowers" characterizes nature in terms that veer toward both the divine and the technological, describing flowers as "the wondrous mechanism of the Almighty."[37] This turn reimagines resemblances between the natural and the contrived.

The juxtaposition by which the *Christian Recorder*'s discussion of Emerson's writing on nature and technology is situated literally alongside this celebration of nature gives some small idea of the newspaper's variety of interests. "Emerson's New Poems" and "The Utility of Flowers" both appeared in a section labeled "The Home Circle," which appeared on the issue's final page, where readers also encountered advertisements and a poem titled "My Mother." The "Home Circle" for this issue also included pieces about work ethic, homeopathic medicine, religious aphorism, and an essay of "Encouragement to Sunday-School Teachers." Nestled in this section of what we must also continually remember was a Black Christian publication, conversations about nature and aesthetic appreciation were framed as partaking in a sort of divine machinery. My final section turns to the theological connections between nature and networks in this context.

"Greet the Glad Miracle": Emersonian Engagements and Black Theology

Black engagements with Transcendentalism may, of course, translate elevation's spiritual connotations to Black spiritual contexts. While Transcendentalism veered toward nonsectarian understandings of the metaphysical, Black Christianity employed not dissimilar notions of higher law and otherworldly existence as guiding ethical principles and a source of motivation in the face of adversity. Like "uplift," notions of "elevation" were tied to not only self-betterment, but societal betterment, and as such connected individuals to a larger—even otherworldly—sphere. Within an explicitly Christian context, readers might also have interpreted perennial change alongside nature's divinity; a framing of the perennial might be understood as natural evolution toward God's will—or even an eschatological hope for the changes of "morning" or "May."

Such a reading of Black theological and Transcendentalist connections is visible in the writing of Black Transcendentalist Edmonia Highgate. Gardner takes up Highgate's writing in the *Christian Recorder* between 1865 and 1867, exposing the ways that African American women, especially, have been erased from histories of Transcendentalism and the need to look for Black women's voices in further scholarship on this intellectual history.[38] As we turn to Highgate we might also recognize the fact that women were also readers of the *Christian Recorder* and likely encountered Emerson's poetry there. Highgate's writing in the *Christian Recorder* gives an example of how Black Christian women engaged Transcendentalism.

Highgate explores Nature's divine trajectory in an essay, "Truth," appearing in the October 1866 *Christian Recorder*. Highgate writes:

> Nature, all nature, proclaims truth. Her beautiful symbolic forms teach it. Notice with me the doctrine in her consecutive whirls of stars, that are loop-holes in the floor of the Eternal; in those same circles in the layers of the tree trunks; in the corolla; in the arrangement of leaves on the stem and in the leaf-bud; in the wavelets in the stream; in the strata of the various incrustations of the earth; in every stone; in the drops that descend to fertilize the earth; in the formation of the human eye; in magnetism and electricity, and none the less so in the most delicate circlets in the abdominal bud just at a time when the human verges nearest the Divine Creator.[39]

Gardner describes that "Highgate's concept of nature is Emersonian" here, connecting "Truth" to his 1841 essay, "Circles."[40] The truthful perfections Highgate perceives are eternal because they are circular, like the perennial changes of seasons. Like Highgate's and Emerson's circles, these cycles are present in the "symbolic forms" that teach elements of nature and humans alike. Highgate presents truth as natural, and also aligned with a Christian Divine Creator, writing that "Christ said of God, 'Thy Word is truth.'"

As Emerson mixes nature with Biblical allusion in "May-Day," we might also consider how this would have signified for Black Christian readers. Lines like:

> And so, perchance, in Adam's race,
> Of Eden's bower some dream-like trace
> Survived the Flight, and swam the flood,
> And wakes the wish in youngest blood
> To tread the forfeit Paradise,
> And feed once more the exile's eyes

resonate in a racialized theological context here. These evocations of exile and "Flight" are particularly salient in an African American Christian theological tradition that made new meaning of Old Testament histories of slavery, exile, and return. In the African Methodist Episcopal Church's paper, both Highgate's evocation of the Divine and Emerson's allusions to Old Testament scriptures were imbued with Christian meaning.

Emerson's "Flight" here evokes not only that of God's people but also creatures. Though the author praises Emerson's treatment of "inanimate nature" this is not only a depiction of inanimacy. Action attends both Emerson's narrator and the natural subjects they encounter, who also "wish to roam." Particularly fitting for the *Christian Recorder* are these lines:

> The caged linnet in the spring
> Harkens for the choral glee,
> When his fellows on the wing
> Migrate from the Southern Sea;

Caged and free birds are iconic in antislavery and other freedom poetry. Antislavery writers for both children and adults compared Black people and birds—not simply in dehumanizing conflations but in recognitions of human–animal relations via shared natural propensities toward freedom.[41] That birds symbolized freedom renders them also a source for inspiration in Black nature writing. Perhaps most famously, Paul Laurence Dunbar declared, "I know why the caged bird sings, ah me, / When his wing is bruised and his bosom sore,—" in his 1899 poem "Sympathy."[42] In this Black context, Emerson's "caged linnet" may "wish to roam" among a chorus of birds whose captivity or freedom resonated for Black freedom struggles within and beyond slavery. The natural world also held such racialized resonances.

A short story in the June 1, 1867 *Christian Recorder*, which appeared in the issue on the page before "Emerson's New Poems," framed birds as a source of comfort for its readers. "Comfort in Little Things" is a very brief account of a couple who become snowed in in a remote cabin, given as an example of how the heart might be "cheered by trifling incidents, and nerved for strength and endurance." While one encounter with nature here—a pack of wolves nearby—is undoubtedly threatening, it is also an encounter with nature that the woman says "gave me fresh courage." We read that "just then when I felt like giving up entirely, I heard a sweet song—a clear, cheerful piping of a bird. You cannot tell how it thrilled me. I looked from the window, and there right on the corner of our dwelling, it sat caroling just as sweet as if it were June." The bird inspires a hymn. "Said I to my husband, 'If that wee bit of a thing can sing, much more can I.'"[43] The natural is divine and the woman recognizes herself in and of the natural world. This story is not unlike the final lines we read in Emerson's poem in the *Christian Recorder*, in which birdsong also inspires:

> And ever when the happy child
> In May beholds the blooming wild,

And hears in heaven the blue-bird sing,
"Onward," he cries, "your baskets bring—
In the next field is air more mild,
And o'er yon hazy crest is Eden's balmier spring."[44]

Both Emerson's and these birds hearken hope for the coming spring, the latter on the cusp of May and the former in the depths of winter, still a reminder of the inevitable change of seasons.

While nods to the spiritual appear in Emerson's May Day appreciation of nature, they are also present in his musings on the cable. As with Emerson's own volume, the *Christian Recorder*'s context links the natural and technological, presented without opposition. In this context, we see how the paper's readers may well have read religious meaning into the "great news ... For which the world had waited." Emerson calls us to:

> Greet the glad miracle. Thought's new found Path
> Shall supplement henceforth all trodden ways,
> Match God's equator with a zone of art,
> And lift man's public action to a height
> Worthy the enormous cloud of witnesses ...

Alongside the paper's various offerings in which characters consult the Bible, seek the Lord's guidance, and facilitate Christian instruction for children, the "height / Worthy the enormous cloud of witnesses" to which the cable might lift human thought reaches also beyond notions of the device's utility. Reading the "new found Path" of the cable as also, perhaps, fulfilling a religious trajectory, "this triumph of mankind" becomes yet another kind of triumph. I read the religious implications of communication technology here without irony, understanding the various purposes for which readers might have understood this development.

As with articulations of the cable's political uses for conveying information in the Black press and elsewhere, we see here potential purposes for communicating about Christian theology. The *Christian Recorder* situated technological development explicitly alongside its particular religious mission. A piece by Rev. Henry Fowler appearing in March of 1867 discussed "Faith and the Cable."[45] The piece explicitly frames Cyrus W. Field, entrepreneurial creator of the Atlantic Telegraph Company, as a man of "heroic faith" who prayed to see his work carried out and gave thanks to God at seeing its success. Fowler describes the Atlantic cable as a "blessing to the world" and describes this communication technology alongside Christian missionary work.

> Yes, the Christian Church is striving to encircle the earth with the cable of Christian love, to bring all nations into the unity of Christian brotherhood, to declare the Gospel in the one language received by all mankind, to distribute the messages of salvation to every kindred and people and tribe, to every town and hamlet and house, and to every man, woman and child, to every conscience and to every soul. Sublime

purpose! If the Cable parts, a new one must be made! Yes, the old one must be fished up from the depths and be re-united.[46]

What may seem a standard sentiment of Christian brotherhood and connection might be understood differently in a Black Christian context. The "cable of Christian love" that might bring "all nations into the unity of Christian brotherhood" embracing "all mankind" does not simply beg the question of racial inclusion. Rather, on the *Christian Recorder*'s pages, this message of religious unity articulates a form of radical Christian inclusion to which not all US churches subscribed in 1867 (or even later). To understand the cable as a technological facilitator of this particular Christian mission, then, reframes the "sublime purpose!" as a simultaneously theological and political one. As Black people employed various technologies from print to telecommunication toward more racially equitable futures, this imagining of the cable situates these readers' interest within this larger scope of import.

Attending to Emerson in this Black print context, we might understand him both within the specific context of periodicals in which his name and work appeared but also within the broader reach of Black writing with which Black readers engaged. The appearance of "Emerson's New Poems" in the *Christian Recorder* is just one of many smatterings of Emerson's name and work that appeared throughout early African American periodicals. There are likely other apt opportunities in the Black press with which scholars might more closely consider Emerson's resonances for a Black audience. Taking Emerson out of exclusively or even predominantly white contexts, we find for him a broader selection of potential interlocutors. Acknowledging Black readers produces different resonances than those that imagine white writers only in relation to white perspectives. Such an acknowledgement must reach beyond white authors' writing about Black people or about race. To fully examine Emerson within Black contexts we must therefore consider his relationship to Black people beyond conversations about slavery. And in this, we gain a fuller comprehension of not only his work's reach and impact but also its intertextual resonances.

Notes

1. See Nell Irvin Painter, "Ralph Waldo Emerson's Saxons," *The Journal of American History* 95, no. 4 (March 2009): 977–85.
2. Koritha Mitchell, "Identifying White Mediocrity and Know-Your-Place Aggression: A Form of Self-Care," *African American Review* 51, no. 4 (Winter 2018): 253–62, 254.
3. Ijeoma Oluo writes similarly of white men's centering in social justice movements, past and present. See *Mediocre: The Dangerous Legacy of White Male America* (New York: Seal Press, 2021), 47–94.
4. Manisha Sinha, *The Slave's Cause: A History of Abolition* (New Haven, CT: Yale University Press, 2016), 1.
5. For recent work on Black engagement with white intellectual and literary histories see, for example, Carla Peterson, "Mapping Taste: Urban Modernities from the *Tatler* and

Spectator to *Frederick Douglass' Paper*," *American Literary History* 32, no. 4 (Winter 2020): 691–722, and Matt Sandler, *The Black Romantic Revolution: Abolitionist Poets at the End of Slavery* (New York and London: Verso, 2020).

6. See Peter Wirzbicki, *Fighting for the Higher Law: Black and White Transcendentalists Against Slavery* (Philadelphia: University of Pennsylvania Press, 2021), 277–99.
7. See Eric Gardner, "Each Atomic Part: Edmonia Goodelle Highgate's African American Transcendentalism," in *Toward a Female Genealogy of Transcendentalism*, ed. Jana L. Argersinger and Phyllis Cole (Athens: University of Georgia Press, 2014).
8. See Sandler, *Black Romantic Revolution*, 90, 94.
9. This poem was later included in Whitfield's 1853 collection, *America and Other Poems*, and some (revised) lines are recited in Martin Delany's novel, *Blake; or, The Huts of America*, which was serialized in the *Anglo-African Magazine* in 1859 and the *Weekly Anglo-African* from 1861 to 1862.
10. James M. Whitfield, "Self Reliance," *North Star*, December 14, 1849, 4.
11. See James M. Whitfield, *The Works of James M. Whitfield*, ed. Robert S. Levine and Ivy G. Wilson (Chapel Hill: University of North Carolina Press, 2011), 86, n. 57.
12. Wirzbicki, *Fighting for the Higher Law*, 5.
13. Gardner, "Each Atomic Part," 283.
14. Camille T. Dungy, *Black Nature: Four Centuries of African American Nature Poetry* (Athens and London: University of Georgia Press, 2009), xxi.
15. Neither is interest in a Black ecoliterary tradition new. Kimberly N. Ruffin, for example, discusses Maud Cuney-Hare, editor of the 1918 collection *The Message of the Trees: An Anthology of Leaves and Branches*, as an early scholar "whose work facilitates the reclamation of African American ecoliterature." See Ruffin, *Black on Earth: African American Ecoliterary Traditions* (Athens and London: University of Georgia Press, 2010), 14.
16. Dungy, *Black Nature*, xxi.
17. Ibid.
18. "Emerson's New Poems," *Christian Recorder*, June 1, 1867, 88.
19. Gardner, "Each Atomic Part," 284.
20. One example is the paper's notice directing readers to *St. Nicholas* magazine to read Emily Dickinson's poem, "Morning," in the May 21 and May 28, 1891 issues, without excerpting any part of the poem.
21. This piece is unsigned in the *Christian Recorder*; it was probably written by the newspaper's then-editor, James Lynch. On Lynch's tenure as editor and the *Christian Recorder*'s editorial shifts around this time, see Eric Gardner, *Black Print Unbound: The* Christian Recorder, *African American Literature, and Periodical Culture* (New York: Oxford University Press, 2015), 52–56.
22. "Emerson's New Poems."
23. On reading Dickinson within this Black context, see Brigitte Fielder, "Emily Dickinson's Black Contexts," in *The Oxford Handbook of Emily Dickinson*, ed. Karen Sanchez-Eppler and Cristanne Miller (New York: Oxford University Press, 2022), 353–71.
24. "Emerson's New Poems."
25. Rayvon Fouché, *Black Inventors in the Age of Segregation: Granville T. Woods, Lewis H. Latimer, and Shelby J. Davidson* (Baltimore: Johns Hopkins University Press, 2003), 2. In a similar vein, Britt Rusert discusses Black scientific contributions and discourse that "resist the 'object' status of black subjects." See Rusert, *Fugitive Science: Empiricism and Freedom in Early African American Culture* (New York: New York University Press, 2017), 5.

26. See, for example: "The International Telegraph," *Christian Recorder*, November 9, 1861, 174; "The Atlantic Cable," *Christian Recorder*, October 15, 1864, 168; "Where Is the Cable to Rest," *Christian Recorder*, July 29, 1865, 120; and "Progress of Telegraphic Construction," *Christian Recorder*, January 20, 1866, 12.
27. See Christopher Hanlon, "Embodied Eloquence, the Sumner Assault and the Transatlantic Cable," *American Literature* 82, no. 3 (September 2010): 489-518, 502–4.
28. *The Self-Elevator*, March 30, 1853, 1.
29. "Political News," *Christian Recorder*, February 23, 1867, 30.
30. James Redpath, *The Roving Editor, or Talks with Slaves in the Southern States* (New York: A. B. Burdick, 1859), 284.
31. Ibid., 284.
32. Ibid., 286.
33. Louis Chude-Sokei, *The Sound of Culture: Diaspora and Black Technopoetics* (Middletown, CT: Wesleyan University Press, 2015), 7.
34. "The *Atlantic Cable* Has Almost Brought the Extremities of the Earth Together," *Christian Recorder*, May 25, 1867, 83.
35. "Emerson's New Poems."
36. Despite the attribution, this selection of text does not appear in Breck's earlier *The Flower-Garden; Or, Breck's Book of Flowers* (Boston: John P. Jewett, 1851) but in the *New Book of Flowers*. See Joseph Breck, *New Book of Flowers* (New York: Orange Judd, 1866), 13–15.
37. "The Utility of Flowers," *Christian Recorder*, June 1, 1867, 88.
38. In addition to reading "transcendentalist traces" in writing by William Cooper Nell and Edmonia Highgate, Gardner presents Charlotte Forten as another important figure deserving more attention in this history. Gardner, "Each Atomic Part," 278–79.
39. Edmonia Goodelle Highgate, "Truth," *Christian Recorder*, October 27, 1866, 170.
40. Gardner, "Each Atomic Part," 289.
41. I discuss the resonance of birds in antislavery writing in "'Animal Humanism: Race, Species, and Affective Kinship in Nineteenth-Century Abolition," *American Quarterly* 65, no. 3 (September 2013): 487–513, and birds' continuing resonance for Black writing about freedom and futurity beyond the nineteenth century in "'As the Crow Flies': Black Children, Flying Africans, and Fantastic Futures in the *Brownies' Book*," *Journal of the History of Childhood and Youth* 14, no. 3 (Fall 2021): 413–36.
42. Paul Laurence Dunbar, "Sympathy," in *The Complete Poems of Paul Laurence Dunbar* (New York: Dodd, Mead, 1913), 102; originally published in *Lyrics of the Hearthside* (New York: Dodd, Mead, 1899), 41.
43. "Comfort from Little Things," *Christian Recorder*, June 1, 1867, 87.
44. "Emerson's New Poems."
45. Although I am not certain, this author may be Methodist Episcopal bishop Charles Henry Fowler.
46. Rev. Henry Fowler, "Faith and the Cable," *Christian Recorder*, March 16, 1867, 41.

CHAPTER 25

ELLEN TUCKER EMERSON

Portrait of a Daughter as Secretary, Editor, and Biographer

KATE CULKIN

ELLEN Tucker Emerson, the daughter of Lidian Jackson and Ralph Waldo Emerson, has an unusually wordy tombstone. Although Ellen had a "fine mind," it explains, she "cared more for people than for books." "She eagerly helped others," it notes, and was the "comfort" of her parents' "later years."[1] Other tributes appearing after her death on January 14, 1909 echoed the stress on her caregiving over intellectual pursuits. In a eulogy later published in *The Christian Register*, the minister A. W. Jackson explains, "She wrote no 'Consuelo,' no 'Middlemarch,' but in her the Emersonian philosophy of life became flesh and dwelt among us."[2] In an obituary for *Friends' Intelligencer*, Elizabeth Powell Bond, Swarthmore's first Dean of Women, claims, "She has not written books nor made pictures nor statues, but she has lived the best that is in books and in artist's achievements."[3] This emphasis on books she did not write is odd, as most posthumous tributes focus on what a person did achieve. It is even odder in Ellen's case, as she played a significant editorial role in her famous father's later published works and wrote a biography of her mother. In his exploration of Emerson's "late style," Christopher Hanlon notes that contemplating Ellen's contributions brings the "challenge of discerning someone else in the midst who didn't want to be noticed as she assisted her father; someone who worked so as to be forgotten, and who consequentially barely registers in our discussions of nineteenth-century literary history even as she seems to have had a profound effect upon its course."[4] The process of "discerning" Ellen's presence in her father's work and beyond, and discerning why she has been so hard to find, involves unpacking a complex interplay of family dynamics, cultural expectations, archival practices, and scholarly trends that shaped Ellen and her responses to the demands of her unique family, along with how family and scholars documented and remembered her.

Born on February 24, 1839, Ellen was the Emersons' first daughter and second child, arriving three years after her brother Waldo and two years before her sister Edith. She was named for Ellen Tucker, Emerson's first wife who died in 1831. "The little soul was impatient for light and action," her father noted when she was born early, a "fair round perfect child" who was "well contented with her new estate."[5] Young Waldo died of scarlet fever in January 1842, just months after Edith's birth. Emerson scholars stress the tragedy's dramatic effect on Emerson's emotional life and the family dynamics; Robert D. Richardson argues, "Waldo's death made a deep wound in the entire Emerson family, one that never completely healed."[6] While the family did mourn Waldo deeply, that emphasis obscures other family dynamics. These include Emerson's engaged relationships with his daughters and his second son Edward, born in 1844, and the playful family atmosphere documented in Edith and Ellen's correspondence and memoirs of their father.[7] The first step in discerning Ellen and her significance, then, is acknowledging that her life is as important as her brother's death.

Her brother's death did, of course, shape Ellen's childhood and her relationship to her family. "Poor little affectionate Ellen ... Babes need babes to quiet each other & and keep them from tormenting the Universe and she has lost as much as we in her irreparable Brother," Emerson acknowledged in a June 26, 1842 letter to his brother William (*LRWE* 3:68). For a time, grief did sap her parents' attention. Lidian had already struggled with the roles of housewife and hostess for the famous author and mother to small children. Almost three years after Waldo's death, she feared that, through her despair, she had "lost Ellen's most important years," adding, "The other children are of softer material as well as more tender years. Perhaps I can yet take care of them."[8] Lidian also suggested Emerson had to remind himself to care for Ellen as he mourned, writing to him of "the sayings & performances of that 'small mercy' Ellen—for which you sometimes pray to be thankful."[9] Ellen did absorb her parents' distance and later remembered "the miseries between Waldo's death" and Edith's "growing big enough to play with" three years later.[10] In her biography of her mother, Ellen includes the detail that Margaret Fuller "could not get over it that he had died and I was left," indicating the fear the wrong child survived added to "the miseries."[11] Fuller's harsh sentiment stands out in a narrative that otherwise emphasizes friends' and neighbors' kindness, including Ann Keyes's loving care of Ellen the night Waldo died.[12] Ellen carefully crafted the manuscript, and her choice to include this anecdote fifty years later shows its lasting pain. The inclusion may have also been an expression of anger, at Fuller and, more generally, the neglect she suffered. Ellen's complex emotions around Waldo's death, combined with nineteenth-century ideas about femininity, nurturing, and sacrifice, primed her to commit herself to caregiving and prove her worth to her family.

Emerson's attention to his children's education is one way he involved himself in their lives. "The teaching is of something less importance in Ellen's case, that she is a good scholar & will learn easily and anywhere. But I wish she should have a good, reasonable, & well behaved set of schoolmates," he explained to Caroline Sturgis Tappan in August of 1852, when Ellen was thirteen (*LRWE* 8:327).[13] Not satisfied with the Concord options, in 1853 Emerson, in consultation with Ellen and Lidian, sent her to the Sedgwick School, in Lenox, Massachusetts. Emerson recognized his daughter's intelligence and wanted her to learn French and math, but he did not see her education as a path to independence.

Before she left for Lenox, he wrote again to Tappan, "I hate to lose the girl too. Ellen chatters with her mates; with me she is so quiet and intelligent, as no one else is." The statement is touching, with his acknowledgement of his daughter's intelligence and his special relationship with her; it is not the sentiment of a man walled off from his living children by grief. But in the same letter, he noted he was willing to sacrifice a "year of quiet reason" to ensure that "she shall chatter well" (*LRWE* 8:337). While Emerson encouraged friendships between Ellen and the intellectual women in his circle, such as Tappan, and did want his daughter to engage in intellectual conversations, he never envisioned her as a writer or even a teacher or any permanent departure from Bush. Ellen would use her education to "chatter well" as her father's hostess and secretary, roles Lidian largely rejected.

From the beginning, therefore, Ellen's intellectual development was simultaneously linked to and in tension with her role as caregiver. Ellen's formal education continued until 1860, but family responsibilities often interrupted it. In 1854, as she settled in at the Sedgwick School, Emerson informed her, "Your Mother is very feeble; & I doubt much if in October I can spare you to go to school anywhere. I think we shall have to instal you as a housekeeper for a time" (*LRWE* 4:454). Tappan, who lived near the school and had become close to Ellen, protested that Emerson should not interrupt her education; he responded, "Ah, thought I, & where is my house to be in the meantime?" (*LRWE* 4:456). Ellen eventually studied at the Concord School, led by Franklin Sanborn, and the Agassiz School in Cambridge, but the family always weighed time allotted for the classroom against the needs in Bush.

In the negotiations around her education, Ellen's complex relationship to family duty emerges. When preparing to leave the Sedgwick School, she wrote to Lidian, "I am still gladder that I may not go to school this winter, but stay at home and keep house."[14] But to her cousin Charlotte Cleveland, she was wistful, noting, "I am so glad I have known it beforehand, for now I am ready to begin, but if it had been suddenly decided after I got home, alas poor me what should I do!"[15] Each switch between school and home brought on a similar swirl of emotions. She did find ways to stay intellectually engaged, such as rising early to study Greek before beginning her housework.[16] But she knew this was different than a scholarly life. When her formal schooling ended in 1860, Ellen acknowledged "nothing could be so good as to go straight back and continue such a charming life till age made it ridiculous, which it is already perhaps."[17]

One reason Ellen was able to go to school for so long was her partnership with her sister. Edith was only thirteen when Ellen was called home from Lenox. As she grew older, however, Edith shared the workload. For the summer of 1859, the Emersons dismissed their servants to allow Ellen and Edith to practice the full range of housekeeping duties. Ellen at first tackled the cooking, while Edith served as the "chambermaid"; they then switched responsibilities.[18] That fall Edith, now seventeen, took a year off school to serve as Bush's housekeeper, with the family again hiring servants, to free Ellen to be a full-time student at the Concord School; going forward, they shared duties.[19] Edith's 1865 marriage to William Forbes changed the nature of the partnership, but it continued throughout their lives. Ellen regularly decamped to Milton to help care for Edith's children (eventually numbering eight), and Edith intervened when Ellen was overwhelmed or exhausted and participated in all major family decisions. Discerning Ellen's contributions is not possible without also acknowledging Edith's.

Emerson's career and fame meant that Ellen and Edith did more than the regular work associated with running a nineteenth-century household. In addition to cooking, cleaning, sewing, and managing servants, they served as their father's secretaries, hosted a stream of guests, and nursed their mother, including hours spent reading to her. Ellen managed the household accounts when her father travelled. While Emerson gave her credit for being "the best accountant in the house," the job was stressful (*LRWE* 5:152). Much of their correspondence when he was away concerned bills, Ellen pleading for more money as she stretched each dollar. Taking on the running of the household as partners allowed their father time to write and to undertake lecture tours, a critical part of his revision process that was also important to the family finances.[20]

Emerson scholars often quote Ellen's claims she did not read, particularly her father's writing, but the issue is more complex. She did tell her sister of Emerson's work, "The reason I don't read those books is not because they are his, it is because they are books." She, however, followed that dramatic statement with an intellectual autobiography:

> Have I ever looked at one of the great authors of this age or any other, except for special purposes?... With you & Una & Uncle George I have read Tasso & Manzoni, with Aunt Lizzy Dante & Homer; for the High School Class I have read some hundred pages of Carlyle, and once to mother a part of Sartor at her request. My Milton and Shakespeare I got at school & from Father, and so on. In my early days on R.R. journeys I read the French memoirs that my school lessons started me on, Coventry Patmore at Father's desire; and I am acquainted with a dozen devotional books. There is a history of my life's reading... Stories & poems I heard read or have read to mother.

In the same letter she states, "I have yet to open my first book of real reading," which she seems to define as serious study done with no distractions, for no other reason than the life of the mind, and with no social element.[21] Emerson's "privileging of self-reliant, inviolate consciousness as the acme of intellectual integrity" through his most famous works surely shaped this definition.[22] Her responsibilities made that relationship to the written word impossible, as did the fact that discussing books contributed to her enjoyment of them, but that did not make her reading less real. As Phyllis Cole and Jana Argersinger have argued, for nineteenth-century women, largely cut off from institutions of intellectual authority like universities and the pulpit, "the initiating and continuing scene of action was a woman reading, responding, and taking part in conversation, whether directly or through exchange of letters and journals."[23]

When illness forced her to rest, Ellen's intellectual interests surfaced quickly. In an 1866 letter to Grisela von Armin, the wife of the author Herman Grimm, she mentioned identifying Grimm's reference to Emerson in his novel *Unüberwindliche Mächte*. After another denial of having read her father's books, she noted that she "immediately recognized the only sentences of my Father's writing that I know." She had been able to read the book due to being sick in bed, leading her to reflect, to "have a month of solitude and rest in one's chamber is such a pleasure and advantage that it quite repays one for all the derangement of housework."[24] In 1870, when a doctor prescribed "perpetual absence" from Bush to an exhausted Ellen, she stayed with Edith's family for two months.[25] She spent hours with her cousin Mary Watson, reading *Eckermann's Conversations of Goethe*, critiquing Charles Dickens's account of his United States tour, and debating "the woman question," with Ellen opposing suffrage; she also attended Elizabeth Peabody's lecture on kindergartens and participated in a "discourse" on "the Lowell Institute and the Technological School" at a dinner.[26] When given the time, Ellen sought out opportunities for intellectual stimulation.

Ellen's faith is critical to understanding her. "She loved the church, loved traditions as her father could not do. In her religious attitude she was distinctly, some would say extremely, conservative," Jackson writes in his eulogy.[27] Her tombstone declares, "She cherished the old religion." Her devotion should not be mistaken for passivity. Ashley Reed explains, "Critics of women's writing have often taken for granted that religion can serve only as an oppressive force in women's lives rather than a matter of personal choice, an aspect of communal belonging, a vehicle for intellection and self-expression, and a sincere apprehension of the nature of the universe and human existence."[28] Ellen's faith served all of the purposes that Reed outlines.

Ellen announced her intention to join the Unitarian Concord First Parish Church in January 1867. "I do it because I have been taught that it is not the fold of the redeemed … but the Christian school, and to join it is to declare simply that you desire to be a Christian," she explained. For her, being a member of the church was not a sign of submission, but an active, engaged process. Her choice helped her declare a quiet independence from her family. "It gives me access indeed to the Communion table," she noted, which, "may help me … If it does, then indeed, I shall have reason to rejoice that I have entered."[29] Given the critical role that rejection of Communion played in her father's departure from the pulpit, it is notable that Ellen emphasized "access" to it as a benefit of her new relationship to the church.[30] Decades later, as evidence that she was religiously conservative, Jackson noted in his eulogy, "Over passages of her father's writings it was possible to get into smiling debate with her, in which she would criticise him as frankly as she would Addison or Montaigne."[31] Ellen was a dutiful daughter, but she followed her own mind on matters of religion. Ellen, in addition, joined the church soon after Edith had her first child, Ralph, in July 1866. Over Thanksgiving 1866 a post-partum Edith had in fact complained that Ellen prioritized her Sunday school pupils over her family. But as her sister set off on the adventure of marriage and parenthood, instead of stepping away, Ellen formalized her commitment to the church. Rather than submitting to an "oppressive force," joining the church was an act of independence and a path to a life beyond Bush.

Ellen engaged with the world through her faith. Visiting houses of worship was her favorite way to explore, whether in Boston or Egypt. Her letters offer pointed critiques and praise of ministers, sermons, and congregations. In Concord, she helped shape the curriculum of the Sunday school, arguing it should focus on doctrine.[32] Ellen relished attending Unitarian and Sunday school conventions and conferences. After serving as a delegate at the 1878 National Unitarian Conference in Saratoga Springs, New York, she wrote, "The joys of Saratoga socially & intellectually were all that had been promised ... conventions mean work and work enlivened by the gayest play."[33] Distressed by the number of Unitarian ministers who did not identify as Christians in 1881, she reflected, "If the Unitarians don't please me why stay with them? ... I must stay where I belong and hope that the new light the Unitarians need, and that not I alone but most of the people I hear talk feel the need of, will shine in my day."[34] By serving as a delegate, in debates about Concord's Sunday school, and in informal conversations and letters with family members, friends, and fellow congregants, Ellen promoted her vision of Unitarianism, far from someone who merely "cherished the old religion." The intellectual labor of parsing sermons and engaging in doctrinal debates, moreover, helped prepare her for the editing work she took on late in her father's life.

Emerson was "surprised" Ellen had joined the church, telling her, "He should feel as if he abridged his boundless freedom if it were himself, but if I feel no difficulty then there is none."[35] He may have welcomed his daughter's devout nature; he did not want "boundless freedom" for Ellen, after all, on whose work he depended. In 1856, Emerson gave her Coventry Patmore's *The Angel in the House*, around the time he considering withdrawing her from the Agassiz school to serve once again as housekeeper; Ellen remembered, he "said it was a good book for me to read. I found it so," and she referred to it throughout her life.[36] Patmore's poem celebrates a feminine ideal of purity, piousness, and caregiving. Emerson had also quoted the poem in an address to a women's rights convention the year before, as he emphasized women's domestic contributions due to their elevated sensitivity and aesthetic sense (*LL* 2:15–29).[37] Even as her faith gave her some independence, Ellen's vision of faithful womanhood also served her father's needs, and he had reason to encourage it, whether through the gift of Patmore or endorsing her connection to the church.

Beyond the church, Ellen involved herself in the Concord community through reform work and service to the schools. Among other activities, she was involved in the Concord Female Anti-Slavery Society and the Soldiers' Aid Society.[38] She loved these events for their social nature as well as their noble contributions; "we have had such frolicsome afternoons," she wrote of the sewing circles for the 1871 Chicago fire victims.[39] In 1870, she became the first woman to serve on the Concord School Committee, finding the annual examinations and committee meetings full of "so many pleasures!"[40] She missed the comradeship when she stepped down in 1877. "Few relations are more delightful than the relations of a committee among themselves, they are so intimate, and full of the delight of the common work," she explained, mourning that "they fall to pieces in a moment when you leave the committee."[41]

Soon after the Civil War, changes in the family dynamic increased Ellen's workload and led to a new stage in her relationship with her father. Edith married William Forbes on October 3, 1865, and moved to Milton, Massachusetts. While Ellen cherished Will, a loving brother-in-law who proved a great help to his in-laws, she was in tears the day after the wedding at the thought of life without Edith.[42] It does not seem that she wanted marriage for herself—as a teenager, Ellen had already rejected the idea, likely due to a combination of the family responsibility her parents instilled in her and the fact she directed her romantic energies primarily towards women—but feared losing her closest companion.[43] Within ten months, Edith gave birth to her first child, but also made it clear she would stay intimately involved with her birth family. She immediately set up a room for Ellen in her home, and she regularly weighed in on family matters, helped manage care of her parents, and stayed at Bush when Ellen travelled. Still, Edith's marriage and growing family meant the day-to-day responsibility for her parents fell to Ellen. More than once, she had ill-defined health crises that likely were a form of physical and mental exhaustion; inevitably, Edith found a way for Ellen to rest.

As the family realigned, Emerson's memory problems began to shape Ellen's duties. In April 1868, Ellen and Emerson travelled to New York, for his lectures at the Packer Institute in Brooklyn Heights. They headed straight to Henry Ward Beecher's Brooklyn church from their overnight ferry. She was pleased her father enjoyed the sermon, as "there could be no doubt that he had come willingly, for I had from the beginning made such a point of coming that I had given him no smallest chance to be recusant, and had feared secretly it was wholly 'self-sacrifice' for my benefit."[44] Leaving the church, the crowd spotted Ulysses S. Grant outside and took chase. "Father and I joined madly in this pursuit, and ran along, now in the street, now out, like little boys beside the trainers, and one way and another succeeded in seeing his head and shoulders, and, now and then, an uninterrupted glimpse of his face," Ellen reported.[45] (Grant made it to the ferry and took refuge in the ladies' cabin.) Ellen's description of the trip is marked by a new sense of father-daughter adventure, particularly the charming, if bizarre, chase of Grant. More ominously, Ellen registers surprise that Emerson did not remember the way from the ferry to the church. This passing mention of her father's confusion marks the beginning of regular references to his memory loss in the Emerson correspondence. Emerson and Ellen's trip to Vermont's Middlebury College later in the summer was also notable for entertaining escapades along with hints at Emerson's confusion.[46]

These trips formed a bittersweet time for Ellen. Her father's decreasing faculties coincided, for a short window, with father-daughter adventures and his increased attention to her. As focusing on work became difficult, Emerson may have found his mind drifting to what might please his daughter, such as seeing Vermont's beautiful Bellows Falls; indulging her requests, like seeing Beecher, perhaps brought a welcome distraction. Ellen was more likely to accompany him on trips as he grew more confused, in addition, bringing them more shared experiences. The lowering of inhibitions that can accompany memory loss may help explain romps like the chase of Grant, a disturbing sign even if it manifested in a moment of antic joy. Long-term, Emerson's declining memory made him more dependent on Ellen and increased her workload.

Even as the family dynamics grew more complex, the Emersons coalesced around Ellen to support her. On October 24, 1868, they told her "to pack my trunks, settle my affairs, make my will, and go to Fayal on Wednesday 28th to stay till June."[47] Fayal, a

Portuguese island in the Azores, was a popular destination for Americans seeking rest.[48] Ellen had been run down all year, and Edward and Edith "conspired" with their parents on the plan and likely pushed for it.[49] Edith promised she, Edward, and Will would care for their parents, visiting and writing often and making sure Lidian was not "neglected or worried."[50] On Fayal, for the first time since she was fourteen, Ellen's days were her own. She grew close to the family of Charles Dabney, the United States Consul, and spent days walking and reading, including the newly-published *Little Women*.[51] As the end of her stay neared, Ellen looked forward to returning to Concord, "but I hold on here pretty fast too, and grudge to see the days slipping away from me."[52]

Emerson's memory and concentration problems accelerated after her return. As Ronald Bosco explains, "Modern biographers typically date Emerson's decline from the period after Bush burned in July 1872; in fact, however, Emerson entered the 1870s already exhibiting symptoms not only of decline, but also of a rapidly deteriorating ability to write original prose and to organize his voluminous papers for presentations in lectures ... or in publications."[53] Ellen reported to Emerson's doctor that the issue arose around 1866, but it may have been as early as 1864, when Emerson faltered at a Saturday Club lecture.[54] Ellen later told James Elliot Cabot that frustration over her father's decline and his refusal to accept her help with his lectures made her relieved to go to Fayal to escape the situation.[55] She did not document those emotions at the time, perhaps not wanting to acknowledge the decline in her correspondence, often shared in the nineteenth century. But after her return her father's problems appear regularly in Ellen's letters.

In 1870, Emerson struggled with a variety of projects. These include the "Natural History of Intellect" course as part of Harvard's University Lecture series, an introduction to an edition of *Plutarch's Morals* translated by William W. Goodwin, about which Emerson had forgotten, and editing and annotating *Parnassus*, a poetry anthology he had worked on for years with Edith and that Edith was eager to finish. To pile on, he learned Moncure D. Conway, an abolitionist minister he had known since the 1850s, had signed a contract with the British publisher John Camden Hotten to produce a volume of Emerson's unpublished essays. Distraught, Emerson agreed to revise the essays himself, "an act of desperation to retain some degree of control over the publication of his writings."[56] By 1871, Ellen and Edith, along with friends and family, scrambled to help him focus, still with the hope he could recover. Ellen wrote Edith in 1871 that it would be best for Emerson's "peace of mind the sooner you get through Parnassus," adding, "the sharper you drive it up the better."[57] More dramatically, Edith's father-in-law John Murray Forbes, likely in consultation with the three Emerson siblings, invited Emerson on a trip to California in April 1871, with the hopes it would restore him. Members of the party included Edith, who was several months pregnant, and Will; Ellen stayed in Concord with the three Forbes children and ended up nursing Edward through smallpox.[58] The trip did bring Emerson some relief, but any respite from his decline was temporary.

Ellen faced an increased burden in 1872, as Edward moved to Germany to study medicine and the Forbes undertook an eight-month tour of Europe. Declaring her father's memory "entirely gone," she encouraged Emerson to read her his lectures before he delivered them to catch unintentional repetitions, a request he often brusquely rejected. She attended the lectures "in great fear," and in April was horrified when he read the same page twice without noticing.[59] Emerson also struggled to find words, leading to nonsense sentences that Ellen claimed to find funny, but in fact added to her anxiety.[60] The fire in Bush on July 24, 1872 accelerated Emerson's decline, with Ellen telling his doctor that in the aftermath he was incapable of editing his own writing at all.[61]

The family again hoped travel would restore their patriarch's faculties, and in October, Ellen and Emerson set off on a trip to Europe and Egypt with funds donated by friends after the fire.[62] While not without frustrations, the trip provided Ellen ample opportunity to indulge her curiosity about other people's beliefs and establish a deeper intimacy with her declining father. "Never till just these circumstances made it manifest had I imagined what a revealing power there was in acts of worship," she reported from the ship after attending services with Methodists, Baptists, Presbyterians, Quakers, and Mormons.[63] Travelling through England, France, Italy, and Egypt, houses of worship interested her more than museums. After attending a Coptic church service in Egypt, she concluded, "I came away very much puzzled ... and most of all curious to know something about it all."[64] Emerson often accompanied her, leading her to proclaim, "For a whole month Father never missed going to Church on a Sunday!"[65] Although the trip did not cure Emerson, the intense time Ellen and Emerson spent navigating the challenges of travel abroad prepared them to maneuver their next shared endeavor.

Once home, the role of editor became a prominent part of Ellen's duties. Emerson continued to struggle with the essays promised to Hotten, which would become *Letters and Social Aims*.[66] By August 1875, Ellen reported to Edith that the "book no longer seems a great difficulty. Father feels the relief of having given it over to me, he chooses to believe I can do everything and in that belief he is happy."[67] The fact that Ellen's editing work brought Emerson relief indicates how this intellectual labor formed part of her caregiving. Ellen, however, did not feel she could do everything. As Nancy Craig Simmons explains, "the method of repeatedly retooling his materials to new uses had served Emerson well during his long lecture career; for Ellen, however, the shufflings were a nightmare."[68] Even before the trip, she had suggested approaching James Elliot Cabot for the role of literary executor to her father, who was worried in the wake of the fire about his papers' fate.[69] Now, she invited Cabot to help with editing the project, and he spent time in Concord throughout the fall, working with Ellen to arrange the essays, with minor consultations with Emerson. It was finally published in December.

"What a mercy it is that there are women in the world to arrange for men," Elizabeth Cabot, James's wife, quipped as she and Ellen realized that her husband and Emerson had both been fearful to start the collaboration but relieved once it began.[70] She meant that Ellen had arranged for Cabot to assist Emerson, but Ellen was in fact arranging the words of her father as well. Little acknowledged for over a century, scholarship by Ronald Bosco and Joel Myerson, Christopher Hanlon, Nancy Craig Simmons, and Joseph Thomas has illuminated Ellen's significant contributions, especially to *Letters and Social Aims* and *Natural History of Intellect* (1893).[71] Hanlon argues, "The focus

Ellen Tucker Emerson and James Elliot Cabot brought to the process of revising and sometimes recomposing Emerson's words resulted in gnostic groupings of texts within the Emerson canon—essays and reconstituted lectures in which the understanding of three Transcendentalist thinkers merged." That merging made room for recognition of communal thought, as "Ellen mined Emerson's notes and lectures for material, selecting and sometimes accentuating passages that spoke to a more communitarian, cooperative account of intellectual life than Emerson previously emphasized in his published work."[72] Given that so many elements of Ellen's life revolved around collaboration and community—from reading to work for the church, the school committee, and reform organizations to her partnerships with Edith and Cabot—it is not surprising she was drawn to the communal threads in her father's work. While Ellen minimized her own intellectual autobiography because of its social nature, her contributions to her father's essays turned the tables and found ways to honor communal thought.

Even as she directed the emphasis away from intellectual self-reliance in Emerson's work, she rejected public credit for her contributions. She reminded Edith she had been "ridiculously" secretive about her work and demanded Cabot not credit her in print.[73] Her secrecy coincides with her ideas about women's roles. She believed women had more power using their influence on men than they would through their own votes and struggled with women speaking in public.[74] Preserving her father's reputation was part of her motivation, but Ellen was open to acknowledging that Emerson received help, as long as the spotlight did not fall on her. After his death, she asked Cabot that her contributions be attributed to Emerson's "family" in his introduction to the Riverside Edition of *Letters and Social Aims*. She added "There, I'll write you a beautiful little paragraph to show you how I mean. Behold! At length his weariness and the frequent letters of the publishers led his family to ask to see his work. It seemed to shock him at first but the day came when he allowed them to read proof-sheets & manuscripts," adding the family realized Emerson needed help and called for Cabot.[75] Even in rejecting credit, Ellen provided evidence of her contributions, by acknowledging she was capable of drafting "a beautiful little paragraph" that Cabot could claim as his own.

Ellen's desire to subsume her individual contributions under the rubric of family is a key to understanding her approach to her editing work. There was, of course, truth in her attribution. She regularly consulted with Edith and Will, as well as Elizabeth Hoar and others; even as Edith nursed her children through scarlet fever in 1878, for instance, Ellen pestered her to return her and Will's edits to "Fortune of the Republic."[76] Beyond that, her choice to edit her father's writing without public acknowledgement forms part of a larger project of preserving the Emerson family history and shaping the family legacy. She inherited her role of family historian from her great-aunt Mary Moody Emerson, who, along with cousins Hannah Parsons and Charlotte Cleveland, bequeathed Ellen the family papers and many of Moody's almanacs in 1861. Phyllis Cole emphasizes that, in the Emerson family, history was women's work: "These manuscripts had survived in the keeping of daughters and granddaughters ... before now returning with Ellen to Concord. They were coming to Waldo's branch of the family, but for Ellen's continued custodianship and delectation more than her father's."[77] Ellen recorded family oral history in "What I Can Remember of Stories of Our Ancestors Told Me by Aunt Mary Ellen Moody." She also wrote "What I Can Remember About Father," which stressed the role of Emerson's family in his life, and *The Life of Lidian Jackson Emerson*. Along with her siblings, in addition, she worked closely with Cabot on *A Memoir of Ralph Waldo Emerson*, providing him with detailed information and pushing him to emphasize Emerson's personal life. As Robert Habich explains, "Ellen and Edith in their behind-the-scenes maneuverings struggled to rescue their father from an iconic whitewash and quietly asserted the family's prerogatives against Cabot's 'Grecian' resolve."[78]

The biography of Lidian was Ellen's most ambitious historical project, and the professional way she approached it belies the image of the passive, unintellectual, and credit-shirking woman subsumed by service to her father. In August 1895, three years after Lidian died, Ellen set up a two-week writing retreat at the home of Nina Lowell, and once home she continued to set aside time to write.[79] This project too was collaborative; Lowell helped her avoid distractions, and Edith provided feedback, at times challenging Ellen's memory of events. While it was not published during her lifetime, Ellen held readings of the work for family and friends, far from her public denial of her contributions to her father's essays.[80]

Lidian's intelligence, achievements, and influence are central to the biography. Ellen emphasizes that her mother found her spirits lifted when she became intellectually engaged, such as when she attended Bronson Alcott's Summer School of Philosophy, and focuses on her reform work; she expresses regret she did not collect the articles Lidian wrote for the Dumb Animal Society.[81] She includes Lidian's blistering "The Transcendental Bible," written around 1841, which mocks the solipsism she identified in the Transcendental conversations that surrounded her.[82] Ellen links her father's accomplishments to her mother, remembering a time Mary Merrick Brooks declared, "The world little knew how much Mr. Emerson owed to his wife, that he would have been a different man with another woman."[83] Her instinct to protect and promote her father's reputation by hiding her involvement with his essays while making sure they were published and her choice to document and celebrate her mother's accomplishments and influence were part of the same commitment to family forged early in life.

While Ellen's editing work took place behind closed doors, her assistance to her father was clear when Emerson spoke in public. He curtailed his lecture schedule after 1872, but Ellen accompanied him on the public appearances he did make. As Jackson notes in his eulogy, "she became the visible providence of her declining father ... going with him in his lecturing journeys, when, though his mind had lost his grasp, people would still see his face and hear his voice."[84] Jean T. Chapin, in a sketch of life in Concord, remembers, "Miss Ellen always accompanied her father when he spoke, & sat up close to the platform knitting busily while she listened, ready to prompt him if he forgot the word he wished to use."[85] These memories depict Ellen as the calm nurse, even though the fear of her father embarrassing himself caused her great anxiety and she did the intellectual work of helping arrange the lectures. Still, the image of Ellen knitting on the platform while steering her father's lectures back on course serves as a perfect metaphor for the ways in which her caregiving, housekeeping, and intellectual labor were entwined.

While her correspondence includes ample evidence of her contributions, it took almost a century for Emerson scholars to investigate them seriously. Emerson's dementia was known during his lifetime, but a desire to protect his reputation, and avoid wrestling with the complicated authorship of the essays in *Letters and Social Aims* and *Natural History of Intellect*, in part explains the lack of exploration.[86] Ellen's insistence she be omitted from the published record is also a critical reason, of course. It was only when scholars had access to her correspondence that the extent of her participation emerged. The publication of Edith W. Gregg's 1982 edition of Ellen's letters was a critical step, even though Gregg edited the letters more substantially than her introduction indicates and includes no letters after 1892, when Lidian died. The edition's inclusion in the database *North American Women's Letters and Diaries* in 2001 increased access dramatically, and the 2005 deposit of the correspondence into the Houghton Library provided researchers with the unedited and unpublished letters. Another batch of Ellen's letters from the 1860s were donated to the American Antiquarian Society in 2003 and digitized in Alexander Street's *Women's Letters and Diaries* database in 2010. The 2003 deposit of Edith's letters into the Edith Emerson Forbes and William Hathaway Forbes Papers at the Massachusetts Historical Society has illuminated the sisters' partnership.

Made possible by these materials, the swell of interest in Ellen has contributed to and been aided by a growing focus on women and Transcendentalism, which has illuminated the significance of Margaret Fuller, Elizabeth Peabody, Caroline Sturgis Tappan, and Mary Moody Emerson, among others.[87] Women's correspondence, in turn, has been critical to that scholarship. As Cole and Argersinger explain in their introduction to *A Female Genealogy of Transcendentalism*, "A corollary principle is that writing originally intended for private audiences merits consideration equally with published writing, indeed that private and public expression were intimately joined."[88] Ellen left a rich archive, writing long, lively letters that document her family, friendships, reading, reform and editing work, and ideas about religion and women's place in society. She took correspondence seriously, critiquing the letters she received, using an editor's eye long before she became an editor. Her brother praised her ability to create "instantaneous domestic pictures, verisimilitudinous memory-tales" and hoped her letters would be published so, when found a century later, they could "enlighten the world."[89] After Ellen's death, Edith collected her sister's letters in an edited typescript now available at the Houghton.[90] So while Ellen did not want her contributions to her father's essays acknowledged in print, she did feel her life—and that includes her work on those essays—was important enough to document in her letters, and her sister felt those letters were important enough to save.

"When necessity threw it for those few years into my hands I did it as anyone would in my place," Ellen wrote of her editing work in 1883.[91] But of course no one else could have been in her place, not even her siblings. Her education, faith, and family experience, along with cultural expectations, merged in Ellen to prepare her intellectually and emotionally to answer the call of "necessity." She refused credit, but she also left behind the written record that allowed scholars living a century later to understand her significance. The family historian has been written back into history.

Notes

1. Sleepy Hollow Cemetery (Concord, MA), Ellen Tucker Emerson tombstone, personally photographed, August 8, 2008.
2. A. W. Jackson, "Ellen Tucker Emerson," [1909]: 3, Ellen Tucker Emerson Correspondence and Other Papers, circa 1835–1909. *2003M-13. Houghton Library, Harvard University (hereafter *ETE Correspondence*); A. W. Jackson, "Ellen Tucker Emerson," *Christian Register*, January 28, 1909, 104.
3. Elizabeth Powell Bond, "Ellen Tucker Emerson," *Friends' Intelligencer*, February 6, 1909, 82.
4. Christopher Hanlon, *Emerson's Memory Loss: Originality, Communality, and the Late Style* (New York: Oxford University Press, 2018), 45.
5. Ralph Waldo Emerson to Elizabeth Hoar, February 24, 1839 (*LRWE* 2:185).
6. Robert D. Richardson, Jr., *Emerson: The Mind on Fire* (Berkeley: University of California Press, 1995), 359.
7. Edith Emerson Webster Gregg, "Emerson and His Children: Their Childhood Memories," *Harvard Library Bulletin* 28, no. 4 (1980): 407–30.
8. Lidian Emerson to Ralph Waldo Emerson, December 21 [1845], in *The Selected Letters of Lidian Jackson Emerson*, ed. Delores Bird Carpenter (Columbia: University of Missouri Press, 1987), 135.
9. Lidian Emerson to Ralph Waldo Emerson, January 15, 1843, *Selected Letters of Lidian Jackson Emerson*, 116.
10. Ellen Emerson to Edith Forbes, March 22, 1894, *ETE Correspondence*.
11. Ellen Emerson, *The Life of Lidian Jackson Emerson*, ed. Delores Bird Carpenter (East Lansing: Michigan State University Press, 1992), 90.
12. Emerson, *Life of Lidian Jackson Emerson*, 88. For all her reputation for self-sacrifice, Ellen was capable of a sharp tongue, whether it was a withering review of a sermon or expressing her frustration at housekeeping.
13. See also Kate Culkin, "The Education of Ellen Emerson," *The New England Quarterly* 93, no. 1 (March 2020): 74–100.
14. Ellen Emerson to Lidian Emerson, August 6, 1854, *ETE Correspondence*.
15. Ellen Emerson to Charlotte [Haskins Cleveland], September 24, 1854, *ETE Correspondence*.
16. Ellen Emerson to Emma Stimson, October 8, 1854, and Ellen Emerson to Emma Stimson, November 6, 1854 and December 21, 1854, *ETE Correspondence*.
17. Ellen Emerson to [Addie Manning], October 8, 1860, *ETE Correspondence*.
18. Edith Forbes to Suzy Loring, July 18, 1860, Edith Forbes and William Hathaway Forbes Papers; Ms. N-2306, Massachusetts Historical Society, Boston (hereafter Forbes Papers).
19. Edith Forbes to Susy Loring, July 18, 1860, Forbes Papers.
20. Ronald A. Bosco explains that Emerson depended "on the 'congenial' responses from audiences to his continuing work on a lecture in order to bring it to the level of polish required of a printed essay." Ronald A. Bosco, "Historical Introduction," in *Letters and Social Aims*, ed. Joel Myerson (Cambridge, MA; Harvard University Press, 2010), xxxii.
21. Ellen Emerson to Edith Forbes, April 27, 1892, *ETE Correspondence*.
22. Hanlon, *Emerson's Memory Loss*, 23.

23. Phyllis Cole and Jana Argersinger, "Introduction," in *Towards a Female Genealogy of Transcendentalism*, ed. Jana Argersinger and Phyllis Cole (Athens: University of Georgia Press, 2014), 10.
24. The letter published in the first volume of Ellen's correspondence is a draft in pencil. Ellen Emerson to [Grisela Von Armin] Grimm, March 2, 1868, in *The Letters of Ellen Tucker Emerson*, ed. Edith Emerson Webster Gregg (Kent, OH: Kent State University Press, 1982), 1:462.
25. Ellen Emerson to Lidian Emerson, March 19, 1870, *ETE Correspondence*.
26. Ellen Emerson to Ralph Waldo Emerson, March 24, 1870, and Ellen Emerson to Lidian Emerson, March 26, 1870, *ETE Correspondence*.
27. Jackson, "Ellen Tucker Emerson" (*ETE Correspondence*), 6.
28. Ashley Reed, *Heaven's Interpreters: Women Writers and Religious Agency in Nineteenth-Century America* (Ithaca, NY: Cornell University Press, 2020), 2.
29. Ellen Emerson to Haven Emerson, January 18, 1867, *ETE Correspondence*.
30. Richardson, *Emerson*, 125–26.
31. Jackson, "Ellen Tucker Emerson" (*Christian Register*), 104.
32. Ellen Emerson to Ralph Waldo Emerson, January 28, 1867, *ETE Correspondence*.
33. Ellen Emerson to Edith Forbes, September 28, 1878, *ETE Correspondence*.
34. Ellen Emerson to Clara Dabney, July 28, 1881, *ETE Correspondence*.
35. Ellen Emerson to Lidian Emerson, January 5, 1867, *ETE Correspondence*.
36. Ellen Emerson, "What I Can Remember About Father." MS Am 1280.227. Houghton Library, Harvard University.
37. See also Phyllis Cole, "The New Movement's Tide: Emerson and Women's Rights," in *Emerson: Bicentennial Essays*, ed. Ronald A. Bosco and Joel Myerson (Boston: Massachusetts Historical Society, 2006), 117–52.
38. Sandra Harbert Petrulionis, *To Set This World Right: The Anti-Slavery Movement in Thoreau's Concord* (New York: Cornell University Press, 2006).
39. Ellen Emerson to [Mary] Dabney, March 4, 1872, *ETE Correspondence*.
40. Ellen Emerson, February 23, 1871, quoted in Delores Bird Carpenter, "Introduction," in *The Life of Lidian Jackson Emerson*, by Ellen Tucker Emerson, ed. Delores Bird Carpenter (East Lansing: Michigan State Press, 1992), xxxii.
41. Ellen Emerson to [Mary] Dabney, February 28, 1877, *ETE Correspondence*.
42. Ellen Emerson to [Mary] Waterman, January 3, 1866, *ETE Correspondence*.
43. Ellen Emerson to Addy [Abby Adeline] Manning (AM), January 22, 1856, *ETE Correspondence*. For Ellen's focus on women, see Culkin, "Education of Ellen Emerson," 91–92.
44. Ellen Emerson to Edith Forbes, April 20, 1868, *ETE Correspondence*.
45. Ellen Emerson to Edith Forbes, April 20, 1868, *ETE Correspondence*.
46. Bosco, "Historical Introduction," clv.
47. Ellen Emerson to Haven Emerson, [October 24, 1868], *ETE Correspondence*.
48. Daniel Dillard, "'The Delicious Sense of Foreignness': American Transcendentalism in the Atlantic," *American Nineteenth Century History* 14, no. 2 (2013): 209–31.
49. Ellen Emerson to Haven Emerson, November 3, 1868, and Ellen Emerson to [Mary] Waterman, December 10, 1868, *ETE Correspondence*.
50. Edith Forbes to Ellen Emerson, October 30, 1868, Forbes Papers.
51. Ellen Emerson to Emma Stimson Diman, February 16, 1868, *ETE Correspondence*. For the Dabneys in Fayal, see Joseph C. Abdo, *On the Edge of History* (Lisbon: Tenth Island Editions, 2011).

52. Ellen Emerson to Haven Emerson, April 15, 1869, *ETE Correspondence*.
53. Bosco, "Historical Introduction," xxxviii–xxxix.
54. Hanlon, *Emerson's Memory Loss*, 19.
55. James Elliot Cabot's revised notes of interviews with Ellen Emerson, June 1882, bms AM 1280.235 (711), Box 79, Houghton Library, Harvard University.
56. Bosco, "Historical Introduction," xciii.
57. Ellen Emerson to Edith Forbes, February 17, 1871, *ETE Correspondence*.
58. John Murray Forbes, *Letters and Recollections of John Murray Forbes*, ed. Sarah Forbes Hughes (Boston: Houghton Mifflin, 1899), 2:175–77; Brian Wilson, *The California Days of Ralph Waldo Emerson* (Amherst: University of Massachusetts Press, 2022); Ellen Emerson to Edith Forbes, May 13, 1871, *ETE Correspondence*.
59. Ellen Emerson to Edward Emerson, April 15, 1872, *ETE Correspondence*.
60. Ellen Emerson to Edward Emerson, June 5, 1872, *ETE Correspondence*.
61. Joel Myerson, "Textual Introduction," in *Letters and Social Aims*, ed. Joel Myerson (Cambridge, MA: Harvard University Press, 2013), ccxxx–ccxxxi.
62. Ronald A. Bosco and Joel Myerson, *Ralph Waldo Emerson: A Bicentennial Exhibition at Houghton Library, 26 March to 7 June 2003* (Cambridge, MA: Houghton Library of the Harvard College Library, 2003), 46.
63. Ellen Emerson to Lidian Emerson, October 27, 1872, *ETE Correspondence*.
64. Ellen Emerson to Edith Forbes, February 3, 1873, *ETE Correspondence*.
65. Ellen Emerson to Edith Forbes, November 26, 1872, *ETE Correspondence*.
66. Hotten died in June 1873; the firm was purchased by Andrew Chatto and W. E. Windus. Myerson, "Textual Introduction," ccxxvii.
67. Ellen Emerson to Edith Forbes, [August 1875], *ETE Correspondence*.
68. Nancy Craig Simmons, "Arranging the Sibylline Leaves: James Elliot Cabot's Work as Emerson's Literary Executor," *Studies in the American Renaissance* (1983): 343.
69. Ellen Emerson to Edith Forbes, August 22, 1872, *ETE Correspondence*.
70. Ellen Emerson to Edith Forbes, September 8, 1875, *ETE Correspondence*.
71. Bosco, "Historical Introduction," especially xxx–xxxv, xl, cvi, ccii, ccix–ccxiii; Hanlon, *Emerson's Memory Loss*, 1–45; Myerson, "Textual Introduction," especially ccxxvi, ccxxix–cclxiii, cclxxi–ccxlxxxii; Simmons, 335–89; Joseph M. Thomas, "Late Emerson: 'Selected Poems' and the 'Emerson Factory,'" *ELH* 65, no. 4 (1998): 971–94.
72. Hanlon, *Emerson's Memory Loss*, 3, 13.
73. Ellen Emerson to Edith Forbes, September 25, 1875, *ETE Correspondence*; Myerson, "Textual Introduction," ccxl–ccxli.
74. Ellen explained her views aligned with the women in "Talks about the Tea Table" in *Old & New*'s July 1871 issue. Ellen Emerson to Edward Emerson, October 30, 1871, *ETE Correspondence*; Carpenter, "Introduction," xxxi.
75. Ellen Emerson to James Elliot Cabot, August 1, 1883, quoted in Myerson, "Textual Introduction," ccxl–ccxli.
76. Ellen Emerson to Edith Forbes, May 18?, 1878, *ETE Correspondence*.
77. Phyllis Cole, *Mary Moody Emerson and the Origins of Transcendentalism* (New York: Oxford University Press, 1998), 298.
78. Robert B. Habich, *Building Their Own Waldos: Emerson's First Biographers and the Politics of Life-Writing in the Gilded Age* (Iowa City: Iowa University Press, 2011), 106.
79. Ellen Emerson to Edith Forbes, August 30, 1895, *ETE Correspondence*.
80. Carpenter, "Introduction," li–lii.

81. Emerson, *Life of Lidian Jackson Emerson*, 84, 131, 168, 182.
82. Emerson, *Life of Lidian Jackson Emerson*, 81–83. For more see Delores Bird Carpenter, "Lidian Emerson's 'Transcendental Bible,'" *Studies in the American Renaissance* (1980): 91–95.
83. Emerson, *Life of Lidian Jackson Emerson*, 155.
84. Jackson, "Ellen Tucker Emerson," 104.
85. Jean T. Chapin, [Concord in 1875], 1912, Henry W. and Albert A. Berg Collection of English and American Literature, New York Public Library.
86. Bosco, "Historical Introduction," xxxvii–xl; Hanlon, *Emerson's Memory Loss*, 33–36.
87. For a detailed historiography of women and Transcendentalism, see Cole and Argersinger, "Introduction," 7–9.
88. Cole and Argersinger, "Introduction," 11.
89. Edward Emerson to Ellen Emerson, January 26, 1892, and Lidian Emerson to Ellen Emerson, February 15, 1873, quoted in Carpenter, "Introduction," xxi.
90. Edith Emerson Webster Gregg, "Preface," in *The Letters of Ellen Tucker Emerson*, by Ellen Tucker Emerson, ed. Edith Emerson Webster Gregg (Kent, OH: Kent State University Press, 1982), 1:xiii.
91. Ellen Emerson to James Elliot Cabot, August 1, 1883, quoted in Myerson, "Textual Introduction," ccxli.

8

THE MAN OF THE WORLD, OR, READERS, INTERLOCUTORS, NETWORKS

CHAPTER 26

"FLEEING TO FABLES"

Reading Emerson in Literature for Children

KRISTINA WEST

LOOKING FOR EMERSON

It is not particularly unusual for readers to encounter Ralph Waldo Emerson in works of fiction. Such references tend to invoke Emerson's writings to illustrate a point; or alternatively, a fictional character is positioned by the author or assumed by the reader to represent Emerson himself. Laura Dassow Walls, among others, identifies Emerson and Henry David Thoreau as the two lovers of heroine Sylvia Yule in Louisa May Alcott's adult novel, *Moods,* for example; in addition, Alcott quotes Emerson's essay "Experience" at the beginning of her text.[1] Likewise, critics including Rachel McCoppin have read the character of Jim Casey in John Steinbeck's *The Grapes of Wrath* as modelled on Emerson; indeed, Steinbeck seems to espouse Emerson's doctrine of the Oversoul in later chapters of the novel. And in modern fiction, Amor Towles's 2021 novel, *The Lincoln Highway*, cites Emerson's *Essays* as posthumous justification for a father's actions.[2] However, with the sporadic and unconnected nature of such appearances, much analysis of Emerson in fiction is limited either to passing comments in wider author studies or to high school study guides.

Even less attention is paid to Emerson's appearances in fiction written for a child or young adult readership. This blind spot in Emerson scholarship is part of a wider pattern, for despite the close ties between English Romanticism and American Transcendentalism, Emerson has rarely been considered as a writer either for or about children in academic studies of his work. Yet he has been the subject of at least one full-length biography aimed at children, James Playsted Wood's 1964 work, *Trust Thyself: Ralph Waldo Emerson for the Young Reader*, and has appeared in a biographical essay for children written by Louisa May Alcott in 1888. Further, Emerson has been featured in several fictional works for children including a number by Alcott, Canadian author L. M. Montgomery, and late twentieth-century American author Ransom Riggs. And the figure of the child looms paradoxically large in Emerson's works as he labours to define what "man" should be, as he frequently figures the child, in seemingly Romantic terms, as that which man should emulate in its innocence and closeness to nature. Yet Emerson's constructions of childhood were much more nuanced than a simple rehash of English Romantic thought. Across the public works of essays including (but not limited to) *Nature*, "Self-Reliance," and "Experience," and poems such as "The Sphinx," "Threnody," and "Woodnotes 2," as well as the private writings of journals and letters, Emerson regularly engages the figure of the child to reflect on man's fallen state, not simply as an example for man to follow but in a complex engagement between two seemingly disparate states that frequently cross and challenge the boundaries between them.

But what are we looking for, or at, if we attempt to read Emerson in fiction for children? Indeed, why search beyond his own texts at all if it is Emerson we are hoping to find? Although the undertaking of such an analysis necessitates a negotiation of genre between what is understood as fiction and the assumption of a reality or truth conferred by the proper name, searching for Emerson in this way appears to destabilize genre in the very assumption of separations such as "academic" and "literary" writing as well as "adult" or "child" audiences. As Robert D. Habich's work on Emerson's "afterlives" and Paul de Man's work on the problems with autobiography as a genre have made compellingly clear, neither biography nor autobiography can supply a singular, knowable truth of a life. As such, searching for Emerson in fiction, and reading such portrayals *as* fiction, becomes ever more problematic. Additionally, while much has been written by theorists such as Jacqueline Rose and Karín Lesnik-Oberstein on what is at stake when adults write the child in children's fiction, the writing of lived adults into children's fiction is a field that remains relatively unexplored.

I will therefore investigate how such authors of fiction portray Emerson and his writings in relation to child characters and assumed child readers, and how they position such versions or interpretations of Emerson within these structures. I will consider issues of gender suitability—how Emerson is framed in terms of the gender of the child reader both inside and outside of the text—and how such framings are both accepted and challenged across different authors, further considering how each author both promotes and dismisses Emerson's role in the lives of their characters, thereby challenging the role of books and the written word in the lives and education of the young. And in analyzing these iterations of Emersons, this chapter will explore how his presence in these works might further unsettle what we think we know about his own works, and particularly the relationships between child and adult.

"Putting On Airs"

When considering Louisa May Alcott's textual depictions of Emerson, it is easy to fall back on biography: after all, the young Alcott grew up with Emerson as a family benefactor and close friend. Yet to read Alcott's biography into representations of Emerson in her fiction for children risks disenfranchising a reading of Emerson in and of text and in relation to Alcott's child characters and readers, especially as Emerson makes brief appearances in many of her works for children and adults: Jo takes the named Emerson as her example in throwing fan letters in the trash in *Jo's Boys* (1886); "Mountain-Laurel and Maiden-Hair" (1887) contains a section in which two young women discuss their responses to Emerson's works; and the prefatory poem to *Flower Fables* (1854) is taken from Emerson's "Woodnotes".[3] To read each of these instances simply to reflect a lived relationship between Alcott and Emerson is to follow a reductive trend in children's literature criticism, with a critical appeal to the so-called reality of childhood frequently rendering textual childhood as too simple or obvious to read.[4] As such, I will focus solely on Emerson as text in Alcott's works rather than any lived relationship between the two.

The most sustained example of Alcott's textual engagement with Emerson is in her children's novel, *Rose in Bloom* (1876), the sequel to *Eight Cousins* (1875).[5] Rose is visiting the countryside with adopted orphan Dulce when Mac, one of the titular "eight cousins," drops in for a visit. Mac has spent several weeks "tramping" in the hills and has brought several gifts from nature as toys for Rose's orphan girl. Alcott writes: " 'Dearest Nature, strong and kind' knows what children love, and has plenty of such playthings ready for them all, if one only knows how to find them."[6] The inlaid quote is from the poem that precedes Emerson's essay "Experience," in which he claims:

> Little man, least of all,
> Among the legs of his guardians tall,
> Walked about with puzzled look:—
> Him by the hand dear Nature took;
> Dearest Nature, strong and kind,
> Whispered, "Darling, never mind!"
> (CW 3:25)

Alcott has adapted the meaning from Emerson's narratorial attempt to reconcile the child to his seeming lack of importance "among the legs of his guardians tall" and his role in the world of adulthood to position Nature as a guide to children, in the sense of creating a world expressly for them or for how Alcott thinks childhood should be. Yet Alcott leaves the quote from Emerson unattributed, requiring of her reader a knowledge of Emerson's works that is prior to and outside of Alcott's text; similarly, any claim to a shift in context between Emerson's and Alcott's works relies on this prior reading. Can we then, with any justification, claim that Emerson is represented in this text beyond the author's own, if obscured, knowledge of his work? Emerson can only be located in this section in terms of a reading that is also a deferral to something other; an intertextuality that acts to obscure as much as it suggests authorial intentionality.

Positioned here at a later stage of childhood than Rose's young charge, Mac and Rose require a supplement to the "playthings" provided by nature, with books supplied by Alcott as a suitable and valuable tool to replace such toys. Those texts that Alcott values are the poetry of John Keats and works from Henry David Thoreau and Emerson, with such value consisting of an education appropriate to the needs and challenges of each character: for Rose, who was "feeling as if some change were going on in that pleasant sort of pause but [was] unable to describe it," it is the navigation of a period of her life between one state or another for which she has no words of her own; and the books act further to provide a sentimental education as Mac and Rose begin to realize romantic feelings for each other under their influence.[7] As Mac quietly observes Rose, "he felt a curious desire to help [her] in some way, and could think of none better than to offer her what he had found most helpful to himself," and with neither Keats nor Thoreau quite fulfilling this role, Mac chooses Emerson.[8] "Picking up another book, he opened it at a place where an oak leaf lay, and ... said, as if presenting something very excellent and precious, 'If you want to be ready to take whatever comes in a brave and noble way, read that.'" As such, Alcott constructs Emerson's works as a catalyst for the change that accompanies the passage from childhood to adulthood, with Emerson invoked here through those of his writings that position him as teacher but also as conductor from one state to another; that is, away from the childhood with which Alcott's books and this chapter are concerned. Yet this giving of books from the man to the woman also prefigures a concern that runs through this and other portrayals of Emerson in children's fiction: that girls and women need male intervention and suggestion—beyond the male presence of Emerson himself as author of his works—to access Emerson at all. Although Mac's conditional "if" offers Rose a choice, she takes the book as advised, and once she has Emerson's essays, there is no need for another writer: Emerson is the pinnacle of Mac's literary offerings and of Rose's literary needs, and Mac's superior position as the medium between Emerson and Rose is established.

The text's direct engagement with Emerson's words begins with quotes from "Self-Reliance" and "Heroism"; although, at this stage, Alcott leaves these quotes unattributed, again privileging the content of the text above the name of Emerson as writer. Rose reads "here and there"; fragments rather than a consistent engagement with a single text. Alcott therefore positions this uneven engagement as a way for Emerson to be accessed by the young or within an assumption that these quotes are more relevant or helpful in meeting Mac's male desire to help effect the change from child to adult in his female cousin.

The fragments that Rose reads from "Heroism" are focused on the "maiden" and the "fair girl," and are framed as advice by Emerson as well as from Mac, who does not explain them to her, but asks: "You understand that, don't you?" She replies in the affirmative, but leaves Alcott's readers to puzzle out a meaning for themselves without either the guiding male hand or the endorsement of the author; meaning always, therefore, deferred. Rose continues: "I never dared to read these *Essays*, because I thought they were too wise for me," with Mac replying: "I don't ask you to read or understand all of that—don't myself—but I do recommend the two essays I've marked, as well as 'Love' and 'Friendship.' Try them and let me know how they suit." "I fancy this *will* suit," Rose concludes.[9] This conversation between Mac and Rose, while it might appear to focus on the content of Emerson's works, concerns itself rather with the question of Emerson's suitability and/or accessibility for children and young people, but with a further positioning of gender along traditional roles in which the "young man" should prepare himself to act within the wider world and the "girl" should concentrate on her interpersonal relationships. This positioning is reiterated in the following chapter when Alcott claims: "It is not strange that while the young man most admired 'Heroism' and 'Self-Reliance,' the girl preferred 'Love' and 'Friendship,' reading them, over and over," placing Alcott's young characters as submissive to the roles expected of them by society and by Alcott herself in this text, roles that they later assume in their eventual marriage.[10] However, Alcott is also claiming that a merely partial understanding of Emerson is to be expected in young people and is better than none at all. She thereby warns both child characters and readers of the difficulties in reading Emerson, and simultaneously encourages to carry on regardless.

This language of suitability runs throughout the passage, with Rose worrying that Emerson may not be appropriate for her as "Aunt Jessie may think I'm putting on airs if I try Emerson." This comment from Rose signals the first mention of Emerson by name in Alcott's text and unlike Mac's claims to be "with Thoreau," his references to "my Thoreau," and his claiming of Thoreau as his "best friend," Emerson is a writer who must first be tried: he is much less accessible, Rose implies through her equivocations, and so an engagement with him may still lead to failure.[11] But as Rose names Emerson in this tentative, anxious way, she installs a divide between the man and his works, as if Emerson, rather than his works, creates the barrier in Rose's mind. Yet Mac, via Alcott, rebuts Rose's concern: "He has done more to set young men and women thinking than any man in this century at least," with Alcott taking this opportunity to work through arguments for and against young people's engagement with Emerson's works, reflecting or even creating an anxiety around the suitability of Emerson for young readers.[12]

Still, Alcott largely presents Emerson in this chapter through his works rather than through a biographical construction or a fictional (or fictionalized) representation, therefore positioning Emerson's works in terms of value for both child characters and her own readers, with Mac's imperative of "read that" acting as direction to both. However, she challenges her own valuation in other ways. In recommending Emerson's works, Alcott raises further questions about the role of books in the education of children and young people, and particularly the conflict between the didacticism of adult-endorsed and adult-written texts versus the opportunity for young people to learn independently; to "enjoy an original relation to the universe" as Emerson wrote in *Nature* (*CW* 1:7). She further constructs Emerson as a conduit for change, but does so through the quotation of short passages from named essays. Such an engagement with Emerson is as fragmentary as the approach Alcott is suggesting to those young readers who might engage with his works under Alcott's direction—in terms of which essays they might "try" and the appropriate positive response to any such reading—rather than through their own independent study. As such, Alcott both foresees and creates her own difficulties with any such engagement between author and reader, and particularly in reading Emerson. Alcott's validation of Emerson's role as a guide for children is undermined still further in that Mac takes Emerson's place as poet in the text, first guiding and directing Rose, and then putting his own works into her hand and consciousness, with both characters leaving Emerson behind; a construction also used by early twentieth-century Canadian author L. M. Montgomery in her own works for children.

Troubling "The Poet"

L. M. Montgomery's engagement with Emerson's works dates back to her own girlhood, in which she experienced some of the difficulties foreseen by Alcott. An eighteen-year-old Montgomery wrote in her journal for January 1892:

> I went to church this morning, and spent the afternoon and evening reading Emerson's essays. To be interested in Emerson, you must get right into the groove of his thought and keep steadily in it. Then you can enjoy him. There can be no skipping or culling if you want to get at his meaning. I admire and appreciate Emerson, although I do not always understand him—I suppose I am too young. His style is clean, precise, and cold, with all its beauty. I think his ideals are rather impracticable in this sort of a world. He doesn't seem to take "human nature" sufficiently into account.[13]

This journal entry, much like Alcott's claim that Emerson must be "tried" and his suitability assessed, speaks to Montgomery's ambivalent relationship with Emerson and his works from her perspective as a young woman. Her shift from the "I" who went to church to the "you" who might wish to be interested in Emerson creates a distance between Montgomery and her own reading; her own interest, even. Like Alcott's Mac, she employs imperatives to direct an assumed reader—even if, this being Montgomery's journal, the reader might also be the writer—in how to access Emerson, constructing Emerson as that which needs help, advice, and direction: again, one cannot access Emerson unaccompanied as a child or young person. Montgomery shifts back to the personal "I" after this direction, however, to offer a critique that appears to negate her advice, to show that it has already failed, as "I do not always understand him." However, she also claims that "I suppose I am too young," indicating that Emerson's essays were not suitable for young adults in Montgomery's view and at this point of her life. Yet she paradoxically believed that Emerson's poetry had much to offer her child readers when she came to write the *Emily* series many years later.

Montgomery drew on a wide range of literary influences for her children's fiction, including *Jane Eyre*, the Romantic poets, and *Rebecca of Sunnybrook Farm*, and she quoted liberally from these works, sometimes with attribution but frequently without. Yet Emerson is notable for his repeat appearances in Montgomery's *Emily of New Moon* trilogy, which focuses on the girlhood and young womanhood of the titular heroine, an orphan living with her wider family much like Alcott's Rose. Emily is a writer from a young age, with her writing defining her throughout her series, and it is this role and her later role as lover on which Montgomery's engagement with Emerson (like Alcott's) is predicated. At the beginning of the second book in the trilogy, *Emily Climbs*, thirteen-year-old Emily is writing in her journal and remembering a talk with her older friend, Dean "Jarback" Priest. In Emily's recollection, Dean asks:

> "Star, do you know Emerson's lines?" And then he quoted them—I've remembered and loved them ever since.
>
> > "The gods talk in the breath of the wold,
> > They talk in the shaken pine,
> > And they fill the reach of the old seashore
> > With dialogue divine;
> > And the poet who overhears
> > One random word they say
> > Is the fated man of men
> > Whom the ages must obey."
>
> Oh, that "random word"—that is the Something that escapes me. I'm always listening for it—I know I can never hear it—*my* ear isn't attuned to it—but I am sure I hear at times a little, faint, far-off echo of it—and it makes me feel a delight that is like pain and despair of ever being able to translate its beauty into any words I know.[14]

The inlaid quote is taken from Emerson's poem, "The Poet," begun 1831 or even earlier, revised over twenty years, never completed, and not included in the variorum edition of Emerson's poetry; however, it appears in the Appendix of the Riverside Edition of volume 9 of Emerson's *Complete Works*.[15] There are, however, differences between Montgomery's quote and the Riverside Edition: "wold" for "wood," in the first line; the omission of "long" before "reach of the old seashore," and the replacement of "some random word" with "one random word." This named reference to Emerson so early in the second book, as compared to Alcott's later naming of Emerson after both quoting from and naming certain works, establishes Emerson as a presence within the text as writer from the outset of the second book of Montgomery's trilogy: this partial quotation of "The Poet" (though the name of the poem is not given) is anchored to its authorship. Yet, in its differences to the published version of the poem, this quotation could be argued both as Emerson and as not-Emerson in the changes or misquotation from the established text, raising further questions about perspective or who gets to decide on what is, or is not, Emerson and to what extent portrayals of Emerson in fiction are also necessarily fictional portrayals.

Within Montgomery's book, Emerson's lines construct the role of the poet as a conduit between the nature-based gods and man, and also in terms of a power both human and more than human: the "fated man of men / whom the ages must obey."[16] Yet the role of poet is largely out of the poet's control in this partial quotation of Emerson's poem: like the Puritan notion of divine grace, it is the gift of both the gods and fate, with the poet figured as the chosen one. And this opinion is seemingly endorsed by Emily at this stage of her narrative: the role of poet escapes her because she has not been chosen, because "*my* ear isn't attuned to it" (author's emphasis). Yet given that Emily progresses to a successful literary career later in the trilogy, is this an issue of age or of gender, that a female child may only hear a "faint, far-off echo" of what Emerson's adult, male poet is able to hear? As in Alcott's text, where Mac's reading of Emerson promotes Mac to the role of poet later in the text while Rose becomes only the consumer of another man's words, the assumption at this point is that women are barred by gender from ever fulfilling this role themselves. Yet this is Emily's assumption in her role as child as well as girl: like Rose's concern that Aunt Jessie will think her "putting on airs" if she "tries" Emerson, it is Emily's youth that is placing assumed barriers in her way, though based on an understanding of Emerson's male poet—the "man of men"—at its root.

The figure of the poet plays an important role across Emerson's poetry and prose, with his 1844 essay "The Poet" also establishing what Albert J. von Frank calls "Emerson's dramatically aggrandized figure of the Poet" (*CW* 9:xxvii). And the *fort/da* representation of the poet that von Frank recognizes in this essay, with a move from the slightly comic figure like "a secretary poorly taking dictation" from the gods to that of a self-reliant man in charge of his own destiny, structures the course of Emerson's poem. "In a characteristically Emersonian contradiction, what was first impressed in turn impresses" as the Poet becomes "active and heroic," von Frank comments (*CW* 9:xxvii). This shift in the poet's characterization is also accounted for later in the *Emily* trilogy, but not within this quoted section of Emerson's poem, the only one used throughout Montgomery's trilogy. As such, the male poet, who is both passive beneath the power of the gods and of fate and yet still the ideal to which child-Emily strives, remains fixed, with Emily's growth toward womanhood and her powers as writer instead the fulfilment of Emerson's promise.

Emerson's words—both these and others—are repeated and echoed throughout the three texts of this series, and it is worth taking a little time to consider who is speaking them; that is, the various fictional and fictionalized iterations of Emerson that Montgomery employs. This is not to claim that each of the following characters is a biographical portrait of Emerson, but rather that each acts, in some respects, as a speaker of his words and philosophies and as one aspect of Montgomery's representation of Emerson's poet figure. The value of Emerson's words in this text is frequently based on their quotation by Emily herself, either at first hand (although this can still be disputed in that it is Dean Priest who first introduces Emily to Emerson as Mac does for Rose), or in her quotation of others' quotations of Emerson in her journals. Emily is therefore an iteration of Emerson; of Emerson's poet figure; and of the child-reader of Emerson transformed by his words into adult, woman, lover, and finally poet. As with Alcott's Rose, Emerson acts as guide and conductor to the young heroine of this text; yet whereas Emerson is replaced by Mac in Alcott's work, it is Emily herself who takes Emerson's role as the trilogy reaches its climax. However, before this can happen, Emily is confronted with other male representations of Emerson and his textual poet in her life.

The first character in a male tripartite representation of Emerson is Dean Priest, a member of a related "clan" to Emily's family of the "proud Murrays," but one always troubled by his differences, with Priest's academic brilliance, disability, and love of travel all constructed as antithetical to New Moon conservatism, his name also betokening a Protestant religious protectionism that outlaws Catholic notions of worship. Priest befriends Emily when she is twelve and he is thirty-six, and while she sees him as one of the stand-ins for her lost (and also literary) father, he has a romantic, even sexual, interest in her from the outset.[17] Yet despite this seemingly predatory intent, Dean is the initial conduit between Emily and Emerson. This link is first established at the end of the first book in the trilogy, *Emily of New Moon*, in which "a certain line from a poem that Dean had recently read to her ... had captured her fancy. 'Good-bye, proud world, I'm going home,' she declaimed feelingly."[18] Although this quote is unattributed at this point—like Alcott, Montgomery begins with the words, not the writer—already Emerson is constructed in conjunction with Priest; indeed, with no other named source, the words become Priest's. He quotes Emerson again in the section previously discussed, and Emily requotes words from Priest's two Emerson quotes throughout the subsequent books.

Priest remains a complex character in his relationship to Emily and links to Emerson. In the first two books in particular, he is guide, teacher, and poet to the growing Emily, seducing her with words. As the books progress, however, Priest's seeming love for Emily is exposed as jealousy and a desire for ownership that traps Emily into a promise of marriage, eventually leading Priest to deny Emily her earned identity as Emerson's poet figure by his jealous dismissal of her work. One might argue that Montgomery's depiction of the doomed love affair between Priest and Emily is not related to the alignment she creates between Priest and Emerson; and yet, the older male's attempt not just to deny but to destroy the young girl's status as poet—an attempt that leads Emily to burn her first book—is bolstered by Montgomery's selective quoting of Emerson's "The Poet," in which Emily is forever shut out of her vocation by the paradoxically "random" decisions of the patriarchal gods. And that hold over her by the male poet figure is both reiterated and dissolved in that she can only be free of Priest through his belated admission that he lied to her: "Something had happened; she was really free ... Her own woman once more."[19] Despite the dearly-bought freedom that allows Emily to restart her career as a writer and begin to achieve her goals, Priest's hold over Emily is therefore reinstated, even if Montgomery does not construct it that way; for Emily can only write with his approval and benediction, thus reinstating a mastery that Montgomery cannot fully resolve. However, the positioning of Emily here not just as "woman" but as a woman belonging to herself and inhabiting this status not for the first time but as a *return*—"Her own woman once more"—paradoxically also allows Emily to lay to rest the ghost of the male poet that has haunted her since childhood along with the man who had personified that damaging assumption in her life.

While Priest has brought Emily to "The Poet," and thus attempts to deny her identity as writer, schoolteacher Mr. Carpenter rather quotes from Emerson's essay, "Heroism," to reposition him not as exclusionary but as educational and inspirational outside of any claims to gender suitability, telling Emily: "Remember your Emerson—'always do what you are afraid to do.'"[20] While Emerson himself quoted "high counsel that I once heard given to a young person" in his essay rather than claiming this as original advice, Montgomery positions Emerson here as an adviser to young people and his words as relevant to pass from teacher to pupil, especially in terms of Emily's growing status as writer; one that is endorsed, if critically, by Carpenter. Like Priest, Carpenter is figured as an influential character in Emily's life and one whom she trusts implicitly regarding his opinion of her writing talent: unlike Priest, he is almost brutally honest, using Emerson to inspire rather than to deny Emily's ambitions. This quote also suggests that he has spoken to Emily of Emerson before in his advice to "remember." Further, it is "*your* Emerson" (my emphasis) that Carpenter advises Emily to recall: Emerson belongs to Emily here, and perhaps also to youth and learning, as he does not to these men who cannot grow or learn from their mistakes. After all, like Priest both before and after him, Carpenter remains static in his position, and eventually—if by weakness rather than design—fails Emily too when his long-term alcoholism takes its toll and he dies, leaving Emily once again bereft of a father figure and more firmly in the clutches of Priest. As such, another male iteration of Emerson and of Emerson's poet figure is constructed by Montgomery as a failure and as that which Emily must leave behind in her own journey towards literary success.

The final iteration of Emerson in this trilogy is Emily's childhood friend, love interest, and eventual husband, Teddy, although only on a singular and somewhat belated occasion. In *Emily's Quest*, Teddy asks Emily: "Isn't it Emerson who said, 'Always do what you are afraid to do?'" to which Emily responds: "I'll bet Emerson said that when he'd got through being afraid of things. It's easy to be brave when you're taking off your harness."[21] This late engagement between Teddy and Emerson as the trilogy comes to a close is key to understanding the progression of Emerson's role across the three books. While Teddy requotes Carpenter here, this quote is phrased as a question rather than in the imperative used by the schoolteacher. And rather than accepting the Emersonian imperative, Emily answers Teddy's question through unsettling the position from which Emerson was speaking. As such, Teddy's late adoption of Emerson's words is too late: rather than a signal that he is taking over the role of learned, intellectually superior advice-giver in Emily's life, she instead takes that role for herself and fulfils the trajectory of Emerson's poet role to become "active and heroic," as von Frank says, but also, ultimately, self-reliant, with Priest's seemingly necessary permission for her career as poet finally overcome.

If we might read Priest, Carpenter, and Teddy as representations of Emerson in that each quotes his words to Emily with the intention of educating or helping her from a seeming position of authority, it is interesting to note his changing role as Emily grows, not just from child to adult or even from girl to woman, but from one who can never hear that "random word" to an accomplished and successful writer in her own right. The child Emily does not see the deception in Dean's selective quoting of "The Poet," and neither—one might assume—will Montgomery's child readers. Yet as the series progresses and both Dean's intentions and his jealousy of Emily's writing become evident to the reader if not yet to Emily herself, his early assertion that the status as "poet" might only come as a gift of gender and the gods rather than through hard work and dedication is problematized, and Emily grows into the status of poet through her own efforts and in her status as a self-reliant woman. Her seeming final repudiation of Emerson is therefore not a repudiation at all, but rather a sign that she no longer needs the advice of men and that she has used Emerson's words not as an end in themselves but as a means for her own development; a very Emersonian conclusion. This male tripartite representation of Emerson in Montgomery's works reflects the structural development in Emerson's works, with "The Poet" a key example of this approach: it is those who seek to deny that progression and to fix Emily in their own selfish desire of what she should be—to "nail the wild star to its track"—who fail.[22] To return to each man's quoting of Emerson and Emily's repetition of their quoting, while there is no sense in which she is doing her own reading during her childhood in the earlier books, with each man a conduit to and from Emerson but also a barrier between Emily and Emerson, when she finally feels free to criticize Emerson via her own reading of his words, she can both access him first-hand and move beyond him to claim the role of poet for herself.

Emerson's "Peculiar Children"

Emerson's representation in Ransom Riggs's 2011 young adult fantasy novel, *Miss Peregrine's Home for Peculiar Children*, draws attention to a different aspect of the Emersonian child that is also present in both Alcott's and Montgomery's fictional texts. Alcott's heroine Rose, though she may adhere to social conventions in many respects, is yet separated from other children in *Eight Cousins* by virtue of her gender and in her unsettling of that gender role as she grows up. Cousin Charlie denigrates her as a "queer chicken," while her later advocacy for women's roles to extend beyond love and marriage earns her a response from her assembled male cousins of "mingled surprise and amusement."[23] Likewise, Emily is not like other children: in *Emily of New Moon*, home help Ellen says: "The fact is, Emily Starr, you're queer, and folks don't care for queer children."[24] Neither was Emily "a proper child," according to Montgomery, with the extremes of this characterization occurring at the point in each text where she exhibits an uncanny ability to know things she cannot know. Riggs's inclusion of Emerson in works on the "peculiar children" further aligns Emerson—in the imagination of children's authors—with children who deviate from assumed social, physical, spiritual, or even temporal norms.

Miss Peregrine's Home for Peculiar Children is the first in a series of six young adult novels by American author Ransom Riggs. This first novel is set predominantly in a Welsh children's home which inhabits a time loop restricted to 3 September 1940, and which is lived in by a number of children designated in some way as "peculiar": one child is full of bees, another has to wear heavy boots or she will float away altogether, with these peculiarities and others based on photos that the author discovered before writing the book. The photographs suggest that childhood is something that can be fixed and known as such, and yet their subjects are presented as the not-child in that their characteristics are described in terms of the "peculiar": these are not how children should be, with a normative and desired childhood therefore invoked in contrast.

Riggs's first book is prefaced with a quote attributed to Ralph Waldo Emerson, who is named here in full:

> Sleep is not, death is not;
> Who seem to die live.
> House you were born in,
> Friends of your spring-time,
> Old man and young maid,
> Day's toil and its guerdon,
> They are all vanishing,
> Fleeing to fables,
> Cannot be moored.[25]

The poem from which this quote was taken begins Emerson's essay, "Illusions," published in *The Conduct of Life* in 1860 and revised in 1876. Much as in Montgomery's *Emily* books, and to a lesser degree in Alcott's *Rose in Bloom*, these lines are offered without explanation, without context or analysis, but inform the direction of the text in many ways, particularly in the prefatory position which they also hold in Emerson's own work, being both text and extratextual; introductory and seemingly thus offering an access point to the "main" text but also apart, able to be read separately. And as with Montgomery's partial quoting of "The Poet," this quote also constructs a singularity that does not exist in Emerson's full poem, which is constructed in a similarly developmental manner. As such, this quote serves only to unsettle and not to resolve.

Indeed, the poem appears to focus on the nature of illusion, of those things/people that appear to offer a solidity that falls apart when we try to hold it, but also the role we play in our illusions, or how we participate in that which appears to fool or escape us; in the very act of assuming that something is solid, fixed, and known, we create the conditions ourselves from which we can be fooled or left behind. In this quote, Emerson indicates that we need to accept the evanescence of all things, and that this very evanescence *is* what it is. The problem with analyzing Riggs's quoted section of Emerson's prefatory poem—either as a section or in conjunction with the rest of the poem and/or with the essay that follows—is that the analysis always escapes because it is about that very escape: it "cannot be moored." Even the "fleeing to" creates a problem, partly because of the mutable nature of "fables" and partly because it may be "to," but it remains in the movement towards and never arrives. Riggs's construction of the "peculiar children" is interesting to read against this, because in one sense they fit the nature of "illusion," of that which cannot be; and yet they also contradict Emerson's construction because they are "moored" more than any other child has ever been, stuck in a time loop which both protects and confines them in space and time, fixing them as forever child. Yet it also prefigures that the time loop is under threat, at risk of vanishing and "fleeing to fables," becoming just another story, unless the loop is broken by the children rather than by the enemies who want to destroy them.

The name "Emerson" is similarly precarious in this text. The full name of "Ralph Waldo Emerson" used at this early point of Riggs's text in the attribution of the poem is challenged by the "Emerson" who provides the initial mystery in the main work. When the grandfather of teenage boy Jacob dies in mysterious and disturbing circumstances, his last words are: "Emerson—the letter. Tell them what happened, Yakob."[26] Jacob has nightmares after his grandfather's death and is guided by analyst Dr. Golan to work out these last words through investigating who Emerson might be, with Emerson therefore figured as mystery and as that which needs decoding in order for the teenage Jacob to move forwards. Although this might appear as an opposing approach to Alcott and Montgomery where Emerson acted as guide both from and towards a position of knowledge, this iteration of Emerson paradoxically works differently but with the same aim in mind: to educate the young character and reader. Knowing Emerson is all about naming here, but it is a peculiar knowledge, because while Riggs quotes Emerson at length at this initial point of his work, the characters' only engagement with Emerson's works in this text is to dismiss them. Jacob thinks the "Emerson" of the letter might have been one of his grandfather's neighbours, or an old war buddy, but when these theories draw a blank, his analyst suggests that Jacob tries Ralph Waldo Emerson, a "supposedly famous old poet."[27] Despite this paradoxical and ironic "fame," Jacob needs adult direction to discover Emerson—Dr. Golan "wouldn't let me quit"—in much the same way as Emily and Rose needed adult guidance, if with a change in gender. But unlike Rose and Emily, Jacob is not impressed with his reading of Emerson:

> His writing was so dense and arcane that it couldn't possibly have held the slightest interest for my grandfather, who wasn't exactly an avid reader. I discovered Emerson's soporific qualities the hard way, by falling asleep with my face in the book, drooling all over an essay called "Self-Reliance."[28]

While "Self-Reliance" sent Jacob to sleep, he was still "drooling all over" it, with the words' double connotations of sleep and desire. This is an interesting contradiction to both Alcott's and Montgomery's gender constructions, where male figures were required to lead female characters to a (limited and controlled) appreciation of Emerson; here, instead, the boy both rejects Emerson as writer and desires the self-reliance that the essay appears to offer. Jacob's seeming reluctance to move towards this self-reliance, as he attempts both to hold onto his lost grandfather and escape his father, further echoes Emily's return to Emerson even as she appears to reject him. And while Jacob initially refuses to believe that this is the Emerson of whom his grandfather wrote, he discovers his mistake when he is given a copy of *The Selected Works of Ralph Waldo Emerson* as a beyond-the-grave gift from his grandfather, with an inscription on the title page reading: "To Jacob Magellan Portman, and the worlds he has yet to discover—" with Emerson's position as a giver of knowledge in children's literature thereby troubled in that here he is merely a signpost to something other than himself.[29]

This characterization of Emerson also differs from the previous texts in that the name of Emerson acts as a double-blind: while the two seemingly different-named Emersons are eventually resolved as one, it is not the book itself—that is, Emerson's words—that will be of interest to Jacob, but a letter that is secreted inside and which takes Jacob to Wales and on to the home and its "peculiar children." As such, Emerson's role reiterates that of Alcott's and Montgomery's texts in that Emerson acts as a guide and conductor to the young character, and can be left behind when that role is complete, but also rewrites it as it is his name, not his works, that is important and then only as a container for something other; that is, the words of another writer. While Rose and Emily are led by quotations from Emerson's writings, notwithstanding that they are mediated by men in positions of some power, Jacob has no access to the quote from "Illusions" that begins this book, with Emerson's "Self-Reliance" both an absence, in that it is not quoted, and a diversion. As such, rather than fixing Emerson as poet and his writings as a guide to the young if properly mediated and explained, this attribution unsettles Emerson's status as writer and divorces him from the childhood to which he might appear as guide. In many ways, and despite the extensive initial quote, Riggs's Emerson is merely a plot device to be discarded once that goal is achieved: in this way, Riggs effectively silences Emerson as writer. It is, indeed, a peculiar engagement.

In an interview about the inclusion of Emerson in his text, Riggs explains:

> Emerson figured much more heavily into the first draft of *Miss Peregrine*, but his involvement was whittled down quite a bit. Part of that had to do with the story changing direction. In the old version, Jacob met the peculiar children gradually, and it took him several chapters to finally and fully believe they were real. Emerson often speaks about the possibility of fantastic things that exist just out of view, and many of his most famous quotes almost seem to refer directly to the peculiar children. "The power which resides in him is new in nature," he writes in "Self-Reliance" (1841), "and none but he knows what that is which he can do, nor does he know until he has tried." That's certainly true of the children, and of Jacob, too. Then there's this line, from *Nature* (1836): "In the woods, too, a man casts off his years, as the snake his slough, and at what period soever of life is always a child. In the woods is perpetual youth." It's not hard to imagine that Emerson is describing the deep woods surrounding Miss Peregrine's house and its strangely youthful inhabitants.[30]

In this sense, Riggs is claiming, like Alcott and Montgomery, that Emerson is relevant to his young readership, both within and beyond his text: he is inviting his readers to explore Emerson still further. Yet despite Riggs's passive-voiced claim to Emerson's "involvement" in the text—one that suggests that this was out of the author's control, along with the claim that this involvement "was whittled down"—the claim to his book's engagement with Emerson here is a peculiar one too, in that Riggs appears to be claiming that his book preceded Emerson's writings, even if the claim that "Emerson is describing the deep woods surrounding Miss Peregrine's house" is necessarily imaginary. Riggs also quotes from Emerson's essays here, despite their absence from the body of his children's book, with lines from "Self-Reliance" and *Nature* attributed to both author and text, and both quotes read in the context of his construction of a "peculiar" and fictional childhood. It is Emerson's descriptions of "the possibility of fantastic things that exist just out of view" that Riggs both reads and constructs as belonging to childhood, positioning both Riggs's and Emerson's iterations of childhood in opposition to adulthood in their very strangeness.

"Cannot Be Moored"

In my readings of Emerson within fiction for children, the characterization that has emerged across the texts in terms of Emerson's writings and Emerson as writer is that of a relevance to children and young people that might not be assumed given the relative paucity of critical readings of childhood within his own works. Yet this relevance always takes place at a divide in that it takes adult direction, and sometimes interpretation, to bring the child (frequently a child already characterized, in some sense, as peculiar, one that is therefore also the not-child; and also a child divided from other children by gender and gender assumptions) to Emerson: he is not available at first hand and, even in the child's own reading, he remains aloof, with the engagement presenting challenges both within and beyond the reading of his text. Emerson also figures within a heteronormative romantic education, thereby both proving and challenging his relevance to childhood in that it is the transformation from one state to the other that allows a simultaneous development of friendship to romance in these texts, and acting within a discourse of desire both within and beyond romance. As such, Emerson's applicability and relevance to children is always partial and qualified, somehow oblique.

This slippage that we encounter in Emerson's characterization within these fictional works for children also offers an opportunity to return to the figure of the child in Emerson's own texts, where we might read a similar ambivalence. A focus on Emerson's frequent recourse to the child figure in his observations on an ideal manhood reveals a seemingly polarized view in which the idealized, Romantic child who provides a type to which man might aspire is contrasted with the "lost" child of "The Sphinx" and the child denigrated in its contextual alliance as "minors" with "invalids" and "cowards" in "Self-Reliance" (*CW* 9:5–9; 2:28), but with each type destabilized and unmoored both within and between texts, with the Emersonian child thus as "peculiar" as those with whom he is linked in children's literature. Any reading of Emerson in children's literature therefore returns us to a closer exploration of his own engagement with childhood and the structures within his work that these texts have both reflected and failed to simplify.

Perhaps to conclude this investigation of Emerson in children's literature, then, we must return to Emerson's own philosophy of circles and illusion to understand how, in the authors' simultaneous connection and division of Emerson from fictional children and child readers in their works, and the child characters' seeming repudiation of or moving on from Emerson as punctuation to their textual engagement, there is also the negation of that very moving on by the authors themselves, who circle back to Emerson and to his engagement with childhood by the very writing of him into their texts as a young person's guide, with the additional "afterlife" of children's literature as books are read by generation after generation, prompting a similar circularity in our own engagement with Emerson and his works as we too return to ask Emerson's own question in *Nature*: "What is a child?"

Notes

1. Laura Dassow Walls, *Henry David Thoreau: A Life* (Chicago: University of Chicago Press, 2017), 462.
2. Amor Towles, *The Lincoln Highway* (London: Hutchinson Heinemann, 2021), 29–30.
3. Louisa May Alcott, 1886, *Jo's Boys* (London: Collins Classics, 2013), 300; "Mountain Laurel and Maiden-Hair," in *A Garland for Girls* (Boston: Roberts Brothers, 1888), 219–58: 225; *Flower Fables* (Bedford: Applewood Books, 1854), unnumbered. With gratitude to Joel Myerson for his complete list of Emerson's appearances in Alcott's works and for his kind support of this project.
4. See Kristina West, *Louisa May Alcott and the Textual Child* (Basingstoke: Palgrave Macmillan, 2020) for further discussion of this issue.
5. Louisa May Alcott, 1876, *Rose in Bloom* (New York: Puffin Books, 1995).
6. Ibid., 288.
7. Ibid., 262.
8. Ibid., 263.
9. Ibid., 264.
10. Ibid., 269.
11. Ibid., 261–62.
12. Ibid., 264.
13. L. M. Montgomery, *The Selected Journals of L. M. Montgomery*, vol. 1, *1889–1910* (Oxford: Oxford University Press, 1985), 75.
14. L. M. Montgomery, 1925, *Emily Climbs* (London: Puffin Books, 1990), 17–18.
15. Ralph Waldo Emerson, "The Poet," in *Poems: The Riverside Edition* (London: George Routledge and Sons, 1899), 253–63.
16. This appeal to nature, one that also links Priest's quotation of Emerson to the pines under which Emily and Priest were sitting, also connects what is often read as Emerson's Romantic vision of childhood with the critically-read green world archetype of Montgomery's child heroines.
17. Montgomery, *Emily Climbs*, 302.
18. L. M. Montgomery, 1923, *Emily of New Moon* (London: Puffin Books, 1990), 301.
19. Montgomery, *Emily's Quest*, 105.
20. Montgomery, *Emily Climbs*, 19.
21. Montgomery, *Emily's Quest*, 14.
22. See "Threnody," *CW* 9:287–302.
23. Alcott, *Rose in Bloom*, 10.
24. Montgomery, *Emily of New Moon*, 30.
25. Ransom Riggs, *Miss Peregrine's Home for Peculiar Children* (Philadelphia: Quirk Books, 2011), unnumbered; also *CW* 6:164–65.

26. Ibid., 33.
27. Ibid., 46.
28. Ibid., 47.
29. Ibid., 56.
30. http://www.watermarkbooks.com/miss-peregrines-home-peculiar-children-ransom-riggs (interview no longer available).

CHAPTER 27

EMERSON, MELVILLE, FUTILITY

RACHEL BANNER

In terms of offering comment on the relationship between the writings of Ralph Waldo Emerson and Herman Melville, I think it's helpful to first underscore that they did not know each other. The discourse surrounding their writings' possible relations—issuing from me and from past critics—is necessarily speculative and elastic. What critics see between these two is not necessarily true and not necessarily false either; all the commentaries are figments of critical perception, "a train of moods like a string of beads, and as we pass through them they prove to be many-colored lenses which paint the world their own hue, and each shows only what lies in its focus. From the mountain you see the mountain. We animate what we can, and we see only what we animate" (*CW* 3:30). That is to say, if the Emersonian Melville and the Melvillean Emerson that you encounter in this essay fail to cohere, there await other connections no doubt waiting for your animations. Both writers function—as do any worthy objects of cultural criticism—as contested and evolving sites of meaning for critics and readers alike.

Of course there is a great deal linking the two both factually and thematically, which has given rise to decades of literary criticism about how their writings may speak to each other. Both were well-known literary figures at different times in their lives, although Emerson's popularity was certainly more enduring, spanning most of the nineteenth century and on into the twentieth. Melville had a somewhat spectacular fall from literary grace starting in the 1840s, was eventually declared "insane" in a local New York newspaper item, and died in relative literary obscurity.[1] And while the two never had any known personal interactions, Melville did attend one of Emerson's lectures in Boston in the winter of 1848. In a later letter, he declared himself "very agreeably disappointed" in Emerson's plain-speaking lucidity, praising Emerson by classifying him among the fabled "men who dive ... the whole corps of thought-divers, that have been diving & coming up again with bloodshot eyes since the world began."[2] As far as scholars can tell, though, there seems to have been no mutual awareness between these two prolific writers whom a slate of US literary critics would, by the middle of the twentieth century, situate as among the most important American authors in the antebellum US.

That being said, invocations of Emerson, or perhaps more accurately what Emerson had come to stand for by the middle decades of the nineteenth century, surface regularly across Melville's writings. In his 1852 novel *Pierre, or The Ambiguities*, Melville dedicates a robust narrative subplot to a biting critique of a popular philosopher/writer turned lecturer named Plotinus Plinlimmon. Plinlimmon's brand of hypocritical asceticism is Melville's caricature of New England Transcendentalism's progressive subcultural cachet, of which Emerson was very much a figurehead by the early 1850s. Elsewhere in Melville's oeuvre, the chapter in *Moby-Dick* titled "The Masthead" has the narrator teasingly warning owners of whaleships, "Beware of enlisting in your vigilant fisheries any lad with lean brow and hollow eye; given to unseasonable meditativeness ... For nowadays, the whale-fishery furnishes an asylum for many romantic, melancholy, and absent-minded young men, disgusted with the carking cares of earth, and seeking sentiment in tar and blubber."[3] With the narrator Ishmael taking on the perspective of just such a melancholic romantic, the chapter lulls the reader into contemplating the beauty of Emersonian correspondence between self and surroundings—"at last he loses his identity; takes the mystic ocean at his feet for the visible image of that deep, blue, bottomless soul"—and then casually pivots to a declaration that such mysticism while doing a whaler's work will more than likely lead to a fall from the masthead and a watery grave.[4] The chapter's final image of the dreamy young sailor experiencing a Transcendentalist high that causes him to plummet to his death is simultaneously seductive, horrible, and a little bit hilarious. This is itself an apt description of the way Melville tends to most obviously engage the man who would come to be known as the "Sage of Concord." As Melville wrote in the same 1849 letter quoted above, sniping about Emerson's supreme intellectual confidence, "These men are all cracked about the brow."[5]

Twentieth-century literary and cultural critics also tended to locate the core of the Melville-Emerson literary relationship within Melville's restless engagement with Emerson's cultural status and popularity. Much early twentieth-century Americanist literary criticism that explicitly compares the two largely retains the competition narrative, with the critic coming down in favor of only one. Robert Levine, quoting Ida Rothschild, identifies this impulse as the need of scholars to engage fantasies of authority that often manifest as "speculative biographical mythology" meant to position one author over another.[6] In some early twentieth-century criticism, Melville and Emerson are often positioned in an agonistic, oddly personal relation. From the 1920s Melville Revival through the 1950s, prominent literary criticism on the two somewhat aggressively juxtaposes them and then demands answers: *Optimist or pessimist? Transparent eyeball or white whale? Blondes or brunettes?*

That last question derives from Perry Miller's 1953 article "Melville and Transcendentalism," where his analysis of the marriage plot in Melville's 1851 novel *Pierre* segues into a taxonomic use of its two heroines—Lucy, the blonde, blue-eyed, jilted fiancée, and Isabel, the mysterious brunette with mystical guitar skills who is Pierre's live-in lover, common-law wife, and possible biological sister—as a way of diagnosing Melville's fraught relationship to New England Transcendentalism, of whom Ralph Waldo Emerson is Miller's exemplar. Describing Melville's novel with much bombast as, among other things, a "climax of Satanic rebellion," Miller reads the novel as Melville setting out to deliberately "explode the romantic thesis" at the heart of nineteenth-century transatlantic literary culture. Miller's broad point here is that Melville is a crypto-Transcendentalist, with the Satanic excesses of *Moby-Dick* and *Pierre* abetted by some of Emerson's earlier heterodoxies, though Miller positions Emerson's work as comparatively more arid and enervating.

The weird bit is that Miller stages his point via analogizing Emerson's and Melville's writings with the cultural associations attached to the color of a woman's hair.[7] Miller strives to convince readers of the validity of both his literary stakes and his hirsute schematics with the assurance that "today the rivalry of the blonde and dark heroines seems Hollywood type-casting, but then it posed the issue of the nineteenth century."[8] Though he later grudgingly acknowledges that "Transcendentalism seemed obtuse to the problem of the duel between blonde and brunette," this compositional choice compels not because it offers particularly incisive commentary on Emerson or Melville, but because the critic's own cultural situatedness is so evident.

Miller is not an anomaly here. In fact his essay follows earlier work from F. O. Matthiessen in his 1941 book *The American Renaissance* that also devotes a substantial amount of time to "the two girls" from Melville's *Pierre* in crafting a hypothesis about the Melvillean relation to the Emersonian. Matthiessen also uses *Pierre*'s Lucy and Isabel to argue that Melville's art struggled against both mainstream domestic American culture and an American Transcendentalist counterculture that Melville perceived as equally lacking. According to Matthiessen, neither the mainstream nor the counterculture had the ability to account for the existence of human evil and social immiseration that so preoccupied Melville throughout his artistic life.[9] As the chapter progresses, Matthiessen firmly positions himself as Melville's man against Emerson, their critical duel filtered through the apparently irresistible blonde vs. brunette framing. He bluntly states that "at no period, not even in *Mardi*, does it seem right to think of [Melville] as other than a critic of transcendentalism" and by extension, of Emerson's oeuvre.[10] Matthiessen later writes, "Pierre seems to need them both, but far below any conscious awareness he is drawn most naturally to the dark, life-giving forces of Isabel, the forces that were being so atrophied by the incessant pale American search for the ideal."[11] Matthiessen's prose at times projects through Melville's "girls," enacting a neat Sedgwickian homosocial triangulation[12] where he himself takes the role of Pierre, figuring Emerson as poor Lucy—the pallid, Romantic idealist—who cannot hold a candle to the brash, brunette, and altogether more compelling Melvillean Isabel.

I want to note here that I don't summarize these critical accounts to mock them. Personally I am delighted by the notion that critics as esteemed as F. O. Matthiessen and Perry Miller settled on "is s(he) a Jackie or a Marilyn?"[13] as a useful hermeneutic when thinking about the two writers. What I particularly like about the pieces is their shared urgency in identifying which type of literary "girl," Emerson or Melville, ultimately catches and holds the critic's gaze. In the middle of the twentieth century, for these two white men, it seemed to *matter* on an epistemological level which girl/text/author hybrid they would embrace over the other.

Contemporary Emerson critics Randall Fuller and Robert D. Habich[14] rightfully emphasize that enshrined literary figures like Emerson and Melville are always retooled and retrofitted to hew to the cultural vocabularies of each critical generation. Wherever and however one draws interpretive lines connecting Emerson to Melville, that relation is largely the product of textual readings inflected by critical peccadilloes and historical context. While I regrettably cannot in good conscience argue that blonde vs. brunette "poses the issue" of more than a century of Emerson and Melville criticism, I harp on this small thematic concurrence in both critics to emphasize that sometimes the facts about Emerson and Melville are simply not as interesting as what we (critics, students, readers) can make of them together, now, in whatever moment you happen to be reading this.

I think too that there are ethical benefits to thinking about these two writers together beyond what archives and biographers empirically substantiate. In a recent article about contemporary critical "turns" back towards biographical literary criticism—specifically about squaring thematics of sexual abuse in Nathaniel Hawthorne's writings with the possibility that Nathaniel Hawthorne may have been a victim of childhood sexual abuse—Jordan Alexander Stein argues:

> Though scholarly methods of archival recovery and biographical reconstruction dictate that we [contemporary scholars] must be precise, I'm suggesting that such a commitment to the high bar of methodological precision requires scholars to move ... in callous pursuit of our knowledge-making activities, sacrificing our willingness to see the something that the texts manifest. That sacrifice condemns us to not-know something these texts are plainly telling us.[15]

In agreement with Stein, I am not particularly interested in the scholarly-critical impulse to meticulously document and define, in what Stein terms as a strictly "positivist fashion," anything that we claim to *know* about literature. The rigorous demand for proof can sometimes discount and reinforce racial, gendered, and sexual power structures within scholarly critical cultures.

To give just one example, note how David Dowling largely dismisses Elizabeth Renker's scholarship that analyzed Melville's writing in the context of material evidence suggesting he committed domestic abuse. Dowling characterizes the Renker essay thus: "critics have largely been content with the bleak implications of Elizabeth Renker's 1994 essay, 'Herman Melville, Wife Beating, and the Written Page,' which inspired a critical edition on Melville and gender, most of it indicting the author." The footnote to this passage minimizes Renker on the grounds of what Dowling views as unpersuasive documentary evidence. Dowling characterizes Renker's use of a letter by Elizabeth Shaw Melville's brother, Samuel Shaw, referencing the abuse within the Shaw-Melville marriage, as evidence that Renker "can only 'suggest' that Melville actually assaulted his spouse. Renker nonetheless uses this tenuous scrap of historical documentation to launch into an attack on Melville's gender politics, emphasizing the grave, profound, shaping force his spousal abuse had." Renker's work is, in Dowling's note, finally denigrated as a feminist "over-corrective [that] blinds readers to the play, humor, and liberation at the heart of much of [Melville's] fiction that deals with gender."[16] What

Dowling's essay knows is that it must dismiss Renker's claims about the fundamental importance of domestic violence in Melville's art and life. It tries to convince readers that they should "not know" something that the texts (and archive!) gesture towards in order to shore up a particular critical-biographical mythos of Melville as a playful gender theorist.

Turning to Emerson, critics like Christopher Hanlon similarly explore a facet of the Emerson archives that past criticism largely decided to "not know." Hanlon hypothesizes that Emerson's late style is inextricable from his experiences of cognitive dementia and growing reliance on his daughter to compose and edit his writings. Hanlon prods scholars to acknowledge that critical interpretive claims exist always in "varying states of fragmentation," the archives themselves serving as repositories mainly of "discontinuities" rather than coherent narratives.[17] Hanlon's late-style Emerson reminds us that the misbegotten pursuit of locating an idea's original source or stable meaning, in a text or a life, sidesteps the communitarian force of teaching and learning from each other at all.

While it is a worthy and valid goal for scholars and critics to commit to precise fact-based argumentation, I tend to agree with Stein that:

> Sometimes, to be empathetic scholars and teachers and people, we have to commit to accuracy even without the possibility of precision. To imagine instead that our job is to know (and therefore, given our methodological standards, inevitably to deny) the cause of a thematic display of sexual violence like the one that spans Hawthorne's career, rather than to attend to it, perpetuates a kind of cruelty not only toward the object we study but, as I will explain, also to the people we teach.[18]

The rest of this essay builds with Stein's suggestion in arguing that it is a worthwhile experiment for scholars still interested in thinking comparatively about Emerson and Melville to emphasize accuracy over precision. What I mean by this is that we should weight contextual accuracy—a sense that something is true *for this moment*—more heavily than historicist fact or critical histories. In the rest of what follows I argue that an accurate appraisal of "Emerson and Melville now" is one that necessitates being honest about the fact that there may not be (ought there not be?) much future criticism to speculate about at all.

The Accuracy of Irrelevance

In the 1841 essay "Circles," Emerson evinces a casualness with the notion of what a fact is or means. His is a definition that is not beholden to positivist verification. He conceives of all human endeavors as an "apprenticeship to the Truth that around every circle another can be drawn" (*CW* 2:179). Against any human pretensions to stable arrangements of power, Emerson cautions, "There are no fixtures in nature. The universe is fluid and volatile. Permanence is but a word of degrees. Our globe seen by God is a transparent law, not a mass of facts. The law dissolves the fact and holds it fluid." The obvious contradiction here of a supreme power, "holding" the inherently "fluid" and "volatile" world in place as facticity dissolves, at once asserts and undermines the sentence's claim. In both Stein and Emerson, the thing that matters, the truth, is empirically elusive and yet perhaps all the more true for that. In this spirit, I offer a claim that unavoidably undermines itself: first, it is hubristic to write *as if* there is likely to continue to be sustained critical considerations of Emerson and Melville's entwined literary legacy. Second, these writers' shared belief in the futility of their work is a salient legacy for our current historical moment.

As I draft this piece, it seems increasingly unlikely that I am writing towards a future in which any critical mass of readers will think overly much about if and how Emerson and Melville's writings relate to one another. It is a claim born out of the increasingly painful and precarious circumstances for humanities scholars within the strictures of the twenty-first-century university. In the United States in 2022, enrollments of undergraduate majors in English departments consistently trend downwards, tenure-track job postings in the fields and subfields of American literature decrease annually, and underpaid and inherently exploitative adjunct positions proliferate in lieu of stable professorships that allow time for scholars to produce humanistic research.[19] Because these declines in fairly compensated scholarly labor only seem to deepen, it is increasingly clear that even those people who are deeply committed to studying nineteenth-century US literature, let alone these two writers specifically, have a slim to non-existent chance of being able to lead dignified work lives doing such a thing.

These dismal facts about the profession do not begin to encompass the pressures and pain that undergraduate students navigate within and outside of contemporary university classrooms. Many, and perhaps most, US college students today live in a world where they are subject to a great deal of socially-engineered historical pain. Pain that winnows its way into individual lives in precise, harrowingly mundane ways: wildly unaffordable cost of living and college tuition, enormous student debt, getting enough to eat, finding someone to watch the kids, having to help out your parents or siblings or grandparents financially while needing to buy books and do your coursework. And all of this against the background of a now years-long global pandemic, racist policing practices, mass incarceration, proliferating restrictions on abortion rights in the US after the Supreme Court overturned *Roe v. Wade* in June 2022, and the increasingly lively specter of catastrophic and irreversible global climate change.

In the face of such a grim litany, and as a tenured professor at a regional-public university who teaches mostly general education classes in composition and literature, I increasingly doubt that it matters if students read some Emerson and Melville in an introductory literature course.[20] I do *want* my students to encounter these writers. I think both Emerson and Melville are able to illuminate the prehistories of many of the painful circumstances attending our collective life in the early twenty-first-century United States. Their writings, though obviously not *only* or *exclusively* or *eminently* their writings, are key sites from which we can glimpse operative historical, aesthetic, and political energies that still slice into the material circumstances of the present.

And still. It is hubristic and perhaps speaks to a tendency towards over-valorization of our jobs amongst English professors to think that any of my students *need* to contain encounters with Emerson and Melville in the course of their educations. They do not, and this is nothing to grieve. Emerson reminds us in "Circles" that any artwork's descent into irrelevance—his own included—is likely baked in, so to speak, to the structure of US culture: "Our culture is the predominance of an idea which draws after it this train of cities and institutions. Let us rise into another idea: they will disappear ... The new continents are built out of the ruins of an old planet; the new races fed out of the decomposition of the foregoing. New arts destroy the old" (240). Emerson here seems to grant a tacit permission to my frequent doubts about his work's continuing relevance as we move through the decades of the twenty-first century.

The opening gambit of "Circles" is to turn a calm eye to the inevitable destruction, decomposition, and/or disappearance of old cultural material and to insist that this is nothing to mourn. Or, at least that mourning a particular artist's obsolescence is of no ultimate consequence to cultural formations writ large. Is it actually a loss, Emerson's words themselves prod, if students no longer learn about American literature through the lens of a six-man (and one woman) "American Renaissance"?[21] Of course not.

Nina Baym already more than made this point in her classic 1981 essay "Melodramas of Beset Manhood." Baym reminds us that in canonizing Emerson and Melville as exemplars of American literature in the first half of the twentieth century, influential white male critics like Lionel Trilling and Leslie Fiedler helped shape a perception of Emerson and Melville as cultural iconoclasts due to, Baym notes drily, their "modest alienation" from a hyperspecific WASPish ideal of American manhood.[22] Baym's work was followed in the 1990s and early 2000s by a trove of criticism insistent on using Black Studies, feminism, postcolonial theories of empire, and queer theory in their theorizations of nineteenth-century US literature. Work written by invaluable scholars and critics like Hortense Spillers, Toni Morrison, Dana D. Nelson, Ann duCille, Karen Sanchez-Eppler, Amy Kaplan, and Betsy Erkkila to name only a few.

The field of what we think about when we think about nineteenth-century US literature is larger, truer, messier, and more just because of this work that decentered the importance of previously delineated major authors from the period. And no doubt because their scholarship (among others) has been so central to my own training, I have found myself struggling mightily to find value in elaborating on what I happen to see as the relationship between Emerson and Melville's writings *now*, beyond reviewing the critical history of that relationship's creation and maintenance in some earlier American literary scholarship. While it is not my place to declare, nor would I, the dawning irrelevance of their works or critical legacies, neither can I quite countenance their (possibly) declining cultural currency as a serious problem.

When I assign students to read some Melville and some Emerson, their names are generally brand new to most of my students (as indeed they were to me as a college student in 2004). Correspondingly, there is generally little awareness of their writings being considered culturally significant or even compelling. Sometimes, for some students and readers (my past self included), an appreciation grows in the course of reading and study. For most it doesn't. Perhaps as scholars and teachers of these writers today, we can worry less about some critical mass of readers finding these writers culturally important because they likely won't and that is likely fine, if not even for the better. Emerson and Melville themselves suggest such a conclusion. I argue that the most crucial way of conceptualizing Emerson and Melville together now is to take seriously their writings' theorizations of the futility of their own ambitions. I think that the Emerson-Melville relationship of most consequence is one in which scholars acknowledge, as indeed both of their works seem able to do, that many—perhaps most—human enterprises are destined to fail. And more, and that these failures are casual in the sense that maybe not very much of what's lost needs to be grieved.

Failure Artists

It may seem odd to link Emerson and Melville with concepts as passive as futility and failure. These are, after all, canonical US writers who have rightly been analyzed as championing "self-reliance" and/or individualized hypermasculine "isolato" bravado that is inseparable from doctrinaire nineteenth-century US imperialism, misogyny, white supremacy, and other exclusionary power structures. Recall Emerson's sneering retort in the essay "Self-Reliance" in which he chastises various philanthropic movements: "Are they my poor? I tell thee, thou foolish philanthropist, that I grudge the dollar, the dime, the cent, I give to such men as do not belong to me and to whom I do not belong" (*CW* 2:30–31). But as often as Emerson and Melville operate in registers of bombast and (especially in the case of Emerson's early writings and speeches) something that often veers into toxic individualism, there is a lurking sense of imminent and unavoidable failure that propels the best writing from each.

Futility is an interesting heuristic in that it draws attention to a quieter, more fretful and subsequently more intellectually useful sense of these writers for our own historical moment. A moment in which human efforts seem and are so incommensurate with the problems we face on a global scale. It is this sense of futility—the failure of language to express thought, of art to meaningfully have effects, of "souls [to] … touch their objects" as Emerson longs for in the essay "Experience"—*that* paradoxically seems the most fitting version of Emerson and Melville in the twenty-first century. It captures a sense of fated development. As a literary mood, futility is a register in which one can gesture at things that *might happen but will not*, or things conceived of that are destined to *not-be*. Futility as it appears in their writings appeals to the subjunctive imagination but remains fundamentally apprehensive about an idea's ability to hold purchase in the world. Thinking like this asks scholars to sit with the possibility that our diligence and our study and our own critical desires that we bring to their texts may create or reveal nothing. Or at least nothing of lasting importance. Melville and Emerson understand this and, in the moments in which I cleave to their writings most, admit an honest pessimism about what their works cannot do.

A prime example here is perhaps the most well-known and infamous passage from Emerson's essay "Experience." Emerson here veers from an abstracted meditation on human encounters with "disaster" to what can be read as a shockingly casual invocation of his young beloved son Waldo's death from scarlet fever only a few years earlier. Probing what he describes as his fundamentally inaccessible grief over his young son's death, he writes:

> What opium is instilled into all disaster! It shows formidable as we approach it, but there is at last no rough rasping friction, but the most slippery sliding surfaces; we fall soft on a thought. *Ate Dea* is gentle—"Over men's heads walking aloft, / With tender feet treading so soft." People grieve and bemoan themselves, but it is not half so bad with them as they say. There are moods in which we court suffering, in the hope that here at least we shall find reality, sharp peaks and edges of truth. But it turns out to be scene-painting and counterfeit. The only thing grief has taught me is to know how shallow it is. That, like all the rest, plays about the surface and never introduces me into the reality, for contact with which we would even pay the costly price of sons and lovers. Was it Boscovich who found that bodies never come in contact? Well, souls never touch their objects. An innavigable sea washes with silent waves between us and the things we aim at and converse with. Grief too will make us idealists. In the death of my son, now more than two years ago, I seem to have lost a beautiful estate—no more. I cannot get it nearer to me. If tomorrow I should be informed of the bankruptcy of my principal debtors, the loss of my property would be a great inconvenience to me, perhaps for many years; but it would leave me as it found me—neither better nor worse. So is it with this calamity; it does not touch me; something which I fancied was a part of me, which could not be torn away without tearing me nor enlarged without enriching me, falls off from me and leaves no scar. It was caducous. I grieve that grief can teach me nothing, nor carry me one step into real nature. (CW 3:28–29)

The passage stuns. It stuns in its crass real estate metaphor and naked admission of emotional emptiness, and in the way it spirals from a typically pedantic invocation of a Greek goddess to the gutting string of semicolons in the penultimate sentence, in which Emerson admits that with this child's death he has lost the capacity to even conceive of *loss* as an intellectually, let alone spiritually, sufficient concept. The figure of the child, *his beloved child*, materializes to cleave away in a moment—"it was caducous"—leaving Emerson to glumly marvel at his own continued existence.

The stupefying thrum of ongoing existence in the face of disaster is given various shapes: the soft feet of the goddess of ruin as she tiptoes through your life wreaking havoc, the "silent innavigable sea" that washes between us all as we try to communicate and still never manage to touch one another. There is a counterintuitive kind of relation crafted from his naked negative admission, "I grieve that grief can teach me nothing, nor carry me one step into real nature." Perhaps the primary thing joining anyone, the passage ventures, is the ability to survive life's catastrophes until, one day, we don't. He laments the loss of even the idea of a grievable loss that one could theoretically come to grips with. Indeed, the paragraph that immediately follows the quoted passage above positions the search for understanding as a type of farce. It opens with the line, "I take this evanescence and lubricity of all objects, which lets them slip through our fingers then when we clutch hardest, to be the most unhandsome part of our condition." The unwieldy term "unhandsome" punningly rehearses the intrinsic slippage between experience and cognition.

It is *this* Emerson, driven by horror at his child's death to admit that the transience of human existence leaves him bewildered and bereft, who I think today's readers and students can use. Or, more honestly, it is only in this tonal mood that I am able to plausibly invite today's students—who have suffered so much and will likely be asked to suffer more—to find a space to think alongside Emerson.

This is also because its meditations on the ineffectuality of human intellect will nonetheless aim to incite action. The essay reasons thus: if all we wish to know is essentially "unhandsome" to a seeker's grasp, nevertheless we need to cultivate a steadfast obstinacy in the face of this inexorable truth. Emerson turns to the concept of futility to form the crux of this argument:

> But what help from these fineries or pedantries? What help from thought? Life is not dialectics. We, I think, in these times, have had lessons enough of the futility of criticism. Our young people have thought and written much on labor and reform, and for all that they have written, neither the world nor themselves have got on a step. Intellectual tasting of life will not supersede muscular activity. If a man should consider the nicety of the passage of a piece of bread down his throat, he would starve. (CW 3:34)

Note that the passage's animating question—"what help from thought?"—is not ultimately fatalistic. "Life is not intellectual or critical, but sturdy," he writes a few lines further down. In true Emersonian fashion, this reference to a "sturdy" life flies in the face of the opening section's lamentations. To my mind, the essay itself maintains its relevance because of that contradiction: we all will survive until one by one, one day or another, we do not. I read and teach Emerson as advocating that in the midst of that inevitable outcome, we ought at least spend our time trying (and failing) to grasp the ineffable rather than endlessly ruminating on the end that it all must come to.

"Let us treat the men and women well: treat them as if they were real: perhaps they are," he winks towards the end of the essay (*CW* 3:35). In the essay's theorization, we exist always only as momentary possibilities to each other, and since "our office is with moments, let us husband them." The phrasing here—to husband a moment—indexes the essay's most concrete contradiction: that we will not survive, any of us, *and so* we should care: about one another, about the place we live in, and the thoughts we search after. Emerson here posits that we should care in the fleeting moments where the possibility of care arises, as the casual turns ever to casualty.

To my mind, this is the philosophical vein in which Melville and Emerson are most attuned to one another. Melville's oeuvre is a cornucopia of thwarted life's plans and delusions of mastery—or at least escape—that end in disaster on various scales. His writing manifests the sense that although other ways of being in and conceiving of our social world might be possible, those avenues are as potentially foreclosed as they are open. Melville's 1855 story "Benito Cereno" makes this theme salient in its indictment of prosperous global commerce that is undergirded by the structured immiseration of millions of enslaved Black people.

"Benito Cereno" simultaneously conceals and reveals the story of a maritime insurrection of captive Senegalese people onboard a Spanish slaver captained by a man named Benito Cereno.[23] In Melville's story, the uprising of enslaved people is unwittingly halted by the friendly, guileless, and unfailingly racist American ship's captain that drops anchor nearby. Throughout the story, Melville's infamous free indirect discourse is a punishing exercise of narrative sleight-of-hand that confounds readers at every turn, especially when it cajoles readers into thinking we understand what is happening and what it means. The story's final image is one of a resounding and unsettled quiet. Once all are onshore in Lima, Spanish colonial authorities execute the leader of the rebellion, a Senegalese man named Babo. They display Babo's severed head on a pike as a silent and prolific symbol of Anglo-European racial terror:

> Seeing all was over, he [Babo] uttered no sound, and could not be forced to.
> His aspect seemed to say, since I cannot do deeds, I will not speak words.
> ... Some months after, dragged to the gibbet at the tail of a mule, the black met his voiceless end. The body was burned to ashes; but for many days, the head, that hive of subtlety, fixed on a pole in the Plaza, met, unabashed, the gaze of the whites; and across the Plaza looked towards St. Bartholomew's church, in whose vaults slept then, as now, the recovered bones of Aranda;[24] and across the Rimac bridge looked towards the monastery, on Mount Agonia without; where, three months after being dismissed by the court, Benito Cereno, borne on the bier, did, indeed, follow his leader.[25]

Babo's head is the final image of the passage, and it speaks only through silence. The preceding brief narration of his capture and execution emphasizes Babo's practiced refusal to speak. Yet, the final image's brutality repels any easy identification of Babo's silence with an overweening resistant agency. It is, after all, a scene that functions as a terroristic display directed against anyone resisting the regime of Spanish colonial slavery. The head creates a fundamentally apprehensive interpretive space, where any reader's attempted valorization of Babo's silence as resistance risks acquiescence to the racist structures of a society that created the social and legal conditions for the scene to exist in the first place.

This ending ensnares readers in a constricted moment of contemplating white supremacy's legal and lethal outcomes alongside the equally unrelenting force of Black diasporic resistance to these racial capitalist logics. It leaves readers never able to definitively pinpoint the leader that Benito Cereno follows into the grave, and/or given the narration's slipperiness, cognitively unable to determine whether the narrative is ushering us through a repetition-with-a-difference or yet another repetition of a historically familiar, violently racist end to an uprising of the enslaved. In Melville's fictive rendering, Babo's brilliant engineering of the story's hidden insurrection might have succeeded, but then it didn't. The captive Senegalese people might have succeeded in turning the boat back out to sea, but they did not. Similarly, the final image of Babo's head on a pike simultaneously quashes and emphasizes the insurgent agency of the man. His potential is present and brutally excised by the global machinery of racial capitalism and slavery. Babo's resistance was futile; Babo's resistance was fecund.

Another way of saying this is that the teeming silence of the final image matters precisely because of its final failure—which is final, of course, only in hindsight. The knotted intricacy of the text encourages rereading, shoving us back to the start to watch it all play out again. But of course the ending does not change, cannot. Still, "Benito Cereno" insists that readers husband the moments of Babo's insurgent possibility.

Admittedly, this seems an odd pairing with my earlier reading of Emerson's admission of stunned grief over Waldo's death. The two texts are incongruent in terms of content and scope: the small, pitiful stillness of a loved child's death and the gaping, centuries-old horrors of the transatlantic slave trade and anti-Black racism's ongoing depredations. But they are philosophically linked in Melville and Emerson's assertion of the silence that greets us at the sites where acts fail: love alone cannot keep the sick boy alive, nor can Emerson's grief provide any intellectual consolations for the loss. Babo's virtuoso management of the shipboard uprising and its concealment from the US captain does not avert the captives' New World enslavement, hastens his own gruesome death, and makes his corpse into a symbolic reminder of racist state power. And at the heart of both texts is the frailty of the expressive medium itself—language, too, fails. It cannot do or create in the material ways that one sometimes wishes it could.

Kindling

I take a bizarre kind of comfort from the dour synthesis just proposed about what it might mean to think about Emerson and Melville together now. Since I most often reread and think about Emerson and Melville in the context of the classroom, it at least feels most honest to bring these writers before my students in their guises of bitter humility. This is, in part, a way to counter or complicate the masculine bombast and aggrandizing individualism that pervades much of their respective works. It is also, I am self-aware enough to admit, a mode of consoling myself about the consistent flood of bad news about shrinking enrollments and declining funding and ever-tightening labor markets for humanistic programs of study.

Emerson and Melville's writings, at least in the moments I cobble together here, consistently nod to the idea that these things of theirs were not really built to last. Society has moved and will continue to move on from artistic valuations and modes of inquiry deemed culturally important or fashionable. Circles open out onto other circles, and so it goes. Ultimately I urge students—and counsel myself—to take from these old books, these old men, what they can and only what they find useful. And if it turns out, as perhaps it should, that there is not much there for them to use or that what's there for them now seems good only for kindling, then I think that is a usage both fitting and just. At the least I think it is more than fair if these writers come to occupy a auxiliary position in nineteenth-century literary and cultural studies. If these fields are to continue at all, their energy lies in subordinating an older sense of these writers' centrality to an extant body of nineteenth-century Black writings about the repercussions of a US culture where the ideological trappings of whiteness and masculinity predominate. Black women writers who were contemporaries of both Emerson and Melville offer prolific and razor-sharp theorizations of American culture's failures and violences of which both writers can be made example.

I am thinking specifically of Harriet E. Wilson's 1861 autobiographical novel *Our Nig*, which offers an incisive study of the white-racialized gender dynamics that create and sustain violently unjust living conditions for Black girls and women at all levels of the US domestic economy, private and public. The white Belmont men in her novel are thoughtful and eloquent, playful and sometimes kind. They consistently lament the physical and psychological abuses heaped on the quasi-enslaved protagonist Frado. They also do precisely nothing to stop Mrs. Belmont's abuse of Frado, interrogate their role in facilitating it, or assist her in any meaningful way. What Harriet E. Wilson—and writers like Harriet Jacobs, Frances E. W. Harper, and Sojourner Truth—theorize in their written work is that a US artistic culture most attentive to the thoughts and creations of white people in general, and white men particularly, is a culture that metastasizes in its constitutive violences, even as it manifests a willingness to critique the self and/or the prevailing social order. What these Black women's nineteenth-century writings know, and have known, about figures like Emerson and Melville is that they can be understood as mere examples rather than exemplary in the study of US culture and literature writ large. Scholars of both should strive to continue perceiving their texts as formally interesting, philosophically heterodox, funny, smart, and also no more than conduits for some of the worst ideological impulses of their period.

Reading Emerson and Melville in this mood, I'm reminded of a favorite line in Melville's 1855 novella "Bartleby," about a preternaturally ascetic and willfully doomed office worker. In context, it is delivered by "Bartleby" to the story's first-person narrator, a character identified only as the Lawyer, after Bartleby's arrest for vagrancy and before Bartleby's purposeful hunger strike and eventual suicide via starvation in jail. The Lawyer is Bartleby's last known employer, and the Lawyer's convoluted relations with him in their brief time together at work play a not insignificant role in Bartleby's eventual imprisonment and, the story suggests, perhaps his death. Nonetheless the Lawyer follows out his compulsion to visit Bartleby in jail. It is a contradictory attempt to both prolong the stilted intimacies of their (non)relationship and exculpate himself from it. At his approach, Bartleby dismisses the Lawyer with a line both assertive and inchoate.

I deliver it to both Melville and Emerson as I encounter them now: "I know you … and I want nothing to say to you."[26]

Notes

1. Sustained scholarly interest in his works was reinvigorated about thirty years after his death in the 1920s, a period known as the "Melville Revival"—and has remained strong ever since.
2. In a March 1849 letter to Evert Duycinck, Melville gives his fullest impression of Emerson. It's worth quoting in full to grasp the equal measures of repulsion and attraction that seemed to animate Melville's perception of Emerson:

   I do not oscillate in Emerson's rainbow, but prefer rather to hang myself in mine own halter than swing in any other man's swing. Yet I think Emerson is more than a brilliant fellow. Be his stuff begged, borrowed, or stolen, or of his own domestic manufacture he is an uncommon man. Swear he is a humbug—then is he no common humbug. Lay it down that had not Sir Thomas Browne lived, Emerson would not have mystified—I will answer, that had not Old Zack's father begot him, old Zack would never have been the hero of Palo Alto. The truth is that we are all sons, grandsons, or nephews or great-nephews of those who go before us. No one is his own sire.—I was very agreeably disappointed in Mr Emerson. I had heard of him as full of transcendentalisms, myths & oracular gibberish; I had only glanced at a book of his once in Putnam's store—that was all I knew of him, till I heard him lecture.—To my surprise, I found him quite intelligible, tho' to say truth, they told me that that night he was unusually plain.—Now, there is a something about every man elevated above mediocrity, which is, for the most part, instinctually perceptible. This I see in Mr Emerson. And, frankly, for the sake of the argument, let us call him a fool;—then had I rather be a fool than a wise man.—I love all men who dive. Any fish can swim near the surface, but it takes a great whale to go down stairs five miles or more; & if he don't attain the bottom, why, all the lead in Galena can't fashion the plumet that will. I'm not talking of Mr Emerson now—but of the whole corps of thought-divers, that have been diving & coming up again with bloodshot eyes since the world began. I could readily see in Emerson, notwithstanding his merit, a gaping flaw. It was, the insinuation, that had he lived in those days when the world was made, he might have offered some valuable suggestions. These men are all cracked right across the brow …

   Herman Melville, *The Letters of Herman Melville*, ed. Merrell R. Davis and William H. Gilman (New Haven, CT: Yale University Press, 1960), 78, my emphasis.
3. Herman Melville, *Moby-Dick, or The Whale* (1851), ed. Harrison Hayford, Hershel Parker, and G. Thomas Tanselle (Chicago: Northwestern University Press, 1988), 158.
4. Ibid., 159.
5. Melville, *Letters of Herman Melville*, 78.
6. Robert Levine, "Why We Should Be Teaching and Writing about the Literary World's 'Hawthorne and His Mosses,'" *J19* 5, no. 1 (2017): 179–89, 185.
7. Perry Miller, "Melville and Transcendentalism," *Virginia Quarterly Review* 29, no. 4 (1953): 556–75, 558.
8. Ibid., 559.
9. F. O. Matthiessen, *American Renaissance: Art and Expression in the Age of Emerson and Whitman* (Oxford: Oxford University Press, 1941), 484.

10. Ibid., 472, n. 1.
11. Ibid., 484.
12. Eve Kosofsky Sedgwick, Between Men: English Literature and Male Homosocial Desire (New York: Columbia University Press, 1985).
13. Reference to the television series Mad Men, season 2 episode 6 "Maidenform," in which an ad campaign asks consumers to identify as one or the other iconic fashionable woman.
14. Randall Fuller, Emerson's Ghosts: Literature, Politics, and the Making of Americanists (New York: Oxford University Press, 2007); and Robert Habich, Building Their Own Waldos: Emerson's First Biographers and the Politics of Life-Writing in the Gilded Age (Iowa City: University of Iowa Press, 2011).
15. Jordan Alexander Stein, "Rappaccini's Son," J19 9, no. 1 (2021): 145–54, 149.
16. David Dowling, "Parlors, Sofas, and Fine Cambrics: Gender Play in Melville's Narrations," Leviathan 11, no. 1 (2009): 37–54, n. 4 on p. 38. See also Elizabeth Renker, "Herman Melville, Wife Beating, and the Written Page," American Literature 66, no. 1 (1994): 123–50.
17. Christopher Hanlon, Emerson's Memory Loss: Originality, Communality, and the Late Style (New York: Oxford University Press, 2018), 4.
18. Stein, "Rappaccini's Son," 141.
19. I draw here from Kyla Wazana Tompkins's 2021 essay "The Shush," PMLA 136, no. 3 (2021): 417–23, in which she describes the process of forcing herself to write the text of the essay itself (which was commissioned by and eventually published in the journal of literary studies' major professional organization) as the COVID-19 pandemic rages and massive wildfires burn in her home state of California, following the murders of George Floyd and Breonna Taylor by US police in spring and summer 2020. She explains the title term, "the shush," as a psychic project that necessitates "writ[ing] into the heavy quiet that had settled over me. I had to name both the shush of the coerced nondisclosure under which so many of us live our institutional lives and the heaviness of the historical grief that weighs upon those of us who love what we do and who see the world, and our communities, and our institutions and fields and students, who are after all part of the world, suffering" (418).
20. Sociologist of education Sara Goldrick-Rab uses the term "Real College" to delineate the actual experiences of the majority of US college students today from the (now incorrect) assumption that most Americans pursue an undergraduate education from the ages of 18 to 22 while living on campus at a four-year Bachelor's-granting college or university. Her work has focused on student hunger, student debt, and the competing sociocultural demands that most people pursuing college education today increasingly navigate. See Sara Goldrick-Rab, Paying the Price: College Costs, Financial Aid, and the Betrayal of the American Dream (Chicago: University of Chicago Press, 2016).
21. Maurice Lee's recent work about nineteenth-century American literature and canonicity reminds us that in practice the core nineteenth-century US literary canon taught to many college undergraduates may be only marginally more capacious than it was in the first half of the twentieth century. Emerson, Melville, Thoreau, and Whitman were still the most common recurring authors on Lee's 2016 survey of nineteenth-century American Literature undergraduate syllabi. See Maurice Lee, "Introduction: A Survey of Survey Courses," J19 4, no. 1 (2016): 125–30.
22. Nina Baym, "Melodramas of Beset Manhood: How Theories of American Fiction Exclude Women Authors," American Quarterly 33, no. 2 (1981): 123–29, 129.

23. The story is based on the 1805 uprising of a group of Senegalese people onboard a slaveship named *The Tryal*. It was recounted in the 1817 memoirs of American captain Amasa Delano.
24. Aranda is the Spaniard overseeing the transport of the kidnapped Africans to the Spanish colonies of South America, where they would be enslaved for life. Babo and the other captives kill him during the initial uprising onboard Cereno's ship, the *San Dominick*. Afterwards, they mount Aranda's bleached skeleton onto the ship's prow and chalk the motto "Follow Your Leader" underneath it. Aranda's skeleton supplements the ship's original figurehead of Christopher Columbus.
25. Herman Melville, 1856, "Benito Cereno," in *Billy Budd and Other Stories*, ed. Frederick Busch (New York: Penguin Classics, 1986), 159–258, 258.
26. Herman Melville, 1853, "Bartleby, The Scrivener," in *Billy Budd and Other Stories*, ed. Frederick Busch (New York: Penguin Classics, 1986), 1–59, 43.

CHAPTER 28

EMERSON, RHETORIC, AND ORATORICAL CULTURE

ROGER THOMPSON

To read Emerson's writing is to encounter artifacts of an extensive education in the discipline of rhetoric, a field of study that has been taught from ancient Greece up to today. Emerson's body of work contains residue of wide-ranging rhetorical theories and practices that were being systematically advanced, challenged, and rewritten throughout the nineteenth century. Rhetoric, often defined as the art of persuasion, was widely accepted as the foundation of not only exemplary speaking, but writing as well, and students across a young United States were steeped in it. The broad adoption of Hugh Blair's *Lectures on Rhetoric and Belles Lettres* as a writing and speaking primer throughout North America testifies to the influence of classical rhetorical principles on nineteenth-century education, with Blair's conception of literary production built on Greek and Roman treatises on rhetoric.[1] Emerson was introduced to Blair's work while at Harvard, and while he modeled some of his early work on it, he developed pointed criticisms about its value for America and Americans. Indeed, for Emerson, America was a testing ground for a more expansive and inclusive rhetoric. A figure well known to resist traditions, Emerson would himself become one of rhetorical history's most important theorists, a challenger of various traditions who charted a path to a new rhetoric that, on the one hand, appropriated core aspects of classical rhetoric and belletristic ideals while, on the other hand, embracing radical democracy. While the extent of Emerson's own study of rhetoric, stretching from his school years to late in life, has only recently begun to be fully excavated and mapped, a growing body of research positions him as the progenitor of a revolutionary rhetoric that insisted that eloquence was accessible to all people and could be employed by anyone regardless of their level of education or social or cultural background. This inclusive art of rhetoric would be for Emerson the central currency of the great American experiment.

Culture of Oratory

Emerson's interest in rhetoric might best be described as vocational. He was, in many important practical, theoretical, and historical respects, a *rhetor*. As John Jay Chapman wrote long ago in his reflections on various literary giants, "It was the platform which determined Emerson's style. He was not a writer, but a speaker. On the platform his manner of speech was a living part of his words."[2] Despite his well-established place in the American literary canon, Emerson did not, in fact, grow up wanting to be a famous writer, at least not in the sense of how we think of "being a writer" today. Writing as vocation or career, or even the concept of "author" as a producer of literature, is largely an innovation of the eighteenth and, in America, nineteenth centuries, but our portraits of Emerson and our theories of his work and its impact on culture rarely navigate this terrain. There was no dream of being a "writer." Instead, for Emerson there was the dream of being a great orator. Oratory was the vocation for intellectuals and writers. Writing was one vehicle for that vocation, but lecturing was the pathway to financial success, social influence, and even fame.

By the middle of the nineteenth century, lecture halls had become a standard feature of American towns and cities, and they welcomed a broad array of professional orators, scientists, professors, financiers, and others who traveled the country not only to advance their ideas, but to make a living. Lecturing paid well, and the best lecturers were very well paid indeed. By the midpoint of his career, Emerson "was dependent on lecturing for his (and his family's) livelihood," and "his early profits as a lecturer and an author, and his shrewd investment of his monies" meant that by 1851, "he was listed in *The Rich Men of Massachusetts* as possessing $50,000," roughly $2 million in today's currency.[3] He rode the wave of popularity that came from public speaking as a creative force for democratic expression.

In the 1830s, Josiah Holbrook had successfully launched a movement, the Lyceum Movement, which sought to place lecture halls, libraries, and natural history libraries and museums in every small city in America.[4] The establishment of the lyceum lecture circuit was a major development for the country, and it is hard to fully understand American identity or the cultural movements that shaped American identity without an understanding of how the lyceum functioned. The success of the Lyceum Movement might be best compared to the expansion of movie theaters throughout the United States in the middle part of the twentieth century. It was a stunning development and was fueled by expanding literacies, broadening education, entrepreneurship, and the rise of the natural societies, workers' guilds, and, as Holly Jackson has so extensively documented, various communal groups, agitators, and entertainers.[5] With roots in neoclassical traditions of rhetoric, American oratory branched out beyond Enlightenment rhetorical theory to become increasingly democratic, providing access to new ideas and new inventions to small towns and large cities alike. The rapid expansion of lecture halls was a topic of frequent commentary in newspapers, books, and even political campaigns, and it was not always treated as a benefit to the American state. For instance, William Pittenger, one of the many authors who capitalized on the growing lecture industry by producing a handbook on oratory, wrote that by the 1870s:

> The field of instructive lectures is constantly enlarging. In former times they were monopolized by university professors, and very few persons sought to teach the people. But this has changed. There are now many more schools where courses of lectures are given on various topics, and every town of any pretension has its annual lecture course. Even these are not sufficient to meet the increasing demand, and, as every community cannot pay Beecher or Gough from one to five hundred dollars for an evening's entertainment, there is abundant scope for humbler talent. Strolling lecturers, without character or knowledge, reap a rich harvest from the credulity of the people.[6]

Pittenger here questions the character and capability of "strolling lecturers" who travel from town to town earning money despite lack of credibility, and the passage implies a critique of the endlessly expanding space to accommodate them. Pittenger subsequently defends the pseudoscience of phrenology by criticizing the lecture halls that too readily welcome the onslaught of "quacks" who don't really understand the real "science" of it, but his message as it relates to the lecture hall is that the market for lecturers was growing too rapidly and that there was room for improvement through better training of speakers—presumably by reading Pittenger's book and adopting his methods.

Pittenger's volume is just one of hundreds that effectively codified lecture propriety, not only in content, but in form. Prominent and successful speakers, as well as not a few college faculty, raced to publish handbooks, and many sold well. Usually steeped in neoclassical traditions, they relied on well-established rules for not only creating a speech or lecture, but for listening to and understanding them. To learn to lecture or to simply go to a lecture hall for an evening's entertainment was to participate in a collective experience constrained by cultural expectations that were advanced in schools from a very early age. Violation of those expectations usually resulted in a very short lecture career for any offender, further ensuring that conventional oratory remained entrenched and typically unchallenged.

This highly stylized oratorical culture was an important force in American society that would in some respects effectively supplant the church as a community-building force. Michael Halloran and Gregory Clark have described it as perhaps the central cultural phenomenon of the nineteenth century.[7] Orations held a central place in American myth-making from the earliest days of the country, and they could run hours long. Each year on July 4, towns and villages across America held orations to commemorate the founding of the country, most of which compared the United States to ancient Greece (where rhetoric was first taught) and the first formulations of democracy. Orations on George Washington, which were especially common, ensured that American idealism was rooted in a particular time and connected to a particular place and person.

Emerson was a central figure in this culture. He began his career as an orator when he was thirty years old. He had been ordained as a minister in 1829 but preached for barely three years before he broke from the church in 1832, resigned as a preacher, and sailed to Europe. On his return a year later, he delivered his first public lecture on November 5, 1833, at the Masonic Temple in Boston: a talk titled "The Uses of Natural History" and from which parts of his famous first book *Nature* (1836) were drawn. The lecture reflects Emerson's newfound desire to study natural history in order to reveal patterns in nature that illustrated its metaphorical value in explaining the cosmos. The lecture was successful, and Emerson's brother would later write in a letter to another brother, William, that "I was glad to have some of the stump lecturers see what was what and bow to the rising sun" (*LRWE* 1:397n). Emerson rapidly secured invitations for other engagements, with three more booked before the end of 1833, including a well-received one in Concord in December,[8] and eight more in 1834. After middling sales of *Nature* (*CW* 1:6), he devoted more time to his lectures, embracing public speaking as the pathway to both financial and intellectual success. He would go on to give more than 1500 lectures, traveling from New England to the South, and from Europe to the West.

His early lectures demonstrate his awareness of oratorical conventions and the established rhetorical history underlying them. Perhaps most striking among them was a distinction between types of oratory that Emerson found especially well aligned with his spiritual training in the early days of his speaking career. His first works invoked a Platonic vision of language, and Emerson peddled in the same use of the term "rhetoric" as Plato had a thousand years before. "Rhetoric" was pejorative, a method of expression whose primary purpose was ethically empty persuasion and whose primary outcome was ethically spurious action. Plato labelled the art of rhetoric "pastry-baking," likening it to tasty desserts that, while sweet, were empty of nutrition.[9] Emerson shared this skepticism of rhetoric when he first left the pulpit for the podium. In one early lecture, he lists the fine arts that shape human civilization, counting among them the art of eloquence, but in doing so, he says that "I omit rhetoric, which respects only the form of eloquence and poetry" (*CW* 2:44). The notion here is that rhetoric as a craft doesn't fully embrace the powerful truths that eloquence conveys.

Yet, like Plato, he would change course and ultimately reclaim the term, re-inscribing its meaning to reflect his own transcendental idealism and his belief that language, when yoked to truth, transforms into beauty and power:

> In my youth, when the genius of an eminent pulpit orator drew crowds to the church in which he chanced to speak, I used the opportunity to go eagerly with the rest, to drink in that delicious rhetoric which has had no equal in its kind. As others did, I used to bring home, and repeat, and could not repeat enough, the fine sentences that took my fancy. (*LL* 2:101)

The effusive praise of the rhetorical art of sacred oratory here inspired the young Emerson, leading to his own modeling of the performance. Indeed, Emerson paints a picture here of a hypnotic event that influences him and his peers for days afterward, conjuring in them a desire to emulate what they had heard. Strikingly, he calls rhetoric "delicious," recalling the very idea that Plato found objectionable when he first criticized the art. Rhetoric, when done right, aligned with spiritual insight and action.

Emerson's wedding of spiritual truth and rhetoric is important for several reasons. Certainly, it establishes Emerson as descended from Platonic and Neoplatonic rhetorical theories, wherein a true form of rhetoric is juxtaposed with a false form. That true form is marked by beauty, affirmation of truth and goodness, and reliance on the notion of divinity as an animating force of language. More practically, though, Emerson's rhetoric recognized the way that the field of study was being advanced by a wide range of theorists, writers, and speakers, and the way that rhetorical training was imagined to be central to establishing the New Republic. Rhetoric could drive America's ascension to the place that divine providence had intended for it. To invoke one of Emerson's more famous works, "The American Scholar," "A nation of men will for the first time exist, because each believes himself inspired by the Divine Soul which also inspires all men" (*CW* 1:70). As a practiced and widely taught discipline, rhetoric was an important tool in building that vision of a new country because it could be used to foster a sense of divine mission.

That type of certitude in the spiritual destiny of the United States may today sound quaint or even troubling, but it was central to politicians, policymakers, artists, industrialists, entrepreneurs, and a vast army of orators and public speakers who traveled across the continent in the nineteenth century advancing an idealized version of the country. Edward Everett, perhaps the most famous speaker of the period, frequently valorized the founding of America. In "American Manufactures," for instance, he figures the Constitution as a remedy for otherwise trivial failings of any particular citizen:

> But before the inefficiency of this measure had been discovered by experience, a new and unhoped for remedy for their sufferings had been devised. The daystar of the constitution arose; and of all the classes of the people of America to whose hearts it came as the harbinger of blessings long hoped for and long despaired of, most unquestionably the tradesmen, mechanics, and manufacturers hailed it with the warmest welcome.[10]

For Everett, the constitution was a beacon not for noble classes, but for the working class.

Even those who spoke to challenge the supposed virtues of the young nation—and there were many in the midcentury in the lead-up to the Civil War—nonetheless relied on the twin forces of rhetorical idealism and national ascendency to advance their claims. For instance, Frederick Douglass, who spoke pointedly about the failures of the American experiment, argued in one lecture that "interpreted as it ought to be interpreted, the Constitution is a GLORIOUS LIBERTY DOCUMENT." His ultimate point, however, was that the country had failed to enact a just interpretation of it, and instead had driven a wedge between the free population and the enslaved:

> The sunlight that brought life and healing to you, has brought stripes and death to me. This Fourth of July is yours, not mine. You may rejoice, I must mourn. To drag a man in fetters into the grand illuminated temple of liberty, and call upon him to join you in joyous anthems, were inhuman mockery and sacrilegious irony.[11]

The force of Douglass's condemnation of his own audience here gains its power from his reliance on a shared assumption—what rhetoric scholars call an "enthymeme"—that the constitution is a liberating document, even if it had not liberated all people. Douglass's frustration at being asked to deliver a July 4 oration reflects the irony that his invitation to celebrate freedom comes despite the fact that freedom had not yet been extended to all people.

These tropes and figures surrounding American idealism were grounded in long-standing rhetorical practices, conventions, and theories that drew contrasts between faithful adherence to truth and idealism in speech and distortion of it through sophistry and solipsism. To distort or twist the words of the Constitution meant distancing oneself from truth and divine providence, just as speaking empty words separated orators from the truths of the communities they addressed. For antebellum American speakers, it also separated them from American exceptionalism, which envisioned the American state as tool of a universal spirit driving the country to greatness. American idealism emerged from rhetorical traditions that fostered it.

Emerson was in deep conversation with those traditions, and he imagined himself to be one of the people who could help the country in its ascendancy, even if he did fear, like Douglass, that the country was teetering on the brink of a failed experiment. Nonetheless, he aimed to inspire young intellectuals to seek outlets for a message of divine integrity, and arguably the most important of those outlets was the lecture circuit. Lecturing was the force that would usher in change, and in America, the lecture hall was the central battleground for adjudicating that change.

Nonetheless, the traditions of the lyceum frustrated Emerson. In one of the most important declarations of Emerson-as-lecturer, he laments that the lyceum, which promised hope for being something new and wonderful for the American scene, had failed to live up to its potential. "These lectures," he records in his journal in 1840, "give me little pleasure. I have not done what I hoped when I said, I will try it once more. I have not once transcended the coldest self-possession. I said I will agitate there, being agitated myself ... Alas! Alas! I have not the recollection of one strong moment" (*JMN* 8:338–39). The significance of this slim record of Emerson's discontent is twofold. On the one hand, it illustrates Emerson's frustration with himself, but on the other hand, it illustrates what would come to be a lingering problem for Emerson—some of his audiences failing to follow his attempts to agitate for change. Those attempts, ultimately, centered on a desire to transform the lecture circuit itself from a place of practical power to one that yoked action in the world with sublimity and transcendence.

Emerson's Rhetorical Experiment

Several lectures-turned-essays sit at the center of Emerson's conception of rhetoric as agitating for truth to be unleashed into the world and the sublime revelations possible from such transcendence. The most widely discussed and the most developed are his two different published works called "Eloquence." Derived from a group of lectures that are all but impossible to completely reconstruct, the first essay version was published in the *Atlantic Monthly* in 1858 and again in Emerson's collection *Society and Solitude*, and the second was published in *Letters and Social Aims*. Together they represent Emerson's fullest treatment of rhetoric. They also illustrate his more radical thinking on the topic. Ronald A. Bosco and Douglas Emory Wilson have provided textual history of the lectures (*CW* 7:xix), and Jim Warren has provided similar accountings of the complexity of the eloquence "essays" and the lecture folders from which they are constructed.[12] Both were lectures that Emerson gave and reworked multiple times (one being, according to William Charvat, his most popular and frequently delivered lecture), and both illustrate extraordinarily well not only Emerson's trademark style, but his purposeful rejection of more easily recognizable oratorical or homiletic forms.[13]

Before he began lecturing, homiletics shaped Emerson's public speaking. While homiletics is a wide-ranging field of study in its own right, some core features of it emerge not only in Emerson's preaching, but in his later theorizing of the role of the orator in American life. Arguably the most important is his abiding belief in the power of divinity within language. For Emerson, language is holy because it relies not only on spiritual principles in its genesis and organization, but because it manifests divine will *for and within* all people.

This position can be found in some of Emerson's earliest sermons, such as in "But Be Thou an Example of the Believers, in Word, in Conversation, in Charity, in Spirit, in Faith, in Purity" on 1 Timothy 4:12. The sermon traces the importance of manifesting godly behavior in life and in language, and in an especially important discussion as the sermon comes to a close, Emerson details the way that a preacher's "eloquence" moves a congregation to fuller consideration of God's actions in the world. In doing so, he insists that eloquence is best understood as God's actions, not the preacher's. In the face of God's eloquence, conveyed by the preacher to the congregation, "the mask would fall from the face of the hypocrite. The sneer would die on the lip of the sophist—Virtue would prove too awful for the argument of the infidel."[14] The references here to sophists and argument recall concepts with which the audience would have been very familiar—the idea that argumentation, when handled by the unrighteous, devolved into an insidious sophistry that corrupted society. The holy word—the words that preachers might utter when they have given themselves over to God—reveal the pedantry, hypocrisy, and futility of language that has lost touch with divinity.

Sacred rhetoric and homiletics were deeply woven into the fabric of Emerson's education at Harvard, a school which boasted the first endowed chair in rhetoric, the Boylston

Chair in Rhetoric and Oratory. Its first holder, John Quincy Adams, published extended theories on the role of rhetoric and oratory in antebellum America. Emerson would win the Boylston prize in declamation while attending the college, the award named for the chair and an early sign of Emerson's growing mastery of rhetorical communication.

As Michael-John DePalma has shown, however, rhetorical education was pervasive not only at Harvard, but at divinity schools throughout New England, with Austin Phelps at the neighboring Andover Theological Seminary, for example, advancing the idea that rhetoric was empty without alignment with divine purpose and will.[15] That Emerson would himself begin to explore the relationship between language and spiritual truth, then, is hardly surprising. It is a central concern of his, and he never fully departs from this crucial conceptualization of rhetoric as an office of the divine will. For example, in his late lecture "The Preacher," he exhorts his audience:

> Be not betrayed into undervaluing the churches which annoy you by their bigoted claims. They too were real churches. They answered to their times the same need as your rejection of them does to ours. The Catholic Church has been immensely rich in men and influences. Augustine, à Kempis, Fénelon, breathe the very spirit which now fires you. So with Cudworth, More, Bunyan. I agree with them more than I disagree. I agree with their heart and motive; my discontent is with their limitations and surface and language. (CWE 10:227).

Here Emerson relies on the basic dualism that would animate much of his thinking, but in this passage and others like it, he does something that other rhetoricians had been previously unwilling to do: he introduces the idea that the audience itself can adjudicate the virtue of the speaker.

Emerson's belief in democratic access to the divine word is a notable break from a long-standing rhetorical tradition that begins with Plato, one that insists on a dichotomy, implied or otherwise, between those who study and understand the spiritual aspects of language and those who are removed from its power and are susceptible to the distortion of truth. Emerson's early work, like Plato's dialogues, relegate "rhetoric" to nothing more than an unethical veneer of genuine spiritual communication, but Emerson later casts aside the notion of "mere rhetoric" in favor of a democratic concept that equated common expression with divine utterance. Indeed, Emerson's abdication of the pulpit might be provocatively read as a rejection of the lack of access to a spiritualized rhetoric for the "common man." One of his first lectures after he separated from the church was to a society whose founding by "less fortunate" citizens sought to bring education to lower classes, and his sentiment that divine word was written not just in sacred texts, but in nature and in the human spirit, broadened the possibility of participation in spiritual activities far beyond the church doors, effectively launching Emerson into what Jim Warren has called America's culture of eloquence.[16] That culture was expansive and extended well beyond the lecture circuit.

While Emerson saw the potential for the podium to ignite an American intellectual expansion across social classes, he also found other rhetorical modes as promising pathways for change. One particular mode, conversation, he theorized as potentially reshaping culture as extensively as the lecturing, noting that the methods of deliberation in private conversation require a different set of skills than on the podium. Perhaps more importantly, he recognized that conversation as a rhetorical art extended to a wider range of people than public speaking. The lecture circuit was dominated by men, with women sometimes excluded from lyceum events by local rules. In the event that a woman was invited to speak, she was not infrequently advertised as a novel performance or even a sideshow. Because most towns' lecture halls were places of propriety where middle and upper classes might gather to be educated on the latest scientific or cultural development, they typically avoided controversy, and women speakers, as Holly Jackson has shown, were in many regions controversial as public figures in and of themselves simply by the fact of their gender.[17] The result is that the classical genres of communication and the types of rhetorical performances used in lecture halls were rarely part of the education of women, even among more progressive families.

Jane Donawerth has prompted renewed consideration of conversation as a trained rhetorical mode, and she has revealed the ways that conversation, or "parlor rhetoric," enjoys a tradition of its own that sometimes aligns in surprising ways with other rhetorical forms.[18] Parlor rhetoric has received significant attention as a largely forgotten and ignored rhetorical mode since Nan Johnson examined its impact.[19] Similarly, Jacqueline Jones Royster has prompted energetic recoveries of nineteenth-century African American women's rhetorics, a project that continues to fundamentally change our definitions of rhetoric by expanding on notions of conversation and informal, daily communication.[20] Parlor rhetoric rose concurrently with the lecture circuit, yet it presumed an entirely different set of participants, leaders, and contexts. Nonetheless, it became increasingly codified in its form through the use of conduct books that were targeted for women readers. Of course, conversation as a rhetorical mode or dialogue as a foundation of rhetorical theory appears in ancient times, becomes codified in extreme ways in the courtly exchanges of Renaissance Europe, and transforms into a sign of education that became well-entrenched in nineteenth-century theories and handbooks. Still, the nineteenth century, with its rapidly expanding educational systems, proved especially fertile ground for the emergence of new rhetorical modes and the transformation of old ones, and as language instruction became democratized, possibilities for new forms arose simultaneously. Put another way, just as an increasingly educated demographic served as a foundation on which American oratory and the lecture hall could be built, so too did it serve as a foundation for other rhetorical practices in which even more of the population could participate. New theories emerged that challenged notions of race and gender, that suggested the equality of the sexes and races in their capacity to read, write, and speak, and that would lead ultimately to some of the most significant transformations in American culture.

Many of these theories broke explicitly from traditional formulations. Margaret Fuller is perhaps the best example in part because she explicitly names "conversation" as the cornerstone of learning and wisdom and in part because her own writing embodies what a new form of rhetoric, emerging from conversation, would look like. Fuller's own experiment in hosting focused and intentional gatherings to exchange ideas and support the education of women and others would leave a lasting impression on Emerson, and though Emerson's own foray into an official conversation gathering at the invitation of Fuller did not yield the fruit either had hoped for, it clearly planted a seed in Emerson's mind about the limitations of his own ways of knowing and his own ways of describing the world he knew.

It was only after his extensive interactions with Fuller, Elizabeth Peabody, and others who were challenging status quo conceptions of rhetoric that Emerson's insistence on democratic access to expression and participation in public speech became most pronounced. While Emerson virtually always insisted that rhetoric was sharpened or made even stronger by training and education, he maintained a deeply-held belief that any person, regardless of social status, education, or class is capable of profound eloquence. He insists on this feature of rhetoric time and time again, from the earliest part of his career to the latest, and it shapes his views not only on language, but on the way that language shapes people and institutions.

Emerson's rhetorical theory, then, necessitates a radical rethinking of how democratic access to public speech and persuasion might shape a culture. His idealism rests on a sense of transcendence that can be made manifest in the world, but crucially, no single person, group of people, or civic body can lay singular claim to that divine spirit. Instead, each person or group represented one part of a greater whole, and it was only by making room for all parts of that whole to be expressed that anyone could start to make sense of how the divine works in the world.

The Panharmonicon

Emerson actively built a new rhetoric, and he sought some way to explain how it could work. Always keen to exploit a metaphor, he sought language that would capture the diversity of expression that could animate an enraptured audience, and he would find it in a fantastical invention whose creator toured the country demonstrating the innovative device's capacity to amaze large crowds. It was called the panharmonicon, and for Emerson, it perfectly captured the possibility of a democratic rhetoric.[21]

The creation of Johann Maelzel, a nineteenth-century German inventor better known for creating the metronome and the first ever artificial chess player, the panharmonicon was a large mechanical device that was purportedly capable of replicating the sound of any instrument. It unified in a single machine the diverse expressions of different instrumentation, a feature that for Emerson embodied the possibility of democracy. It was a single instrument that sounded best when each individual part of it rang out together and allowed the listener to experience the full richness of the different tones and notes. In using the panharmonicon as his image for an ideal rhetorical theory, then, Emerson broadens the right to eloquence. Just as any person might be trained to play a single instrument to express diversity of sounds, so too could any person become capable of deploying powerful language. Anyone—any single individual—might utter the words that shake the foundations of civilization.

Kenneth Cmiel has provided an astute analysis of this drift toward democratic language in Emersonian thinking, and he illuminates Emerson's full—even if sometimes conflicted—embrace of the common, the mundane, even the brutish, precisely because it reflected the realities of a democratic society, which is at once noble and rough-and-tumble.[22] This is a type of American idealism in its own right, one that insists that a country succeeds only when it acknowledges and supports the honor and integrity of every citizen, no matter how haughty or how base. Panharmony—harmony by and through all—would be the idea that Emerson invoked to describe an ideal, transcendental rhetoric.

The final outcome of that harmonious union of disparate voices was a new purpose for rhetoric. In the field of rhetoric, purposes are called "offices," and even today, the offices primarily discussed are those theorized by Cicero in ancient Rome. Emerson's rhetorical education was steeped in Ciceronian rhetoric, with even Hugh Blair's rhetoric reliant on it. Emerson read Cicero directly throughout his life, and indeed, he frequently figures Cicero as the prime example of exceptional eloquence. Cicero famously posited three "offices" of rhetoric—core purposes for which language was used. For Cicero, the duty of the orator was either 1) to teach, 2) to move, and/or 3) to entertain. A speaker's organization, delivery, and even diction was shaped by the stated office.[23]

Emerson's vision of Ciceronian eloquence, however, was influenced by St. Augustine's re-examination of Cicero in the *De doctrina Christiana*.[24] Augustine assigns very specific styles to each office, so that the duty "to teach" was linked with a more lowly style than the duty "to persuade," which Augustine insists would require a grand style. Such conflation of style and purpose would have been impossible for Emerson to avoid in his readings of Augustine, as Augustine not only states them explicitly, but also embodies them in texts like *The Confessions*, where it is only through the grandiloquence of the Bible that Augustine is converted from pagan to Christian.

While Emerson did not in wholesale fashion adopt Augustine's take on Cicero, he did attach divine significance to language, wedding the worlds of rhetoric and faith and expanding rhetoric's potential in the world. Indeed, Emerson effectively posits a fourth office to rhetoric, one derived from this yoking of spiritual wisdom with practical craft. That office might best be called "to transform" or "to inspire," and the image of the panharmonicon perfectly captured for him the ability of a speech to transform listeners.

Emerson's insistence that the true rhetoric does more than simply persuade, teach, or entertain is grounded on his idealized version of the individual's potential for transformation into someone entirely new. Under the influence of divinity and acting on the whispers of a deity, Emerson's individual is capable of being fundamentally changed from brute selfishness, pedantry, or sophistry into a being aware of their place in a cosmic order. That awareness, granted through connection to nature, experiences of love, and the power of language (whether written or uttered), inevitably changes the fundamental character of the person. The person is, in other words, inspired to be different, transformed into someone new.

Such figuring of a person as becoming entirely new under the influence of language aligns with certain Christian traditions, especially those based heavily on Biblical hermeneutics. Many Protestant traditions, no less so than in many Catholic traditions, posit a Holy Book as a vehicle of transformation such that the written word of God fundamentally remakes those who read it. It may be through revelation of divinity or the inspiration of holiness that fosters the change, but the core feature remains the same: the words utterly change the person into a new being, one more closely connected to a deity. The godhead becomes manifest in that person.

Emerson invokes this power repeatedly, and it explains how Emerson's democratic values connect to his spiritual yearning. "To transform" or even "to inspire transformation" functions outside the typical offices described by many rhetorical theorists. It suggests that rhetorical power is available to every person. It turns rhetoric away from solely mediated exchanges between a priest and parishioner, a speaker and a listener, or a teacher and a student toward something enacted through individual power. While persuasion may help generate the action a speaker or writer might want from their audience, transformation requires an abandonment of a previous version of the self in order to live in a new version, a version that can only be embodied by embracing the wide range of voices surrounding everyone. For Emerson, the hope of an American rhetoric was that it lifted all people, regardless of social status or standing, and advanced a revolutionary transformation of a society into a holy chorus of diverse voices. That vision—fully accessible and fully accessed by any person, regardless of class or caste—is the heart of Emersonian rhetoric, and it is the feature that makes Emerson's theory not only democratic, but American. If, as Emerson asserted in his first "Eloquence" essay, "probably every man is eloquent once in his life" and even untrained speakers can "hurl a sentence worthy of attention," it was not because such individuals were lucky (*CW* 7:30). It was because they, like anyone else, shared in the divine will that was making the dream of a new nation a reality, as imperfect as it might be.

Notes

1. Hugh Blair, *Lectures On Rhetoric and Belle Lettres*, ed. Linda Ferreira-Buckley and S. Michael Halloran (Carbondale: Southern Illinois University Press, 2005).
2. John Jay Chapman, *Emerson and Other Essays* (New York: AMS Press, 1899), 33.
3. See "Historical and Textual Introduction" of *LL* 1:xix.
4. Carl Bode, *The American Lyceum* (New York: Oxford University Press, 1956).
5. Holly Jackson, *American Radicals: How Nineteenth-Century Protest Shaped the Nation* (New York: Crown, 2019).
6. William Pittenger, *Oratory Sacred and Secular: Or, the Extemporaneous Speaker, with Sketches of the Most Eminent Speakers of All Ages* (New York: Samuel R. Wells, 1875), 125.
7. Gregory Clark and S. Michael Halloran, *Oratorical Culture in Nineteenth-Century America: Transformations in the Theory and Practice of Rhetoric* (Carbondale: Southern Illinois University Press, 1993).
8. Albert J. von Frank, *An Emerson Chronology*, 2nd edition, 2 vols. (Albuquerque: Studio Non Troppo, 2016), 152.

9. Plato, *Gorgias*, ed. Donald J. Zeyl (Cambridge: Hackett, 1987), 464d.
10. Edward Everett, *Orations and Speeches on Various Occasions*, vol. 2 (New York: C. C. Little and J. Brown, 1850), 86–87.
11. Frederick Douglass, *The Oxford Frederick Douglass Reader*, ed. William L. Andrews (New York: Oxford University Press, 1996), 116.
12. Jim Warren, *Oratory and Reform in Antebellum America* (University Park: Pennsylvania State University Press, 1999), 45.
13. William Charvat, *Emerson's American Lecture Engagements: A Chronological List* (New York: New York Public Library, 1961), 19.
14. Ralph Waldo Emerson, *The Complete Sermons of Ralph Waldo Emerson*, vol. 1, ed. Albert J. von Frank (Columbia: University of Missouri Press, 1989), 75.
15. Michael-John DePalma, *Sacred Rhetorical Education in 19th-Century America: Austin Phelps at Andover Theological Seminary* (New York: Routledge, 2020).
16. Jim Perrin Warren, *Culture of Eloquence: Oratory and Reform in Antebellum America* (University Park: Penn State University Press, 1999).
17. Holly Jackson, *American Radicals: How Nineteenth-Century Protest Shaped the Nation* (New York: Crown, 2019).
18. Jane Donawerth, *Conversational Rhetoric: The Rise and Fall of a Women's Tradition, 1600–1900* (Carbondale: Southern Illinois University Press, 2011); and "Nineteenth-Century United States Conduct Book Rhetoric," *Rhetoric Review* 21, no. 1 (2002): 5–21.
19. Nan Johnson, *Gender and Rhetorical Space in American Life, 1866–1910.* Carbondale: Southern Illinois University Press, 2002.
20. Jacqueline Jones Royster, *Traces of a Stream: Literacy and Social Change among African American Women* (Pittsburgh: University of Pittsburgh Press, 2000).
21. Roger Thompson, *Emerson and the History of Rhetoric* (Carbondale: Southern Illinois University Press, 2018), 110–15.
22. Kenneth Cmiel, *Democratic Eloquence: The Fight over Popular Speech in Nineteenth-Century America* (Oakland: University of California Press, 1991).
23. Marcus Tullius Cicero, *On the Ideal Orator*, trans. and ed. Jakob Wisse and James M. May (New York: Oxford University Press, 2001).
24. St. Augustine, *De doctrina Christiana*, trans. and ed. R. P. H. Green (Oxford: Clarendon Press, 1996).

CHAPTER 29

LYDIA JACKSON EMERSON

RANDALL FULLER

So persuasive and relentlessly canonical are "Self-Reliance," "The Over-Soul," and "Circles," that it has long been acceptable practice to read *Essays: First Series* entirely on their terms. But Emerson's first collection is anything but monologic, as the author makes clear in his title: the book is a *series*, from the Latin *serare*, a chain joined together, a marriage of disparate ideas, each link reverberating with the others, each in correspondence and conversation. The essay on "Love," which is the fifth in the sequence and three after "Self-Reliance," is a statement that largely refutes the martial pronouncements of the earlier essay. To read "Self-Reliance" without "Love" is to risk ignoring an interplay, a dialogue: the circuit between the isolate individual and the individual's inescapable reliance on others. Love forms attachments, Emerson writes; it reveals the importance of "social instincts," delights in "perfect equality" (*CW* 2:102).

Much of "Love" was written from passages Emerson inscribed in his journal about his wife, Lydia Jackson Emerson, a woman characterized by generations of biographers as woefully ill-prepared for her husband's philosophy and fame.[*] For Ralph L. Rusk, writing in 1949, Lydia Emerson was afflicted with "imaginary ills" that were likely the result of "her unconscious protest against a philosophy that she was unable to live up to," while for Megan Marshall, more recently, she is best understood as an oppressed housewife who "sought refuge in illness and, when well, in an obsessive attention to the details of housekeeping."[1] These portraits, not so much wrong as partial, tend to caricature a deeply complex woman who exerted enormous influence on her husband's thinking. They are uniform in their descriptions of a depressive invalid overwhelmed by domestic responsibilities and deeply unsympathetic to her husband's individualism. It is certainly true that Lydia penned the most searing and insightful critique of Transcendentalism ever written from within the movement, a satire of its excesses and hypocrisies that combined her talents for humor and her astringent acuity. She called it

---

[*] Because it was Emerson who famously "renamed" Lydia as Lidian, and because she clearly felt uncomfortable with the new appellation for years, signing letters to family as "Lydia," I have chosen to use her given name.

her "Transcendental Bible," and her husband, skewered by the document, was nevertheless able to laugh at and even appreciate her observations. To consider Emerson's life and work without a full appreciation of his wife is like reading only the canonical portions of the *Essays*—certainly possible, even heuristically satisfying, but also certainly incomplete. That Emerson appreciated his wife's provocations and counterexamples is clear in a letter he wrote to Carlyle in 1838: "My wife Lidian ... keeps my philosophy from Antinomianism."[2]

* * *

Her father was a captain of industry. Charles Jackson owned a large counting house at the end of the wharf at Plymouth, Massachusetts and a small fleet of ships that imported goods from around the world. Lydia, born on September 20, 1802, believed he "was the most dignified person she ever saw"; from him she inherited her height, her oaken majesty, her flair for the histrionic.[3] Lucy Cotton Jackson, two years older than her husband, was also from an old Plymouth family, but hers was ministerial rather than commercial: her great-great-grandfather was the Puritan divine, John Cotton, and her father, also John Cotton, had preached in nearby Halifax for two decades before poor health forced him to resign and return to Plymouth. There he was locally famous for his huge library of Greek and Latin books.

The Jacksons were prosperous, which meant that Lydia and her older sister Lucy were educated in a series of academies for young women. But their formal education ended in the summer of 1818, when Lydia was sixteen and when both her parents died within the span of a few months. Lydia and her siblings (a brother, Charles T. Jackson, later a physician and inventor, was the youngest child) each inherited fourteen thousand dollars, a substantial sum, but less than anticipated (fraud was suspected). For the next decade or so, Lydia inhabited a room in the family house overlooking the sea. According to her oldest daughter, Ellen Emerson, who would serve eventually as her biographer and factotum family historian, "Mother's Plymouth life was exactly to her taste. She loved perfection and exquisite order and with her small space of one room to care for and her command of her own time she was able to have it."[4]

In 1821, when Lydia was nineteen, she contracted scarlet fever. Without treatment (and there was no treatment), the bacteria could migrate to a patient's lungs and kidneys. It could also cause rheumatic fever. In Lydia's case, it left her physically diminished for the rest of her life; "her head was hot ever after, and she never was so well in other ways."[5] Of equal concern was her spiritual health; reared in the Calvinist tradition, she had grown up with a terror "of death and future punishment."[6] As a teenager she began to feel the gnawing of spiritual hunger, and at twenty-three she underwent the first of several profound religious experiences. "It seemed to her that she entered into a new state in those weeks," Ellen reported, "and that dimly all her future was shown to her and she was mercifully prepared for all that was to come."[7]

Soon she led a Sunday school class for young women. She also attended lectures on chemistry and traveled to Boston to take riding lessons (where another student was Emerson's first wife, Ellen). Mostly, though, she read: novels by Maria Edgeworth and

Sir Walter Scott, sermons by Joseph Stevens Buckminster. She rejoiced when the *North American* magazine attacked James Fenimore Cooper, whose writings she enjoyed but thought "deserve more censure than praise."[8] She also tackled the massive *Institutes of Natural Philosophy*, a scientific work by the English Unitarian William Enfield, telling a friend that "if it is fit to use at Cambridge"—meaning Harvard—"it will answer for me."[9]

In 1833, under the guidance of George Bradford, she took up German, absorbing the poetry of Herder and Schiller as well as Goethe's formative novel, *Wilheim Meister*, from which she never tired of reciting.[10] Without quite knowing it—without even knowing the term—she was becoming a proto-Transcendentalist. She was drawn to the movement's ideas and ideals the way most people are drawn to any new set of beliefs: tentatively, haphazardly, feeling their way in stages toward a philosophy that accords with their experience. At age thirty, her life involved study and friends; conversations about philosophy and literature; spiritual searching; and just enough money to be independent. That's when she met Emerson.

* * *

Theirs was an unusual courtship. Lydia first saw the young minister in 1832, while visiting her sister Lucy in Boston. After the sermon she "found herself leaning eagerly forward, and as she looked back on the whole dear & beautiful service and noticed that now she felt tired of her position she [realized] she must have taken it when the minister said his first words and had been too much absorbed to move from beginning to end." A strange feeling swept over her, and she said to herself, "That man is certainly my predestined husband."[11] Two years later, Emerson visited Plymouth, where he delivered two sermons in the First Parish Church. When the first one was over, a friend approached Lydia and asked how she liked hearing her own ideas preached in public: "What Mr. Emerson said was just what you always say."[12] At some point the two were introduced. Emerson later described the meeting in fairy-tale language in his journal, his language shifting from the past to the present tense at the moment the lovers gaze upon one another for the first time: "It happened once that a youth and a maid beheld each other in a public assembly for the first time. The youth gazed with great delight upon the beautiful face until he caught the maiden's eyes. She presently became aware of his attention, and something like correspondence immediately takes place.... Presently their eyes met in a full, searching, front, not to be mistaken glance. It is wonderful how much it made them acquainted."[13]

In January 1835, Lydia had a premonitory vision. She stood on the staircase of her family home, dressed in bridal white, while Emerson escorted her down the stairs. A few weeks later, she saw his face again, "very beautiful ... gazing at her, just for a moment."[14] Soon after, she received a letter from him: "I am rejoiced in my Reason as well as in my Understanding by finding an earnest and noble mind whose presence quickens in mine all that is good and shames and repels me from my own weaknesses. Can I resist the impulse to beseech you to love me?" (*LRWE* 7:232). It was a wedding proposal, couched in the language of Coleridge and Kant.

She invited him to Plymouth, where she sat in the parlor with her eyes closed, determined not to look at his imploring eyes while she told him she had never managed a household and "should not be a skillful mistress of a house and that it would be a load of care and labour from which she shrank and a giving up of an existence she thoroughly enjoyed and to which she had become exactly fitted ... [and that] she could not undertake it unless he was sure he loved her and needed her enough to justify her in doing it..." Emerson later called this episode "that catechism with the closed eyes," but apparently his response was satisfactory, because when she at last looked at him and apologized for her uninteresting conversation, he exclaimed, "Uninteresting! It is heaven." At that moment "his eyes seemed to her to be like two blue flames."[15]

* * *

The familiar story about her name change is that Emerson disliked the New England pronunciation that inserted an "r" between two vowel sounds. (*Lydiar* Emerson grated on his poet's ear.) She grudgingly accepted the change, signing her name "Lydia" to her family and friends, "Lidian" to his. But that wasn't the only alteration he insisted upon. In an early letter, Emerson praised Concord and said, "I must win you to love it" (*LRWE* 1:434–35). Lydia, who loved Plymouth, hoped he "would consent to come to Plymouth to live."[16] But he remained adamant.

Lydia took these changes in stride, developing from them a philosophy of marriage that she outlined to her new friend in the Transcendentalist coterie, Elizabeth Palmer Peabody: "The conjugal union—is strengthened and perfected and made productive of mutual goal by the very dissimilarity of the natures thus joined by the order of Providence." A perfect marriage, she believed, entailed radically divergent natures, each person compensating for and correcting the faults of the other. "Only when the differing spirits thus joined co-operate with Providence—conform to Divine Order ... harmony and mutual improvement is the result."[17] Her faith in the interdependence of dissimilar personalities was bolstered by her reading of Emanuel Swedenborg. Emerson, who had been introduced to the Swedish mystic by his Aunt Mary Moody Emerson years earlier, found his interest reinvigorated during their engagement. Lydia, who had been reading his works "for the last year or two," took Swedenborg's ideas quite seriously.[18] Two especially appealed to her. The first was his belief that the only obstacle to a perfect society was preoccupation with *self*, which Swedenborg called the *proprium* and which he considered "nothing but evil, and the falsity therefrom."[19] The other idea had to do explicitly with marriage and appeared in his work of 1768, *Wisdom's Delight in Marriage: ("Conjugial") Love*, published in Latin and written, like the Bible, in chapters and verses. The book advanced the idea that earthly marriage was a preparation for "spiritual nuptials," a heavenly union of truth and goodness that would last an eternity.[20]

In her letter to Peabody, Lydia affirmed that God had created each person with unique strengths and weaknesses so that he "should consider himself as part of a great whole," and she repeated her belief that "Our individual being ... is not complete in itself—was not created with chief reference to itself." This was in opposition to Emerson's belief that he lived in "the age of the first person singular" and that the independent self, funded by divinity, was the primary unit of importance. But to Lydia, the difference in opinion only advanced her point; she and Emerson were to be "united for the purpose of correcting each other's defects and supplying each other's deficiencies."[21]

* * *

A few days after her wedding to Emerson, Lydia wrote her sister to describe her happiness. Then she tried to inoculate herself from the fear that such good fortune could not last forever. "Disappointment in some form probably awaits us—and let it come—if our God will. It is a medicine salutary as bitter."[22] The first calamity came on May 9, 1836, when Charles Emerson died. The death of Emerson's younger brother brought Lydia closer to his fiancée, Elizabeth Hoar, who soon became a permanent fixture in the Emerson household. The two women participated in the antislavery cause together, each subscribing to *The Liberator*, each attending lectures by the celebrated Grimké sisters and, in 1837, each joining sixty other women to create the Concord Female Anti-Slavery Society.

Lydia's enthusiasm for abolitionism created tension from an unexpected quarter. In a journal entry written soon after the Grimkés' visit that grappled with his wife's outrage over slavery, Emerson wrote, "Lidian grieves aloud about the wretched negro in the horrors of the middle passage; and they are bad enough. But to such as she, these crucifixions do not come. They come to the obtuse & barbarous to whom they are not horrid but only a little worse than old sufferings" (*JMN* 5:382). The sentiment would eventually make its way from journal to print; in "The Tragic," written for *The Dial* in 1844, he noted, "A tender American girl doubts of Divine Providence whilst she reads the horrors of 'the middle passage': and they are bad enough...."[23] More notoriously, in "Self-Reliance," he argued, "If an angry bigot assumes this bountiful cause of Abolition, ... why should I not say to him, 'Go love thy infant; love thy wood-chopper: be good-natured and modest ... and never varnish your hard, uncharitable ambition with this incredible tenderness for black folk a thousand miles off. Thy love afar is spite at home'" (*CW* 2:30). Many readers have taken this passage to reveal a cruel streak inherent in Emersonian individualism, an indifference to suffering and a dismissive attitude toward projects of social justice. But Emerson's point was that while we *should* feel sympathy and outrage on behalf of the oppressed, it is also possible to mime such feelings—and to do so is to create falsehood and self-division, a betrayal of one's authentic personality.

In the journals he nevertheless struggled with his wife's perspective, entering imaginatively (as she encouraged him to) into the conditions of enslaved people. "The fury with which the slaveholder & the slavetrader defend every inch of their plunder, of their bloody deck, & howling Auction," he wrote soon after the previous entry, "... the loathsome details of the kidnapping; of the middle passage; six hundred living bodies sit for thirty days betwixt death & life in a posture of stone & when brought on deck for air cast themselves into the sea" (*JMN* 5:440). Lydia's example worked in other ways, too, often as a subtle corrective to his most extreme ideas. "In company with a lady," he acknowledged, "it sometimes seems a bitterness and unnecessary wound to insist, as I incline to, on the self-sufficiency of man" (*JMN* 12:181). Another time, when Elizabeth

Hoar spoke to him about her continued grief over Charles's death, he refused on principle to commiserate. "It seems to me as if what we mainly need," he explained to himself, "is the power of recurring to the sublime at pleasure." Written in pencil, in Lydia's hand, was an addendum: "I'll tell you what to do. Try to make Humanity lovely unto itself" (*JMN* 5:489–90, see footnote).

Her influence was most apparent in another issue then roiling the nation. In April 1838, she wrote her sister, "Doing good you know is all out of fashion, but there happens just now to occur a case so urgent that one must lay aside for awhile all new-fangled notions." She was referring to the federal government's decision to remove Cherokee people from their ancestral lands and to relocate them in the west. Encouraged by his wife, Emerson reluctantly agreed to address a protest meeting in Concord and to write a letter to President Van Buren condemning "so vast an outrage upon the Cherokee Nation." Lydia also urged her sister to persuade friends in Plymouth to raise the issue with "the gentlemen most likely to care that something be done."[24] Her strategy of domestic influence got results: a petition from Plymouth's prominent politicians and businessmen opposing Cherokee removal was soon addressed to Congress.

Despite these victories, there were trials in the marriage. The responsibilities of running a large household were particularly overwhelming to Lydia. Once she dreamed she had died and was lying in her coffin in the parlor when she noticed the carelessness of the servants; she abruptly sat up and scolded them. These domestic pressures only increased as Emerson vaulted into national prominence; on the weekend he delivered "The American Scholar" address, for instance, she was "honoured," as she drily informed Peabody, "with the opportunity of ministering to the earthly comfort of the whole transcendental coterie."[25] But the conventional account that she felt imprisoned by domestic duties and overshadowed by her charismatic husband isn't entirely accurate, either. Lydia and Emerson shared much that was private—pet names, personal references, ironic wit, and a shared erotic passion. "O I could live upon memory alone might I select the *blessed* hours and moments of the Past," she wrote him, referring at least in part to previous intimacies.[26] Even her sister expressed discomfort at the sexual current that passed between them when they looked at one another. Moreover, Lydia was proud of her husband's success and her ability to influence him. A year and a half after their wedding, Emerson stepped outside and stood in the snowy yard, gazing up at the field of stars. Then he returned to his study to record his thoughts. "My gentle wife has an angel's heart," he wrote, "& for my boy, his grief is more beautiful than other people's joy" (*JMN* 5:454). He was referring to the single greatest fact of their married life, an event that bound Lydia and Emerson more closely than ever. It was the birth of a son.

* * *

Everyone who saw the infant Waldo Emerson described him as beautiful, angelic. When the Reverend Ezra Ripley came for a visit and placed the baby face down in his lap, he raised the child's undershirt. Asked whether anything was wrong, Ripley pulled down the shirt and said he had been told "the child of this couple would probably have wings."[27]

The pregnancy had been arduous, with Lydia spending entire weeks in bed. At one point, Emerson grew so alarmed that he summoned Concord's leading physician, Dr. Josiah Bartlett, telling him, "It does not seem just that the Mother should have so much pain and suffering and the Father none." Bartlett replied: "She is repaid. She has the pleasures of lactation." But Lydia's suffering was psychological, too; according to her daughter, "When a baby was born or a person died in Plymouth, it was the custom for the children all to go in to see the baby or the corpse; the first was amusing, the latter was considered impressive. It would keep the children in mind that they must prepare for death."[28] The association of birth and death was further reinforced when Lydia was in her twenties and attending the lying-in of an aunt. Asked to hold the child, she took it and sat by the fire. The infant died in her lap; the next morning the mother died, also.

The arrival of Waldo would alter the dynamics of the household. Emerson had completed *Nature* during Lydia's pregnancy, and the book is full of references to infancy and childhood. "The lover of nature," he declared, "is he ... who has retained the spirit of infancy even into manhood." The stars awakened in an adult "the simplicity of his childhood," the sun shone "into the eye and the heart of the child" (*CW* 1:9), and the abundance of nature caused the jaded city-dweller to perceive things anew, as "he saw and heard them in his infancy" (*CW* 1:21). In the woods, Emerson wrote, an adult "is always a child" (*CW* 1:10), and he even traced language to its infancy where, he claimed, poetry was found. With the arrival of a son, Emerson was astonished by the transformation of his world, and especially by the change he discerned in Lydia, who held the baby in her arms and nursed him, creating a bond the father could only imagine. "Babe & the mother together" formed a Renaissance picture, he wrote, the child's "tiny beseeching weakness ... compensated so perfectly by the happy patronizing look of the mother, who is a sort of high reposing Providence toward it— ... they make a perfect group" (*JMN* 5:234–35).

Lydia, too, subscribed to a Romantic, Wordsworthian notion of childhood, believing her baby was closer to God because unspoiled as yet by society. "Every day a child presents a new aspect," she told Emerson, "... as the face of the sky is different every hour, so that we never get tired" (*JMN* 5:234). She begrudged leaving Waldo for even a moment, aware that he grew "so fast that each look is new & each is never to be repeated" (*JMN* 5:300), and her correspondence was now filled with descriptions of the child: "In the morning, while I am in the room next to Waldo's nursery, dressing myself—I hear a sweet little voice talking—and I think somebody is there with Baby—he seems so sociable."[29] So smitten was she with her son, she sometimes sought to minimize her feelings. "I do not myself think him so very uncommon," she wrote her sister. "He is a fine child but there are hundreds of fine children in the world." Trying to protect herself against her greatest fear, she compared him to her sister's children, saying, "I do not know that I love Waldo any better than I did Frank or Sophia. I loved them with *all* my heart. [But] I think I should feel more if Waldo were to die than if one of yours had died."[30]

The child's first years were clamorous, eventful. "All sorts of visitors with new ideas began to come to the house," Lydia's daughter later wrote, "the men who thought money was the root of all evil, the vegetarians, the sons of nature who did not believe in razors nor in tailors, the philosophers and all sorts of come-outers."[31] Frequent guests included Elizabeth Peabody, Bronson Alcott, and George Bradford. In 1837, Lydia began inviting a young man to dinner because he had walked to Boston—twenty miles—to hear her husband speak; soon she was reporting that her husband had taken to Henry David Thoreau "with great interest & thinks him uncommon in mind & character."[32] Another houseguest was Margaret Fuller, who had been recommended by Elizabeth Peabody. "Miss Fuller is with us now," Lydia wrote her friend, "—and you will be glad to hear we find real satisfaction—Miss F. Mr E. & myself—in our intercourse with each other."[33] In November 1839, Lydia began rising before dawn each Wednesday in order to attend Fuller's famous Boston conversations, designed "to ascertain what pursuits are best suited to [women] in our time and state of society, and how we may make best use of our means of building up the life of thought upon the life of action."[34]

By the time Lydia began attending Fuller's talks, another occupant had entered the Emerson household: Ellen Tucker Emerson was born on February 4, 1839, with Lydia and her husband "both rejoicing at the fulfillment of our strongest earthly wish."[35] As with her earlier pregnancy, she suffered considerably—so much so that she asked her mother-in-law to take over housekeeping chores. But in other ways the second birth was different. This time it was *she* who named the child, albeit in honor of her husband's first wife.[36] "Lidian, who magnanimously makes my gods her gods," Emerson wrote, "calls the babe Ellen. I can hardly ask for more for thee, my babe, than that name implies" (*JMN* 7:170).

It was during this baby's early months that he began work on the essay on "Love," a summation of his feelings for his second wife. Emerson extolled the "private and tender relation of one to one, which is the enchantment of human life," and called romantic love "a certain divine rage and enthusiasm, [which] seizes on man[,] ... works a revolution in his mind and body; unites him to his race, pledges him to the domestic and civic relations, carries him with new sympathy into nature ..." (*CW* 2:99). In many ways, this was a reformulation of Lydia's "theosophy of marriage," her belief in the interdependence of dissimilar personalities. Emerson made his debt to her beliefs even more explicit in another passage: "In the particular society of his mate [a lover] attains a clearer sight of any spot, any taint, which her beauty has contracted from this world, and is able to point it out, ... to indicate blemishes and hindrances in each other, and give to each all help and comfort in curing the same" (*CW* 2:106).

* * *

"For five years Mother said she and Father were getting more & more married all the time," Ellen Emerson wrote. "They were as happy as it was possible to be."[37] Then something changed; cracks began to emerge in the marriage. Lydia and Emerson expressed their dissatisfaction in different ways, but by 1841 the marriage had entered a period of strain. "He is not happy as formerly I suspect," Mary Moody Emerson told Elizabeth Hoar, speaking of her nephew.[38] Emerson's dissatisfaction is apparent in his journals. "Swedenborg exaggerates the circumstance of marriage," he wrote. "One to one, married and chained through the eternity of ages is frightful beyond the binding of dead and living together." Lydia's unhappiness appears primarily through the recollection of others. Starting in 1841, Ellen Emerson reported, and "for the next thirty years sadness was the ground-colour of her life."[39] Part of the malaise was spiritual. "In 1841, Mother waked to a sense that she had been losing—had lost—that blessed nearness to God in which she had lived so long, and she never regained it."[40] This loss, however, was related to her husband, who had increasingly shed all religious affiliation. Despite her "theosophy of marriage," Lydia had thought she and her husband shared the same religious beliefs; according to her daughter, "now it was clear to her that he was not a Christian in her sense of the word, and it was a most bitter discovery."[41]

Her sadness was compounded by the sense that she was undervalued by many in the Transcendentalist circle. Always sensitive to slights, she was acutely aware of those who did not regard "her as anything but the housekeeper."[42] The only clue Lydia left about her feelings is a document written in pencil on a single sheet of paper. It is a manifesto of sorts, a personal credo, a work often referred to as her "Transcendental Bible." It is also the most scathing criticism of the movement written by an insider.

Many readers encountering Transcendentalist writing for the first time are struck by its sense of liberation. All traditions are to be held up to scrutiny; social conventions and religious orthodoxy are to be discarded; the individual, endowed with godlike judgment, is encouraged to make a clean break with the past, to reimagine a newfound heaven on earth. But all of this ignores a crucial fact: human life is collective; people need one another. Lydia believed that human growth depended upon a deep connection to others. Drawn all her life to the weak and disenfranchised—to the enslaved and the impoverished, to vulnerable animals of all kinds—she understood that in any society some people will require more help and care than others, that some will necessarily enlist our compassion. Sympathy, in this context, is not weakness, but the prerequisite for a flourishing society.

Her "Transcendenta Bible" attacks the movement's tendency to deploy the sanctity of the self—Swedenborg's *proprium*—as an excuse for bad behavior. While Emerson's followers were busy gazing inward, the rest of the world seemed beneath their concern. ("Queenie says, 'Save me from magnificent souls,'" Emerson once wrote of his wife. "'I like a small common sized one'" [*JMN* 8:242].) Lydia's work is written in the style of Proverbs, much in the spirit of Swedenborg, and it is meant to critique, through Blakean paradox, the core tenets of the "New Thought." She reveals the hypocrisy and even mean-spiritedness that sometimes guided Transcendentalism's practitioners, ventriloquizing the airy pronouncements of her husband and his followers: "Never hint at a Providence, Particular or Universal," she wrote under the heading of "Whole Duty of Man."[43] "It is narrow to believe that the Universal Being concerns itself with particular affairs, egotistical to think it regards your own." This was a swat at Emerson's insistence on an impersonal deity. It was also a parody of Transcendentalist style, which often affected such breezy proclamations—in this case, that it was possible to replace a personal God with one's own personality. Lydia was suggesting that egotism was the original sin of Transcendentalism, that it had replaced God with Self, the same point Hawthorne would make contemporaneously in "Egotism; or, the Bosom-Serpent."

But it was in the next section—"Duty to Your Neighbour"—that she launched her most caustic attacks. These proverbs, loosely collected as an "Abstract of New Bible," were aimed at the selfishness she believed was the natural byproduct of unchecked egotism:

> Loathe and shun the sick. They are in bad taste, and may untune us for writing the poem floating through our mind.
> Scorn the infirm of character and omit no opportunity of insulting and exposing them. They ought not to be infirm and should be punished by contempt and avoidance.
> Despise the unintellectual, and make them feel that you do by not noticing their remark and question lest they presume to intrude into your conversation....
> If any seek to believe that their sorrows are sent or sent in love, do your best to dispel the silly egotistical delusion....
> Let us all aspire after this Perfection! So be it.

Ellen Emerson, the family's historian, grew up hearing about this document, which her father called "The Queen's Bible," but it was not until much later that she discovered her mother's manifesto among family papers. One evening she brought it into her father's study and read it aloud to both parents. "Father laughed all the way through and said 'Yes, it was a good squib of your Mammy's.' Mother at once fell into the strain of it and made a few remarks on those views and those times."[44] This retrospective view suggests the "Transcendental Bible" was meant as entertainment, but in so doing it glosses over the disappointment that prompted Lydia's work in the first place—disappointment in her marriage, her circumstances, the premises upon which her husband had constructed his intellectual life. The "Bible" is in many ways a direct response to Emerson's essay on "The Transcendentalist," where he announces that "the height, the deity of man is to be self-sustained, to need no gift, no foreign force. Society is good when it does not violate me..." (*CW* 1:203–4). And it was written soon after the greatest tragedy to afflict Lydia and her husband.[45]

* * *

Waldo Emerson died from the same disease Lydia had contracted at nineteen: scarlet fever. Six weeks earlier, she had given birth to a second daughter, Edith. On the evening the boy died, the grieving mother held the tiny infant in her lap by the fire while Emerson and his mother sat in the room consoling her. Throughout their conversation, Lydia "kept stretching 'way over to look at something behind [Edith's] little head, and smiling most rightly at it. There was nothing there but the bedstead. Mother hoped it was the angel Waldo smiling to his innocent little sister still able to see him."[46]

Later that night, she collapsed. "Grief, desolating grief came over me like a flood—," she wrote her sister, "and I feared that the charm of earthly life was forever destroyed."[47] Her despair was soon compounded by Emerson's departure, barely two weeks after the calamity, to deliver a series of lectures. "Have the clouds yet broken, & let in the sunlight?" he wrote her while gone, clearly worried. "Alas! Alas! that one of your sorrows, that our one sorrow can never in this world depart from us!" (*LRWE* 3:11–13).

Seven months later, when Margaret Fuller arrived in Concord for one of her annual visits, she found that "all things looked sad."[48] Sophia Hawthorne, recently arrived in the village with her husband Nathaniel, thought the same. Visiting the Emerson household, she found the bereaved woman "very ill with ague accompanied with fever. She took tons of calomel and now walks abroad but is exceptionally feeble and paler than snow."[49] In addition to fever, Lydia was also suffering the aftereffects of dental surgery, which she treated with opium. "She does look very ghostly now," Fuller wrote in her journal, "as she glides about in her black dress, and long black veil."[50] Fuller also recorded an incident that suggests the strain still felt in the Emerson household. She had refrained from visiting Lydia's room, "simply because I was engaged all the time and kept expecting to see her down stairs. When I *did* go in, she burst into tears, at sight of me, but laid the blame on her nerves, having taken opium &c." Embarrassed, Fuller was uncertain whether to stay or leave, when Lydia said something that "made me suppose she thought W[aldo]. passed the evenings in talking to me, & a painful feeling flashed across me, such as I have not had, all has seemed so perfectly understood between us."[51] Was Lydia jealous? This was Fuller's interpretation, although it seems more likely the grieving mother simply wanted her feelings acknowledged by her often self-centered houseguest. Lydia was clearly in some distress during Fuller's visit, but the letters she wrote her husband after their son's death paint a different picture than that of a jealous spouse. Those letters are punctuated with affection, railery, occasional ebullience, as well as the ever-recurring ache of their shared misfortune.

"My turn of expression is so happy," Lydia wrote Emerson in January 1843, one year after the boy's death, "that I think you must believe the time of my breaking forth into verse is at hand."[52] For his part, Emerson's letters were invariably tender and solicitous. In February 1842, acutely aware that he had left her during her greatest sorrow, he begged, "Write to me quickly that you are all well." When her letters were not forthcoming (their correspondence often crossed or was delayed during his peregrinations), he miserably wondered if her silence was meant "to punish my philosophy?" (*LRWE* 3:12, 18). She replied with affection and reports of their surviving children—of Edith, for instance, she said she could not remember "such intelligent looks" and had never "heard such gay laughs from *any* baby her age."

Both frequently returned to their loss. "It is true that the Boy is gone," Emerson wrote, a month after Waldo's death, "the far shining stone that made home glitter to me when I was farthest absent—for you & I are passing, and he was to remain…" (*LRWE* 3:12). On a visit to Boston in January 1843, Lydia wrote, "I was thinking of Waldo my Husband and of Waldo in Heaven. The sacred anniversary of my (virtual) marriage and the sickness and death of my first-born—brought realities near to me and the pangs of bereaved affection were lost in hope and trust."[53] Moments of despair remained. In 1843, Lydia went into Emerson's study and wrote the following in his journal: "Dear husband. I wish I had never been born. I do not see how God can compensate me for the sorrow of existence" (*JMN* 8:365).

That same sorrow animates Emerson's most famous essay from this period, "Experience," lines of which are interwoven with his shared life with Lydia. "Where do we find ourselves?" the essay begins, then deploys an image with special resonance for his wife. "We wake and find ourselves on a stair," Emerson writes, alluding to Lydia's marriage vision as well as to Swedenborg's stairway to heaven; "there are stairs below us, which we seem to have ascended; there are stairs above us, many a one, which go upward and out of sight" (*CW* 3:27). Characteristically, Emerson's answer to the numbness of grief is a return to the self, "the solitude to which every man is always returning" (*CW* 3:49). Lydia's response was altogether different. She opened herself to her pain, to sharing it with her husband. In February 1843, she wrote a description of Ellen, who was "a year in advance of Waldo in reading." But the reference to the boy prompted fresh anguish. "Torn is my heart as I write that cherished name. The wound of separation is as fresh as it was a year ago. At least it seems so to me. I am bruised in heart—and cannot be healed by Time. Only a new spiritual experience can bring balm to that wound."[54]

In the end, grief brought them together. Emerson's journal contains no more slighting references to marriage; his correspondence, now addressed to a "dear Wife" (*LRWE* 3:129), is filled with praise for her letters, "so generous & so true to what is best in my wife. Such thoughts so deep & pure, enrich the reader & the writer, and the world is better for them" (*LRWE* 3:138). He assured her "that I am the same aspiring all-loving person whom you have known so long" (*LRWE* 3:144), and wanted her to know how "very refreshing it is to me to know that I have a good home, & so much truth & honor therein…" (*LRWE* 3:129–30).

Lydia continued to endure bouts of grief and poor health. There would be no healing from the death of her son, only the daily heroics of carrying on; she oversaw her three children's education and directed Henry Thoreau in various tasks about the house. Having supplanted the sainted Ellen Louisa Tucker in her husband's affections, she had somehow become Lidian instead of Lydia, yet without sacrificing herself. Her continued centrality to Emerson is apparent in a letter he wrote her describing a small lecture hall in New York. "I see not how it will hold people enough to answer any of my profane & worldly purposes … and then for sacred purposes of influence & provocation why we know that a room which will hold two persons holds audience enough: is not that thy doctrine, O unambitious wife?" (*LRWE* 3:21).

* * *

Toward the end of January 1843—a year after her son's death—Lydia traveled to Boston. The ostensible purpose of the trip was to visit her brother and sister-in-law. But she had another motive, as well. "I went on *Wednesday* and it was partly because I hoped to be able to get to the conversation of 'the wise men' that I chose that day." This group, apparently a mixture of male and female Transcendentalists, had gathered to discuss Bronson Alcott's plans to create a "new Eden" at Fruitlands. "When I found myself seated in the midst of the company of disciples I was very happy," Lydia wrote Emerson, "and even said to myself This is like Heaven. And why was I so happy? Not at what I heard for it was [what] I had heard much—though that was good. It was because I saw so many angels at once, and remembered there were more, elsewhere." The next day, Fuller paid her a formal visit, and Lydia felt gratified by the younger woman's "reverence for you." That evening she attended one of Fuller's conversations, and again there was a feeling of warm sociability. "Every body who loves my husband likes to meet my husband's wife— and it is dear to me to be recognized as belonging, in any sense, to him."[55]

A year later, Mary Moody Emerson wrote to say, "I have often thought of your strong reliance in affliction on a *particular* providence," referring to Lydia's belief that suffering was sent by a watchful, personal God.[56] The two women discussed a range of ancient and recent authors, including Plotinus, Madame de Staël, Jean Paul Richter, and Ralph Cudworth; they each read John Ruskin's *Modern Painters* and Robert Chambers's early work of proto-evolutionary theory, *Vestiges of the Natural History of Creation*.[†] But not all of their talk was about books and ideas. In 1848, Aunt Mary wrote to express her pleasure that her nephew had moved "beyond the mists & rainbow visions of transcendental philosophy (however it has truths of nature) and once more mingle[s] with the woes & cares of *practical* life"—a development she attributed in large part to Lydia.[57] And two years later, she wrote about a recently married friend: "If ever a happy girl is to be pitied it is the first year of leaving a good home & mother. After that the yoke becomes easier and bye & bye after a few years dragged out in mutual efforts for the pocket prosperity they become necessary to each other."[58] Thinking she had overstepped with this comment, she quickly wrote another letter asking Lydia to excuse her "raving letter" about the "dark side of matrimony."[59] This prompted a response:

"You ask if I think what you said about marriage in general true," Lydia began. "It is I am sure both true and false—that is it is most true of marriage without love—and I suppose the majority of marriages are so ... not many, I half believe, are capable of love." But there were exceptions, marriages of the sort described by Swedenborg in *Conjugial Love*. "A true husband is incomparably more than father mother & early home to the true wife's heart. A true marriage is a 'perfect freedom'[,] there is no *yoke* there. But the yoke of an unfit marriage may I should say be more galling and degrading than that of the Negro Slave. Unless her children bind her, a true woman should quietly slip her neck out of the snarl."[60] Lydia had certainly sacrificed portions of herself when she married Emerson—she had sacrificed home, name, even health to become his wife. And it was true she was disappointed by his "heresies," which clashed with her belief that the road of salvation lay through Christ. But she had not slipped the yoke. In their shared suffering

---

[†] That Lydia kept current on the latest intellectual developments is evident in a letter she wrote in 1864 to her son Edward: "What I have this eveg. been thinking of is, That it seems to me two of our modern Infidel Philosophies—(with Infidel *tendencies,* is the *best* I can say of them) nullify each other—Certain Rationalists (or whatever they are called), believing that the universe is a machine set a-going ages since, and then left to itself to grind on at its own stupid will,—and who shrink from nothing so much as the idea of Providence [and] say, that nature is reckless of the Individual but careful to preserve the Type [and] The Darwinians whose Philosophy seems to me—to use an old expression—'The latest form of Infidelity—' say on the contrary that there *are* no fixed types—but that one type is perpetually shading— blending, into another, so that all creatures beast bird and fish, came from one germ or monad—making *itself* first one thing and then another, till it became Monkey and then Man!"

she believed she had found a "true husband … incomparably more than father mother & home."

She nevertheless remained a sharp-eyed critic of their union. Writing in 1866 to her son Edward, she confessed, "Your father is called a great philosopher and your mother styles herself a Christian—but such instances of content and equanimity one may look for in vain at 'Bush' Hall."[61] Another time, writing to Emerson, she expressed her own painful sense of unworthiness: "God be merciful to me—dwindled to nothing. … I dared to marry you, simply because I believed that my Creator and Redeemer, who had as I believed destined me for union with you, would enable me to be to you—"[62] The rest of the letter is missing.

Sometimes she wished for greater agency, for the ability to influence national events. Discussing the plight of Native Americans with her oldest daughter, she admitted, "Now I wish I could speak for these Modocs in every paper in the land—I don't do it for a good reason—chief of which is, that I am nobody & editors would not publish any thing I wrote. Another, that I don't know well enough how to write English not to make myself ridiculous—and if I published in my language how would Papa like that? I have done enough in that line already."[63] But this characteristic self-deprecation ignores the pervasive influence she exercised over her husband.

Lydia's insistence on sympathy for the most oppressed served as a constant goad and counterweight to his individualism, and her expressions are sprinkled throughout his writing. As a mutual friend said, "Mr. Emerson wouldn't be the man he is if it wasn't for Mrs. Emerson. People have no idea how much he owes his wife." He relied on her as a sounding-board and compass; he respected her literary judgments. "Father has come to my room several times a day lately to talk over his Dartmouth Oration," she wrote their children, "with which I was well pleased."[64]

At the end of "Experience," Emerson concluded his meditation on the irrefragable givenness of circumstances with a resurgence of hope: "Never mind the ridicule, never mind the defeat: up again, old heart— … there is victory yet for all justice" (*CW* 3:49). Nearly three decades after the essay was written, Lydia wrote her surviving son Edward when Emerson was suddenly called away to Chicago, exclaiming: "Up heart—and bear it."[65] Was she quoting from her husband's essay, or had Emerson borrowed one of her characteristic sayings with which to conclude his essay? Like much that occurs behind the closed doors of a marriage, it is impossible to say. The two of them had grown entangled, their personalities intertwining and permeating each other. Like the essays on "Self-Reliance" and "Love," they stood distinct and conjoined, mutually influencing one another, less, somehow, even incomplete, without the other.

Notes

1. See Ralph L. Rusk, *The Life of Ralph Waldo Emerson* (New York: Columbia University Press, 1949), 358; and Megan Marshall, *The Peabody Sisters: Three Women Who Ignited American Romanticism* (Boston: Houghton Mifflin, 2005), 335.

2. Charles Eliot Norton, ed., *Correspondence of Carlyle and Emerson*, 2 vols. (Boston: James E. Osgood, 1883), 1:161.
3. This, as so much of my account, is based upon the biography of Lydia's life that was posthumously written by her eldest daughter, Ellen Tucker Emerson, *The Life of Lidian Jackson Emerson*, ed. Delores Bird Carpenter (Boston: Twayne Publishers, 1980), 15.
4. Ibid., 37.
5. Ibid., 19.
6. Ibid., 10.
7. Ibid., 41.
8. Lidian Jackson Emerson, *The Selected Letters of Lidian Jackson Emerson*, ed. Delores Bird Carpenter (Columbia: University of Missouri Press, 1987), 12.
9. Ibid., 5.
10. Ibid., 42.
11. Ibid., 43.
12. The friend is unidentified; ibid., 47.
13. Ralph Waldo Emerson, *Journals of Ralph Waldo Emerson, 1820-1872*, ed. Edward Waldo Emerson and Waldo Emerson Forbes (Cambridge, MA: Riverside Press, 1910), 3:436.
14. Emerson, *Life of Lidian Jackson Emerson*, 47.
15. Ibid., 48.
16. Ibid., 50.
17. *Letters of Lidian Jackson Emerson*, xxiii.
18. Ibid., 27.
19. Emmanuel Swedenborg, *A Compendium of the Writings of the Theological and Spiritual Writings of Emmanuel Swedenborg*, 2nd ed. (Boston: Crosby and Nichols, and Otis Clapp, 1854), 281.
20. Ibid., 292.
21. Lydia Jackson Emerson to Elizabeth Palmer Peabody, July 28, 1835, in *Letters of Lidian Jackson Emerson*, 29.
22. Lydia Jackson Emerson to Lucy Jackson Brown, September 16, 1835, ibid., 33.
23. Ralph Waldo Emerson, "The Tragic," in *The Dial* 4, no. 4 (1844): 520.
24. Lydia Jackson Emerson to Lucy Jackson Brown, April 23, 1838, in *Letters of Lidian Jackson Emerson*, 74.
25. Ibid., 57.
26. Lydia Jackson Emerson to Ralph Waldo Emerson, July 18, 1841, ibid., 96.
27. Emerson, *Life of Lidian Jackson Emerson*, 70.
28. Ibid., 15.
29. Lydia Jackson Emerson to Sophia Jackson Brown, August 19, 1837, in *Letters of Lidian Jackson Emerson*, 56–57.
30. Lydia Jackson Emerson to Lucy Jackson Brown, sometime after October 31, 1836, ibid., 50–51.
31. Emerson, *Life of Lidian Jackson Emerson*, 79–80.
32. Lydia Jackson Emerson to Lucy Jackson Brown, April [1838], in *Letters of Lidian Jackson Emerson*, 73.
33. Lydia Jackson Emerson to Elizabeth Palmer Peabody, [Late July, 1836], ibid., 49.
34. Margaret Fuller, *The Letters of Margaret Fuller*, ed. Robert N. Hudspeth, 6 vols. (Ithaca, NY: Cornell University Press, 1983–1994), 2:87.
35. Lydia Jackson Emerson to Lucy Jackson Brown, fragment, 1838, in *Letters of Lidian Jackson Emerson*, 81.

36. Emerson, *Life of Lidian Jackson Emerson*, 77.
37. Ibid., 79.
38. Mary Moody Emerson to Elizabeth Hoar, April 8, 1841, in Emerson, *The Selected Letters of Mary Moody Emerson*, ed. Nancy Craig Simmons (Athens: University of Georgia Press, 1993), 427.
39. Emerson, *Life of Lidian Jackson Emerson*, 84.
40. Ibid., 83.
41. Ibid., 79.
42. Ibid., 130.
43. The "Transcendental Bible" is transcribed in Emerson, *Life of Lidian Jackson Emerson*, 81–83; see also Delores Bird Carpenter, "Lidian Emerson's 'Transcendental Bible,'" Studies in the American Renaissance (1980): 91–95.
44. Emerson, *Life of Lidian Jackson Emerson*, 83.
45. When exactly Lydia's "Transcendental Bible" was written is a matter of some speculation. Ellen's recollections are unclear, but she mentions that it was written while Lydia visited her brother Charles T. Jackson. This visit occurred in 1843.
46. Emerson, *Life of Lidian Jackson Emerson*, 88.
47. Lydia Jackson Emerson to Lucy Jackson Brown, February 4, 1842, in Letters of Lidian Jackson Emerson, 104.
48. Joel Myerson, "Margaret Fuller's 1842 Journal: At Concord with the Emersons," *Harvard Library Bulletin* 21, no. 3 (July 1973): 320–40, 322.
49. Sophia Peabody Hawthorne to Mrs. Eliza Palmer Peabody, September 1 and 2, 1842, Sophia Peabody Hawthorne collection of papers, New York Public Library.
50. Myerson, "Margaret Fuller's 1842 Journal," 339.
51. Ibid., 331.
52. Lydia Jackson Emerson to Ralph Waldo Emerson, January 10, 1843, in Letters of Lidian Jackson Emerson, 113–14.
53. Lydia Jackson Emerson to Ralph Waldo Emerson, January 30, 1843, ibid., 120.
54. Lydia Jackson Emerson to Ralph Waldo Emerson, February 17, 1843, ibid., 129.
55. Lydia Jackson Emerson to Ralph Waldo Emerson, January 30, 1843, ibid., 120.
56. Mary Moody Emerson to Lydia Jackson Emerson, March 3, 1844, in Letters of Mary Moody Emerson, 457.
57. Mary Moody Emerson to Lydia Jackson Emerson, January 28, 1848, ibid., 503.
58. Mary Moody Emerson to Lydia Jackson Emerson, June 26, 1850, ibid., 518.
59. Mary Moody Emerson to Lydia Jackson Emerson, July 26, 1850, ibid., 521.
60. Lydia Jackson Emerson to Mary Moody Emerson, August 11, 1850, in *Letters of Lidian Jackson Emerson*, 174.
61. Ibid., 247.
62. Ibid., xxv.
63. Ibid., 309.
64. Mrs. Nathan Brooks, quoted in Emerson, *Life of Lidian Jackson Emerson*, xiv.
65. Ibid., xxv.

9

THE POET, OR, FROM COMMONPLACING VERSE TO POETIC PRINT CULTURE

CHAPTER 30

METAMORPHOSIS AND TRANSCRIPTION

Emerson's "The Poet" and the Question of Form

MEREDITH L. MCGILL

Emerson's essay "The Poet" (1844) is a rare example of a text that is frequently taught, but seldom studied and widely misunderstood. A staple of the American literature survey, the essay is usually called on to bridge the gap between Emerson's Transcendental philosophy and Whitman's radical poetic practice. Emerson is praised as a theorist but criticized as a poet who could not live up to his own ambitions, a prophet who called for an original American poetry that he himself could not produce.[1]

Subtending this familiar tale about the disappointment of Emerson's verse is a hierarchical account of genre whereby the conventionality of Emerson's poetry serves only to emphasize the adventurousness of his prose. Dan Chaisson's 2015 *New Yorker* review of Albert J. von Frank's edition of the poetry shows this critical common sense in action. For Chaisson, the "listless," "mediocre" poems that often serve as epigraphs to Emerson's essays "make for a strangely rigged contest between turbocharged prose and the rickshaw verse it ostensibly reveres." Chaisson's solution, finally, is to dismiss Emerson's poetry altogether; through an act of generic transubstantiation all too common in Americanist literary criticism, he asserts that all that remains valuable in Emerson's writing can be found in the essays: "his quicksilver prose *was* poetry."[2]

There is a lot that is wrong with this story—not least, as Jay Grossman showed us years ago, that it glosses over significant differences between Emerson's and Whitman's poetics in the interest of telling a coherent story about theory and practice. This received wisdom about Emerson has been largely produced by what Grossman has identified as the composite figure "Emerson/Whitman," in which, like type to antitype, Emerson's poetic theory is embodied in and completed by Whitman's poetry.[3] Having Whitman too much in mind as the *telos* of Emerson's poetic theory, we both misread the theory and unnecessarily drive a wedge between Emerson's theory and his poetic practice—his writing of poetry, but also his mentoring of younger poets such as Henry David Thoreau,

Jones Very, and William Ellery Channing; his keeping of commonplace books; his use of poetry in his lectures, essays, and interlocking series of journals; his translations of verse; and his anthologizing of English poetry. A "Whitmanian" reading of Emerson's essay "The Poet" takes formal innovation—Whitman's breaking of the metrically regular line—as the Emersonian experiment Emerson himself was not bold enough to try. Such a reading focuses on Whitman's absorption of the voices of the American people and the American landscape into his capacious poem as a fulfillment of Emerson's desire for a poet who could "chant our own times and social circumstance" (*CW* 3:21) and notes Whitman's careful self-positioning as the representative poet whom Emerson describes.

But this composite figure Emerson/Whitman distorts Emerson's poetic theory in a number of ways. First, by emphasizing formal innovation we misread Emerson's antiformalist commitment to form. While Emerson is disdainful of adherence to convention, including poetic conventions, and abhors modes of repetition that calcify into unthinking routine, he considers the perception and articulation of forms to be the central duty of the poet. Emerson is not, as he is frequently represented to be, hemmed in by form. Indeed, one of the reasons he is attracted to poetry, in theory and in practice, is the opportunity it affords him to think in a sustained way about questions of form. The innovation he celebrates in poetry has less to do with novelty than with the poet's uncanny attunement to metamorphosis, the transformation of already existing forms. Reading "The Poet" through a Whitmanian lens not only causes us to focus too narrowly on the poetic line as stand-in for larger questions about form, it also makes Emerson's poetic theory seem more nationalistic than it actually is. In calling for a poet who could "chant our own times and social circumstance," Emerson is more interested in contemporaneousness—poetry written today or poetry of the past that retains present power—than he is in literary nationalism.

In this essay I will argue that we have misread Emerson's "The Poet" by yoking the essay to Whitman's verse and reading it as a founding text of modernist poetic experimentation. Emerson's assertion in this essay that "language is fossil poetry" is widely quoted, but taken as a whole, "The Poet" aligns poetry not with the language experiments that are so important for modernism but with a preternatural sensitivity to form; his is not an expressive theory but a mimetic one, rooted in Neoplatonism. Emerson wrote "The Poet" in the midst of a period of great productivity as a poet and as a reader, translator, editor, and prospective anthologist of poetry. Taking a broader view of Emerson's poetic practice into account can help us better understand his poetic theory and discern how his poetics and his practice richly informed one another.

Emersonian Commonplaces

Much of Emerson's thinking about poetry in the early 1840s was shaped by his friendship with Henry David Thoreau, whom Emerson regarded as a promising poet and whose literary career he worked hard to promote.[4] Poetry is very much on both Emerson's and

Thoreau's minds in these years. In November 1841, Emerson delivered the first version of a lecture that laid the groundwork for his essay "The Poet."[5] Emerson had been encouraging Thoreau's development as poet since the late 1830s, and over the objections of Margaret Fuller, sponsored the publication of a number of Thoreau's poems in *The Dial* (1840–44).[6] Both men were busy copying poems and fragments of poems into their journals in this period, and embarked on the anthology of English poetry either as a collaborative project or as a way for Emerson to help Thoreau launch his career as a man of letters. This plan was quickly derailed, however, most immediately by the double tragedy of the death of Thoreau's brother John and the death of Emerson's son Waldo in January of 1842, and, over time, by Thoreau's decision to transform himself from an aspiring poet and editor of poetry into the author of hybrid texts such as *A Week on the Concord and Merrimack Rivers* (1849) and *Walden* (1854).[7] I want to dwell on the complex conjuncture of Emerson's and Thoreau's interest in poetry around the commonplace book that formed the basis of the projected anthology—a text shared between them—to consider what the practice of commonplacing might tell us about Emerson's emerging theories of poetry.

Emerson's commonplace books—of quotations and passages for declamation, as well as a poetry notebook titled "OP" for "Other People," one called "Parnassus," and another called "Parnassus Scraps"—have largely been neglected by scholars despite the rich account they give us of the range of Emerson's reading and of what Emerson and Thoreau valued in the poetry they read. Despite the extraordinary editing projects that have brought us the sixteen-volume *Journals and Miscellaneous Notebooks* and the three-volume *Topical Notebooks*, Emerson's commonplace books of poetry have not been edited and made available to scholars. This exclusion from the corpus says more about what critics value in Emerson than about what Emerson himself valued. The logic of this exclusion is clear: this poetry is not original to Emerson.[8] Emerson's poetry commonplace books are comprised of handwritten versions of a wide range of already printed texts, combined with scraps of newspaper poetry and poems enclosed in letters, which are either pasted or tipped into the volume. Preparing a scholarly edition of these books can seem superfluous, particularly since Emerson published an authorized version of his commonplace books as *Parnassus* in 1874. And yet, *Parnassus* is a much belated version of the commonplace book that was actively shared between Emerson and Thoreau in 1841. Reading it as an 1870s text erases both Thoreau's collaboration in the work of commonplacing, and his importance to Emerson's thinking about the cultural place of poetry in the early 1840s.[9]

Commonplacing as a cultural practice can be traced to the classical conception of *topoi*, rhetorical strategies designed to ensure that an orator always had enough to say about his topic. According to Mary Thomas Crane, Renaissance humanists redefined the abstract Aristotelian "places" (which were categories of relationship such as opposition, adjacency, correlative ideas, the relation of part to whole) as textual fragments suitable for gathering, and promoted the keeping of commonplace books as the best way of understanding and putting to use the classical past.[10] Textualizing the commonplaces—transforming them from places in the mind to places in a text—gave them cultural specificity; these were no longer abstract and portable modes of relation, but rather a shorthand for the prevailing cultural code.

Commonplace books are a mode of cultural transmission that allows for the deracination and reframing of cultural authority. As Crane argues, in the Renaissance, they were a primary tool for making classical antiquity accord with modern consensus. Perhaps because commonplacing is a technology for time-travel, Crane's description of the hallmarks of Renaissance commonplacing rings remarkably true to nineteenth-century practice. Commonplaces tend to be already framed as quotable, ready to be plucked, favoring brevity, prescriptiveness, and a strong sense of closure. Although commonplacing is performed by individuals, it is anti-individualistic insofar as it highlights the means by which subjects, understood to be plural and iterable, are produced. Commonplace books provide a storehouse of texts through which experience can be managed and understood. Emerson famously referred to his own journals as a "Savings Bank" (*JMN* 4:250), depositing thoughts and excerpts from his reading so he could draw on them later for his lectures and essays.

Less clearly an instrument for moderns to grapple with the ancients (although still a site for the construction and contestation of authority), nineteenth-century commonplace books nevertheless display an achronicity that offers powerful resistance to the reading norms of historicist literary criticism. For example, Emerson's commonplace books of poetry employ multiple modes of organization, none of them chronological. In "OP," Emerson organizes poems loosely into clusters by author with blank pages between them, though here, and in "Parnassus," he also juxtaposes poems by different authors with anonymous poetry and with "authored" poetry copied over without attribution. Importantly, the blank pages allow for later insertions earlier in the volume, making it impossible to read the text within an evolutionary schema; it is impossible to know what Emerson's commonplace book looked like at any one time, what it included and what was added later. Like the published volume *Parnassus*, which is organized topically, with poems assembled under headings such as "Nature," "Human Life," "Intellectual," "Contemplative," "Heroic," and so forth (followed by an author index), commonplace books eschew literary history understood as chronology. Received literary hierarchies are also put into question in the democratizing space of the page. While Emerson most often copies over complete poems, he doesn't respect the formal boundaries of the poems he copies, creating, for example a much-truncated version of "Tintern Abbey" that makes its way into the published edition.[11]

None of the criteria Foucault borrows from St. Jerome to describe the conditions of modern authorship pertain here: there is neither a constant level of value, nor conceptual/theoretical coherence (the topical organization and headings are supplied later); Emerson's commonplace books are marked by stylistic diversity and temporal incoherence, both in textual terms, and in terms of the life of the writer.[12] Just how thoroughly these books resist our conventional ways of understanding literature became apparent to me when I ran across a series of excerpts in "Parnassus" that reflected on death and loss: first, a passage from Shakespeare's *Macbeth* (1623), describing how death has purchased an enviable immunity for Duncan; then an excerpt from Coleridge's translation of Schiller's *Wallenstein* (1800) beginning, "He is gone, he is dust—;" followed (on the next page) by an anonymous epigram: "Whatever fortunes wait my future toils / The *beautiful* is vanished—and returns not."[13] I found myself fighting off the conviction that Emerson had copied these poems in the months following his son Waldo's death, struggling against my desire for the couplet to be Emerson's own (it is Coleridge's Schiller, an unidentified excerpt from *Wallenstein*). But no such anchoring subjects or events are available to the readers of a commonplace book.[14]

Many of Emerson's commonplace book entries thematize their own fragmentary status. The selection Thoreau copied begins with a meditation by Sir Walter Scott on the piecemeal persistence of song: "Fragments of the lofty strain / Float down the tide of years / As buoyant on the stormy main / A parted wreck appears," and includes a meditation on the creepily enduring power of a generic and deracinated "verse" (an unmarked excerpt from Wordsworth's "Upon the Same Occasion" [1819]), an extract on extracts from Byron's *Don Juan* (1824), a selection on the recycling of clothing by Herrick, and so forth.[15] The detachment of these poems and fragments from their contexts makes them more noticeably self-reflexive; they are granted the authority they wield by the act of copying itself. Importantly, these instances of poetic reproduction are both highly personal and non-proprietary, themselves open for copying. While an entry might honor the genius of a particular poet—not everything, after all, gets copied into a commonplace book—commonplacing is an appropriative practice that acknowledges that poetry lives in a culture only by virtue of its repetition.

Emerson's interest in the contemporaneity of poetry helps to reconcile his poetic theory with the practice of commonplacing. With Whitman's example and Emerson's strictures against copying in "Self-Reliance" in mind, we have misread "The Poet" as an expressive theory and underplayed the importance of mimesis to his theory and practice of poetry. Americanists could all probably cite chapter and verse from "Self-Reliance" (1841): "Insist on yourself; never imitate. Your own gift you can present every moment with the cumulative force of a whole life's cultivation; but of the adopted talent of another, you have only an extemporaneous, half-possession" (*CW* 2:47). But an "extemporaneous half-possession" is precisely what Emerson values in poetry. Emerson celebrates both the extratemporal experience of lyric transport, embodied in the timelessness of his commonplace miscellanies, and the half-possession which is characteristic of the writing and the reading of poetry—the externality of poetic inspiration to the poet himself, who experiences it as transient, nonproprietary, but also the multiple acts of appropriation that are necessary for poetry to retain its power.

Emerson's poetic theory may accurately be described as an expressive theory so long as we acknowledge that he understood both reading and listening as fundamentally expressive acts. Take, for example, his definition of "expression" from the 1841 lecture "The Poet." Emerson begins with a sense of urgency retained in the published essay: "Expression;—all we do, all we say, all we see, is that, or for that." And yet he turns for his example to an audience-eye view of Niccolò Paganini's and Marie Taglioni's artistry: "What is the origin of our enjoyment but an apprisal of our own power;—that the range of human articulation reaches higher and lower than we had yet found, and every hearer goes away to copy or appropriate to himself as far as he can the new art?" (*EL* 3:350). He continues with an account of performance as a kind of surrogacy, explaining the lure of Taglioni: "But what is her charm for the spectators other than this, that she dances for them, or they dance in her feet, not being … able to dance themselves? We must be expressed" (*EL* 3:351).

If in his lecture Emerson defines the consumption of art as a mode of expression, in his essay "The Poet" he describes *poesis* as transcription rather than an independent act of making:

> The sea, the mountain ridge, Niagara, and every flower-bed, pre-exist, or super-exist in pre-cantations which sail like odors in the air, and when any man goes by with an ear sufficiently fine, he overhears them, and endeavors to write down the notes without diluting or depraving them. (*CW* 3:15)

The transformation of nature into poetry is only part of a larger process of metamorphosis to which the poet is uniquely attuned. In one of the most memorable figures of the essay, Emerson argues that poetry lies embedded in ordinary language and in ordinary labor: "Being used as a type, a second wonderful value appears in the object, far better than its old value, as the carpenter's stretched cord, if you hold your ear close enough, is musical in the breeze" (*CW* 3:8). Invoking the "carpenter's stretched cord" as a kind of working man's Aeolian harp, Emerson suggests that we need only sharpen our attention to transform routine acts of measuring into musical measures ("if you hold your ear close enough"). But he also implies that poetry exists in the world independently of our perception; this music is produced regardless of our willingness or ability to hear it. For Emerson, the poet's "better perception" enables him to stand "one step nearer to things" than the ordinary man: the poet "sees the flowing or metamorphosis; perceives that thought is multi-form; that within the form of every creature is a force impelling it to ascend into a higher form; and, following with his eyes the life, [the poet] uses the forms which express that life, and so his speech flows with the flowing of nature" (*CW* 3:12). Emerson here calls not for a revolt against form but for a higher consciousness of it, with poetry aspiring to the "self-regulated motion" (*CW* 3:13) of the natural world.

What I want to emphasize is how well and how easily Emerson's poetic theory accommodates a copybook understanding of poetic history. In "The Poet," Emerson describes poetic transmission as a kind of transplantation that allows for the accidental survival of some poems and not others; the poet is compared to "a poor fungus" that shakes down "countless spores, any one of which, being preserved, transmits new billions of spores" (*CW* 3:13). In his famous account of language as the "archives of history," Emerson acknowledges that language is also "a sort of tomb of the Muses"; the accrual of tropes through history shakes them free of their "poetic origin" (*CW* 3:13). But it is the partial and fragmentary nature of poetic inheritance that allows poems and poets to achieve a kind of contemporaneity, to "chant our own times and social circumstance" despite their importation from ancient history and from foreign places. In another striking figure, Emerson describes the "rich poets" such as Homer, Chaucer,

Shakespeare, and Raphael as mirrors "carried through the street, ready to render an image of every created thing" (*CW* 3:23). Mimesis, conventionally aligned with the realist novel, is here produced by the fragmentary, mobile nature of poetic tradition; it is extemporaneity that allows for contemporaneity.

Stone by Stone

I have argued that in order to understand the high value Emerson placed on poetry—his lifelong investment in the imitation, translation, editing, and commonplacing of poems, his drafting, redrafting, and publishing of his own verse in periodicals and books, and his painstaking revision of his published and unpublished poetry—we need to look beyond his empowering of Whitman's bold break with genteel poetic norms and the legacy of what will come to be known as "free verse." Using Whitman's experiments with the poetic line as a gauge by which Emerson's poems invariably fall short keeps us from seeing Emerson's own complex wrestling with poetic form, which at times serves as an apt vehicle for conveying intimate resonances between man's consciousness and the natural world, and at others, as a bracing reminder of the impossibility of realizing his poetic ideals. Moreover, regarding Emerson's poetry through the lens of modernist dissatisfaction keeps us from perceiving how thoroughly his poems are *themselves* infused with disappointment, frequently thematizing the inevitable failure of art to live up to his aims for it.

It is easiest to see Emerson's exploration of the capacities and limits of poetic form in poems that explicitly reflect on these questions, such as his early *ars poetica* "The Snow-Storm" (*Dial* 1 [January 1841]: 339). In this poem, the "north wind" that drives the storm takes on many of the characteristics of Emerson's ideal poet: it violently interrupts the workaday world, defeating the human drive for productivity; it displays superhuman power derived from mysterious, undiscernible origins; and it demonstrates a wild, playful, and disruptive energy, overturning human priorities and hierarchies:

> Come see the north wind's masonry.
> Out of an unseen quarry evermore
> Furnished with tile, the fierce artificer
> Curves his white bastions with projected roof
> Round every windward stake, or tree, or door.
> Speeding, the myriad-handed, his wild work
> So fanciful, so savage, nought cares he
> For number or proportion. Mockingly,
> On coop or kennel he hangs Parian wreaths ...
> (*CW* 9:90)

Emerson initially represents the storm's artwork as a secondary effect; the north wind depends on the built environment of the farm for its artistic flourishes, dignifying outbuildings such as the coop and kennel with ornaments reminiscent of the finest sculptural marble. But this "fanciful" creative force is also a "savage" one, disregarding human needs as it transforms the landscape.

Emerson's play with meter in these lines reinforces the alien power of the storm, tacitly contrasting it with the tameness of his own poetic efforts. For instance, line 15 interrupts the smooth iambic pentameter of the previous line with the trochaic foot "speeding," then has trouble reestablishing a regular iambic rhythm, concluding with a set of evenly stressed syllables. Line 16 is similarly hard to scan, toying with triple meter and concluding, in parallel with the previous line, with the defiant "nought cares he." The contrast between the storm's indifference to human order and Emerson's deference gets played out metrically in line 17, which returns to regular iambic pentameter, forcing the poem's own concern with "number and proportion" conspicuously into view as an object of critique. This is a metrically regular poem that mocks its own rule-following.

Like the ideal poet, the north wind can make extraordinary beauty suddenly visible in an ordinary landscape as the snowdrifts reveal invisible correspondences: "A swan-like form invests the hidden thorn" (*CW* 9:90). These insights are, however, as fleeting as they are compelling. The poem concludes with the sudden departure of the storm, leaving "astonished Art / To mimic in slow structures, stone by stone, / Built in an age, the mad wind's night-work, / The frolic architecture of the snow" (*CW* 9:90; ll. 27–28). The secondary work of the storm is given primacy by the poem's end; it is the human artist who is forced to imitate nature's "frolic architecture," not in a comparable fit of wild inspiration but painstakingly slowly, "stone by stone."

"The Snow-Storm" gives an account of *poesis* as metamorphosis and transcription, one that is very much in line with Emerson's thinking in "The Poet" and with his broader poetic practice. The north wind produces flashes of insight for the spectator, new perceptions of the intimate relations between utility and ornament, beauty and danger, kennels and statues, swans and thorns. But these insights are, like the storm itself, transient and nonproprietary. Aesthetic experience in the poem is produced by an estrangement from the ordinary and the dramatic transformation of the familiar landscape, a figurative correlative for the logic of deracination and reframing that underwrites the work of commonplacing. Finally, in "The Snow-Storm," imitation is the engine of art-making, both for the north wind, which models creativity as a kind of transformative secondarity, and for the human spectators, left to approximate "the mad wind's night-work" with a deliberateness that is hopelessly inadequate to its object. John Greenleaf Whittier quoted the first stanza of "The Snow-Storm" as an epigraph to his popular narrative poem, "Snow-Bound: A Winter Idyl" (1866), giving Emerson's poem a second life by aligning it with postwar nostalgia for an idealized, rural New England. But Emerson's poem moves quickly past the scene where Whittier's poem will spend most of its time—with the household huddled around the "radiant fireplace." Emerson is less interested in the domestic scene (which he enigmatically describes as a "tumultuous privacy") than he is in the gulf between nature's transformative power and the ponderousness of human attempts to keep pace with it. The poem leaves us with an epitaphic moment reminiscent of John Milton's sonnet "On Shakespeare," which may well have been a source for a number of Emerson's figures and phrases.[16] In "The Snow-Storm," the beholders of the storm's remains are abstracted and petrified into "astonished Art," coming to resemble the very stones they will use to build their replica of and monument to the creative force of the natural world.

An Architecture of Its Own

Emerson's "The Poet" begins with a complaint about criticism, arguing that the practice of aesthetic judgement has been reduced to the mere application of "rules and particulars" to works of art: "Men seem to have lost the perception of the instant dependence of form upon soul. There is no doctrine of forms in our philosophy" (*CW* 3:3). If Anglo-American criticism disappointed him with its vulgar empiricism, the Platonic tradition on which he drew for many of his ideas about art didn't give him much guidance in thinking about poetic form. Platonic forms take discernible shape—enough to be the source of imperfect copies and provocative resemblances—but they are necessarily immaterial, beyond the limits of the sensible.[17] While references to the fecundity and variety of natural forms abound in Emerson's poetry and prose, there is no doctrine of forms in Emerson's poetics, either.[18]

Emerson's most famous critical pronouncement from "The Poet" insists on the priority of the ideal to the material, of thought to poetic form, raising the stakes for both poets and critics: "For it is not metres, but a metre-making argument, that makes a poem;—a thought so passionate and alive that, like the spirit of a plant or animal, it has an architecture of its own, and adorns nature with a new thing" (*CW* 3:6). That Emerson strives to produce poems with highly specific, individualized structures and styles has proved difficult for twentieth- and twenty-first-century readers to perceive, despite his assertion that the poet's imagination is an active, creative force that joins in the natural proliferation of diverse forms. The problem is not that his poetry is too derivative but rather that it is not derivative enough easily to be placed into recognizable lineages and traditions.

The best readers of Emerson's verse have long remarked on its astonishing formal variability, whether understood in terms of genre, theme, line, rhyme, or tone. For example, Lawrence Buell long ago called attention to Emerson's interest in "prosodic experiment: the roughening and breaking and shifting of meters."[19] Barbara Packer has noted Emerson's innovation at the level of line and stanza, calling attention to how often his verse paragraphs contain "lines of varying lengths," employing rhyme, but in a disarmingly provisional manner: "the rhyme scheme that obtains in one verse-paragraph may be discarded in the next."[20] Paul Kane offers a taxonomy for understanding "the breadth of his poetry in the formal terms of genre," dividing Emerson's poems into twelve general classes: philosophic, political and public poems; prophetic or bardic poems; mediative poems; elegiac poems; didactic poems; rambles; gnomic poems; dramatic monologues; love poems; translations; and squibs.[21] Saundra Morris emphasizes the "tonal variety and instability" of the corpus, noting how often the poems incorporate dialogue and multiple voices that they fail to situate or reconcile.[22]

Given the formal experimentation and remarkable variability of Emerson's poetic corpus, it is striking that most anthologies and criticism of Emerson's poetry, including this essay, gravitate towards the poems written in blank verse.[23] What would it take for critics to tackle the full range of Emerson's poetry with the kind of seriousness the essays have long drawn? To begin with, the failure of Emerson's metamorphic verse to live up to our expectations should cause us to question the expectations we bring to the study of nineteenth-century American poetry. Why is it that Emerson's deliberately unsystematic method is acceptable—even admirable—in his prose but can only be seen as a liability in his poems? We should allow the often rebarbative strangeness of Emerson's poetry to disarm our assumptions about what could be accomplished with the tools of metrically regular verse, asking whether and how Emerson's shifting rhyme schemes and sometimes jolting, irregular lines align with, strain against, complicate, or defeat the poem's and the poet's aims. Like "The Snow-Storm," many of Emerson's poems are tantalizingly self-reflexive, including meditations on the poetic line, on rhyme and rhythm, on figure and form. Rather than elaborating an Emersonian poetics that is realized elsewhere, and by others, we need to tease out the poetics that is carried out in his poems, often in frustrating and inconclusive fashion.

Finally, we need to consider whether Emerson's poetic idiosyncrasies are deliberate forms of resistance to the emergent norms of romantic poetry, including that of the lyric speaker. One of the most challenging aspects of Emerson's verse is the refusal of many of his poems to index an autobiographical persona like the one that launches Whitman's "Song of Myself," one that we have retrospectively come to expect as the source and value of Romantic-era poetry. M. H. Abrams's summary of the features of the genre he calls the "greater romantic lyric" illustrates in brief how far from this norm most of Emerson's poetry wanders. For Abrams, the greatest Romantic-era English poems, including Samuel Taylor Coleridge's "Frost at Midnight," William Wordsworth's "Tintern Abbey," and Percy Bysshe Shelley's "Ode to the West Wind" "present a determinate speaker in a particularized and usually localized outdoor setting, whom we overhear as he carries on, in a fluent vernacular, which rises easily to a more formal speech, a sustained colloquy, sometimes with himself or with the outer scene but more frequently with a silent human auditor, present or absent."[24]

By contrast, many of Emerson's poems offer us not a determinate speaker but an abstract and often unlocatable one. Poems such as "Xenophanes" or "Pan" are not spoken by their title characters, rather, they work through an idea associated with these philosophic or mythological figures. Like "The Sphinx," which, as Saundra Morris and others note, stands guard over Emerson's first volume of verse, warning readers of the difficulty ahead, the point of view from which Emerson's poems emerge is often deliberately inaccessible, conspicuously ancient, obscure, or foreign. Speech in these poems frequently shifts along with metrical patterns and rhyme schemes; it remains difficult to pin down. Poems such as "Alphonso of Castile" and "Mithridates" begin with first-person declarations made by obscure historical figures, offering their savage critiques or runic wisdom at an estranging distance from the contemporary world, to which they both do and don't refer. Even the pairs of "Merlin" and "Woodnotes" poems, which come closest to Abrams' norm, barely fit the pattern. "Merlin" 1 and 2 are elaborately metapoetic and hover indeterminately between the first and third person (whose poetics are these?), while "Woodnotes 2" begins with a warning against identifying the pine tree's speech with the poet's own: "So waved the pine-tree through my thought, / And fanned the dreams it never brought" (103). Tellingly, in his *Selections from Ralph Waldo Emerson* (1957), Stephen E. Whicher trims "Woodnotes 1," beginning his excerpt with the seemingly autobiographical second section ("And such I knew, a forest seer"), overriding the opening lines of the poem that insist on the temporal dislocation of the bard, "Born out of time" (*CW* 9:93).

In excerpting the poem so as to create a lyric speaker who just might be Emerson himself, Whicher follows the example of Thoreau, who includes selections from "Woodnotes 1" as an epigraph to the "Thursday" chapter of his *A Week on the Concord and Merrimack Rivers* (1849) so as to suggest that he himself is Emerson's "forest seer." Perhaps, rather than apologizing for Emerson's verse or normalizing it, creating a lyric speaker who provides a bridge to Emerson's biography, we should follow the tracks and traces of our own critical acts of commonplacing, measuring the distance between the purposes to which we have put Emerson's verse and the creative acts of time travel implicit in a poetry that addressed the exigency of the present moment through complex acts of decontextualization and readdress.

Notes

1. This way of understanding Emerson's work has a long history, stretching back at least as far as F. O. Matthiessen's *American Renaissance: Art and Expression in the Age of Emerson and Whitman* (New York: Oxford University Press, 1941). In an insightful overview of Emerson's poetry, Matthiessen cites a passage from Emerson's essay on "Europe and European Books" describing the poet as an "electric rod" mediating the real and the ideal. But he can't keep himself from offering a damning summary judgment: "There could hardly be a more exact description of what Emerson's poetry was not than this, which was of course written by himself" (54).
2. "Ecstasy of Influence: Ralph Waldo Emerson's American Poetry," *The New Yorker*, September 7, 2015.
3. See Jay Grossman, *Reconstituting the American Renaissance: Emerson, Whitman, and the Politics of Representation* (Durham, NC: Duke University Press, 2003), especially 75–115. A comparable theory/practice distinction structures many accounts of Emerson's relationship with Thoreau, where Thoreau's *Walden* is taken as the practical realization of Emerson's ideas about self-reliance.
4. Most of this section is taken from my essay "Common Places: Poetry, Illocality, and Temporal Dislocation in Thoreau's *A Week on the Concord and Merrimack Rivers*," *American Literary History* 19, no. 2 (2007): 357–74.
5. Emerson delivered a lecture called "Nature and Powers of the Poet" at the Concord Lyceum on November 3, 1841 and repeated it (as part of a lecture series) in Boston on December 16, 1841, in Providence on February 12, 1842, and in New York on March 5, 1842, where, critics speculate, Whitman may have heard it. A few passages from this early lecture appear in the

published essay "The Poet" (*Essays: Second Series* [1844]); portions are also siphoned off into the late essay "Poetry and Imagination" (*Letters and Social Aims* [1875]). The manuscript of "Lecture 3: The Poet" has been reprinted in *EL* 3:347–65.

6. Fuller published four of Thoreau's poems—"Sympathy," "Nature Doth Have Her Dawn Each Day," "*Sic vita*," and "Let Such Pure Hate Still Underprop"—in her two years as editor of *The Dial*. Emerson, by contrast, published eight of Thoreau's poems in the October 1842 issue, his second after taking over editorship of the journal. For the history of Thoreau's submissions to *The Dial*, see Walter Harding, *The Days of Henry Thoreau: A Biography* (Princeton, NJ: Princeton University Press, 1982), 113–20.

7. For Emerson's and Thoreau's projected anthology, and Emerson's sponsorship of Thoreau's career as a poet, see Robert Sattelmeyer, "Thoreau's Projected Work on the English Poets," *Studies in the American Renaissance* (1980): 239–57 and "'When He Became My Enemy': Emerson and Thoreau, 1848–9," *New England Quarterly* 62, no. 2 (June 1989): 187–204.

8. Phyllis Cole reviews the editorial principles that have guided the production of Emerson's standard works and argues for a "more interactive, socialized construction of authorship" (268) in "The New Emerson Canon," *Resources for American Literary Study* 37 (2014): 259–71. Christopher Hanlon takes up this challenge in his reading of the collaboratively produced Natural History of Intellect (1871) in *Emerson's Memory Loss: Originality, Communality, and the Late Style* (New York: Oxford University Press, 2018).

9. For a detailed account of Emerson's collaboration with his daughter Edith Emerson Forbes in the publication of the 1874 *Parnassus*, and the importance of this volume to Emerson's late essays "Poetry and Imagination" and "Quotation and Originality" (*Letters and Social Aims*, 1876), see Ronald A. Bosco, "'Poetry for the World of Readers' and 'Poetry for Bards Proper': Poetic Theory and Textual Integrity in Emerson's *Parnassus*," *Studies in the American Renaissance* (1989): 257–312.

10. Mary Thomas Crane, *Framing Authority: Sayings, Self, and Society in Sixteenth Century England* (Princeton, NJ: Princeton University Press, 1993). For the historical development and architectonics of Early Modern commonplace books, see also Ann Moss, *Printed Commonplace-Books and the Structuring of Renaissance Thought* (New York: Oxford University Press, 1996). For some splendid examples of commonplace books throughout history, see the exhibition catalog edited by Earl Havens, *Commonplace Books: A History of Manuscripts and Printed Books from Antiquity to the Twentieth Century* (New Haven, CT: Beinecke Rare Book and Manuscript Library, 2001).

11. See Ralph Waldo Emerson, *Parnassus* (Boston: James Osgood, 1875), 29. Emerson begins his excerpt from the poem with the didactic turn toward the end, "I have learned / To look on Nature, not as in the hour / Of thoughtless youth" (ll. 88–89), but cuts the passage off before Wordsworth completes his string of metaphors, severing the phrase "the anchor of my purest thoughts" (l. 109) from what follows: "the nurse / The guide, the guardian of my heart, and soul / Of all my moral being (ll. 109–111). Numerous other poems make their way into print in conspicuously truncated form. For instance, Shelley's "To a Sky-Lark" consists of the eighth stanza only (36), while his "The Cloud" becomes a three-stanza poem, beginning with the second stanza, skipping to the fourth and then concluding with the final stanza (46–47). Tennyson's "Ode to Memory" is reprinted as "Memory" and is reduced to ten lines taken from the third stanza (92), while William Cullen Bryant's "Thanatopsis"—marked as an excerpt in this case by the insertion of ellipses—begins with line 17, after the invocation of the "still voice" (168).

12. For Foucault's elaboration of these criteria, see "What is an Author?" in *The Foucault Reader*, ed. Paul Rabinow (New York: Pantheon Books, 1984), 101–20.
13. Ralph Waldo Emerson, "Parnassus," Houghton MS Am 1280H, 36–37, Houghton Library, Harvard University.
14. It is this illocality—the creation of a common place that is nowhere in particular—that, I argue, proves most seductive to Thoreau as he wrestles with the relation of locality to textual authority in *A Week*. See McGill, "Common Places."
15. For a facsimile text of Thoreau's transcription of entries from Emerson's commonplace books, see Henry David Thoreau, *Thoreau's Literary Notebook in the Library of Congress*, ed. Kenneth Walker Cameron (Hartford: Transcendental Books, 1964), 53–76. For a transcription of these entries, see Kenneth Walker Cameron, *Transcendental Apprenticeship* (Hartford: Transcendental Books, 1976), 209–12.
16. Milton describes a hypothetical monument to Shakespeare as "the labor of an age," while in "The Snow-Storm," any human imitation of the "north-wind's masonry" would similarly be "built in an age." Milton asserts that readers "in our wonder and astonishment" have erected a "live-long monument" to Shakespeare's genius. While the work of Emerson's storm-poet is conspicuously ephemeral, his poem ends on a deflationary note that echoes Milton's struggle with Shakespeare's influence: "our fancy of itself bereaving / Dost make us marble with too much conceiving." For Paul de Man's influential reading of the work of prosopopoeia in Milton's poem, see "Autobiography as De-Facement," *Modern Language Notes* 94, no. 5 (1979): 919–30.
17. For a helpful exploration of the "paradox of Forms" (76) in Platonic and Neoplatonic thought, see James I. Porter, "Plato and the Platonic Tradition: The Image Beyond the Image," *Yearbook of Comparative Literature* 56, no. 1 (2010): 75–103.
18. Lawrence Buell comes closest to identifying what an Emersonian doctrine of forms would look like, emphasizing the importance of "microcosmic form" in his essays; see Buell, "Emerson and the Idea of Microcosmic Form," in *Literary Transcendentalism: Style and Vision in the American Renaissance* (Ithaca, NY: Cornell University Press, 1973), 145–65. Vivian Hopkins explores Emerson's thinking about organic form in *Spires of Form: A Study of Emerson's Aesthetic Theory* (Cambridge: Harvard University Press, 1951), 64–146.
19. Lawrence Buell, "The American Transcendentalist Poets," in *The Columbia History of American Poetry*, ed. Jay Parini (New York: Columbia University Press, 1993), 97–119: 117.
20. Barbara Packer, "American Verse Traditions, 1800–1855," in *The Cambridge History of American Literature*, vol. 4, ed. Sacvan Bercovitch (New York: Cambridge University Press, 2004), 11–144: 99.
21. Paul Kane, "Ralph Waldo Emerson," in *Encyclopedia of American Poetry: The Nineteenth Century*, ed. Eric L. Haralson (Chicago: Fitzroy Dearborn Publishers, 1998), 141–50: 146.
22. Saundra Morris, "'Metre-Making' Arguments: Emerson's Poems," in *The Cambridge Companion to Ralph Waldo Emerson*, ed. Joel Porte and Saundra Morris (New York: Cambridge University Press, 1999), 218–42: 224.
23. Emerson's blank verse poems include "The Rhodora," "The Snow-Storm," "Pan," "Xenophanes," and the first part of "Hamatreya"; these are among the most frequently anthologized of his poems.
24. M. H. Abrams, "Structure and Style in the Greater Romantic Lyric," in *The Correspondent Breeze: Essays on English Romanticism* (New York: Norton, 1984), 76–108: 76–77.

CHAPTER 31

EMERSON'S MUSES, POETS, AND PERSONS FROM *THE DIAL* TO *THE ATLANTIC MONTHLY*

ELIZA RICHARDS

SCHOLARSHIP from the last three decades reclaiming—and critiquing—Emerson as a writer engaged with social reform rarely addresses his poetry, even though many of the poems treated political issues (both in explicit and encoded ways), evoked a powerful public response, impacted understandings of historical events, and influenced later writers.[1] On the other hand, studies of Emerson's poetry have long foregrounded his formal, philosophical, and spiritual commitments without considering historical contexts that include slavery and the US Civil War. Saundra Morris, the scholar who has written most extensively on Emerson's poetry in recent years, has noted the persistent tendency to cordon off the poetry from the prose and has stressed the importance of integrating the poetry into the developing critical narrative of Emerson's increasingly explicit political engagements; her essays advocating such an approach merit attention.[2] In short, studies of Emerson's political engagements slight the poetry, while studies of the poetry slight Emerson's political engagements. This is more an indication of the literary-critical field than of a generic split in Emerson's writings.

This essay tracks a transformation in Emerson's poetry and poetics from his publications in *The Dial* in the early 1840s to his publications in *The Atlantic Monthly* between 1857 and 1867. I argue that Emerson increasingly imagined poetry as a socially engaged form, distinct from prose, with its own affordances. Poetry has long been understood to hold special visionary power. For Emerson, compressed, aphoristic riddles and paradoxes encrypted within lineated structures of patterned sonic repetition invoke a muse—defined variously but always encompassing a higher moral, spiritual power—that is inaccessible in prose. Emerson frankly states in his notebooks and elsewhere that he is insufficiently gifted as a poet to gain that access, but he nevertheless, for the public good, dramatizes muses speaking. In the *Dial* years, the poems repeatedly stage a drama between an ineffective poet and the elusive power of universal spirit or soul that the true poet could harness. In the *Atlantic Monthly* poems, published across the US Civil War, Emerson leaves behind this agonistic drama of the poet trying and failing to express divine knowledge. Influenced by abolitionism and intensifying sectional conflict, he turns more directly to intervening in current events with the power of moral suasion. In these later poems he stages muses speaking without a poet's company; or, alternatively, accepting the poet's limitations, Emerson speaks as "himself," a limited poet, who is explicitly not a "true" poet.

Toward the end of his essay "The Poet" (1844), Emerson admits that the figure he has been celebrating does not currently exist: "I look in vain for the poet whom I describe" (*CW* 3:21). Sharon Cameron has centered this problem in her critique of what she has influentially identified as Emerson's "impersonality":

> While the poet is not visible, the one who calls him into being is precisely visible as a presence whose rhetoric fails ... For, on the one hand, the reference for the speaking voice is the unemancipated person who anticipates the poet. But on the other, the poet being evoked also seems referenced to the subject position we call "Emerson." The one who calls for the poet, who calls the poet forth, is the one who knows enough of bondage not to be wholly or even mainly defined by freedom. Thus the essay charts two positions and has a double voice.[3]

Emerson's failure to summon the impersonal authority that draws on "a power that transcends all limits of privacy," for Cameron, lies paradoxically in the writer's inability to convincingly summon the sense of his own person.[4] The essay's "double voice" demonstrates that Emerson cannot or will not inhabit the personality that would enable him to enact the "task of ravishment" he sets for himself and his readers, whereby a person's boundaries are shattered by impersonal, emancipating forces.[5]

How Emerson's personal "vacancy" appears in his poems is left to speculations, for like most recent critics Cameron does not mention Emerson's poetry, even while discussing his conception of "The Poet."[6] The most sustained studies of Emerson's poetry—by Hyatt Waggoner and R. A. Yoder, for example—are more than four decades old. A more recent turn to what has been called "historical poetics" and an increase in critical attention to nineteenth-century US poetry has not impacted a widespread tendency to ignore his poetry, despite its powerful influence on American literary history and its prominent place in nineteenth-century US culture. Perhaps the most important contribution to the study of Emerson's poetry in the past two decades is the publication of *Poems: A Variorum Edition*, edited by Albert J. von Frank and Thomas Wortham. In the "Historical Introduction," von Frank takes issue with formulations like Cameron's, insisting that "it is a mistake ... to be scandalized by the gap between theory and practice, promise and performance" because poetry for Emerson is "necessarily a useful betrayal of the ideal"; most importantly, Emerson found a way "of representing the importance of the process and what was at stake in its conduct (*CW* 9:xix, xvii, xxx).

I suggest that "The Poet" is not so much double-voiced as voiced by an orator who seeks to bring "the poet" into being through a process of presenting to the reader contradictory formulations that build in power and surge to a commanding exhortation at the end of the essay:

> Doubt not, O poet, but persist. Say, "It is in me, and shall out." Stand there, balked and dumb, stuttering and stammering, hissed and hooted, stand and strive, until, at last, rage draw out of thee that *dream*-power which every night shows thee is thine own. (CW 3:23)

The non-existent poet Emerson apostrophizes does not to me "[seem] referenced to the subject position we call Emerson." Emerson addresses any reader, including himself; he taunts readers so that "rage" will finally fuel an outpouring of pure poetry wherever it might erupt. If we all only "persist" strenuously enough, for long enough, someone will express the "*dream*-power" that we experience "every night" while we are sleeping but as yet cannot access while awake. Emerson is included in that "we" who must accept as an article of faith that such power can be drawn out of a present-day person in "America" as it has in other times and places. The place of personhood in Emerson, in other words, is occupied by the reader. The reader's person may be implied, but Emerson's pestering harassment of this person is certainly perceptible: his goading may annoy us sufficiently that we wish that someone among us would stop "stuttering and stammering" and start speaking in dream language. This proposition counters Cameron's claim that there is no person at the center of Emerson's impersonality: the person is the reader, whose conversion is Emerson's—the insufficient poet's—vocation. Often charged with having an emotional vacuum at its core, Emerson's poetic emptiness generates a place for the reader's emotional response.

Like Whitman, who may have learned to harry the reader from such addresses, Emerson exhorts anyone who might be reading or listening to become not "barrows" or "pans" but "children of the fire," and speak as the muse (*CW* 3:xx). For ideally the muse would not inspire the poet: the muse would be the poet, and the poet would be the muse. "*Dream*-power" is shared power, channeled through individuals, but not itself individual. If the poet could be the muse, "he" (for Emerson it is a "he") could in turn directly inspire readers, cutting out the stammering, stuttering middleman of the poet, as we understand that romantic, lyric figure, altogether. Taking seriously Emerson's attempts to invoke unmediated poetic utterance can help us understand his poetry not as a failed version of what he achieves in his essays, nor as a collection of abstract, ineffective moral proclamations, nor as a jumble of semi-intelligible aphorisms, but as a sustained effort to figure a muse—the true poet *is* the muse—who has no need for a garden-variety poet like Emerson or anyone else he has "looked in vain for" in "America," where "we have yet had no genius." Experimenting with these figurations repeatedly in his poems, from those published in *The Dial* from 1840 to 1844 and collected in *Poems* (1846–47), to those published in *The Atlantic Monthly* from 1857 to 1867 and collected in *May-Day and Other Pieces* (1867), Emerson foregrounds muses as superior, prophetic beings in conflict with the inadequate poet that they bypass, displace, criticize, undermine, or dismiss. This dynamic, even antagonistic relation between muse and poet distinguishes Emerson's poetry from many of his contemporaries and underpins an oracular, "orphic tradition" of American poetry.[7]

In his historical introduction to *Poems*, von Frank notes a curious fact:

> During the *Dial* years (1840–1844) Emerson published two dozen poems in that journal, then not a single one in any magazine until 1857, when *The Atlantic Monthly* was founded. This thirteen-year interval included, of course, the publication of *Poems* in 1846 first in London then a fortnight later in Boston, but the fact is that Emerson would not submit his poems to any journal not closely identified with the Transcendentalists. If between 1844 and 1857 no such journal existed, he was perfectly content to let his poems quietly accumulate in the notebooks. (CW 9:lxii)

The thirteen years of nonpublication is curious, as is Emerson's careful selection of two specific outlets for his poetry, but his publishing decisions suggest more than a preference for Transcendentalist affiliation, especially with regards to *The Atlantic Monthly*. Indeed, the two magazines are vastly different. *The Dial* was a specialized journal, circulating among a small group of like-minded intellectuals, with around three hundred subscribers at its peak, Emerson serving as the editor from 1842 to 1844.[8] Introducing the first issue in July 1840, Emerson specified its lofty goals of elevating readers by leading them away from "desultory" human affairs toward communion with the natural world. The editors' "wish" was:

> ... to give expression to that spirit which lifts men to a higher platform, restores to them the religious sentiment, brings them worthy aims and pure pleasures, purges the inward eye, makes life less desultory, and, through raising man to the level of nature, takes away its melancholy from the landscape, and reconciles the practical with the speculative powers.[9]

The practice of moral strengthening relies upon turning away from politics, commerce, and other daily involvement in "life." Evoking the image of the sundial as a kind of moral compass, Emerson hails the journal's "cheerful rational voice amidst the din of mourners and polemics."[10] The journal thus channeled a sort of high Transcendentalist discourse—focused on readings in Goethe and Swedenborg, for example—that would reflect the relative calm prior to the more intensely politicized years surrounding the annexation of Texas.

The Atlantic Monthly, on the other hand, was launched not as a Transcendentalist endeavor, but as a magazine devoted to showcasing national intellectual excellence on topics ranging from science, to politics, to the arts. Its editor, James Russell Lowell, announced in the first issue, in November 1857, that "in politics, *The Atlantic Monthly* will be the organ of no party or clique, but will honestly endeavor to be the exponent of what its conductors believe to be the American idea"; it aligns itself with "that body of men which is in favor of Freedom, National Progress, and Honor, whether public or private." The founders included Lowell, poet Henry Wadsworth Longfellow, doctor and writer Oliver Wendell Holmes, and Emerson. Those listed as "interested in the enterprise" included Herman Melville, Nathaniel Hawthorne, John Greenleaf Whittier, William Cullen Bryant, and Lydia Maria Child.[11] While not explicitly partisan, from the start the magazine promoted progressive Northern causes. Child and Whittier were prominent abolitionists, Lowell proclaimed support for Republican presidential candidate Abraham Lincoln, the writers were almost entirely Northern, and the magazine quickly became one of the most influential publications supporting the Union cause during the Civil War. Circulation of the magazine topped 32,000 by 1861 and 50,000 by 1866, more than one hundred times the circulation of *The Dial* at its peak.[12] While *The Dial* rejected political engagement as a form of corruption that would compromise individual moral purity and spiritual transcendence, *The Atlantic* was explicitly nationalist from the outset and engaged directly with current social debates. Though sympathetic to Transcendentalist ideals, the founding editors did not identify themselves or the magazine with a Transcendentalist strain of inquiry. *The Atlantic* was more intellectually heterogeneous, politically engaged, and ambitious in terms of seeking a broad American readership.

That Emerson embraced *The Atlantic*'s vision from the outset indicates the extent to which his ideas about political engagement had changed, a transformation charted in Len Gougeon's *Virtue's Hero*, which tracks Emerson's increasing rejection of his 1840s position that people needed to undergo individual spiritual and moral transformation before social and political ideals could be actualized.[13] That Emerson published his prose and poetry in *The Atlantic* indicates that he sought a broad sympathetic readership for his work in both genres as a way not only to present ethical viewpoints on slavery and the Civil War, but to convert his readers to abolitionism and the Union cause (which Emerson cast as one). Stepping aside as a compromised earth- and language-bound poet and presenting the unmediated speech of the muse in his *Atlantic* poems, Emerson forges an oracular poetry fueled by a potent universal spiritual force, one influenced by his "orientalist" readings of sacred Hindu texts and Persian poetry, especially Hafiz. If Emerson retains the certainty that "the one thing of value in the universe is the active soul" because the active soul can discover absolute truth, his sense of the political urgency of helping readers access that truth shifts into a far more pragmatic and applied mode during the Civil War period (*CW* 1:56).

"The Higher Tone of Criticism" in the *Dial* Poems

In the note from "The Editors to the Reader" that prefaces the first issue of *The Dial: A Magazine for Literature, Philosophy, and Religion*, Emerson proclaims that the progressive "spirit of the time" is "in every form a protest against usage, and a search for principles." That protest adopts the "higher tone of criticism," since the kind of expression it summons does not yet exist. This "higher tone" offers a "comparison of the record with nature, which at once shames the record and stimulates new attempts."[14] Readers of *The Dial* may benefit "from the experience and hope of spirits which are withdrawing from all old forms, and seeking all that is new somewhat to meet their inappeasable longings": the editors, in short, "hope to draw thoughts and feelings, which being alive can impart life."[15] Articulating such thoughts and feelings is not so simple, however, because human language almost never approaches nature, much less expresses it. And yet expression, where "poetry finds its origin," is "a primary impulse in nature." "Expression is prosperity": without it "I must disappear, and the brute form must crowd the soul out of nature."[16] The restorative, life-preserving, enspiriting function of expression conflicts with the limitations of language; those limitations are felt most strongly in poetry because poetry is, for Emerson and others of his time, the most exalted form of expression. Emerson severely limits his canon of true poets; only a handful of historical people, including Shakespeare, Plato, Milton, Homer, Chaucer, and Swedenborg, have succeeded (Emerson's list varies, but Shakespeare remains preeminent). No one in Emerson's own historical time, including himself, has yet shown himself to be capable: "For this present, hard / Is the fortune of the bard, / Born out of time," begins "Woodnotes 1", published in *The Dial* in October 1840 (*CW* 9:93). In his notebooks in 1859 Emerson writes "I am a natural reader, and only a writer in the absence of natural writers. In a true time, I should never have written."[17] He clearly includes himself in his insistence that, while poets must assert the soul's survival through poetry, they almost certainly fail to write lasting words.

Dramatizing most poets' failure to be true poets, and including himself among those ranks, Emerson's poetry in *The Dial* repeatedly dramatizes a poet's struggle with linguistic limitation, staging his failed attempts to speak for and with "nature," "the muse," "truth," and underlying spiritual and moral "principles." Within the poems a poet encounters a muse that stands apart, present, yet inaccessible. Rather than cooperating with the poet, the muse (much like "Emerson" in "The Poet") taunts him, finding him inadequate, measuring the space between "the record" and "nature" in "the higher tone of criticism." The antagonism of the muse is striking, and it fuels the poet's attempt to write a poem in spite of his lack of inspiration in order to urge others to complete his failed task. They may be "balked and dumb, stuttering and stammering, hissed and hooted," but he hopes that "rage will draw out of" some future poet the vision whose existence is proven by dreams (*CW* 3:23). Because the poet is uninspired, or only partially inspired, his poems are notably and self-consciously at a loss for words.

In "The Snow-Storm," for example, published in *The Dial* in January 1841, the "night-wind," an inspiration with no need for a human vessel, performs his "artistry" while the poet reports on the event for the readers he apostrophizes. The force of the muse works all around the poet without penetrating him sufficiently to lift his metaphors above the mundane world of practical matters that he wishes to transform. The poet looks on as the wind whips the snow into whimsical concoctions that momentarily occupy a farmer's practical built landscape. Protesting mere "usage," the north wind "curves his white bastions with projected roof / Round every windward stake, or tree, or door" (*CW* 9:90). "Mockingly," he "hangs Parian wreaths on coop or kennel," ornately decorating humble structures and placing beauty above daily material needs and routines: feeding chickens so they can be eaten, feeding dogs so they can guard herds or hunt to feed the farmer. The wind stops all human commerce and communication as well by "filling up the road." Forcing a break in transactional thinking, the night-wind:

> Leaves, when the Sun appears, astonished Art
> To mimic in slow structures, stone by stone,
> Built in an age, the mad wind's night-work,
> The frolic architecture of the snow.
> (*CW* 9:90)

On the one hand, Emerson's point is clear, simple, and didactic: Art can only "mimic" nature imperfectly and laboriously. But the poem's insistent architectural metaphors trouble the simplicity and suggest that the humans are left to mimic a natural mimic. The speaker's architectural and decorative metaphors paradoxically suggest that the "mad wind" can do no more than elaborate on and "mock" human constructions— creating a "projected roof" on "every windward stake," hanging "Parian wreaths" on "coop or kennel," adding a "tapering turret" to the gate. If the snow is truly inspired, then it is the poet who fails to summon the language necessary to convey the force of "the mad wind's night-work" as any more than a series of decorative, unnecessary and insignificant elaborations on human constructions. Emerson's theory of art does not usually depend on mimesis or mimicry (though like his contemporaries he is preoccupied with the relationship between imitation and originality): he seeks the new, the unspoken, the unrevealed. Why, then, would Art bother to adorn human structures with mockingly mimetic versions of the same? Through a process of rational speculation the reader must conclude that the snow's performance exceeds the poet's powers of expression. This sort of dead end is a feature of Emerson's instructive, obstructive poetry of the period. The poem implicitly but clearly asks a more capable poet to write a better poem by taunting the reader with verbal limitations. Recognizing the problem, someone else may be better able to draw the night wind into his poem and exceed the dead-end architectural and decorative metaphors that "The Snow-Storm" employs.

Other *Dial* poems take this taunting of the poet by the muse to greater extremes, intensifying the staged, dramatic quality, and formally structuring the antagonism in terms of dialogue. In "The Sphinx," for example, published in January 1841, muse and poet confront each other and reach an enigmatic standoff. Having long awaited "a seer," and becoming impatient, the Sphinx talks to herself at the outset of the poem, complaining of humans' inability to integrate themselves with natural harmonies, which she describes at length. Only "man crouches and blushes / Absconds and conceals"; he "poisons the ground" he walks on. The metapoet we might call "Emerson," who narrates the encounter between muse and poet, intervenes to tell us that "cold shuddered the sphere" when "the great mother spoke" (*CW* 9:6). This speaker, the writer of the poem, does not play a part in the action. He observes the muse talking to herself while the poet who is a character in the poem overhears her. This metapoet plays a tiny onstage role, quite different from "a poet" whom he "heard" "cheerfully answer" the Sphinx in a cheeky, disrespectful manner, negating her formulations: her "dirges / are pleasant songs" to this poet (*CW* 9:7). This cheerful poet tells the Sphinx that her disgust with his unnatural nature misses the point of human existence. Unlike "Sea, earth, air, sound, silence, / Plant, quadruped, bird" who are "stirred" by "one deity" (*CW* 9:6), the human evolves eternally, knowing that "the heavens that now draw him" will be insufficient once he finds them (*CW* 9:7). In keeping with the "eterne alternation" (*CW* 9:8) that the poet espouses, he directly counters the Sphinx's harmonious, stable vision of a world plagued by the human misfit with an endless spiritual questing narrative: "Profounder, profounder, / Man's spirit must dive" (*CW* 9:7). The poet's dimeter lines, gathered in octets in which the second and fourth, and the sixth and the eighth lines rhyme, mimic the Sphinx's rhythmic mystical chant, underscoring his recognition and absorption of her perspective into his own vision, which he brashly posits as a broader, more capacious worldview than the oracle's own. Underscoring his feat of perfect formal mirroring, the poet then moves to uneven trimeter lines when he tells the Sphinx that she is losing her touch: "Dull Sphinx, Jove keep thy five wits". The Sphinx, in the same meter (indicating a second reversal where she adopts the poet's speech form), tells the poet he is deluded: she is his spirit that he has refused to recognize by reinforcing division and opposition rather than synthesis and integration. The human's questing is a function of "time," which is "the false reply". The metapoet then breaks in to describe the Sphinx's vivid metamorphosis and disappearance, leaving the debate at a standoff, though the Sphinx has the last word: "Who telleth one of my meanings / Is master of all I am" (*CW* 9:8). Whether the poet or the metapoet has told a meaning, or whether the Sphinx won the debate is up to the reader to decide, though the question is more or less undecidable, since Emerson has balanced the possibilities, proposed a riddle, and disabled a solution. He does so in order to provoke readers into deeper involvement in the question of the relationship between human transformation and realization—"clothed eternity"—and eternity, history and spirit. Saundra Morris, who has interpreted "The Sphinx" in a far more sustained way, stresses this poem's importance as a "threshold poem" (Morris coins this term), which Emerson placed in the beginning of three collections of his poetry to serve as a "guide."[18] He does so, she argues, because the poem foregrounds "undecidability" and "the difficulties of self-expression," central preoccupations for Emerson.[19] But while Morris identifies "an allegory of split subjectivity," I read "The Sphinx" as an impossible encounter between an all-knowing inhuman force and a time-bound, language-bound, relatively ignorant poet.[20] The encounter is explicitly and self-consciously orchestrated by a third figure, Emerson the metapoet, not as an allegory, but as an articulation of a nearly insurmountable circumstance: the poet's almost universal inability to access cosmic insight. The particular poet engaged in dialogue with the Sphinx is especially inept, not even recognizing what he does not know.

The muse's even more excessive taunting of the poet extends to 383 lines in "Woodnotes 2," published in *The Dial* in October 1841. The poet restricts his own speech to four italicized lines that serve as an epigraph for a pine tree's harangue:

> *As sunbeams stream through liberal space,*
> *And nothing jostle or displace,*
> *So waved the pine-tree through my thought,*
> *And fanned the dreams it never brought.*
> (CW 9:103)

Admitting failure from the start—the pine tree fans dreams that never arrive in the dreamer's "thought"—the poet does not even try to speak in his own person in the poem proper. Nevertheless, the tree demands the poet's silence, as if human speech were harmful and even sacrilegious: "Speak not thy speech my boughs among," "talk no more with feeble tongue" (*CW* 9:108). Instead the poet translates the pine tree's goading invitation to evolve beyond human limits and speak the universal language of poetry that "waves" the tree. Three times in 383 lines, the poet interjects brief, non-committal phrases—"quoth the pine tree" twice, and "once again the pine-tree sung"—underscoring his incapacity to do more than listen and try to convey the pine tree's message (*CW* 9:103, 104, 108). Of course, the quoted speech is not the pine-tree's; it is the poet's attempt to stage the tree's nonlinguistic apostrophe to the poet, an apostrophe that fails to summon a response just as all apostrophes fail, by definition: though intended to animate the poet, the tree's apostrophe mutes and deadens him. The poet's English translation fails because the tree's "rhymes," composed of wind playing through boughs, are universal; they are understood in all languages around the globe, because they are nonlinguistic:

> Come learn with me the fatal song
> Which knits the world in music strong,
> Whereto every bosom dances,
> Kindled with courageous fancies.
> Come lift thine eyes to lofty rhymes,
> Of things with things, of times with times,
> Primal chimes of sun and shade,
> Of sound and echo, man and maid,
> The land reflected in the flood,
> Body with shadows still pursued.
> (CW 9:109)

The poet's translation of nature's rhymes into poetry's rhymes necessarily fails: they are a weak metaphor or symbol for a truer language. Once again, a poet stages his distance from a muse that should be inspiring him: instead of speaking through him, the pine tree charges him with inadequacy. "Unbound, unrhymed," "misplaced, mistimed," the poet can only imagine the tree pitying his incompetence and lack of creative potential.

The muse's apostrophe ("But though, poor child!"), translated by the poet himself, deadens rather than enlivens him: he demonstrates to the reader that he cannot do more than narrate his repeated failure to be inspired by the pine tree's song (*CW* 9:109). That charge results in the despairing epigraph that prefaces the poem.

These poems and others from the 1840s are formally experimental in ways that underscore the poet's failure to achieve a nearly impossible ideal, even while charging readers—potential poets—to continue trying to discover a way to rhyme language with nature. The poems seek to generate a sense of camaraderie in the reader and a desire to accomplish what the poet cannot, to prove the pine tree wrong when it says that "there lives no man of Nature's worth / In the circle of the earth" (*CW* 9:110). The central drama is the human poet's failure to become one with his muse, envisioned variously, but always appearing as a moral, spiritual truth that endures eternally via, paradoxically "rushing metamorphosis." The snow and the pine tree are themselves poets conveying a song—"the mystic song / Chanted when the sphere was one"—that will outlast them; the Sphinx is a metamorphic force that endures without needing human recognition. The poet figure's uninspired poems are grounded in conventional forms of rhyme, stanza, and meter; they disrupt these constraints with off rhymes, varying line lengths, additional stresses, rhythms that work against the meter, and other clunky interventions. This awkwardness conveys impatience with linguistic limitation, but it rarely conveys the impression of a snowstorm's force or a pine tree's melody or a Sphinx's otherworldliness. Most of all, these poems are about the poet's inadequacies. Their redundancy, self-involvement, and awkwardness, however, do not reflect Emerson's failure to accomplish something else. He successfully conveys this particular point: that the muse cannot speak unhampered through the poet, and that the poet is ineloquent as a result.

The Muse Speaks in the *Atlantic Monthly* Poems

Emerson's *Atlantic Monthly* poems show far less concern with staging the poet's incapacities. Muses cease to criticize poets for their inability to experience and utter spiritual truth, and the metapoet, or displaced lyric figure of Emerson, who orchestrates these dramas but rarely enters into them, often disappears entirely. These shifts emerge in part from Emerson's changing response to major historical events, primary among them slavery and the Civil War. The poet is no longer the main problem; or rather, he is a problem that will never be solved. Taunting, mocking, shaming, urging, and encouraging had not succeeded in producing the emergence of the true American Poet, notwithstanding the work of Thoreau, Whitman, Very, and other talented poets who responded to Emerson's call. In most of Emerson's poems published between 1857 and 1865, individual, social, and political moral failures are the muse's target of criticism, rather than the poet's aesthetic and spiritual shortfalls. Though the figure of the muse is Emerson's necessarily imperfect linguistic construct, he no longer draws attention to the inadequacies of his artistry in poems where the muse speaks. He redirects his energies to presenting potent, persuasive powers of moral justice, speakers—distinctly not Emerson—that declare true terms of judgement to readers, thereby seeking to stimulate moral insight and practical action. This strain in Emerson's poems is familiar from his earlier work as well, but it takes on new urgency and specificity in this period.[21]

The four poems published as a cluster in the first issue of *The Atlantic Monthly* (November 1857)—"The Romany Girl," "The Chartist's Complaint," "Days," and "Brahma"—signal this shift. In all but "Days," where an Emerson-like figure condemns himself for losing sight of his cosmic aspirations, the speaker is a dramatic persona that speaks from a position of moral authority, addressing contemporary American injustice in slightly veiled ways. "The Romany Girl," speaking with authority forged through living outdoors in the natural world without material possessions, charges "pale Northern girls" who "wear out in-doors [their] sickly days" with assuming a false position of superiority over impoverished women with darker, sun-touched skin (*CW* 9:421). Summoning the visionary powers that are stereotypically associated with Romany people, Emerson's "girl" claims the power of truth-telling:

> You doubt we read the stars on high,
> Nathless we read your fortunes true;
> The stars may hide in the upper sky,
> But without glass we fathom you.
> (*CW* 9:421)

Fathoming without the need of any physical apparatus—telescope, microscope, crystal ball—the visionary speaker conveys Emerson's critique of genteel Northern white women—a group associated with abolitionism in the period—a critique that targets racialized prejudice. Published during the period of Bleeding Kansas, when fights over slavery fueled the start of civil war, "The Romany Girl," in an understated way, locates the force of moral justice in marginalized people of color and charges well-to-do Northern white women—regularly associated with Christian virtue—with racial and socioeconomic discrimination.

In "The Chartist's Complaint," Emerson sides with laborers, the poem's title signaling approval of workers' rights protests in London in 1848, protests that extended to violence. Oddly, aside from the title, as von Frank notes, "English politics are nowhere to be seen"; nor is the shift to industrial labor that motivated Chartism (*CW* 9:430). In the context of *The Atlantic* in 1857, especially with the poem's evocation of agricultural labor, readers would understand the "Chartist" speaker to be charging plantation owners with the exploitation of enslaved workers. The speaker condemns the enormous gap between the "humble farmer," for whom light serves only as a "laborer's lamp," and the "rich man," who revels in the "treacherously bright" "amber mornings" that illuminate "his planted isle where roses glow" (*CW* 9:431). The indictment of Beauty as complicitous in the exploitation hints at why most of Emerson's poems are not "beautiful," in a recognizably romantic sense: he associates cultivated beauty with moral corruption. The division is so extreme that the Chartist can only imagine that "Day" is schizoid, possessing "two faces." He is at such a loss to fathom the distinctly human injustice that he uses Day as a scapegoat: a "treacherously bright" "sycophant" that enables inequality. The speaker goes so far as to ask Day and its Sun to return to "chaos" and leave the world without light. The poem's vagueness allows this "complaint" to speak for all for whom the Day serves only as a "laborer's lamp." The title, on the other hand, suggests that Emerson supports class and caste rebellion, including the kind of violent slave revolt that John Brown tried to stage in 1859, which Emerson did indeed support explicitly in his lecture at Tremont Temple (*CWE* 11:265–73).

The fourth poem of the cluster, "Brahma," has often been interpreted in isolation as a cryptic, befuddling, and even incomprehensible aphoristic conundrum; but read in the context of the other three poems and its historical moment, it can be understood as a formulation that situates social conflicts in relation to a cosmic moral principle, inscrutable in human time but operable nevertheless. Just as the Romany girl and the Chartist voice their complaints, Brahma begins with a provocation:

> If the red slayer think he slays,
> Or if the slain think he is slain,
> They know not well the subtle ways
> I keep, and pass, and turn again.
> (CW 9:365)

The supernatural power unnecessarily qualifies the "slayer" as "red," concisely summoning the stereotypical figure of a Native American warrior, a literary figment that helped justify and displace US imperial violence onto its target. But the "red slayer" could also be one who slays "red" people, or anyone who kills and has blood on their hands. Brahma seems to assert indifference to cycles of violence, regardless of who slays or who is slain, because the distinction is illusory from this higher power's perspective. His more "subtle ways" involve keeping, passing, and turning; assessing, equating, or inverting opposites: "far" is "near," "forgot" is remembered, "shadow" is "sunlight." Because "Brahma" and not Emerson speaks, however, what appears to be amorality or abnegation of moral judgement is more likely the invocation of an unreadable, omniscient moral power. The poem concludes with this challenge to the reader:

> But thou, meek lover of the good!
> Find me, and turn thy back on heaven.

Only if we understood the "meek lover of the good" and "heaven" as real and laudable is it wrong to turn our backs. If instead we understand meekly loving good in order to gain entrance to heaven as self-serving, immoral behavior, then it is right to turn one's back on heaven, and to recognize one's self-justifications as myopic. "Brahma" asks readers like the Northern white woman in "The Romany Girl" or the "rich" in "The Chartist's Complaint"—figures aligned with readers of magazines like *The Atlantic*—to "fathom" themselves, or at least to understand that self-righteousness grounds and justifies immoral, self-serving acts. Only Brahma knows, but we would do well to cease to understand morality within a tainted Christian framework that is used to such brutal ends as justifying US slavery and try on this orientalist thought experiment instead.

In "The Test: *Musa Loquitur*," published just a few months before the beginning of the Civil War, Emerson highlights in the very title the muse's direct speech and his aesthetic experiments with sidelining "the poet" as well as what I have called the metapoet, the person who wrote the poem. Emerson told James Russell Lowell, the *Atlantic*'s editor, that this riddle poem had a simple answer, which he could provide for the next issue. According to Emerson, "The Test" "admits, like other riddles, of several solutions. Mine is, five national poets, Homer, Dante, Shakspeare (sic), Swedenborg, and Goethe" (quoted in *CW* 9:409). But the poem's "simple" meaning is not so obvious. "The Solution" was never published in *The Atlantic* and was only completed in 1866, in time for inclusion in *May-Day*. Readers did not have the benefit of Emerson's answer, and they may have arrived at "several" other "solutions". The metaphoric structure, moreover, exceeds the simplicity of the "answer" and poses additional riddles that the reader must try to solve: the metaphors suggest sectional conflict. I quote the poem in full:

> I hung my verses in the wind;
> Time and tide their faults may find.
> All were winnowed through and through;
> Five lines lasted sound and true;
> Five were smelted in a pot
> Than the South more fierce and hot.
> These the Siroc could not melt,
> Fire their fiercer flaming felt,
> And their meaning was more white
> Than July's meridian light.
> Sunshine cannot bleach the snow,
> Nor Time unmake what poets know.
> Have you eyes to find the five
> Which five thousand could survive?
> (*CW* 9:409)[22]

According to Emerson's comments, the muse proclaims that all "verses" should serve as transmitters for immortal truth, but the number of poets who "know" and deliver what "last[s] sound and true" is five in five thousand. More precisely, if one attends to the phrasing of the poem and not Emerson's gloss, only five out of five thousand "lines," regardless of the author, "could survive": verses were "winnowed" until only "lines" remained. The rare success in poetic survival is known only by the muse: the rest of us must wonder if we "have" the "eyes to find the five." Because the muse does not stipulate what the truth consists of, "finding" the answer would not reveal the truth, especially since the five lines would presumably be fragments of a larger whole. Seeking a truth outside the poem, moreover, would distract the reader from the timebound qualities of the poem itself; it is a riddle posed at the advent of the war in metaphors evocative of violent sectional conflict. The verses are "hung" "in the wind" like flags, which are shredded. The smelting process evokes forging metal weapons and making ammunition. Southern heat is the muse's crucible: "South" is capitalized, suggesting sectional conflict. Her meaning is "white," and whiteness is pure truth; or perhaps truth is the true whiteness between two whitenesses, the Southern and the Northern varieties: in Emerson's notebooks as well as his poems of this period he posits a moral geography, where Northern climates, cold, and snow are more conducive to cultivating moral force than warmer climates. Finally, only five lines "survive" the winnowing process: the other 4995 "lines" will die, as if the lines were made up of soldiers fighting a bloody war of attrition. Overtly, this is a metaphor for true poetry outlasting the present moment, but the phrasing doubles to suggest that "what poets know" is analogous to what few principles could survive a war.

These "universal" or dislocated proclamations precede and prepare for the more grounded, explicit engagements of Emerson's muses during the US Civil War. Scholars have sought to explain why "The Boston Hymn," a poem Emerson first read publicly on January 1, 1863 to celebrate the Emancipation Proclamation and then published in the *Atlantic* in February, is spoken by "God," who addresses the "watching Pilgrims"; but as we have seen, Emerson's anachronistic setting and selection of God as the orator is less an exception than an extension of his earlier work. While the poem presents a scene in which "the word of the Lord" "came" to the "watching Pilgrims," many aspects of the poem work against a consistent, literal reading of this scenario. Just as the Romany girl seems to address antebellum American white women, and the Chartist demands a fair principle of equal land and labor ownership in what could be an American agrarian setting, "God" too crosses time and political circumstance to address the current moment. He is never, moreover, explicitly Christian: his angel's name is "Freedom," and he advocates for a version of the nineteenth-century ideology of Manifest Destiny: "Lo! I uncover the land / Which I hid of old time in the West." That ideology is radically revised, however, in that it is underpinned by a principle of racial equality:

> Come East and West and North,
> By races, as snow-flakes,
> And carry my purpose forth,
> Which neither halts nor shakes.
> (CW 9:383)

God conspicuously leaves "South" out of his cardinal equation, and he dissolves the westward expansion that he declared part of his "purpose" earlier by calling all directions to gather, disorienting readers from the nationalist geography that seemed to be quite clear. God embodies a democratic principle, in short, and he calls for corrections of and reparations for inequality in a new version of "Columbia" in which "the slave is owner," "poor men can govern," there are no "masterships," and the "humble" "shall rule." God is a new God, and the Pilgrims are new Pilgrims. The aspect of this God-muse that derives from the Puritan God is righteous anger and retribution. He issues a warning in the final stanza:

> My will fulfilled shall be,
> For, in daylight or in dark,
> My thunderbolt has eyes to see
> His way home to the mark.
> (CW 9:384)

Like Brahma, God is a cosmic moral principle. Perhaps to avoid the broad response of ridicule and incomprehension that Brahma inspired, Emerson makes plain the identities of the slayer and the slain and the consequences of defying this God's will.

Emerson's "Atom in Full Breath"

Emerson's experiments with lyric self-negation that stage powerful, omniscient muses of moral truth, bypassing the poet and speaking directly to readers, end with "Boston Hymn." The last two poems he published in *The Atlantic* during the Civil War take different approaches to the poet's necessary limitations: Emerson finally embraces and comes to terms with them. "The Titmouse" dramatizes this encounter with human frailty in the context of the Civil War. While critics have praised the poem as one of Emerson's most successful, they have not noted the sustained martial metaphors that would have been vibrantly noticeable to readers of *The Atlantic* in May 1862, a time when many Northern poets publishing there and in other periodicals were saturating their purportedly peaceful nature poems, about watching leaves turn red in autumn or observing a snowstorm, for example, with ominous undertones and oblique expressions of horror about violence taking place in Southern locations remote from the landscapes they described.[23] "The Titmouse" engages in this practice by playing out the poet's wartime meditations about his previous attempts at staging enormous cosmic forces that dwarf and threaten humans with punishment for moral violations. Instead, Emerson in his own person, a human, aging poet, walks "three dangerous miles" toward home in freezing winter weather, fearful that he will be "embalmed by purifying cold": his expressions of vulnerability and immersion in the scene starkly contrast with the removed, disembodied, completely safe spectator in "The Snow-Storm." In "The Titmouse," snow, wind, and freezing temperatures are a "foeman" with "a million arms to one" of the speaker's, who has no idea how to "fight" against such an adversary. Emerson's martial metaphors both mock the smallness of the struggle—walking three miles home in the cold—and emphasize the danger of the situation, which is both incomparable and similar to the mortal threats of mass warfare.

In this state of extreme vulnerability, he comes to appreciate the "titmouse dimension." A small bird's cheerful song and "gymnastic play" inspires Emerson to keep walking and reassures him that he will survive. The titmouse—"this poet," "this scrap of valor," this "little savior"—causes him to realize that "no virtue comes with size":

> The reason of all cowardice
> Is that men are overgrown,
> And, to be valiant, must come down
> To the titmouse dimension.
> (CW 9:441)

Emerson had long encouraged his readers to expand toward the infinite: though he seeks and encourages the escape from individual personhood, rarely does he ask humans to shrink in physical size and attend to tiny beings. This shift from macro-muses to a micro-muse, an "atom in full breath," abnegates the enormous metaphysical abstractions Emerson had previously caused to speak. This muse simply says, in human translation, "Good day, good sir!" and shows no fear of the vast world, the freezing cold, or his own limited powers of oral expression, the repeated "chic-chic-a-dee-dee!"

"The Titmouse" suggests that this shift in scale and "dimension" arises from the unfolding experience of mass warfare in which soldiers are small moving parts in an enormous, life-threatening system and have little control over their destiny. Emerson casts the bird as a tiny soldier in "dare-devil array," a "scrap of valor" "hurling defiance at vast death," singing "battle-numbers bold." The titmouse's courage highlights Emerson's "weak behavior" and causes him to realize that "the soul, if stout within, / Can arm impregnably the skin": the soul's armor can protect Emerson from "polar frost." In this poem, unlike the others I have discussed, he never reaches for an overarching moral power or a cosmic principle to give his struggle with proper conduct and mortality meaning: the tiny bird itself is the "antidote to fear." An "atom in full breath," a simple, natural, enlivened part of the material universe, conveys enough vibrancy in the face of overwhelming odds to help the poet home. The poem concludes by making the bellicose language explicit and putting Caesar's words in the bird's mouth to bolster the poet's own courage: "*Paen! Veni, vidi, vici.*" Emerson convincingly and movingly expresses the same kind of courage more directly and less playfully in "Terminus," published in *The Atlantic* in January 1867, where he acknowledges his dwindling poetic powers, the natural process of aging, and his awareness of moving toward the end of a life that did not measure up to his earlier, humanly impossible expectations (*CW* 9:469).

Emerson recasts the titmouse in human terms in the last poem he published during the war in *The Atlantic*. "Voluntaries" commemorates the deaths of white commander Robert Gould Shaw and 116 members of the Massachusetts 54th, the first free Black Northern army regiment, in the Battle of Fort Wagner on July 18, 1863. Twenty-five-year-old Shaw was the son of Emerson's friend Francis George Shaw, who attended Harvard with Emerson's younger brothers, and who asked his son to lead the regiment. In a badly planned maneuver that the regiment knew was almost certain to fail, Shaw led his regiment across a beach and climbed a thirty-foot-high Confederate fortification on Morris Island while facing constant, direct fire from above. Shaw and William Carney, an African American flag bearer, made it to the top before Shaw was killed. The mythology surrounding the battle coalesced almost immediately in popular media. The regiment's willingness to die for their freedom and their country proved (for the moment—this continuously needs to be reproven) that Black American manhood was a reality deserving of full citizenship. It also provided evidence that morally upright white Northern men were willing to sacrifice themselves for the sin of enslavement and for long-term inaction in the face of a moral crime. And it demonstrated that Black and white men could work together in common cause, with the significant requirement that the white man was a singular leader, and Black men were cooperative followers. Shaw is the titmouse in Emerson's poem; he is "the youth" who replied "I can" when "Duty whisper[ed]" (*CW* 9:392). The presence of the Black men is only implied, as a mass of volunteers (evoked by the title, which primarily signifies a dirge). Carney's presence disappears in the image of a single "stainless soldier on the walls": Shaw becomes the white figure of Duty's sacrifice, eclipsing Black agency and courage. Along with other poems of the period that follow the same pattern, Emerson's diminishment of Black courage and elevation of Shaw's white, Northern leadership—Shaw belongs to "a virtuous race / Clinging to a colder zone"—contributed significantly to forging the myth of the Battle of Fort Wagner in popular perception. It is not a coincidence, and perhaps too obvious to note, though the repeated acknowledgement does little to rearrange the story, that John Brown, Robert Gould Shaw, and Abraham Lincoln are all commemorated as white martyr figures who offered their lives to free enslaved people, while Black Civil War heroism persists largely in anonymity. It is a recalcitrant formulation, evident in the "Shaw" monument on the Boston Commons and elsewhere.[24] The persistence of the narrative is an unfortunate tribute to the influence of Emerson's poetry. "Voluntaries" is perhaps the most politically and culturally influential poem Emerson ever wrote. The power derives in part from his balancing the oracular voice of the muse with his own human voice. And yet his attempt to reclaim a human higher moral ground relies on the erasure of African Americans' decisions to fight for freedom and equality, their courage in confronting lethal force, and their willingness to collaborate and cooperate with white Northern officers, which also carried serious risk of betrayal.

Conclusion

Emerson's dramatizations of tensions between poet and muse increasingly assume an applied political force. In the 1840s the *Dial* poems repeatedly foreground the maladjustment between poet and various configurations of the muse; Emerson the poet stands at an additional remove from the conflict in the role of orchestrator. By 1857, when Emerson begins publishing in *The Atlantic Monthly*, and throughout the Civil War period, the muse speaks to the reader without the intervention of a poet. The benefit of this unmediated address is fundamentally moral. By providing a dramatic stage from which universal moral powers speak to readers, Emerson seeks to change their understanding of their actions in a transient, physical world by placing them within a broader, universal frame. Like abolitionist poets John Greenleaf Whittier and Frances Ellen Watkins Harper, Emerson strives to articulate a "higher law" in poetic form to effect political change: to end slavery, and to inspire Union soldiers to fight and sacrifice their lives in service of that goal.

When Emerson tries to reconcile an awareness of human vulnerability and immersion in timebound political struggles with his goal of achieving transcendent moral insight, a limitation emerges: these poems demonstrate that, when applied to historical circumstances, Emerson's figurations of morality are geographically and racially informed and determined. His racialized climatic romanticism allows him, for example, to construe the American flag as a symbol of white Northern moral superiority: the stars are "snowflakes," the stripes are the Northern lights. (This kind of racialized and climate-bound symbolism is widespread in the time—artist Edwin Church's "Our Banner in the Sky" [1862] also envisions the aurora borealis as the American flag.)[25] Emerson recognizes and complicates his own affirmations of white Northern superiority in "Voluntaries," for example, by insisting that people from Southern latitudes have "avenues to God / Hid from men of Northern brain," indicating that all "races" and dwellers in all climates must be comprehended to fully understand universal moral truth (CW 9:391). These kinds of racialized distinctions and affirmations, versions of which appear in Emerson's notebooks and other writings, underscore both a desire and an incapacity to recognize accomplishment regardless of race—to summon the image of William Carney beside Robert Gould Shaw on top of the battlement, for example, as Currier and Ives did in a popular print (approximately 1863).[26] That incapacity disables his ability to convincingly affirm a higher moral truth. Here, in his inability to reconfigure historically embedded, systemic racialized thinking, and not in his experiments at locating personhood in his readers, the limitations of Emerson's impersonality emerge. His alliances with whiteness stymy his attempts to invoke an all-inclusive, impersonal moral force. Emerson indicates an awareness of this problem without being able to solve it. The presumably white speaker of "The Titmouse" could be understood as facing the threat of a frozen, lethal landscape of racialized whiteness. The unalloyed whiteness of snow is an immobilizing, deadening and deadly figure in this and other poems written by Northern white poets in the period, but it is also, at the same time, a metaphor for moral superiority. Momentarily immobilized in "The Titmouse," Emerson articulates a fear of being buried by sheer whiteness; he doesn't, however, move beyond that fear to imagine a diversified landscape: the bird rescues him from that line of thought. That returns us to Emerson's repeated invocations of muses that assume a "higher tone of criticism," one that charges him, along with the poets and readers he inspires, to read his poems, recognize his limitations, and continue his work of imagining a future that moves closer to inclusive moral truths.

Notes

1. The groundbreaking anthology Ralph Waldo Emerson, *Emerson's Antislavery Writings*, ed. Len Gougeon and Joel Myerson (New Haven, CT: Yale University Press, 1995), for example, does not include Emerson's poems; nor does Emerson, *The Political Emerson*, ed. David Robinson (Boston: Beacon Press, 2004); *A Political Companion to Emerson's Writings*, ed. Alan Levine and Daniel S. Malachuk (Lexington: University Press of Kentucky, 2011); or *The Emerson Dilemma: Essays on Emerson and Social Reform*, ed T. Gregory Garvey (Athens: University of Georgia Press, 2001). Len Gougeon discusses the poems in his touchstone book *Virtue's Hero: Emerson, Antislavery, and Reform* (Athens: University of Georgia Press, 1990).
2. Recent studies of Emerson's poetry that focus on philosophy and spirituality include Stephen Cushman, "Transcendentalist Poetics," in *The Cambridge Companion to Nineteenth-Century American Poetry*, ed. Kerry Larson (Cambridge: Cambridge University Press, 2012), 76–93; Paul Kane, "Emerson and Hafiz: The Figure of the Religious Poet," *Religion and Literature* 41, no. 1 (Spring 2009): 111–39; Saundra Morris, "Through a Thousand Voices: Emerson's Poetry and 'The Sphinx,'" in *Emerson's Prose and Poetry*, ed. Joel Porte and Saundra Morris (New York: Norton Critical Edition, 2001), 777–90. In later essays, Morris discusses Emerson's 1867 collection *May-Day* as a response to the US Civil War. See Morris, "Metre-Making Arguments," in *The Cambridge Companion to Ralph Waldo Emerson*, ed. Joel Porte and Saundra Morris (Cambridge: Cambridge University Press, 1999), 218–42; and Morris, "Whim Upon the Lintel: Emerson's Poetry and a Politically Ethical Aesthetic," *Nineteenth-Century Prose* 40, no. 2 (2013): 189–218. Major studies of Emerson's poetry include Hyatt Waggoner, *Emerson as Poet* (Princeton, NJ, 1974), R. A. Yoder, *Emerson and the Orphic Poet in America* (Berkeley: University of California Press, 1978).
3. Sharon Cameron, *Impersonality: Seven Essays* (Chicago: University of Chicago Press, 2007), 103.
4. Cameron, *Impersonality*, 89.
5. Cameron, *Impersonality*, 94.
6. Cameron, *Impersonality*, 94.
7. See Yoder, *Emerson and the Orphic Poet*.
8. Information on *The Dial* found at *The Walden Woods Project*, https://www.walden.org/what-we-do/library/thoreau/index-of-individual-contributors/. Accessed April 14, 2024.
9. Ralph Waldo Emerson, "The Editors to the Reader," *The Dial* 1, no. 1 (1 July 1840): 1–4, 3–4.
10. Emerson, "The Editors to the Reader," 4.
11. Quoted in Susan Goodman, *Republic of Words: The Atlantic Monthly and its Readers, 1857-1935* (Lebanon, NH: University Press of New England, 2011), 6.
12. Statistic from *Illustrated Civil War Magazines* website, accessed June 20, 2020, https://www.lincolnandthecivilwar.com/SubLevelPages/AtlanticMonthly.asp.
13. Emerson, *Emerson's Antislavery Writings*; Gougeon, *Virtue's Hero*; Emerson, *The Political Emerson*.
14. Emerson, "The Editors to the Reader," 3.
15. Emerson, "The Editors to the Reader," 4.
16. Quoted from Emerson, 1841 lecture on poetry in von Frank, "Historical Introduction" (*CW* 9:lvi–lvii).
17. *Emerson in His Journals*, ed. Joel Porte (Cambridge, MA: Harvard University Press, 1982), 483.

18. Morris, "Through a Thousand Voices," 780; see also Morris, "The Threshold Poem, Emerson, and 'The Sphinx,'" *American Literature* 69, no. 3 (September 1997): 547–70.
19. Morris, "Through a Thousand Voices," 778.
20. Morris, "Through a Thousand Voices," 782.
21. See Derrick Spires, *The Practice of Black Citizenship: Black Politics and Print Culture in the Early United States* (Philadelphia: University of Pennsylvania Press, 2019), for an incisive discussion of the question of what to "do with the White people," raised by Black activists, specifically in the *Anglo African Magazine* directly before the US Civil War (161). This essay attempts to delineate both Emerson's affiliations and extreme limitations with respect to this question.
22. The text of the poem follows *The Atlantic* publication, January 1861 (85): see notes for version "A" (*CW* 9:410).
23. For a discussion of these disfigured "nature" poems, see Eliza Richards, *Battle Lines: Poetry and Mass Media in the US Civil War* (Philadelphia: University of Pennsylvania Press, 2019), chapters 1 and 2.
24. On the diverging traditions of Black and white poetic memorializations of the Battle of Fort Wagner, see Richards, *Battle Lines*, chapter 3: "'To Signalize the Hour': Memorialization and the Massachusetts 54th."
25. George Fredrickson, in *The Black Image in the White Mind: The Debate on Afro American Character and Destiny, 1871-1914* (Middletown, CT: Wesleyan University Press, 1987), coins the term "racial romanticism": Laura Dassow Walls discusses racialized scientific contexts for Emerson's thinking in *Emerson's Life in Science: The Culture of Truth* (Ithaca, NY: Cornell University Press, 2003).
26. Currier and Ives, "The Gallant Charge of the 54th Massachusetts Regiment," National Museum of American History. https://americanhistory.si.edu/collections/nmah_448713. Accessed April 14, 2024.

10

"ME" AND "NOT-ME," OR, EMERSONIAN EMBODIMENTS, AFFECTS, INTIMACIES

CHAPTER 32

"NATURE ABHORS THE OLD"
Emerson's Transcendental Ageism

SARI EDELSTEIN

"In twelve days, I shall be nineteen years old; which I count a miserable thing. Has any other educated person lived so many years and lost so many days ... mine approaching maturity is attended with a goading sense of emptiness and wasted capacity" (*JMN* 1:133). Emerson goes on to deprecate his vanity as childish, telling himself he "may quite as well resume the bauble & rattle ... picturebook in hand instead of Plato and Newton." Drawn from his commonplace book, *The Wide World*, which he kept almost religiously for much of his life, this passage displays Emerson's use of age as a benchmark for self-assessment.[1] Indeed, just as he scrupulously monitored his weight ("stable at 144"), Emerson often relied on the numerical metric of age to calibrate his intellectual progress and discipline himself. But perhaps even more significantly, it reveals that from the time he was a teenager, Emerson was anxious about aging and worried he was getting old too quickly. Such private concerns about growing older situate Emerson as part of a culture-wide turn toward "age consciousness" and the pathologization of older people that arose with antebellum economic and social transformations.[2] Emerson's theories of individualism and self-reliance, which presume able-bodiedness and youth as neutral, baseline statuses, contributed powerfully to the valorization of youth and heroic autonomy that took hold in his era and remain with us today.

It is perhaps surprising that so little scholarly attention has been paid to Emerson's relationship to age, but the silence on this subject may have been how Emerson wanted it. Scholars seem to have inherited his fraught relationship with aging, studiously avoiding an engagement with his late life. Not until the publication of Christopher Hanlon's watershed *Emerson's Memory Loss* in 2018 have scholars confronted directly the realities of Emerson's dementia; on the contrary, his old age and cognitive decline have largely been repressed by a critical establishment wedded to the very tenets of self-reliance that Emerson himself so famously articulated.[3] As Hanlon powerfully observes, Emerson's old-age debility and dependence, especially on his daughter Ellen, threatens to fracture the iconic Emerson, sage of Concord, alone and inspired in his private study. Hanlon's project has opened up the possibility of reading age critically in Emerson's work and of seeing his oeuvre as participating in the neoliberal logics of individualism. In the pages that follow, I hope to cast Emerson's preoccupation with age into relief and to show how aging represented a perpetual specter that threatened the power of autonomous white masculinity. Indeed, Emerson's work contributes to the very sanctification of youthful autonomy that vexed him throughout his life and would condition the response to his own career, resulting in a "reticence concerning Emerson's very late work" and reticence about old age in US literary studies more generally.[4] Putting age at the center of a reading of Emerson, the patron saint of self-reliance, also reminds us that growing older can cast into disorienting crisis the terms by which white masculinity defines itself as self-directed and contained.

Over the last decade, critical age studies has emerged as a flourishing interdisciplinary field that examines how age acquires meaning through narrative and culture. Once overlooked as a worthwhile site of scholarly interest, age and aging have become critical vectors for thinking about race and lifespan inequality; dependence and the gendered dimensions of care work; and the unequal distribution of seemingly natural life-stage statuses. Scholars in this field have revealed how chronological age operates as a biopolitical tool and a locus of social demarcation. Margaret Gullette has influentially argued that mainstream American ideas about aging are premised on a "decline narrative" that naturalizes a telos whereby aging is synonymous with a range of losses, including the loss of creativity, cognition, and mobility.[5] Such "decline narratives" reinforce capitalist values, such as productivity and efficiency, and pathologize repose, slowness, and need.

When read through the lens of critical age studies, Emerson's work becomes legible as a key discursive force in the production of the age norms that anchor industrial capitalism. Beyond the embrace of youth and childhood characteristic of Romanticism, Emerson deploys generalizations about the life course that shore up notions of old age as the opponent of individualism and independence, thus setting the terms for contemporary notions of "successful aging."[6] In the pages below, I focus first on his commonplace books and then on a selection of essays that span his career, moving from "Self-Reliance," to "Circles," to "Old Age." By tracking Emerson's engagement with age through these classic essays, Transcendentalism emerges as a youth discourse as his oeuvre associates aging with psychic and physical deficits.

On one hand, growing older seemed to offer Emerson the promise of personal development, as his journal entry above suggests, a usable datapoint for measuring the cultivation of the self. That is, one could acquire greater self-knowledge with age and develop one's intellect, but it also more forcefully raised the threat of dependence and frailty, the nightmarish antithesis of self-reliant manhood. It may have been his youthful bout with blindness that exacerbated the horrors of aging. For a full year of his life, when he was just twenty-two years old, Emerson "went dark," as Louisa Thomas puts it, and ceased writing in his journal. As she writes, "An anxiety over blindness and an obsession with sight subsequently haunts Emerson's work."[7] Along with blindness, the specter of old-age cognitive and material disability haunted Emerson, threatening to undermine his identity as a writer and intellectual, and eventually prophesied his fate.

Emerson's journal serves as a repository for his age anxieties and a venue for developing his personal feelings about the passage of time to broader philosophies about how to age well. At thirty-six years old, he writes, "We ought never to lose our youth ... In all natural and necessary labors as in the work of a farm, in digging, splitting, drawing water, a man always appears young—is still a boy ... He is still a youth. But if his work is unseasonable, as botany & shells or the Greek verbs at 80 years of age ... we say Go up thou baldhead!" (*JMN* 7:283–84). The injunction that one "ought never to lose our youth" suggests that it is a status retained through action and engagement rather than a fixed biological state. And the description of some work as "unseasonable" buttresses notions of age normativity, naturalizing the correspondence between specific behaviors and specific life stages.

Throughout the entries in the 1830s, Emerson links old age with a kind of spiritual degradation while youth is the shorthand for an active, agential existence. For example, in 1840, he writes, "*Old Age*. Sad spectacle that a man should live and be fed that he may fill a paragraph every year in the newspapers for his wonderful age, as we record the weight and girth of the Big Ox or Mammoth girl. We do not count a man's years until he has nothing else to count" (*JMN* 7:361). Even though Emerson himself recorded his weight and age regularly in his commonplace books, the idea of a superannuated man is rendered here as a grotesque spectacle, obsessed with the mere accomplishment of staying alive rather than with living in a fuller sense.

These entries suggest that aging was a chronic menace to Emerson's identity, linked with fears of stagnation, ossification, and decay. In an entry in 1840, he goes so far as to wonder: "Is it possible that a man should not grow old? I will not answer for this crazy body" (*JMN* 7:250). He imagined, or idealized, the self as separate from the body, a division he would cling to until his own later life. In 1842, he writes, "After thirty a man wakes up sad every morning excepting five or six until the day of his death."[8] Here, the very fact of aging is a source of lamentation, connected with loss and decline, and as if to stave off such sadness, he contemplates the divide between his physical self and his sense of an interior and unchanging spiritual age, noting that "within I do not find wrinkles and used heart, but unspent youth" (*JMN* 15:416). Again, he wishfully imagines age outside of material terms, divorcing the physical body from the mind. In these dualist formulations, youth is always the privileged status, the key idiom of a Transcendental way of being. The dissonance between his wrinkles and his "unspent youth" suggests his desire to retain a status connected with power and vitality even as he implies that perhaps his own youthfulness may have been squandered in "unseasonable" work, a life of inaction and study.

Given the tenor of these journal entries, it is no surprise that the essays and public lectures delivered during these same years offered Romantic valorizations of youth and linked aging with disability. In *Nature*, for example, he famously writes, "Few adult persons can see nature" (*CW* 1:9). Adulthood here is linked with a form of blindness, an incapacity for divine revelation or intuition; one is disabled by adulthood, and growing older is an affliction rather than a coming into greater knowledge or self-awareness. Emerson affirms Romantic conceptions of childhood as a special status exempt from the straitening forces of received wisdom and institutional education.

Further, Emerson's Transcendental ideal specifically defined white boyhood as the most desirable cultural position, a position of utter autonomy, free of the encumbrances of others and of the body itself. As a result, the philosophy held special appeal for young people; David Dowling notes that the "the transcendental youth movement" was dubbed "Emerson mania" and describes Emerson's complicated relationship with mentoring the many young people that flocked to him.[9] Recall that for Emerson a "lover of nature" is one who has "retained the spirit of infancy even into the era of manhood." As he explains, "In the woods too, a man casts off his years, as the snake his slough, and at what period so ever of life, is always a child. In the woods is perpetual youth" (*CW* 1:10). Repeatedly, he associates aging and adulthood with inhibition and entrenched thinking, but he posits that one can "slough" these years and return to youth through experiences in the natural world. In other words, aging itself is unnatural and undesirable. He fantasizes youth as a volitional state of mind, a form of consciousness, and imagines one can shed years and return to youth in the right circumstances and with the right disposition. Old age is fundamentally incompatible with this Transcendental vision. Because it is a status that impedes the possibility of the "transcendental eyeball," necessarily lodging one in the body, old age is a discrete subject position in a way that his idealized, unmarked notion of youth ostensibly is not.

Emerson elaborates this perspective even more fully in "Self-Reliance," which celebrates youth as that stage of life most conducive to independent thinking and nonconformity. "Infancy conforms to nobody: all conform to it, so that one babe commonly makes four or five out of the adults who prattle and play to it" (*CW* 2:28–29). Here, infancy is not associated with weakness or dependence but on the contrary with the disruptive power to make others childish and to unsettle social norms. He celebrates "youth and puberty" for their "own piquancy and charm" and cautions: "Do not think the youth has no force, because he cannot speak to you and me. Hark! in the next room his voice is sufficiently clear and emphatic. It seems he knows how to speak to his contemporaries. Bashful or bold, then, he will know how to make us seniors very unnecessary" (*CW* 2:29). In this scenario, young people communicate in a different register; he imagines a generational divide that makes old and young people unable to communicate with one another. "Seniors" do not even speak the same language as younger people, a communication breakdown that ultimately makes them obsolete.

Emerson proceeds to describe "the nonchalance of boys who are sure of a dinner, and would disdain as much as a lord to do or say aught to conciliate one, is the healthy attitude of human nature. A boy is in the parlour what the pit is in the playhouse; independent, irresponsible, looking out from his corner on such people and facts as pass by, he tries and sentences them on their merits, in the swift, summary way of boys, as good, bad, interesting, silly, eloquent, troublesome" (*CW* 2:29). Like the "pit in the playhouse," this idealized boyhood represents a status untainted by social norms or the impositions of conventional thinking. Significantly, Emerson genders youth, as young girls were not granted this same freedom, and while he doesn't specify this irreverent, "irresponsible" boyhood as white, certainly Black boys were not granted the sort of social latitude that Emerson takes for granted in this idealization of boyhood.[10] Indeed, the "nonchalance of boys who are sure of a dinner" indicates that he was thinking exclusively of privileged boys from the middle and upper echelons of the social strata, unconcerned about their next meal or their seat at the proverbial table.

As a glimpse at these canonical essays makes clear, age operates as a key index for Emerson in his theorizations of self-reliance and Transcendentalism; more precisely, it serves as a sort of shorthand for a value system that idealizes youth and saddles old age with a host of negative associations. The notion that one should refrain from "dragging about the corpse of memory" suggests that the struggle of aging is that it tethers one to the weight of past identities and prior forms of knowing; thus, the challenge of aging is to remain new to oneself, resisting the pull to remain consistent with younger selves (*CW* 2:33). It is not merely that old age is linked with the retrospective sanctification of the "fathers" and the "dry bones of the past"; it is more broadly correlated with intellectual stagnation and institutional thinking (*CW* 1:3).

One context for Emerson's thinking about age and the life course is the shifting cultural landscape in which he entered adulthood and old age. Over the course of the nineteenth century, mainstream US culture witnessed a seismic shift in the political and cultural significance of age. Such a deficit model of aging became especially widespread in the middle of the nineteenth century with the rise of industrial capitalism, mass media, and advertising. The demographics of the nation transformed to include an unprecedented number of people over sixty, a significant precursor to the "graying" of the American population so often discussed in our own historical moment. Along with this demographic change, the nineteenth century saw the rise of age-graded schooling, age-specific medical treatments, and the emergence of a commodity and periodical culture that enshrined age as socially meaningful. Age segregation and the move away from multigenerational contexts were core components of modernization.

The US census reveals this profound change in thinking about the human life course: the 1790 census simply recorded whether free white males were older or younger than sixteen (and significantly did not even ask women and people of color to report their ages), while the 1850 asked individuals to report a specific numerical age. With this addition as a primary identifier on the census, age was enfolded into a governmental project of tabulating citizens' biopolitical information. As Judith Treas writes, chronological age became the "linchpin of a host of standards for stratifying individuals in a uniform fashion—a practice that gives rise to the standardization of the life course."[11] What seemed like a new datapoint for establishing individual identity actually served to plot individuals along normative developmental trajectories; indeed, the ostensibly democratic project of the census enlisted the populace in age awareness, making individuals complicit in the project of monitoring and acting their ages. That the first commercial birthday cards were printed in the US just a few decades later suggests the extent to which observing numerical age became an essential aspect of social identity as well as an industry.[12]

Popular iconography stressed the linear path of development, as if to remind Americans that life cycles remained constant in spite of uncertainties in social and political life. Along with Thomas Cole's popular *Voyage of Life* series (1842), Nathanial

Currier, George Cram, and James Baillie were just a few of the artists to depict the stages of life in series that naturalized assumptions about the life cycle, including that one should progress according to a timeless, linear model of development and that manhood should be a period of physical and spiritual testing. Such images were posted on bedroom walls and printed as broadsides, and in the words of one historian, the popularity of this theme reveals "just how obsessed Americans really were with the life cycle during the middle decades of the 19th century."[13] As critic Thomas Cole puts it, "This iconography of the life course reveals the middle-class quest for a normal life course, increasingly defined in terms of health and material self-reliance."[14]

Beginning in the first decade of the nineteenth century, age, rather than property ownership, became the relevant qualification for voting (for white men) and age-segregated institutions such as convalescent homes and children's hospitals became mainstays of the American cultural landscape.[15] The nineteenth century also gave rise to what we now call the "cult of youth" and to an anxiety about old age that David Hackett Fisher refers to as "gerontophobia," displacing a longstanding tradition of reverence for older people.[16] Old age was increasingly regarded as a medical condition; one late-nineteenth-century medical researcher described old age as "an infectious, chronic disease."[17] In his 1858 bestselling treatise, *Medical Common Sense*, Dr. Edward Bliss Foote went so far as to caution readers about the dangers of exposing children to prolonged physical contact with people of advanced age: "When, by contact for long nights with elder and negative persons, the vitalizing electricity of their tender organizations is given off, they soon pine, grow pale, languid and dull, while their bed companions feel a corresponding invigoration."[18] Thus, the older people could supposedly sap the strength and vitality from children by sheer proximity.

In the face of a rapidly industrializing economy, old age became a liability rather than a benefit in a workplace that came to value expertise and professional credentials over experience and seniority. Enjoining older people to resist dominant understandings of old age as a time of loss and estrangement from mainstream culture, poet Lydia Sigourney asks in 1856, "Is it worthwhile to be so much shocked at the circumstance of becoming old? Is it a mark of excommunication from our race?"[19] As it turns out, for many, especially marginalized people, aging *was* a kind of excommunication. By the end of the century, "senescence," a synonym then for old age, was considered "a distinctive and debilitated state of existence," in the words of historian Carole Haber.[20]

The professionalization of medicine, along with the rise of social science, catalyzed a shift in the way Americans understood and experienced aging. As W. Andrew Achenbaum notes, "With growing frequency after the Civil War, Americans began to challenge nearly every favorable belief about the usefulness and merits of age."[21] As older people lost their utility to the prevailing economic system, the aging body came to be seen as a sign of failure and a site of revulsion.[22] We might therefore see the second half of the nineteenth century not only as the era in which institutional care emerged for the aged but also as the era in which ageism itself was institutionalized.

Many writers found creative ways to resist or revise the age discourse circulating in popular culture, highlighting the instability of age as a reliable metric. Frederick

Douglass famously lamented how the institution of slavery eroded the meanings of age. Of his white enslaver's son, he wrote in *My Bondage and My Freedom* (1855), "He could grow, and become a MAN; I could grow, though I could not become a man, but must remain, all my life, a minor—a mere boy."[23] As Douglass makes clear, slavery severs aging from the opportunity for self-development and from the rights of adult citizenship; his autobiographies upend naturalized ideas about youth and old age, both of which are revealed as meaningful only in relation to race and gender. The literature of slavery repeatedly exposes age as a vector of power, a site through which enslavers could ascribe value to enslaved people's lives and delimit the category of the human as a white category. Certainly Emerson's anti-developmental fantasies take on a more complex light when considered in relation to those excluded from political and social forms of adulthood.

Nineteenth-century women writers were keenly aware of how age norms also served to uphold gender-based forms of injustice, drawing attention in particular to what Susan Sontag would eventually dub the "double standard of aging," an ideology that links male aging with prestige while it correlates inversely to women's diminishing value. Sontag's theorization of age and gender, written at the height of second-wave feminism, articulates a political concern that germinated over a century earlier and preoccupied Emerson's Concord neighbor and acolyte, Louisa May Alcott. Consider Jo March's lament in *Little Women* (1868): "At twenty-five, girls begin to talk about being old maids, but secretly resolve they never will be. At thirty they say nothing about it, but quietly accept the fact."[24] Through Jo's reflections, Alcott points to how the failure to comply with heteronormativity can render a woman prematurely "old," as the pejorative term "old maid" penalizes women for noncompliance with the dual codes of age and gender. While Emerson claimed that a man was more likely to be "sad" after turning thirty, his melancholic reflection obscures the fact that white male aging typically bolsters prestige and political recognition.

Indeed, where women writers and writers of color acknowledged age ideology as a disciplinary force linked with the maintenance of gender and racial hierarchies, white male writers largely clung to and helped concretize normative understandings of age. Henry James, for example, reinforced the doctrine that older women should remain out of public life with his unflattering caricature of the politically engaged Miss Birdseye in *The Bostonians*, a pathetic symbol of obsolescence and exhaustion. And conversely sixty-two-year-old Walt Whitman added a line in the 1881 edition of *Leaves of Grass* describing himself as "thirty-seven years old, in perfect health," wishfully identifying himself with robust youth.[25]

But it was Emerson who laid the groundwork for these visions of aging; perhaps more than any other writer, his work codifies age as a site of diminishing returns, consecrating youth as a form of capital and a resource that should be safeguarded. In an effort to reconcile himself with the phenomenon of aging—and to retain the power of youth— his essays often fantasize about how to extend youth into old age and expound on the capacity for willpower to delay or even circumvent the material realities of aging. In "Circles," published in 1841, Emerson posits a vision of growth as expansion through its central motif of the circle, a theory of development linked with expansion and dilation, and yet such development is explicitly divorced from aging. As Emerson puts it, "old age seems the only disease: all others run into this one. We call it by many names,—fever, intemperance, insanity, stupidity, and crime: they are all forms of old age: they are rest, conservatism, appropriation, inertia, not newness, not the way onward. We grizzle every day. I see no need of it" (*CW* 2:188–89). This gerontophobic screed directs its ire at those who have fallen victim to old age through their own ineffective lifestyles; he sees their resignation to these "forms of old age" as failures of will, signs of lethargy, rather than aspects of varied human experience. Old age, in Emerson's estimation, is something that one can avoid with enough grit; indeed, there is "no need of it," and no need of "rest."

By defining "old age" specifically as "not newness," Emerson squarely positions it against Transcendentalism, commonly known as "the Newness," and thus reinforces the idea that only through the relentless action and ambition of boyhood can one access an original relation to the world and to the divine.[26] Significantly, Emerson believed that aesthetic encounters had the capacity to take us out of the quotidian, "hodiernal" circle and put us into contact with new ideas and other minds. As he writes, the poet "smites and arouses me with his shrill tones, breaks up my whole of habits, and I open my eye on my own possibilities" (*CW* 2:185). Literature can thus wield a kind of anti-aging power, disrupting the psychic effects of aging even if they cannot offset the corporeal ones.

Such a perspective led Henry David Thoreau to declare eighty-one-year-old Mary Moody Emerson "the youngest person in Concord."[27] For Thoreau, like her nephew Emerson, this impressive intellectual woman remained "young," precisely because of her intellectual and psychic vivacity. As Emerson elaborates in "Circles": "Whilst we converse with what is above us, we do not grow old; but grow young. Infancy, youth, receptive, aspiring, with religious eye looking upward, counts itself nothing, and abandons itself to the instruction flowing from all sides. But the man and woman of seventy assume to know all, they have outlived their hope, they renounce aspiration, accept the actual for the necessary, and talk down to the young … This old age ought not to creep on a human mind" (*CW* 2:189). To avoid the "creep" of old age, one must remain a perpetual student, capable of surprise, open to learning from others.

Later in "Circles," this philosophy of aging comes into fuller view. He writes, "People wish to be settled: only as far as they are unsettled is there any hope for them" (*CW* 2:189). Whereas earlier in his life, in his commonplace books, he had expressed the possibility that getting older should mean accruing more knowledge, here he rejects this idea and instead advocates a Romantic embrace of unknowing. "I cast away in this moment all my once hoarded knowledge, as vacant and vain. Now, for the first time, seem I to know any thing rightly" (*CW* 2:189). Here the ideas that were percolating in "Self-Reliance" and *Nature* reach their full development; he articulates "hoarded knowledge" and experience as impediments to insight, emphasizing instead a desire to remain uncertain and aware of the limits of one's own knowledge.

As the essay progresses, Emerson continues to articulate a vision of life premised on drawing new circles, abandoning prior selves, not ossifying into an unchangeable, fixed identity. Such a vision theoretically allows for extended youth and the potential to hold onto the privileges of youth indefinitely. Of "Circles," Ronald A. Bosco observes that

"Emerson dismisses all negative connotations typically associated with a culture's or an individual's advancing years. Believing that cultures do not necessarily decline with age, he argues that with cultures as with men, there has to be a 'proportion between the designs of [each] and the length of [their life]'" (*CW* 7:lviii). Bosco sees the essay as engaging with an extended metaphor for the nation as it matured through war as well as a reflection on Emerson's own aging. And yet, here we can see Emerson's profound idealism at play, as he underscores again the notion that one might think oneself out of aging, disability, senility.

"Circles" thus reads age as a malleable status, one that can be evaded through adopting a position of perpetual unknowing and unsettling, but it nonetheless affirms youth as the only desirable status. Furthermore, despite the essay's reliance on circles as the operative non-linear metaphor and symbol for the life course, it denies the materiality of the body, even as it begins with the eye as the central and primal circle. Despite Emerson's embrace of circular and the cyclical here, he ultimately hierarchizes the stages of life and elides the material realities of aging. Indeed, Emerson seems to be suggesting that if one tries hard enough, one can perhaps outwit the forces of aging that lead to dullness and stagnation, affirming historian David Hackett Fisher's observation that "Americans like to act like aging is a form of voluntary action."[28]

By the time Emerson wrote "Old Age," which he delivered as a lecture in 1861 and published in the *Atlantic* the following year, he was fifty-nine years old, only a few years away from the onset of the dementia that would characterize his final decade. "Old Age" reveals Emerson reckoning with the repressive cultural discourses he helped to invent and circulate. While it is clear he no longer sees aging as merely a "state of mind" the way he did in "Circles" or as a disease or lethargy of the spirit, the essay never fully accepts the somatic realities of aging or sees Emerson fully reconcile himself to inhabiting the category of old age. Instead, he wrestles with the very discourses he put into place, grappling with how to redeem an aspect of human existence he spent most of his career degrading.

"Old Age" begins by clarifying that the appearance of old age itself should not automatically confer respect, as the visible signs of old age do not always correlate to wisdom. As he explains, "the venerable forms that so awed our childhood were just such impostors ... Nature is full of freaks, and now puts an old head on young shoulders, and then a young heart beating under fourscore winters" (*CW* 7:160). As he writes, "For if the essence of age is not present, these signs, whether of Art or Nature, are counterfeit and ridiculous: and the essence of age is intellect" (*CW* 7:160). Thus, Emerson theorizes age again as a psychic state, divorced from the physical body, observing that nature lends us "masks" but "all is not Age that wears them." This seemingly anti-essentialist perspective makes "Age" a status of power and intellect, not merely the inevitable honorific bequeathed by the passage of time.

The essay exudes a kind of troubling recognition that old age is a marginalized status and that one cannot evade its public meanings or avoid being interpellated by it, even by maintaining openness and receptivity. He writes, for example, about how old age is unwelcome and unappreciated in urban spaces and public venues:

> Age is comely in coaches, in churches, in chairs of state and ceremony, in council-chambers, in courts of justice, and historical societies. Age is becoming in the country. But in the rush and uproar of Broadway, if you look into the faces of the passengers, there is dejection or indignation in the seniors, a certain concealed sense of injury, and the lip made up with a heroic determination not to mind it. (*CW* 7:161–62)

Emerson acknowledges that older people are socially ostracized; for him, aging represents a check on a previously limitless mobility and universal acceptance. While "youth is everywhere in place," a kind of passport to move freely through all spaces, "age, like woman,—requires fit surroundings" (*CW* 7:161). This linkage of aging with womanhood reveals the extent to which he fundamentally saw "old age" as linked with a more circumscribed life and a loss of privilege. Moreover, Emerson's articulation of the social geography of old age and his sense of older people as out of place in the public sphere, that it "requires fit surroundings," aligns with the coextensive prohibition of disabled people in the labor market and the public sphere; people with visible disabilities were simultaneously cast "as morally questionable dependents in need of permanent rehabilitation to achieve 'self-care' and 'self-support,'" as Sarah Rose puts it.[29] When read alongside "Self-Reliance," "Old Age" reminds us of how aging alters one's social orientation and can impel a belated political awakening, rupturing the ease of inhabiting an invisible white male body in an era of profound racial and sexual injustice.

For Emerson, the entrance into old age not only challenged his capacities for self-reliance but troubled his identity as a writer, thinker, and individual. As older Americans became subjects of social organization and medical scrutiny, they were cast as a uniform group. As Stephen Katz writes, "technologies of differentiation constituted the elderly as a kind of population-subject."[30] As the nineteenth century progressed, older people were rendered valueless in profit-driven economies. Sonia Kruks puts it in terms of seriality: "Each isolated and each 'the same,' the elderly are passively unified by the social institutions and practices that serialize them in the collective of the 'aged.'"[31] Kruks's formulation reveals how growing old involves conscription into an externally imposed category. For the foremost voice of individualism, this ascription of old-age identity concerned Emerson because, as with any ascribed identity, it colonizes one's self-perception and individual identity.

In "Old Age," Emerson seeks to redeem some aspects of growing older, enumerating its ostensible benefits, but his often sardonic tone mainly ends up reifying the age-based stereotypes he found imprisoning. He notes, for example, that "the passions have answered their purpose"; "success more or less signifies nothing"; one has found expression and a keener sense of attention and ability to complete tasks (*CW* 7:164). Emerson observes that young people are often restless, with "an excess of sensibility" (*CW* 7:166), but he binarizes age, describing older people as staid and stalwart. "In old persons, when thus fully expressed, we often observe a fair, plump, perennial, waxen complexion, which indicates that all the ferment of earlier days has subsided into serenity of thought and behavior" (*CW* 7:166). With this characterization of "plump" and "waxen" old people, Emerson universalizes old age as a status of complacence, unmarked by class, race, or gender, affirming the increasingly popular idea that old age was ideally a period of resolution rather than experimentation and discovery.

His journal entries from this same time period also lament that old age signifies the loss of vim and intellectual vigor: "The grief of old age is, that now, only in rare moments, ... can we attain those enlargements and that intellectual elan, which were once a daily gift ... old age brings along with its ugliness the comfort that you will soon be out of it—which ought to be a substantial relief to such discontented pendulums as we are ... old age. 'Tis proposed to call an indignation meeting."[32] Emerson observes that the intellectual "elan" he took for granted is more elusive, and his proposed "indignation meeting" suggests his rage at getting old, his frustration with its loss and limitations and attendant indignities, and the realization that even his body can become vulnerable, frail, and impossible to transcend.[33] Emerson is angry about how little affordances the world makes for those who prefer rest or require assistance, the very aspects of aging he claimed he could avoid through force of will in "Circles."

In "Terminus"—his last published poem but likely written in his forties—Emerson invokes the "voyage of life" imagery that was so pervasive in popular iconography of the life course:

> It is time to be old,
> To take in sail:—
> The god of bounds,
> Who sets to seas a shore,
> Came to me in his fatal rounds,
> And said: "No more!"
> (*CW* 9:469–70)

Emerson envisions the onset of old age akin to entering the harbor, taking down the sails, coming back to shore. The "time to be old" is the end of adventure and danger, and more than this, it means giving up creativity. As he writes, "Fancy departs: no more invent" (*CW* 9:470). Just as in "Old Age," he reinforces the notion of old age as a period of retreat and disengagement, not only for himself, but more broadly.

And yet the departure of "fancy" need not characterize late life; such elegies for creative thought suggest the extent to which Emerson internalized—and reinscribed—the disdain for older people circulating in periodicals and mainstream culture. Indeed, his point of view in this elegiac poem echoes George Miller Beard's view of old age in his bestselling book *American Nervousness* (1888), which equates aging with the loss of innovative thinking. Beard claimed he was the "first to make the discovery of the law of relation of age to work." He writes: "I find no record of any very important invention conceived and developed after the age of 60. Edison with his three hundred patents, is not the only young inventor. All inventors are young."[34] Such a view is the logical endpoint of Emersonian thinking that connects adulthood with blindness and a loss of creative vision.

More than once, Emerson asked, "Is it possible a man should not grow old?" Responding to this question has become the province and preoccupation of Google scientists and "longevity experts," who sell millions of books promising to offer the right diet and exercise plans and project-driven retirement lifestyles to stave off the effects of aging. Emerson's age anxiety was linked to the external, material aspects of aging but also to his fear of psychic dulling, interior and intellectual stagnation; aging, for Emerson, was most pernicious as a thief of perception and insight. To lose one's vision and capacity for new insights was ultimately to become irrelevant, making old age and its attendant disabilities the singular threats to Emerson's otherwise guaranteed ability and permission to speak and move freely and without assistance.

Ultimately, his own doctrine of self-reliance and radical individualism helped to put in place the foundations of what gerontologists now call "successful aging," an aspirational ideal which celebrates a version of getting old defined by activity, self-disciplining, and independence. Such a neoliberal accomplishment recuses the state or even the private family from providing care or resources and instead applauds the individual for aging without debility and dependence. This version of aging necessarily reads as "unsuccessful" those forms of aging that require assistance, entail repose or stillness, and do not resemble youth. According to this ethos, successful aging is best understood as the rejection of aging, a sort of paradoxical denial of change itself.

It is this vision of autonomous liberal selfhood that made Emerson's own anxieties so profound and that conditioned the critical response to his work. Only recently have scholars moved past euphemizing or ignoring his dementia to consider his old-age writing as a form of commentary on the models of strident individualism that are the hallmarks of his most well-known essays. Scholars, including Christopher Hanlon, Phyllis Cole, and Nikhil Bilwakesh, have considered the communal production of Emerson's final publications as incitements to rethink notions of textual authority and authorial intention that revere individual genius and solitary creation.[35] This long overdue critical engagement with Emerson's late life and recognition of his reliance on an intimate network of editors and collaborators illuminates how Emerson himself was mired in the legacy of his most celebrated postulations. Further, such readings of late Emerson invite us to consider alternative models of old age creativity and relationality. For example, Swedish gerontologist Lars Tornstam's theory of "gerotranscendence" offers an alternative to Emersonian Transcendentalism that sees old age not as the endpoint of insight but rather as a time of dawning awareness and potential new affinities across temporalities and generations.[36] As scholars return to Emerson in the wake of critical age studies and disability studies, methodological turns that have exposed conventional thinking about bodies through the logic of biocapitalism, Emerson's age discourse warrants renewed attention for how it entwines Transcendental thinking with normative visions of the life course and exposes the valorized youthful subject as a disciplinary fiction with particular stakes for white masculinity.

Notes

1. Of this same passage, Julie Ellison notes that Emerson's "self-loathing is expressed in the image of himself as an old man with a baby's playthings and in the savage precision with which he summarizes the motives of his 'brilliant visions of future grandeur.'" See Ellison, *Emerson's Romantic Style* (Princeton, NJ: Princeton University Press, 1984): 31.
2. See Howard Chudacoff, *How Old Are You?: Age Consciousness in American Culture* (Princeton: Princeton University Press, 1989), 20.
3. In *The Collected Works of Ralph Waldo Emerson* (2010), Ronald Bosco and Joel Myerson treat Emerson's aphasia and memory loss more directly than previous biographers and scholars. For a scholarly analysis of Emerson's dementia in relation to processes of composition, see Nikhil Bilwakesh's "Emerson's Decomposition: *Parnassus*," *Nineteenth-Century Literature* 67, no. 4 (2013): 520–45.
4. Christopher Hanlon, *Emerson's Memory Loss: Originality, Communality, and the Late Style* (New York: Oxford University Press, 2018), 19.
5. Margaret Morganroth Gullette, *Aged by Culture* (Chicago: University of Chicago Press, 2004), 13.
6. For a popular discussion of "successful aging," see Daniel Levitin's 2020 New York Times bestseller, *Successful Aging: A Neuroscientist Explores the Power and Potential of our Lives* (New York: Dutton, 2020).
7. Louisa Thomas, "Emerson's Eyes," *Sewanee Review* 125, no. 4 (Fall 2017): 822–32, 823.
8. Ralph Waldo Emerson, *Emerson in His Journals*, ed. Joel Porter (Cambridge, MA: Harvard University Press, 1982), 142.
9. David Dowling, *Emerson's Protégés: Mentoring and Marketing Transcendentalism's Future* (New Haven, CT: Yale University Press, 2014), 11.
10. Of nineteenth-century girlhood, Melanie Dawson notes that "because girls are encouraged to act out scenes of maturity, take on domestic duties, and develop self-monitoring skills, girlhood appears nearly indistinct from womanhood." See Melanie Dawson, "The Miniaturizing of Girlhood: Nineteenth-Century Playtime and Gendered Theories of Development," in *The American Child: A Cultural Studies Reader*, ed. Caroline Levander and Carol Singley (New Brunswick: Rutgers University Press, 2003): 63–84, 66.
11. Judith Treas, "Age in Standards and Standards for Age: Institutionalizing Chronological Age as Biographical Necessity," in *Standards and Their Stories: How Quantifying, Classifying, and Formalizing Practices Shape Everyday Life*, ed. Martha Lampland and Susan Leigh Star (Ithaca, NY: Cornell University Press, 2009): 65–88, 87.
12. I do not mean to suggest that age was meaningless before the nineteenth century. Eighteenth-century Americans unevenly relied on age qualifications for militia duty and jury service, and many Americans recorded their births, deaths, and developmental benchmarks like marriage in family Bibles. Holly Brewer's *By Birth or Consent: Children, Law, and the Anglo-American Revolution in Authority* (Chapel Hill: University of North Carolina Press, 2005) examines the construction of childhood in relation to the shift from status as the basis of political authority to consent. See also Corinne T. Field and Nicholas L. Syrett, eds., *Age in America: The Colonial Era to the Present* (New York: New York University Press, 2015).
13. Michael Kammen, "Changing Perceptions of the Life Cycle in American Thought and Culture," *Proceedings of the Massachusetts Historical Society* 91 (1979): 35–66, 45.

14. Thomas Cole, *The Journey of Life: A Cultural History of Aging in America* (Cambridge: Cambridge University Press, 1992), 111.
15. On the democratization of voting, see Jon Grinspan, *The Virgin Vote: How Young Americans Made Democracy Social, Politics Personal, and Voting Popular in the Nineteenth Century* (Chapel Hill: University of North Carolina Press, 2016). On the establishment of Philadelphia's first home for the elderly, see Carole Haber, "The Old Folks at Home: The Development of Institutionalized Care for the Aged in Nineteenth-Century Philadelphia," *Pennsylvania Magazine of History and Biography* 101 (1977): 240–57.
16. See David Hackett Fisher, *Growing Old in America* (New York: Oxford University Press, 1977), 113. While most historians agree that what we now call "ageism" was firmly in place by the turn of the twentieth century, there is some disagreement about when and why this view of elderly people as burdensome and unappealing first arose. For an overview of the scholarship on old age in the US, see Carole Haber and Brian Gratton, *Old Age and the Search for Security: An American Social History* (Bloomington: Indiana University Press, 1994).
17. Elie Metchnikoff theorized old age as pathological; he coined the term "gerontology" in 1903. Quoted in W. Andrew Achenbaum, *Crossing Frontiers: Gerontology Emerges as a Science* (New York: Cambridge University Press, 1995), 30. Thomas Cole notes, "In England and America, the word 'senile' itself was transformed in the nineteenth century from a general term signifying old age to a medical term for the inevitably debilitated condition of the aged" (196). See also Carole Haber, *Beyond Sixty-Five: The Dilemma of Old Age in America's Past* (New York: Cambridge University Press, 1985).
18. Edward Bliss Foote, *Medical Common Sense* (New York: Published by the author, 1868), 46.
19. Lydia Sigourney, *Past Meridian* (Hartford, CT, 1857), 21.
20. Carole Haber, *Beyond Sixty-Five: The Dilemma of Old Age in America's Past* (Cambridge: Cambridge University Press, 1983), 4.
21. Andrew W. Achenbaum, *Old Age in the New Land: The American Experience Since 1790* (Baltimore: Johns Hopkins University Press, 1978), 40.
22. Jane Gallop observes that "in the current moment, the worship of the reproductive future might in fact devalue old people even more than it does queers." Gallop, *Sexuality, Disability, and Aging: Queer Temporalities of the Phallus* (Durham, NC: Duke University Press, 2019), 11.
23. Frederick Douglass, *My Bondage and My Freedom* (New York: Penguin, 2003), 224.
24. Louisa May Alcott, *Little Women* (New York: Penguin, 2000), 440.
25. As David S. Reynolds notes, "In 1881, readers knew well enough that Walt Whitman was neither thirty-seven nor in perfect health." Reynolds, *Walt Whitman's America: A Cultural Biography* (New York: Vintage, 1995), 535.
26. See Dowling, *Emerson's Protégés*, 10–11 and 26–27 for a discussion of this term.
27. See Noelle Baker and Sandra Petrulionis, "Mary Moody Emerson Was a Scholar, a Thinker, and an Inspiration," *Humanities* 38, no. 1 (Winter 2017).
28. Fisher, *Growing Old in America*, 129.
29. See Sarah Rose, *No Right to be Idle: The Invention of Disability, 1850–1930* (Chapel Hill: University of North Carolina Press).
30. Stephen Katz, *Disciplining Old Age: The Formation of Gerontological Knowledge* (Charlottesville: University Press of Virginia, 1996), 76.

31. Sonia Kruks, "Simone de Beauvoir: Engaging Discrepant Materialisms," in *New Materialisms: Ontology, Agency, and Politics*, ed. Diana Coole and Samantha Frost (Durham, NC: Duke University Press, 2010), 258–80, 273.
32. Emerson, *Emerson in his Journals*, 516.
33. Ibid., 517.
34. George Miller Beard, *American Nervousness* (New York: G. P. Putnam's Sons, 1881), 237.
35. Phyllis Cole, "The New Emerson Canon," *Resources for American Literary Study* 37 (2014): 261–73.
36. Lars Tornstam, "Gerotranscendence: The Contemplative Dimension of Aging," *Journal of Aging Studies* 11, no. 2 (Summer 1997): 143–54.

CHAPTER 33
....

APHASIC ETYMOLOGY

A Disability Poetics and the Emerson-Whitman Connection

....

DON JAMES MCLAUGHLIN

FEW relationships of influence between American writers have received as much attention as the connection between Ralph Waldo Emerson and Walt Whitman. From their first epistolary encounter, both foresaw the possibility of such a future. When Whitman sent the Concord philosopher a copy of his inaugural 1855 edition of *Leaves of Grass*, the recipient responded with a staggering concentration of quotable praise. "The most extraordinary piece of wit and wisdom that America has yet contributed," Emerson called it in a letter of gratitude dated July 21, ". . . I rubbed my eyes a little, to see if this sunbeam were no illusion."[1] Whitman put the flattery to good use. By October 1855, the savvy self-promoter had arranged for Emerson's letter to be printed in the *New York Tribune*. Copies of the letter began to appear pasted to the front or back endpaper of first editions.[2] The genealogy seemed to Whitman a natural fit. As John Townsend Trowbridge would recall the poet telling him in Boston in the spring of 1860, Whitman felt that reading Emerson, whose essays he carried to work in a pail beside his lunch in Brooklyn in 1854, had expedited self-discovery: "I was simmering, simmering, simmering; Emerson brought me to a boil."[3] Curiously, this same 1860 excursion to Boston, taken to prepare the third edition of *Leaves* for publication with Thayer & Eldridge, marks also the occasion Whitman and Emerson became most acutely aware of their differences. As *Leaves* grew more vocal in its celebration of sex, in the newly integrated "Enfans d'Adam" and "Calamus" clusters especially, Emerson urged the poet to reconsider—as Whitman records, "asked whether I could consent to eliminate certain popularly objectionable poems and passages."[4] Whitman tells us in another published account, "I felt down in my soul the clear and unmistakable conviction to disobey all, and pursue my own way."[5] These two nodes, of public praise in 1855 and diverging paths five years later, have structured the extraordinary body of scholarship interested in the significance of their bond, from F. O. Matthiessen to Harold Bloom,

Jay Grossman to Jacques Rancière. The inadvertent consequence is that one of the most meaningful Emerson-Whitman encounters, their successive meetings at Emerson's house in Concord, September 17–18, 1881, seven months before Emerson's death, has been all but fully eclipsed.

This essay rereads the Emerson-Whitman connection by looking backward, through the lens of their final meeting. I propose that the final meeting sheds light on, and provides a fitting culmination for, a relation that had from its initiation been founded partly on a disability poetics scholars have neglected. In remembrance of their last meeting, Whitman notes Emerson's minimal speech: "the best of the present occasion (Sunday, September 18, '81) was the sight of E. himself. As just said a healthy color in the cheeks and good light in the eyes, cheery expression, and just the amount of talking that best suited, namely, a word or short phrase only where needed, and almost always with a smile."[6] Readers familiar with Emerson's biography will intuit that Whitman is partly referencing his former mentor's experience of dementia, which scholars today believe had likely progressed to Alzheimer's disease. As Christopher Hanlon traces in *Emerson's Memory Loss: Originality, Communality, and the Late Style* (2018), Emerson began to deal increasingly with aphasia, an inability to summon desired speech, by 1864, and would display a loss of memory so great by 1872 that his daughter Ellen feared it had become "entire." It has been difficult to discern the exact nature of Emerson's memory loss in the last two decades of his life, in part because contemporaries and subsequent critics guarded this knowledge, from each other and themselves, through delicate euphemism.[7] Indeed, nineteenth-century accounts set in motion a tradition of omission that has, until recently, continued to cloud Emerson studies. As Hanlon explains, wherever scholars come across revealing details, such as Ellen's report that when a fire consumed their family home, "The Bush," her father began throwing rescued belongings back into the blaze, such "anecdotal evidence of Emerson's senility jars the critical apparatus ... it unsettles a tacit agreement among so many commentators that the available facts concerning Emerson's derangement in late life shall not be addressed in a plainspoken way."[8] For anyone who has experienced memory loss, personally or with a loved one, these manifestations of stigma and uncertainty around representation will resonate. This uncertainty has also made scholars less likely to take interest in the final, in-person Emerson-Whitman encounter.

The theme of memory's fallibility and its capacity to be reconceived within a collective frame can be followed across Emerson's career before he began to regret his personal lapses in memory openly. In a luminous close reading of textual variants in Emerson's "Eloquence," Hanlon explores how the essay stages a complex relationship between orator, audience, and speech, lauding at some moments the "power to master other people with words," leaning elsewhere into a "view of oration *and* of textuality that is more communal," even at home with "a certain estrangement from his own words."[9] Fittingly, revisions to "Eloquence" in later versions, prepared by Ellen and Emerson's literary executor James Elliot Cabot, appear to enact this very thematic tension in the form of editorial praxis.[10] Hanlon reveals how a line excised from Emerson's 1847 manuscript for the essay's first publication reappears in an 1875 printing arranged by Ellen and

Cabot. "In moments of clearer thought or deeper sympathy," the resuscitated line asserts, "the voice will attain a music and penetration which surprises the speaker as much as the auditor; he also is a sharer of the higher wind that blows over his strings. I believe that some orators go to the assembly as to a closet where to find their best thoughts."[11] Was this reclamation Emerson's preference? Or an executive decision made by Ellen? Not all questions raised by these textual recoveries can be answered. What we may conclude is that such editorial renewals enabled a performance of remembering as a collaborative, de-individualized endeavor. To illustrate this point, Hanlon observes Ellen's message to her sister Edith, "Father exclaimed yesterday, 'Correcting these proofs is work that pays well. Selections made long ago, and forgotten, keep rising, each as fresh as a star.'"[12] This communal reformulation of the meaning of memory reveals how such concerns had been lurking at the heart of Emerson's project from the outset.

Building on Hanlon's work, this essay proposes a strain of thought in Emerson's corpus, both prior to and during his profound memory loss, which I describe as "aphasic etymology": a studied devotion to the depths of linguistic meaning invested in reckoning consciously with our inability to excavate all that we are trying to express. I track this career-long interest in verbal estrangement through the essay that left its greatest impact on Whitman, "The Poet" (1844), where Emerson argues that all language, originating first as poetic expression, then representing gradually the burial and disappearance of these inaugural poetic embers, progresses toward collective memory loss. In this respect, "The Poet" makes room for a social model of aphasic etymology, directly citing the "fossil poetry" embedded in language as a kind of forgetting commons (*CW* 3:13). We do our best to use words for purposes of expression, but, consistently, our words fall short of reminding us of their founding *raison d'être*. Whether consciously or not, the human mind experiences communication as a persistent grappling with impasses separating speech and meaning. We crave forms of recollection that reach into deep time and return to us the pictorial catalyst impelling a word's spectacular materialization. "Poetry" is the name we give to the mechanism of accessibility that enables traversal of these distances.

In the body of this essay, I unfold Emerson's aphasic etymology in "The Poet" to offer what I hope will make for an original contribution to our understanding of Emerson's relationship with Whitman. As noted above, this scholarship has been vast. Matthiessen helped cement a familiar understanding of their relation in *The American Renaissance*, writing, "Whitman set out more deliberately than any of his contemporaries to create the kind of hero whom Emerson had foreshadowed in his varying guises of the Scholar and the Poet."[13] Grossman has revised this narrative with attention to the dissonance that structured their dialogue. In an extensive study revolving around Whitman's recurring replays of the disagreement in Boston Common, Grossman proposes, "Emerson's and Whitman's differences about the sexuality of the 'Enfans d'Adam' cluster might be reimagined not as a mere conflict of 'taste' or 'literary measurements,' but rather as a defining disagreement sufficient to undo the claims of a supposedly foundational Emersonianism in the first place."[14] Bloom comes close to introducing something like a shared disability poetics in his elevation of anxiety as a normal affective dynamic that illuminates the reciprocal indebtedness among writers. Advocating a method of "kenosis," taken from Christian theology to mean renunciation of divinity in the embrace of precarious embodiment, Bloom urges, in partial reference to Emerson and Whitman, "We need to stop thinking of any poet as an autonomous ego, however solipsistic the strongest of poets may be. Every poet is a being caught up in a dialectical relationship (transference, repetition, error, communication) with another poet or poets."[15]

While finding each of these interventions instructive, I argue that readings predicated on the compulsion to seek or reject hierarchy (or, relatedly, a search for origins) stand to benefit from a divergent orientation, namely the aphasic etymology we find in "The Poet." To be sure, a visceral demand of memory loss is the way it decentralizes a priority of origins, generating radical ambiguity about the value of a pristinely recuperable past. There are silences that shroud, but epiphanies about the irrelevance of exactitude to numerous modes of meaningful interaction also flourish in these experiences. Dignity, care, and connection in facing memory loss necessitate a deviant navigation of the proximity of past and present. In deprivileging matters of synchrony or discord in the Common for the sake of inhabiting together a forgetting commons, the meanings of "connection" and "encounter" are liberated to accommodate a range of intimacies otherwise precluded.

Emerson and Disability

Scholars have found competing, sometimes contradictory perspectives on disability across Emerson's corpus. In *Extraordinary Bodies*, Rosemarie Garland-Thomson presents an incisive critique of the logic of Emersonian individualism, as revealed in essays from "Self-Reliance" (1841) to "Fate" (1860).[16] Quoting the 1847 edition of "Self-Reliance," Garland-Thomson notes the way Emerson's idealized liberal selfhood at once rejects and relies for its own definition on the presence of the disabled. "Unlike the supposedly inviolable real 'men,' who act as 'guides, redeemers, and benefactors' capable of 'advancing,'" she states, "Emerson's disparaged and static 'invalids' are banished 'in a protected corner.'" Quoting from "Fate," she explains further, "The 'blind,' the 'halt,' and the 'invalids' Emerson enlists to define the liberal individual by opposition are, above all else, icons of bodily vulnerability."[17] The consequence is that Emerson makes this ostracized vulnerability necessary for the hermetically capable self to exist as such. Stanley Cavell has discussed how Emerson's related appropriation of the amputee in "The American Scholar," as a counterintuitive metaphor for the sacrifices endured by would-be individuals subordinated to society—"distributed to multitudes ... so minutely subdivided and peddled out," as though "amputate[d] from the trunk"—gave Friedrich Nietzsche precedent for doing the same in *Thus Spake Zarathustra*. Where Emerson uses the phrase "walking monsters," Nietzsche's German has been translated as "inverse cripples."[18] Building on this scholarship, David T. Mitchell and Sharon Snyder propose that these moments in Emerson and his interlocutors reveal a literary tradition that "fixate[s] upon [the] defining disruptive potential" of "aberrant bodies" "as critical to their challenge of cultural beliefs."[19]

While Mitchell and Snyder do not concern themselves at length with Emerson, this greater point they make (regarding the work of Montaigne and Nietzsche) is especially helpful for thinking through aspects of Emerson's thought that appear incommensurable. For Mitchell and Snyder, work that evinces the untenable repression of bodily alterity, in material and abstract spaces alike, may simultaneously "provide possibilities for a more thoroughgoing revision of societal precepts about the fiction of the normative body and the necessity of physical and attitudinal accommodation."[20] Emerson epitomizes this tension. Throughout his oeuvre, one finds that puffed up virility and self-aggrandizing compensation for the weakness of others often dissolve abruptly into the most intricate interdependencies and shared incapacities, among these a persistent interest in the intimate affinities linking debility and creativity.

The purpose attributed to the eponymous archetype of "The Poet" exemplifies this tendency. The essay makes one of its most provocative turns in comparing poets to etymologists. "The poets made all the words, and therefore language is the archives of history, and, if we must say it, a sort of tomb of the muses," Emerson explains.

> For, though the origin of most of our words is forgotten, each word was a stroke of genius, and obtained currency, because for the moment it symbolizes the world to the first speaker and to the hearer. The etymologist finds the deadest word to have been once a brilliant picture. Language is fossil poetry. As the limestone of the continent consists of infinite masses of the shells of animalcules, so language is made up of images, or tropes, which now, in their secondary use, have long ceased to remind us of their poetic origin. (CW 3:13)

Decades before Emerson would begin to struggle with dementia (in a publicly concerning form, at least), he argues here that collective memory loss serves as the very landscape of language. Disability studies scholars have urged critics to interrogate facile extrapolations of illness and disability into metaphor; thus, I want to be clear that I do not mean to invoke aphasia in an exclusively or even predominantly figurative manner here. Rather, I believe "The Poet" directs attention to the way Emerson sometimes approached human relationships to language like a disability theorist. To think of language as a vessel of ever-unfolding memory loss, in a literal sense, resonates with what is known in scholarship as the "social model of disability," meaning a framework that locates incapacity as a feature of shared environment and societal systems.

Scholars usually contextualize this passage within a tradition of Romantic theories of language and poetry. Emerson takes partial inspiration from August Wilhelm Schlegel in this respect, who saw language as a "great, unfinished poem in which human nature is expressed." By this, Schlegel meant that language first emerges through a palpable intimacy between sign and signified. Thus, the German poet also understood language to inhere in a phenomenology of perpetual bereavement. As Schlegel explains, "Language loses part of its original force, which is grounded in the necessary relation between the sign of the message and its signified," the more systematic it becomes.[21] "Just as the unlimited qualities of manifold nature are impoverished and become stripped terms, so the living plenitude of sounds dwindles to become a dead letter."[22] Even so, language remains, for Schlegel, textured by the power of poetry to resuscitate these earlier affinities. "Hidden" within one may find "the deep, irresistible, unrestrained language of nature, unlimited in its restraints," Schlegel says; "it has to be hidden in there: only this makes poetry possible. He is a poet who not only discovers the invisible deity, but also knows how to reveal it to others, and the degree of clarity to which this can still occur in a language, determines its poetic force."[23] Emerson pictures language in a comparable state: a "tomb of the muses" where the treasure of nature's inceptive relation to language will stay buried, beyond reach of consciousness, until the poet rediscovers and reacquaints their audience with it.

In an effort to "scrutinize" and reconsider presumptions about Romanticism's interest in spiritualizing nature, Tristram Wolff has challenged critics to do justice to a pervasive tradition of "Romantic inorganicism."[24] "Romantic organicism" designates "a mode of attachment to matter, or 'motive for metaphor'" that "did not deaden or still, but to the contrary mobilized the world by reimagining physical forces and categories like motion, causation, and agency as, yes, spiritual, but also partly perspectival, cultural, and rhetorical."[25] An astounding study of transatlantic exchange, which has as its horizon an interest in confronting environmental impasses in the present by resuturing linguistics and geology in criticism, Wolff's essay takes particular interest in Romantic intrigue in what he terms "stone speech," meaning both rocks that talk and the transmutation of words into geological forms. Turning briefly to Emerson's account of language as fossil poetry, Wolff observes, "Whether built by natural or cultural process, these Emersonian images share an evident interest in conceiving language as externalized in slowly changing material forms."[26] Wolff does not connect Emerson or this greater tradition of thought to disability studies directly. Nonetheless, he concludes with a reflection that brings us closer to appreciating why Emerson took the step of combining these ideas with a disability poetics emanating from collective memory loss. In his conclusion, Wolff proposes, "It would be remarkable if we learned to feel our own insensibility" "as deeply as some Romantic poets seem to have done ... by training attention on the relations that bind us to others and environments, or to worlds we feel as exterior."[27] For Emerson, poetry encourages attention to relations otherwise remote to us, by disinterring, so to acknowledge, our mutual embeddedness in insensible forms.

What is meant by this phrase "disability poetics"? Orchid Tierney has proposed that "a disability poetics makes possible multifarious forms of poetic invention, while challenging received cultural assumptions about bodily functionality."[28] Tierney continues, "There is no one size fits all when it comes to poetry, cognition, and embodiment. A poetics—and politics—of disability ... is inventive, radical, and intensely critical of cultural practices that measure, classify, and stigmatize disabled figures."[29] In his essay "Crip Poetry, or How I Learned to Love the Limp," Jim Ferris accentuates the power of a disability poetics to induce "a transformation in consciousness, not only the consciousness of the poet and the reader, but the potential to transform the world, to make the world in which we live roomier, not only more transparent and known, but to make space in the imagination, and so in the culture, for the wide and startling variety of rich and fulfilling ways that real people live and love, work and play."[30] Disability poetics destabilize, destigmatize, deindividualize, then remake, reopen, and reimagine.

One finds these orientations at the center of Holly J. Hughes's anthology *Beyond Forgetting: Poetry and Prose about Alzheimer's Disease* (2009), a collection devoted to centering the humanity and experiences of people living with Alzheimer's disease and their loved ones. Speaking in the preface of her relationship with her mother, who lived with Alzheimer's from her late sixties until her death in 2001 at the age of seventy-five, Hughes recalls, "We did something unexpected, Mother and I: we moved beyond forgetting. Each day I bent my imagination, which had formerly been reserved for the classroom and the page" to reconsider "the best way to carry each hour, each day, each season."[31] For Hughes, this bending of the imagination means allowing one's own mind to be touched by both the "haunting" pain of the disease and its capacity for "unlikely beauty," "moments of grace" gleaming "even in the darkest stretches."[32] Hughes's poem "The Bath" conveys the affordances of this deconstructed experience of time with arresting simplicity. As Hughes draws a bath, her mother realizes it is meant for her. "Oh no, she says, drawing her / Three layers of shirts to her chest, / Crossing her arms and legs. / Oh no, I couldn't, she repeats, / Brow furrowing, that look I now / Recognize like an approaching squall."[33] With a desire to alleviate her mother's anxiety, Hughes recalls, "I abandon reason."[34] The daughter enters the bath instead, "completely, slipping down until / Only my face shines up, a moon mask."[35] "Interested now / In this turn of events," her mother stays. The poem continues:

> Will you wash my back, Mom?
> So much gone, but let this
> Still be there. She bends over
> To dip the washcloth in the still
> warm water, squeeze it,
> lets it dribble down my back,
> leans over to rub the butter pat
> of soap, swiping each armpit,
> then rinses off the suds with long
> practiced strokes. I turn around
> to thank her, catch her smiling,
> lips pursed, humming,
> still a mother with a daughter
> whose back needs washing.[36]

Released from expectation, "The Bath" remakes memory in an unpredictable form. The speaker lets go of the idea that care can only be unidirectional at this stage in the history of their relationship. Sensing that maybe her mother would prefer the chance to occupy the role of caregiver in the moment, Hughes surrenders to the potential opened by a once-familiar dynamic. Together, the bath and "The Bath" recover and remake the meaning of "wash," a "brilliant picture" "symbolizing" a shared "world" for speaker and hearer.

Readers may not be conditioned to think of "The Poet" in these terms. And yet, the argument I am making, that Emerson reconceives poetry as a mechanism of accessibility, parallels other influential readings. In *Aisthesis*, Rancière does not center accessibility, but his reading enhances our understanding of this theme. The poet "is the one to reattach words to things, and thus inform his contemporaries of a common wealth, that of the universal soul which exteriorizes itself in the material world," he writes. "He is a complete man only by his capacity to attach each particular sensible form and each word of language to the breath of the whole. And he draws this power only from his ability to nourish himself with the potential latent in collective experience."[37] As Branka Arsić elaborates in a discussion of Rancière's reading of Emerson, "Because poetry is not invested in articulating the experience of the world by accessing it through a privileged site—the exceptionality of the poet's mind, the 'essential' historical position of the bourgeoisie in the new modern world, etc.—the poetry advocated by Emerson finds everything and everybody equally relevant for the ways of modernity."[38] When we ground this perspective on the dependency of the poet upon collective consciousness in Emerson's interpretation of language as a forgetting commons, the centrality of an embodied, social model of cognitive accessibility to the meaning of poetry becomes indispensable. One is reminded of Travis Chi Wing Lau's elegant insistence, "Disability poetics creates a collective experience of shared uncertainty, of contingency in the face of disability's vicissitudes."[39]

Positioning these ideas as inextricable from a disability poetics at the center of "The Poet" allows us to understand better the unique contribution Emerson makes to nineteenth-century theories of poetic language. On the one hand, as Melanie Maria Lörke notes in her illuminating study, Emerson builds on impassioned portraits of poets as sources of creation found in the likes of William Blake and Percy Bysshe Shelley, reliably "invok[ing] the climactic apotheosis of the poet whose imagination," being in a liberated state of dynamic "flux," manages to "find the magic word to unlock the world for men."[40] And yet, as Lörke proceeds to show, this magic for Emerson is just as soberingly elusive. Flux can disempower. In Emerson, the "limitlessness of language" can also impede "the poet's capacity to see and transmit truth with it."[41] The same "fluidity" of "becoming" that permits recuperation of material occasions for language risks dissolving the subject into "incoherence."[42] In Lörke's words, "Emerson describes a process that takes the self, usually contained by bodily boundaries, apart by categories of time and space."[43] Such is the state of language that demands from Emerson an aphasic etymology.

APHASIC ETYMOLOGY IN WHITMAN

We know that Whitman took this precise piece of Emersonian philosophy to heart. At the close of his essay "Slang in America," Whitman paraphrases "The Poet" directly:

"The science of language has large and close analogies in geological science, with its ceaseless evolution, its fossils, and its numberless submerged layers and hidden strata."[44] Still, scholars have yet to ask how Whitman, in modeling himself early on as an answer to Emerson's call, integrated the theme of collective memory loss into early editions of *Leaves*. In fact, the clearest emblem of this influence of "The Poet" is among the most iconic elements of the 1855 edition. Ironically, this same emblem will probably be considered by critics an unlikely place to go for locating a disability poetics in Whitman's early work. I'm speaking of Whitman's *yawp*, as in, "I too am not a bit tamed … I too am untranslatable, / I sound my barbaric yawp over the roofs of the world."

The reason readers of Whitman tend to be fond of this line is the same reason it possesses a fundamental connection to Emerson's account of the poetic origins of language: it sounds made up. That is, it does the work Emerson tells us poets do: "For, though the origin of most of our words is forgotten, each word was a stroke of genius, and obtained currency, because for the moment it symbolizes the world to the first speaker and to the hearer."

Some caveats are needed. As Ed Folsom has shown in his meticulous study of the yawp, the term is indebted to Whitman but does not originate with him. In antebellum America, *yawp* appears in newspapers as a slang term meaning an incomprehensible bark, yelp, or (especially) a bird's squawk, connected to a slang term for the orifice capable of producing such a sound, one's *yap* (a spelling that could also serve as a variant form of *yawp*).[45] As Folsom notes, this is particularly significant since the preceding adjective *barbaric* has comparable roots in "echoic language," meaning language created from imitating sound.[46] Folsom explains, "*Barbaric* goes back to Latin, Greek, and ultimately Indo-European roots that are themselves echoic, imitative syllables of what rude and uncivilized and primitive peoples (those who spoke neither Latin nor Greek) sounded like to 'civilized' ears: *barbarbarbar*."[47] Thus, when Whitman uses *yawp* he not only means to catapult slang—a form of speech that thrives precisely because it signals openly the pleasure of taking language into one's own hands—into a more robust set of associations. More fundamentally, the word appeals to him because it encodes Emerson's theory about the origins of language in its echoic derivation.

Interestingly, as defined by the *Oxford English Dictionary*, *yawp* is no mere shout of hubris. As the *Etymological Dictionary of the Scottish Language* put it in 1825, *yawp* may be defined as "the cry of a sickly bird, or of one in distress."[48] At first glance, this definition may seem a far cry from the mood of *Leaves*, but, in fact, it is the shriek of a hawk to which Whitman is comparing himself at this juncture in "Song of Myself": "the spotted hawk swoops by and accuses me … he complains of my gab and my loitering." Here resides a disregarded genealogy of the yawp. Consider Allen Ginsberg's adaptation of Whitman's guttural rooftop cry in "Howl," a poem that maintains ecstatically the centrality of disabled bodyminds to the inception of liberatory language: "the best minds of my generation destroyed by madness," "yacketayakking screaming vomiting whispering facts and memories and anecdotes and eyeball kicks and shocks of hospitals and jails and wars," "who howled on their knees in the subway and were dragged off the roof waving genitals and manuscripts."[49] Inhabiting a terrain of collective memory loss, Whitman and future reimaginings of the yawp harness the creative power of flux and incoherence in tandem, transforming language and reader through an aphasic etymology that reminds us, albeit always incompletely, of the purpose of language to build intrinsic, corporeal connections between word and world.

September 17–18, 1881

This relation between Emerson and Whitman becomes personal in their final meeting. In a series titled "How I Get Around and Take Notes" (1881–1882), published in Jeanette Gilder and her brother Richard Watson Gilder's newly founded magazine *The Critic*, Whitman reflects on the history of his relationship with Emerson in light of their reunion. A mix of unorthodox criticism and journal entries documenting Whitman's playful adaptation of contemporary physical therapy techniques in the great New Jersey outdoors, in the wake of his partial paralysis by a stroke in 1873, "How I Get Around at 60, and Take Notes" presents one of the most compelling experiments of Whitman's own late style. A criticism that wallows in idleness, it shows us a portrait of Whitman as disability theorist. Ambivalent about committing to the genre of *The Critic*, the poet spends most of his time indulging in peripheral wanderings, granting vulnerable glimpses into his process of getting ready to write—how he moves, the physical pain he endures, what he receives from the natural world as a disabled writer, and what he contributes to it.

Interestingly, it is the fifth installment, featuring multiple segments on Emerson, that comes closest to a work of extended criticism. Yet even here the experimental nature of Whitman's idle criticism becomes starkly, evocatively disorienting. In fact, the clearest example of literary criticism Whitman introduces in the series is neither his own, nor is it articulated as such. It arrives when Whitman recalls the evaluation of the 1860 edition of *Leaves* Emerson gave him twenty-one years ago. Returning to the poet during his visit to Boston in October 1881, the scene materializes as an act of remembering. Upon revisiting Boston Common, Whitman tells us in the present tense that he spends "a good deal of time on the Common, these delicious days and nights—every mid-day from 11.30 to about 1," where he recognizes individually all "the old elms along Tremond and Beacon Streets" and has "come to a sociable-silent understanding with most of them, in the sunlit air (yet crispy-cool enough)," while "saunter[ing] along the wide unpaved walks."[50] Abruptly, we travel back in time to be with Emerson in 1860, a mental transport visualized by the section title's dash: "Boston Common—More of Emerson." Two decades ago, Whitman explains, Emerson had read the third edition of *Leaves of Grass*, featuring the controversial "Enfans d'Adam" cluster. He was not pleased with the turns Whitman was taking. "During those two hours, he was the talker and I the listener," Whitman remembers.[51] "It was an argument-statement, reconnoitering, review, attack, and pressing home (like an army corps, in order, artillery, cavalry, infantry), of all that could be said against that part (and a main part) in the construction of my poems,

'Children of Adam.'"[52] Emerson's evaluation rained down from all sides. Whitman could say little in return.

But the meditation takes a turn. With a fragment at once affectionate and utterly opaque, Whitman starts to disclose what the conversation meant to him: "More precious to me than that dissertation—(I only wish I had it now, verbatim)."[53] Whitman elaborates:

> It afforded me, ever after, this strange and paradoxical lesson; each point of E.'s statement was unanswerable, no judge's charge ever more complete or convincing. I could never hear the points better put—and then I felt down in my soul the clear and unmistakable conviction to disobey all, and pursue my own way. "What have you to say then to such things?" said E., pausing in conclusion. "Only that while I can't answer them at all, I feel more settled than ever to adhere to my own theory, and exemplify it," was my candid response. Whereupon we went and had a good dinner at the American House.
>
> And thenceforward I never wavered or was touched with qualms (as I confess I had been two or three times before).[54]

At first glance, the entry seems to represent an opportunity for Whitman to make his peace with Emerson's disapproval, maybe also to wrest his reputation from the shadow of Emerson's famous letter of recommendation. Whitman had long outgrown his early need for an advocate. Yet we should also note, considering the way Whitman narrates the exchange in "How I Get Around at 60, and Take Notes," that it is precisely the things Whitman does not say, the distinctions he resists drawing, that make the meditation meaningful. In fact, Whitman's reminiscence hinges not on any modicum of actual content (readers are fully blocked from the substance of Emerson's critique, in this recounting), but rather on the oxymoronic admission that the very irrefutability of Emerson's reproach became the catalyst to Whitman's decisiveness.

This nostalgia-inducing disentanglement stages a particular kind of revolt in the pages of *The Critic*, as if to assert that the genre known as criticism—designed to evaluate and influence aesthetic appraisal—is always intrinsically, at least partially, self-undermining. The capacity for self-determination in Whitman is equally undermined by the memory: after all, it is only the rebuke of his mentor that at last frees him of his inhibiting "qualms." Whitman's self-duplication in response, in the positions of adherence to his theory and self-exemplification, a literal doubling down, becomes meaningful to Whitman to the extent that it also makes space for a strangely enabling parenthetical aside—"the dissertation—(I only wish I had it now, verbatim)." As a mirror of Whitman's lingering anxiety, a manifestation of potential retaliations threatening to thwart the purpose of *Leaves of Grass*, Emerson's criticism gives Whitman a counterintuitive stability of meaning otherwise evasive.

What will it be like to be together again? Whitman's interplay of memory and its expurgation as context for the 1881 reunion foregrounds this familiar question. Much has happened. What remains? What can we summon from the past to make our next meeting momentous? Whitman sets the scene by emphasizing Emerson's and his own silence in comparison to the other guests. "Never had I a better piece of luck befall me: a long and blessed evening with Emerson, in a way I couldn't have wished better or different," Whitman says.[55] What follows is striking for the parallels drawn between Emerson's silence, inflected by his dementia, as well as Whitman's own insecurities amid the gathering of esteemed visitors.

> For nearly two hours he has been placidly sitting where I could see his face in the best light near me. Mrs. S.'s back parlor well fill'd with people, neighbors, many fresh and charming faces, women, mostly young, but some old. My friend A. B. Alcott and his daughter Louisa were there early. A good deal of talk. ... (No doubt I seemed very stupid to the room-full of company, taking hardly any part in the conversation; but I had 'my own pail to milk in,' as the Swiss proverb puts it.) My seat and the relative arrangement were such that, without being rude or anything of the kind, I could just look squarely at E., which I did a good part of the two hours. On entering he had spoken very briefly, easily and politely to several of the company, then settled himself in his chair, a trifle pushed back, and, though a listener and apparently an alert one, remained silent through the whole talk and discussion. A lady friend quietly took a seat next him to give special attention.
>
> And so, there Emerson sat, and I looking at him. A good color in his face, eyes clear, with the well-known expression of sweetness and the old clear-peering aspect quite the same.[56]

The image of Whitman feeling "stupid" next to loquacious Alcotts is amusing. But once again, the implication seems to be that Whitman is taking a cue from Emerson, wanting to partake of the mood surrounding Emerson's minimal speech. One cannot help but wonder if Whitman cites the proverb about having one's "own pail to milk in," in part, because the imagery bookends a relationship that had begun with a pail, the one he had used to carry Emerson's essays alongside his lunch in Brooklyn.[57]

These themes, too, the benefits of economical language, and of honoring an unconquerable mystery in one's confidants, can be found in Emerson's earlier writings. "Reverence is a great part of it," Emerson states in the 1841 essay "Friendship." "Treat your friend as a spectacle. Of course he has merits that are not yours, and that you cannot honor, if you must needs hold him close to your person. Stand aside; give those merits room; let them mount and expand. ... To a great heart he will still be a stranger in a thousand particulars, that he may come near in the holiest ground" (*CW* 2:123). An earlier line in "Friendship" carries a certain prophecy. "How many persons we meet in houses, whom we scarcely speak to, whom yet we honor, and who honor us!" Emerson had written. "How many we see in the street, or sit with in church, whom, though silently, we warmly rejoice to be with! Read the language of these wandering eye-beams. The heart knoweth" (*CW* 2:113).

These last exchanges Whitman and Emerson shared contain the accrued significance of an aphasic orientation toward language. Whitman's own disabled criticism in the pages of "How I Get Around at 60, and Take Notes" achieves one of its great contributions at this juncture. Whitman cherishes the final meeting, in which the words did not come, for either of them, because it captured something the poet had long before absorbed from Emerson, regarding the relationship between poetry and the forgetting commons of which language is made. The earlier theorization of poetry as a mechanism of accessibility, answering an ever-unfolding aphasic present by which meaning is negotiated, is revealed in the last Emerson-Whitman encounter to encompass a proleptic orientation toward a future conversation that will have already happened. The quiet that Whitman meditates on in Emerson's presence becomes a sign of transfers of meaning that have had the privilege of accumulating—which, like the "infinite masses of the shells of animalcules" buried in the "limestone of the continent," have since become foundational sediment. No reciprocal power of recollection is required for this relational accumulation to be substantive.

There is additional value to the 1881 encounter depicted in *The Critic*. In the essay *Nature* (1836), Emerson explains, "It is not words only that are emblematic; it is things which are emblematic." For this reason:

> Every appearance in nature corresponds to some state of the mind, and that state of the mind can only be described by presenting that natural appearance as its picture. An enraged man is a lion, a cunning man is a fox, a firm man is a rock, a learned man is a torch. A lamb is innocence; a snake is subtle spite; flowers express to us the delicate affections. Light and darkness are our familiar expression for knowledge and ignorance; and heat for love. Visible distance behind and before us, is respectively our image of memory and hope. (CW 1:18)

This formulation deepens our understanding of the Emersonian relationship between poetry and the origins of language. Poetry not only inheres in the fidelity of a word to the image it names; poetry attests further to extra-lingual correspondences between mind and environment. In desiring to contribute to Emerson's comfort, by honoring Emerson's way of being in the room, Whitman saw in the space they delineated together something akin to a poem, a state of mind still worthy of emblematic reflection. The visible distance before Whitman becomes the sign of a hope exceeding the confines of memory, hope located in what Hughes describes as an "odd dignity" compatible with gentle proximity and adaptive affection.[58]

Notes

1. "[Letter, Ralph Waldo Emerson to Walt Whitman]," July 21, 1855, Library of Congress, Library of Congress, https://www.loc.gov/item/mcc.012/. Accessed January 1, 2021.
2. Nicole Gray, "Introduction to the 1855 *Leaves of Grass* Variorum," *Walt Whitman Archive* (2020), accessed January 1, 2021, https://whitmanarchive.org/published/LG/1855/variorum/intro.html#n12.

3. "Reminiscences of Walt Whitman," *Atlantic Monthly* 89 (1902): 165–66. See also William Sloane Kennedy's *Reminiscences of Walt Whitman* (London: Alexander Gardner, 1896).
4. Horace Traubel, *With Walt Whitman in Camden*, vol. 1 (Boston: Small, Maynard, 1906), 51.
5. Walt Whitman, *Specimen Days, and Collect* (Philadelphia: David McKay, 1882–83), 191.
6. Ibid., 190.
7. Christopher Hanlon, *Emerson's Memory Loss: Originality, Communality, and the Late Style* (Oxford: Oxford University Press, 2018), 18–19.
8. Ibid., 20–21.
9. Ibid., 9, 11, 9.
10. Ibid., 10–11.
11. Quoted in Hanlon, *Emerson's Memory Loss*, 10–11.
12. Quoted in Hanlon, *Emerson's Memory Loss*, 11.
13. F. O. Matthiessen, American Renaissance: Art and Expression in the Age of Melville (Oxford: Oxford University Press, 1941), 650.
14. Jay Grossman, *Reconstituting the American Renaissance: Emerson, Whitman, and the Politics of Representation* (Durham, NC: Duke University Press, 2003), 81.
15. Harold Bloom, *The Anxiety of Influence: A Theory of Poetry* (New York: Oxford University Press), 91.
16. Rosemarie Garland-Thomson, *Extraordinary Bodies: Figuring Physical Disability in American Culture and Literature* (New York: Columbia University Press, 1996).
17. Ibid., 42.
18. Stanley Cavell, *A Pitch of Philosophy: Autobiographical Exercises* (Cambridge, MA: Harvard University Press, 1994), 46.
19. David T. Mitchell and Sharon Snyder, *Narrative Prosthesis: Disability and the Dependencies of Discourse* (Ann Arbor: University of Michigan Press, 2000), 66.
20. Ibid., 93.
21. Quoted in Melanie Maria Lorke, *Liminal Semiotics: Boundary Phenomena in Romanticism* (Berlin: De Gruyter, 2013), 70.
22. Ibid., 70.
23. Ibid., 71.
24. Tristram Wolff, "Romantic Stone Speech and the Appeal of the Inorganic," *ELH* 84 (2017): 617–47: 618.
25. Ibid., 619.
26. Ibid., 625.
27. Ibid., 640.
28. Orchid Tierney, "Amodern 10: Disability Poetics," *Amodern* 10 (December 2020), https://amodern.net/article/amodern-10-disability-poetics/ Accessed May 14, 2021.
29. Ibid.
30. Jim Ferris, "Crip Poetry, or How I Learned to Love the Limp," *Wordgathering* 1, no. 2 (2007): par. 5, https://wordgathering.syr.edu/past_issues/issue2/essay/ferris.html. Accessed May 14, 2021.
31. Holly J. Hughes, "Preface," *Beyond Forgetting: Poetry and Prose about Alzheimer's Disease* (Kent, OH: Kent State University Press, 2009), http://www.beyondforgettingbook.com/preface.html. Accessed January 15, 2022.
32. Ibid.
33. Holly J. Hughes, "The Bath," *Beyond Forgetting: Poetry and Prose about Alzheimer's Disease* (Kent, OH: Kent State University Press, 2009), 119–21.

34. Ibid.
35. Ibid.
36. Ibid.
37. Jacques Rancière, *Aisthesis: Scenes from the Aesthetic Regime of Art*, trans. Zakir Paul (London: Verso, 2013), 63–64.
38. Branka Arsić, "Poetry as Flowering of Life Forms: Rancière's Reading of Emerson," *Textual Practice* 30, no. 4 (2016): 551–77: 561–62.
39. Travis Chi Wing Lau, "The Crip Poetics of Pain," *Amodern* 10 (December 2020), https://amodern.net/article/the-crip-poetics-of-pain/.
40. Melanie Maria Lörke, *Liminal Semiotics: Boundary Phenomena in Romanticism* (Berlin: De Gruyter, 2013), 92.
41. Ibid., 93.
42. Ibid., 94.
43. Ibid., 94.
44. Whitman, "Slang in America," in *Complete Prose Works* (Philadelphia: David McKay, 1892), 408.
45. Ed Folsom, "Translating Walt Whitman's 'Barbaric Yawp.' Introduction," *Comparative Yearbook* 4 (2013): 255–63: 257.
46. Ibid., 256.
47. Ibid., 256.
48. Quoted in Folsom, 259.
49. Allen Ginsberg, *Howl and Other Poems* (San Francisco: City Lights Books, 1956), 9, 10, 12.
50. Whitman, "How I Still Get Around and Take Notes (No. 5)," *The Critic*, December 3, 1881, 331.
51. Ibid., 331.
52. Ibid., 331.
53. Ibid., 331.
54. Ibid., 331.
55. Ibid., 330.
56. Ibid., 330.
57. Relevant to the method I am calling aphasic etymology, it is worth noting the puzzling revelation of a 1906 study titled *Walt Whitman and the Germans* that its author could not locate any source for the allegedly Swiss proverb in either the *Swiss Idiotikon* or "any other collection of German proverbial sayings." Richard Henri Riethmueller, *Walt Whitman and the Germans: A Study* (Philadelphia: Americana Germanica Press, 1906), 9.
58. Hughes, "Preface," http://www.beyondforgettingbook.com/preface.html. Accessed January 15, 2022.

CHAPTER 34

FROM ICONOCLAST TO ICON

The Public Intellectual as Celebrity

BONNIE CARR O'NEILL

> Everywhere he appears as an alternate iconoclast and renovator. He breaks the old idols, and shows how new ones can be made. Not by handicraft and joinery, but by the plastic agency of great ideas.[1]

TAKEN from a profile of Ralph Waldo Emerson published in the newspaper *Banner of Light* in 1861, this passage captures the dissonance of Emerson's celebrity. In labeling Emerson an iconoclast, author George S. Phillips refers almost exclusively to Emerson's early career. When he first emerged in the public consciousness in the 1830s, Emerson's defiance drew attention and audience. The author of *Nature* (1836), a notorious address at Harvard's Divinity School (1837), and "Self-Reliance" (1841) was labeled a pantheist and an atheist; his ideas promised "a revolution in all the offices and relations of men" that threatened the social order (*CW* 2:44). But by the time Phillips published his profile of Emerson in 1861, Emerson was so widely known that his ideas no longer held the same power to shock. Yet for many, his unconventional thinking reflected an intellectual power beyond that of the average American. Never mind the fact that Emerson consistently emphasized every individual's capacity for what he called genius; Emerson was celebrated as *a* genius—the living embodiment of superlative intelligence. His iconoclasm is one sign of his ability, but, integrated into the fuller portrait of his life and accomplishments, it no longer scandalized to the same degree. The iconoclast was now an icon and the subject of critical and biographical sketches like this one in the *Banner of Light*. Phillips's biographical sketch of Emerson is one of many such pieces, which simultaneously acknowledge Emerson's intellectual rupture with convention and reflect his institutional stature in contemporary celebrity culture.

Emerson's transition from iconoclast to icon occurred sometime in the 1850s, the decade in which the early interest in his novel insights and manner of expression had gone mainstream. To an extent, Emerson himself encouraged his changed public identity by intentionally appealing to as large an audience as possible. In this middle phase of his career, he published books, like *Representative Men* (1850) and *English Traits* (1856), designed to attract a greater readership than his more overtly philosophical early essays. His public lecturing at the time took a similar turn, addressing popular topics—domesticity, wealth, and manners, for example, as well as the lectures on England that he later revised for *English Traits*. Emerson extended his lecture tours to frontier cities, venturing ever further west thanks to expanding rail, stage, and steamboat routes. Lecture appearances and their accompanying newspaper write-ups, in addition to book reviews that quoted heavily from his writings, reproduced Emerson's image far and wide. In emphasizing Emerson's deliberate appeal to popular interest, I want to de-emphasize his longstanding reputation for aloofness, reserve, and intellectual isolation. Likewise, I am revising the critical timeline that emphasizes his apparently epiphanic awakening to the antislavery cause circa 1847. In my reading, Emerson's antislavery speeches fit into the larger trajectory of Emerson's self-fashioning as a public intellectual. As he crafted a career that appealed to the widest possible audience, Emerson conscientiously developed his image as an embodiment of intellectual power at once unique to him yet accessible to all.

The celebrity image is not simply a visual representation. According to Richard Dyer, the celebrity or "star image" is "a complex configuration of visual, verbal, and aural signs,"[2] the totality of the representations of that figure across media. As it is multiplied, Sharon Marcus points out, the celebrity image becomes more familiar to more people, yet paradoxically "by virtue of being multiplied, celebrities come to seem unique, their apparent singularity is *intensified* by copying."[3] A public individual cannot call himself an icon; as with the star, "icon" is an identity bestowed by observers.[4] To call an individual an icon is to reduce and enlarge him simultaneously. He is a symbol, representing specific qualities or ideas made legible in his image. At the same time, the icon experiences an enlarged public image. The celebrity portraits of Emerson that emerged in the popular press in the 1850s attempt to both humanize the icon and take critical account of his work. They attest to Emerson's significance as a man of letters and philosopher; he was the nation's intellectual leader, and his iconoclasm paradoxically contributed to his iconic status.

Emerson consistently called himself a scholar, and his work coheres with modern understandings of the public intellectual as he brings his skills as a scholar and critic to bear on subjects of widespread interest and importance. Emerson seems to live up to Edward Said's credo for the public intellectual: "Never solidarity before criticism."[5] From the moment he stepped down as pastor of Boston's Second Church in 1832, independence was crucial to Emerson's self-fashioning; as a self-employed freelance lecturer and author, he declined most political associations and nurtured instead ad hoc networks of supportive friends and associates. But as his fame intensified during the 1850s, the urgency of the antislavery effort pulled Emerson deeper into the political mainstream. To be clear, though he occasionally shared the stage with activists like Wendell Phillips and William Lloyd Garrison, Emerson never formally linked himself to organized politics or activist movements. But his celebrity—the sheer scale of his increasing renown—signified beyond such movements. His intellectual stature was such that his appearance alongside the activists underscored their credibility and moral authority. Nonetheless, in the 1860s, he welcomed the institutional recognitions he increasingly received, and in 1862 he attained the superlative honors of delivering a lecture at the Smithsonian and meeting President Abraham Lincoln at the White House. The fact that these Washington, DC events were facilitated by his longtime friend, Senator Charles Sumner, indicates not only Emerson's own achievement, but also the way individual celebrity leavens itself, as publicity and exposure yield further access, opportunities, and privileges. Thus while Emerson fulfilled Said's mandate—"never solidarity before criticism"—by the 1860s, he could hardly be called an outsider. As a celebrity, he was not entirely independent; he relied on and lived in the public's esteem.

Interestingly, the decade in which Emerson's celebrity reached its zenith is the same period scholars have identified with his maturation as an abolitionist. The intersections between his celebrity and political activism invigorates scrutiny of his racial views, as these two modes of publicity, celebrity and intellectual, each carry different expectations and standards of judgment. Emerson's own apparent ambivalences have made him elusive: on the one hand, Emerson supported antislavery, excoriated the Fugitive Slave Law, and advocated equal rights for Black Americans; on the other hand, he wrote appreciatively of the Anglo-Saxon as the future of America. As Cornel West puts it, Emerson's understanding of race and history "can easily serve as a defense of Anglo-Saxon imperial domination of non-European lands and peoples."[6] Celebrity studies, I suggest, offers a way not simply to think through the contradictions in Emerson's writings and his critical legacy, but to recognize and account for their relevance to his cultural stature. It does so by distinguishing the Emerson image, the image of the public intellectual in a celebrity culture. In shaping this essay, I head each section with an epigraph that relates to the Emerson image. Just as Emerson's audience encountered him as an image, lacking direct access to the man himself, so do we. In this light, celebrity studies offers a useful approach to the contradictions of Emerson's reputation and politics.

THE SANE MAN

> Society at all times have the same want, namely, of one sane man with adequate powers of expression to hold up each new object of monomania in its right relations.... But let one man have so comprehensive an eye that he can replace this isolated wonder in its natural neighborhood & relations, it loses instantly all illusion, and the returning reason of the community thanks the monitor. (*JMN* 9:197)

In this 1845 journal passage, Emerson condenses several ideas that are key to his thinking about popular culture and power. Foremost, he emphasizes the singular individual—here, the "sane man," but elsewhere the representative man, the poet, or the scholar—who is distinguished by his influence over a public body. That power derives from his "powers of expression," the eloquence through which he is able to reveal powerful truths—"facts amidst appearances," as he says of the scholar's office nearly ten years earlier (*CW* 1:62). Here, "appearances" take the form of monomania, the deranged fascination with a singular object idea, shared by the masses out of all proportion with the object's actual significance. Emerson perceives that significance is relational: the sane man recalibrates popular perception by restoring objects to their "right relations" to one another. To do this work, the sane man must remain indifferent to popular fascinations. His sanity derives from the aloofness that sets him apart from "the community" he addresses and grants him the comprehensive perspective truth requires.

In his portrait of the sane man, Emerson describes the public intellectual he sought to be, an individual who assumes a stance of intellectual and affective independence in order to see and speak the truth about contemporary society. Indeed, Lawrence Buell identifies Emerson as "the first modern American public intellectual."[7] The word "modern" is more important here than "first": Emerson crafted a career as a self-described scholar in response to the challenges of his moment, specifically, the social reorganization wrought by industrialization and the affective pressures of nationalism and sectional politics. "The American Scholar" remains the foundational expression of Emerson's ideals for the scholar as one who turns from his private study to public action. The lecture reflects on the ways modern capitalist society reshapes the scholar's work: when all the functions of a society are divided among different classes, the scholar becomes the "designated intellect." As Buell explains it, "in the emerging industrial economy of Emerson's day, mental and manual labor were becoming both more divergent and more routinized."[8] Emerson's answer to this problem is deliberately inexact, Buell posits: the scholar's public actions must be adapted to circumstance and context even as they serve to liberate.

Indeed, Emerson came to accept the professionalization of his literary labors. From about 1850 onward, Buell argues, he retained a sense of "solidarity" with the members of the newly professional classes who flocked to his lectures.[9] Other pressures on the scholar proved less easy to resolve, however. While industrialization separated the scholar from other kinds of workers, the affective pull of both nationalism and political sectionalism countered the rhetorical weight of the scholar's speech. In a climate where all are called to stake their political positions, the public intellectual must take special care not to become an instrument of factions.

In identifying Emerson as a public intellectual, Buell makes a move not unlike my own discussion of Emerson's celebrity: he adapts to a nineteenth-century figure a concept developed in twentieth-century media and political culture. In this context, the public intellectual maintains an attitude of skepticism, contrarianism, and even outrage in the face of powerful ideological forces. Julien Benda addresses this idea in his influential work *Treason of the Intellectuals* (1937). Writing in the aftermath of the First World War and amid fascism's rise, Benda scornfully describes the "clerks," contemporary intellectuals whose nationalist passion prevents them from pursuing universal truth: "The modern 'clerk' is determined to have the soul of a citizen and to make vigorous use of it. ... To have as his function the pursuit of eternal things and yet to believe that he becomes greater by concerning himself with the State—that is the view of the modern 'clerk.'"[10] Benda evokes the ideal of the intellectual as a perpetual outsider, allegiant only to truth. Edward Said, a writer similarly concerned about the intellectually damaging effects of nationalism, upholds and emulates Benda's vision of "the intellectual as a being set apart, someone able to speak the truth to power, a crusty, eloquent, fantastically courageous and angry individual for whom no worldly power is too big and imposing to be criticized and pointedly taken to task."[11] The public intellectual is "someone whose whole being is staked on a critical sense."[12] Casting his allegiance only with the truth he represents in his work and in his person, the public intellectual depersonalizes the truth and, as a result, universalizes it.

Applied to Emerson, Said's ideal of the public intellectual as a perpetual outsider gets complicated. Emerson remained skeptical of the main political movements and associations and urged a more comprehensive cultural analysis: "Each 'Cause,' as it is called,—say Abolition, Temperace, say Calvinism, or Unitarianism,—becomes speedily a little shop, where the article ... is now made up into portable and convenient cakes, and retailed in small quantities to suit purchasers," he facetiously laments in "The Transcendentalist" (*CW* 1:211). Outsiders to mainstream discourses, Emerson's Transcendentalists resemble the sane man he describes in the 1854 journal: they reject political movements as monomanias, disconnected from universal law. Amid the humanitarian and political crises wrought by slavery, however, Emerson had to find a way to engage with movement politics. His 1844 antislavery speech "An Address ... on the Anniversary of the Emancipation of the Negroes in the British West Indies" opens by confessing his reluctance: "I might well hesitate, coming from other studies, and without the smallest claim to be a special laborer in this work of humanity, to undertake to set this matter before you; which ought rather to be done by a strict cooperation of many well-advised persons; but I shall not apologize for my weakness" (*CW* 10:301). He begins his 1854 "Seventh of March Speech on the Fugitive Slave Law" with a similar statement: "I do not often speak to public questions; they are odious and hurtful, and it seems like meddling or leaving your work" (*LL* 2:333). Putting his ambivalence on record, Emerson acknowledges his struggle to reconcile political immediacy with his self-understanding as a scholar.

Emerson's confessed ambivalence reveals the conflict at the center of his vocation, as his mandate for critical detachment collides with the affective power of moral truth. In the "British West Indies" speech, for example, he urges rational calm: "In this cause, we must renounce our temper, and the risings of pride" (*CW* 10:302). But reason only carries one so far. Not the brain, but "the blood is moral: the blood is antislavery: it runs cold in the veins: the stomach rises with disgust, and curses slavery" (*CW* 10:304). It seems that Emerson's larger struggle was not with his own political views, which were as impassioned as anyone's, but with his public identity. As even a casual reader of the journals recognizes, Emerson kept abreast of politics, and according to Barbara Packer, "Emerson's spirits rose and fell with the state of political affairs in the nation" (*CW* 6:lx). For much of his career, those shifting moods primarily governed his private experience. But following the 1844 West Indies speech, Emerson spoke out on behalf of antislavery and other political causes more readily than at any time in his career. He publicly protested the Fugitive Slave Law in a speech he delivered numerous times between 1851 and 1855. In 1856, speaking at a fundraiser to support—that is, to arm—free-soilers in Kansas, he excoriated the politics of territorial expansion: "*Manifest Destiny, Democracy, Freedom*, fine names for an ugly thing. They call it otto of rose and lavender,—I call it bilge water" (*CW* 10:373). He continued speaking against slavery until the Emancipation Proclamation was issued in 1863. As important as his appearances at such venues, Emerson's nonappearance before the New Bedford Lyceum in 1846 was a protest against the lyceum's refusal to allow Black people to attend lectures and evidence of Emerson's awareness of his own cultural power, as he leveraged his public image for political effect.

Rather than thinking about Emerson as a celebrity activist, however, I think it is more productive to think of him as a person who operated in, responded to, and was shaped by celebrity culture, just as he operated in, responded to, and was shaped by the industrial capitalist economy from which celebrity culture emerged. Emerson's discussion of the sane man suggests his awareness of the challenges. Like his scholar and poet, the sane man represents a fantasy of public intellectualism that remains free of celebrity culture's trappings. Since no one, not even Emerson, can excuse himself from the dominant culture, the sane man's posture is necessarily oppositional, even radical. Whereas Emerson's sane man models rational detachment, celebrity culture is motivated by affect—specifically, the affective responses that follow a presumption of familiarity among the audience as it regards the celebrity image. Insofar as the sane man operates independently of the personal public sphere's affective forces, he models a freedom that is not political but intellectual and psychological. In other words, by imagining the ideal of sanity, Emerson provides a means of recognizing its opposite, in the form of monomanias and improper relations—and, thereby, a measure of public actors in the personal public sphere that celebrity culture generates.

The Celebrity Image

> He is the most natural man in America. True, among men he is odd. He is so unfortunate as to have his time in an age, when to be true to himself and faithful to his own nature, must forever separate him from his fellows, must consign him to the lot, and doom him to the blackened and opprobrious character of "impostor" and "monster," must single him out and set him apart for the unmingled and unmeasured abhorrence of the great body of the race. Emerson was destined to be a true man, and in that he was destined to be odd.[13]

Celebrities are always odd. The nature of celebrity is monstrous, outsized, endlessly analyzed yet ultimately unknowable. In this profile essay, the writer associates Emerson's strangeness with his authenticity: he shows his true self in a world of sham and artifice. Emerson's realness breaks conventions, but it alone does not make him an iconoclast. When I call Emerson an iconoclast, I mean it in one specific way: he broke with conventional American Protestantism. The break occurred in phases. First, he resigned his pulpit at Boston's Second Church, an act which he justified in his Lord's Supper Sermon as not only a disagreement with church doctrine but more specifically, a sense of personal dissatisfaction with the minister's offices. Next, his publication of *Nature* offered a philosophy that many contemporary readers saw as pantheistic. Most notoriously, however, his 1837 "An Address" at the Harvard Divinity School brought condemnation for Emerson and the "New School in Literature and Religion" that he represented. According to Andrews Norton, the "disciples" of this movement "disavow learning and reasoning as sources of their higher knowledge.—The mind must be its own unassisted teacher."[14] Led by Norton, Boston reviewers tore into Emerson and his ideas. Norton himself emphasized Emerson's insult to Harvard Divinity School and the clergy. Other reviewers, guided by their readings of *Nature* and familiarity with Emerson's public lectures, engaged more fully with Emerson's ideas. Among such critics, Orestes Brownson offers perhaps the most trenchant critique of Emersonian individualism at the time. Emerson, he says, assumes everyone can recognize their higher nature without benefit of role models or examples: "We must take none of the wise or good, not even Jesus Christ as a model of what we should be. We are to act out ourselves."[15] Emerson's philosophy replaces Christ with the self, but it offers no assurance that the self will fulfill moral duty. Inevitably, Brownson says, the result is "a deification of the soul with a vengeance"—solipsism and heresy.[16]

In the Divinity School "Address" controversy, Emerson became the subject of public discussion and debate, and the authority he claimed in delivering the lecture diminished as others assumed interpretive authority over his ideas and image. Emerson's meaning—any celebrity's meaning—is neither permanent nor assured, because his image is always subject to analysis and interpretation. Moreover, as the herald of a "new school" of thought, Emerson incurred the notoriety that comes with major cultural shifts.[17] Throughout Emerson's writing life, his most serious detractors return to his religious errancy. An 1861 review of *Conduct of Life* calls Emerson's philosophy "pantheistic," and offers a critique reminiscent of Brownson's 1837 comments: "Mr. Emerson is not the teacher the world wants.... his philosophy of life is too narrow and too frigid, for it cuts it off from personal relations with the Father of all, and from the powers of the world to come. He sinks life into the purely subjective element out of which it springs... We find in this book truths such as elevate through sham and pretense... But he has not seen the face of God in Jesus."[18] The passage's notion of a personal relationship with God or an individual experience of Jesus, central to liberal Protestantism, is in fact closer to Emerson's views of spiritual experience than its writer recognizes. But the writer objects primarily to Emerson's unwillingness to separate the deity from human experience, to see it as a fact external to selfhood. A decade later, reflecting on Emerson's cultural influence, the *Methodist Review* printed a two-part critical evaluation of his work that approaches this idea, but ultimately rejects it. "Despite occasional appearances to the contrary," it argues, "Emerson distinctly and unhesitatingly rejects the Christian conception of God, and his relation to the universe."[19] Critical essays like these demonstrate that Emerson retained his reputation for religious iconoclasm throughout his career. For his detractors, Emerson warranted serious attention precisely because of his popular appeal, which threatened to spread his particular form of irreverence and undermine Christianity in the nation.

While these critics aimed to point out Emerson's error, they could not counter the appeal of his iconoclasm. His defenders acknowledged his unorthodoxy—and they loved him for it. Amid the crisis over the Divinity School "Address," G. T. Davis captured the enthusiasm of the young men Emerson attracts:

> Something is due to his personal manners, much to the peculiar characteristics of his style as a writer and as a lecturer; but still more to his independence, to the homage he pays to the spirit of freedom. Our young men have grown weary of leading strings. They are dissatisfied with the tyranny which custom, conventionalism has exercised over them. ... It is as the advocate of the rights of the mind, as the defender of personal independence in the spiritual world, not as the Idealist, the Pantheist, or the Atheist, that he is run after, and all but worshipped by many young, ardent and yet noble minds.[20]

The idea that Emerson was "worshipped" by his admirers was not likely to appease critics such as Andrews Norton, but it captured the parasocial connection Emerson's most ardent admirers felt for him.[21] Emerson toppled the icons not only of Christianity but of culture itself. His works and person appealed to a generation's desires for spiritual and intellectual freedom. In this reading, Emersonian philosophy does not lack a role model for virtuous action; Emerson himself provides the model, though Emerson would object to such a claim upon himself.

From our current vantage point, the "worship" of Emerson in 1837 presages his celebrity that develops over the next decades. By the 1850s, profiles of Emerson began to appear in mainstream periodicals. Biographical sketches, sometimes accompanied by drawn portraits of Emerson, repeated details of his early life and career—his education at Harvard; his ministry at and resignation from Boston's Second Church; major speeches and publications, including the Divinity School "Address" and ensuing controversy; his marriages and home life. As a genre, profiles of public figures in mainstream periodicals rely on the repetition of these biographical details to generate a sense of familiarity among readers even as they "elevate" their subjects above those readers.[22] The image that emerges is static. The 1855 Emerson is, in some way, the 1837 Emerson, the renegade philosopher quarrelling with Christianity. That quarrel seemingly never ends, though it loses some of its force as Emerson's reputation as both a gentleman and an intellectual power takes hold. An 1860 biographical sketch demonstrates the complexity of Emerson's image in the period of his greatest celebrity. Reprinted in several periodicals, the piece narrates a visit with Emerson in his home:

The door at the right now opens, and we are face to face with the great transcendentalist. There is a smile about his mouth, a pen behind his ear, and two or three daubs of ink on as many of his fingers; but holding out both his hands to us, and saying: "Come in, come in; I am glad to see you," he leads the way into his study.[23]

Whether or not this piece is based on an actual visit to Emerson's home matters less than that the profile effectively brings readers into Emerson's presence, into his home. From this friendly welcome, the "great transcendentalist," as the profile calls Emerson, accedes to an interview. He obligingly describes his work habits: he writes in the mornings, when "the intellect is fresh and the spirits elastic," and "never after dinner, if I can help it." These quotidian details help to humanize the Sage of Concord, even as the piece affirms Emerson's stature as "one of the crowned heads of literature." But the piece is not all praise. Ultimately, the writer weighs in on Emerson's religious failings with a quote from Goethe's *Faust*: "thou hast no Christianity," he says of Emerson, the allusion to one of his literary heroes only slightly tempering the judgment.[24]

Profiles and biographical sketches like these are valuable records of Emerson's celebrity image, revealing how criticism of Emerson's ideas dovetailed with criticism of his character in the mass media. They also demonstrate the interrelations of celebrity culture and public intellectualism. Unlike book reviews or lecture notices, which respond to specific cultural events, periodical sketches originate with the premise of public interest in the subject. They both respond to and reinforce the subject's significance. Emerson's significance derives from his ideas, which the sketches in turn associate with his physical person and character. Edward Said claims the public intellectual is a representative figure whose purpose is to represent the universal truth that guides him.[25] That representation is a matter of expression as well as of character, occurring in his outsider status and in his work. In this representative effort, he abstracts the personal or physical self to reveal the universal truth he expresses. But celebrity culture refuses that abstraction. It regards the public intellectual as the physical representative, the embodiment, of ideas. The public intellectual is therefore subject to double mediation, that of print culture and of his own body, as both interpose between universal truth and the audience.

In short, the mass media environment in which the public intellectual operates challenges his efforts to remain independent of dominant cultural paradigms. In Emerson's case, the effort to represent universal truth was made more difficult by the celebrity culture's particularizing tendency. Nowhere is all of this clearer than in Theodore Parker's 1850 review of *The Complete Writings of Ralph Waldo Emerson*. Although technically a book review, the essay offers a lengthy defense of Emerson against his detractors. Parker builds a case for Emerson's significance as a philosopher and social critic in terms that evoke the public intellectual. At the same time, however, he engages some of the same particularizing analysis that is common to the celebrity culture. After an extended opening discussion of the limitations of criticism, he turns to Emerson, suggesting that the critics are not able to properly comprehend his work. He emphasizes Emerson's intellectual independence: "Emerson is neither a sectarian nor a partisan, no man less so; yet few men in America have been visited with more hatred,—private personal hatred, which the authors poorly endeavored to conceal, and perhaps did hide from themselves. The spite we have heard expressed against him, by men of the common morality, would strike a stranger with amazement, especially when it is remembered that his personal character and daily life are of such extraordinary loveliness."[26] The personal vitriol Emerson receives is inappropriate on two grounds, Parker avers: first, as he is unaffiliated with party or sect, his ideas do not invite rancor. Second, his "personal character and daily life" belie the disapproval he receives. These two claims are slightly at odds, as Parker both objects to and practices personal criticism of his subject. Parker's Emerson represents both universal, because nonpartisan, truth, and the particular example of virtue. Parker's goal may be to distinguish the real Emerson he knows from the image of Emerson, but he unwittingly engages a trope of celebrity journalism, associating his subject's private experience with his public expressions.

Notwithstanding this lapse into the personal, the piece as a whole emphasizes Emerson's universalizing tendencies. "Mr. Emerson is the most American of our writers," Parker claims; "the Idea of America, which lies at the bottom of our original institutions, appears in him with great prominence."[27] Parker clarifies that Emerson stands for shared ideals such as "the idea of personal freedom, of the dignity and value of human nature, the superiority of a man to the accidents of man."[28] Institutional concerns of "the state, the church, society, the family, literature, science, art," even America itself, "all of these are subordinate to man" in Emerson's thinking.[29] Parker's defense of Emerson hinges on important distinctions between particular and universal: though Emerson is independent of church and its doctrines, for example, his works are "eminently religious."[30] The ideal American, Emerson also "criticizes America often; he always appreciates it; he seldom praises, and never brags about our country."[31] Because his reading is borderless, "he has a culture quite cosmopolitan and extraordinary in a young nation like our own."[32]

Straining to bring nuance to critical discussions of Emerson, Parker demonstrates the strange predicament of the public intellectual. His access to mass culture gives him significance, but his work requires him to defy the culture's interpretive practices. Rhetorically, his task is not impossible, but it is costly in the sense that he risks misunderstanding and personal vitriol. This is because the Emersonian public intellectual promotes fidelity to truth amid a celebrity culture dominated by forms of affect. Idolizing Emerson as "the most American of our writers," Parker attempts to circumvent the debates over Emerson's significance: Emerson contains multitudes. By generalizing Emerson as a representative of the nation itself, Parker anticipates a generation of biographers who, after Emerson's death, sought to "detranscendentalize Emerson by distancing him from philosophical extremism and redeeming him as an exemplary American" as Robert Habich puts it.[33] But Emerson's own ambivalence about what America is and who it is for complicates that claim, as does his image as the embodiment of idealized intellectualism.

THE CRITICAL IMAGE

> Fame casts an anticipatory chill over our current efforts because it awakens expectations that can never fully be met.[34]

> Much of his popularity grew out of his ability to mirror and to orchestrate the thinking of his age: as a mirror, he reflected back familiar notions already accepted, if only tacitly, by educated Americans; as an orchestrator, he arranged simple thoughts into elaborate, memorable performances.[35]

These two reflections on Emerson's celebrity interest me for different reasons. The first, from Robert Richardson's biography of Emerson, glosses Emerson's essay "Character" in the effort to account for the writer's attitude toward his public stature. According to Richardson, fame "was a problem Emerson had been preparing for," and so he was unbothered when it arose in the 1850s.[36] As Richardson reads it, Emerson's analysis of fame shows his understanding of both the public's interpretive power and its estrangement from famous men—ideas he would have gleaned from his own experiences in the public eye and his studies of great men of the past. Emerson responded to his fame well because he recognized that his public image was distinct from his actual self.[37] Nell Irvin Painter offers a different response to Emerson's fame. Regarding him as a mirror for his audience of educated white people, she makes a case not for the *what* but the *how* of Emerson's cultural influence. Emerson influenced his society because he was popular—or, rather, he influenced his society via his popularity, his celebrity, which, Painter argues, derived from his appeal as a spokesman for whiteness in works like *English Traits* and his popular lecture "The Anglo-American." Thus, in Richardson's reading, fame was a nuisance, a tax Emerson paid for greatness. For Painter, Emerson's popularity gave philosophical sanction to white supremacist ideology. In Richardson's reading, Emerson retained the public intellectual's detachment; in Painter's, Emerson abandoned truth's universality and joined the party of whiteness.

The contrast between these two critics invites further consideration of how criticism responds to celebrity. Although Painter's version of Emerson derives from her readings of specific texts, she associates his significance with his celebrity. Painter's examination of Emerson stands out to me as one of few that attempt to account for his celebrity as a rhetorical instrument. Setting aside the important topic of Emerson's racial views—the subject of a significant and growing body of scholarship, including works by some contributors to this volume[38]—Painter is alert to the ways that celebrity amplifies the speaker's voice. Her argument assumes an affective dynamic between the speaker and his audience. Whereas her reading prioritizes racial affinity as the crucial element, my examination of contemporary periodicals underscores Emerson's appeal as a cultural and religious renegade. In both readings, Emerson's influence on audiences may be understood with reference to modern ideas of fandom. Lawrence Grossburg explains fandoms as affective communities in which "fans actively constitute places and forms of authority (both for themselves and for others) through the mobilization and organization of affective investments. By making certain things or practices matter, the fan 'authorizes' them to speak for him or her, not only as a spokesperson but also as surrogate voices (as when we sing along to popular songs)."[39] Building on Grossburg's idea, Emerson served as a cultural savings bank in which his increasingly national audience invested its values and ideas of itself. Those values and ideas were not uniform, as our previous discussion of periodical profiles indicates, but the act of investing occurred through the distribution of individual and collective attention to the celebrity image and the interpretive acts that inevitably followed.

Second, Richardson's analysis suggests that Emerson understood something of how this burgeoning fan culture worked, in that he recognized publicity's tendency to refract his image. Or, put another way, he understood his image to be mediated, so that even as he strove to represent himself as authentically as he could, he could not control audience's responses to him. Living peacefully in and with that tension between public identity and private selfhood may be the apex of sanity.

In a celebrity culture where audiences invest their feelings—themselves—in public figures, can the celebrity himself retain the detachment and independence that public intellectualism requires? Emerson's placid demeanor may suggest he stayed aloof, but a journal entry from his 1848 England visit hints at the pressure to satisfy the crowd: "Happy is he who looks only into his work to know if it will succeed, never into the times or the public opinion; and who writes from the love of imparting certain thoughts & not from the necessity of sale—who writes always to *the unknown friend*" (*JMN* 10:315). Discipline and independence require him to seek the ideal audience, an "unknown friend," yet Emerson knew who his friends were. His 1847–48 trip to England, for instance, gave him a star's-eye view of English society; in addition to his lecture engagements, he maintained a busy social life visiting with leading writers and cultural figures, whom he carefully listed in his journal (*JMN* 10:361–62). Back in the US, the commercial successes of the 1850s led to cultural prominence: he lectured before President Lincoln in 1862; the following year, he served on the Board of Visitors at the US Military Academy in West Point, New York. Although he resented the length of that appointment—the anticipated two-day visit stretched to nearly two weeks—it nonetheless reflected his reputation and resulting demand for his presence. In 1864, he was elected to the American Academy of Arts and Sciences, and in 1867, thirty years after his polarizing "Address" at Harvard's Divinity School, his alma mater welcomed him back to deliver another Phi Beta Kappa address. He was made an overseer of the college and served in that role enthusiastically, thus concluding his long estrangement from the nation's premier educational institution.

Emerson's acceptance by major institutions reveals the convergence of his intellectualism, celebrity, and Americanism. In his public appearances of the 1850s and 1860s, as Emerson strove to meet the political moment, he also attempted to answer the demands that arise from the curious mixture of celebrity and public intellectualism. Among his chief subjects in this period were not only slavery but also national character and cultural power. This move is part of his larger intellectual shift toward determinism from the mid-1850s on and especially during the Civil War years. He understood the war itself as an epic conflict between moral forces on one side and brutality, or the Fall, on the other. In his popular speech "Fortunes of the Republic," for instance, he advised his listeners, "We are in these days settling for ourselves and our descendants questions, which, as they shall be determined in one way or another, will make the peace and prosperity, or the calamity of the next age" (*LL* 2:322). As he put it in a prior address for the Fast Day declared by Lincoln in April of 1862, the question will not be settled only through violence or political maneuvering: "Even in war, which is the organization of brute force, moral force is immensely the stronger of the two" (*LL* 2:281). In practical terms, this result will settle the question of national identity. "We are coming,—thanks to the war,—to a nationality," Emerson says in "Fortune of the Republic" (*LL* 2:327). The war "shall restore intellectual and moral vigor to these languid and dissipated populations" by resolving the moral problem of slavery, "which was harming the white nation more than it was harming the black," according to Emerson (*LL* 2:327, 330).

The idea that slavery hurts white people more than those who are oppressed by its brutal system can only make sense in light of Emerson's interest in moral character as the wellspring of national identity. The moral character of Black Americans was not tested by slavery, but all of white America was implicated in slavery's injustices. For Emerson, national character remained unsettled, constantly and gravely tested by slavery and capitalism, by party and section, and his inquiries into the relationships between individual and cultural power took on new moral exigency. Even the potentially great men were unable to affect change single-handedly. For example, he writes that Lincoln "is not free as a poet, to do as he pleases, but in a position of great responsibility, barricaded all 'round by stern conditions" (*LL* 2:278–79). Lincoln is bound by human law, with its moral compromises and legal restraints. Resolution is possible only when individuals align themselves with moral law.

Importantly, Emerson reframed the scholar's vocation in response to the crisis. Always interested in the ways the scholar engages actively in the shared cultural life, he now charged the scholar to provide the intellectual and moral grounding for a revivified democracy. Addressing on separate occasions the students of Dartmouth and Waterville (Bates) Colleges, for example, Emerson exhorts intellectual and moral vigor: "Gird up the loins of your mind. Every principle is a war-note. See on which side you are. A scholar defending the cause of slavery, of arbitrary government, of monopoly, of the oppressor, is a traitor to his profession. He has ceased to be a scholar. He is not company for clean people" (*LL* 2:313). The scholar is to serve not nation or party but moral law, justice, and humanity. His argument identifies a politically neutral intellectualism as personally degrading in its immorality. In this way, he extended the battle front to the personal conscience of young intellectuals and, through their effort and example, all Americans.

In this moment, Emerson anticipates Said's credo and sets it before the college students as a guide not just to critical thinking but to ethical citizenship. The work he proposes is both intellectually detached and personally felt. Rhetorically, it is a remarkable moment, in which the celebrity speaker reverses the affective dynamic between himself and his audience. That is, using his status as a celebrated public intellectual to establish the very terms of scholarly engagement, he redirects the young scholars' gaze from himself, as the embodiment of intellectualism, and back upon themselves. He declines to provide the surrogate voice for admiring fans, and instead requires them to speak for themselves—and for justice.

(ICON)OCLAST

> The above portrait of Mr. Emerson, we are sorry to be obliged to say, is not a very good one. The daguerreotype from which it was drawn was not a happy likeness, and does not give one a true impression of its subject.[40]

Written as a footnote, this acknowledgement accompanies a picture of Emerson in the *American Phrenological Journal*. The drawing is placed prominently above an essay titled "Ralph Waldo Emerson. Phrenology, Physiognomy, Biography, and Portrait." The entire essay is interesting as a specimen of uniquely nineteenth-century celebrity journalism, blending phrenological analysis with the now-familiar biographical and critical sketch. But that footnote tells another story, the story of the celebrity image as the distorted representation of a representation. In the mirror of celebrity, the individual we seek both appears before our eyes and recedes endlessly, a reflection of a reflection. The important question is not "which is the real Emerson?" but "what do these images contain?" The celebrity image is capacious, and it tolerates illusion, disagreement, contradiction, and paradox equally. Emerson, the iconoclast, was also an icon. My essay's title suggests that Emerson's popular reputation transformed over time, the icon ironically toppling the iconoclast. That's not quite true. Instead, the icon absorbs the iconoclast; they merge into the composite and variegated celebrity image.

A public intellectual in an age of celebrity, Emerson presumed to evade illusion by standing aloof from the popular fascinations. "Never solidarity before criticism"—yet Emerson attempted to forge solidarity with truth and others who pursue it. In his vocation as a public intellectual, Emerson claimed independent critical judgment. His self-positioning could not entirely account for the critical practices that celebrity culture engenders, and so he too had to "stand by his order" (*LL* 2:311). Both contemporary and critical responses to Emerson benefit from acknowledging how celebrity culture tends to freeze the subject into a single image subject to multiple interpretations. Seeking the divine within the self and the universal law that pervades nature, Emerson apparently toppled the American Christian theology, according to some contemporary readers. At the same time, Emerson himself became an object of secular worship for a generation grown impatient with the ways of the past. These are not responses to contradictory messages Emerson delivered, but divergent interpretations of the same materials Emerson provided. Criticism, too, responds to and generates images of Emerson in the effort to answer the urgent and complex questions his works raise. A scholarship that recognizes the ways celebrity culture functions is able to account for the extraliterary rhetorical practices at work in both Emerson's self-presentation as it changed over time and in audiences' diverse responses to him.

Notes

1. George S. Phillips, "Critical and Biographical Sketch of Ralph Waldo Emerson," *Banner of Light* 9, no. 23 (August 31, 1861): 1.
2. Richard Dyer, "Stars as Images," in *The Celebrity Culture Reader*, ed. P. David Marshall (New York: Routledge, 2006), 153.
3. Sharon Marcus, *The Drama of Celebrity* (Princeton, NJ: Princeton University Press, 2019), 127. Emphasis in original.
4. On the ability of audiences to interpret celebrities, see Dyer, "Stars as Images," and Marcus, *Drama of Celebrity*, as well as P. David Marshall, *Celebrity and Power: Fame in Contemporary Culture* (Minneapolis: University of Minnesota Press, 1997), and Chris Rojek, *Celebrity* (London: Reaktion, 2001).
5. Edward Said, *Representations of the Intellectual: The 1993 Reith Lectures* (New York: Pantheon, 1994), 32.
6. Cornel West, *The American Evasion of Philosophy: A Genealogy of Pragmatism* (London: Palgrave Macmillan, 1989), 34.
7. Lawrence Buell, *Emerson* (Cambridge, MA: Harvard University Press, 2003), 9.
8. Buell, *Emerson*, 42.
9. Buell, *New England Literary Culture* (Cambridge: Cambridge University Press, 1986), 62.
10. Julien Benda, *Treason of the Intellectuals*, 1928, trans. Richard Aldington (London: Routledge, 2017), 30.
11. Said, *Representations of the Intellectual*, 8.
12. Said, *Representations of the Intellectual*, 23.
13. "Ralph Waldo Emerson," *Marietta Collegiate Magazine*, November 1, 1855, 184.
14. Norton, "The New School in Literature and Religion," in *Emerson and Thoreau: The Contemporary Reviews*, ed. Joel Myerson (Cambridge: Cambridge University Press, 1992), 33.
15. Brownson, "Mr. Emerson's Address," in *Emerson and Thoreau: The Contemporary Reviews*, 43.
16. Brownson, "Mr. Emerson's Address," 43–44.
17. According to Chris Rojek, in celebrity culture, "notoriety is often associated with shifts in aesthetic culture" because the work of the individual in question destabilizes established values and norms (176). Rojek writes of aesthetics, but I propose a clear analogy to the intellectual shifts Emerson represents.
18. "Ralph Waldo Emerson and his Writings," *Christian Review* 26, no. 106 (October 1861): 653.
19. "Ralph Waldo Emerson," *Methodist Quarterly Review* 27 (1875): 190.
20. Davis, "Review of Divinity School Address," in *Emerson and Thoreau: The Contemporary Reviews*, 40–41.
21. On the link between celebrities, religion, and the parasocial, see Rojek, *Celebrity*, 52.
22. For a relevant discussion of early twentieth-century celebrity profiles, see Leo Lowenthal, "The Triumph of Mass Idols" (1944), in *The Celebrity Culture Reader*, 124–52. On the celebrity profile as a means to "elevate" the celebrity, see Rojek, *Celebrity*, 75.

23. "Ralph Waldo Emerson," *Household* 2, no. 11 (November 1869): 199.
24. "Ralph Waldo Emerson," *Household*, 199.
25. Said, *Representations of the Intellectual*, 11.
26. Parker, "The Writings of Ralph Waldo Emerson," in *Emerson and Thoreau: The Contemporary Reviews*, 228.
27. Parker, "Writings of Ralph Waldo Emerson," 228.
28. Parker, "Writings of Ralph Waldo Emerson," 228.
29. Parker, "Writings of Ralph Waldo Emerson," 229.
30. Parker, "Writings of Ralph Waldo Emerson," 233.
31. Parker, "Writings of Ralph Waldo Emerson," 229.
32. Parker, "Writings of Ralph Waldo Emerson," 230.
33. Robert Habich, *Building Their Own Waldos: Emerson's First Biographers and the Politics of Life-Writing in the Gilded Age* (Iowa City: University of Iowa Press, 2011, 10.
34. Robert D. Richardson, Jr. *Emerson: The Mind on Fire* (Berkeley: University of California Press, 1995), 525.
35. Nell Irvin Painter, *The History of White People* (New York: Norton, 2010), 185.
36. Richardson, *Emerson*, 523.
37. On the split between the Emerson image and the man himself, see my *Literary Celebrity and Public Life in the Nineteenth-Century United States* (Athens: University of Georgia Press, 2017), especially chapter 3.
38. See, for example, work by Len Gougeon, Christopher Hanlon, Philip Nicoloff, Martha Schoolman, and Laura Dassow Walls, as well as relevant discussions in Buell's *Emerson*.
39. Grossburg, "Is There a Fan in the House? The Affective Sensibility of Fandom," in *The Celebrity Culture Reader*, 587.
40. "Ralph Waldo Emerson. Phrenology, Physiognomy, Biography, and Portrait," *The American Phrenological Journal* 18, no. 3 (March 1854): 53.

CHAPTER 35

EMERSON, RELUCTANT FEMINIST

LESLIE ELIZABETH ECKEL

Ralph Waldo Emerson's relationship to the women's rights movement in the nineteenth century, otherwise known as the first wave of feminism, is defined by a series of refusals: to fully acknowledge the influence and leadership of the women who lifted up his circles of family and friends, to advocate for women at the conventions that empowered them in Massachusetts and beyond in the 1850s, to listen thoughtfully to women's own ideas about their futures, and to acknowledge the problematic intersections of femininity with other forms of socially enforced subservience, such as slavery, poverty, and immigrant status. By the time Emerson accepted Paulina Wright Davis's second invitation to address the Woman's Rights Convention in Boston in 1855, he had already turned her down along with her colleague Lucy Stone once, with the excuse that he was too busy compiling the *Memoirs of Margaret Fuller Ossoli* (1852), a tribute to his close friend and co-editor of the Transcendentalist periodical *The Dial* that probably harmed Fuller's reputation more than it celebrated her achievements. When Emerson stood up at the 1855 convention, he scoffed that women "embellish trifles" even as he affirmed, "Woman is the power of civilization" (*LL* 2:21, 18).

At this moment, when Emerson was both agitated and vocal about the urgency of abolishing slavery, he held in his hands Fuller's *Woman in the Nineteenth Century* (1845) as well as the first volume of English writer Coventry Patmore's soon to be infamous narrative poem *The Angel in the House* (1854–62). Although Emerson quoted Patmore's poem in his address, he failed to mention Fuller's manifesto, which argues that women must transcend the social roles prescribed for them as daughters, wives, and mothers to release their potential. In contrast, *The Angel in the House* ingrains a vision of women as virtuous helpmeets for moony men, for which Patmore would be admired by the Pre-Raphaelites but mocked by Virginia Woolf and Charlotte Perkins Gilman in the early twentieth century.[1] Shockingly, Emerson was torn between these two futures for women, and it is this struggle that I want to revive and interrogate as one source among many of the misunderstandings, conflicts, and failures in the pursuit of women's rights that still shape our collective experiences well into the twenty-first century. In a *New York Times* opinion written on Emerson's bicentennial in 2003, Adam Cohen describes Emerson as both a "great" and a "pernicious" thinker, suggesting, "Emerson the secular preacher still matters not because he has all the answers but because he so intriguingly reflects who we actually are."[2] In that spirit, I want to argue that it is as much Emerson's deep doubts about women's private identities and public roles as it is his faith in their goals of revolution that invite us to confront the ways in which we take gender equality for granted even now, as women continue to be marginalized, disbelieved, and restricted, especially in the ongoing #MeToo movement, the theft of girls' educations worldwide, and the erasures of reproductive rights in the US Supreme Court's 2022 ruling on Dobbs v. Jackson Women's Health Organization.

Ever since Emerson shared his views of women at the Woman's Rights Convention in 1855, critics have been split on whether he truly sympathized with the feminist cause. In a letter acknowledging his speech, activist Caroline Healey Dall observes, "some of the papers thought it doubtful whether you were for us or against us." While Davis invited him to speak with the assumption that "your heart is with us," Emerson ended up hedging his bets on women, which Dall realized could "lure the conservatives" to their cause, as Emerson's leading reputation by that point guaranteed sharper attention from newspapers.[3] As scholars have devoted their energies over the past two decades to uncovering the Transcendentalists' contributions to social and political movements, from antislavery to environmentalism to utopian radicalism, a consensus has emerged that Emerson, Thoreau, Fuller, the Alcotts, and others are far less stodgy than we might think. Instead, many agree that their words and actions are more fundamental to progressivism, anticolonialism, and an understanding of the Anthropocene than twentieth-century Americanists, once fascinated by their New England intellectualism, realized. While Thoreau is well known for his acts of resistance to the state that landed him in jail and for his fearlessness in support of John Brown's militant takedown of Southern slavery, scholars have recognized that Emerson's commitment to advocacy for Indigenous people and critique of racist laws dates back to the 1830s.[4]

The key issue of women's rights is still a thorn in Transcendentalism's side. However, this deficit in Americanist scholarship has been shrinking thanks to a growing variety of critical approaches to and editions of Margaret Fuller's writings as well as Jana Argersinger and Phyllis Cole's essential 2014 collection *Toward a Female Genealogy of Transcendentalism*. Despite the copresence of many innovative and assertive women in Emerson's circles, the "doubtful[ness]" of his audience in 1855 persists in the scholarly debate about his support for women's rights. This debate is polarized, with some contending that Emerson was fully invested in the evolving goals of the movement and others concluding that he was entirely "antifeminist".[5] Fewer readers occupy the middle ground that I wish to explore here, although I seek to build on work by Phyllis Cole and Christopher Newfield that discusses how Emerson's ideas served women well despite his personal "limits."[6] Len Gougeon contends that Emerson's advocacy for women gained strength along the same timeline as his antislavery activism, but as I have argued elsewhere, assumptions about gender roles and identities in the nineteenth century actually could be more intractable than racial ideologies, and like many of his peers, Emerson struggled to think differently about gender.[7] The history of US suffrage bears this out, as the women's rights movement did not achieve its goal of full citizenship for women until 1920, whereas African American men could vote from 1870 onward, even if state laws undermined those rights in ways that still disenfranchise people of color today. By placing Emerson's 1855 address on women's rights in a broader context, including his journals and notebooks as well as other writings published during his lifetime, I want to argue that women were always secondary and relational in Emerson's thought. Outwardly, his world was ruled by "representative men" (as the title of his 1850 book suggests), not leading women. He most often spoke about women's struggles for equal participation with unforgivable hesitation. His words may have been the gateway to self-reliance for women, but they were explicitly meant for men. Emerson's halfhearted advocacy for women's rights proves that even the nineteenth century's most fervent proponent of individualism could not transcend the ideology and institutions that upheld gender inequality.

In her 2014 manifesto *We Should All Be Feminists*, Chimamanda Ngozi Adichie recalls just how hard it is to "unlearn" the lessons she has absorbed about who women must be and what feminism means. She contends, "The problem with gender is that it prescribes how we should be rather than recognizing how we are. Imagine how much happier we would be, how much freer to be our true individual selves, if we didn't have the weight of gender expectations."[8] Adichie's desire for all "to be our true individual selves" surely aligns with Emerson's statement of purpose as a leader who intends not "to bring men to me, but to themselves" (*JMN* 14:xiv). Yet, this "problem with gender" Adichie identifies is a vivid part of our twenty-first-century reality, and we need to recognize that Emerson is partly responsible for that struggle. In the rest of this chapter, I want to examine three stages of Emerson's thinking about women: the reductively figurative roles they play in his early essays and the romance with his first wife Ellen, the multidimensionality of his engagements with women in fact, including Margaret Fuller and his second wife Lidian, and the kind of female future he envisions through his association with the women's rights movement and the world it promises to create. In doing so, I hope to set aside the feminist Emerson might have been in order to reveal the more complex human whose ideas haunt us now.

Feminine Figures

In the early years of his career, up to and including *Essays: First Series* (1841), Emerson developed the contradictory and troubling views of women that would restrict his public statements on women's rights throughout the 1850s and 1860s. On the one hand, he adored his first wife, teenage bride Ellen Louisa Tucker, whose death from tuberculosis left him unmoored and ready for an entirely new career outside the church. He paid tribute to his freethinking aunt Mary Moody Emerson in his journals, whose formative influence Cole illuminates in her landmark study *Mary Moody Emerson and the Origins of Transcendentalism: A Family History* (1998). His journals also chronicle the growth of his friendships with Margaret Fuller, Elizabeth Hoar, Caroline Sturgis and others such as Sarah Ripley who attended Transcendental Club meetings and co-founded utopian communities like Brook Farm. Emerson reflects on his marriage to second wife Lydia Jackson Emerson (whom he patriarchally renamed Lidian) and their parenting of two daughters, Ellen and Edith, along with two sons, Waldo and Edward. Despite the inspiring presence of these women and girls, Emerson spoke of women in stereotypical terms in his journals and the published writings that drew from that "Savings Bank" of ideas, including "The American Scholar" and "Self-Reliance," which are most often quoted and taught in classrooms now (*JMN* 4:xiv). These early women of Emerson's are metaphors, either idealized or demonized figures of femininity that push men to realize their "genius," never human beings allowed to grow fully into themselves.

Emerson's first wife Ellen is a curiously overlooked figure who played a significant role in both his lived experience and the growth of his literary imagination. While Emerson spent only three years with her in his twenties, her image stayed with him always, and the inheritance Emerson received from her estate made possible his philosophical explorations and gradual shift to a self-defined career as author and lecturer. In his eyes, Ellen is otherworldly, even in life, for "she has the purity & confiding religion of an angel." In the midst of writing a sermon in 1829, Emerson swoons over Ellen, declaring, "I do dearly love you" (*JMN* 3:149, 153). Their spiritual connection helped him envision the union of souls many Transcendentalists hoped could improve marriage as an institution, one of the many unjust systems of their era which they sought to interrogate. After Ellen's death, this ideal of marriage reappears in Emerson's essay "Love" (1841) as a kind of radical vision, "a love which knows not sex, nor person, nor partiality, but which seeks virtue and wisdom everywhere, to the end of increasing virtue and wisdom." It is fascinating to observe Emerson's figuration of Ellen as both an idealized, "angel[ic]" woman and a spur to his thinking about how women and men could surpass "sex" entirely as they attain greater "virtue and wisdom." During her life and beyond, "Ellen's beauty & love & life" heightened the contrasting views Emerson developed in his journals and essays of women, who either could rise to Ellen's stature in his estimation or fall to the level of scorn (*JMN* 4:263).

Given his worship of Ellen as his "angel," Emerson's insulting writings concerning women come as a shock as his characterizations of women swing between extremes. "Women generally have weak wills," he writes in 1834, "sharply expressed perhaps, but capricious unstable." Emerson goes on to say that "the perfection of female character seldom existed in poverty," narrowing his vision of ideal womanhood even further to an elite class of female counterparts (*JMN* 4:256–57). Although Emerson imagines that women might take the lead in social settings, in his mind, they do so in highly codified ways, always within the private, domestic sphere assigned to them by nineteenth-century gender ideology. He explains, "The rare women that charm us are those happily constituted persons who take possession of society wherever they go & give it its form[,] its tone. If they sit as we sit to wait for what shall be said we shall have no Olympus. To their genius elegance is essential" (*JMN* 4:299). While such female figures possess their own "genius," a keyword in "Self-Reliance" that releases the divine energy within each individual, their contributions uphold and improve the "form" and "tone" of the social order rather than transforming it, as a true Transcendentalist would seek to do. In a far more disturbing journal entry in 1835, Emerson puts women in their place, labeling a woman victimized by male sexual aggression in an imagined scenario as a "worthless slut," shaming words that are painful to read and impossible to forget in the longer arc of Emerson's advocacy for women (*JMN* 5:22). Taken together, Emerson's characterizations of women in his journals reveal his uncertainty and discomfort with women more broadly. While Ellen remains his "sweet friend, wife, angel," an ethereal model of femininity after whom he names his first daughter, Emerson seems as likely to acknowledge women as shaping forces as he is to cast them aside.

Emerson's unpredictable attitude toward women in his journals forms an intriguing backdrop to his double-edged engagement with and erasure of women from his most memorable public writings in the 1830s and early 1840s. In private, Emerson seems aware of the limits set on women's lives, objecting to the message they receive that "marriage is nothing but housekeeping & that Woman's life has no other aim" (*JMN* 4:351). His own home and domestic relationships continue to be sources of joy and comfort for him, and he reflects, "the garden & the family, wife, mother, son, & brother are a balsam. There is health in table talk & nursery play. We must wear old shoes & have aunts & cousins" (*JMN* 5:474). Yet, when he steps forward to give his address on "The American Scholar" and later, composes "Self-Reliance," he leaves women at home, doing them harm by erasing their presence in print. As he speaks on "The American Scholar," Emerson addresses an all-male audience, participating in patriarchal systems that excluded women from higher education before the Civil War. Emerson's writing does nothing to mitigate such exclusion, with his focus on the ideal of "Man Thinking," his vision of the (presumably white, male) scholar as universally representative ("he is the world's eye. He is the world's heart"), and his relentlessly gender-specific pronouns (*CW* 1:62). Women are nowhere to be found in Emerson's vision of intellectual growth, which we often ask students to overlook, if not accept, in ways that we ourselves have been dulled into believing are inevitable for a nineteenth-century thinker. In an 1842 journal entry, Emerson explains, "A highly endowed man with good intellect & good conscience is a Man-woman & does not so much need the complement of Woman to his being ... as another' (*JMN* 8:175). Although Emerson's vision of the ideal "Man-woman" appears to be inclusive, his choice to subsume "Woman" into this hybrid figure effectively renders women invisible and makes them accessories to lesser men. Margaret Fuller surely was aware of what her new friend was writing and proclaiming, as her friendship with Emerson grew from 1836 onward, and Fuller instructed him in German while they exchanged books on Goethe, who makes an appearance in "The American Scholar," although neither Fuller herself nor any other woman does (*JMN* 5:319).

It is important to recognize the significant absence of women from Emerson's foundational statements on nature, intellect, religion, and self-reliance. Most scholarship on Emerson and women's rights has focused on contextualizing his 1855 speech on

"Woman," zeroing in on those moments when he addresses women and their concerns directly. While I share this interest in Emerson's most visible commentaries, I believe that it is equally valuable to realize that the times when he diminishes or excludes women are just as important to his overall impact on the evolution of feminism. When he had a choice, especially early on, Emerson most often decided not to speak up for women. In his journal entries from 1838–39, Emerson demonstrates an awareness of the women's rights movement as well as the strong opinions held by his female friends. He observes that there is "a good deal of character in our abused age. The rights of woman, the antislavery,—temperance,—peace,—health,—and money movements; female speakers, mobs, & martyrs, the paradoxes, the antagonism of old & new." Later, he notes that Elizabeth Hoar insists he "add the topic of the rights of Woman; & Margaret Fuller testifies that women are Slaves" (JMN 7:6, 48). While Emerson is exhilarated by the possibilities of his time, which he celebrates in "The American Scholar" as "the age of Revolution; when the old and the new stand side by side, and admit of being compared," he also seems overwhelmed by its multiple pathways to reform and does not exactly, as he suggests, "know what to do with it" (CW 1:67).

In "Self-Reliance," Emerson prioritizes the inspiration and independence of men, reducing women to merely "feminine" energies that hold men back. David Leverenz's work in *Manhood and the American Renaissance* illuminates the ways in which "Emerson's early essays proclaim an explicit rhetoric of man making" as they "insist on manly power as the essence of mental energy and rail against what society does to manhood."[9] As focused as he is on shoring up manliness, Emerson once again sidelines women throughout the essay, mentioning them only in specific relation to men: "I shun father and mother and wife and brother, when my genius calls me"; and in perceived opposition to them, when the "feminine rage" of the "cultivated classes" prevents men from becoming truly self-reliant. While it is helpful to note that Emerson wrote this essay partly in self-defense after facing criticism for his defiant "Divinity School Address" (1838), the extent to which he genders his detractors by assigning them traditionally feminine traits—"decorous and prudent," "timid," and "vulnerable"—points to a habit of sidelining women and what they represent when he himself is under threat (JMN 7:xi). In this passage, Emerson also antagonizes "the ignorant and the poor," which emphasizes both the limits and the costs of Emerson's empowering theory of self-culture (CW 2:30, 33). Scholars have become accustomed to calling out Nathaniel Hawthorne's sexist mindset in his tirade against bestselling female authors as "that d—d mob of scribbling women" and to acknowledge the immateriality of women in Herman Melville's fiction, but somehow Emerson has been given the benefit of the doubt. Emerson plays both sides, figuring women as enemies at the same time that he is praising Lidian as "my gentle wife . . . [with] an angel's heart," commenting on the progress of women's rights, and partnering with Fuller to edit *The Dial*, which he hopes will "go straight into life with the devoted wisdom of the best men & women in the land" (JMN 7:388). If Emerson were the oblivious Abel Lamb of Louisa May Alcott's utopian satire "Transcendental Wild Oats" (1873), who did not realize his wife Hope was sustaining Fruitlands while he and his fellow philosophers "build castles in the air," he might be forgiven.[10] With the evidence of Emerson's admiration for and collaboration with women, however, his pattern of dismissing them in writing demands further investigation.

Women in Fact

At the midpoint of his career, from the publication of *Essays: First Series* in 1841 up to his 1855 address at the Woman's Rights Convention, Emerson no longer marginalized women but rather acknowledged them directly as partners, friends, and colleagues. With rare exceptions, Emerson's women returned to their bodies from the figurative realm to which he relegated them as virtuous "angels" or representatives of social conformity. Thus, I agree that Emerson's views evolve along the positive lines that Christina Zwarg, Len Gougeon, and Armida Gilbert have traced, especially through his conversations and professional collaborations with Margaret Fuller.[11] Despite such progress, Emerson's reluctance to let go of some sexist assumptions and his condescending pity for women disqualify him from what Gougeon identifies as "the vanguard of women's rights advocates," the leading edge of feminist thought and activism by men at midcentury that Phyllis Cole credits instead to William Henry Channing, Theodore Parker, and Thomas Wentworth Higginson.[12] I want to focus here on Emerson's expressions of ambivalence toward women in his circles as well as on his insistence that women are fundamentally different from and subordinate to men; in his mind, they are the helpers and the influencers, not the seekers of their own truths.

In "New England Reformers," a lecture Emerson included in *Essays: Second Series* (1844), he assesses "the great activity of thought and experimenting" that drove multiple reform movements in this crucial decade of the 1840s. One avenue of reform that hit especially close to home for Emerson was the formation of utopian communities by fellow Transcendentalists such as George and Sarah Ripley and Bronson and Abba Alcott. Although their endeavors intrigue him in theory, in practice, "their reliance on Association" clashes with his belief in the primacy of individual reform, for "society gains nothing whilst a man, not himself renovated, attempts to renovate things around him." These utopian communities draw together "men and women of superior talents and sentiments," allowing for communication and interaction between separate spheres and serving as laboratories for reimagining gender, which Holly Jackson has explored in her work on American radicalism (*CW* 3:149, 154–56).[13] While Emerson's friends were experimenting with gender identities and relations in real time, he went inward, thinking these matters through on his own and in "strange, cold-warm, attractive-repelling conversations with Margaret, whom I always admire, most revere when I nearest see, and sometimes love" (*JMN* 8:109). Fuller pulls Emerson in even as he pushes back, and she demonstrates women's capabilities as she rejects his lagging, two-dimensional views of women. As early as the 1830s, Emerson notes the way Fuller antagonizes him by asking, "Who would be a goody that could be a genius?" (*JMN*

5:407). In response to such prodding, and likely to his tangled feelings for Fuller herself, Emerson starts speaking of female "genius," opening up that key term of male empowerment from "Self-Reliance" to women as well. Although he recognizes this potential in women, Emerson insists that it is secondary to men's ambitions, as "Woman should not be expected to write or fight or build or compose scores, she does all by inspiring man to do all . . . She is the requiring genius." Women's creativity is limited to "inspiring" men, a distinction Emerson later emphasizes in his statement, "The Muse is feminine. But action is male." While the gender dynamics Emerson imagines might seem harmless and romantic, in fact, they have serious political consequences for women and the rights of citizenship they are starting to demand in the 1840s and 1850s. As he ponders the power of voting, Emerson explains, "Each of us, [men] . . . has at home in the shape of woman (who is naturally good) a directing conscience to hold him to the right." If "good" women are there to influence men, why would they need the vote for themselves?

Despite the frustrating limits of his vision, Emerson's progress in thinking about women's "genius" and women's rights is especially remarkable in the years leading up to 1845, when Fuller published *Woman in the Nineteenth Century*, a book that expanded her 1843 *Dial* essay "The Great Lawsuit: Man *versus* Men. Woman *versus* Women" into a feminist manifesto, the first to appear in the United States. Above and beyond other women in his Transcendentalist circles, including Hoar, Sturgis, the Peabody sisters, Sarah Ripley, Sarah Freeman Clarke, and Anna Barker Ward, Emerson celebrated Fuller for "the firmness with which she treads her upward path," by which "all mortals are convinced that another road exists than that which their feet know" (*JMN* 8:368). In his eyes, Fuller is an innovator, carving out her own "path" and then turning it into a "road" for others to follow. On this point, Emerson turned out to be exactly right. A brief study of some of Fuller's key statements in *Woman in the Nineteenth Century* seems essential here, as they help illuminate how conventional and even conservative Emerson was at this stage in his understanding of women and their hopes.

While Fuller agreed with Emerson that women's and men's fates were intertwined— "they are two halves of one thought"—she insisted that total equality replace women's deference to men. Fuller argues, "We would have every arbitrary barrier thrown down. We would have every path laid open to woman as freely as to man." Fuller is aiming to lift women out of the shadows to which Emerson relegates them in "Self-Reliance," especially in her persona of Miranda, who models a distinctly female "self-reliance" and enables Fuller to crack open that core Transcendental concept and make it much more inclusive.[14] While Fuller's feminism is not quite intersectional in the terms we might wish it to be in the twenty-first century, she comments on the historical marginalization of women alongside the oppression of Black and Indigenous people—"what has been done towards the red man, the black man"—showing an awareness that sexism, racism, and white supremacy often go hand in hand.[15] Finally, while Emerson upholds the gender binary that divides humanity into male and female, Fuller sees it as a false matrix. She contends, "Male and female represent the two sides of the great radical dualism. But, in fact, they are perpetually passing into one another. Fluid hardens to solid, solid rushes to fluid. There is no wholly masculine man, no purely feminine woman."[16] In this moment, Fuller reaches far beyond Emerson's fixed ideas about gender as she articulates male and female identities "passing into one another" as well as more "fluid" gender expressions that we have come to understand and accept in the twenty-first century. As Cole suggests, Fuller found ways to transcend gender, whereas Emerson, despite his progress in thinking about the subject, did not.[17]

I believe that part of what held Emerson back on women's rights was his lifelong practice of writing down and retooling provocative statements by others for his own use. We often think of Emerson as an incredibly original, oracular thinker (as in that unfortunate, undying phrase "the sage of Concord"), but that is not in fact the case; he quotes others frequently and weaves their words into his writings, sometimes without fully acknowledging their influence. He details this strategy in "Quotation and Originality," an essay in one of his final books, *Letters and Social Aims* (1875). While Emerson's writing process may have allowed him to create new intellectual structures by building on older foundations, it also perpetuated sexist opinions from previous generations: the very trap he urges others to avoid in *Nature* and "The American Scholar." For instance, in his journal, Emerson records quotations from Plato's works that refer to women as "fraudulent" and charge them with "imbecility," and in other entries, he repeats an idea of woman as a "snare" who must be protected from her "savage pursuers" (*JMN* 11:444, 31). These patterns of literary misogyny become more problematic when they affect the way Emerson treats women in fact. In his journal, Emerson records the condescending words of a male journalist who told Fuller that "in everything they [women] wrote, said, or thought, they were thinking of a husband" without responding to or refuting that assumption in any way (*JMN* 11:433). Later, in the "Margaret Fuller Ossoli" notebook he used to draft his contributions to her *Memoirs*, Emerson echoes the journalist's insult as he reflects, "The unlooked for trait in all these journals to me is the Woman, poor woman: they are all hysterical. She is bewailing her virginity and languishing for a husband" (*JMN* 11:500). After years of praising Fuller's intelligence and individuality, Emerson's choice to transform his friend into generic "Woman" with a capital W, a "poor woman" who should be pitied and then dismissed, is truly disturbing.

The instability of Emerson's views of women continued into the 1850s, after Fuller's untimely death and in the years leading up to his address at the Woman's Rights Convention in Boston. On the one hand, Emerson affirms the movement's goals of "equal rights of property & right of voting," which seems like a great leap forward in aligning previously separate spheres (*JMN* 11:444). That word "equal" is surely the result of his collaborations with Fuller and other women in the 1840s, including Elizabeth Hoar, who, according to Emerson, claims "a woman may speak, & vote, & legislate, & drive coach, if only it comes by degrees" (*JMN* 13:245). In supporting women's contributions to the public good, however gradual, he is listening to women themselves, fulfilling a promise he made a decade earlier:

> Man can never tell a woman what her duties are ... No. Woman only can tell the heights of feminine nature, & the only way in which man can help her, is by observing woman reverentially & whenever she ... speaks from herself & catches

him in inspired moments up to a heaven of honor & religion, to hold her to that point by <hearty &> reverential recognition of the divinity that speaks through her. (JMN 8:381)

Here, Emerson recognizes women as the arbiters of their own fates, the channels of that "divinity" which enables self-reliance. Men now play the secondary roles Emerson usually assigns to women, as they are the ones "observing" and supporting women in their pursuits, helping them realize their best selves. Again, it is both heartening and exasperating to see Emerson articulating for himself the kind of respectful approach to women's self-determination that Fuller and others were hoping he would express in public. While Emerson was capable of such "reverential" treatment, his years of reading and revivifying poisonously sexist material kept pulling him in the opposite direction, resulting in such regrettable statements as "the Woman's Convention should be holden in the Sculpture Gallery" and the ultimate zinger, "Few women are sane" (*JMN* 11:444–45). Unfortunately, these ideas are not momentary relapses in the upward trajectory of Emerson's views, but he carries them forward into his defining statement on women's rights in 1855.

Female Futures

Paulina Wright Davis invited Emerson to speak at the Woman's Rights Convention in 1855 with great expectations. She explains, "From your well-known antecedents we have taken it for granted that your heart is with us, and that you have a message which will aid, cheer, and strengthen us in progress toward perfect freedom and the highest right." If Davis had caught Emerson in one of those "inspired moments" he evoked in his journals, when he meant to "aid, cheer, and strengthen" women, her trust would have been better placed. However, even though Emerson was writing and speaking in an abolitionist vein that year, presenting his lecture on "American Slavery" in six different venues and declaring his opposition to this "system" of injustice, he was unwilling to do the same for women. Instead, Emerson's address was far more ambivalent and left muddled impressions on listeners, as Caroline Healey Dall pointed out in her response to him. Emerson recognized the "complicity" with punitive racism that the Fugitive Slave Law had made impossible for him and other Northerners to ignore, but he struggled to understand the systemic advantages of being male and failed to critique that form of injustice when he stood on the podium.[18] I call Emerson's speech a failure because he knew better about women and had said so in his journals, because he did not express the support for women's self-reliance that Fuller had demanded a decade earlier in *Woman in the Nineteenth Century*, and because he presumed to state both what women wanted and what they could achieve: an irritating move that we in the twenty-first century call "mansplaining." While Emerson built upon the 1855 address with a post-Civil War "Discours Manqué. Woman," which was published only after

Emerson's death (in the 1884 *Miscellanies*, where Emerson's son Edward titled the original speech "Woman"), and he updated his words for the 1869 anniversary celebration of the New England Women's Suffrage Association, he himself was more than a feminist *manqué*. Emerson's 1855 address and the texts that extend its claims reveal that while he was conscious of standing on the cusp of a new era of gender relations, he chose to prioritize tradition over innovation, betraying both himself and women in the process.

At first, Emerson celebrates women's rights as a leading issue of the times and seems ready to contribute to this revolution. In an opening sentence that surely thrilled his audience, he proclaims, "Woman is the power of civilization," putting the key element of "power" from "Self-Reliance" into women's hands. Part of women's power is seeing what is to come, according to Emerson, for "they are more delicate than men, and, as thus more impressionable, they are the best index of the coming hour." He affirms, "Any remarkable opinion or movement shared by women will be the first sign of revolution." Emerson leaps ahead of the curve in his implication that "the future is female," as Hillary Clinton declared after the Women's Marches lifted women's spirits and prospects worldwide in the wake of the 2016 elections. Still, his language both empowers women and stereotypes them as "more delicate than men" and "more impressionable," reminding us that he has not left sexist judgments behind.[19] In Emerson's mind, women always exist in relation to men; if they are to vote, they can clean up the mess of "election frauds and misdeeds" that men have made, but they will be tempted to "lose themselves eagerly in the glory of their husbands and children" (*LL* 2:18–19). Such retrograde beliefs in women's secondary status further separate Emerson from the radical origins of the slogan "the future is female," which arose, as journalist Katie Mettler explains, from 1970s "lesbian separatism, a school of feminist thought that promotes the complete isolation of lesbians from men and heterosexuals, either temporarily or permanently."[20] Emerson's understanding of women's identities is entirely heteronormative, and he never allows them space to develop alternative modes of being, doing, and loving. In contrast, Fuller explores in *Woman in the Nineteenth Century* what might happen if "Woman, self-centered, would never be absorbed by any relation …": a possibility that Emerson forecloses.

While gathering his thoughts for this address in his journals, Emerson promises solidarity. "And the new movement is only a tide shared by the spirits of man & woman," he writes, "& you may proceed in a faith that whatever the woman's heart is prompted to desire, the man's mind is simultaneously prompted to execute" (*JMN* 14:13). Emerson suggests that he is willing to follow women's lead, and he believes that women and men can do this "shared" work "simultaneously." On the other hand, his words leave the impression that it is up to women to "desire" and men to do, or "execute," and therefore, women cannot take action by themselves. This internal debate haunts Emerson throughout the address, where he echoes the demands of feminist organizers for "the right to education; to avenues of employment; to equal rights of property; to equal rights in marriage; to the exercise of the professions; to suffrage"—some of which carried forward into feminism's second wave in the 1960s and 1970s—but undercuts them by validating antifeminists who claim that "the best women do not wish these things." Emerson makes the rhetorical blunder of giving too much time and credence to those who object to women's empowerment without dismissing them, continuing a habit that became problematic in his journals. Such heightened attention to conservative arguments is more than just a structural mistake, though, as Emerson allows them to delay his own advocacy for women, concluding, "I do not think it yet appears that women wish this equal share in public affairs. But it is they, and not we, that are to determine it." He expects that women might be ready to articulate their position "in a few years" (*LL* 2:25–26, 28). It is truly stunning to imagine Emerson standing in front of an audience of women and men who have been demanding an "equal share in public affairs" and making this kind of oblivious statement. Christopher Newfield contends that Emerson's "misogyny" is devastating precisely because it is insidious; his patriarchal impulses travel "not through abuse but affection, an affection that remains coercive nonetheless."[21] In that spirit, I would add that Emerson's effort to protect women, to call for a retreat just when they are forging ahead, significantly weakens their mission. Instead of obliviousness, therefore, Emerson's attempt to "mansplain" women's rights to his audience at the Woman's Rights Convention is a kind of rhetorical violence, much worse than his odious comment earlier in the address that women "embellish trifles."

While she herself did not coin the term "mansplain," Rebecca Solnit argues in her 2008 essay "Men Explain Things to Me" that this longstanding social pattern "trains us in self-doubt and self-limitation just as it exercises men's unsupported overconfidence." It turns out that mansplaining does not just make women roll their eyes and move on, but it feeds what Solnit identifies as "a war within herself too," as women internalize doubts about their capacities for self-determination.[22] That is the most problematic legacy of Emerson's reluctant feminism; his perpetual ambivalence about women who follow their own internal compass toward the lives they want to lead turns out to be infectious. Although feminist leaders like Julia Ward Howe took up Emerson's words and used them to power the women's rights movement beyond the Civil War, Todd H. Richardson's work on the *Woman's Journal*, which was published by Howe, Lucy Stone, and Thomas Wentworth Higginson together with the Boston-based American Woman Suffrage Association, has revealed the extent to which their forward-looking Emerson bore little resemblance to the man they had encountered in fact.[23] In subsequent statements such as the 1869 "Discours Manqué. Woman" and an 1881 piece in the *Woman's Journal* titled "Mr. Emerson and Woman Suffrage," Emerson did write with more sympathy for women and greater faith in the leadership they had demonstrated in the antislavery movement and during the war, granting that woman "is entitled to demand power which she has shown she can use so well" (*LL* 2:17–18). Still, Emerson's progress on women's rights continued to be incremental, his ideas contradictory, and his judgments oppressive, as in his claim that women's suffrage could balance out "the uneducated emigrant vote … representing a brutal ignorance and mere physical wants." In Emerson's mind, women possess his own sense of moral superiority, with "the virtues, the aspirations … the purest of the people," and he still defines them in the narrow, idealized terms he used to describe his "angelic" first wife Ellen and other women in his family. Emerson assumes such women would look and act like him, for he says, "certainly all my points would be sooner carried in the State if women voted."[24] These "new women" are not yet practitioners of self-reliance, but avatars of Emerson's own.

Emerson and Twenty-First Century Feminism

By digging deep into Emerson's private histories with individual women as well as his broader, public statements about women's identities and capacities, I have sought to investigate the patriarchal structure of his thinking. His boldest theories of reshaping culture by going inward and then turning self-reliance outward claim to be universal, yet they explicitly exclude women, keeping them silent and disembodied. When Emerson is ready to grant power to women, he does so in limited, often patronizing ways, and even the boldest among them—women like Margaret Fuller, Paulina Wright Davis, Caroline Healey Dall, and Lucy Stone—are left hoping for more, depending on his lukewarm affirmations to validate their claims to full citizenship. If it sounds as though I am making a case against Emerson, that is true to some extent, as his failures to advocate for women and their rights are seriously disappointing. However, I believe it is crucial to keep Emerson in the picture as we work to understand nineteenth-century culture and its legacies today. To return to Adam Cohen's point that Emerson is relevant in the twenty-first century "not because he has all the answers but because he so intriguingly reflects who we actually are,"[25] I want to emphasize that we must keep thinking and writing about Emerson's relationships with women and others marginalized both in his time and in our own. His ideas about gender roles are inadequate, unsettling, and harmful, and therefore they demand that we interrogate our own assumptions about how gender works.

Emerson's outsized influence on American literature courses and the field of nineteenth-century American literary studies is unlikely to shrink anytime soon, yet there are important ways of decentering him in the interest of greater inclusion and further critical discoveries. When we teach Emerson, especially his theory of self-reliance that runs through so many of his writings, we can keep him in conversation not only with men in his circles such as Henry David Thoreau, who turned such ideas into powerful political resistance against state-sponsored injustice, but with others both in and beyond Concord who challenged Emerson and reimagined self-reliance on their own terms. What does self-reliance look like for Frederick Douglass, for Margaret Fuller, for Harriet Jacobs, for Jane Johnston Schoolcraft? Instead of relentless self-assertion, it might be mutual aid through education, women's efforts of self-cultivation apart from men, the creation of more equal marriages and families, or a balance between self-reflection and cultural belonging. In an age of extreme partisanship and disinformation, it is especially important to ask students to think critically about missing pieces, lingering prejudices, and alternatives to that tenacious Emersonian individualism which often perpetuates systems of social and economic inequality.

In reflecting on Emerson's habit of talking over women while claiming he was listening to them, it is necessary to consider Rebecca Solnit's point about how this tradition "opens up space for men and closes it off for women, space to speak, to be heard, to have rights, to participate, to be respected, to be a full and free human being."[26] Again, these were spaces and freedoms Emerson was demanding for himself and other men but reluctant to offer women, as though they were his to give in the first place. These silences, Solnit believes, then become opportunities for further oppression, for erasure, for violence against women and anyone who lives outside the gender binary. While Margaret Fuller released that binary in her assertion that male and female "are perpetually passing into one another. Fluid hardens to solid, solid rushes to fluid. There is no wholly masculine man, no purely feminine woman," Emerson found comfort in it.[27] The women he celebrated were a select few, and the feminism they advanced turned out to have exclusionary tendencies as well, as recent critics of "white feminism" such as Koa Beck have argued. This culturally approved and commodified feminism still prioritizes what Beck, who identifies as a "biracial queer woman in a siloed world," calls "self-empowerment" over the fundamental needs of diverse collectives.[28] What Emerson gives to and takes from women over the course of his career insists that we keep engaging him in conversation, for better, and sometimes, for worse.

Notes

1. Charlotte Perkins Gilman, 1891, "An Extinct Angel", in *The Yellow Wall-Paper, Herland, and Selected Writings* (New York: Penguin, 2009), 163–65; Virginia Woolf, "Professions for Women," in *The Death of the Moth, and Other Essays* (London: Hogarth Press, 1942).
2. Adam Cohen, "It's Emerson's Anniversary and He's Got 21st-Century America Nailed," *The New York Times*, 4 May 2003, www.nytimes.com/2003/05/04/opinion/editorial-observer-it-s-emerson-s-anniversary-he-s-got-21st-century-america.html.
3. For Dall's and Davis's letters, see *LL* 2:15. For Dall's reflection on Emerson's "lure," see Phyllis Cole, "The New Movement's Tide: Emerson and Women's Rights," in *Emerson Bicentennial Essays*, ed. Ronald A. Bosco and Joel Myerson (Boston: Massachusetts Historical Society, 2006), 117–52, 138.
4. David M. Robinson includes Emerson's 1838 letter to President Martin Van Buren protesting the forced removal of the Cherokee people in *The Political Emerson* (Boston: Beacon Press, 2004), 27–32. For a comprehensive study of Emerson's engagement with the antislavery movement, see Len Gougeon, *Virtue's Hero: Emerson, Antislavery, and Reform* (Athens: University of Georgia Press, 1990).
5. For a positive view of Emerson's commitment to women's rights, see Len Gougeon, "Emerson and the Woman Question: The Evolution of His Thought," *New England Quarterly* 71, no. 4 (1998): 570–92. Jamie S. Crouse highlights Margaret Vanderhaar Allen's assertion that Emerson is "anti-feminist" in Allen, *The Achievement of Margaret Fuller* (University Park: Pennsylvania State University Press, 1990). See Crouse, "'If They Have

a Moral Power': Margaret Fuller, Transcendentalism, and the Question of Women's Moral Nature," *American Transcendental Quarterly* 19, no. 4 (2005): 259–79, 264.
6. Cole, "New Movement's Tide," 120. See also Christopher Newfield, "Loving Bondage: Emerson's Ideal Relationships," *American Transcendental Quarterly* 5, no. 3 (1991): 183–93.
7. Leslie Elizabeth Eckel, "Gender," in *Ralph Waldo Emerson in Context*, ed. Wesley T. Mott (Cambridge: Cambridge University Press, 2014), 188–95.
8. Chimamanda Ngozi Adichie, *We Should All Be Feminists* (New York: Anchor, 2014), 38, 34.
9. David Leverenz, *Manhood and the American Renaissance* (Ithaca, NY: Cornell University Press, 1989), 45.
10. Louisa May Alcott, "Transcendental Wild Oats," in *The Portable Louisa May Alcott*, ed. Elizabeth Lennox Keyser (New York: Penguin, 2000), 538–52, 543.
11. See Zwarg, *Feminist Conversations: Fuller, Emerson, and the Play of Reading* (Ithaca, NY: Cornell University Press, 1995); Gougeon, "Emerson and the Woman Question"; and Gilbert, "Emerson in the Context of the Woman's Rights Movement," in *A Historical Guide to Ralph Waldo Emerson*, ed. Joel Myerson (Oxford: Oxford University Press, 2000), 211–49.
12. Gougeon, "Emerson and the Woman Question," 582; Cole, "New Movement's Tide," 120.
13. For more on utopian experimentation with gender roles, see Holly Jackson, *American Radicals: How Nineteenth-Century Protest Shaped the Nation* (New York: Crown, 2019), 142–57.
14. Margaret Fuller, *Woman in the Nineteenth Century*, in *The Essential Margaret Fuller*, ed. Jeffrey Steele (New Brunswick: Rutgers University Press, 1992), 245, 260, 262.
15. Fuller, *Woman*, 253. For a critique of Fuller's limited activism for the rights of African Americans, see Katherine Adams, "Black Exaltadas: Race, Reform, and Spectacular Womanhood After Fuller," in *Toward a Female Genealogy of Transcendentalism*, ed. Jana L. Argersinger and Phyllis Cole (Athens: University of Georgia Press, 2014), 399–420.
16. Fuller, *Woman*, 310.
17. Phyllis Cole makes this point about Fuller in relation to other feminists, not Emerson himself. See "Woman's Rights and Feminism," in *The Oxford Handbook of Transcendentalism*, ed. Joel Myerson, Sandra Harbert Petrulionis, and Laura Dassow Walls (Oxford: Oxford University Press, 2010), 220–40, 228.
18. Paulina Wright Davis to Emerson, June 7, 1855, and Caroline Healey Dall to Emerson, October 7, 1855, quoted in *LL* 2:15. See also Emerson, "American Slavery," in *LL* 2:2.
19. See also Crouse, "Moral Power," 265.
20. Katie Mettler, "Hillary Clinton Just Said It, but 'The Future Is Female' Began as a 1970s Lesbian Separatist Slogan," *The Washington Post*, 8 February 2017, www.washingtonpost.com/news/morning-mix/wp/2017/02/08/hillary-clinton-just-said-it-but-the-future-is-female-began-as-a-1970s-lesbian-separatist-slogan/.
21. Christopher J. Newfield, "Loving Bondage: Emerson's Ideal Relationships," *American Transcendental Quarterly* 5, no. 3 (1991): 183–93, 184–85.
22. Rebecca Solnit, *Men Explain Things to Me* (Chicago: Haymarket, 2014), 4.
23. Todd H. Richardson, "Publishing the Cause of Suffrage: The *Woman's Journal*'s Appropriation of Ralph Waldo Emerson in Postbellum America," *New England Quarterly* 79, no. 4 (2006): 578–608, 581.

24. Emerson, *A Reasonable Reform* (New York: National Woman Suffrage Publishing, n.d.), 2–4. Bosco and Myerson note that this pamphlet reprints "Mr. Emerson on Woman Suffrage" from the *Woman's Journal* (March 26, 1881). See *LL* 2:18.
25. Cohen, "It's Emerson's Anniversary."
26. Solnit, *Men Explain Things to Me*, 14.
27. Fuller, *Woman*, 310.
28. Koa Beck, *White Feminism: From the Suffragettes to Influencers and Who They Leave Behind* (New York: Atria Books, 2021), xv, xviii.

CHAPTER 36

EMERSON AND THE WILDNESS OF FRIENDSHIP

EDUARDO CADAVA

How could one agree to speak of this friend? Neither in praise nor in the interest of some truth. The traits of his character, the forms of his existence, the episodes of his life, even in keeping with the search for which he felt himself responsible to the point of irresponsibility, belong to no one. There are no witnesses.... We must give up trying to know those to whom we are linked by something essential; by this I mean we must greet them in the relation with the unknown in which they greet us as well, in our estrangement. Friendship, this relation without dependence, without episode, yet into which all of the simplicity of life enters, passes by way of the recognition of the common strangeness that does not allow us to speak of our friends but only to speak to them, not to make of them a topic of conversations (or essays), but the movement of understanding in which, speaking to us, they reserve, even on the most familiar terms, an infinite distance, the fundamental separation on the basis of which what separates becomes relation.

Maurice Blanchot, "Friendship"[1]

I do then with my friends what I do with my books.

Ralph Waldo Emerson, "Friendship" (*CW* 2:126)

Epitaphs

WHAT can friendship be if, as Maurice Blanchot suggests, we can never understand or speak of the friend? What can it be if it begins, not in an experience of familiarity and communion, but in an experience of strangeness, of distance and separation? What would an encounter be, and is it even possible? What would it mean to think about the time of a friendship—about the time that composes a friendship, or about the time that touches it, belongs to it, even makes it possible? Is there a time for friendship, a time that summons friendship, a time that, touching every dimension of the experience of friendship, also keeps this experience from remaining the same from one moment to the next? For Ralph Waldo Emerson, the possibility of such a time—of a time that also suggests the passing of time—had to be thought beginning from the date of May 9, 1836. On that day, at that time, the person in whom he had found both a brother and a friend, his brother Charles, died. For Emerson, the possibility of a time for friendship requires thinking of the relationship between this time and the death of an other. We could even say that death is what makes the thought of time possible, even if this thought is, at this very moment, at the time of his brother's death, perhaps the most difficult and disconcerting element of Emerson's mourning—and not only because, for him, "the event of death is always astounding," "our philosophy never reaches it, never possesses it" (*JMN* 5:415) but also because, for him, his brother Charles was, in the felicitous phrase with which John Michael has described Emerson's sense of Charles, "like no other."[2]

If Charles was like no other, it is certainly because of what Emerson perceives to be his special talents as well as the special intimacy that Emerson believed they shared, but it also is because his own sentiments and thoughts also belonged to Emerson. "The eye is closed that was to see Nature for me, & give me leave to see," Emerson writes a few days after Charles's death (in an echo of Montaigne's sentiments in his own essay on friendship, also written after the death of his friend, Étienne de la Boétie), "besides my direct debt to him of how many valued thoughts,—through what orbits of speculation have we not traveled together, so that it would not be possible for either of us to say, This is my thought, That is yours" (*JMN* 5:152 and 151). If we listen closely to him here, we can hear a declaration of his love of Charles and his sense that his identity is both constituted and deconstituted by their relation, and, thinking about his friendship, we can imagine him even telling the dead Charles this:

> I begin, my dear Charles, I begin in relation to you, in relation to the beginning that you are for me, in relation to what you "give me leave to see." I begin with the trace of this relation that, because it suggests everything I am saying here, already implies my correspondence with you, my being with an other, my being with you. What our friendship has taught me is that I begin only on the condition that I am not alone, that I see through the eyes of another, that I have no self but the self that disappears in its relation to an other, in this instance, "you." I approach myself as I think of you, but I know that, with your death, but also in your life, the self I approach is lost and cannot be found. As a result, I experience the madness of a single desire: to affect time with time, and with the hope that I may yet live to archive the music of my relation to you. I cannot live without you, Charles, and, with your death, I am no longer myself, even though I know that, even before your death, and because of our friendship, I already was not myself. If I have been wounded by your death—if it has pierced me and struck me—it is because this wound already was "mine," already was the signature of my relation to you. Your death has been added to my life, even

if, from the very beginning, it already was there. No longer simply alive, but not yet dead, at the threshold of life and death, I offer you these thoughts on our friendship, on friendship in general, in the hope that they can suspend and derange time, and that, confessing my enduring friendship, my enduring wound, they can transform your corpse into a body I can cite and recite, again and again, into a body I can incorporate into the body of my writing.

Indeed, as numerous commentators have noted, Charles's corpse is everywhere in *Nature*—which Emerson was completing when Charles died. As Emerson writes in his essay, "Nature always wears the colors of the spirit. To a man laboring under calamity, the heat of his own fire hath sadness in it. Then there is a kind of contempt of the landscape felt by him who has just lost by death a dear friend. The sky is less grand as it shuts down over less worth in the population" (*CW* 1:10–11). The horizon closes in on the eye that views it, he suggests, and the expanse of the sky descends and seals death in the landscape, even generalizing it across nature and all of its inhabitants, in particular human ones. "All things perish," he tells us elsewhere, "all are the partakers of this general doom but man is the prominent mark at which all arrows are aimed. In the lines of his countenance it is written 'that he is dying,' in a language that we can all understand" (*JMN* 3:73).

This is why, repeatedly in *Nature*, the reader comes upon a corpse—which is Charles and not Charles at the same time—and on the unresolved problem of relation that this corpse represents. As Michael has put it, "the problem of the relation to the NOT ME in *Nature* is complicated by the dead body in the landscape and the question of how to view it.... Emerson's figurative language tends to transform all of nature into the corpse it contains. Nature not only contains the 'sepulchers of the fathers,' that Emerson in his introduction says we build; it is itself a kind of tomb."[3] This is why, Emerson notes, in a passage about Sir Thomas Browne's 1658 *Hydriotaphia; Urn Burial*, "All history is an epitaph. All life a progress toward death. The [sun] world but a large Urn. The sun in his bright path thro' Ecliptic but a funereal triumph ... for it lights men & animals & plants to their graves" (*JMN* 3:220). According to Emerson, the world of *Hydriotaphia* is one in which everything passes away, in which all life progresses toward death. It tells us that there can be no history that is not a history of death—that is not a history of its own death. To be more precise, the true history of the past is the one that is always in a state of passing away. This is why "all history is an epitaph." *Nature* teaches us, in other words, that death and life are inseparable from one another, and this lesson is the key to the questions raised by the corpse in *Nature* and the body of Emerson's work in general. Nevertheless, as Emerson notes in his journals, again speaking of Charles's death but also of death in general:

> We are always at the beginning of our catechism; always the definition is yet to be made. What is Death? I see nothing to help beyond observing what the mind's habit is in regard to that crisis.... After I have made my will & set my house in order, I shall do in the immediate expectation of death the same things I should do without it. But

more difficult is it to know the death of another. ... So with the expectation of the death of persons who are conveniently situated, who have all they desire, & to whom death is fearful, [one] looks in vain for a consolation. In us there ought to be remedy. There ought to be, there can be nothing, to which the soul is called, to which the soul is not equal. And I suppose that the roots of my relation to every individual are in my own constitution & not less the causes of his disappearance from me. (JMN 5:415–16)

As Michael notes, this haunting, moving passage joins "Emerson's own death with the death of another, a 'he' who can only be Charles,"[4] but who also figures the mortality of the friend in general, a mortality that, even before the other dies, is linked to his relation to others, a relation that prevents him from remaining identical to himself and that therefore disappears him. The fact that it is precisely his relation to the other that prevents him from remaining simply "himself" accounts for Emerson's suggestion that the traces of others are rooted in our own constitution and this relationality deconstitutes both the self and the other and, in so doing, announces the other's death, even if this death remains inscrutable, just as ours does.

Infinite Remoteness

The singularity that defines Charles's existence (Charles is like no other) is at the same time, then, the knowledge of an encounter and a relation (Charles is like no other because he is very much like Emerson). Indeed, after the death of Charles, Emerson's journals consistently record his sense that the loss of his brother-friend represents a loss of his own self. He comes to experience his mortality by way of his brother-friend's death, by what this death communicates of his brother-friend's mortality. This mortality is not unrelated to his understanding of the worth of his brother-friend. What becomes apparent is that this brother-friend—the one Emerson believed he knew—can no longer be found in any other, and not even in the memory of his closest other, Emerson himself. For Charles's papers revealed him to be neither the thinker nor the optimist that Emerson believed him to be. In reading Charles's writings, Emerson comes to understand that he never really knew Charles, that he never understood him, and this fact is more devastating to him than Charles's death itself.[5] Indeed, what Charles's death suggests to Emerson is the utter inaccessibility of our friends. When he writes "Friendship," he takes his point of departure from this recognition and, in so doing, he seeks to understand what friendship can be if we can never know the other. This is why he later suggests that to "a great heart [the friend] will be a stranger in a thousand particulars" (CW 2:123).

That the friend is a figure of the unknown is confirmed by the little fable with which Emerson begins his essay. The fable suggests that the first experience of friendship is, in his words, "the palpitation which the approach of a stranger causes" (CW 2:113). This palpitation implies that the first impulse toward friendship occurs in the body: it emerges involuntarily, and before any act of cognition or representation. Nevertheless, if Emerson's stranger is, as he tells us, a "commended stranger," the responsibility for this figure of foreignness is assigned to the household by an unnamed other and this helps explain why the household responds to the stranger even before his arrival. Since "of a commended stranger, only the good report is told by others," "only the good and new is heard by us," the commendation prevents the stranger from being entirely a stranger—it alters the stranger's strangeness—even as it preserves the stranger's alterity. "Having imagined and invested him," however:

> We ask how we should stand related in conversation and action with such a man, and are uneasy with fear. The same idea exalts conversation with him. We talk better than we are wont. We have the nimblest fancy, a richer memory, and our dumb devil has taken leave for the time. For long hours we can continue a series of sincere, graceful, rich communications, drawn from the oldest, secretest experience, so that they who sit by, of our own kinsfolk and acquaintance, shall feel a lively surprise at our unusual powers. (*CW* 2:114)

Indeed, everything in this encounter seems to promise an experience of friendship—until, that is, the stranger begins to speak, somewhat in his own idiom: "But as soon as the stranger begins to intrude his partialities, his definitions, his defects, into the conversation, it is all over. He has heard the first, the last and best he will ever hear from us. He is no stranger now. Vulgarity, ignorance, misapprehension are old acquaintances" (*CW* 2:114).

It would seem that the possibility of friendship ends at the very moment the stranger is no longer a stranger, at the very moment when, through a process of familiarization that corresponds to a process of reading and interpretation, we regard "his partialities, his definitions, his defects," when, that is, we say: "He is no stranger now. Vulgarity, ignorance, misapprehension, are old acquaintances." The fable not only uncovers our own "partialities," "definitions," and "defects"—this is its beauty and wonder—but also signals the death rather than the birth of relation. While the stranger as stranger here marks the limit of friendship, the interruption of friendship, he at the same time exposes the "hearts" that greet him in their strangeness. If the passage points to the death of the other as other, it also signals the preservation of the other as other, since, as he puts it later in the essay, every encounter confirms the other's "infinite remoteness" (*CW* 2:116). Indeed, as the fable suggests, the very moment we believe we know the other, there is no chance for friendship. This is why Emerson insists on dissociating friendship from knowledge, transparency, or communion. Friendship never occurs without the marking of a certain strangeness, and, indeed, this strangeness belongs to its very structure. This is why, Emerson suggests, the stranger "stands to us for humanity" (*CW* 2:114): we always remain strange to ourselves and to each other. As the essay proceeds, this fable of the conditions of friendship in general is elaborated in different contexts and, although its elements get dispersed throughout the essay, they can be followed, like a kind of red thread, as they increasingly become more forceful. The stranger not only marks the limit of friendship, but he at the same time suggests the alterity without which friendship is impossible. He represents humanity because he figures, in his strangeness, what is common to all our relations: the strangeness of our being-in-common. What we share is our incommensurability with one another. Recalling that the essay is written after the death of his brother-friend, the suggestion seems to be that we know friendship only when we experience the impossibility of knowing the other, the impossibility of communion or immanence (the self-presence of individuals to one another in and by their relation) before the dead other. According to this scheme, the nature of friendship—what we might call, following Blanchot, "a relation without relation"—is understood as double and contradictory, or, in Emerson's words, as "a paradox of nature" (*CW* 2:120). Requiring "that rare mean betwixt likeness and unlikeness, that piques each with the presence of power and of consent in the other party," Emerson's conception of friendship leads him to be "equally balked by antagonism and by compliance." "Let him not cease an instant to be himself," Emerson says of the stranger-friend he has before him, "the only joy I have in his being mine, is that the *not mine* is *mine*" (*CW* 2:122). This means, among other things, that friendship has nothing to do with possession, at least as we generally understand it. Friends can never be possessed, and this is why "the condition which the high friendship demands, is, the ability to do without it" (*CW* 2:123). We must be willing to let our friend go, to say "farewell" to him, in order not to surrender to the temptation of believing that we can comprehend him, that we can appropriate him and make him ours. The first law of friendship is to respect the other's "infinite remoteness," to understand that the other always will exceed our understanding. In Emerson's words, "I cannot make your consciousness tantamount to mine," but, he adds, "these things may hardly be said without a sort of treachery to the relation" (*CW* 2:116).

This does not mean, however, that, from the very first moment in which we are touched by the other, moved by him, even altered by him, we do not retain a trace of him, a relation to him, but rather that, even though this trace of the other comes to inhabit us, it simultaneously exceeds us. "My friends have come to me unsought," Emerson tells us; "by oldest right, by the divine affinity of virtue with itself, I find them, or rather not I, but the Deity in me and in them derides and cancels the thick walls of individual character, relation, age, sex, circumstance, at which he usually connives, and now makes many one" (*CW* 2:115). This trace of the other within me—this Deity that is in me but also transcends me, that is "mine" but also "not mine"—suggests that, as soon as the self encounters an other, the self is no longer who or what it was before the encounter and therefore the encounter "itself" names a kind of death. This experience of living at the threshold of death and life is another name for the experience of friendship—for what takes place in our relation to the one we come to love. From the very moment in which the self is touched or moved by the other, it is broken into by the other, inhabited by the other, and therefore no longer simply "itself," since the walls that helped define its borders have been canceled by its relation to the other. To put this another way: within the experience of relation, within an experience in which the self and the other come to inhabit each other, neither the self nor the other can return to himself: the self and the other deconstitute one another precisely in their relation. Their relation names a "one" that shatters the identity of each, and that "itself" also is shattered, fragmented, and never self-identical to itself because it already is "many." In Emerson's words, "In good company, the individuals merge their egotism into a social soul exactly coextensive with the several consciousnesses there present" (*CW* 2:122). If friendship is, as Werner Hamacher says of history (among other things, Emerson's essay seeks to delineate not only the history of friendship but also the way in which friendship comes to us *as* history), "a relation to the other as a finite other, then it is a relation to a self-altering other, to the withdrawal of the other, and is therefore a self-altering, self-withdrawing relation."[6] This is why, Emerson suggests, "the higher the style we demand of friendship, of course the less easy to establish it with flesh and blood. We walk alone in the world. Friends, such as we desire, are dreams and fables" (*CW* 2:125). Or, as he puts it just before, "Late,—very late,—we perceive that no arrangements, no introductions, no consuetudes or habits of society, would be of any avail to establish us in such relations with them as we desire,—but solely the uprise of nature in us to the same degree it is in them; then shall we meet as water with water; and if we should not meet them then, we shall not want them, for we are already they" (ibid.). If Emerson suggests that he is not in need of an other, it is because the other is already in him and because—from the moment they encounter one another—neither he nor the other are any longer simply "themselves."

As he puts it in relation to Charles, emphasizing the play between knowing the other and "the occult hereditary sympathy" that exceeds what he can know: "I have felt in him the inestimable advantage, when God allows it, of finding a brother and a friend in one. The mutual understanding is then perfect, because Nature has settled the constitution of the amity on solidest foundations; and so it admits of mercenary usefulness & of unsparing censure; there exists the greatest convenience inasmuch as the same persons & facts are known to each, and an occult hereditary sympathy underlies all our intercourse & extends farther than we know" (*JMN* 5:151–52).

"Thine ever, or never"

This interplay between what is mine (what is in me) and what is not mine (what is in me that is not me and that therefore prevents me from being just "me")—an interplay Emerson registers earlier in his essay and to which he refers as "inward irradiations" (*CW* 2:113) in order to suggest a movement that simultaneously moves inward and outward—is linked to Emerson's sense of the relations that both separate and attract a self and an other involuntarily (each of which is already, as he puts it, "several"). Having read Goethe's *Elective Affinities* in the spring of 1837, Emerson suggests that these affinities draw us to the other without our knowing how and why; they name a force that, attracting us to the other, nevertheless acts independently even of our perception. As Branka Arsić has noted, if "love is blind," it is because in Emerson it becomes a fable ("love is fabled to be blind," he notes in a journal entry from April 1837), not because "he wants to restore the power of vision to it but because it is not related to visual perception at all."[7] Rather, it is tied to "the power of electivity": as he notes in his journals, "love is not an ophthalmia but an electuary" (*JMN* 5:294). That love is not an ophthalmia means that it does not belong to the order of vision, but rather to what we see without seeing, even in an elective way.

But, as always in Emerson, election is never something that originates in the self. "'Tis fine for us to speculate and elect our course," he tells us in his essay "Fate," "if we must accept an irresistible dictation" (*CW* 6:2). In other words, if we are moved by another person without knowing why, it is largely because of this force of dictation: one reason why we can never know the other, why we can never touch the other, is that our access to him is entirely mediated by a network of unforeseeably mediated relations. Emerson confirms this in the very act of writing his essay since it proceeds by way of citation: his effort to think about the nature of friendship is mediated by the history of friendship, and by the history of efforts to think about friendship. But how are we to think about the time of an essay that presents itself as a kind of anthology, a reservoir of anecdotes, sayings, proverbs, on friendship in particular and on relation in general? What is the time of an essay which, without naming everyone it cites, evokes and recirculates passages from Emerson's own previous letters, lectures, journals, and poems, as well as from the Bible, Plutarch, Milton, Shakespeare, Montaigne, Goethe, to name only a few of the authors to whom he alludes in his essay? What is the time of an essay that conjures not only the words of the living and the dead but also the dead as the living, as what survives through the act of writing that Emerson's essay is? Every citation declares the death of what is cited, and every survival in citation is the survival of one that is dead, one that absents itself, withdraws, disintegrates and, slipping away from its own control and the control of every possible other, is altered. If "Friendship" is a literary history of the surviving dead, of linguistic phantoms and shadows, it also is a history of friendship, a history of the place of death within the structure of friendship, a history of history *as* friendship. It is a history of what cannot enter history, a history in which, as Emerson writes in his essay "Love," "we must leave a lingering adherence to facts, and study the sentiment as it appeared in hope and not in history" (*CW* 2:100).

This is why friendship can never be brought under a concept. Indeed, the first thing to notice about Emerson's essay is its title. The title does not say that the essay is "On Friendship" or "Of Friendship"; simply titled "Friendship," the essay presents itself *as* "Friendship," as an example of friendship. Friendship cannot be thought about. It cannot be articulated in a series of propositions or theses. This essay is not an essay on friendship as a real, empirical "theme" or "referent" but rather of friendship as the athematization or withdrawal of theme or referent. The suggestion would seem to be that we cannot read "Friendship" until the surface intelligibility of the essay's language is shaken and we follow not the content, the propositions or statements that comprise the essay, but the very movement of its language as it opens to what is other. In its citationality, the essay speaks its language as immediately other. It is different from itself in each of its utterances—and not only because of its constant citation—and, in this self-differentiation, it stages within the very movement of its language what it wants to suggest about the way in which relationality deconstitutes the self—whether it be the self of a friend or a sentence, or even of a word. Neither the essay nor the experience of friendship are self-identical to themselves. This is not to say that the opening onto thought, onto the other, onto language, and onto friendship are not one and the same—for each announces a relation to something other than what it is in order to suggest what makes any relation to beings in the world possible, the very structure of representation. Rather, what Emerson defines as friendship lies at the limits of language—it could even be said to be the origin of language. As Emerson tells us, "the scholar sits down to write, and all his years of meditation do not furnish him with one good thought or happy expression; but it is necessary to write a letter to a friend,—and, forthwith, troops of gentle thoughts invent themselves, on every hand, with chosen words" (*CW* 2:113). He suggests what such a letter might look like when, later in the essay, he writes:

> every man passes his life in the search after friendship, and if he should record his true sentiment, he might write a letter like this to each new candidate for his love:
> DEAR FRIEND:—
> If I was sure of thee, sure of thy capacity, sure to match my mood with thine, I should never think again of trifles in relation to thy comings and goings. I am not very wise; my moods are quite attainable; and I respect thy genius; it is to me as yet unfathomed; yet dare I not presume in thee a perfect intelligence of me, and so thou art to me a delicious torment. Thine ever, or never. (*CW* 2:117)

Emerson beautifully draws out the significance of such correspondence—of the coming and going of the friend, of the friend's incomprehensibility, and of the impossibility of possession, even when we remain touched, inhabited, and altered by the other—when he adds: "I will owe to my friends this evanescent intercourse. I will receive from them, not what they have, but what they are. They shall give me that which properly they cannot give, but which emanates from them. But they shall not hold me by any relations less subtile and pure. We will meet as though we met not, and part as though we parted not" (*CW* 2:126). Within the experience of friendship, he suggests, within this experience of existing at the threshold of life and death, we "will meet as though we met not" because we can never fully know the other, and we will "part as though we parted not" because, from the moment we are touched or moved by the friend, we will remain inhabited by his trace, and therefore never be free of this relation.

Star Friendship

This play between proximity and distance is confirmed and elaborated in a beautiful passage in Nietzsche's *Gay Science* (a book whose epigraph comes from Emerson and whose title is taken from Emerson's late 1872 essay "Poetry and Imagination"—in the essay, Emerson says that "poetry is the *gai science*"). There, in a passage that points to the distance on the basis of which relation is both possible and impossible, Nietzsche writes of what he calls "star friendship":

> Star friendship.—We were friends and have become estranged. But this was right, and we do not want to conceal and obscure it from ourselves as if we had reason to feel ashamed. We are two ships each of which has its goal and course; our paths may cross and we may celebrate a feast together, as we did—and then the good ships rested so quietly in one harbor and one sunshine that it may have looked as if they had reached their goal and as if they had one goal. But then the almighty force of our tasks drove us apart again into different seas and sunny zones, and perhaps we shall never see one another again,—perhaps we shall meet again but fail to recognize each other: our exposure to different seas and suns has changed us! That we have to become estranged is the law *above* us; by the same token we should also become more venerable for each other—and the memory of our former friendship more sacred! There is probably a tremendous but invisible stellar orbit in which our very different ways and goals may be included as small parts of this path,—let us rise up to this thought! But our life is too short and our power of vision too small for us to be more than friends in the sense of this sublime possibility.—Let us then believe in our star friendship even if we should be compelled to be earth enemies.[8]

If we are to believe Nietzsche, the history of friendship could be said to begin with the stars, and with ships that move underneath them, and across shifting, moving seas. Like Emerson, who in a letter from January 24, 1843 writes that "the first two friends must have been travelers" (*LRWE* 7:521), Nietzsche suggests that friendship requires a going outside of oneself, a leaving of what is familiar, an experience of strangeness and defamiliarization. It also requires a capacity to alter in relation to change and transformation. This relation that emerges only in order to vanish, this oscillation between proximity and distance, can be read under the light of the stars, under the light of the innumerable suns that cast their light on us. This light, which in a flash travels across thousands of light years, figures an illumination in which the present bears within it the most distant past and where the distant past suddenly traverses the present moment. This emergence of the past within the present, of what is most distant in what is closest at hand, suggests that starlight—and even star friendship—appears only in its withdrawal. Friendship, too, can only be friendship when it is the withdrawing trace of its own transience. Only when it is no longer friendship—that is to say, no longer an empirical, historical fact among others—can it survive as friendship. Like the friendship that bears a relation to what is no longer there, to what, having changed in time, can no longer even be recognized, starlight names the trace of a celestial body that has long since vanished. For Nietzsche, the friend, the experience of friendship, is, like the star, always a kind of ruin. That the friend can never remain identical to himself, is never revealed as such, means that he always is inhabited by a certain distance or darkness, is always a stranger—to us and to himself. All stars, and, by implication, all friends, are always in the process of vanishing and fading away. They are always already dying, and most of them perhaps already have died. Like the diminishing light of the stars, the friend is a commemorative sign of what is no longer there. The friend tells us that, because of the fleetingness and shortness of life, it is with loss and ruin that we have to live. But who is the friend? Who is he? Who is it? Who, from the moment when all the categories and all the axioms that have constituted the concept of friendship in its history are threatened by ruin: the subject, the person, presence, communion, proximity, and, of course, the dead brother who touches everything?

What is accented in both Nietzsche and Emerson is the distance, the separation or discrepancy, which structures and forms the basis of relation in general. Friendship is a thing of distance, a thing of the future. If Nietzsche exhorts us in *Thus Spake Zarathustra* to flight from our neighbor and "to love of the farthest,"[9] Emerson encourages us to "even bid our dearest friends farewell," to "defy them, saying, 'Who are you? Unhand me: I will be dependent no more.' Ah! seest thou not, O brother, that thus we part only to meet again on a higher platform, and only be more each other's, because we are more our own? A friend is Janus-faced: he looks to the past and the future. He is the child of all my foregoing hours, the prophet of those to come, and the harbinger of a greater friend" (*CW* 2:126). For both thinkers, this distance, this "farewell," permits the relation to an other, since, without it, there would be no interval or gap across which a relation could be formed with this other. This is why, for Emerson, the condition of relation is that "there must be very two, before there can be very one." "Let it be an alliance of two large, formidable natures, mutually beheld, mutually feared," he goes on to say; "let him be to thee forever a sort of beautiful enemy, untamable, devoutly revered, and not a trivial conveniency to be soon outgrown and cast aside" (*CW* 2:123–24). That the friend is "untamable" and inappropriable, that he is the figure of the foreign and the unpredictable, means that the relation itself can never be stable. It is because "the law of nature is alternation for evermore" that, for Emerson, the laws of friendship require that we "should never fall into something usual and settled, but should be alert and inventive" (*CW* 2:116, 121).

This alertness and inventiveness—always seeking to remain faithful to what is always about to vanish, to what never remains the same from one moment to the next, to what, touched by time and language, can never be self-identical to itself—is what, for me, remains the signature of the "one" (this "one" who is always "more than one") to whom this essay is dedicated, and for whom it is written, and written in the name of this wild thing that Emerson calls, even knowing that it cannot be named, "friendship."

Distance and Absence

In closing, I want to turn to another instance and version of what Emerson means by this wildness of friendship. I want to turn to a photograph that was sent to me, in the form of a missive, as I was first beginning to write about Emerson's essay. I want to offer my response to it, a response that, beginning with the photograph, actually begins elsewhere, in the relation with the friend who sent it to me, but not only with her, since I can always only begin with Emerson, even if he remains unnamed in this correspondence, and with the network of relations that make and unmake me at every moment.

"Love begins with a *bench*."[10] This is the first line of Hélène Cixous's brief story, "Hiss of the Axe," and it refers to the way in which Marina Tsvetaeva reads the story of the relation between Tatiana and Onegin in Pushkin's story, *Eugene Onegin*. The love of which the narrator speaks—in particular, Tatiana's professed love for Onegin, but, more generally, all love—is a love that begins in distance and absence, in separation and loss, and is confirmed and lost at a bench. We are told that, before arriving at the bench, Tatiana had run through the meadow, the little wood, the branches, and the flowers and, at the very moment in which she can no longer run, can no longer flee from the one she suspects is not following her, she collapses "onto the bench." It is the bench at which Marina stops, one hundred years later, under the influence of Pushkin's story. It is the bench on which Tatiana waits for Onegin, having fled from the one for whom she waits. She can flee no more, and, most importantly, she can no longer flee from what Onegin comes to tell her. He finds her at the bench, but doesn't sit down beside her because everything is already over. She stands up from the bench and, while they are both standing next to one another, the standing already signals their separation. In front of the bench, Onegin tells Tatiana that he cannot be happy and that, if he permitted himself to be close to her, his love would stop. He tells her that he can only love her from a distance. "If I were to love," he says, "it would be from afar, once in awhile, separately."[11] Marina reads these lines and reads them in relation to the bench, but also in relation to her own relationship with Rilke. This is love, she thinks, a bench, on which Tatiana sits and Onegin does not, and from which, no longer able to stand the dissolution of her love, Tatiana stands up to listen to Onegin declare his inability to be with her, to sit with her on this bench of love.

But the narrator reminds us that, before the bench, there was the running, and that, before the running, there was the letter that Tatiana wrote to the one she loves. "This has been decreed from on high," she writes, "it's heaven's will. I am *yours*." Tatiana tells Onegin that she is his to give and that, if he replies, he will return her to herself. But "the letter arrives too late. … When Onegin finally receives it, ten years have gone by, Tatiana is on the other side."[12] This is love, too, the narrator tells us: the letter that never arrives on time, that always arrives in accordance with a different temporality. This is what happens with Marina, too, who sends a letter to Rilke after he has died, and who continues to dedicate to him the writings she writes after this death, writings she also calls "letters." She had begun writing to him in May of 1926 and continued to do so for more than six months. She was in exile in France and he was dying in Switzerland. They never meet, but they fall in love with one another through their correspondence, they become close in relation to the distance that separates them. Before the first letter is sent, however, Marina already loves Rilke, already loves his poetry, which she identifies with him (in her first letter to him she even claims that his name is a poem). On her end, the correspondence only intensifies and makes more legible what already was there. Like the bench that watches over the assertion and dissolution of love, the distance that separates Marina and Rainer can only insist on their absence from one another. In a letter of June 3, 1926, Marina writes: "Now it is over. It doesn't take me long to be done with wanting. What did I want from you? Nothing. Rather—around you. The longer, the worse. Without a letter—without you; with a letter—without you; with you—without you. Into you! Not to be.—Die! This is how I am. This is how love is—infinite time. Thankless and self-destructive. 'I do not love or honor love,' says one of my lines.... So, Rainer, it's over. I don't want to go to you. I don't wish to want to."[13] In love with Rilke before the correspondence, during the correspondence, and even after his death, Marina discovers that love comes with absence and distance. Whether she receives a letter from Rilke or not, whether she is with him or not, she remains without him. This is love, she says: the experience of loss and absence. Love begins with a *bench*—with an *empty* bench, with what Henry James once called "a bench of desolation."[14] This is why, we might say, love is always mourning for lost love and this also is why, as Tatiana and Marina suggest, every letter is always a love letter, especially the letter that begins with a bench.

This is confirmed in Samuel Beckett's remarkable little story, "First Love." The narrator of Beckett's story confesses that he identifies his beloved with a bench. As he tells us, recalling his first experience of love, "Her image remains bound, for me, to that of the bench, not the bench by day, nor yet the bench by night, but the bench at evening, in such sort that to speak of the bench, as it appeared to me at evening, is to speak of her, for me. That proves nothing, but there is nothing I wish to prove. On the subject of the bench by day no words need be wasted, it never knew me, gone before morning and never back till dusk."[15] The beloved is a bench, and the bench is the beloved, but this identification only takes place at dusk, at twilight, at the moment of the transit between light and darkness. This identification takes place, in other words, in a moment that we might call "photographic," the moment in which light is interrupted by darkness, by the click of the camera. If it is true that love begins with a bench, in this instance love begins with a photograph of a bench, a photograph that captures the moment between the coming and going of lovers. Moreover, this coming and going, of Beckett's narrator but also of the bench and beloved of which he writes, identifies the bench as a site of appearance and disappearance. The three clusters of flowers that seem to sit on this photographed bench, almost as if they were growing from it, evoke another text by Beckett. Indeed, Beckett's *Come and Go* also is organized around a bench, a bench on which three childhood friends sit beside one another many years later. Flo, Vi, and Ru, wearing colorful full-length coats, all dulled over time, are effectively three faded flowers, something that a draft headed "Scene 1" confirms when it suggests that Flo, Vi, and Ru began their life as Viola, Rose, and Poppy.[16]

I have received this photograph as a kind of archive, as an anthology (the word "anthology" comes from the Greek *anthologia* and means "flower-gathering," or a collection of flowers). This link between texts and flowers, between photographs and anthologies, is, for me, an invitation to begin a correspondence with my friend, to see how it might blossom, to see how it might serve as a kind of benchmark of our friendship, and to see how, like the trees and foliage that surround this bench, this correspondence and friendship might grow. If, as Emerson writes in "Nominalist and Realist," "truth sits veiled there on the Bench, and never interposes an adamantine syllable" (*CW* 3:145), it is because things change and metamorphose, because they never remain the same from one moment to another. I send this missive, then, which, like all missives—including the one Emerson imagines sending to his friend—comes from its destination, from the bench I have been permitted to imagine and on which I sit with the promise of a friendship whose wildness makes it the only friendship worthy of the name "friendship," a friendship that, as Emerson and Nietzsche tell us, loves what is most surprising, what is most unpredictable, what is, in other words, the future.

Notes

1. See Maurice Blanchot, "Friendship," trans. Elizabeth Rottenberg, in *Friendship* (Stanford: Stanford University Press, 1997), 289 and 291.
2. See John Michael, *Emerson and Skepticism: The Cipher of the World* (Baltimore: Johns Hopkins University Press, 1988), 89. I am throughout indebted to Michael's lovely reading of Emerson's essay. Although I revisit several of the same Emersonian passages he does, I trust that I have recontextualized and even renewed their significance.
3. Ibid., 88.
4. Ibid., 94.
5. Michael makes this point as well. Ibid., 91.
6. Werner Hamacher, "History, Teary: Some Remarks on La Jeune Parque," trans. Michael Shae, in Yale French Studies 74 (1988): 85.
7. Branka Arsić, *On Leaving: A Reading in Emerson* (Cambridge, MA: Harvard University Press, 2010), 184.
8. Friedrich Nietzsche, *The Gay Science, with a Prelude in Rhymes and an Appendix of Songs*, trans. Walter Kaufmann (New York: Vintage Books, 1974), 225–26.
9. Friedrich Nietzsche, *Thus Spoke Zarathustra: A Book for All and None*, trans. Adrian del Caro (Cambridge: Cambridge University Press, 2006), 44.
10. Hélène Cixous, "Hiss of the Axe," trans. Keith Cohen, in *Stigmata: Escaping Texts* (New York: Routledge, 1998), 42.
11. Ibid.
12. Ibid., 43 and 45.
13. Boris Pasternak, Marina Tsvetayeva, and Rainer Maria Rilke, *Letters: Summer 1926*, trans. Margaret Wettlin, Walter Arndt, and Jamey Gambrell (New York: New York Review of Books, 2001), 162–63.
14. Henry James, "The Bench of Desolation," in *The Turn of the Screw, The Aspern Papers and Other Stories* (London: Collins, 1956).
15. Samuel Beckett, "First Love," in *First Love and Other Shorts* (New York: Grove Press, 1994), 19.
16. Samuel Beckett, *Come and Go*, in *The Theatrical Notebooks of Samuel Beckett: The Shorter Plays*, ed. S. E. Gontarski (London: Faber and Faber, 2020).

AFTERWORD

RALPH WALDO EMERSON TRANSFIGURED

CORNEL WEST

THIS marvelous gathering of essays brought together by the visionary Christopher Hanlon poses three fundamental questions of life and death in our bleak times. First, how does the rich legacy of the great Ralph Waldo Emerson provide intellectual and existential weaponry in our battles against major contemporary catastrophes such as ecological collapse, US imperial breakdown, postmodern cultural decay, and global south despair? Second, can our creative appropriations of the variegated work and witness of Ralph Waldo Emerson authorize a credible and better future—without fetishizing futurity itself? Third, do we have the individual and institutional capacities to forge the requisite improvisational modes of being-in-the-world to save the world and the human species from destruction?

During the first centenary of Emerson's birth in 1903, two of the most influential and important American philosophers—William James and John Dewey—gave two monumental public lectures on the perennial and practical impact of Emerson's thought. At that historical moment, the prevailing catastrophes consisted of European, US, and Japanese imperialisms expanding and clashing (with impending world wars), American robber barons in the driver's seat of the domestic economy alongside white patriarchal terrorism targeting Black, Brown, and Indigenous peoples. William James—a wealthy yet self-fashioned intellectual with no BA, MA, or PhD (only an MD) who helped lead the anti-imperialist league (along with the inimitable Mark Twain) and mentored the even greater W. E. B. Du Bois—spoke from Emerson's hamlet in Concord, Massachusetts on May 25 exactly one hundred years after Emerson's birth.

William James's words were intimate and intense. He was speaking of his personal godfather whom he had encountered on numerous occasions in "Mr. Emerson's room"—the guest room of the James family's Washington Square house in New York City. The iconoclastic Henry James, Sr.—father of William, Henry, Alice, Garth, and Robertson and husband of Mary Robertson Walsh—was married by the mayor of New York City in Washington Square and remained a good friend of Ralph Waldo Emerson.

William James's address at the Concord Centenary begins with a moving meditation on "the pathos of death" that tends to reduce "the whole of the man's significance ... into a mere musical note or phrase suggestive of his singularity." And though Emerson "is now dust ... the soul's note, the spiritual voice, rises strong and clear above the uproar of the times, and seems securely destined to exert an ennobling influence over future generations."[1]

James spent months reading and rereading much of the corpus of his godfather Emerson for his eulogy-like speech. He once noted that a "motto for my philosophy" came from Emerson: "We are born believing. A man bears beliefs as a tree bears apples" (CW 6:108). We are reminded of George Santayana's famous words about James's personal religion—"He did not really believe; he merely believed in the right of believing that you might be right if you believed."[2] For James, like Emerson, existential integrity and personal moral authority trumps theoretical veracity and impersonal ethical doctrine. James says to his Concord audience about Emerson:

> 'Stand by your order,' he used to say to youthful students; and perhaps the paramount impression one gets of his life is of his loyalty to his own personal type and mission. The type was that of what he liked to call the scholar, the perceiver of the truth; and the mission was that of the reporter in worthy form of each perception ... This duty of spiritual seeing and reporting determined the whole tenor of his life.[3]

James suggests that Emerson's response to the catastrophe of his day—especially the US enslavement of Black people—was shaped by his unique spiritual calling and personal temperament. Emerson indeed was a genuine abolitionist who shared the progressive platforms with Frederick Douglass, yet stood firm that "I have quite other slaves to face than those Negroes to wit, imprisoned thoughts far back in the brain of man, and which have no watchman or lover or defender but me."[4]

James applauds this "fidelity to the limits of his genius" though it "must often have made him seem provokingly remote and unavailable," yet "the faultless tact with which he kept his safe limits while he so dauntlessly asserted himself within them, is an example fitted to give heart to other theorists and artists the world over."[5] We know that one such theorist and artist was Friedrich Nietzsche whose discovery of Emerson's writings in the spring of 1861 inspired and instructed him for the rest of his life. Emerson, Pascal, and Montaigne were Nietzsche's constant intellectual interlocutors until his breakdown. His first public reference ("Fate and History") to Emerson sounds like a note from James's songbook: "And do not events provide, as it were, only the musical key of our lot while the strength or weakness with which it affects us depends merely on our temperament. Ask gifted physicians, Emerson says, how much temperament decides..."[6]

James concludes that Emerson was first and foremost "an artist whose medium was verbal and who wrought in spiritual material." Yet, "his optimism had nothing in common with that indiscriminate hurrahing for the Universe with which Walt Whitman has made us familiar ... Emerson was a real seer" who "could perceive the full squalor of the individual fact, but he could also see the transfiguration."[7] James then goes on to give a fascinating example of a "present-day agitator against our Philippine conquest" whom Emerson regards as "a tedious bore and canter" while also "the axis around which the Universe revolves passes through his body where he stands."[8] James is convinced "that posterity will reckon him a prophet" with his "words ... certain to be quoted and extracted more and more as time goes on, and to take their place among the Scriptures of Humanity."[9] Lastly, James addresses Emerson directly as my "beloved Master. As long as our English language lasts men's hearts will be cheered and their souls strengthened and liberated by the noble and musical pages with which you have enriched it."[10]

At the very day and moment James was bringing to a close his eloquent eulogy of his godfather Emerson in Concord, John Dewey was commencing his uncharacteristically lyrical reflections on "Emerson—The Philosopher of Democracy" at the University of Chicago. In opposition to those who deny that Emerson is a philosopher—either because he is "a mere writer of maxims and proverbs, a recorder of brilliant insights and abrupt aphorisms" or "because he is more than a philosopher ... He would work ... by art, not by metaphysics, finding truth 'in the sonnet and the play' "[11]—Dewey admits that Emerson called himself:

> "in all my theories, ethics, and politics, a poet." ... His own preference was to be ranked with the seers rather than the reasoners of the race, for he says, "I think that philosophy is still rude and elementary; it will one day be taught by poets. The poet is in the natural attitude; he is believing; the philosopher, after some struggle, having only reasons for believing ..." To Emerson, the perception was more potent than reasoning; the deliverances of intercourse more to be desired than the chains of discourse; the surprise of reception more demonstrative than the conclusions of intentional proof.[12]

Yet Dewey is not impressed by "hard and fast lines between philosopher and poet, yet there is some distinction of accent in thought and of rhythm in speech." He boldly proclaims that "looked at in the open, our fences between literature and metaphysics appear petty—signs of an attempt to affix the legalities and formularies of property to the things of the spirit."[13]

Dewey claims that Emerson assesses any philosophy or poetry by "the test of trial by the services rendered the present and immediate experience."[14] This evaluation is grounding in the doings and sufferings of everyday people that find "truth in the highway, in the untaught endeavor, the unexpected idea ... versions of Here and the Now, and flow freely."[15] Like the tormented T. S. Eliot's Pascal or the adorable Stanley Cavell's Emerson, Dewey's Emerson combines a serious and substantive wrestling with skepticism within a real and reverent faith. For Eliot, this faith is Christian, for Cavell, it is perfectionist, and for Dewey, this faith is democratic through and through.

> Against creed and system, convention and institution, Emerson stands for restoring to the common man that which in the name of religion, of philosophy, of art, and of morality, has been embezzled from the common store and appropriated to the

> sectarian and class use ... For such reasons, the coming century may well make evident what is just now dawning, that Emerson is not only a philosopher but that he is the Philosopher of Democracy ... But at least, thinking of Emerson as the one citizen of the New World fit to have his name uttered in the same breath with that of Plato, one may without presumption believe that even if Emerson has no system, none the less he is the prophet and herald of any system which democracy may henceforth construct and hold by, and that when democracy has articulated itself, it will have no difficulty in finding itself already proposed in Emerson.[16]

There is no doubt that this is John Dewey in his sublime mode and majestic mood. Never in his nearly countless volumes does he soar like this. Emerson indeed has electrified his soul and emancipated his pen. And there is a bit more to come.

> We are moved to say that Emerson is the first and as yet almost the only Christian of the Intellect. From out such reverence for the instinct and impulse of our common nature shall emerge in their due season ... a philosophy which religion has no call to chide and which knows its friendship with science and with art ... Before such successes, even the worshipers of that which today goes by the names of success, those who bend to millions and incline to imperialisms, may lower their standard, and give at least a passing assent to the final word of Emerson's philosophy, the identity of Being, unqualified and immutable, with Character.[17]

These two magnificent encomiums to America's premier man of letters both ring true and ring hollow. William James's poignant words cut to the heart and bone, yet they move too quickly from the massive heartaches and broken bones on the underside of European modernity and US imperial subjugations. Even Emerson's grand essay on "Montaigne; or the Skeptic" in *Representative Men* (1850) ends on a blue note.

> Things seem to tend downward, to justify despondency, to promote rogues, to defeat the just, and, by knaves, as by martyrs, the just cause is carried forward. Although knaves win in every political struggle, although society seems to be delivered over from the hands of one set of criminals into the hands of another set of criminals, as fast as the government is changed, and the march of civilization is a train of felonies, yet, general ends are somehow answered ... But the world-spirit is a good swimmer, and storms and waves can not drown him. (CW 4:104)

William James's most famous student and subsequent teacher—the greatest public intellectual in US history, W. E. B. Du Bois—gets to the heart of European darkness and American brokenness in "The Souls of White Folk" (1920).

> As we saw the dead dimly through rifts of battle-smoke and heard faintly the cursings and accusations of blood brothers, we darker men said: This is not Europe gone mad; this is not aberration nor insanity; This *is* Europe; this seeming Terrible is the real soul of white culture—back of all culture—stripped and visible today. This is where the world has arrived,—these dark and awful depths and not the shining

and ineffable heights of which it boasted. Here is whither the might and energy of modern humanity has really gone.

Du Bois continues his profound and persuasive challenge to Emerson and James—especially in regard to any form of American exceptionalism that excuses American imperial crimes against humanity.

> It is curious to see America, the United States, looking on herself, first, as a sort of natural peacemaker, then as a moral protagonist in these terrible times. No nation is less fitted for this role. For two or more centuries America has marched proudly in the van of human hatred—making bonfires of human flesh and laughing at them hideously ... rather a great religion, a world war cry: up white, down black; to your tents, O white folk, and world war with black and particolored mongrel beasts![18]

John Dewey's eloquent hymn to the poetic genius and philosophic subtlety of Emerson's writings rings true, yet he moves too quickly to grandiloquent claims about Emerson's philosophy of democracy given Emerson's own "test of trial" tied to the concrete lived experiences of genocide, enslavement, deportation, Jim Crow terror, of people of color and white revolutionary dissenters.

Du Bois continues:

> America, Land of Democracy, wanted to believe in the failure of democracy so far as darker people were concerned. Absolutely without excuses she established a caste system, rushed into preparation for war, and conquered tropical colonies. She stands today shoulder to shoulder with Europe in Europe's worst sin against civilization. She aspires to sit among the great nations who arbitrate the fate of "lesser breeds without the law" and she is at times heartily ashamed even of the large number of "new" white people whom her democracy has admitted to place and power.[19]

Over half a century later, the culminating figure of the grand Emersonian tradition, the American Montaigne of the twentieth century—the great James Baldwin—concluded in *No Name in the Street* (1972):

> All of the western nations have been caught in a lie, the lie of their pretended humanism; this means that their history has no moral justification, and that the West has no moral authority. Malcolm, yet more concretely than Frantz Fanon ... made increasingly articulate the ways in which this lie, given the history and the power of the Western nations, had become a global problem, menacing the lives of millions.[20]

It is not surprising to see the focus on Herman Melville in our time (more so than Emerson)—and his great legacy that goes through Eugene O'Neill, William Faulkner, Robert Penn Warren, and culminates with Toni Morrison. I tried to lay bare both traditions in *Democracy Matters* (2004). But it received little traction. Times have changed.

I remain deeply committed to the dialectical interplay and dialogical intercourse of the Emersonian and Melvillean streams in the prophetic American traditions. I think the greatest artistic and existential breakthrough in the catastrophic twentieth century—the Black musical tradition, especially of gospel, blues, jazz, rhythm and blues, house, and hip-hop—gives us some sense of the weaponry we need in the face of our multiple catastrophes, some different experiences of time (like swing) that authorize different and better futures (Afro-Futurism as prologues to various World-futures) and build capacities—of self and societies—for mature improvisational ways of seeing, feeling, hearing, and acting that shatter dogma and domination in truthful, beautiful, and loving ways. Any wise and credible way of acknowledgment, resolution, pursuance, and psalm—the great Coltranean project—must pass through the Emersonian brook of fire and Melvillean rose garden of thorns. I have in mind much of what the great Toni Morrison says in *The Sources of Self-Regard* (2019):

> That egalitarianism that places us all ... on the same footing reflected for me the force of flight and mercy and the precious, imaginative yet realistic gaze of the black people who (at one time anyway) did not anoint what or whom it mythologized.[21]

In our grim and dim times, I find the Emersonian fortitude and Melvillean fructitude—best embodied and enacted in the Black musical tradition of blues, swing, and improvisation—constitutive of being a small force for good. So I salute Brother Ralph Waldo Emerson—alongside Ralph Waldo Ellison—even as we transfigure them!

Notes

1. William James, "Address of William James," in *The Centenary of the Birth of Ralph Waldo Emerson*, ed. John Shepard Keyes (Boston: Riverside Press, 1903), 67.
2. George Santayana, *Character and Opinion in the United States* (New York: Scribner's, 1922), 77.
3. James, "Address," 68–69.
4. Quoted in James, "Address," 69.
5. Ibid., 69–70.
6. Quoted in Daniel Blue, *The Making of Friedrich Nietzsche: The Quest for Identity, 1844–1869* (Cambridge: Cambridge University Press, 2016), 134.
7. Ibid., 75–76.
8. Ibid., 76.
9. Ibid., 77.
10. Ibid.
11. John Dewey, 1903, "Emerson—The Philosopher of Democracy," in *The Essential Dewey*, ed. Larry A. Hickman and Thomas M. Alexander (Bloomington: Indiana University Press, 2009), 2:366.
12. Ibid., 366–67.
13. Ibid., 367.
14. Ibid., 368.

15. Ibid., 369.
16. Ibid., 369–70.
17. Ibid., 370.
18. W. E. B. Du Bois, 1920, "The Souls of White Folk," in *W. E. B. Du Bois: A Reader*, ed. David Levering Lewis (New York: Henry Holt, 1995), 470.
19. Ibid., 470–71.
20. James Baldwin, 1972, *No Name in the Street* (New York: Knopf Doubleday, 2013), 85.
21. Toni Morrison, *The Sources of Self-Regard: Selected Essays, Speeches, and Meditations* (New York: Knopf Doubleday, 2019), 192.

Index

For the benefit of digital users, indexed terms that span two pages (e.g., 52–53) may, on occasion, appear on only one of those pages.

Tables are indicated by an italic *t* following the page number

abolition xvi, 60, 67–68, 71, 81, 108–9, 111–12, 139, 140–47, 154, 161, 171, 177–79, 180–81, 184–86, 194, 195, 197–200, 204, 210, 214, 224, 225–26, 233, 236, 242, 248, 288–90, 304, 408, 409–11, 416, 493–94, 520–21, 536–37, 577, 598–99
   Black abolition 141–42, 408, 409–11, 417
   British abolition 140, 197–200, 289
   Carlyle's response to 201–4, 233–34, 289–90, 408, 577–78
and Emerson's 1844 Address concerning 71–74, 140–41, 142–44, 145, 146, 152–56, 177–78, 180, 194–95, 197–200
   and Emerson's 1851 Address concerning 142–43, 180
   and Emerson's 1854 Address concerning 180, 204, 211, 249–51, 365, 577–78
   and Emerson's 1855 Address concerning 180, 225–26, 249–51, 598–99
   Emerson's shifting attitudes concerning 60, 67–68, 71, 81, 139, 140–41, 142, 161, 177–79, 194, 197–98, 204, 248, 493–94, 524, 575, 577–78, 598–99, 620
   and gradualism 144–47, 150
   and immediatism 142–43, 577
   versus reconstruction 177–78, 179–81, 185–86
   scholarship assessing Emerson's involvement with 71–74, 108–9, 140–43, 144–45, 178–80, 194, 224–26, 408, 409, 416, 575
aging 534, 535, 543–46, 547, 548, 552–54

and idealized youth 543–44, 545–46, 547, 548, 551, 552, 554
Alcott, Bronson 284, 299–300, 324–25, 383–84, 385, 386–87, 404, 435, 495–96, 500–1, 569, 590, 595–96
Anaxagoras 20, 87, 88, 92–95, 97, 98, 101
Anaximenes 20, 87, 92, 93–94, 97
Arsić, Branka 109, 115, 246, 264–65, 355, 565, 611–12
Atlantic Monthly, The xviii, 23, 185, 215, 291–92, 482, 520–21, 522–24, 529–32, 533, 534, 535–37, 551
Alcott, Louisa May xiv, 443–51, 453, 454, 455, 456–57, 590, 594–95
   Little Women 431–32, 549
Apess, William 161–62, 163, 165–66, 170–73, 174
   and abolitionism 171

Baldwin, James 38–40, 253–54, 623
Beecher, Henry Ward 428–31, 478
Berlant, Lauren 38–39, 246, 252–53
Biden, Joseph Robinette 217–19
Bloom, Harold 136, 334, 558–59
Borges, Jorge Luis xv–xvi, 125–27, 136
Bosco, Ronald A. 384, 385, 399–400, 401, 402, 403–4, 405, 432, 433–34, 482, 550–51
Brown, John 67–68, 180, 194, 242, 249–50, 360–61, 368, 408, 530–31
   see also Emerson, Ralph Waldo, "Address at the John Brown Relief Meeting" (18 November 1859); speech at the John Brown Relief Meeting at Salem (6 January 1860)
Bryant, William Cullen 523–24

Buell, Lawrence xiii–xv, 18–19, 107–8, 225–26, 241–42, 316–17, 334, 358, 364, 515, 576

Cabot, James Elliot 181, 182–83, 184–85, 186–87, 353–54, 373–74, 376, 398, 400, 432, 433–35, 559–60
Cameron, Sharon 20, 41, 55, 64–65, 66–67, 109–10, 246–47, 264–65, 521, 522
capitalism xvi–xvii, xviii–xix, 4–5, 10, 12, 38, 43, 47, 49, 144–45, 261–65, 262, 263, 264–65, 266–67, 268, 269–74, 279, 280–83, 284, 286–87, 288–89, 290, 291, 292, 297–98, 299, 302, 303–5, 576, 578, 585
  and climate change 38, 43, 48, 49, 64–65
  and extraction 12, 15, 38
  and slavery 10, 144–45, 231
  see also Marx, Karl
Carlyle, Thomas xvi, 8, 97–98, 125–26, 193–95, 196, 197–98, 200, 201–5, 323, 359–61, 400–1, 428, 489–90
Carson, Rachel xv, 19–20, 22–25, 26, 28–31, 56
Cavell, Stanley 40, 60–61, 66–67, 243, 561–62, 621
Channing, William Ellery 315, 338–41, 342, 381, 404, 507–8
Child, Lydia Maria 523–24
Christian Recorder, The 409, 410, 412, 413–17, 418, 419, 420, 421–22
Civil War, US xvi, 8–9, 12, 177–84, 185–87, 188–89, 195, 204–5, 208–9, 214, 221, 222, 254, 262–63, 279–80, 291–92, 408, 430–31, 480, 520–21, 523–24, 529–30, 532–34, 535–37, 548, 550–51, 573–85, 593, 600–1
Clarke, James Freeman 376, 385
Clarke, Sarah Freeman 596
Clarkson, Thomas 154, 155, 198
climate change
  and the Anthropocene xv, 3–4, 9, 20, 37–38, 46, 48–49, 50, 62–63, 86–87, 92, 94, 95, 97, 101–2, 590
  and "Build Back Better" 217–19
  and despair 6–7, 9, 16, 36–38, 39–41, 42–43, 46–49, 50–51
  and energy xv, 4–6, 7–9, 10, 11, 13
  and fossil fuels xiv, 3, 4, 5, 6–7, 8, 10, 11, 14, 291

  and infrastructure 4–7, 9, 10–16, 40–41, 213, 215–16, 291, 301–2
  and "Resources" 8–9, 11–12
Cole, Phyllis 334, 364, 376, 384, 405, 428, 436, 554, 590–92, 595, 596–97
Coleridge, Samuel Taylor 97–98, 376, 381, 382, 386, 388, 491, 510–11, 516
commonplace books see commonplacing
commonplacing xviii, 372–73, 374–76, 378–81, 382, 383–84, 385–90, 507–11, 513, 514–15, 517, 543, 545, 550
Cooper, Anna Julia 224–25, 234, 237

Dall, Caroline Healy 590, 598–99, 601
Davis, Paulina Wright 589, 590, 598–99, 601
Descartes, Renee 86–87, 95–96, 360–61
Dewey, John 224–25, 619, 621–22, 623
Dial, The xviii, 299, 302, 304–6, 372–73, 383, 412, 493, 508–9, 520–21, 522–28, 589, 594–95, 596
Dickinson, Emily xiv, 101–2, 414–15
Dimock, Wai Chee 74–75, 81, 86–87, 364
disability
  and aphasia 559, 562, 569–70
  and Emerson's memory 431, 432–33, 436, 464, 543–44, 551, 554, 559–60, 561, 562, 568–69
Douglass, Frederick xvi, 141, 145–46, 224–28, 233, 234–35, 236, 237, 303, 410, 480–81, 548–49, 601, 620
Du Bois, W.E.B. 224–25, 228–34, 236, 237, 248–49, 619, 622–23

Eddy, Mary Baker 325–26, 342
Edwards, Jonathan 333, 360–61
Emerson, Charles 165, 378, 398, 493–94, 605–8, 611
Emerson, Edith 242, 384, 385, 398, 400–1, 425–26, 427–28, 429, 430–32, 433–35, 436, 498, 499, 559–60, 591–92
Emerson, Edward Bliss 385, 398, 405
Emerson, Edward Waldo 181, 376, 398, 399, 402, 405, 425–26, 431–33, 502, 591–92, 598–99
Emerson, Ellen (née Ellen Louisa Tucker) 91–92, 242, 282–83, 374, 405, 425–26, 490–91, 500, 591–93, 600–1

Emerson, Ellen Tucker xvii–xviii, 181, 182–83, 184–85, 186–87, 353–54, 398, 405, 425–37, 490, 496–97, 498, 500, 543–44, 559–60, 591–92
Emerson, Lidian (née Lydia) Jackson xviii, 250–52, 303, 306–7, 381, 398, 404–5, 425, 426–27, 431–32, 435, 436, 489–502, 591–92, 594–95
  and activism 250–51, 493–94
  and depression 307, 426, 498–99
  and "Transcendental Bible" 435, 489–90, 497–98
Emerson, Mary Moody xvii, 242, 334, 372–73, 375–76, 377–81, 379*f*, 380*f*, 382–83, 384, 387, 388–90, 398, 404, 405, 434–35, 436, 492, 496–97, 501, 550, 591–92
Emerson, Ralph Waldo
  works
    "Address at the John Brown Relief Meeting" (18 November 1859) 249–50
    "An Address delivered in the Court-House in Concord, Massachusetts, on 1st August, 1844, on the Anniversary of the Emancipation of the Negroes in the British West Indies" 71–74, 75, 77–78, 81, 83, 139–41, 142–44, 145, 146, 152–56, 177–78, 194–95, 197–200, 201, 224, 225, 226–28, 232, 233–34, 237, 289–90, 408, 577–78
    "Address to the Citizens of Concord" 142–43
    "The Adirondacs" 409, 413, 414–16
    "American Civilization" (also "Civilization at a Pinch") 185–86, 215–16, 217, 220
    "The American Scholar" xii, 60–61, 101–2, 115, 117–18, 189, 227, 231, 243, 284, 285–86, 291–92, 301–2, 309, 322–23, 373–74, 480, 494, 561–62, 576, 591–92, 593–94, 597
    "American Slavery" (also "Lecture on Slavery" Jan 1855) 180, 225–26, 249–51, 598–99
    "The Anglo-American" 204, 583
    "Anti-slavery Speech at Dedham" (1846) 289, 290
    "Behavior" 243–44, 270–71
    "Boston Hymn" 208, 209, 212–13, 215, 219–20, 533–34

"Circles" xii, 7–8, 11, 15–16, 25–26, 27, 36, 43, 47, 48–49, 58–59, 60–61, 109, 113–14, 142, 189, 286, 419, 464–65, 466, 489, 544, 549–51, 553
"Climacteric" 50
"Compensation" xi, 20–21, 26–27, 59–60, 67–68, 177, 189, 328–29
The Conduct of Life xvi–xvii, 49, 50, 54–55, 58–59, 208–9, 213, 216–18, 221, 261, 262–68, 269–74, 286, 290–92, 355–56, 399–400, 454, 579–80
"Divinity School Address" 21, 212, 243, 251–52, 323–24, 326–27, 338–39, 343–44, 363–64, 594–95
"Each in All" 296, 383–84, 386–87
"The Emancipation Proclamation" 177–78, 218–19
English Traits 3–4, 192–94, 195, 199, 204–5, 208–9, 210, 214–16, 217, 221, 224, 356, 366, 399–400, 573–74, 583
"Eloquence" 164, 319, 482, 487, 559–60
"Experience" 20, 27, 39–41, 42, 50–51, 57–59, 65–67, 87, 90, 92, 93–94, 178–79, 189, 304, 358, 361–62, 443–44, 445, 467–69, 500, 502
"Fate" 228–29, 234, 237, 247–48, 263–65, 328–29, 352, 404, 561–62, 612
"Fortune of the Republic" 8, 186–88, 189, 204–5, 221–22, 434–35, 584–85
"Friendship" 60, 241–42, 244, 245–46, 247, 358, 389, 446–47, 569, 605, 608–13, 615
"The Fugitive Slave Law" (1854) 204, 211, 249–51, 365, 577–78
"The Heart" 243–44
"Hamatreya" 44–45, 45
"Heroism" 355–56, 446–47
"History" 21, 60–61, 62, 355–56, 362
"Lecture on the Times" 250–51, 301, 356
Letters and Social Aims 109, 222, 356, 384, 398, 404, 434, 436, 482, 597
Letter to Martin Van Buren on Cherokee Removal xvi, 64, 161, 162–63, 164, 170, 174, 211–12, 217, 301, 494
"Love" 245–48, 358, 389, 446–47, 489–90, 496, 502, 592, 612
"May-Day" 409, 413, 414, 415, 416, 419–21

Emerson, Ralph Waldo (*cont.*)
 May-Day and Other Pieces (1867) 409, 522–23, 532
 "The Method of Nature" 27–28, 45–46
 Natural History of Intellect 129, 181, 398, 400, 402, 404, 432, 433–34, 436
 Nature (1836) xii, 5, 18, 26, 27, 54–56, 59, 60, 62–63, 71, 87, 99–102, 109, 119, 129, 161–62, 189, 227–28, 234–36, 237, 242, 244–45, 246–48, 340–41, 353, 355–56, 372, 373–74, 447–48, 456–58, 479, 489–90, 545, 546, 550, 570, 573, 578–79, 597, 607
 Nature (1844) 7, 21, 58, 59
 "New England Reformers" 244, 288, 303–4, 595–96
 "Old Age" 404, 544, 551–53
 "The Over-Soul" 20–21, 22, 27, 60, 114–15, 246–47, 340, 341, 489
 Parnassus 373, 384, 385, 386, 432, 509, 510
 "Parnassus" 510–11
 "Perpetual Forces" 181–85, 186–87, 291–92
 "The Poet" (essay) xviii, 7, 23–24, 25, 60, 117, 129, 134, 135, 241–42, 450, 507–9, 511–13, 515, 521–23, 525, 560–61, 562–63, 565–66
 "The Poet" (poem) 449, 451–53, 454
 "Politics" 117, 209, 242, 248, 249, 250–51, 254, 304
 "Power" 49, 90–91, 208–9, 216–17, 263–64, 273, 274
 "Prudence" 7, 286–87
 "Quotation and Originality" 109, 362, 384, 597
 Representative Men 125–26, 297, 308–9, 342–44, 352, 356, 359–60, 361–62, 399–400, 573–74, 590–91, 622
 "Resources" 8–9, 11–12, 402
 "Self-Reliance" xii, 7–8, 54–55, 101–2, 109, 112, 117, 139, 189, 220, 236, 243, 247–48, 281–82, 296, 300–1, 308, 327, 351–52, 358, 443–44, 446–47, 455, 456–57, 467, 489, 493, 502, 511, 544, 546–47, 550, 552, 561–62, 573, 591–93, 594–96
 speech at the John Brown Relief Meeting at Salem (6 January 1860) 242, 249–50

 "The Sphinx" xviii, 101–2, 443–44, 457, 516–17, 526–27, 529
 "The Snow-Storm" 513–15, 516, 525–26, 534
 "Success" 11, 12, 244–45, 404
 "Swedenborg; or, The Mystic" 342, 343–44 (*see also* Emerson, Ralph Waldo, *Representative Men*)
 "Thoreau" 281
 "The Tragic" 493
 "Water" 19, 21, 22–23, 24, 26
 "Woman" 233–34, 589, 590, 593–94, 595, 599–600
 "Woodnotes" poems 443–45, 516–17, 524–25, 528
 "Works and Days" 11
 "The Young American" 11–12, 304–5
Emerson, William 384, 398–99, 426, 479
Everett, Edward 166–67, 279, 280–81, 480

Faraday, Michael 54–55, 56–57, 58–59
free love movement 296–97, 306–7, 310
 and Emerson's relationships with women 306–7, 308
 and women's rights 307, 310
 and Transcendentalism 306
Foucault, Michel 265, 352, 510–11
Fourier Charles xvi–xvii, 125, 296, 297, 298, 300–1, 302–6, 307–10
 see also free love movement
Fremont, John C. xvi, 208–13, 214, 216, 217–18, 249–51, 408, 575
Fugitive Slave Law of 1850, 178–80, 194, 204, 211, 288, 577–78, 598–99
 see also Emerson, Ralph Waldo, "The Fugitive Slave Law"
Fuller, Sarah Margaret xiv–xv, xvii, 54–55, 241–42, 251–52, 284, 307, 360–61, 372–76, 377f, 378, 382–84, 385–90, 426, 436, 484–85, 495–96, 499, 500–1, 508–9, 589–92, 593–97, 598–99, 601, 602

Garrison, William Lloyd 142–43, 148–49, 150, 154–55, 171, 177–79, 233, 250–51, 300, 303, 408, 574–75
Gates, Henry Louis 226–27, 228–29
Gougeon, Len 71, 178–79, 194, 200, 211, 225–28, 410–11, 524, 590–91, 595

Grimké sisters (Angelina and Sarah) 250–51, 493

Haitian Revolution 143–44, 146, 147–49
 and coverage in *The Liberator* 149–50
 and *Emancipation in the West Indies* (Thome and Kimball) 150–52
 and *The West Indies in 1837* (Sturge and Harvey) 150, 152–53
Hanlon, Christopher 208–9, 286, 353–54, 373–74, 381–82, 386–87, 408, 416, 425, 433–34, 464, 543–44, 554, 559–60, 619
Harper, Francis Ellen Watkins 177–78, 411, 472, 536–37
Hawthorne, Nathaniel 281–82, 335, 360–61, 381, 463, 464, 497, 523–24, 594–95
Hawthorne, Sophia Peabody 499, 596
Hickman, Jared 140–42, 144–45, 147, 148–49, 151
Higginson, Thomas Wentworth 595, 600–1
Hoar, Elizabeth 434–35, 493–94, 496–97, 591–92, 593–94, 596, 597
hooks, bell xvi, 129, 252–53
Hopkins, Pauline (*Contending Forces*, 1900) 224–25, 232–36, 237
Huidobro, Vicento xv–xvi, 127, 130–31, 133–35, 136
Humboldt, Alexander von 55–56, 360*f*, 360

Insko, Jeffrey xi, 71–73, 74, 80–81, 142–43, 144–45, 150, 154–56, 178–79, 198–99, 289

Jacobs, Harriet 472, 601
James, William 60, 224–25, 343
 on Emerson 619–21
Jefferson, Thomas 155, 164–65, 337
Jordan, June xvi, 252

Kateb, George 334, 335, 336–37, 338–39, 344

Lee, Maurice 49, 71, 178–79, 281, 389
Liberator, The 148–50, 225–26, 493
Lincoln, Abraham xvi, 181, 182, 185–86, 188–89, 194, 208–9, 210, 211, 212, 215, 217–21, 222, 523–24, 535–36, 574–75, 584–85
Lima, José Lezama xv–xvi, 127, 130–31, 133–34, 135

Longfellow, Henry Wadsworth 373–74, 404, 523–24
Lyceums 4, 11–12, 97–98, 196–97, 224, 225–26, 411, 483–84, 562–63
 Lyceum movement 477–78, 481
Lyell, Charles 74–80, 81, 83

Márti, Jose xv–xvi, 107–21
Marx, Karl xvi–xvii, 261–62, 263, 264, 265–67, 268, 269–71, 272–73, 274, 280–81, 282, 286–87, 299
 works
  Capital xvi–xvii, 268, 286–87
  Communist Manifesto 280–81
  Grundwisse xvi–xvii, 269–70

Matthiessen, Francis Otto xiii, 309–10, 334, 364, 462, 558–59, 560–61
Melville, Herman xiii, 101–2, 126–27, 241–42, 288, 319, 335, 402–4, 460–68, 470–73, 523–24, 594–95, 623
 works
  Bartleby, the Scrivener xiii, 472–73
  "Benito Cereno" 470–71
  Moby-Dick xiii, 288, 319, 461–62
Miller, Perry 326, 333, 364, 461–62
Myerson, Joel 399–400, 402, 404, 405, 408, 433–34

Nietzsche, Frederick 131, 561–62, 613–15, 620

Parker, Theodore 241–42, 337–40, 360–61, 408, 581–82, 595
Patmore, Conventry 428, 430, 589–90
Paz, Octavio xv–xvi, 127, 131–33, 135, 136
Peabody, Elizabeth 304–5, 381, 402, 428–29, 436, 485, 492–93, 494, 495–96, 596
Peabody, Elizabeth Palmer 304–5, 381, 428–29, 436, 485, 492–93, 494, 495–96, 596
Phillips, Wendell 177–78, 225–26, 250–51, 408, 574–75
Plato 24, 87, 112, 179–80, 246–47, 358*f*, 358, 362–64, 367–68, 376, 377–78, 479–80, 483, 524–25, 543, 597, 621–22
Poirier, Richard 109, 110–11, 224–25, 316–17

Reynolds, David 316–17, 318

Riggs, Ransom xviii, 443–44, 453–57
Ripley, George 167, 299–300, 301, 303, 305–6, 595–96
Ripley, Sarah 387–88, 591–92, 595–96
Rowe, John Carlos 49, 178–79, 181–82, 188, 225–26, 261–62, 305–6, 309–10

Said, Edward 201, 574–75, 576–77, 581
Santayana, George 136, 620
Schoolman, Martha 71–72, 178–79, 289–90, 408
Socrates 89, 359, 367–68
  see also Plato
Spiller, Robert E. xii–xiii, 399, 402
Stone, Lucy 589, 600–1
Stowe, Harriet Beecher 38–39, 151, 334, 339, 362
Sturgis, Caroline 241, 242, 253–54, 307–8, 375–76, 383–84, 386–87, 426–27, 436, 591–92, 596
Sumner, Charles 180, 184, 210, 211–12, 574–75
  caning of 210
Swedenborg, Emmanuel 100, 112, 315–16, 324–25, 340, 342, 343–44, 358f, 359, 362–63, 492, 496–97, 500, 501–2, 523, 524–25, 532

Tarbox (Methodist minister) 315–16, 324–27, 328–30
Taylor, Edward Thompson 167, 315–16, 317, 318–23, 324–25, 329
Thales 20, 87, 88, 90–92, 96, 97, 101–2
Thoreau, Henry David 12, 18–19, 101–2, 171, 182–83, 281, 286, 292, 302, 341, 353, 356, 360–61, 368, 385, 402, 404–5, 408, 412, 443, 445–46, 447, 495–96, 500, 507–9, 511, 517, 529–30, 550, 590, 601
  works
    Walden 353, 412, 508–9
    A Week on the Concord and Merrimack Rivers 508–9, 517

Walker, David 10, 141–42
Walls, Laura Dassow 7, 56–57, 59, 75–76, 81, 86–87, 94, 99, 200, 352, 381, 443
Ward, Anna Baker 596
Washington, Booker T. xvi, 224–25, 230–33, 234
West, Cornel 56–57, 63–64, 178–79, 224, 301, 575
Whicher, Stephen E. 179, 188, 402, 516–17
Whitman, Walt xviii–xix, 101–2, 112, 126–27, 177, 250, 281, 319, 507–8, 511, 513, 516, 522–23, 529–30, 549, 558–59, 560–61, 565–70, 620–21
Whittier, John Greenleaf 208, 210, 211, 213–14, 215–16, 374–75, 514–15, 523–24, 536–37
Wilberforce, William 154–56, 198
women's rights movement xi, 49, 67–68, 224, 310, 383, 387–88, 430, 589–91, 598–601
  Emerson and 430, 599–601
  Emerson's attitudes toward women 591–98, 601–2
  Ellen Tucker Emerson and, 434–35
  and free love movement 307, 310
  scholarship assessing Emerson's involvement with 49, 224, 590–91
Wordsworth, William 359, 362, 381, 495, 511, 516